PSYCHOLOGY

A SCIENTIFIC STUDY OF MAN

FILLMORE H. SANFORD

UNIVERSITY OF TEXAS

SECOND EDITION

PSYCHOLOGY
A SCIENTIFIC STUDY OF MAN

WADSWORTH PUBLISHING COMPANY, INC.
BELMONT, CALIFORNIA

Psychology: A Scientific Study of Man
Second Edition
Fillmore H. Sanford

Sixth printing: July 1969
© *1961, 1965, by Wadsworth Publishing Company, Inc., Belmont,*

L.C. Cat. Card No.: 65-14316
Printed in the United States of America

PREFACE

DECISIONS, DILEMMAS, SEQUENCES, AND GRATITUDES II

As the first edition of this book was on its way to press early in 1961, the present writer, as author of record, composed a preface designed to convey to students and teachers of psychology a useful feeling for the nature of the book and an informative exposure to some of the decisions leading to its content and scope. Evidence indicated that the 1961 screed did communicate something, probably something useful. Hence it is repeated here, in an edited, extended, and naturally, a vastly improved form. The revised book is, hopefully, different from its precursor; but the aspirations and problems in producing it are not much changed.

The production of an introductory textbook in psychology is a rich, varied, and protracted experience. It involves quiet adventure, frustration, pleasure (perhaps of a masochistic sort), grim persistence, puzzles, insights, and a feeling—probably lifelong—of a lack of closure. It also involves decisions—thousands of decisions. Any introspectively inclined author may wish to deal in his preface with the innumerable events transpiring within his skin as the project moved along. But he needs to suppress such impulses; it seems better to deal only with the decisions. To do so will require both fewer paragraphs and less spiritual nudity than to engage in detailed introspection; and, in comparison with an account of peregrinations through the byways of inner life, his preface has a greater chance of being useful to someone.

Decisions

There were decisions about intellectual level, about style, about length, about inclusions and exclusions; about sequences, organization, slant, approach; and, at a more molecular level, about such details as phrases, figures of speech, and punctuation. Some of these decisions were made deliberately, perhaps even logically; they appeared to flow with some inevitability from certain explicit notions about the field of psychology and from a reasonably clear sense of pedagogical strategy. Other decisions simply happened. They came as surprises to the author, sometimes bringing what felt like pleasurable insight, sometimes inserting a disagreeable dissonance into the project. By the time the writing stopped (a book is never finished), decisions had been made, overtly or covertly; and the present book is the result.

Perhaps the best way to deal with these decisions is not to catalog them, but to back away from them and to set down some of the larger dilemmas that led to the many detailed commitments.

Dilemmas

Here, then, are some of the author's dilemmas. They are presented in the form of two-pronged caveats, which the author formulated for himself as he went along.

1. Write a unified book—give it a plot; let each chapter have a subplot; give every unit a beginning, a middle, and an end—*but* remember coverage, and let not the yen for coherence select *out* significant content.

2. Write a sequential book, with chapter building on chapter—*but* remember that your logical sequence may be another's chaos.

3. Emphasize a general and informed appreciation of the broad field of psychology; try to help the student see psychology in its intellectual and social context—*but* remember that the student should also learn detailed facts, technical methods, precise vocabulary.

4. Emphasize a mature scientific attitude toward problems of behavior, for that may constitute psychology's greatest contribution—*but* remember to cover technical content in some depth.

5. Articulate the book to the arts and sciences curriculum—*but* attract

as many majors as you can and help prepare them for further courses in psychology.

6. Emphasize the ideas that you'd like your son and daughter to carry with them the rest of their lives—*but* remember that the field of psychology is broad and that one man's importances may be another man's trivia.

7. Teach the substance, significance, and great intellectual challenge of psychology, and teach it with confidence—*but* remember that psychology is a young science and in many areas incompletely formed; so teach it with humility and, without diffidence or apology, take the student into your confidence.

8. Help the student see that psychology is the most exciting and most challenging of all scientific fields—*but* stay in perspective, for it is only one of man's ways of studying man.

9. Represent every special segment of psychology as best you can, for there is intellectual excitement for somebody in every one of them—*but* don't write a catalog.

10. Write in a sprightly style—*but* watch your dignity; the text writer's role is a stuffy one.

11. Write concretely; remember James and Boring—*but* remember that every informality will irritate someone and that figures of speech, however pleasant, are inherently imprecise.

12. Write personally; the author is an individual and students are people—*but* textbook authors should be essentially anonymous, and personality is an intrusion.

13. If a sentence comes out with a bit of humor in it, let it alone; laughing and learning are not incompatible—*but* keep humor relevant and nondistracting and do not poke hostile fun at anybody; be friendly to anyone who has the good sense to learn something about psychology.

14. Don't clutter up the text with the trappings of scholarship—*but* remember that psychology *is* a scholarly field with a rich literature and that undocumented statements are taboo.

15. Write directly to students as you know and like them—*but* remember that you are the instructor's servant; don't interfere with his role and his function; also remember that the instructor is a gatekeeper who decides whether you shall have any access at all to his students.

16. Maintain high intellectual standards; never talk down, predigest, or oversimplify—*but* remember the average student, for he is in the vast majority and will rule the world; write to the student where he is and bring him, if you can, to where you want him to be.

17. Don't be hesitant to speculate a bit, interpret a bit, or even preach a little on the virtues of science and education—*but* remember to label clearly any departure from the evidence or from established theory.

18. If you find yourself with a novel approach, either to content or to method of presenting it, follow your inclinations; there is plenty of room and perhaps even need for change in our established ways of handling introductory psychology—*but* remember that the accepted approaches have much to recommend them, and that human tolerance for novelty, even of high quality, is finite.

These, then, are the larger and more significant dilemmas faced in the creation of this book and its revision. Obviously, none of the conflicts was permanently paralyzing, for the book was published and now is revised. Actually, almost all of the dilemmas started out as aspirations—aspirations entertained with enough naive optimism to allow the project to get started, but transformed into conflicts when one grim reality after another inserted itself into the process. In most cases, the sentiments appearing in front of the *buts* in the foregoing list are the ones the author held and holds most dear and the ones he hopes have won out—albeit narrowly—over the tough opposition.

Sequences

This second edition of the book, in much the same way as the first, is intended to proceed from perspectives to methods to specific fields and specific problems—such as motivation, sensation, and learning—and on to the molar fields of personality, adjusting, and social psychology. The author has found this sequence pedagogically workable; and it has some logic about it, too. But it is by no means the only feasible sequence. The book can be assigned in other sequences, particularly when the instructor furnishes a bridging context.

Major Changes for Second Edition

There can be no doubt that both psychology and its students are more advanced than in 1961. Thus, the present revision deals with many topics which, because they are either new or more salient than before, were not included in the earlier edition. Also, there are new examples of old points; that is, recent research is used to illustrate or to document a point. In addition, there have been changes, hopefully for the better, in the arrangement of chapters. One major change brings the nervous system up front, where, with some apology, the earlier edition did not choose to place it. The author has reached the conclusion that the nervous system is more interesting than it used to be; new methods and a wealth of new knowledge have seen to that. Along with the moving of the nervous system, a good deal more material is included, in appropriate chapters, on physiological factors in behavior. Finally, in accordance with the suggestions of numerous instructors, the earlier two chapters on motivation have been combined into one, as have the two chapters on sensation. These developments, along with an attempt to tighten and shorten introductory and transitional material, may have increased somewhat the intellectual level of the book; there is probably more substantive content per page.

Research Readings and Bibliographies

At the end of each chapter in this edition, there are supplementary materials of two kinds: (1) research abstracts and (2) a bibliography of suggestions for further reading.

The items in each bibliography have been selected on the dual basis of relevance for the subject matter and intelligibility for students who have taken seriously the parts of the text for which the materials are judged relevant.

The research reports were selected with two purposes in mind: (1) to help the student penetrate deeper into some limited aspect of the material covered in a given chapter; (2) to give the student an intimate exposure to and feeling for the nature of psychological research as it actually occurs and as it is reported in the scientific literature. For the most part, these research reports are abstracted versions of published articles. Not all psychologists would agree that each of the selected research papers is of first significance for the science. Not all would agree either that every one of the research projects is a prime example of the best possible research design. The aim is to present a representative selection of research reports, each one of which is intelligible and, in some important way, informative.

Gratitudes

When an author sends off the final proofs of a textbook, his greatest gratitude, flowing out to the world at large, is for the fact that the project has reached a stopping place. But there are many other gratitudes he wants to express. Of course, he really cannot. Even were he sure he is not merely sharing the blame, he could not capture in words his own grateful impulses or state accurate facts about who has helped how much and in what way. He who keeps one end in view makes all things —and all people—serve. The author has used people, sometimes when they knew it not, and sometimes perhaps with self-seeking inconsiderateness, in getting the book done. He has used students by the hundreds. He has used his colleagues, his neighbors, and even a goodly number of total strangers who happened to wander into his office just as he finished a paragraph that had to be read, while hot, to some pair of human ears.

There is genuine gratitude to all these people. They will be thanked, appropriately and personally, whenever and if they can be found.

The following professors read all or part of the manuscript of the first edition at one or more stages and offered much valuable criticism: Kenneth E. Clark, University of Rochester; L. E. Cole, Oberlin College; I. E. Farber, University of Illinois; Paul R. Farnsworth, Stanford University; Eugene Galanter, University of Washington; Harry F. Harlow, University of Wisconsin; George Kelly, Ohio State University; F. Kodman, Jr., University of Kentucky. The following professors gave special help on certain chapters: James Deese, The Johns Hopkins University, on the learning chapters; Howard Gilhousen, University of California, Los Angeles, on the motivation chapters; Elizabeth B. Hurlock, University of Pennsylvania, on the development chapter; Daniel Katz, University of Michigan, on the social psychology chapter; and S. S. Stevens, Harvard University, on the theories of people and sensation chapters.

To help guide the author in the task of revising the book, the following professors reviewed the first edition and offered valuable suggestions for the development of the second edition: Mark K. Allen, Brigham Young University; Carson Bennett, Ball State University; Henry Borow, University of Minnesota; Erle Kirk, Foothill College; Charles A. Knehr, Hunter College; Garvin McCain, Arlington State College; Marilyn Rigby, St. Louis University; John J. Rooney, La Salle College; William Stratford, Weber College; and Thomas Turnage, University of Maryland.

After the manuscript for the second edition was drafted, the following professors gave special help on certain chapters: Neil Bartlett, University of Arizona, on the motivation, emotion, perception, and sensation chapters; David Birch, University of Michigan, on the motivation and emotion chapters; Judson S. Brown, University of Oregon, on the motivation and emotion chapters; L. E. Cole, Oberlin College, on the psychoses and neuroses chapter; James A. Dyal, Texas Christian University, on the learning chapters; Frederick R. Fosmire, University of Oregon, on the psychoses and neuroses chapter; William L. Hays, University of Michigan, on the methods chapter; Elizabeth B. Hurlock, University of Pennsylvania, on the development chapter; George A. Kelly, Ohio State University, on the personality chapter; Geoffrey Keppel, University of California, Berkeley, on the higher mental processes chapter; Thomas K. Landauer, Stanford University, on the learning chapters; Brendan Maher, University of Wisconsin, on the psychoses and neuroses chapter; Melvin Manis, University of Michigan, on the higher mental processes chapter; Albert Pepitone, University of Pennsylvania, on the social psychology chapter; Jessie Rhulman, University of California, Los Angeles, on the adjustment chapter; Dorothy Rogers, State University of New York at Oswego, on the development chapter; Mark R. Rosenzweig, University of California, Berkeley, on the nervous system chapter; Pauline S. Sears, Stanford University, on the development chapter; James P. Thomas, University of California, Los Angeles, on the sensation and perception chapters; Ralph H. Turner, Oberlin College, on the social psychology chapter; Leona E. Tyler, University of Oregon, on the methods chapter; and Edward L. Walker, University of Michigan, on the learning chapters.

Many colleagues at the University of Texas were especially and tolerantly helpful with the preparation of the book's first edition. Heading this list are the names of John Capaldi and Bert Forrin. In the work on the revision, often more demanding and less rewarding than labor on a first edition, other colleagues at Texas went far beyond the ordinary demands of colleagueship, and a number of graduate students when asked to go one mile went much more. The former list is led by Demetrios Papageorgis and Edwin I. Megargee. The second-miling students were Hugh Poyner, Carleton Johnson, Ben Clopton, Tom Bourbon, and Sue Seitz.

Something very special, such as the arranging of a co-authorship, ought to be done about the contribution to the enterprise made by the writer's wife. If anybody needs someone with the capacity to read an improbably strange chirography, and to do remarkably good typing, who is knowledgeable about bibliographic work and eagle-eyed at proof reading, and if someone wants them all combined with both nurturance and wisdom, he can look elsewhere; the writer's wife will be taking a rest.

NOTE TO THE STUDENT

The student who reads this book may profit by a word on what kind of experience the author has tried to arrange for the reader. Of course, no writer knows exactly what he is doing when he produces a book. When a student reads it, he brings his own unique interests and backgrounds to the situation; the intellectual events that then transpire have never happened before. A large measure of unpredictability is involved. Still, authors do try to predict what the reader will find most interesting; they also try to arrange sequences of ideas so that a reader may have an increased chance to profit—and in some measure enjoy himself—from exposure to a book.

The attempt here has been to write a textbook with something of a plot. The plot has subplots and interlocking underlying themes, and it may take some sudden, perhaps disturbing, turns; therefore, the author thinks that the student who understands the plot may have an easier and more satisfying experience than if he treated the book as a catalog or compendium of subject matters. So, some coaching. Read the first chapter for the major substantive plot line and the second chapter for a major secondary methodological theme. Then turn, in sequence, to the outlines and introductory pages of each of the other chapters. These introductory materials furnish a general framework into which the content of the book can be placed, a framework which may give an added increment of meaning to each of the substantive subdivisions.

It was the author's hope that each of the chapters might also have both plot and unity. This was probably an impossible aspiration for dealing with such a broad and variegated field; it did result in an attempt to write chapters that are organized, first, for reading and, second, for studying. If the author has had any success in this attempt, the student may profit from reading a chapter in its entirety and then coming back later to pay special attention to what he wishes to understand more fully or to learn more thoroughly.

Each chapter has a brief summary at its end. It is hoped that these summaries, together with the glossary at the end of the book,* will supplement the cursive text material in such a way that the student has, first, a general grasp of the content of a chapter and, second, an easy access to key points and to explicit definitions of technical terms.

A number of students who have read the manuscript have commented, some wryly, on the extensive vocabulary, both technical and nontechnical, in the book. As for the technical vocabulary, there is and very probably should be no way an author can avoid its use. An introductory course in any scientific discipline must deal with the language that is crucial for that field. Eventually, perhaps, teaching machines can be used to help the student learn, quickly and painlessly, the technical vocabulary necessary for intelligent reading in a field. For the time being, however, more conventional methods are necessary. In the present book the attempt has been to define technical words through their use in context. The author has a cantankerous objection to the procedure of jerking himself to a stop for a definition in the middle of a page that seems to be going well. So, the hopeful attempt has been to define the words by context as ideas are developed, leaving more precise definitions to the glossary in the back of the book. The student can obviously profit from intensive study of the glossary.

As for use of nontechnical words that may be beyond the student's present vocabulary, the author takes a similar stand. He justifies the use of his own natural vocabulary as necessary if he is to make the best sense he can of his material—and he probably gives in to a schoolteacherish impulse to have students learn some good English words even while studying psychology. The rule he has tried to follow, however, is again a rule of context; if a relatively rare word seems really necessary, either for self-expression or for increasing the precision of meaning, the rule has

---

* Words that appear in the glossary are set in **bold face** the first time they appear in a chapter.

been to use it in such a way that the reader will not necessarily have to look it up in order to get the sense of the paragraph in which it occurs.

The author hopes mightily that his efforts will make it possible for students to understand and appreciate the field of psychology—a field which he himself finds inherently exciting and which seems to have a significant contribution to make in the advancement of the human enterprise.

CONTENTS

2 THEORIES OF PEOPLE—Continued

PART TWO

BIOLOGICAL FOUNDATIONS
OF BEHAVIOR

FIGURE CREDITS

The figures not accompanied by a credit line came from the following sources:

Allison Laboratories, Inc.: Fig. 10–8.
Walter Barnes Studio: Figs. 7–2, 7–5, 9–8, 10–1, 11–6, 15–6.
British Information Services: Figs. 2–1, 8–15.
A. Devaney, Inc.: Fig. 9–5.
James Esten: Fig. 5–10.
Ewing Galloway: Figs. 1–4, 8–8.
Grason-Stadler: Fig. 12–7.
Dr. Harry Harlow: Figs. 3–6 (photo by Sponholz), 8–10.
Dr. Keith J. Hayes: Figs. 1–2, 3–16.
The Library of Congress: Figs. 1–6, 6–1 (left photo), 11–7, 15–8, 18–2.
Dr. Neal Miller: Fig. 16–2.
National Aeronautics and Space Administration: Fig. 13–14.
The National Audubon Society: Fig. 3–7 (photo by Tom McHugh).
Dr. James Olds: Fig. 4–16.
The Psychological Corporation: Figs. 2–5, 2–8, 5–2, 5–4, 5–6.
Science Service, Inc.: Fig. 12–1.
Dr. B. F. Skinner: Fig. 13–13.
The Standard Oil Company of New Jersey: Figs. 15–7, 18–6.
D. H. Stoelting Co.: Fig. 5–5.
Texas State Department of Public Safety: Fig. 9–3.
The University of Texas News and Information Service: Fig. 6–1 (right photo).
University of Texas Visual Instruction Bureau: Figs. 2–6, 13–1.
Western Design: Fig. 13–15.
Wide World Photos: Figs. 3–1, 6–15, 15–4, 18–14.

PART ONE

INTRODUCTION

OUTLINE / CHAPTER I

I. THE SUBJECT MATTER OF PSYCHOLOGY

   A. Organisms
      1. All organisms are composed of protoplasm
      2. All organisms are irritable
      3. All organisms perform the basic physiological functions
      4. All organisms have ancestors
      5. All organisms have a capacity for growth
      6. All organisms tend to maintain a constancy of internal conditions
      7. All organisms are biological systems

   B. Human Organisms
      1. Language in Animals and Men
         a. Animal language
         b. Complexities of human language
      2. Reasoning in Animals and Men
         a. Reasoning in animals
         b. Reasoning in human beings
      3. The Accumulation of Culture
         a. Animal culture
         b. Human culture
         c. Man and freedom
         d. The soul: man and animal

   C. Human Beings in Particular Cultures
      1. Cultures Differ
      2. Cultures Change
      3. Effect of American Culture on the Individual

   D. Recapitulation

II. THE PSYCHOLOGICAL PROCESS

   A. Psychological Process and Development

   B. The Content of Psychology

   C. Historical Approaches to the Psychological Process
      1. Structuralism
      2. The Functional Approach
      3. Behaviorism and Gestalt Psychology
      4. Freud and Psychoanalysis

   D. Modern Approaches to Psychological Processes
      1. Present-Day Segmentation
      2. Holistic Approaches
      3. Physiological and Neurological vs. a Psychological Approach

III. SUMMARY

IV. SUPPLEMENTARY READING: WILLIAM JAMES AND MODERN PSYCHOLOGY

CHAPTER 1

KNOWING THE HUMAN BEING

Among the most universal and most engrossing of all human pursuits is the attempt to understand the human being. Philosophers, poets, theologians, humanists, historians, political scientists, sociologists, anthropologists, biologists, physiologists—all study man and cast into print the results of their observations. The butcher, the baker, the candlestick maker —all study man and use the results of their study as the basis for conducting their daily lives. Each of us, in his own way, has studied human beings. And each of us has his own view of man. On the basis of what we have learned, we can predict, sometimes with great success, what people will do.

This book deals with the *psychologist's* attempt to understand man. Because the psychologist approaches things in his own particular way and because he tries to operate within the strict rules governing scientific inquiry, his attempts to know man are different

from those of the philosopher or poet or novelist; different also from those of the sociologist and anthropologist. And his efforts lead him down roads and into byways that may seem strange to the man of practical affairs. His methods and his factual results will not substitute for the philosopher's approach or for his general insights into man. Nor can psychology now replace the everyday wisdom by which the world's affairs are run. But books are written and courses are given in the belief that what the psychologist has to say may add both precision and richness to the philosopher's paragraphs, and may contribute in some measure to the wisdom with which the educated man will live out his life.

This first chapter tries to present a broad view of the enormous, intricate, and often humbling problem that confronts psychology. Succeeding chapters will then deal with slices and aspects of the general problem.

Figure 1–1. MAN STUDIES MAN. *Many men, from many vantage points, study man and make predictions about him.*

THE SUBJECT MATTER OF PSYCHOLOGY

What is the basic problem of psychology? One good way to approach this question is to imagine ourselves in a guessing game, such as the old game of twenty questions, in which we are given successive cues about the identity of a hidden object. Each cue, as it comes, gives us some scientifically sound information about the object. Each succeeding cue gives us more specific knowledge—so that, as we go along, we should come closer and closer to an accurate description of the hidden object. And perhaps we will be able to make better and more meaningful statements about how it came to be what it is.

Such a guessing game is essentially a game of categories. Each cue will place our object in a category—animal, vegetable, or mineral, for example. When we know it is assigned to one category and not another, we gain knowledge about it and we have expectations about what it is like and what it does. If it is a mineral, we think of metals and expect it to be mined and not eaten. If it is a vegetable, we

are inclined to think it is more edible than malleable. And so on. If we know it to be vegetable, then we seek within the large category *vegetable* for smaller and more precise categories into which we can place it. Is it, in fact, edible or inedible? Is it green, yellow, red, or blue? Is it large or small? Is it oriental or occidental? And so on. Eventually we may come very close to a description of the particular vegetable in question.

In dealing with the mystery object concerning us here, we will place it in a series of categories, each category somewhat narrower than the one preceding it. Each new category gives us new expectations about the object. Some of our expectations are probably unsupported by evidence, while others are backed by scientific fact. At the end of our exercise we may or may not be able to describe our mystery object, may or may not be able to account for it. We shall see.

ORGANISMS

If we know that our object is an **organism,** we know a number of important things about it—and about what it is not.

All organisms are composed of protoplasm. **Protoplasm,** an organized solution of chemical compounds, is the physical basis of life. The chemical compounds in protoplasm are found also in nonliving objects, but only in protoplasm are they organized in mysterious solutions in the way that constitutes life.

All organisms are irritable. In contrast to inanimate objects, organisms can respond to events and processes outside themselves. They are able to sense external events, to register changes in the environment. In simple animals, this registering is crude and lacking in precision. In more complex animals, structures such as eyes and ears do a highly specialized job of registering events in the external world.

All organisms perform the basic physiological functions. All organisms take in some kind of nourishment, digest it, circulate it, eliminate waste products. And all organisms reproduce. The lowly **amoeba,** with its unicellular simplicity, performs all these functions and, in so doing, evidences a basic characteristic of life. Man performs all these functions and, in so doing, takes on a basic kinship with all things that are living.

All organisms have ancestors. Though what we call life presumably had a beginning, sometime and somewhere, without benefit of conventional ancestors, all living things now can pretty well be assumed to have come from forebears very much like themselves.

All organisms have a capacity for growth. For all protoplasmic units new material is taken in and converted to growth—either through cell expansion or cell division. If we know that our object is an organism, then we know that it has a future in which it will grow and a past through which it has developed.

All organisms tend to maintain a constancy of internal conditions. All organisms conform to the principle of homeostasis, the principle that describes their tendency to respond in ways that keep their internal conditions steady and stable. If external conditions produce internal imbalance, the organism attempts to restore balance and stability. The **paramecium,** for example, will avoid both total darkness and bright light. Apparently, a subdued light best maintains its internal balance. In more complicated forms of life, more intricate behavior can be used to preserve internal stability. If the human body is chilled, for example, it tries to raise its temperature by shivering; if it is hot, it perspires.

All organisms are biological systems. By definition, organisms are organized. Any organism may be seen as having separate parts. But the parts are integrated and interwoven in function so that events in one part affect the whole. The whole in turn influences the function, and the very existence, of the part.

The organism considered as a whole has properties in its own right which cannot be explained merely by considering the sum of the properties of its individual parts. From this standpoint it is difficult or impossible to understand the whole organism by analyzing its parts, for such a procedure destroys the organization which is the basic part of life (Hickman, 1955, p. 112).

These, then, are some of the things we know about an object that is an organism.

Whatever kind of organism it is, amoeba or ape or man, it is *composed of protoplasm,* it is *irritable* and it *senses its world,* it performs certain *basic physiological functions,* it *grows,* it *probably maintains homeostasis,* it has *ancestors,* and it is an *organized system.*

If our object were a paramecium, one of the simplest of all organisms, the job of describing it might seem relatively simple. Perhaps we can say that the most significant thing about a paramecium is that it is an organism. We would not be likely to say that about a man —at least not to his face. But were our object a paramecium, we would still need to know his particular size, shape, and structure and the particular ways in which he carries out the functions common to all organisms. We would want to know his particular manner of sensing the world. We would want to know his behavioral traits—how he reacts in the presence of light, heat, gravity, contact, and so on. And if we were going to *explain* him, we would have to understand how his system operates. We would have to understand life processes. But our object is not a paramecium. Our task becomes even more difficult.

HUMAN ORGANISMS

When we know that our object is a human organism, we make an enormous jump forward —and an enormous jump into complexity. Man has "known" a great deal about himself ever since he learned to speak and to write down his ideas. This knowledge was firmly embedded in his view of things—so firmly that the certainty of it has been perhaps the greatest barrier to the development of a systematic scientific study of man. Science is largely a questioning, based on curiosity. Certainty—even demonstrably false certainty—kills curiosity, stifles observation, and leads man to defend the answers he has rather than to seek new ones which he may find uncomfortable. We are therefore recipients of a great array of insights, beliefs, dubious certainties, and shared superstitions about the nature of man.

Only recently has man applied to his study of himself the methods that have given him such impressive knowledge of the physical world with which he contends. The science of man is a recent arrival on the stage of history. Man understood much about the stars and planets centuries before he knew that his own blood circulates. And he began to study his own body long before it occurred to him that he could make scientific sense out of the workings of his mind. Man's attempt to garner scientific knowledge about himself is thus a recent development in his intellectual history. There exists nevertheless an impressive array of scientific knowledge of the human being.

What do we know, then, when we have established that our object is a human organism? At the outset, of course, we know that man has all the characteristics of other organisms: he is irritable, he probably has some homeostatic tendencies, he has ancestors, etc. In addition, most of us have a pattern of beliefs and attitudes that constitutes our ideology of man. Most of us believe that man has characteristics not found in any other organism, that he has traits and capacities not shared with lower animals. Perhaps our appreciation of the true nature of man can be advanced by a look at evidence bearing on the current ideology of man.

Let us examine the following frequently encountered assertions about man:

1. Man is the only organism that has a language.
2. Man is the only organism that can reason.
3. Man is the only organism that accumulates a culture.
4. Man is the only organism that is free.
5. Man is the only organism with a soul.

Language in Animals and Men

If we know that our mystery object is human, we know that he probably produces and reacts to those noises, signs, and writings that we call language. As an adult he can speak many thousands of separate words. He can combine these words into an almost infinite variety of sentences and paragraphs. And he can respond differently to a great variety of noises and signs and writings produced by his fellows. *His use of language is perhaps his most intricate and his most uniquely human behavior.* By learning and using language, he brings into his present world events long past. He can model his behavior upon that of Sir Walter Raleigh, or he can learn directly from the writings of Galileo. In planning his day, he can take into account events of the moment in Egypt or China or perhaps on the moon. And through putting words to imagined coming events, he can project himself forward in time, guiding himself into his own future. Such is the power of language. However, we cannot jump to the conclusion that man is the *only* organism using language.

Animal language. Animals communicate. Bees, for instance, communicate with one another in highly complicated ways. Von Frisch (1950) noticed that if bees found a rich supply of food at a distance from the hive, they would come back home and perform an intricate dance. After watching this dance, other bees then could head forth directly toward the source of food and find it with little or no exploration. Von Frisch discovered that the bees danced more rapidly if the food was close at hand than if it was far away; by certain directional cues in their dance, the returning bees also could tell their colleagues the direction in which to fly to find the food. Von Frisch himself learned the language of bees so well that by watching the dance of returned foragers he could tell accurately where his research assistant had placed the supplies of sugar the bees were "talking" about to their co-workers.

Many other animals use what appears to be language. The young chick runs to the place it sees its mother pecking; after awhile, if the mother has consistently clucked whenever she found something worth pecking, the chicks will "listen" to the cluck and go where it tells them to. In a fight, one dog responds rapidly to what another dog begins. Such behavior is very similar to the human response to a balled fist or bared teeth. It is a "conversation of gesture" (Mead, 1934). Apes make a wide variety of sounds and communicate with one another not only by physical gestures but by vocal gestures, warning one another of danger, announcing the presence of food, or asking the help of a friend in pulling in a weighted, food-bearing box too heavy for one ape alone (Köhler, 1925).

Is this language? In one sense it clearly is. Such gestures constitute a very simple emotional or expressive language. The organism, man or animal, that uses such language is responding to the immediate demands of a situation. His associates soon learn that the gesture or the cry is associated with a situation—a snake, a hawk, a tempting pile of grain, the presence of a lion or a fresh kill—and behave toward the *sign* of the situation much as if it were the situation itself.

Complexities of human language. Man, probably because of the peculiarities of the human nervous system, can and does learn a much more intricate language. In addition to gestural or expressive language, he uses **propositional language** (Cassirer, 1933). He not only can cry out in the presence of a snake; he can run around a corner and state the proposition that a snake lies coiled under the third mulberry bush from the fence. The stating of the proposition to one of his kind who has learned the same language enables that one to react to the snake at a distance. He can test every phase of the proposition if he cares to take a look. Or, if he wishes to accept the proposition as a true representation, he can begin reacting in what he regards as a suitable way. He can fetch his gun. Or, if he is sufficiently afraid of snakes, he can disappear forthwith into the next county.

We might say that bees too use a propositional language—in effect, one bee states a proposition concerning a distant supply of nectar. But the human use of propositional language takes on new dimensions of complexity, dimensions that add a mighty versatility to human adjustment. Human communicators use **concepts** and **symbols** in ways other organisms cannot. Human beings not only can use signs and signals to tell where there is honey; they can talk *abstractly* about honey as a sweet or as a member of an abstract class of foods. They can talk about what they would do if there were no honey there. Because symbols can be divorced from the concrete or physically present reality to which they refer, their use empowers the human individual not only to report but to summarize and to imagine, to rearrange in his mind a world which to lower animals must remain immutably fixed.

There are other cardinally significant aspects of human language. Not only is there an array of symbols, but these symbols are shared—many people accepting a symbol as signifying the same idea. Such sharing of symbols is necessary if there is to be communication between individuals. It will not be meaningful to most American college freshmen, for example, to be warned that there is a *Pferd* in the closet; only Germans have the shared belief that *Pferd* means horse.

Further, intricate human communication depends on a *system* of shared symbols, on *rules*, or *conventions*, with respect to the use of symbols. For example, in the English language the phrase "horse eats" means something quite different from "eats horse." Those who wish to communicate with one another need to know the same meaning for the symbols they use and need to adhere to certain conventions about the order and arrangement of the symbols. There must be a syntax—a grammar. Animals are not able at all to *talk about talking.* They have no grammar, no stable rules for the proper formulation of statements. And, finally, animals cannot *deliberately invent an abstract language*—such as algebra or calculus —that has no simple and concrete reference to the world as most of us know it.

By knowing, then, that our organism is man, we know he has a language, that he uses to his advantage symbols of things not present, that he states propositions, that he shares symbols and grammar with his fellows; that he can, in a way not known to lower forms of life, manage his affairs through the use of the experiences occurring to others far removed in time and space.

The mere knowledge that human beings in general use language, however, does not tell us about the *particular linguistic behavior of our particular human being.* We do not know *what* language he speaks. We do not know *how well he speaks* whatever language he speaks. We do not know with whom he is in linguistic contact. We do not know the processes whereby our individual—or others like him—comes to possess particular linguistic abilities and skills. Nor do we know how his verbal behavior intertwines with his other behavior.

Reasoning in Animals and Men

Man has long been convinced that he is set apart from all other creatures and brought closer to the gods by his ability to think, to reason. There is some scientific justification for this belief; for man, by virtue of his capacity to use abstract symbols, can achieve a unique form and degree of mastery of his world. He can deal with events long past, engage in flights of fancy, entertain hypotheses contrary to fact, observe the world and find in it the elegant simplicities that constitute the basic laws of science. He can solve problems without appearing to move a muscle, and through the use of mathematical formulas he can calculate the distance between stars.

To be human is to be able to think. How far does this capacity remove us from other organisms which we choose to regard as lower forms of life?

Reasoning in animals. One key aspect of thinking is the ability to react to events (**stimuli**) not physically present. If an animal responds to a signal that is no longer there, then the animal must be responding to some *representation*, some *symbol* of that signal. The symbol must be stored in his nervous system.

If we place a desired bone on the other side of a wire fence from a desirous dog, the dog will seek the bone in the most direct way he deems possible—he heads straight through the fence. A dog that is not very bright may keep trying the direct approach until he is worn out, or until the fence comes down. But dogs do not often do that. They have the capacity to turn their backs on the bone, run many yards away from it, and then come back around the end of the fence. This detour behavior cannot happen unless the dog carries with him some image or symbol or representation of the bone he is not actually seeing.

Figure 1–2. SUBHUMAN PROBLEM SOLVING. *Chimps have the capacity to solve problems. Here the chimp must use the candle to burn the string to open the door to secure reward.*

This seems to be behavior of quite a thoughtful kind.

Young children—even very bright young children—have difficulty with such detour tasks. A 13-month-old child has difficulty turning his back on a chair and then sitting down on it. Very often the child will get himself in the proper landing position but then look between his legs to see where the chair went. By re-establishing direct sensory contact, he can respond to the chair. He often is unable to respond to it in the absence of such direct contact.

Can dogs think? It looks as if they can. They can handle problems of detour. Early students of the behavior of apes (Yerkes, 1943; Köhler, 1925) report many instances of what appears to be thinking in these animals. If a banana is placed outside the chimpanzee's cage, beyond arm's reach, the chimp will soon learn to fasten together a pair of sticks furnished him and use them to rake in his food. Or the ape will stack up a number of boxes, one upon the other, so that he can reach a banana far above his head. This appears to be thoughtful behavior.

Reasoning in human beings. With reasonable safety we can assume, however, that man's thinking is quite different from that of animals, that it leads him on to a highly in-

Figure 1–3. SUBHUMAN PROBLEM SOLVING. *Detour behavior requires some form of thought or some representation of the world.*

tricate manipulation of his world. We need only to be reminded of the problem-solving activity of Galileo, Newton, Harvey, and Einstein—and of ourselves—to be rightly convinced that man's reasoning ability is real and unique. But to know only that it is there and that it is intricate is, of course, to know very little about it. We still don't know *how well our particular individual thinks, what he thinks about, how he came to learn to use his head,* or *how his thought processes are interrelated with the rest of his behavior.* To give him a good description, then, we need to know more about him *as an individual* and about the *processes,* including thought processes, by which he came to be himself and by which he will live through his future. By placing our individual in the category "human with thought," we gain knowledge. But we have a long way to go in our tasks of (a) describing and (b) accounting for our individual.

The Accumulation of Culture

Man, to a much greater extent than any other organism, lives in a world which he him-

self has created. If we know, then, that our individual is a human being, we can infer that he was born into a world which has been to a large extent fashioned, structured, interpreted, and organized by his ancestors. And we can be sure that since his birth his elders have been busy seeing that he knows, understands, and appreciates the man-made world into which he has been thrust.

Though a new-born animal comes into a nest or a burrow or a hive built before his birth, and though the social animals, such as ants and bees, are born into elaborate organizations, we cannot accurately say that animals accumulate either a material or a social culture.

Animal culture. Perhaps we had better examine this matter a bit if we are to understand the alleged uniqueness of man. In a way, young animals are indeed born into a world fashioned by their progenitors. Harvester ants, for example, build underground granaries and stock them with millet or wheat. These storehouses are carefully constructed and well drained. If, by accident, the stored grain becomes damp, it is hauled into the sun to dry. New-born ants inherit a share of this wealth (Morley, 1954).

Similarly, the fungus-growing ants plant and cultivate mushroom gardens. The queen ant, in setting up a new colony, plants mushroom spores in a bed of chewed leaf mold and fertilizes this garden with her own excreta. When her offspring come along, they are set to work tending and extending the garden. They bring in leaves and chew them to make mulch for the mushroom beds, which are constantly replanted and extended. New-born ants thus inherit cultivated farmlands.

Ants also are born into elaborate social organizations. Most ant colonies have a caste system consisting of the queen, workers, soldiers, and sometimes slaves. The single newborn ant, then, if he is born into a going colony, is surrounded by a social structure in which he must find his place and make his way.

What is the difference between the ant's culture and human culture? Perhaps the clear-

Figure 1–4. ANT REAL ESTATE. *In a sense, the social insects have a culture and a social organization; but there is no evolving of culture over time. Here is the elaborate nest built by duck ants.*

est distinction is to be found in the fact that when a newly fertilized queen ant leaves a colony to strike out on her own, she and her offspring will soon set up a culture, both material and social, exactly like the culture the queen left behind her. Soon the new colony, without any action from the queen, will behave exactly like the old colony. The culture does not change from one generation to another. As far as we know, harvester ants have been behaving just like harvester ants for millions of years. They seem to learn nothing from their neighbors the honey-pot ants or the army ants. And, though ants can learn, they apparently do not pass along to their young the results of their learning. Thus, ant culture *does not accumulate* or progress.

Higher animals—rats, dogs, apes—do not demonstrate the elaborate social organization

that characterizes ants and bees. Few animals are born into a world structured and arranged by their forebears. In a way, each new-born animal, other than the human one, starts from cultural scratch. Young animals do learn from their wise and experienced elders; canaries, for example, that are raised with chicks will tend to chirp rather than sing, taking on the "cultural" ways of their adopted peers. However, the accumulation of material possessions or wisdom from one generation to another is very meager, if it occurs at all. A present generation of chimpanzees behaves pretty much like the generation of its great-great-great-great-great grandfathers.

Human culture. What is required, then, for the true accumulation of culture? How does it come about that we live in a world so vastly different from the world of the cave man or, for that matter, so markedly different from the horse-and-buggy life of our own grandfathers or great grandfathers?

First, there must be *material creation.* Man builds. Animals build too—nests, burrows, hives. But man builds more *elaborately*, because he has mastered tools and has learned the power of cooperation and division of labor. Man builds more *permanently.* He often builds with a deliberate eye on future generations. The millions of man-hours required to build the Cathedral of Notre Dame were not invested in the interest of immediate shelter from the rain or even for a place to worship next month or next year. There had to be a vision of the future.

In order to build deliberately for the future, there must be the ability to *conceive of the future.* The future is an abstract idea and can be dealt with only by an organism with the capacity to think in terms of abstract symbols. Man has that capacity. Through it he is able to create material objects that enrich or cripple the lives of his grandchildren's grandchildren. Man also builds immaterial things—he builds a philosophy, a science, a literature, an art. And he builds, often without deliberation, an elaborate social organization. Some of this immaterial building is done with an eye to posterity. Much of it, perhaps, is not. It represents the products of man's attempt to see his world, to express himself, to solve his urgent problems. But all of these creations *can be preserved and passed along. Language* is the *principal preservative.* Whatever can be spoken can be passed along from the old to the young. Whatever can be written can be passed along, with great precision, from one century or one era to another.

Man, then, with the capacity to create and to cast his creations into words and symbols, can accumulate a culture—material and immaterial. The new-born infant in any generation comes into a world structured, interpreted, and preserved by his forebears. But how does the infant take into himself all the creations of his ancestors? That, of course, is an enormous question and one with which we must valiantly contend later on. At the moment it needs only to be made clear that (a) man does, in some degree, take into himself his cultural heritage and (b) he is able to do this largely through the acquisition of language. He can, through language, be informed, enriched, educated, and sometimes misled and endangered by the experiences, insights, inventions, and bigotries recorded by persons long dead.

To know that our individual is surrounded by a culture—things, ideas, social arrangements—tells us something highly significant about him. But this knowledge raises at least as many questions as it furnishes answers. We do not know *what culture* surrounds him. We do not know the *processes* by which he relates to his culture, by which he comes to share the values and attitudes and habits of his elders, or by which he resists the pressures to conformity and strikes out on his own unique pursuit of the human adventure.

Man and Freedom

It has been frequently asserted that man is free, that he freely wills his own behavior, that he freely chooses between good and evil. Other organisms, by contrast, are most generally seen as *determined,* as bound by instinctual necessities to behave in certain fixed and predictable ways.

As man watches himself, as he experiences intent and the directionality of his behavior, as he now savors a future he is only beginning to fashion, it is almost inconceivable that he can regard himself as a passive tool of cause and effect. But is he indeed free? Is he free in a way animals are not free? Is he free in a way not known by atoms and molecules?

Perhaps the deep question of freedom can best be approached by asking questions of a different sort. Let us ask whether man is predictable. Can we predict what he will do under certain known circumstances? Can we predict his behavior as well as we can predict the behavior of worms or ants or molecules or chemical compounds? And if we can predict his behavior, can we then maintain that he is free?

Man's behavior can, in fact, be predicted, sometimes with great precision. We can predict that if we flash a light in someone's eye, the pupil will contract. Is he then free *not* to give a reflex response when stimulated appropriately? We can also predict with a known degree of accuracy that if a student performs in a certain way on an intelligence test he will also perform in a certain way on an hour examination. Is he free to perform at a Phi Beta Kappa level in an hour exam if his intelligence is that of an idiot? The question of freedom vs. **determinism** takes on such a form.

Man's behavior is predictable, at least in part—and there's the rub. If behavior is not entirely predictable, then there is room for a belief in freedom—a freedom of some kind existing in some degree. We know also that atoms are imperfectly predictable. There is now no way of knowing exactly what an individual atom will do or exactly where it will go. As Heisenberg (1958) has pointed out, there is no possible way of knowing what an atom—or a worm or a man—would be doing if it were not under observation. So there is room for the principle of freedom.

The scientist, however, in his professional behavior, acts as if he does not believe in freedom. In his constant seeking for cause-and-effect relationships, in his search for predictability, he acts as if nothing were free to go its own way, including human beings. Thus, whatever his philosophical convictions, he adopts determinism *as a strategy or a policy.* He *acts as if* the behavior of man and of his world were determined by natural laws and as if it were possible for him to formulate those natural laws in such a way that all is predictable.

The philosophical problem of man's freedom remains with us. But that problem need not be finally settled before the scientist goes to work. The scientist knows that there are predictions, even about people, that he can learn to make. And he follows as a working strategy, *but not necessarily as a final truth,* the principle of determinism.

We cannot know, then, on scientific evidence whether man is free. We similarly cannot know, once and for all, that man's behavior is determined.

How about the *relative* freedom of men and animals? Here again we encounter a philosophical problem, the answer to which requires other than scientific evidence. Let's see where we get, however, if we try to define freedom itself in scientific or naturalistic terms. One way to deal with the question is to define freedom in terms of the varieties of responses an organism can make in a given situation. In any behavioral situation we can estimate with some discrimination the number of different responses a dog or a man has the capacity to make. The dog, being relatively more bound by inborn patterns, has relatively few responses he can make. The man, by contrast, can conceivably make any one of a large number of responses. His repertoire of possible behaviors is large. In this sense he is more free. And if we wished to make him freer still, we would do what we could, through education and training, to increase the variety of possible discriminations and behaviors at his disposal.

The Soul: Man and Animal

Since the dawning of man's self-consciousness he has been possessed of the notion that he is something more than mere body, more than physically tangible matter. In various times and in various cultures, man has conceived of both himself and animals as having a nonmaterial nature as well as a material one.

In some present-day cultures we can find a belief in animism—in the nonphysical, nonmaterial nature of man, of animals, and sometimes of inanimate objects as well. Since the ancient Greek philosophers, however, Western man has been inclined to think that he alone has a soul and that animals, being further from the gods, are creatures of instinct and nature.

As with freedom, it is almost inconceivable that man should have failed to conceive of soul. His observations of the differences between life and death, his awareness of the seeming rationality of his own behavior led to the concept of a soul. Now, in actuality, does man have a soul? Animals? These questions are not answerable by science. If the soul is defined as unobservable and immaterial, then science, being bound to direct observations of the material universe, has nothing to say about the soul. If the soul is defined in terms of ability to think, to feel, to be conscious, then the soul is a naturalistic and psychological matter. With respect to this we can draw some distinctions between men and other organisms.

Is the soul immortal? This is a question clearly beyond the ken of science. There is no way to observe beyond mortality and no way, within science, to infer immortality from known and observable events. A belief in the immortality of the soul lies in the area of faith. It is not a matter of scientific knowledge.

To know that our mystery organism is a human being is to bring to mind a wealth of knowledge, theory, belief, and superstition. We can know a great deal about the complexity of man's organic nature and about the potential complexity of his behavior. We know he can use language, can think, can create, can absorb and hand down culture. We cannot finally know, on purely scientific grounds, whether he is free or whether he has an immortal soul.

If we wish to push further toward details in our search for the unique attributes of man, we can find, and demonstrate to be true, that man is the only organism with a thumb set so that it can oppose four fingers. We can know also that he is the only organism that blushes. We can know that he, more than any other higher animal, is free of body hair. We can know that he is the only organism that makes love the year around.

By placing our individual into the category "human," we can attribute to him many traits and capacities known to characterize mankind in general. But human beings vary enormously. No two of them are alike. We have a long way to go before we can put down a full and accurate description of our particular human being. And if we wish to go beyond description and into an *accounting for,* our road goes on and on into the distance.

HUMAN BEINGS IN PARTICULAR CULTURES

We have seen that it is a uniquely human thing to be born into a cultural setting whose shape and nature has been determined by the accumulated and recorded experiences of many generations of living, striving, thinking, feeling, building, speaking, and writing people. But to know merely that our mystery person was born into a human culture is to possess very inadequate knowledge. We need to know *what culture.* Cultures vary widely, so that practices and patterns approved in one may horrify people in another. And any given culture changes over a period of time. The behavior of even their immediate elders can shock members of a succeeding generation, and vice versa.

We know, both from common-sense observation and from the extensive studies of cultural anthropologists, that individual participants in a given culture tend to believe similarly, to like and dislike the same things, to hold similar values, to develop the same habits, attitudes, and goals. So if we know the characteristics of the culture into which our individual was born, we can, with some degree of safety, infer a good deal about him.

Cultures Differ

Each culture has its own particular characteristics. Let's look at the behavior of the Tchambuli, a tribe of dark-skinned people liv-ing in New Guinea (Mead, 1935). Tchambuli men, to be real men, must excel in artistic activities. The men spend most of their time at ceremonial activities. They work tirelessly to perfect their dancing, to make beautiful ceremonial masks, to polish their flute playing. Each man is an artist. He carves or paints or plaits. And while working at these manly pursuits, the men gossip and rail like fishwives at one another.

The women, meanwhile, are busy making the world go round. They care for the children, prepare the food, and take care of all gardening and fishing. When they have time, they manufacture mosquito bags for sale to other tribes. The women are hearty, easy-going people, full of self-reliance and initiative. They regard men as the weaker sex. Men are a little afraid of women, having to look to them for support. They would like some female authority and power, but this is only a wistful hope.

To see quite dramatically that cultures vary, all we have to do is imagine a red-blooded, self-made, sports-loving, hard-living, big-chested American male suddenly set down among the Tchambuli and put under pressure by the native-born citizens to "act like a man."

Cultures Change

We need only think about the lives our grandfathers lived in their youth to be convinced that cultures do change. Of course, changes over so short a time may be relatively superficial—mainly changes in the array of machines and gadgets rather than in basic aspects of life. If one looks at gadgetry alone, the cultural change in half a century is enormous. Our recently acquired planes, rockets, computers, and bombs, our enormous array of domestic electrical devices and labor-saving mechanisms make a deep impression on anyone who grew up fetching water from a well, traveling by horseback, reading by kerosene lamps, or washing clothes on a flat rock in the creek.

With the advent of new machines, there must be new habits, attitudes, and values. But many scholars have observed that material culture changes more rapidly than does immaterial culture. How much change has there been, for example, in our attitudes toward women, the home, children, marriage, religion, and government? The invention of the hydrogen bomb without the concurrent invention of social and governmental machinery to control its use has led to the sobering observation that physics and death have a head start on social science and life. The explosion of the first atomic bomb on Hiroshima changed instantaneously the whole world of man, raising for the first time the stark question of man's ability to prevent his own obliteration from the face of the earth. How much change—progress—has there been since Hiroshima in man's ability to live amicably with himself?

But there are perceptible changes over time in the nonmaterial aspects of culture. Since 1900, for example, there has been very appreciable change in what is allowed, and expected of, the American woman. And, conversely, of the American male. How many American fathers changed how many diapers in 1900 as compared with today? How many American fathers in 1900, as compared with today, fed infants? With the invention and perfection of bottle feeding—with the bottle, by its nature, an extension of the hand rather than of the breast—men became as competent and as eligible as women for baby feeding. And, for varied reasons, many men became willing to share in the chores and responsibilities of child rearing. Women, meanwhile, have moved more frequently out of the traditional feminine role into factories, offices, professions, and politics. Grandfather, or anyone with grandfather's slant on things, may still cling to the belief that woman's place is in the home, preferably pregnant and barefooted, and may have great difficulty in reconciling himself gracefully to the trend toward mutual responsibility of the sexes. But grandfathers are in the minority.

Effect of American Culture on the Individual

All right. We have seen that cultures differ. And we have seen that any one culture changes over a period of time. We know that the particular individual we are considering was born and raised in America. What does this mean? What do we know about our individual when we know he is an American?

At one level we know immediately certain things about him. We know that he probably speaks English, that he probably has had at least a few years of public education, that he probably can read and write. We know that he generally wears clothes rather than a breechclout, and we can make some good guesses about the kinds of clothes he wears. We know that he probably has a familiarity with automobiles, airplanes, refrigerators, radios, and central heating. He probably has heard of the New York Yankees, Notre Dame football, Lyndon Johnson, and Elizabeth Taylor.

But what about deeper aspects? What about personality and character? We strongly suspect that most Americans, in their psychological characteristics, are quite different from the Tchambuli or Mundugumor. What is the American character, if there is any such thing?

We know that there is great cultural variation in America. Texans are not quite the same as Vermonters, and Virginians differ from North Carolinians. A man of Polish descent may have more in common with his cousin in Warsaw than with his neighbor in Detroit. But can we ignore these differences, back off to a distance, and see the general characteristics of the American culture or the "American national character"? Some social scientists think so, and they have tried it. David Riesman (1955) has described the American tendency toward "other-directedness," seeing a decline in our time of the self-determined individuality of the "inner-directed" man and an increase in our tendency to direct our lives by what others are doing and by what others expect of us. F. S. C. Northrop (1946), a philosopher, has observed the flavor given to the American culture by Thomas Jefferson's acceptance and translation of the individualistic philosophies of Locke and Hume. Wolfenstein (1951) has noted our "fun morality"—a morality that makes it almost as obligatory to have fun as to do something useful. Charles Morris (1956), another philosopher, has seen the American way of life as Promethean, with touches of the

Christian and the Apollonian. The Promethean way of life emphasizes the conquest and organization of the environment through science and technology. The Christian way of life puts value on the purifying of self for spiritual values, while the Apollonian seeks the conservation of traditional values.

Many other writers (De Tocqueville, 1956; Gorer, 1948; Commager, 1947; Bryce, 1908; Laski, 1948; Veblen, 1945) have tried to cast into words the character of American culture. In some ways the most satisfactory and most complete job was done by Robin Williams, Jr. (1951), when he set down the following list of "major value orientations" in America:

1. A stress on achievement and success.
2. A stress on activity and work.
3. A tendency to view the world in moral terms.
4. Humanitarianism.
5. A stress on efficiency and practicality.
6. A belief in progress.
7. A valuing of material comfort.
8. An avowal and (to an extent) the practice of equality.
9. An avowal and (to an extent) the practice of freedom.
10. An emphasis on external conformity.
11. A belief in science and in secular rationality.
12. A stress on nationalism and patriotism.
13. A stress on democracy.
14. A belief in the value and the dignity of the individual personality.
15. A belief in racism and in group superiority.

If we accept Williams' list as valid, then we will guess that our particular individual is likely to possess these value orientations. He is likely to strive for success, to be moral, to be humanitarian, efficient, practical, fond of material comfort, nationalistic, and so on. Or at least he will probably support, believe in, defend all these things as good.

But even if we were sure that these are the true American traits, we could not apply this knowledge to a description or explanation of any single person. There is a great range of individuality within a culture. Group differs from group. Subculture differs from subculture. Greenwich Village bohemians are not like the Boston Brahmins. Ranchers are not like bankers. Individuals, within groups and within subcultures, differ from one another. No two men share precisely the same history.

We have seen some of the characteristics that are common to all organisms, some that are common to most human beings, some that may be common to many Americans. But we do not yet have the knowledge enabling us either to describe intimately or to account for this particular individual under consideration.

RECAPITULATION

We started this chapter with the stated intent of trying to see what psychology is. Where are we now? Everybody knows that psychology deals with human beings. So far we have been dealing mostly with human beings. Have we been dealing with psychology?

We have dealt some with *biology*. We looked at the general characteristics of organisms—characteristics that hold for every human being. To say it differently, we put our individual in a biological category and imputed to it the characteristics common to all others in that category. By this exercise we learned that a living organism is irritable, performs physiological functions, and has ancestors, the capacity for growth, and a homeostatic relation to its environment.

Then we placed our organism in the human category and searched a bit for the unique attributes of humanness: the possession of language, the capacity to reason, and the possession of a culture richly fashioned and structured before his time.

When we put our human into a cultural setting, we were dealing with *anthropology— cultural anthropology*. We know that our organism, humanly equipped with language and the capacity to reason, tends to have characteristics in common with those who share his culture. He handles his physiological processes, his growth, his irritabilities, and his homeostasis one way in one culture, in other ways in other cultures. When we place him in the cultural category "American," we can make some pretty shrewd guesses about many aspects of his behavior. But we still are dealing with very broad categories. All we have learned is true of our particular human being, but we still cannot describe the particular individual we are dealing with. We might continue our present procedure almost indefinitely by placing our individual in additional biological and sociological categories. We might say that he is male, white, 18 years old, of German descent, of the lower middle class, Protestant, and the son of specified parents. Each new categorization brings additional knowledge. But we still do not know how our particular individual employs his human capacities in his attempt to achieve organismic survival in a particular cultural setting. So we clearly cannot say how he became what he is, nor can we predict what he will do the next minute or tomorrow or next year. In other words, we have little real knowledge about him as a person. And we have learned almost nothing about the *processes whereby he got to be the sort of person he is.*

We do not know whether he is friendly or hostile, optimistic or pessimistic, bright or dull, aggressive or passive, neurotic or well adjusted, athletic or scholarly, ambitious or lazy, tenacious or easily discouraged, quiet and introverted or as outgoing as a trumpet. We do not know his motives, his interests, his values, his goals, his aspirations. And we do not know *how* he became the kind of person he is, or *why* he will probably behave in a certain way tomorrow. He remains an integer, an abstraction, a mystery. *We have not dealt with his psychological attributes. And we have not dealt with the psychological processes involved in his development or in his present behavior in his present environment.* We have missed something—something very crucial for our describing and understanding of a human being.

THE PSYCHOLOGICAL PROCESS

Since the day he was conceived, things have been happening to our individual. And he has been happening to things. He has been caught up, day and night, month by month in a process of interaction with his environment—a dynamic, flowing, evolving process extending from conception to death. He experiences his world and responds to what he experiences. He changes from day to day and from year to year—changes in ways that enable him better to contend with the physical and human environment around him.

This process is similar, in some respects, for all organisms. But human organisms pursue it beyond the capacity of lower forms of life. For all human organisms the process is similar, but Americans go about it in a way the Tchambuli would regard as very strange. And white, middle-class, Protestant Americans pursue it in ways different from other American groups. For any child, the process is structured by his own heredity and by the behavior of his parents toward him. But two children of the same parents may be quite different in the ways they experience the world and respond to it. We will not fully understand our individual unless we can understand the *processes* involved in his interaction with his environment. And that is what psychology is about.

PSYCHOLOGICAL PROCESS AND DEVELOPMENT

Psychology, as science, is concerned primarily with *general* processes—with the understanding of the processes whereby living organisms interact with their environments; the processes involved in the complex transformation of a helpless, largely formless infant into a mature and functioning adult; and the processes whereby the adult, a product of his psychological history, lives from one day to another.

We have dealt in very general terms with the psychological process. Now let us look at it more closely. Psychologists view the process as one in which

A restless (motivated) organism
Senses the world around him,
Interprets it,
Responds to it, and

Responds to the results of his
own response.

Perhaps the clearest and purest example of this process is that of a restlessly hungry infant who, in his random thrashing, comes in contact with a breast, starts sucking, and experiences a relief of hunger. In the early days and weeks of life, this process is vague and undifferentiated. The infant is so helpless that the mother must take charge of almost all phases of the process. She responds to the infant more than the infant responds to her. The baby's hunger is real and urgent. But his sensing of the world is blurred and fuzzy. He has little experience to use in his interpretation of the world. All breasts look alike, and probably like nothing much. He will suck at anything suckable. But once he experiences a satisfaction of his hunger, something has happened to him, something permanent. He is never the same again, for he has lived through a bit of his own history; he has begun to make connections between his inner restlessness, his behavior, and his world. The evolving, flowing, interweaving process of living has started.

Later—by the age of 3, say—when the child has already accumulated a past, this past, combined with the development of his body and his nervous system, has brought about vast changes in the process of living. Now, when he is hungry, he is not just vaguely hungry for something in general. He is hungry for something specific. His experience with his world has led him to be hungry for a cookie, or maybe a peanut-butter cookie. His world is now much clearer and richer to him, for his sensory mechanisms have ripened and he has had several years' experience in living. He can now sense his way to the kitchen and interpret his way to the red box containing precisely what he wants. The process now is well along. There still is in it the element of restlessness, of want, of need, of motive. There is a sensing or registering of the world. There is an interpretation of things, a perceiving of objects and of people. There is response. And there is response to response—a registering and interpreting of the results of what he does. All of these subprocesses are involved in the basic process of living. But during any sequence of behavior, the influence of the past can be seen.

His restlessnesses have been altered by experience—by learning. Restlessnesses do change. Hunger changes from an amorphous discomfort to a yen for olives or pheasant under glass or raw fish. And hunger becomes entwined with other restlessnesses, so that there is not mere hunger, nor an appetite for a favorite dish, but a seeking out of a certain prestigeful restaurant and of certain company with which to dine.

His sensing of the world has also changed. The basic processes of registering the world have not altered essentially, but he has become *selective* about what he sees and hears and feels and smells, and his interpretation of his world has changed mightily on the basis of his experience. If he is an Arab, for example, his world contains perhaps twenty-seven different kinds of camels. If he is an American, all camels, and perhaps dromedaries, too, will look alike to him—but he will recognize a dozen-odd varieties of automobiles which would seem bewilderingly similar to the Arab.

His responses, too, have changed marvelously. He has learned, through practice, many skills, many highly developed sequences of behavior occurring as interwoven parts of the ongoing process. And he has learned language. He has learned to put the world into words. He has learned to put words to his own experiences of the world, and he has learned about the experiences of other speaking organisms in other times and other places. And he reasons. And he solves problems.

THE CONTENT OF PSYCHOLOGY

Psychology deals with all phases of the psychological process. In subsequent chapters we will study the development—the biological development—of the individual and look at the ways in which the process is affected by the physical and biological maturity of the organism. We will deal with restlessnesses, with the motives of men, and with the emotions that are interconnected with motives. We will deal with the processes whereby the organism senses the world, the ways in which he translates into experience events outside his skin. We will deal with perception (or the interpretation of what the senses bring into the organism), with responses, and with the ways in which new responses are affected by responses to previous responses. We will deal with language and thought as they interweave with all phases of the process.

In addition, we will look at the results of the psychological process—at the differences among individuals who for some years have lived in and through the process. Relatedly we look at personality, at the characteristic ways the whole organized process now functions for the individual. And because the process in one individual is drastically affected by other people, we study social behavior, seeing the process in a social setting.

HISTORICAL APPROACHES
TO THE PSYCHOLOGICAL PROCESS

In the next chapter, we will talk about the way the "man in the street" views the psychological process, and we will compare that view with the approach of the psychologist. Before getting into that discussion, however, let us look first at the way the process has been viewed in the past—psychology does have a history—and by various modern psychologists.

Structuralism

In 1879 a professor of philosophy at the University of Leipzig established a small laboratory for the purpose of preparing demonstrations on sensation, to help illustrate his lectures. That development has come to be regarded as the founding of the first psychological laboratory, and that date has been widely accepted as the birthday of scientific psychology (Miller, 1962). The professor, Wilhelm Wundt, is regarded as a —if not *the*— founder of the new discipline. But that historic date and that founder both had a history.

As early as 1862, seventeen years before he had his little laboratory at Leipzig, Wundt stated that there could be a science of mind and, furthermore, that he fully intended to build one. The work done in Wundt's laboratory, and by his students there and elsewhere for the next half century, has been described as structuralism, the attempt to study the structure of mind. The structuralists analyzed the elements of consciousness, studied the ways in which these elements are connected, and attempted to state the laws of connection.

Now, in looking backward, we can make a case for the inevitability of Wundt. He almost had to happen. John Locke, a century and a half before, in 1690, had published *An Essay Concerning Human Understanding*, in which he told the world that experience and observation (sensation) lie at the root of all knowledge. This emphasis on sensing, which came to be known as British empiricism, led to philosophical associationism, an attempt to deal with the *elements* of mind (ideas) and with the laws governing the association of ideas. Thus, one of Wundt's historical roots goes back to the British empiricists and associationists. Another runs back to positivism as formulated in the mid-nineteenth century by the French philosopher Auguste Comte (1798–1857). In his *positive philosophy,* Comte took the position that every aspect of man's life can profitably be studied through the application of the scientific approach. Comte, incidentally, is often regarded as the father of social psychology (Allport, 1954) because of his stated belief that social phenomena, like all other human phenomena, can be approached scientifically. Accompanying these philosophical movements in Wundt's historical background was a third development, a scientific one. Wundt, trained in medicine, served for a time as an assistant at Heidelberg to the great physiologist Hermann von Helmholtz. And he knew about the work of Gustav Fechner, a former physicist, who as early as 1850 was working out his own ideas about the relations of sensations to changes in physical stimuli (see pp. 313–315).

All these influences were there in the mind of Wundt (Boring, 1929; Miller, 1962). But it was uniquely Wundt who deliberately set about pursuing the explicitly stated goal of creating an experimental science of psychol-

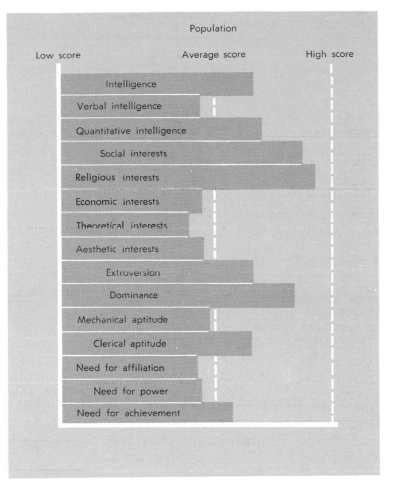

Population

Low score   Average score   High score

Intelligence
Verbal intelligence
Quantitative intelligence
Social interests
Religious interests
Economic interests
Theoretical interests
Aesthetic interests
Extroversion
Dominance
Mechanical aptitude
Clerical aptitude
Need for affiliation
Need for power
Need for achievement

Figure 1–5. PSYCHOLOGICAL CHARACTERIZATION
—A PSYCHOGRAPH. *Psychological tests describe
the individual and show how he differs from
others in the same social categories. Long
bars here indicate high scores. When we
engage in psychological characterization, we
are describing the outcomes of the psychological processes as represented in the present
characteristics of the human system.*

ogy. This aspiration he set down for himself
in his 1862 book, *Contributions to the Theory
of Sensory Perceptions*, and reiterated it in
1874 in the first of many editions of his famous
Physiological Psychology. A number of the
British and American students who went to
Leipzig to study with Wundt carried the
Wundtian structuralism away with them. One
of these students, E. B. Titchener, a native of
Britain, later came to the United States and for

many years headed the psychological laboratory at Cornell University.

Structuralism, then, was the first "school" of
scientific psychology. The prime method of
Wundt and his students and successors was
that of *introspection*—of observing mind from
within. By the introspective procedure, which
is still employed in a number of fields of modern psychological research, the experimenter
exposes the subject to a physical stimulus or
to an array of stimuli; the subject analyzes very
meticulously the state of his awareness and reports to the experimenter the results of that
analysis.

The Functional Approach

Structural psychology never really caught on
in America. At the time Wundt's books and
students were crossing the ocean, the most influential American philosophers, William James

and John Dewey, were caught up in values and ideas that rendered them unenthusiastic about the structuralists' ideas and concerns. James, for instance, after studying reports of the painstaking experimental work going on in Wundt's laboratory, made the observation that such a science could not have been invented in a country whose citizens could possibly be bored. And in responding to what he thought was the lack of incisiveness and organization in Wundt's theoretical system, qualities making the system very difficult to attack or destroy, James remarked: "Cut him up like a worm and each fragment crawls." For more details about James, see the biographical excerpt at the end of this chapter.

James and Dewey, under the influence of C. S. Peirce, the founder of American **pragmatism,** were more interested in how mind functions than in how mind is structured. *Philosophical pragmatism* represented an approach to the meaning of truth, an emphasis on the practical or pragmatic consequences of stating a definition or of entertaining belief. This philosophical pragmatism, in the hands of James and Dewey, became psychological **functionalism,** in which there is an emphasis on how things work, and on the experimental approach to all kinds of practical questions.

The functionalists, instead of studying the mental structure of fully formed human minds, studied such things as the behavior of animals in puzzle boxes, the mental functioning of normal and retarded children, and problems involved in the measurement of intelligence. One can see how such a functional, "practical" kind of psychology might find in America a compatible soil. One writer observes: "By the time of Wundt's death in 1920 the purely introspective, experimental science he had founded in Leipzig was merely a small part of, and had been overshadowed by, the larger and more pragmatic American science of psychology. Ten years later the victory of the functional psychologists was complete. In the U. S. today functional psychology *is* psychology" (Miller, 1962, p. 66).

Behaviorism and Gestalt Psychology

Both the structuralists and the functionalists took explicit positions concerning the proper subject matter of psychology. Two other "schools" of psychology, although each tended to emphasize certain areas of investigation, were characterized primarily by their divergent stands concerning the proper way to study whatever it is that psychology studies.

Behaviorism, an approach coming into view early in the twentieth century and associated initially with the name of J. B. Watson, grew naturally out of American functionalism. Where functionalism de-emphasized mind as the focal subject of psychology, Watson went one step further and recommended that mind be eliminated entirely from the concern of the scientist. Psychology, he contended, should confine itself to what can be seen, to observation of stimuli and of the observable behaviors associated with the stimuli. If anyone wishes to study sensation, let him avoid the befuddling and picayune procedures of introspection and observe instead what kinds of discriminating responses the subject, animal or human, can and does make.

Today much of American psychology is both functional and behavioristic. Although psychologists do not abjure, not as much at any rate as Watson would like, the making of inferences about mental processes that may intervene between stimulus and response, there is a widespread tendency to accept the position that behavioral data are the basic data of science.

Gestalt psychology, a "school" originating in Germany early in the twentieth century and imported into the United States in the thirties, commends a certain approach to the study of both mind and behavior. And the commended approach emphasizes the organization, patterning, and wholenesses in nature; it opposes what it considers the atomistic, strained, artificial analysis of mind and behavior into tiny unnatural elements.

The Gestalt psychologists—and the leading names here are those of Max Wertheimer, Wolfgang Köhler, Kurt Koffka, and Kurt

Lewin—have had their greatest influence in the fields of perception and higher mental processes. For instance, in emphasizing that natural wholes must be dealt with as wholes rather than broken down into atomistic elements, they point out that when we hear a melody in one key and then in another we still recognize the melody in spite of the fact that the separate sensations of pitch all change. There is a pattern, a Gestalt, there; and these natural patterns, in perception, in problem solving, in behavior, should not be insulted by strained and profitless reduction to artificial elements.

Both behaviorism and Gestalt psychology have had marked influence on American psychology. Perhaps it is accurate to say that both movements died of success, for there are no longer to be found any violently partisan "schools." Psychologists still differ decidedly in their interests, in their preferred approaches and methods, and in their ideas about the best ways to think about behavior and the most profitable ways to conduct research upon it. Psychology can now be accurately described as a *behavioral science;* perhaps that is the accomplishment of the behaviorists. But psychology is a behavioral science that is still interested in understanding the processes that occur between stimulus and response, and it remains hospitable to Gestalt ideas when these are supported by evidence.

Freud and Psychoanalysis

Another mighty intellectual stream that has influenced modern psychology sprang up in Europe at about the same time that structuralism was in flower there and functionalism was coming into its own in the United States. That was the stream of psychoanalytic thought, with Sigmund Freud as its first and most influential formulator and spokesman. But as with other "firsts" in history, Freud too had historical ties to major intellectual trends occurring before his time. He was committed to the views, advanced in the 1850s by Comte, that science can be brought to bear on human affairs and that human behavior makes sense

—that cause-and-effect relationships maintain in human life. He also was an admirer of Helmholtz, the physiologist. And, as a physician and neurologist, he became interested in the peculiar symptoms of individuals who would now be described as emotionally disturbed or mentally ill. In 1895 he and a colleague, Breuer, wrote a book, *Studies on Hysteria,* in which they attempted to show that the very peculiar behavior of disturbed people was subject to cause-and-effect relationships. From this beginning, Freud went on to create an elaborate theory of the organization of personality, a theory that has had enormous influence in the Western world on the presently prevailing view of man and his nature. Freud also invented the technique, as separate from the theory, of **psychoanalysis;** this is a technique widely employed today in the treatment of mentally disturbed people.

The psychoanalytic stream of theory, though it has been subjected to many attempts at revision, is still very much alive today and, both in history and in the present, is the most highly visible attempt to deal with the whole individual as an organized system interacting with its environment. We can refer, then, to the psychoanalytic influence in psychology as the *holistic* influence. It was also the first *dynamic* psychology, in that it conceived of human life not in terms of the relatively static structures of mind, but in terms of strong forces, often primitive, animalistic, and unconscious, that were involved in the adjusting of the individual. We also can regard psychoanalysis as a way of thought that attempted for better or worse to see whole, and from a scientific perspective, the nature of human nature.

Modern Approaches to Psychological Processes

In viewing the psychological process, we have already tended to break it down into segments—into motivation, sensation, perception, learning, etc. It is almost inevitable that we do this, for the scope and complexity of the process make it presently very difficult

Figure 1–6. THE FIRST PSYCHOANALYTIC THEORIST. *Sigmund Freud, 1856–1939.*

to conceive of it as a unitary phenomenon and to talk about all of it at once.

In the chapters that follow, we will likewise need to follow the segmental approach in order to come to grips with the problems, facts, concepts, and theories that fascinate psychologists. But we need to bear in mind that any segmentation is probably an insult to nature. Everything is related to everything. To study learning, for example, as if it were not intimately connected with motivation and perception would be like studying a carburetor as if it were the only part of an automobile. While the study of the inner life of a carburetor may be a thoroughly justifiable occupation, such a focus will not reveal much of the total organized process that makes a car go.

Present-day segmentation. Today nobody very seriously holds forth that any one seg-

ment of the psychological process is *the* segment. Today we have specialists rather than school men. One psychologist may devote his entire scientific career to the study of the inner ear. Another studies learning, and another the relation between behavior and processes in the brain. Though any given psychologist may believe that his own line of research is the one most likely to advance the science, few will espouse the proposition that the study of segments is the study of the total process, and few will hold that one approach or one method is the only true one.

Holistic approaches. We pointed out earlier that no one has found a way to talk, in simple and inclusive terms, about the whole psychological process. There are no general laws bearing grandly and simply on the process in its entirety. A number of theorists, in addition to Freud and other psychoanalytically oriented writers, have attempted to deal with the organism or the person as a whole.

The **holistic psychologists** are those who study personality, and most personality psychologists assume that the personality exists as an organized whole, as a single system—a system separated from its environment; a system composed of interrelated elements or systems; a system that—as a *whole* system—interacts with its environment (N. Sanford, 1963). Whether or not we think of systems and subsystems in dealing with the interaction of the organism with its environment, it will often be useful to keep in mind a distinction between "process psychologists" and "organism psychologists." Although the same individual psychologist may sometimes study processes and at other times devote himself to observations of the person or the whole organism, it is generally true that students of processes and students of organisms are quite different people with differently constituted curiosities.

Physiological and neurological vs. a psychological approach. If we choose, we can view the psychological process in neurological and physiological terms. Every time the organism senses the world, interprets it, responds to it, and feels a satisfaction or dissatisfaction with the results of its response, its body and its nervous system are involved. Its motives may be conceived as physiological imbalances. And every experience, every act, is mediated by neurological events in the brain and in the nervous system.

Much psychological research, some of which we will examine later, is directed at the discovery of the relation between experience and behavior on one hand, and underlying physiological or neurological processes on the other. A study of these underlying processes may eventually yield a science of behavior. At the moment, most psychologists study behavior itself, rather than processes underlying it. The psychological approach is one that seeks to find lawful relations between stimulus and response, between behavior and behavior, between past events and present behavioral consequences. The present book will be, in this sense, a psychological book. But where there are neurological and physiological data relevant for psychological phenomena, these will be dealt with.

SUMMARY

1. In his attempt to understand the mystery of himself, man has followed many roads to knowledge and belief. Psychology represents one of these roads, only recently traveled. Down this road there is the promise of a systematic scientific knowledge of human behavior.

2. We can come to intellectual grips with the nature of psychology by accepting the dual challenge of (a) describing completely and (b) accounting for or explaining a single individual.

3. We know first that this individual is an organism. Because it is an organism we know that it is composed of protoplasm, that it performs certain physiological functions, that it is irritable, that it has ancestors, that it grows, that it operates according to the principle of

homeostasis, and that it is an organized system.

4. When we know we are dealing with a human organism, we can ascribe to it the attributes that are common to all members of the human species. The most significant of these for our purposes are (a) the capacity to use language, (b) the capacity to reason, and (c) the capacity to accumulate both a material and an immaterial culture. As we go deeper into psychology we will come upon more detailed exposure to the attributes of the human organism.

5. When we learn that our human organism is an American, we take a large step toward knowing him, for a man is known by the culture he espouses. Knowing the traits of the American culture, however, even if that were really possible, would not tell us about the characteristics of any particular American. Americans differ from Americans.

6. We come closer to a knowledge of an individual by learning that he belongs to certain biological and sociological groups.

7. All our biological, sociological, and anthropological information leaves us yet a long way from a description of this particular person. We are an even greater distance from the sort of understanding that will let us say how he came to be the person he is, while his brother and his friend are so different. Nor can we predict with any certainty at all whether tomorrow he will be stupid or intelligent, ambitious or lazy, interested in medicine or plumbing, a liberal or conservative, sane or psychotic.

8. If we are going to deal with the behavioral characteristics of our individual and if we are going to predict him, we need to go beyond the facts of biology, genetics, anthropology, and sociology. We need to understand the psychological process, the process of interaction with the environment, the process that begins at conception, rooted in heredity, and continues ceaselessly until death.

9. We need to understand the organismic restlessness with which life begins. We need

to understand how the irritable organism senses and interprets the world, how it responds to it, how it registers the satisfaction or dissatisfaction following upon a response. We need to know how its behavior changes over time, so that through living it comes to live differently.

10. Psychology can be defined as the study of this lifelong process, as a search for the laws and regularities that appear in the individual's interaction with the world about him.

11. In the past, psychologists have taken various views of the psychological process. The structuralists dealt with sensation and consciousness. Behaviorists dealt almost exclusively with response. Gestalt psychologists specialized in perception. The functionalists, more than the others, emphasized the necessity of looking at the whole process, viewing it as a process of adjustment. The psychoanalysts, beginning with Freud, also concerned themselves with general adjustment and with aspects of the whole psychological system, but with a special focus on emotional difficulties.

12. Modern psychologists tend to specialize in one or more segments of the psychological process but are generally aware of the segmental nature of their problems. And today's psychologists tend to work at the psychological rather than the physiological or neurological level of analysis.

SUPPLEMENTARY READING

WILLIAM JAMES
AND AMERICAN PSYCHOLOGY *

William James . . . the frontiersman of American psychology . . . wrote like a novelist, lectured like a witty after-dinner speaker, conversed like a Bohemian cafe-sitter, and lived like a civilized man. James was far removed from the

---

* Abridged from John K. Winkler and Walter Bromberg, "A Psychological Prima Donna" in *Mind Explorers,* Chap. 8, pp. 146–183. Copyright, 1939, by Harcourt, Brace & World, Inc., and reprinted with their permission.

queer, one-sided laboratory scientist, the naive experimenter with his head in a test tube and his feet in unpolished boots. He was a man who sparkled, yet still ran deep. A man who could live and write psychology as he did could easily capture the hearts of his countrymen—and guide them painlessly into the maze of psychology and its problems. . . .

Opportunity [for James] came in the form of the Thayer expedition. Louis Agassiz was planning a trip to Brazil for the purpose of collecting zoological specimens. James saw him at once. Could he come along? "Well, yes, but what we need is zoologists." "But let me go as the party philosopher!" They set sail for Brazil in April 1865. More experience, more human contacts, a serious illness in Rio de Janeiro, and a chance to think and learn.

With Agassiz was Bishop Alonzo Potter and his third wife. The spirit of this scientific company was predominantly religious. Sunday sermons were the regular order of life aboard ship. James listened to everything. "I heard," he wrote, "the Bish. tell them that they must try to imitate the simple child-like devotion of our great leader. They must give up pet theories of transmutation, spontaneous generation, etc., and seek in nature what God put there rather than derive systems of human imagination." Long discussions of science and religion were the order of the day. James was a little amused when he saw Agassiz, the impeccable scientific observer, weep at the conscience-rending conflict. Agassiz, who loved concrete fact, joined the Bishop in defending the Church against the advance of evolution and materialism; and James himself was striving for harmony with the intellectual world with which the Bishop was at odds. Traditional religion could not make peace with science. Man could not become indifferent to his ultimate destiny; he could not deny the intelligence of God, even if he could accept the biology of Darwin. The human mind, if it was simply a mechanism, had to be in tune with a divine universal scheme of reality. . . . This conflict between religious principles and science must have sunk deeply into James' consciousness. . . .

In the depths of Brazil, when Agassiz was busily classifying snakes, William observed the abundance of resources spread out to meet the simple needs of a simple people. The intricate social order from which he derived sprang to his mind in contrast. "The idea," he wrote to his mother, "of people swarming about as they do at home, killing themselves with thinking about things that have no connection with their merely external circumstances, studying themselves into fevers, going mad about religion, philosophy and such, seems almost incredible to me." These speculations did not lead to any solution; James returned to his feverish world in the same dilemma as when he had left it. His tie with religion was too strong to be broken by the tuggings of a distraught youthful mind. The materialistic philosophy of the evolutionist Herbert Spencer, in which he steeped himself, was hardly more satisfying than the opiate of religion. . . .

Now James became an active psychological writer and controversialist. It was his intention to ally psychology with physiology and neurology, having read and admired Charcot's and Janet's handling of hysterical cases. But James was constitutionally unable to bring about the marriage of his own philosophical deductions to cold laboratory and clinical work. He had too little actual knowledge of experimental work in the first place, and, in the second place, he had nothing but dislike for laboratory work. James's bias was more on the side of the British introspectionists. But monism, the explanation of things physical and mental by *one* principle, annoyed him; it was vague. He wanted psychology to get close to life. The philosophy of Spencer was a feeble monster alongside James's army of the "data of life."

As for the name of his doctrine, James was little concerned. Later it was to be the philosophy of pragmatism. "Pragmatism," explained a commentator on James, "is not a philosophy, but only a working theory, an attitude of utility, a method rather than a system." James himself said truth was only the expedient in our way of thinking, just as right as the expedient in our way of behaving. For the present he *felt* his new pragmatic philosophy, and gloried in being able finally to work.

James's thinking was becoming clearer and bolder, and his friend Charles Peirce, a brilliant mathematical mind, gave him courage to think. It was Peirce who had observed the practical aspect of the experimenter's attitude toward observed phenomena. He explained how a scientist's acceptance of a workable hypothesis could change the course of scientific thought. James drew heavily on Peirce's concept and made it the basis of his definition of truth, which he said means agreement with reality. This was where James ruffled the tempers of philosophers who labored with their God, the idea of "Absolute Truth." James swept it all aside. Truth was determined by *practical consequences.* That was the

essence of Pragmatism, James's most enduring contribution to philosophy.

A workable philosophy, a charming wife, a busy, happy life—James had left behind forever the slough of despair through which he had passed. Academic circles outside of Cambridge began to hear of James. *Mind,* an English journal, published his papers, and in 1878 he contracted with Henry Holt for a textbook on psychology to be delivered in two years. It was 1890, however, before *The Principles of Psychology* saw the printing presses. Writing this work proved to be a laborious and torturing process for James, but the two volumes established the work as a classic. The material was vivid and real; his principles of psychology were helpful in everyday life; the writing was literature. People were astounded at his clarity. Psychology had never been like this. When a reader asked for the James book, a witty librarian countered, "Do you mean the psychologist who writes novels or the novelist who writes psychology?" The professional psychologists weren't so sure about James's work. Stanley Hall of Clark University was contemptuous because there was nothing in the books about genetic psychology. Lincoln Steffens the journalist, then a student with Professor Wundt in Leipzig, brought the volumes to the German dean of experimentalists. Wundt read them at one sitting and brought them back to the laboratory with a grave air. Steffens looked at him quickly: "How did you like it?" Thoughtfully the Professor replied: "It is literature, it is beautiful, but it is not psychology."

James returned the compliment. He had little patience with experiment or experimentalists. They didn't understand a real "mental" psychology. He scoffed at their method of studying isolated bits of mental life. This "microscopic psychology" was leading the younger men astray, taking them away from the heart of the subject. "The simple and open method of attack having done what it can, the method of patience, starving out, and harassing to death, is tried; the Mind must submit to a regular siege . . . There is little of the grand style about these new prism, pendulum, and chronograph-philosophers. They mean business, not chivalry." Mental life, full of thoughts, feelings, memories, habits, and mixed spiritual and corporeal experience, was beyond experiment.

James deplored the new complications which experimentalists were introducing into an already complicated subject. "This method taxes patience to the utmost and could hardly have arisen in a country whose natives could be *bored*. Such Germans as Weber, Fechner, and Wundt obviously cannot; and their success has brought into the field an array of younger experimental psychologists, bent on studying the *elements* of the mental life, dissecting them out from the gross results in which they are embedded, and as far as possible reducing them to quantitative scales." James could not restrain his indignation at this piecemeal psychology. Fechner, through laborious testing, had demonstrated what he called the *law of psychophysic*. This law states that when we increase the strength of a sensory stimulus, for example touch, the strength of the sensation we perceive increases as the logarithm of the exciting cause. Fechner's law became gospel for more than twenty years for German experimenters, who checked it in every conceivable way for every kind of sensation. To James, the outcome of all this work was "just nothing."

James's idea of the proper subject matter for psychological study was mental life as a whole— i.e., the stream of consciousness itself. But how to attack it? What does a nonexperimental psychologist do anyhow? Where does he work, what does he work with? Chiefly, the introspectionist thinks —he thinks while sitting, lying, walking, lecturing to classes, arguing with friends, listening to music. He has no set work time, but is at his desk for hours raptly reading articles and books that come pouring in. He reads experimental reports, surveys of work done, novels, and especially the writings of his own critics. His job is to test both new and old ideas found in scientific articles against his theories of how the mind works. Then he sets out to modify his own theories or refute another's. He examines his own stream of consciousness as it passes by, trying to plumb its depths first in himself, then in his colleagues, his wife, the janitor or his students. . . .

What did James ponder over? For one thing, he thought about whether there was an "unconscious" mind or not. Many psychologists discredited the idea, but James felt there were excellent reasons for assuming its presence. One proof could be seen in the learning of any skilled activity. When a person learns to drive a car he studies his every movement with care and anxiety. Soon the movements become automatic. What originally required full conscious attention is carried out on an unconscious level. A similar thing happens when the solution of a vexing question that we "sleep on" overnight is obvious in the morning. Everyone has had the surprising experience of suddenly mastering a complicated muscular movement, such as a dance routine, after a long rest following weeks of practice, when hard practice itself has been unavailing. Learning how to skate in the summer or how to swim over the winter involves apparently some muscular learning or coordination that goes on without our conscious attention to the process. When attention is diverted or an object once thought of is forgotten, some portion of our mental apparatus still continues its activity; it is this process that really is the "unconscious." Automatic decisions that we make by the thousand daily are made with a part of our deciding apparatus other than the conscious *attending* part. Our daily conduct, observed James, is in accordance with our total mind-drift, which is never clearly before us. . . .

Others wanted to know truth for its own sake, but James, utilizing his old friend Pierce's idea that truth must be tested by investigation, asked other questions. A religious precept, a philosophical concept, a moral preachment, had to be looked at in this way: "What sensible difference to anybody will its truth make? How will truth be realized? What experiences will be different from those which would obtain if the belief were false? What, in short, is the truth's cash value in experimental terms?" Why talk of "absolute" truths or ideas in a world that is always changing and striving? This in a nutshell is the philosophy of pragmatism.

SUGGESTED READINGS

Berelson, Bernard, ed. *The behavioral sciences today.* New York: Basic Books, 1963.

Boring, E. G. *A history of experimental psychology*, 2nd ed. New York: Appleton-Century-Crofts, 1950 (1929).

—————. *Psychologist at large, an autobiography and selected essays of a distinguished psychologist.* New York: Basic Books, 1961.

Freud, Sigmund. *A general introduction to psycho-analysis.* New York: Boni and Liveright, 1920 (reprinted by Washington Square Press, 1960).

Marx, M. H., and W. A. Hillix. *Systems and theories in psychology.* New York: McGraw-Hill, 1963.

Miller, George A. *Psychology: The science of mental life.* New York: Harper and Row, 1962.

Postman, L. J., ed. *Psychology in the making: Histories of selected research problems.* New York: Knopf, 1962.

Sanford, F. H., and E. J. Capaldi, eds. *Advancing psychological science. Vol. I: Philosophies, methods, and approaches.* Belmont, Calif.: Wadsworth, 1964.

Winkler, J. K., and Walter Bromberg. *Mind explorers.* New York: Reynal and Hitchcock, 1939.

OUTLINE / CHAPTER 2

I. EVERYMAN'S PSYCHOLOGY

   A. Need for a Theory of People

   B. Sources of the Theories We Live By
     1. We Learn from Our Culture
     2. We Learn through Experiments
     3. Our Theories Differ
     4. Our Theories Make a Difference

II. EVERYMAN'S PSYCHOLOGY AND THE PSYCHOLOGIST'S PSYCHOLOGY

   A. Evaluation vs. Objectivity

   B. Casual vs. Controlled Observation
     1. Observations in Daily Life
     2. The Scientist's Controlled Observations
       a. Naturalistic observation
       b. Clinical observation
       c. Survey observation
       d. The experimental method

   C. Casual vs. Sophisticated Use of Language
     1. Language of Fact and Language of Opinion
     2. Language of Fact and Language of Constructs
     3. Rules for the Use of Constructs
       a. Naturalistic constructs
       b. The law of parsimony
       c. Operational definitions
     4. Facts and Constructs in Use
     5. The Body of Constructs of a Science

   D. Prediction and Process
     1. Molar and Molecular Approaches
     2. Psychology and the Understanding of Processes

   E. The Implicit-Explicit Dimension
     1. Private Meanings
     2. Personal Perceptions
     3. Unconscious Meanings

   F. The Dimension of Precision

   G. Finality-Tentativeness

III. WHY STUDY PSYCHOLOGY?

   A. Psychology as Liberal Education

   B. Careers in Psychology

   C. Psychology and Everyday Decisions

IV. SUMMARY

V. RESEARCH REPORTS

CHAPTER 2

THEORIES OF PEOPLE

In Chapter 1 we dealt with man's age-old problem of knowing himself, and we tried to sketch out a general view of what psychology, as science, conceives that problem to be. We ended with a description of the psychological process and with a discussion of some of the ways in which that process can be viewed. The task psychologists have chosen for themselves is the scientific understanding of that process. Through the use of a wide variety of methods, approaches, stances, and slants, psychologists seek to make meaningful statements about the ways in which the motivated organism senses the world, interprets it, responds to it, and changes.

Psychologists are not alone in seeking to understand the psychological process. Everybody joins this enterprise; for, in a world full of human behavior, none of us can survive or thrive without some understanding of that behavior, without some ability to predict what

people will do. In a way, then, every man is a psychologist—at least a part-time psychologist. And in his dealings with the psychological process, the part-time psychologist—the man in the street—has a kinship with the full-time psychologist.

There are some very real differences, however, between the layman's psychology and the psychologist's psychology. Though the science of psychology is closer to "common sense" than are many other scientific disciplines, there are times when the psychologist will depart so far from conventional ways of thinking about people that he appears to the layman to be talking gibberish in a strange world of his own.

In this chapter we will examine the psychologist's way of studying the psychological process and make some comparisons between his way and the layman's way. Such a comparison should render more meaningful and more rewarding the study of the psychologist's efforts to make scientific statements about the psychological process—efforts that may seem to the layman sometimes eminently sensible, sometimes strange, sometimes exciting, sometimes trivial.

EVERYMAN'S PSYCHOLOGY

NEED FOR A THEORY OF PEOPLE

Each of us needs to predict what people will do. People constitute so significant a part of the world in which we live that we probably could not tolerate life if they were constantly surprising us. We are so dependent, particularly when we are young, that we could not have any sense of safety at all—or lay any plans whatsoever—if we could not rely on the people around us to behave in certain ways at certain times. What would the 2-year-old baby do if he had not the knowledge that his mother would turn up at regular intervals with food? What would the adult do if, on a certain day, all his friends suddenly became enemies, all conservatives became liberals, all girls took up football and all boys knitting? And what would he do if he found himself behaving in ways totally unexpected?

Each of us, then, needs a "theory" [1] to help us predict what people will do. In our dealings with people around us, we learn those things that lead us to what one writer (Miller, 1958) has termed the "minimization of surprise."

---

[1] Those who are familiar with the varied use of the concept "theory" in scientific literature may be somewhat puzzled by the way the term is used here and throughout this chapter. It will be used to mean a more or less organized, a more or less explicit, a more or less inclusive view of human behavior—"a general point of view," "a general schema," or "a general frame of reference." Feigl (1951), a philosopher of science, has described as follows the use of the term "theory" in scientific circles: ". . . by a 'theory' in the empirical sciences we may mean anything from a style or jargon of mere description, from a mere classification, inventory or typology to a full-fledged hypothetico-deductive system; from a bold guess or a suggestive working hypothesis, a program of research, to an elaborate model in either analogical or purely abstract mathematical terms." It may be unfortunate to add to such confusion by using "theory" in yet another way, but convenience will be served thereby.

SOURCES OF THE THEORIES WE LIVE BY

We Learn from Our Culture

We talked in Chapter 1 about some of the prevailing notions on what it means to be a human being. We saw that some of these ideas or beliefs are grounded in scientific evidence and that others, if they are accepted, must be supported on other than scientific grounds. At any time in any culture there is a prevailing ideology of man—a prevailing pattern of beliefs widely shared by people. Each of us tends to accept these beliefs, making them a part of our own view of ourselves and of others. We saw in Chapter 1 some of the beliefs, some of the working theories, that many Americans share. And we saw also that such people as the Tchambuli have un-American theories about proper ways for men and women to behave.

Each of us, then, by virtue of having grown up in a certain culture, has been exposed to the prevailing ways that culture has evolved for thinking about man. Often, such exposure has meant adoption of the approved behaviors, for there are mighty forces that move us to take on the ways of our elders. The behaviors and views that have evolved over eleven or twelve years of childhood experience are no longer adequate for a world that now expects adult behavior. So, with our knowledge of human ways, we experiment, and through experiment—sometimes planned, sometimes happening when we are not ready—we learn about our own behavior and its consequences. We try behavior on like a garment, for size and fit, and experimentally watch the reactions of our parents or our peers. If we are girls, we experiment with lipstick and high heels and tones of voice and mannerisms and attitudes. If boys, we experiment with smoking and ways of handling cars and tones of voice, mannerisms, attitudes. Some experimental gambits pay off well. They are stamped in. Others are dropped as worthless.

One form of psychotherapy is based on the deliberate conduct of "experiments" with new and different ways of behaving (Kelly, 1955). In this therapeutic procedure a troubled stu-

Figure 2–1. EXPERIMENTATION. *Through experimenting with adult ways, the child learns a theory of correct, incorrect, rewarding, and unrewarding behavior.*

dent may be coached to act as if he were the "Abraham Lincoln type." In this acting, this experimenting, he may find new and rewarding ways of behaving that will become a lasting part of his personality, replacing behaviors that formerly caused him discomfort and trouble.

We Learn through Experiments [2]

Although we have taken uncritically unto ourselves much of the wisdom and nonwisdom

of the ages, we also learn from experience. Much of our learning from experience is essentially an *experimental* learning, a learning that approaches in form and quality the learning that scientists try to arrange for themselves.

One essence of an experiment is the yen to find out "what would happen if." Most of us, many times in life, have tried the experimental approach to human behavior and have learned from it. The young child, for example, experiments with parents when he "tests limits." His mother may say, "If you go out of the yard, I'll punish you." While the child probably does not say out loud to himself that he will now design and conduct an experiment, he does experimentally test reality by going out of the yard, perhaps just to see what will happen. The results of the experiment help him predict in the future whether his mother means what she says. Perhaps, through further experiments, he finds that his mother means what she says when she speaks in one tone of voice but that in other tones she is really not serious.

Our Theories Differ

Since each of us was born unique and has had his own particular experience with people, each of us will have his own particular theory of people. The individual theories found in the same culture or the same community or the same family can be expected to have a good deal of similarity, but within these similarities individuals differ widely. All of us learn, of course, that most people most of the time will stop at red lights, will drive on the right-hand side of the road, will have breakfast every morning, will at least act as

---

[2] As with the concept of theory, we are here using the term "experiment" in a way that will run somewhat counter to its habitual use in scientific articles. The definition here is: *An experiment is any attempt to manipulate some part of the world so that we can learn more about it.* By employing such a definition, we bring science and intelligent common sense close together. In so doing, we follow the thinking of Bridgman (1945) when he says: "The scientific method, as far as it is a method, is nothing more than doing one's damnedest with one's mind, no holds barred." And we are close to the stand of Warren Weaver (1955), who, in addressing a national scientific body, said: ". . . the impressive methods that science has developed . . . involve only improvement —great, to be sure—of procedures of observation and analysis that the human race has always used. . . . In short, every man is to some degree a scientist."

if they love their mothers. But some of us develop an exceptionally keen ability to understand people, to predict what they will do under certain circumstances. One may be able to write a novel, presenting in paragraphs of great insight and seeming validity the whole history of an intricate human personality contending with its world. Another may develop special insights enabling him to sell almost anybody almost anything or to persuade millions of people that the earth is square and does not move.

Sometimes we learn very peculiar and erroneous things. We may learn, for example, that all authority is bad, that all parents, teachers, policemen, and leaders are to be distrusted. Or we may learn that all authority is good—to be respected, deferred to, believed implicitly. If our learned view or theory of authority takes either of these extreme forms, our predictions about authority are likely to be less than perfect.

Again we may learn, on the basis of our unique experience, that people in general dislike us, are hostile, and must constantly be appeased. If we learn such a theory, if it becomes deeply embedded in our psychological marrow, then we may spend a lifetime trying to please everyone. Or we may learn an opposite orientation—that all people are wonderful and all of them like us. Such a theory will probably lead to quite different behavior, and perhaps also to disillusionment; for sometime, somewhere, we will encounter a clearly and pervasively hostile person.

Figure 2–2 presents evidence of individual differences in theory. Students in an introductory psychology class were asked to fill out a form indicating their general attitudes and beliefs about people. They could do this by making checks along the lines presented in the figure. On the *good–bad* line, for example, a mark to the left, toward good, indicates a belief that people in general are good. *X* represents the answers of one student; *O* represents the answers of the student sitting next to him in class. One student says that people are good, pleasant, and friendly. The other says that they are neither good nor bad, neither pleasant nor unpleasant, neither friendly nor unfriendly,

but that they are disorganized and tend to be both dull and submissive. The excerpted research material at the end of the present chapter bears on individual differences in theories of the nature of human nature.

Our Theories Make a Difference

The theories of man that we have evolved, either deliberately or through the powerful accumulation of experiences of which we are dimly aware, are related to our behavior toward people. One illustration will help make this point clearer. In a study dealing with attitudes toward authority (Sanford, 1950), 963 Philadelphia people were asked whether they agreed or disagreed with the following statements:

"Human nature being what it is, there must always be war and conflict."

"The most important thing a child should learn is obedience to his parents."

"A few strong leaders could make this country better than all the laws and talk."

"Most people who don't get ahead don't have enough will power."

"Women should stay out of politics."

When the data were in, several things became clear about the nature of personal theories and about their influence on behavior. For one thing, people who agree with one of these statements tend, generally, to agree with them all. And those who disagree with one are inclined to disagree with them all. Why this should be so is a subject for psychological speculation, but the fact is there and leads to the notion that our little theories are systematically organized into larger theories.

There is also evidence that those who agree with these statements behave in a way that is different from those who disagree. Those who disagree, for example, volunteer for community service more frequently than those who agree. They also have a different pattern of personal worries, they admire a different group of heroes, they vote for a different kind of community leader.

Along this general line, suppose the founding fathers of this country had not held the view that human nature is rational and per-

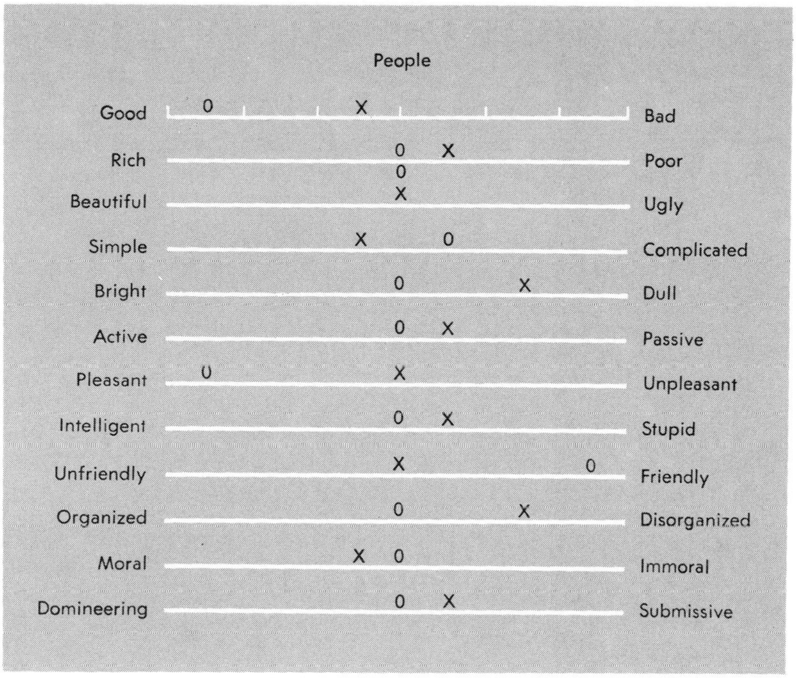

People

Good	O		X			Bad
Rich			O	X		Poor
Beautiful			O / X			Ugly
Simple		X		O		Complicated
Bright			O		X	Dull
Active			O	X		Passive
Pleasant	O			X		Unpleasant
Intelligent			O	X		Stupid
Unfriendly		X			O	Friendly
Organized			O		X	Disorganized
Moral		X	O			Immoral
Domineering			O	X		Submissive

Figure 2–2. ONE WAY TO MAKE A "THEORY"
EXPLICIT. *An individual reveals his theory of
people when he completes a form such as this
one. He reacts to "people" by making marks
on each of a number of bipolar dimensions.
The O's above represent the marks made by
one student; the X's, the marks made by
another. The two sets of marks indicate two
different orientations to people. This form
is an adaptation of a procedure, known as the*
semantic differential, *widely used to explore
the world of meaning. (Osgood, 1952.)*

fectible. Suppose, instead, that they had joined
with Thomas Hobbes in the sour belief that
the natural state of man is a state of war of
everyone against all; that the life of man, in
Hobbes's words, is "solitary, poor, nasty, brut-
ish, and short." Thomas Jefferson and his colleagues obviously did not hold such a belief.
Therefore, instead of designing a state for
man the beast, they wrote a constitution designed for men of rationality and good will.
The views of John Locke and Rousseau seem
to have been more influential than those of the
"pessimistic" social philosophers. On a somewhat less grand scale of speculation, one writer
(Allport, 1954) holds that the early and

chronic American belief in the possibility of
solving human problems and in the improva-
bility of the human state—"American melior-
ism" is the phrase—made it possible for
psychology, particularly social psychology, to
thrive in this country as it has in no other.

We are not really justified here in concluding that one's theory *causes* behavior. Nor do
we know for sure that a change in theory
will produce a change in behavior. But it is
almost inconceivable that a man's view of
people is totally inconsistent with his behavior
toward people. There is much evidence to the
contrary.

EVERYMAN'S PSYCHOLOGY
AND THE PSYCHOLOGIST'S
PSYCHOLOGY

The psychologist's present theories differ in
many salient ways from the theory of any of
us. In subsequent chapters we will deal with
the puzzles, researches, and tentative theories
that psychology has evolved. Now, however,
we will look at the way in which a full-time
psychologist tries to think and behave and

Figure 2–3. EVALUATION. *Adjectival evaluation is everywhere.* (Austin *[Tex.]* American Statesman. *Tm. Reg. U.S. Pat. Off.—All rights reserved. Copr. 1961 by United Feature Syndicate, Inc.*)

write as he plies his chosen trade. And we will contrast and compare his approaches with those employed by most of us most of the time. We can do this by talking about *characteristics of problem-solving activity,* and set down as these characteristics a number of dimensions of problem-solving activity. These dimensions, for the most part, can be thought of and will be dealt with in relatively clear-cut bipolar terms. We will consider (1) evaluation vs. objectivity, (2) casual vs. controlled observation, (3) casual vs. sophisticated use of language, (4) the study of prediction vs. the study of process, (5) implicit vs. explicit knowledge, (6) precise vs. unprecise procedures, (7) finality vs. tentativeness of attitude.

EVALUATION VS. OBJECTIVITY

Living is full of evaluating. Living is making choices, liking and disliking, approaching and avoiding. We *must* evaluate, for we have to do something about events, about people and their acts. And doing something is most often an encouragement or discouragement, an approval or disapproval, a going closer or a retreating farther. In dealing with the daily problems of living, we evaluate many, many times every day. Often, we simply cannot observe calmly or neutrally before we leap into a solution. Most of the problems we confront, most of the decisions we make are handled—must be handled—on the basis of quick and prelearned evaluation.

If the student wishes to convince himself of the evaluative nature of his living, let him count the evaluative adjectives in the last letter he wrote home. How much purely objective reporting of events did the letter contain? How many statements of preference?

The ease and primacy of evaluation can be illustrated by the following incident. Students in a class in psychology were asked (a) to listen to a brief account of a man who murdered his wife and then committed suicide, and (b) to write down the first words that occurred to them. Most of the words listed were evaluative adjectives: *terrible, distressful, pathetic, horrible, tragic, bad, sad.* These words all describe the students' feelings about the act, not the act itself.

The students used other evaluative words also. There were religiously evaluative ones, like *sinful, ungodly,* and *hell-inviting.* There were socially evaluative ones—*criminal, illegal,* and *irresponsible.* Few students were inclined to give relatively neutral and objective adjectives, such as *fatal, mortal, bloody, violent, extreme.*

Some of the time, however, all of us can take and have taken an objective stance with respect to people and their behavior. We can observe, can contemplate calmly, can try out alternative views and ideas before we face the necessity to act. On these occasions we come close to the habits the scientist has tried to build into himself—the habits that science, as an institution, demands of its adherents.

Evaluation is natural and often necessary. Evaluation is a friend of action. But it is an enemy of science.

Scientific observation is, ideally, observation without evaluation. Science aspires to **objectivity.** The scientist, as such, tries to look at the world as if he had no emotion, no biases, no prejudices. He tries, while at work, to see the world as if it had no goodness or evil, no beauty or ugliness, no joy or sadness. He wants to see objectively, neutrally, what is there. His language of observation is cold language. He talks about the bare presence or absence of things; the length, height, weight of things; the speed, the distance, the sight and sound and feel of things. The language of scientific observation and interpretation has no beauty except the beauty that one might see in man's elegantly simple scientific representations of nature.

Objectivity, as opposed to evaluation, is a characteristic of the scientific approach to behavior. All psychologists at work try to be objective, to avoid quick evaluation, to keep in check the human tendency to see a desired rather than a real world. Of course, not all psychologists are objective all of the time, even in their laboratories. They, too, become personally involved in their theories and are by

Figure 2–4. EVALUATIVE GEOGRAPHY. *Where objectivity is low, the observer sees the world in ways highly subjective and evaluative. Here is a lesson in "psychological geography." (Adapted with permission of John Randolph.)*

no means walking embodiments of Olympian objectivity. Furthermore, although the scientist tries to be objective, he is not a neutrally passive observer of the human scene. He rearranges things, sometimes quite actively and even courageously, in order to learn about them, in order to see "what will happen if." And, after work, of course, he must live and survive in a real world of responsibilities, evaluations, preferences, and decisions.

While at work, the psychologist is surrounded by safeguards that tend to preserve objectivity. To be sure that he sees something that is actually there, and not a figment of his desires, he follows certain standard techniques of observation. He makes *repeated observations* of the same event. He calls in other observers to watch, to be sure he is not imagining something, for he has been taught that his own perceptions may fool him. He is alert to poor **sampling**, to the danger that what he sees in a few people will not be true of many people. Much of psychological methodology consists of devices to ensure objective observation. Many of these devices anyone can use if he wishes to be sure he is observing what is actually there and not engaging in too early evaluation and interpretation—or reading into the world some creation of his own nervous system. There are many times, perhaps, when any educated man wishes to talk the "language of observation." At such times he may find useful some of the psychologist's techniques.

CASUAL VS. CONTROLLED OBSERVATION

Few problems, either practical or scientific, can be solved without observation. Sherlock Holmes, Nero Wolfe, and other great fictional detectives were represented as problem solvers who relied mightily on processes within the confines of their own heads. But no problem concerned with events in the physical world or with the behavior of human beings was ever solved without observations of fact. Both Holmes and Wolfe were meticulous observers as well as thinkers. Not even Einstein could have spelled out a theoretical formula unless he had put his fertile mind to work on the observations of fact furnished him by hundreds of experimental physicists. Nor can we deal with the practical problems of diurnal existence, except by the veriest of arbitrariness, unless we "encumber ourselves with fact."

We have emphasized that objectivity is vital for science. And we talked briefly about some of the factors helping the scientific investigator maintain objectivity. But objectivity in observation is not enough. There must be precision, relevance, completeness.

Observations in Daily Life

In the hundreds of decisions each of us makes in a week—whether to have the car greased, to go to the movies, to buy a two-ring or a three-ring notebook—observation, even though it may be objective, plays a relatively minor role. We have lived and learned, and we make many of our routine decisions automatically. We do not examine carefully the state of actual lubrication of the knuckles and joints of the car. We do not read all the reviews of all the movies presently available to us, nor do we calculate exactly the relative distances to the Strand and the Paramount. We do not bother to collect facts about the relative convenience and durability of a three-ring vs. a two-ring binder. If we do any relevant observing before jumping to action in any of these cases, the observation is very casual. "It's about time for a grease job." "This movie sounds good." "This is a nice-looking notebook." And life goes on.

When we come to more important decisions, however, we become more conscious of data. We frequently will seek facts, will make careful observations, and will weigh the evidence as best we can. "Shall I send my son to this public school or to that private one?" Although some parents may make such a decision without either observing or thinking, many other parents will seek, through careful observation, data to help them predict which course of action will yield results most to their future liking. They may seek evidence about the particular pattern of their child's abilities. They may examine carefully the two schools and the alternative sets of teachers. They may measure distances, calculate dollars, and assess how the parents in the two schools will behave in the parent-teacher organizations. In making the prediction that they will like School A better than School B, these parents bring into the process all the facts they think are relevant. In so doing, they draw close to the narrow path the scientific investigator tries to walk. For parents, careful observation is only intelligent common sense. For the scientist, careful observation is the same thing, except that the scientist has evolved some refinements that are not known to most parents. And the scientist is interested in predicting not what *he will like* but what *will be* or what, precisely, *will happen.*

The Scientist's Controlled Observations

The best-known method the scientist has evolved for making his observations is the *experiment,* about which we will talk later. The experiment can be thought of as a highly contrived and deliberate way to observe the world and to learn about it. The scientist uses other methods also, methods calculated to reveal the facts he needs if he is to build a solid, public, and systematic picture of the way the world works.

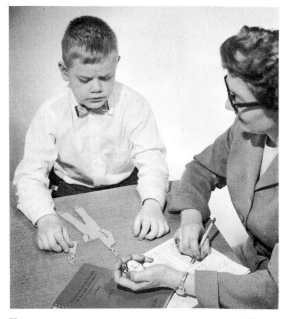

Figure 2–5. CONTROLLED OBSERVATION. *The psychologist constantly tries to make objective and controlled observations.*

Naturalistic observation. Naturalistic observation is observation of things as they naturally happen. We cannot always control nature or bring it into the laboratory. We have to take it the way it is. If the psychologist is interested, say, in aggressive behavior in children, and if he wishes to free himself from all his preconceptions, he may do well to sit in a corner of a nursery school and observe carefully for a few days all the behavior of all the children, taking notes on what he sees and hears and on what hunches occur to him. This would be naturalistic observation aimed at *finding an* **hypothesis** about what leads to aggressive behavior.

If he finds such an hypothesis, he can use naturalistic observation to test his hunch— to *test an hypothesis*. Perhaps his hypothesis says that frustration leads to aggression, that when a child seeks something—a toy or a first turn in a game—and is prevented from having what he wants, then he will show aggression. He will hit somebody, or he will break up the furniture or smear the walls. The psychologist can test this hypothesis by observing the course of natural events in the nursery school and carefully recording who is frustrated and who aggresses against what or whom. If the investigator is sufficiently ingenious, he may also find a way to take his hypothesis into the laboratory and arrange more precise ways of looking at the relation between frustration and aggression. We will have more to say about that later.

Clinical observation. Clinical observation is observation of an individual for purposes of alleviating a trouble. The psychologist or psychiatrist who is interested in helping the individual with a psychological problem needs to observe that individual with meticulous and insightful care if he is to know what the problem is and if he is to be of any help in alleviating it.

The psychologist—the therapist—will soon have hunches or hypotheses about the problem. He may use *diagnostic tests* or a *standard interview* to help him formulate his hypotheses.

And he may conduct an experiment. He has an hypothesis—say, that this individual needs to learn to express and to accept his strong

dislike of his father. Then as he works to bring about this expression and this acceptance, the therapist observes to see whether progress in these directions leads to alleviation of the problem the client brought in.

The clinical method is used also in circumstances other than those closely connected with the treatment of disturbed individuals. A case can be made that the entire psychoanalytic theory of personality is based on Freud's clinical observations. And clearly any psychologist since Freud who wishes to study personality relies on his own clinical observations of himself and of other individuals. Certainly we cannot yet formulate a comprehensive theory of personality on the basis of experimental data and mathematical formulations.

Survey observation. If you wish to know how your friends voted in the last election, the simplest way to find out would be to ask them. Or if you wish to know how they feel about funds for foreign aid, you might follow the same procedure. You will be conducting a survey.

A good deal of psychological research is conducted through the survey method of observation—*a method designed to see a selected variety of people responding to the same stimulus.* Usually, surveys are confined to verbal responses to questions. The question may be part of an interview, a questionnaire, or an attitude scale. Or, occasionally, we may wish to use a psychological test, such as a test of intelligence, on a large population. This, too, can be classed as survey observation.

Though anybody can, and many people do, conduct surveys, there are a number of rather technical precautions to be observed if the survey is to make any sense. The problem of getting *strictly comparable data* from every person questioned is difficult to lick. The question may be asked with one tone of voice one time and with a different intonation another. Or different respondents may put different meanings on the same question. When this happens, we are not observing what we have set out to observe.

Another problem is that of *sampling*. If we

Figure 2–6. PSYCHOLOGICAL OBSERVATIONS. *Top: Clinical observation of a child in a playroom. Middle: Research on an objectively scored inkblot test of personality. Bottom: Observing subject's responses to carefully timed and measured auditory stimulus.*

are interested in knowing the taste of a soup, we seldom taste *all* of it before rendering a judgment. We want to know about it all, but we want to "study" only a sample. The prob-

lem is to see that the sample is a good one. So we stir the soup first, thereby increasing the likelihood that a spoonful of it contains the same proportion of salt, pepper, meat, barley, and tomatoes as does the whole pot. In other words, we try to make a spoonful a *representative sample.* The man who conducts a survey follows an equivalent procedure so that he can talk with reasonable assurance about many people on the basis of data from a sample of them. If he selects his sample properly, he can "taste" that sample and thereby know, within specified limits, about his whole pot of people. The precise procedures he follows will be dealt with later.

The experimental method. Of all the methods employed in scientific inquiry—or for that matter, in intelligent problem solving anywhere—the experimental method of observation is most to be recommended. More than any other method, it can bring us close to the precise and definite knowledge we need for clear solutions to problems.

The experimental method, however, cannot always be employed. We cannot, for obvious reasons, experiment on brain damage in human beings. The Nazis are reputed to have conducted such experiments, but not with the approval of the civilized world. Often, too, we cannot experiment because we do not know precisely what we are experimenting upon. For *an experiment demands an hypothesis.* It demands that we spell out precisely, in logical terms, the things we are going to watch. The psychologist interested in aggression in children can observe only at random until he gets a hunch about what relates with what. If he can state his hunch clearly, he has an *hypothesis.* If he can state his hypothesis in *clear, well-defined,* and *testable* form, then he can experiment.

An hypothesis comes in an *if–then* form. The experimenter, whether he is in a scientific laboratory or in a kitchen, says, "It seems to me that if I do A, then B will happen." Or "I'll bet that if A changes, B also changes." To be able to run an experiment now, he needs to define both A and B and find some way of measuring both.

This procedure—or this *thinking* part of

the experiment—is similar to experiments we run every day. We may say, "If I spank baby George, he will not chew on cigarette butts again." So we spank him. And for an hour or two he stays entirely away from ash trays. But he comes back. So we measure out a slightly larger dose of spanking. He abjures cigarette butts for a longer time. We have demonstrated a relationship between a defined treatment and a behavior. So, we are all right until the youngster again chews on a second-hand cigarette, looks us in the eye, and in a way almost explicit asks to be spanked again. Such a development clutters up the simplicity of the relationship we have demonstrated and demands that we revise our hypothesis. So we revise our hypothesis and try another experiment to test it. Perhaps we now try reasoning with the child.

When the scientific investigator can *state an hypothesis, define his* **variables** (the definable and manipulable behavior he is interested in knowing about), and find a way to *control* at least one of them, he is in a position to arrange some experimental observation. Let us consider the psychologist interested in aggressive behavior. His general hypothesis is that *frustration leads to aggression.* He defines frustration as the blocking of motivated behavior. He defines aggression as attack on objects or people. Now, if he can arrange some frustration for his children, he can observe whether or not aggression happens. If he produces changes in his *independent variable* (frustration), he should get changes, he thinks, in the *dependent variable* (aggression). He uses a fence to separate children from toys with which they have been playing. This is frustration. He thinks he will now see aggression. He does. The children attack the fence and each other. He has observed, experimentally, a connection between frustration and aggression. He has not demonstrated that differing amounts of frustration lead to differing amounts of aggression. Or that frustration always leads to aggression. But he has a good hypothesis. If he can then find ways to measure the amount of frustration and the amount of aggression—and if he can vary, in ways he chooses, his independent variable, all the while watching his dependent variable—then

he can tie down pretty precisely the connection between frustration and aggression.

CASUAL VS. SOPHISTICATED USE OF LANGUAGE

A subtle but nonetheless major aspect of thought, scientific and practical alike, involves the use of language. If we are going to make sense out of our observations and if we are also going to communicate sensibly the sense we make, then language must be used carefully and in what is often a highly self-conscious manner. In this respect a cardinally important thing for us to know is whether or not at any given time we are talking the language of data on the one hand, or, on the other, one of several other kinds of language including (a) the language of opinion and (b) the language of **constructs.**

Language of Fact and Language of Opinion

We have said that, like any intelligent person with a problem, the scientific investigator observes the facts before he flies off into conclusions and solutions. But what is a fact? This, on the face of things, is a silly question. But it is not so silly that philosophers and scientists have given up worrying about it.

Let us try this as a provisional definition: *A fact is a perceptual relation between an observer and an event.* Where does such a definition take us? When I say, "That Cadillac is chartreuse," do you accept it as a factual and established matter that the car really is chartreuse? You'd better not. For what I really am saying, whether I know it or not, is something like this: "In the prevailing conditions of lighting and distance and with my eyes and brain and attitudes toward Cadillacs working the way they were at the time, I made the judgment that the car was chartreuse."

What would happen if the situation changed? What would happen if my eyes were working peculiarly at the moment? What if I were color-blind? And what would you conclude if you brought in other observers and found that only four out of six of them agreed on the color of the car?

Take another example. Suppose a friend of yours sees a purple rabbit on the ceiling of his room. How can you decide whether the rabbit is really there? You can call in other observers. If they all see the rabbit, and you do not, you have a problem. If none of them— if none out of 6,742 of them—sees the rabbit, then you conclude that your friend has a problem.

Single observations do not establish facts. *Private* observations do not establish facts either. What we want, if we are going to be absolutely sure of a fact, is repeated observations on the part of many observers. Similarly, *opinions* do not establish facts. An opinion is an evaluation, a *personal* relation between an

Figure 2–7. DANGERS OF A SINGLE OBSERVATION. *What is an elephant like? Single observations by fallible observers can be misleading.*

observer and an event. Opinions generally are flavored with **emotion**—which is fine, unless we confuse facts and opinions. When I say, "Alaska is a wonderful state," I am not really talking about Alaska. I am talking about me —about my evaluations of Alaska. That is all right, too, until some Texan takes issue with me, with both of us thinking we are arguing about Alaska instead of ourselves, that we are talking facts rather than our personal evaluations.

We have to revise our definition to read: *A fact is an agreed-upon perceptual relation between an observer and an event.* Such a definition will serve us very well, will help us determine whether or not someone whose

voice we hear or whose words we read is using the language of fact or the language of opinion.

Science, in the strict sense, has no commerce with opinions and evaluations. Its primary language is instead the language of fact, of observation. In psychology, the primary language of science is the language of behavior, for behavior is what psychologists observe. But science is by no means fact alone, nor is the language of either science or psychology restricted to a traffic in direct observations. Scientists talk about interpretation, explanation, theory. And when they talk about such matters, they depart from the language of observation into other kinds of linguistic procedures.

Language of Fact and Language of Constructs

In the realm of facts, we deal with what can be felt, heard, seen, smelled, or tasted— by more than one well-equipped nervous system. But facts do not organize or interpret or explain themselves. So when the scientist wishes—as he so often does—to concern himself with more than mere facts, he does so through the use of the *language of constructs,* or the *language of intervening variables.* And when he steps over into this linguistic realm, he must tread with care, for not only is it a realm of great promise but one in which it is easy to stumble.

Scientific investigators are concerned with relationships between or among facts. In order to specify the nature of the relationship between two observable events, they frequently will *invent* or *infer* something—a construct or an intervening variable—that must be there to account for the relationship that is observed. Sir Isaac Newton observed a variety of facts about the behavior of bodies in space; he then invented the construct of gravity to account for what he saw. He never saw gravity; nor has anyone else. It is a construct—referred to variously as an *hypothetical* or *theoretical* or *logical* construct or as an *intervening variable.* In the natural sciences such constructs have become thoroughly familiar—so familiar, in fact, that we are often inclined to regard them as actual things rather than as linguistic inventions of scientists. We are familiar not only with the constructs of gravity and gravitational fields but also with vectors and valences and recessive genes and a number of unobservable hypothetical entities on the inside of the atom.

In psychology, too, there is heavy reliance on constructs to deal with observed relationships. We can examine the nature of these psychological constructs by examining the matter of hunger. While each of us has had what seems to be some direct and intimate experience with his own hunger, we have never observed directly the hunger of anyone else. We observe behavior in the presence—or absence —of food. We hear talk about food and can observe a change in the restlessness of an individual's behavior as he approaches the established time for his dinner. And if we arrange ways to observe the contractions of his stomach and the chemistry of his blood, we can have further factual data of relevance for what we call hunger. But we do not observe hunger. We invent it or infer it to account for relationships among observables. The same goes for such matters as *intelligence*, or *attitude*, or *motive*, or *trait*, or *personality*, or for any one of very many terms psychologists use.

Every construct in psychology is intended to deal with a relationship between or among observed facts. Some refer to relationships between *observed antecedent conditions* on one hand and *overt behavior* on the other. Others deal with the relationship between *observed behavior* on one hand and *other observed behavior* on the other. Generally speaking, the former relationships are described as S-R (stimulus-response) relationships, the latter as R-R (response-response) relationships. An example of an S-R relationship and of a construct to deal with it is, again, hunger. We observe antecedent conditions, such as prolonged food deprivation. Then we place the deprived organism in the presence of food. He eats, and he quiets down after he eats. Quite comfortably we use the construct of hunger to tie together the facts we observe. There is observed deprivation, which leads to unobserved hunger, which leads to observed eating responses and

to observed evidence of satiation. Another example of a construct in an S-R relationship is furnished by an instance of what we regard as simple learning. We expose an experimental animal to a buzzer in his ear and then quickly give him an electrical shock on his paw. When the buzzer-and-shock (S) comes, the animal withdraws his paw (R). Later, after a few repetitions of the buzzer-shock stimulus, the buzzer alone leads to a withdrawal of the paw. The S-R relationship has changed. We account for the change in terms of learning—a construct.

In response-response relationships, constructs also come into play, both in technical psychological circles and in everyday life. We observe responses on a test of a certain kind, infer that the individual is characterized by intelligence (a construct), and predict that this intelligence will lead to subsequent responses of a certain kind in another situation. Much of our everyday psychology involves our observations, casual or otherwise, of R-R relationships and our attempts, justifiable or not, to apply constructs to what we observe. We readily—perhaps too readily—apply the constructs of bright or stupid or extroverted or lazy and expect our friends to behave in accordance with the constructs we have inserted between those R's that we have observed and the R's we expect to see tomorrow.

Science, of course, thrives on constructs. It is not far wrong to regard science as an organized system of logical constructs. The scientist observes facts aplenty. But his real thrill and his real progress often come only when he invents a logical construct that fits the observed facts and allows him to build larger and more inclusive bodies of knowledge.

Rules for the Use of Constructs

As he goes about the business of fitting constructs to relationships among facts, the scientific investigator tries to keep himself in line with certain rules that seem likely to help make the best scientific sense.

Naturalistic constructs. First, he confines himself to naturalistic constructs, to constructs phrased in terms of natural and worldly forces. In the scientist's view, the world makes sense; it runs in an orderly and lawful manner, and the scientist believes that man, if he goes about it right, can see the sense the world makes—can, if he's bright and persistent, set down the laws by which the natural world works. The scientist does not, by his own ground rules, bring in factors and forces from other worlds to help him account for the events he sees. He does not think in terms of leprechauns, witches, demons, spirits, souls, or mysterious essences. He conceives of the insane person, for example, as a disorganized personality rather than a bedeviled unfortunate. He sticks to *naturalistic* constructs.

The law of parsimony. Related to the scientist's preference for naturalistic constructs is his attempted adherence to the **law of parsimony,** the law insisting that in the use of constructs, as elsewhere in science, all unnecessary complications be avoided. Other things being equal, the principle holds, the simplest is the most elegant. This principle, though first formulated by William of Occam (1280–1349), came prominently into the thinking of psychologists around the turn of the present century, when Lloyd Morgan, an eminent researcher and theorist, insisted that unnecessarily complex constructs not be used in accounting for the behavior of animals. Actually, he was arguing against **anthropomorphism**—the imputing of human traits to animals—in his insistence on parsimonious procedures. He wrote, "In no case may we interpret an action as the outcome of the exercise of a higher physical faculty, if it can be interpreted as the outcome of one which stands lower in the psychological scale" (Morgan, 1899, p. 59).

The law of parsimony says, in general, that we do not employ mysterious and complex constructs when simple ones will do. We do not talk of a soul if a personality will do, nor of a mind if a habit will do, nor of free will if a motive will do, nor of insight if a simple learned response will do.

Operational definitions. The scientist also tries to define every construct in terms of the observable events to which it is related. This emphasis on explicit definition is generally referred to as **operationism.** The genesis of that term can be found in the following brief passage from a physicist (Bridgman, 1927) who was an early and influential proponent of the principle: "To find the length of an object, we have to perform certain physical operations. The concept of length is therefore fixed when the operations by which length is measured are fixed: that is, the concept of length involves as much as and nothing more than a set of operations . . ."(p. 5).

We can give a construct a clear definition by relating it either to the antecedent conditions or to the observed responses—or to both. In experimental situations we can make hunger explicitly and operationally meaningful by describing in detail the *operation* of food deprivation. The experimental rats, we say, were deprived of food but not of water for a period of 18 hours and 22 minutes before beginning the experiment. Later we can say, and properly so, that our "hungry" rats, with their hunger clearly defined, behaved in specifiable ways in learning a maze; after an average of twenty trials they came out of the starting box, with a measured delay, and ran with a measured speed toward the food box and made a counted number of wrong turns in doing so.

The constructs used in dealing with R-R relationships also can be defined in operational terms. If we are conducting an experiment on problem solving and wish to talk about intelligence, we report that the intelligence of our experimental subjects, "as measured by Form B of the 1939 edition of the Stanford-Binet test of intelligence," was indicated by a mean IQ of, say, 120. The construct of intelligence as used in this experiment is thus clearly defined in terms of the operations used in measuring it.

Although there is room for debate about the desirability of saying that the meaning of a construct is "as much as and nothing more than" a set of operations, few psychologists will want to argue against the importance of (1) knowing the difference between facts and constructs and (2) defining constructs as clearly as we can in terms of observable conditions or observable behaviors or both.

Facts and Constructs in Use

In the actual wrestling with a problem, the scientific investigator, like any intelligent person, mentally weaves back and forth between facts and constructs, between observation and hunch, between definition and redefinition. He studies facts, tries a tentative construct, observes more facts to see whether they fit the construct, revises his construct, looks at more facts—perhaps gained through an experiment —redefines his construct, and so on. This process, of course, the student may recognize as the basic research process of stating and testing, restating and retesting hypotheses; here the process is described in the language of fact and construct.

Eventually the researcher hits upon a construct that makes sense in the light of all the facts he can observe. So he publishes his research. Then other scientists, if they are curious, bring in other facts. The construct is further revised, and relations between it and other constructs (e.g., the relation between frustration and aggression) are studied. In all of science there are no final constructs. Even the construct of gravity, which did so much to help man understand his physical world, is under revision by those scientists who are probing the inner life of atoms. The construct of phlogiston is long outmoded.

Sigmund Freud (1915), writing in a way surprisingly at variance with the prevailing view of his orientation, described as follows this interweaving of facts and constructs:

[Constructs] must at first necessarily possess some degree of indefiniteness; there can be no question of any clear delimitation of their content. So long as they remain in this condition, we come to an understanding about their meaning by making repeated references to the material of observation from which they appear to have been derived, but upon which, in fact, they have been imposed. Thus, strictly speaking, they are in the nature of conventions—although everything depends on their not being arbitrarily chosen but determined by their having significant relations to the empirical material, relations that we seem to sense before we can clearly recognize and demonstrate them. It is only after more thorough investigation of the field of observation that we are able to

formulate its basic scientific concepts with increased precision and consistency over a wide area. Then, indeed, the time may have come to confine them in definitions. The advance of knowledge, however, does not tolerate any rigidity even in definitions.[3]

The Body of Constructs of a Science

In Chapter 1 we gained an exposure to constructs in various fields of human science. There were biological constructs and sociological constructs. There was the anthropological construct of culture pattern. And there were psychological constructs: the broad constructs of motivation, emotion, sensation, perception and learning, and the somewhat more limited constructs of personality traits, intelligence, and so on. As we go on into the content of modern psychology we will deal with a wide variety of constructs, and with the facts upon which they are based. A science is known by the constructs it keeps, and to know psychology is to know its constructs.

PREDICTION AND PROCESS

Because we need to predict the behavior of ourselves and of others, our usual tendency in trying to deal with human behavior is to seek bare *prediction* without much concern for *process*. If we push the accelerator, the car speeds up. If we flash a light in the eye, the pupil contracts. If we score below a certain level on an intelligence test, we will probably flunk out of college.

If the car speeds up every time we push the accelerator, we may never have a practical need to understand the processes whereby the

---

[3] Freud, 1915 (1957), p. 117. By permission of the Hogarth Press.

There is much controversy among psychologists and philosophers of science concerning operationism and the necessity to keep constructs or concepts very closely and rigidly tied to facts. This tolerant view expressed by Freud and quoted above is one that Carnap, a leading philosopher of science, now seems to accept. Carnap (1956) says, "Today I think, in agreement with most empiricists, that the connection between the observational terms and the terms of theoretical science is much more indirect and weak than it was conceived either in my earlier formulations or in those of operationism." This is the same Carnap who earlier seemed to feel that Freud was polluting the language of science with meaningless phrases.

pushing and the speeding are connected. But let the predicted relationship once break down, so that we push the pedal and the car gives only a disgruntled belch. What do we do? Nothing very useful, unless we understand something about the processes whereby the pedal is related to the carburetor, to the gas line, to the tank, to the intake manifold, to the firing chamber, to the valves, to the spark plug, to the distributor, to the coil, and to the battery. By pushing an accelerator, we trigger off an elaborate and organized sequence of interlocking events, the failure of any of which will break down the frequently observed and heretofore predictable relationship between pedal and motion. This process is equivalent in many respects to the psychological process we described in Chapter 1.

Similarly, we can predict that a light flashed in the eye will lead to the contraction of the pupil. There seems to be a very stable relation here between stimulus and response. But the neurological process involved between the light and the contraction is of a very elaborate and still somewhat mysterious kind. The light gets itself translated, by receptors in the eye, into a nervous impulse. The nervous impulse travels over certain neural paths to a certain part of the brain. Here there is a connection made between the incoming neuron and an outgoing one. The impulse goes back to the muscles of the eye and triggers off a muscular response. If we are to have a complete understanding of this phenomenon, we need to know everything about all phases of the process. And this is what the scientist most often seeks—knowledge of process, not just knowledge of those predictable connections between an *A* and a *B*.

Molar and Molecular Approaches

Most of our practical predictions about people are made on the basis of observations and ideas at a **molar** level—a relatively gross level of observation and conceptualization. We observe accelerators and carburetors rather than electrons and molecules. When we concern ourselves with processes, however, we often get ourselves involved in a **molecular ap-** **proach** to the world. Our everyday psychology tends to be a molar psychology. We observe gross behaviors and we think of motives, attitudes, and personality traits. Much of scientific psychology, too, is at the molar level—at least, the part of psychology that many students find most interesting. But psychology, as it delves beyond practical prediction and explores for knowledge of process, will turn molecular also.

Figure 2–8. PREDICTION. *The Bennett Hand-Tool Dexterity Test, used to predict success on certain jobs.*

Psychology and the Understanding of Processes

Applied psychology, like common sense, is more concerned with prediction than with process. Many psychologists work to make immediately useful predictions. They want to find ways of predicting performance in college, or in flying airplanes, or in typing, or in operating a lathe. Or they wish to know what kind of practice leads predictably to the most rapid learning. And they achieve considerable success in such attempts. But the core of psychological science is concerned with the understanding of processes. The study of these processes, a study that goes wherever the scientist's curiosity may lead it, produces a vast array of results. To illustrate this, a specimen list of titles of psychological papers is included below. These papers, along with hundreds of other papers, were presented at the 71st annual meeting of the American Psychological Association in Los Angeles in 1964—a conclave attended by about 10,000 psychologists.

Correlates of paired-associate learning in children. John C. McCullers

A study of consensus among classroom informants. Richard Bloom, James Dunn, and William C. Morse

Psychiatric hospital effectiveness: Replication on a sample three years removed. Leonard P. Ullman

Effects of number of training trials upon the development of a secondary reinforcer with children. Norman Klass, Helen Wilson, and Joseph B. Sidowski

Classification of achievement profiles of socially maladjusted pupils. Donald A. Leton

Interpersonal values of United States Air Force Academy cadets. Lyle D. Kaapke

The effect of monocular light stimulation on the perception of the body midline: A developmental study. Kenneth T. Chandler and Marjy N. Ehmer

Visual perception and ocularmotor skills in reading readiness. Donald A. Leton and Margaret H. Jones

Anxiety, stress, and Wechsler subtest performance. James A. Dunn

Dimensions and criteria of talented behavior. Carson McGuire, Earl Jennings, A. C. Murphy, and Ray Whiteside

A method for studying sensitivities to implied meanings. Norman D. Sundberg

Learning set as a determinant of perceived cooperation and competition. Olga V. Vegas, Ronald L. Frye, and Frank P. Cassens

Clinical correlates of ulcerative colitis in children and adolescents. Karol Fishler and Allan E. Edwards

Operant conditioning of the Indian elephant (Elephas maxima). Leslie H. Squier

The development of visual evoked responses in the human infant. R. J. Ellingson

Reactivity patterns in bilateral electrodermal activity. Joan F. Dixon, Theodore R. Dixon, and John A. Stern

Group cohesiveness of a simulated thirty-day space flight. Bernard Borislow

Programming reinforcement schedules with an on-line digital computer. Bernard Weiss and Victor Laties

Personality changes associated with college attendance. Walter T. Plant

Longitudinal investigation of intellectual function following unilateral temporal lobectomy. Manfred J. Meier and Lyle A. French

The development of correction scores for a biographical inventory to predict success in science. Robert L. Ellison and Calvin W. Taylor

Self-starvation caused by "feeding center" self-stimulation. Aryeh Routtenberg

The facilitating effects of food set and food deprivation on responses to a subliminal food stimulus. Carol M. Gordon and Donald P. Spence

Shirtsleeve spacesuit effects on human performance. George E. Hanff

Tactual discrimination learning in monkeys with frontal lesions. Martha Wilson and Marlene Oscar

Effects of age and stimulus size on perception. James A. Thomas and Don C. Charles

Single-cell analysis of brightness and hue discrimination. Russell L. DeValois, Gerald H. Jacobs, and Israel Abramov

Persistence of escape responses shocked during extinction. Robert M. King and John P. Seward

The effects of instructions and changes in outcome probabilities on three-choice decisions. Richard G. Swensson and Kenneth M. Michels

Structural factors in verbal behavior. Howard R. Pollio

Response availability, stimulus similarity, and familiarization in auditory identification learning and transfer. A. M. Barch and J. R. Levine

Effects of different kinds of feedback on achievement in a multiple-cue probability learning task. Frederick J. Todd and Kenneth R. Hammond

Number and size of unrewarded blocks as determiners of resistance to extinction. Glenn D. Jensen

Activity of rabbits, guinea pigs, chicks, hamsters during food and water deprivation. Byron A. Campbell, Nelson F. Smith, and James R. Misanin

Evidence suggesting the acquisition of a simple discrimination during sleep. Harold Weinberg

Basal conductance levels and galvanic skin responses of normals and alcoholics. Kenneth Woodrow and Stanley Coopersmith

The perception of off-size versions of a familiar object under conditions of rich information. Samuel Fillenbaum, H. Richard Schiffman, and James Butcher

Some context effects in magnitude estimation. F. Nowell Jones and Morris J. Woskow

Above-threshold differences in the discriminability of changes in values, and concept formation. J. Peter Denny and Judy Kaas

THE IMPLICIT-EXPLICIT DIMENSION

Very few of us can put into words all the things we know and believe about people in general or about ourselves. We probably know a good deal more than we can say. And we believe many things that we cannot—or will not—say out loud.

The scientist is in much the same position. He, too, has hunches and feelings and intuitions too fuzzy or too subtle to put into words. But *he cannot create science until he can make explicit what he knows.* For science, by definition, is public. Intuitions and feelings and impulses can be private, but scientific observations must be open to public view so that they can be checked and tested. And scientific interpretations must be stated explicitly so that they can be examined critically by any interested person.

Why is this? Is public knowledge better than private knowledge? Is stated knowledge better than concealed knowledge? For purposes of living, perhaps not always. But for purposes of science, yes. And we can make a case that no knowledge is genuine knowledge unless it can be stated openly and clearly.

Scientists have widely adopted a number of strategies that seem to help in the accumulation of knowledge. The techniques and procedures of observation mentioned earlier may be thought of as strategies for gaining knowledge —objective, tested, trustworthy knowledge that can be shared by any well-equipped person who wishes to look and learn. The strategy of publication—making knowledge explicit— is a further attempt to ensure that knowledge is sound. Only by making his observations and interpretations explicit and public can the scientist have real assurance that what he thinks he knows is not a product of his own imagination.

And only through publication *can scientific knowledge be cumulative.* Science is a social process. Scientific investigators teach one another. One man in one country in one century, if he publishes his findings, touches other men in other countries in other centuries. A second man, having learned, can then add his bit to the store of knowledge. Private knowledge, by contrast, cannot be taught; it can only be learned.

It may well be, as Tennyson complained, that the net of language is so crude that the more delicate human thoughts forever escape. But the reality remains that neither poet nor scientist can share his insights with another unless he can cast into symbols the subtleties registered by his own brain. Language is the bridge to the lonesome island of the single human mind.

The scientist is committed to the creation of knowledge that can be publicly stated and explicitly tested. In his commitment he has no license to belittle other kinds of knowledge, unless they are falsely advanced as public and explicit. But in value, in attitude, in method, and in the institutionalizations of science, he is committed to those strategies he believes likely to create a public and explicit understanding of the world.

In this commitment the scientist is joined by many nonscientists. In a way, the philosophers share his commitment and his aspiration. The philosophers aspire to conceive in the broadest terms the nature of man and of man's world. And they aspire to write it down, so that their own insights may be shared—may be tested by anyone who wishes to work out his own cosmology.

All of us who hope to become educated men aspire also to work out our own view of the world and of our place therein, to state it in terms sufficiently explicit to live by. While we may not always wish to make public our own personal cosmologies, our own theories of ourselves and of our fellow men, many of us strive to cast into words and paragraphs our own philosophies of life. Once we succeed, even tentatively, we possess a general set of principles by which we can live with some consistency.

Though we cannot put into words everything we "know," privately, about the world, there is good reason to believe that what we "know" has an important hand in shaping what we do. Our theories of ourselves and of others are interwoven with many unspoken knowledges, many highly personal and unique interpretations of the world, many conclusions that may be partially or totally unconscious.

Private Meanings

Each of us interprets the meaning of an object or a word in terms of our own unique experience with that object or word. If we carefully examined each of a hundred students to find the meaning of the word "scientist," for example, we would probably find one hundred different meanings. There would be some similarity among all of the meanings, but each person would bring in his own personal associations and his own unique imagery. To one, a scientist is a glamorous figure in a white coat speaking a strange but fascinating language about the things he and only he can see in test tubes and under electron microscopes. To another, the scientist is a very peculiar bird who closets himself all day in a dingy back room, worrying about the left front foot of a white rat while he should be out in the real world doing something useful.

Each word we use or hear has to us a meaning that, in some respects, is private. We can appreciate the difficulties that arise when we try to talk to one another about scientists, communists, democracy, or motherhood. And we may appreciate also some of the procedures scientists employ in the valiant attempt to communicate with precision, so as to create a truly public knowledge.

Personal Perceptions

Closely related to the privacy of meaning we give to words is the privacy—the uniqueness—of the ways in which we see physical objects. We tend to see the world not as it actually is but as we are.

A classic example of the private nature of perception is found in what is called the **autokinetic phenomenon** (Sherif, 1936a). If we place an observer in a room totally dark except for one small stationary point of light, and ask him to stare at the light, he will "see" the light move. One subject will see it move through a wide arc, while for another it moves only a very small distance. We must conclude that processes within ourselves determine what is seen.

An illustration closer to life is given by an experiment (Bruner and Goodman, 1947) in which "rich" boys and "poor" boys were asked to look at a half dollar and later to duplicate its size. The "poor" boys produced larger circles than the "rich" boys. We are inclined to conclude that fifty cents occupies a larger and more luscious place in the private life of the "poor" boys.

If we are to make sound public statements about a fifty-cent piece, we need procedures to rule out the privacy of perception.

Unconscious Meanings

When we interpret the world or respond to it or make statements about it, we may be doing so on the basis of meanings of which we are unconscious. We do some of our learning about the world before we have developed the ability to put words to our experience. The knowledge we have about mothers, for example, is knowledge we have been acquiring since birth. It is based on a very wide and extended experience. These experiences have been both pleasant and unpleasant—sometimes extremely pleasant, sometimes extremely unpleasant. Mothers furnish food and comfort and love. They also furnish deprivation and discipline and denial and punishment. Our knowledge of mothers, then, should be a very complicated knowledge, with all this past experience there to back it up. But that is not the way things tend to operate. There are many pressures at work, both within us and outside us, to make us forget or repress unpleasant experiences. So now our knowledge of mother may be disproportionately full of sweetness and light. The accumulated experience that might round off our knowledge and make us much less favorably disposed toward mother is unconscious. Such knowledge does not show up in what we say about mother. But it does influence our *working theory* of mother. It does influence what we *do* about mother. The process of psychotherapy may be conceived as an exercise in making explicit those experiences and conclusions that are locked in unconsciousness.

All in all, then, the wise man, when he is trying to solve problems in the real world, will have a healthy skepticism of his own private meanings, his private perceptions. If he wishes to make public, objective, and testable statements about the world, he may do well to adopt procedures ensuring that he does not mistake private knowledge for public knowledge.

THE DIMENSION OF PRECISION

Inquiries into the nature of man vary in precision—precision of observation and of report. The investigator who wishes to make scientific statements about human behavior will, if he possibly can, avail himself of the power inherent in mathematical language. It is often said, especially in justifying college courses in algebra and calculus, that mathematics is the language of science. Why should this be so? What are the virtues and strengths of mathematics—of ordering, counting, scaling, calibrating?

Perhaps a good illustration of the power that

man gained when he learned to number and to count is to be found in Hogben's (1937) account of the Egyptian priests and their Nilometers. The temples of Egypt were equipped with devices—Nilometers—for measuring very precisely the rise and fall of the Nile River. These devices were carefully hidden from the people. The priests, reading their measuring devices, made careful records of the rise and fall of the river and were able to predict with mysterious accuracy the coming of floods. Knowledge, quantified, was power. In this case it was power carefully guarded and used in ways not all of us would approve—to fool people.

The inherent power of quantification can be illustrated again quite simply. First, there is the power of *precision*. Here the essential point is illustrated by the difference between "some" and, say, "23." To know that "some" of something is somewhere may be sufficient. We can and do live with imprecision. But if both "some" and "23" apply to the days we have to live, the difference between the two terms becomes quite significant. Quantitative knowledge is very much the clearer and more precise knowledge.

Then there is the potential power that comes when we use *mathematical* models to express the relationships of the world. When we use a mathematical model properly, we gain gratuitous knowledge. The philosopher Whitehead (1925) illustrates this very simply:

It is a general abstract truth of pure mathematics that any group of forty entities can be subdivided into two groups of twenty entities. We are therefore justified in concluding that a particular group of apples which we believe to contain forty members can be subdivided into two groups of apples of which each contains twenty members.[4]

Once we count our apples accurately, we can apply what we know about arithmetic to

---

[4] From *Science and the Modern World* by Alfred North Whitehead, p. 33. Copyright 1925 by The Macmillan Company, copyright renewed 1952 by Evelyn Whitehead, and used by permission of The Macmillan Company, New York, and the Cambridge University Press, London.

the apples. If we slice each in half, we will have eighty slices. If we have four people wanting our apples, an equitable distribution of them will give each person ten, and so on. When we properly fit a fact into the language of mathematics, the language itself then takes over to add to our knowledge, often in highly significant ways.

S. S. Stevens (1951) makes this point in a much more sophisticated way:

When this correspondence between the formal model and its empirical counterpart is close and tight, we find ourselves able to discover truths about matters of fact by examining the model itself. Thus we calculate the flight of a bullet or the course of a comet without laying hands on either. And we are awed by the prodigious power of mathematics to see what is beyond our own vision.[5]

We all quantify, perhaps a great deal more than we are aware. We live in a world of clocks, calendars, speedometers, scales, calorie charts, interest rates, course grades, and football scores. But we are not able, most of us, to think quantitatively about human behavior. We fall back on "some" and "few" and "many." Or we say simply, without any attempt at quantification, that people are smart, or crude, or pretty, or boisterous, or maybe demented or extroverted. The use of such language leads to knowledge of only a limited kind.

Precise measurement is a vital aspiration and an essential achievement for an advancing psychological science. However, there is little merit in precision for its own sake. Not all measurements are equally valuable, and someone who runs about measuring things at random is not likely to make major contributions to knowledge. One of psychology's best writers (Miller, 1962) puts it this way:

A blind faith that measurement is necessarily a good thing, that someday somebody will provide a theory to explain every conceivable measurement we might make, completely ignores the delicate play between observation and analysis. Outside of a supporting framework of problems,

facts, and theories measurement is empty; inside such a framework it may unlock the secrets of the universe.

FINALITY-TENTATIVENESS

Scientists have learned the advantages of tentativeness. They learn it from their own experience and from reading the history of science. They know by experience that their own research results may be outmoded tomorrow. They know that next week someone may come along with a newly invented—and vastly better—way of explaining the very thing they have spent many years wrestling with. For explanations *are* invented, and men are highly inventive beings, likely at any time, if fed more facts, to hit upon new ways of conceiving those facts. Science is a pursuit, not an accumulation.

C. D. Darlington, an English man of science, stated in 1948:

Scientific discovery is often carelessly looked upon as the creation of some new knowledge which can be added to the great body of old knowledge. This is true of the strictly routine discoveries. It is not true of the fundamental discoveries, such as those of the laws of mechanics, of chemical combination, of evolution, on which scientific advance ultimately depends. These always entail the destruction of old knowledge before the new can be created.[6]

Darlington goes on to talk about ways in which we can escape, in intelligent inquiry, the strong arm of routine custom and frozen modes of thought. He ends by saying, "We need a Ministry of Disturbance, a regulated source of annoyance; a destroyer of routine; an underminer of complacency."

John Dewey (1911), making the same point, but more gently, observes that ". . . science is a pursuit, not a coming into possession of the immutable; new theories as points of view are more prized than discoveries that quantatively increase the store at hand."

The term "scientific humility" is sometimes used to describe a mature disinclination to

---

[5] Reprinted by permission from S. S. Stevens, *Handbook of Experimental Psychology*, Copyright 1951, John Wiley & Sons, Inc., p. 2.

[6] By permission of the Conway Memorial Lecture Committee, South Place Ethical Society, Conway Hall, London, W.E. 1.

accept as final the knowledges that are merely current. It is to be doubted that all scientists are humble, that scientists always regard what they know as being tentative knowledge only. But many scientists, and many wise laymen, though they seek to secure final and everlasting knowledge, know in their personal depths that final knowledge is unobtainable. On the day man is convinced he has final knowledge, science will die—and so will all other forms of curiosity and inquiry. The possession of knowledge is stagnant, but the gaining of knowledge is a high pursuit.

WHY STUDY PSYCHOLOGY?

We have defined psychology as the scientific study of the lifelong process we outlined in Chapter 1. We have seen that each of us, in his own way, has studied this process for many years, and each of us has evolved for himself a working psychological theory to guide his own life. We have seen in this chapter some of the similarities and differences between the everyday study of human behavior and the scientific study of the same thing. In the next eighteen chapters we will be concerned with the results obtained, the difficulties encountered, and the problems raised as psychologists try to come to grips with the over-all psychological process, as they try to create an inclusive scientific theory that is better than the theories we all presently live by. Now the large question arises: Why should the part-time psychologist spend a semester or more studying what thousands of full-time psychologists do and have done? There are several answers to this question. Some perhaps are more practical than others.

PSYCHOLOGY AS LIBERAL EDUCATION

We saw in Chapter 1 that each individual human being is born into a cultural setting. His world has been structured by the work and wisdoms, the foolishnesses and failures of his forebears. It is the theory behind liberal education that the individual human being, as he seeks solutions to new problems and as he

pursues the goal of enriched human existence, does well to know and to appreciate both his cultural heritage and his current environment.

Psychology in the past fifty years has become a firmly established part of man's intellectual heritage. And, as an advancing scientific discipline, psychology is a significant factor in present-day existence. Thus, courses in psychology take their place alongside courses in mathematics, physics, art, history, and literature. Psychology, like these other courses, contributes to the liberal education of students.

What can psychology actually contribute to the education of an individual? We could confront such a question more profitably, perhaps, if we could agree on what a good education is and what a liberally educated person is like. These are questions, questions both of value and of fact, that might well absorb us for years. We will confront some of them again (Chap. 17). At the moment we can only raise the questions and suggest one format within which they might well be faced. According to one psychological writer on higher education (N. Sanford, 1962), the "highly developed" personality is both *complex* and *whole*.

The highly developed person is . . . complex in the sense that he is possessed of many parts or elements having different functions and standing in different relations one to another, and he is integrated in the sense that all of the parts have the possibility of communication with all the others. In the face of some adaptive requirement the highly developed individual can bring to bear all of the resources that he needs, but no more than he needs, thus meeting fresh situations in ways that will develop him further while permitting him to go on being himself.

CAREERS IN PSYCHOLOGY

Though it can be argued that no man can be well educated without some knowledge of what 20,000 psychologists are doing and have done, such an argument is likely to seem fuzzy and abstract to some students. Liberal education is not easy to sell. A more practical reason for studying psychology is the possibility of finding therein a professional career. The present demand for psychologists far exceeds the supply. It seems a safe assumption that American society will continue to demand the service of those who can either create, teach, or apply psychological knowledge. There will continue to be demands for psychologists in clinics, hospitals, industrial settings, governmental agencies, military installations, courts, prisons, medical schools, law schools, secondary schools, and other settings where a professional psychological competence can contribute to the solution of human problems. If present trends continue, there will also be an increasing number of research opportunities. And the demands for teachers of psychology will probably go up at least proportionately with increased college enrollments. Materials at the end of the present chapter contain information about the numbers and kinds of psychologists.

Since matters bearing on a career are very practical matters indeed, any student who is thinking of becoming a psychologist will find the introductory course a practical one. The practicality is there even if the course helps the student decide *not* to become a psychologist.

Since many people still do not know the difference between psychologists and psychiatrists, it may be worth a few lines here to clarify the distinction. All of those who have earned the title of psychologist (people in some states can and sometimes do take on the title without having earned it) have had graduate study in a university of recognized standing. The holding of the Ph.D. degree from such an institution is the preferred indication of competence, though not all psychologists gain that degree.

Psychiatrists are those who have been trained first as physicians in medical school and who then, through continuing experience as psychiatric residents in a mental hospital setting and often also through special experiences such as a training analysis with an established psychoanalyst, move on to specialized practice with emotionally disturbed individuals. There are certain treatments, such as the use of drugs, that only the psychiatrist and not the psychologist is equipped to administer. However, clinical psychologists and psychiatrists often work side by side in hospitals,

clinics, and other practice settings, and they often do very similar things in both diagnosis and treatment.

The diversity of psychologists' professional as well as scientific endeavor can be inferred from a look at the following list of officially organized divisions of the American Psychological Association. Each of these divisions has its own officers, its own bylaws, its own membership requirements; and, with the help of central coordination, each one stages an annual program of papers and symposia.

Division of General Psychology
Division of the Teaching of Psychology
Division of Experimental Psychology
Division of Evaluation and Measurement
Division of Physiological and Comparative Psychology
Division on Developmental Psychology
Division of Personality and Social Psychology
The Society for the Psychological Study of Social Issues
Division on Esthetics
Division of Clinical Psychology
Division of Consulting Psychology
Division of Industrial Psychology
Division of Educational Psychology
Division of School Psychologists
Division of Counseling Psychology
Division of Psychologists in Public Service
Division of Military Psychology
Division on Maturity and Old Age
The Society of Engineering Psychologists
National Council on Psychological Aspects of Disability
Division of Consumer Psychology
Division of Philosophical Psychology

PSYCHOLOGY AND EVERYDAY DECISIONS

Perhaps the best way to assess the possible worth of a course in psychology is to examine the effect such a study may have on the decisions—decisions about people—each of us will make during the rest of his life.

Let us say that each of us makes fifty decisions a day. That makes 18,250 decisions in 365 days. In fifty years, each of us will make a total of 912,500 decisions. These will be little decisions about ourselves, about our children, our friends, our customers, our clients, our neighbors. Each decision will affect the welfare of someone. Some decisions, if we take a position of great responsibility, will affect the lives of hundreds of thousands of people. If we grant that one decision can be better than another, then anything that increases the quality of a decision takes on vast significance. Particularly is this so if we multiply our 912,500 individual decisions by 200,000,000 people, obtaining a total of 182,500,000,000,000 decisions by American people during the next fifty years of our national existence.

Suppose we are sure we know how to influence the decisions people make about people. How can we be sure that we exert our influence for the better? What is *the better*? That, of course, is a question of values, and hence it is a matter that falls outside of science. But decisions also involve predictions.

When we decide to do *A* rather than *B, we are predicting that A will lead to something we will like better*. We decide to spank a baby, marry a girl, buy a car, enter law school, or cast our vote for the opposition candidate on the basis of our predictions that our actions will have certain consequences and that we will like them. What people *should* like is not the province of knowledge and the scientific approach. However, science is concerned with predictions about future likes and dislikes. Whether a man *should* like obedient children is not in the area of psychology. But whether spanking will produce obedience is a psychological matter. And whether the man who now likes obedient children will continue to like obedient children—that is a psychological matter also, and potentially a scientific one.

There are a number of aspects of psychology, as a scientific discipline, that would seem reasonably sure to have a bearing on the quality of decisions a person makes.

First *there are the facts of psychology*. The following chapters will contain many facts about many facets of human behavior. Not all of these facts will have an immediate bearing on practical decisions, for the scientific investigator does not run his life in the pursuit of facts of immediate utility. He studies processes, and follows where his curiosity leads him. But a knowledge of the relevant facts should contribute at least a modicum to the quality of the student's future decisions.

A working familiarity with the *constructs of psychology* should also influence future decisions. Much of the learning in our introductory course is the learning of a vocabulary—a vocabulary of the basic constructs of psychological science. The naturalistic and relatively parsimonious constructs of psychology can often usefully be substituted for the common-sense constructs which many people use. There is utility in thinking in terms of frustration rather than meanness, **Intelligence Quotient** (IQ) rather than stupidity, regression rather than childishness, frames of reference rather than points of view, retroactive inhibition rather than failure to learn, etc.

A knowledge of the *theories* and *working hypotheses* of psychology will also affect future decisions, probably for the better. A theory represents, among other things, one way of looking at and interpreting events. Each of us, as we have seen, has his own general theory, evolved over a period of time. The psychologist's theories may often run counter to student theories. Exposure to new theories may cause discomfort and confusion, but the exposure will also supply the thoughtful student with alternative ways of viewing and interpreting human behavior. Other things being equal, the man with two ways of interpreting an event is more likely to find a *good* way of interpreting it than is the man who knows, very incontrovertibly, only one way. Perhaps this is an argument for enlightened confusion as the stuff out of which wisdom is made.

In addition to facts, constructs, and theories, the *methods* of psychology should make a contribution to the quality of a student's decisions. Not that all students will or should learn to conduct psychological research. But, in line with the major burden of the present chapter, any person faced with a decision can profit from controlled observation, an objective attitude, an ability to distinguish between facts and opinions, an increased ability to use the power of quantification, and an attitude of tentativeness. Someone has observed that the outstanding characteristic of a good psychologist is that *he has learned to learn about be-*

havior. Perhaps the highest aspiration for an introductory course in psychology is that it should help students learn to learn.

SUMMARY

1. Every individual is, in a sense, a part-time psychologist; he observes people and, with some success, formulates his ideas about them.

2. Each of us needs a "theory" of people if we are to make necessary predictions about them.

3. Our "theories" of people probably stem from the prevailing ideology of man, from our individual experiences and "experiments."

4. Each of us has his own personal "theory," and there is some evidence that our "theories" make a difference in our behavior.

5. Although everyone is something of a psychologist and everyone has his own theory of human behavior, not many of us as laymen adhere to the rules or employ the techniques of the scientific psychologist.

6. Scientific psychology aspires to objectivity of observation, and there are a number of established techniques to help ensure objectivity. These include repeated observations and precise control of sampling.

7. Scientific psychology employs, wherever possible, controlled rather than casual observations. The scientist may employ naturalistic observations, clinical observations, survey observations, or highly structured experimental observations, with explicit hypotheses and controlled observations of ways in which dependent variables change with changes in independent variables.

8. Science employs both *the language of fact* and *the language of logical constructs* in attempts to account for relations between fact and the language of constructs. A fact is an agreed-upon perceptual relation between observers and an event. Constructs are terms that are invented in the attempt to deal with the variables that may intervene between S-R facts or R-R facts.

9. Constructs as used in psychology are naturalistic and are employed with an eye to operational definition and the law of parsimony. A study of psychology involves a study of an interlocking body of psychological constructs.

10. Basic science is concerned not only with prediction but also with a complete understanding of process. An immediate concern with prediction characterizes common sense and applied psychology, and most often leads to a molar rather than a molecular approach to problems of behavior.

11. Psychologists employ a richly varied research attack upon the psychological process, an attack varying from the molecular to the molar, from the neurological to the purely psychological, from the rigorously experimental to the insightfully clinical, from the pure to the frankly applied.

12. Science is, by definition, public; it must be so if it is to be testable and if it is to accumulate. Each of us has private perceptions, private and sometimes unconscious meanings. Science remains explicit and public.

13. Science strives for precision both of observation and of report. Precision in observation and report, and the precision and power that can inhere in the use of mathematical models, can contribute both to the attainment and the communication of knowledge.

14. Science is tentative. It is a seeking rather than a final knowing.

15. There is value in liberal education, and in psychology as a part of the arts and science curriculum. A knowledge of the facts, theories, hypotheses, methods, and constructs of psychology can contribute to the quality of everyday decisions involving oneself and others.

RESEARCH REPORTS

THE FIELDS OF PSYCHOLOGY [*]

In early 1962 the American Psychological Association, in association with the National Science

[*] Robert F. Lockman, An empirical description of the subfields of psychology, *Amer. Psychologist*, 1964, 19, 645–653.

Foundation and the National Scientific Register, mailed questionnaires to the 19,370 psychologists who were then members of the Association. These questionnaires sought and obtained data on a variety of aspects of the scientific and professional lives of psychologists. In reporting one analysis of the data from this survey, Lockman gives a tabulation of the primary specialty reported by the first 9,521 psychologists who returned their completed questionnaires. The analyst satisfied himself that the psychologists on whom he tabulated data constituted a good and usable sample of the total population of APA members. His data are presented in the following table.

ENUMERATION OF PSYCHOLOGY RESPONDENTS' PROFESSIONAL IDENTIFICATION

PROFESSIONAL IDENTIFICATION	TOTAL NUMBER
Clinical psychologist	3,441
Experimental psychologist	1,210
Counseling psychologist	1,000
Industrial psychologist	866
Educational psychologist	731
School psychologist	633
Social psychologist	527
Engineering psychologist	293
Psychometric psychologist	248
Developmental psychologist	201
Personality psychologist	198
General psychologist	30
"Other" psychologist	11
Social scientist	36
Physiologist	21
Statistician	6
Pharmacologist	5
Numerical analyst	3
Operations researcher	3
Industrial and "Other" engineer	2
Ecologist	1
No report	55
Total	9,521

SOURCES AND KINDS OF GRADUATE DEGREES IN PSYCHOLOGY [*]

Each year the American Psychological Association collects and publishes information about graduate programs in psychology and about scholarships, fellowships, and assistantships available

[*] Sherman Ross and Robert F. Lockman, Survey of graduate education in psychology, *Amer. Psychologist*, 1964, 19, 623–628.

to graduate students. In 1963, in connection with its annual collection of these kinds of data, the Association also asked 186 departments of psychology, all known to offer graduate work, to report on the number and kinds of graduate degrees the departments had granted. Information was received from all but four departments. Analysis of the data showed that, during the academic year 1962–63, 99 departments granted a total of 880 doctoral degrees while 158 departments granted 1,796 master's degrees. The following table presents figures on the master's and doctoral degrees granted by the 27 departments granting the largest number of master's degrees.

The same researchers tabulated the data on the fields of specialization in which the degrees were

MASTER'S DEGREES AWARDED BY THE LARGEST DEPARTMENTS IN ACADEMIC YEAR 1962–63

DEPARTMENT	MASTER'S DEGREES AWARDED	DOCTORATES ALSO AWARDED
Columbia University (Teachers College) Foundations and Psychological Services [a]	86	45
Temple University	50	6
Purdue University	45	40
Fordham University	38	13
Ohio State University	33	22
San Jose State College	31	—
Boston University	27	12
Kansas State Teachers College	27	—
Western Michigan University	23	—
Columbia University	23	9
University of Minnesota	20	22
City University of New York	20	—
San Francisco State College	20	—
University of California (Los Angeles)	20	10
University of Missouri (Education) [a]	19	—
Hofstra University	18	—
State University of Iowa	17	21
University of Massachusetts	17	16
University of Colorado	17	5
University of Illinois	16	15
Catholic University	16	6
University of Michigan	15	43
Michigan State University	15	18
Western Reserve University	15	15
University of Pittsburgh	15	11
University of Hawaii	15	2
Kent State University	15	—

Note.—N = 27.

[a] *All others are departments of psychology.*

granted. These data on doctoral degrees are presented in the table below.

KINDS OF GRADUATE DEGREES GRANTED IN
PSYCHOLOGY IN ACADEMIC YEAR 1962–63

| | DOCTORATES | |
AREA OF SPECIALIZATION	N	%
Clinical	320	36.4
Experimental	257	29.2
Social and personality	84	9.5
Industrial	46	5.2
Counseling and guidance	43	4.9
Educational	36	4.1
General	28	3.2
Developmental	20	2.3
Psychometrics	19	2.2
School	15	1.7
Engineering and human factors	2	0.2
Unspecified and others	10	1.1
Total	880	

Note.—Data from 180 of 186 departments.

EMPLOYERS OF PSYCHOLOGISTS *

In 1963 the American Psychological Association published a booklet, *A Career in Psychology*, giving assorted information about psychologists and about the paths to, nature of, and rewards for psychological work. Among the information presented was that of the employers of psychologists, shown on the graph below.

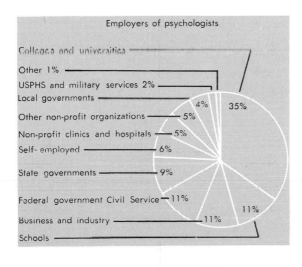

Employers of psychologists

Colleges and universities — 35%
Other 1%
USPHS and military services 2%
Local governments — 4%
Other non-profit organizations — 5%
Non-profit clinics and hospitals — 5%
Self-employed — 6%
State governments — 9%
Federal government Civil Service — 11%
Business and industry — 11%
Schools — 11%

---

* Sherman Ross and Robert F. Lockman, *A Career in Psychology* (Washington, D.C.: American Psychological Association, 1963).

MEASUREMENT OF PHILOSOPHIES OF HUMAN NATURE *

In this study, Wrightsman created a test to measure some broad aspects of the individual's philosophy of human nature. First, after analyzing a wide range of writings on the nature of human nature, he defined six basic bipolar dimensions with respect to which philosophies of human nature vary:

1. Trustworthiness: possession of moral, honest, and reliable characteristics.

2. Altruism: unselfishness, sincere sympathy, and concern for others.

3. Independence: maintenance of one's own convictions in the face of society's pressures toward conformity.

4. Strength of will and rationality: understanding of one's own motives, and control over one's own actions.

5. Complexity: the extent to which a person is complex and hard to understand or simple and easy to understand.

6. Variability: extent of individual differences in basic nature and the basic changeability in human nature.

It was the investigator's intent to create six psychological tests to determine the individual's "score" on each of these six aspects or dimensions of human nature. He also wished to test a number of hypotheses, which he describes as follows:

1. Females will possess more favorable views of human nature than will males. Females are also expected to view human nature as more complex than are males.

2. Students from Fundamentalist religious backgrounds will possess more unfavorable

---

* Lawrence S. Wrightsman, Jr., *Psychol. Report,* 1964, 14, 743–751.
The abstracts of research reports, here and at the end of other chapters, are not intended to represent the "classics" of the literature. Rather, they are typical, recent contributions of relevance for topics dealt with in a given chapter. The student is invited not only to see close up some of the research literature of psychology, but to concern himself with ways in which the research might be sharpened, clarified, extended—or refuted. The research reports will be presented with more technical detail in the later chapters of the book.

views of human nature. In other words, the Calvinist view of the basic perversity of man will be revealed in the view of human nature held by persons of Fundamentalist background.

3. Persons dissatisfied with their present self-concepts will possess unfavorable views of human nature.

4. Various students' views of human nature will be related to the favorability of their evaluations of the instructor of their class.

5. Philosophies of human nature, as revealed by this instrument, will be related to other measures of attributes of human nature—specifically, political cynicism, Machiavellianism, and faith in people.

For each of the dimensions described above, the experimenter constructed what amounted to a short psychological test (employing methods described in Chap. 5). These six tests, combined into one paper-and-pencil form, were administered first to 260 college students and later to 200 additional ones. The tests themselves were "tested" (cf. Chap. 5 for discussion of split-half and test-retest reliability) and found to be usable. On this matter of the usefulness of the tests, there was evidence, for example, that the individuals who indicated on one occasion that people are trustworthy, altruistic, and independent were also very much inclined to have the same convictions on a later occasion. Similarly, subjects who felt that people are trustworthy or altruistic in one situation felt that people are also trustworthy or altruistic in another situation; that is, these views of human nature tend to be general and consistent views for the individual.

Perhaps the finding that individuals do have characteristic, lasting, and consistent philosophies of human nature was the most significant result of this study. But there are also data that bear on the hypotheses with which the researcher began his study. Female students *were* more favorable than males in their view of human nature. Students at one college where there prevails a strong Fundamentalist-religious atmosphere *were* significantly less favorably disposed than students at other colleges toward the nature of human nature. Students who on an appropriate test indicated an unhappiness with themselves *were* inclined to be unfavorable in their general views of mankind. Students who were more favorably disposed toward human beings in general were also more favorably disposed toward the particular human being who was their instructor in the psychology course. Finally, the students' views of human beings, as those views were tapped by the test created for this study, were in general theoretical agreement with the students' scores on other psychological tests (see discussion of the construct validity of psychological tests, pp. 131–132).

SUGGESTED READINGS

Anastasi, Anne. *Fields of applied psychology.* New York: McGraw-Hill, 1964.

Clark, K. E. *America's psychologists.* Washington, D.C.: American Psychological Association, 1957.

Conant, J. B. *On understanding science.* New Haven: Yale University Press, 1947.

Hayakawa, S. I. *Language in thought and action.* New York: Harcourt, Brace and World, 1949.

Marx, Melvin H., ed. *Theories in contemporary psychology, including original papers contributed by leading psychologists.* New York: Macmillan, 1963.

Miller, G. A. *Mathematics and psychology.* New York: Wiley, 1964.

Osgood, C. E. *Method and theory in experimental psychology.* New York: Oxford University Press, 1953.

Sanford, F. H., and E. J. Capaldi, eds. *Advancing psychological science, Vol. I.: Philosophies, methods, and approaches.* Belmont, Calif.: Wadsworth, 1964.

PART TWO

BIOLOGICAL
FOUNDATIONS
OF BEHAVIOR

OUTLINE / CHAPTER 3

I. THE HUMAN INFANT

    A. The Neonate's Biological History

    B. Characteristics of the Human Neonate
       1. Dependency
       2. Absence of Instincts

II. INHERITED CHARACTERISTICS

    A. Inheritance of Physical Traits

    B. Inheritance of Learning Capacity

    C. Inheritance of Intelligence

    D. Inheritance of Susceptibilities

    E. Interaction of Heredity and Environment: Case of Shorty

III. CONGENITAL FACTORS

    A. Physical Effects

    B. Emotional Effects

    C. Prenatal Learning

IV. GENERAL DIMENSIONS OF DEVELOPMENT

    A. Cephalocaudal Sequence

    B. Proximal-Distal Sequence

    C. Differential-Integration

V. DEVELOPMENT IN SPECIFIC AREAS

    A. Motor Development

    B. Language Development

    C. Emotional Development

VI. GLANDULAR PROCESSES IN DEVELOPMENT

VII. MATURATION AND LEARNING

VIII. EFFECTS OF EARLY EXPERIENCE

    A. Effects of Early Sensory Experience

    B. Effects of Early Physical Stimulation

    C. Effects of Early Child-Parent Relationships

IX. SUMMARY

X. RESEARCH REPORT

CHAPTER 3

THE
DEVELOPING
ORGANISM

We have defined the psychological process, have viewed it against some perspectives, and have considered the general nature of the scientific approach to the study of psychological phenomena. We now will do well to focus on the biological organism that enters into the psychological process.

In such a focus we shall not attempt to cover or even to recapitulate the content of modern biology, since our primary concern is with the *behavior* of the organism rather than with physiological or neurological structures or functions. However, as we have seen, the psychological process always occurs against a background of physiology and neurology; behavior remains rooted in biological processes, and psychology is closely interrelated with biology.

*In this chapter we shall deal with the general biological attributes of the human organ-*ism—*particularly those attributes that are laid down in human heredity and that unfold during the period of human development—and with their effect on the ways in which the organism senses external events, interprets them, responds to them, and learns from its own experience.*

THE HUMAN INFANT

We can begin our study of human development by looking for a moment—and from a certain point of view—at the new-born human infant, the **neonate.** Because it is an organism, the human infant can be counted on to grow and develop. Because it is a human organism, it can be counted on to grow and develop as human rather than as ape or monkey or owl or crayfish. The nature and sequences of human development, from conception to death, will have a significant role in determining the form and sequences of the behavior we see as the motivated organism finds its way in its world.

Table 3–1. THE STAGES OF DEVELOPMENT

Neonate	From birth at full term to end of 1st postnatal month
Infant	From 1 month until walking (15 or 16 months)
Toddler	From 15 or 16 months to about 2½ years
Preschool Child	2½ years until entry into the first grade
Child in Middle Years	6 to about 12 years
Adolescent	Pubescence to social maturity

The human neonate, when he takes his first breath and begins his separate and separated psychological life, triggers diverse reactions among the people around him. To the physician who delivers him he may represent the successful completion of a very difficult case. To his mother he is the object of wondrous maternal affection. To his father he represents a new responsibility, and perhaps, too, he constitutes welcome evidence of the father's true effectiveness as a male. To his older brother he may be a threat and an interloper into the sibling's heretofore cozily monopolistic hold on the attention and the affection of his parents.

In addition, the human infant has his own attributes. We are likely to think first about the psychological future of this bundle of potentialities. In any particular neonate we may have the next Churchill or the next Hitler or the next Einstein or the next member of the mentally deficient branch of the Kallikak family. Twenty years from the instant of birth, this individual may be accepting the office of president of his college class or may be led toward the intake desk of the mental hospital.

In our fascination with this psychological

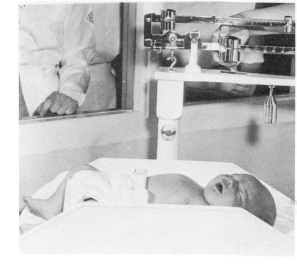

Figure 3–1. NEW-BORN BABY. *When the dependent, incomplete human individual weighs into the world, he has behind him a long biological history; in front of him is a future of biological development. He will through growth come into his own particular biological inheritance.*

future, we are likely to overlook the fact that the individual already has a history, a *biological history,* which at the time of conception not only recedes into the distant past but also has already cast into final form some aspects of the psychological future. The individual also has a *biological* future as well as a psychological one. The neonate is not yet a fully formed biological organism. It is not yet biologically ready to register its world accurately or to respond except very inaccurately to it. It cannot yet appreciate Prokofiev or master the simple rigors of toilet training. It must ripen—and it will. Its nervous system, its glandular system, its skeleton, and musculature must all come into their biological inheritance before the organism can successfully assimilate its social inheritance. It will grow and develop until it reaches maturity. Then it will begin the process of aging, a process bringing about a decline in many of its biological capacities. At any stage of its life, on any day, what the organism does, what it *can* do, depends in some measure not only on its biological history but also on the particular stage of its biological development.

The human infant may be viewed as the latest event in an aeon-long sequence of biological events. The sequence may be viewed in three ways: (1) as an evolutionary sequence, (2) as a sequence within the human species, and (3) as a sequence involving the **genes** and **chromosomes** of a direct line of ancestors.

Viewed against a Darwinian perspective, the human neonate has an *evolutionary history* extending back in time to the first trace of life in the primordial sea. The infant has life. It is an organism, with a kinship to all other organisms (see Fig. 3–2).

The individual neonate also has a *species heredity*. It is human and thereby is the potential possessor of all the limitations and capacities that human flesh is heir to. It cannot fly unaided through the air, nor by its own native devices can it breathe under water. It cannot stand on the ground and nibble leaves from the tops of trees. It cannot hunt with the hawk, run with the cheetah, or lift with the elephant. But it is heir to a nervous system that has enabled its forebears, through invention, to adapt to the environments of both birds and fish; and it can be expected to achieve a mastery of its world far surpassing that determined by the native endowments, however impressive, of the hawk, the cheetah, the giraffe, or the elephant.

Most important for the problems of psychology, the neonate has its own *individual heredity*. As we shall see, the individual has inherited certain traits, capacities, and limitations from his human ancestors, and this inheritance has an important effect on his later behavior.

The life of the human individual begins when a germ cell (**spermatozoon**) from the father unites with an egg (**ovum**) from the mother to form a combined cell, or **zygote**. (See Fig. 3–3 for a depiction of early cell development.) When this event occurs, much of the life of the human individual is already determined, for the chromosomes he gets from his father and those from his mother decide in a very large measure the kind of individual this one will be. He will, of course, be human. It is now determined that he will be an individual with a certain size and shape of body, certain color of eyes and hair, a certain facial configuration, a certain complexion. He will begin the psychological process with certain limitations and endowments.

With respect to the total number of hereditary **traits**, the influence of the individual's mother and the influence of his father are approximately equal; for his *chromosomes*, the carriers of heredity, come equally divided from either side of the family. Since the human germ cell contains 46 ordinary chromosomes (including two sex-determining chromosomes), the new individual receives 23 from his father and 23 from his mother (one sex chromosome each from both his father and

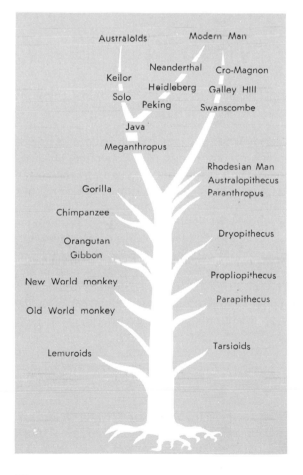

Figure 3–2. THE EVOLUTIONARY HEREDITY OF THE SPECIES. *An evolutionary tree of the primates.*

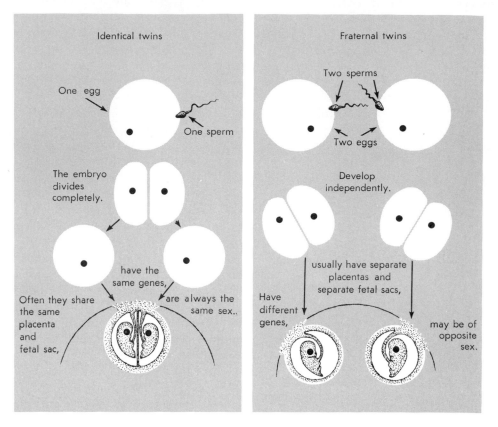

Identical twins

One egg

One sperm

The embryo divides completely.

have the same genes,

Often they share the same placenta and fetal sac,

are always the same sex.

Fraternal twins

Two sperms

Two eggs

Develop independently.

usually have separate placentas and separate fetal sacs,

Have different genes,

may be of opposite sex.

Figure 3–3. HEREDITARY MECHANISMS: FRATERNAL AND IDENTICAL TWINS. *Fraternal twins are produced when two separate ova are fertilized at the same time. Identical twins occur when one fertilized ovum divides.*

mother). Therefore, there is a *double set* of chromosomes in each cell—22 *pairs* of ordinary chromosomes in addition to the sex-determining ones. The new individual's mother and father also, of course, have had an heredity. Both have received half of their chromosomes from each of their parents. The chance then becomes one in four that the new individual will have any given chromosome in common with any one of his four grandparents. Similarly, there is one chance in eight that he may inherit a chromosome from any one of his great grandparents. And so on.

Consider the trait *eye color*. Each pair of chromosomes contains parts, called *genes*, that are responsible for particular traits. It is believed that the pair of genes responsible for eye color lie in a specific pair of chromosomes;

and each gene is located normally at a corresponding position in its respective chromosome. Each chromosome pair in any particular germ cell may possess similar genes (both bearing, for example, brown-eyed determiners or blue-eyed determiners), or the chromosomes may carry opposing genes (the one bearing brown- and the other blue-eyed determiners). In the cell division involved in the maturation of the germ cell, the paired genes separate, so that only one of any pair of genes is retained in the mature germ cell, and passed on to the zygote.

Furthermore, these traits are classified as **dominant** or **recessive**; since brown eye color is dominant and blue eye color is recessive, an individual who receives a gene for brown eyes from one parent and a gene for blue eyes from the other parent will have brown eyes. If both parents have only brown genes, the progeny will have only brown eyes; or if the parents have only genes for blue eyes, their offspring will all have blue eyes. But if each parent carries both brown and blue genes, the possible results are more varied. Figure 3–4 shows the resulting possible combinations. Figure 3–5 depicts the inheritance of red hair (a recessive trait) over three generations.

cell, or in an egg cell, the potential variation in heredity is even more enormously increased.

This kind of computation underscores the individuality of the single human organism.

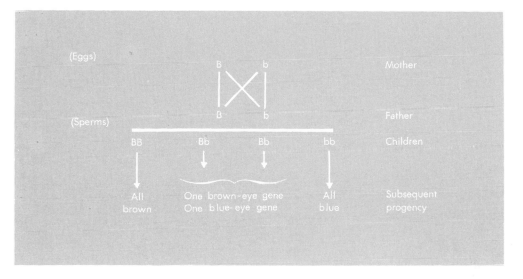

Figure 3–4. INHERITANCE OF BROWN AND BLUE EYES. *B — brown eyes; b = blue eyes.*

These statistical computations do not mean, however, that we can predict with any certainty just what will be the precise characteristics of the new individual. Theoretically, the 23 chromosomes coming from his father could occur in any one of 2^{23} or 8,388,608 different combinations. Any father, then, has more than 8,000,000 different combinations of characteristics to pass along to his children. The same situation exists, of course, for the mother. When one of 8,000,000 combinations of chromosomes in the sperm gets together with one of 8,000,000 possible combinations in the ovum, the resulting event has a very great rarity about it. Theoretically, any two parents have a pool of about 150 trillion trait combinations, differing in some measure from each other in their inherited pattern of chromosomes. This figure becomes even greater when we recognize that the genes, the basic determiners of heredity, do not always stay put in the chromosomes that carry them. Chromosomes may exchange genes. If genes *cross over* from one chromosome to another in a sperm

When he is born, unless he has an identical twin, there has probably never been another organism exactly like him. It can safely be said, for example, that the events transpiring when any student reads these paragraphs are unique in history; for not only has there never been an organism quite like him but, by the time he can read, he has lived through a unique pattern of life events.

CHARACTERISTICS OF THE HUMAN NEONATE

Dependency

One of the outstanding characteristics of the human neonate is his great helplessness and dependency. In muscular control he is greatly limited and incompetent. When he moves, he tends to move all over. There are no precise reachings or graspings—only general undifferentiated movement. His sense organs are similarly formless and limited. Though the pupil of his eye will automatically expand and contract as the intensity of light changes, the infant, as far as anyone can tell, has very little of what we would recognize as sensation. He

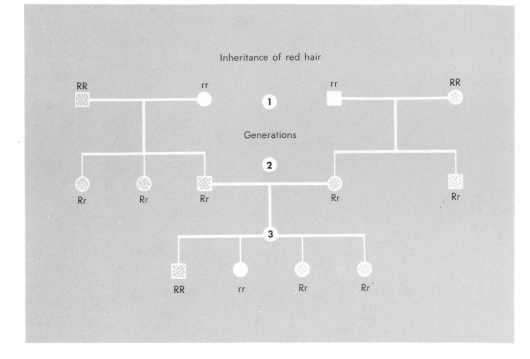

Figure 3–5. INHERITANCE OF RED HAIR. *Red hair is a recessive trait. In the diagram, all second-generation offspring have one dominant gene (R) and one recessive (r). If generation three follows laws of chance perfectly, one quarter will be RR, one quarter rr, and one half Rr. Circle = female; Square = male; Solid = red hair.*

cannot yet follow a light with the movement of his eyes or head, for example. Although he does respond to loud noises, his auditory life is probably very vague and limited. When he responds emotionally to such stimuli as loud noises or the sudden withdrawal of support, he again responds all over with something that can best be described as general excitement. Specific emotions, such as fear or anger or happiness, cannot yet be observed.

Because of these limitations, the human infant—more than any other animal—is completely dependent on other organisms for his survival. The lemur, for example, is dependent on outside assistance for, at the most, a few days. At the end of that time, he is ready to pursue what seems to be an independent life. The young monkey is dependent only for a few weeks (see Fig. 3–6). The infant chimpanzee remains with his mother three to six months. By contrast, at what age is the human being ready to stand on his own feet and make his own way in the world? At 6 years? At 12? We do not know the age at which the human young might, in a natural environment, demonstrate surviving independence. We know that in our culture most young people do not achieve genuine independence until they are in their late teens or beyond. Actually, many individuals have difficulty in making a transition from the period in life when dependency is rewarded to a later period in which it is not rewarded at all or is even punished (Stendler, 1954). And some human organisms never really achieve *psychological* independence from parental care, being prone to run home to mother in times of stress or pressure long after they have reached biological and chronological maturity.

If one wishes to speculate, he might make the case that this protracted period of human dependency has a great deal to do with the forms of human existence in the various cultures of the world. A protracted dependency means a long exposure to educative adults.

Figure 3–6. EARLY SELF-SUFFICIENCY. *Monkeys attain self-sufficiency early. Compared to long-dependent human infants, monkeys are able, after a few weeks, to shift for themselves and soon can contend with laboratory problems.*

It means at least the opportunity to learn an accepting or a rejecting orientation toward other human organisms. It may mean that in any one culture there is a great tendency for the younger generation to copy the older one. This would not be the case if our young left home at age 4 or 6 or 10. However such speculation may run, the human infant is a dependent organism and remains so for a relatively long time.

Absence of Instincts

Relating closely to the protracted dependency of the human infant is the fact that, compared to other forms of life, he seems to be lacking in **instincts.**

The term *instinct* generally refers to an unlearned pattern of goal-directed behavior that can be counted on to appear under set circumstances in all members of a particular species. These patterns generally have a great biological utility for the organism, contributing cardinally to its survival. A swallow, for example, does not have to live through an elaborate and laborious process of learning in order to build a nest (Fig. 3–7). With no experience in nest building and without ever having seen another swallow in its life, the bird will, when the time comes, build a nest as other swallows have done since swallows have existed. Similarly, the trapdoor spider builds his ingenious home in ways apparently dictated by inherited patterns in his nervous system. He does not learn his architecture from his elders. As a matter of fact, despite romantic writings about the ways mother bears and she wolves educate their young, the human organism is the only one that deliberately sets out to teach its offspring how to live.

In contrast to other organisms, the human infant does not appear to have this preformed and unlearned repertoire of responses with which to meet the demands of the world. He is equipped only with a few relatively simple **reflexes,** a number of which are present before actual birth (Hooker, 1943). If his lips are touched, he will—particularly when he is hungry—give a sucking reflex. If a bright light is flashed in his eyes, he will blink by reflex. If an object is placed in his palms, he will close his fingers around it. He will respond automatically, with vague behavior that seems generally uncomfortable, to loud sounds. He also has what is known as a **Babinski reflex:** if the sole of his foot is scratched, his toes will move outward and upward. (This reflex, however, disappears very soon after birth.) When compared with the relatively rich repertoire of elaborate instinctive behaviors of lower-animal forms, this native equipment of the human being seems very meager. Not only is our infant almost completely dependent on his outside world, but he also faces what to him must sometimes seem to be the grim and discouraging necessity to *learn* his ways out of dependency.

We might conceive this absence of instincts as one of the misfortunes burdening humankind. On the other hand, the absence of instincts does represent a prime human freedom. The human being, without the fixities of instinctive patterns, is free to learn. As he goes about the business of meeting his biological needs for food and warmth and survival, he

Figure 3–7. INSTINCTIVE BEHAVIOR. *Lower animals are equipped with instinctive behavior patterns. The cliff swallow builds its characteristic nest without having to learn from its elders.*

can learn almost any form of behavior that is prevalent in his social environment or that becomes necessary for the advancement of his own comfort. He has learned his way off the earth and into orbit, and perhaps soon he will be pursuing his fate on other planets and in other worlds.

That, then, is the human infant—a relatively formless, helpless, unorganized being, possessed of a few reflexes and a very vague awareness of events about him. To dramatize a bit at this point, we might reflect on the contrast between this dependent bundle of potentialities on one hand and the fully mature, fully competent, fully organized, fully realized, keenly and analytically conscious, marvelously active adult human being on the other—the human being whose life is characterized by elaborate habits, skills, attitudes, values; who loves and hates; who thinks and explores and creates; who has taken into him-

self the best of his own culture and who in wonderfully unanticipated ways takes hold of his world to revise it, to change it, to move it ahead toward the realization of human goals.

On a more prosaic level we can say that this small organic system, the neonate, is now ready to begin its psychological history. Its biological ripening will continue into adulthood. And accompanying the unfolding of the infant's biological potentialities is always his psychological interaction with his environment. Our study of psychology will focus on the psychological history of the organism and on the processes by which that history is possible.

INHERITED CHARACTERISTICS

At the moment of conception, many characteristics of the human individual are fixed for all time, remaining throughout life essentially independent of environmental influences. Other attributes of the new zygote, though also determined by hereditary mechanisms, must be regarded as capacities or limitations or susceptibilities rather than fixed characteristics; for they show themselves only through the organism's interaction with the environment.

Generally speaking, heredity provides an over-all program for the developing organism; the fulfillment of that program depends on the kind of environment he faces and the ways in which he interacts with that environment. A leading theorist (Hunt, 1961) has pointed out that in the first half of the present century psychologists generally—sometimes perhaps unconsciously—were committed to the view that intelligence and other attributes are rigidly fixed at birth and that development is predetermined. Hunt, however, emphasizes the relatively great influence of environmental factors (his book is entitled *Experience and Intelligence*) in all phases of human development. Today, the environment-heredity question still produces lively controversy and productive research (Chap. 7).

We need to exercise considerable care in our attempt to deal with allegedly inherited characteristics and with ways in which these characteristics are influenced, if any, by environmental pressures and processes.

INHERITANCE OF PHYSICAL TRAITS

In the zygote's particular configuration of genes and chromosomes, a blueprint of the future physical characteristics of the human individual are laid down. As he lives out his life, we can see the unfolding of his racial and ancestral inheritance. His height and general bodily contours, within relatively narrow limits, are set. His facial appearance, the color of his eyes, the color, texture, and distribution of his hair, and other physical characteristics are set and are not amenable to influence by the ordinary forces of the environment (see Figs. 3–4 and 3–5).

These inherited physical characteristics determine much of the psychological future of the individual. Obviously, the boy who inherits a large and well-coordinated body will not only be able to play football but will also probably be placed under environmental pressure to do so. The person with red hair will similarly encounter in his social environment certain pressures and expectations that are reserved for redheads; these will influence his adjustment perhaps in significant ways.

INHERITANCE OF LEARNING CAPACITY

That such a thing as capacity to learn is inherited is suggested by an experiment (Tryon, 1940) in which a deliberate attempt was made to breed a strain of rats very good at running a maze and another strain of rats very poor at this performance. The experimenter started with a large population of male and female rats. Each one of these animals was run for nineteen trials through a relatively long maze containing food at its end. After the nineteen trials, the experimenter selected the rats who were "brightest" and the rats who were "dullest" at this chore, with brightness and dullness defined in terms of number of errors committed while running the maze. Then bright males were mated with bright females, and the dull with the dull. Those who showed only average capacity to run the maze were excluded from the experiment. When the offspring of these experimental matings were available, they in turn were tested in the maze. Again, after testing, bright males were mated with bright females and dullards with dullards. This procedure was continued for eighteen generations of rats.

By the ninth generation there seemed to be almost entirely separate strains with respect to the capacity to learn this kind of task (Fig. 3–8). The experimenter could by then take any young rat from his bright strain and be very safe in betting that that one would learn the maze better than any young rat picked from any mother in the dull strain.

The capacity for the rapid learning of a maze, then, seems to be determined by heredity. But that this capacity is not a *general* capacity to learn is indicated by further experimentation with these same animals. Searle (1949) tested these two strains on a variety of other learning tasks. He found that the "bright" maze runners were not equally bright on all other learning tasks. Nor were the dull ones dullards across the board. The variety of the rat's intellectual capacities has not been thoroughly traced out, and so we do not know what pattern of abilities we can expect by heredity; but that some learning capacities are open to hereditary influences seems well established.

INHERITANCE OF INTELLIGENCE

The research literature amply indicates that there is a significant hereditary factor in individual intelligence (Chap. 7). Perhaps the clearest evidence comes from studies of **identical twins.** Such twins, called *monozygotic* twins because they come from the same fertilized egg, have in all respects an identical heredity (see Fig. 3–3). If intelligence is an inherited trait, then, they should have identical intelligence. Or, to state it differently, the differences in intelligence between identical twins should be much less than the differences between **fraternal twins,** who do not have

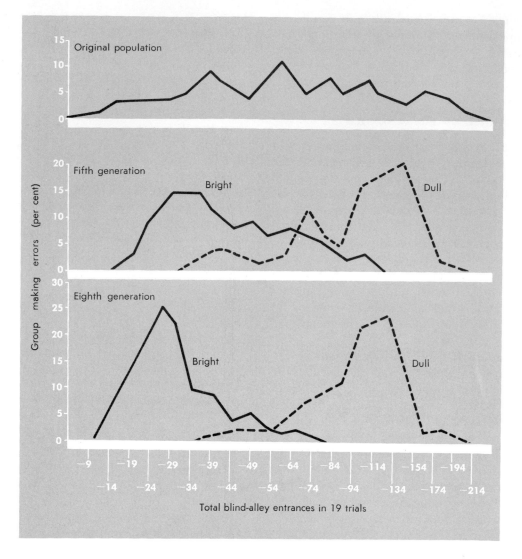

Figure 3–8. THE INHERITANCE OF LEARNING CAPACITY. *When "bright" rats are bred with "bright" rats and dull with dull for nine generations, the result is two almost separate populations of rats. In the charts here, the height of the curve represents the per cent of the rats making the number of errors (i.e., blind-alley entrances) indicated on the baseline of the curve. By the ninth generation, for example, a large percentage of the bright rats were making about 30 errors in 19 trials, while a larger percentage of the dull rats were making about 135 errors in 19 trials. (Tryon, 1940, page 113, Part I; by permission of National Society for the Study of Education.)*

identical heredity. Also, identical twins should be more similar in intelligence than pairs of brothers or pairs of sisters born to the same parents. These statements assume, of course, that environmental influences are held constant in each case. The literature bears out the general conclusion that the tested intelligence of identical twins tends to be very similar, and more similar than that of fraternal twins or the tested intelligence of other brothers and sisters.

A dull identical twin is very likely then to have a dull co-twin, and a bright identical twin is likely to have an almost identically bright co-twin. This is fairly convincing evidence that one's intellectual capacities are, to a large extent, determined by heredity. Although environmental influences can change the tested intelligence of an individual, it is a moderately safe estimate that the intelligence with which an individual first enters the psychological process is an inherited attribute.

INHERITANCE OF SUSCEPTIBILITIES

There is also fairly definite evidence that individuals inherit *susceptibilities* of one kind and another—for example, susceptibility to schizophrenia, a form of mental illness. One study (Kallmann, 1953) found that if one of a pair of identical twins developed **schizophrenia**, the chances were 86 in 100 that the other twin would develop the same mental disorder (Fig. 3–9). By contrast, if one fraternal twin developed schizophrenia, the chances were only 14 in 100 that his twin would develop the same disease.

Such evidence, it needs to be remembered, does not mean that we can make the general statement that mental illness is inherited. In Kallmann's study, 14 of 100 identical twins did *not* develop schizophrenia along with their identical siblings. Also, identical twins, more than most of us, live in highly similar environments, facing perhaps the same kinds of environmental stresses. Although the twins in Kallmann's study were separated at an early age, experiences before they were separated—during the first year or so of life—may have been very significant in producing schizophrenia.

INTERACTION OF HEREDITY
AND ENVIRONMENT:
THE CASE OF SHORTY

The following case of Shorty illustrates the way in which constitutional and biological factors in the person interact with environmental influences to produce a pattern of adjustment of a certain form and flavor.

Shorty appeared at the Institute for Child Study at Oakland as one of a number of children who were being followed over a seven-year period. As his name implies, he was short and stocky. In addition, his rate of growth was slow; and although he was quite unconscious of this at the start, it finally became the central factor in his development. Shorty had always been a bundle of energy; even as a small tot he would disappear for the day, wandering down to the wharfs or railroad yards, sometimes getting lost in his absorption with noise, machines, motion. At eleven he was spending his out-of-school hours at a busy intersection, selling papers, hopping on the running boards of passing cars, relishing the traffic, the banter, the give-and-take scuffles with the other boys. His frank friendliness made him one of the most popular boys of his grade, and, whenever a group gathered, Shorty would be in the center of it, full of suggestions. This was more apt to be true when things were in a disorganized phase; when they settled down to more organized activities Shorty was less in evidence. When he came to the clinic, at the beginning of the study, there was little that was noteworthy save possibly his high metabolic rate and a slight boisterousness and mischievousness that threatened to disrupt the institute. His intelligence was above average (IQ 128) and his school work was passable, although Shorty was always more interested in activity than in the steady application of effort.

It was not really until senior high school that Shorty's difficulties were precipitated, although there had been a steadily mounting disparity between his development and that of his peers. The youngsters in the high-school club rooms began to make disparaging remarks about his personal appearance, which had not hitherto bothered them; and his rowdyism and clowning now annoyed them. While his pals were shooting up inches in height and their voices and other secondary sex characteristics were changing into those of young men, Shorty remained the little boy. At the clinic he stretched upward, when his height record was taken, visibly attempting to make a better record; and he inquired of the physician whether there was not some medicine that he could take to grow tall. In the gym he took to hanging from the bars, hoping to stretch out his inadequate stature. He found that he was not chosen for games, that he could not compete physically (and this was the field where he had excelled). Worst of all, while he remained—like most preadolescents—interested mainly in masculine companionship, his pals "went soft," hung around the dance floor where

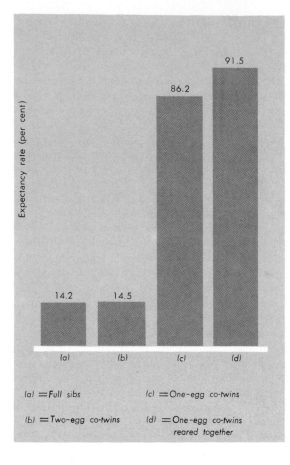

Figure 3–9. INHERITANCE OF SCHIZOPHRENIC
TENDENCY. *If schizophrenia occurs in one of
a pair of randomly selected and unrelated
people, the chances are less than 1 in 100
that the other member of the pair will have
the disease. By contrast, if one member of a
pair of identical twins has schizophrenia, the
chances are 86.2 in 100 that the other twin
will also have the disease. The greater the
similarity in heredity, the greater the chance
that the second member of a pair will have
schizophrenia if the first member does.*
(Kallmann, 1953. From Heredity in Health
and Mental Disorder. *Franz J. Kallmann,
copyright* © *1953. W. W. Norton & Company Inc.*)

the girls danced to the music of the phonograph.
While they spruced up in appearance, danced,
dated, played kissing games, Shorty remained
the small boy whose imagination prompted him
to shut off the phonograph, steal the ice-cream at

the party, interrupt the more adult atmosphere
with pathetic clowning. Shorty was not wanted.

At home he became difficult, morose, quarrelsome. A sullen aloofness replaced his frankness.
His school work declined. Then there was a brief
period in which a "jalopy" assembled from junk-
yard parts took all of his interest; but aside from
his discovery of two cronies who shared in this
project his social adjustment did not improve. An
episode of teasing and hazing in the shop, in
which his lack of masculine development played
a central part, precipitated a state that almost
bordered on the psychotic. He accused his shop-
mates of stealing the key to his car, called the
police, who, in turn, accused Shorty of being the
ringleader in some serious thieving then going on.
He was taken to a detention home and in his
frantic resentment at the false accusations and
misunderstandings behaved in such a fashion that
he was diagnosed as schizophrenic. An intelligence test administered at this time classified him
as of borderline intelligence (IQ 78).

Rescued by an understanding counsellor, Shorty
was put on a new schedule of work, made into
an athletic manager (which utilized many of his
talents and provided a substitute satisfaction for
his frustrated ambitions). His long-delayed
growth carried him (at 15) into the adulthood too
long postponed; and with a little better insight
into his own needs and with new heterosexual interests that carried him back into group life,
Shorty became an average adolescent (Stolz,
1940, pp. 405–411).

In the story of Shorty we can see in personal
form what would otherwise remain a statistical
item in a chart of growth indices. To describe
him as in the lower quartile in stature does not
adequately indicate what this lag in growth
can mean to an active boy who has the human
desire to be popular. There was nothing wrong
with Shorty's growth except that he was "out
of phase" both intellectually and physically.
Placed with his intellectual peers, he was physically and socially retarded; placed with his
physical peers, he would have been bored intellectually. While Shorty could not analyze
his difficulties, he could *feel* them, and the
violence with which he rejected his role convinced one examining physician that his intelligence was deficient and that he was border-
ing upon a psychosis.

CONGENITAL FACTORS

We have said that the psychological life of the individual can be regarded as beginning at birth. This is not quite accurate. Before birth, the human infant has lived for approximately nine months in the relatively simple environment of its mother's womb. Events impinging upon it there can have a hand in its readiness, at birth, to begin pursuing the psychological process.

PHYSICAL EFFECTS

Although the nervous system of the mother is not connected with that of the **fetus,** and although the mother's blood does not flow directly through the child's circulatory system, there is an exchange of nutrient and other materials between the two systems. Therefore, changes in the mother's blood stream, produced by a diet or perhaps by emotional experiences, can affect the unborn child. If the mother has diabetes or high blood pressure, or if she takes large doses of barbiturates, the unborn child can be fatally affected. Thalidomide taken by the mother can produce drastic fetal deformity. If the mother has syphilis, the brain of the infant may be damaged by the time it is born. And nutritional factors, such as vitamin deficiency, can affect the general health of the baby.

EMOTIONAL EFFECTS

What about the *psychological* condition of the mother and its effect on the fetus? We know (see Chap. 9) that emotions such as fear and anger produce definite physiological changes in the body. Such a knowledge leads to questions about the effect of the mother's psychological experience on the fetus. Although there is little clear evidence on this in human beings, an experiment with rats relates directly to the topic.

One experimenter (Thompson, 1957) housed a group of female rats in a double-compartment box. In one compartment, the rats received a strong shock every time a buzzer

sounded. The rats soon learned to avoid the shock by opening the door between the two compartments and escaping from the shocking side of the box to the safe side. The rats were then mated. As soon as they became pregnant, they were again exposed to the buzzer. But now the door was locked, and they could not escape to the safe side of the box. Even though they received no shock under their changed conditions, this experience was a very trying one for the mothers, arousing considerable anxiety. The experimenter assumed that this kind of experience would generate "free-floating" anxiety, which would produce changes in the rats, and that these changes would, in turn, be transmitted to the fetuses.

To pursue this study, the experimenter devised tests whereby he could compare the behavior of rats from the anxious mothers with the behavior of a control group of rats from mothers who had had a less stressful pregnancy. The experimenter knew, from other experiments, that frightened or anxious rats, if placed in a large open area, will move around relatively little. Frightened rats do not explore. Thus, his "open-field" test could be used to examine the anxiety of the two groups of rats. He conducted his test when his rats were between 30 and 40 days old and again when they were 130–140 days old. The offspring of anxious mothers were decidedly less inclined to explore in the open-field situation than were the offspring of the nonanxious mothers (Fig. 3–10, Test A). This difference between the two groups, the experimental and the control, lasted on into the adulthood of the rats.

In a second test, the experimenter measured the emotionality of the rats by noting the time it took them to open the door of their cage and start down a runway to a known source of food. Each member of both these groups of rats was deprived of food for 24 hours in order to ensure that it would have considerable interest in some form of nourishment. The rats born to the anxious mothers were significantly more hesitant in leaving their cages than were rats in the control group (Fig. 3–10, Test B).

Did the hormonal changes produced in the mothers by an emotional experience produce

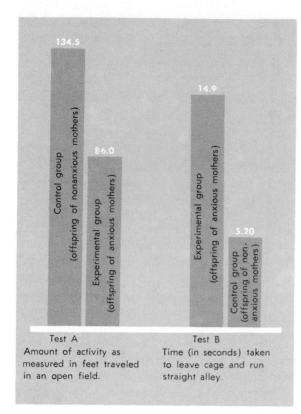

Test A
Amount of activity as
measured in feet traveled
in an open field.

Test B
Time (in seconds) taken
to leave cage and run
straight alley.

Figure 3–10. INHERITED EMOTIONALITY. *Rats born to mothers who had been made anxious were less inclined to explore an "open field," more hesitant to leave home cage to explore. (Adapted from Thompson, 1957.)*

lasting changes in the physiology of the off-spring? We cannot say this for sure. Perhaps the fetal rats heard the same buzzer that their mothers did and consequently developed some emotional reaction. But whether the effect was produced on the young rats by the sound of the buzzer disturbing them or was produced through the mediation of changes in the hormonal activities of their mothers, the influence of prenatal experience seems clearly demonstrated by this experiment. A more recent follow-up study (Ader and Belfer, 1962) supports such a position.

The same conclusion may be drawn from another research in which emotionality in rats was measured by the amount of urination and defecation in an open-field situation (Hall, 1938). The experimenter placed 145 rats in the open field, finding that they differed greatly in the duration of the resulting increased emotionality. Some seemed very unemotional even on the first day while others continued for twelve days to urinate and defecate at an increased rate when placed in the open field. The experimenter then mated the seven most emotional pairs and, for comparison, the seven least emotional pairs. When the offspring, 75 of them, were placed in the open field, 88 per cent of the total instances of emotional behavior of the kind measured occurred among the offspring of the emotional parents.

Also, there is evidence (Thompson, 1962) that when pregnant rats are crowded, given tranquilizing drugs, exposed to irradiation, or given adrenalin, the eventual behavior of the offspring is significantly affected. Apparently, then, emotionality in rats can be inherited. But we are still not safe, of course, in assuming that the same or similar relationships hold for human beings.

PRENATAL LEARNING

There is some evidence that the fetus learns before birth. For example, although fetuses will sometimes move with considerable vigor when loud sounds are made close to the prenatal abode, they will not ordinarily respond to a vibrator applied to the mother's abdomen; however, they can *learn* to respond to the vibrator. In one experiment (Spelt, 1948) the vibrator was applied to the abdomen for five seconds, and during the interval of application a loud clang was sounded nearby. After fewer than 100 paired presentations of the vibrator and the sound, the fetuses being tested responded to the vibrator alone. The conclusion is that they had learned, by association of these stimuli, to respond to the vibrator. The data from a similar experiment are presented in (Fig. 3–11).

Such experiments demonstrate that the fetus can learn. No experiments, however, have demonstrated that the fetus ever learns very much or retains after birth what it has learned. Other studies (Marquis, 1931; Wenger, 1936) dealing with the learning of very young post-

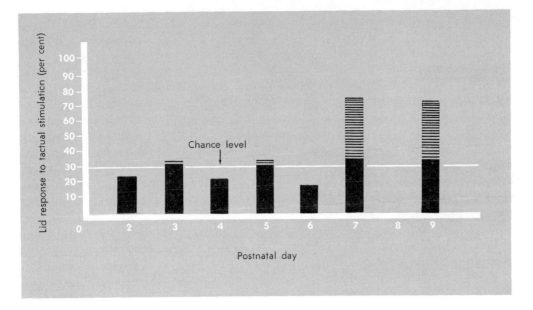

Figure 3–11. CONDITIONED RESPONSES IN
INFANCY. *When a light is flashed in an infant's eye, there is an automatic blink. When the light is repeatedly paired with a vibrator, the vibrator alone will produce a blink on about the seventh day of life. This is a form of learning known as conditioning. Before the seventh day, the blink occurs about 29 per cent of the times the vibrator is presented, but this is a matter of chance; the infant is blinking about 29 per cent of the time anyhow (Wenger, 1936; by permission of The State University of Iowa.)*

natal infants suggest strongly that the nervous system simply is not sufficiently ripe during the prenatal period to register much in the way of outside stimulation. It is not able to make the connections between stimulus and response that are necessary for the alteration of behavior on the basis of experience.

GENERAL DIMENSIONS OF DEVELOPMENT

In observing the development of the infant, we can see four general trends in his biological ripening: the **cephalocaudal sequence**, the **proximal-distal sequence**, differentiation, and integration.

CEPHALOCAUDAL SEQUENCE

In both form and function the infant shows a *cephalocaudal*, or head-to-foot, progression. At two months after conception, the fetus is about 50 per cent head, with the rest of the body barely developed at all. At birth the infant is about 25 per cent head, and the rest of him is evenly divided between trunk and legs. The normal adult is only about 12 per cent head, with half of him running to legs and about a third to trunk. There are very different growth rates for the different parts of the body. The head grows very rapidly in the early stages of the fetal history and, by the time birth occurs, has already achieved something over 60 per cent of its total growth. The trunk comes next in growth rate. By the end of the second year of life, it is about half as large as it will ever be. During the second year the legs and arms begin to grow in earnest, reaching a halfway mark in their total growth in about the fourth year.

Behavioral response goes along with the cephalocaudal sequence of physical development. If placed face down in its crib, the infant can raise its head before it can raise its shoulders, and it can move its shoulders before it can lift its stomach off the bed.

PROXIMAL-DISTAL SEQUENCE

Accompanying the head-to-foot progression in physical growth is the progression from growth in the central parts of the body to growth in the peripheral parts. For example, the trunk and shoulders develop first; then the arms, legs, fingers, and toes begin their real growth. Behavior of the infant similarly shows a central-to-peripheral development. The following observations of the sensorimotor achievements of the infant (Gesell and Amatruda, 1947) illustrate both the cephalocaudal and the proximal-distal sequences in behavior.

4 weeks—Control of eye movements; ability to follow an object visually.

16 weeks—Ability to balance head.

28 weeks—The hands can be used to grasp and manipulate objects.

40 weeks—The trunk is under control, enabling the child to sit and crawl.

52 weeks—The legs and feet are under control, enabling the child to stand and cruise around.

In all of the infant's movements these two general sequences can be observed. The infant first learns to move its head. Then his purposeful movements stem almost entirely from the shoulder and the pelvis. Later there comes movement at the elbows, wrists, knees, and ankles. When the infant first reaches for something, he reaches with his shoulder and elbows; only later does he begin to use his wrists and fingers in any adaptive way. The actual grasping and manipulation of an object represents a relatively late achievement. And, of course, the use of the legs and feet in walking must wait also a relatively long time for the necessary structural development.

DIFFERENTIATION—INTEGRATION

Over a period of time one can observe a general and gradual narrowing down and refinement of behavior. In the first days of its life the neonate, when it responds at all, responds all over. There are massive, all-inclusive patterns of behavior. If you gently prick the neonate's finger, for example, he is almost as likely to move his shoulder and head as he is to move his hand and arm. He thrashes. Later, he will move the stimulated arm and nothing else. Still later, he may move only the finger to which the stimulation is applied. This process is *differentiation*.

After behavior has reached a certain stage of differentiation and refinement, we can observe in the infant the tendency to *integrate* small and unitary responses into larger and more useful patterns of behavior. When the neonate is hungry, his behavior is characterized by mass action; that is, he thrashes his head, arms, and legs and cries. After some differentiation, he may give different sorts of cries for different degrees of hunger. Then integration sets in. The infant now can put together separate responses into large and useful sequences of behavior. First he learns to reach for the bottle and to apply it, with a good aim, to his mouth. Later, in a systematic search for the cookie jar, he may combine a whole array of well-integrated responses.

Both differentiation and integration can be observed in the emotional as well as the motor development of the child (see Chap. 10). The new infant has only one massive emotional tune to play. Later on, he can be observed to respond in one way when he is happy and in another when he is unhappy or afraid or angry. As he develops, there is still further differentiation, until he comes to live the varied emotional life of the adult. There is also an integration of emotional responses into patterns. By the time adulthood is reached, emotions tend to be highly patterned—for example, the frustration-hostility-anxiety-guilt pattern, which has been widely studied by psychologists and will concern us later.

DEVELOPMENT IN SPECIFIC AREAS

All of the general sequences in maturation can be observed if we focus specifically on a particular kind of behavior and watch it over a period of time. In locomotor behavior, for example, we can see the cephalocaudal sequence and the proximal-distal sequence. We also see both differentiation and integration.

MOTOR DEVELOPMENT

During its first few days of life the neonate will spend most of its time in the fetal position. After three or four weeks it can hold up its head. After two months it can raise its chest from its bed. At 4 months it can sit with support. At 5 months it can reach out and, with fair success, grasp objects. Such sequential development (shown in Fig. 3–12) continues through the creeping stage, which occurs at about 10 months, to the walk-alone

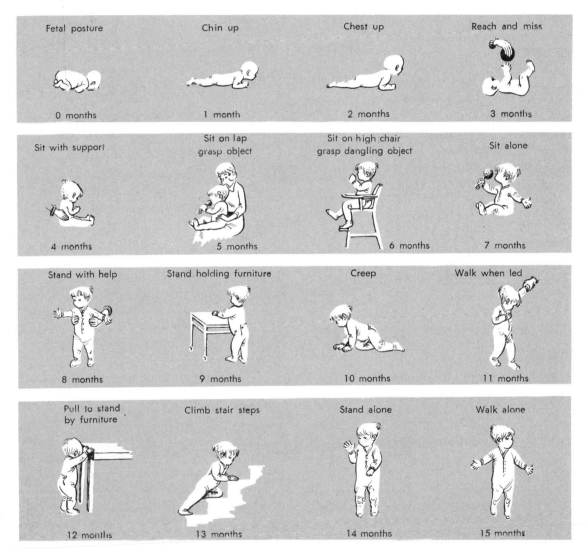

Figure 3–12. THE MOTOR SEQUENCE. *Most infants follow a definite sequence of motor development, although there are relatively wide individual differences on the age at which any given behavior appears. (Adapted from Shirley, 1933; by permission of the University of Minnesota Press.)*

stage, which occurs at about 15 months.

These are the "normal" sequences in motor development: most children most of the time follow such a sequence. Not all children, however, follow precisely this sequence. Some may, contrary to the popular expectation, walk before they crawl. And the ages at which individual children enter into any one of the developmental stages may vary widely. Though the "average" child walks alone at 15 months, some children may accomplish this feat as early as at 10 or 11 months while others may not make it until the ripe age of 18 months or 2 years.

LANGUAGE DEVELOPMENT

The infant can be counted on to emit a variety of vocal sounds very early in life. By the time he is 6 months old, he very probably has spontaneously voiced all the sounds occuring in any language known to man. At about this time he begins to put unitary sounds into patterns and to babble, repeating over and over patterns of sounds that seem to strike his fancy. But he has not yet begun to connect sounds with events either inside or outside himself—an activity that will continue throughout his life. The first recognizable word, a sound showing a definite and predictable connection with an object or event, occurs at about 10 months (Fig. 3–13). By the age of 15 months, the average child probably uses a vocabulary of about two dozen words. After that age, he moves rapidly toward the acquisition of a full vocabulary. At about 18 months his nervous system has ripened sufficiently to make linguistic behavior possible for him in his now more complex and demanding social world. By the time he is 6 years old, he has a *passive* vocabulary (including words he can understand) of around 5,000 words and an *active* vocabulary (words he can use correctly) of half that number (Table 3–2). By the time he is 20, his passive vocabulary will include, on the average, around 50,000 words, while he is able to use correctly around 10,000.

Actually, of course, we can bring very little evidence to bear on the biological processes involved in the development of language. The organism does go through a biological ripening—and later, a decay—that affects all its behaviors. With respect to symbolic and conceptual behaviors we can see only external expressions of the ripening: the increas-

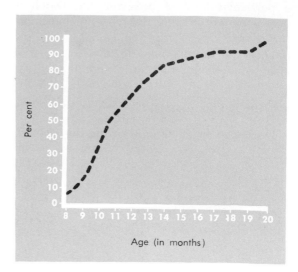

Figure 3–13. AGE OF APPEARANCE OF FIRST WORD. *The graph shows the per cent of children at a given age in months who have uttered their first word. (Adapted from Bühler, 1931.)*

ing variety and complexity of symbolic and linguistic responses.

Recent years have seen a surge of promising research and theory building in areas having a direct relevance for the development of linguistic skills. One theorist-researcher, for example (Hebb, 1949, 1955), has talked in semifigurative terms about "cell assemblies" and "phase sequences" that must be developed through both a biological ripening and a psychological experiencing, with the ripening and the experiencing necessarily scheduled and programmed in a certain way, before the organisms can handle the intricate problems involved in symbolic responses and problem-solving behavior. Another writer (Hunt, 1961) stresses that the right experience must occur at the right developmental phase if the "information-processing" functions are to develop properly. In making his point, he cites extensive evidence concerning the great importance of early experience in the later capacity of the organism, human and otherwise, to make the delicate discriminations and subtle responses involved in such higher mental proc-

Table 3-2. INCREASE IN SIZE OF VOCABULARY WITH AGE

| AGE | | NUMBER | AVERAGE | NUMBER | |
YEARS	MONTHS	OF CASES	IQ	OF WORDS	GAIN
	8	13		0	
	10	17		1	1
1	0	52		3	2
1	3	19		19	16
1	6	14		22	3
1	9	14		118	96
2	0	25		272	154
2	6	14		446	174
3	0	20	109	896	450
3	6	26	106	1,222	326
4	0	26	109	1,540	318
4	6	32	109	1,870	330
5	0	20	108	2,072	202
5	6	27	110	2,289	217
6	0	99	108	2,562	273

*At the tenth month the active vocabulary of the average child is one
word. At two years the average is 272 words. By the sixth year,
the average has risen to 2,652 words. (Smith, 1926; by
permission of the State University of Iowa.)*

esses as symbolization, concept formation, and problem solving. Later on, we will examine some of the research on the effects of early experience (pp. 83–90).

EMOTIONAL DEVELOPMENT

We have pointed out earlier that the processes of differentiation and integration can be seen clearly in the development of emotional behavior. Specific data on emotional development are presented in the discussion of emotions (Chap. 9).

GLANDULAR PROCESSES IN DEVELOPMENT

The body's system of **ductless** or **endocrine glands**—which secrete assorted *hormones* into the blood stream—has a significant role to play not only in the development of the organism but also in its daily functioning (Fig. 3–14).

The most important glands in the regulation of bodily development are (1) the **pituitary,** located in the head; (2) the **thyroids,** found at the stem of the neck; (3) the **adrenals,** on the surface of the kidneys; and (4) the sex glands or **gonads** (**ovaries** in the female and the **testes** in the male).

THE PITUITARY

Among the hormones produced by the pituitary gland is the *growth hormone*, which controls the rate and amount of development in the bones, muscles, and internal organs. If the pituitary functions normally, the individual comes into his normal physical inheritance. But if the pituitary for some reason

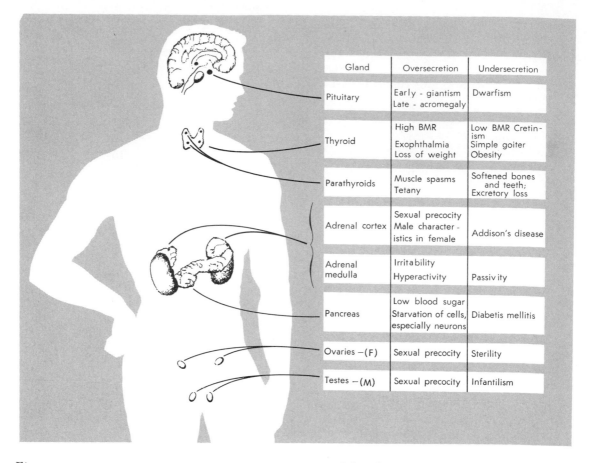

Gland	Oversecretion	Undersecretion
Pituitary	Early - giantism Late - acromegaly	Dwarfism
Thyroid	High BMR Exophthalmia Loss of weight	Low BMR Cretinism Simple goiter Obesity
Parathyroids	Muscle spasms Tetany	Softened bones and teeth; Excretory loss
Adrenal cortex	Sexual precocity Male characteristics in female	Addison's disease
Adrenal medulla	Irritability Hyperactivity	Passivity
Pancreas	Low blood sugar Starvation of cells, especially neurons	Diabetis mellitis
Ovaries —(F)	Sexual precocity	Sterility
Testes —(M)	Sexual precocity	Infantilism

Figure 3–14. GLANDULAR PROCESSES IN
DEVELOPMENT

begins to function abnormally, development can show drastic results. A shortage of the growth hormone early in life results in **dwarfism,** an underdevelopment of the bones. If there is an early overabundance of the growth hormone, the individual may grow into **giantism**—an excess in height and skeletal size without accompanying strength. If there is an oversecretion of the pituitary growth hormone after development is well along, the result is **acromegaly,** a disorder characterized by an unevenness of growth in various parts of the body: greatly enlarged hands or long, dangling, ape-like arms; a greatly enlarged chest cage; or a very prominent jutting of the jaw.

The pituitary also produces hormones that stimulate the production of hormones in other glands—most notably, the glands controlling sexual development. If this pituitary stimulator does not flow until late, sexual maturity is delayed. If it flows too early and too abundantly, we may find the 8-year-old developing a deep voice, pubic hair, and other signs of full sexual maturity.

THE THYROID

Thyroid secretions, interacting with the secretions from the pituitary gland, directly affect growth rates and appear to have some indirect effects on sexual development. Thyroid secretions have their most direct effect on the growth and functioning of the nervous system. The condition known as **cretinism,** involving both a kind of dwarfism and a deficiency in intelligence, is due to early malfunctioning of the thyroid. If severe thyroid deficiency occurs early in life, the development of the brain itself seems to be permanently impaired. If the disorder comes after as much as two years of life, there is a good chance that thyroid treatments can prevent permanent impairment.

THE ADRENALS

Besides bearing a significance for emotional behavior (Chap. 10), the *adrenal glands,* particularly through the production of sex hormones known as *adrenal* **androgens,** have a hand in regulating secondary sex characteristics—pubic hair, pitch of voice, etc. These androgens, appearing shortly before adolescence, work in conjunction with other sex hormones in the male to control the adolescent lowering of voice and the mature distribution of bodily hair. An oversupply of adrenal androgens may produce the phenomenon of **virilism.** In either men or women virilism may be seen in an excessively heavy beard or an unusually deep voice. If these androgens do not appear, on the other hand, there will be a delay in the development of mature sexual characteristics.

THE GONADS

The testes in the male and the ovaries in the female have not only a direct reproductive function but also the function of regulating sexual development. Although some gonadal hormones are produced during childhood, these glands begin their major maturational function at age 13 or 14 in boys and at 11 or 12 in girls.

In males, when the testes begin to produce *testicular androgens,* there is not only a rapid maturation of sexual organs but also the appearance of such *secondary sexual characteristics* as pubic hair and deep voice. Boys spurt up in height, increase in strength, and find themselves, sometimes to their considerable surprise, possessed of sexual motivation.

When the female is 11 or 12, her *ovaries* begin to produce two hormones: **estrogen,** the hormone controlling the growth of sexual organs and secondary sexual characteristics; and **progestin,** the hormone producing internal changes in the reproductive organs. When the estrogens begin to flow there is the development of breasts, a growth of pubic hair and a widening and rounding of the hips. Later, the reproductive organs themselves are ready for full functioning and pregnancy becomes possible.

Both boys and girls secrete male and female hormones, but in different ratios. After puberty the ratios generally change so that males produce relatively more male hormones and females produce more female hormones.

MATURATION AND LEARNING

The interaction between biological processes and psychological processes comes sharply into focus if we look at such behaviors as walking or talking and ask whether these behaviors, say at age 2, are primarily the products of biological maturation or the products of learning. Does the infant walk at a certain age because he has had enough experience with walking or simply because his body and nervous system have ripened sufficiently? Or both?

The classic experiment on maturation and learning (Carmichael, 1926) was carried out on two groups of tadpoles hatched in the laboratory. One group, the **control** group, was allowed to live and develop normally. The experimental group was placed in a solution containing the drug **chloretone,** which has the capacity to stop all muscular movement without interfering with normal processes of growth.

After the tadpoles in the control or undrugged group had been swimming (practicing?) for five days, and the experimental tadpoles had been immobilized for the same length of time, the experimental tadpoles were taken out of their immobilizing solution and put into ordinary water. In thirty minutes, according to the observer, the experimental tadpoles were swimming just as well as their more experienced companions. Conclusion: The swimming response occurs at its fixed stage in maturation, regardless of learning.

The role of maturation in human performance is clearly illustrated by a study of bladder control in identical twins (Hilgard, 1932). One twin, beginning at 3 months, was given by its mother a very attentive training in bladder control. For fifteen months, the twin maintained a record of about 20 per cent successful performance. Then, when he was 18 months old, the per cent of success shot up sharply. Such a result might be easily interpreted as a pay-off for all the effort of training. After success with this twin, his co-twin, for the first time, was put in training.

After very few days of training, the untutored twin was performing just as well as his twin. The reasonable interpretation is that maturation must reach a certain stage before bladder control can be achieved, regardless of the amount of training. The same kind of interpretation seems to fit the data on climbing behavior (Fig. 3–15).

Further examples of the effect of maturation on learning are given by two studies in which young chimpanzees were adopted and raised in psychologists' homes (Kellogg, 1933; Hayes, 1951). In the first of these cases (Kellogg's), a

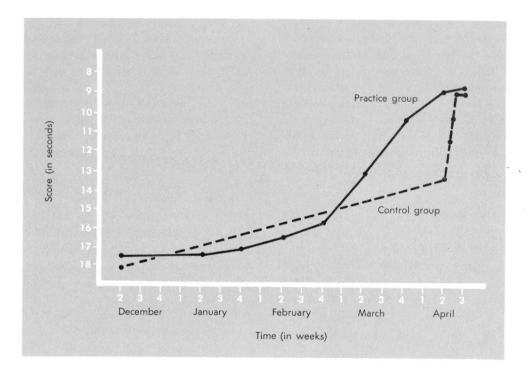

Figure 3–15. MATURATION AND LEARNING IN CLIMBING. *One group of eight preschool children was given twelve weeks of training in climbing, January to April; a matched group of eight was given only one week of training at the end of the sixteenth week of the experiment. This one week of practice, when maturation had proceeded sufficiently, brought the second group up to the proficiency of the first. (From Hilgard, 1932; reproduced by permission of* The Journal Press.)

7½-month-old chimp named Gua was brought into the home and raised along with Donald, the 9-month-old son of the psychologist. For the next eight months Gua and Donald were given equally affectionate care and training. Gua soon began to surpass Donald in ability to perform civilized acts: to use a spoon, to drink out of a cup, to run up and down stairs, to control both bladder and bowels, and to respond to spoken words. By the time Donald was 18 months old, however, he had come into his own, and now surpassed Gua in

Figure 3–16. AN ADOPTED CHIMP. *Vicki was adopted into a psychologist's family and raised as if she were a child. She developed many skills at a relatively early age because of rapid motor maturation. (Hayes, 1951; Courtesy, Dr. Keith J. Hayes.)*

everything but physical strength and agility.

Apes, having a life span approximately one third that of humans, mature more rapidly and reach the peak of maturation relatively early. The earlier maturation of Gua gave her an initial superiority over Donald. But Donald caught up. And because his maturation was that of a member of his own species, it carried him further than Gua toward the eventual mastery of such skills as those involved in language. (It is not a general biological rule that early maturation means a short life span. The elephant, for example, matures rapidly *and* lives a long life.)

The central principle emerging from this and other studies of maturation and learning is that *the stage of maturation limits what the organism can learn.* If maturation has not progressed far enough, no learning, or very little learning, can occur. There is obviously little point in trying to teach the 6-month-old

child either to control his bladder or to play the violin.

The brain centers controlling urination are not functional as early as at 6 months of age (McLellan, 1939). Also, when adults receive brain injury to certain areas of the cortex, they demonstrate a childish lack of urinary control. Injuries to lower centers do not produce the same results. The cortex, then, must ripen before bladder control can be achieved.

There is evidence that no part of the cortex, the highest center of the brain, is functioning very much as early as the sixth month (Conel, 1939). But when maturation—the unfolding of the biological inheritance—has prepared the way, then learning can take hold, to sharpen and coordinate behaviors and to bring into the world of the individual that social inheritance which, blended with his biological inheritance, makes him into an adult personality.

EFFECTS OF EARLY EXPERIENCE

There can be no doubt that those biological factors showing themselves in maturational sequences help to determine the behavior we see. The development of the organism has a great deal to do with the development of behavior. But the experience of the organism —its psychological life—also and obviously has a role in the development of behavior. Much of the science of psychology concerns itself with the understanding of ways in which today's psychological life structures tomorrow's behavior. Learning is pervasive. We shall not here attack the very large problems of learning or of personality development. It will be both possible and proper, however, to examine some of the evidence showing the effects of very early experience on the development of behavior. And perhaps we may find also that psychological factors influence not only subsequent psychological factors but *biological development* as well. We know that psychological processes can produce active physical damage to the body (Chap. 9). Can psychological factors also arrest or misdirect biological development?

EARLY SENSORY EXPERIENCE

Most of us are quite willing to accept the notion that our ability to tell the difference between Bach chorales and Beethoven symphonies, though probably influenced by heredity, is primarily an acquired perceptive ability. But what about the ability to tell the difference between a square and a triangle? We tend to assume that such an ability is automatic and unlearned. There is evidence to the contrary.

There is on record (Von Senden, 1932) the clinical history of a number of people who were born with cataracts and who had their cataracts removed only after reaching adulthood. Such people, deprived of early visual experience, may never come by some of the visual skills we take for granted. They seem to experience little difficulty in registering colors, but they do have great trouble responding to visual patterns. They may need months to learn the visual difference between squares and triangles. One girl, of normal intelligence, could not learn over many months of training to recognize visually more than three of all her circle of acquaintances.

Experiments with animals reared in darkness from birth (Riesen, 1949, 1951) show similar debilitating and long-lasting effects on visual functioning. The normal chimpanzee by the age of 16 months makes excellent use of vision and learns readily to respond to new visual stimuli brought into his environment. He can learn easily, for example, to avoid a new object brought into his visual world if, every time he approaches it, he receives a small shock. By contrast, his cousin, reared all his life in the dark, must be shocked day after day before he learns that the new object is indeed a new object and a dangerous one. It takes the visually inexperienced chimp weeks of normal contending with a lighted environment before he shows signs of being able to see the difference between a friend and a total stranger.

Other researches show similar results for other senses. In one experiment (Nissen, Chow, and Semmes, 1951) chimps were raised for two and a half years with cardboard tubing constantly around both hands and feet, so that they could not experience tactual stimulation. When this tubing was removed, the chimps were given a test requiring them, without their being able to see their hands, to reach for food with the hand that was touched. The experimenter would touch the left hand; and the chimp, if he learned properly, would reach to the left and receive the food. Normal chimps learn this problem in about 200 trials. The chimps deprived of early tactual experience could not learn this relatively simple chore during 2,000 trials. And while normal chimps react quite vigorously to a pinch on the hand or foot, the tactually underprivileged chimp had great difficulty in locating the pinched spot unless he had his eyes to help him. Also, the sensorily deprived chimps did not seem to mind very much being pinched.

Generally speaking, enriched early sensory experiences increase an animal's later capacity to solve problems that require discriminations similar to those involved in the early experience. For example, in one experiment (Gibson and Walk, 1956) the investigators raised one group of rats in cages decorated with black metal cutouts of triangles and circles, while the control group grew up in ordinary nondecorated laboratory cages; later, when both groups were required to learn to solve a problem involving triangles and circles, the rats who had had the "casual" experience with their wall decorations were relatively superior at the task.

The same relationship holds also for higher animals. For example, Rhesus monkeys who were born in their natural habitat exhibit more exploration, vocalization, and acrobatics in a novel situation than do monkeys raised in the laboratory nursery (Mason and Green, 1962). The nursery monkeys engaged in more self-directed behavior, such as clasping, sucking, and crouching. Similarly, chimpanzees reared in perceptual and social isolation during their first two years show definite consequences;

they react timidly to novel stimuli and resort often to rocking, swaying, and head banging. Wild-born chimps, by contrast, explored novel objects boldly, rarely engaging in stereotyped behavior (Menzel, Davenport, and Rogers, 1963).

Such evidence strongly indicates that early sensory experience has significance for later sensory functioning. It seems that normal sensory experience is necessary for normal development. Certainly, there is evidence, clear for animals and suggestive for human beings, that the nature of early sensory experience bears importantly on the nature of later sensory and perceptual functioning. There is as yet no complete understanding of the details of the relationship between early sensory experience and later functioning. Nor is there any knowledge of what may be the neurological or physiological mechanisms involved.

EFFECTS OF EARLY PHYSICAL STIMULATION

There are a number of researches indicating that the early physical experiences of animals have a lasting effect on their development— and perhaps even on their survival.

One experimenter (Bovard, 1958) found that rats who are stroked and petted a great deal as they are growing up are more likely than their nonhandled controls to survive a severe operation.

Along the same line (Weininger, 1956), rats who have been handled a great deal show an increased toughness in the face of another kind of environmental stress: a drawn-out period of immobilization without water. Handled rats showed appreciably less heart and gastrointestinal damage as a result of this trying experience. On an even more drastic test, the handled rats survived without either food or water an average of over fifty hours longer than did the unhandled control group.

The weight of the evidence continues to indicate that early stimulation—even if the stimulation involves stress—produces increased resistance to adult stress. For example, infant rats who are moved around in their nests appear, at the age of 80 days, relatively willing to explore a strange area, while an unstimulated control group is hesitant to explore at all (Meyers, 1962). Rats who receive electrical shocks in infancy recover more quickly from adult shocks than do matched unstimulated animals (Lindholm, 1962).

We might interpret the foregoing experiments on rats in terms of *deprivation* in the lives of the unhandled rats. We might say that they were deprived in infancy of experience having somehow a considerable relevance for later survival. An experiment on dogs (Thompson and Heron, 1954) approaches specifically this matter of deprivation. In this research a group of puppies was raised for the first seven and a half months in almost complete isolation from outside stimulation and from contact with human beings. Their cage was lighted, but they could not see out of it. Human contact was there only momentarily, at feeding time. When compared to a control group of dogs, these restricted animals were significantly inferior on a variety of "intelligence" tests. They were less able to learn mazes, less able to "remember" where objects or food had been placed, less able to pay attention, and less inclined to think that human beings were good things to have around. Such effects seemed to be relatively permanent.

What about the effects of similar deprivations on the development of human beings? Of course, there can be no experimental deprivation of human infants, but there have been studies of institutionalized children, children deprived of normal experience and normal human contact during early life. The most noteworthy—and also the most controversial—of these are the studies conducted by Spitz (1953), who observed children in two institutions. In one of these institutions, a foundling home, infants who had been removed from their mothers soon after birth were observed intensively during the first three months of their lives, and periodically thereafter. During the first year of life, the infants' contact with the nurses was minimal, there being only one nurse for eight children. The children were kept in cubicles that served to cut down the stimulation reaching them, and often bed sheets were hung over the sides of their cribs to increase even further their encapsulation from the world. The children had no toys, and their own hands and feet were the only objects they had to play with.

Spitz reported that these deprived children showed what he called *anaclitic depression* or *hospitalism*. There was a slowing of normal development—they could neither sit nor walk at the usual ages. They were weepy and sad, sitting for long hours with immobile, expressionless faces. They would rock back and forth for long periods of time, play with their genitals a great deal, and engage often in fecal play. They would either scream at the appearance of strangers or show a great friendliness to strangers and a fear of inanimate objects in their environment. There seemed to be also a retardation of actual physical development and an increased susceptibility to disease. During an epidemic of measles, 23 out of 88 young children in one institution died, in spite of proper medical care and excellent sanitary conditions.

Spitz (1955, p. 453) came to the following conclusions from his studies:

1. Affective interchange is paramount, not only for the development of emotion itself in infants but also for the physical and behavioral maturation and development of the child.
2. This affective interchange is provided by the reciprocity between the mother (or her substitute) and the child.
3. A child deprived of this interchange has a serious, and in extreme cases, a dangerous handicap for its development in every sector of the personality.

By no means all psychologists are willing to join with Spitz in these sweeping conclusions. The research procedures employed were far from ideal in control and precision, and the method of reporting the research has also been criticized. The following is an example of the sort of criticism that has been made of the original work.

It is regrettable that he did not note the absence or frequency of congenital abnormalities in the two institutions, the birth condition of the infants, evidence of syphilis in the mothers or other health conditions which might be relevant, and that he did not note what if any effects such factors might have had on his findings (Pinneau, 1955, p. 433).

The general area of investigation obviously needs and deserves further attention. And, as with other problems where research must be clinical rather than experimental, knowledge of demonstrable soundness will be difficult to obtain. Meanwhile, unless we discount entirely the observations of Spitz and of others who have obtained similar—and similarly controversial—results (Bowlby, 1951; Ribble, 1944; Fischer, 1952), we would do well to put at least tentative credence in the proposition that restrictions and deprivations in infancy, of human beings as well as of animals, can have drastic effects on development. A further and more recent research in this area is presented at the end of the present chapter.

EFFECTS OF EARLY CHILD-PARENT RELATIONS

Another line of research having obvious significance for the development of animals and potential implications for human development deals with the early phases of child-parent relations and the effect upon later behavior of the infant's early experience in this respect.

One major facet of research in this area deals with the phenomenon of **imprinting,** or the relatively strong and suddenly established attraction of the infant organism either for its natural mother or for any large, moving object to which it is exposed. Many young animals, particularly birds, have an instinctive tendency to follow the mother about very persistently. When the natural mother is the object of this attachment, all is well. But the tendency can be released by any one of a variety of moving objects, including decoys and research scientists (Lorenz, 1937; Hess, 1958, 1962; Jaynes, 1956, 1957), and the tendency is more likely to be released at one particular time—a critical period—than at another. For ducklings, imprinting on a wooden decoy duck occurs most predictably during the period from 13 to 16 hours after birth (Hess, 1958). New Hampshire red chicks will become imprinted on a moving green cardboard cube during the first 54 hours of life, but not after that period (Jaynes, 1956, 1957).

How long do the imprinted responses persist? For how many days or months will the laboratory duckling, once imprinted, follow a decoy duck or an experimenter? Apparently, the imprinted response—like any learned response—must be rewarded, must result in food or some other desirable commodity for the imprinted animal; or in time (after about six or seven days for Peking ducklings) the response will not be given (Moltz and Rosenblum, 1958).

There is now little or no evidence that either imprinting or critical periods of learning can be found in human infants.

Another line of research on filial development has explored the behavior of young monkeys toward artificial mothers that were experimentally substituted for natural mothers (Harlow, 1962; Harlow and Zimmerman, 1959). In these studies young monkeys at ages of 6 to 12 hours after birth were taken away from their natural mothers and were raised under controlled conditions with substitute mothers. For some monkeys, the substitute mother was constructed of heavy wire. For others, the mother was a piece of wood covered with terry cloth. Each mother was built so that "she" could feed the infant through a nipple.

The two groups of monkeys were observed over a period of time in a variety of situations. When given a choice between fondling the wire mother and the cloth mother, the young monkeys preferred the cloth mother regardless of which mother had been feeding them. When the young who had lived with the cloth mother were exposed to a fearful object, they ran and clung to "mother"; the infants of the wire mothers, by contrast, would not clutch mother but would try to hide and would clutch

themselves, rocking and fussing. Also, the children of the cloth mothers, after clinging in fear for awhile to the terry cloth figure, would eventually turn loose in apparent security and begin to examine the originally frightening object in the cage. The monkeys with wire mothers showed no such investigative behavior.

Figure 3–17. RESEARCH ON THE NATURE OF LOVE FOR MOTHER. *Research on infant monkeys has revealed a great deal about the nature of the relationship of young organisms to their mothers. In Dr. Harry Harlow's laboratory, young monkeys were trained to live with artificial mothers. They got their food from "wire" mothers. But they did not develop any affection for their wire mothers, preferring the more cuddly artificial mothers who were wrapped in towels. The research suggests the psychological importance of physical contact with a mother that "feels right."*

Such studies have at the moment no clear implication for human development. They do raise fascinating and significant questions, however, and already suggest critical-mindedness in the face of prevailing assumptions about certain aspects of human development. It has long been an accepted idea, for example, that the fact that the mother feeds the child has a central and significant bearing on the child's development of mother love. These researches cast doubt on this notion.

SUMMARY

1. The organism grows and develops over time; the nature and sequences of development help determine the nature and sequences of behavior seen in the psychological process.

2. The human infant has a biological history, a biological and psychological future.

3. On the historical side, the human infant has an evolutionary heredity, a species heredity, and an individual heredity, all represented in the pattern of his genes and chromosomes.

4. His heredity gives the human individual a similarity to other organisms but also a uniqueness.

5. More than other kinds of organisms, the human neonate is relatively dependent and his behavior relatively free of instinctual determination.

6. The individual inherits physical traits, capacities, and susceptibilities; and his inherited characteristics have both direct and indirect effects on his behavior.

7. There is evidence that organisms inherit the capacity to learn; and the human capacity to behave intelligently has a strong hereditary component.

8. There is evidence of an inherited susceptibility to schizophrenia.

9. Hereditary and environmental factors interact in many ways to produce the patterns of adjustment we observe.

10. Emotional experiences on the part of mother rats during pregnancy produce emotionality in the offspring.

11. The organism develops in accordance with a cephalocaudal sequence, a proximal-distal sequence, and sequences of differentiation and integration.

12. There are normal sequences with respect to motor development, language development and emotional development. All individuals follow similar sequences but each at his own rate.

13. The functioning of the ductless glands —especially the pituitary, the thyroid, the adrenals, and the gonads—influences significantly the growth of the individual.

14. Learning of certain tasks and skills cannot occur until maturation has readied the organism; the stage of maturation determines what the organism can learn.

15. Early sensory and perceptual experience, or the lack of it, has a bearing on mature sensory and perceptual abilities.

16. Early physical experiences, such as handling or isolation or stress, have definite effects on the later behavior of animals.

17. There is evidence, though somewhat controversial, that infants deprived of early love and attention show severe personality disturbances.

18. The timing and nature of early child-parent relationships can affect development; at certain critical periods young animals tend to become imprinted on large moving objects, tending to follow these objects about as if they were mothers.

19. Research on the effect of artificial experimental mothers suggests the importance of the feel of the mother in the developing attachment to her; infant monkeys with "wire mothers" behave quite differently from those with "cloth mothers."

RESEARCH REPORTS

RETARDATION IN INSTITUTIONALIZED CHILDREN [*]

This paper presents data concerning behavioral development among 174 children, aged 1 to 4 years, in three institutions in Tehran. In Institutions I and II infant development was greatly retarded, while children in Institution III were much less retarded. Of 90 children in Institution I between the ages of 1 year and 2.9 years, only 8 per cent could walk alone; of 33 children in Institution II, only 15 per cent could walk alone. Of 51 children studied in Institution III, 20 of those were between the ages of 1 and 1.9; of those 20, 15 per cent could walk alone. Of the 31 children in Institution III between the ages of 2 and 2.9 years, 94 per cent could walk alone.

The following interpretations are offered for these differences in behavior. In Institutions I and II there was little or no handling of the children; they were placed supine in their cribs and left there until they could learn to move about. They were not taken out and carried about, nor were they even placed prone so that they could lift their heads and shoulders. In Institution III, on the other hand, the children were frequently handled, propped in the sitting position, and placed prone. Thus, the retardation of subjects in Institutions I and II is thought to be due to the restrictions of certain kinds of learning situations. These interpretations seem to be congruent with results of other studies of environmental deprivation.

The children in Institutions I and II, where there were few if any visitors, were extremely shy of the experimenters and cried when they came in. Institution II had had a few more visits than Institution I, and the children were not as shy as in I. Institution III had numerous visitors, and the children responded to the experimenters immediately. In all three institutions, after the experimenters had been there awhile, the children responded to them more than when they first came in.

In Institutions I and II, where children were not helped or propped up, they did eventually learn to sit up and move around but were apt to scoot

along the floor, by sitting and pushing or pulling themselves rather than crawling. Therefore, they had difficulty in pulling themselves to a standing position. The researcher believes that the lack of a *learning* experience, at the time necessary to facilitate the proper sequence of motor development, had a negative effect on motor development.

EFFECTS OF DEPRIVATION ON MONKEYS [*]

Although animals appear to have relatively complete patterns of instinctive behavior, there is abundant evidence that early experience—or the lack of it—can have a highly significant effect on later behavior. The present study—by Seay, Alexander, and Harlow—deals primarily with the maternal behavior of Rhesus monkeys who were deprived in infancy of contact with their mothers and with their peers. The study also looks at the social development of the infants produced and mothered by these motherless mothers (MM's).

The subjects for the present study were four motherless mothers—MM's—and their infants. The four MM's were selected from a group of 51 original unmothered females involved in a larger series of studies of maternal behavior. These unmothered females had turned out to be inept and ineffective in sexual behavior: only twenty of the original unmothered females became inseminated, even under optimal conditions; nine of the twenty delivered infants at the time of the study. The first four of these infants were the primary subjects of the present study. All four had been raised in deprived conditions: two were raised with cloth-mother surrogates for six months, then housed individually in wire cages for an additional year; the other two were housed individually in bare wire cages until approximately 2 years of age. Matched with these MM subjects, for purposes of control, were four feral mothers and their infants, all of whom were observed under identical conditions.

All mother-infant pairs were housed in separate compartments of a cage. Next to each cage was a playpen area; a small opening from the cage to the playpen permitted the infant, but not its mother, to enter the playpen.

All of the infant-mother pairs were placed in

[*] Wayne Dennis, Causes of retardation among institutional children: Iran. *J. Genet. Psychol.*, 1960, 96, 47–59.

[*] Bill Seay, Bruce K. Alexander, and Harry Harlow, Maternal behavior of socially deprived rhesus monkeys, *J. abn. soc. Psychol.*, 1964, 69, 345–354.

the living cages on the day of delivery and thereafter were observed at regular intervals over a period of time. A check list of 96 behavioral items was used during the regular periods of observation. For these categories of observation the experimenters report satisfactory levels of interobserver reliability.

The study yielded quantitative results, for both MM's and feral mothers, on such matters as frequency of the cradling of infants, infant-mother ventral contact, rejection of the infant by the mother, frequency of crying by the infant, frequency of infant-to-infant oral contact during play, and frequency of infantile play.

All four motherless mothers, the experimenters report, were totally inadequate—so much so that the experimenters believe none of the infants would have survived without intervention by the laboratory staff. Two of the four MM's were violent and abusive, while the other two were primarily indifferent and withdrawn. The most abusive mother, MM-63, initially abandoned and retreated from her infant, so that the staff had to hand feed the infant and place it in an incubator for several hours before returning it to its mother. By the third day after birth, the mother passively accepted the baby to the breast, but thereafter any attempt to move or hand feed the baby led the mother to violent attacks on the infant. She would crush its head and body against the floor and jump up and down on it. However, this mother did nurse the baby and did demonstrate more cradling than the other three MM's.

Each of the other MM's displayed equivalent but different inadequacies in their patterns of maternal behavior. One, whenever she observed an emotional disturbance on the part of her infant, somersaulted across the cage violently, appearing to the experimenters as if at any moment she would crush the infant.

Examples of the quantitative results of the study are as follows. With respect to the *frequency of mother-infant cradling*, the feral mothers scored 77, by the system used, whereas the MM's scored 24. With respect to the frequency of *infant-mother ventral contact*, feral mothers scored 88; MM's, 32. On *frequency of rejection*, the feral mothers scored zero, while the MM's scored at approximately five rejections per thirty-minute period.

With respect to social development of the infant, the offspring of the MM's seemed to develop just as successfully as did the offspring of feral mothers. Though the MM group of youngsters demonstrated some peculiarities in social development (for example, they tended to mouth other monkeys with a relatively great frequency) they seemed, after a short period of time, to develop quite normally.

When these MM's had second offspring, their maternal behavior approached that of normal mothers.

On the basis of their results, the researchers hypothesize that maternal behavior of the Rhesus monkey is made up of many innate and learned components and that the absence of early social experiences prevents these components from becoming easily integrated into an effective pattern.

SUGGESTED READINGS

Carmichael, Leonard, ed. *Manual of child psychology*, 2nd ed. New York: Wiley, 1954.

Erikson, E. H. *Childhood and society*, 2nd ed. revised and enlarged. New York: Norton, 1963.

Fuller, J. L., and W. R. Thompson. *Behavior genetics.* New York: Wiley, 1960.

Hayes, Cathy. *The ape in our house.* New York: Harper, 1951.

Hurlock, E. B. *Child development*, 4th ed. New York: McGraw-Hill, 1964.

McCandless, B. R. *Children and adolescents: behavior and development.* New York: Holt, Rinehart and Winston, 1961.

Simpson, G. G. *The meaning of evolution: A study of the history of life and of its significance for man.* New Haven: Yale University Press, 1949 (reprinted 1960).

Stevenson, H. W., ed. *Child psychology,* the sixty-second yearbook of the National Society for the Study of Education, Part I. Chicago: National Society for the Study of
Education, 1963.

OUTLINE / CHAPTER 4

I. INTEGRATED BEHAVIOR

II. RECEPTORS, EFFECTORS, AND CONNECTORS

    A. Receptors
    B. Effectors
    C. Connectors

III. LEVELS OF INTEGRATION IN BEHAVIOR

IV. THE NERVE CELL (NEURON)

V. NEURAL TRANSMISSION

    A. The Neural Impulse
    B. Synaptic Transmissions

VI. MAJOR DIVISIONS OF THE NERVOUS SYSTEM

    A. Central and Peripheral Systems
    B. Somatic and Autonomic Systems
    C. Central Nervous System

VII. THE CEREBRAL CORTEX

VIII. EVOLUTION OF THE NERVOUS SYSTEM

IX. VERTICAL AND CONCENTRIC ANALYSIS OF THE BRAIN

    A. Reticular Formation
    B. Limbic Systems

X. NEURAL PHENOMENA IN INTEGRATED RESPONSE

    A. Synaptic Summation
    B. Alternative Nerve Pathways
    C. The Dendritic Potential

XI. BRAIN FUNCTIONS IN PSYCHOLOGICAL PROCESSES

    A. Motor Functions
    B. Linguistic Functions
    C. Functions of the Reticular Formation
    D. Functions of the Limbic System

XII. ADDITIONAL AREAS OF RESEARCH

XIII. SUMMARY

XIV. RESEARCH REPORT

CHAPTER 4

BIOLOGICAL BASE FOR INTEGRATED BEHAVIOR

INTEGRATED BEHAVIOR

As the **organism** makes its way in life, it does so as an *integrated system of specialized parts*. Events of one kind at one time and place lead to responses of another kind at another time and place. For example, the **receptor** mechanisms in the eye of the individual register electromagnetic waves of a certain length; and then occurs a whole sequence of behavior, which succeeds in guiding his car into traffic. Similarly, the receptors for smell respond to subtle chemical changes in the environment, and the whole organism is involved in a speedy retreat from a skunk—or, years later, in the invention of a deodorizing agent to be applied to victims of skunks' ire; the **hypothalamus,** a part of the brain, reacts to changes in the chemistry of the blood, and soon all the resources of an experienced and thoughtful system are skillfully invested in

the procuring of food. All behavior, even a behavior as simple as the blink of an eye or the jerk of a knee, is organized, is in some measure integrated. The integration is more dramatic, of course, when the behavior increases in complexity, involving many sensory events, much intervening interpretation, and then a complicated sequence of coordinated responses; but wherever behavior occurs, organized systems do the behaving.

Characteristics of the organism's own structure contribute to the integration of behavior. Its skeletal and muscular structure is unified within the confines of a skin. Its blood stream is an integral and integrating system, functioning for the whole body in distributing nutritive matter, circulating **hormones,** removing waste. And, of special concern for the psychologist, its nervous system, by conducting messages and making connections, makes possible a behavioral organization of marvelous complexity—a complexity that is as yet entirely unduplicated by any machines that human nervous systems have invented.

physiological processes underlying every **sensation**, every **perception**, every thought, every action of the organism, will contribute signifi-

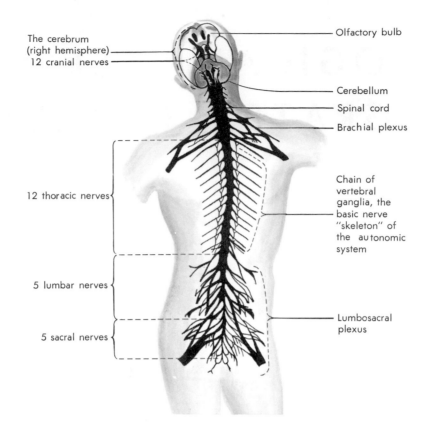

The cerebrum
(right hemisphere)
12 cranial nerves

Olfactory bulb

Cerebellum

Spinal cord

Brachial plexus

12 thoracic nerves

Chain of vertebral ganglia, the basic nerve "skeleton" of the autonomic system

5 lumbar nerves

5 sacral nerves

Lumbosacral plexus

Figure 4–1. THE NERVOUS SYSTEM. *In this drawing the head is tilted back, so that the base of the brain is shown.*

Many people, including many psychologists, feel that we really can never "explain" behavior except through an understanding of **neurology** and physiology. Others take the view that there can indeed be a science based on systematic observations of behavior, followed by meticulous delineation of the necessary explanatory **constructs**—which may or may not be neurological or physiological.

We need not here take a stand on either side of this issue. No one, perhaps, has the wisdom to predict the form a science of psychology will take in another generation or another half century. It seems very sensible to follow the policy that a knowledge of the neuro-

cantly to our full understanding of the psychological process. Furthermore, study of the structure and functioning of the nervous system, which occupies many psychologists, becomes perhaps not only desirable but also highly exciting in the light of recent researches. These researches suggest that the nervous system serves not only to conduct and to connect, thereby making behavior possible, but also to *initiate* behavior—so that perhaps we must view the organism not merely as a creature of **stimulus-response** connections but as an active agent possessed indeed of a mind of its own.

In this chapter we shall review the structures of the nervous system, shall see its major functions in bringing about the integration of behavior, and shall look briefly at the facts and implications of some recent researches on the role of the nervous system in complex behaviors. In succeeding chapters we shall concern ourselves further with neurological and physiological aspects of such matters as motivation, emotion, sensation, and learning.

RECEPTORS, EFFECTORS, AND CONNECTORS

The nervous system is an organization of special cells. In order to see in functional context these cells and this organization, we need to understand the way the nervous system articulates with other special cells and special systems. Of particular interest to the student of behavior are the **receptor** cells and structures and the **effector** cells and structures.

RECEPTORS

All organisms possess various highly specialized cells with the capacity to respond to energy changes in the environment, and to translate physical and chemical events into neural events. In Chapter 10 we will discuss receptors and sensory processes in some detail. Here, we need only make the point that the organism maintains contact with its environment, both external and internal, through its sensory receptors. Without sensory input, there could be no **adjusting.**

EFFECTORS

Nor can there be adjusting without the effectors, the cells and structures with which the organism responds. For vertebrates, the effector structures include *muscles* and *glands*.

Muscles

The human body contains three kinds of muscles. There are the **striated** (or **striped**) **muscles,** given a striped appearance by alternating, differently colored bands. These so-called "**voluntary**" muscles, expanding and contracting in response to **nerve impulses,** are involved principally with the movement (and rigidity) of the skeleton. The **smooth muscles,** more primitive spindle-shaped structures, control the movements of digestion and bring about the expansion and contraction of the blood vessels. The **cardiac muscle,** similar in many respects to the striated muscles, is found only in the heart. It must perform its cycle of contraction-relaxation about eighty times a minute throughout life, or the organism is in trouble. Smooth and cardiac muscles are often called "**involuntary.**"

Glands

The glandular effectors, of as much significance in adjusting as the muscles, are of two types: (1) **duct (exocrine) glands,** such as those of the digestive tract, which feed their secretion through ducts directly into the various organs of the body; (2) **ductless (endocrine) glands,** which secrete various chemical substances directly into the blood stream. Chapter 3 reviewed the role of the ductless glands in development, and Chapter 9 describes some of the functions of ductless secretion in emotional reaction.

CONNECTORS

The student of behavior who concerns himself with the neurophysiology of the organism naturally is interested in both receptors and effectors; but he is more interested in a third class of structure, the **connectors.** Here we are building toward a focus on these connectors—the cells and structures that bridge the gap between receptors and effectors; we have moved toward our focus through a quick look at the cells and structures on either end of the neural processes.

LEVELS OF INTEGRATION IN BEHAVIOR

Behavior always involves an integrated series of events. Receptors do not simply register energy changes and quiet down. Events lead to events that lead to events. The integrations we observe and wish to understand in terms of neural processes come at various levels of complexity.

There are relatively simple and unconscious processes, known as **reflexes,** in which stimuli lead quickly and automatically to unvarying responses. A light is flashed, and the eyelid closes. Brightness increases around us, and the pupil contracts. Figures 4–2 and 4–3 illustrate very schematically the kinds of neural circuits involved in simple integrations.

grations that may involve minutes or hours or days or months of integrative activity between receptor action and effector action. Such integrations involve the storage of past input, the interpretive rearrangement of things, a "mulling over" of various inputs, and, in the end, the eventual adaptive behavior. It is these integrative processes of discrimination, interpretation, memory, learning, and problem solving that are of particular interest to the student of human behavior.

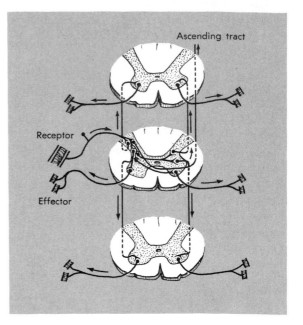

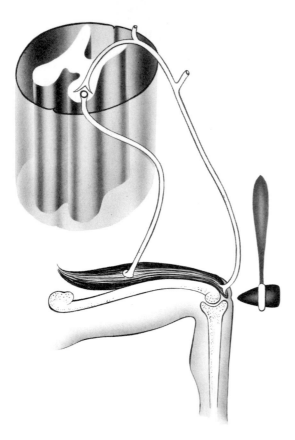

Figure 4–2. REFLEX ARC. *A schematic illustration of the neural connection in a simple reflex.*

Figure 4–3. SPINAL CONNECTIONS. *Diagram of connections by which impulses from a receptor reach motor neurons of various levels on both sides of the spinal cord. Arrows indicate direction of conduction. (From Gardner, 1958,* Fundamentals of Neurology, *3rd Ed., Philadelphia: W. B. Saunders Company.)*

There are more complex integrations, which involve relatively elaborate but still relatively automatic and unconscious responses. There is the **startle pattern,** for example (Chap. 9). There is walking, maintaining balance, breathing—each requiring the integration of stimuli in sequences, and responses in patterns.

At a still more complex level, there are inte-

THE NERVE CELL (NEURON)

The *nerve cell,* or **neuron,** the bit of protoplasm having the specialized capacities to become irritated and to conduct, constitutes the structural unit of the nervous system. Each neuron has a **cell body** built around a **nucleus.** Each neuron also has two kinds of elongated fibers: **dendrites** and **axons.** The cell receives stimulation through its dendrites or cell body and passes its nerve impulses along the axon (see Fig. 4–4) to effectors or to other neurons. A neuron usually has several dendrites but only one axon.

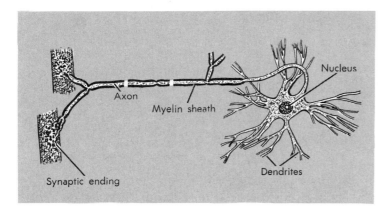

Figure 4–4. THE NERVE CELL. *A diagrammatic representation of structural features of nerve cells, as determined by biochemical and cytological studies.*

Neurons come in a variety of forms (see Fig. 4–5). *Sensory* and *motor neurons* (transmission neurons), which lead from the sensory receptors to the spinal cord and from the spinal cord to the effectors, are structures with short dendrites and long axons that end in endbrushes. In addition, *connecting* or *correlating neurons,* found in the brain and in other nerve centers, have a sometimes elaborately ramified pattern of dendrites that can make contact with a whole network of other cells.

All axons and dendrites have retaining membranes, and all that serve a transmission function, except those of the smallest diameter, have a white, fatty coating known as the **myelin sheath.** The connecting and correlating neurons, which are often not myelinated, constitute the gray matter of the nervous system.

NEURAL TRANSMISSION

THE NEURAL IMPULSE

Once stimulated—in whatever way is adequate for it—the nerve cell sends neural impulses along its fibers. These electrochemical impulses travel along nerve fibers in a way roughly analogous to the traveling of an electrical impulse along a wire. Every neuron, in its existing state at any given time, needs a stimulus of a certain magnitude if it is to respond by sending down its length the propagated electrical disturbance that is a neural impulse. Neurons differ with respect to the magnitude of the **threshold** stimulus. However, the magnitude of the impulse does not vary with the magnitude of the stimulus: once the neuron fires, it fires with all its might. This all-or-none phenomenon prevents our accounting for the increased intensity of a sensation in terms of larger impulses arriving over sensory nerves. Also bearing on the general question of excitability—and also raising difficulty for theories of sensation—is the fact that a nerve fiber will not fire impulses beyond a certain rate, no matter how intense the stimulus. Once a neuron fires, it is, for a brief interval, functionally out of commission. During an *absolute refractory phase* it will not fire, no matter what. Then, during a *relative refractory phase,* it will fire if the stimulus is sufficiently strong, yielding some increase in the frequency of impulses per second in the face of

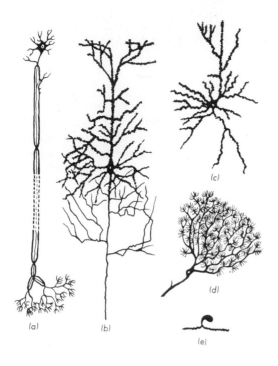

Figure 4–5. TYPES OF NERVE CELLS. *Different types of neurons in nervous system: (a) motor neurons of spinal cord, (b) neuron of motor area of brain, (c) short connecting neuron, (d) bushy cell found in networks of neurons, (e) bipolar neuron of sensory neurons. (From Evans,* Starling's Principles of Human Physiology, *12th Ed., 1956, London, J. and A. Churchill.)*

more intense stimulation. These facts about the limitations of neural transmission mean that the increased intensity of a stimulus can be represented in the nervous system only by (a) a limited increase in the rate of firing of individual neurons and (b) the firing of additional neurons.

SYNAPTIC TRANSMISSIONS

Neurons transmit electrical impulses. But the neural transmission involved in the simplest behavior comprises more than the dendrite and axon of a single neuron. Many neurons and many fibers are involved. Some of these may lie side by side in a single bundle of fibers, and many may be firing simultane-

ously. Others are involved sequentially; neurons connect with neurons which connect with neurons. The connection is not accomplished, however, by anatomical continuity. The sequential neurons do not touch one another. But they do make contact—through a junction called a **synapse.** At the synapse, the neural impulse passes from the axon of one neuron to the dendrites of another. The transmission is probably accomplished by a chemical substance, which is produced by one neuron and stimulates the other. The crossing of the synapse is, compared to the speed of the nervous impulse, a slow process. It is also an irreversible process. Where a nerve impulse may travel either way on a nerve fiber, it will cross a synapse in only one direction. It travels always from the axon of one cell to the dendrites of another.

MAJOR DIVISIONS OF THE NERVOUS SYSTEM

CENTRAL AND PERIPHERAL SYSTEMS

The human nervous system may be divided, structurally, into two parts—the **central nervous system** and the **peripheral nervous system.** The central division includes the brain and the spinal cord; the peripheral nervous system includes all the cell bodies and nerve fibers outside the brain and the spinal cord. The peripheral nerves function to bring messages from the receptors and to pass messages along to the effectors. The central structures serve to coordinate, connect, and integrate incoming and outgoing messages.

SOMATIC AND AUTONOMIC SYSTEMS

The whole nervous system can be viewed from another point of view and divided according to the part of the body served. From this angle, there is a **somatic nervous system** and an **autonomic nervous system,** each having both central and peripheral components.

The Somatic System

The somatic system includes the nerve cells and fibers serving the receptors and the muscles. This system includes the 12 **cranial nerves,** which have their central terminations inside the cranium; and the 31 pairs of **spinal nerves,** which connect at regular intervals with the spinal cord. The cranial nerves function primarily in connection with the receptors and effectors located in the head: smell, vision, taste, and the movements involved in speech and chewing. The **vagus nerve** is the only one of the 12 that extends beyond the confines of the cranium; it serves the heart, blood vessels, and viscera. Each of the spinal nerves has both a receptor and an effector branch. The receptor or sensory branch carries messages from the receptors of the skin, muscles, tendons, joints, and the internal organs; the motor or effector branch controls the striated muscles of the arms, legs, and all the body from the neck down. Each sensory spinal nerve connects with the spinal cord through a **ganglion,** a small center of neurons and synapses lying outside the spinal cord.

The Autonomic System

The autonomic nervous system—which, like the somatic, has both central and peripheral components—is concerned with internal adjustments. Its primary connections are with internal effectors: the smooth muscles of the intestines, the urogenital tract, and the blood vessels; the endocrine glands and the cardiac muscle.

The autonomic nervous system is divided into two parts; the sympathetic and the parasympathetic systems. (Fig. 4–6.) Each in its own way serves the ends of survival and adjustment.

The sympathetic system—connecting with effectors in the heart, the liver, the stomach, the intestines, the blood vessels throughout the body, the medulla of the adrenal gland, and the sweat glands—serves a *mobilizing function.* When it is activated, as in an emotional emergency, a variety of bodily functions go on an emergency footing: there is sweating, constriction of blood vessels, dilation of the bronchioles of the lungs, release of stored sugar in the liver, acceleration of the heartbeat, and inhibition of activity in the stomach and the intestines. All of these

changes—and they tend to occur together—equip the organism for emergency activity. It readies itself, apparently, for a vigorous attack on an enemy or a rapid retreat from one. (See Chap. 9.)

The parasympathetic system—connecting with many of the same organs served by the sympathetic system—is a *system of maintenance.* For example, it sends the messages necessary to maintain a normal heart rate and to produce salivary and other digestive secretions that facilitate digestive movement from the esophagus to the upper colon.

Although opposed in function, the two branches of the autonomic system function in an interlocking manner to maintain an internal environment best suited for the survival of the organism in both the ordinary routine and in the emergencies of living.

CENTRAL NERVOUS SYSTEM

The **central nervous system,** to which we shall return for detailed attention, consists of the spinal cord and the several divisions of the brain.

The spinal cord is the transmission pathway to and from the brain, handling all messages from receptors and to effectors except those carried by the cranial nerves. Its principal function, then, is conduction. In addition, however, it does some simple integration; for many reflex actions involving automatic connection between receptors and effectors, the connecting or integration of sensory with motor messages occurs in the spinal cord.

Proceeding upward from the spinal cord to the top of the brain we find five distinct divisions: *myelencephalon, metencephalon, mesencephalon, diencephalon,* and *telencephalon.*

Myelencephalon

The **myelencephalon,** often called the medulla, connects the spinal cord to the brain. Many nerve tracts pass through the medulla on the way to higher brain centers. It is not, however, merely a way station; it contains centers which control breathing, heartbeat and blood pressure. An injury to one of these centers is fatal.

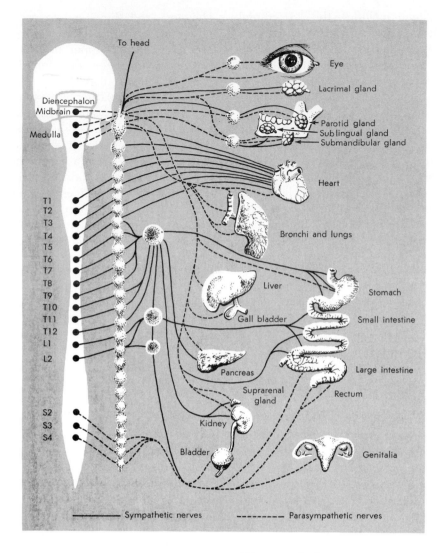

To head

Diencephalon
Midbrain
Medulla

Eye

Lacrimal gland

Parotid gland
Sublingual gland
Submandibular gland

Heart

Bronchi and lungs

T1
T2
T3
T4
T5
T6
T7
T8
T9
T10
T11
T12
L1
L2

Liver

Stomach

Gall bladder

Small intestine

Pancreas

Large intestine

Suprarenal
gland

Rectum

Kidney

S2
S3
S4

Bladder

Genitalia

———— Sympathetic nerves   --------- Parasympathetic nerves

Figure 4–6. AUTONOMIC NERVOUS SYSTEM.
*Diagram shows principal neural pathways of
the two branches of the autonomic nervous
system and the organs to which they connect.*

Metencephalon

The **metencephalon,** the second division of
the brain, consists principally of the **cerebellum** and the **pons.** The cerebellum has as its
chief function the receiving and relaying of
both incoming and outgoing messages having
to do with motor coordination. The pons, located in front of the cerebellum, is also primarily a transmission center, but it functions
in addition as the center for the sensation from
and movement of the mouth and face.

Mesencephalon

The **mesencephalon,** often called the midbrain, is a relatively small bridge between
lower and higher brain centers and serves
mainly as a passageway. The *tectum,* or roof,
of the mesencephalon, however, has some
primitive function in vision and audition.

Diencephalon

When we come to the **diencephalon,** we
encounter more complexity both of structure
and function. The **thalamus** and the **hypothalamus** are its principal parts although it also
contains the **pituitary gland,** structures known
as the **mammillary bodies,** and the optic
tracts.

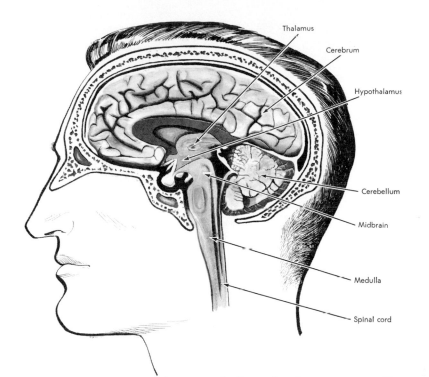

Figure 4–7. MAJOR PARTS OF THE BRAIN (1). *Major parts of the brain and their location within the skull.*

The thalamus is a relay station between the spinal cord and the lower centers of the brain on one hand and the various parts of the telencephalon located above it. Of primary importance among its various subdivisions are the **lateral geniculate body,** relaying messages from the eye, and the **medial geniculate body,** which serves a similar function for auditory messages.

The hypothalamus, which connects directly with the higher brain centers, the pituitary gland, and the vital center of the medulla, is the primary control center for autonomic functions: hormonal secretion; metabolism; the physiological activities associated with hunger, thirst, and sex; and emotional responses throughout the body. It integrates the autonomic messages into patterns that create the internal environment of the organism.

Telencephalon

The **telencephalon,** the highest part of the brain, consists principally of the two hemispheres of the cerebrum and the two olfactory bulbs. The latter are small structures lying just above the olfactory receptors. The cerebral hemispheres and their covering, the **cerebral cortex,** in many respects constitute the "true" brain; here is the part of the nervous system involved in the truly psychological and, in many respects, the truly human functions of the human being.

Of particular recent interest has been a part of the telencephalon known as the **septal areas.** These areas are underneath the frontal part of the cortex, lying deep in the center of the brain in close proximity to the structures of the diencephalon.

Also of particular interest is the **amygdala,** a special group of cells buried in the fore part of the cortex, spatially on a level with the lower part of the diencephalon. The amygdala and the septal areas, recent research has shown, are deeply involved, along with the diencephalon, in the control of emotional and motivational processes. The gross anatomy of the brain is represented in Figures 4–7 and 4–8.

THE CEREBRAL CORTEX

There are two hemispheres of the cerebrum; each hemisphere is covered by cortex, and

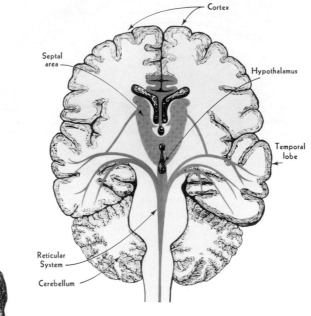

Figure 4–8. MAJOR PARTS OF BRAIN (II). *A diagram showing parts of brain receiving primary attention in recent research on motivation and emotion. This diagram shows a cross section of the brain as seen from behind, with the section made on a line beginning at the top, in front of the ears, and continuing through the ears toward the spinal cord.*

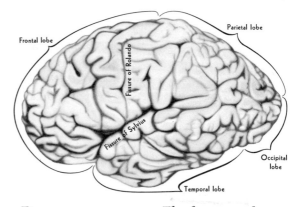

Figure 4–9. THE CORTEX. *The fissures and lobes of the cerebral cortex. The left hemisphere is shown.*

the two are connected underneath by the **corpus callosum,** made up of tracts joining the two hemispheres.

The geography of each hemisphere is described in terms of *fissures* and *lobes.* There are two main fissures, which serve as landmarks in locating the lobes. There is the **fissure of Rolando,** a central fissure, a deep groove running from a midpoint at the top of the center and extending downward and forward. A second major groove is the **fissure of Sylvius,** or *lateral fissure,* beginning on the ventral, or underneath, side of the hemisphere and running upward and toward the rear.

The **frontal lobe** of each hemisphere includes all the cortex lying in front of the central fissure of Rolando above the fissure of

Sylvius. The **parietal lobes** extend from the central fissure about four fifths of the way around the cortex, where they join the **occipital lobes** at the rear of the brain. The **temporal lobes** lie beneath the fissure of Sylvius and, with respect to the skull, beneath those areas designated as temples.

The cortex contains many different kinds of nerve cells and a great number of fibers. A large proportion of its cells connect only with one another and not directly with lower parts of the brain or lower parts of the nervous system.

Below the cortex, making up the corpus callosum, is a large mass of fibers—white because they are myelinated—serving connective functions. The long **commissural fibers,** having cell bodies inside the cortex, connect one side of the cortex with the other. The **association fibers** are relatively short fibers serving also as internal connectors in the cortex. The **projection fibers** carry impulses to and from the cortex. Those carrying impulses downward from the cortex may run to any one of the lower parts of the brain and, in some cases, to spinal cells. The projection fibers coming into the cortex arise almost exclusively in the thalamus, connecting there with fibers running to and from the various parts of the body.

If we examine functions of the cortex, we get a more detailed map than that depicting only fissures and lobes. The surface of the structure contains (1) a *motor* area and a related *premotor* area, concerned with the control of muscular movements; (2) a *somesthetic* area, upon which are projected the sensations from the body senses; (3) an area of *visual projection;* (4) an area of *auditory projection;* and (5) various *association* areas. The so-called association areas are not involved directly in sensory or motor functions and have been regarded as the areas in which complex connections are made.

In general terms, the cortex functions to control all processes occurring in structures beneath it. It is the principal center for sensory discrimination, for control of muscular movement, and for the elaborate associative processes involved in learning, memory, perception, and thought.

EVOLUTION OF THE NERVOUS SYSTEM

All organisms have special cells that can be irritated by the environment and that can transmit messages from one part of the system

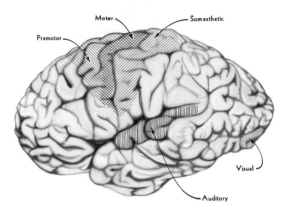

Figure 4–10. SENSORY PROJECTION AREAS. *Drawing indicates the sensory projection areas of the cortex. Direct stimulation of these areas will produce sensory experience; injury will produce sensory malfunctioning. Drawing is of a lateral surface of the left hemisphere.*

to another. In the lower animals, these cells are organized into relatively simple systems. The jellyfish, for example, has a diffuse nerve net, in which there can be no very specialized conduction; when it is "irritated" by a stimulus, it is irritated all over. And the jellyfish has no central nervous system for the conduction, storage, or integration of neural messages. Many organisms, by contrast, have highly differentiated systems with pronounced central development. As we move up the evolutionary continuum, we find three developments: **ganglionic organization, encephalization,** and, later, **corticalization.** We can look briefly at each of these ontological processes. In the diffuse nerve net of the jellyfish, any nerve connects with all nerves. Specific response to specific stimulus is impossible. Insects, by contrast, have *ganglia,* or small centers in which specific nerves connect with specific nerves. Nerves from one segment of the body connect together in one center, or ganglion, where there can be specific connection with other nerves.

When we move up the scale to vertebrates, we find advancing *encephalization* of the nervous system; the major ganglion, or connection center, comes to be located at the head end of

(a)

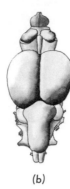
(b)

(c)

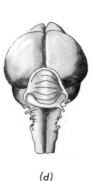
(d)

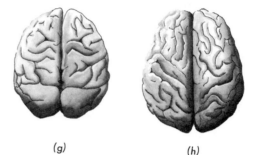

(e)   (f)   (g)   (h)

Figure 4–11. EVOLUTION OF THE BRAIN. *Comparative development of the brain in vertebrates: (a) dogfish, (b) salmon, (c) alligator, (d) pigeon, (e) rabbit, (f) dog, (g) chimpanzee, (h) man. (From* A Textbook of General Physiology *by P. H. Mitchell, Copyright 1948; by permission of McGraw-Hill Book Co., Inc.)*

the organism. And when we get as high as the alligator, for example, we find the beginning of corticalization—the development of higher brain centers that take over increasing control of all neural functions. This latter evolutionary trend is of most interest to students of human behavior, for it is the advanced corticalization of the human brain that makes possible the behavior we regard as most consummately human.

The degree of *corticalization* of an organism depends upon the proportion of its nervous system that is occupied with the carrying out of routine behavior. In lower animals, the entire nervous system is involved in handling the receptor-effector connections necessary to breathe, digest, move, and reproduce. There

is little nervous system "left over" for more complex functions. The ready-made, predetermined connections keep the organism functioning and surviving—unless its functioning depends on memory for past events or the capacity to solve a novel problem. Such complex neural functions become more and more possible as there is more corticalization, as more of the nervous system is free from the inexorable assignment of carrying routine messages over fixed channels. Man, representing the highest stage of corticalization, has neural structures still available, after routine demands are met, for the functions that we regard as most characteristically human: learning, thought, symbolic processes.

The relative corticalization of an organism's nervous system cannot be measured by the size of the brain alone but by the relative size of the brain and the spinal cord. The size of the spinal cord varies with the size of the animal; the larger the animal, the more routine work there is for the nervous system to do. The alligator, for example, has a relatively large spinal cord for handling routine connections, and the lower parts of the brain are also relatively well developed, but it has only a rudimentary forebrain or "new brain"—the part of the brain, the cerebrum, that becomes greatly enlarged in higher animals. The alligator's brain barely outweighs its spinal cord. The brain of the chimpanzee is approximately 15 times as heavy as the spinal cord. The human brain, running much more prominently to cerebrum, is 55 times as heavy as the spinal cord. The human organism, then, has brain to spare for other functions in addition to such routine functions as breathing, eating, moving, and mating.

Perhaps of equal significance is the *increased cerebral control* in human beings of lower kinds of neural activity. In mating behavior, for example, the human being is not a creature of automatic responses and patterns of responses. One wayward idea can vastly facilitate sexual behavior or inhibit it entirely (Chap. 8). The cortex is also necessary for any kind of human sensory discrimination. Animals with the cortex removed can still make crude visual discriminations on the basis of processes at subcortical levels; but if a human being has his visual cortex removed, he becomes totally blind. Corticalization involves a moving upstairs of the centers of control for neural functioning.

VERTICAL AND CONCENTRIC ANALYSIS OF THE BRAIN

For the past hundred years the brain has been studied in terms of *horizontal* analysis, with structures at one level examined as they relate anatomically to structures at the same level. The foregoing description of the brain has been essentially a horizontal one, following in format the evolutionary history of the brain. In recent years, by contrast, there has been a trend toward a *vertical* and *concentric* analysis. The thinking is in terms of vertical systems, involving structures and processes at more than one horizontal level. And there have been studies that differentiate between the

core of a structure—for example, the mesencephalon—and the more peripheral areas of the same structure. This development has led one writer to use the phrase "concentric nervous system" to refer to the newer view of neural organization (Pribram, 1960). It seems likely that the neurophysiology and the neuropsychology of the future will take on a more vertical and concentric flavor.

RETICULAR FORMATION

In recent years one vertical network that has been defined, both anatomically and functionally, is the reticular formation. This is a network of cells deep in the center of the brain, extending from lower to higher centers. It includes the core of the brain stem and the posterior part of the hypothalamus. The reticular formation is connected with, but not a part of, the neural trunk lines carrying direct sensory and motor messages to and from the brain center (see Fig. 4–8).

We shall return later to the function of the reticular formation. We point out here, as evidence of its general significance, that lesions in it tend to produce apathy and sleepiness, while direct stimulation arouses the brain for activity.

LIMBIC SYSTEMS

The limbic systems are another set of vertically defined structures. These are functional circuits connecting higher with lower segments of the cortex and extending downward to subcortical parts of the brain. Three limbic circuits have been defined. One of them apparently has to do only with the olfactory function. Another, though anatomically defined, has a function as yet essentially unknown. The other, referred to as Limbic System II, is a neural circuit of fibers starting in the midbrain and running to the hippocampus, to the amygdala, to the hypothalamus, and upward to the septal area. The fibers return to the reticular formation. The septal area and the reticular formation are diagrammed in Figure 4–8. Limbic System II functions in the facilitation and control of emotion (Chap. 9) and is involved in recent work, of great potential significance for understanding motivation, on self-stimulation of the brain. This matter will concern us later in the present chapter.

NEURAL PHENOMENA IN INTEGRATED RESPONSE

The basic paradigm for neural activity in a simplified stimulus-response sequence is as follows: (1) A physical stimulus strikes a receptor. (2) The receptor stimulates the dendrites of a sensory neuron; a nerve impulse travels up the **afferent** (incoming) fiber to the endbrush. (3) The impulse crosses the synaptic junction and stimulates the dendrites of a connector neuron in the spinal cord. (4) The impulse passes across another synapse from the connector neuron to the dendrites of an **efferent** (outgoing) neuron. (5) The impulse passes along the efferent fiber to its endbrush. (6) An effector—a muscle or gland—responds. Such a process, though obviously intricate when we consider its details, is still a vastly oversimplified model of what actually occurs even in the simplest reflex act. There are a number of known processes which add to the complexity of the simplest neural events, serving to make the nervous system more difficult to understand but more understandably capable of handling the humanly intricate integrations of behavior.

Among the known facts of neural circuits and networks are the following:

SYNAPTIC SUMMATION

The impulse reaching a synapse from a single fiber may not bridge the synapse, but two or more impulses arriving within a very brief period of time may do the job. Thus, although one stimulus—applied, for example, to one area of the skin—may not produce a response, a second stimulus—applied nearby and simultaneously—will carry the impulse across the synapse. Synaptic summation does not occur unless the two impulses arrive within about 15 milliseconds of each other.

ALTERNATIVE NERVE PATHWAYS

It probably never occurs that a chain of a single afferent neuron, a single connector neuron, and a single efferent neuron functions to carry a neural message. Many, probably hundreds of nerve fibers are involved in even the simplest sensory-motor arc. Each of the many incoming fibers can make connections with many connector fibers; and each of these, particularly if the higher nerve centers are involved, can make connection with many efferent fibers. Such a proliferation of possible pathways from stimulus to response makes possible a very great variety of responses to the same stimulus—particularly if the connector neurons of higher brain centers are involved.

THE DENDRITIC POTENTIAL

Until recently, it was the prevailing view that the nervous system was essentially inert, becoming active only when stimulated through the activity in the receptors. The nerve fiber, with its own characteristics, would fire an all-or-none impulse of a certain magnitude and with a certain speed when it was adequately stimulated. A pattern of fibers, each behaving in an all-or-none manner, carried the impulses involved in a sensory-motor integration. Recent research has altered this view and has raised many problems for both the neurophysiologist and the psychologist. For example, in exploring **electroencephalographic** phenomena, two groups of researchers (Bishop and Clare, 1952; Li, Cullen, and Jasper, 1956) found that some of the electrical events recorded from the brain are independent of the number of impulses generated by the neurons they were sampling. The EEG recordings changed for areas of the brain rich in dendrites, indicating that the *dendrites themselves carry an electrical potential*—a steady state of excitability. Not enough is yet known about these matters to understand their implications, but it does appear that the discovery of the **dendritic potential** may revise notions about many aspects of neural functioning. Perhaps the all-or-none law will have to be revised in favor of a view that allows for a graded response on the part of a neuron. The evidence also suggests that the brain is always active, not only because of transmitted impulses but because a different kind of electrical activity is constantly going on (Hebb, 1955).

BRAIN FUNCTIONS IN PSYCHOLOGICAL PROCESSES

A great deal is known and more is being learned about the brain functions involved in the psychological processes with which we are familiar. Recent improvements in techniques make it possible to stimulate electrically or to destroy precisely located parts of the brains of animals, and to record accurately both the electrical and behavioral results. Also, the human brain, in connection with necessary brain surgery and through advancing technology, has been studied with increased precision and thoroughness. All this knowledge adds to the completeness of our understanding of psychological process as we know it; it also may bring about drastic revisions in our conventional ways of conceiving some of the basic psychological functions (Bruner, 1957; Miller, Galanter, and Pribram, 1960).

Later on, when we study motivation (Chap. 8), emotion (Chap. 9), sensation (Chap. 10), and learning (Chap. 12 and 13), we will examine in some specific detail the neural events that underlie the behavior we study when we focus on each of these segments of the psychological process. For the present we have aimed to achieve an overview of neural and physiological processes. For the remainder of the present chapter, we will deal with some areas of neuropsychological research that do not fall appropriately into any of the areas into which the field of psychology is customarily divided.

MOTOR FUNCTIONS

Through research methods similar to those used in exploring the sensory functions of the brain, motor areas have also been mapped. The primary motor areas are located just in front of the fissure of Rolando and extend around the two hemispheres. The areas of the body are represented there in a crisscrossed and approximately upside-down arrangement. Stimulation on the left side produces movement of muscles on the right, and vice versa. The toes and feet are moved by stimulation at the top of the arc, while movement of the tongue and jaw are produced by stimulation of areas far down toward the fissure of Sylvius.

There is, in addition to the primary motor areas, a *premotor* area lying just forward on

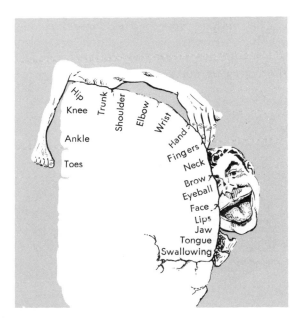

Figure 4–12. MOTOR PROJECTION. *As in somesthetic projection, areas of the cortex are involved in motor control of the various parts of the body. The schematic body here is drawn so that its size is proportional to the size of the area of cortex upon which it is projected. (Penfield and Rasmussen,* The Cerebral Cortex of Man, *Copyright 1950; reproduced by permission of The Macmillan Company.)*

the cortex. The function of this area is not well understood. It is known, however, that damage in this area produces an awkwardness of movement, whereas destruction of the motor areas produces paralysis.

With respect to both sensory and motor functions, there is a duplication—a mirror duplication—of the two hemispheres of the cortex, with the right side of the structure relating to the left side of the body and vice versa. For functions in the middle of the body, such as those involved in speech, one side of the cortex is *dominant*—it takes over control from the other. In right-handed people, the left hemisphere is ordinarily the dominant one, taking over control not only of the midline functions but probably controlling also both sides of the body.

LINGUISTIC FUNCTIONS

The various speech functions—speaking, reading, writing, the recognition of spoken words—involve large and scattered areas of the cortex. It makes immediate sense, in the

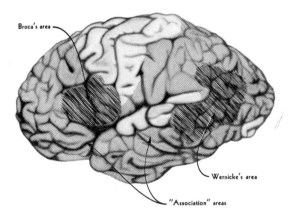

Figure 4-13. SPEECH AREAS. *Drawing of the lateral surface of one hemisphere of the cortex, showing (a) two areas of the brain involved in the control of speech and (b) the so-called "association" areas.*

light of what we already have learned about the brain, that so complex an array of sensori-motor functions should involve a number of different parts of the brain. And it should surprise no one that little is known about the neural processes involved.

There is some evidence, however, about localization, and about the kinds of linguistic disorders produced by brain damage. Direct stimulation of the brain in an area in front of the fissure of Rolando and just above the fissure of Sylvius produces long vowel-like sounds in conscious patients undergoing brain surgery. Vocalization of a repetitive kind has also been produced by direct stimulation of (1) an area of the frontal lobe and (2) several points in the parietal lobe. If a patient is set to counting, the counting is interrupted by stimulation of certain areas on either side of the fissure of Rolando (Penfield and Rasmussen, 1950). Such evidences may be taken to indicate the diversity of cortical involvement in the motor act of speaking. The involvement is probably at least as complex in other facets of linguistic behavior.

Brain damage can produce a variety of disorders of speech. There can be sensory **aphasia,** the inability to understand written or spoken language, or motor aphasia, the inability to speak or to write—either of which can be caused by damage in appropriate areas of the cortex.

FUNCTIONS OF THE RETICULAR FORMATION

We have seen that receptor input into the central nervous system serves two functions: a cue function and an arousal function. Input from both the surface and the visceral receptors sets off processes in the reticular formation which project in a diffuse way onto the cortex, there facilitating neural response to the cue projections (Moruzzi and Magoun, 1949; Lindsley, 1951). Apparently, the cortex will not respond as the cortex should unless it is first aroused by messages reaching it through the reticular formation. Direct electrical stimulation of the reticular formation produces a "waking" EEG pattern of activity in the brain. Injury to the structure abolishes the "waking" EEG and produces apathy, lethargy, or sleepiness in behavior (Lindsley, 1951). In one study—a direct experimental demonstration of the arousal or facilitating effects of reticular activity—monkeys, trained to discriminate objects, made fewer errors, had shorter reaction times, and required briefer **tachistoscopic** exposures when given electrical stimulation in the reticular formation (Fuster, 1958). On a similar task for human subjects, chlorpromazine, which is known to affect the reticular formation, produced an impairment (Primac, Mirsky, and Rosvold, 1957).

These and many other facts about the functioning of the reticular formation have clear implications for understanding motivated behavior. The phenomenon of arousal itself—and the absence of arousal—may be viewed as a motivational matter; but there are other implications also.

According to one theorist (Hebb, 1955), the organism not only seeks arousal but functions poorly without it. And there is evidence that organisms find inactivity distasteful; they seek puzzles, mild threats, excitement, and exposure to the world. Perhaps, then, there is a physiological basis for an exploratory or curiosity or problem-seeking motive (see Chap. 8). As for the matter of malfunctioning in the

absence of arousal, there is the recent evidence from studies of the strange phenomena of *sensory deprivation.*

The best-known experiment dealing with sensory deprivation was one in which college students, for the handsome reward of $20 a day, were paid to do nothing (Bexton, Heron, and Scott, 1954). The subjects in this study were placed in an isolated room, in which they were made comfortable and were fed upon request but could see, hear, speak, feel, and do very little. For periods of up to eight hours, the subjects were quite willing and able to continue the experiment. After awhile, however, they developed an extreme need for stimulation of almost any kind. They were allowed, on request, to hear a talk prepared for young children on the evils of alcohol. Some subjects asked to be exposed to this stimulation as many as twenty times over a thirty-hour period. Others repeatedly asked to hear a recording of an old stock-market report. One subject, in spite of a dire need for money, soon gave up the $20 a day to take a manual job at $7. Furthermore, after five hours or longer of this sensory deprivation, the subjects' nor-

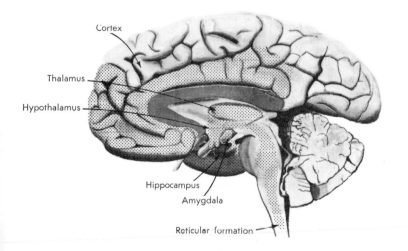

Figure 4–14. THE BRAIN AND EMOTION. *The shaded areas in the drawing above represent the principal structures involved in the integration and control of emotional responses. (From Lindsley, 1951; by permission of John Wiley & Sons, Inc.)*

mal intellectual functioning appeared to be impaired. They were less able to follow a line of logical reasoning, scored lower on intelligence tests, and reported that for periods of up to 24 hours after the deprivation experience they could not concentrate on their studies.

FUNCTIONS OF THE LIMBIC SYSTEM

It is clear, then, that the functioning of the reticular formation must be taken into account in putting together the complete picture of motivated behavior. The same goes for the limbic system, a vertical system of structures extending from the septal area to the amygdala. There have been a large number of recent studies of the system as it relates to emotional and motivational processes of the body and, on the other hand, to the cortical centers of control above it.

Perhaps the most significant of these researches are those showing that direct electrical stimulation in Limbic System II appears to be pleasurable, serving as a direct reward for certain forms of behavior (Olds and Milner, 1954). The experimental demonstration of this kind of effect occurred more or less by accident. A rat, being studied in connection with another problem, had tiny electrodes embedded in a part of its septal area. It was given a few bursts of electrical current before it began the experiment proper. The experimenter noticed that the rat demonstrated a peculiar interest in the place in an open field at which it had received the shock. It would come back to the "shock place" to sniff around, spending more of its time there than elsewhere (Olds, 1955). This bit of serendipity led to a systematic exploration of the then strange phenomenon and to what may be a major breakthrough in physiological psychology.

In following up this matter, the experimenters planted electrodes in various parts of the rat's brain, arranged things so that in a **Skinner box** the rat could press a lever and give himself a brain shock. There was a record of the rat's self-stimulating behavior and a postmortem study of the exact septal area spot at which the electrodes had been placed. Some of the rats would press the self-stimulating lever up to 5,000 times an hour for several hours. They appeared in some cases to prefer the brain stimulation to food, even though they had been starved. With the bar pressing used as a measure of the pleasure of the self-stimulation, it was found that pleasure varied systematically with the part of the limbic system stimulated.

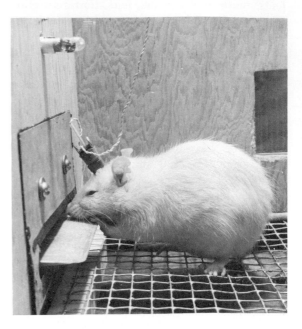

Figure 4–15. SELF-STIMULATION OF THE BRAIN. *With tiny electrodes buried in the septal areas of the brain, rats will repeatedly give themselves electrical stimulation by pressing a switch.*

Those who have carried further this line of investigation have shown that *prolonged* stimulation of the limbic system is sometimes painful and avoided (Delgado, Roberts, and Miller, 1954). Rats, in an apparatus where they could press a lever to turn on a shock or turn a wheel to remove it, would first press the lever and then, after awhile, turn the wheel to remove the shock.

We have evidence here that direct stimulation of certain parts of the brains of rats apparently has an effect similar to the rewards and punishments used as reinforcers in motivated learning. What has this to do with human motivation? We obviously cannot now say. It can be counted on, however, that these phenomena will be thoroughly explored in other animals and perhaps in man. And our eventual full accounting for motivated behavior will include these now not fully appreciated phenomena.

The data bearing on the function both of the reticular formation and of the limbic system are being fused into a general theoretical picture of neural functioning in both emotion and motivation (Hebb, 1955; Olds, 1956). In the simplest—and perhaps too simple—terms, we can say that the theory runs as follows: Arousal, up to a certain point, is rewarding and facilitating, but beyond a certain level is painful and disruptive. Incoming stimuli may set off neural circuits or "cell assemblies," which lead to pleasure or pain and to response of some degree of organization. When behavior leads to a flow of incoming stimuli that produce pleasure, then behavior stops, for the organism has what it wants; when the original stimuli, or the stimuli produced by behavior, are painful, behavior continues, through the activation of alternative sequences of "cell assemblies," until the pleasure-producing stimuli are produced to replace the pain. Such a theory is now plausible but very tentative. Research and speculation continue.

ADDITIONAL AREAS OF RESEARCH

Among the additional research problems on which progress has been made—and will continue—may be listed (a) chemical factors in brain functioning and (b) the brain and intelligence. These areas of advancing knowledge obviously belong in a thorough treatment of the neural and physiological basis of behavior. But like many nutritious topics, they cannot be covered in an introductory text. The student may do well to remember, however, that the brain is constantly bathed in a flow of blood, and there are many ways in which the chemistry of the blood influences the electrical activity of the nervous system. Perhaps anesthesia is the most impressive example. Also the brain must be regarded as the seat of intelligence; its chemistry, metabolic and otherwise, affects the kind of functioning required for intelligent behavior. For example, some forms of mental deficiency are closely related to malfunctioning metabolism. Also, the nature and extent of damage to the brain affects

tested intelligence. Here these matters can only be catalogued.

SUMMARY

1. Behavior, even of the simplest kind, is integrated; the nervous system is the major instrument of integration of behavior.

2. Some psychologists are inclined to "explain" behavior in terms of neural activity. Others tend to ignore the nervous system while they study overt behavior. Almost all will agree that a knowledge of neurophysiological processes can contribute to our understanding of the organism.

3. The organism is able to engage in integrated behavior through the functioning of receptors, effectors, and connectors; the nervous system's primary function is that of connecting.

4. Receptor cells in the various sense organs function to translate physical and chemical events into neural events; the effector cells in muscles and glands translate neural events into response.

5. Behavior occurs at various levels of integration, from the simple reflex to complex problem solving.

6. The structural unit of the nervous system is the nerve cell, or neuron, composed of a cell body, an axon, and dendrites; there are transmission neurons and connecting or correlating neurons.

7. The stimulated nerve sends neural impulses along the nerve fiber and across a synapse, where junction is made from the axon of one cell to the dendrites of another. A neural impulse occurs if stimulation is above the neuron's threshold. The nerve impulse travels in general accordance with the all-or-none law. After a neuron is stimulated, during an absolute refractory phase, it will not fire impulses. During a relative refractory phase, it will fire if the stimulus is sufficiently strong.

8. There are central and peripheral components of the nervous system; the entire system, viewed in another way, can be divided also into a somatic system and an autonomic system. The somatic system includes the 12 cranial and the 31 spinal nerves. The autonomic system, concerned primarily with internal adjustments, is composed of the sympathetic system and the parasympathetic system, with the former functioning primarily in emotional situations and the latter in routine maintenance.

9. The central nervous system is composed of the spinal cord and the brain, which has five major divisions—the myelencephalon, metencephalon, mesencephalon, diencephalon, and telencephalon. The thalamus and hypothalamus; parts of the mesencephalon, the cerebral cortex, the septal areas, and the amygdala; and all parts of the telencephalon are of particular interest to psychologists.

10. The surface of the cerebral cortex is divided by the fissure of Rolando, or central fissure, and the fissure of Sylvius, or lateral fissure; each of the two hemispheres of the cortex is divided into lobes—the frontal, temporal, parietal, and occipital.

11. The cortex can also be roughly mapped in terms of the localization of function; there are motor areas, premotor areas, somesthetic areas, areas of visual projection, areas of auditory projection, and various association areas.

12. The evolution of the nervous system has been characterized by progressive ganglionic organization, encephalization, and corticalization. The human organism is characterized by great cortical control over all lower neural processes.

13. A new trend in the study of the nervous system has emphasized the vertical and concentric analysis both of structure and function; recent research has thrown light on the functioning of the reticular formation and the limbic system.

14. The detailed analyses of neural processes underlying integrated behavior have revealed phenomena of synaptic summation, alternative nerve pathways, and a persisting dendritic potential.

15. The cortex contains relatively specific areas of motor as well as sensory projection. Direct stimulation of specific areas produces muscular movement, and injury produces paralysis.

16. Large and scattered areas of the cortex are involved in linguistic functions. Brain injury in the areas concerned with linguistic function produces aphasia, which may be motor or sensory or both.

17. Recent research involving the reticular formation and the phenomenon of arousal is throwing new light on motivational processes; there is evidence that the organism does not function well unless incoming sensory impulses, diffused by the reticular formation, arouse the brain; there is evidence that the organism actively seeks arousal when input is below a certain minimum and that sensory deprivation produces disturbance of mental functioning.

18. Recent research involving the limbic system has shown that rats will, apparently with pleasure, give themselves repeated small electrical charges in the septal area; however, prolonged stimulation is apparently painful. Such results as these, along with the data on arousal, will perhaps find their way into a new and comprehensive theory of motivation.

RESEARCH REPORT

One line of research having a direct bearing on neural functioning concerns the capacity of simple organisms, possessed of simple nervous systems, to learn from experience. The research paper reprinted here describes, in what seems to be a very successful nontechnical manner, a series of experiments that began with psychologists' curiosity about the learning capacity of worms and that then led, as experiments often do, into some unusual and fascinating discoveries and puzzles. The student should be warned that some of the reported research is still controversial.

MEMORY TRANSFER THROUGH CANNIBALISM IN PLANARIANS [*]

The research that I am going to outline today had its start several years ago, and I trust you will allow me to give you a few of the pertinent background details, if only to convince you that our work is more serious than it sometimes sounds, and of sufficient scope at least to approach respectability. It was in 1953, when I was a graduate student at the University of Texas, that a fellow student, Robert Thompson, suggested to me that we attempt to condition a planarian, or common flatworm. Having avoided the rigors of introductory Zoology up to that point, my only prior experience with worms had been at the business end of a fishing pole. I soon discovered, however, that fishing worms are round, while planarians are flat. Planarians are also usually less than an inch in length, and rather interesting in their own right.

Flatworms occupy a unique niche on the phylogenetic scale, being the lowest organisms to possess bilateral symmetry, a rude form of encephalization, and a human, synaptic-type nervous system. According to some psychological theories—the ones that postulate that learning is a matter of reshuffling connections among neurons—the planarian should be the lowest organism to be able to demonstrate "true" learning. As far as we knew in 1953, no one had ever demonstrated unequivocally that these organisms could indeed be trained. Since then, of course, we have discovered the usual obscure reference that antedates our work by 30 years—it appears in Dutch and was published in a little-read European journal [1]—but I am not at all sure that even this knowledge would have deterred us. At any rate, Thompson and I set out in 1953 to attempt classical conditioning in planarians.

Imagine a trough gouged out of plastic, 12 inches in length, semi-circular in cross-section, and filled with pond water. At either end are brass electrodes attached to a power source. Above the trough are two electric light bulbs. Back and forth in the trough crawls a single flatworm, and in front of the apparatus sits the experimenter, his eye on the worm, his hands on two switches. When the worm is gliding smoothly in a straight line on the bottom of the trough, the experimenter turns on the lights for three seconds. After the

light has been on for two of the three seconds, the experimenter adds one second of electric shock, which passes through the water and causes the worm to contract. The experimenter records the behavior of the worm during the two-second period after the light has come on but before the shock has started. If the animal gives a noticeable turning movement or a contraction prior to the onset of the shock, this is scored as a "correct" or "conditioned" response.[2]

From this brief description of the experimental paradigm, many of you will recognize that Thompson and I were attempting to establish a form of Pavlovian conditioning in our experimental animals (Group E), and, according to our data, we were successful. Planarians occasionally give a mild and presumably innate response to the onset of the light, even when it has not been previously paired with shock, so we ran a control group that received just trials of photic (light) stimulation (Group LC); we also ran a control group that received just shock, occasionally interspersing a test trial of light alone (Group SC). All animals were given 150 trials. Over that period of time, as Tables I and II show, the experimental animals, which received light paired with shock, showed a significant increase in responsivity, while the control groups showed either no change at all or a significant decline.

Hence Thompson and I concluded that we had accomplished what we set out to accomplish—namely, we had proven that worms could be conditioned.[3]

Those of you who have ever chopped up a planarian in a Zoology course will know that these

Table I

MEAN TURNS, CONTRACTIONS, AND
COMBINED RESPONSES ON THE FIRST 50 AND
LAST 50 TRIALS FOR GROUPS E (EXPERIMENTAL)
AND LC (LIGHT CONTROL)

Group	Response	First 50 Trials	Last 50 Trials	Diff.	p
E	Turns	12.6	16.6	4.0	.01
	Contractions	1.2	5.0	3.8	.01
	Combined	13.8	21.6	7.8	.01
LC	Turns	11.7	7.6	−4.1	.01
	Contractions	0.6	2.1	1.5	
	Combined	12.3	9.7	−2.6	

[*] Abridged from James V. McConnell, Ph.D., J. Neuropsychiat., 3, Supp. 1 (Aug. 1962), 42–48. (The author's references appear on page 117.)

Table II

Response	First 15 Test Trials	Last 15 Test Trials	Diff.*
Turns	5.4	4.2	—1.2
Contractions	0.2	0.4	0.2
Combined	5.6	4.6	—1.0

* *None of the differences is significant at the .05 level of confidence.*

animals have enormous powers of regeneration. A large specimen may be cut into perhaps fifty pieces, each of which will eventually regenerate into a complete organism. It was while we were running that first experiment that Thompson and I wondered aloud, feeling rather foolish as we did so, what would happen if we conditioned a flatworm, then cut it in two and let both halves regenerate. Which half would retain the memory? As it happened, we never got around to performing that experiment at Texas, for Thompson received his doctorate soon after we finished our first study and went on to Louisiana State University and bigger and better things—namely, rats. When I went to the University of Michigan in 1956, however, I was faced with the difficult problem that in the academic world, one must publish or perish. The only thing I knew much about was flatworms, so I talked two bright young students, Allan Jacobson and Daniel Kimble, into performing the obvious experiment on learning and regeneration.

Kimble, Jacobson, and I did the following. We took our experimental animals and trained them to a criterion of 23 responses out of any block of 25 trials. When they had reached this criterion, we assumed that they were properly conditioned and immediately cut them in half across the middle. Head and tail sections were then put in individual bowls and allowed about 4 weeks to regenerate. At the end of this period, these experimental animals (Group E) were retrained to the same criterion, and savings scores calculated. We also ran a group of worms which were cut, allowed to regenerate, and then were conditioned for the first time—this to tell us if cutting and subsequent regeneration in any way sensitized the animals to conditioning (Group RC). Another control group was conditioned, then allowed to

rest uncut for a month before being retested (Group TC)—this to tell us how much forgetting we could expect in our experimental animals had we not cut them in half.

In all honesty I must admit that we did not obtain the results we had expected. We had assumed that the regenerated heads would show fairly complete retention of the response, for, after all, the head section retained the primitive brain and "everybody knows" that the brain is where memories are located. And, as Tables III, IV, and V indicate, the heads did show just as much retention as did the uncut control animals. We had also hoped, in our heart of hearts, that perhaps the tails would show a slight but perhaps significant retention of some kind, merely because we thought this would be an interesting finding. We were astounded, then, to discover that the tails not only showed as much retention as did the heads, but in many cases did much better than the heads and showed absolutely no forgetting whatsoever. Obviously memory, in the flatworm, was being stored throughout the animal's body, and as additional proof of this we found that if we cut the worm into three or even more pieces, each section typically showed clear-cut retention of the conditioned response.[4]

Table III

NUMBER OF TRIALS TO CRITERION FOR GROUP E
(EXPERIMENTAL)

S	Original Training	Retest Head	Retest Tail
E1	99	50	51
E2	191	37	24
E3	97	48	72
E4	83	35	44
E5	200	30	25
M	134	40	43.2

Table IV

NUMBER OF TRIALS TO CRITERION FOR
GROUP RC (REGENERATION CONTROL)

S	Head	Tail
RC1	134	150
RC2	188	179
RC3	276	85
RC4	395	300
RC5	250	325
M	248.6	207.8

Table V

NUMBER OF TRIALS FOR GROUP TC
(TIME CONTROL)

S	Original Training	Retest
TC1	123	24
TC2	153	25
TC3	195	62
TC4	131	43
TC5	325	45
M	185.4	39.8

It was at this time that we first postulated our theory that conditioning caused some chemical change throughout the worm's body, and it was also about then that Reeva Jacobson came along to help us test what seemed at the time to be rather an odd hypothesis. She took planarians, cut off their tails, and conditioned the heads before any regeneration could take place. Then she let her animals grow new tails. She next removed these new tails and let them grow new heads, ending up with apparently completely re-formed organisms. These total regenerates, as we called them, were then tested for any "savings" of the original conditioning. By now we knew what to expect from planarians, and so we weren't too surprised when Reeva's regenerated flatworms showed a significant retention of what the original organism had learned. True, as Table VI suggests, these total regenerates did not demonstrate the complete retention that our original animals had shown, but they did remember enough so that our hypothesis seemed vindicated.[5]

Table VI

NUMBER OF TRIALS TO CRITERION FOR
TOTALLY REGENERATED ANIMALS

S	Original Training	Retest after Total Regeneration
1	200	166
2	325	143
3	300	220
4	327	51
5	75	62
6	381	94
mean	268	122.7
SD	102	60

By now, worms were in the *Zeitgeist*. Edward Ernhart, working with Carl Sherrick at Washington University, demonstrated not only that flatworms could learn a two-unit T-maze, but also that this maze habit was retained by their animals following cutting and regeneration. Again, the tails remembered at least as much as did the heads.[6] Ernhart is perhaps most famous, however, for a more recent study of his. If one takes a flatworm and splits the head straight down the middle, time and time again, the two halves will not heal together but will each regenerate into a complete head. One ends up, then, with a two-headed worm. Ernhart compared the length of time it took two-headed animals to be conditioned with the length of time it took one-headed (or normal) animals to reach the same criterion and found that he had validated an old aphorism—two heads are indeed better than one.[7]

Roy John and William Corning, working at the University of Rochester, became quite interested in the chemical theory of learning about this time, and undertook one of the most spectacular pieces of research yet to come from any worm laboratory. John reasoned that learning in flatworms had to be mediated, at least in part, by some molecular change within the organism's cells. Since Hydén had found changes in RNA in nerve cells as a result of experience,[8] John believed that RNA might be implicated in learning and retention in planarians. So he and Corning conditioned a number of flatworms, cut them in half, and let them regenerate in a weak solution of ribonuclease, which breaks up RNA. When they compared their experimental animals with a number of controls, they found evidence that the experimental heads were relatively unaffected by the ribonuclease, while the tails showed complete forgetting. The tails could be retrained, but it took approximately as long the second time as it had the first.[9]

Ralph Gerard, the noted neurophysiologist, interprets the data as follows: There are probably two distinct but related physiological mechanisms for learning in planarians. The first such mechanism is the familiar one of neural interconnections which are reshuffled in the brain due to the animal's experiences—the so-called circuit-diagram model, if I may be permitted the analogy. Structural changes in the neural pathways in the brain would presumably not be altered by ribonuclease, which accounts for the fact that the Rochester head-regenerates showed no real forgetting. The second type of memory mechanism, however, involves a change in the coding of the RNA molecules in the cells throughout the worm's body.

Presumably whenever the animal learns, the RNA is altered appropriately so that when regeneration takes place, the altered RNA builds the memory into the regenerated animal right from the start. If the RNA were destroyed by the ribonuclease, it is likely that the DNA in the cells would replace the lost RNA, but this replacement RNA would not carry the changed code since the DNA was presumably unaffected by the learning.[10]

If all of this sounds rather complex, you must forgive me. I am not at all sure that at this early date we have more than the vaguest notion just how learning could affect RNA nor how, much less why, this altered RNA might build the memory into the regenerating tissue. The important thing to remember is that John's hunch that RNA might be involved in memory seems to have been substantiated.

Before further discussing RNA and memory, I should like to detail, briefly, some other research that Roy John and Bill Corning, at Rochester, and my own group of worm runners at the University of Michigan and at the Britannica Center in Palo Alto, have been pursuing jointly. In 1957, when we got our first results on retention of learning following regeneration, and came up with our chemical hypothesis, it seemed to us that we might be able to transfer a memory from a trained animal to an untrained animal if we could somehow get the right chemicals out of the first worm and into the second. We spent several years trying to test this admittedly wild notion without much success. First we tried grafting the head of a trained animal onto the tail of an untrained planarian, but this never worked very well. If one reads introductory zoology texts, one often gets the notion that this little operation is most easy to perform. Sadly enough, the best average on record is three successes out of 150 attempts [11] and we simply did not have 150 trained heads to waste. We tried grinding the trained worms up and injecting the pieces into untrained animals, but we never could master the injection techniques. It was only some time after we began this work that it occurred to us that we could let the animals do the transferring for us. For, under the proper conditions, one worm will eat another. And since planarians have but the most rudimentary of digestive tracts, there seemed an excellent chance that the tissue from the food worm would pass into the body of the cannibal relatively unchanged.

So, with Barbara Humphries as our chief experimenter, we conditioned a number of worms,

chopped them into small pieces and hand-fed the pieces to untrained cannibals. We also took the precaution of feeding a number of untrained worms to untrained cannibals for a control or comparison group. Our first pilot study gave us such unbelievable results that we immediately instituted several changes in our procedure and repeated the study not once, but four times. And each time the results were quite significant—and still rather unbelievable. I should mention before going any further that the chief procedural change we made was the institution of a "blind" running technique which helped guard against experimenter bias. Under this blind procedure, the person actually training the worms never knows anything about the animals he runs—we follow an elaborate coding system in which each animal's code letter is changed daily. The experimenter then doesn't know which animal is in which group, nor even which animal is which from day to day. Thus, as far as we could tell, we could not have unconsciously tampered with the data.

The results of this work, as Table VII shows, were somewhat startling. In all five studies, it was clear that the cannibals which had fed on trained worms gave approximately half again as many conditioned responses during the first days of training as did the cannibals which had fed on untrained worms. In our studies, the differences between the two groups tended to disappear after the first few days as the control animals approached criterion. The experimental animals were presumably so close to criterion right from the start that the slope of their learning curve was much less than that of the controls.[12, 13] . . .

Now, if we had been the only ones to have obtained such results, our findings might be dismissed as the achievement of crackpots. Luckily for us, Corning, Karpick, and John instituted their own program of cannibalism shortly after we did and so far have run two large and very well-controlled studies, both using the blind technique, and have obtained results which are essentially identical to ours.[14]

And, as if this were not enough, our work has just been replicated by a high school student. . . .

Frankly, we are not quite sure where all of this work leaves us—except that we are most definitely out on a limb of some kind. At the moment, a number of laboratories around the country are starting investigations into the biochemistry of learning, using planarians as their tools. Specifically, several of us are attempting to extract RNA, DNA, and other biochemicals from conditioned

Table VII

NUMBER OF RESPONSES IN FIRST 25 TRAINING
TRIALS FOR CANNIBALS FED CONDITIONED
PLANARIANS (EXPERIMENTALS) AND FOR
CANNIBALS FED UNCONDITIONED
PLANARIANS (CONTROLS)

Number of Responses in First 25 Trials

Experimentals	Controls
4	1
6	1
7	3
8	4
8	4
8	4
9	5
10	5
10	5
10	6
11	6
12	6
13	6
14	7
14	7
15	10
15	10
15	11
15	11
17	16
18	22
19	
mean 11.73	7.14

worms to feed to untrained cannibals. If we can show, for example, that RNA and only RNA causes the memory transfer, we can surely hope to determine the subtle molecular differences between "trained" and "untrained" RNA. If this could be done, we would be one step closer to cracking the problem of the molecular properties of memory—perhaps a giant step closer at that, particularly if it turns out that teaching the animals different sorts of habits causes different sorts of changes in the RNA molecules. But perhaps that is too much to hope for at the present.

Now, in conclusion, let me attempt to tie all of this research together. We have shown that planarians are capable of learning, that this learning survives cutting and regeneration, that the memory storage mechanism has a biochemical component (probably RNA) which is widely distributed throughout the animals' body, and that learning seems to be transferrable from one animal to another via cannibalistic ingestion. If memory in

higher organisms is also mediated via biochemical changes, and if these changes are specific to the habits learned, we might eventually discover a substance (probably RNA with a deliberately modified structure) which would facilitate learning if it were incorporated into animal or human bodies. If so, the research we have been doing with our lowly flatworms may have practical consequences we never dreamed of when we began our work some nine years ago.

REFERENCES

1. Van Oye, P.: *Natuurwetenschappelijk Tijdschrift,* 2:1–9, 1920.
2. McConnell, James V., Cornwell, P. R., and Clay, Margaret L.: *Amer. J. Psychol.,* 73:618–622, 1960.
3. Thompson, Robert, and McConnell, James V.: *J. Comp. Physiol. Psychol.,* 48:65–68, 1955.
4. McConnell, James V., Jacobson, A. L., and Kimble, D. P.: *J. Comp. Physiol. Psychol.,* 52:1–5, 1959.
5. McConnell, James V., Jacobson, Reeva, and Maynard, D. M.: *Amer. Psychologist,* 14:410, 1959 (abstract).
6. Ernhart, E. N., and Sherrick, C., Jr.: "Retention of a maze habit following regeneration in planaria (*D. maculata*)," Paper read at Midwestern Psychological Association, St. Louis, May 1959.
7. Ernhart, E. N.: *Worm Runner's Digest,* 2:92–94, 1960.
8. Hyden, Holgar: In Farber, Seymour M., and Wilson, Roger H. L. (eds.), *Control of the Mind,* McGraw-Hill, New York, 1961.
9. Corning, W. C., and John, E. R.: *Science,* 134:1363–1365, 1961.
10. Gerard, Ralph: Personal communication, 1961.
11. Kenk, Roman: *J. Exp. Zool.,* 87:55–69, 1941.
12. Humphries, Barbara M., and Jacobson, Reeva: *Worm Runner's Digest,* 3:165–169, 1961.
13. McConnell, James V., Jacobson, Reeva, and Humphries, Barbara M.: *Worm Runner's Digest,* 3:41–47, 1961.
14. Corning, W. C., Karpick, R., and John, E. R.: Personal communication from E. R. John, 1961.
15. Jacobson, Allan L.: "Learning in Flatworms and Annelids," *Psychol. Bull.,* in press.

MATERIAL BASIS OF MEMORY [*]

In this study, Hartry, Keith-Lee, and Morton attempted to replicate McConnell's experiment (in the paper quoted above). They used four groups of planaria: (1) a group conditioned in the McConnell manner, (2) a group exposed to light but not conditioned, (3) a group exposed to shock but not to light, (4) a group handled

[*] A. L. Hartry, P. Keith-Lee, and W. D. Morton, "Planaria: Memory transfer through cannibalism" reexamined, *Science,* 1964, *146,* 274–275.

as were the conditioned worms but not given the conditioning regimen. All of these groups were then fed to other planaria.

Through a highly controlled procedure involving care, perhaps even more elaborate than McConnell's, to ensure against unconscious bias on the part of the experimenters, these researchers found that naive planaria who had eaten conditioned planaria learned more rapidly than did naive planaria who had not been fed and not been stimulated. Whereas the latter took a mean of 153.9 trials to reach the specified criterion of learning, the cannibalizing planaria took a mean of only 67.5 trials. But when naive planaria were fed unconditioned planaria, *they also showed sharply increased efficiency in learning.* When naive worms ate the experimental worms that had been exposed to light, they took a mean of 58 trials to reach the learning criterion. The equivalent figure for planaria that ate handled planaria was 60.8; for those who ate other completely naive planaria, the comparable mean was 90.

While these data do not disprove the notion of memory transfer through cannibalization, they do cast doubt on the idea that the transfer is as direct as McConnell was tempted to believe it to be. These three experimentalists suggest that nutritional or metabolic factors must be taken into account.

NEUROLOGY OF MEMORY [*]

In this inclusive and theoretical article, the eminent physiologist R. W. Gerard summarizes several lines of evidence bearing on the material or structural basis of memory. These evidences relate to central problems of the foregoing two research reports, to the general facets of neural functioning that have concerned us in the present chapter, and to the problems and phenomena of learning that we will confront in some detail in Chapters 12 and 13.

In searching out the nature of the material basis of memory, Gerard cites a number of lines of evidence and argument, including the following:

1. In the process of development, the environment exerts its influence on an initially amorphous and plastic nervous system. The environment must exert this influence during certain specified intervals, or the influence will be ineffective. Imprint-

---

[*] R. W. Gerard, The material basis of memory, *J. verbal Learning and verbal Behavior,* 1963, **2**, 22–33.

ing, for instance (see pp. 86–87), occurs only within specific time limits. Similarly, if a newborn goat is removed from its mother for a half hour immediately after birth, the mother will not accept the kid as her offspring; some essential interaction between the two systems did not occur during a crucial period.

2. There must be a certain kind and amount of perceptual experience if the individual is to develop normal perceptual responses. (Some of this evidence is presented on page 84 of the present text.)

3. General evidence on the learning history of great athletes suggests that motor patterns must be formed early if the athletes are to function at their best; few great athletes began to practice late in life. Relatedly, the young can easily learn to make speech sounds that are very difficult or impossible for an equally naive and equally intelligent adult. Certain habits, the argument goes, are built into the structure of the individual; often the presence of one habit makes impossible the learning of another.

4. Hamsters, after learning a simple maze, were cooled to 5°C, at which temperature there is no discoverable activity in the brain, and then were warmed up and retested on the maze; they performed as well as before freezing. These results are interpreted to mean that memory is based on a structural change in the brain rather than on a dynamic and ongoing process.

5. A cat's optic nerve was operated on so that the left eye was connected only to the right brain, and the right eye only to the left brain; the cat's left eye then was taught a discrimination. The cat later made the discrimination with its right eye when the corpus callosum, connecting the two hemispheres, was intact. When this structure was cut, the right eye could not perform. This is taken as evidence that a structural neural change is produced by experience.

6. If hamsters being taught to run a maze were given an electroconvulsive shock after each learning trial, learning still progressed satisfactorily if the shock came an hour or more after the trial. But if the shock was administered at intervals less than an hour after the learning trial, learning became poorer. If the shock came within 15 minutes of the trial, no learning occurred. Such data are taken to mean that the structural changes in learning take time; if there is no time for the change to "set," then the change is erased by electroshock and no learning occurs.

Gerard uses these and related evidences, including data from the studies of planaria, first to argue for a structural basis of memory and then to trace out some of the functional facets of structural changes. He also makes a practical argument for the importance of rich and early experience in the normal development of the individual.

SUGGESTED READINGS

Fulton, J. F. *Physiology of the nervous system,* 3rd ed. rev. New York: Oxford University Press, 1949 (1938).

Gardner, Ernest. *Fundamentals of neurology,* 4th ed. Philadelphia: Saunders, 1963 (1947).

Hebb, D. O. *The organization of behavior: A neuropsychological theory.* New York: Wiley, 1949.

Hernández-Peón, Raúl, ed. *The physiological basis of mental activity: Proceedings of a symposium held in Mexico City, 1961.* New York: American Elsevier Publishing Co., 1963.

Magoun, H. W. *The waking brain,* 2nd ed. Springfield, Ill.: Thomas, 1963.

Rosenblith, W. A. ed. *Sensory communication.* Cambridge: MIT Press; New York: Wiley, 1961.

PART THREE

METHODS IN PSYCHOLOGY

OUTLINE / CHAPTER 5

I. HISTORY OF PSYCHOLOGICAL MEASUREMENT

II. RULES FOR ACHIEVING PRECISION

    A. Define the Variable

    B. Think of Continua Rather Than Categories

    C. Make Objective Observations

    D. Consider the Norm

    E. Remember Sampling

    F. Check the Reliability of Observations

    G. Check the Validity of Observations

III. THE CREATION OF PSYCHOLOGICAL TESTS

IV. KINDS OF PSYCHOLOGICAL MEASURES

    A. Psychological Measure of Enduring Attributes
       1. Intelligence Tests
          a. Binet
          b. Stanford-Binet
          c. The Wechsler scales
          d. Group tests of intelligence
       2. Factors in Intelligence
          a. Performance tests
          b. Factorial studies
       3. Reliability of IQ Tests
       4. Validity of Intelligence Tests
       5. Interim Synopsis

    B. Other Tests of Enduring Attributes of Behavior
       1. Tests of Specific Abilities
       2. Differential Aptitude Tests
       3. Tests of Achievement
       4. Tests of Interests
       5. Self-Report Tests of Personality
       6. Projective Tests of Personality
       7. Interviews

V. SUMMARY

VI. RESEARCH REPORTS

CHAPTER 5

TESTS AND MEASUREMENTS IN PSYCHOLOGY*

In this chapter we will study some of the problems of observation and measurement that are encountered whenever anyone tries to make precise statements about behavior. And we shall study some of the solutions that psychologists have found for these commonly encountered and sometimes difficult problems. For the present, and for illustrative purposes, we shall deal almost exclusively with the procedures psychologists follow in attempting to establish "response-response" relationships—relationships between certain groups of behaviors (such as those occurring while we are administering a test of mechanical aptitude) and certain other groups of behaviors (such as those occurring on a job that demands mechanical aptitude). Later, we shall contend with procedures involved in making statements

about stimulus-response relationships, statements in which there may be quantification of physical variables, such as the wave length of light, or the energy of a sound, as well as quantitative statements about psychological or behavioral variables, such as hue or loudness. In general terms, the requirements for precise observation and precise report are similar for the two general kinds (R-R and S-R) of psychological data.

Most of us now take for granted the results that have come from man's successful quantification of events in the physical world. We wake up in the morning to check a numbered calendar, look at a quantified clock, eat a calculable number of calories cooked at a controlled temperature, drive to school at a measured rate of speed, walk to a numbered room on a numerically designated floor, sit in the third seat in the fifth row and turn to page 74, exercise 2, in the text. In human dealings

---

* Edwin I. Megargee assisted materially with the revision of this chapter.

with human behavior, by contrast, we still lean more naturally to quality than to quantity; we speak of sorts more readily than of amounts. And even when we do find it desirable to observe more meticulously or to speak in more precise terms, we have only a language of estimate and approximation at our disposal.

Can we achieve quantitative precision in recording, accumulating, and analyzing data on human behavior? Psychologists are committed to an affirmative answer to this question and have written many volumes dealing with the desirability of quantification and with the techniques for the appropriate achieving of it.

HISTORY OF PSYCHOLOGICAL MEASUREMENT

The search for meaningful quantification in the area of psychology—or for that matter, in the whole area of human behavior—came relatively late in the history of science. A scientific concern with the physical world, and attempts to make mathematical statements about it, came much earlier. And progress in analyzing man, either as a biological structure or as a behaving organism, was comparatively slow. When Sir Isaac Newton was formulating in mathematical terms his world-shaking laws of physics, it would have been rare to find anyone going even so far as to engage in the simple counting of specifically defined instances of human behavior. It was 142 years after Newton's death that Sir Francis Galton (1869) published his first ideas about classifying and measuring the natural gifts of man; and not until ten years later did Wundt's Leipzig laboratory get actively and systematically about the business of applying quantitative methods in the analysis of psychological phenomena. After still another decade, Galton (1888) published his then highly novel ideas about quantitative "co-relations" between and among measurable attributes of man. Galton, talking about "anthropometric data," was in-

terested in the precise measurement of such a variable as the height of men and in the relative frequency with which men of any given height were found in the population; he also was fascinated by the fact that there is a systematic and mathematically describable co-relation (now called correlation) between the height and the weight of men or between the height of a man and the length of that man's arm. Two years later, James McKeen Cattell (1890), an American who had been a student in Wundt's laboratory, for the first time in history used the concept of mental tests. Soon thereafter, Joseph Jastrow set up an exhibit at the 1893 Columbian Exhibition in Chicago, inviting visitors to record their performance on such variables as sensory and motor reaction times and to compare their scores with the average of the performances of others who had taken the test. Some years later, as president of the American Psychological Association, Jastrow made an eloquent case that his colleagues would find highly rewarding the attempt to measure human intelligence (Jastrow, 1894).

Psychological measurement, then, has had a short history. But during that history there have been valiant and often highly sophisticated attempts to bring into the study of psychological matters all the advantages that inhere in the use of a mathematical language. These attempts range from the simple enumeration of psychological items to the more intricate techniques of dealing with variable data and with matters of probability. And in more recent years psychologists have become involved with the still more elaborate mathematical formulations of learning phenomena, and with the relatively intricate psychological adaptations of such recent developments as game theory, information theory, and decision theory. Also there has come the use of electronic computers not only to analyze psychological data but to simulate such intricate behavioral processes as problem solving, so that those processes can be studied in the computer as if the computer were human (Green, 1963; Miller, 1964).

RULES FOR
ACHIEVING PRECISION

In trying to go beyond the limitations inherent in qualification, psychologists have evolved a number of rules, procedures, and concepts designed to increase the sense and precision of their statements about behavior. These procedural matters, though they can become quite intricate in their technical application, are, at core, common-sense rules for the precise description of human behavior. The procedures can be learned and, in a general way, used by anyone who wishes to make highly accurate statements about the behavior of human beings.

In the following pages we will examine a number of these procedural ideas. We shall try, first, to see each procedure or rule in its most general form, and then we shall go into the more technical use of these ideas in psychological research.

DEFINE THE VARIABLE

We cannot talk intelligently or precisely about anything until we can define the thing we are talking about. Suppose that you, with an air of great objectivity, report to me your considered conclusion that your friend Irma is brilliant. I, in the role of psychologist, have the immediate impression that you are doing very much what the psychologists try to do when they create tests to measure such attributes of behavior as intelligence or extroversion or dominance. You have observed behavior, you have assigned a summary **construct** to that behavior, and, at least by indirection, you are making a comparison between Irma's behavior and the behavior of other people you have observed. I also may have a fairly strong suspicion that, in your "testing" of Irma's behavior, your procedures might—both in justice to Irma and in the interests of science—be considerably improved.

My first detailed concern might well be with definition. What do you mean by *brilliant*? In contending with this question, which you might at first regard as stupid, you would be forced eventually *to talk about behavior*. You would have to describe the ways in which allegedly brilliant people behave, and you would have to put a descriptive finger on the actual behaviors of Irma, the behaviors you are summarizing by the use of a construct.

It is a rule of science—and of good common sense—that constructs must be firmly and properly tied to observable behavior. If our terms are not defined, then we will find ourselves playing some Alice-in-Wonderland game of words, without reference to the real world of observable and reportable events. Until you describe the behavior of Irma and until you convince me that the construct *brilliant* is the best way to summarize that behavior, then I am free to conclude that your use of the term *brilliant* has more connection with your feelings about Irma than with a known attribute of Irma's behavior.

In measuring, testing, and characterizing human beings, *we must start always with observable behavior*. If there is no observable behavior, then the constructs we use cannot make scientific sense. There is no known psychological test for *immortality*, for example. What behavior would we observe? What observable behavior lies behind such adjectives as *spiritual* or *ethereal* or *angelic* or *avaricious* or *stingy* or *supercilious*? Throughout this book, we will be forced to concern ourselves with matters of definition. Whether we talk about complex constructs (the hunger motive, repression, hostility, acquisitiveness, intelligence) or apparently simple aspects of behavior (reaction time, discrimination of pitch, visual acuity, operant conditioning, span of attention), we face the problem of tying our words precisely and meaningfully to observable behavior.

We must keep a clear eye on actual behavior, then, if we hope to make good and accurate sense when we talk about people. One way to achieve such a focus on behavior might be to focus on *adverbs* and to use adjectives sparingly. It is our ingrained habit to apply adjectives to people. We chronically and forever describe whole human beings. A man *is* aggressive, or intelligent, or dominant, or shy, or expansive, or introverted. For purposes of science and sense, however, it is probably better to say that a man *behaves* aggressively, or intelligently, or expansively, or in an introverted manner. Adverbs give us less paralytic fixity than do adjectives, and keep us closer to the reality of observable behavior. To say that Irma *behaves* brilliantly, rather than that Irma *is* brilliant, keeps us thinking about behavior and makes it more likely that we will ask useful and answerable questions about when and where and under what circumstances she behaves brilliantly. If we say that Irma *is* brilliant, we blanket her by a construct—one that suggests, probably wrongly, that all of her behaviors all of the time are occurring in a brilliant manner.

THINK OF CONTINUA
RATHER THAN CATEGORIES

A second general rule for creating precise sense about human behavior is to *think of continua rather than of categories.* To the mind that is straightjacketed by habits of categorical thinking, the world is remarkably simple. Things are either black or white, right or wrong, beautiful or ugly, pleasant or unpleasant. There are no borderline cases in a world so simply sliced. There are no maybe's. When such a way of thinking is applied to human behavior, it yields the conviction that the world is full of people who are either bright or dull, tall or short, fat or thin, extroverted or introverted, dominant or submissive. By such categorical thought, people fall into mutually exclusive conceptual pots. No middle ground and no gradations. Everything is neat—erroneously and dangerously neat.

Perhaps such a simple view of people is adequate if we want to know only whether to approach or avoid people. But if we want to understand people, we do well to cultivate the notion *that people vary along a continuum with respect to almost any attribute we wish to name.* Most people are neither tall nor short; most people fall somewhere on a continuum from very tall to very short. And a great num-

ber of people will be of average height. Most people are neither bright nor dull; again, each individual falls at some point on a continuum from very bright to very dull. And if we actually measured brightness and dullness, we would find the largest number of people falling approximately midway between brightness and dullness. The three drawings in Figure 5–1 present an illustration of the category vs. continuum question.

Later, we will have occasion to examine the **normal distribution curve,** which describes with considerable accuracy and great utility the distribution of height, weight, speed, intelligence, and so on, in a population. At the moment we can accept as a fact of nature that, with respect to many characteristics, most people distribute themselves along the "average" portion of the curve. If we think in terms of continua, our attention is sharpened so that we cannot merely observe whether a person is extroverted or introverted, intelligent or unintelligent, but we can prepare ourselves for talking about *how* intelligent, *how* introverted.

MAKE OBJECTIVE OBSERVATIONS

When you tell me that Irma is brilliant, especially if you tell me in an emotional manner, I somehow get the feeling that you are not describing Irma's behavior so much as you are expressing a feeling about Irma. You like her. That's my first conclusion. And, if I'm wise, I make no conclusion at all about Irma. If I go on trying to be wise, and if I really am interested in Irma's alleged level of intelligence, I will do what I can to get other observers to take a look at Irma. For, as we have seen (Chap. 2), a fact is an agreed-upon perceptual relation between observers and an event. The perceptual relation between you and Irma may, for some reason, be determined more by you than by Irma. If we are to gain precise knowledge, we need neutral, unbiased, unemotional, *objective observations.*

We also need *noninterpretive* observations. If an investigator should send 43 psychology students over to observe Irma's brilliance, he would probably get 43 different reports.

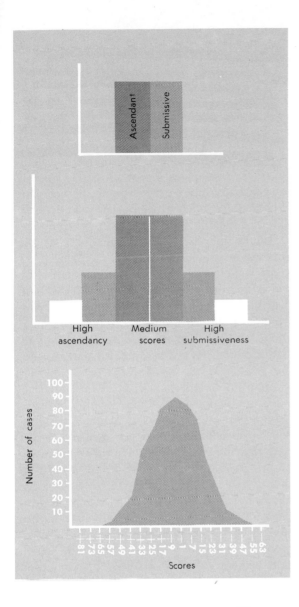

Though each student may be emotionally neutral and a fairly good observer of behavior, each—perhaps observing slightly different behavior, and having a slightly different personal meaning for the word *brilliant*—would interpret his evidence in a slightly different way. The investigator would do much better to tell his students exactly what behavior to observe. Each observer then could probably report precisely how many digits Irma could repeat after they were read to her, or exactly how accurately and quickly she could solve a problem of logical reasoning, or exactly how many of a list of words she could define accurately. There is not much room here for either interpretation or misinterpretation.

If we are going to make good and precise sense, then, in our measuring of behavior, we must rely on *emotionally neutral* and *noninterpretive observations of actual behavior*. We often ensure the neutrality of observation by having a number of observers, whose biases, if any, can be counted upon to cancel one another out. And we avoid the necessity of having our observers make intricate interpretations on the spot. We arrange to have them report the actual behavior they see, and we equip them with needed aids to observation, such as stop watches or foot rulers.

If we exercise proper care in assigning the world *brilliant* to Irma, we will do some of the things the psychologist does on creating a test to measure behavior. Once he has defined, at least tentatively, the variable in which he is interested, the psychologist arranges for the objective observation of an array of behaviors that he believes to be related to the variable he has in mind. If he is interested in making a paper-and-pencil test of intelligence, for example, he arranges for people to behave toward a number of items arranged on a piece of paper. He observes these behaviors objectively. If he can make a case that some behaviors can legitimately be called intelligent and others unintelligent, or less intelligent, then he is on the road to creating a psychological test.

One additional caution is needed, however, if there is to be certainty and sense in observing and interpreting behavior, especially

Figure 5–1. CATEGORIES VS. CONTINUA. *If we think in black-white categories, we make only crude discriminations, as in the top figure above. If our categories are finer, as in the second figure, our discriminations can be more precise. But if we deal with continua (which are often represented as series of very fine categories), then our discriminations and our characterizations can be very precise. The graph at the bottom presents the distribution of scores for 600 women on the Allport-Vernon Ascendance-Submission Scale. (From Ruggles and Allport, 1939; by permission of the American Psychological Association.)*

if we are going to compare individuals with one another. There must be *standardized conditions of observation*. If we are going to compare your intelligence with that of Irma,

Figure 5–2. STANDARDIZED CONDITIONS OF OBSERVATION. *The psychologist attempts to make precise and noninterpretive observations under standardized conditions.*

we would not make the mistake of observing your behavior while you are riding horseback chased by a swarm of bees and comparing it with Irma's behavior while she is sitting calmly in an armchair. We must do everything we can to ensure that you are both responding to the *same events in the same kind of situation.*

CONSIDER THE NORM

When we deal with adjectives, we almost always make relative judgments. Whenever we make a judgment about an attribute of an individual, we are in some way comparing that individual's height or weight or intelligence or introversion with something that we accept subjectively as an average for the population we know. When we say that Irma is brilliant, we are making some kind of judgment, implicitly at least, about Irma's comparative position on some kind of a scale. We might even go so far as to give Irma a quantitative score on some personally con-

ceived scale of intelligence, and report with an air of great assurance that she scores 171 on our test. Such a statement, despite its quantitative form and its air of assurance, is completely meaningless until we know something about who else scores what on the same test or about the particular behaviors that lead to particular scores. Perhaps almost everyone in Irma's high school scores above 171 on this test; perhaps only 4 per cent score higher than 171. In each instance, Irma's score has a vastly different meaning. If, for the test in question, we know the scores of all members of the population of which Irma is a member, if we know something about the **norms,** about the ways that other members of the population distribute themselves on the continuum with which we are dealing, then our judgment about Irma's brilliance, whether quantitatively stated or not, takes on a much clearer meaning.

Such judgments are almost always relative. A six footer on a basketball team impresses nobody; set him down in a village of midgets, and he becomes a colossus. Hence, to get data that may make relative judgments meaningful, good and useful tests are *standardized;* that is, the test is administered to a large number of people and their scores are recorded in such a way that an individual's score can be compared with the scores of a known group. If the test is to measure high school achievement level, for example, it is composed of items of varying degrees of difficulty dealing with the content of the typical high school curriculum. Some of the items almost any high school senior knows. But the whole array of items are chosen so that no high school senior knows them all. If the test were then administered to every high school senior in the country, we would have *national norms* on the test. We would know how many seniors got 99 per cent of the items, how many got 50 per cent, how many got 10 per cent, and so on. The scores of individual seniors can then be compared with scores for the total population of seniors. The student's scores on such tests are most often expressed in **centiles.** If he scores at the ninety-ninth centile, this means that 99 per cent of the total group scored lower than he. If he scores at the tenth centile, 90 per cent of the seniors scored higher than he, and only 10 per cent scored lower.

If such a test were given only to high school seniors planning to go to college, or to a population of seniors averaging B or better in their classes, then the norms would change; and the score of the individual would have to be interpreted accordingly.

In following the procedures here referred to as *standardization,* we are creating an **ordinal scale,** a scale allowing us to arrange individuals in a series from highest to lowest with respect to the attribute we are considering. This relatively crude kind of scale has some inherent limitations (Stevens, 1951). It does not allow us, for example, to say that the individual who scores at the eightieth centile is twice as high as the one who scores at the fortieth. Nor does it allow us to say that the individual at the eightieth centile is half way between the individual at the ninetieth and the individual at the seventieth. Ordinal scales allow us to talk *only about ranks.* If we wish to state *how far apart* two individuals are—if we want to *interpret* accurately differences in scores—we must see to it that our test is an **interval scale** rather than an ordinal scale. The thermometer is a good example of an interval scale; the distance from 50 to 55 degrees is the same as the distance from 55 to 60 or 75 to 80. Psychologists do construct and use interval scales—for instance, to measure the strength of an attitude or the pitch of a tone. But for the present we will concern ourselves primarily with ordinal scales.

REMEMBER SAMPLING

Another general intellectual rule concerning the use of either professional or nonprofessional testing of human attributes requires us to remember that *almost always we are dealing with only a sample* of the behaviors or of the people in which we are interested. We never have access to all the behaviors an individual emits, nor to all the individuals who emit the behavior that concerns us. Most often, out of necessity or by design, we confront samples—often relatively small and sometimes very inadequate samples—of behavior.

It is inherent in the nature of psychological testing that we examine a sample of behavior and try to make meaningful statements about many behaviors not yet observed. Most often, we study a sample of behavior at a present time and try to make statements, with a known degree of certainty, about an array of future behaviors. This, of course, is one of the principal reasons for psychological tests. We give an individual an "intelligence test" that lasts thirty minutes or an hour, and we make the best statements we can about future behaviors in a wide variety of unobserved situations, all requiring intelligent behavior. Often, psychologists do make statements, with some degree of justification and a known degree of probable accuracy, about thousands of items of behavior that have not yet occurred. In selecting the samples of behavior to be observed and in making their predictions on the basis of these samples, psychologists adhere to some fairly definite rules, which we will consider later (Chap. 6).

CHECK THE RELIABILITY OF OBSERVATIONS

A crucial matter in the design and use of any psychological test is the general question of *consistency* or *stability.* If an individual, observed or tested repeatedly in exactly the same way, performs in much the same way each time, we say the test or the observation has high **reliability.** If there is instability or inconsistency from one observation to another, or from one scoring to another of a test, then the observation or the test is characterized by low —or certainly lower—reliability.

In addition, there must be *inter-observer* or *inter-scorer reliability.* Two or more observers, viewing the same situation at the same time, must agree on what they have observed. If two judges agree that an individual who is observed by both does indeed give one of three possible correct definitions of a word, then we have inter-observer reliability. If the two judges disagree, we have trouble. Similarly, we have trouble—and low inter-scorer reliability—when those administering a test do not agree on the scores to be assigned. That such a problem is by no means imaginary is illustrated by a study (McCarthy, 1944) in which three trained people scored independently the drawings produced by a large number of children who took the Goodenough Draw-a-Man Test of Intelligence (Goodenough, 1926). All three of the scorers worked with a clear and objective system of assigning scores to the children. However, they still failed to achieve anything close to perfect agreement; for about 25 per cent of the children there was a disagreement among the three judges of a year or more of mental age. Another study (Cattell, 1937) showed that two experts, administering to children a standard individual test of intelligence, disagreed by as much as 40 IQ points —enough to make the difference between "normal" and "very superior" or between "normal" and "retarded" intelligence—in their scores for the same individual.

The question of reliability includes also a concern for a test's *stability over a period of time.* Minor variations over time can be expected, even if we have a good test and even if we are testing a stable and well-defined attribute of behavior. However, if we are to put credence in our test score, there needs to be evidence that the test tests the same thing on different occasions. Even in observing a single simple attribute, such as weight, we suspect that either our scales or our eyes are behaving peculiarly, unreliably, if the 100-pound individual we weigh today weighs 165 tomorrow. In more intricate observations, such as those involved in administering a personality or an achievement test, we cannot say that we are observing an enduring attribute of an individual's behavior unless we achieve relatively high *test-retest* or *repeat reliability.*

Because familiarity with the test may influence scores on second testing, many tests are published in two alternate and comparable forms, so that test-retest reliability can be calculated without the influence of familiarity. But if the relationship between today's score and that of next week approaches **randomness,**

approaches a level we might well expect if chance alone were involved, then our repeat reliability sinks toward nonexistence and our test becomes meaningless. (See the research report at the end of the present chapter for an account of a relatively new departure in the testing field, one in which there are repetitive measures of changing attributes of behavior.)

A further aspect of reliability may involve the question of *consistency from one part of a test to another.* We often want to know whether a test is testing the same thing throughout itself. Let us say that we construct 100 items for an objective test on introductory psychology; and then, after shuffling the items, we divide them into two subtests of 50 items each. When we administer these two subtests, we naturally expect that any given student will perform at about the same level on one as on the other. If this indeed does occur when we give the test to students, then we are assured that the 100-item test has satisfactory *split-half reliability:* there is consistency from one part of it to another. If there is a strong tendency for individual students who make A on one subtest to fail the other, split-half reliability is low, and there may be something drastically wrong with our test.

If we choose to concern ourselves with the observation and testing of enduring attributes of individual behavior, we must, in the interest of making the most accurate possible statements either over the back fence or in the clinic, concern ourselves with matters of consistency in our observational and testing procedures. Except in very special circumstances, we want high internal consistency. In the vast majority of situations of the sort we are dealing with, we can say that if there is no consistency to be found, there is no sense to be made. In both a technical and nontechnical sense, a useful and meaningful psychological test is one with respect to which there is good (a) inter-observer reliability, (b) repeat reliability, and (c) split-half reliability.

CHECK THE VALIDITY OF OBSERVATIONS

Both in the technical business of making psychological tests and in our daily characterizing of people, we need to consider the **validity** with which we operate. We need to know whether we are measuring—or testing or observing—what we think we are measuring and how well we are doing so. Whereas reliability is concerned with the general matter of consistency, validity involves the general matter of meaningfulness. Once we succeed in making a reliable observation or in setting down a reliable test score, we still face the key question of what it means, if anything.

Perhaps we can best attack this question of the meaning of a test by returning to a consideration of Irma's tested intelligence. Assuming that we have created a reliable test, how do we know that the test tests "intelligence"? There are several ways of confronting this question. We might assert that the test, just on the face of things, is an intelligence test, for responses to its various items obviously require the functioning of intellectual processes. We would, in such a case, be saying that the test has *face validity;* it obviously tests what it purports to test. But we are on shaky grounds if we rely on appearances alone in determining the meaning of a test score. We cannot be sure about validity until we have examined the *empirical validity,* as contrasted with the *face validity,* of the test. There are two principal ways to check on the empirical, the coldly factual, validity of the intelligence test of Irma or of any other test of anybody else. We can determine its *concurrent validity,* or its *predictive validity,* or both. And the process of examining either or both is a process of studying the relation of Irma's performance on the test to her performance in another situation in which intelligent behavior is called for. As her acquaintances, we "measure" her intelligence by observing a sample of her behavior and by reporting our observations as indicating "brilliance." When we do this, we are, in effect, making an as yet unsupported assertion about the validity of our observations. Implicitly, we are asserting that in nontest situations in the present, Irma's behavior will be of the same intellectual level, and such an assertion deals with the *concurrent validity* of our "test." We may be implying also that Irma's behavior in future nontest situations will be such as to be

properly described as brilliant. If so, we are assuming that our test has *predictive validity.* We can check on validity, either concurrent or predictive, by observing Irma's behavior either in other nontest situations today or in nontest situations in the future.

For actual psychological tests, procedures for examining either concurrent or predictive validity are the same, in form if not in degree of precision, as that outlined in the case of Irma. In actual practice there is a careful definition of a *criterion,* thought to be related to the test performance, and there are attempts to measure performance on that criterion. Then there can be, for large numbers of individuals, a computation of the precise relation between performance on the test and performance on the criterion. If we are working on a test of mechanical aptitude, for example, we may administer the test to 500 men, making the prediction that, when these men are actually on the job, those who score high on the test will also score high on a measure of proficiency on the job. Then, if possible, we put all 500 men to work on a job requiring mechanical aptitude, measuring as precisely as we can how long it takes each man to reach a certain and specified level of skilled performance on the job. If our predictions are good, the test has a known level of predictive validity and, under proper conditions, can be used in the future to select individuals for jobs requiring mechanical aptitude.

We may also bring light to the question of a test's meaningfulness by examining its *construct validity.* The construct validity of a test refers to all available evidence, direct and indirect, that the test does indeed measure the construct or trait—e.g., intelligence, mechanical aptitude, or introversion—that it is supposed to measure. If it is a test of intelligence, we say, then scores on it ought to have a similarity to scores on other tests of intelligence. And if it is a test of intelligence, then, by all that we know about intelligence, scores on it ought to increase with age. These and other procedures can help determine the construct validity of a test—can help make a test score meaningful by examining the psychological company that score keeps.

For an account of one such study of con-

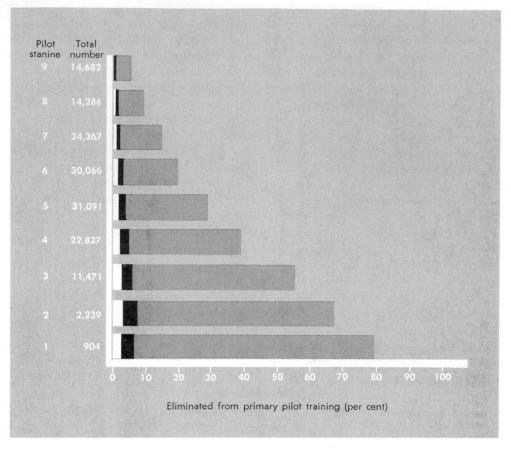

Pilot stanine	Total number
9	14,682
8	14,286
7	24,367
6	30,066
5	31,091
4	22,827
3	11,471
2	2,239
1	904

Eliminated from primary pilot training (per cent)

Figure 5–3. VALIDITY OF PSYCHOLOGICAL TESTS. *A good illustration of the validity and the usefulness of psychological tests is given by the above data on the relation of test scores to elimination from flight training in the Air Force in World War II. The stanine is a weighted composite score on a battery of tests used to select aviators. The black area indicates the per cent eliminated for physical or administrative reasons; the white area, those eliminated at their own request; the gray area, those eliminated for flying deficiencies. The graph shows that less than 10 per cent of those who scored in the top stanine were later eliminated during primary training; of those scoring in the lowest stanine, nearly 80 per cent were later dropped from primary training. Scores, then, do predict the criterion and hence have a known validity. (Staff, Psychological Section, Office of the Surgeon, Headquarters, AAF Training Command, 1945; reproduced by permission of the American Psychological Association.)*

struct validity, see the research excerpt at the end of the present chapter.

THE CREATION OF PSYCHOLOGICAL TESTS

So far in this chapter, we have taken the stance that basic ideas in psychological testing and measuring are not particularly intricate and that what the psychologist does professionally in measuring behavior is similar, at core, to what the intelligent student does—or can do—in observing and characterizing behavior. The successful scientific measurement of behavior, however, and the creation of a useful psychological test require some highly inventive and often extremely technical applications of the basic principles enumerated above. Even the creation of a workable questionnaire is much more intricate than many perpetrators of questionnaires seem to realize.

Suppose, for example, we undertook to create a relatively simple kind of psychological test—an achievement test. To keep matters close to home, let us select the job of constructing a test to measure the academic achievement of students of introductory psychology. The steps in constructing such a test are outlined below.

1. Create a large number of objective items covering the content of the course.

2. Check the items with a panel of instructors in introductory psychology, selecting those that the instructors agree are appropriate for the content of the course.

3. Administer the whole battery of items to large numbers of students in a properly chosen sample of colleges and universities.

4. Discard all items that are too easy or too hard. There is no point in having an item that everyone misses or that everyone can answer. It contributes nothing to the test.

5. Check each item for correlation with the total score on the test. We do not want items that A students miss and D students find easy.

6. Check the test for internal consistency. Run a split-half-reliability study to see whether the test agrees with itself and is measuring the same thing throughout.

7. Check the test for repeat reliability. Do high-scoring students rank high and low students rank low on a second testing or on an equivalent form?

8. Check the test for validity. Does it rank high those who, on other grounds, should rank high? How does it correlate with grade-point average in similar courses? How does it correlate with grades on other kinds of examinations in psychology?

9. Standardize the test. Administer it to a national population of students so that the score of any student can be compared with the performance of all other students or with the performance of all other students in selected kinds of institutions.

KINDS OF PSYCHOLOGICAL MEASURES

PSYCHOLOGICAL MEASURES OF ENDURING ATTRIBUTES

It is possible, if we follow the principles and procedures discussed in the foregoing pages, to create a psychological measure of almost any attribute of behavior that strikes our curiosity. However, the best-known and most widely used psychological measures deal with what we choose to regard as relatively enduring attributes of the behavior of individuals, patterns of behavior that will occur in future situations. Tests of intelligence are designed to predict behavior in school; tests of clerical or mechanical aptitude predict success on a job; tests of neurotic tendency predict the quality of future adjustment. (See Fig. 5–3.)

Although not all psychological measurement is concerned with complex patterns of behavior occurring in complex environmental situations—in the vast majority of laboratory studies, for instance, the researcher is interested in relatively restricted S-R relationships that occur in special and limited situations—at the moment we confine ourselves to a study of the various kinds of tests of enduring attributes of the behavior of individuals.

Intelligence Tests

Binet. Perhaps since the beginning of civilization men have been judging the ability of other men to learn rapidly and to solve problems, but the idea of a test of such capacities came only recently into man's conception of man. We saw earlier that the term "mental test" was used for the first time in psychological literature by James McKeen Cattell in 1890, and that in the same decade Joseph Jastrow was beginning to concern himself with what might be regarded as psychological tests. Not until 1905, however, did anyone succeed in making a test that would now be recognized as a test of **intelligence.** In that year Alfred Binet, responding to an earlier request of the

French Minister of Public Instruction, came up with the idea that one could measure the difference between the behavior of feeble-minded children and normal children and thus differentiate between poor students of low ability and poor students who behaved badly simply because of poor instruction. Binet believed that these matters could be subjected to quantitative treatment, and that measurements of such functions could be used in the actual planning of school programs. Working with a physician, Theodore Simon, Binet set about the task of creating an intelligence test (Binet and Simon, 1905).

In tackling their novel project, Binet and Simon first collected a number of problem situations, or "test items," which they planned to try out on a variety of children. They assumed that, for instance, the average 5-year-old child could solve problems that the 4-year-old would find over his head and, by the same token, that the average 4-year-old could outperform most of his juniors. To support this line of thinking, the two investigators found that the average 5-year-old could, for example, count four coins but could not point out his right hand and left ear. Relatedly, the average 12-year-old could put into one sentence three different words given him but could not cite three differences between a king and a president. And so on. By this procedure, then, they could confront any child with an array of problems, watch and record the child's performance, and then compare that individual's performance with the performance of a number of children of the same age. If the 5-year-old child was able to handle problems at the 7-year level, then Binet assigned the 5-year-old a **mental age** (MA) of 7. And if the 7-year-old flunked the 7- and 6-year problems but solved the 5-year ones, he was assigned a mental age of 5. By the same procedure, Binet could compare the behavior of mentally defective children with that of normal children, assigning each, regardless of chronological age, a mental age around which his school experience could be planned.

Binet's first test, though a giant step beyond the casual observation and subjective judgment of intelligence, was still a relatively crude instrument. In 1911, however, shortly after Binet's death, there appeared a revised and standardized version, which met a number of our modern criteria of a good test (Binet and Simon, 1911). But Binet still did not concern himself directly with the key problems of reliability and validity.

Stanford-Binet. Soon after Binet's work, several American psychologists became interested in the problem of measuring intelligence. The first was H. H. Goddard (1911). Another was Lewis M. Terman, a psychologist at Stanford University. Using adaptations of Binet's items and others, Terman tested a large number of American children and, in 1916, published the *Stanford Revision of the Binet Tests* (Terman, 1918).

Since it would not make sense to compare the behavior of a 7-year-old in France with that of a 7-year-old in America, Terman clearly had to **standardize** the test on American children and establish American *norms* with respect to which the individual child could be judged. The 1916 Stanford-Binet, as it came to be called, was widely used for twenty-one years in measuring the intelligence of children.

But the Americanized Binet test still had some shortcomings. There was only one form of it, for one thing. This made it impossible to retest the same child after a short interval in order to examine the reliability of the measurement. In actual testing, if the examiner feels that the child, through fear or other emotional blocks, is not performing at his best, he may wish to repeat the test under different circumstances. Because of the practice factor, it is not desirable to use precisely the same items. An alternative yardstick, one like the first in all essential aspects but containing different items, therefore is useful. Also, the 1916 test did not adequately test either very young children or adults. It did not have enough data on the very young to furnish good norms. And its hardest items were too easy for many adults—making it difficult, for

Table 5–1. SOME ITEMS FOR VARIOUS AGE LEVELS FROM THE BINET-SIMON INTELLIGENCE TEST OF 1911

Mental Age 1 and 2 Years:
Move lighted match slowly before child's eyes. Full credit given if eyes follow light for briefest period.

Mental Age 3 Years:
Show me your nose. Show me your eyes. Show me your mouth.

Mental Age 4 Years:
Show child a pen knife saying, "What is that? What is it called?" Then show penny and finally key, asking same questions. Names of three objects required.

Mental Age 5 Years:
Draw a square 3 to 4 centimeters in diameter with ink and ask the child to copy it, giving him pen and ink to do so.

Mental Age 6 Years:
Draw a diamond figure with ink and ask the child to copy it, giving him pen and ink for the purpose.

Mental Age 7 Years:
"Take this key and put it on that chair; bring me that book lying on the table and open the door." Repeat these directions distinctly twice.

Mental Age 8 Years:
"I want you to count backward from 20 to 0. Like this—20—19—18." This must be accomplished in 20 seconds. One error allowed.

Mental Age 9 Years:
"What is a fork?" "What is a table?" "What is a chair?" "What is a horse?" "What is a mama?" Definitions superior to use are required.

Mental Age 10 Years:
"I am going to read you some sentences; in each one of them there is something foolish or absurd. You listen carefully and tell me each time what it is that is foolish." "The body of a young girl cut into 18 pieces was found yesterday. People think that she killed herself."—"What is foolish in that?". . .

Mental Age 12 Years:
"Find the sentences which these words make. Fix the words in their proper order."
(a) At-country-we-for-started-hour-an-the-early.
(b) Teacher-I-to-my-exercise-asked-my-correct.
(c) Defends-a-his-dog-master-good-bravely.

Mental Age 15 Years:
"I am going to say seven numbers. Listen well and repeat them exactly. 4-9-2-6-5-3-7; 9-3-5-1-8-2-6; 2-7-4-9-3-8-5." One success in three required.

Adult:
"What is the difference between laziness and idleness?" "What is the difference between event and advent?" "What is the difference between evolution and revolution?" Two correct responses required.

example, to measure the difference between superior adults and very superior adults.

Many of these shortcomings were removed in the 1937 revision of the Stanford-Binet. Two equivalent forms were created, so that it became possible to check the reliability of an individual's score. Items and adequate norms were furnished for very young children, so that it became possible to compare the behavior of an individual 2-year-old with the behavior of his peers. And the test was extended toward the upper levels of difficulty, so that it became possible to test superior adults.

The 1960 revision combines into one scale the best items from the two earlier forms of the test. It also eliminates from the older scale the items that had become obsolete because of cultural changes. For example, items involving models or pictures of stoves were more difficult for children in the 1950s than for the youngsters of the 1930s (personal correspondence, Merrill, 1960). The new scale (called the L-M scale because it combines the old L and M alternate forms) works better than the old in testing adults and also remedies certain technical difficulties in the older form (Terman and Merrill, 1937, 1960). But again no alternative form is available.

The Stanford-Binet not only introduced the measurement of intelligence into America but injected into the technical vocabulary of psychology a term—invented in 1910 by a German psychologist, William Stern—that soon became a well-worn part of everyman's lexicon: the **intelligence quotient,** or IQ. The IQ is a relation between the chronological age and the mental age of the individual. In brief, it is expressed as follows:

$$IQ = \frac{MA}{CA} \times 100$$

If the 6-year-old child (CA = 6) performs as well as the average 6-year-old in his culture (MA = 6), his IQ will be exactly 100. He will have, then, average intelligence. If his CA is 6 but his MA is 9, then his IQ will be 150, or decidedly above the normal or average intelligence for 6-year-old children. If our

test is valid, then our 6-year-old first-grader should be able to handle intellectual tasks at the level of 9-year-old third-graders.

The IQ has been a useful notation in that it represents, regardless of age, the individual's relative standing in a group. However, beginning with the 1960 version of the Stanford-Binet, the term *deviation IQ* has been used with increasing frequency. The deviation IQ, as computed, de-emphasizes the age factor (ratio of mental to chronological age) and emphasizes the deviation of the individual's score from the mean (average) score of the group with which he is being compared. For children, the appropriate comparison is made between the individual's score and the scores of a large number of other individuals of the same chronological age. For adults, where it never did make good sense to divide the MA by the CA to get an IQ, the deviation IQ can be a score that compares the individual with any group on which scores are available, such as all high-school graduates or all college seniors or all members of a sample of adults carefully chosen to represent the total population of adults.

Soon after Terman transplanted the Binet test, many people in this country, both psychologists and laymen, became interested in intelligence testing. Perhaps the American emphasis on individual achievement and success produced a ready public acceptance of the idea that intellectual capacities can be measured, and that the measurement can be used to predict success in certain activities. At any rate, psychologists soon produced a variety of other tests of intelligence, and the testing of intelligence became quite widespread in schools, in industry, in clinics, and in the military.

The Wechsler scales. In 1939 David Wechsler (Wechsler, 1958) developed an intelligence test known as the Wechsler-Bellevue Scale, a scale including both verbal and performance tests and intended for use in the diagnosis of clinical cases in mental hospitals. The test was used widely during and after World War II in hospitals and clinics. In 1949, the test was

Table 5-2. STANFORD-BINET ITEMS, 1960 REVISION *

Year IV-6

2. OPPOSITE ANALOGIES I

Procedure: Say:

(a) "Brother is a boy; sister is a . . . . . ."
(b) "In daytime it is light; at night it is . . . . . ."
(c) "Father is a man; Mother is a . . . . . ."
(d) "The snail is slow; the rabbit is . . . . . ."
(e) "The sun shines during the day; the moon at . . . . . ."

Year VI

5. OPPOSITE ANALOGIES II

Procedure: Say:

(a) "A table is made of wood; a window of . . . . . ."
(b) "A bird flies; a fish . . . . . ."
(c) "The point of a cane is blunt; the point of a knife is . . . . . ."
(d) "An inch is short; a mile is . . . . . ."

Year VII

5. OPPOSITE ANALOGIES III

Procedure: Say:

(a) "The rabbit's ears are long; the rat's ears are . . . . . ."
(b) "Snow is white; coal is . . . . . ."
(c) "The dog has hair; the bird has . . . . . ."
(d) "Wolves are wild; dogs are . . . . . ."

Year XII

2. VERBAL ABSURDITIES

Procedure: Read each statement, and after each one, ask, "What is foolish about that?" The response is frequently ambiguous. If it is not clear that the subject sees the absurdity, say, "Why is that foolish?"

(a) "Bill Jones' feet are so big that he has to pull his trousers on over his head."
(b) "A man went one day to the post office and asked if there was a letter waiting for him. 'What is your name?' asked the postmaster. 'Why,' said the man, 'you will find my name on the envelope.'"
(c) "The fireman hurried to the burning house, got his firehose ready, and after smoking a cigar, put out the fire."
(d) "In an old graveyard in Spain they have discovered a small skull which they believe to be that of Christopher Columbus when he was about ten years old."
(e) "One day we saw several icebergs that had been entirely melted by the warmth of the Gulf Stream."

* *Some items from the* Stanford-Binet Intelligence Scale, *Revised Edition.*
(Terman and Merrill, 1960. Boston: Houghton Mifflin. Reproduced by permission of the publisher.)

revised for use with children and made available as the Wechsler Intelligence Scale for Children (WISC) (Wechsler, 1949). In 1955 (Wechsler, 1955), a revision of the adult scale was completed—the Wechsler Adult Intelligence Scale (WAIS). Figure 5–4 shows an individual taking one part of the WAIS.

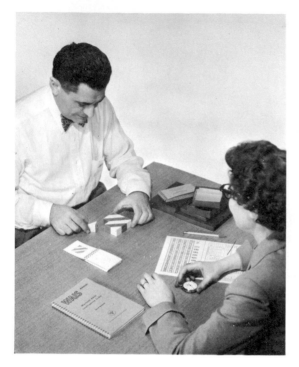

Figure 5–4. TESTING ADULT INTELLIGENCE. *An adult being administered the block-design subtest of the Wechsler Adult Intelligence Scale (WAIS).*

The Wechsler scales differ from the Stanford-Binet in several respects. First, there is a greater emphasis on performance items. Second, the items are arranged in subtests of various definable types, each subtest containing items of various levels of difficulty. Because the items are grouped into various subjects, it is possible to score an examinee separately on Information, Comprehension, Digit Span, Similarities, Arithmetic, and Vocabulary (all part of the verbal scale), and on Picture Arrangement, Picture Completion, Block Design, Object Assembly, and Digit Symbols (all part of the performance scale). Also, these scales sample the same types of behavior at each age level. This is not true of the Stanford-Binet, in which there may be relatively more performance items at one age level and more verbal items at another.

There have been a number of attempts to use the profile of scores on the Wechsler scales for diagnosis of emotional as well as intellectual traits of individuals. These attempts have not met with marked success (Cronbach, 1960).

Group tests of intelligence. The first group test of intelligence was developed by the military. Some military leaders in World War I became convinced that it would be useful to know the intelligence of military inductees so that (a) the very dull could be spotted and (b) any inductee could be placed in a military assignment for which his intellectual capacities suited him. A group of psychologists (assigned, incidentally, to the Sanitary Corps) went to work on the problem. The Stanford-Binet, because it had to be administered individually and by a specially trained tester, was obviously unsuited to the speedy testing of millions of men. The psychologists therefore adapted a test earlier constructed by Otis (Freeman, 1939) and produced the *Army Alpha Test of Intelligence* (Yerkes, 1921), a paper-and-pencil test that could be administered to large groups of men. After it was developed and tested, it was used widely in the assignment of military personnel. Many of our fathers and grandfathers had their military careers—and perhaps their lives—determined by this test.

There are a number of other group tests of intelligence in use today. These are all paper-and-pencil tests requiring the testee to read, to follow instructions, to solve problems of logic or mathematics or of visual arrangement of printed figures. Widely used group tests of intelligence include the Scholastic Aptitude Test (College Entrance Examination Board, 1956), the California Test of Mental Maturity (Sullivan et al., 1951), the College Qualification Tests (Bennett et al., 1957), the Miller Analogies Test (Miller, 1950), the Otis Quick-Scoring Mental Ability Tests (Otis, 1937, 1939), and a number of others. Group tests often are designed to predict a very specific criterion. A good group test of academic aptitude, for example, can predict better than can individual tests of general intelligence the academic behavior of students; we would not expect the performance items on either the Stanford-Binet or the Wechsler to relate highly with grades in highly verbal college courses.

There are also disadvantages in group tests. For one thing, if there is no examiner in close contact with the individual being tested, there is no way to tell if the latter is trying as hard as he can, or if he is very tired or has a broken pencil. Thus, his score on the test may be low simply because he did not exert maximum effort. Also, the group test does not allow for the observation of the more subtle and qualitative aspects of the individual's performance, aspects that may be very important to the clinical psychologist.

Factors in Intelligence

Both Binet and Terman seemed to assume that intelligence is a distinct entity: that is, when individuals are confronted with a variety of problems, one person, they assumed, would be behaving intelligently if he could solve the problems well and speedily; another person would behave unintelligently, solving problems poorly and slowly. Intelligence, then, was defined as one's manner of behaving in the face of a variety of problems. However, the problems posed by both Binet and Terman, particularly for people at the higher age levels, were mostly verbal items, requiring the individual to read or listen to words and to behave accordingly. The Binet and Stanford-Binet tests, then, operating on a verbal definition of intelligence, *may not* be testing any general, all-purpose attribute of the individual's behavior. Perhaps the individual who cannot handle words with very much skill *can* skillfully handle problems involving mechanics or visual arrangements, such as those depicted in Figure 5–5. If we test such an individual in a purely verbal way and say that he scores at a certain level on general intelligence, then we are using our construct of general intelligence in an improper way. The equivalent procedure would be to call a person athletically inept just on the basis of his lack of skill at quoits.

Some skepticism about the proper definition of general intelligence led to the discovery that people who do well on one test of intelligence do not necessarily do well on another. One test may emphasize verbal performance, while another may deal more heavily with tasks involving the manipulation of objects. We can see the possibility of added precision and sense when we are able to distinguish between intelligence on verbal items and intelligence on performance items. We are more discriminating in our observations of behavior and more precise in our assigning of constructs. We begin to see the necessity of pointing out our methods of observation before we assign interpretation to behavior. We can see why, for example, the careful clinical diagnostician always reports what IQ was found *on what test*. And we may now see some sense in the often quoted statement that "intelligence is whatever it is that intelligence tests test."

Performance tests. A number of **performance tests** have been devised to test those individuals whose scores on verbal tests, either for an obvious deficiency in language or for some other reason, may be suspect. Performance tests can be given without verbal instructions, and they require perceptual and motor responses rather than linguistic behavior. The test may include, for example, a *form-board* task, wherein the subject is required to place variously shaped objects in an incomplete jig-saw picture. The Arthur Point Scale Performance Test (Arthur, 1947) is one such performance test, designed for children from the ages of 3 to 15. There are a number of others.

Factorial studies. Continuing skepticism about the propriety of assigning blanket terms to all the problem-solving behaviors of individuals has led to a number of *factorial studies* of intelligence. These studies, using an intricate statistical device known as **factor**

Figure 5–5. A PERFORMANCE TEST. *The Arthur Point Scale Performance Test, designed for children between the ages of 3 and 15 years.*

analysis, have tried to find out which problem-solving behaviors of individuals tend to group themselves together in such ways that we can talk not about the intelligence but the intelligences of individuals. Factorial studies have shown that a number of so-called factors, or *primary mental abilities,* may underlie the problem-solving behaviors of individuals. These primary abilities or factors include *reasoning ability, ability to handle spatial problems, numerical ability, perceptual speed, rote memory,* and *verbal ability.*

If we constructed separate tests to measure each of these primary abilities, the individual might score high on some of them and low on others. Actually, people who score high on tests of general intelligence, such as the Stanford-Binet, tend to score high on all the primary abilities. Those scoring low on a test of general ability tend to score low on all the separate factors. But people of average intelligence may show a wide variation from one factor to another, making it sometimes precarious to describe individual intelligence by means of a cover-all term such as "an IQ of 110."

Reliability of Intelligence Tests

We have seen that no test of intelligence can be useful unless it yields a reliable measure, unless the results obtained on one occasion are essentially the same as results obtained on another. We cannot here go deeply into the technical data on the reliability of the various tests of intelligence. It will perhaps be enough to state that before any test is made available for general professional use, it is thoroughly tested for reliability. And the results of reliability studies are given to potential users of the test so that they can know how much credence to give the results obtained. Generally speaking, we can have confidence that an IQ reported by a competent examiner using an established test will not vary more than two or three points from the IQ reported by the same or a different examiner using the alternative form of the test on a different occasion. The reliability of group tests of intelligence tends to be, in the main, similarly satisfactory. The level of confidence in the reliability of a test can be vastly greater than we can accord to impressionistic judgments. One is not justified, however, in accepting as completely and finally "true" the results of any single exposure to any single test of intelligence.

Validity of Intelligence Tests

If a test has no reliability, then it cannot be useful in measuring stable attributes of individuals; for it is not actually measuring anything. Neither can it be useful unless it is *valid,* unless scores on it relate meaningfully with performance on a criterion in which we are interested.

The question of the validity of intelligence tests is a fairly intricate one (Chap. 7). We can make the summary statement here, however, that the existing tests have been studied for validity and there can be reasonably good assurance that, on the average, the individual who behaves intelligently on a test will behave intelligently in other situations. It can be clearly demonstrated, for example, that scores on a carefully constructed intelligence test relate significantly to performance in school. But test scores cannot by any means predict perfectly how any given individual will perform in school or college; factors other than intelligence enter into success in school achievement or in any other achievement anywhere. We can be quite confident, however, that the individual with an IQ of 60 will have great difficulty in graduating from high school.

We shall return in Chapter 7 to a fuller consideration of intelligence. How is intelligence distributed in the population? How does it vary with age and sex and race? Is it inherited or acquired? How much, if any, can intelligence be changed by environment? What is the relation between intelligence and creativity? Once we have instruments for the accurate measurement of intelligence, it becomes possible to deal with these and related questions. We shall do so.

Interim Synopsis

Before going on to other aspects of measurement, it may be well here to recapitulate briefly. We started our approach to problems of measurement by a look at our everyday characterizations of people. We settled on Irma's perceived brilliance as an example. Then we drew comparisons between our everyday "tests" of people and the more careful and more precise tests that psychologists create and use. We have dealt primarily with tests of enduring characteristics of the behavior of individuals. Because tests of intelligence were the first tests created and are so widely used, we chose to examine these tests as examples of the problems of test making and test use. We have seen that Binet, Terman, Wechsler, and others who have been curious about intelligence have encountered and have overcome many of the problems of precise characterization of behavior. They have encountered problems of definitions, of establishing and examining continua, of maintaining objectivity, of maintaining reliability, of establishing norms, of making valid predictions

about behavior. As a result of all this concern, and of all the research involved, it is now possible for us to examine Irma's behavior and to say something much more discriminating than "brilliant" or "stupid" about attributes of her behavior. Such a hard-won ability may be worth the trouble it has entailed if, either for reasons of utility or of decency, we wish to be accurate in characterizing people or if, for reasons of plain curiosity, we wish to know more about the intellectual facets of human behavior.

OTHER TESTS OF ENDURING ATTRIBUTES OF BEHAVIOR

Psychologists have created a wide variety of tests to measure a wide variety of enduring attributes of the behavior of individuals. If we can define an attribute of behavior—such as clerical aptitude, or neurotic tendency, or ascendancy, or finger dexterity, or visual acuity—and if individuals differ with respect to that attribute, then we can, at least theoretically, make an instrument to measure it. We follow the rules we have laid down above, we use our ingenuity, we check for the reliability and validity—and we have a test. The creation of a truly useful test may, of course, take many years of highly intelligent and concentrated work. But it can be done if the two conditions stated above are met.

Each of us, of course, will continue our daily "testing" and characterizing of people and we will make moderately accurate predictions about them. But when there is a need for highly accurate measurement, and when decisions must be made, as in clinical diagnosis of the mentally disturbed or in the counseling of a college student or in vocational guidance, a wide variety of solidly useful measuring devices are needed. Many are available.

Tests of Specific Abilities

None of the widely used tests of general intelligence will describe accurately all the **aptitudes** or potentialities of a person. We have seen that even within the area of intellectual capacity individuals may differ widely with respect to the pattern of primary abilities. They also differ widely with respect to many other abilities and aptitudes that are not involved in problem-solving ability but that still have a significant bearing on vocational or other performance. There are a variety of tests of motor abilities, for example. The Minnesota Rate of Manipulation Test (Ziegler, 1939) is one of many such; the Crawford Small Parts Dexterity Test (see Fig. 5–6) is another (Crawford, 1949). This test requires the subject, working as rapidly as he can, to fit rounded blocks into rows of 2-inch holes in a board. Then he is required, also rapidly, to turn each block over in its hole. His score is a speed score. People who score high on this test are also rated high for their speed as packers of facial tissues. (We say that the test was *validated* against a *criterion* of rated speed on this particular job.) When people who take this test are scored later on the speed with which they can assemble electrical pull-sockets, the validity is not so high. Apparently, tests of speed of simple movements do not do well in predicting speed of complex movements.

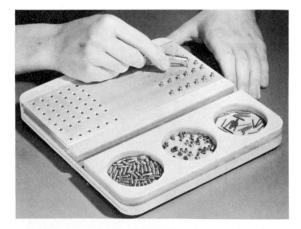

Figure 5–6. a test of motor ability. *The Crawford Small Parts Dexterity Test, used in predicting success on jobs requiring manual dexterity.*

Tests of complex coordination are also used in the attempt to predict performance on jobs requiring complex muscular performance. The Bennett Hand-Tool Dexterity Test (Bennett, 1947), for example, requiring the subject to perform some standard operations with wrenches and screwdrivers, predicts fairly well the future performance of machinists.

In addition to these tests of motor abilities, there are tests of mechanical aptitude, mechanical comprehension, artistic ability, visual abilities, and hearing abilities. Each of these tests of special abilities can be of use in the practical business of vocational guidance or in selecting people for the performance of certain specialized jobs.

Differential Aptitude Tests

A number of tests, widely used in connection with vocational guidance, test a variety of abilities that have relevance for vocational performance. The best-known and most widely used are the General Aptitude Test Battery (GATB) and the Differential Aptitude Tests (DAT). The GATB, developed by the U.S. Employment Service, contains both paper-and-pencil tests and apparatus tests to measure nine factors: not only the intellectual factors such as general reasoning ability and numerical aptitude but also such factors as manual dexterity and motor coordination (Dvorak, 1947; USES, 1958). The DAT measures eight factors deemed to be important in vocational performance. The test includes the usual intellectual factors but also has subtests on mechanical comprehension and clerical speed, accuracy, and spelling (Bennett et al., 1952, 1959).

Tests of Achievement

Employing methods similar to those used in constructing intelligence tests, psychologists have created a number of **achievement tests** to measure with some precision the results of learning experience. Properly designed and properly standardized achievement tests can compare quite accurately the individual's knowledge of French or mathematics or any chosen subject with the knowledge possessed by a known national population of students at the same academic level. Such carefully constructed and carefully standardized tests can very usefully supplement the often subjective and unreliable tests administered by teachers. Among the widely used achievement tests are the California Achievement Tests (Tiegs and Clark, 1951), the Iowa Tests of Educational Development (Lindquist, 1948), and the Metropolitan Achievement Tests (Hildreth, Bixler, et al., 1951).

Tests of Interests

For a number of reasons, psychologists have become interested in the measurement of interests. It makes immediate sense to expect that a person's persisting tendency to be interested in certain objects or activities has a bearing on such things as what college courses

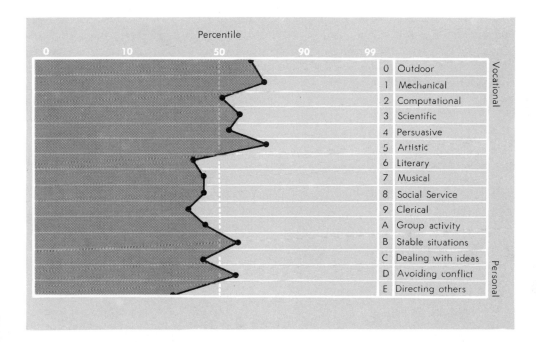

Figure 5–7. PROFILE OF INTERESTS. *A specimen profile of interests, as measured by the Kuder Preference Record. The scores for the individual in this schematization furnish a statistical comparison of his interests with those of people in various lines of work. This individual shows a relatively high interest in mechanical and artistic work, in stable and nonconflictful situations. He has relatively little interest in literary or clerical matters and is low in interest in directing others. This profile is similar to that of many carpenters. (Reproduced by permission of Science Research Associates.)*

he might pursue with most vigor and what occupation he should choose. The Strong Vocational Interest Blank (Strong, 1951) and the Kuder Preference Record (Kuder, 1953) are the two most widely used measures of interests. Through the use of an interest test, it is possible to compare an individual's interest in, say, literary activities with the strength of this interest found in a total population (see Fig. 5–7). It is also possible to compare a person's pattern of interests with the pattern of interests of the successful practitioners of architecture, medicine, law, accountancy, etc. Such a comparison can be useful in vocational choice.

Interest tests, like some other psychological tests, require an honest attempt on the part of the subject to report accurately on his behavior and his feelings. The results of interest tests, like the results of any self-inventory, are relatively meaningless if the subject deliberately or through lack of insight, or for any other reason, fails to answer truthfully.

Self-Report Tests of Personality

A variety of tests have been devised to measure such enduring aspects of the behavior of the whole person as *neurotic tendency, extroversion-introversion, ascendance-submission,* or his relative strength of adherence to economic, social, political, and other patterns of values. (See Fig. 5–8.) Most of these **per-**sonality tests are of the *self-report* type; that is, instead of the actual observation of the behavior of the subject, these tests require the subject to answer questions about his behavior and his feelings.

The behavior being observed in such tests, then, is indirect behavior; the person reports on what he has done, what he would like to do, how he feels, and how he would like to feel. Such tests are useful only if he says similar things on different occasions (reliability), and if what he says in the test situation has a meaningful relation to what he does in other situations (validity). The reliability of such tests is generally good. These tests seem to tap persisting attributes of behavior. But psychologists continue to have long and hot arguments about the validity and usefulness of self-report personality tests. Many researchers are more comfortable with direct observations.

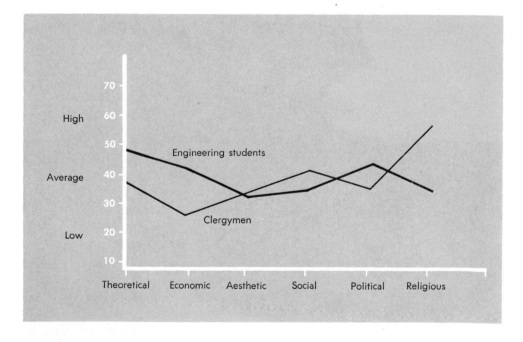

Figure 5–8. PROFILE OF VALUES. *Scores on the Allport-Vernon-Lindzey study of values for 508 engineering students and 26 clergymen. (Reproduced by permission of Houghton Mifflin Co.)*

of behavior than with observation of a subject's observations of his own behavior.

Such devices as the Minnesota Multiphasic Personality Inventory (Minnesota Multiphasic; Gough, 1953) and the California Personality Inventory (Gough, 1957) are widely used to uncover possible personality trends or disorders that may need further investigation. These personality inventories, incidentally, illustrate very clearly the empirical approach in test construction. Items are selected for the tests and are combined into scales not on the basis of any preconceived ideas about what items have what kind of psychological meaning but instead on a purely factual basis. They are items that people known to be disturbed answer one way, while normal subjects answer another. An item is a good item if it contributes to making of the prediction that the man who creates the test wishes to make. One of the creators of the MMPI, for example, reports that he does not know the "meaning" of any single one of hundreds of items on the test (Hathaway, 1964).

Projective Tests of Personality

There have been a number of attempts to handle personality measurement in ways that overcome the disadvantages of self-report techniques, so that an individual's behavior can be directly observed and assigned to its proper place on a standardized continuum of behaviors. The most widely used personality tests that rely on direct observations of behavior in a standardized situation are the various **projective tests**. These tests, the best known of which are the **Rorschach** Inkblot Test (Rorschach, 1942; Klopfer and Kelley, 1942; Beck, 1944) and the **Thematic Apperception Test** (TAT) (Murray, 1938, 1943), require the subject to respond directly, in the presence of the examiner, to standard stimuli that are presented to him. The Rorschach employs a standard set of inkblots. The TAT uses a set of twenty pictures, each of which might be interpreted in a variety of ways. On the Rorschach the subject is asked to report what he sees in each of the inkblots. The TAT asks him to tell a story around each of the TAT pictures. His responses, it is assumed, are determined not so much by the picture or the blot as by forces within himself. In other words, he *projects* into vague and unstructured stimuli his feelings, his worries, his ways of seeing the world. The way one man sees an intricate inkblot will differ very much from the way another man sees and interprets the same thing. And, the theory goes, one man tends characteristically to see many inkblots in the same way; further, his characteristic way of perceiving is indicative of his characteristic way of living. The same theory goes for TAT. The man who looks at twenty pictures and tells repeated stories about the meanness of a father is probably projecting, whether he knows it or not, a vital concern over his relations with his father.

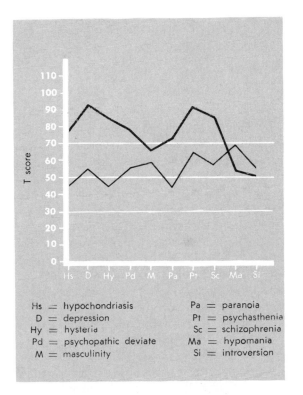

Hs = hypochondriasis
D = depression
Hy = hysteria
Pd = psychopathic deviate
M = masculinity

Pa = paranoia
Pt = psychasthenia
Sc = schizophrenia
Ma = hypomania
Si = introversion

Figure 5–9. MINNESOTA MULTIPHASIC PERSONALITY INVENTORY. *The heavier line represents the profile of a 38-year-old man admitted to a psychiatric hospital after his second suicide attempt. The lighter line represents the profile of an undergraduate student in psychology without known gross psychopathology.*

Figure 5–10. STIMULUS CARD FOR PROJECTIVE TEST. *In a projective test, the subject projects his own personal dispositions onto a relatively unstructured object, so that what he "sees" is determined mainly by forces within himself.*

These and other projective tests present difficult problems of reliability and validity. Though the tests can be "scored," the scoring remains a relatively subjective and interpretive matter. Two scorers of the same responses do not always agree on the scores. The projective tests continue to be widely used, however, in diagnosis of emotional disturbance; they serve to supplement other sources of diagnostic information about the person. There is at the end of this chapter an account of one research study of the validity of the projective test.

An adaptation of the TAT method has been successfully used for measuring an individual's achievement motivation (n ach). Four stimulus pictures are used, and the stories are scored for the number of themes or ideas stressing high standards of excellence or the desire to do well. The scoring procedure yields high reliability, and the meaningfulness of the score for achievement motivation has been repeatedly demonstrated (McClelland et al., 1953). Similar procedures can be used to measure the individual's power motive

and the motive of affiliation (Atkinson, 1958).

A test that promises to combine the sensitivities of the Rorschach test with the precision and objectivity of modern **psychometric** methods is the Holtzman Inkblot Test (Holtzman, 1961). In the construction of this test, 90 inkblots that met the criteria of good test items were selected from a very large number of inkblots. These 90 were divided into two sets of 45 each, to yield alternate forms of the test. The subject gives one response to each of the blots. The responses are objectively coded, and the individual is given a score on each of 22 variables. His scores can be compared precisely with the scores of known standardization groups. The scores of a college student, for example, can be compared with the scores of other college students or with the performance of a group of schizophrenic patients.

Interviews

Psychologists and many other people interested in understanding and predicting behavior frequently use the interview as a procedure for gaining information. It may be questioned whether a discussion of the interview properly belongs in a chapter on measurement, for an interview is not likely to yield precisely quantified data on anything. But the interview is a standard procedure in the practice of clinical psychology and psychiatry, and most employers would feel helpless unless they could use an interview in deciding whether or not a candidate is suitable for a given job.

In the attempts to understand and treat personality disorders, psychologists and psychiatrists undoubtedly can gain a great deal of information through the interview. They can, if they wish, ask any of the questions occurring on any of the self-report tests of personality. They then have not only the answers to these questions to work with, but they can also observe the whole individual—his style of speaking, his facial expressions, his gestures, his nervousness or calmness—as he talks. All this constitutes a rich flow of information. But what can the interviewer do with all this wealth? He can and does formulate for himself a picture, a theory, of a personality. Sometimes such theories have great plausibility and are adopted with great certainty. But what about the reliability and validity of such theories?

Anyone conducting an interview is at least skirting the dangers inherent in casual observations of behavior. The interviewer may easily succumb to the **halo effect,** the tendency for a favorable or unfavorable impression on one trait to spread to judgments on other traits. The person who is socially poised and attractive, for example, is sometimes likely to be given a wrongfully favorable judgment on intelligence. The hostile, unattractive person may be given a negative "halo," which leads to unfavorable judgments of his ability.

Also the phenomenon of **stereotypy** may enter into interviewing. We tend to carry in our heads preconceived pictures or *stereotypes* of the behavior of people of a given race or religion or hair color or size. These ready-made judgments may clutter up our ability to judge what is actually there, to observe the behavior of *this particular* redhead or Irishman or minister or Negro or New Yorker and make reasonable judgments about him.

There are some techniques that can be used to increase the trustworthiness of judgments based on interviewing. We can use *standardized interviews* to be sure that every applicant for a job or every clinic patient we interview is exposed in the same way to the same questions. We can contend with the halo effect by judging one trait at a time. We can devise careful *rating scales* for recording our interpretive judgments. And, best of all, we can go next door and get our colleague to conduct the same interview to see whether he reaches the same conclusions. If he does, we are inclined to give increased trust to our own judgments. If he does not, then we are in trouble, but a very healthy kind of trouble and one we perhaps should cultivate.

Studies of the reliability of interviews do not furnish grounds for a firm general faith in the procedure. However, when the technique is used with care, it can serve as the basis of good predictions (Yonge, 1956). And before anyone becomes too skeptical of the method, it might be well for him to remember that the widely used individual tests of intelligence are, in essence, only highly standardized interviews.

SUMMARY

1. A rigorous seeking for precision often sets the psychologist apart from the layman and the literary artist; tests and measurements are employed widely to ensure precision both of observation and of report.

2. Only in the last century has man tried to apply quantitative methods in the study of his own behavior; pioneers in psychological quantification included Galton, Wundt, and Cattell.

3. There are a number of procedural rules for increasing the accuracy of statements about human behavior; in their most technical form, these rules apply to the construction of actual psychological tests, but in their most general application they can serve all of us as guides to good sense in talking about human individuals.

4. To achieve precision it is necessary to define the variable in terms of observable behavior.

5. In the use of psychological constructs or of everyday adjectives, it is useful to bear continua in mind; there are dangers in categorical thinking.

6. To ensure accuracy, we need objective and noninterpretive observations, observations repeated in standardized conditions of observation.

7. In the world of testing, all is relative; a score must be interpreted in terms of comparison with the distribution of scores obtained by the members of a designated group of individuals. We need to think in terms of norms.

8. Psychological testing characteristically involves the observation of a sample of behaviors of a sample of individuals. It becomes a matter of considerable importance not only to remember the fact that we are sampling, but to understand the techniques for selecting samples to study.

9. A psychological test is probably useless unless it is characterized by reliability, unless it consistently measures the same thing. A test may be checked for split-half reliability or repeat reliability; the former refers to internal consistency, the latter to consistency over time.

10. The concept of validity refers primarily to the ability of a test to measure what it is supposed to measure; the validity of a test is described most generally in terms of the relation between test scores and some external criterion of performance. A test can have concurrent validity or predictive validity or both; and if scores on the test make theoretical sense, the test is said to have construct validity.

11. To create an ideal instrument for measuring performance in introductory psychology would require technical steps to ensure definition, objectivity, reliability, validity, and standardization.

12. Psychologists have created a large number and variety of tests to measure the enduring attributes of individual behavior. The most widely used of these tests are tests of intelligence.

13. Intelligence tests were invented by Binet, refined by Terman and others, and have been widely employed in many practical settings.

14. The intelligence of an individual may be described in terms of IQ or in terms of scores on standardized tests.

15. The Stanford-Binet test is an individual test, revised in 1960 to cover ages up to 18.

16. The Wechsler tests, the WAIS and the WISC, are also individual tests, putting greater emphasis than the Stanford-Binet on performance and arranging items by types rather than by age level or level of difficulty.

17. Group tests of intelligence, beginning with the Army Alpha of World War I, are available and widely used.

18. The analysis of factors in intelligence has made possible a more precise definition and measurement of the individual's intellectual performance.

19. Intelligence tests are sufficiently reliable and sufficiently valid in predicting such criteria as college grades as to be widely useful and widely used, but no test score should be accepted as absolutely final or as absolutely valid.

20. There is available a wide variety of tests of relatively enduring attributes of the individual; these include tests of motor abilities, of differential aptitudes, of achievements, of interests, and of temperamental and personality traits.

21. Projective tests, including the Rorschach, The Thematic Apperception Test, the Holtzman Inkblot Test, and others, are employed to test attributes of which the individual may be unaware or about which he cannot speak.

22. The interview is often used to assess the attributes of the individual, but it must be used with great care if its inherent disadvantages are to be overcome.

RESEARCH REPORTS

ON THE VALIDITY OF A PROJECTIVE TEST [*]

Mussen and Naylor administered ten cards of the Thematic Apperception Test (TAT) to 29 lower-class boys who were being detained in a juvenile home for various acts of delinquency. Each TAT was scored for the amount of aggression expressed by the hero of the story and the amount of punishment inflicted on the hero by those in the environment. The researchers reasoned that there should be a direct relation between the amount of aggression on the TAT and the amount of aggression shown in overt behavior, but that there should be an inverse relation between the amount of punishment a boy projected into his TAT stories and the amount of overt aggression he displayed.

Each day for two weeks, the cottage attendants filled out reports on the amount of aggression shown by the 29 boys. They also filled out weekly ratings of aggressive behavior on the part of each boy.

As predicted, there was a significant tendency for those who were high on TAT aggression to be high also on overt aggression, while those who expressed little aggression in fantasy tended to be low on overt aggression (see accompanying table).

| | | FANTASY AGGRESSION | |
		No. S's with High Scores	No. S's with Low Scores
OVERT	High	12	3
AGGRESSION	Low	6	8

There was also some tendency for those who had high punishment scores relative to their aggression scores to be somewhat less aggressive than those who had punishment scores that were low relative to their aggression scores. This trend, however, did not reach statistical significance.

---

[*] Paul Mussen and H. Kelley Naylor, The relationship between overt and fantasy aggression, J. abn. soc. Psychol., 1954, 49, 235–240.

A STUDY OF CONSTRUCT VALIDITY [*]

The authors noted that people who are high on the psychaesthenia scale of The Minnesota Multiphasic Personality Inventory (MMPI) are said to be characterized by ". . . vacillation, excessive doubt, worry, lack of confidence, and mild depression." On the other hand, those who are high on the hypomanic scale are ". . . active, enthusiastic, confident, aggressive, and expansive." The researchers reasoned that the two kinds of individuals should differ in the confidence with which they could make simple decisions.

Having at their disposal 1,200 MMPI's completed by students at the University of Alabama, the psychologists selected sixteen subjects who had high scores on the psychaesthenia scale and fourteen who had high scores on the hypomanic scale of the inventory. Fifteen control subjects with neutral MMPI's were also selected.

Each subject was given eight weights in random order, ranging in weight from 92 grams to 108 grams. His task was to decide whether each was heavier or lighter than a 100-gram standard weight. If he was unable to decide, he was allowed to say he was uncertain. The authors predicted that those who were high on the psychaesthenic scale would show the most uncertainty, while those who were high on the hypomanic scale would show the least uncertainty. The predictions were borne out; the sixteen psychaesthenic subjects had a mean uncertainty score of 41.9, the fifteen neutral controls had a score of 31.0, and the fourteen hypomanics had a mean score of 20.1. When this difference was statistically tested, it was found to be statistically significant (see tests of statistical significance, pp. 168–173).

REPETITIVE MEASUREMENT [†]

A novel development having relevance for psychological testing concerns the use of tests not to establish stable scores for enduring attributes but to secure meaningful scores for attributes that

---

[*] Albert V. Griffith, Harry S. Upshaw, and Raymond D. Fowler, The psychaesthenic and hypomanic scales of the MMPI and uncertainty in judgments, J. clin. Psychol., 1958, 14, 385–386.

[†] L. J. Moran and R. B. Mefferd, Jr., Repetitive psychometric measures, Psychol. Rep., 1959, 5, 269–275.

change from day to day. For this purpose a pair of researchers developed a large number of alternative forms of a word-association test that could be scored in terms of the "relatedness" of an individual's responses. The test was administered every day to a number of patients in a mental hospital. Also, the clinical staff made daily ratings of the degree of the illness of the patients. Pre-sented below are data for one patient over a 240-day period during which both tranquilizing drugs and shock therapy were administered. The scores on the repetitive tests generally agreed with the independently made ratings of illness. However, the test scores usually indicated changes in degree of illness several days before the changes became apparent in clinical ratings.

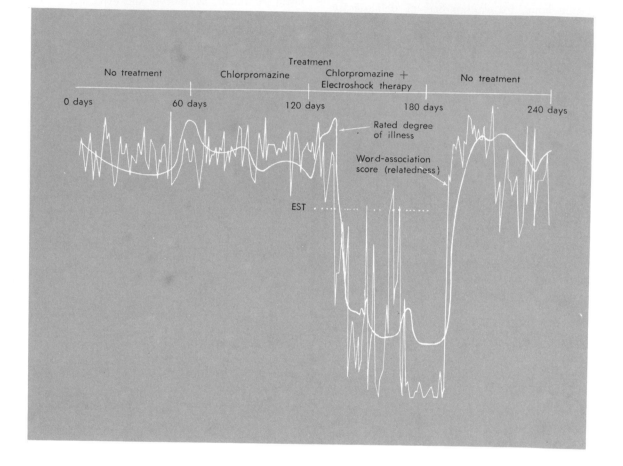

SUGGESTED READINGS

Anastasi, Anne. *Differential psychology: Individual and group differences in behavior,* 3rd ed. New York: Macmillan, 1956.

—————. *Fields of applied psychology.* New York: McGraw-Hill, 1964.

Barnette, W. Leslie, Jr. *Readings in psychological tests and measurements.* Homewood, Ill.: Dorsey, 1964.

Chauncey, Henry, and J. E. Dobbin. *Testing: Its place in education today.* New York: Harper and Row, 1963.

Cronbach, L. J. *Essentials of psychological testing,* 2nd ed. New York: Harper, 1960 (1949).

Tyler, Leona E. *The psychology of human differences,* 2nd ed. New York: Appleton-Century-Crofts, 1956 (1947).

OUTLINE / CHAPTER 6

C H A P T E R   6

EXPERIMENTAL DESIGN AND PSYCHOLOGICAL STATISTICS*

So far, in dealing with measurement, we have concentrated on a molar approach rather than a molecular approach to the problem of making statements about the behavior of individuals, and we have focused on response-response relationships. Psychologists, almost as much as laymen, want to be able to understand and predict relatively widespread and significant behaviors. But the creation of tests of molar traits and abilities by no means occupies all psychologists all of the time; a concern with more molecular variables and with stimulus-response relationships, the kinds of variables and relationships most often involved in experiments in psychology, is at the very core of the science. In trying to deal accurately with either R-R relationships or S-R relationships, the researcher encounters a

variety of problems of quantification. Some of these involve highly specific behaviors, such as the blink of an eye; some involve behaviors more difficult to observe and define, such as aggression; some involve readily specifiable aspects of the stimulus situation, such as a sound stimulus of a certain intensity, while others may treat so subtle and troublesome a matter as group atmosphere.

Look for a moment at the kinds of questions research psychologists pose for themselves. Does the hungry rat learn a maze more or less rapidly than the well-fed rat? Does the anxious sophomore perceive objects as accurately as does his nonanxious colleague? Does the individual student learn a list of nonsense syllables more rapidly if he works on the whole list all at once or takes it a part at a time? Does the animal who has learned to push a lever to receive a pellet of food push more rapidly under conditions of regular or

---

* Carleton Johnson assisted materially with the revision of this chapter.

irregular reward? At what age are children able to tie their shoes with a measured degree of skill? What differences in sensation are produced as we change the frequency of the stimulating sound from 1,000 to 1,200 vibrations per second? Does a person have a longer-lasting afterimage from a bright light or from one not so bright? Do frustrated children aggress against one another more than children who are not frustrated? Can a person react more quickly to an auditory or to a visual stimulus? And so on, for thousands of additional questions.

When any such question is opened to research attack, we encounter problems of definition and quantification. Often these questions are just as knotty as those we face in trying to measure intelligence or neurotic tendency. Look at some of the terms that must be defined and measured in the above list of questions if we ever are going to get good answers:

Hunger	Sensation
Speed of learning	Long-lasting afterimage
Anxiety	Frustrated children
Accuracy of	Aggression
perception	Reaction time
Regular reward	Auditory stimulus
Irregular reward	Visual stimulus
Skill at tying shoes	

Some of these terms—these **variables**—can be defined and measured quite readily. We can, for example, define very precisely the nature of an auditory stimulus. There are electronic devices that will, at the turn of a dial, produce a sound of any intensity or frequency the experimenter may want. Simple. But what about measuring the resulting sensation so that we can state exactly the relation between a change in stimulus intensity and a change in reportable sensation? We immediately run into a problem of measurement sufficiently subtle to challenge the best mathematical minds in all of psychology. For many years, psychologists have been trying to create *psychophysical scales*, scales to measure the *dimensions of perception*, to cope with such problems.

Let us go back for a moment to reaction time. Suppose the United States Air Force wants a psychologist to determine whether a bomber pilot will react more quickly to an auditory or to a visual emergency signal. It is a fairly simple matter to record by a timer the interval between the sounding of a buzzer and the pushing of a button. But trouble sets in when we discover that the same subject does not always have the same reaction time in the same situation. So we get from him a variety, or distribution, of reaction times to sound. How do we decide his "true" reaction time? We want to compare this distribution to the distribution we get when we set him to responding to a flash of light. How do we make a meaningful and precise statement when we are comparing one distribution of responses (reaction times to an auditory stimulus) with another distribution of responses (reaction times to a visual stimulus)? This is the kind of measurement problem requiring a statistical approach. We shall soon face up to such a matter.

STATISTICS IN PSYCHOLOGICAL RESEARCH

In the preceding chapter we dealt with psychological tests and measurements almost as if there were no such thing as **statistics.** The larger problems in the assessment, characterization, and measurement of behavior are not really mathematical or statistical problems. They are mainly problems in straight thinking. But if we aim higher than plain good sense, aspiring to all the precision we can get, then statistical approaches become vitally necessary in treating most kinds of data with which psychologists deal.

The professional psychologist must have a competence in statistical thinking and a skill in using statistical tools if he is to carry out research of his own or to read what his colleagues write. The introductory student must have some competence in statistical thinking and some knowledge of statistical concepts if he is to grasp very many of the facts and principles that will be coming his way for the

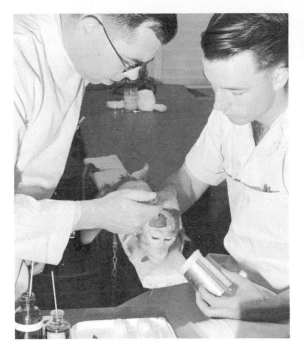 

Figure 6–1. LABORATORY MEASUREMENT.
Definition, design, control, measurement, and recording characterize laboratory research.

remainder of the semester. Statistics has become the quantitative language of psychology, and to talk psychology without statistics would be like talking English without adverbs; it could be done, but only haltingly.

To say that some knowledge of statistics is needed to talk and read psychology is not to say that we need to learn mathematics before heading into the later chapters in this book. Though the student who has a quantitative bent may profitably tangle with the mathematics underlying the frequently used statistical tools, a knowledge of mathematics is not necessary for the understanding of the few basic statistical ideas needed for good thinking and intelligent reading in the psychological area. The student who turns a little pale at the mention of math may comfort himself—a little arithmetic and a clear head will see him through the remainder of this chapter.

We had a brief look earlier at the troubles one can have in determining so simple a matter as the reaction time of a single individual. And if we want to talk about the reaction time of individuals in general, we face even more

serious problems. We need many observations of many behaviors of many individuals—and therein lies the necessity of statistics. *Statistics*, in its essence, *is a body of techniques for arranging, organizing, examining, and interpreting data*—numbers of observations or numbers of behaviors or numbers of individuals. An important function of statistical procedures is that they may help us estimate the wisdom of decisions made on the basis of variable and limited data.

THE PROBLEM OF VARIABILITY

OBSERVATIONS VARY

Although each of us may feel quite competent to determine the true length of a line or the true height of a man or the true loudness of a sound, we may find that others do not agree with our estimate. If you wish to examine the problem of the "true" length of a line, simply sit where you are and estimate the width of a door frame across the room. Now ask someone else to sit in your seat and do the same thing. If you brought in twenty people, you would probably get a distribution of estimates something like that accumulated in a similar "experiment" and presented in Figure 6–2. Thirty-two people estimated the length of a line on the blackboard. Their estimates varied from 32 to 39 inches; nine estimated 36 inches.

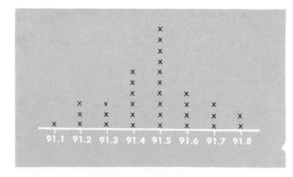

Figure 6–2. OBSERVATIONS VARY. *Estimated length (in inches) of a line drawn on a blackboard. Each* x *represents one estimate by one subject.*

In essence, when you estimate the length of a line, you are making a measurement. It's a crude measurement, right enough, but still a measurement. But it seems impossible by so crude a procedure to determine the true length of the line. So, let us try a better measurement. Let us get our thirty-two people to use a meter stick and *actually* measure a line. When we do this, we get the data presented in Figure 6–3.

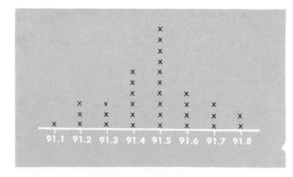

Figure 6–3. MEASUREMENTS VARY. *Length of line is measured in centimeters. Each* x *represents one measurement by one subject.*

We still get a distribution of measures. What is the true length of the line? Is one of these observations any better than any other? Can we throw out as unqualified observers all those who do not agree with the experimenter —who was *sure* the true length was 91.6 centimeters?

There are two points to this kind of exercise. First, no matter how precise our measuring device, we probably would not get precisely the same measurements from different measurers who use it. Also, if we arranged things so that a single measurer were not caught in the social necessity to agree with himself, we would probably get an array of slightly different measurements from the same measurer using the same instrument. Second, most of the measurements in psychology are made without the aid of any micrometrically precise instruments. The measurements thus can vary over a large range.

All right. Observations vary. We clearly need a way to talk about distributions of measures, about arrangements of data showing both the possible measurement values that might have occurred and the number of times each actually did occur.

BEHAVIOR VARIES

An individual's behavior may vary over a wide range when he is trying to give the same response in the same situation. In complicated activities such as in golf or bowling, we expect fairly wide variation. Presented in Figure 6–4

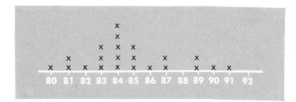

Figure 6–4. BEHAVIOR VARIES. *Golf scores obtained by one player in 22 successive 18-hole games.*

are the scores for 22 games of golf played on the same course by one chronic amateur golfer. How good a game does he shoot? What should his handicap be? If he's out to win a bet from you, he'd like to bet that he'll score lower than 91. If *you* are betting, a good deal would be to bet that he will score 80. He appears to have only one chance out of 22 of doing so. But what constitutes a fair bet?

INDIVIDUALS DIFFER

Not only does the behavior of one individual vary from time to time, but individuals also differ one from another. Individuals differ with respect to almost any human attribute we wish to talk about. They differ in physical attributes: height, weight, pigmentation, speed; size of head, foot, neck, or waist. They differ with respect to physiological attributes: metabolic rate, blood pressure. They differ in the persisting molar attributes of behavior: intelligence, mechanical ability, interests. They differ in hundreds of molecular behaviors: reaction time, speed of reading, memory for nonsense syllables, pitch discrimination, trials needed to learn a maze.

Rarely, if ever, can we talk quantitatively about an attribute or a behavior of more than one person, or for that matter of more than one organism, without needing to refer along the way to a group of which they are a part. And often we will want to talk about groups themselves. We want to talk about the intelligence of a group of boys and compare it with that of a group of girls. Or we want to talk about the neurotic tendency of a group of only children as compared with that of a group of children from large families. Or we want to compare the pitch discrimination of a group of musicians with that of a group of nonmusicians. Or we want to compare the maze-learning speed of a group of anxious rats with that of a group of nonanxious rats. Always we have distributions to contend with. How do we talk about distributions? And how do we compare one distribution with another?

DESCRIBING DISTRIBUTIONS

VISUAL DESCRIPTIONS

One way to deal with a distribution of measures is to look at it. We can plot our array of measures so that we can see all measures simultaneously and, if we wish, make a visual comparison between two or more distributions. We have already seen examples of distributions of data—measurements of length of a line, reaction time, golf scores.

Plotting of Data

Almost any array of data can be plotted against coordinates so that, at a glance, we can see a whole array of measures. We mark off on the **abscissa**, or the horizontal line, the units of measurement we are using—meters, inches, seconds, grams, IQ's, or whatever. On the **ordinate**, the vertical line, we mark off frequencies with which measures occur in the group of measurements or the group of people we are using. Most generally, we are plotting *how many* against *how much*. (See Fig. 6–5.) How many people in one group have how much intelligence? How many estimate the length of a line to be how much?

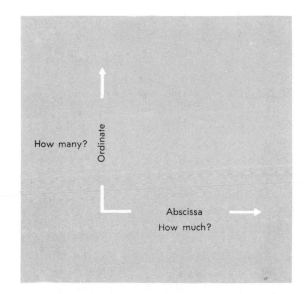

Figure 6–5. PLOTTING OF DATA

To see how a **frequency distribution** is made, we can use data on the reaction time of 1,000 male applicants for mechanical jobs (Fessard, 1926). On the abscissa we lay out step-intervals of 10 milliseconds each. The first step-interval includes all measurements falling from 125 to 134.9 milliseconds. The second interval includes measurements from 135 to 144.9 milliseconds. And so on, until there are intervals to include every measurement obtained. On the ordinate we lay out a series of numbers beginning with zero, spacing them so that the distance between two numbers is proportional to the difference in their values. We can now plot our data in the form of a *histogram*, or bar graph, with the height of each bar representing the number of individuals who have reaction times included in each of our step-intervals. (See Fig. 6–6.) Thus, out of our 1,000 people, 30 have reaction times between 125 and 134.9 milliseconds; 174 of them fall between 165 and 174.9 milliseconds; and, on the slow end of this distribution, 25 fall between 205 and 214.9 milliseconds.

If we wish, and if our timing device is sufficiently sensitive, we can use smaller step-intervals on the abscissa and thereby add precision to the presentation of the data. We might wish to use intervals of 5 or 2 or 1 millisecond, for example. And we can plot the distribution by using narrower bars or simply by placing dots at the appropriate places and connecting those dots with a continuous line,

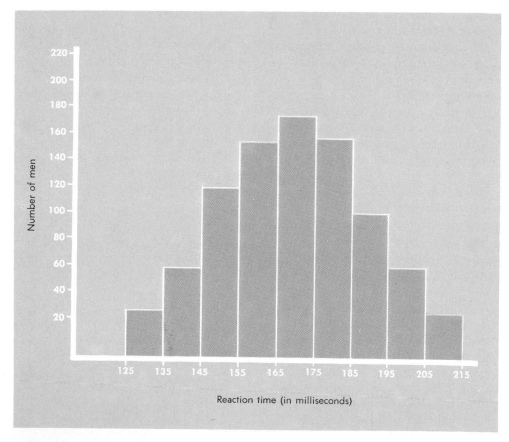

Figure 6–6. A FREQUENCY DISTRIBUTION. *A frequency distribution of the reaction times of 1,000 French males. (Fessard, 1926; by permission of* L'Année Psychologique.)

thereby constructing a *frequency polygon.* Throughout the present book there will be many occasions to study frequency distributions of data.

Kinds of Distributions

As we pointed out earlier, most human characteristics—such as height, weight, IQ, reaction time, running speed, or distance jumping—tend to fall into symmetrical distributions, with relatively many individuals or measures falling in an "average" range and relatively few at the extremes on either side of the middle. The distributions presented in Figures 6-6 and 6-7 tend to be such bell-shaped distributions. Such a symmetrical distribution frequently approximates a theoretical, or ideal, curve—the **normal distribution,** to concern us later.

Though many sets of measurements may distribute themselves in symmetrical bell-shaped fashion, there are exceptions. We sometimes find **skewed curves,** where measures, instead of being grouped in the middle, are grouped at one end or the other of a continuum. Then, too, there are **bimodal curves,** which fall into two bell-shaped groups on the two sides of the mean. Or in some cases we may get **J-shaped curves,** such as that in Figure 6-8 and again in Figure 6-9. Often, a knowledge of the shape of a distribution will prevent errors in interpreting the data. For example, we say that in a certain array of measures an individual falls at precisely the midpoint of the abscissa: this fact would have one meaning for a bell-shaped curve and quite a different one for, say, a **U-shaped curve** like one of those in Figure 6-8.

If the psychologist running the reaction time study for the U.S. Air Force were to put both his data on auditory-signal reaction time and on visual-signal reaction time on the same coordinates, we would find overlapping distributions, such as presented in Figure 6-10. Here the same display presents two distributions for visual comparison. We can see the difference between the measured reaction times; a similar arrangement would similarly display differences in intelligence, or any other aspect of two contrasting groups.

Sometimes, when we are concerned with differences between groups, a quick inspection of the two distributions is enough to sat-

isfy us that a difference exists. With the results presented in Figure 6-10, do you think the Air Force would be willing to spend $50,-000 more per bomber to equip it with an auditory emergency signal rather than a visual emergency signal? Here we can see a difference, but we are not yet equipped to say we can safely base a decision on it.

MATHEMATICAL DESCRIPTIONS

Measures of Central Tendency

If we are going to do something more useful and more communicable than merely inspect our data, we need quantitative rather than visual procedures. We need to describe our data, for one thing, in terms of *central tendency.* We can substitute a succinct bit of arithmetic for such an awkward term as "bunched in the middle." We can compute the **mean** of the distribution. This figure, better known as the average, is computed by the familiar schoolroom procedure of adding up the total of all the measurements and dividing by the number of cases. Or we can find the slightly less familiar **median**—the 50 per cent point or middle point in the distribution, the point separating the upper half from the lower half of the distribution. Or we can put a finger on the **mode,** the most frequently occurring measure in the distribution.

For bell-shaped distributions such as the normal curve, the mean, median, and mode coincide (see Fig. 6-11). However, when a distribution is *skewed* (with subjects piled up more on one side than the other of the mean), the three measures no longer coincide. Two skewed distributions, and their measures of central tendency, are pictured in Figure 6-12. If a distribution is skewed, there is a need for care in interpreting whatever statistic is used as a measure of central tendency. The mean, median, and mode by no means coincide; and, if the mean is used, we should remember that in skewed distributions the mean can be strongly influenced by the presence of extreme cases in the distributions.

The *mean, median* and *mode,* then, are all

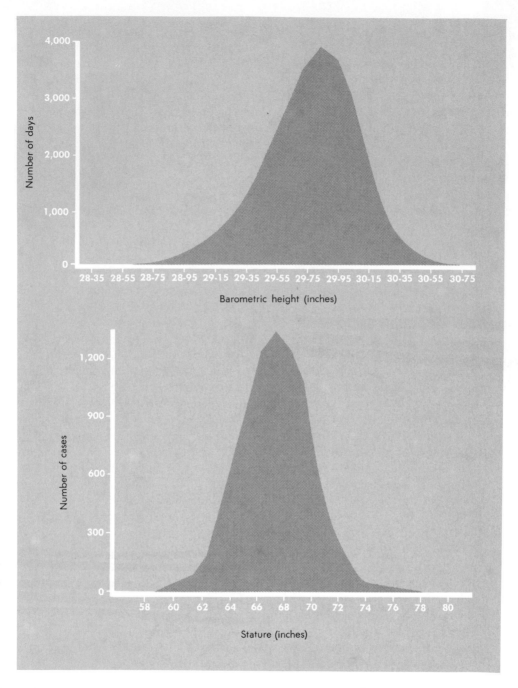

Figure 6–7. BELL-SHAPED DISTRIBUTION CURVES. *The curve on the top shows a distribution of barometric height at Greenwich, England, on alternate days from 1848 to 1926. The bottom curve presents the distribution of height in inches for 8,585 adult males born in the British Isles. Both distributions are of the symmetrical bell-shaped form, in which frequencies decrease to zero on either side of the central maximum. (Reproduced from* An Introduction to the Theory of Statistics, *by G. A. Yule and M. G. Kendall, 14th Edition, 1958, Charles Griffin & Co. Ltd., London, England; by permission of authors and publishers.)*

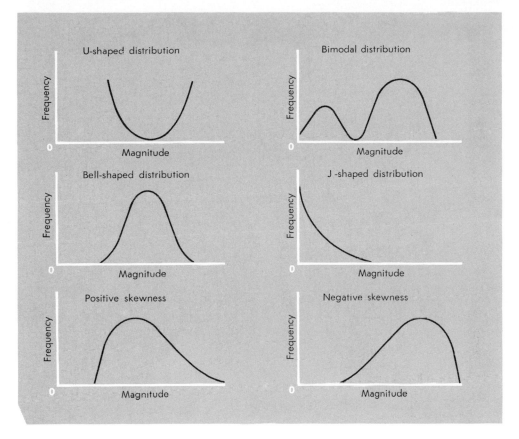

Figure 6–8. TYPES OF FREQUENCY-DISTRIBUTION
CURVES

measures of the central tendency of a distribution. But even though such a measure is an improvement over casual inspection, it still does not allow us to summarize and communicate all the information in the distribution. Two distributions may have precisely the same mean or median or mode and nonetheless describe quite different arrays of data. To describe our array of measures, then, we need not only a measure of central tendency but also a way of describing accurately the **dispersion** of data around that central tendency.

Measures of Dispersion

We may describe a frequency distribution by specifying how "scattered" or "spread out"

or, as statisticians say, how *dispersed* the distribution is. For example, of the two distributions in Figure 6–13, Distribution II is obviously the more dispersed.

There are a number of ways to obtain a number to describe the amount of *dispersion* a distribution exhibits. The simplest is a statement of *range*—the difference between the highest and lowest score in a distribution. For example, the range in Distribution II of Figure 6–13 is 60 (130 — 70). In Distribution I, the range is only 20 (110 — 90). A group with a mean IQ of 110 and a range of 65 to 150 is obviously different from a group with a mean IQ of 110 and a range from 100 to 120.

A more commonly used measure of dispersion, used when the mean is the measure of central tendency, is the **standard deviation** or *sigma* (written σ). The standard deviation represents not merely the spread of the distribution, as does the range, but the degree to which scores are clustered around the

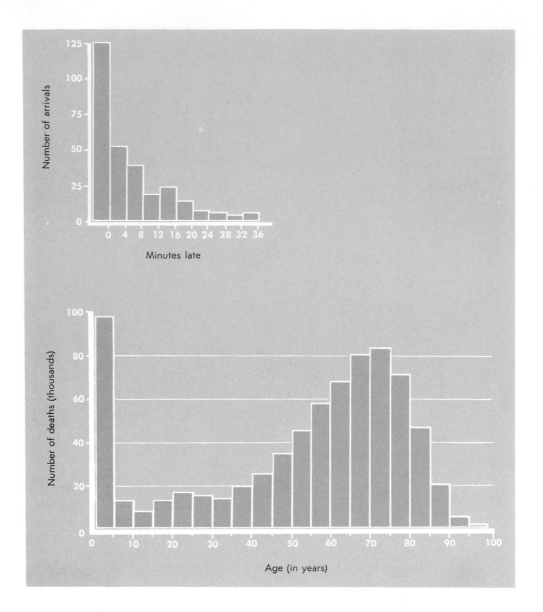

Figure 6–9. KINDS OF DISTRIBUTIONS. *The bottom curve, depicting a distribution of the age at which death occurs, is a negatively skewed curve. The curve on top is an extremely skewed curve known as a J-curve. Such a curve is frequently found when measures are made of conformity behavior; most people conform to an established norm while relatively few are nonconformist. This particular J-curve describes the time of arrival at church; many arrive on time, but some arrive late. (The bottom curve reproduced from* An Introduction to the Theory *of Statistics by G. A. Yule and M. G. Kendall, 14th Edition, 1958, Charles Griffin & Co. Ltd., London, Eng.; by permission of authors and publishers. Curve on top adapted from Allport, 1934; by permission of The Journal Press.)*

mean. The standard deviation is a measurement of distance along the base line of a distribution curve. To compute the sigma of a distribution (a chore we will not undertake here), we need to take into account the

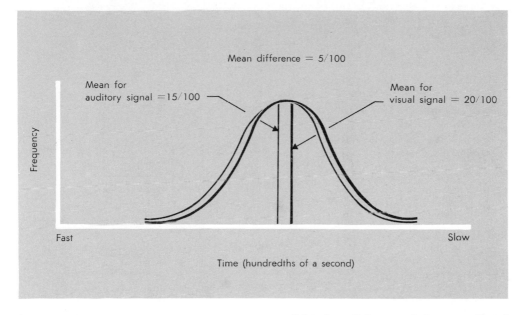

Figure 6–10. OVERLAPPING DISTRIBUTIONS.
Simple reaction times to an auditory and to
a visual emergency signal. The curves overlap
to such an extent that it is difficult to tell
whether there is a significant difference
between them.

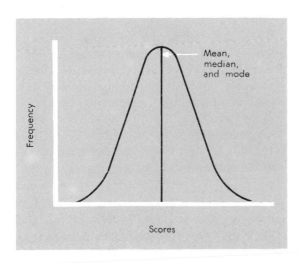

Figure 6–11. MEAN, MEDIAN, AND MODE IN
NORMAL DISTRIBUTIONS. In normal distributions,
the mean, the median, and the mode coincide.

squared differences between each score and
the mean of the distribution. When we do
this according to formula, we have a very

useful index of the variability in a distribution.
The relation of the standard deviation to the
areas under the normal curve is visually presented in Figure 6–14.

For a normal distribution, approximately 68
per cent of the cases fall within one standard
deviation of the mean, either above or below it
(written $\pm 1\sigma$); 95 per cent fall within $\pm 2\sigma$,
and essentially 100 per cent of the measures
fall within $\pm 3\sigma$ of the mean. This measure
of dispersion has a great usefulness in further
statistical operations on the kinds of distribution data psychologists work with. When we
say, for example, that our mean for a set
of 100 measurements of intelligence is 96 and
the standard deviation is 8.2, we are describing with considerable economy the data we
have gathered, and we are setting the stage
for a meaningful quantitative comparison of
one distribution with another.

EXPERIMENTAL DESIGN
AND PROBLEMS
OF INFERENCE

Ultimately, in psychological measurement,
we run into the crucial question of deciding
what to measure. And we also soon come face
to face with the difficult question of knowing,

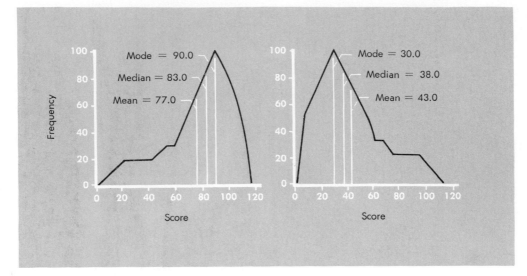

Figure 6–12. MEAN, MEDIAN, AND MODE IN SKEWED DISTRIBUTIONS. *In skewed distributions, the mean, the median, and the mode do not coincide.*

at the end of an experiment, whether we have measured what we think we have measured and whether the relation between the variable we are manipulating (the independent variable) and the variables we are observing (the dependent variables) is what we think it is. In contending with these vitally important questions, we need to deal with matters of **experimental design** and statistical inference.

On the question of what to measure, we have to deal first with *hypotheses*—with the questions we wish to ask of our research. The creative psychologist is known by the hypotheses he keeps. He soaks in the knowledge of the particular field that strikes his curiosity. He somehow gets an idea about an unanswered question that is crucial for that field. He reads and thinks and talks and gets a hunch about a significant relationship. He may run an exploratory study to get preliminary data on the question he has in mind. Then he states his hypothesis in a clear and testable form. He is ready now to attempt the experimental verification of his hypothesis.

Once the hypothesis is stated, the psycho-logist must think of experimental design—of ways of ensuring that the data he plans to collect truly bear on the relationship he wishes to study. He must find a way to be sure that he has *controlled* all, or at least as many as possible, of the factors that might affect the dependent variables in a significantly biasing manner. He then can manipulate the independent variable or variables and watch the results.

Let us return again to our hypothetical problem in which the United States Air Force has asked a psychologist to determine whether a bomber pilot can react more quickly to a visual or an auditory emergency signal. The experimenter selects ten pilots and determines their reaction time to the visual signal. He selects another ten pilots and determines their reaction time to the auditory signal. He finds that the pilots receiving the auditory emergency signal react faster than the pilots responding to the visual emergency signal. That's that, he may say. The hypothesis is proved. But if he does say that and does report his study in the scientific literature, he will be laughed at. Why? He has clearly not designed an experiment that will justify the statement that pilots can react faster to an auditory signal than to a visual signal.

The unanswered questions about such an experiment include the following:

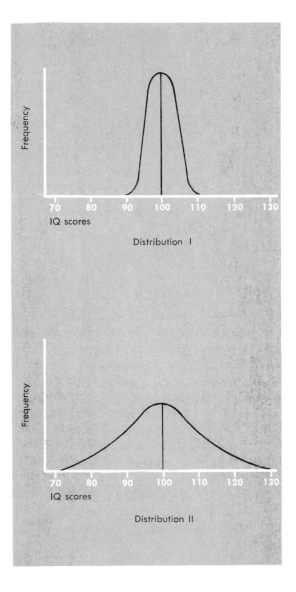

Figure 6–13. DIFFERENCES IN DISPERSION OF
FREQUENCY DISTRIBUTIONS

1. How do we know that one group of pilots
   might not have been older than the others,
   and hence had slower reaction times—or
   faster?
2. How do we know that one group of ten
   subjects did not have more pilot experience,
   and hence more efficient reaction times, or
   perhaps more deliberate reaction times?
3. How do we know that one group of pilots
   might not have had longer arms, allowing

them to reach the switch more rapidly, or
perhaps interfering with their reaction times
due to cramped space?

Is the measured change in the dependent
variable due—and due only—to the changes
deliberately produced in the independent
variable? We cannot say. The experiment is
almost impossible to interpret unless we can
rule out or in some way account for the effects
of other "nuisance" variables that might be
producing the observed result. We clearly
need procedures to rule out the possible effects of such variables as age, experience, and
size, and of any other variable that might influence the results of our experiment.

As an example of the problem of control in
research, suppose some preliminary data show
that students who take an introductory psychology course have higher grades in subsequent academic work than do students who do
not take the course. Some people might think
immediately that students learn something in
psychology that contributes to their general
academic effectiveness. Maybe they are right.
How might we examine the hypothesis? We
(1) think of all the factors that might be accounting for such a result and (2) find ways
to **control** for them so that we can watch the
variable in which we are interested.

On the face of things, each of the following
alternative hypotheses may be just as reasonable as the one we are interested in testing:

1. More girls than boys take psychology, and
   girls tend to make better grades.
2. Older students tend to take psychology, and
   older students make better grades on all
   courses.
3. Students who take psychology have personality attributes that contribute to good academic performance both before and after
   taking psychology.
4. Students who take psychology are more intelligent than students who do not and hence
   make better grades.
5. Students who take psychology have been in
   college longer and hence make better grades
   in subsequent courses.

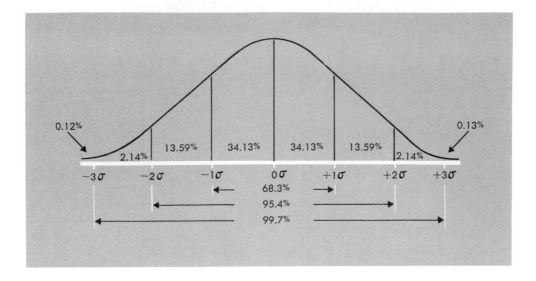

Figure 6–14. STANDARD DEVIATION IN A NORMAL DISTRIBUTION

6. Students who take psychology choose easier courses later and hence make better grades.

To test our original hypothesis, we need a way to see whether the independent variable —the study of psychology—can produce results in line with our hypothesis when these other possible variables are controlled. How do we control? One obvious way is to use a *control group*—a group like the experimental group in every significant respect except that it is *not* treated by our independent variable. We choose two groups that are *matched* with respect to sex, age, potentially significant personality traits, intelligence, length of time in college, and curriculum choice. We measure the academic performance of the two groups before the experiment begins. We measure again after one group has taken psychology. If now we find a genuine difference between the two groups, we have reasonable assurance that taking psychology has made a difference. Of course, being sure that an obtained difference is genuine, rather than merely a chance difference, requires statistical assessment of our data.

The student who can set up an experiment properly, taking into account all these varia-

bles, is well on the way to an understanding of experimental design and an appreciation of the care, the inventiveness, and the plain hard work involved in making scientific statements about anything. If such an understanding and such an appreciation happen to "take," happen to become a part of a student's intellectual personality, it is a good bet that the student will forever be less inclined to make unsupported and unsupportable statements of alleged fact.

But there is still more trouble in store for the Air Force experiment. Let us say we do in fact succeed in designing a proper experiment using these two groups of pilots, a properly designed experiment exercising proper experimental control. We still are not really interested in talking about only ten pilots or even twenty pilots. We want to talk about *all* pilots. Can we make statements about all pilots on the basis of studying just ten? Maybe so. But maybe also such an *inference* from ten to all would be no safer than saying "all Indians walk in single file, because I saw one once and he was in single file."

The problem here is a problem of *statistical inference*. We will not dig deeply into this matter, but we can illustrate the problem and its solution by suggesting that we compare the results we have obtained with the results we might have obtained *by chance alone*. If there is a good possibility that accidents in the selection of our pilots are determining the results we get, then we are properly wary in making everlasting statements about all pilots everywhere. There are ways to compare the results of an experiment with the results that might be expected by chance. Through such comparisons of the actual data with chance results, we know what *statistical inferences* we can make from a small group to a large group or from a few observations to many. We must involve ourselves, then, in statistical matters if we are to know what our experimental results are saying.

SAMPLING AND INFERENCE

Psychologists try to make meaningful statements about *all* members of the population they study, whether the population is of rats or parakeets or mental defectives or schizophrenics or of all human beings everywhere. The term **population** refers to a well-defined group of individuals or of observations, with each member of the group possessing in common a definable quality or pattern of qualities. Actually, however, it is rarely possible to deal with whole populations; there must, for practical purposes, be a **sampling** of the population in which we are interested. Psychologists work most frequently with samples. If a psychologist is interested in the difference between male and female performance on a test of spatial intelligence, he selects a *sample* of 10 or 100 or 1,000 men and a similar number of women as subjects in his research. He hopes to be able to perform measures on his sample and to infer accurately from his actual measures to the measures he would theoretically get if he had the time and patience to measure each of 160,000 or 160,000,000 men and an equal number of women.

The same thing holds for populations of measurements. There is rarely or never the time to make a million measurements of the reaction time of a single individual. If one undertook such a chore he would end with what might be the "ultimate" distribution for measurements on that one person. How do we

infer, and with what degree of confidence, from a sample to a total population? That sort of question is the central one in *inferential statistics*.

The use of inference from a sample to a population involves a comparison of obtained results with the results that might have occurred by chance alone. Suppose we believe that we have found a person who is gifted with some strange ability to call the fall of coins. So we bring him into the laboratory and set him to the task of calling "heads" and "tails" as we flip coins for him. We know that by chance—by the "law of averages"—he ought to be right 50 per cent of the time. There are only two ways a coin can fall; so on any given flip the chances are 50-50 that it will fall heads or tails. We flip away and collect data. At the end of an hour of such research, we find that our subject has made 100 calls and that he has been right 55 times—five more than the value expected by chance. Have we shown that he has some unusual ability, or can we call our results accidental? Suppose we run another, ungifted, subject through 100 flips and find that he calls correctly 49 times. Is the difference of 6 between the two subjects a genuine difference or is it an accident? Do we endow our first subject with extrasensory perception? Or do we say he had a run of luck?

We can get at such a question by flipping thousands of coins and counting the number of times out of 100 flips a subject or many subjects score 55 or more correct calls. We would find that out of thousands of such experimental runs, a result of 55 or better would occur once in approximately six runs of 100 flips each. This is a matter the student can demonstrate for himself if he has the time and the patience. Or if he trusts mathematics, he can, through the application of the **binomial theorem,** compute a distribution of frequency with which correct calls of 51, 52, 53, etc., will occur. Such a computation, yielding a theoretical curve of *normal probability*, will show the same distribution of results we get if we actually flip thousands of times.

Thus, through either the experimental or

Figure 6–15. SAMPLING. *Research often requires systematic sampling of a population. Making statements about a population on the basis of measuring a sample involves statistical inference.*

mathematical construction of a "true" distribution curve, we can determine what results occur by chance alone, and we can say with relative certainty how often 55 or more correct flips out of 100 would occur by chance alone. The fact that we can expect such results, in the long run, to occur by chance about once every six times keeps us from making any startling conclusions upon getting such results from a subject.

Similarly, we can calculate, either by flipping or by computing, how often differences of six or more would occur between any two runs of 100 flips. We find out that such a difference would occur by chance alone twice in every three pairs of runs. So what do we make of our obtained difference between our "gifted" caller and our "normal" caller? Very little indeed. As a matter of fact, nothing at all. By general agreement, psychologists do not pay attention to experimental results that

could occur more than five times out of a hundred times by chance alone. Such a convention is known as the 5 *per cent level of confidence* or the 5 *per cent level of significance.*

STATISTICALLY SIGNIFICANT VS. CHANCE MEASURES

In many research situations it is possible, through proper experimental design and through proper statistics, to compare obtained results with results that can be expected by chance. And no result is paid attention to unless it is due to something other than chance.

Let us return once more to our hypothetical U.S. Air Force study. You will recall that the Air Force was unwilling to authorize the expenditure of millions of dollars to convert a particular emergency system from visual to auditory on the basis of inspection of the data in Figure 6–10. They hesitated to make this change because the differences in reaction times to the two different signals were so close that the obtained difference might have occurred by chance. If the two curves had been completely separated, as in Figure 6–16,

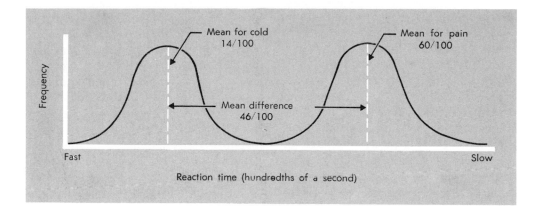

 contains the following labels:

Frequency

Mean for cold
14/100

Mean for pain
60/100

Mean difference
46/100

Fast

Slow

Reaction time (hundredths of a second)

Figure 6–16. NONOVERLAPPING DISTRIBUTIONS.
*Simple reaction times to a pain stimulus and
to a cold stimulus. Interestingly, people react
faster to cold.*

the differences between them would probably
not have occurred by chance alone. Fortu-
nately, when distributions overlap, as in Figure 6–10, the differences between their means
can be tested for *statistical significance,* to
determine how often a difference this large
would occur by chance. The most frequently
used statistic for a mathematical comparison
of the difference between two means is the
"t" statistic. The "t" statistic utilizes the *means,
standard deviations,* and sample sizes of both
samples in its computation.

If our psychologist were to compute a "t"
statistic, and if he found a difference so large
that it would occur by chance only five times
or less in a hundred, he might well then
recommend the conversion of this particular
emergency system.

We have seen that almost every time the
psychologist wishes to measure something,
he has to deal with a distribution. He rarely
can make anything out of a single measurement of a single behavior of a single individual. He has to handle distributions. In order
to do so, he must have some *descriptive statistics.* These can be visual devices for inspect-
ing distributed data. Or they can be, and
often need to be, mathematical descriptions
of central tendency and dispersion. The *mean*

and the *standard deviation* are vital statistical
concepts for describing psychological data.

Not only is it necessary to make precise descriptions of distributions but also to make
sound inferences from small numbers of measurements or small numbers of people to large
numbers of measurements or large numbers of
people. Inferential statistics deals with such
matters. Through known and tested procedures, we can infer, with a known degree of
confidence from a small sample to the population from which the sample is drawn. But
this is possible only by comparing the results
we actually obtain with the results we might
expect by chance; statistical inferences are
made concerning obtained measures only
when there is justification. These ideas constitute the heart of psychological statistics.
The actual application of statistics to problems
of research will require, of course, considerable keenness in selecting the best statistical
tools for the particular problem at hand as well
as good skill at mathematical computation.
But the student who gets the basic ideas in
descriptive and inferential statistics is fairly
well equipped to read psychological literature—and perhaps to think a bit more carefully about everyday problems that are statistical in nature.

CORRELATION

Many research problems call for the use of
correlational techniques. We may wish to

know, for example, how mechanical intelligence is related to verbal intelligence, how athletic ability is related to scholastic ability, how speed of reading is related to retention of material read, how speed of auditory reaction time is related to visual reaction time, how age is related to visual activity, how neurotic tendency is related to academic achievement, or how speed of learning is related to strength of achievement motivation. These and many similar problems can be approached through correlation, through the study of the relationship between measures of one variable and measures of another. During the later chapters of this book, there will be numerous occasions to refer to correlational data. We can see both the nature and usefulness of correlational techniques by returning to our earlier consideration of reliability and validity.

RELIABILITY OF TESTS

In dealing with reliability of a test, we are interested in the capacity of the test to measure repeatedly the same thing. One way to calculate the reliability of a test is the straightforward procedure of administering it to a number of subjects and then, after an interval of time or by use of an alternate form, administering it in the same way to the same people. Do the same people tend to get the same rank on the retest? Or, more precisely, *how great* is the tendency for the same people to achieve the same ranks? We can compute a **coefficient of correlation** to answer the latter question. The technique is designed for just such a problem.

To examine the amount of relationship between scores on the test and those on the retest (few if any tests yield perfect reliability—one in which every person receives precisely the same relative position every time), the simplest procedure is to compute a *rank-order correlation* between the two sets of scores. Let us say, in order to use the simplest example, that we are using ten subjects in our test-retest study. On the first test we can rank their scores from highest to lowest, as in Figure 6–17. Then we make a similar rank order for the scores of the same people on the retest. If the highest person on the first test is highest on the second, the second highest again second highest, and so on, with the lowest on the first scoring lowest on the second, then we obviously have a close relationship between the two sets of scores; and we begin to think the test is highly reliable. If, however, we get a rank order on the second test like that at the right-hand side of Figure 6–17, where there is no clear tendency for rank on the first test to go with the same or similar rank on the second, then we begin to think of tearing up our test. Its repeat reliability begins to look very low or nonexistent.

Although we would not often use a sample of only ten cases as a basis for inferring how a thousand cases might turn out, the nature of a correlation can be seen here. The closeness of the relationship between scores on Test I and Test II can be stated in precise terms. Our first column of ranks for the second test would yield a *high positive* correlation, stated as +.90. If the ranks on the second test are the opposite of ranks on the first test, so that rank 1 on the first test goes with rank 10 on the second, rank 2 with rank 9, and so on for the ten cases, with high ranks on the first test going consistently with low ranks on the second test and low first ranks with high seconds, we would have a *negative* correlation. A perfect negative correlation would be stated as −1.00. Actual correlation coefficients vary, then, from +1.00 through 0 (no relationship at all) to −1.00.

This oversimplified example reveals the kind of relationship expressed in a coefficient of correlation. The rank-order correlation is fairly frequently used in actual research (yielding a coefficient known as rho or ρ). But a preferred method of computing a coefficient is the **product-moment** procedure, yielding a figure written as r. Such a procedure is often a more precise one in that it deals with actual scores rather than with the relatively crude matter of ranks. But the principle

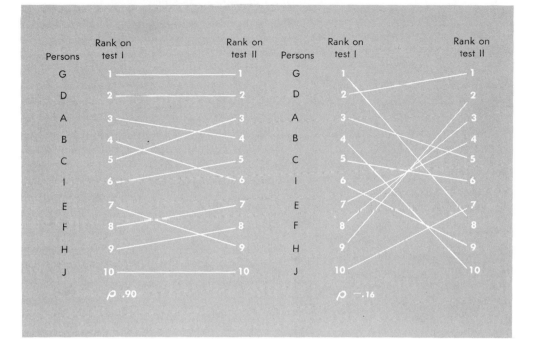

Figure 6–17. A RANK-ORDER CORRELATION. *A rank-order correlation coefficient, or rho, describes the similarity of ranks on two tests or two sets of measures. The chart on the left represents a high positive rho. The chart on the right represents a negative relationship. The method of computing the latter is indicated below:*

$$= 1 - \frac{6(192)}{10(99)}$$

$$= 1 - \frac{1,152}{990}$$

$$= 1 - 1.16$$

$$\rho = - .16$$

Persons	Rank on Test I	Rank on Test II	D	D²
A	3	5	—2	4
B	4	10	—6	36
C	5	6	—1	1
D	2	1	1	1
E	7	4	3	9
F	8	3	5	25
G	1	8	—7	49
H	9	2	7	49
I	6	9	—3	9
J	10	7	3	9
				$\Sigma D^2 = 192$

$$\rho = 1 - \frac{6 \Sigma D^2}{N(N^2 - 1)}$$

remains the same. Measures at one time relate to measures at another, and the amount of relations can be stated in precise terms.

VALIDITY OF TESTS

When we deal with the validity of tests, our central question concerns the relation between scores on the test and scores or measures on an independent *criterion.* We say that if a test of intelligence is valid, it ought to relate to performance in school. So we *validate* our test against a *criterion* of academic grades. We compute a coefficient of correlation between the two sets of measures and find the corre-

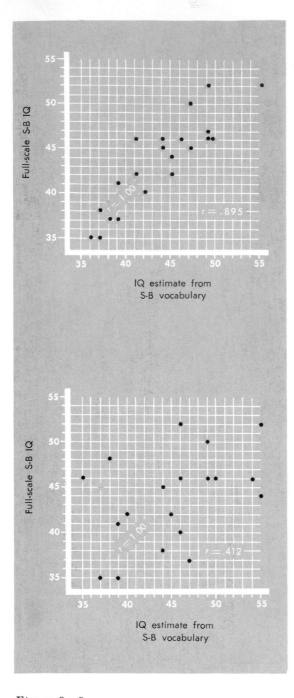

a tendency for the estimate to fall close to the full-scale scores. The correlation between the two measures is .895. A perfect positive correlation would be represented by a scatter plot in which the dots fall on a straight diagonal line.

In the lower scatter diagram are results obtained when IQ estimated on vocabulary items is plotted against full-scale IQ measurement made after an interval of nine years. The correlation between the two measures is .412.

The figures below give the formula and the actual computations involved in obtaining the quantitative statement of the relationship depicted in the upper scatter plot.

Full-Scale S-B IQ	IQ Estimate from S-B Vocabulary (high r)
47	49
35	37
46	49
40	42
52	55
46	41
42	45
35	36
38	37
42	41
41	39
52	49
37	38
46	46
46	44
45	44
44	45
46	49
50	48
45	47
$\Sigma X = 875$	$\Sigma Y = 881$
$\Sigma X^2 = 38{,}755$	$\Sigma Y^2 = 39{,}305$

$$r = \frac{N\Sigma XY - \Sigma X \Sigma Y}{\sqrt{N\Sigma X^2 - (\Sigma X)^2}\sqrt{N\Sigma Y^2 - (\Sigma Y)^2}}$$

$$= \frac{20(38{,}978) - (875)(881)}{\sqrt{20(38{,}755) - (875)^2}\sqrt{20(39{,}305) - (881)^2}}$$

$$= \frac{8{,}685}{97.34 \times 99.69}$$

$$r = .895$$

Figure 6–18. PRODUCT-MOMENT OR PEARSONIAN *r. When twenty adult inmates (IQs ranging from 35 to 55) of a school for the mentally defective are given IQ's estimated on the basis of the vocabulary items on the Stanford-Binet Scale and then, after a month, are given the complete scale, results like those in the upper scatter plot are obtained. There is clearly*

lation to be +.65. So we say our test has just that *coefficient* of *validity* with respect to grades.

CORRELATION AND PREDICTION

If two variables are correlated, then we can measure one and predict, with *some* degree of certainty, what the measurement of the other will be. We know that the correlation between height and intelligence, for example, is about +.12 (this is *not* a hypothetical case; there actually is a correlation). How well can we predict intelligence by measuring height? Not very well at all. The positive correlation, however, means that there is some tendency for tall men to score higher than short men on intelligence tests. If we measured a thousand men on both height and intelligence, and (1) divided the thousand into two equal height groups—a tall group and a short group—then (2) divided them into two intelligence groups—a high group and a low group—we could see how many of our tall people were also in the high-intelligence group. We would find that 265 of our 500 tall people were in the high-intelligence group, while 230 of the 500 short people were there. This is not a striking relationship. But it is precisely the magnitude of the relationship signified by an r of +.12.

Table 6–1. CORRELATION AND PREDICTION

CORRELATION COEFFICIENT	PER CENT OF TOP HALF OF FIRST TEST WHO WILL FALL IN TOP HALF OF SECOND
.00	50
.10	53
.20	57
.30	60
.40	63
.50	67
.60	70
.70	74
.80	79
.90	85
.95	91
1.00	100

Take another example. Many studies have found that intelligence test scores correlate as high as +.70 with college grades. An r of .70 means that if we tested 1,000 people on both intelligence and grades, we would find that, of the 500 who scored in the top 50 per cent on intelligence, 370 would score in the top half on college grades. These computations may serve to give concrete meaning to the r's we encounter in psychological literature. Table 6–1 gives a more complete picture of the kinds of predictions that can be made from r's of various magnitudes (Chesire, Saffir, and Thurstone, 1933).

CORRELATION AND CAUSATION

A correlation coefficient tells us only that two things vary together. It does not tell us that variation in one causes variation in the other. Height does not necessarily cause intelligence nor intelligence height, even though the two are correlated. The per capita consumption of whiskey in the fifty states of the union is positively correlated with the average salaries of school teachers in these states. The birth rate in Belgium over a number of years is correlated with the number of storks nesting on chimneys. Athletic ability shows a slight positive correlation with intelligence. What causes what? We are clearly not justified in jumping to causal conclusions from every correlational fact we run across. But r means covariation. And covariation *may be* produced by the influence of one variable on another. Or it may be produced by some factor influencing both variables in the same way. With respect to intelligence and height, for example, one might suspect a common factor of health. Healthy, well-fed people may show a slight tendency to be both a bit taller and a bit brighter than unhealthy, ill-fed people. And perhaps the year's weather in Belgium has a simultaneous influence on the nesting of storks and the production of babies. Similarly, perhaps, both teachers' salaries and consumption of alcohol vary with the general level of prosperity in the various states. Correlation coefficients present only facts. Facts do not explain themselves.

SUMMARY

1. Psychological measurement requires clear definition, clear experimental design with proper controls, and, often, statistical inferences.

2. Statistical procedures and statistical thinking in psychology are necessary because observations vary, behaviors vary, and people vary; there is the frequent necessity to talk about distributions.

3. Distributions may be described graphically through the plotting of data, or mathematically through the computation of measures of central tendency and dispersion.

4. Distributions will vary widely in shape, but in many instances data are distributed in such a way as to yield a symmetrical, bell-shaped curve approximating in form the theoretical normal probability curve.

5. Special problems of interpretation arise when two distributions of data overlap.

6. The mean, median, and mode are three measures of central tendency, with the mean the most commonly used of the three.

7. The dispersion in a distribution is measured in terms of the range or, more frequently, in terms of the standard deviation; the standard deviation or sigma (σ) is a measurement of distance along the base line of a distribution curve and is a useful index of the variability in a distribution.

8. Experimental design refers to the procedure whereby the researcher ensures that the results he observes are due to changes in a specified variable or variables rather than to other factors that, unless he has controlled for them, may be producing the results.

9. Statistical inference refers to the process whereby the researcher, on the basis of a few measures or a few cases, can make statements of a known degree of probable accuracy about many measures or many cases.

10. Psychologists often wish to make statements about a population on the basis of studies of a sample of that population; the safety of an inference from a sample to a population can be calculated by comparing obtained results with the theoretical results that can be expected on the basis of chance alone.

11. If an obtained result might have occurred by chance alone 5 per cent or more of the time, the obtained result is regarded as not meeting the criterion of statistical significance.

12. The correlation coefficient is a measure of the amount of covariation of two variables. A correlation coefficient of $+1.00$ represents perfect covariation, with positions on the first test or variable agreeing perfectly with positions on the second test or variable. A zero correlation signifies no covariation at all. Negative coefficients express a negative covariation.

13. The existence of a correlation between two variables does not by any means always signify that there is a cause-and-effect relationship.

SUGGESTED READINGS

Green, B. F. *Digital computers in research: An introduction for behavioral and social scientists*. New York: McGraw-Hill, 1963.

Hays, W. L. *Statistics for psychologists*. New York: Holt, Rinehart and Winston, 1963.

McNemar, Quinn. *Psychological statistics*, 3rd ed. New York: Wiley, 1962 (1949).

Winer, B. J. *Statistical principles in experimental design*. New York: McGraw-Hill, 1962.

OUTLINE / CHAPTER 7

C H A P T E R   7

INTELLIGENCE*

In the history of their attempts to measure the individual's personal characteristics, **intelligence** was the first relatively enduring attribute of behavior that psychologists tackled. And now it is perhaps the most frequently measured attribute. Over the years there has been accumulated an extensive body of knowledge about intelligence and its measurement; now we can ask and at least sometimes answer questions about the alleged roots of intelligence in heredity, about its constancy or inconstancy over time, about its distribution in the population, about its relation to various kinds of achievement, and so on. In the asking of such questions and in the search for answers, perhaps there can be an advancement of learning not only about this significant aspect of behavior but also about both

the pleasures and pitfalls that can be involved in applying some of the psychological methods confronted in the last two chapters.

FOLKLORE AND DEFINITION OF INTELLIGENCE

FOLKLORE OF INTELLIGENCE

Accompanying the advance of scientific knowledge of intelligence there has developed also an extensive folklore about the whole matter. Almost everyone now knows about intelligence and its testing, but many people "know" things that are wrong or partially wrong. We might explore the prevailing folklore about intelligence by administering the following true-false test to a representative sample of men in the street.

---

* Edwin I. Megargee assisted materially with the preparation of the revision of this chapter.

T F	1.	Intelligence is inherited and is not changed after birth.
T F	2.	Intelligence does not increase beyond the age of 13.
T F	3.	A high intelligence quotient is an assurance of high achievement.
T F	4.	Individuals with exceptionally high intelligence quotients are likely to be emotionally disturbed or queer.
T F	5.	Blondes are less intelligent than brunettes.
T F	6.	The white race is demonstrably superior to the Negro in intelligence.
T F	7.	People with extremely high IQ's are likely to be sickly.
T F	8.	Any person with a normal IQ of 100 can pass college courses.
T F	9.	A person with an IQ above 120 rarely flunks out of college.
T F	10.	Men are superior to women in intelligence.
T F	11.	Football players tend to be low in intelligence.
T F	12.	Almost all mentally retarded children are placed in institutions.

We would probably find in the general population—and maybe even among students in introductory psychology—some persons who would check one or more of these statements as true. They are all more false than true.

This chapter will deal with a number of aspects of the scientific literature on intelligence. In doing so, its aims will be multiple. In the first place, the treatment of the topic of intelligence will serve to illustrate the application of some of the methods of psychological measurement. Second, the chapter will illustrate for the student the kinds of knowledge that can become available on any psychological variable which can be defined and measured. In the third place, there is a practical goal: a reasonably accurate knowledge of the facts in this whole area can be commended to any future parent or teacher or administrator or, for that matter, to any citizen whose increased knowledge of psychological matters has a bearing on the welfare of us all.

DEFINITIONS OF INTELLIGENCE

For a long time it was fashionable to set down as a definition the statement that *intelligence is what the intelligence tests test*. This definition has the virtue of emphasizing that intelligence is a **construct** and that we need to keep in mind the operations—the tests—we employ to give the construct a clear meaning. But this definition still leaves us hanging in mid-air; we want to tie ourselves to something more substantive.

Actually, there may not be available to us a single definition of intelligence that is much more satisfactory than that given above. We can, of course, specify the various items that appear on intelligence tests and can describe the responses the tests elicit. Such a procedure can add definitional clarity. For example, we say that in taking an intelligence test an individual is confronted with an array of tasks involving such processes as the solving of problems, the perception of relationships, the use of symbols, the processing of information in general, and the understanding of spoken and written language. And then we define intelligence in terms of the specifiable quality or level of his responses to these items.

We can shorten this consideration into the definition that *intelligence is an inferred and relatively enduring attribute of the behavior of an individual, an attribute relating to the individual's capacity to respond successfully to a variety of perceptual, cognitive, and verbal problems*. This definition will prove workable for most purposes. But we will probably have an increased chance of understanding recent research on intelligence if we make a basic distinction recommended some years ago by one of psychology's most thoughtful writers (Hebb, 1959)—that is, that the term intelligence has had *two* separable meanings: (1) Intelligence (Intelligence A) is an *innate potential* to develop and to grow into a given capacity to function intelligently. (2) Intelligence (Intelligence B) is an *average level of performance or comprehension* at a specified time in the developmental history of the individual. Intelligence B is the intelligence we infer from observing the individual's behavior in the presence of a variety of intelligence test items. Intelligence A is a more difficult thing to come to grips with. And the question of the relation of Intelligence A to the more easily inferrable Intelligence B is a difficult one, to which we will do well to devote some attention.

IS INTELLIGENCE INHERITED OR ACQUIRED?

In drawing a distinction between Intelligence A as an innate potential and Intelligence B as a current level of performance, and then in asking about the relation between A and B, we are, of course, involving ourselves in the old and often noisy debate on the issue of nature versus nurture in intelligence. Many laymen believe, and some psychologists act as if they also believe, that intelligence is primarily innate—it is all Intelligence A—and that Intelligence B is but an obvious expression of the present stage of development of Intelligence A. Others, both within and without the field of psychology, have tended to discount hereditary factors and to emphasize the role of experience in the development of intelligence.

It is a matter of great practical significance to know whether intelligence is cast into its final form at the time of conception or whether experience during life has something to do with it. If intelligence is strictly determined by the genes, then perhaps we will reconcile ourselves as gracefully as we can, and as may be demanded, to our own intelligence or to that of others for whom we have some concern. Or perhaps we will take steps to see that, through selective breeding, the intelligence of future generations is increased. If, on the other hand, intelligence can be raised or lowered by environmental influences, then most of us, because we place a positive value on high intelligence, want to do what we can to avoid experiences that may lower intelligence and to cultivate those that may increase it.

In facing the nature-versus-nurture question, the psychologist first of all removes the "versus" from it and asks simply, "What is the *relative contribution of hereditary and environmental factors* to intelligence?" This question can be approached in a variety of ways through several logics. It has been.

Bearing on the heredity-environment question are a number of lines of investigation, each of which deserves attention. Among these are the studies of family resemblance in intelligence, the related studies of the intelligence of fraternal and identical twins, studies of foster children, studies of the effects of special environments or of special experiences, and studies of the constancy or inconstancy, over the years, of intelligence test scores. We will examine at least some specimen investigations in each of these areas.

FAMILY RESEMBLANCE

If intelligence is determined primarily by hereditary factors, we reason, then there should be family resemblance in intelligence just as there are family resemblances in eye color and height and strength, which are known to be directly influenced by hereditary factors. A number of studies show decided family resemblances in intelligence. One typical research (Conrad and Jones, 1940), for example, found a correlation of .49 between the IQ's of parents and their children, and also between the IQ's of **siblings** (children of the same parents). By comparison, the correlation between a group of randomly selected adults and a group of randomly selected children would be zero. Another study (Newman, Freeman, and Holzinger, 1937) found a correlation of .63 between the IQ's of **fraternal twins** (as compared with the r of .49 mentioned above). IQ's of a certain magnitude, then, tend to run in families. But why should there be a higher correlation between the intelligence of fraternal twins, whose heredity is no more similar than that of any other pair of children of the same parents, than there is between siblings? Perhaps the greater similarity between fraternal twins must be explained by the greater similarity in their life-long experiences. Their very simultaneity may add to the similarity of the treatment they receive at the hands of their parents, siblings, and friends. This notion immediately suggests the possibility that all family resemblances in IQ may be due to similarities in environment. Bearing on this point, there is a higher correlation on intelligence between siblings approximately ten years old—$r = .62$—than between siblings approximately four years old —$r = .40$ (Jones and Conrad, 1954). It appears that the longer children live in the same environment, the more similar they become with respect to intelligence.

On the basis of these data, we clearly cannot say that intelligence is either hereditary or environmentally determined. We see evidence that both nature and nurture are influential.

Of some relevance for the heredity-environment question are studies that show a positive correlation between the socioeconomic status of the parents and the intelligence of children (Havighurst and Janke, 1944; Janke and Havighurst, 1945). The higher IQ's are found among children whose fathers are professional men or leading businessmen. IQ's are lower when the fathers are semiprofessional people, proprietors of small businesses, or skilled or white-collar workers. Lower still are the scores of children of the semiskilled or unskilled la-

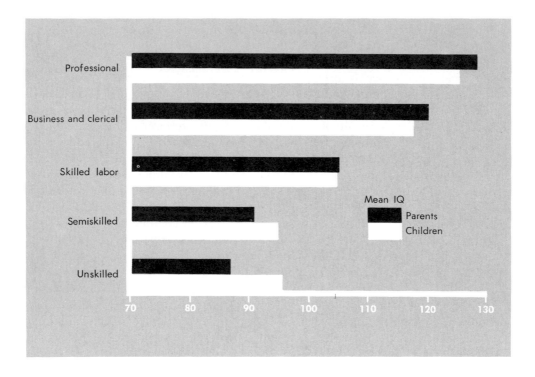

Figure 7–1. PARENTAL PROFESSION AND CHILDREN'S IQ. *The intelligence of children varies with the profession of the parent. The intelligence of parents and children over 12 years was measured by the Army Alpha test; the intelligence of children under 12 was measured by the Stanford-Binet. (Outhit, 1933; reproduced from the* Archives of Psychology.)

borers. Lowest are those children whose fathers are in a laboring or semiskilled occupation and who also have a poor reputation in the community. Additional data on these relationships are to be found in Figure 7–1.

Similar results have been found in other studies. In one, for example (McNemar, 1942), the mean IQ's of children of professional men ranged from 114.8 to 117.5, with the mean varying somewhat from one age group to another. For children of day laborers, by contrast, the means varied from 93.8 to 97.6.

Here again, the facts are clear, but their interpretation is difficult. Do children from more stimulating homes have higher test scores? Is environment a major factor? Or is it that more intelligent people choose or are more able to enter the "higher" occupations and *also* produce more intelligent offspring? If so, heredity would be the principal determiner.

TWIN STUDIES

The existence of identical twins is a fortunate thing for psychological science. Since they come from the same fertilized ovum, their heredity is identical. Any differences between such twins must, therefore, be due to environmental factors. Although it is not always a simple matter to determine with absolute certainty whether twins are indeed identical in all respects (Woodworth, 1941), twins have been used in a number of lines of research where it is important to hold constant all hereditary factors. By *co-twin control*, one of a pair of twins can be regarded as a member of the experimental group, while the other is a member of the control group.

In the matter of intelligence, the research logic when using identical twins is clear: If intelligence is set primarily by the genes, then any pair of identical twins, whatever the difference in their experience with the environment, should have identical intelligence. This is an eminently testable hypothesis.

Identical twins are very similar in intelligence. One study, for example (Newman et al., 1937), found a correlation of .88 between the IQ's of identical twins. The comparable correlation for fraternal twins is .63.

To push this kind of analysis further, we can examine the effect of environment on intelligence if we hold heredity constant (by studying identical twins) and vary the environment. Such a research is made possible because not all pairs of identical twins are reared in the same home. When there are measurements of the intelligence of identical twins who are reared apart, the correlation

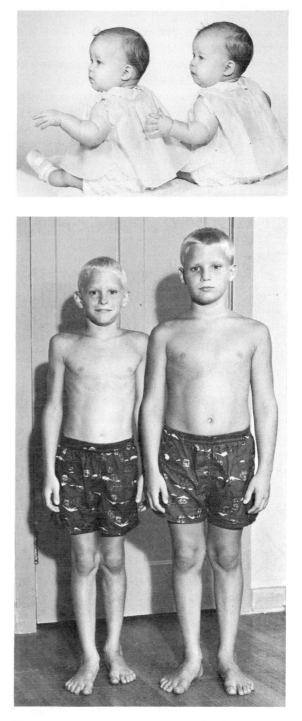

Figure 7–2. TWIN STUDIES. *Twins, both fraternal and identical, have been widely used in research with heredity-environment questions. Fraternal twins, as on the bottom, are not identical in heredity; they are simply simultaneous siblings.*

drops from the .88 reported above to .77 (Newman et al., 1937). The difference between the two coefficients gives evidence of an environmental factor. And there is indication that the environmental factor can exert a very large influence. The IQ's of identical twins reared apart have differed as much as 24 points (Newman et al., 1937). Figure 7–3 presents a brief summary of data on family resemblances in intelligence.

of their biological fathers was .40. By contrast, the correlation of the children's IQ's with the educational level of the foster mothers was .02, and it was .00 with the educational level of foster fathers. Heredity clearly seems to be a strong factor. But we still cannot discount the importance of environment. The researchers just cited "measured" adopted parents' intelligence indirectly, by educational level, and found that adopted children do not take on

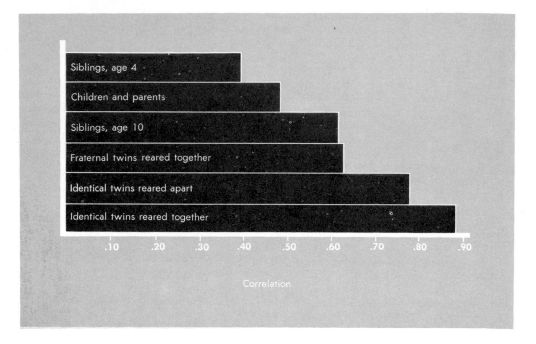

Figure 7–3. FAMILY RESEMBLANCES IN INTELLIGENCE. *The similarity in intelligence varies with similarity of heredity and similarity of environment. The data here come from a number of separate studies cited in the text.*

STUDIES OF FOSTER CHILDREN

Further evidence can be obtained on the heredity-environment question if we study children who have been adopted in infancy. In one study of 100 adopted children (Skodak and Skeels, 1949), the correlation between the intelligence of the children and that of their biological mothers was .44. The correlation of the children's IQ's with the educational level

a similarity to the intelligence of their adopted parents. Other studies, however, reported a growing similarity to the intelligence of the adopting parents (Skeels, 1938; Skodak, 1939; Skodak and Skeels, 1945). And a further study (Skodak, 1950) showed that when two children, unrelated to each other, are adopted into the same home in infancy, they are as similar in intelligence ($r = .65$) as are pairs of natural siblings. We infer that living in the same environment helps produce similarities in intelligence.

So far, then, we have evidence that the level of intelligence of an individual is significantly determined by hereditary factors but that there are also some environmental influences operating.

INFLUENCES OF SPECIAL ENVIRONMENTS

If there is environmental influence on intelligence, then we should be able to find out what particular environmental experience is effective and in what way it is effective. Do intellectually stimulating environments raise intelligence test scores? How much? Do impoverished environments depress IQ's? How much? A number of researchers have tackled these problems.

They have found, for instance, that children who attend nursery school—presumably a more enriched environment than the homes from which the children have come—have higher IQ's than children who do not attend. Results from such studies are not interpretable, however, unless we know something about the intelligence of the children when they entered nursery school. Perhaps only more intelligent parents from the higher socioeconomic groups send their children to nursery school.

In a project designed to bring adequate controls into the study of effects of school on intelligence, Wellman (1940) matched a group of 34 children who attended a nursery school with a control group of 34 from the same community who did not attend school. She tested all 68 children in the fall and again in the spring. Between the two testings, the group attending school gained an average of 7 IQ points, while those not attending lost an average of 3.9 points. Such results seem to show a significant influence of experience on intelligence. But such a conclusion is not completely justified. The factor of parental decisions, as mentioned above, was not controlled. Also, perhaps the in-school subjects benefited from practice at taking tests similar to the intelligence tests or from increased comfort in the presence of the person giving the test.

Other studies seem to confirm the general finding that school increases intelligence test performance. For example, one investigator (Lorge, 1945) compared the intelligence test scores of thirty men at age 34 with the scores of the same men at age 14. Then he divided his subjects into two groups: those who had continued schooling through relatively many grades, and those who had continued through relatively few grades. When matched with respect to test scores at age 14, the group continuing in school scored, on retest, significantly higher. Again, there is an apparently positive effect of schooling.

A very dramatic report of the apparent effects of living in a stimulating environment (Skeels and Dye, 1939) concerns the change in IQ of two children who were transferred from an orphanage to a home for the mentally retarded. One of the children was 13 months old, the other 16 months, at the time of transfer. Both had IQ's of 46, and both were retarded also in physical and motor development. They were placed in a ward with mentally retarded girls, aged 18 to 50 years, many of whom became attached to the babies and paid them a great deal of attention. At the end of six months, when the two youngsters were retested, the IQ's were 77 and 87. After a year, they were 100 and 88. After the "clinical surprise" entailed in these data, the investigators arranged to transfer a number of retarded children, from 1 to 10 years of age, into similar environments. Of a total of thirteen children who were given an experience like that of the first two, all showed gains in IQ, with the gain ranging from 7 to 58 points. These data indicate that a stimulating environment can increase intelligence. Additional data on this point are presented in Figure 7-4.

There is consonant evidence that depressing environments can have the reverse effect. Canalboat children (Gordon, 1923) and backwoods children (Sherman and Key, 1932) seem to show considerable retardation. Such studies as those of Spitz (1953, 1955) and Dennis (1960) show severe developmental retardation in children who are deprived of normal contact with mothers or mother substitutes during the early months of life. Presumably, but not yet demonstrated conclusively, developmental retardation includes retardation in intelligence.

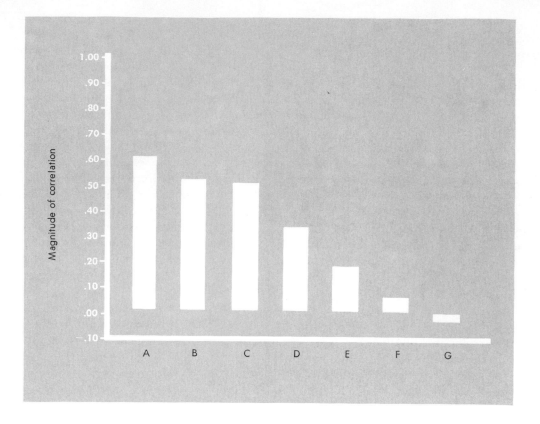

Figure 7–4. SPECIFIC ENVIRONMENTAL FACTORS IN INTELLIGENCE. *Research has helped specify the nature of the stimulation in stimulating environments. A, mother's education; B, father's education; C, opportunity for use of constructive play materials; D, number of hours adults spend daily with child; E, number of playmates in home; F, number of hours father reads to child; G, nutrition index. (Adapted from Van Alstyne, 1929.)*

EXPERIENCE AND INTELLIGENCE: STUDIES OF ANIMALS

A number of investigations conducted with animals appear to bear directly on the question of whether or not early experience has an effect on later intellectual development. Since it is easier to control the early environment of animals than of human subjects (for example, animals can be raised in complete darkness for years if the experimenter needs to do so), the results of these researches are often more interpretable than are those deal-

ing with effects of enriched or deprived early environments on human infants.

A part of one study will illustrate the kind of evidence that has been accumulating in this area since the first deprivation study was done (Hebb, 1949). In the project in question (Thompson and Heron, 1954), two groups of dogs were raised quite differently during the period between their weaning and the time they were 8 months old. One group of thirteen, raised in ordinary wire cages in a laboratory, had relatively little contact either with other dogs or with human beings. To match each of the dogs in this group, a litter mate was taken away from the laboratory and raised as a pet in an environment considerably more enriched than that of a wire mesh cage in a laboratory. Between the ages of 8 and 18 months, the enriched and domesticated dogs took up residence again with their laboratory siblings. At the end of eighteen months, each of the twenty-six dogs was given a variety of "intelligence tests." One of these required that the dog, who could see food through a

Figure 7–5. PARENTAL ATTENTION. *Among the intellectually stimulating experiences is that of receiving adult attention. Other things being equal, children who are often read to will show greater intellectual growth.*

wire screen, turn his back on the food and run away from it in order to circumvent a barrier and get at it. Each dog, after adequate preliminary experience in the test room and with similar but less challenging problems, was given five trials on this barrier test. The dogs who spent their early months in the caged and impoverished environment averaged 72.1 seconds to solve the problem and reach the food. By comparison, the pet dogs averaged 29.4 seconds.

The pet dogs also showed superiority in other tests that seemed to involve intellectual functions. For example, on delayed-reaction tests, the dog saw the experimenter place food behind a screen and was held back for various intervals before he was allowed to go to the food if he could "remember" where it was placed. The pet dogs were significantly superior to the caged dogs in this test.

Numerous results such as these have led one writer (Hunt, 1961) to state that certain kinds of early experiences are vitally necessary if the organism, including perhaps especially the human one, is to develop its intellectual capacity. If the requisite experience is not there at the propitious time, certain crucial learning processes do not occur, and, as a result, there may be a permanent impairment of functional intelligence. Not yet available,

of course, is a full array of data on what kinds of experiences—or deprivations—at what stages of development have what effects on what kinds of organisms.

These results are consonant with those of the study abstracted at the end of the present chapter (Goldfarb, 1955).

CONSTANCY OF THE IQ

Of direct relevance for determining whether intelligence is innately fixed or is substantially a product of experience is the old question of the constancy of the IQ. If intelligence is fixed, the individual's level of intellectual functioning should remain constant throughout life; if we could test the intelligence of a thousand infants at birth and retest them at intervals throughout life, we should not, except for errors of measurement, find changes with time in the relative position of individuals. The person who started life one sigma above the mean should remain one sigma above the mean, even though he and all of his contemporaries do obviously show a developmental increase in level of intellectual functioning. This is a matter that can be examined in the light of fairly abundant available evidence, but evidence that is unfortunately not always of pristine clarity.

RELIABILITY OF TESTS

Over brief periods of time, intelligence test scores do not change very much. This is, of course, another way of saying that intelligence tests have high test-retest reliability. And they do indeed. The test-retest reliability of the Stanford-Binet, though it varies somewhat with the IQ level (Table 7–1), is most frequently found to be around 90 or above (Terman and Merrill, 1937; Thorndike, 1940). Even on children less than 1 year old, a population very difficult to test meaningfully, a test-retest reliability, with the second test coming after a three-month interval, has been found to be as high as .81 (Bayley, 1940).

These levels of reliability testify to the short-term constancy of the IQ. So do data (Fig. 7–6) on the correlation between the

Table 7-1. RELIABILITY OF STANFORD-BINET

IQ LEVEL	INDEX OF RELIABILITY
130 and over	.898
110–129	.912
90–109	.924
70–89	.945
Below 70	.982

The correspondence of scores on forms L and M of the 1937 Revision of the Stanford-Binet is indicated, for various IQ levels, by the correlation coefficient at right. (Terman and Merrill, 1937; by permission of the Houghton Mifflin Co.)

two forms of the Stanford-Binet. Scores obviously do not change very much by the week or by the month. But what about constancy over longer periods? Is there the kind of birth-to-death constancy one would expect if intelligence were innately fixed and development inexorably predetermined? The evidence speaks in the negative.

MEASURED CHANGES WITH AGE

Intelligence, whether conceived as Intelligence A (inherited potential) or as Intelligence B (present functional level) obviously changes with age. Most children can handle problems this year that were beyond them last year. There is evidence also that they change in other than this developmental sense. Individual IQ's change; that is, the individual's level of functioning, when compared with that of his peers, changes—sometimes quite dramatically.

In the research reported above (Bayley, 1940) on the reliability of infant tests of intelligence, where the test-retest reliability was .81 after three months, the comparable correlation based on comparable procedures dropped to .39 after twenty-one months and to .22 after thirty months. By the time the children (originally tested before they were 1 year old) had reached the age of 6 years, the correlation between test and retest had virtually disappeared altogether.

Similar results are reported in reviews of research on people in their teens and in young adulthood (Thorndike, 1933, 1940). Where the short-term test-retest constancy (reliability) is high for these subjects, .89, the correlations between the original test and later tests tend to fall, though not as sharply as with young children. After a ten-month interval, the correlation drops from .89 to .87; after thirty months it is .81, and after five years it falls to .70. In individual cases, the change in IQ over a period of years may amount to as much as 46 points (Hilden, 1949). And nearly 10 per cent of one group, tested over an eighteen-year period, changed by as much as 30 points (Honzik, Macfarlane, and Allen, 1948).

PERSONALITY FACTORS AND CHANGES IN INTELLIGENCE

Tested intelligence tends to move upward in an intellectually stimulating environment. But given what appears to be an equally stimulating environment, some children show an increase in IQ while others do not. The personality factors associated with increase were delineated in a study (Baker, Sontag, and Nelson, 1958) of 140 children, who were repeatedly tested on intelligence and other variables from age 6 to 10. The children who showed an IQ increase between 6 and 10 years of age differed in personality from those who decreased over the same period. The children who increased tended to be (1) more competitive, (2) less emotionally dependent on their parents, (3) more likely to solve problems than to avoid them, (4) less well behaved at home, (5) more often engaged in self-initiated activities, (6) more able to work without being prodded or urged by their teachers, (7) more satisfied with their work itself than with praise from others, and (8) more inclined to express hostility toward their brothers and sisters.

In this study it was also found that boys are more likely than girls to show an increase in tested intelligence over time—probably because of the social pressure on girls to assume a feminine role, which does not call for the conspicuous use of intellectual skills.

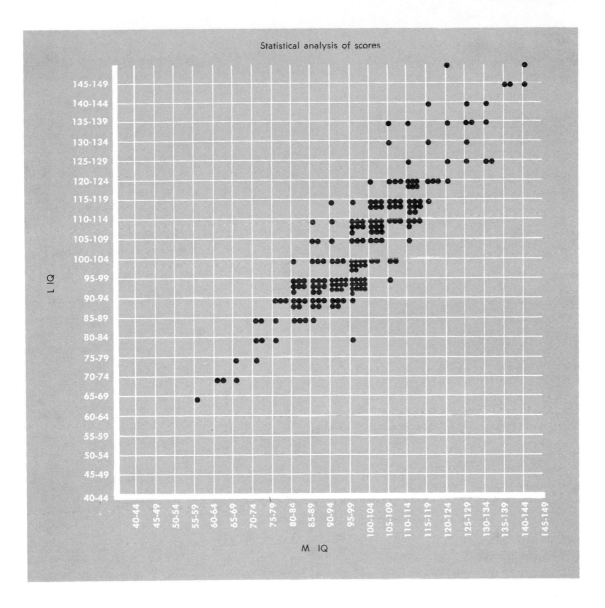

Figure 7–6. STANFORD-BINET RELIABILITY. *When scores on the L-form of the Stanford-Binet are plotted against the scores on the alternate M-form, the above scatter plot is obtained. (Terman and Merrill, 1937; reproduced by permission of Houghton Mifflin Co.)*

That intellectual functioning is entwined with the adjustment of the whole person seems clear. But do the relationships reported here mean that certain children—namely, those who have hereditarily determined temperamental traits of a bustling and active na-

ture—"profit" more from environmental opportunities? Or do parental and other environmental forces operate to suppress both the intellectual and nonintellectual activities of some children and stimulate those of others? Both factors could be operating, but there is much related evidence indicating the powerful influence of the home environment and parental attitudes on many phases of personality development.

The following case, although highly unusual, gives concrete illustration of ways in which personality factors enter into intellectual performance.

The Case of Danny:
Personality Factors in Intellectual Performance

Danny was born January 15, 1929. He entered kindergarten at the age of 5 years and was such a misfit that after a few weeks he was given a Binet test. The following are records of the four tests given before the end of grade 6, with the date of test, chronological age, mental age, and IQ.

2-2-34	Age 5-0	MA 4-2	IQ 82
5-9-35	Age 6-4	MA 6-2	IQ 98
6-8-37	Age 8-5	MA 9-4	IQ 111
12-3-40	Age 11-11	MA 15-9	IQ 132

The first test showed such mental immaturity that Danny was excluded from kindergarten for a year. The next year he moved into another school district. This time his Binet score seemed normal; and in September, in spite of his lack of social adjustment, he was placed in the first grade. The teachers complained that Danny seemed to live in a world of his own, was noticeably poor in motor coordination, and had a worried look on his face most of the time. The mother was called in, and only then was light thrown on his peculiarities.

The mother explained that while Danny was still a baby his father developed encephalitis. In order for the mother to work, they lived in the grandparents' home, where Danny could be cared for. Danny's grandfather was a high-strung, nervous old gentleman, who was much annoyed by the child's noise and at times expostulated so violently that Danny became petrified with fear. The grandfather's chief aim was to keep things quiet and peaceful at any cost. When Danny was excluded from kindergarten, the mother took him from the grandparents' home.

The next few years were a period of educational, social, and emotional growth for the starved child. He amazed his teachers with his achievement. He became an inveterate reader and could solve arithmetic problems far beyond his grade level. He was under a doctor's care much of the time and was also treated by a psychiatrist because of his marked fears. He made friends with boys in spite of physical inferiority (from Lowell, 1941, pp. 341–356).

INTELLIGENCE IN LATER LIFE

It is a widespread general belief that older people are not so "bright" as they once were; and a number of research studies seem, on the surface at least, to support this common-sense contention. In the extensive testing program during World War I, scores on the Army Alpha Test steadily decreased from young groups of 20 years or less to older groups of up to 50 and 60 years of age. The following table presents typical data (Yerkes, 1921):

Age	Average Score
20	150
20–24	146
25–30	143
31–40	133
41–50	125
51–60	120

The same trend was found among the citizens of nineteen New England villages (Jones and Conrad, 1933). The decline, which is not pronounced in such well-practiced skills as vocabulary, is most apparent where the tests require response to novel situations. Such results have been interpreted as support for the old saw "You can't teach an old dog new tricks."

The two studies cited above, as well as some more recent ones (Tyler, 1956) reporting very similar results, are **cross-sectional** studies. They are carried out by finding a group of 20-year-olds, a group of 30-year-olds, a group of 40-year-olds, and so on, and testing them all *at the same time* on the same test or test battery. When another approach, the **longitudinal** one, is employed, different conclusions emerge—conclusions more to the liking of older people. The longitudinal approach is essentially that employed in the previously reported studies, in which the same group of individuals was followed for a period of years. When this approach is used with adults, intelligence is *not* found to diminish with age —at least not through middle age. When the test scores of a group of middle-aged people were compared with the scores they themselves made thirty years earlier as college freshmen, the middle-aged scores were *higher* on every subtest of the Army Alpha except that dealing with arithmetic (Owens, 1953). Other studies (Bentz, 1953) yield similar results. There is evidence, however, that when longitudinal studies are carried into the years beyond middle age, they reveal a later decline in intelligence.

Why such a discrepancy between cross-sectional and longitudinal studies, and which set of results do we accept? These are questions that cannot now be finally answered, for there are possible sources of bias in each approach. In the cross-sectional approach, it is difficult to gain assurance that all groups being compared are equal in relevant educational opportunity. In the longitudinal approach, there needs to be certainty that those who drop out of the continuing study are not in some biasing way different from those on whom longitudinal data can be gathered; also, it must be determined that the test used has not become outdated, or that "revised" forms are not producing errors of measurement.

There is no incontrovertible evidence that intellectual capacity changes significantly during the mature years.

INTERIM SUMMARY: NATURE AND NURTURE

There is an accumulation of evidence, then, that experience affects the development of intelligence. Certainly, either stimulating or depressing environments can have an effect on tested intelligence (Intelligence B), the functional intelligence that has most to do with the problem solving that occurs outside the testing situation. There has been a recent tendency (Hunt, 1961) to turn away from the view that intelligence is fixed (and all development predetermined) to the view that experience, if it occurs at a developmentally propitious time and in the proper sequences, can be of great significance in determining the intelligence with which the individual regards the events in his world.

If one wishes a simple general statement on the nature-nurture issue in intelligence, the assertion that seems best to fit the facts is as follows: Genetic factors are involved in determining intelligence in that there are hereditarily imposed limits beyond which environmental factors are ineffective; but within hereditarily defined limits, environment—

experience—can exert significant influence on the individual's functional level of intelligence. In other words, Intelligence A, the innate potential for development, is real in that it imposes limits on development; but Intelligence B, the present level of functional intelligence, can be significantly influenced by factors other than Intelligence A.

DISTRIBUTION OF INTELLIGENCE IN THE POPULATION

THE NORMAL CURVE

Intelligence tests are so designed that intelligence is normally distributed (p. 159) in the total population; that is, distributed so that many people have "average" intelligence and few have either very high or very low intelligence. Those who create intelligence tests assume that the attribute is normally distributed, as are such attributes as height and weight. Tests are so devised that, when they are used on a large population, the resulting distribution takes on the essential form of the bell-shaped curve.

In a sense, then, it is not very meaningful to talk about the distribution of intelligence in the population, for we will be talking only about details of the curve of normal distribution. However, when percentages and labels are attached to these details, they take on some meaning.

THE IQ CATEGORIES

The various words used to describe levels of intelligence can be defined with reasonable accuracy in terms of ranges of IQ (Terman and Merrill, 1937). The *normal* category, which embraces 50 per cent of the population, includes IQ's from 90 to 110. Anyone with an IQ of more than 110 is in the upper fourth of the population. IQ's from 110 to 120 place a person in the *superior* category; from 120 to 130, in the *very superior* category; and from 130 to 140, in the *near-genius* category. IQ's over 140 are placed in the *genius* category, a category including less than 1 per cent of the population.

On the other end of the continuum, Terman and Merrill place the *dull normals,* with IQ's between 80 and 90; the *borderline mentally deficient,* between 70 and 80; and the *mentally deficient,* with IQ's of 70 and below. Those in the **mental deficiency** category who have IQ's between 50 and 70 are termed morons.

til recent years, by many others, are now falling into disfavor. The preferred terms for levels of retardation, in descending order of severity, are *mild, moderate, severe,* and *profound.* These descriptive terms, not tied specifically to IQ ranges, are used in the literature produced by the President's Commission on Mental Retardation and, recently, in the scientific literature. Similarly, the terms *mentally deficient* and *genius* are now going out

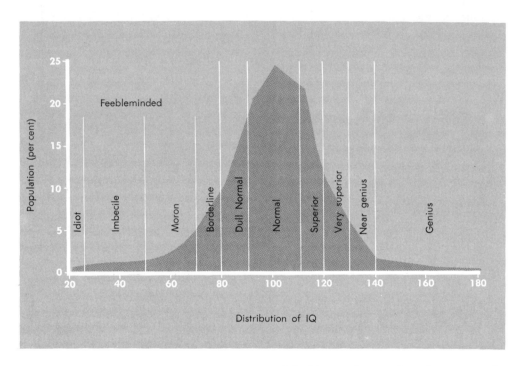

Figure 7–7. DISTRIBUTION OF IQ IN POPULATION. *Scores on the Stanford-Binet Scale are normally distributed in the population. The figure presents the names conventionally given those who score within certain ranges. Also one can read the percentage of the population falling within each range. See the text for a caveat about the changes in terminology for these categories. And see Table 7–2 for the current terms for describing the mentally handicapped. (Terman and Merrill, 1937; reproduced by permission of Houghton Mifflin Co.)*

The older terms **idiot, imbecile,** and **moron,** used by Terman and Merrill in 1937 and, un-

of fashion and may, in a few years, disappear from the technical literature.

MENTAL RETARDATION AND MENTAL DEFICIENCY

About 3 per cent of people in the population have IQ's of less than 70 and are regarded as **mentally retarded.** The President's Commission on Mental Retardation reported in 1963 that every five minutes one person is born mentally handicapped or destined to become so, and that 126,000 such individuals are being born each year.

Many individuals with IQ's of 70 or below

are able, especially with some skillful training, to make their independent way in the world. Others are relatively unable to function unaided in the modern world and need special assistance, sometimes for long periods of time, either at home or in special institutions. The amount and kind of special education or special assistance needed will vary with the level of IQ and with other characteristics of the individual.

Special schools and institutions for the mentally defective endeavor to teach the individual the personal and social skills necessary to care for himself. The less severely deficient are taught the vocational skills necessary to find and hold a job in the community. The schools sometimes score marked success in preparing the higher-grade defective for useful and satisfactory life in the community (Hegge, 1944).

A number of authors (Masland, 1958; Sarason and Gladwin, 1958) point to the need for making a clear distinction between the *mentally deficient* individual and the *mentally retarded* one. Mental deficiency refers to actual intellectual defects produced by hereditary factors, disease, or injury. Mental retardation refers to the failure of an individual—because of an emotional disturbance or lack of opportunity to learn—to utilize or express his native gifts. The mentally retarded individual may often show marked intellectual improvement if personal problems are alleviated or if he is placed in a stimulating environment.

In recent years there has been concrete and encouraging progress toward an understanding of some of the factors that produce mental deficiency. And the new emphasis noted earlier on the role of experience in the development of intelligence leads some observers (Hunt, 1961) to an optimism that we can arrange for children, whatever their innate potential, the kind of experience that is most conducive to the fullest possible development. This latter line of thinking, and the research it will stimulate, holds out hope for the prevention of mental retardation and perhaps also for increasing success in helping those already retarded.

One recent and noteworthy research advance in the area of mental deficiency has involved increased knowledge of individuals who are born with phenyketonuria (known as PKU), a condition in which there is an inability to break down phenylalanine, an amino acid component of all proteins (Jervis, 1954, 1959). This innate peculiarity, occurring about once in every 25,000 births, produces a metabolic disturbance that results in the production of a toxin; the toxin in turn—probably by interfering with the growth of the normal coating of nerve fibers—interferes with the development of the brain. Doctors now can diagnose this condition at birth by the simple expedient of placing ferric chloride on a wet diaper and seeing whether or not a bright green is produced as the ferric chloride interacts with phenylpyruvic acid secreted in the urine. If the defect is present, brain damage can be averted if the child is placed for a period on a diet low in phenylalanine.

Also it has recently been determined (Lejeune et al., 1959) that one kind of mentally deficient individual (the Mongol) is born with an extra chromosome, a fact that is leading to further research in hereditary mechanisms on enzyme systems and cellular metabolism.

INTELLIGENCE AND PERFORMANCE

We know now a good deal about the hereditary and environmental factors in intelligence, about its relative constancy over time, and about its distribution in the population. And we know that extremely low intelligence renders an individual incapable of self-sufficient life in the community. We all believe that the possession of normal or better-than-normal intelligence is a good thing. But what does a certain score on an intelligence test really mean? The student may recognize in this question a return to the problem of *validity* of intelligence tests—the problem of the relation between scores on intelligence tests and various *criteria*, either concurrent or in the future, of intelligent behavior. In the following paragraphs, we confront the general question of the meaning of intelligence test scores. We do so by examining the nontest behavior, or selected nontest behaviors, of individuals who score at various levels on intelligence tests. We begin by looking at the behavior of people who score extremely low and extremely high on tests.

BEHAVIOR OF THE MENTALLY HANDICAPPED

In dealing earlier with mental deficiency, we began to see some of the behavioral consequences of low intelligence. The individual who is severely retarded or defective cannot care for himself in the normal situations of everyday life. He needs special care, and, if he is to gain any kind of self-sufficiency, he has to have special, and often prolonged, training.

Perhaps a clearer notion of the behavior of the mentally handicapped can be gained from the following description of the work they can do (Cronbach, 1960).

The adult with an IQ of 40 can mow lawns, handle freight, do simple laundry work.

With an IQ of 50, an adult can do rough painting, simple carpentry, domestic work. A child with an IQ of 50 can profit from special classes in regular schools.

An adult with an IQ of 60 can repair furniture, paint toys, and harvest vegetables.

At the 70 level, an adult can set and sort type, and do farm work. A child at the same level can do average fifth-grade work, but probably no more.

Table 7–2 presents another description of the performances that can be expected of the mentally handicapped, along with the current descriptive terms used in referring to these individuals.

BEHAVIOR OF THE INTELLECTUALLY GIFTED

The behavior of the mentally deficient contrasts very dramatically with the behavior of those who score at exceptionally high levels on tests of intelligence. In order to build a perspective on the meaning of intelligence, we will do well to look at the sometimes astounding behavior of the intellectually gifted.

Through an analysis of biographies and autobiographies of eminent men of history, and through a comparison of their recorded behavior with that of gifted children of the present, it is possible to make meaningful estimates of how these famous men would have scored had IQ tests been available in their day. John Stuart Mill, for example, is estimated to have had an IQ of 190. At the age of 3, he began the study of Greek under his father's tutelage, and from then to the advanced age of 9 he continued regular reading and reporting upon the Greek classics. At 7 he read Plato in Plato's own language. He began Latin at age 8, and before age 9 he was reading original Latin works. Also at 8 years he began his study of geometry and algebra, and at age 9 went on to conic sections and spherics. He wrote a history of Rome when he was 6½, and at 12 began to assist in correcting the proof of his father's history of India (Cox, 1926).

In Table 7–3, the estimated IQ's represent the mean of the ratings of three judges. The ratings, based on extensive biographical and autobiographical material, are estimates of the individual's IQ at age 17.[1]

The following poem was written by Thomas Chatterton [2] at age 10 years, 2 months.

On the Last Epiphany, or Christ Coming to Judgment

Behold! just coming from above,
The judge, with majesty and love!
The sky divides, and rolls away,
T'admit him through the realms of day!
The sun, astonished, hides its face,
The moon and stars with wonder gaze
At Jesu's bright superior rays! . . .

---

[1] Data here are reprinted from *Genetic Studies of Genius*, Vol. II, "The Early Mental Traits of Three Hundred Geniuses," by Catherine Morris Cox, Stanford University Press, with the permission of the publishers, Stanford University Press. Copyright 1926 by the Board of Trustees of the Leland Stanford University.

[2] *Ibid.*

Table 7–2. DESCRIPTIONS OF THE MENTALLY HANDICAPPED

	PRESCHOOL AGE 0–5 MATURATION AND DEVELOPMENT	SCHOOL AGE 6–21 TRAINING AND EDUCATION	ADULT 21 AND OVER SOCIAL AND VOCATIONAL ADEQUACY
Profound	Gross retardation; minimal capacity for functioning in sensorimotor areas; needs nursing care.	Obvious delays in all areas of development; shows basic emotional responses; may respond to skillful training in use of legs, hands, and jaws; needs close supervision.	May walk, may need nursing care, may have primitive speech; will usually benefit from regular physical activity; incapable of self-maintenance.
Severe	Marked delay in motor development; little or no communication skill; may respond to training in elementary self-help—e.g., self-feeding.	Usually walks, barring specific disability; has some understanding of speech and some response; can profit from systematic habit training.	Can conform to daily routines and repetitive activities; needs continuing direction and supervision in protective environment.
Moderate	Noticeable delays in motor development, especially in speech; responds to training in various self-help activities.	Can learn simple communication, elementary health and safety habits, and simple manual skills, does not progress in functional reading or arithmetic.	Can perform simple tasks under sheltered conditions; participates in simple recreation; travels alone in familiar places; usually incapable of self-maintenance.
Mild	Often not noticed as retarded by casual observer, but is slower to walk, feed self, and talk than most children.	Can acquire practical skills and useful reading and arithmetic to a 3rd to 6th grade level with special education. Can be guided toward social conformity.	Can usually achieve social and vocational skills adequate to self-maintenance; may need occasional guidance and support when under unusual social or economic stress.

Adapted from a report of the President's Commission on Mental Retardation, 1963.

At age 10, Ralph Waldo Emerson[3] wrote "The History of Fortus; a Chivalric Poem." The last eight lines of the work are as follows:

. . . Six score and twenty thousand 'gan the fray,
Six score alone survived the dreadful day.
Ah! hear the groans of those that bled
In that sad plain o'erlaid with dead.
Fortus, who would not quit the field,
Till every foe was forced to yield,

[3] Cox, *Genetic Studies of Genius.*

To tender pity now transformed his wrath,
And from the bloody field pursued his path.

Such precocity, of course, is very rare. But many gifted children of today demonstrate Mill-like behavior at an early age and go on through life showing exceptional behavior. The best-known and most thorough study of the gifted was begun in 1921 by Lewis M. Terman and continued for many years by Terman and his associates (Terman and Oden,

Table 7-3. ESTIMATED IQ'S OF EMINENT MEN

EMINENT MEN WITH EXCEPTIONALLY HIGH IQ'S

Name	Estimated IQ	Work
Adams, J. Q.	165±4	American Statesman
Bentham, Jeremy	180±4	English Writer
Chatterton, Thomas	170±4	English Writer
Coleridge, S. T.	175±4	English Writer
Grotius, Hugo	185±5	Dutch Statesman
Leibniz, G. W.	185±5	German Philosopher
Macaulay, Thomas	180±4	English Writer
Mill, John Stuart	190±4	English Philosopher
Pascal, Blaise	180±5	French Scientist
Pope, Alexander	160±4	English Writer
Schilling, F. W.	175±4	German Philosopher
Voltaire	170±5	French Writer

EMINENT MEN WITH NONEXCEPTIONAL IQ'S

Name	Estimated IQ	Work
Bunyan, John	105±10	English Writer
Cervantes, Miguel de	105±10	Spanish Writer
Cobbett, William	105±9	English Writer
Dryden, John	125±9	English Writer
Faraday, Michael	105±10	English Scientist
Grant, U. S.	110±7	American Soldier
Jackson, Andrew	110±8	American Soldier
Lavoisier, A. L.	120±10	French Scientist
Luther, Martin	115±10	German Religious Leader
Madison, James	120±9	American Statesman
Rembrandt	110±9	Dutch Artist
Saint-Cyr, L. de Gouvion	105±10	French Soldier
Swedenborg, Emanuel	115±10	Swedish Religious Leader

1947). Terman selected 1,500 children with IQ's of 140 and above, and began the study that was to follow them into adulthood.

The children selected on the basis of high intelligence turned out to be exceptional in other respects. Their weight at birth was above average. They were, on the average, more than an inch taller than their less gifted colleagues of the same age. At the time the testing began, most of them were a grade ahead of their age group in school. They showed clear superiority also in leadership and social activity. Such data explode the myth that high intelligence is connected with peculiarity or weakness. There seems to be a tendency for many highly regarded human attributes to come in the same package.

What about the adult achievement of these gifted children? Do the gifted "burn out," as the common belief has it, or does high intelligence generally lead to high achievement? Terman's gifted children far exceeded any average group in such criteria of achievement as advanced academic degrees, listings in *Who's Who* and *American Men of Science*, number of publications, amount of income, and occupational level. Also, perhaps indicating a superior emotional adjustment, relatively few of these people were divorced. But not all of Terman's bright ones went on to glowing achievement. Not all of them went to college; some turned instead to nonprofessional careers. Of those who did go to college, not all by any means had distinguished records. In a study of the personality difference between those of his sample who "succeeded" and those who did not, it became evident that such factors as perseverance, self-confidence, and integration toward goals are intimately involved in achievement.

INTELLIGENCE AND SCHOOL SUCCESS

Intelligence tests were first invented for predicting success in school. And they are most frequently used today in connection with decisions on placement in school and on admission to institutions of higher learning. The question of the relation between test scores and academic success continues to interest both researchers and those who must make practical decisions about the educational future of individuals.

A number of studies have reported the average IQ's of individuals who successfully reach the various education levels. One investigator (Wrenn, 1949) reports that the average Stanford-Binet IQ was 118 for college freshmen, 123 for graduated seniors, and 141 for those obtaining the Ph.D. degree.

After reviewing many studies of intelligence tests as predictors of school success, one author (Tyler, 1956) reports a range of correlations running from .40 to .60. Correlations of these magnitudes signify a clear and definite relationship between IQ and academic performance. When tests with these coefficients of validity are in competition with casual judgments on the part of parents or teachers, then they succeed conspicuously. There is by no means perfect validity here, however. Obviously, many bright people do not do well in school and many not-so-bright manage to handle school work successfully. The student with a high intelligence is not assured of automatic academic success, nor should the student who scores at an undistinguished level toss himself into the slough of despond. Factors other than intelligence obviously contribute to academic success.

Perhaps the factors of perseverance, self-confidence, and integration toward the goal are significant here too (Terman and Oden, 1947).

There are a number of difficulties in predicting school success from intelligence tests. For one thing, not all tests correlate equally well with academic performance in various subjects. For example, the Otis Intelligence Test correlates .74 with grades in English, .68 with algebra grades, .30 with Latin grades, and .28 with German grades. Such research findings, though they clarify the relation between tests and performance, raise as many questions as they answer. What *does* relate significantly with success in Latin and German? In addition, the tests usually do not permit long-range predictions of school success. Tests given this year predict performance this year—correlations running as high as .80 (Bayley, 1949)—better than they will predict performance further in the future. If we measure IQ in the first grade and then, when our subjects are in college, run a correlation between these early IQ's and college grades, the relationship is likely to be small. One author (Travers, 1949) reports a correlation of .21 in just that situation.

Intelligence tests, then, can predict academic success—but not perfectly. Although they do predict more successfully than any other single test, judgments about future academic performance probably should not be made on the basis of intelligence tests alone. Any counseling psychologist, dealing with a student who needs academic or vocational counseling, wants to know the student's IQ. But he will also want much other information—information about motivations, interests, work habits, special abilities. Academic achievement involves the whole person, not just his IQ.

The growing body of literature dealing with academic achievement also suggests that factors other than intelligence are involved both in ordinary achievement and in what is regarded as highly creative activity. One such study (Gough, 1955) related college performance and personality attributes. In this study, a large number of gifted students were administered a comprehensive personality inventory. Half of these students had achieved conspicuously, and half had achieved less than normally would be expected. The two groups, the overachievers and underachievers, differed significantly in their test results with respect to four personality dimensions: delinquency, social responsibility, academic motivation in high school, and academic motivation in college. These results led the investigators to the following conclusions:

1. The constructive use of personal talent and genius is part of a larger context of socialization within the individual.
2. Academic achievement among intellectually gifted persons is a form of social behavior.
3. Academic underachievement among intellectually gifted persons is a form of social behavior.

There are additional data in Chapter 8 showing a positive relationship between the individual's score on a test of need for achievement and his academic performance both in high school and college.

INTELLIGENCE AND OCCUPATIONAL SUCCESS

There has been extensive use of psychological tests in the assessment and selection of people who are candidates for various kinds of jobs and professions. Both in mass selection procedures, such as those employed in selecting from among thousands of enlisted men those to be sent to officer-candidate school, and in vocational counseling, wherein the counselor and the client attempt to gain a full picture of the client's capacities and inclinations, tests of intelligence figure prominently. There can be no doubt that some lines of work require higher intelligence than others. And there can be no doubt that the individual without the minimal requisite intelligence for a given line of work is in for trouble—and so is his employer.

The general relationship between intelligence and occupational performance can be seen in data relating intelligence to the prestige or social status of various occupations.

The occupations carrying the greatest prestige, such as medicine, banking, or science, tend to be populated by people of the highest intelligence. People of lower intelligence are found in the occupations of lower prestige. One investigator (Ball, 1938) found correlations of .57 and .71, in two groups, between intelligence tested in childhood and the rated prestige of the occupations the individuals entered. In the face of such data, do we say that the brighter people had sense enough to choose the more prestigeful and generally more rewarding occupations? Or do we take the position that the more prestigeful professions actually demand more intelligent behavior? We probably would incline toward the latter interpretation, but the bare correlations do not give a definitive answer.

A more thoroughgoing study in the same area related scores on the Army General Classification Test to the civilian occupations followed before military service by 18,782 Air Force enlisted men (Harrell and Harrell, 1945). The scores for accountants, lawyers, and engineers were in the upper ranges. Machinists, foremen, and sales clerks fell in the middle ranges. Farmers, miners, and teamsters averaged relatively low. Similar relationships were found in connection with the use of the Army Alpha in World War I (Yerkes, 1921). A more recent study is reported in Table 7–4.

INTELLIGENCE AND CREATIVITY

There is abundant evidence that factors other than intelligence enter into human performance. Since the middle of the 1950s there has been a large and regularly enlarging volume of research on creativity—on its nature, on factors that contribute to it, on ways to measure it, on ways to predict it, and, of direct concern for us in the present context, on its relation to intelligence.

If you were to ask the next dozen students you see what they think is the relation between intelligence and creativity, most of them would probably say that the two are closely related. Probably not so many would think that college *grades* and creativity are related, for many students, particularly those

Table 7–4. INTELLIGENCE AND OCCUPATIONS

OCCUPATION	MEDIAN SCORE AGCT	OCCUPATION	MEDIAN SCORE AGCT
Accountant	129	Locomotive Fireman	108
Student, Medicine	127	Student, High School	
Chemist	127	Vocational	108
Student, Chemical		Sheet Metal Worker	106
Engineering	125	Riveter, Pneumatic	106
Auditor	124	Brakeman, Railway	105
Stenographer	122	Structural Steel	
Pharmacist	121	Worker	104
Draftsman, Mechanical	120	Plumber	103
Salesman	115	Automotive	
Store Manager	115	Mechanic	102
Embalmer	114	Chauffeur	100
Student, High School		Hospital Orderly	99
Academic	113	Tailor	97
Shipping Clerk	111	Truck Driver, Light	95
Stock Clerk	110	Longshoreman	95
Machinist	110	Barber	93
Policeman	109	Teamster	87
Telephone Operator	109	Farm Worker	86
Machinist's Helper	108	Lumberjack	85

Scores on the Army General Classification Test for 81,553 white enlisted men in World War II were related to 227 civilian occupations from which they came. The table above gives a sample of data from the study. (After Stewart, 1947. Adapted with permission from Occupations.)

who live with C's and D's, cherish the idea that "grinds" have neither much intelligence nor much creativity but manage by stolid persistence to join the grim group at the A end of the grading curve. Such students may have some empirical considerations going for them. We have seen that the correlation between IQ and grades is not excessively high, and that other factors enter into academic performance. There is also some evidence that neither the ability to get good grades nor the ability to score high on an intelligence test is closely related to an individual's capacity to achieve the significantly original or to create what one writer has called "effective surprise" (Bruner, 1962).

What is creativity? This question is still troublesome, even after a decade of research on what everybody agrees probably should be termed creativity. Creativity, although now a highly valued quality, is also an elusive one. What do highly creative people *do*? And what do they do, if anything, that sets them apart from the noncreative people? Or from highly intelligent people?

One investigator (Guilford, 1950) suggests that we can approach this problem by making a distinction between two basic intellectual processes: *convergent* thinking and *divergent* thinking. This discussion is stated by two other psychologists as follows:

The one mode [convergent] tends toward retaining the known, learning the predetermined, and conserving what is. The second mode [divergent] tends toward revising the known, ex-

ploring the undetermined, and constructing what
might be (Getzels and Jackson, 1962, pp. 14–15).

The second mode, the *divergent* mode, is
presumably descriptive of the cognitive style
of the creative individual.

If such a distinction is meaningful, then we
ought to observe differences in what convergent and divergent thinkers actually do. Getzels and Jackson explored these differences
by administering to more than 500 public-
school students, in grades 6 through 12, tests
of intelligence and a battery of five "creativity
tests": (1) a word-association test, in which
the student was asked to give as many definitions as possible for fairly common stimulus
words; (2) a test for "uses of things," in which
the subject (S) was asked to give as many
uses as he could for familiar objects such as
"bricks"; (3) a "hidden-shapes test," which
required the S's to find geometric figures hidden in more complex figures; (4) a fables
test, where the S was asked to furnish a last
line to an incomplete fable; and (5) a "make-
up problems" test, in which the S was given
a number of paragraphs containing a good
deal of numerical information and was asked
to make up as many mathematical problems
as he could, using the available information.

The authors report small correlations between scores on these tests and regular intelligence tests. Such results were confirmed
by another investigator (Torrance, 1960),
who reported mean correlations between
these five Getzels-Jackson tests that varied,
according to the group and the intelligence
test used, from .16 in one group to .32 in another—all relatively low.

So there is not much tendency for individuals to score at the same level on "creativity
tests" and on tests of intelligence. Does behavior in nontest situations relate to these
facts about scores? The two investigators went
at this problem by selecting a group of students who were in the top 20 per cent on the
"creativity" tests but *below* the top 20 per
cent in IQ; then, on a number of variables,
they compared this high-creativity group with
a group of 28 who scored in the top 20 per
cent on IQ but below that level on the "crea-

tivity" tests. This high-intelligence group contrasted in a number of ways with the high-
creativity group. The two groups, in spite of
a difference of 23 points in mean IQ's, performed equally well in school. The high-
intelligence students tended to be more highly
approved by their teachers and were more
"success oriented" than were the high-creativity students. The high-creativity students also
showed significantly more freedom, more originality, more humor, more incongruity, more
violence, and more playfulness than did the
high-intelligence group in their responses to
projective tests.

Such evidence begins to bring meaning to
the concept of creativity and to indicate that
it is not closely related to conventionally
measured intelligence. A good deal of work has
been done on the defining of creativity (Torrance, 1962; Taylor, 1964) and on the construction of tests to measure it (Torrance,
1962). One writer (Torrance, 1962) lists 84
personality characteristics that, according to
various researchers, distinguish the creative
from the noncreative individual. Another
writer (Gough, 1964) summarizes what he
sees as consistent findings in all this literature:

1. Creative thinking is flexible thinking.
2. Perceptions and associations of the creative
   person tend toward the less common, the
   less typical.
3. The creative individual shows a concern for
   form and elegance, a concern that carries
   him beyond mere correctness and accuracy.
4. The creative personality is intuitive and
   empathic; he is psychologically minded.
5. The creative personality is open rather than
   judgmental; the creative person perceives
   much before making up his mind and takes
   delight in the novel.
6. The creative personality is aesthetically
   sensitive.
7. The creative personality is emotionally and
   socially sensitive.
8. The creative personality is a complex personality.

The likelihood that an individual will make
a creative contribution to the human enter-

prise depends, obviously, on an array of psychological traits, many of which are not yet clearly identified. Also, of course, achievement depends on environmental factors such as opportunity and stimulation. A recognition of the complex array of factors involved in creative accomplishment can lead to an appreciation of the fulsome intricacy of the human being's intellectual life and at the same time put into perspective the IQ variable. Intelligence test scores relate meaningfully to many facets of human performance. But they by no means explain all that is good and valuable—and creative.

SEX DIFFERENCES IN INTELLIGENCE

Opinions run strong on the question of the relative intelligence of men and women. Are there facts that may be brought to bear on this particular skirmish in the "battle of the sexes"? Psychologists have tackled the problem, but, as is so often the case, the best answer now available is complex—an answer that does not stifle debate but may, instead, advance productive discussion.

DIFFERENCES IN GENERAL INTELLIGENCE

Studies comparing men and women, or boys and girls, on *general intelligence* most often have uncovered negligible differences. A Scottish research, for example (Scottish Council for Research on Education, 1949), found the average IQ of boys to be four points higher than that for girls on an individually administered test. When the same subjects were given a group test, the girls exceeded the boys by an average of two IQ points. Such differences, though statistically significant, cannot be given practical significance—especially when they are contradictory. On the matter of over-all general intelligence, the discovered differences between males and females are likely to be due more to the tests than to actual differences between males and females.

SPECIFIC DIFFERENCES

When we refine our question and ask whether there are qualitative intellectual differences between men and women, we get a different answer.

On the 1937 Stanford-Binet (from which were eliminated those items showing large sex differences), girls were found to do better on tasks involving language, aesthetic matters, and social skills. Boys were better on mathematical, mechanical, and absurdity items (McNemar, 1942).

On the matter of verbal skills, a number of studies have found that girls are superior to boys. That this difference may be a matter only of verbal fluency is indicated by a study (Terman and Tyler, 1954), in which boys and girls were equal in size of vocabulary and ability to comprehend written material, but differed appreciably in speed of reading. The girls could read more rapidly.

In a study comparing primary mental abilities of boys and girls (Havighurst and Breese, 1947), a battery of tests was administered to a large number of Midwestern 13-year-olds: girls outdid boys in *number, verbal fluency, reasoning*, and *memory;* boys scored better on problems of spatial relationships. A similar study in Massachusetts (Hobson, 1947) reports similar results. Girls again were superior in verbal fluency, reasoning, and memory; boys were superior in space. There were no differences in ability to handle problems of numbers.

We are relatively safe in concluding, then, that males show a superiority in dealing with problems of space, while females perform better in memory, reasoning, and verbal fluency. There is some evidence that girls are more intelligent in matters of aesthetics and social skills, and that boys are better on mechanical problems. In *over-all measures of intelligence, there are very probably no important differences.*

SEX AND ACHIEVEMENT

On the basis of the data on sex differences in intelligence, we might expect men and women to achieve equally high but qualitatively different goals and positions in the world's affairs. Of course, our expectations would be more confident if intelligence were the *only* determiner of achievement. We know it is not. And the great discrepancy between the achievement patterns of men and women gives us further evidence that factors other than IQ enter into an individual's success in handling life's challenges.

Females consistently outscore males in achievement in school. One author (Tyler, 1956), summarizing the evidence on this point, writes as follows:

It is recognized that girls are less frequently retarded [below "normal" expectations] and more frequently accelerated than boys. More of them receive high marks and fewer of them receive unsatisfactory marks. When batteries of achievement tests rather than school ratings are used to evaluate school performance, the differences are less marked but are still, on the whole, in favor of girls.[4]

Such an observation is consonant with the fact that girls mature—intellectually, educationally, and physically—more rapidly than boys, and in any grade in school can be expected to outperform boys because of greater maturity, not because of inherent differences in intellect.

When we examine achievement beyond school and college, defining achievement as outstanding accomplishment in the fields of science, arts, and letters, quite a different picture emerges. Very few women are listed among the world's great achievers. For example, only 32 women are listed in a 1903 catalog of the 1,000 most eminent people in the world (Cattell, 1903). Nor do women occupy much space in lists of geniuses (Ellis, 1904), or in *Who's Who*. And the title of the volume *American Men of Science* speaks for the rarity of female accomplishment in scientific endeavor.

In sheer intelligence, women have as much capacity as men for achieving. Why do they not achieve? We may take the stand that the gifted woman who raises a family with great skill and wisdom does actually score a cardinal achievement, and that it is a commentary on the man-dominated state of the world that such achievements are not visibly recognized. Or we may find more reasonable the position that the female role in Western civilization is so defined and restricted that women are trained, in subtle ways, to stick to the gentler, less competitive, and less visible activities. Many women themselves accept such a definition of their proper ladylike role in life. We must list social expectancies—both what we expect of ourselves and what others expect of us—as a significant factor in individual achievement. (See Chap. 19.) Of course, we must not forget that women do bear children. But cultures differ widely with respect to the amount of time the mother is expected to devote to the intimate care of children. Perhaps the coming century, with the increasing emphasis on creative achievement, will move more women out of the home, out of the standard American female's role, and into activities where more visible achievements are possible.

RACE DIFFERENCES IN INTELLIGENCE

Discussions of racial differences in intelligence have probably been characterized by even more heat and less light than have living-room debates on the superiority of one sex over the other. Thinking about any aspect of the whole question of racial superiority or inferiority is beclouded by ethnocentrism, by the very human but sometimes regrettable tendency of most of us to assume automatically that our own group—our church, our state, our nation, our culture, our race—is inherently and incontrovertibly better than any other. When ethnocentrism is strong, facts are relatively powerless, and the logic of feeling replaces the logic of intellect.

Psychologists have accumulated an extensive array of facts having relevance for the question of racial differences in intelligence.

---

[4] From *The Psychology of Human Differences* by Leona E. Tyler. Copyright 1956, Appleton-Century-Crofts, Inc., p. 249.

Before becoming involved with these facts, however, we will do well to re-examine briefly the nature of an intelligence test and to look at some of the problems encountered when we wish to compare the intelligence of one group with that of another.

BACKGROUND CONSIDERATIONS

An intelligence test is a carefully selected array of items or problems. The items are selected so that individuals of the same age and with the same opportunity to have become familiar with the content of the items will find some of the items easy and some difficult. Two six-year-old boys, for example, confront a test item concerning cups, saucers, and spoons. One boy solves the problem; the other does not. We can assume that the one who solves it is, at least on that item, more intelligent than the one who fails, *provided* the two boys (a) are equally familiar with these objects, (b) are equally interested in them, and (c) are equally motivated to solve problems presented them by adults. If the two boys are not equally familiar with dining implements, then their behavior may not be related entirely to intelligence. If one, for some reason, has a deep-seated dislike of cups, saucers, and spoons, something other than intelligence may show through his response. And if one boy is compliant where the other is rebellious in the presence of an adult examiner, these nonintellectual factors will influence test performance. When a psychologist constructs an intelligence test, he selects items that are known, on the whole, to be equally familiar and equally interesting to all members of the population he wishes to test. And, at least in administering individual tests, the skilled examiner can often handle the problem of differential test motivation. Intelligence tests work. They succeed in comparing the responses of one individual with the responses of another and in assigning a meaningful, though relative, quantitative index of intelligence to each individual.

Now let us see what problems are encountered when we ask a six-year-old from another culture to solve a problem involving the din-ing tools familiar in our own. That youngster is faced with a foreign language, a foreign adult, and with objects he may never have seen. His behavior can obviously not be compared in intelligence with the behavior of the two other children.

One can see the problems involved when anyone wants to make comparisons of one cultural group with another. Attempts are being made to create tests by which cross-cultural comparisons can be made, but the assignment is a troublesome one (Davis and Havighurst, 1948).

This summary obviously suggests that there are difficulties in comparing the intelligence of one group with another. We touched upon some of these difficulties when we examined the differences between males and females. Boys and girls, by training and perhaps by nature, have different familiarities and different interests. Tests that are designed for use on both boys and girls, however, can control for these two factors so that the test responses, whether by boys or girls, can reveal intelligence rather than something else.

EVIDENCE ON RACIAL DIFFERENCES IN INTELLIGENCE

Now, against this background, let us look at the data on racial differences in intelligence. Most of the research in this area has been concerned with the difference between Negroes and whites in the United States. The first of these studies, conducted during and not long after World War I, yielded a consistent over-all result: whites have a higher average IQ than Negroes (Yerkes, 1921; Garth, 1925). Many people are inclined to accept these results as proving what they knew all along—that whites, by nature, are intellectually superior to Negroes. Then came studies that investigated regional variations in average IQ scores. These studies brought some confusion to the issue. It was found, for example, (1) that Northerners scored higher, on the average, than Southerners; (2) that within any region whites scored higher than Negroes; and (3) that Negroes from such states as New York, Ohio, and Illinois scored higher than whites from Arkansas, Kentucky, and Missisippi (Benedict and Weltfish, 1943; Tyler, 1956). Data on the latter point are presented in Table 7–5.

Philadelphians scored much as they had in the first grade, with a 9A mean IQ of 93.7. It seems clear that the school environment in Philadelphia produced these changes in the

Table 7–5. ARMY ALPHA SCORES FOR SOUTHERN WHITES AND NORTHERN NEGROES BY STATES

WHITES		NEGROES	
State	*Median Score*	*State*	*Median Score*
Mississippi	41.25	Pennsylvania	42.00
Kentucky	41.50	New York	45.02
Arkansas	41.55	Illinois	47.35
Georgia	42.12	Ohio	49.50

(Reprinted with permission from Negro Intelligence and Selective Migration, *Otto Klineberg, Columbia University Press, 1935.)*

How might we account for such results? An obvious hypothesis is that such differences reflect different amounts of education. An investigation bearing directly on this notion (Lee, 1951) showed that Southern-born Negro children, after moving into Philadelphia schools, showed consistent gains in IQ. This investigator measured the intelligence of a control group of Negro children who were born in Philadelphia and who had entered the Philadelphia schools at the beginning of the first grade. The experimental group consisted of Negro children who had recently moved, or who moved during the study, from Southern states and entered the Philadelphia schools. Measurements on both the control and experimental groups were made at five grade levels between the first and ninth grades. During their first year, the children who moved from the South and entered school were, at every grade level, lower in IQ than Negroes who had started school in Philadelphia. The longer the Southern children stayed in the Philadelphia schools, the higher their IQ's became. A Southern-born group entering in 1A had an average IQ at that time of 86.5. The native Philadelphia group in grade 1A had a mean IQ of 92.1. But by grade 9A, the Southern-born group had risen to an average of 92.8, whereas the

test scores of the newcomers. The data in Table 7–6 give related evidence on the effects of a stimulating environment on Negro intelligence. Table 7–7 presents data on general geographical differences in intelligence.

Such evidence demonstrates that educational experience makes a difference in Negro scores on IQ. Our earlier data (p. 183) support the conclusion that stimulating environments can raise the IQ and that depressing environments may lower it. But are all the measured differences between whites and Negroes due to different education or to differentially stimulating environments? Or is there room for evidence of an hereditary difference? Such questions cannot be given final answers.

We might approach the question not on the basis of presently demonstrable fact but on what seems most likely in the light of all we know about the matter. We know that stimulating environments and good educational opportunities do make a difference in tested intelligence. We know that familiarity with and interest in the content of intelligence tests can influence the intelligence test scores of individuals. We recognize the possibility that Negro children being tested by white researchers may show a resentment that will adversely affect performance. These factors seem to many psychologists (Klineberg, 1935; Benedict and Weltfish, 1943) sufficient grounds to account for all obtained differences between races. But such a stand is one that can be reversed by new and keenly relevant facts —if and when they can be set down.

Table 7–6. STANFORD-BINET INTELLIGENCE QUOTIENTS OF NEGROES AND LENGTH OF NEW YORK RESIDENCE

GROUP	NUMBER	AVERAGE IQ
Less than 1 Year	18	82.6
1–2 Years	17	84.5
2–3 Years	19	83.0
3–4 Years	22	85.9
More than 4 Years	21	87.7
New York born	50	89.3
All Southern born	97	84.9

Data based on a study of 147 ten-year-old Negro boys. (Reprinted with permission from Negro Intelligence and Selective Migration, *Otto Klineberg, Columbia University Press, 1935.)*

Whether or not there is a native difference between Negroes and whites, between Northerners and Southerners, between Ohioans and Mississippians, it should be remembered (1) that obtained differences are relatively small and (2) that when we compare the distribution of intelligence in one population with its distribution in another, there is in the groups we are considering always a sizable overlap; the brightest people in the lower group are generally far higher in IQ than are the dullest people in the other.

SUMMARY

Table 7–7. INTELLIGENCE AND GEOGRAPHICAL REGION

AREA OF RESIDENCE	PER CENT OF FRESHMEN EXCEEDING CRITICAL SCORE
New England	54
Middle Atlantic	60
East North Central	55
West North Central	57
South Atlantic	40
East South Central	32
West South Central	39
Mountain	52
Pacific	55
Territories	25
All areas	53

After World War II hundreds of thousands of college students were given intelligence tests to

1. Intelligence is probably the best defined and most thoroughly studied of the enduring attributes of human behavior; there is a body of scientific knowledge concerning it.

2. Intelligence may be defined as an inferred and relatively enduring behavioral attribute relating to an individual's capacity to solve a certain variety of problems.

3. An intelligence test is a device for eliciting responses to a wide variety of problems of a verbal, perceptual, and symbolic nature, and for comparing (a) the responses of one individual at different times and (b) the responses of one individual with those of another.

4. The term intelligence is frequently used with two separable meanings: (a) an innate potential and (b) an average level of

performance or comprehension at a specified time. The two usages should not be confused. It is the latter usage that refers to the intelligence that intelligence tests test.

5. Bearing on the relative contribution of heredity and environment to the tested intelligence of the individual are facts showing family resemblance in intelligence, a greater resemblance between identical twins than between other siblings, and a greater resemblance between identical twins reared together than identical twins reared apart.

6. Evidence showing the contribution of environment to tested intelligence includes (1) a decreased similarity of identical twins reared apart, (2) a similarity that increases with the length of time adopted children live with adopting parents, (3) the positive effects of a stimulating environment, and (4) the negative effects of deprived environments.

7. Within hereditarily defined limits, environmental factors can exert significant influence in determining tested intelligence and the effectiveness of intellectual functioning.

8. Early experience can have an apparently lasting effect on the problem-solving capacities of animals; stimulating environments lead to better later performance.

9. Tested intelligence may vary from one time to another because of technical factors in the design and administration of tests.

10. Although tested intelligence is relatively constant over time, there are changes of significant magnitudes. Tested intelligence tends to increase with education and as a consequence of living in a stimulating environment. Personality factors are involved in the improvement or decline in intelligence.

11. Cross-sectional studies of intelligence show a decline of intelligence with age; longitudinal studies do not yield the same results.

12. The terms idiot, imbecile, moron, borderline deficient, dull normal, normal, superior, very superior, near genius, and genius are defined in terms of ranges of IQ; the percentage of the population in each category is known.

13. There is a meaningful distinction to be made between primary mental deficiency, based on heredity, and secondary deficiency, caused by injury or disease. Also a distinction needs to be made between the mentally deficient and the mentally retarded.

14. Recent research has shown a relationship between metabolic processes (PKU) in the infant and early brain damage. This form of mental handicap can be prevented.

15. Meaning of tested intelligence may be made clearer if we observe the behavior of the mentally deficient on one hand, and of intellectually gifted individuals on the other.

16. Intellectually gifted children tend to be superior also with respect to social criteria. They are more likely to be leaders, achievers, and adjusters.

17. Intelligence predicts school success; correlations between IQ and academic achievement vary from .40 to .60. Such correlations are sufficiently high to be very useful but are not so high as to exclude other factors as predictors of school success. Personality factors are involved.

18. Intelligence test scores relate meaningfully to occupational success; again, however, other factors are clearly involved.

19. Factors other than intelligence enter into creative achievement. There is little if any correlation between scores on tests of intelligence and tests of creativity. Research efforts are revealing differences in the thought patterns of convergent as contrasted to divergent thinkers and are discovering some delineable characteristics of creative individuals.

20. There are no significant differences between the sexes with respect to over-all intelligence. Men do better on some tests; women, on others.

21. Men and women differ widely with respect to level of achievement in areas where

intellectual ability clearly contributes to performance. Social and personality factors are involved in sex differences in achievement.

22. Possible innate differences in intelligence between racial or cultural groups are at present very difficult to examine.

23. On present tests, whites on the average score higher than Negroes; Northern whites score higher than Southern whites; and, in some instances, Northern Negroes score higher than Southern whites.

24. When Southern Negro children move into Northern schools, their IQ's increase.

25. Obtained differences between racial and geographical groups are small, and distributions are characterized by overlap.

RESEARCH REPORTS

RESEARCH ON CONSTANCY
OF INTELLIGENCE *

The accompanying table presents data obtained from repeated administration of the Wechsler Intelligence Scale for Children (WISC) to 65 educable mentally retarded boys. The mean time between the first and second administrations of

the list was 12 months, with a range from 2 to 32 months. The mean time between the second and third administrations of the test was also 12 months, with a range of 9 to 15 months.

There were no statistically significant differences in scores on the VQ (the verbal parts of the test) between either the first and second or first and third administrations. The only statistically significant differences occurred between the first and second administrations on the score for performance items (PQ) and on the full scale (FS).

EARLY DEPRIVATION
AND LATER INTELLIGENCE *

In this general paper Goldfarb summarizes some of his work, which he had spread out over some ten to fifteen journal articles. His basic study was as follows: Fifteen pairs of children, ranging from 10 to 14 years of age, were compared on a number of measures. Their mean age at the time of comparison was 12 years and 3 months. Both children in each pair had been separated from their families in the early months of infancy.

One member of each pair was reared in an institution until about age 3 and then was placed in a foster home; the other child had been raised continually in the foster home. The foster homes of both the institutional and the continuous chil-

REPEATED WISC MEASUREMENTS

	ADMINISTRATION 1 MEAN CA 10–1			ADMINISTRATION 2 MEAN CA 11–1			ADMINISTRATION 3 MEAN CA 12–1		
	VQ	PQ	FS	VQ	PQ	FS	VQ	PQ	FS
M	74.09	74.57	71.65	75.43	81.68	76.23	76.40	85.51	78.80
Range	55–89	50–97	56–87	53–99	53–111	52–101	58–101	55–120	57–100
SD	8.01	11.04	8.12	10.29	13.28	10.36	9.76	13.94	11.11

CA = *Chronological Age*
VQ = *Verbal Quotient*
PQ = *Performance Quotient*
FS = *Full-scale score*

cable mentally retarded boys. The mean time between the first and second administrations of

* Roger Reger, Repeated measurements with the WISC, *Psychol. Reports*, 1962, 11, 418.

dren were equal in every respect. Moreover, the true mothers of the institution-reared children tended, if anything, to be somewhat superior to

* William Goldfarb, Emotional and intellectual consequences of psychologic deprivation in infancy: A re-evaluation, in E. Hoch and J. Zubin, eds., *Psychopathology in childhood* (New York: Grune & Stratton, 1955), Chap. 7, pp. 105–110.

the true parents of the children reared in foster homes.

During their first nine months, in order to prevent infection, the institutionalized babies were kept singly in separate cubicles. They had brief and hurried contact with adults only when their physical needs for food and clean clothes were met. During the next two years, their environment was only slightly less impoverished. Physically, the institution was as good as or better than the foster homes. Thus, the major experimental difference between the two groups was on the amount of deprivation in infancy.

When tested later in life, the institution children were found to be retarded intellectually; they showed a distinctly impaired conceptual ability. There was a generalized state of intellectual and emotional impoverishment and passivity. They were hyperactive, restless, and generally deficient in impulse control and inhibition. Despite insatiable demanding of affection, they had no genuine attachments. They were also less socially mature.

More detailed data on 15 experimental (institutionalized during their first three years) children and 15 control children are presented in the accompanying table.

DIFFERENCES BETWEEN 15 INSTITUTIONALIZED AND 15 NONINSTITUTIONALIZED CHILDREN

FUNCTION TESTED OR RATED	TEST OR RATING METHOD	RESULTS EXPRESSED AS	RESULTS	
			INST. GROUP	CONT. GROUP
Intelligence	Wechsler	mean IQ	72.4	95.4
Ability to conceptualize	Weigl-Vigotsky	mean score mean score	2.4 0.5	6.8 4.7
Reading	standard tests	mean score	5.1	6.8
Arithmetic	standard tests	mean score	4.7	6.7
Social maturity	Vineland Scale completed by caseworkers	mean social quotient	79.0	98.8
Ability to keep rules	frustration experiment	number of children	3.0	12.0
Guilt on breaking rules	frustration experiment	number of children	2.0	11.0
Capacity for relationships	caseworker's assessment	number of children	2.0	15.0
Speech		number of children up to average	3.0	14.0

Note: In all differences shown, p < 0.01.

CREATIVITY AND SENSITIVITY TO PERIPHERAL STIMULI [*]

In this study, the authors tested their hypothesis that highly creative people are sensitive to a wide range of stimulation from the environment and are better able to make practical use of peripheral stimulation that other people tend to ignore.

Using a well-known test of creativity, they selected three groups of students: one highly creative, one moderately creative, and one minimally creative. Each group memorized a list of 25 common words. They were told that the purpose of the task was to see how well they could memorize in the presence of distracting stimuli. The distractions consisted of 25 other words being played over a tape recorder while the students were trying to learn the list.

Next, the subjects were given a series of anagrams to solve. The solutions to ten of the anagrams were words that had been on the list the

[*] Gerald A. Mendelsohn and Barbara Griswold, Differential use of incidental stimuli in problem-solving as a function of creativity, *J. abn. soc. Psychol.*, 1964, **68**, 431–436.

subjects had memorized. The solutions to ten other anagrams were words that had been spoken on the tape recorder as a "distraction." There were also a number of anagrams of equal difficulty for which no words had appeared on either list. The subjects had no idea that the two tasks were related or that words from the learning task would serve as solutions for the anagrams.

The authors reasoned as follows: If it is true that highly creative people make better use of peripheral information, then the highly creative people should show superiority in solving the anagrams whose solutions had appeared on the list to be memorized, even when there is control for the ability to solve anagrams. They also pre-dicted that, with anagram-solving ability controlled, the highly creative subjects would do better on the anagrams whose solutions had been presented as part of the distraction on the tape recorder. Both hypotheses were confirmed.

The authors checked to see whether the highly creative subjects simply had better memories. They found, however, that all of the subjects were equal in their recall of the neutral words they had memorized. The authors therefore concluded that the superior problem solving of the highly creative subjects was due not to superior memories or to better basic ability, but rather to their ability to use incidental stimuli, which others are apt to ignore or overlook.

SUGGESTED READINGS

Getzels, J. W., and P. W. Jackson. *Creativity and intelligence: Explorations with gifted students.* New York: Wiley, 1962.

Hunt, J. McV. *Intelligence and experience.* New York: Ronald, 1961.

Jenkins, J. J., and D. G. Paterson, eds. *Studies in individual differences: The search for intelligence.* New York: Appleton-Century-Crofts, 1961.

Pinneau, S. R. *Changes in intelligence quotient: Infancy to maturity.* Boston: Houghton Mifflin, 1961.

Taylor, C. W., and Frank Barron, eds. *Scientific creativity: Its recognition and development.* New York: Wiley, 1963.

Terman, L. M., et al. *Genetic studies of genius.* Stanford, Calif.: Stanford University Press, 1925–59. 5 vols.

Terman, L. M., and Maud A. Merrill. *Stanford-Binet intelligence scale: Manual for the third revision, form L-M.* Boston: Houghton Mifflin, 1960.

Wechsler, David. *The measurement of adult intelligence,* 4th ed. Baltimore: Williams and Wilkins, 1958.

PART FOUR

SEGMENTS OF THE PSYCHOLOGICAL PROCESS

OUTLINE / CHAPTER 8

I. DEFINITION OF MOTIVES

II. THE WORKING OF MOTIVES

    A. Motivated Behavior Is Instigated
    B. Motivated Behavior Is Directional
    C. Motivated Behavior Is Selective
    D. Motivated Behavior Is Satiable

III. MOTIVES AS CONSTRUCTS

IV. MOTIVES AND INSTINCTS

V. PHYSIOLOGICAL MOTIVES

    A. Hunger
      1. Conditions of Arousal
      2. Selective and Directional Behavior
      3. Satiation
    B. Thirst
      1. Conditions of Arousal
      2. Selective and Directional Behavior
      3. Satiation
    C. The Sex Motive
      1. Instigation of the Sex Motive
      2. Selective and Directional Behavior
      3. Satiation
    D. Pain as a Motive
      1. Neural Processes
      2. Pain as an Activator
      3. Pain and Previous Experience
    E. Exploration and Problem Seeking: An Unlearned Motive

VI. PSYCHOLOGICAL MOTIVES

    A. The Need for Achievement
      1. Measurement of Achievement Motive
      2. Conditions of Arousal
      3. Selectivity and Directionality
      4. Achieving Societies
    B. Other Psychological Motives
    C. Unconscious Motives

VII. CLASSIFICATION AND CRITERIA FOR MOTIVES

    A. Hierarchy of Motives
    B. Dependable Motives

VIII. HUMAN MOTIVES AND "HUMAN NATURE"

IX. SUMMARY

X. RESEARCH REPORTS

CHAPTER 8

MOTIVES

If we are interested in understanding all we can about the behavior of the organism as it adjusts to its environment, we almost inevitably must be concerned with motives, with those conditions of the organism that seem to impel it to persistent goal-seeking behavior. The psychological process involves a *motivated* organism that senses, interprets, and learns about the world.

All laymen and most psychologists think quite naturally in terms of motivating conditions that "cause" behavior. The nature of these "causal" factors may be seen, perhaps, in the principle of **homeostasis**, considered earlier (Chap. 1). We saw that all organisms seem often to show the tendency to maintain a constancy of internal conditions; paramecia move away from too much light, and human beings sweat when they are overheated. These apparently simple homeostatic reactions, if we look at them objectively, may

furnish a model for thinking about motives in general. It is inherent in the nature of life, apparently, either through internal processes or through changes in the environment, that an organism gets itself occasionally in an imbalance. Then it does something about its imbalance. It does something by triggering off mechanisms, such as sweating or shivering, that tend with a degree of automaticity to produce the desired situation. Or it moves its body. Or it battles the environment it finds not to its liking. When the paramecium moves away from light or the human being sweats in conditions of heat, an automatic mechanism functions to change the conditions of the organism. In more elaborate circumstances, such as human hunger, the condition may be remedied through laboriously learned and very intricate behaviors, such as the hunting and cooking of a big-horn sheep or the seeking out of an Italian restaurant.

In some respects we can think about paramecia and hungry humans in the same sense. And perhaps we can think about gregarious or status-seeking or ambitious individuals in a similar way. Imbalances lead to actions to restore balance. Although it may be difficult for us to conceive of a burning ambition in the same terms that we use for the relief of a pain or the relief of a hunger or a thirst or the removal of an irritation, it may be generally helpful to do so. As we will see, the "deficit-removing" motivating conditions are probably not the only motivating conditions that seem to characterize human beings; for some psychologists believe there are "growth motivations" as well as deficit motivations. The deficit-removal model may nevertheless be a good one with which to begin. By using it, we can make some general sense of the phenomena occurring when a living organism, responding either to external or internal conditions, behaves in such a way as to bring about a state of affairs which it seems to like better.

A number of aspects of observable behavior lead us almost inevitably to formulate motivational constructs to "explain" that behavior. First, it is easy to observe the *variety of behaviors* that seem to be involved in the attainment of a single goal. If we deprive a dog of food and then place the food on the other side of a fence where it can be seen and smelled but not easily approached, the dog will employ a wide variety of responses in an effort to relieve his hunger. He may scratch under the fence, climb over it, circumvent it, attack it; he may sit up in a begging position, howl, and do perhaps other things—all, apparently, in an effort to obtain the food. In the face of all this variety of behavior, we may naturally say that the dog has a hunger motive and is interested in obtaining food.

Another aspect of behavior that leads to formulation of the notion of motives is the fact of the *triggering action* of **stimuli**; small changes in the external world set off what seem to be relatively enormous responses in an organism. For example, the tinkle of a bell or the flash of a signal light can, under some

circumstances, produce very vigorous behavior on the part of an organism that is poised to eat or to flee. We are likely to account for the relative vigor of the behavior in terms of the condition of the organism itself, rather than to impute cause to the small amount of physical energy transmitted as stimulus to the eye or ear. Again, we think in terms of motivating conditions. It also occurs sometimes that the action of the organism remains steady in the face of changing stimuli. The thirsty man behaves the same in response to many varied signs of water; in such a case we quite naturally think that the motive causes behavior.

Both psychologists and laymen, we have said, think naturally in terms of motivational conditions of the organism. Also, we have said that it is a *motivated* organism that registers and interprets events in its outside world and that learns its way through the problems that world presents to it. In the latter connection, we can point out that motivation constitutes a segment of the psychological process as we have conceived it. It is a segment that can be studied in relative isolation from other segments, but we should remember that such isolation has an artificiality about it; for motivational phenomena are intricately related with all other segments of the psychological process. For example, our motives influence both what we sense and how we interpret what we sense; the hungry man, as compared to his satiated friend, is more likely to register the smell of food on the fire and is likely to interpret that smell as something edible. Similarly, the ambitious man may perceive his friends as stepping stones to his own success, while the more affiliative man will see them in a warmer and more affectionate light. Then, too, a man's motives will mightily influence his learning; he is most likely to learn those habits and skills that lead to the satisfaction of his motives. In this chapter we will deal with the nature of motivation, trying to see what motives are, how they work, and how they are interrelated with other segments of the psychological process as the organism interacts with its environment.

DEFINITION OF MOTIVES

We can define a **motive** as *an energizing condition of the organism that serves to direct that organism toward a goal or goals of a certain class.*

In dealing with motives defined in such a manner, we will need to distinguish between the term "motive" and some related terms that appear in the psychological literature. The term "motive" is sometimes used almost interchangeably with the terms "need" and "drive." Most frequently, however—and this will be the usage adhered to in the present book—the term "need" refers to deficiencies of substances the organism needs for survival or to excessives of substances that jeopardize survival. "Need," then, is primarily a biological concept. The organism, for its survival, may be in fairly desperate need to take in calories, but it still may not be motivated for food; for there can be conditions under which the need for calories does not arouse any kind of food-seeking behavior, does not direct the organism to a goal. The term "drive" is most frequently used to refer to those motives of the organism that are closely related to biological needs. These are also called "primary motives," and this category most frequently includes the motives of hunger, thirst, sex, the need for air, the need for rest, the need to escape pain, the need to eliminate waste, and perhaps others. These motivating conditions, then, can be referred to as "drives" or "primary motives," or as "physiological motives." Here we shall use the latter term to refer to those conditions that seem to energize behavior and that seem closely related to the biological needs of the organism. The general term "motive" is used to include those motivational conditions that are described as more *psychological* in nature. These motives, also sometimes called "secondary" or "derived" motives, include those motivating conditions referred to as **gregariousness, aggressiveness, affiliativeness, acquisitiveness,** the **achievement** motive, the need for power, the need for **status.**

In our treatment here, then, we will talk about motives and about the things that all motives seem to have in common. We shall make the distinction between physiological motives and psychological motives and will deal with a number of motives that fall under each of these headings.

THE WORKING OF MOTIVES

We define a motive as an energizing state. A motive is a restlessness, a lack, a yen, a force. Once in the grip of a motive, the organism does something. It most generally does something to reduce the restlessness, to remedy the lack, to alleviate the yen, to mitigate the force. It behaves. It moves through its environment toward those objects or situations or conditions that seem likely to alleviate its deficits and meet its needs. There are a number of facets of such motivated behavior that we can observe. Let us set them down explicitly.

MOTIVATED BEHAVIOR IS INSTIGATED

Something sets off the sequence of behavior. The instigator may be either a *deficit within the organism* or some external object—an *incentive*—that serves to trigger the sequence of behavior. The ravenously hungry man is in the grip of internal urgencies. They will move him. The moderately hungry man, by contrast, may continue playing golf until he passes by the refreshment stand. The incentive smell of a frying hamburger will trigger the hunger drive. To be most sure of ourselves in talking about a motive, we need to be able to define its conditions of arousal.

MOTIVATED BEHAVIOR IS DIRECTIONAL

Once a motivated sequence is set off, behavior carries the organism toward or away from something. It moves toward the satisfying and away from the painful or undesirable. When we can see directionality, and see what it is directional *toward*, we know more about the motive that is at work.

Figure 8–1. MOTIVATED BEHAVIOR IS SELECTIVE. *(Reprinted by permission of the Hall Syndicate, Inc. All rights reserved.)*

MOTIVATED BEHAVIOR IS SELECTIVE

Once a motivated sequence of behavior has begun, it tends to take over the whole organism. It registers and interprets only those parts of the world having a relevance for its needs; the hungry man develops a keen sensitivity to signs pointing the way to a restaurant and loses some awareness of pretty girls or sunsets. The experienced organism selects those routes and those locations known to hold forth promise of satisfaction; the thirsty man heads for the spring rather than the putting green. Only those skills and habits are activated which in the past have helped the organism achieve satisfaction.

MOTIVATED BEHAVIOR IS SATIABLE

Motivated behavior leads to a goal. The goal may be an object, a situation, or a changed condition of the organism. Once the goal is reached, behavior changes. The restlessness and the stewing cease, at least for awhile, and the organism gives behavioral signs of satisfaction. The well-fed rat does not explore for food. (It may explore, as we shall see, but it explores for reasons other than hunger.) The sexually gratified organism at least temporarily shows a decreased interest in members of the opposite sex.

The satisfaction of psychological motives should, at least theoretically, lead to observable signs of satiation. If the motivating condition is rooted in a deficit, behavior is directed to the removal of that deficit; and when the deficit is removed, we naturally expect a quieting down of behavior. But is the ambitious man ever satisfied with his achievements? When does the acquisitive man acquire enough? What satisfied behavior can we observe? Is there a cessation of ambitious behavior? Does acquisition stop? Or have such motives escaped somehow from the functional rules applying to biological motives—rules saying that deficits lead to goal-seeking behavior and that achieving a goal reduces motives and puts an end to seeking? The question

Figure 8–2. DEFICIT AND SATIATION. *(Austin [Tex.] American Statesman, Tm. Reg. U.S. Pat. Off.—All rights reserved. Copr. 1960 by United Feature Syndicate, Inc.)*

of satiation of our psychological motives is an involved one and one that will concern psychologists for a long time. At the moment we simply raise this question and make the point that unless we can see signs of satiation after a goal has been reached, we are not completely sure that the motive whose effects we think we have been watching is the one that is actually at work. We shall return to this matter when we consider the psychological motives in more detail.

MOTIVES AS CONSTRUCTS

Whether we talk in standard English about the motives of our friends or deal in scientific terms with the motives of organisms, we should bear in mind that motives are **constructs** rather than facts. When we talk about specific motives, then—hunger, thirst, sex, ambition, gregariousness, acquisitiveness—we are using constructs. That is, we are going beyond observed facts and are summarizing, interpreting, and sometimes translating observed facts into terms that, for one reason or another, we find more convenient. No one ever observed in anyone else such a thing as hunger or a sexual impulse or ambition. All we observe is behavior. We see restlessness and seeking and the reaching of goals and the quieting down of the organism. We *infer* motives. For instance, we can observe that a person has been without food for ten hours, that he shows an increasing sensitivity to pictures of food, that he sees reminders of food where the well-fed person sees something else entirely. We can see him seek a restaurant, we can see him eat, and we can see a decrease in restlessness. We infer, with considerable confidence, that a hunger motive was in full operation. But we have not seen hunger.

The same situation maintains for other alleged motives. Take jealousy. No one ever saw it. We see certain situational conditions. We see a senior dance all evening with a freshman's date. We see the freshman's behavior. It may be highly visible or audible behavior, standing out clearly in this particular setting. When we tell someone about the freshman, we summarize what we have seen in the situation and in his behavior by saying that he was jealous. But *we* create the summary. Jealousy is a construct. And the use of constructs should, in the interest of making the best sense about the world, proceed according to certain rules that enable us to tie our constructs to our facts and to recognize when we depart so far from facts that we are talking not much sense at all.

We have considerable confidence in using motivational constructs such as hunger and thirst, because we can observe the antecedent condition, the *conditions of arousal*. We take away a man's food or water, and we are quite sure we can produce a certain kind of behavior that, without fear of controversy, we can call hunger or thirst. And, if we go about it right, we can observe the physiological processes involved in arousal. Then, in addition, we can observe the *selectivity and directionality of the behavior of the organism*. We can see the increased sensitivity to sights and sounds and smells and signs of food, and we can see movement toward food. We can see eating. And *we can see obvious signs of satiation*. The construct of hunger seems a safe construct to use. It is so safe that we can and do create the motive experimentally by depriving the organism of food or water—assuming thereby, and with reasonable safety, that we can observe in action the behavioral consequences of a motive.

The motive of jealousy, on the other hand, presents some problems of definition. So does any motive of the social or psychological sort —jealousy, ambition, acquisitiveness, gregariousness, the need for security. In our use of these constructs, we rarely have the certainty and comfort that come from complete and concrete observation. We cannot always observe the precise conditions of arousal. We cannot always describe accurately the behaviors involved, for the jealous man or the gregarious man or the ambitious man has many different ways of behaving as he pursues his goal—and no two jealous men or ambitious men will behave in precisely the same way. And we cannot at present relate these complex motives to physiological or neurological processes. Although we know a good deal, as we will see, about the processes in the blood and the brain that are involved in such a motive as hunger, we have not been able to find an ambitious pattern in the brain or a gregarious contraction of the gut. So that when we use such terms as ambitious and gregarious—and we will—we are removed somewhat from the comfort and certainty of precise and concrete definition. When I tell you that Henry is ambitious, I am giving you a highly interpretive statement; and I am running the risk that had you seen the same conditions and behaviors that I saw, you would have interpreted quite differently, seeing not ambition but competitiveness or aggression or the need for security. This is a matter to which we shall return.

MOTIVES AND INSTINCTS

During the foregoing talk about motivation, many students may have wondered about the absence of any mention of **instinct**. This term at one time had wide currency in psychological literature, and we still often hear the word in everyday talk about behavior. In psychological circles today, however, there is only very skittish mention of instincts. The term has had a long and sometimes emotional history. We need not go into that in detail here. But perhaps we do need to account for the infrequency with which the concept of instinct is mentioned in an introductory textbook.

An instinct, as defined by McDougall (1908)—leading proponent of the instinct theory of behavior—*is an innate disposition which determines the organism to perceive or to pay attention to any object of a certain class, to experience in its presence a certain emotional excitement, and to act or have an impulse to action which finds expression in a specific mode of behavior in relation to that object.* McDougall's instincts, by such a definition, have much in common with latter-day motives. There is a disposition (a condition) of the organism to perceive the world in a selective way and to pursue, directionally, an adaptive line of behavior. But the instinct theory deals in *innate* dispositions—dispositions allegedly born into all members of a species. This assumption of *innate* conditions

of the organism, particularly of so elaborate a kind, brought the instinct theory into disrepute. Evidence from anthropologists threw grave doubt on the universality, among all men in all cultures, of McDougall's instincts. The idea of *learned* motives rather than innate motives was then more attractive to psychologists. Also, there was criticism of the instinct theory on the basis of its circularity. One writer had this scathing paragraph to offer (Holt, 1931):

Man is impelled to action, it is said, by his instincts. If he goes with his fellows, it is the "herd instinct" which actuates him; if he walks alone, it is the "anti-social instinct"; if he fights, it is the instinct of pugnacity; if he defers to another, it is the instinct of self-abasement; if he twiddles his thumbs, it is the thumb-twiddling instinct; if he does not twiddle his thumbs, it is the thumb-not-twiddling instinct. Thus everything is explained with the facility of magic—word magic (p. 4).

Such criticisms led to a marked reaction against the instinct theory. Psychologists still use the term *instinctive behavior* to refer to apparently inborn sequences of unlearned behavior—such as nest building among birds. But they consider it both against evidence and against the **law of parsimony** to account for human behavior in terms of innate and highly elaborate dispositions. They prefer to think in terms of conditions (often learned) of the organism that lead, with selectivity and directionality (often learned), to goals (also often learned).

When we deal with psychological motives, we will see some evidence bearing on the alleged universality of such "instinctive" dispositions as McDougall's acquisitiveness and self-assertion.

PHYSIOLOGICAL MOTIVES

We have defined a motive as a condition of the organism, a condition that serves to direct that organism toward a certain goal. A physiological motive, then, is a motive wherein the condition of the organism can be clearly traced to physiological states, to tissue needs.

In dealing with what is known about physiological motives, we shall focus here on hunger, thirst, sex, and pain. The research literature on these motives will enable us to see how internal conditions of the organism affect its external behavior and will let us have a look at the ways in which learning and motivation are interrelated.

HUNGER

Any organism, including man, gets hungry. When the state of hunger arises, there will probably be activity. If there is opportunity at all, the organism will take food. And when it has taken food, its pattern of activity will change—unless something not normal is going on.

This relatively simple sequence of events may seem strange to those of us who are accustomed to being hungry for specific kinds of foods—olives, artichokes, crepes suzette—in specific circumstances and at predictable times, and may not help us directly account for the fact that a primitive man may crave young dog en casserole, while the very thought of such a delicacy turns the stomach of a modern American. But the basic simplicities are nonetheless there, and essentially in the form we have described.

Conditions of Arousal

In examining the *conditions of arousal of hunger*, we look first to *internal conditions*, internal physiological or neurological factors and processes that arouse the organism to specific kinds of action, and for previously established habits that serve its motives. Next we look for *incentives*, for the external objects or situations that have the capacity to trigger the goal-directed sequence of behavior.

Internal conditions and processes in hunger. It was long thought that contractions of the stomach produced the awareness of hunger in man and at the same time brought forth the accompanying seeking for food. There obviously is a relation between the stomach contractions and food-seeking activity. This relationship was first demonstrated as early as 1912 (Cannon and Washburn). People who had gone without food for a length of time were required to swallow a balloon, which was then inflated in the stomach; consequently, any time the stomach muscles contracted, the balloon would then contract—making it possible to measure by sensitive recording devices the timing and extent of activity in the stomach muscles. The subjects in this experiment were asked to press a key whenever they were consciously aware of being hungry. (See Fig. 8–3.) The results of the experiment showed almost an exact correspondence between the vigorous contractions of the stomach muscles, recorded through the balloon, and the conscious experience of hunger.

This and subsequent experiments seemed to indicate very clearly that the experience of hunger and the ensuing food-seeking activity are both "caused" by stomach contractions. But not so. If we assume that stomach contractions "cause" the awareness of hunger and food-seeking activity, then we must assume that the nerves in the stomach somehow communicate with the brain and set the brain to work—not only to register the awareness of hunger but also to get the organism busy seeking food. But an ingenious experiment knocks this assumption in the head (Morgan and Morgan, 1940). An experiment on hungry rats demonstrated that when the sensory nerves connecting the stomach with the brain are cut, the food-seeking activity of the rat remains essentially the same. We would naturally assume, under the older theory, that the rat's brain "reads" his stomach and, on the basis of this reading, knows that he is hungry. So he seeks food. Now, we intervene between the brain and the stomach, cutting the sensory nerves that convey messages from the stomach to the brain. The rat still gives us evidence of being hungry. Therefore, he must be "reading" some other kinds of cues.

Other studies support the notion that stomach contractions alone do not furnish the physiological basis for hunger. For example, in one study (Keys et al., 1950), a number of subjects were kept on semistarvation diets for

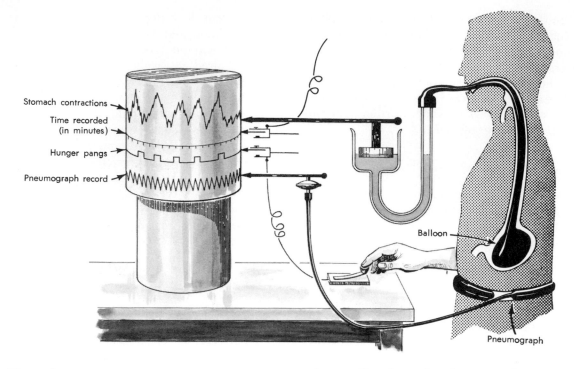

Stomach contractions

Time recorded
(in minutes)

Hunger pangs

Pneumograph record

Balloon

Pneumograph

Figure 8–3. MEASURING STOMACH
CONTRACTIONS. *An apparatus like that above,
once a subject has swallowed a balloon, has
been used to record stomach contractions and
the conscious awareness of hunger pangs.*

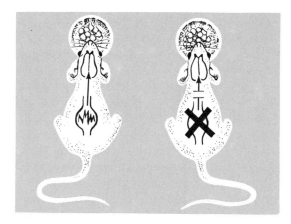

Figure 8–4. THE SEARCH FOR PHYSIOLOGICAL
BASES OF HUNGER. *When the vagus nerve is
cut, the rat's brain cannot respond to contractions of his stomach. Yet he still acts hungry.*

a long period of time. These people experienced hunger pangs even when they were
taken off the diet and given a full meal. And

other studies show that the stomach can contract persistently without there being present
any conscious experience of hunger.

If the experience of hunger, and the activity of food seeking, is not set off by stomach
contractions, what does do the triggering?
One may think, in the face of such a puzzle,
that possibly the brain somehow "reads" the
chemical state of the blood. That such a process is likely is indicated by an experiment
(Tschukitschew, 1930) in which blood trans-
fusions from hungry dogs to well-fed dogs
made the well-fed dogs start looking for food.
This kind of evidence suggests that food
deprivation produces some kind of deficit in
the blood stream; as a result, we get stomach
contractions as well as a direct effect on the
brain, a direct effect leading to food-seeking
behavior and, in human organisms, to the
awareness of hunger.

So we know fairly certainly that the brain
is responding directly to blood chemistry.
But how? Some studies indicate that the
hypothalamus, a small structure at the base
of the brain, is involved. In one study, electrical stimulation of the lateral part of the hypothalamus caused even the satiated animals to
eat (Andersson, Jewell, and Larsson, 1958).

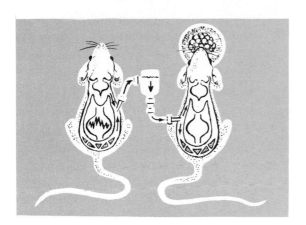

Figure 8–5. THE SEARCH FOR PHYSIOLOGICAL BASES OF HUNGER. *When blood from a hungry rat is transferred to the system of a well-fed one, the well-fed one starts eating.*

If this lateral portion of the hypothalamus is removed, **aphagia** (loss of all appetite) results (Anand and Brobeck, 1951). A center of satiation is indicated too. If the *ventromedial hypothalamus* is stimulated, even a hungry animal stops eating, while the removal of this structure causes **hyperphagia,** pronounced overeating (Hetherington and Ranson, 1940). Thus, we see that specific parts of the brain are sensitive to bodily conditions, such as the amount of sugar in the blood, and are involved in directing behavior in the appropriate directions.

There are two general theories about the brain's response to conditions of the blood: the *glucostatic theory* and the *thermal theory.* The glucostatic theory holds that receptors in the hypothalamus respond to relatively short-term variations in available blood glucose. The thermal theory maintains that cells in the hypothalamus respond to subtle changes in temperature, which are related to food deprivation and food intake. Neither theory accounts for all known facts, and neither is universally accepted (Cofer and Appley, 1964).

Specific hungers. Though we cannot trace at the moment the precise physiological and neurological mechanisms involved in the hunger drive, we can see how complicated the whole process is by examining the behavior of children and animals when they are suffering from specific dietary deficiencies. In an early experiment it was found (Davis, 1928) that children, when given a wide choice of food, would choose over a long period of time what was essentially a balanced diet. No one had to worry about the child's getting the "right" foods. He did it by himself when given a choice. As a matter of fact, one of the children had a case of rickets at the beginning of the experiment. Over the next few months, this child selected large quantities of cod liver oil, a substance containing liberal amounts of Vitamin D, the specific for the curing of rickets. This experiment demonstrates the wisdom of the organism—a physiological wisdom that leads it to secure for itself a balanced diet.

One implication here is that we do not have to worry ourselves sick about the eating habits of our children—provided we can (a) make available to them a wide choice of foods, (b) refrain from injecting psychological and emotional factors into the process of eating, and (c) tolerate the mess. However, after learning has taken place, we cannot trust a person to select for himself the ideally balanced diet. The foods used in the experiment cited above were all unseasoned and, we may infer, all equally attractive or unattractive on the basis of taste alone. We do not know what might have happened if ice cream or sugar cookies had been on the menu. In this connection, an experiment on rats (Wilder, 1937) demonstrated that rats can be trained to prefer and seek out foods that are not "good" for them.

The early experiments on children were followed by more systematic ones on dietary deficiencies in rats. In one experiment, for example (Harriman, 1955), a group of ten rats was given an adequate diet, while an experimental group of ten rats was given a diet deficient in Vitamin A. The vitamin deficiency was built up over a period of 22 days. Later, those rats deficient in Vitamin A, when given a choice, ate large amounts of a food containing Vitamin A. Those without the vitamin deficiency continued a normal diet. Similar

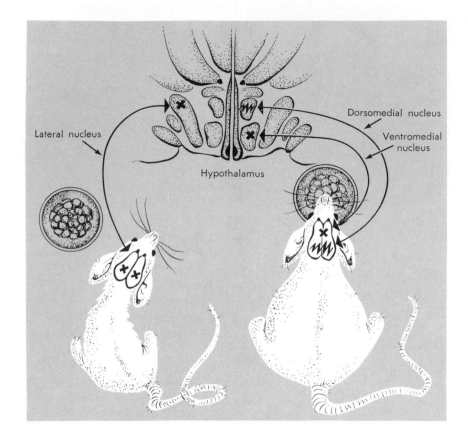

Figure 8–6. THE SEARCH FOR PHYSIOLOGICAL
BASES OF HUNGER. *Both stimulation (repre-*
sented by the jagged lines in the drawing)
and destruction (represented by the crosses)
of the hypothalamus can affect eating behavior.

results obtain for the behavior of rats with a
salt deficit. (See Fig. 8–7.)

Again, we do not know the precise physiological and nervous mechanisms involved in
this primitive wisdom of the organism. We do
know, however, that *taste receptors* are somehow involved in the process (Richter, 1943).
We know that if we cut the taste receptors in
rats, rats lose the tendency to select a balanced diet.

Incentives to hunger. What are the external
objects and situations that seem to set off a
hunger motive or a food-seeking sequence of
behavior? If we wanted to stimulate the appe-

tite of a Zuñi or a truck driver or a cocker
spaniel, what might we do? In general terms,
of course, the incentive to hunger is obviously
food. But there are foods and foods, and individual appetites vary widely.

As is the case with other physiological motives, we learn when to seek food. We learn
when a motive should turn itself on. Many nu-
tritionists observe that it would be generally
better for us if we ate five times a day rather
than the conventional three times. But most
of us learn to eat on schedule. Infants, as most
parents know, can be trained to eat at times
that are convenient for the parents. The child
involved in such dietary education may put up
some resistance for awhile, but environmental
factors generally bring his physiological inclinations into line. Within limits, he learns to
be hungry at the "proper" time. Such learning makes possible the institution of family
meals, and allows restaurants to predict the
necessary increase in the number of waitresses

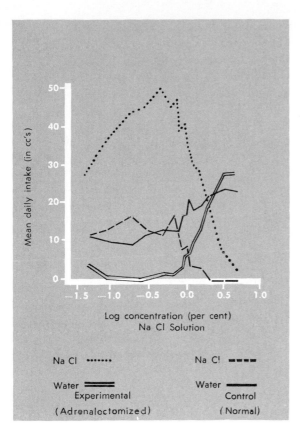

Mean daily intake (in cc's)

Log concentration (per cent)
Na Cl Solution

Na Cl ••••••   Na Cl ━ ━ ━

Water ══════   Water ━━━━
Experimental   Control
(Adrenalectomized)   (Normal)

Figure 8–7. SPECIFIC HUNGERS. *Rats with a salt deficit will drink salty water. The curves above show the intake of fresh and salty water by normal rats and rats who have had the adrenal glands removed, an operation creating a salt deficit. (Bare, 1949; reproduced by permission of the American Psychological Association.)*

required from 11:30 to 1:00 on any given day.

Food-seeking behavior among human organisms seems to be triggered by a wide variety of external cues. Similar triggering occurs among animals. They, too, learn when to seek food. It appears that the animal's physiological processes learn to tell time, responding on schedule to external cues of some sort. In one experiment (Lawrence and Mason, 1955), one group of rats was fed regularly every day, while a second group was fed irregularly. Over a period of 27 days, the rats who were fed at the same time every day ate appreciably more than those fed at irregular intervals. One is inclined to think that the regular rats have had their physiological processes trained to respond to definite time cues. When the learned time comes, there is some sort of readiness to eat, which leads to more eating than if the food is unexpectedly made available.

Human beings not only learn when to eat. They also learn what to be hungry for. Most people in our culture, for example, learn a hunger for scrambled eggs and bacon and apple pie and roast beef. Few Americans will find themselves having food fantasies about horse steak or snails or raw fish or fried grasshoppers or human flesh. And certain combinations of food are abhorrent to us—such as a half grapefruit topped by a fried egg and a maraschino cherry. The foods that might be quite adequate to meet nutritional needs are not always the foods that will necessarily be selected for the diet in a given society.

Eating behavior can be triggered not only by time cues and by varied objects that have come to have appetitive significance; it can be set off by the eating behavior of others. If hens are fed in groups of three, they eat almost twice as much as when they are fed individually. And if a thoroughly fed hen is suddenly exposed to the grain pecking of a hungry hen, the well-fed animal will start in again and eat upwards of 25 per cent as much as she ate originally. If three hungry hens are set to eating in the cage of the satiated hen, the satiated hen will eat around 50 per cent as much as she did originally (Bayer, 1929).

Rats demonstrate similar behavior (Rasmussen, 1936; Bruce, 1941), and casual observation leads one to believe that human beings are also socially facilitated in their eating habits. The fat man is probably most likely to break his diet if he dines with gourmands. The child who is finicky about food at home often eats like a healthy animal if on a cook-out with the scout troop. We are fairly safe in concluding that social situations can have a decided incentive effect on the eating behavior of organisms.

Figure 8–8. SOCIAL INCENTIVES TO EATING. *When a well-fed hen is surrounded by hungry hens busily eating, the well-fed animal will eat again—up to 50 per cent as much as she had eaten originally. The same kind of social incentive probably works on children. The watermelon-full youngster will probably have some more if his friends start eating in his presence.*

Selective and Directional Behavior

We have defined a motive as a condition of the organism that serves to direct the organism to a certain goal. In an early experiment on the effects of motivation on perception (N. Sanford, 1936), students deprived of food for a few hours demonstrated a clear tendency to "read" certain suggestions of food into the environment. When they were shown ambiguous blobs and vague forms, hungry students tended to see food while well-fed students gave a variety of interpretations.

Perhaps the most dramatic experimental demonstration of the way hunger directs the behavior of the organism took place in the studies of semistarvation carried out by the University of Minnesota shortly after World War II (Keys et al., 1950; Guetzkow and Bowman, 1946). In these studies a number of students who volunteered for the experiment were then subjected for 24 weeks to a semi-starvation diet. Whereas the normal diet of these people included an average of 3,492 calories a day, the semistarvation diet—made up mainly of bread, macaroni, turnips, cabbage, and potatoes—provided only 1,570 calories a day.

The changes in behavior were dramatic. The men developed a single-minded preoccupation with food. They talked about almost nothing else. They read about food. They studied cookbooks and collected recipes. The more intellectual ones studied dietetics and agriculture. Several of them seriously considered giving up their vocational plans and began to think about pursuing the art of cookery as a career. The insistent hunger motive simply took over the intellectual and emotional life of these subjects.

Also, pronounced personality changes took place. Sexual urges almost disappeared. The men lost interest in their girl friends, and a number of courtships simply ended. They seemed unable to express any kind of affection. They became humorless (more likely to be irritated than amused by events in their environment), apathetic, and gloomy. Nobody seemed to like anybody very much, and tactlessness replaced social sensitivity. There were general feelings of inferiority and of depression. On intelligence tests there was some decline in the general level of performance—probably because the men were unable to think about anything but food, and could not become involved in the non-nutritious business of scoring on a test.

Such data can supplement meaningfully the experience each of us has with his own hunger pangs. When there are changes in the chemistry of the blood, changes brought about by the absence of food intake, the brain responds in such a way as to increase our sensitivity to certain food-relevant stimuli in the environment. Even before we are aware that we are hungry, we show an increased sensitivity to signs and reminders of food. If we are on an automobile trip, we become unusually aware of the number of restaurant signs on the road. We may see a steer not as a sign of animal life, but as the source of steaks. Conversation, along about mealtime, can be depended on to direct itself to the general subject of eating. The organism, we can say, is *selectively registering* those aspects of the world having most to do with its internal motivated state. Sooner or later we become keenly conscious of being hungry. When we do, all the resources of the nervous system, all of its stored experience with food-getting activities, come into play. We devote ourselves to the business of securing food. The brain serves as a filter, letting in relevant stimuli and keeping out those that have nothing to do with our needs (Deutsch and Deutsch, 1963).

In this selectivity of awareness, incidentally, we can see clearly the way in which motivation, as one segment of the psychological process, becomes intertwined with other segments of the process. Just as we saw, a few pages back, that learning—learned incentives—is involved in the operation of a motive, here we cannot ignore the effects of motivation on perception.

Satiation

Generally speaking, the well-fed organism stops eating and stops searching for food. The full stomach stops its contractions, and, in due time, the body chemistry rises to a well-fed and satiated state. Such is the normal course of events. But we know that well-fed animals will eat further if hungry animals start eating. And we know that many human beings will eat when there is no simple physiological need for it. The number of overweight people in our population testifies against the simple and direct physiological control of eating behavior (even though physiological factors can and do produce nutritional disturbances). We are led to the notion that, for many people, eating is not alone a matter of meeting physiological urgencies but also has psychological significance. Food comes to stand for something other than nourishment. The "problem eater" —who gorges himself all day long on any comestibles he can lay his hands on—seems to be following the dictates of some involved psychological motive that cannot be allayed

by a balanced blood chemistry. His hunger is a psychological hunger, or perhaps a "brain hunger," not now directly connected with bodily deficits and surfeits.

THIRST

Conditions of Arousal

Generally speaking, the history of the search for an understanding of thirst has paralleled the history of the investigation of hunger. Just as the early theorists held that food-seeking behavior was instigated locally by contractions of the stomach, the prevailing early theory (Cannon, 1918) was also one of local instigation; the salivary glands, when they fail to provide sufficient fluid to moisten the mouth and throat, produce a discomfort, which results in the feeling of thirst and which leads to the seeking of water. This early theory produced a good deal of research. Two recent writers (Cofer and Appley, 1964) cite a number of studies in which drugs (principally pilocarpine, which stimulates salivation) have been used to examine the relation between salivation and the water intake. If dry local tissues in the mouth set off water-seeking behavior, the reasoning goes, and if a given drug stops salivation, then an injection of the drug should produce increased water intake. The results of these studies are variable, and allow of no simple statement to the effect that increased salivation reduces water intake or that decreased salivation increases water intake.

Other tests of the same hypothesis involved the extirpation of the salivary glands of animals. If these glands are removed, salivation cannot occur and water intake, the thinking goes, will go up. Two studies have independently indicated that such is not the case (Montgomery, 1931; Gregerson, 1932). Also it has been pointed out (Cofer and Appley, 1964) that many animals, such as water animals and birds, do not have salivary glands, so that this mechanism could by no means be one that functions for all organisms.

Again as in the case of hunger, the cutting

of the nerves to the specific mechanisms hypothetically triggering thirst should have a definite effect on water intake. Experiments reveal that such an operation has no effect on dogs' water intake, either for normal dogs or for animals suffering from a disease that made them drink abnormally large amounts of water (Bellows and Van Wagenen, 1939).

There may be a relation between salivation and water intake, but the facts indicate that the relation is not primarily—or at least necessarily—involved in instigation of water intake. What then does set off the intake of water? There is some evidence (Verney, 1947) that a **hormone** secreted by the posterior **pituitary gland** is involved in the regulation of the body's water balance. This finding has led its founder to formulate a theory holding that there are *osmoreceptors* in the central nervous system that respond to the osmotic pressure of the fluid that surrounds them: they swell when water is plentiful and contract when it is not, thus serving as sensory receptors which can set off water-seeking mechanisms.

Generally speaking, there is a relation between deficit in body water and resulting drinking behavior. It's a fairly straightforward matter to deprive laboratory animals of water for a period of time and then to observe the efforts they will exert to secure water. Such efforts are systematically related to the period of deprivation. But the general and undifferentiated deficit of water does not seem to be the critical factor in thirst and in drinking. Special characteristics and distribution of body fluids have something to do with water-seeking behavior. A number of experiments have indicated that the salt content of the blood has a bearing on water intake. For example, a number of different sodium chloride solutions were injected into the stomach of rats and observations made of the amount of bar pressing for water the rats would demonstrate (O'Kelley and Falk, 1958).

A number of experimenters have worked to find out the precise areas of the brain that are involved in the thirst motive. Two researchers, in a series of experiments (Andersson and McCann, 1955), found that very small injections of a sodium chloride solution into a certain precisely located area of the goat's hypothalamus (in the medial hypothalamus proximal to the third ventricle) produced drinking—not only of water but of urine as well. Electrical stimulation of the same area of the goat's brain also produced drinking (Andersson and McCann, 1955), while injections of tiny amounts of distilled water into the same area of the cat's hypothalamus decreased intake of water (Miller, 1957).

It is clear that certain structures in the hypothalamus are involved in the instigation of the motive of thirst. These structures can be located with considerable precision, but the exact processes and mechanisms involved in the instigation and control of water intake are not yet known.

Selective and Directional Behavior

There can be little doubt that when the animal is deprived of water, or when there is the proper configuration of circumstances within the body to set off the motive of thirst, the animal will work to get water, if work is necessary, or that there will be an activation of learned habits that have proved to be effective in the past in getting it. Although the research demonstrations of these phenomena have not been carried out as thoroughly as they have with hunger, there seems not much reason to doubt that both selectivity and directionality of behavior do characterize the operation of the motive of thirst.

Satiation

As with hunger, when the deficits that lead to water-seeking behavior are taken care of, the animal stops drinking. But there remains some question about how the animal "knows" that its water balance is in good shape. The research on this point has been far from conclusive. Does the animal stop drinking when the dryness of the mouth is removed? Apparently not; when local dryness is overcome, animals continue to drink (Bellows, 1939). It has been demonstrated that introduction of water directly into the stomach will, after a period of time, bring a halt in water intake (Solarz, 1958). There seems to be evidence that animals who have water injected directly into their stomachs will demonstrate satiated responses but that animals who have had their water through their mouths more dependably show signs of satiation. In one experiment on the latter point (Miller, Sampliner, and Woodrow, 1957) three groups of rats, all of whom had learned to press a bar to receive water, were observed as they worked to receive water (a) after having 14 cubic centimeters (cc's) of water directly injected into their stomachs or (b) after drinking 14 cc's by mouth or (c) after no water had been given, so that they were in a state equal to that of the other two groups before those two groups were given water. During an eighteen-minute test the rats who had had no water drank 21 cc's, the animals who had been directly watered in the stomach drank 16 cc's, and the mouth-watered rats drank 6.7 cc's. It appeared that water received through the mouth is more likely to produce satiation.

There is evidence also that stomach distension has a role in the instigation of thirst or at least in the control of drinking. For example, one investigator (Adolph, 1950) found that stomach distension stopped immediate drinking in a number of animals but that it did not interfere with the drinking of dogs and rabbits unless the distension was extreme. In the latter two animals, a cutting of the nerve to the brain led the animals to overdrink. For some animals, distension of the stomach serves to stop the intake of water.

THE SEX MOTIVE

The sexual motive, like the hunger motive, can be demonstrated to rest on physiological processes—on conditions within the organism that increase its readiness to pursue a certain course of behavior. Sex, like hunger, can "take over" the organism, rendering it very sensitive to certain sex-relevant stimuli in the environment, directing its behavior toward objects and goals that will reduce the motivating condition. And, as with hunger, the sexual motive is encompassed by learning; we learn when to be sexually aroused and toward what.

There are differences, of course, between the hunger motive and the sexual motive. They rest on different physiological processes. But perhaps a more pronounced difference lies in the fact that hunger is a *vital motive*, while sex is not. If the hunger motive is not satisfied, the organism perishes. The same cannot be said for the sex motive, for the human being can live out his span of life without ever experiencing any sexual satisfaction. He cannot live without eating—or without satisfaction of the other vital physiological motives, such as thirst, the need for air, and the need for rest.

Another major difference between the phenomena associated with hunger and those with sex is the difference in the way society behaves toward the two motives. We talk quite freely about hunger and about food. We write cookbooks and circulate recipes. There are newspaper columns on cookery and on dieting. And we express food-seeking behavior quite openly. We have banquets and feasts and morning coffees and afternoon teas and cocktail snacks. We have pie-eating contests and cake sales. Our talk about sex and our behavior with respect to the expression of this motive are appreciably different. However, although the hunger motive, in the abstract, has had a mighty hand in determining the affairs of mankind, the sexual motive—though not vital, and though not so openly recognized—is perhaps at least equally influential in human behavior.

Instigation of the Sexual Motive

Though knowledge of the physiology of sex is incomplete, it is very clear that the sexual motive is grounded in physiological processes. Changes within the organism lead to restlessness, to a sometimes elaborate courtship, and to the consummatory sexual act, provided it can be arranged. The external incentive to the sexual behavior sequence is most frequently a member of the opposite sex; but, as we will see, there are wide variations within species and among individual members of the same species as to what constitutes a sexually attractive object.

Sexual physiology of the male. The secretions of the pituitary gland have a developmental hand in the sexual behavior of the male. If the pituitary gland is removed before puberty, a male animal or a male child will not develop either the *secondary sexual characteristics* (deep voice, pubic hair, etc.) or the primary sexual abilities. Occasionally, when the pituitary is overactive, an 8- or 9-year-old boy may show *puberty praecox*, an unusually early sexual maturity. When in the course of normal development the testes are developed and begin their functioning, these glands serve two functions; they secrete **androgens** into the blood, and they generate **sperm.** It is the androgens that concern us here. The sperm have an obvious biological function, but the androgens in the male blood constitute a major dynamic factor in sexual motivation, though the pituitary secretions continue to exercise some indirect control.

The strength of male sexual motivation is related to the quantity of androgens secreted into the blood. But the quantity of androgens is by no means the only determiner of sexual motivation. Generally speaking, androgens are most plentiful in human males in the late teens. This is also the time of the greatest sexual urgency. The concentration of androgens falls off after the age of about 20, and so does apparent urgency of the sexual motive. Kinsey et al. (1948) report that the average frequency of the coital act drops from four per week for the late teens to three times per week at 30, two at 40, and something less than one at 60 (Fig. 8–9). Such a drop in frequency seems likely to be associated with a drop in the secretion of androgens. To be sure of this, however, we would have to determine whether men of all ages are equally exposed to equally potent sexual stimulation.

The androgens are not the only determiners of sexual motivation; for when these hormones are absent (through removal of the testes), there may be little or no change in established sexual habits. Castrated dogs may persist in both sexual interest and ability for two years

or more—provided castration occurs *after* sexual maturity. Castrated human males may live out their lives with no noticeable falling off in sexual motivation—except, of course, that castration removes the possibility of reproduction. It seems to be clear, then, that once the sexual motive has been developmentally established, its dependency on androgens is diminished considerably. It must be that the brain, acting in some independence of hormones, becomes sexy. And if this is so, then the learned component of sexual motivation takes on greater significance.

Sexual physiology of the female. Pituitary secretions, as with males, are also involved in the sexual development and behavior of the female. The pituitary controls the ripening of both the primary and secondary sexual characteristics of the female. Once the ovaries develop, they begin secreting **estrogens,** which influence the sexual urge. In lower animals, the female's receptivity to males is almost entirely a captive of the rhythms of estrogens and the estrous cycle. Most female animals, with straightforward biological functionality, are most receptive to males during the period of ovulation, the period at which offspring are most likely to be initiated. Receptivity falls off during those periods of the month when there is no ovum to be fertilized. Human females, however, report a quite different schedule of sexual desire, with receptivity lowest during the ovulation period and highest shortly after and shortly before menstruation (Ford and Beach, 1952).

Neural processes. The neural mechanisms in sexual behavior appear to be more intricate than are those for hunger and thirst. In the female guinea pig, for example, the back part of the hypothalamus and the mammillary bodies that lie close by are necessary for sexual functioning (Dempsey and Rioch, 1939). When lesions completely destroy these areas and, with them, sexual motivation, no amount of injected hormones will reactivate an interest in sex (Brookhart and Dey, 1941). Moreover, removal of the cortex will abolish sexual behavior in the rat and cat but not in the

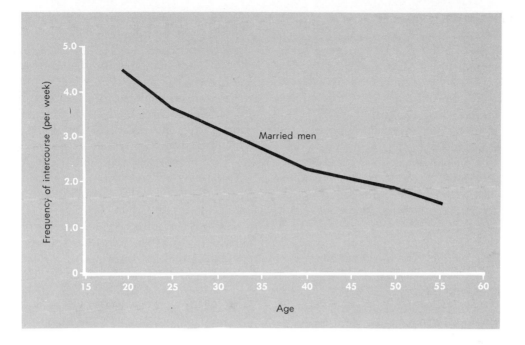

Figure 8–9. INDIVIDUAL DIFFERENCES IN
MOTIVATED BEHAVIOR. *There are wide
individual differences in behavior springing
from a motive. At least some of such
differences probably can be attributed to
individual differences in motive strength.
(A. C. Kinsey, W. B. Pomeroy, and C. E.
Martin,* Sexual Behavior in the Human Male.
*Philadelphia: W. B. Saunders Co., 1948. By
permission.)*

rabbit (Beach, Zitrin, and Jaynes, 1956). Increased sexual behavior has been produced
by both electrical and chemical stimulation.
These and other results leave in doubt the
specific brain mechanisms involved in sexual
motivation. One writer (Rosvold, 1959) concludes that mechanisms may differ from one
sex to another of the same species, and that
we cannot generalize from species to species.

Sexual incentives. The evidence that human beings are not so tightly bound to their
sexual hormones leads to the possibility that
learning plays a prominent role in sexual
motivation of human beings. So does the evidence bearing on the wide range of individual differences in sexual behavior. Kinsey

(1948) found that the frequency of coital acts
varied, in his sample of married males, from
more than one per day to less than one per
year. And the modal frequency in this culture,
of three times a week, contrasts with a modal
frequency of once a day or more in other societies (Ford and Beach, 1952).

One need cite no erudite reference as evidence of this wide variation—within a culture and cross-culturally—with respect to
what and who is sexually attractive. An extreme case in point is the incidence of homosexuality in our culture. Kinsey and his associates estimate that up to 30 per cent of the
males in their sample have achieved ejaculation at one time or another as the result of
contact with other males. Four per cent of
the male population is estimated to be chronically homosexual. Kinsey and his people also
report that 90 per cent of their males and 60
per cent of their females give a history of
masturbation. The incentives to sexual activity, then, can vary widely. So can the form of
sexual behavior. At any instance of the arousal
of a sexual motive we can look for certain
physiological conditions and for certain
learned situational factors that can trigger the
sequence of sexual behavior.

Selective and Directional Behavior

Sex operates much as does hunger in making the organism selective in his perceptions of his world and directional in his behavior. The sexually aroused man will demonstrate a certain indifference to peanut butter sandwiches if there is a pretty girl around. And there are instances in which a man, probably because his physiological urges have been enhanced enormously by learned motivational factors, may come down with the Don Juan syndrome, making a life's work out of the pursuit of women.

Satiation

Normally, the primary biological goal for the sexually driven male is orgasm or ejaculation. When the male achieves this, he at least temporarily loses both sexual interest and sexual ability. After recovery from the effects of copulation, there is apparently no increase in the organism's sexual motivation that is proportional with the period of deprivation. Certainly this holds for rats. In a study of sexual behavior in the male rat (Warner, 1927), experimental animals were first allowed two hours of free copulation and were then segregated from females. Then each animal was placed in a test situation for a twenty-minute period, and the experimenter counted the number of times he crossed an electrified grid in order to get to a female. After six hours of deprivation, the male rats were willing to cross the grid on the average of about four times. After twenty-four hours of deprivation, this crossing increased to an average of about fourteen times. But after 24 hours and up to 25 days of deprivation, the number of crossings did not increase. In a related study it has been shown (Beach and Jordan, 1956) that of male rats who have copulated to the point of exhaustion, less than 10 per cent show copulation and ejaculation after one day, approximately 75 per cent show the same behavior after three days, almost 90 per cent both copulate and ejaculate after six days.

The phenomena of satiation and of deprivation are not so clear in the case of the female. In subhuman organisms, the estrous cycle has a significant bearing on the sexual activity and on satiation in the female. In one experiment (Bermant, 1961), female rats in estrus were trained to press a bar in order to obtain a male. In the experimental procedure, after one male had copulated, he was removed from the female's cage and, whenever the female pressed the bar, was replaced by another. There was no evidence in this study that the act of copulation decreased the female motivation.

There is no direct evidence bearing on the relation of orgasm to sexual satiation in the human female. In their study, Kinsey and Gebhart (1953) found that about 25 per cent of the women interviewed in their sample, though they said they had enjoyed the sex act, reported that they had not experienced orgasm. And among women who do experience orgasm, there is little known either about the underlying physiological processes or about its effect, if any, in reducing sexual motivation.

Individuals, both human and otherwise, differ widely in the duration of satiated behavior following the sex act. The facts on the frequency with which the act is accomplished are relevant here (see Fig. 8–9). One is led toward the belief that the sex act, as in the case of Don Juan, may take on very appreciable psychological as well as physiological significance. Perhaps the accomplishing of the sex act comes to stand for satisfaction of other, nonphysiological, motives. In some respects, then, the sexual motive may be as psychological as it is physiological in nature.

PAIN AS A MOTIVE

Pain is one of the more potent motivating conditions we encounter. In dealing with pain, we skirt the area of reflexes, but avoiding pain involves more than jumping from a pin prick; it includes the sometimes elaborate treatment of a burn or the limp and the disinclination to walk with a sprained ankle. With pain, more clearly than with hunger, sex, and thirst, the dominant goal of the motivated behavior is the reduction or elimination of the stimulus conditions. Whereas other motivations normally arise periodically or in prescribed situations, pain is often an instantaneous, unexpected occurrence; and its avoidance is necessarily high in the hierarchy of things that are relevant for the continued well-being of the organism.

Neural Processes

Pain results from damage or inflammation of tissues or from stress. Any one of a number of events can start pain receptors sending impulses to the spinal cord, which may provide a return route to the muscles, in the case of a reflex, or transmit the message to higher centers. If the latter occurs, the organism will become aware of persistent pain and may engage in more complex behavior in order to rid itself of pain. Pain fibers go to many centers of the midbrain area. It is thought that impulses reaching certain *thalamic centers* cause the sharp-pain sensation, while lower sites in the midbrain are centers for persistent, gradual pain (Magoun, 1963). If strong stimulation of an injured tooth is involved, impulses reach the midbrain region where some varieties of anesthetics probably do their work in blocking pain (Kerr, Haugen, and Melzack, 1955).

Pain as an Activator

Since the organism must react promptly to painful stimuli, it is not surprising that pain registers in the midbrain, near the top of the reticular formation in the brain stem. The reticular activating system arouses those higher centers involved in the intricate behavior often necessary for the reduction of pain. If flight is a good idea, the reticular "command center" is able to mobilize the heart muscles, glandular excretions, etc., so that a quick escape is possible. If some thought is necessary, the cerebral cortex and other higher centers also come under the control of the reticular formation. In any event, the "starter button"—in the reticular forma-

tion—is one of the first stops for pain impulses.

Pain and Previous Experience

We have all seen people "take something for a headache" or medicate themselves to prevent sunburn. The reduction or avoidance of pain is biologically a natural reaction, but learning often modifies the behavior of a pained person. Additional pain may be endured at the present, for example, to avoid greater pain later; we will suffer the pain of having a tooth filled in order to prevent the greater future pain of having the tooth pulled. Drugs may be taken to stop pain which otherwise would have to be endured. In each case the "natural" behavior is suppressed or supplemented.

Some cultures do not accept the showing of pain. Our culture holds that men should have greater pain-enduring capacities than women, even though the evidence indicates that women have greater tolerance of pain. Parents teach their children the culturally proper attitudes about pain, and perhaps also, without deliberate intent, they teach the young some highly individual and idiosyncratic responses to pain. The **sadist** and the **masochist** demonstrate two extremes in individual reactions to painful experience in others and themselves. Pain, like hunger, thirst, and sex, is colored by earlier experience and by social pressures.

EXPLORATION AND PROBLEM SEEKING

There is another apparently unlearned motive of some consequence for the affairs of the organism. This is the exploratory or curiosity motive. Though there are no known physiological deficits or tissue needs involved in this motive, recent evidence clearly indicates it to be a factor in behavior.

It has long been observed that animals devote a good deal of time and energy to the investigation of new and strange objects in their environment. Monkeys, for example, will sniff, pull, push, handle, and paw a strange object put in their cage. If a door is inserted in an opaque monkey cage (Butler and Alexander, 1955), monkeys will open the door with considerable frequency, visually exploring the outside world. Such behavior seems to have no connection with any tissue needs of the organism. The animal simply explores its world. It explores more if the world contains many and complex objects (Berlyne, 1955). It explores more if it is young than if it is old (Welker, 1956). It explores less if it is afraid (Montgomery and Monkman, 1955). Monkeys raised with soft artificial mothers are more active in an open field than monkeys raised with hard artificial mothers (Harlow, 1960b). There is conflicting evidence on the relation of exploration to hunger, but in general the research literature furnishes grounds for at least a tentative postulation of an exploratory motive.

Figure 8–10. EXPLORATORY BEHAVIOR. *Animals, like human beings, seem to have an incapacity to do nothing. They are curious, will manipulate objects, and will explore in the absence of any obvious biological deficits.*

Related to this exploratory behavior are some other behaviors similarly having no "practical" connection with physiological deficits. If hungry rats are trained to run both a simple maze and a complicated one in order to get food and then are given a choice as to which maze they will use, they tend to choose the complicated one (Dember, Earl, and Paradise, 1957). And if they have a choice between running (a) a maze with food at a known place at its other end and (b) a maze in which they have to search for food after they have reached the end, they will choose the latter. What goes on here? It seems that rats are, in some sense, *seeking* as well as solving problems. There is evidence of similar behavior on the part of other animals. An early investigator (Romanes, 1912) reported that one of his monkeys worked for two solid hours to unlatch a trunk containing nuts, in spite of the fact that he was all the while surrounded by nuts. And monkeys, apparently just for the fun of it, will learn to unhook a series of hasps on a door (Harlow, Harlow, and Meyer, 1950). Such behavior seems to be related to the propensity of human beings to seek out puzzles, to set up problems in order to solve them, to make trouble for themselves in order to gain the satisfaction of overcoming troubles. Perhaps we need to postulate, in addition to the exploratory motive, a *problem-seeking motive*—another motive that rests on no demonstrable physiological deficit, that has no obvious "practical" significance in maintaining the organism, but a motive that may have considerable significance in human affairs.

It has been pointed out (Cofer and Appley, 1964) that the increasing amount of evidence in favor of exploratory or curiosity drives bears on the continuing controversy between those who regard motivation as a *conservative* or *homeostatic* phenomenon and those who see importance also in *growth-oriented* motives.

PSYCHOLOGICAL MOTIVES

When we move from a study of physiological motives to a consideration of psychological or social motives, we are moving toward a concern for even more intricate and involved behaviors than those associated with hunger, sex, and other conditions closely related to tissue needs. Many students may feel that now we are approaching "real" psychology, a psychology dealing not with hungry men or thirsty men or men driven by any of those biological urges which are shared with other animals, but men of full-blown human complexity, men who love and strive and hate and fight, men who read the past and project their plans into years not yet arrived, men who create and destroy, men who sacrifice for the welfare of others and who die in the defense of ideals, men who shape the world and make human history.

When we see these consummately human behaviors, we are inclined to seek their causes. We want to know why some men love when others hate; why some build and others destroy; why some pursue high ideals while others seek worldly power; why some court the approval of their fellows while others aggress against all mankind. And when we seek for causes, we think naturally of motives, energizing factors within the person leading him to seek his goals and advance his purposes.

In considering the so-called psychological motives, our first problem—and perhaps it is the most troublesome and significant problem facing psychology today—is the problem of relating the motives of the adult person to the biological and psychological history of that person. We can see no evidence whatsoever that the human infant has an acquisitive motive. But some adults hoard. We can see in the infant no need for achievement nor any status drive. But adults strive for high standards of performance or spend decades in the apparent effort to outdo their fellows. How does this happen?

We also face a semantic problem: What should we call these nonphysiological motives? Here, we have used the term "psychological motives"; the term may often be used interchangeably with "social motives." The motives we wish to consider—such as gregariousness, the achievement motive, the status motive—are all clearly psychological in the sense that they are not rooted in presently discoverable tissue needs of the organism. Also, they are all social in that they tend most generally to be involved in the individual's relations with other individuals and not with impersonal objects in the environ-

ment. Here we will use the term "psychological motives" because it is more general and more inclusive than the term "social motives."

Another problem that psychologists debate among themselves concerns both the scientific propriety and the intellectual utility of trying to talk at all about these psychological motives. Do we need such constructs as acquisitiveness or the power motive to deal with human behavior? And even if we need them, can we use them with enough precision to enable us to make meaningful statements?

These are all legitimate questions, and they suggest the appropriateness of caution in dealing with the constructs we refer to as psychological motives. The position here, however, is that we can profitably attempt to define and discuss psychological motives; and that it is a legitimate—if precarious—scientific endeavor to observe behavior and to make inferences, through due process, about the kinds of constructs we need to deal with the behavior we observe. In engaging in such a process, we will do well to remember, of course, that constructs are invented; and we can have only very limited assurance that we have captured in our net of constructs the best of all possible ways either to describe the nature of man or to account for his observable behavior. But science is a seeking more than it is a finding, and man's attempt to build a science of himself has only a short history—but a long future.

We have defined a motive as an *energizing condition of the organism serving to direct that organism toward a certain goal.* Psychological motives, then, become conditions of the organism—conditions that are not demonstrably physiological—that direct the organism toward certain goals.

We have employed, in connection with the physiological motives, the procedure of observing (a) the conditions of instigation and arousal of the motive, (b) the directionality and selectivity of the motive, and (c) the evidence of satiation.

Observations under these various rubrics serve to help us be sure we are justified in using a particular motivational construct,

They also help us in getting a full picture of the working of a motive once we believe it to be in action. This system of observing will also help, perhaps, as we examine some of the motivational constructs of a psychological sort and try to see how they operate. Our procedure will be to examine the question of achievement as a motive, using this motive first and others later to illustrate the problems and the knowledge we encounter as we study the motivational segment of the psychological process.

THE NEED FOR ACHIEVEMENT

We can inject ourselves into the problems of dealing with psychological motives by first considering one on which a great deal of research has been focused and about which we now know a great deal. That is the *achievement motive,* or the **need for achievement,** referred to in the literature and in the following paragraphs as **n ach.** In our review of the research on the *n ach,* we perhaps can see the kinds of investigations that must be carried out if we are to advance beyond the merely plausible in dealing with any psychological motive that we assume to be of great significance for understanding human behavior.

The *n ach* may be defined, in our terms, as *an energizing condition of the organism leading it in many situations to seek high standards of performance.* Since the late 1940s, this condition, or postulated condition, of the organism has been studied intensively—first by a small group of psychologists at Wesleyan University (D. C. McClelland, J. W. Atkinson, R. A. Clark, and E. L. Lowell, 1953) and then by an expanding number and variety of researchers (Atkinson, 1958; McClelland, 1961). We now know a good deal about the ways in which *n ach* can be defined and measured, about ways in which it is acquired, and about its operation both in individual life and in the lives of whole societies.

This whole research enterprise has not only a direct relevance for our understanding of the complex matter of human motivation but can serve as an example, a case study, of the

way in which a science advances. For progress toward an understanding of this one facet of motivation was possible because the researchers were able to combine in a series of investigations many facts, ideas, and methods already in the body of psychological literature. When the researchers began the attack on the achievement motive, they had at their disposal a basic array of experimental data. They knew about the conditions of internal and external arousal, about directionality and selectivity of motivated behavior. They knew a great deal about the basic laws of learning. They knew about Freud and his emphasis on the significance of fantasy life. They knew about projective tests and about the rigorous requirements of sound test construction. And they had at their disposal a knowledge of experimental design. From one point of view, the story of the research on the achievement motive is an account of a scientific adventure —an adventure into the unknown, starting from a base of prior knowledge and undertaking to extend that knowledge so that future researchers can set out from a more advanced station.

Measurement of Achievement Motive

The achievement motive can be defined and measured. The method that has been successfully used for its measurement is an adaptation of the **Thematic Apperception Test** procedure (p. 145). Through the use of two of the TAT pictures and two additional ones, all designed to bring out the individual's attitudes toward achievement, it is possible to make a quantitative and reliable assessment of the need to achieve (McClelland et al., 1953). The four pictures used in the measurements represent (1) a work situation, showing men at a machine; (2) an academic situation, showing a boy at a desk; (3) a father-and-son picture; and (4)a boy apparently daydreaming. Subjects were asked, in responding to the pictures, to tell what is happening at the moment, what led to the present situation, what is being thought, and what the outcome will be. The individual's response can be scored in terms of the number of achievement ideas or themes his stories contain. The following story, for example, illustrates a high achievement response to the picture of the daydreaming student (this subject, it also can be noted, expresses themes that suggest a fear of failure):

This chap is doing some heavy meditating. He is a sophomore and has reached an intellectual crisis. He cannot make up his mind. He is troubled, worried.

He is trying to reconcile the philosophies of Descartes and Thomas Aquinas—and at his tender age of 18. He has read several books on philosophy and feels the weight of the world on his shoulders.

He wants to present a clear-cut synthesis of these two conflicting philosophies, to satisfy his own ego and to gain academic recognition from his professor.

He will screw himself up royally. Too inexperienced and uninformed, he has tackled too great a problem. He will give up in despair, go down to the Goodyear and drown his sorrows in a bucket of Piel's (McClelland et al., p. 336).

By contrast, there is a response of another subject to the same picture, a response illustrating little concern with achievement.

This poor boy is now worrying about something he has done recently. He is probably wondering why he did it.

This boy has probably had his first sexual intercourse with a girl after which he was then given a lecture on V.D.

He is probably thinking about why he has done "this awful deed" (so they say).

He will probably say to himself that it was wrong to do what he did and that he won't do it any more (*ibid.*, p. 361).

There is abundant evidence, as we shall see, that scores on this projective test do indeed tap an underlying condition of the organism—an underlying condition which, when aroused, leads the individual to strive toward excellence in performance. It is significant that the projective procedures used to measure the motives are getting at an aspect of personal motivation of which the individual may not be aware. When subjects are given a questionnaire on their desire for achievement, their overt answers do not agree very closely with the themes emerging in response to the pictures (DeCharnes et al., in McClelland [ed.], 1955). The individual who consciously reports himself concerned with achievement puts emphasis on deference to expert authority and on conformity. The high achievers on the projective test, by contrast, emphasize there the matters of effectiveness and striving. It is also apparently true that one's associates are unable to rate the achievement motive. One study (French, 1958) found essentially no correlation between peer ratings on achievement motivation and a projective measurement of the motive. It seems to be the case that the "common sense" assessment of the achievement motive somehow misses the psychological mark. The projective measurements of the achievement motive, however, do predict achieving behavior.

Conditions of Arousal

The evidence on the learning of the achievement motive points directly to the nature of childhood training. Adult individuals high in *n ach* were subjected as children to relatively rigorous independence training. The mothers of men high in *n ach*, for example, reported that they expected their children at a relatively early age to have mastered such independent behavior as obedience to traffic lights when out alone, undressing and going to bed alone, ability to entertain themselves, ability to earn their own spending money and to choose their own clothes. The mothers of men low in *n ach* reported that they expected the same independent performances, but at *a significantly later age* (Winterbottom, 1953). Also mothers who reported that they gave rewards of physical affection—kissing and hugging—for independent achievement had sons who scored twice as high on tests of *n ach* as did mothers who reported no physical affection for independent behavior (Winterbottom, 1953).

It seems to be the case that the relatively demanding parent who "kicks the child out of the nest" at an early age, making him fly by himself, and who then rewards independent

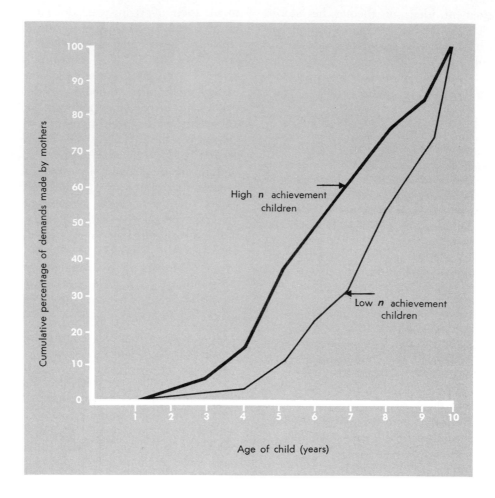

Figure 8–11. INDEPENDENCE TRAINING AND
NEED FOR ACHIEVEMENT. *Mothers of subjects
with high achievement motivation report
that they demanded independent behavior
at an earlier age than do mothers of subjects
low in* n *achievement. As the arrows in the
above chart indicate, of all the independence
skills expected of a child by the time he is
10, the mothers of high scorers expect 60
per cent of them to be mastered by age 7.
The mothers of low scorers are less demanding, expecting only 30 per cent of the
independence skills to be mastered by age 7.
(From McClelland et al.,* The Achievement
Motive, *1953, p. 300; by permission Appleton-
Century-Crofts, Inc.)*

behavior is, intentionally or otherwise, teaching the child a need for achievement.

Consonant results have been obtained from
studies of achievement motivation in primitive
cultures. In those cultures where there is early
and rigorous independence training of children, the adults are achievement-oriented.
Where the independence training is late and
casual, adult achieving is less emphasized.
Navaho youngsters, for example, are pushed
early and vigorously toward high standards
of independence; Navaho adults are strivers
(McClelland and Friedman, 1952).

We are fairly safe in concluding that some
individuals, through childhood exposure to
parental reward and punishment, learn an enduring tendency to strive for excellence and
to meet high standards of performance.

There is evidence that the achievement
motive is aroused by situations of an ego-
involving nature, by situations in which the

individual's self-respect is challenged. In one experiment, for example (Atkinson, 1950), subjects who were measurably high and low in *n ach* were asked to work on a series of paper-and-pencil tasks; only about half of the tasks could be completed in the allotted time. Under one condition, a "relaxed" condition in which the subjects were asked informally to "try out some tasks," the subjects low in *n ach* finished more tasks than did those who scored high. Apparently, in the relaxed situation those without strong need for achieving are motivated to be pleasant, cooperative, and deferent. They do well not out of a need to achieve but for other reasons. When the conditions were changed, however, and the subjects were told the tasks measured such things as intelligence and executive capacity, the subjects high in *n ach* significantly outstripped the others.

Selective and Directional Behavior

There is evidence that the achievement motive, once learned and once aroused, (1) leads to a selective perception of relevant segments of the environment and (2) gives behavior a direction toward the goal of meeting standards of excellence.

An experiment on the speed with which achievement-oriented words are recognized will illustrate the selective influence of the motive (McClelland and Liberman, 1949). The experiment involved a procedure whereby words on cards could be exposed to subjects for very brief intervals and a measurement made of the duration of exposure necessary for each subject to recognize each word. One group of words, including "mastery," "success," "perfect," had a positive relevance for achievement. Another group of words, including "failure," "unable," "obstacle," was negatively relevant for achievement. A third group contained only neutral words. The results showed that subjects high in *n ach* were relatively quick to recognize words having to do with positive achievement. Those scoring low on *n ach* recognized neutral words just as quickly as they did any of the words,

positive or negative, relating to achievement. The subjects receiving medium *n ach* scores were particularly quick in recognizing the words having negative bearing on achievement. (Fig. 8–12.) This latter finding the experimenters interpreted in terms of a pronounced fear of failure on the part of those having a moderately strong achievement motive.

On the question of directionality of behavior a number of researches demonstrate that individuals measurably high in achievement motivation behave in marked contrast to those who are low. In one experiment (French and Thomas, 1958) a group of highly intelligent subjects were divided into those high and low in *n ach*. Then all subjects were given a very difficult intellectual problem to solve, a problem having several acceptable solutions. The high scorers worked at the problem, on the average, twice as long before giving up as did the low scorers. They were also much more successful in finding solutions. For the high scorers, there was a correlation of .36 between success on the task and a test of intellectual ability. For those low in the need to achieve, there was no relationship between ability and performance.

Both on simple tasks in the laboratory and in more complicated human endeavors, those who score high on *n ach* outperform those who are low. With intelligence held constant, those high in the achievement need outperform the lows in solving arithmetic problems; and high scorers do significantly better at a laboratory task of unscrambling scrambled words (Lowell, 1952). (See Fig. 8–13.) With intelligence held constant, those high in *n ach* make higher grades in high school (Sadacca, Ricciuti, and Swanson, 1956). A similar relationship holds for performance in college. In one study (Morgan, 1951), a number of students, all scoring very high on the ACE test of academic aptitude, were divided into two groups on the basis of actual grades achieved in university courses. The academically gifted who had made high grades were also high in achievement motivation. The gifted ones who received lower grades were significantly lower

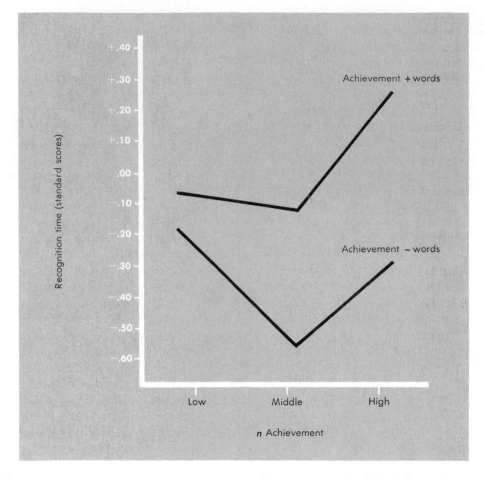

Figure 8–12. NEED FOR ACHIEVEMENT AND PERCEPTION OF WORDS. *Subjects high in achievement motivation are quicker to recognize positive achievement-related words, tachistoscopically presented, than are subjects low in achievement motivation. On negative achievement-related words, low scorers on* n *achievement are as quick as or quicker than high scorers. (From McClelland et al.,* The Achievement Motive, *1953, p. 259; by permission Appleton-Century-Crofts, Inc.)*

in achievement motivation. Ability alone does not guarantee academic success.

Achieving Societies

Research on the achievement motive has gone beyond a concern with the function of this motive in the life of the individual and has begun an exploration of the achievement motive as it functions in whole societies. The general question in this research venture has been: "What happens in a society if large numbers of individual members are highly motivated to achieve?" Such a question becomes amenable to research attack (a) when the achievement motive is measurable and (b) when techniques are invented for measuring certain social phenomena. Both these criteria seem to have been met in a number of studies of "achieving societies."

One such study (McClelland, 1958) related the achievement motivation of ancient Greeks to the economic activity of the Greek society. Achievement motivation was "measured" by counting the number of achievement themes occurring in comparable samples of literature from three periods of Greek history: (1) the

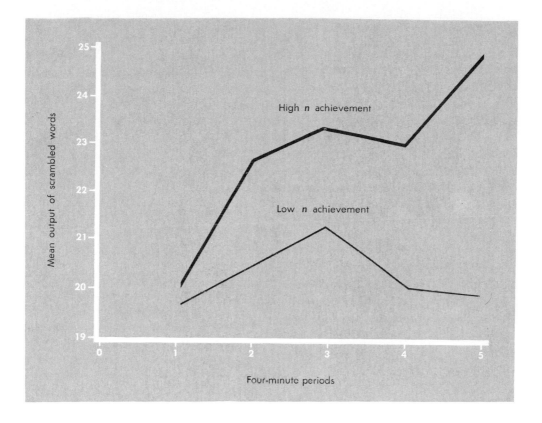

Figure 8–13. NEED FOR ACHIEVEMENT AND PERFORMANCE. *Mean output of scrambled words per four-minute period for subjects with high and low* n-*achievement scores. (McClelland et al.,* The Achievement Motive, *1953, p. 231; by permission Appleton-Century-Crofts, Inc.)*

period of growth, 900 B.C. to 475 B.C.; (2) the period of climax, 475 B.C. to 362 B.C; and (3) the period of decline, 362 B.C. to 100 B.C. As an index of economic activity, the size of the Greek area of trade was used. It was found that achievement themes were significantly more frequent in the period of growth than in either of the other periods, and that during the period of growth there was great increase in the Grecian area of trade, which reached its maximum about 450 B.C. By the time the area of trade had reached its maximum, however, achievement themes in Greek literature had greatly fallen off. From 450 B.C. onward,

there was a decline both in the trade area and in achievement themes in the literature. (See Fig. 8–14.)

Similar studies have related the frequency of achievement themes in English ballads to an index of economic growth across several centuries of English history. More extensively, other studies have analyzed the achievement themes appearing in primary school readers of 25 different countries in 1925 and in 1950, and have related this index of achievement motivation to indices of economic development (McClelland, 1961).

There seems little doubt that when many individuals in a society are highly motivated to achieve—a condition we may view as a product of certain child-rearing practices—that society will demonstrate relatively vigorous economic growth.

It seems a reasonable interpretation that economic development in a society is brought about by individual entrepreneurs who are motivated to achieve and who take those lim-

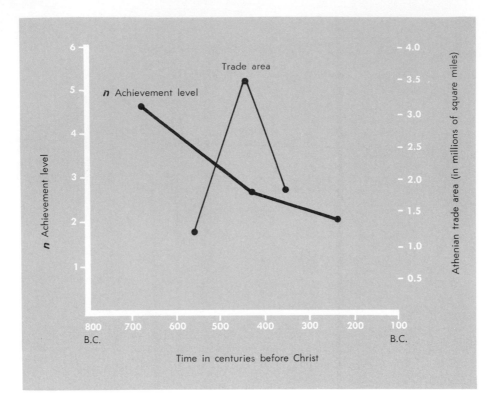

Figure 8–14. ACHIEVEMENT MOTIVATION AND AREA OF TRADE IN ANCIENT GREECE. *Average* n *achievement level plotted at midpoints of periods of growth, climax, and decline of Athenian civilization as reflected in the extent of her trade area (measured for sixth, fifth, and fourth centuries only). The* n ach *level is measured in terms of the achievement images in Greek literature during these periods. (From McClelland in J. W. Atkinson, ed.,* Motives in Fantasy, Action, and Society, *1958; reproduced by permission of D. Van Nostrand.)*

ited and calculated risks that are most likely, in the gross, to lead to realistic success. But how does it happen that many individuals simultaneously learn a need to achieve? We go back to the evidence on independence of training of children. In the period of early development in Greece, for example, there was little in the way of stable urban society;

a relatively nomadic way of life prevailed. The children of nomads are not likely to be long pampered—they must learn at an early age to carry their own weight and to shift for themselves. They tend to grow into achieving adults. When the Greek society became more stable, more "civilized," children had things easier. Frequently they were reared by slaves who, in order to keep their jobs, might be expected to discourage childhood independence rather than to encourage and reward it. A likely result is a population of adults who are not characterized by high achievement motivations. Such reasoning is, of course, speculative. We can say only that it is consonant with the data; it does not follow inexorably. One might nevertheless extend the speculation further and raise questions about such matters as the effect of present child-rearing practices on the achievement motivation of future adults in this society. And what about independence training in our kindergartens and primary grades? In a way the teachers of young children are professional child rearers. Do they encourage independence or do they, like the Greek slaves, tend to foster dependence?

OTHER PSYCHOLOGICAL MOTIVES

There have been attempts to create complete lists of psychological motives. We need not here try to review the various catalogues of motives. It will be enough to set down a list of those frequently posited by psychologists. Such a list includes:

Acquisitiveness
Need for security
Need for status
Need for autonomy
Need for affiliation
Need for achievement
Need for dependency
Need for aggression
Need for power
Need for nurturance

There have been successful attempts, using procedures similar to those employed in work on the achievement motive, to measure the need for affiliation (Shipley and Veroff, 1952) and the need for power (Veroff, 1957). In studies of motivation in whole societies (McClelland, 1961), the two motives of achievement and power have been explored as they relate to the life of nations.

Along a somewhat different line, a series of experiments has traced out some details of the way in which the affiliative motive functions (Schachter, 1959). For example, subjects who were highly anxious in an experimental situation were more likely than their non-anxious fellows to prefer human company while they waited for awhile in the experimental situation. Similarly, affiliative desires increase with increasing hunger. These and related experimental facts led the researcher to state the general hypothesis that underlying the subjects' tendency to seek the company of others were more basic needs for

anxiety *reduction* and for *self-evaluation*. In other words, in the views of this experimenter, the individual has a need not only to reduce anxiety but also to obtain social evaluations of the appropriateness and propriety of his own reactions.

Another line of development is exemplified by a recent theoretical formulation (White, 1959, 1963) maintaining that human beings have a highly significant *effectance motive*. This motive, seen as having no relation to biological imbalances and no simple way of being satiated, has as its function that of obtaining competence in dealing with the environment. Such a line of theoretical development, relating in some ways to the research on the exploratory and curiosity motives mentioned earlier, is continuing and doubtlessly will be subjected to laboratory tests.

We might go on here and for many pages in the consideration of psychological motives that have attracted the attention of psychologists. Actually, such motives may better be considered when we deal with matters of adjustment, of mental health, and of personality in the later chapters of the present book. The same holds, of course, for the consideration of the psychoanalytic theory of motivation.

UNCONSCIOUS MOTIVES

There was occasion earlier to refer to **unconscious motives**—motives that clearly influence behavior but that are wholly or partially beyond conscious awareness. If we observe carefully the behavior of an individual over a period of time, and hit upon the best motivational constructs to account for what he does, we may find it necessary to posit some motives of which the individual is partially or totally unaware. If for some reason we confront the person with our inference, he may deny with great vigor that he owns any such motive. In our desire to believe in our own rationality, many of us have a bilious resentment against the idea that we are moved by forces beyond our consciousness. But if we can tolerate the notion of unconscious motive, we may even find ourselves searching for possible unconscious factors behind some of our own more puzzling and apparently inconsistent behavior.

Evidence is strong in support of the concept of unconscious motives. And the idea is rendered more plausible to us if we realize how much of our behavior occurs without our awareness. We are seldom aware of the movement of our feet as we go downstairs. And if we focus our attention on these ordinarily unconscious movements, bringing them into consciousness, we are likely to stumble. It is possible to drive for an hour through heavy city traffic without being aware of a single movement and without being able later to recall a single stop or start or turn. Routine behaviors become automatic and unconscious, ticking off like clockwork while we are thinking about things miles away.

Motives, too, can operate at unawares. One dramatic illustration of this can be produced by the use of hypnosis. If a subject is deeply hypnotized and given the suggestion that when he wakes up he will have a strong hostility to his teacher, some unusual but psychologically meaningful events will transpire. The subject will demonstrate the hostility, all right. He may argue very disagreeably with the teacher. He may whisper audibly during crucial parts of the lecture. He may scribble nasty comments to his fellow students. And he will not have the slightest idea why he is engaging in this unusual behavior. If asked about it, he will make up some plausible reasons: "I'm just irritable today, I guess," or "I just never liked that fellow. He parts his hair wrong."

An actual experiment of this sort is reported by Erickson (1939). We can quote one of Erickson's descriptions:

The subject was told during hypnosis that he felt antagonistic, resentful and jealous of Dr. D., and that this emotional state would persist after he was awakened. He was also told that after awakening he would try to be courteous and acquiescent toward Dr. D. in every way and

would appear to be willing to do anything requested of him.

After being awakened the subject seemed to be entirely at ease; he responded courteously to some casual remarks addressed to him by Dr. D. Presently Dr. D. asked him if he would mind changing his seat. The subject replied certainly not, that he would be delighted, but that *he* was quite comfortable where he was; if, however, it would make *Dr. D.* more comfortable, he would be delighted to change his seat. The request was repeated, whereupon the subject arose and asked Dr. D. to designate the precise chair in which he was to seat himself. He walked over toward the designated chair but asked Dr. D. if perhaps a certain other chair might not serve even better since the reason Dr. D. had given for his request was that he was not quite in full view of the audience. When Dr. D. insisted that the designated chair was the better one the subject, with great courtesy, still questioned, seeming nevertheless most willing to do precisely what was desired and to be hesitant only about seating himself before he was absolutely certain of Dr. D.'s wishes. After much insistence by Dr. D. that he seat himself the subject agreed that the chair indicated was precisely the one that he ought to sit in and proceeded to do so, but as he did so he moved the chair about six inches to one side and shifted its position so that it faced in a slightly different direction. Immediately upon seating himself he turned and politely asked, "Is this the way you would like to have me?" After a few moments of casual conversation Dr. D. found fault with his position and asked him if he would mind taking his original chair. He rose promptly, said that he would be delighted to sit anywhere that Dr. D. wished but that perhaps it would be better if he sat on the table, and offered to move the designated chair to any desired spot, suggesting some clearly unsuitable positions; finally, when urged insistently to sit in the chair he again had to move it.

The motives we learn can operate similarly. The man who protests a great fondness for his father may behave in such a way that we are forced to the conclusion that he has considerable unconscious hostility toward the gentleman. He conspicuously forgets appointments with his father. He remembers his father's birthday a week late. He avoids contacts with his father. He tends to stutter when he's talking to his father but to no one else. He behaves toward his own children in ways almost ostentatiously different from his father's ways. And in the stories he writes and publishes there are frequent occasions in which somebody's father has gory accidents or suffers sore indignities. We are very inclined to say that his hostile feelings for his father are repressed—removed from consciousness—but nevertheless are affecting his behavior. We will consider more thoroughly these unconscious processes when we have a look at the reactions to frustration and conflict (Chap. 15).

CLASSIFICATION AND CRITERIA FOR MOTIVES

THE HIERARCHY OF MOTIVES

Two authors have in recent years stressed the idea, consonant with but not explicitly supported by data, that human motives can be arranged in a hierarchy from stronger and lower at one end to weaker and higher at the other (Maslow, 1954; McGregor, 1960). Such an idea has a significance both for a theoretical and a practical approach to motivation and commands attention here.

The hierarchy as originally described (Maslow, 1954) is as follows:

1. *The physiological needs,* hunger, thirst, air, etc.

2. *The safety needs,* the need for freedom from threat or danger, the need to ally oneself with the familiar and the secure.

3. *The belongingness and love needs,* the need for affiliation, for belongingness, for acceptance.

4. *The esteem needs,* the need for achievement, for strength, for competence, for reputation, for status or prestige.

5. *The need for self-actualization,* the need for self-fulfillment, to realize potentialities, to become what one is capable of becoming.

6. *Cognitive needs,* the need to know and understand, curiosity, the need to understand the mysterious, the need to tackle the unknown.

7. *Aesthetic needs,* the need for symmetry, order, system, and structure.

Figure 8–15. HIGHER-ORDER MOTIVATION? *Some psychologists believe that creative work will be most likely when there is a freedom from the lower and stronger motives; that the well-fed, well-housed, personally and socially secure individual is the one most likely to explore and to create. Photograph above shows Henry Moore, eminent British sculptor, at work.*

This approach to motivation has it that the lower needs, in the face of deficits, are the more potent needs. The ravenously hungry man or the man with a shortage of air will seek above all else to remove these deficits. He has and can have no concern for the higher needs, often not even the safety needs. We saw, in the studies of the semistarved (pp. 222–223), that prolonged deficit of food produces a mighty preoccupation with the removal of nutritional deficits. Similarly, if a man feels threatened, or in psychological danger, he must devote his energies to the achieving of security, showing little or no concern for the higher and more social needs. In order for the motives of a self-actualizing kind to become activated and to lead to behavior, the theory goes, there must be a freedom from deficits, a freedom from the potent necessity to seek physiological goals or safety goals or even the social goals of love and belongingness. Necessity, this theory has it, is not the mother of invention. Certainly not the grim necessity of sheer survival or the necessity of finding enough food. Freedom from deficit must precede invention and creativity—which grow out of the cognitive and aesthetic needs.

Proceeding from this general view of the hierarchy of motives, the second author cited above (McGregor, 1960) has pointed out that in the management of human affairs, in industry and elsewhere, efforts to create the conditions under which the higher motives can become activated may have mighty consequences for the level and quality of human productivity and creativity.

Although many students may join with those psychologists who resonate favorably to the theory of the hierarchy of motives—the theory does take what may be described as a pleasant, optimistic and perhaps humanistic stance on the nature of human nature—there is not much hard evidence to support the hierarchical view. The view has a plausibility about it, and we can bring to it a variety of supporting observations found in everyday life; nevertheless, the theory must be held only tentatively.

DEPENDABLE MOTIVES

A study of motivation has a relevance for the answers to our large and encompassing questions about the nature of human nature. Is war inevitable? Is man by nature aggressive? Is man by nature better suited to a capitalistic or a communistic way of life? If we choose to confront such basic questions—and why not?—we need to know what motives we can count on being there in the behavior of any man anywhere.

One psychologist (Klineberg, 1954) has developed a procedure for examining the *dependability* of human motives, for examining the question of whether a motive can be depended upon to be there, once we know the organism to be a human being. The procedure calls for the study of evidence to see whether it fits the following three *criteria of dependability*.

1. *The criterion of animal continuity.* Is there evidence that animals, particularly the apes, demonstrate the sort of behavior in which we are interested? In the light of what we know about evolution, our confidence in the existence of a given motive is increased if there is evidence that it appears below man in the animal hierarchy.

2. *The criterion of biochemical or physiological bases.* Biochemical or physiological evidence of a condition within the human organism gives us greater confidence that the motive will appear in all human organisms. If it is rooted either in structure or in physiological function, we believe it to be species-determined rather than culture-determined.

3. *The criterion of universality.* Does the behavior in which we are interested appear in all individuals in all cultures? Evidence that the behavior occurs universally, in spite of wide variations in cultures and in individual experience within cultures, gives us faith that the behavior, and the motive lying behind it, is truly fundamental to human nature.

A dependable motive, in Klineberg's terms, meets all three of these criteria. We need to bear in mind, perhaps, in dealing in this way with motives, that we are using "dependability" in a highly specific sense. Here the concept has a meaning of a dependable attribute of universal human nature. Every one of us can have motives that are dependable in another sense; they are dependably ours and can be depended upon to guide our behavior. But our motives may be unique to us, or unique to our own culture and thereby lacking dependability of the sort Klineberg deals with.

Actually, very few of the psychological motives that concern us in our culture meet these criteria of dependability.

HUMAN MOTIVES AND "HUMAN NATURE"

In many of our more philosophical moods, we find ourselves inclined to make cloud-high generalizations about human nature. In our yearning to see man clearly and to see him whole, we often find ourselves thinking of human behavior in terms of those motives that are common to all men everywhere. Certainly if we knew for sure what motives, physiological and psychological, are found in all members of the human species, we would be in a good position to make some sound general statements about one very vital aspect of universal human nature. We know that it is human nature to breathe, to eat, to mate, to escape pain. But these biologically rooted elements of humanity are not the ones we find most intellectually nutritious when we wrestle with the larger problems of man's nature. We want to make statements about man's natural gregariousness or his natural aggressiveness or the pervasiveness of the profit motive.

All of our consideration of the psychological motives of man adds up, among other things, to what may be no more than an enlightened confusion about the use and usefulness of motivational constructs. Psychologists are in continuing debate about the best ways to conceive motivation. With considerable frequency they have to leave the discussion table to pursue research in this difficult and still confused area. What might the beginning student get out of all this? Of what value is enlightened confusion? One very important benefit might well be an adaptive hesitancy to make easy interpretations of the motives of friends—or of oneself. To characterize a person as status-driven, or acquisitive or dominant or aggressive is to assume quite a license. Such an act of characterization—or explanation—presupposes very careful observation of a great deal of behavior, a carefully wrought interpretation, and an examination of the factual justification for the positing of a persisting condition of the organism about which we speak. Most of us, whether novelists

or teachers or salesmen or politicians or parents or poets, can probably profit by increased accuracy and humility in our interpretations of human motives.

And most of us, as individuals concerned with our own personalities, can usefully apply even greater caution to our characterizations of ourselves. While each of us, in a way, is the world's greatest expert on himself, each of us also is likely to be short in objectivity when it comes to observing and interpreting his own behavior, when it comes to putting a descriptive finger on his own true motives.

An illustration of ways in which assumptions, commonly shared or otherwise, about motivation can influence behavior is presented in an analysis of two "theories" of motivations prevalent today in American industry. The author describes the two prevailing theories [2] as follows:

Assumptions in Theory X: The Traditional View

1. The average human being has an inherent dislike of work and will avoid it if he can.

2. Because of this human characteristic of dislike of work, most people must be coerced, controlled, directed, threatened with punishment to get them to put forth adequate effort toward the achievement of organizational objectives.

3. The average human being prefers to be directed, wishes to avoid responsibility, has relatively little ambition, wants security above all.

Assumptions in Theory Y: The Integrative View

1. The expenditure of physical and mental effort in work is as natural as play or rest.

2. External control and the threat of punishment are not the only means for bringing about effort toward organizational objectives. Man will exercise self-direction and self-control in the service of objectives to which he is committed.

3. Commitment to objectives is a function of

---

[2] By permission from *The Human Side of Enterprise* by P. McGregor, pp. 33, 34, 47, 48. Copyright, 1960. McGraw-Hill Book Co., Inc.

the rewards associated with their achievement.

4. The average human being learns, under proper conditions, not only to accept but to seek responsibility.

5. The capacity to exercise a relatively high degree of imagination, ingenuity, and creativity in the solution of organizational problems is widely, not narrowly, distributed in the population.

6. Under the conditions of modern industrial life, the intellectual potentialities of the average human being are only partially utilized.

It is easy to visualize the stern and directive administrative behavior of foremen, managers, parents, teachers or deans who adhere to Theory X. Quite different behaviors—and perhaps presently fairly unusual behaviors—follow from the espousal of Theory Y. The industrial organization, for example, that tried to implement Theory Y in its structure and functioning would be regarded, initially at least, as mildly insane. But some companies are moving in the Y direction. Perhaps it is the direction in which lies greatly enhanced human effectiveness in an affluent society.

SUMMARY

1. If we are going to understand the psychological process, we almost inevitably must concern ourselves with motives, for it is a *motivated* organism that senses, interprets, and learns about its world.

2. In thinking about motivating conditions, we might do well to adopt as a tentative model that of homeostasis, or the tendency of an organism to maintain a constancy of internal state.

3. The use of motivational constructs to "explain" behavior seems necessary when we consider the variety of behaviors that are involved in the attainment of a single goal.

4. Similarly, when we see that large and sometimes violent responses are set off by relatively small stimuli, we very naturally infer the existence of motivating conditions in the organism.

5. Motivation may be regarded as one segment of the psychological process, but it must be viewed as a segment that interacts intricately with other segments, such as sensing, perceiving, and learning.

6. A motive is an energizing condition of the organism that serves to direct that organism toward a goal or goals of a certain kind. The general concept of motive is distinguished from the more biologically oriented concept of "need"; it is used to include "drive," as well as both physiological and psychological motives.

7. Our confidence in using a motivational construct is greatest if we can observe (a) conditions of arousal, (b) selectivity and directionality of behavior, and (c) satiation. We can use these three rubrics in analyzing the working of a motive once we have reason to believe the motivational construct is justifiably employed.

8. Motives are constructs. They are inferred from observed behavior. We never see hunger or jealousy; we see only behavior and relations among behaviors. We infer motives and think of them as "causes" of behavior.

9. The concept of motive has almost entirely replaced the concept of instinct in human psychology. The preference is for learned rather than elaborate innate patterns of motivated behavior.

10. Physiological motives are those motives which are closely related to the physiological needs of the organism. This class of motives, often referred to also as primary motives or drives, includes the motives of hunger, sex, thirst, the need for air, and the need to escape pain.

11. The condition of arousal of the hunger motive includes internal conditions and external incentives; the internal processes in-

volve the reaction of the hypothalamus to the chemical state of the blood. Stomach contractions are also involved but are not essential for the arousal of food-seeking behavior.

12. There is good evidence that special areas of the hypothalamus are involved in the arousal and control of the hunger motive. Direct electrical stimulation of certain structures will cause even a satiated animal to eat, while stimulation of other areas will cause a hungry animal to stop eating.

13. The exact nature of the process whereby the brain responds to blood chemistry is not known.

14. Research on specific hungers shows that both rats and children will, given free choice, select food that compensates for specific dietary deficiencies.

15. Incentives to hunger include a wide variety of food objects for which preferences have been learned. Also there are temporal cues and social factors involved in the arousal of hunger. The selectivity and directionality involved in hunger can be seen in the influence of hunger on perception and in the way semistarved subjects are almost entirely preoccupied with food.

16. Normally, the well-fed organism stops eating and loses interest in food; but eating in some cases takes on a psychological function, and satiation is no longer a matter of removing simple physiological deficits.

17. The motive of thirst is aroused when the water balance of the body sets off certain neural mechanisms. Water intake is related to, but is not precisely controlled by, the dryness of oral tissues. Instead, some receptors, perhaps osmoreceptors in the hypothalamus, apparently respond to the level and the chemical constitution of the body's water.

18. The areas of the brain involved in the control of water intake have been traced down and are to be found in a narrowly confined area of the hypothalamus.

19. Generally speaking, the animal stops drinking when its water level has reached a certain point, and when the constitution of the water is of a certain kind. But the control of water intake is not a simple matter. Apparently, in ceasing its water intake, the organism senses the level and chemical constitution of the body's water and also responds to conditions in the mouth. Also the distension of the stomach has a role in the cessation of water intake.

20. The sex motive is in some ways similar to both the hunger and the thirst motives. It stems from physiological processes and results in behavior that is selective and directional. But sex is not a vital motive and, unlike hunger or thirst, is given a great deal of social restriction and control.

21. The internal processes of the sex motive involve the secretion of androgens for males and estrogens for females, but for human organisms strength of sexual motivation is not entirely bound to sexual hormones.

22. There are wide variations, from culture to culture and from individual to individual, in the frequency of sexual activity and in the incentives that set off sexual interest.

23. With respect to selectivity, directionality, and satiation, the sexual motive operates much as does hunger or thirst. With respect to satiation, there are again cases in which the removal of simple physiological deficits does not remove sexual interest and activity. The strength of sexual motives for animals is not proportional, over a period of time, to the period of deprivation of sexual activity.

24. The avoidance of pain can be a very strong motive in human behavior, but it differs from other motives in that it becomes a motive as a result of sudden changes in the environment. Pain arises as a result of actual damage or inflammation of tissues or from a variety of stresses. It easily and quickly serves as an activator of many neural circuits that can be involved in the removal of a noxious stimulus.

25. Behavior, in the face of pain, is influenced by past experience.

26. In addition to the physiological motives

based on obvious biological needs, there is increasing evidence that there are also exploratory or problem-seeking motives.

27. Psychological motives are energizing conditions of the organism that function in many ways as do physiological motives; however, these motives cannot at the moment be related to any kinds of biological or physiological imbalances in the organism. Psychological motives are more likely than physiological motives to be learned.

28. An examination of the research on the achievement motive illustrates many aspects, problems, and challenges in psychologists' attempts to deal with psychological motives.

29. An analysis of the psychological problem of psychological motives presents difficult problems of definition, classification, semantics, and analysis.

30. The achievement motive has been measured through a specialized use of Thematic Apperception Test procedures.

31. The achievement motive is learned by children who are given early independence training and who are rewarded for independent achievement.

32. The achievement motive is aroused in situations that challenge the individual or bring about ego involvement.

33. The selectivity of perception of those high in the need for achievement is shown by the great speed with which they perceive achievement-relevant words.

34. In a wide variety of situations in which the reward is the attainment of high standards of performance, subjects high in need achievement outperform those who are low.

35. There is evidence that societies differ in the prevalence of a high need for achievement among their citizens and that those societies in which many individuals are high in need achievement are likely to show vigorous economic development.

36. It seems reasonable that child-rearing practices prevalent in a society influence the level and prevalence of achievement motivation in that society. There has been research on the measurement of the power motive and of an affiliative motive and experimental work on other motives, including the functioning of the need for affiliation; but for most of the psychological motives there remain difficult problems of definition and classification and measurement.

37. When we observe the behavior of human individuals, we are sometimes unable to account for the behavior we see except in terms of unconscious motives—motives that the individual cannot report upon or describe and the existence of which perhaps the individual will deny.

38. The existence and functioning of unconscious motivational states can be demonstrated and examined through the experimental use of hypnosis.

39. Both physiological and psychological motives may, perhaps with intellectual profit, be thought of as falling into a hierarchical arrangement extending from lower and stronger motives, such as hunger and thirst, to higher and weaker motives, such as cognitive and aesthetic needs.

40. The hierarchical view of motivation has it that the higher and weaker motives can become aroused and can direct behavior only when the lower and stronger motives have been satisfied.

41. A motive can be judged in terms of the likelihood that it constitutes a dependable part of universal human nature. If a motive is (a) found in subhuman organisms (characterized by animal continuity), (b) rooted in discoverable physiological processes, and (c) found universally in all human beings and in all cultures, it may, in the present terms, be said to be dependable.

42. Few if any of the psychological or social motives on the grounds of biological, physiological, psychological, and anthropological evidence can be judged to meet all three criteria of dependability.

43. In our everyday appraisal of human

motivation, we may tend to place an emphasis on deficits, on the alleged inclinations to avoid work and to dodge responsibility. On the other hand, we may adopt what has been termed the "integrative view" of motivation and hold that work and responsibility are not avoided but are sought out and that self-direction, imagination, and commitment to objectives can be expected of most human beings.

RESEARCH REPORTS

FACTORS CONTROLLING FOOD INTAKE [*]

There is continuing research to discover the mechanisms involved in the regulating of food intake. It has been known for some time that lesions in the ventral medial hypothalamus of the rat produces hyperphagia or an increased food intake. Initially, after such a lesion, there is a "dynamic" phase in which the animal shows a very high intake of food, eating as much as two or three times what he did before the operation. After awhile, however, as the animal gains more and more weight, food intake decreases and eventually reaches a "static" phase, in which food intake returns to what it was before the operation.

In this study, Corbit and Stellar investigated these phenomena, studying systematically (a) the effect of stimulus properties of food and (b) the degree of obesity of the rat, as these variables affect food intake. They measured food intake and body weight of rats as the sensory properties of the diet were varied; also, they presented the experimental animals with the same diet at times when their body weights were very different.

In the experiment concerning us here, nine female adult rats were divided into an experimental group of five and a control group of four animals. Body weights and food intake were measured before the experiment began. The five experimental animals underwent a delicate operation, in which a direct current of precisely controlled magnitude was passed through the tip of a stainless-steel electrode for 20 seconds, thereby destroying a small area of tissue in the region of the ventral medial nuclei of the hypothalamus

[*] John D. Corbit and Eliot Stellar, Palatability, food intake, and obesity in normal and hyperphagic rats, J. comp. physiol. Psychol., 1964, 58, 63–67.

of each of the animals. After the experiment was done, the precise location of the lesion was verified through histological examination of the tissues affected.

After surgery, the operated animals were allowed free access to Purina laboratory chow and water for from 9 to 16 days to determine whether or not they demonstrated hyperphagia. After it was determined that the rats did demonstrate hyperphagia, their body weights were reduced by reducing food intake until body weights reached preoperative levels. Then food intake of both the experimental and control animals was restricted to 13 grams of pellets per day for 75 days; following this period of controlled food intake, all animals, the experimental and control alike, were given free access to a series of diets in the following order: (1) Purina laboratory chow powder, (2) Purina laboratory chow pellets, (3) a high-fat diet, (4) Purina laboratory chow pellets again, and (5) a mineral-oil diet. Water was always available in any quantity the animals desired. During this part of the procedure, each animal continued to receive a given diet until its body weight reached a steady state—asymptote. After body weight had leveled off in this manner, the animal was presented with the next diet in the series. When placed on the initial diet with Purina powder, the hyperphagic rats and the normal rats showed about the same food intake and gained at approximately the same rate. When the diet was changed, in the second phase, the operated animals for a definite period showed a *vastly increased intake of food* and an accompanying gain in body weight. After their weight increased an appreciable amount, their intake of pellets declined so that it was not very much higher than that of the normal rats. During this period the normal rats gained a bit in body weight but did not show any increase in intake of food.

On the third phase of the study, when the animals were given free access to a high-fat diet, the hyperphagic rats showed a similar pattern of eating. Initially, they increased very appreciably in their caloric intake and began to gain weight at a rapid rate. After weight had gone up, however, the intake of food declined. The normal rats, by contrast, showed a very constant intake of the high-fat diet and a fairly constant gain in weight over the period of this phase of the experiment.

The fourth and fifth phases of the experiment yielded similar results. As the diet was changed, the caloric intake of the hyperphagic rats jumped to a relatively high level and stayed there until body weight began to rise appreciably. As body weight went up, caloric intake went down.

The experimenters conclude from these results that the animals with lesions of the central medial hypothalamus are more reactive to the stimulus properties of food than are normal animals. The researchers also conclude that some correlate of obesity exerts an inhibitory effect on food intake. Throughout the experiment the hyperphagic animals, when they gained weight, showed an accompanying decrease in caloric intake until, at a "static" phase in the experiment, food intake reached such a level that further gain in weight did not occur. Also the experimenters point out that during the second exposure to pellets, the animals took in fewer calories of pellets than they did when first exposed to pellets. The second exposure to pellets came at a time when both the hyperphagic animals and the normal animals were relatively very obese. These facts lead the experimenters to speculate that the central nervous system is somehow sensitive to some correlate of obesity. There may be some afferent signal, they say, arising from adipose tissue, or perhaps some factor in the blood varies with the amount of stored fat and gives the nervous system signals. Or, in line with other theoretical trends, they state that the inhibitory effect of obesity may be connected with thermal events in the central nervous system.

TEMPERATURE AS A MOTIVE [*]

A large proportion of the experimental work on motivation has dealt with hunger, sex, and thirst. In this study, Howard shows that the temperature motive can be used in experimental work on animal behavior and that rats' motivated behavior, originally set off in the interest of escaping cold and approaching warmth, can be instigated by stimuli that have been *associated with* the experience of cold.

This researcher used as subjects thirty female hooded rats, approximately 90 days of age. These thirty were divided into three groups of ten rats each. The basic apparatus used in the research was a box, approximately 10 inches square and 8 inches high, that had formerly been a picnic chest. The chest was refrigerated in such a way

that its temperature could be controlled. A hole approximately 2½ inches in diameter was cut in the top of the chest; attached to this hole was a piece of cloth, which was allowed to hang down within easy reach of a rat in the chest itself. The members of one of the three groups of rats were put into the cold box when it was at a temperature of 20°F. The second group was placed in the box when it was at a temperature of 40°F., and the third group when the box was at room temperature—75°F. Every one of the rats, when placed in the insulated chest, readily grasped the cloth and climbed out into a box above it, which was maintained at room temperature. Each of the animals in each of the groups received 15 trials per day. There was a recording of the time elapsed between the rat's insertion in the refrigerated chest and his entry into the box above it.

Throughout the experiment, the animals who were put into the colder box escaped most rapidly; the animals who were put into the 40° box, less rapidly; and the animals who were placed in the room temperature box, much less rapidly still. Cold is clearly the motivating condition. Apparently the colder the animal is, the more strongly he is motivated to do something about it.

In addition to this straightforward kind of finding, the experiment showed that the animals learned to avoid the cold box even when it was not cold. After each animal had had 35 trials in his respective experimental group, the temperature of the lower box was changed to 75°, or room temperature. The results during this testing period are presented below.

Previous experience of animals	Mean time in seconds of escape from 75° chest
With 20°	149.64
With 40°	210.06
With 75°	259.49

These results (showing statistically significant differences between each of the three groups) led the researcher to conclude that the animals who had experienced cold in the experimental box had learned an "acquired temperature response" to the cues in the refrigerated chest. Thus, we can say that environmental cues, having been associated with motivating conditions, were sufficient to set off motivated behavior, even in the absence of the original motivating condition. Animals escaped from the chest as if it were still cold: those who had experienced it

---

[*] Thomas C. Howard, Conditioned temperature drive in rats, *Psychol. Reports,* 1962, **10**, 371–373.

as a very cold chest escaped from it as if it were very cold; those who had experienced it as moderately cold escaped from it as if it were still moderately cold; and so on.

THE AFFILIATIVE MOTIVE [*]

Among the findings reported by one experimenter out of a systematic series of studies of affiliative behavior (Schachter, 1959) was that subjects (college students) who are either first-born or only children in their families differ in affiliative behavior from those subjects who come later in the birth order; the first-born and only child, when they have to wait for a feared coming event, show a relatively strong preference for spending the frightening interval with company. Such a finding suggests either (a) that people who are first-born or an only child may somehow learn a stronger affiliative motive or (b) that they learn a certain set of behaviors, not learned by others, which they employ in a situation such as that presented by the experiment. The research reported here attempts to bring data to bear on the question: Is the behavior only specific behavior, or is it best thought of as arising from an affiliative motive? The attempt here is to measure directly the affiliative motive for first-born and later-born subjects.

Subjects employed in the research were 42 individuals, all volunteers, who ranged in age from 11 to 62 years, with a median age of 20 years. Of the subjects, approximately half were in the first-born group and half were later-born. The groups were matched with respect to sex. Each subject was tested individually by responding to three Thematic Apperception Test pictures that had been previously used in attempts to measure the need for affiliation (n aff). In the testing procedure, each picture was presented for twenty seconds. The subject was then given four minutes to write a story, guided by the standard "four questions": (a) What is happening? Who are the persons? (b) What has led up to this situation? That is, what has happened in the past? (c) What is being thought: What is wanted? By whom? (d) What will happen? What will be done? These stories were scored blind; that is, without the scorer's knowing the identity of the subject or whether or not the subject was first- or later-born. The scoring involved the assessment and tabulation of affiliative themes occurring in the projective stories.

The scores on the need for affiliation for the first- and later-born subjects were examined in a variety of ways and were found, with respect to any criterion that could be established, to differ significantly. It became very clear that first-born subjects had higher scores on need affiliation on this TAT procedure. They saw significantly more themes of relevance for affiliation. First-born subjects also varied one from another more extremely than did the later-born subjects, a fact which made difficult a statistical comparison of the two groups. The table below is a quick comparison of the need-affiliation scores of all subjects, all female subjects and then of all male subjects.

This particular experiment did not include any attempt to validate the TAT score for the affiliative need. It remains conceivable, then, that the first-born people have learned specific behaviors with respect to the telling of projective stories, and that the later-born people have not learned these particular behaviors. It may be simpler and more straightforward, however, to interpret these results in terms of a motivational condition of the organism.

EXPLORATORY BEHAVIOR AND CURIOSITY IN CHILDREN [*]

A number of researches, both on animals and on human subjects, have indicated that in the absence of any strong and specific needs organisms will engage in exploratory behavior and, further, that there seem to be grounds for regarding curiosity or, perhaps more accurately, a need for variation as an energizing condition that arouses exploratory behavior.

The present report concerns the work of two experimenters, Pielstick and Woodruff, who have tried to find out, for human subjects, whether age and intellectual ability have a bearing on exploratory behavior.

The study selected as subjects 64 children, half of them from the second grade and half from the sixth grade of six randomly selected elementary schools in DeKalb County, Illinois. The mean chronological age of the younger group was 8 years, 4 months and of the older group, 11 years, 11 months. Sixteen of the children in each

[*] William N. Dember, Birth order and need affiliation, J. abn. soc. Psychol., 1964, 68, 555–557.

[*] N. L. Pielstick and A. Bond Woodruff, Exploratory behavior and curiosity in two age and ability groups of children, Psychol. Reports, 1964, 14, 831–838.

RELATIONS BETWEEN BIRTH ORDER AND N AFF SCORE

N AFF	ALL SUBJECTS		FEMALES		MALES	
	First-born	Later-born	First-born	Later-born	First-born	Later-born
High	18	5	12	2	6	2
Low	4	17	2	12	2	6

group were well within the average range of mental ability (with Binet IQ's of 92 to 108). The IQ's of the other sixteen of each group were at least two sigmas above the mean (132 and above).

Each of the 64 subjects in the experiment was brought into a room in a mobile laboratory where he could be exposed to a range of stimuli and could be observed through a one-way mirror. When first brought into the experimental room, the subject was asked to be seated at a table containing a kaleidoscope, a box containing four wire puzzles, a partially assembled 500-piece jig-saw puzzle, a children's book written in Russian, and a "novel object" (a 10-inch-high triangular structure, painted brown and yellow, the likes of which the children had very probably not seen before). When the child was seated at the table, the experimenter who had ushered him in excused himself, giving the subject permission to "spend his time with the objects" on the table. The experimenter was gone for seven minutes, during which the observer, located behind the one-way mirror, watched and recorded the behavior of the child in relation to the curiosity-arousing objects.

After seven minutes, the experimenter re-entered the lab and instructed the child in the use of the tachistoscope, a device for exposing slides for set periods of time. The array contained 24 prepared slides, representing eight common objects, with each object depicted at three levels of complexity. That is, a house was drawn with one or two or three degrees of complexity of detail; the simplest drawings were merely outlines, while the most complex drawings approached photographic quality of detail.

The experimenters were curious first about the relation of age and mental ability to manifestations of curiosity in the children. Neither variable, under these experimental conditions, seemed to be influential. The amount of time the children spent with the various objects to which they were exposed varied from object to object but not with either ability or age. For all subjects taken together, the mean time spent with the jig-saw puzzle was significantly greater than the mean time spent with any of the other objects. There were also no differences with respect to either age or intelligence ability when the objects were grouped into categories. The authors regarded the book and jig-saw puzzle as objects giving opportunity for expression of *epistemic curiosity*, curiosity directed at knowing more about something; they regarded the mirror and the novel object as opportunities for expressing *perceptual* curiosity, while the kaleidoscope and the wire puzzles were classed as objects providing opportunity for expressing *manipulative behavior*. The younger and the older children did not differ significantly in frequency or in extent of behavior in any of these categories. Nor were there differences with respect to intellectual level. There were some differences, however, with respect to behavior on the tachistoscopically exposed slides. Generally speaking, the younger children exposed more slides more frequently than did the older children. Also, the more gifted children of both age groups tended to expose more slides than did the less gifted. In all four groups the children tended to take more frequent looks at the more complex drawings. The researchers point out that the older children may have shown less curiosity here simply because they had had more experience with the objects shown on the slides.

SUGGESTED READINGS

Brown, J. S. *The motivation of behavior.* New York: McGraw-Hill, 1961.

Cofer, C. N., and M. H. Appley. *Motivation: Theory and research.* New York: Wiley, 1964.

Ford, C. S., and F. A. Beach. *Patterns of sexual behavior.* New York: Harper, 1951.

McClelland, D. C. *The achieving society.* Princeton: Van Nostrand, 1961.

McClelland, D. C., J. W. Atkinson, R. A. Clark, and E. L. Lowell. *The achievement motive.* New York: Appleton-Century-Crofts, 1953.

Murray, H. A., et al. *Explorations in personality: A clinical and experimental study of fifty men of college age.* By the workers at the Harvard Psychological Clinic. New York: Oxford University Press, 1938 (reprinted 1953).

Young, P. T. *Motivation and emotion: A survey of the determinants of human and animal activity.* New York: Wiley, 1961.

OUTLINE / CHAPTER 9

I. EMOTIONS AND MOTIVES

II. WHAT ARE EMOTIONS?

    A. Emotions as Conscious Feelings
    B. Emotion as Response
      1. External Response
      2. Internal Response
      3. Recording of Internal Responses

III. CONDITIONS OF AROUSAL OF EMOTION

    A. Fear
    B. Anger
    C. Annoyance
    D. Happiness and Other Pleasant Emotions

IV. THEORIES OF EMOTION

V. EMOTIONS AND MALADJUSTMENT

    A. Phobias
    B. Psychosomatic Reactions

VI. EMOTIONS AND THE PERSON

    A. Emotions and Personality
    B. The Development of Emotion
      1. The Emotions of the Infant
      2. The Emotions of the Adolescent
      3. Emotional Maturity

VII. SUMMARY

VIII. RESEARCH REPORTS

CHAPTER 9

EMOTIONS

When we see an organism sensing, interpreting, and in ever changing ways responding to its environment, we ordinarily "explain" what we see in terms of the organism's **motives.** We define motives as activating conditions leading, through selective and directed behavior, to goals. But we cannot account for the energies of the organism entirely in terms of its motives. In the grip of a hunger motive, the organism may on one occasion seek food in fear and trembling, while in a different situation he may forage with what appears to be exultant and optimistic joy. The energy aspect of his motivated behavior is quite different in the two situations. The emotions—the fears, angers, and joys—that accompany motivated behavior need to be understood if we are to deal most intelligently with that behavior.

Emotions, like motives, are constructs. We observe behaviors and feel that we need to infer or invent constructs to account for what we observe. We concern ourselves here with emotional behaviors and with the special constructs employed to deal with these behaviors.

EMOTIONS AND MOTIVES

It will be helpful to think of emotions as accompanying motivated behavior. Rarely do human beings seek goals without fear or joy or happiness or jealousy or anger accompanying that seeking. We live our daily lives in the midst of what may feel like a whole and ever changing symphony of emotional experience. We probably are more aware of our emotions than we are of our motives themselves.

Emotions accompanying motivated behavior may *facilitate* that behavior. The basketball player happily anticipating victory seems

253

to play with his greatest skill. Emotions may, on the other hand, *interfere* with behavior. The violently angry man is not the one best equipped to repair a watch or to solve a problem in calculus.

Sometimes, emotions may function as motives. Once an emotional state has been firmly connected by experience to an object or situation, that emotion also meets our definition of a motive—*a condition of the organism leading it, through selective and directive behavior, to seek certain goals.* The person who has developed an overriding fear of high places and a deep anger at women can be depended on to guide his behavior as if the absence of both high places and women were goals devoutly to be wished. In this case, the association of an "unpleasant" emotion with objects or situations causes avoidance, while a contrasting association of a "pleasant" emotion might have caused the active seeking of specific objects or situations. As with a motive, we can see the conditions of arousal of these states, can see selectivity and directionality of behavior, and can observe a change in behavior once women and high places have been escaped. For these reasons emotions cannot always be separated from motives; sometimes they are the epitome of motives.

WHAT ARE EMOTIONS?

In spite of the vividness of our personal knowledge of emotions, it is very difficult to put down an objective definition of the term. We "know" more than we can say about emotions for when we try to look at them they turn out to be enormously complex.

EMOTIONS AS CONSCIOUS FEELINGS

When a man is angry, he knows it. He feels angry, and he can, unless he is too angry, tell you something about the extent and flavor of the anger he feels. He also knows and can report upon his depression, his joy, his anxiety, his fears, his jealousy, his happiness, or upon his joyous anger or his pleasant thrill of fear or his heady mixture of hostility and af-

fection. Emotion is subjective experience. As such, it is rich, varied, concrete, and personal—but very difficult to define or study. The difficulties can be illustrated by one study (Nafe, 1937) in which observers often described "pleasant" emotion as a "bright pressure-like" sensation while "unpleasantness" was a "dull pressure." Along the same lines, it has been found (Hoisington, 1928) that these "pressures" were usually located in the abdominal region for unpleasantness and near the upper part of the body about the shoulders for pleasantness. These reports were not emotions but verbal descriptions of them, apparently descriptions of sensory images of internal processes.

A man can report introspectively that now he is gripped by anger, now inundated by fear. But we cannot know that two people who report an anger are reporting the same thing or that one anger is the same as another in the same person. And, of course, we are utterly unable to study the conscious emotions, if any, of an earthworm or a cat. Animals cannot report their feelings, so we must study their emotions through the observation of nonverbal behavior. We infer emotions in animals because of observable behavior analogous to what we believe to be emotional behavior in human beings.

Data on the conscious and reportable aspects of human emotion are reported in a study of the emotions of aviators who had just returned from combat missions (Shaffer, 1947).

REPORTED SYMPTOM	PER CENT OF 4,504 AVIATORS REPORTING
Pounding heart	86
Muscular tenseness	83
Irritability	80
Dryness of throat and mouth	80
Cold sweat	79
Butterflies in stomach	76
Feeling of unreality	69
Frequent urination	65
Trembling	64

SYMPTOM	PER CENT REPORTING
Confused and rattled	53
Feeling weak or faint	41
Poor memory for what happened on mission	39
Feeling sick to stomach	38
Poor ability to concentrate	35
Wetting or soiled pants	5

All these were effects noted during or soon after a combat mission. There were also some reportable delayed effects frequently noticed.

SYMPTOM	PER CENT REPORTING
Tired out	92
Restlessness	89
Feeling depressed	80
Jumpy at loud or sudden noises	76
Grouchiness	65
Poor appetite	63
Bad dreams	58

EMOTION AS RESPONSE

While we can learn something about emotions by studying the conscious reports of people who have them, there are great limitations inherent in introspective data. We want to study responses—physiological and behavioral responses—that occur along with subjective reports of emotions. To do so, we must turn from the study of conscious experience to other observations.

External Response

The angry man is himself the only one who can know for sure what he feels. But we all can know what he *does* under specified conditions when we observe him from the outside. When we observe his behavior, we can then, if we are careful, justifiably apply such constructs as anger or fear to describe his internal states, which we cannot see.

In lower animals, emotional responses appear to involve readymade behavioral patterns that often need only be triggered off by appropriate external **stimuli.** The cat cornered by a barking dog, for example, will crouch in fear, growl, lower its ears, raise its back, and lash its tail. All cats will behave very similarly in the same situation. (See Fig. 9–1.) As a matter of fact, the cat can be made to behave in this manner through the direct stimulation of specific parts of its **hypothalamus** (Lashley, 1938). Actually, the hypothalamus is probably only a triggering mechanism for such emotional behavior, since the emotional behavior obtained by such stimulation stops abruptly when the stimulation ceases (Masserman, 1943, 1946), whereas normal emotional behavior dies away slowly, as if a "balance" were slowly being regained. Other parts of the brain are also clearly involved in emotion. Areas of the cerebral cortex seem to exert both excitory and inhibitory influences on "rage" mechanisms; for example, dogs with the cerebral cortex removed show a rage response at the slightest touch, a phenomenon indicating that the intact cortex may inhibit rage responses (Young, 1962). Lesions in the **rhinencephalon** have been shown to make formerly vicious animals docile (Schreiner and Kling, 1956).

In animals, the relatively fixed patterns of what seems to be emotional response have direct value for survival. One can see that the emotional cat is behaving in a self-preservative way. She is prepared to defend herself. Even the animals that "freeze" in terror may be engaging in biologically sensible ways: in a predatory world, movement is sometimes dangerous, while doing nothing is relatively safe —particularly for the animal possessed of protective coloration.

In human organisms there appear to be relatively few fixed behavioral patterns of emotional response. The startle pattern is one of the few exceptions. If we casually observe a person when he is startled by such a sudden change in his environment as the shot of a gun, we may see him do a variety of startled and perhaps startling things. But if we use high-speed movie photography, so that we can later see the behavior in slow motion, certain relatively invariable responses are seen in

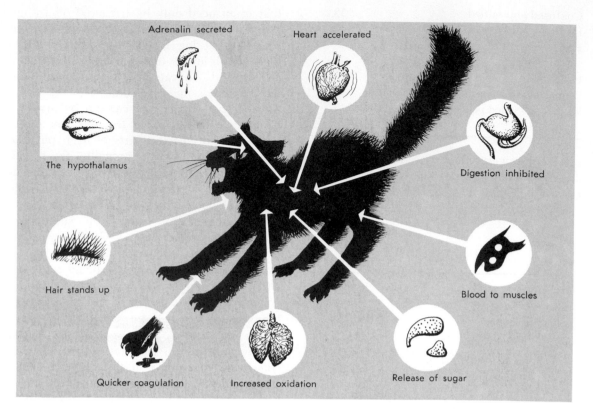

Labels on figure: Adrenalin secreted · Heart accelerated · The hypothalamus · Digestion inhibited · Hair stands up · Blood to muscles · Quicker coagulation · Increased oxidation · Release of sugar

Figure 9–1. EMOTION AS RESPONSE. *When there is a direct stimulation of a certain area of the cat's hypothalamus, there is a "sham-rage" response, including both internal and external responses. There is a diffuse discharge in the sympathetic nervous system—including the increased production of adrenalin, which, in turn, produces changes in the endocrine balance of the blood.*

most subjects (Landis and Hunt, 1939). There is an immediate closing of the eyes. The mouth widens as if to bare the teeth. The head and neck come forward a bit. The muscles of the neck stand out. (See Fig. 9–2.) Such a pattern we may wish to interpret as an evolutionary carry-over of a primitive and instinctive mechanism of self-preservation. The organism seems to be preparing itself to repel attack.

For the most part, the external responses of the human organism are learned behaviors. We learn what to do and what face to put on when we are angry or sad or annoyed. If we learn well enough to imitate deliberately the expressions and gestures that are current in our culture, then we can become professional actors. In other cultures, the learned expressions of emotion may be unrecognizable to us. For instance, Klineberg (1938) found that the Chinese culture has expressions for anger, fear, surprise, worry, and disappointment which our society would confuse with very different emotional expressions.

Though human beings have few built-in patterns of external emotional response, there are some involuntary processes in emotion that can be observed through their effect on behavior. These processes illustrate, incidentally, the *activating* role of emotions, a matter that will concern us later.

The person gripped by a strong emotion can *exert energy over a longer period of time* than is normal for him. The football player who has practiced only on offense can, when angry at the enemy and adaptively fearful of impending defeat, play a whole game. The phenomenal endurance of those angry men who survived the march of death after the Japanese victory at Bataan is testimony to the

Figure 9–2. EMOTION AS RESPONSE. *The startle pattern is an automatic response involving a variety of interrelated movements. The automatic pattern, partially depicted here, is typically followed by a more obvious learned response.*

effects of strong emotions.

Emotion also enables the individual to *exert great energy for a brief period of time.* "Superhuman" efforts are likely to occur at times of emotional emergency.

A highly emotional state also *increases the indifference to pain.* The professional boxer during the excitement of battle pays no heed to cuts and bruises which in the calm of the dressing room give him excruciating pain.

Though there has been little or no systematic research on the role of emotion in athletic performance, there can be little doubt that emotional factors very often spell the difference between victory and defeat in athletic contests. Particularly in football, a game that may be described as a 60-minute emergency, the team's emotional readiness bears on its performance. The complacent team, the "fat, dumb, and happy" team, simply cannot exert

its greatest effort. The "fired-up" team, by contrast, can move mountainous guards and contain or sink a fleet of fast backs, perhaps playing far over its own head in the crucial game of the season.

One football player describes his game-time feeling in this way:

I knew we were going to tear them apart. We all came close to hating them. Not real hatred, I guess, but they came on the field so smug and so confident. The things they had been saying about us in the papers made us all mad. And we were sort of scared of them too. They were good. There's no denying that. Real good. There wasn't a one of us who didn't realize that we could get ourselves clobbered if we let down for a minute. So, I, at least, was both mad and scared, if that's possible. And I guess it is. I started really sweating about an hour before the game. Nervous as a cat. I guess you could tell by the smell that we were ready to play. Everybody was sweating, I guess. You could see that we really had our game faces on. We clobbered 'em. *Clobbered* 'em.

Football coaches are keenly aware that the team's performance can vary widely according to its emotional readiness. They use various stratagems to bring their players up to the proper emotional state. Some rely heavily on the "pep talk" before the game and between halves. Others avoid oratory and locker-room histrionics in the conviction that the danger of saying the wrong thing is greater than the likelihood of saying anything effective. They rely on the events of the week, sometimes the carefully arranged events of the week, to produce the desired combination of fear, anger, and provisional optimism. They depend on their players to read the newspapers, and when the coach talks to reporters he is also talking to his players, trying to produce in them just the right pattern of emotions. Coaches are haunted by the fear that the team will be "flat," undercharged, too confident.

Other sports require different kinds of emotional readiness. Basketball coaches, though they also fear overconfidence, do not want in their players the high-voltage do-or-die emotionality that serves the football player so well. Basketball is a more delicate game, requiring a fine touch and precise coordination. One basketball coach, in an effort to prevent his team from becoming too emotionally worked up before game time, kept on the squad one youngster who was a miserably poor basketball player but a fine comedian. This fellow's antics in the locker room served to relax the team and send it to the floor with just the right combination of emotions. Though the comedian never scored a basket, he probably contributed a great deal to the team's undefeated season.

In many sports, the so-called "good competitor" is the athlete whose emotional reserves are released in the presence of the opposition. In one college, for example, there were two men on the track team who ran the 440-yard dash. During routine workouts, the taller and more graceful of the two runners almost always made the better time and almost always, when the two ran in the same race, could win by a yard or two. In official meets, however, things worked differently. Nine times out of ten the short, ungainly runner could beat his colleague. The competitive situation seemed to bring out extra effort. His teammate did not respond in the same way to the increased tension of official competition.

The changes produced by such emotions as fear and anger are highly adaptive in emergency situations. The organism is better equipped to fight or to flee. The primitive survival value of strong emotion, for animals and in the more animal-like activities of man, seems clear. But in many of the more intricate behaviors required of a civilized man, strong emotion serves no useful purpose. In fact, strong emotion has a decidedly disruptive effect on the more intricate or intellectual of human pursuits. The chess player who loses his head also loses the game, and "stage fright" can produce almost paralytic inability to perform.

Internal Response

Emotion is an intricate phenomenon in that it involves so many functions and structures of the organism. There is an all-over involvement in an emotional response, and the stronger the emotion, the more evident this generality of involvement. Along with the conscious feelings and overt responses, there are a multitude of intricate neurological and physiological processes that we need to know about if we are to understand emotions. Some of the phenomena that have been used in the study of emotions include heart rate, skin resistance, breathing rate, stomach and intestinal motions, chemical changes in the blood and the saliva and the urine, skin sweating, metabolic rate, color of the skin, amount of salivary secretion, muscle tension, tremor, eye blink and eye movement, blood pressure, and pupillary response (Lindsley, 1951).

The autonomic nervous system plays a prominent role in emotional behavior, since it has to do with the maintenance of the internal environment. In emotional phenomena, the sympathetic nervous system—concerned mainly with the expenditure of bodily energy—is often much more active than the parasympathetic system, which is concerned with the conservation of bodily energy. Activity in the sympathetic system accounts for increased heart rate, adrenal output, increased blood pressure, stoppage of salivation, and other signs of, say, stage fright or other emotion (Morgan and Stellar, 1950). In a strong anger response, for example, the medulla of the adrenal gland, a structure located near the upper end of each kidney, secretes adrenalin into the blood stream. This secretion, when it reaches the liver, causes sugar to be released into the blood stream, enabling the body to exert greater energy and to resist fatigue. Also, in anger, there are changes which make the blood clot more readily, increase blood pressure, increase the pulse rate, enlarge the air passages into the lungs, enlarge the pupils of the eye, produce sweating, and bring about other related changes. Such changes, it can be seen, do a remarkable job of preparing the body for primitive emergency. There is greater strength, greater endurance, quicker removal of waste products through faster breathing and more forceful circulation of the blood. There is more resistance to bleeding and to pain. All these reactions are very adaptive, at least for primitive emergencies. But, as we shall see, these physiological changes can also produce some fairly grave trouble for the organism.

Recording of Internal Responses

Through a number of special devices, it is possible to record and to study the internal changes that occur in emotional response. Such recordings have been made for a variety of research purposes in order to trace the internal story of emotional response. They have also been made for other reasons—for example, the detection of lying.

The galvanic response. When an emotion occurs and when, due to glandular responses, there is an increased sweating, minute changes occur in the electrical properties of the skin. The tissues actually generate a small voltage of their own; and there is a change in the electrical resistance of the skin. Consequently, a small, externally applied current flows differently when an emotion occurs. These changes, known as the **galvanic skin response** (GSR), can be measured quite accurately by measuring either the change in the skin voltage (Tarchanoff method) or the skin's resistance to an externally applied current (Féré method).

Blood pressure. Changes in blood pressure can be measured with fair accuracy and sensitivity by the *sphygmomanometer.* The family doctor in measuring blood pressure will frequently use the familiar pressurized band around the arm and the *stethoscope* to listen for the pulse at the wrist. Laboratory devices are available to register and record over long periods of time the ups and downs in blood pressure, so that even small and momentary changes in pressure can be observed.

Breathing pattern. The *pneumograph*—a rubberized tube (for circling the chest) connected to a recording pen—is used to record changes in the depth and the pattern of breathing. Although the dramatic gasp we frequently see in real or make-believe emotions is probably a learned and perhaps a deliberate response, emotion does produce small involuntary changes in the breathing pattern even when there are conscious efforts to conceal it. The pneumograph records these subtle variations over a period of time.

Heart activity. The rate of heartbeat increases in emotional situations and may be measured by the *electrocardiograph* (EKG). The "pounding heart" in strong emotion is a familiar experience and is a measurable reality. The EKG has not yielded reliable data, however, for weak emotions.

The lie detector. The lie detector, more technically known as the **polygraph recorder,** records simultaneously the GSR, the blood pressure, and the breathing pattern (see Fig. 9–3). In most cases, for people accustomed to telling the truth, even a small lie produces an emotional twinge—a "twinge of con-

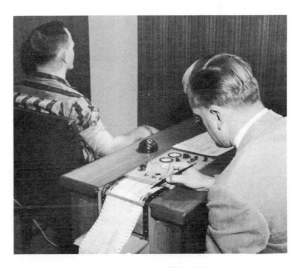

Figure 9–3. THE "LIE DETECTOR." *The polygraph recorder, registering changes in the GSR, in heart action, and in breathing, is used to detect subtle emotional responses, including those that generally occur when a subject is lying.*

science." The twinge becomes more pronounced if there is great personal significance attached to the lie—if, for example, serious personal guilt or a ten-year jail sentence is involved. The polygraph recorder picks up these twinges, great or small, and records them on a moving tape. The skilled technician can read these records and, with considerable success, tell when an individual is lying.

The lie detector is not infallible. Its results are not admissible as evidence in court unless both sides to a controversy agree that the results should be used. In the hands of a skilled technician, however, the polygraph can succeed in up to 90 per cent of the cases in telling which of two suspects is lying and which is telling the truth (Ellson, 1952). Reliability of such a magnitude makes the device a useful aid in police work.

The operator of the polygraph can compare the individual's emotional responses to neutral questions with his responses to "guilty" questions. Or, after he establishes a "baseline" response for each of two suspects, he may compare responses of the two to questions—about the murder weapon or an address—which can be known only to the guilty person.

Frequently, the device is used to narrow the list of suspects. For example, the individual who is thought to know the location of a body or a truckload of stolen furs may be rigged into the recorder and confronted with a map of the city. As the operator's pointer, going over the map, touches closer to the crucial location, the suspect's guilty knowledge, if he has any, will speak through his emotions, even though he says not a word. There have been a number of successful uses of this procedure in actual police practice.

Brain potentials. In its normal and usual state the brain serves to connect incoming stimuli with stored past experience and with nerve fibers running to the glands and muscles of the body. When the brain is carrying on these functions in a calm and relaxed way, it emits "brain waves" with a frequency of about ten oscillations per second. This normal pattern of the *brain potential* is known as the **alpha rhythm.** This rhythm of tiny electrical impulses can be amplified and recorded on a device known as the **electroencephalograph** (EEG), which reads the impulses coming from electrodes fastened to the scalp (see Fig. 9–4).

Under a number of conditions the *alpha rhythm* is replaced by other rhythms, and a record of these electrical events can tell us a good deal about the functioning of the brain. When the organism is asleep, the alpha rhythm is replaced by a slower oscillation. Thus, the EEG can be used to measure both the reality and the depth of sleep. When there is epilepsy or brain damage, the alpha rhythm is also affected in characteristic ways, making the EEG an important diagnostic device. Of most direct concern to us here, however, is that under conditions of excitement and emotion the alpha rhythm gives way to a pattern of *smaller* and more *rapid* oscillations. Though the EEG has not been used for such practical purposes as catching liars, it is used in studying emotion and a variety of other phenomena.

CONDITIONS OF AROUSAL OF EMOTION

As with our study of motives, we can learn about emotions by observing the conditions under which they occur. Though the literature does not give us complete and detailed information about what kinds of situations arouse what kinds of emotions, we can nevertheless pursue with some profit this line of attack.

FEAR

A fear response is evoked, quite naturally, by threatening situations. In animals, the threats are generally clearly interpreted as threats to life and limb, and the fearful response is often set off by stimuli that do not have to be learned. Young geese, for example, will flee in noisy terror from a cardboard profile of a hawk fastened to the fence of their pen (Tinbergen, 1951). In young children, by contrast, threats to physical survival have little or no emotional effect (Jersild, Markey, and Jersild, 1933). This is a vivid

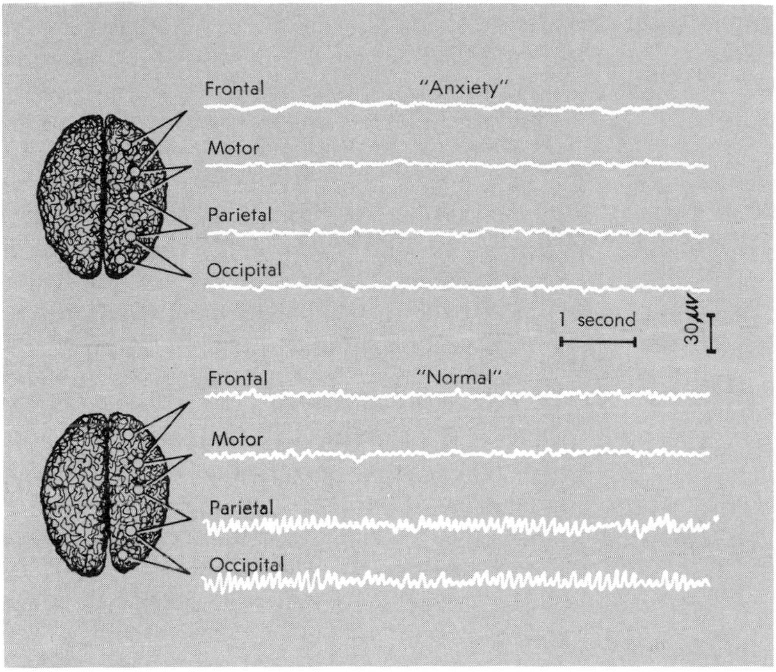

Figure 9–4. ELECTROENCEPHALOGRAMS. *EEG records for an anxious and a normal subject. In states of anxiety the well-regulated alpha rhythm often is absent. (From Lindsley, 1948; by permission of McGraw-Hill Book Co.)*

example of the relative dependency of the young human organism; it must be protected for a relatively long period from the hostilities of the environment. Babies often respond with what appears to be fear, however, to loud noises, to the sudden withdrawal of support, and to a variety of strange sights and sounds. As the child grows older, it begins, probably through adaptive learning, to respond less to noises, to falling, and to strangeness—none of which has yet greatly hurt it. It responds with greater frequency to animals as fearful objects (Jersild, Markey, and Jersild, 1933).

As children grow into adolescence and maturity, a different and wider variety of objects and situations evoke fearful responses. As time passes and learning progresses, stimuli of symbolic and psychological significance take on fearfulness. In one study, for example (Anastasi, Cohen, and Spatz, 1948), college girls reported that their most frequent fears

centered around (1) school work, (2) possible loss of prestige, (3) illness and physical danger. The fact that only 17 per cent reported fears in the third category may be taken as a commentary on the difference between the emotional life of children and adults, and between that of symbolizing man and non-symbolizing animals.

For the human adult fear may be evoked by numerous situations that, either in reality or in imagination, appear threatening to physical or psychological well-being. A fear of something that might be harmful requires the capacity for symbolic representation of things, and the ability to respond in the present to something not yet here. Most adult fears, then, require both symbolic processes and learning. And such a civilized fear as that aroused by possible loss of prestige requires also, of course, that the individual shall have learned a status motive.

ANGER

Anger is most often aroused in human beings by the thwarting of motivated behavior. Children will readily burst forth with anger

Figure 9–5. EMOTIONAL RESPONSES ARE LEARNED. *Few children fear snakes; many adults do—whether the snake is dangerous or not.*

when their relatively simple motivated behavior is blocked—when food is denied, when toys are taken away, when they are pushed or held back. Adults react similarly, but in more sophisticated ways and for more intricate reasons. College girls reported bursts of anger to be most frequently produced by interference with their plans (Anastasi et al., 1948). Also, the girls were angered by their own feelings of inferiority and by their felt deficiencies in school work. College men apparently behave similarly. One study (Meltzer, 1933) found that they most frequently became angry when their motive of self-assertion was somehow blocked. The most frequent stimulus for their anger, and the chief targets for the venting thereof, were other people.

Because of the great frequency with which human motives are thwarted and because of the variety and significance of behavior in the face of **frustration,** we shall return in Chapter 16 to a fuller consideration of these matters.

ANNOYANCE

Annoyance seems to be best described as a mild kind of anger. Annoyances are most generally passing spurts of emotion, leading to no intense feelings and most often to no violent action. Sometimes, however, what appears to be a picayune annoyance can set off an emotional explosion. In such cases the annoyance is probably serving only as a trigger, igniting pent-up emotions that are due to other causes.

What is annoying? That depends on the person. Perhaps it is accurate to say that a man is known by the annoyances he keeps. Most of us, however, are more annoyed by the behavior of people than by inanimate objects. In one study (Cason, 1930), 654 people who were asked to report their annoyances set down a total of over 18,000. Approximately 10,000 of these concerned people's behavior. The behaviors most frequently found annoying were the following:

1. A person blowing his nose without a handkerchief.
2. A person coughing in one's face.
3. A person cheating in a game.
4. A woman spitting in public.
5. A child being treated harshly.

The study reporting these results was conducted in 1930. Since annoyances probably change as culture changes, one might not find the same pattern of annoyances today. But the behaviors reported in the early study will still probably have considerable annoyance value.

Though we are most frequently annoyed at people, inanimate objects can also be annoying. Some sounds appear, for example, to have an inherent capacity to annoy people (Kryter, 1950). Sounds of high pitch are more likely than low-pitched tones to set off the small anger reaction that is annoyance.

HAPPINESS AND OTHER PLEASANT EMOTIONS

Not much is known about the situations conducive to happiness, joy, elation, and other pleasant emotions. These emotions have a very real subjective existence but are difficult to define in objective terms and hence are difficult to study systematically. Generally speaking, pleasant emotions accompany the busy and successful pursuit of goals. One group of graduate students, for example, reported that their greatest happiness came from successful working at their chosen studies (Washburn, Deyo, and Marks, 1924). It is perhaps not far wrong to say that happiness occurs when the individual is active in the pursuit of a goal and is anticipating success. Thus, happiness may have much to do with the anticipation of desired future events.

Love, another pleasant emotion (and one the poets tell us can make the plain girl beautiful and the lout a gentleman), may be regarded as the emotion that (1) accompanies, or has grown out of, satisfying contact with the mother, or mother figure and (2) accompanies or grows out of successful operation of the sexual or maternal motives. In infancy the child derives basic satisfaction from his mother's fondling, feeding, and cuddling. These basic satisfactions are accompanied by pleasant physiological processes of an emotional nature. In time, through associational learning, the mere sight of the mother evokes the emotion originally connected with the basic physiological satisfactions. Harlow (1960a) suggests four or five affectional patterns, such as the affection of infant for mother, child for child, heterosexual affection, maternal and paternal affection.

In a more general sense, we probably feel affection for any person or object associated in our experience with the satisfaction of our motives. We feel affection, for example, for the person whom we see as contributing to our self-assertion or to our achievement or to our needs for independence, self-sufficiency, and autonomy.

THEORIES OF EMOTION

Although it may be profitable to describe emotion as conscious experience, to talk about it in terms of either overt or physiological response, or to describe as best we can the conditions under which emotions are aroused, none of these efforts comes anywhere near either explaining emotion or dealing with emotional phenomena in terms that can be described as theoretical. There is, in fact, no single and accepted explanation of emotion. There have been, however, a number of attempts at theoretical formulation of emotional phenomena, attempts to put into one interrelated set of propositions something more than descriptions of facts. These theoretical attempts vary in tone, in focus, and in scope; one theory, for example, attempts to relate the conscious experience of emotion with the physiological events thereof, while another may deal almost exclusively with interrelated physiological and neurological phenomena.

The oldest theory of emotion, the James-Lange theory, was introduced around the turn of the present century. It deals with the relation between our feeling of emotion and the body's emotional reactions. In essence, the theory has it that our felt emotions are perceptions of bodily reactions in certain stressful situations: "We are afraid because we run, are angry because we fight." More prosaically stated, we are angry because our muscles are tense, because "fighting responses" are occurring in the autonomic nervous system, and because the whole body is equipped to attack. By contrast, another situation produces a smiling face and a relaxed body; so we are happy. The James-Lange theory, then, gave physiological processes the central, primary role of preparing the organism for action, while the conscious "feeling" is left to take care of itself. There have been objections to this formulation, because studies showed that animals deprived of sensory impulses from body structures still exhibit emotional behavior. Many took such evidence to refute the theory, but Hebb (1958) points out that the animals' deprived senses may have precluded his *feeling* of emotion without destroying the animals' capacity to behave emotionally. Thus, we cannot test the theory on animals, for they cannot verbalize their feelings, cannot report on conscious experience. The theory has been superseded, but not disproved.

A second early theory of emotion, the Cannon-Bard theory, attempted to formulate in general terms some of the newly discovered physiological evidence on emotion. Cannon (1927) originally formulated the theory, stressing the brain processes involved; and Bard (1934) elaborated upon it. The theory holds that the situation sets off a sequence of neural processes, a sequence involving an interaction of the **thalamus** and the **cerebral cortex.** Both the pattern of emotional behavior and the experience spring from the emotion itself—which is conceived as a neural response.

A more recent theory of emotion (Lindsley, 1951) is referred to as an *activation* theory and deals primarily with the processes whereby neural structures are activated in emotional situations. Perhaps the mechanisms and sequences spelled out in this theory can best be seen in the processes involved in the startle response, which is a complicated reflex action having a good deal in common with fear. When a sudden loud stimulus is generated, auditory impulses pass to the auditory cortex by way of the **pons,** the midbrain, and the **medial geniculate body** of the thalamus. On its way this pattern of impulses activates the reticular formation, which in turn "arouses," through its projection fibers, the cortex. Behaviorally, there is a flexion of a number of muscles of the body. There are two components to the neural message reaching these muscles: one of these reaches the muscle one tenth of a second after the intense stimulus, the other after a full second. Presumably, the latter impulses come to the muscles not directly through lower brain centers but through more involved circuits, perhaps in the thalamus and cortex. The eye blinks even sooner than the skeletal muscles respond, while the galvanic skin response is slow. These and similar facts are taken to show that there is a *hierarchy of reflex adjustments* in the startle response: at one level there are quick and automatic reflexes, such as muscular response and the eye blink; at a higher level, probably in the thalamus, there are slower automatic (and autonomic) responses. There is also cortical activity, probably facilitated by arousing impulses from the

reticular formation; this cortical activity results in delayed messages that are sent only after there is a conscious recognition of the significance of the stimulus.

Similar processes and sequences are theoretically involved in such emotions as fear and anger. There is a *sequential activation of a hierarchy of circuits.* Some lower circuits or centers produce the more immediate and automatic motor and visceral responses. Activation of the reticular formation arouses the cortex. The cortex produces an awareness of the situation and, much evidence shows, can control processes occurring in lower brain centers.

There has been a good deal of other research on the nature of the brain processes involved in emotion and some accompanying theory-like speculations. For example, two investigators (Klüver and Bucy, 1937) found that when the **temporal lobes** of the cerebral cortex of wild monkeys were removed, the animals became remarkably tame. The animals showed no fear and could not be made angry. Emotions were alien to them. In consideration of these and other findings, Papez (1937) proposed specific circuits in the brain for a new theory of emotion, which gave the **limbic system** a major role; and MacLean (1960) said that the limbic system might serve as a "visceral brain" where the experience of everyday life is expressed as "feeling," while the neocortex takes care of the more "intellectualized" aspects of experience. The "visceral brain," it is suggested, expresses itself with an "organ language" rather than through the more symbolic responses occurring in the cortical areas.

EMOTIONS AND MALADJUSTMENT

We have pointed out earlier that by no means all emotions all of the time contribute usefully to the quality of the civilized **adjustment** of the human being. Though emotions can and do often facilitate ongoing behavior, they can also cause trouble. The individual can learn emotional responses that are clearly awkward or inconvenient or sometimes downright debilitating. Also, he can get himself into situations producing persisting emotions, which, in turn, through lasting physiological processes, can interfere seriously with the normal functioning of his body.

PHOBIAS

A **phobia** is an unreasoning fear—a fear that does not make sense when first appraised. All of us probably have emotional quirks that might be referred to as small or "normal" phobias—little fears that interfere at least mildly with the process of daily living. Women are supposed to fear mice to an extent far beyond the capacity of mice to do anybody any actual harm. Many people fear snakes so much that even a picture of an innocent garter snake can produce an emotional willy-waw. Others are emotionally repelled by the very idea, for example, of eating horse meat, even though in many parts of the civilized world horse roast is a delicacy. Through association—sometimes far-fetched and symbolic association—stimuli and situations now present bring forth emotional responses once reserved for other stimuli and other situations long past. The violent emotional response to one snake long ago now springs forth for any snake or even at the mention of the word. We learn emotional responses or have them impressed upon us by situations which we cannot always control. And not always is our learning of a sort that can be regarded as sensible.

Of more significance for living than these everyday miscarriages in emotional response are the genuine phobias—the extreme, irrational, and often unconsciously rooted fears of harmless objects or situations. The psychological literature records many kinds of phobias. There are, for example, *acrophobia*, the fear of high places; *agoraphobia*, the fear of open spaces; and *claustrophobia*, the fear of closed places.

Phobias are learned—learned sometimes in relatively strange and intricate ways.

George Q., a senior in college, reported to the clinical psychologist in the student health center with what appeared to be a case of fairly severe agoraphobia. He experienced a violent fear, with sweating, shortness of breath and rapid heartbeat, every time he found himself in the middle of a room, in a wide street or in open places between buildings on the campus. He found it necessary, when walking to class, to stay as close to buildings as possible, preferably close enough to touch the wall. Occasionally, when the sidewalk ran from one building to another, he would run, in near panic, from one building to the security of the other. When inside of buildings he had to stay as close as possible to walls. He had to drop one class where, by an alphabetical seating plan, he was placed in the middle of the room.

After several hours of probing for the source of this fear, the clinical psychologist was able to put together the following account of events. When George was about 5½ years old, he and his mother drove his father to the airport to catch a plane. Shortly before leaving home, his father and mother had what George saw as a violent argument. George, a highly emotional witness to the argument, had attacked his father, biting, scratching, kicking, and screaming. He was promptly and decisively punished. At the airport he was still in a highly charged state of emotion. He remembers wishing, with a glow of satisfaction in the fantasy, that his father's plane would crash, carrying his father to a horrible flaming death. George was told to sit in one place while his parents went to see about the tickets. Still seething, George wandered away, soon finding himself out in the middle of a runway. A large plane took off, coming close enough to George to give him a paralytically severe fright. Panic set in. George ran senselessly around the expanse of the airport until his father caught him and carried him back to the building. His fear of the plane, his hostility toward his father, his guilt at wishing his father dead, his feeling of foolishness at having wandered into danger—all this added up to an intolerable emotional experience. In time George forgot, or repressed, the whole episode. But during the last semester of his senior year there was a strong conflict with his father over George's marriage

Figure 9–6. PHOBIAS. *Phobias, or unreasoning fears, come in a variety of forms.*

plans. The earlier experience was reactivated, but without actual memory of it. Open spaces, presumably spaces similar to the airport, began to set off the emotional response to the earlier experience.

PSYCHOSOMATIC REACTIONS

Another way in which emotions can and do interfere with adjustment is by lasting too long. The psychological changes in emotion contribute very helpfully to response in emergency. But if the emergency lasts a long time,

so do the physiological processes that underlie emotion—and they start doing actual damage to body tissues, producing **psychosomatic** symptoms.

Studies on stress in animals have demonstrated clearly that prolonged emotional response can harm tissues. In one experiment (Brady, 1958) two monkeys were put in an apparatus side by side, and each was given an electric shock every 20 seconds. One of the monkeys had in front of him a lever which, if pushed at the right time, would save both animals from the shock. If he pushed it at the wrong time or failed to push it at all during the 20-second interval, both monkeys received a shock. The monkey who simply sat there with no decisions to make seemed to suffer

Figure 9–7. PSYCHOSOMATIC REACTIONS.
*Protracted emotional response can produce
physical symptoms and actual damage to body
tissues. Psychosomatic reactions include
asthma, migraine, obesity, high blood pressure,
neurodermatitis, and other disorders.*

very little from the whole experience. He was free from responsibility and stress. The responsible or administrative monkey, by contrast, developed a severe stomach ulcer after three weeks and died.

In human beings, prolonged **stress** may be produced by clearly definable environmental situations. A company executive may experience weeks and months of stress during a prolonged emergency in his organization. A

student may suffer from a prolonged and perhaps justified fear of failure. And a combat infantryman may be under great stress for weeks at a time. These protracted emergencies, producing emotionality, can and frequently do produce psychosomatic disorders, including physical damage to tissues.

Frequently, prolonged stress is due more to factors within the individual than to objective and outside emergency. There may be a persisting anxiety, for example, wherein the individual is constantly caught up in fear without knowing exactly what it is he is afraid of. Or prolonged periods of resentment and hostility may be produced by internal psychological dynamics of which the individual is not completely aware (pp. 446–447). Persisting emotion, however produced, can bring about psychosomatic disorder. It has been demonstrated that peptic ulcers, migraine headaches, dermatitis, colitis, obesity, high blood pressure, and asthma are due in part to emotional disturbances. And it is fairly well established that a large proportion of the patients seen by the medical profession are suffering from symptoms emotionally produced or facilitated.

The way in which emotional factors can produce somatic damage is illustrated by the research on peptic ulcers. Ulcers form because of persisting overactivity and oversecretion in the stomach and, probably, a predisposition of certain people toward developing them. Normally, when all is well with the organism, the stomach goes actively to work only when a meal is being digested. Once the stomach has completed its work, passing its contents on to the small intestine, it comes to rest. In certain emotional conditions, however, acid secretions continue to pour into the stomach. These secretions can, in time, produce inflamed craters in the wall of the stomach. Peptic ulcers can become so severe as to lead to serious internal bleeding.

The direct connection between stomach acids and the formation of ulcers was demonstrated in the case of a man whose esophagus had been so badly burned by scalding soup that it was permanently closed (Wolf and Wolff, 1942). Doctors had to make a surgical opening directly into his stomach so that he could be fed. It then became possible to observe directly a part of the lining of the stomach. At one time, a small erosion or abrasion occurred in this part of the lining. This small erosion was artificially kept moist by gastric juice. After four days the erosion had become a painful ulcer. When the ulcer was covered so as to protect it from gastric juice, it quickly healed.

The vagus nerve is responsible for the oversecretion of gastric fluids (Gellhorn and Loofbourrow, 1963). When its influence is eliminated, gastric secretion in ulcer patients is reduced so that in about 90 per cent of the cases the ulcers are healed. Much of the extra gastric secretion in ulcer patients is at night. Dragstedt (1956) found the night secretion to be up to twenty times greater in ulcer patients than in normal persons.

Why should the stomach work overtime? And how is this disorder connected to the emotional life of the individual? These are questions to which there are no clear answers. It is apparent that there *is* an emotional factor. Ulcers most frequently occur in men under tension—generally, driving and ambitious men. At one time the malady was called "Wall Street stomach" because of its frequency among business executives. But by what intervening mechanisms does tension lead to an overactive stomach? One theory (Alexander, 1934) has it that ulcers occur in ambitious, aggressive men who, underneath, have a longing to be supported, cared for, and loved. This unconscious and denied need for dependency, the theory goes, somehow triggers off the digestive mechanism associated with being fed.

This plausible theory, however, is not supported by the facts (Wolf and Wolff, 1942) concerning the flow of gastric juices in the man, mentioned earlier, who had a direct opening into his stomach. His juices flowed more vigorously when he was feeling angry and resentful, becoming particularly plentiful on the occasion of his being fired from a job. When he experienced fear or sadness, by contrast, his gastric acidity fell off.

The emotional factor seems to be clearly there in producing ulcers, but neither the physiological nor psychological processes involved are yet understood. Among the facts that will have to be considered in writing the full scientific story of peptic ulcers are the following:

1. Peptic ulcers occur much more frequently in men than in women.
2. Ulcer patients tend to be slender, fragile, above average in height, and below average in weight (Draper, Dupertuis, and Caughey, 1944).
3. Acute attacks of gastric pain in ulcerated patients are set up by the following events (Draper, et al.):
   a. Conflict with a mother or a mother figure.
   b. The pregnancy of one's wife or the birth of a baby.
   c. Events that create a sense of failure.
   d. An extreme sense of guilt over sexual relations.
4. Some cases of ulcer clear up rapidly when the patient rests and is attentively cared for in the hospital.
5. Some ulcer cases have been cured through psychotherapy, which seemed to help the patient understand and accept his needs for dependency.

With respect to high blood pressure, or *hypertension*, the physiological connection between emotion and body change appears more direct than with ulcers. An increase in blood pressure is a predictable consequence of anger. To account for continuing high blood pressure, then, we search for psychological factors that can produce a persisting emotional state. Research has not yet explored fully this question, but there are some illustrative cases that at least suggest the kinds of psychological situations that can produce lasting anger and resentment. One such case is presented by Saul (1939).

Miss D., in her early twenties, was the sole support for her mother and younger sisters, quietly sacrificing her own life to care for her family.

Her mother was very solicitous of Miss D.'s welfare, feeding her and tenderly caring for her. This Miss D. liked. As a matter of fact, her dreams and fantasies suggested that she wanted more tender, loving care than she was receiving, but at the same time she felt a bitter resentment that she was so submissive to her mother. Her anger at her mother needed to be controlled carefully. She also had strongly hostile feelings toward her boss. She would often and easily boil with anger at his irritating ways. Her blood pressure was dangerously high. Apparently, in this case, the lasting anger works very similarly to the normal spurts of anger we experience in everyday life. Miss D.'s persisting anger arose out of conflicts within her own personality. She found herself acting submissively and actually wanting submissiveness. But she also resented submissiveness and turned her anger on those to whom she found herself submitting. This lasting psychological knot kept her blood pressure high.

The evidence for the other psychosomatic disorders takes a form similar to that presented here for ulcers and hypertension. The connection between emotion and the disorder cannot be denied. But we have no complete knowledge of either the physiological processes involved or the specific psychological factors that set off the physiological events.

EMOTIONS AND
THE PERSON

In thinking about emotions we can adopt several approaches. We can study the conscious experience associated with emotion. We can focus on the physiological processes involved. We can study the ways in which the nervous system functions. Or we can study emotional behavior, concerning ourselves with what responses are likely to occur in what situations. Each of these approaches is thoroughly legitimate, and each can contribute to our understanding. An additional point of view involves a study of emotion and the over-all adjustment of the individual. We can think of the individual as an organized system and can concern ourselves with the ways emotional responses interweave themselves with the total organization of personality. In a related approach we can think of the *differences between individual systems* with respect to emotions. We come close to this kind of approach, of course, when we deal with emotion and maladjustment.

EMOTIONS AND PERSONALITY

There have not been many psychological studies of emotions from the standpoint of personality. As we shall see, studies of personality, though they do not deny the significant role of emotions in the organization of the individual life, tend to concentrate on other aspects of behavior. From casual observation, however, we can convince ourselves that each individual has his own characteristic way of living his emotional life; both the situations that arouse his emotions and the way he expresses them are quite personal and quite characteristic of his way of meeting his environment.

We learn what objects, people, values, situations to be emotional about. And each of us learns differently. One man's fear is another's anger, and my affections are your indifferences. Life may teach me a pervasive timidity, while you may learn a happy and secure optimism. Or one of us may come down with such a phobia that the whole tenor of our adjustment is affected. Such was the case with William Ellery Leonard, who, in his book *The Locomotive God* (1927), describes how a fear of locomotives dominated much of his life.

Each of us has not only his own personal catalogue of emotional stimuli but also his own characteristic ways of expressing emotion. We could probably describe ourselves and our friends with respect to such dimensions of emotionality as the following:

Deep	Shallow
Strong	Weak
Rich	Meager
Broad	Narrow
Open Expression	Restrained Expression
Controlled	Impulsive
Appropriate	Inappropriate

Were we to take seriously the description of such general aspects of the individual's emotions, we would, of course, encounter ticklish problems of definition, of measurement, and of **reliability.** The literature does not give us much help with such problems. But the enumeration of these possible dimensions of emotional life may still assist somewhat in our organization of our observation of personality.

THE DEVELOPMENT OF EMOTION

While the literature does not spell out for us the dimensions of adult emotional life, it does give us some information about the individual's emotional development.

The Emotions of the Infant

An early comprehensive study by Bridges (1932), involving protracted observation and tests of many infants, traced the history of emotional development during the first two years. At birth and during the first few weeks of life, the infant emotes all over whenever it emotes at all, and any emotional situation evokes about the same response as any other. This characteristic emotional state, observed on a variety of occasions, is one of *undifferentiated excitement.* By three months, maturation, learning, and differentiation have proceeded to an extent allowing the infant to express general distress in some situations and general delight in others. He persists also in showing sometimes the pattern of general excitement. By the time the child is 2 years old, he has developed sufficiently—through both maturation and learning—that he can, at least in the eyes of an observer, express fear, disgust, anger, jealousy, distress, excitement, delight, joy, elation, and affection for both adults and children.

A study with dogs has shown that if the animals spend their early life in isolation from the usual sources of stimulation, they grow up to make inappropriate emotional responses to ordinary stimuli (Melzack, 1954). There is the implication here that learning to emote correctly is a necessity for the developing organism.

Figure 9–8. DIFFERENTIATION OF EMOTION. *As the individual develops, affection for other children comes later than affection for adults.*

The Emotions of the Adolescent

A number of writers have made observations about the intense emotional lives of adolescents. When the individual has ended —or partially ended—the relatively uncomplicated years of childhood and when he has just entered—or partially entered—the role of self-sufficient adult, he is in a confused and precarious situation. His childish behaviors are no longer adequate, nor are they tolerated. Secure and comfortable adult ways have not yet been learned. Life can be something of a mess, and heightened emotionality can be expected. One psychological writer (Hurlock,

1953) has described the emotional life of the adolescent as characterized by intensity; lack of control; inconsistency; prevalence of long-drawn-out emotions, or moods; the growth of such sentiments as patriotism, loyalty, and reverence.

Emotional Maturity

Some adults may be accurately characterized as living childish or adolescent emotional lives. We all know adults who demonstrate a childish lack of control or an adolescent inconsistency in their emotional behavior. But most adults have lived and learned enough to lead less precarious, less frantic, and more adaptive emotional lives. Although there is no explicit agreement among psychologists as to what constitutes true emotional maturity, most of them will probably feel that the desirable emotional life should be characterized by the following:

1. *Appropriateness of emotion.* The mature adult does not rage at gnats nor shout joyous exultation at a funeral. His emotional response is appropriate to the stimulus situation, and his expression of his feelings shows an awareness of social proprieties.

2. *Emotional control.* Maturity, in many of its aspects, implies control. There is the control involved in delayed gratification of needs now felt. There is the control of impulses which, in the child, would lead to immediate overt behavior. And there is the control that holds in or defers or tones down emotional flares so that expression can be made more consonant with the person's way of life and with the demands of a specific situation.

3. *Richness and variety and differentiation.* Many observers will hold that the emotionally mature person lives a richly varied emotional life. In contrast to the infant's global and emotional excitement, the mature adult experiences highly differentiated emotions, varying perhaps from righteous indignation to exquisite disgust, to wry enjoyment, to delicately subtle aesthetic pleasure. Emotions accompany motivated behavior. As motives mature and differentiate, leading to a wide variety of interests and values, the concurrent emotions take on subtle shadings, thereby enriching life.

No psychologist would equate emotional maturity with the absence of emotion. As a matter of fact, too flat an emotional life is often regarded as a sign of serious maladjustment. Emotion, in the healthy adult, will occur. The problem of achieving emotional maturity is not a matter of stamping out emotions or of denying emotions—even the very strong and very unpleasant ones. It is a problem instead of learning to live with emotions, of learning to keep them within reasonable bounds and of turning them, whenever possible, to the ends of integral survival in a complicated world.

SUMMARY

1. Emotions accompany motivated behavior; the effect may be facilitating or interfering.

2. Emotions may also serve as motivational factors, as conditions of the organism leading it to seek the presence or absence of certain goals or states.

3. Emotions are represented to us as conscious feelings; they may also be viewed as response, both internal and external.

4. The energizing effects of emotions include their capacity to permit (1) the exertion of energy over a longer period of time, (2) the exertion of greater energy over a short period of time, and (3) an increased indifference to pain. These effects can be seen in the more violent athletic activities.

5. The internal changes in emotion are mediated by the autonomic nervous system; these changes, involving first the secretion of adrenalin, include the release of blood sugar, the tendency of the blood to clot more readily, an increase in blood pressure, an increase in

pulse rate, an increase in air flow into the lungs, enlarged pupils, and increased sweating.

6. The galvanic skin response, heart activity, and breathing activity all give cues about internal change in emotion; these three effects are recorded on the lie detector or polygraph recorder.

7. Changes in brain potentials, recorded on the electroencephalograph, may also indicate emotional processes.

8. As for conditions of arousal, fear is a response to a threatening situation, with the nature of threat most often a learned matter; anger is a response to thwarting situations; and annoyance appears to be a mild form of anger. The conditions of arousal of such emotions as happiness and jealousy are not easily described with precision.

9. The early James-Lange theory of emotion held that conscious experiences of emotion arise as perceptions of bodily reaction: "We are afraid because we run." The Cannon-Bard theory and the more recent activation theory both deal with the neurological process involved in emotion; the latter theory holds that emotion involves a sequential activation of a hierarchy of neural circuits.

10. Emotional responses may be maladaptive responses. Phobias are unreasonable fears that may interfere with normal adjustment; and psychosomatic reactions, produced by long-continuing emotions, may produce actual damage to the body.

11. Peptic ulcers, one of the frequent psychosomatic symptoms, are produced by a variety of persisting emotional conditions which result in a malfunctioning of the secretions of the stomach.

12. Each individual has his own characteristic mode and pattern of emotional response.

13. The emotional responses of the infant show a developmental sequence, beginning with undifferentiated excitement and continuing with a variety of distinct emotional responses.

RESEARCH REPORTS

ULCERS AND EMOTION [*]

There have been a number of studies of the kinds of stress that produce ulcers in animals. One stress that has been used successfully and often with rats is to immobilize the animals for a long period so that they cannot move at all, and at the same time deprive them of food and water. Such restraint produces what is apparently anger; and the continuation of this stress, along with deprivation of food and water, for a period of 20 to 48 hours is often enough to produce gastric ulcers. Another extensive literature concerns the effects of the so-called tranquilizing drugs on hypertension and emotional disorder. One of these tranquilizing drugs, reserpine, has found wide use in the fields of internal medicine and psychiatry. From the literature on the effects of reserpine, one might well expect that administration of the drug would reduce any tendency to ulceration. But there is evidence also in the literature that large doses of reserpine may actually encourage ulceration.

In the experiment reported here, Hartry examined the relation between reserpine and ulceration in rats. She attempted to produce ulcers in experimental animals by restraining them for a period of 48 hours while also depriving them of food and water. The restraint was accomplished by inserting the rat in a very small cage, constructed of mesh hardware cloth in the shape of a half cylinder that was 7 inches long, 2½ inches wide at its maximum width, and 1½ inches high. The animals in the control groups were kept in larger cages, allowing relatively free movement.

The subjects for the experiment were 28 female rats, 100 to 120 days old, distributed among four groups. The groups were as follows: (1) seven rats were subjected to 48-hour restraint, combined with hunger and thirst; (2) seven rats were subjected to 48-hour restraint, with accompanying

[*] Arlene L. Hartry, The effects of reserpine on the psychogenic production of gastric ulcers in rats, *J. comp. physiol. Psychol.*, 1962, **55**, 719–721.

hunger and thirst, but were injected intramuscularly with reserpine (0.1 mg. per kg. of body weight) just before they were immobilized and again 24 hours after immobilization; (3) seven rats, a control group for the effects of reserpine, were injected on the same schedule and level of dosage as the second group above, but each of these rats was unrestrained, being placed instead in a larger control cage; (4) seven rats, serving as a control group for the effects of hunger and thirst, were merely placed individually in control cages and subjected to 48 hours of hunger and thirst.

At the end of the experiment, the rats were sacrificed in accordance with established procedure and their stomachs stored, being made available for later examination. At the time of inspection the stomachs were pinned on cork boards in such a manner that the entire inner surfaces of the stomachs were visible. Each stomach was inspected by three judges using a hand lens; and each judge tallied, without knowing anything about the prior experience of the rat, the number and size of the ulcerated areas. Although the judges did not always reach perfect agreement as to whether an ulcer was present or absent, the reliability of the judgment was sufficiently high to allow an interpretation of the results. Statistical analysis of the data shows that there are significant differences between the groups in the number of rats developing ulcers.

Of the 14 rats subjected to the prolonged stress, half developed ulcers during the 48-hour period. Of the rats in the control group who received neither stress nor drugs, none developed an ulcer. It seems clear that stress of this kind does produce ulceration. That reserpine itself, in the dosages employed, assists in the formation of ulcers is indicated by the fact that of the rats who were treated with reserpine before and after the stressful period, six out of seven developed ulcers. Of those who did not receive stress but were given the drug, one out of seven developed an ulcer. Although the numbers of rats are small, the results indicate with statistical significance that both stress and reserpine contribute to ulceration.

Supporting data are obtained when there is a rating of size of ulcers produced in the four conditions. The ulcers occurring in the stomachs of the animals who had received both stress and reserpine were on the average about five times larger than the ulcers appearing in rats who had received the stress but who had received no drugs.

EMOTION AS RELATED TO PERCEPTUAL, SENSORY, AND COGNITIVE FUNCTIONING [*]

The series of experiments concerning us here explored systematically the relationship between intensity of stress or emotion on one hand and, on the other, the degree of physiological activation as well as effects on some psychological variables. Used in the series of experiments were novice participants in the sport of parachuting. In basic design, the series of experiments measured the physiological factors associated with the emotion of making a parachute jump, studied these processes as the time of the jump approached, and related the amount of physiologically and subjectively indicated stress to a wide variety of responses, varying from simple sensory responses to fairly complex cognitive processes.

The subjects for the series of experiments were 27 college students who were in training in various sports-parachuting centers in the Boston area. They were rewarded for participating in the research program by having their expenses paid in the training course up to and including their second parachute jump. All subjects had made one or two parachute jumps before testing and had agreed to make at least one more jump as part of the research program. A control group of 27 subjects was selected from students in an introductory course in psychology at the University of Massachusetts.

All 27 parachutists were tested three times: once on the day of a jump, once on the day before a jump, and once two weeks before a jump. The testing procedure on each of these days was arranged to include such internal checks and balances as to ensure good experimental design. On each of the three days of testing, each of the 27 experimental subjects was given a word-association test and a test to determine the variations in his auditory threshold (or the intensity of the smallest sound stimulus he reported being able to hear). On the days these subjects actually made a jump, they were also given a projective test, involving TAT-like responses to a number of pictures, one of which had a limited relevance for parachute jumping and one of which had very

[*] Walter D. Fenz, Conflict and stress as related to physiological activation and sensory, perceptual, and cognitive functioning, *Psychol. Monog.*, No. 585. 1964.

direct and obvious relevance for parachute jumping. While the subjects took these tests on each occasion, their galvanic skin responses were continuously recorded, with the recording being made from the index and middle finger of the nondominant hand. Also, after each response on the word-association test, their auditory thresholds and their reaction times to the association words were recorded.

In connection with the word-association part of the testing, each subject responded on each of the testing days to one of three matched lists of stimulus words. Each of these matched lists contained several different kinds of words. On each there were, first, neutral words—a number of which were given at the beginning of each word list to establish a general level of performance. Also on each list there were words of three degrees of relevance for parachuting (the relevance of the words was determined by the subjects themselves on the basis of standard scaling and scoring techniques): words of low relevance, such as "sky" and "swift"; words of medium relevance, such as "aircraft" and "opened"; and words of high relevance, such as "rip-cord" and "parachute." Each list also contained anxiety words, such as "hurt" and "kill."

With respect to the auditory threshold, each subject was given some preliminary training in judging the presence or absence of an audible tone in his ear. He was asked to put on earphones and then was asked to practice making a judgment as to whether or not he could hear a sound as he himself turned the intensity up so that it was just barely audible, or down so that it was not audible at all. The subject was asked to make such a determination of auditory threshold immediately after each response on the word-association test.

GSR and relevance of stimuli. As the data in Figure 1 show, the parachutists clearly responded with a greater GSR to anxiety words than to neutral words, and the magnitude of the GSR response increased with the degree of relevance of the stimulus words. The control group responded with a greater GSR for anxiety words than for neutral words, and gave no difference in response to words of low or medium or high relevance. To words of medium and high relevance, the experimental subjects responded much more strongly on the day of the jump than they did on the day before the jump and, similarly, more strongly on each of these days than they did at the testing time two weeks before the jump. When tested two weeks before the jump, they seemed to show some tendency to respond less emotionally than did control subjects to anxiety words, to neutral words, and to words of low relevance for parachuting. This difference is a statistically significant one and, the experimenter suggests, may be a personality difference between those who are interested in parachuting and those who are not.

Auditory threshold. With respect to auditory threshold, the parachutists demonstrated a higher threshold on the day of the jump than they did the day before a jump and appreciably higher on both days than on the day of testing two weeks before a jump. These data are presented in Figure 2. Members of the control group showed a slightly higher threshold when such a measure was taken after anxiety words than when it was taken after neutral words, but they showed no change in auditory threshold with the words of varying degrees of relevance for parachuting.

Reaction time. The experimental subjects varied from situation to situation in reaction time to stimulus words. On the day of a jump, there

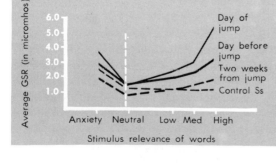

Figure 1. GSR of parachutists and control Ss.

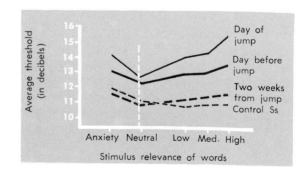

Figure 2. Auditory threshold of parachutists and control Ss.

was a significant difference in reaction time for neutral words and reaction time for highly relevant words. The difference was less but still statistically significant on the day before a jump and still significant at the testing two weeks before. No reliable differences of this kind occurred for the control subjects.

Emotion and perception. It was possible to tabulate the frequency with which the stimulus words in the word-association test were correctly perceived. If the subject reported that he had not heard a word or, when questioned, indicated that the inappropriate response stemmed from a failure to perceive correctly, then it was fairly clear that misperception was occurring. The results presented in Figure 3 show that the experimental subjects on the day of a jump—as com-

pared with the control subjects—had a marked tendency to misperceive both anxiety words and neutral words. Also, on the day of the jump—as compared to the testing on the day before the jump or the testing two weeks before the jump—there was a greater inclination to misperceive anxiety words and some tendency to misperceive neutral words. But on the day of the jump there seemed to be some manner of "sharpening" of the perceptions of the experimental subjects; the perception of relevant words was relatively very keen.

Thematic responses and emotion. Analyzing the scores to the responses to thematic pictures, the experimenters found that on the day of a jump parachutists produced strong approach responses to parachuting. Also, they explicitly denied any fear of parachuting, and few if any fear responses occurred in stories told—even in connection with the picture having high relevance for parachuting. However, when compared with the control group, the experimental subjects produced a relatively high number of fear responses to pictures having nothing to do with parachuting. Such a finding inclines the experimenters to an interpretation involving a defense mechanism, in which there is a displacement of anxiety from an explicit and immediate situation to situations removed from the immediate.

This series of experiments extends to a study of memory as it is affected by stress and goes on to explore the relation between the self-ratings of their feelings by experimental subjects and the relation of subjective feelings to physiological indicators.

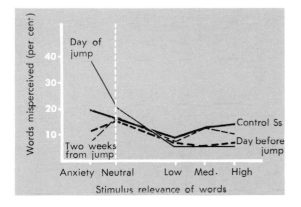

Figure 3. Misperceptions of parachutists and control Ss.

SUGGESTED READINGS

Candland, D. K., ed. *Emotion; bodily change, an enduring problem in psychology: Selected readings.* Princeton: Van Nostrand, 1962.

Cannon, W. B. *Bodily changes in pain, hunger, fear and rage,* 2nd ed. New York: Appleton, 1929 (1915).

Grinker, R. R., and J. P. Spiegel. *Men under stress.* Philadelphia: Blakiston, 1945.

Hess, W. R. *Diencephalon: Autonomic and extrapyramidal functions.* New York: Grune and Stratton, 1954.

Plutchik, Robert. *The emotions: Facts, theories, and a new model.* New York: Random House, 1962.

Reymert, M. L., ed. *Feelings and emotions: The Moosehart Symposium.* New York: McGraw-Hill, 1950.

OUTLINE / CHAPTER 10

I. BIOLOGICAL ROLE OF SENSORY PROCESSES

II. PSYCHOLOGICAL ASPECTS OF SENSORY PROCESSES

III. HEARING

    A. Stimulus for Hearing
    B. Structure of the Ear
    C. Hearing Defects
    D. Auditory Discrimination
        1. Loudness Discrimination
        2. Pitch Discrimination
        3. Tonal Mixtures
        4. Sound Localization
    E. Theories of Hearing
        1. Telephone Theories
        2. Place Theories
        3. Present Theory

IV. VISION

    A. Stimulus for Vision
    B. Structures of the Eye
    C. Defects of Vision
    D. Visual Discriminations
        1. Hue
        2. Brightness
        3. Saturation
        4. Sorting in the Dark
        5. Form Discrimination
        6. Brightness Discrimination
            a. Brightness and wavelength
            b. Theory of brightness discrimination
        7. Visual Acuity
        8. Color Vision: Hue Discrimination
            a. Color mixture
            b. Theories of color vision
            c. Color blindness

V. OTHER SENSES

    A. Taste
    B. Smell
    C. Cutaneous Senses
    D. Sense of Position in Space
    E. Kinesthesis: The Sense of Active Movement

VI. SUMMARY

VII. RESEARCH REPORT

CHAPTER 10

SENSATION

The living, motivated **organism** senses the world, interprets it, responds to it, and then responds to the consequences of its own response. In order to survive, the organism must be able to sense and interpret the world around it. It would not be able to do anything about its motives, nor to know perceptions, nor to change its behavior on the basis of experience unless it were able, through its senses, to keep itself in intimate touch with the environment in which it lives. In the present chapter, we shall deal with the processes whereby the organism senses or registers environmental events, trying first to see those processes in biological perspective and then examining in some detail the factors involved in, and aspects of, the human capacity to make sensory **discriminations.**

BIOLOGICAL ROLE OF SENSORY PROCESSES

The organism must register the world in order to respond to it, and the capacity of the organism for varied response is limited by its capacity for varied registering. From a biological point of view, the scope of an organism's life is largely determined by what it can sense.

Take the ordinary wood tick, for example. The wood tick is not equipped by nature to see sights or to hear sounds. It does have, however, a sensitivity to light and dark and warmth, and a capacity to register the smell of butyric acid that emanates from the skin glands of mammals. At a certain stage in its development the female tick, reading the photosensitivity of its skin, crawls toward the light high up on a twig and remains there until a warm-blooded animal passes by. When the tick senses butyric acid, it drops. If it then registers the proper sensation of warmth, it digs in for a feast. If it falls on a cold surface, it begins all over again its trip toward the

writer's estimate of the way the same scene appears to a fly and to a human being. The fly's eye, containing few sensitive elements, cannot register fine details—a fact of considerable benefit, incidentally, to the spinners of spider webs.

Other organisms may have special sensory

Figure 10–1. ORGANISMS DIFFER IN SENSITIVITY. *A human view and a fly's view of the same scene. Because its eye has fewer receptors per area, the fly is not able to register fine detail.*

light, to try its luck once more. Ticks have been known to hang, essentially in suspended animation, for as much as 18 years—waiting, we are inclined to say, for that crucial smelly sensation to trigger adaptive action. Once the tick finds a warm-blooded host, she gorges herself. Then she falls to the ground, lays her eggs, and dies (Von Uexküll, 1934).

The tick's sensory life, then, includes only light and darkness, one crucial smell and a sense of temperature. Most of us would regard this as a highly unsatisfactory sensory exposure to the world. But for the tick's way of life it is adequate, and in some ways quite impressive. However, although its sensory equipment enables the tick to make certain delicate adjustments, it also limits drastically the kinds of adjustments the tick can accomplish.

As we go up the evolutionary scale, sensory mechanisms become more varied and in many cases more sensitive. Flies, for example, have relatively well-developed eyes, enabling them to make fairly fine visual adjustments. But the fly's eye is still far below human standards of sensitivity. Figure 10–1 presents one

gifts not known to human beings, but the human organism seems to be marvelously well equipped to register his world. The human ear can register vibrations of air particles ranging in **frequency** from 16 to 20,000 per second. And if the ear were just a bit more sensitive than it is, it would hear the constant sound of air particles bumping busily and randomly into one another. Its range of **auditory** sensitivity is impressive; the loudest sound the ear can register without injury is perhaps a hundred trillion times more violent, in physical energy, than the smallest perceptible sound.

The human eye, sensitive to the electromagnetic radiation known as light, can register the flare of a match 50 miles away. It can also respond to the brilliance of a noonday sun, a stimulus a thousand million times as intense as the flare of the match. In its capacity for fine discrimination, the eye can register a stimulus occupying only 1/500,000 of its total sensitive surface. This represents a capacity, under proper conditions, to see a telephone pole 45 miles away or a wire 1/16 inch in diameter from a distance of 440 yards.

Through taste buds located on the tongue, the palate, and the cheeks, we can register a rich variety of tastes. Through **olfactory** organs at the top of the nasal passage, we can respond to a great variety of smells. In addition to these more vivid and well-known sensitivities, we also have the capacity to respond, through the operation of special receptors, to touch, pressure, pain, warmth and cold, movement in space, and the movement of our own muscles.

We may rightly regard the human organism as the possessor of an impressive array of sensitivities. But it is *not* sensitive to all energy changes in its world. The eye, sensitive as it is, registers only a small proportion of the **wavelengths** in which electromagnetic waves are known to occur. We cannot directly sense gamma rays, X rays, ultraviolet rays, radar waves, radio waves, or the waves of ordinary A-C circuits. Of this vast array of wavelengths of electromagnetic energy, varying from 10^{-14} to 10^8 meters in length, the human eye can register only a very small proportion—those waves whose length falls between 16 and 32 millionths of an inch (Fig. 10–2). For all the waves to which we are not sensitive, we must use translating devices if they are to come to our sensory awareness. Man has invented such things as X-ray photography, radar scopes, radios, and television receivers to transform into visible or audible forms those electromagnetic waves that are beyond his natural ken.

The eye, though we may regard it as remarkably sensitive, is also limited in its ability to see *tiny* objects. It cannot see all the things its owner may want it to see. Man has invented microscopes and telescopes to bring small and distant objects up to a size that the eye can deal with.

In hearing, there are also limits. The human ear cannot register molecular vibrations more rapid than 20,000 per second. Beyond that frequency, the vibrations are called ultrasonic —beyond direct human sensibility. Dogs, however, have the capacity to respond to vibrations that are beyond the human limit. This makes it possible to use ultrasonic dog-calling whistles which rend the neighborhood air without disturbing the tranquility of the neighbors. Certain moths register frequencies as high as 100,000 per second, perhaps even higher. Such sensitivity can be of considerable utility in steering them away from the very high-pitched cries of predatory bats.

Other animals are also superior in sense of smell and sensitivity to movement. Dogs can trail a rabbit through a thicket or a raccoon through the woods—sensory feats in

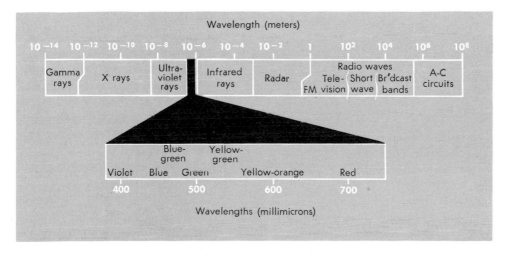

Figure 10–2. THE VISIBLE AND INVISIBLE SPECTRUM. *Electromagnetic waves are as short as 10^{-14} meters and as long as 10^8 meters. The visible part of this spectrum is a narrow band of wavelengths around 10^{-6} meters. This visible spectrum is usually described as extending from 390 to 760 millimicrons.*

which man would probably have to bow to the beagle. Hawks are renowned for their sensitivity of vision, particularly for vision of movement, and horses have remarkably keen vision for movement at the edges of the visual field. Horses can come closer than human beings to seeing behind themselves, making the use of blinders desirable if we want a horse to be undistracted by goings-on far to his right and left.

Generally speaking, although he may have to defer to the dog in hearing and take second place to the hawk and the horse in sensitivity to movement, man is biologically equipped with great sensory versatility. Over the millennia he has evolved the particular sensitivities with which he is now equipped and which, if we choose to regard it so, make his sensory life richly varied. If we wish to cultivate a fantasy by extending human evolution a few million years ahead, we can imagine the way the world will appear to the organism whose sensitivities have been extended. Why not a human being with a direct sensitivity to radio waves, making it possible to experience radio and television programs without the help of electronic gadgets?

PSYCHOLOGICAL ASPECTS OF SENSORY PROCESSES

So far, we have dealt broadly with the biology of sensing and have not come to grips with the truly psychological aspects of sensory processes. The psychologist is interested in what sensations the organism can report or—to say the same thing in a more behavioral way—what discriminations it can make so that it can adjust its behavior according to the sensory messages it receives. He also wants to know how these possible discriminations relate to physiological processes in the receptors, in the nervous system, in the brain; and to physical or chemical events outside the organism.

In order for a sensation to occur, there must be first a *stimulus*—some physical event in the world. There must also be **receptors**—specialized sensitive cells that can respond to the stimulus. There must be processes whereby the responding receptors change physical events—such as light waves or sound waves—into neural events, into *nervous impulses*. There must be a **central nervous system** that translates neural events into awareness, and, if there is to be muscular response to the in-coming signals, the nervous system must also make connections between the incoming sensory messages and the nerves running to the body's **effectors**—its muscles and glands.

In a nutshell, the sequence from stimulus to receptor to sensory nerve to the central nervous system to effector contains the story of sensation. In that sequence there are some intricacies and still some mysteries that fascinate the psychologist.

In confronting the intricacies of sensation, we will first study in some detail the two senses, hearing and vision, on which there has been the greatest research and about which we know most. Then we will consider some of the many other senses—smell, taste, touch, etc.—that man uses in interacting with his environment.

HEARING

Although we are highly conscious of vision and, in our daily lives as well as in our poetic literature, make much of the eye as the "window of the soul," the sense of hearing is in many ways the human being's most vital channel of interaction with the environment. The human individual who is born deaf is under perhaps more of a handicap than is the congenitally blind, because he cannot learn the symbolic uses of sound in language—and spoken language is vital in the life of so conspicuously social a being as man. Even the individual who becomes deaf after he has thoroughly learned the symbolic uses of sound still has great difficulty with communication, for the most skilled lip reader fails to respond to the subtle tonal inflections of human speech.

STIMULUS FOR HEARING

The physicist will report that sound is a form of energy, that it consists of waves of changing pressure. The psychologist will point out that sound is a sensation aroused when sound waves stimulate the auditory sense organ and send impulses up the eighth nerve to the auditory portion of the cortex.

Sound is both of these things, of course, and the old question "If a tree falls in the forest with no one there to hear it, is there a sound?" is a question of semantics.

The physical stimulus for sound consists of vibrations of air particles—a series of *condensations* and *rarefactions* of these air particles striking the eardrum. Normally, the particles are distributed fairly evenly in air space and move about in a random fashion. If we sit in a soundproof room and if nothing is done to disturb the normal distribution and movement of air particles, the only sounds we can hear are those produced by our own muscular activity and by the flow of blood through the vessels in and around our own ears. If there is an explosion in the room, or the drop of a pin, things change. A force is applied, in all radial directions, to the air particles surrounding the physical event. This force pushes the nearby particles away, pressing them against their next neighbors, which in turn push still other molecules that surround them. This *condensation* of molecules is followed by a *rarefaction* as the molecules spread out again, returning the particles to their normal distribution. The result of this series of condensations and rarefactions is the sound stimulus: a propagated change in the density (and therefore in the pressure) of any medium, including air, water, and solids, that can contract and expand. Such propagated changes are usually spoken of as sound waves, for they progress like waves and, when diagrammed, are usually and appropriately drawn in the form of waves.

The traveling back-and-forth pressures that are **sound waves** vary in *frequency*, in *complexity*, and in *amplitude*. (See Fig. 10–3.)

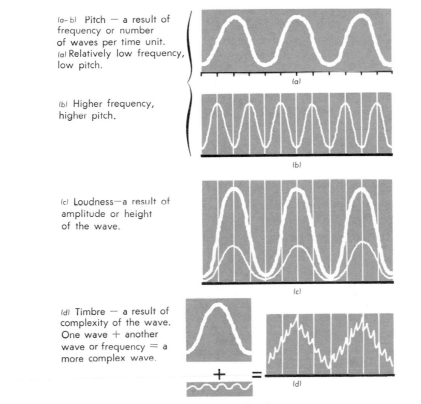

(a–b) Pitch — a result of frequency or number of waves per time unit.
(a) Relatively low frequency, low pitch.

(b) Higher frequency, higher pitch.

(c) Loudness—a result of amplitude or height of the wave.

(d) Timbre — a result of complexity of the wave. One wave + another wave or frequency = a more complex wave.

Figure 10–3. THE STIMULUS FOR SOUND. *The stimulus for hearing varies in frequency, in amplitude, and in complexity. Variations in frequency relate to psychological variations in pitch; variations in amplitude, to loudness; and in complexity, to timbre.*

The frequency of sound waves is measured in *cycles per second* (cps). We can tap a particular tuning fork, for instance, that goes through these back-and-forth motions 16 times per second, setting up a 16-cps pattern in the air. This is heard as a very low tone, lower than the deepest bass voice and the lowest steamboat whistle. A lower frequency would probably be inaudible to the human ear. Similarly, when sound waves go above 20,000 cycles per second, they go beyond the sensitivity of even the most ardent hi-fi fan. Beyond that frequency, the waves may be good for dogs, for cleaning delicate instruments, and for killing bacteria; but they are no good for human hearing.

The physical stimulus for sound also can vary in *complexity*. Most sounds we hear are the result of a complex pattern of waves, a pattern containing many different frequencies, striking the ear. Even musical instruments of the highest quality do not emit *pure tones*— or one frequency at a time. The flute comes close to producing only one frequency at a time, but even there some complexity exists. (See Fig. 10–4.) Pure tones are rare in nature,

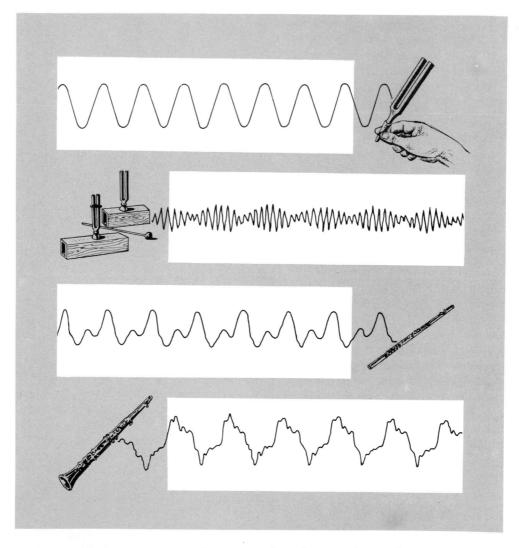

Figure 10–4. THE STIMULUS FOR SOUND. *A representation of the form of sound waves produced by various instruments. (Adapted from Miller, 1937; by permission of The Macmillan Company.)*

but they can be produced at will by the use of electronic sound generators in the laboratory.

The intensity of the sound stimulus corresponds to the *amplitude* of the back-and-forth vibrations. The amplitude of a sound wave is diagrammatically represented by the vertical distance between the wave peaks. If we strike a tuning fork a very gentle blow, its tines will vibrate gently and through a small amplitude. If we strike it a resounding whack, its vibrations, without change in frequency, will be more violent, covering a wider back-and-forth amplitude. The traveling pattern of condensations and rarefactions will then behave accordingly.

The intensity of the sound stimulus is measured in **decibels** (db). The decibel scale is a logarithmic scale, which can begin with the weakest sound pressure or intensity the ear can hear and go upward in a logarithmic manner. In such a scale the point of zero decibels is placed arbitrarily wherever we want it. It is convenient and conventional to set the zero point at or near the weakest sound the human ear can hear, a point usually fixed at 0.0002 dynes per square centimeter. A sound ten times as forceful as the sound of zero decibels falls at 10 db. A sound of 40 db is 10,000 times as forceful as the weakest sound; a sound of 60 db, the approximate level of ordinary conversation, is 1,000,000 times as strong; and a sound of 100 db—say, the noise of a passing locomotive—is 10,000,000,000 times as strong as the weakest sound we can hear. (See Fig. 10-5.) The ear can register sounds up to 125 or 130 db; but when sounds approach that intensity, they begin to pain the ear and, if they go higher, will produce actual damage to the hearing mechanisms.

STRUCTURE OF THE EAR

The ear is composed of three parts, each of which serves a vital function in transforming pressures in the air into auditory sensations (see Fig. 10-6). The *outer ear*, the visible part of the hearing mechanism, is not very impressive, except perhaps to the romantically inclined, in either shape or function; it serves merely to funnel sounds down the external **auditory canal** to the **eardrum**, a thin membrane at the end of the canal. The *middle ear* is more mechanically intricate. Within it there is a system of bones known as the

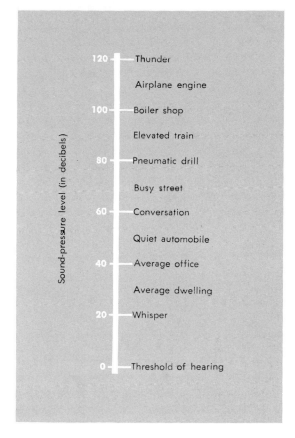

Figure 10-5. THE DECIBEL SCALE. *The decibel scale, representing here the sound-pressure level of various familiar sources of sound. (Adapted from Stevens and Davis, 1938; by permission of the authors and John Wiley & Sons, Inc.)*

malleus (hammer), the *incus* (anvil), and the *stapes* (stirrup). These bones are hinged into a system of levers, so that movement of the eardrum is transmitted to the *oval window*, the membranous opening into the *inner ear*. It is in the inner ear that both structure and function become truly intricate.

In the inner ear there are three fluid-filled canals in what is called, because of its spiraling snail-shell shape, the **cochlea**. The oval window leading from the hinged bones of the middle ear is in contact with this fluid. Separating the **cochlear canal** (the center of the three canals) from the *tympanic canal* (see Fig. 10-7) is the **basilar membrane**, on which is

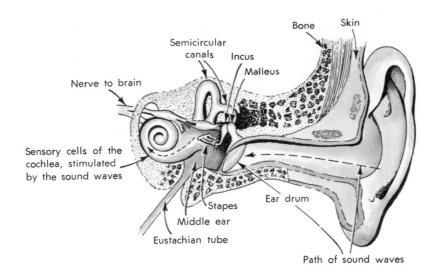

Figure 10–6. THE STRUCTURE OF THE EAR. *A diagram of the structure of the ear, indicating the course of the sound wave from the external ear, to the eardrum, through the ossicles of the middle ear, to the oval window of the cochlea.*

located the **organ of Corti** containing the *hair cells,* the specially endowed structures that translate physical stimulation into neural activity. When the bones or **ossicles** of the middle ear transmit movement through the oval window into the fluid of the cochlear canal, this movement in turn moves the basilar membrane, which moves the hair cells of the organ of Corti.

The way in which this energy is transferred in the inner ear can be compared to the snapping of a rope. As the movement travels like a wave the length of a rope, so does a wave of energy travel along the basilar membrane as if the membrane were a miniature rope. The result is a movement and a bending of the hair cells on the organ of Corti. As the hair cells are moved, they stimulate the fibers of the eighth nerve, which serves the organ of Corti. From this stimulation come the neural impulses that we interpret as sound. Move-

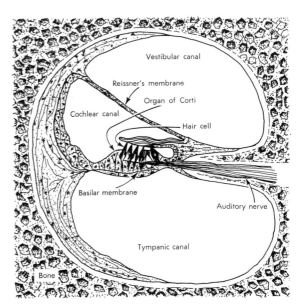

Figure 10–7. THE COCHLEA. *A diagram of a cross section of the cochlea. The receptors for sound are located in the organ of Corti on the basilar membrane which extends from the oval window of the cochlea to its end.*

ment of the stapes against the oval window serves also to send eddy currents through the fluids (**perilymph** and **endolymph**) that fill the cochlea. The movement of these fluids "dampens" or retards the movement of the basilar membrane.

After the ear has registered this physical input and has transformed it into nervous impulses, what does the auditory nervous system do with it?

The eighth nerve passes into the skull at a point very near the cochlea. Once inside, the nerve fibers from the cochlea branch so that some of the fibers from each of the two cochlea of the two ears terminate on cells in the *olivary nucleus,* on the same side of the head as the cochlea from which they arise. The rest of the fibers cross through the brain stem and terminate on cells in the olivary nucleus on the opposite side of the head.

Fibers go from each of the olivary nuclei to other specific centers on their way to the auditory cortex. There are many places in this system where information from the two ears may be compared, combined, enhanced, or reduced, a fact of considerable import for the understanding of ways in which we use two ears to locate the direction from which a sound comes. A long and exciting tradition of research has centered about efforts to determine which functions are performed at each of the stations of the auditory system.

HEARING DEFECTS

A number of structural defects can damage human hearing. *Conduction deafness* can be produced by some defect in the system of bones and membranes that conducts pressure changes from the outside air to the inner ear. If the external canal is plugged with wax, as frequently happens, sound waves are not conducted properly into the auditory system. Similarly, if the eardrum is broken or there is some defect in the **ossicles** of the inner ear, sound waves will not be adequately transmitted to the place where they can trigger off nervous impulses. Conduction deafness can often be remedied by devices that amplify or magnify sound vibrations and transmit them directly through the bones of the skull to the inner ear. Other hearing aids simply amplify the sound stimulus so that it can be sent through regular channels with enough force to overcome structural difficulties.

Figure 10–8. MEASURING HEARING LOSS. *The audiometer is used to measure the threshold of hearing throughout the range of audible frequencies.*

Perceptual deafness (formerly called "nerve deafness") is another matter. This kind of deficiency in hearing results from damage to the nerves themselves or to the delicate mechanisms in the cochlea. Most frequently, the person with a loss of auditory discrimination is unable to hear the high-frequency sounds or is able to hear them less well than he can hear low sounds. Such deafness leads to particular difficulty in hearing speech sounds, for the crucial clicks and hisses and many of the tones of speech are of relatively high frequency. The individual with perceptual deafness may be unable, for example, to distinguish between such words as "ice" and "eyes" or between "seal" and "zeal."

There are also cases of *central deafness,* most frequently caused by damage to auditory structures of the brain; and cases of *hysterical deafness* or *functional deafness,* produced by psychological or emotional factors rather than discoverable brain damage.

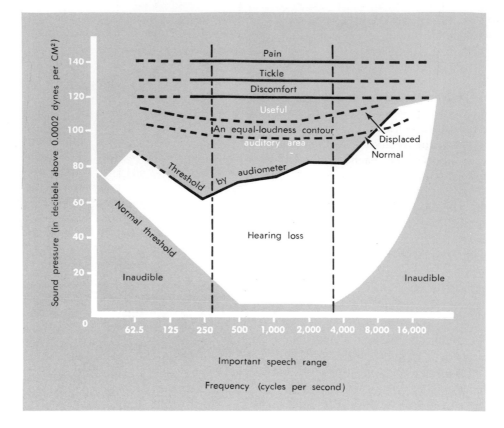

Figure 10–9. HEARING LOSS. *A diagram indicating (1) the point at which various sound frequencies can be just barely heard by the normal ear (normal threshold); (2) the raised threshold for various frequencies characterizing one kind of deafness; and (3) the thresholds of discomfort, tickle, and pain. The curves showing equal-loudness contours indicates that the perceived loudness of a tone varies with the frequency of that tone. (Davis, 1947; reproduced by permission of Holt, Rinehart & Winston, Inc.)*

AUDITORY DISCRIMINATION

The psychology of hearing begins, as we have seen, with a consideration of the auditory discriminations the individual can make —namely, his responses to frequency (**pitch**), amplitude (loudness), and complexity (**timbre**). Of these discriminations, loudness and pitch will concern us most. Additional psychological phenomena—beats, masking, etc.

—will also concern us at least briefly, for these do enter into our auditory lives and do fascinate the auditory theorists. Also we will consider the ways in which the organism locates the source of sounds.

Loudness Discrimination

The sensed loudness of a sound stimulus varies with the intensity of the stimulus. There is no auditory sensation at all, of course, unless the intensity of the stimulus is at or above the **absolute threshold.** And for intensities above the absolute threshold, the relation between intensity of stimulus and loudness of sound— phenomena involving *relative* rather than absolute sensitivity—becomes fairly intricate; at least, there is no simple one-to-one relationship there. With respect to the absolute threshold for sound, we have already seen that the smallest pressure the ear can register is about 0.0002 dynes per square centimeter, a pressure slightly larger than that created by the spontaneous collisions of the molecules of the air at ordinary temperatures. This minimal pressure, however, is not the same for all frequencies of sound. If we test across various frequencies for the absolute threshold of hearing, we find a distribution of thresholds (see Fig. 10–10; also Fig. 10–9). The ear, though still marvelously sensitive at all audible frequencies, is most sensitive to frequencies around 1,800 to 3,000 cps, and less sensitive to either high or low frequencies. In a communication system, then, where every iota of transmission energy is at a premium, tones of 1,800 to 3,000 cps would have, by our data, the greatest chance of being heard.

tionship between physical events on one hand and sensory or psychological events on the other. For a long time psychologists have been fascinated by this nonlinearity and have worked not only to describe the relationship precisely but to account for it. A brief history of the research on this phenomenon is presented at the end of the present chapter. In simplest terms we can say that large increases in physical energy do not produce equally large increases in sensation; generally speaking, a small increase in the energy of a weak stimulus will lead to a noticeable difference in sensation, while only a relatively large increase in the energy of an already strong

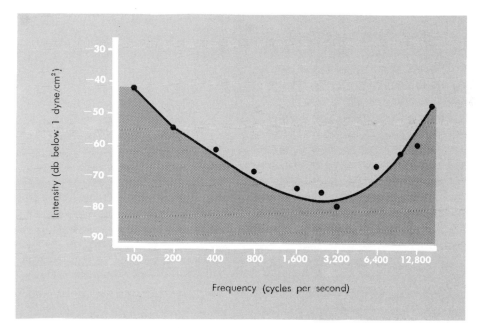

Figure 10–10. ABSOLUTE THRESHOLD FOR SOUND. *The smallest physical intensity of sound that can just barely be heard (the absolute threshold for sound) varies with the wavelength of the stimulus. The greatest sensitivity is for stimuli with a frequency around 3,000 cps. (Sivian and White, 1933; reproduced by permission of the authors and the* Journal of the Acoustical Society of America.*)*

When we come to study the *relative* sensitivity of the auditory mechanism, we encounter the basic phenomenon of a nonlinear rela-

stimulus will produce a noticeable difference in sensation. This general kind of relationship holds not only for audition but for other senses as well.

Pitch Discrimination

As in its reaction to intensity, the human organism refuses to respond with copycat directness to changes in frequency. If we ask an experimental subject to listen to one tone and then to select a tone that is twice as high in pitch, and if we do this throughout the range of audible frequencies, we can systematically relate the psychology of pitch to the physics of frequency. If in constructing a **pitch scale** in this manner, we plot **mels**, or units of pitch, against frequency, we get the function presented in Figure 10–11. The curve there is based on the arbitrary procedure of assigning the figure of 1,000 mels to the frequency of 1,000 cps. The curve tells us clearly that there is no one-to-one relationship between frequency at the eardrum and pitch in the brain. Whereas a 1,000-mel pitch is produced by a 1,000-cycle stimulus, a 2,000-mel pitch takes a stimulus of 3,120 cps.

logue four additional psychological phenomena in audition—phenomena that will need to be accounted for in the final theory of hearing.

Beats. If two tones, almost the same in frequency, are heard at the same time, we will hear a periodic rising and falling of the intensity of the total sound. This "beating" of the total pattern will come with a frequency equal to the difference between the frequencies of the two primary tones. If one tone is 120 cps and another is 122, we will hear two

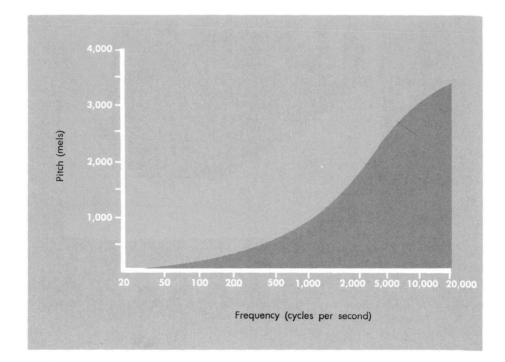

Figure 10–11. THE PITCH SCALE. *Pitch, a psychological variable measured here in mel units, varies systematically with the physical frequency of the stimulus. (Stevens and Volkmann, 1940; reproduced by permission of the* American Journal of Psychology.)

Tonal Mixtures

In addition to the primary matters of loudness and pitch, we ought here at least to cata-

beats per second. If the second tone is 125 cps, we hear five beats per second. This phenomenon relates to the physical fact that, when two tones of different frequency reach the ear simultaneously, the condensation phase of one wave will occur periodically at the same time as the rarefaction phase of the other. When this occurs, the two waves tend to cancel each other out. Just as frequently, the two waves will reinforce each other—with both being in the condensation phase at the same time. When this occurs, there is an increase of sensed intensity.

Masking. Some tones will serve to blot out or mask other tones if they are simultaneously present. But there is an asymmetry here. Low tones mask high tones better than high tones mask low tones. The best masking tones, if one wishes to jam a radio broadcast or blot out conversation, are complex tones or tones containing a great variety of frequencies. The sounds emitted by propeller-driven aircraft are such effective masking sounds that highly intricate procedures are needed to shield the pilot's ear from them so that they will not mask vital radio communication.

Difference tones. If two tones, too far apart in frequency to produce noticeable beats, are heard at the same time, a third tone, with a pitch corresponding to the difference in frequency of the two tones, will also be heard. If one stimulus is at 500 cps and the other is at 700, we hear both these tones and, in addition, a difference tone of 200 cps.

Summation tones. Sometimes we hear tones that are the sum of the frequencies of the two primary stimuli. For instance, our two tones of 500 and 700 cps will, under some circumstances, produce a summation tone of 1,200 cps.

Sound Localization

The fact that we have more than one ear is a matter of considerable importance for survival and of cardinal importance for determining where a sound comes from. The mechanical and neurological events occurring in one ear occur, in essentially the same way and at essentially the same time, in the other ear. We have to say "essentially" here, however, for the processes in the two ears are rarely, if ever, identical. Most frequently, sound waves from the same source do not reach the two ears at precisely the same time. For example, if the stimulating vibrations come from a source to our right, they must travel around the head to reach the left ear. And in the

process of getting around the head, the sound wave may also be reduced a bit in intensity, and the stimulus hitting one eardrum may be in the middle of a rarefaction phase while its counterpart for the other ear may be in the middle of condensation. We then say that the sound wave at one ear is not in *phase* with that at the other.

The two ears, then, receive stimulation that can differ in *time of arrival*, in *intensity*, and in *phase*. These are the aspects of the stimulus out of which the organism must create its judgments of the direction from which sound comes. If we had only one big ear located in the middle of the forehead, the perception of the direction of sound would be very difficult.

It has been shown that differences in the time of arrival are especially important in determining the location of high-frequency tones, since high-frequency tones (above 4,000 cps) seem to be partially "blocked" by the head, while low-frequency tones are not. Phase differences give important cues for low frequencies (Stevens and Newman, 1936). For locating sounds with frequencies between 2,000 and 4,000 cps, neither differences in time of arrival nor phase differences are effective; hence, sounds in this range are difficult for human beings to localize.

It is interesting to note, by comparison, that many lower animals (birds, rodents, insects, etc.) give their warning cries in frequencies in the 2,000–4,000-cps range and that the calls of the young are in the same range, while calls serving to inform other animals of the location of the caller (mating cries, cries to announce the location of food) often sweep up and down across the high and low frequencies, thereby taking advantage of both intensity and time of arrival as cues to localization.

THEORIES OF HEARING

Scientists who are curious about the phenomena of hearing, like scientists who are curious about anything else, seek the simple and inclusive statement that fits all the facts, that "explains" all phenomena. Such a statement constitutes a theory. The auditory theorists face the task of fitting together all the facts about auditory experience and of relating these facts systematically to facts of structure, nerve, and brain. The ultimate theory of hearing, then, will have to show how pitch, loudness, timbre, masking, beats, difference tones, and summation tones are all related to, or made possible by, events in the ear and/or events in the auditory nerve and/or events in the brain's auditory centers. At present, there is no such theory. But a number of varied and ingenious attempts have been made. The student, though his own curiosity may not be uncontrollably committed to problems of audition, may do well to follow for a bit the paths the scientists' curiosity travels.

Historically, theories of hearing have turned out to be theories of pitch alone. These theories fall into two categories: (1) *frequency* or **telephone theories** and (2) **place theories.** The telephone theories have as their basic tenet the notion that the auditory nerve, reacting to events in the inner ear, carries to the brain neural impulses corresponding in frequency to the frequency of the sound stimuli reaching the ear. The nerve itself, then, acts like a telephone line, faithfully carrying frequency messages to the brain. Place theories, by contrast, maintain that the brain gets its cues to pitch not from the frequency of neural impulses reaching it but from nervous impulses arising from *certain places* in the inner ear.

Telephone Theories

The telephone theorists got their greatest boost when Wever and Bray (1930) measured what has come to be known as the "cochlear microphonic." Through some ingenious surgical and electronic work, they managed to "plant" an electrode—a wire that picks up electrical potentials—just ouside the cochlea on the auditory nerve and to listen to the electrical pattern (just as a radio or a telephone allows you to listen to an electrical pattern). They even talked into a cat's ear in one room and listened in the next room to the amplified output of the cat's auditory nerve.

The sounds coming through the loudspeaker were so faithful a reproduction of the sound reaching the cat that a listener could recognize the voice of the talker.

The "Wever-Bray effect" would have represented a great and simple victory for the telephone theorists except for some firm facts of neurological life. According to students of neurophysiology, a **nerve fiber** cannot produce a complicated pattern of electrical frequencies. Each single nerve fiber can send along only occasional **nerve impulses.** When the fiber is rested, it may transmit as many as 1,000 impulses per second. But when it tries, it cannot handle more than perhaps 200 impulses a second (Derbyshire and Davis, 1935). And each impulse, at whatever rate impulses come, is much like any other impulse. The nerve fiber fires or fails to fire by the **all-or-none principle.**

Wever, facing these facts, formulated the **volley theory**—a theory that nerve fibers operate in an alternating fashion, so that a group of nerve fibers, working together and taking turns, can send relays of impulses along the auditory nerve at very high frequencies. This theory had plausibility and was used in support of the telephone theory of hearing. But it also ran into trouble. Later research made it clear that even bundles of nerve fibers cannot carry impulses at a faster rate than about 3,000 or 4,000 a second. And still lower limits are set when the impulses must pass through the relay station of a **synapse,** where one nerve fiber connects to another.

What, then, were Wever and Bray hearing from the cats? It seems probable that they were listening not only to a pattern of neural impulses on the auditory nerve, but also to some electrical activity within the cochlea itself. The hair cells apparently were producing electrical processes—cochlear microphonics—which "leaked out" and were picked up by Wever and Bray. The evidence seems to indicate, then, that though a telephone theory may work for low frequencies, some other explanation must be found for the higher pitches; the nerve simply cannot, like a telephone, handle frequencies as high as the ear can hear them.

Place Theories

Quite a few years before the volley theory was developed, the great physicist, physiologist, and psychologist Hermann von Helmholtz studied a basilar membrane and made an educated guess about what happens to it when a sound stimulus comes along. Seeing that the membrane was wider at one end than at the other, he conceived it to be and to operate like a harp: fibers of varying lengths were strung across it, long ones at the far end and short ones at the base; and each fiber was ready to vibrate with sympathetic resonance when "plucked" by a sound stimulus of the proper frequency.

Again a plausible idea. But as is so often the case, plausibility ran into difficulty when confronted with fact. It became clear that for the basilar membrane to operate in accordance with the simple selective resonance with which Helmholtz endowed it, fibers at one end of the membrane would need to be about 1,000 times larger than the fibers at the other end. They clearly are not, and that reality takes care of any simple resonance theory.

But perhaps the mass of the fibers, as well as the length, has something to do with this selective resonance. Harps and piano strings do vary in mass as well as in length. Again, facts kill off plausibility. The fibers of the basilar membrane do not vary enough in mass to allow mass to be a significant factor. What about tension? It, too, has a hand in the tuning of a harp and perhaps determines the "tuning" Helmholtz suspected in the basilar membrane. One ingenious researcher (Békésy, 1928) undertook to measure the tension across the various parts of the basilar membrane. He punctured the membrane and examined the size and shape of the tears produced by the puncture. If the holes were round, the reasoning went, there would be equal tension in all directions. If the holes were oblong, there would be more tension in one direction than in another. If the holes were small, there would be little tension; if large, a lot of tension. The holes were universally round and small. There clearly seems to be only negligible tension on any part of the basilar membrane.

Present Theory

One present version of the place theory maintains that when a sound stimulus enters the basilar membrane, it sends a *traveling wave* down the length of the cochlea, much as one sends a wave down a rope by "snapping" one end of it. That such a phenomenon occurs has been demonstrated (Békésy, 1928). This traveling wave may involve the whole membrane; but, the theory goes, the differing *stiffness* of the parts of the membrane allows one part of it to vibrate more vigorously than others to a stimulus of a particular frequency. A stimulus, then, of 1,000 cps would involve all of the membrane from the oval window to those fibers which respond most resonantly to this particular frequency. The wave tends to die out beyond that point. A stimulus of a different frequency would produce a different pattern of vibration on the membrane. The principle of place is thus re-established—at least until something better is discovered. Though some theorists still have reservations about the role of stiffness, the evidence on traveling waves is widely accepted.

According to the traveling-wave theory, then, a sound enters the ear as a variation in air pressure and shakes the eardrum, which wiggles the three little bones of the middle ear; the footplate of the stirrup rocks in and out of the oval window and displaces some fluid which, on its way toward the round window, vibrates the basal end of the basilar membrane and starts a traveling wave. At the place of maximum membrane vibration, the hair cells send out an electrical pattern and set off the nerve fibers that carry the message—a message indicating the particular spot on the membrane that has been stimulated. And there you have it—a revised place theory of pitch.

Now we have two theories: a telephone theory for low frequencies and a place theory for high frequencies.

Licklider (1951), dissatisfied with the low-frequency theory as it stood, tried to devise a simple method for translating *rate*-of-nerve-firing into *place*-of-nerve-firing and succeeded quite well. By so doing, he made it possible to describe both the volley and the traveling-wave theories as a single place theory—but in this case, the "place" is further toward the brain than Helmholtz might have liked.

At the moment, then, we can say that pitch is represented (more or less) by a place in the auditory nervous system. Loudness, which we have not considered here in detail, can be accounted for fairly well by the total number of nerve firings that take place. Most of the other phenomena of hearing are unaccounted for. But research continues apace.

VISION

STIMULUS FOR VISION

The stimulus for vision is constituted of electromagnetic waves—waves that vary in length from about 16 to 32 millionths of an inch. Most frequently, these wavelengths are measured in *millimicrons* ($m\mu$), a millimicron being one thousandth of a *micron*, which is one millionth of a meter. The range of wavelengths to which the eye is sensitive runs from about 400 to about 800 millimicrons. Figure 10–2 illustrates the place of these wavelengths —called the *visible spectrum*—in the total range of electromagnetic waves, called the *electromagnetic spectrum*. If the light hitting the eye is around 400 $m\mu$ in wavelength, we experience violet. If it is at the long end of the visible spectrum, from 700 to 780 $m\mu$, we experience red. In between violet and red, as the wavelength increases, come blue, green, yellow, and orange. Below the violet are the ultraviolet wavelengths, and beyond the reds, at around 780 $m\mu$, are the infrared wavelengths.

The stimulus for vision varies in both **intensity** and **complexity.** Intensity is physically represented by the amplitude of the wave, of whatever length, striking the eye. Generally speaking, we register this physical intensity as brightness. *Complexity* refers to the mixture of wavelengths hitting the eye. We rarely see pure or uncomplex light waves in daily life. White light or sunlight is a very complex light, containing all the visible wavelengths. The light coming to us from the objects we see is almost always reflected light, and very few objects reflect only one wavelength of light. We can, however, create relatively pure or uncomplex stimuli through the use of a prism, which breaks up the sun's light into the component wavelengths and spreads them out to create the colors of the rainbow.

The eye and the nervous system, responding to these physical dimensions of the stimulus, create for us the wealth of visual experience with which we are accustomed to living.

STRUCTURES OF THE EYE

The specialized cells that respond to the visible spectrum are two microscopically small structures located in the **retina**, a layer of sensitive cells lining the eyeball. The retina contains approximately 115,000,000 **rods** and 6,500,000 **cones.** Rods are shaped like tiny cylinders; cones, as their name implies, are conical or tapered in shape. Stimulation of the rods and cones leads to stimulation of the **optic nerve**, which runs to the brain. Through a complex photochemical process within the rods and cones, electromagnetic waves are transformed into nervous impulses.

From a stimulus that varies in wavelength, complexity, and amplitude and from receptor cells of two types, the organism creates a visual experience containing innumerable colors, and an almost infinite variety of shapes, sizes, brightnesses, and saturations. The psychologists who study vision have undertaken the very challenging task of explaining how this is done. A little later we shall look at some of their efforts.

Not only do we need specially endowed receptors if we are to have visual experience but also, if our experience is to be most useful to us in moving around in a lighted world, we need a special structure to keep the receptors working at their best. The eye is just such a structure, evolved over millions of years as a camera-like device that focuses light on the most sensitive part of the retina. The **lens**

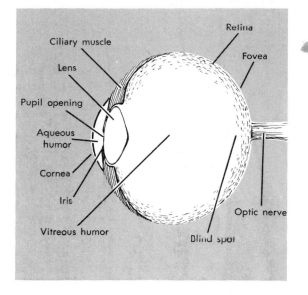

Figure 10–12. STRUCTURE OF THE EYE. *Light enters the eye through the cornea, pupil, and lens. The iris, the colored part of the eye, opens and closes to regulate the size of the pupil and the amount of light entering the eye. The lens changes in shape through the action of the ciliary muscles in order to focus light on the retina, where the receptors are located.*

and the **cornea** focus the incoming pattern of light waves as close as possible to the **fovea**, the part of the retina containing the most receptors per area. **Ciliary muscles** attached to the lens adjust its shape according to the distance of an object, so that the object is in clear and continual focus on the retina. For distance vision the lens is pulled into a thin shape. For near objects, the lens thickens. When the lens is working properly, the object we view, whether far or near, is brought into focus on the retina. (Incidentally, the object is always focused *upside down.* Yet we see things "right side up." To account for this strange event, we need to go beyond stimulus, receptors, and structure into purely psychological matters.)

Of considerable significance for the sensing organism is the fact that it has two eyes, essentially identical, functioning in the same way. The presence of two eyes, set slightly apart, means that the organism is receiving

two slightly different images on its two retinas. This **retinal disparity** is translated into sensations (or perceptions) of depth and distance. The one-eyed organism is at a disadvantage in judging distance and in telling the difference between two-dimensional and three-dimensional objects.

DEFECTS OF VISION

The lens does not just sit there, like the fixed lens of a camera. It must **accommodate** its shape to the distance of the objects in view. If it fails in accommodation we are in for trouble. When, with advancing age, the lens hardens so that it cannot change its shape, a condition known as **presbyopia**, a special form of farsightedness, occurs. The presbyopic person cannot focus clearly on near objects, and must wear glasses that come to the aid of the lens, doing for it what it can no longer do for itself. Figure 10–15 diagrams some forms of visual defects.

There are other ways in which the lens may not function properly, but this time through no fault of its own. The whole eye may be shaped in such a way that the lens is unable to focus light precisely on the retina. If the distance from the lens to the retina is too short, the lens will focus at a point behind the retina, making near objects appear fuzzy. Such a person is *farsighted*. He is able to see far objects but not near ones. If the eye is shaped so that the distance from the lens to the fovea is too long for the normal capacity of the lens to handle, then light is focused in front of the retina, producing *nearsightedness*. Near objects can be seen clearly, but the lens is unable to thin out enough to bring far objects into clear focus. The right kind of correction in glasses can remedy either of these conditions, clearing up vision and reducing the eyestrain produced when the eye muscles try to make the lens do the impossible.

Another structural defect in the eye, **astigmatism**, is generally caused by an irregularity in the shape of the cornea, the transparent outer membrane of the eye. Irregularities in the cornea will bend incoming light in various ways so that the lens receives an irregular

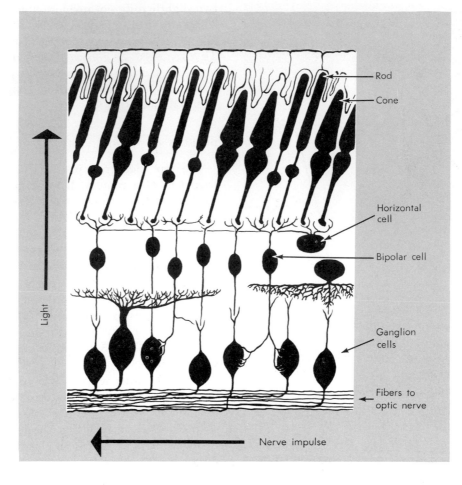

Rod

Cone

Horizontal cell

Bipolar cell

Ganglion cells

Fibers to optic nerve

Light

Nerve impulse

Figure 10–13. STRUCTURE OF THE RETINA. *The rods and cones, the two kinds of receptors for light, appear in the retina, the light-sensitive lining of the back of the eye. These receptors respond to light waves and set up impulses in the nerve cells. The receptors are more densely packed around the fovea, area of greatest sensitivity in the daylight.*

image to pass along to the retina. This defect can also be corrected by properly ground glasses which compensate for the eye's irregularities.

VISUAL DISCRIMINATIONS

As with hearing, the *psychology of* vision, as contrasted with its physics or its physiology, concerns itself focally with the visual discriminations the organism is capable of making. Primary dimensions of visual experience are **hue, brightness,** and **saturation.** We will be concerned with the relation of these sensory dimensions both to dimensions of the stimulus and to aspects of structure. Further, we will concern ourselves with the psychological and practical matters of visual acuity and of form discrimination.

We can get ourselves involved in these phenomena by thinking about the concrete aspects of a laboratory job of sorting colored disks. If a human subject with normal vision were given a million paper disks of many, many colors and all possible shades between pure black and pure white, he could sort them in a variety of ways. And if we can describe his sorting behavior under varying circum-

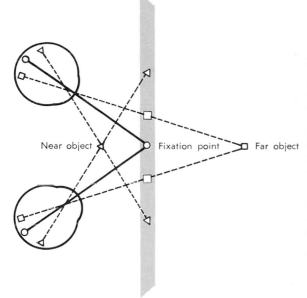

Figure 10–14. BINOCULAR VISION. *When the two eyes are fixated on a single object, each eye receives a slightly different image of the object. This retinal disparity furnishes an important cue for the perception of depth and distance. The effect can be duplicated by the old-fashioned stereopticon or by modern "three-dimensional" photography.*

stances, we will have described all the psychological dimensions of visual sensing. First we ask that the sorts be made in bright daylight.

Hue

In many ways the simplest sort will be on the basis of the hue of the disks. Our subject might organize his hue sorting around the color arrangement of the visual spectrum, with violet at one end and red at the other. He could put all the violet disks in one series of piles beginning with deep violet and running over to bluish violet. Then might come the blues, the greenish blues, the greens, the yellowish greens, the yellows, the oranges, and the reds. He would, of course, put in a separate pile all the black, white, and gray disks—the achromatic disks that have no hue at all.

Brightness

The next-easiest sort would be on the basis of the brightness of the disks. Perhaps in carrying out this set of discriminations, the subject would do well first to sort his achromatic disks, creating a series of piles running from the brightest white through the light and dark grays to the blackest black. Then he could match the brightness of the colored or chromatic disks, regardless of their hue, with the various achromatic ones. Some red disks, some blue ones, some yellow ones, and so on, would go into a pile very close to the white pile, for their brightness might be almost the brightness of white. Other chromatic disks would be very close to black in their lack of brightness.

Saturation

A more difficult sort, but one still quite possible for the human subject, would be on the basis of *saturation*—the hueness—of various disks. A saturated color is one free of whiteness. To make a saturation sort, it would be necessary to put our disks again in hue piles and then sort within each hue for saturation. Among our reds, for example, there would be some that seem verily and purely red. Others would have varying degrees of gray, or white, in them. The reds characterized by great redness, whatever the particular shade of red, are saturated colors. Those with much whiteness, whatever the particular hue of the bit of redness involved, would be relatively unsaturated. Pink is unsaturated red. This saturation aspect of colors is not so obvious to most of us as hue and brightness, but it still contributes significantly to the nature of our visual experience.

Sorting in the Dark

Now if we placed our subject in total darkness, he could, of course, not sort at all. But if we gave him a little light, and left him alone for half an hour, he could begin to do some sorting; he would adapt to the dark, and in 30 to 40 minutes his eyes would become 100,000

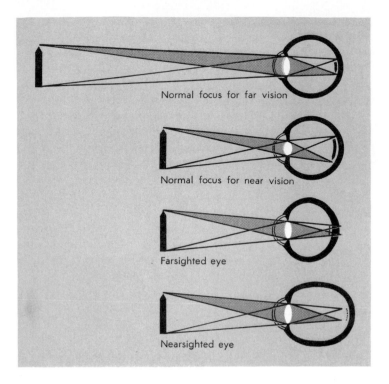

Normal focus for far vision

Normal focus for near vision

Farsighted eye

Nearsighted eye

Figure 10–15. STRUCTURAL DEFECTS IN VISION. *Normally the cornea and the lens focus incoming light precisely on the retina, whatever the distance of the object viewed. When there is an incapacity to focus near objects, with the point of focus falling behind the retina, there is farsightedness. When there is a relaxing and thickening of cornea and lens, far objects are focused in front of the retina. This is nearsightedness—only near objects focus precisely so that vision is clear.*

times as sensitive as they were in daylight, able to see brightness of very minute magnitudes (see Fig. 10–16). He would not be able to sort now on the basis of hue. No hues can be seen in very dim illumination. He could sort only on the basis of brightness, and a large number of the less bright disks would all look alike; for brightness discrimination would be poor under conditions of reduced illumination. If we compared his darkness sorting of brightness with his daylight sorting, we would notice some other discrepancies. Some of the colors lose brightness at night more markedly

than do others. In low illumination, reds tend to blacken out more than do blues. This is known as the *Purkinje phenomenon,* to be discussed later. (See Fig. 10–17.)

Form Discrimination

If on each of our disks there was a small dot, with the dots varying from microscopic proportions to the size of a golf ball, we could get a sort on the basis of form discrimination and could use the accuracy of the sort as a measure of the subject's visual acuity. He could not sort the microscopic dots, of course, since they would be below the *absolute threshold* for acuity, but he could do a very delicate and precise job of sorting the remaining dots if the lighting conditions are good. If we reduce illumination, form discrimination rapidly deteriorates. But if the subject can still see some forms, he would find that he sees better if, instead of looking directly at a dot, he looks slightly to the side of it. Where lights are low, the contrast between the dot and its background can be seen better with off-center vision.

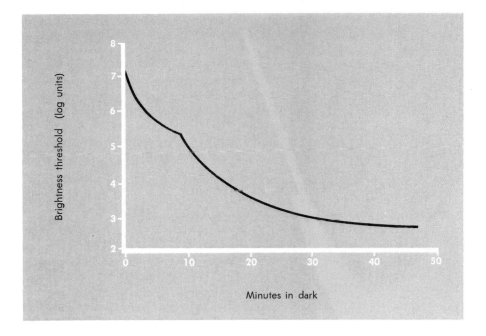

Minutes in dark

Figure 10–16. TYPICAL DARK-ADAPTATION CURVE. *If a subject is placed in total darkness after having been in bright illumination and is asked to register the weakest (threshold) stimulus he can, he initially can see only a relatively strong stimulus. But as time passes, the sensitivity of the eye increases tremendously. The typical curve for the threshold drops rapidly at first, then flattens out, then drops again after eight or ten minutes. The shape of the curve suggests that there are two separate adaptation processes involved.*

Through the mind's-eye completion of our task, we can perhaps gain a good and concrete understanding of the psychological dimensions of the visual process. We now will do well to return to consider in greater depth some of these dimensions and to see what progress can be made toward a general theory of visual phenomena. We will return first to a study of brightness, then will consider further matters of acuity, and then will turn to the intricate question of hue or, more generally, of color vision.

Brightness Discrimination

Brightness and wavelength. If we explore more thoroughly the facts of brightness discrimination, we will find that the sensitivity for brightness varies with the wavelength of the stimulus—just as, in audition, sensitivity to intensity varies with the frequency of the stimulus. If we conduct our measurement in the conditions of light prevailing when the sun is a few degrees below the horizon (at a few minutes after sunset), we find that the eye is relatively insensitive to very short (violet) and very long (red) wavelengths, and relatively more sensitive to middle (greenish) wavelengths. Now, having in mind our knowledge that the eyes work differently in low illumination, we decide to repeat our experiment after the eye is adapted in a condition of total darkness. We expect to get greater sensitivity. We do. But the sensitivity curve shifts. Now the greatest sensitivity is at 505 millimicrons rather than at 555, where it was in the daylight conditions. This is the **Purkinje shift.**

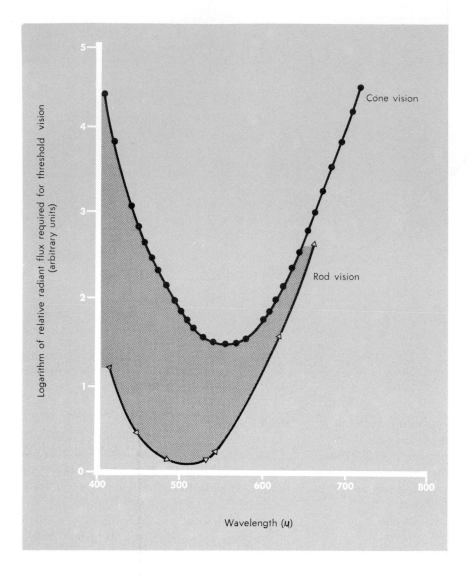

Cone vision

Rod vision

Wavelength (μ)

Logarithm of relative radiant flux required for threshold vision
(arbitrary units)

Figure 10–17. TWO VISIBILITY CURVES. *If we ask a subject, in conditions of reduced illuminations, to report the weakest light he can see while he is looking straight ahead and if we vary systematically the wavelength of the light, we find he is most sensitive to wavelengths around 550 millimicrons. If we keep everything else the same and ask him to observe stimuli that are about 20 degrees off center, we get a curve like the lower one here. Sensitivity is greater. It is also different now, in that the point of greatest sensitivity falls around 505 millimicrons. (Chapanis, 1949; by permission of the author.)*

Theory of brightness discrimination. These facts about brightness discrimination are accounted for by the **duplicity theory of vision.** According to this theory, the cones of the retina, in the presence of light stimulation, function mainly to mediate the sensing of chromatic stimuli, while the rods, insensitive to hue itself, are very sensitive to achromatic stimuli. The curve for **dark adaptation** is explained in terms of the increased sensitivity of both rods and cones when illumination is reduced: the break in the curve (Fig. 10–16) is produced at the point where the cones have reached their maximum sensitivity. After that

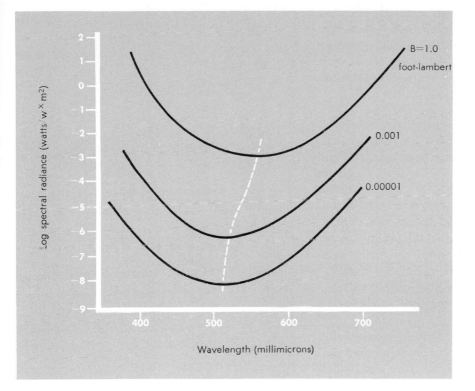

Figure 10–18. EQUAL-BRIGHTNESS CONTOURS.
*If we place a subject in illumination equal to
that prevailing at sunset and ask him to make
judgments about the brightness of stimuli of
various wavelengths, the results are represented in the top curve here (B = luminance).
Stimuli of long and short wavelengths must
be more physically intense than stimuli in the
middle ranges if they are to be seen as equally
bright. In other words, the sensitivity of the
eye is greatest under these conditions for
wavelengths around 540 or 550 millimicrons.
When we reduce the illumination, the areas of
greatest sensitivity shift toward the short
wavelengths. The middle curve shows results
obtained when the illumination is equivalent
to that of a quarter moon. The bottom curve
represents results (absolute thresholds) in
conditions of total darkness. The student may
wish to relate these data to those presented in
Figure 10–17. (From Judd, 1951, after Weaver,
1949; by permission of John Wiley & Sons,
Inc.)*

point, the rods continue to gain in sensitivity.

The two curves showing how sensitivity
varies for different wavelengths (Fig. 10–18)
are also accounted for by the duplicity theory.
The daylight curve is a *cone curve*. The twilight curve is the *rod curve*. When illumination
is reduced, the cones soon cease to function
effectively, but the rods, in a sense, come into
their own.

The rods and cones are distributed differently on the retina. *The fovea contains only
cones.* In regions close to the fovea, there are
both rods and cones, with the cones becoming
less frequent the further we move away from
the fovea. *At the edges of the visual field,
there are only rods.* You can test this by holding colored pencils or disks at the ear and
slowly bringing them forward while the eye
is focused straight ahead. At first, though the
object can be seen, it has no hue. As it comes
closer to the center of the visual field, where
the cones are, it takes on its color.

The duplicity theory is being re-examined
in view of the difficulty of distinguishing rods
and cones by shape alone. Furthermore, there

is good evidence that rods, contrary to earlier theory, may play a role in color vision. We cannot here evaluate all the evidence bearing on this theory, but we can accept it at least tentatively as one way to account for the facts we have seen.

Visual Acuity ✳

We pointed out earlier that the eye can see the equivalent of a wire ¼ inch in diameter at a distance of 440 yards. Such fine discrimination of form can occur if the structure of the eye is normal (not nearsighted, astigmatic, or farsighted), if the conditions of illumination are ideal, and if the eye is looking straight ahead. Through highly refined experimental techniques, it is possible to trace out in considerably more detail the facts of visual acuity for form.

The most widely used device for measuring visual acuity is the **Snellen chart,** a chart containing rows of letters of varying size, which the subject or examinee is asked to read from a standard distance, usually 20 feet. If, at 20 feet, he can read the letters that the "average" person can read at that distance, he is said to have 20/20 vision. If he reads at 20 feet what the average person can read at 100 feet, his vision is relatively very poor and is described as 20/100. If he can read at 20 feet letters that come clear to the average person only if that person moves up to 10 feet, then his vision is above average and is given the designation of 20/10.

For detailed experimental work on visual acuity, researchers generally prefer to use **Landolt rings,** circles of various sizes containing breaks of various widths. These stimuli do not require a knowledge of the alphabet, and they allow more precise control than does the use of printed letters (see Fig. 10–19).

Acuity and position on retina. With the aid of stimuli like the Landolt rings, it is possible to map out precisely the relation of visual acuity to the place the light strikes the retina. A curve presenting such a map of acuity is presented in Figure 10–20. The greatest acuity

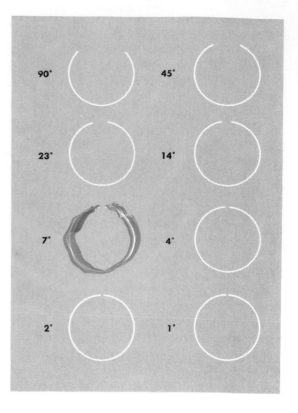

Figure 10–19. LANDOLT RINGS. *Variations in the width and location of the break in the rings make it possible to measure very precisely an individual's ability to see fine detail. The use of rings such as these instead of letters gives assurance that factors of familiarity and meaningfulness are not influencing the measure of acuity.*

occurs in the fovea, and acuity falls off rapidly on both the nasal and temporal sides. This curve is accounted for by the fact that visual receptors are tightly packed in the fovea (where there are only cones) and fall off in frequency per unit area as we move away from the fovea. We think of the analogy of a photographic film with its sensitive elements very close together at its center but more scattered at the periphery. Such a film would yield a picture with fine detail at the center but considerable fuzziness of detail at the edges of the picture.

There is no vision at all in that part of the retina where the optic nerve enters the eye-

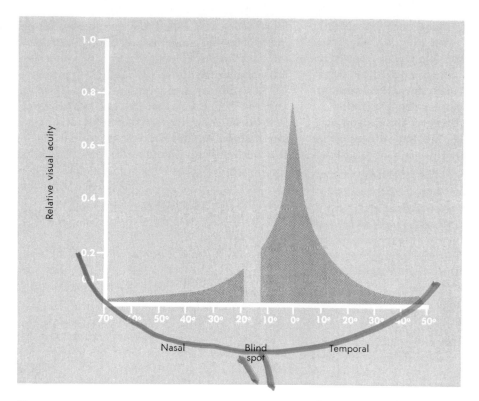

Figure 10–20. ACUITY AND POSITION ON RETINA. *Visual acuity varies with position on the retina, being greatest in the fovea, where receptors are densely packed. There is no vision at all in the blind spot—the place at which the optic nerve enters the retina.*

ball. This area is known as the blind spot (see Fig. 10–21).

Acuity and illumination. Illumination engineers have worked out very carefully the conditions of lighting that lead to the greatest acuity and the least eyestrain. Generally speaking, acuity increases with the amount of contrast between the object and its background. It is affected for the worse by glare. Acuity usually increases with the amount of illumination. The more light there is, the smaller the pupil becomes and the sharper is the focusing of objects. Even a person with poor vision can read fine print if he uses "an artificial pupil" such as a pinhole, holding the pinhole close to the eye and viewing the print through it.

Figure 10–21. THE BLIND SPOT. *The blind spot can be demonstrated if one closes his left eye and looks steadily at the cross with the right, then moves the page slowly away until the picture on the right disappears.*

Color Vision: Hue Discrimination

Color mixture. The basic processes in color vision can be understood most clearly, perhaps, if we talk about the sensing of pure colors—colors having only one wavelength. Actually, of course, we rarely or never see pure colors in everyday life. Most objects reflect and most lights emit a mixture of wavelengths. Out of these mixtures, the organism creates its world of color. The psychological effects of mixing wavelengths have been very systematically worked out, and the essential phenomena of color mixture can be presented in terms of the **color wheel** (Fig. 10–22).

four colors are called the **psychological primary colors** because they cannot be analyzed into any other colors. Colors (wavelengths) intermediate to these psychological primaries can also be arranged on the solid. If we select any two colors that are not exactly opposite to one another on this solid and if we mix them in equal proportions, we get a color that lies between them on the rim of the solid. For example, a mixture of red and yellow

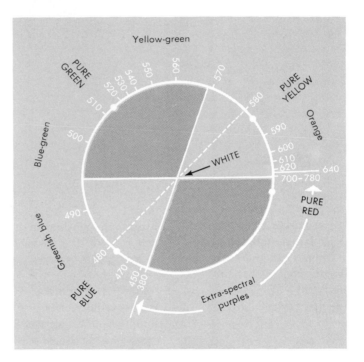

Figure 10–22. THE COLOR WHEEL. *The color wheel represents graphically a number of psychological relationships among hues. Points opposite one another on the unshaded parts of the wheel represent complementary hues; if they are mixed, they will yield a neutral gray. If two hues around the perimeter of the wheel are mixed, the result will be a hue falling between the two. Saturated mixtures fall at or near the perimeter of the wheel; unsaturated ones closer to the hub. The shaded areas have no complementary wavelengths in the visible spectrum.*

Around the outside of the wheel are arranged the four psychologically irreducible colors of red, blue, green, and yellow. These

yields orange; a mixture of blue and red will produce purple. A number of wavelengths on the wheel, if mixed with the wavelengths exactly opposite them, will yield an achromatic gray. These are called **complementary colors.** In experience, they seem to cancel one another out in a way that removes all saturation. Some wavelengths, indicated by shaded areas on the chart, do not have single complementary wavelengths. These wavelengths will still yield an achromatic gray, however, if they are mixed with two, or more, appropriately chosen other wavelengths.

The color wheel can be used also to predict the *saturation* of a mixture of equal portions of two colors. If a line drawn between two points on the rim comes close to the center of the solid, the *saturation* of a mixture will be close to the saturation produced by complementary colors—zero. If the line stays near the rim, the saturation will be relatively high. The obtained hue, then, is the hue on the rim that is perpendicular to the midpoint of the connecting line.

If colors are mixed in other than equal portions, the obtained hue will fall proportionately between the two wavelengths entering into the mixture. If there are three parts of red to one part of yellow, for example, we draw a line from red to yellow and put a perpendicular one fourth of the way from red to yellow, extend it to the rim, and get a very reddish orange (of high saturation).

These laws of color mixture, first worked out by Sir Isaac Newton, obtain only when we *additively* mix colors, when we add one wavelength of light to another—as by projecting lights on a screen. These neat regularities do not hold for mixing paints or pigments, as any amateur painter is likely to have discovered. Paints absorb wavelengths as well as reflect them. To predict what color will turn up when we mix paints, we have to be able to subtract the wavelengths that are absorbed by the component pigments.

It must be borne in mind that we are dealing with color mixture seen from a *psychological* point of view. The primary colors are psychologically primary in that they appear to the eye to be unanalyzable. *Physical primaries* are the colors that cannot be produced by mixing any other colors but, when mixed themselves, can produce all colors. The physical primaries for the mixing of lights are *green, red,* and *blue.* For mixing pigment, the physical primaries are *red, blue,* and *yellow.* The four irreducible psychological primaries are, by comparison, *yellow, blue, green,* and *red.* The color solid also summarizes the change of brightness, from black to white, which is represented along the vertical dimension.

Theories of color vision. How does the organism tell the difference between a red stimulus and a green or blue or yellow one? Here, our established knowledge runs thin. The most widely accepted theory, known as the **Young-Helmholtz theory,** says that there are three kinds of cones on the retina, each sensitive to a different wavelength of light. When all kinds of cones are stimulated equally, we see white. When one kind of cone is stimulated, we see red. Another kind yields blue, and another yields green. All the colors we see can be created out of mixtures of these three colors, and presumably they are produced by various mixtures of response from three kinds of cones.

Although the Young-Helmholtz theory, postulated in its first form in the early 1800s, and since revised by Hecht, is still the color theory in vogue, there are many others that merit consideration. Some of these have been inspired by the difficulties of fitting the color yellow into the Young-Helmholtz theory. Yellow, the least saturated (i.e., having the most white) color, is a primary hue; and yet it cannot be derived from any combination of the three primary colors for which there are receptors, according to Young-Helmholtz. Yellow cannot be derived from red and green, nor from green and blue, nor from red and blue. Furthermore, there are those with red-green blindness who see yellow. Hering (1878; 1964 ed.) hypothesized three chemical substances in three types of cones: a white-black substance in one type of cone, a yellow-blue substance in another, and a red-green substance in a third. The breaking down (catabolism) of these substances was supposed to yield one type of sensation (white, yellow, red), but a building up (anabolism) of the same substances was supposed to yield the opposite sensations. Light exciting both catabolic and anabolic activities in the white-black substance would result in gray.

The problem created by this theory seems greater than the problem it purports to solve. Each cone must somehow distinguish between catabolic and anabolic activities, and the nerve fibers leading from the cones must carry two different kinds of impulses. This theory, then, goes against the *law of specific energies*—the law stating that any given nerve cell fires only in its own particular way—but, because that law is in question in several areas, Hering's theory is at least plausible.

The sensation of yellow has prompted still another theory. Christine Ladd-Franklin (1929) advanced the theory that red, green, yellow, and blue all have distinct receptors. She theorized that, initially, visually sensitive organisms possessed only achromatic rods, which later differentiated to form primitive yellow and blue receptors. Still later, red and green receptors evolved from the yellow-sensitive cones. If this theory holds, some of the difficulties of accounting for red-green color blindness and the phenomenon of yellow can be accounted for.

A more recent investigator, Ragnar Granit (1959), using electrophysiological techniques, has stimulated very small areas on the retina and recorded resulting electrical activity in cells upon which several cones converge. He has found three kinds of structures: (1) *scotopic dominators* (rods), receptors maximally sensitive at 500 mμ; (2) *photopic dominators* (some cones) structures maximally sensitive at 560 mμ (the Purkinje shift again); and (3) *photopic modulators* (other cones), which are sensitive to very narrow frequency ranges. Granit attributes the experience of *hue* to the activity of *modulators* and that of *brightness* to the activity of *dominators*.

Granit's theory has some advantage over other color theories in accounting for chromatic summation, a phenomenon of considerable significance for theory. We saw earlier that saturation varies with intensity. A special case of the relation between saturation and intensity is chromatic summation: As the area of a stimulus is reduced to a very small size, saturation decreases toward gray. This fact offers problems for the Young-Helmholtz or the Ladd-Franklin theory, but not for Granit's. Since the white dominators have a wider sensitivity range than the more specialized modulators, a reduction of the area of stimulation decreases the probability of contacting the less numerous modulators and hence "whitens" the sensation.

Whatever is made of the new facts of color vision and whatever are the processes in the retina, there must be a translation of light waves into neural impulses that travel along the optic nerve to the visual centers of the brain. There is an accumulation of knowledge about the nature of the photochemical processes and about the nervous impulses going to the brain. It remains a mystery, however, as to just what happens in the brain to yield the experience of red on one occasion and blue on another. Just what is the brain reading? All it has to work on is a pattern of nervous impulses coming to it with certain speeds and certain frequencies and over certain fibers. Out of these messages, the brain somehow creates color vision.

Color blindness. If the subject we put to sorting a million disks were not possessed of normal color vision, he would have difficulty doing the chore we have assigned him. If he were completely color blind, of course, he could not make the hue sort at all. There are relatively rare cases of totally color-blind people, generally albinos, who see no hues at all and whose visual world is composed entirely of blacks, whites, and grays of different degrees of brightness. Such a person could sort in terms of brightness, perhaps with less difficulty than could a normal subject, but hues would be meaningless to him.

Much more frequent, occurring in about 4 per cent of the population, is an inherited form of **color blindness** known as **dichromatism.** The dichromat is sensitive to only *two* colors, *blue* and *yellow*. On our sorting task, such a person would find it next to impossible to deal with disks of red, green, bluish greens, and violets. There are at least two distinguishable types of dichromats. One type, the **deuteranope,** cannot discriminate *red* and *green* hues but is able to handle brightness discriminations throughout the spectrum. Another type, the **protanope,** has brightness difficulty as well as hue trouble. When he comes to our red disks, he may classify them as black. (See color plate 1 for a specimen item on a test of color blindness.)

In addition to these forms of actual color blindness, there are a number of *color weaknesses*, which would produce definite but relatively subtle difficulties in the task of sorting hues. These color weaknesses need not interfere significantly with visual discrimination and may not ever come to light until the individual tackles some such sorting chore as we have assigned him or until he is given careful tests of color vision.

The theories of color vision advanced by Ladd-Franklin and Granit are better able to cope with color blindness than are other theories. Granit would account for particular types of color blindness on the basis of the failure or defectiveness of the modulator cells responsible for the color sensations involved. Ladd-Franklin, with her evolutionary theory, is better able to account for the genetic basis of color blindness than are most other theorists. Color blindness, in her theory, represents a failure of the genetic material of the individual to reproduce the more recently differentiated color receptors.

OTHER SENSES

TASTE

Stimulus

When we turn from vision and hearing to other sensitivities of the human organism, our knowledge becomes sparse. In taste, for example, a sense that has a direct bearing on both the fact and the enjoyment of survival, we are not yet able to say much more than that chemical substances in solution are the functioning stimuli. We do not have systematic knowledge about ways in which taste stimuli vary. Hence, it is difficult in this sensory area to control experimentally the stimulus we may wish to study. Cooking remains either a matter of routine habit for the dull cooks, or a matter of high art for the culinary genius.

The Receptors

The receptors for taste are groups of specially constructed cells grouped together in taste buds. Normally there are 245 of these buds located on the top and sides of the

tongue and, more sparsely, at the back of the mouth and in the throat (see Fig. 10–23). There are four basic tastes: sour, sweet, salt, and bitter. Receptors for the sour taste are located mainly along the sides of the tongue. Sweetness is best experienced by the tip of the tongue. Salt receptors are at the top and the sides of the tongue, and the bitter-sensitive areas are at its base.

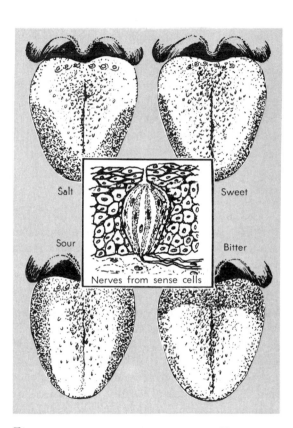

Figure 10–23. RECEPTORS FOR TASTE. *Taste buds, the receptors for taste, are located principally on the tongue. Receptors especially sensitive to sweet are at the tip of the tongue; for salt, somewhat farther toward the back; for sour, along the two sides of the tongue; and for bitter, at the base.*

This classical description of the four basic tastes has led to theories concerning four types of taste-specific receptors. Recent electrophysiological work (Beidler, 1961; Pfaffman et al., 1961) has shown that one nerve fiber may respond to several types of taste stimuli, with different fibers responding to different patterns of the four common "basic" stimuli. Work with the electron microscope has revealed that there is only one kind of taste cell, but that it undergoes a constant process of change through continuous degeneration and multiplication. Thus, sensitivity to different patterns of taste stimulation might be a consequence of the stage of change a cell has reached when it is excited.

All taste receptors operate with reduced sensitivity after smoking or other prolonged stimulation. Smokers who give up the habit often find that foods now taste so good that the habit of overeating easily replaces the habit of smoking. Old people do not taste as keenly as do younger people, and children, with all taste buds functioning fully, apparently have very active taste lives.

SMELL

The intimate details of our **olfactory** life—the life of smell—are no better known than are those for taste. We still do not understand fully the actual stimuli involved, nor the way in which chemical events are translated into consciousness or into signals—for tracking a rabbit or trailing the odor of French perfume or finding a seafood restaurant.

That we can smell a full and rich variety of smells is beyond doubt. We know that we are somehow able to translate into experience, and if necessary into action, chemical events in the vicinity of the nose. We know, too, that the sense of smell is significant for life—particularly in the life of animals, for the ability to respond to smells has a direct bearing on whether the animal will find a meal or be one.

There have been some recent advances in knowledge of brain structure involved in smelling. (See Fig. 10–24 for a depiction of olfactory receptors.) In lower animals, the olfactory lobe of the brain is well developed, tending to dominate other structures. As one moves up the phylogenetic scale, the olfactory lobe becomes reduced in size, until, in man,

it is only a small part of the total mass of the brain. The sense of smell also plays a lesser role in the life of man than in that of animals. The older olfactory structures have, in man, gone to form part of the rhinencephalon, or phylogenetically "old brain," as compared with the more highly evolved neocortex. This **rhinencephalon** in man is considered to be vital to emotional experience (MacLean, 1964).

Stimulus

We know that the stimuli to smell are molecules in the air emanating from volatile chemical substances. And we know that, for some substances, an almost infinitesimal concentration of molecules is enough for the organism to smell. Artificial musk, for example, can be smelled when there is only four hundred thousandths of a millionth of an ounce of it in a liter of air.

In spite of the everyday attempts to create pleasant smells and to avoid or obliterate the smells we do not like, there still is very little solid knowledge about what chemical substances in what form or quantity are registered by the human nose.

On the psychological side, there have been attempts to make systematic classifications of smells. The best known of such systems classifies smells according to six fundamental qualities: spicy, burnt, resinous, fragrant, ethereal, and putrid. Another system employs the four fundamentals of acid, burnt, fragrant, and goaty (or, more properly, capric). Still another (Pfaffman, 1960) shows that human beings can identify 16 odor qualities. Such systems, of course, are not systems for classifying chemical stimuli. They are psychological systems attempting to impress order on the sensations of subjects who have been exposed to different forms of stimulation.

The Receptors

The receptors for smell are located in two small areas at either side of the roof of the nasal passage (Fig. 10–24). In order to bring stimuli to these receptors, we often need to sniff, since the sensitive areas are a bit off the beaten track used routinely in breathing. In olfaction, as in taste, the concentration, manner of presentation, and duration of presentation of the stimulus compounds all have profound effects on the sensations of the subject.

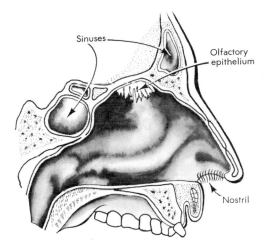

Figure 10–24. RECEPTORS FOR SMELL. *The receptors for smell are located at the top of the nasal passage in the olfactory epithelium, where they can be stimulated by molecules "sniffed" past them.*

The processes involved in changing chemical events into the sensation of smell are not understood. One line of research suggests that it is a process involving infrared radiation rather than chemical reactions (Beck and Miles, 1947). The theory here is that the olfactory receptors give off a variety of infrared wavelengths, that a particular kind of molecule passing by the receptors absorbs a particular pattern of wavelengths, that the receptor elements emitting the absorbed wavelengths will thereby lose heat, and that this loss of heat is translated into neural impulses which go to the brain.

An experiment with honey bees (Miles and Beck, 1949) suggests that infrared absorption does have something to do with smell. In this experiment, two airtight chambers were filled with gaseous honey. One chamber had a window made of a crystal, which allowed the passage of infrared rays. The window of the

other box had a piece of ordinary glass, which does not pass infrared radiation, between the crystal window and the honey. Under experimentally controlled conditions, bees demonstrated a great deal more interest in the window through which infrared rays could pass. This experiment has not been replicated.

Many other theories have been advanced (Davis and Taylor, 1959; Wright et al., 1956) to account for olfactory stimulation. They consider the shape, size, and chemical activity of the stimulus compounds as being vital to the initiation of activity in the receptor.

CUTANEOUS SENSES

The **cutaneous senses**—the skin senses—are the relatively less appreciated group of senses enabling us to experience pressure, pain, cold and warmth, and other sensations.

It was once firmly believed that there were specific receptor organs for each of the "basic" skin senses, but a mass of recent work has challenged this viewpoint.

It has been shown that touch sensations may be produced by all of the morphologically different "receptors"—not by just a few.

Some structures, such as the *basket nerve endings* at the roots of hairs and the encapsulated Pacinian corpuscles, seem to be especially sensitive to touch; but they do not hold exclusive rights to the neural interpretation of touch stimuli.

Pressure

Pressure sensitivity is not the same for all parts of the body. If we stimulate the skin by applying the end of a fine hair with a known degree of pressure, we find **pressure spots.** Presumably these are spots immediately above a receptor so sensitive that even a microscopic bending of the skin makes an impression on the receptor. Such pressure spots appear to occur more frequently where, handily enough, we are most likely to need a delicate sense of touch. There are 135 pressure spots per square centimeter, for example, on

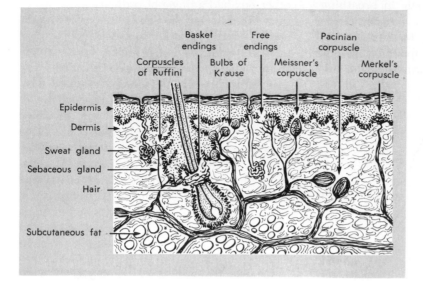

Figure 10–25. SKIN RECEPTORS. *A representation of a section of the skin, showing the receptors for warmth, cold, touch, pressure, and pain.*

the ball of the thumb, but only about 10 in a square centimeter on the upper arm.

The phenomenon of **adaptation** is very pronounced for the sense of pressure. After a relatively short time we stop sensing a stimulus that is steadily applied. In a matter of seconds our awareness of an object touching us may disappear entirely. If you wish to be aware of the pressure exerted by your clothes, for example, you will find it necessary to move or to wiggle so that the pressure moves from receptors that are adapted to others that are still ready to respond.

Pain

The actual stimulus to pain is probably the destruction of nerve tissues produced by blows, cuts, needle pricks, burns, or other insults to the tissues. The receptors for pain are the **free nerve endings** widely but unevenly distributed throughout the body. We can map the skin's pain spots just as we can its pressure spots, except that for pain we use a sharp needle. There are about 230 pain spots per square centimeter on the neck, 60 in an area

of this size on the ball of the thumb, and 50 on the bottom of the foot.

The biological significance of pain is considerable. It serves as a warning to the organism that injury or destruction may be on the way. People who are born without the capacity to experience a pain—and there are such cases—are not at all as fortunate as they may seem to be. Though their lives are free of bodily pain, this freedom means that they can bruise or cut themselves dangerously and not know it, and they may not know they are being severely burned until they smell burnt flesh.

Temperature

The stimulus to sensations of warmth and cold is the application to the body of a temperature that is above or below the **psychological zero point** of temperature. The skin normally has a temperature around 90° Fahrenheit. Stimuli warmer than that will generally be experienced as warm, and those colder will be experienced as cold—with 90° stimuli leading to no experience of either warmth or cold. The psychological zero point, however, is not a constant point. If the hand is placed for awhile in water of 100° Fahrenheit, the psychological zero point soon becomes 100° also, with temperature above that point producing the sensation of warmth and tempera-

TEST FOR COLOR BLINDNESS

*Sample plates from a color blindness test. Persons with normal vision
see a number in each of the designs. Red-green defectives cannot see the
numbers. (Reproduced by permission of the author of the Dvorine-Pseudo-
Isochromatic Plates, published by the Scientific Publishing Co.,
Baltimore, Maryland.)*

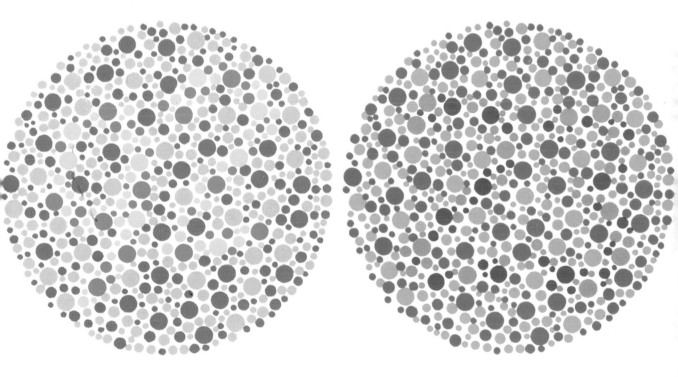

PLATE I

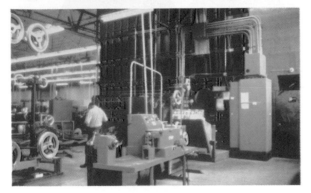

COLOR IN USE

Color can be used to conceal the unattractive, to highlight the attractive, to make essential and significant items stand out from their background, to assist in the fine visual discriminations that are required in industrial and other operations. The effective use of color also has been shown to improve morale and performance. (Reproduced by courtesy of Raychem Corporation.)

PERCEPTION OF COLOR

The human organism "takes many things into account" in interpreting its world. Here, the two blue triangles are the same in every respect. But the perceiver, automatically "taking into account" the background of the triangles, sees the triangles as different.

PLATE IV

ture below yielding cold, while stimuli of exactly 100° will be felt as neither warmth nor cold. Thus, the body does not respond like a reliable thermometer to temperatures impinging upon it.

Not much is known about the receptors for warmth and cold. For a long time it was thought that some fairly complex structures, known as **Krause end bulbs**, were the sole receptors for cold and that other structures in the skin, known as **Ruffini cylinders**, handled warmth. But when stable cold and warm spots are located, cut out, and studied under the microscope, only free nerve endings are found in many places (Dallenbach, 1927).

It has not been finally established, however, that free nerve endings are the receptors for temperature changes. There is some reason to believe that the free nerve endings in and near the blood vessels of the skin may be the mechanisms involved (Nafe, 1934). When the temperature of the skin is raised, blood vessels are dilated. Lowering the temperature constricts them. This dilation and constriction very probably is registered by nerve endings in the muscles around the blood vessels, and this process may be the basis for temperature sensation.

Not all areas of the skin register temperature. As with pressure and pain, there are definite spots of sensitivity. And the spots sensitive to warmth are different from the spots that are sensitive to cold. This fact presents some difficulty for the blood-vessel hypothesis.

Neurology and Skin Senses

A recent study (Winkelmann, 1960) suggests that what were once thought to be specific receptors seem to be modifications of nerve fibers that are associated with the different regions of the skin in which they are found, rather than with distinctly different functions. Some of the types of "end organs" have even been shown to be nothing more than degenerating nerve fibers.

Studies of free nerve fibers in the cornea of the eye (Weddell et al., 1960) have shown that these pain fibers subserve the entire gamut of cutaneous sensitivities and are the only receptors present. The fibers are also in a constant process of degeneration and regeneration, much as are the taste receptors on the tongue.

A recent summary of research (Bishop, 1956) indicates that the kind of sensation coming from a given nerve fiber is related to the size of the fiber. Small, slowly conducting fibers tend to be associated with sensations of diffuse pain, temperature, "crude" or nonlocalized touch, and vibration. Larger, more rapidly conducting fibers tend to be related to sensations of precisely localized touch, "sharp" pain, and fine discrimination of contours.

The small-fiber system is called the *lateral-column system*, for it projects up the sides of the spinal column to the thalamic region. The large-fiber system is known as the dorsal-column system and runs up the dorsal pathways of the spinal cord. The latter is apparently the "younger" system, in an evolutionary sense (Mountcastle, 1961; Wall, 1961).

SENSE OF POSITION IN SPACE

One of the senses we are likely to take most for granted, unless of course we become dizzy or car sick, is the *static sense* or *sense of passive movement*. We are equipped to respond, sometimes consciously but most often with reflex automaticity, to changes in our position in space (from the upright to the not-so-upright, for example, or the change from front-facing to side-facing) and to changes in the rate of movement through space. The stimulating condition for these sensations is the movement of the head, movement most often accompanied by movements of the body.

The receptors for these movement stimuli lie in a part of the inner ear known as the semicircular canals. There are three of these canals in each ear, with each canal in the three essentially perpendicular to each of the others, so that they fall into three planes. At the base of each canal there is an enlargement, called the *ampulla*, containing hairlike structures. The canals and the ampulla contain a liquid known as *endolymph*. When the head turns to right or left or is bent forward or thrown back, this movement displaces the endolymph and produces movement in the *hair cells*. This movement is translated into nervous impulses.

The hair cells respond not only to the rotation of the head but also to changes in the acceleration of rotation. If one sits blindfolded in a rotating chair spinning at a certain speed, and if the speed of the chair is slowed, the sensation will be one of rotating in the opposite direction. The reducing speed lets the displaced liquid of the semicircular canals begin to return toward its original position. This movement stimulates the hair cells in a way opposite to the stimulation produced by the original rotation.

The dizziness occurring after rotation is due, at least in part, to what seems to be a built-in connection between the eyes and the events in the semicircular canals. After a rapid rotation the eyes show a rapid movement known as *post-rotational* **nystagmus.** This movement makes it difficult to get a visual orientation in space and, coupled with the other effects in the inner ear, can produce stumbling and staggering. Dancers, through practice, can learn to control both nystagmus and dizziness.

Sensitivity to movement in a back-and-forth, up-and-down, or right-and-left direction, as opposed to rotational movement, stems from the **vestibule,** a double-sac structure at the base of the semicircular canals. The vestibule too is filled with a syrupy liquid and contains hairs, with **otolyths**—small calcium particles —on their ends. Movement of the head results in the movement of these otolyths. Their movement, in turn, is translated into neural impulses.

Both the semicircular canals and the vestibular mechanisms are involved in our control of bodily position. As we move about, or are moved, the continuing flow of nerve impulses from these receptors makes it possible to maintain balance, direction, and uprightness. Also, when there is unusual stimulation of these receptors, some people get *motion sickness,* an unpleasant and little understood malady affecting many people in boats, planes, trains, and automobiles.

KINESTHESIS: THE SENSE OF ACTIVE MOVEMENT

The static senses respond to our bodily movement, enabling us to deal with balance, acceleration, and rotation whether we ourselves initiate the movement or whether it is initiated for us. Were these senses all we had for dealing with movement, however, we would be very helpless; for we would not be able to locate for ourselves any part of the body or to tell, without using our eyes, what the body is doing at any particular time. Every time we move a muscle, a whole wave of sensory information flows to the brain, making possible the skilled coordination of muscular movements. The importance of this kind of sensory input is dramatically illustrated by the difficulties of those who do not have it. There is a disease known as **tabes dorsalis,** which involves a destruction of the neural tracts carrying muscular sensations to the brain. With this disease, an individual can still move his muscles, for the pathways running to them are intact. But he cannot control his movements except by watching very carefully what he has just done. If he shuts his eyes, he cannot walk. Nor can he stand erect with his eyes shut, for what we know as standing involves a constant pattern of leaning a bit one way, correcting for it, leaning the other, correcting for it, and so on. Such small, speedy, and constantly needed correctives cannot be made on the basis of visual and static sensations alone. If the damage in *tabes dorsalis* is high up in the nervous system, the individual is unable to touch his face or his ear without watching carefully his every move; if the damage is in the brain itself, the delicate muscular coordinations necessary for speech become difficult, and the patient's speech may become almost completely unintelligible.

The pressures produced by stretching or bunching muscles and by movement in tendons and joints are registered by a variety of receptors. *Free nerve endings* in the muscles appear to be receptors for muscular stretch. Specialized structures known as **Golgi tendon organs** record the stretching of tendons, and other structures in the lining of the joints assist in the registering of movement.

We have seen already that the sensory life of the human organism is by no means limited to the traditional five input channels. Although there is incomplete knowledge about the particular mechanisms and processes involved in all the sensibilities the organism needs and uses in its adjustments to life, we do know something about the variety of sensory input and about sensation's general role in behavior. But we still have not completed the picture of the organism's sensory input.

The organism needs to know what goes on in its deep insides—and, at least to some extent, it does know. It has *organic sensitivities* enabling it to know some things about events in its internal organs. The stomach and the esophagus can clearly register warmth and cold. We do not know how this is managed, but it occurs. There is also a registering of internal pain and of internal pressure, but again there is no knowledge of the precise way in which these sensations come about. Questions about these organic sensitivities obviously have a relevancy for the daily welfare of the organism. They also arise when we tackle the task of understanding the mechanisms of motivation. How does the brain know when the organism is hungry or sexually aroused or thirsty? Such questions need to be answered if we are to have a complete knowledge of the processes of motivation.

SUMMARY

1. The motivated organism, in order to survive, must register changes in the external world, and the complexity of its adjustment is often determined by the adequacy of its capacity to sense.

2. The human organism is equipped to register vibrations of air particles ranging in frequency from 16 to 20,000 cps. It can register a light stimulus occupying 1/500,000 of the surface of the eye, and it can register a rich variety of smells, tastes, touches, pressures, pains, temperatures, and movements.

3. The human organism is *not* sensitive to supersonic vibrations nor to a large variety of electromagnetic waves lying outside the visible spectrum; it cannot compete with certain other organisms in olfactory sensitivity or in visual sensitivity to movement. The human organism is uniquely able, however, to translate physical events into what is for him sensible.

4. The conditions of sensation include a stimulus, a specialized receptor, and a central nervous system; processes from the stimulus through the central nervous system lead to response through the effectors.

5. The stimulus of sound is initiated by a series of condensations and rarefactions of particles at the eardrum; the physical stimulus can vary in frequency, amplitude, and complexity.

6. The intensity of the sound stimulus is measured in terms of a logarithmic decibel scale.

7. The auditory receptors are hair cells in the organ of Corti in the inner ear; the structure consists of the external ear, the middle ear, and the inner ear, wherein lies the cochlea with its tympanic canal and basilar membrane.

8. The malfunctioning of auditory structures can produce conduction deafness, in which the sound stimulus does not adequately reach the basilar membrane; or discrimination deafness, involving an injury to nervous mechanisms.

9. The major psychological dimensions of auditory sensation are pitch, loudness, and timbre; additional psychological phenomena include beat, masking, difference tones, and summation tones.

10. The absolute threshold for auditory intensity varies with the wavelengths of the stimulus, with the greatest sensitivity falling

between 1,800 and 3,000 cps. There is a non-linear relation between stimulus intensities and sensory intensities.

11. Pitch discrimination is not a one-to-one relationship between sensation and stimulus; the pitch scale, plotted in mels, describes the sensed pitch as a function of the frequency of the stimulus.

12. Historically, the theories of hearing have been either frequency theories or place theories.

13. The telephone or frequency theory was initially forwarded by the discovery of electrical discharges thought to be from the auditory nerve (cat experiment), and by the invention of the volley theory. The electrical discharges turned out to be cochlea microphonics, however, and the volley theory not wholly adequate.

14. Place theories, requiring that the basilar membrane vibrate in one place for one frequency and another for a different frequency, are not able to account for auditory phenomena involving high frequencies.

15. The prevailing modern theory is one in which principles of place and principles of frequency are combined.

16. The stimulus for vision is constituted of electromagnetic waves extending from 400 to about 800 millimicrons in length; the stimulus varies in wavelength, amplitude, and complexity. The presence of two eyes, creating retinal disparity, facilitates the perception of three-dimensionality.

17. The receptors for vision are the rods and cones in the retina; the structures of the eye function much as does a camera to focus light waves on the retina, with structural malfunctioning resulting in nearsightedness, farsightedness, or astigmatism.

18. The human subject can make visual discriminations of hue, brightness, and saturation. He also discriminates form, and his discriminations are different if we lower the level of illumination in which he works.

19. In conditions of dark adaptation, the sensitivity of the eye increases by 100,000 times; the shift in brightness sensitivity as illumination goes down is not the same for all wavelengths. This is the Purkinje effect.

20. The duplicity theory of vision involves the idea that the rods and cones function differently, with the cones mediating mainly the chromatic stimuli and the rods the achromatic ones. The theory accounts for many experimental facts.

21. Visual acuity, measured by such devices as Landolt rings, varies with position on the retina and with conditions of illumination.

22. In color vision, hue varies with wavelength, brightness with intensity, and saturation with the complexity of light waves.

23. The psychological effects of mixing wavelengths of light have been systematically described. There are four psychological primaries; there are complementary colors; there are additive mixtures. Physical primaries must be considered in mixing pigments.

24. Dichromatic color vision, in which there is sensitivity to only two colors, occurs in about 4 per cent of the population. Such a person cannot discriminate reds, greens, bluish greens, and violet. Other kinds of color blindness are deuteranopia and protanopia.

25. The Young-Helmholtz theory of color vision has it that there are three kinds of cones, each kind responding to a different wavelength of light; new experimental results cast doubt on the older theory and suggest that color vision is produced by an interplay of long and short wavelengths of light.

26. The stimuli to taste are chemical substances in solution; the receptors are taste buds, distributed principally on the tongue. Not a great deal is known about the processes involved in the sensation of taste.

27. The stimuli to smell are molecules emanating from volatile chemical substances; the olfactory receptors are specialized structures in the top area of the nasal passage. There

is some evidence that the process of smelling involves infrared radiation.

28. The human organism can sense pressure, pain, warmth, and cold—each through receptors in the skin and underlying tissues.

29. Position in space is sensed through processes involving the movement of fluids that stimulate hair cells in the semicircular canals.

30. The sense of active movement, or kinesthesis, involves a registering of pressures produced by the bunching and stretching of muscles.

31. There are a variety of sensory messages flowing from organic processes in the body, but the details of these sensory structures and functions are not yet known.

RESEARCH REPORT

HISTORY OF RESEARCH
ON RELATIVE SENSITIVITY

More than a hundred years ago, Gustav Fechner, a young and distinguished physicist at Leipzig University, resigned his professorial chair because of illness. For the next decade he almost completely disappeared from the intellectual world upon which he had made such an impression as a young man. Then he reappeared, in the guise of a philosopher. In 1848 he began publishing a series of philosophical treatises dealing with the relations of mind and matter. Neither his scientific colleagues nor the world of philosophy paid him much mind. After his fourth philosophical work failed to arouse the sleeping public, he produced another in which he said, "I now say a fifth time, 'Steh' auf!' and, if I live, I shall yet call a sixth and a seventh time, 'Steh' auf!' and always it will be but the same 'Steh' auf!' " (Boring, 1929, pp. 269–270).

Fechner reports that while lying in bed one morning in 1850 he suddenly hit upon an idea about the way to awaken the sleepers to the significance of his philosophy. He would hit them with scientific evidence. He would go back to the laboratory and demonstrate experimentally the

relation of mind and matter. His subsequent experimental work, though it convinced none of his colleagues that he really had created what he described as an "exact science of the functional relations or relations of dependency between body and mind" (p. 271), did represent the beginning of a new science of psychophysics.

The basic idea with which Fechner worked was that sensations (mind) could be measured and precisely related to a measurable physical stimulus. The way to measure sensation, he held, was through working with what has come to be called *just noticeable differences* (jnd's). If the ear is exposed to the least intense stimulus, for instance, it can register (at the absolute threshold), and if the intensity of the stimulus is increased, the observer sooner or later will register a jnd— a sensation just noticeably different from the one at the absolute threshold. If stimuli of slightly greater intensities than that producing this new sensation are then exposed, another jnd will be registered. For very low intensities, Fechner found, a very small increment of intensity will produce a jnd in sensation; but for stimuli of higher intensity, a larger increment is necessary to produce a difference in sensation.

What excited Fechner was the fact that there is a constant relation, whatever the intensity of the stimulus, between the intensity already there and the intensity that needs to be added to produce a jnd. He stated this fundamental relation in this formula:

$$dS = C\frac{dR}{R},$$

where dS is the increment in the sensation, C a constant of proportionality, and R the stimulus. By this formula a jnd at low intensities is produced by a change in R—say, from eight to twelve units of intensity. At a level of forty units of intensity, the same *proportional* change is necessary to produce a jnd. Thus at that level we need twenty additional units of intensity to produce a jnd. We can say that at one level we need only four units of physics to produce one unit of psychology, but at the higher level we need twenty units of physics to produce one unit of psychology.

Fechner went on to state his relationship in logarithmic terms, as follows:

$$S = K \log R.$$

Fechner named this law after E. H. Weber, an anatomist and one of his teachers at the University of Leipzig. For awhile it was called "Weber's Law" but has come to be called the *Weber-Fechner law*. This law Fechner regarded as the fundamental solution to the philosophical problem of the relation of mind and body. We use it here to illustrate the fact that the human organism, in registering outside stimuli, does not in any simple way merely mirror physical events. Psychological events—sensations or discriminations—are related to physical events, but the or-

Workers in psychophysics, though they still do not all agree on either the necessity or the method of tearing down Fechner's bold structure, have belabored it mightily. Recently, through new ideas and new approaches to measurement, it has been possible to state in relatively simple terms a *power law* (see figure) describing the relation between subjective magnitudes and stimulus magnitudes (Stevens, 1957). The power law was derived not by having subjects judge what consti-

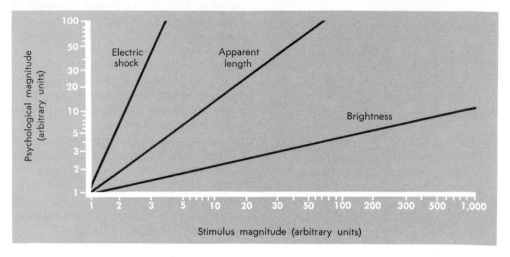

THE POWER LAW IN PSYCHOPHYSICS. *The power law states that equal stimulus ratios produce equal subjective or psychological ratios, with the ratios varying from one sensory area or modality to another. Physical events and psychological events are systematically related. (Stevens, 1959; reprinted by permission of* Daedalus, the Journal of the American Academy of Arts & Sciences, *Fall 1959, pp. 611–617.)*

ganism intervenes in intricate ways between the external energies and the psychological event. This matter of the relation between changes in the external stimulus and changes in sensation continues, of course, to be a basic concern of sensory psychologists. Although Fechner fathered the field of psychophysics, his scientific descendants, while respecting his originality, have forcefully rejected many of his ideas, including the notion that sensation can be measured in the way Fechner believed—by counting its constituent units, its jnd's.

Near the end of his career, Fechner wrote (1877): "The tower of Babel was never finished because the workers could not reach an understanding on how they should build it; my psychological edifice will stand because the workers will never agree on how to tear it down."

tutes a just noticeable difference in a sensation; instead, when presented a variety of different intensities, they were asked to judge the intensity of the resulting sensations. Subjects can make such judgments, although sometimes under protest. When they do, it becomes possible to compare the ratio of the intensity of any two stimuli with the subjective ratio of the two sensations produced. The power law, derived from such judgments, states that *equal stimulus ratios produce equal subjective ratios*. This means, in effect, that there is a relatively simple proportionality between the input of stimulus intensity and the reported magnitude of the sensation. The proportionality differs from one sensory area to another, but the basic nature of the relationship seems to hold, with satisfying simplicity, for all sensory processes when the stimuli can be quantitatively scaled for intensity. With respect to brightness, for example, sensations grow less rapidly than the growth in the stimulus. But for reaction to electric shock, sensations grow more rapidly than does the energy put into the organism.

In general mathematical terms, the power law can be stated $\psi = K\phi^n$, with ψ = magnitude of sensation, K = a constant, ϕ = the magnitude of the stimulus intensity and $n =$ an exponent that varies from one sense modality to another. For brightness .33 is the approximate value of the exponent. For the sensed intensity of electric shock, 3.5 is the exponent. If the power functions are plotted with logarithmic scales on both the ordinate and abscissa, straight lines of varying degrees of slope are obtained.

Whether or not the student has the background to grasp the mathematics in this matter, the basic relationship should be clear—physical events and psychological events are systematically related. The relationship is not as Fechner thought it, but it is there, and its discovery is a psychological discovery.

SUGGESTED READINGS

Bartley, S. H. *Vision: A study of its basis.* New York: Van Nostrand, 1941.

Broadbent, D. E. *Perception and communication.* New York: Pergamon Press, 1958.

Davis, Hallowell, and S. R. Silberman, eds. *Hearing and deafness* (rev. ed.). New York: Holt, Rinehart and Winston, 1960 (1947).

Rosenblith, W. A., ed. *Sensory communication.* Cambridge, Mass.: MIT Press; New York: Wiley, 1961.

Stevens, S. S., and Hallowell Davis. *Hearing: Its psychology and physiology.* New York: Wiley, 1938.

OUTLINE / CHAPTER II

I. ATTENTION AND SET ; PRINCIPLES OF SELECTION

    A. Kinds of Sets
        1. Motor Set
        2. Perceptual Set
        3. Mental Set
    B. Factors Producing Set
        1. Situational Factors
        2. Motivational Factors
        3. Stimulus Factors
            a. Intensity of stimulus
            b. Size of stimulus
            c. Change
            d. Repetition
    C. Neurological Processes in Attention

II. PRIMITIVE PERCEPTUAL ORGANIZATION

    A. Kinds of Organization
        1. Grouping
        2. Closure
        3. Figure-Ground Effect
        4. Constancy Phenomena
    B. Perception of Depth and Distance
        1. Monocular Cues
        2. Binocular Cues
    C. Learning in Primitive Organization

III. SYMBOLIC FACTORS IN PERCEPTUAL ORGANIZATION

    A. Intellectual Contexts
    B. Emotional or Motivational Contexts
        1. Organic Need and Perception
        2. Personality and Attitudinal Factors
            a. Personal values
            b. Perception of threatening words
            c. Personality and perception: The Witkin experiments
        3. Social Factors in Perception
    C. Perception and Remembering

IV. THEORIES OF PERCEPTION

    A. Neural Theories, Behavioral Theories, Gestalt Theories
    B. Adaptation-Level Theory

V. SUMMARY

VI. RESEARCH REPORT

CHAPTER 11

PERCEPTION

In order to behave in ways that will satisfy its motives, the human **organism** must maintain an intimate contact with its **environment.** Such a contact is made possible by the organism's array of specialized **receptors.** These receptors respond, each in its own way, to external energies and set in motion the processes whereby physical and chemical events are translated first into **neurological** and then into psychological events. This responding and this translating must occur if the organism is to interact with its environment. The elimination of any sense modality interferes seriously with the functioning of the organism. The elimination of all sensing would make life itself impossible. But sensory processes, however necessary they are for survival, are not sufficient for the guidance of motivated behavior in a world so full of physical and chemical events to which the organism is sensitive.

Behavior cannot occur in an organized way unless the individual can *select* from among the **stimuli** impinging on him those stimuli that have a relevance for his needs. In addition, he must be able to *organize* those stimuli, to bring meaning to the barrage of naked physical stimuli striking his receptors.

In this chapter we shall examine first the phenomena of *selection*—specifically, *attention* and *set* as selective principles. Then we shall study the principles of *primitive organization*, going on from there to examine some of the more involved processes whereby, in our efforts to make meaning out of our sensory experience, we bring our past experience symbolically or conceptually to bear in creating a world in which future behavior can occur.

ATTENTION AND SET: PRINCIPLES OF SELECTION

Because we can sense only a limited range of the physical energies in the world (we cannot, for example, respond to radio waves or to the supersonic vibrations of air particles), we are by nature selective in our orientation to the environment. But we must also select *from among* those physical stimuli that we *can* register at any given moment. For example, consider all the sensations occurring at this moment while you have been engrossed in your reading. Start with the feet: is there a pressure from shoes and hose? Are the legs registering a pressure where they touch the chair? What about the pressure from a sore spot anywhere? Is there a feeling of eye strain? Now look and listen. Are there noises from the people next door, from the heating system, the cooling system, the refrigerator, cars in the street, planes in the air, or mice on the stairs? Now think of all the things that must have been registered on your **retina** as you occasionally have lifted your eyes to think—or perhaps to lead a bit of fantasy life while doing your homework. All of these stimuli have been having their way with your sense organs and your nervous system. But if you have been paying close attention to words on a page, all these stimuli have been selected out. You have shut yourself off from some stimuli and opened wide your input channels to others. You have yourself *set* to respond to the words on this page, just as the sprinter poised for the starter's gun is ready for, or open to, a signal, and the hungry man has a perceptual readiness for restaurant signs.

However, certain events may, by their nature as stimuli, *select themselves into* your perceptual life and distract you from your reading. Other things being equal, the sound of a cannon is more likely than the sound of a refrigerator to attract your attention.

In dealing with selective phenomena in perception, we use the term *attention* to cover all aspects of the selective process. The term **set** refers to *specific* factors or processes within the individual that bear on what he shall attend. In studying the processes of attending—the selective processes in perception—we study factors in the individual—factors of set—that serve a selective function. We also study those stimuli that can, in relative independence of the individual's set, insert themselves into his experience; some stimuli are inherently attention-getting.

In a way, each of us may be said to be known by the sets we keep; for, as we live out our motivated lives, we learn which stimuli to watch for and which we can safely ignore.

KINDS OF SETS

Motor Set

In many specific situations our muscles are tuned up and ready to react as soon as we receive an appropriate signal. When we are in a hurry to keep an appointment, for example, and are stopped by a red light, the break-releasing muscles and the accelerator-pumping muscles are tense and ready, and the input channels are wide open to receive the green signal. On every offensive play in a football game, eleven patterns of muscles are tensely set for the quarterback's signal. In a laboratory experiment, the subject is set by the experimenter's instructions to say "Constantinople" or "Father Sigmund" or to press a lever when he sees a certain pattern of lights before him.

In all motor sets there is an anticipation of a sensory experience to come and a readiness to respond when it does come. Most often, we speak of motor sets as they apply in specific and contained situations such as those described above. But perhaps, if we explore far enough, we could find that each of us has lifelong motor sets learned somewhere in the past. We know of cases in which ex-soldiers, twenty years after combat experience, still fall to the ground at the sound of an explosion or seek cover at the sound of a plane. Perhaps there are counterparts to these sets in the habit systems of many of us.

One interesting aspect of a motor set is its likelihood of misfiring. When the muscles are primed for action and the sensory channels are open, it is easy for a wrong signal to set off the response. The motorist at the traffic light or the track star on the starting blocks are both likely to go into action if anyone says a loud "boo." The football player who goes offside is often reacting with the right response to the wrong signal. A sound or a movement from the opposition will sometimes achieve the same results as the proper starting signal from the quarterback.

Perceptual Set

Often the individual assumes a definite readiness to perceive a certain stimulus or

Figure 11–1. PERCEPTUAL SET. *Children at a movie demonstrate a readiness to perceive: all input channels are open.*

stimuli of a certain class. Such a readiness is termed a *perceptual set.* The hungry man seeking a restaurant has a perceptual set that increases his likelihood of seeing restaurant signs and decreases his likelihood of noticing signs announcing the presence of photography shops or the availability of dancing lessons.

Mental Set

Mental set, a term referring to a selective process influencing the way we think about a given problem, will concern us more intimately when we come to a discussion of thinking (Chap. 14). However, we can quickly illustrate the phenomenon by asking a series of questions about pronunciation:

1. How do you pronounce M-a-c-t-a-v-i-s-h?
2. How do you pronounce M-a-c-d-o-n-a-l-d?
3. How do you pronounce M-a-c-b-c-t-h?
4. How do you pronounce M-a-c-h-i-n-e-r-y?

If you pronounced the *M-a-c* in (4) as you did in (1), (2), and (3), you have been cap-

tured by a mental set, producing *MacHinery* rather than the more conventional *machinery.*

FACTORS PRODUCING SET

A number of factors can produce these sets or these readinesses to perceive and respond. There are *temporary* or *situational factors,* such as the quarterback's anticipatory signals or the experimenter's instructions. There are more lasting *motivational conditions* of the organism, such as hunger or thirst. Also, certain properties of the *stimulus* itself—its intensity or its repetitiveness, for example—will demand the organism's attention. In addition, the kind and level of activity in progress in the organism at any given time, the *adaptation level* (see pp. 339–340), will have an effect on the selective and other aspects of perception.

Situational Factors

In experimental situations the instructions of the experimenter can produce perceptual sets. As early as 1904, the German psychologist Külpe demonstrated that different perceptions result from different instructions. In his study he used three-letter nonsense syllables printed in different colors and with differing spacing of the letters. These were presented to a number of subjects by means of a **tachistoscope** (a device whereby stimuli may be exposed for brief and exact intervals). Each subject was instructed to report on just one of the following aspects of the stimulus: (a) number of letters, (b) color of the syllables, (c) patterning of the letters, (d) identity of the letters. The investigators found that subjects most often and most accurately reported the aspects they were set to perceive as a result of the instructions they received. When they were quizzed on features of the stimulus other than the one mentioned in the instructions, their reports were far less accurate. For example, subjects set to count the number of letters or to observe their arrangement were generally unable to report the colors of the letters. Many even believed the letters had not been colored.

Motivational Factors

The hungry man, we have seen, is sensitive to stimuli related to food. It is the nature of psychological life that motivational tensions increase the organism's sensitivity to stimuli which, his past experience has told him, have a relevance for his needs. The retired traffic policeman and his aesthetically inclined wife attend different aspects of Paris. Advertisers, well aware of the more common motive-produced sets of the buyers, use bikini-clad beauties to advertise products that have no logical connection with uncovered female pulchritude. The girl is there to attract attention, to capitalize on the sets of potential consumers. The advertiser's hope is that once attention is attracted, the desired message can be got across.

Stimulus Factors

If we can arrange it so that motivational factors in set or in attention are held constant, we will find that some external stimuli have a marked capacity to attract attention (or to produce a set to perceive).

Intensity of stimulus. Other things being equal, a more intense stimulus will demand attention. As advertisers know, the loud sound and the bright light take precedence over less intense stimuli. Table 11–1 presents data on this point.

Size of stimulus. Other things being equal, the larger of two visual stimuli will attract more attention. Advertisers vie with one another to construct the largest signs on Times Square. Data in Table 11–2 support the idea that size gets attention. Sometimes, however, in a perceptual world of elephants, the mouse may stand out.

Change. The outstanding mouse in a field of elephants emphasizes the principle that a break in monotony is perceptually demanding. The single minnow breaking the surface of a lake takes on a perceptual potency out of proportion to its size. The orator who suddenly whispers, the gentle long-suffering mother

Table 11–1. ATTENTION AND INTENSITY OF STIMULUS

PERCENTAGE OF PEDESTRIANS STOPPING TO VIEW WINDOW DISPLAY	
Illumination of Display (in Foot Candles)	Percentage of Pedestrians Stopping
15	10
30	12
50	15
65	17
85	19
100	21

An observer counted the number of pedestrians who stopped at a lighted display window in a store. The brighter the window, the larger the percentage of passersby who stopped. (Burtt, 1938.)

Table 11–2. ATTENTION AND SIZE OF STIMULUS

Relative Size of Stimulus	Relative Amount of Attention
1.00	1.00
1.80	2.78
3.00	2.51
5.00	2.10
8.80	3.55
34.80	8.32

Amount of attention increases with size of newspaper advertisement. The increase in attention is not proportional, however, to the increase in size. A 34-fold increase in size gave only an 8-fold increase in attention. (Adapted from Strong, 1915.)

who suddenly shouts, the one chair that is moved in a familiar room—these are all attention-demanding stimuli because they represent a change from constant sameness.

Perhaps a good illustration of the factor of

change or variation in attracting attention is the story of the lighthouse keeper who lived for twenty years hearing his warning cannon fire automatically on the hour every hour all night long to warn ships away from the rocks. One night the cannon failed to fire. The keeper waked with a start and shouted, "What was that?"

A more quantitative illustration comes from a small study of the number of people stopping to view a window display. When the display was stationary, 6 per cent of the passersby stopped. When the display was mounted on a rotary pedestal, 45 per cent stopped (Printers' Ink, 1932).

Repetition. Other things being equal, the repeated stimulus will come through to attention better than one presented only once or twice. There is a limit, however, to the strategy of repetition. After awhile, change becomes much more effective than repetition—a fact that some people wish were brought more repetitiously to the attention of commercial advertisers.

NEUROLOGICAL PROCESSES IN ATTENTION

Some recent work (Hernández-Péon, Scherrer, and Jouvet, 1956) has uncovered evidence bearing on what occurs in the nervous system when the organism is attending. Tiny electrodes were attached to the nerve leading away from a cat's inner ear. While the cat was exposed to an auditory stimulus, the **nerve impulses** flowing along the ear were of one distinct pattern. When two mice in a closed bottle were put in the cat's cage, the auditory responses from the cochlear nucleus were greatly reduced. When the mice were removed, the nerve began responding as it had before. When fishy smells were piped through a tube into the cat's cage, again there was a suppression of the response on the auditory nerve. When the attention-getting smells were removed, the auditory response again returned to normal. These results suggest the operation of neural inhibitory mechanisms that assist in the exclusion of certain sensory messages.

PRIMITIVE PERCEPTUAL ORGANIZATION

In dealing with set and attention, we faced the question of what stimuli, from among all those available to it, the organism lets into itself. When we turn to matters of organization, we deal with the question of *what the organism does with the sensory data* it has admitted into its processes of adjusting. Think for a moment about visual experience. If you look about you now, you bring to your retina a pattern of electromagnetic energies. If we leave this pattern at the retina, instead of following it as it is translated to sensation, it has no psychological meaning whatever. When the pattern reaches the brain, it becomes sensation. At that point it could, theoretically, remain bare sensation. We could—and perhaps the visually inexperienced infant *does*—see the pattern solely as **hues, brightnesses,** and **saturations.** But we do not. We see a world of three dimensions. We see some near objects and some far objects, some objects as standing out and others as background, some objects grouped and others disparate. The organism does something to *organize* the psychologically meaningless retinal image.

Certain organizing processes—processes that lend meaning to incoming data—seem to occur widely in human nervous systems and are relatively independent of past experience or motivational tensions. These are referred to as *primitive processes of organization.*

The **central nervous system** does not merely register in a passive way the raw sensory data flowing to it. It does something. Taking into account all the sensory data coming to it, it creates a definite organization. Perhaps the best illustration of the active role of the central nervous system can be gained from the area of illusions—of false interpretations, misleading organization, of sensory data. One of the simplest of the known illusions is the Müller-Lyer illusion (Fig. 11–2). In the Müller-Lyer illusion, the interpretation is demonstrably at variance with the interpretation made under other more "normal" conditions—such as those we employ when we actually

Figure 11–2. MÜLLER-LYER ILLUSION. *The two horizontal lines are precisely equal in length. They occupy precisely the same space on the retina. Yet, when imbedded in different setting, the lines appear of different lengths. Incidentally, chickens also see these as different in length (Révész, 1937), demonstrating that primitive perceptual processes occur in other than human nervous systems.*

measure both lines. Below, we shall describe briefly some of the phenomena of primitive perceptual organization.

KINDS OF ORGANIZATION

Grouping

A simple kind of perceptual organization is that of grouping, of perceiving some things as together and others as separate. When three

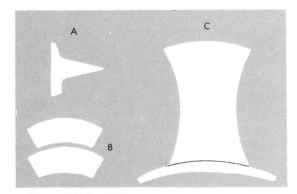

Figure 11–3. OPTICAL ILLUSIONS. *Because of the way the human being is "programmed," he sometimes sees the world erroneously. In A, the length of the nose is the same as the height of the figure. In B, the top arcs are the same length. In C, the height of the hat and the width of the brim are the same.*

piano notes are sounded with brief intervals between and then a fourth note comes after a more protracted interval, the three equal-interval notes are grouped and the fourth appears to be isolated. Sense of time comes into the bare auditory experience, and thereby grouping occurs. Similar groupings are found in the visual field. Objects or stimuli that are near together, are similar in appearance, fall into a symmetrical pattern, or continue a form or sequence toward completion, tend to be grouped together.

Closure

The organism tends sometimes to create wholes where there are none, to "close in" gaps in sensory data. If we briefly expose a curved line, which, except for a small segment, makes a circle, it will be perceived as a complete circle. The same goes for an almost complete square or the almost complete drawing of a familiar figure.

Figure-Ground Effect

As we look around us, the objects of which we are aware stand out as figures against a ground. The book stands out against the table on which it rests, words stand out against the page, the shriek of terror stands out against the noise of city traffic. There seems to be no immutable physical reason why objects should stand out against their backgrounds. Why should not the wall be the impressive thing and the picture on it insignificant? The organization of the environment into figure-ground relations is a feat of the nervous system. Figure 11–5 presents an opportunity to observe a relatively strange figure-ground phenomenon.

Constancy Phenomena

Clearly illustrating the fact that the nervous system is not passive in the presence of sensory data are the various phenomena showing our tendency to bring perceptual constancy to an inconstant world. Look at your friend a hundred yards across the campus. Then watch him as he comes closer and

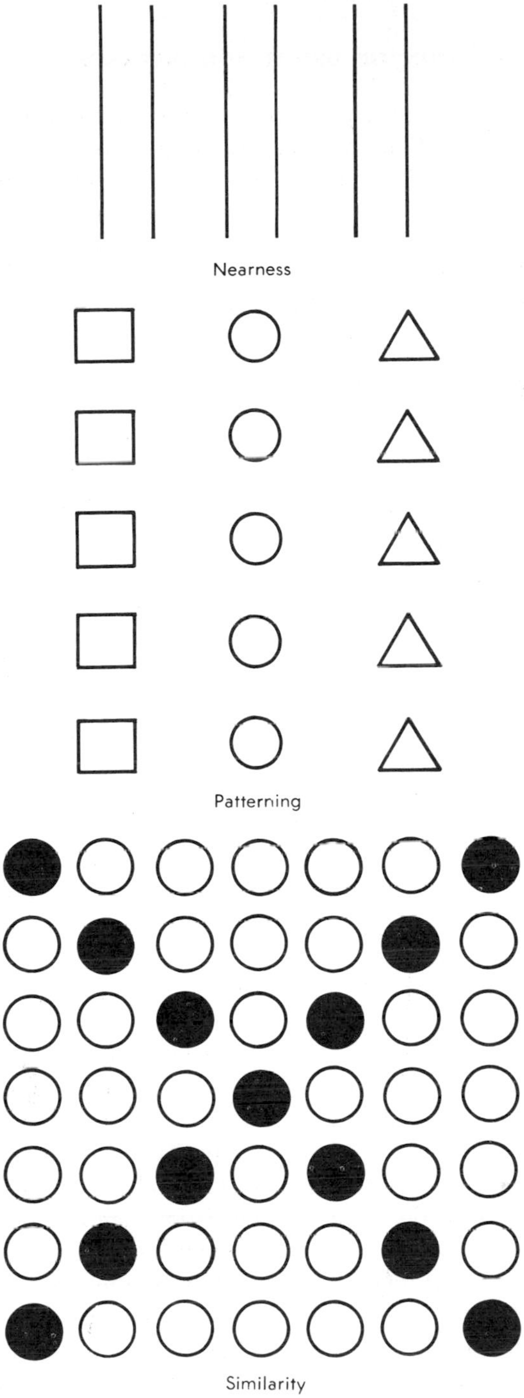

Nearness

Patterning

Similarity

Figure 11–4. PERCEPTUAL GROUPING. *In our perceptions we group environmental objects according to psychological principles of nearness, similarity, and patterning. It is difficult to see six individual lines in the top drawing, or either columns or rows in the middle, or rows in the bottom one. We can overcome the natural tendencies to group, but it takes deliberate effort.*

closer to you. The space he occupies on your retina when he is face to face with you is perhaps a thousand times greater than the space he filled at a distance. But his perceived size does not change that much. As perceivers we take many things into account and produce a size constancy in the face of a drastically changing pattern of stimuli. What can happen when there is no such taking-into-account is illustrated in Figure 11–6. That size constancy is a fairly elaborate taking-into-account has been demonstrated by an experiment (Holway and Boring, 1941) in which subjects were required to judge apparent size —first with both eyes and with all cues, and next with one eye and a reduction of miscellaneous cues. When objects are seen with one

Figure 11–5. FIGURE AND GROUND. *Most often the white in this drawing will be seen as figure. However, if one looks long enough, the black becomes figure and the white, ground.*

eye through a long tube that drastically narrows the field of vision, size constancy does not maintain; objects are seen at their "true" size—a size directly proportional to the size of the image on the retina. Another study (Zeigler and Leibowitz, 1957) shows that children more than adults tend to judge the size of objects according to the actual size of the retinal image. Adults, apparently, take into

Figure 11–6. CAMERAS KNOW NO CONSTANCY. *The image on the retina is essentially the same as the image caught by a camera; the human perceiver, however, takes into account many things beyond the capacity of a camera. In reacting to such a scene in actuality, we see the apple as small and the girl as large. The camera obeys the laws of physics rather than the laws of psychology.*

account more cues in bringing perceptual order into their world.

There is a perceptual constancy of shape as well as size. Tilt a dinner plate so that its retinal image is an ellipse; it is perceived as having a constant roundness. Also there is **brightness constancy.** Snow still appears white when the actual brightness of it is vastly reduced at night. Again the nervous system takes into account a variety of sensory data and organizes the psychological world. Further, there is **color constancy.** Grass is seen as green, and as the same green, in both sunlight and shade. Or—more impressively, perhaps—the colors of the world remain relatively unchanged even though we may view them through rose-colored or green-tinted glasses.

PERCEPTION OF DEPTH AND DISTANCE

We live in a perceptual world of three dimensions. Our space and the objects in it have depth, and some objects are nearer than others. Yet our two retinas are two-dimensional. The nervous system, again by a taking-into-account, creates psychological depth where physiologically there is none.

Monocular Cues

There are a number of cues for the perception of depth. If only one eye is open, there is a registering of *shadows* and *brightnesses* that helps give objects the appearance of depth. There is a taking-into-account of the relative *clearness* of near objects or of nearer parts of large objects. This cue is called **aerial perspective.** There are cues to be gained from movement, for as we close one eye and move the head from side to side while looking at a scene, near objects and distant objects do not appear to move to the same extent. Also, if one object moves in front of another (creating interposition), we know that the moving object is closer and that the world has depth.

Only recently has the role of this relative "movement" of objects been experimentally explored. In one experiment it was possible to remove or to hold constant all cues to depth perception except the cue of **motion parallax** —the cue furnished us as we travel along a road and see objects move past us at different velocities. If two objects in the laboratory are placed at the same distance from a subject but made to move at different velocities across the visual field, the object with the greater velocity is perceived as nearer (Gibson, Gibson, Smith, and Flock, 1959). The telephone pole zipping by the train window is seen as closer than the herd of cows that "moves backward" slowly as we move down the tracks.

Another cue, **linear perspective,** is very important for the artist who wishes to paint depth into a two-dimensional canvas. Linear perspective can be experienced by looking down a railroad track: the rails appear closer together as they recede into the distance.

When we look at a scene, we take into account the cues coming from the relative size of the retinal images of objects. The artist, in dealing with perspective, takes into account our takings-into-account and creates the illusion of depth. An additional monocular cue is probably given in the eye itself by **accommodation** —the change in shape of the **lens** as an object comes closer or as we change focus back and forth from distant objects to near ones. There is probably a registering in the central nervous system of the **kinesthetic** cues coming from the activity of **ciliary muscles.** Cues from accommodation, however, work only for relatively near objects.

Figure 11–7. LINEAR PERSPECTIVE. *The apparent convergence of lines is a cue to depth and distance perception. Also, there is a change in texture as the distance increases. This also is taken into account when we perceive depth and distance.*

Binocular Cues

The nervous system, in creating depth, also takes into account the slightly different arrays of data coming from two separate eyes. Because the two eyes are slightly separated in space, each gets a slightly different image of any object or scene. This is known as **retinal disparity** and is perhaps the most significant cue in depth perception. (Retinal disparity can be mechanically arranged by having two cameras take slightly different pictures of the same scene. When, through a viewing device, one of these pictures is presented to one eye and one to the other, the result is a photograph appearing to have realistic depth.)

Other binocular cues—cues coming from two eyes—arise from *convergence.* Convergence refers to the "aiming" of the two eyes at near and far objects. If the object is near, the eyes turn inward in order that both may focus on it. If the object is at a distance, the line of sight is more nearly parallel. Again, sensory impulses from the muscles involved probably give cues to be used in the perception of depth and distance, particularly for objects relatively near.

LEARNING IN PRIMITIVE ORGANIZATION

We have tended to describe the processes of primitive organization as if they automatically occur whenever the normal human nervous system is exposed to incoming stimuli. Perhaps they do. But perhaps also we must define the "normal nervous system" as one that has had at least a minimal experience at perceiving. We saw earlier (Chap. 3) that people who were blind from birth but had cataracts removed in adulthood have lasting difficulty in handling some perceptual problems (Von Senden, 1932). In reviewing the clinical data on such people, one writer (Hebb, 1949) suggests that these inexperienced adult perceivers have no real difficulty in perceiving "unity"—they can perceive that an object is a unitary thing standing out as a figure from its background—but in dealing with "identity," in recognizing an object as a member of a class of objects. They cannot easily identify the faces of their friends. Nor can they identify triangles and circles except after long practice. Such an interpretation suggests that the more primitive perceptions are unlearned, but that any perception requiring context is influenced by learning. Perhaps we innately can know that something is there, but we must learn what it is.

Researches in which animals are deprived of sensory (and perceptual) experience for a period of time and then tested for perceptual skill (Riesen, 1949, 1950; Nissen, Chow, and Semmes, 1951) show that perceptually deprived animals (e.g., raised in darkness for many months after birth) cannot learn ordinary perceptual tasks that seem to be easy for normal aniamls. Chimps deprived of visual experience or given only very limited exposure to light are slow to show a blink response to a moving light, slow to follow with their eyes a moving person, and relatively unable to fixate steadily the image of a stationary person (Riesen, 1950). Ringdoves reared without visual experience are inferior to normal birds on visual discrimination (Siegel, 1953). Pigeons whose eyelids were sewn together before they naturally opened showed, six weeks later when they were permitted to see, a tendency to assume strange postures and to bump into objects that normal pigeons easily avoid (Mowrer, 1936). The same sort of behavior characterizes rabbits who are reared in the dark and then brought into the light (Goodman, 1932). There is evidence that early deprivation of visual experience actually prevents normal physiological development of visual mechanisms (Brattgard, 1952; Riesen, 1951).

Rats, in contrast to apes, pigeons, rabbits, and ringdoves, do not appear to suffer so extensively from deprivation of visual experience. Rats reared in darkness are, when exposed to normal visual conditions, able in a short time to make size, brightness, and pattern discriminations (Hebb, 1937ab).

We naturally expect that learning is significantly involved in the more complex forms of perception, where symbolic context enters the process; but we see also that, even with respect to primitive perception, learning is important. Just what kinds of perceptual organizations may be regarded as innately determined and what kinds are influenced by learning remains to be clarified. With respect to the more elaborate and more symbolic processes through which we give meaning to the world, by contrast, it is not to be questioned that the role of learning is significant. Though we *may* need to learn that an object is present, we surely *must* learn that it is beautiful or small or a table or a hippopotamus.

SYMBOLIC FACTORS IN PERCEPTUAL ORGANIZATION

We have seen that in the process of bringing so-called primitive organization to the world of sensory data, the human nervous system, in impressively elaborate ways, takes into account many discrete bits of information and creates organization, creates a kind of primitive meaning. These primitive meanings make possible a primitive kind of adjustment. The organism can know what are objects and what are not; it can know about depths, distances, groups, figures, and grounds.

One might wish to think of the intellectual nakedness and emotional dullness of a life conducted in a world organized only at the primitive level. Such an imagining is very difficult and perhaps a bit repulsive, for our adult worlds are replete with objects that have rich meanings, both intellectual and emotional, and we generally like it that way.

As life advances, objects, events, and situations take on more and more meaning for us. As adults, we still receive sensory data. Our habits of attention, our lasting sets, may operate to exclude some stimuli and especially to facilitate the incoming flow of other data. We must, however, still have sensory contact with the environment. We continue to organize our external world in accordance with the primitive principles by which the nervous system operates. But now, when we face any object or event or person or situation, the meaning it has for us is a vastly enriched meaning. The nervous system has stored up a vast amount of past experience, which, in the face of a stimulus situation, becomes the context or *apperceptive mass* that is taken into account in perceiving the meaning of any stimulus object or situation. The world becomes organized, not only in a primitive way, but in terms of meanings—meanings based on the past experience of the perceiving individual.

A recent writer (Bruner, 1957) suggests that in our attempts to make meaning for ourselves, we not only select what events we shall attend but "recode" events, sometimes in oversimplified form, into our own categories of experience. Consider the 4-year-old who views a Rembrandt painting on the wall of a museum. He can see that it is an object at a certain distance, that it appears as a figure against a ground, that it is two-dimensional, that it has a squareness about it. He can also take into account, perhaps, the fact that adults are more interested in it than he; so it becomes to him an "adult-world" object. Now, for comparison, consider the perceptions of the same stimulus by a senior major in the Department of Fine Arts. All the primitive organizations are there, but so is an array of knowledge. There is knowledge about the painter, about his techniques, about his preferences and aspirations as an artist. There is knowledge of color, of perspective, of anatomy. All this is a context now for the incoming sensory data. But there is more. There are attitudes, perhaps strong ones, concerning Rembrandt, concerning paintings that are liked by the common people or concerning representational art in general. These attitudinal factors also furnish the context against which the incoming sensory data are now interpreted.

We organize our environment—initially a physical, then a sensory environment—into a world that has rich psychological meaning for us. It is full of organized objects and events that are beautiful or ugly, good or bad, positive or negative, objects to be approached or to be avoided. The perceived world of each of us, then, is a world primitively organized in ways that are dictated primarily by the fact of our human nervous system; but it is also a world organized in accordance with the symbolic background or context each of us brings to the interpretation of the primitively organized events.

Perhaps the difference between primitive organization and the more elaborate symbolic organizations can be illustrated in the following way: First, look at Figure 11–8. On the

basis of primitive process, you tend immediately to see simple lines. All of this is primitive organization. Now read the words that go with the drawings and see how the meaning is changed. The whole experience is now organized in a more meaningful way.

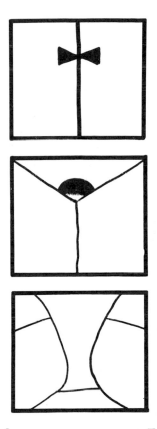

Figure 11–8 THE ROLE OF CONTEXT. *Each of these droodles represents (a) sensory input and (b) simple perceptual organization. A third dimension of perception enters when some intellectual context is supplied. The words that go with the drawings are:* (top) *"Man in tuxedo who stood too close to the front of an elevator."* (middle) *"Husband as seen by wife at breakfast."* (bottom) *"Two fat ladies on a bus fighting for the same seat." From* The Rich Sardine, *by Roger Price. Copyright 1954 by Roger Price, by permission of Simon & Shuster, Inc.*

When we try to understand the perceptual life of a human individual, then, we must deal with the context—the intellectual context and the emotional or motivational context—that is taken into account in assigning a meaning to a piece of the environment. Perceptual organization at this level becomes a matter of assigning meanings to the objects, events, situations, and people in the environment. Or, to say it differently, we selectively perceive objects and assign them to categories of meaning which we already have evolved for ourselves.

INTELLECTUAL CONTEXTS

Although it is probably impossible to separate "intellectual" factors from "emotional" factors in the context against which objects are perceived, we can make at least a theoretical distinction that may be of some utility. Intellectual factors in perception involve the classification of an object or event into our existing categories of experience. If such a classification, or the attempt to achieve such a classification, is not influenced by emotion or bias, then we refer to the process as an intellectual one. Should we, during a walk in the woods, pick up a circular stone with a pair of entwined snakes carved on its surface, our first concern might be to locate the object in our context of knowledge. We know about the history of the region and something about the domestic and economic practices of the primitive tribes who earlier inhabited the area; we know that there is such a thing as archeology and that the nearby university has an anthropology department and an archeologist in it. All this knowledge leads us to interpret the stone as a potentially significant artifact from an ancient culture and leads us to save it for the university archeologist. The intellectual context available leads eventually to an attitudinal interpretation: it may be a valuable stone.

We may compare this perceptual process with that of another woods-walker who, upon finding this stone, interprets it immediately in the light of a violent antipathy to anything having to do with snakes and throws the stone down a ravine.

Both individuals have brought perceptual order into their worlds, but the order, the meaning, was quite different. One individual brought to bear a rich intellectual context and the other perceived almost solely on the basis of an attitudinal or motivational context. In the instance of the second perceiver, the object, in spite of the variety of categories into which one might place it, is very quickly assigned to a category "snakes" and the response that stands ready for snakes is quickly elicited. No problem.

An illustration of the role of intellectual context in perception is provided by a study showing that the speed with which a word is recognized when it is focused on a screen for varying but very brief intervals is proportional to the frequency with which that word appears in standard printed English (Howes and Solomon, 1951). The intellectually familiar is perceived rapidly.

To think that the intellectually familiar is perceived more fully and more richly seems obvious. Educators may perhaps be said to engage in the attempt to enrich the intellectual apperceptive mass of the student, who will spend the rest of his life interpreting the objects and events of his world. The teacher of art would be harshly disappointed at the student who saw a Renoir or a Utrillo as merely a square block. The biology instructor who finds a student responding to an amoeba or the brain of a frog simply as a "mess" would feel that he had added little intellectuality to the student's apperceptive mass. The psychology instructor who did not somewhat enrich or perhaps "encumber with fact" his students' perceptions of morons, or aggressors, or introverts, or of man himself would probably feel himself a failure.

EMOTIONAL OR MOTIVATIONAL CONTEXTS

In discussing motivation (Chap. 8) we saw that a condition of motivated tension in the organism has the effect of (1) increasing the sensitivity to those stimuli having a relevance for the satisfaction of the motive and (2) of determining the way in which the individual perceives ambiguous stimuli. The hungry individual thus not only selects stimuli to attend

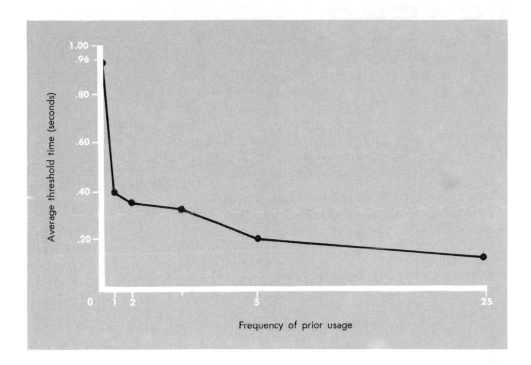

Figure 11–9. FAMILIARITY AND PERCEPTION. *Words occurring more frequently in prior usage are perceived more rapidly when they are exposed tachistoscopically. The curve shows a decrease in the number of seconds required to recognize a word as the frequency of prior usage of that word increases. (Solomon and Postman, 1952; adapted by permission of the American Psychological Association.)*

but interprets available stimuli in the light of his own tensions.

The connection between motivational tensions and perceptual processes makes possible the use of **projective tests.** In the presence of an amorphous or ambiguous inkblot or picture, the individual's perceptions are almost solely determined by his own needs; so we can use his "projected" perceptions as evidence bearing on the nature of his own personal dynamics.

Organic Need and Perception

We saw earlier that students deprived of food tended to see food where there was none and that semistarved subjects began to organ-

Figure 11–10. PROJECTIVE PERCEPTION. *The state of the organism often determines what will be seen in ambiguous situations. The hungry perceiver here will probably see a steak.*

ize their whole lives and their whole world around the theme of eating (Keys et al., 1950). Other studies reinforce the evidence

TSAEKS

Figure 11–11. PROJECTIVE PERCEPTION. *A game of anagrams. What words are created out of these letters probably will be a function of the needs of the perceiver.*

on the role of organic motives in perceptual life. One of these directly supports the finding that, after a period of hunger, subjects read food into ambiguous drawings (Levine, Chein, and Murphy, 1942). Another study showed that hunger has a tendency to increase the apparent size of food objects (McClelland

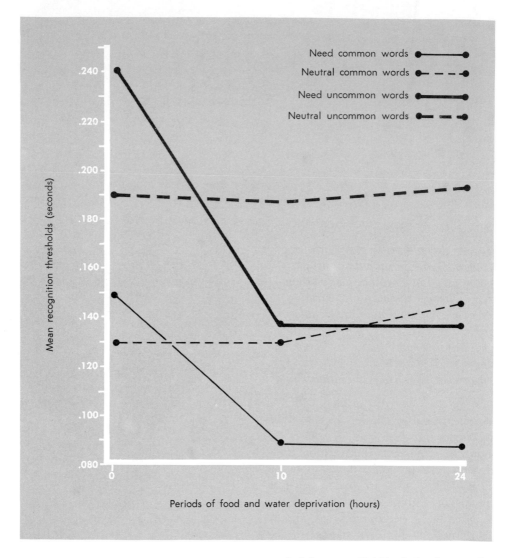

Figure 11–12. NEED AND SPEED OF PERCEPTION. *Hungry and thirsty subjects recognize food and water words more rapidly than they do neutral words. Also, as hunger and thirst increase, hunger words (need words) are recognized with increasing speed. (Wispe and Drambarean, 1953; by permission of the American Psychological Association.)*

and Atkinson, 1948). A further study (Wispe and Drambarean, 1953) divided 60 subjects into three groups, one of which was deprived of food for 10 hours, another was deprived for 20 hours, while the third served as a control group and was not deprived of food. All subjects were given very brief (tachistoscopic) exposures to a number of words, half of which

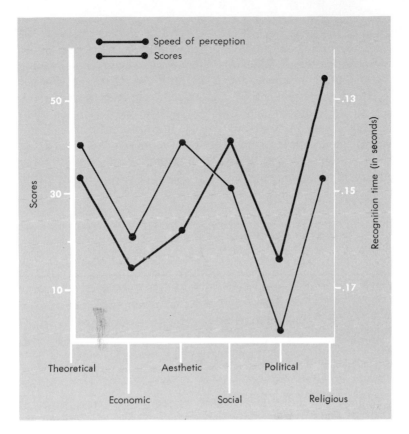

Figure 11–13. PERSONAL VALUES AND PERCEP-
TION. *Personal values relate to the speed with
which words are perceived. When this subject
is presented words relating to the six values,
he perceives more rapidly the words relating
to those values in which he scores relatively
high. (Postman, Bruner, and McGinnies, 1948;
reproduced by permission of the American
Psychological Association.)*

were related to hunger and thirst and half of
which were neutral. The three groups did not
differ in the quickness with which they could
perceive the words not related to hunger or
thirst; but the deprived subjects perceived the
need-related words appreciably more quickly
than did the control group.

Personality and Attitudinal Factors in Perception

The whole individual, with his personal pattern of needs, interests, and attitudes, undertakes to make organized perceptual sense out
of his environment. And the sense—or nonsense—he makes is related to characteristics
of his own system.

Personal values. In a study of values and
perception, Postman, Bruner, and McGinnies
(1948) administered the Allport-Vernon scale
of values (see p. 144) to a group of students,
deriving a score for each on interests in religious, social, economic, aesthetic, political,
and theoretical matters. They then exposed
the subjects for very brief intervals to words
in each of the areas of interest. The purpose
was to discover whether the student with, for
example, a strong value investment in the religious area would more quickly recognize
the words having a religious implication. The
results were positive. Subjects with a dominant religious interest would recognize on
very brief exposure such words as "priest" or
"minister" while taking longer to recognize
economic words such as "cost," "price," or
"bonds."

A later investigation of the same hypothesis (Postman and Schneider, 1951) showed that this relationship between personal values or interests and the perception of words does not hold when the words relating to each of the value areas are all very simple and familiar. The relationship seems to hold only for less common words. The fact that personal values seem to influence the perception of uncommon words but not of common ones has been interpreted (Bruner, 1957) to mean that the individual, in dealing with an array of common words, is perceiving in the interest of the "requirement that surprise be minimized." He tries to anticipate what is coming. When the word is rarer, the subject gives up trying to predict what it is and his values take over to make "his" words, words relating to his values, more readily perceptible.

Another experiment (Bruner and Good-

Table 11–3. THE EFFECTS OF CHANGE IN CLASSIFICATION LISTINGS OR TITLE IN SALES OF BOOKS

FORMER TITLE OR CLASSIFICATION	LATER TITLE OR CLASSIFICATION	ORIGINAL SALES PER YEAR	LATER SALES PER YEAR
What the Editor's Wife Is Thinking About	*Marcet Haldeman-Julius' Intimate Notes on Her Husband*	"almost zero"	16,000 copies in 1927
Poems of Evolution	*When You Were a Tadpole And I Was a Fish*	2,000	7,000
A Guide to Rabelais (classified: "Doors to New Worlds")	*How to Enjoy the Humor of Rabelais* (classified: "Cultural Helps")	"around the zero mark"	13,000 copies in 1927
Poems of Holmes (classified: "Poetry")	*One Hoss Shay and Other Poems* (classified: "Humorous Verse")	3,000	almost 7,000
Euphorian in Texas (classified: General Fiction)	*Euphorian in Texas: An Unconventional Amour* (classified: Love)	very few	22,000 in 1927
Sarah Bernhardt's Philosophy of Love	*The Code of a Parisian Actress*	14,000 in 1926	29,500 in 1927
Loyola: Founder of the Jesuits	*The Jesuits: Religious Rogues*	8,000	34,000 in 1927

An illustration of ways in which the labeling—the arranging of motivational context—can influence the reaction to an object is furnished by data on the effects of affixing new titles to books that had not sold well. The table above gives sales records of a number of Haldeman-Julius "Little Blue Books" before and after the indicated change of title. (From The First Hundred Million *by E. Haldeman-Julius. New York: Simon and Schuster, 1928, Chapter IX, "What a Change of Scenery Will Do," pp. 163–178.)*

man, 1947) reflects again the relation between value and need on one hand and perception on the other. In this study, two groups of 10- and 11-year-old children, one group from prosperous homes and one group from a slum area, were brought into the laboratory and asked to adjust the size of a controllable opening to the size of various coins. When asked to adjust a diaphragm to the size of a remembered nickel or dime or half dollar, all the children tended to overestimate the size

of the coins, with the overestimation increasing with the increased value of the coin. The poorer boys, however, overestimated to a greater extent than did the boys from more prosperous families—perhaps because perceived size is related to perceived value, and the psychological value of the coins was greater for the poorer boys. (See Fig. 11–14.)

This kind of perceptual phenomenon is further illustrated by a research (Ashley, Harper, and Runyon, 1951) in which subjects were

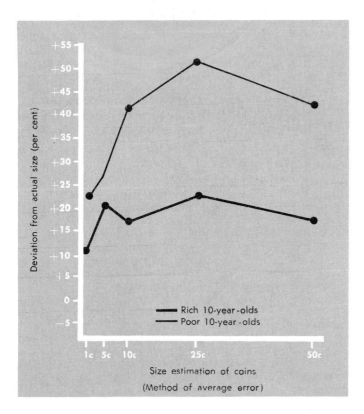

Figure 11–14. MOTIVATIONAL FACTORS AND PERCEPTION. *While all boys tend to overestimate the size of coins, poor boys overestimate more than do well-to-do boys. The top curve above represents the size estimation made by poor 10-year-old boys, when asked to adjust a circle of light so that it was the same size as a designated coin. The bottom curve shows the results from well-to-do boys. (Bruner and Goodman, 1947; reproduced by permission of the American Psychological Association.)*

hypnotized and given posthypnotic suggestions, with one group being told that they were poor and another that they were rich; the subjects who were "poor" tended to overestimate the size of coins more than did the "rich" subjects—results consonant with those obtained from subjects more validly poor and rich.

Perception of threatening words. That inner forces influence the perception of words is suggested by evidence (Bruner and Postman,

1947; McGinnies, 1949) that threatening words and taboo words create perceptual difficulty for the individual. We appear to "block" on words that are threatening, requiring a longer tachistoscopic exposure to recognize them. This research has led to the concept of *perceptual defense*, the tendency of the individual to close the perceptual door to those aspects of the world he finds intolerable. There is no final evidence, however, that perceptual defense is a real phenomenon. Perhaps the subjects were simply unfamiliar with the taboo words. Another experiment suggests just that (Solomon and Howes, 1951). The unfamiliar takes longer to recognize. Or perhaps the subjects show not so much a hesitancy to recognize dirty or taboo words as a hesitancy to pronounce them or to give external evidence that they possess a knowledge of "bad" words.

Personality and perception: The Witkin experiments. Over a period of some years, Witkin (1954) and his research associates conducted an elaborate series of experiments designed to explore the relationship between personality factors and perceptual processes. The experimenters designed a number of perceptual tasks on which they could measure their subjects' performance. Then perceptual performance was related to data from an array of personality tests.

The ingenious perceptual tasks designed for the research involved, for the most part, problems of the relationship between an object and its perceptual field. The subject was asked, for example, to sit in a gray room with walls outlined in white; while he was in this unstructured situation, the subject's chair would be tilted or the whole room would be tilted. The subject was asked to judge when his body was upright by reading cues from his own body and ignoring the sometimes confusing visual cues. Another task involved the ability to see a figure embedded in another figure. The primary dimension of these perceptual performances was the subject's ability to respond to *segments* of the perceptual experience rather than to the whole. The *field-dependent* subject could not easily, for example, see the embedded figure or report accurately on his up-

Figure 11–15. NAPOLEON AND HIS TOMB. *An imbedded figure. Neither the figure of Napoleon nor his tomb initially stands out in a clear figure-ground perspective. Both, however, eventually can be seen. Individuals differ in the ability to find such embedded figures and there is evidence that such differences are related to personality variables. (Fernberger, 1950.)*

rightness in a visually tilted world. The *field-independent* observer could do so.

The field-dependent perceiver and the field-independent perceiver differed with respect to a number of personality variables. Among these were the following:

1. Field-dependent perceivers tended to be more passive, dependent, and submissive.
2. Field-dependent subjects showed more fear of their own sexual and aggressive impulses.
3. Field-dependent subjects showed more anxiety.
4. Field-dependent subjects showed lower self-esteem, less self-acceptance.
5. Field-dependent subjects showed a lower evaluation of their bodies.

These results we may take as evidence that the individual's way of perceiving his world is intimately intertwined with his whole way of facing life. The research in this area has been expanded (Witkins et al., 1962) and will concern us later (Chap. 16).

Social Factors in Perception

In our dealing with emotional and personality factors, we are, in a way, accumulating documentation for the general position that we see the world not as it is but as we are. We select and we organize in terms of our own needs and tensions. In a sense, then, each of us lives in a world of his own creation. But we also live in a world founded and patterned by the views of our fellows, for our perceptions are conspicuously open to social influences. Perhaps, then, there is some justification also for the statement that we see the world not as it is but as *others* see it.

An important part of the socialization process, which brings each of us into full membership in our culture, is training in ways to perceive the world. The native of South Africa and the native of South Bend, walking side by side in New York, would obviously not perceive the same things nor place the same interpretations on the things they simultaneously view. Anthropologists have reported that members of some cultures seem deficient, by our standards, in the perception of color, being unable to make fine distinctions in the blue-green segments of the spectrum. This finding probably would not surprise many American women, who are already quite convinced that the male is seriously deficient in his ability to perceive the subtle shades of female attire. Along a different line, one writer (Whorf, 1940) suggests that the form of a language influences the ways in which a people interprets the world; the Hopi, for example, having no past or future tense for their verbs, are much more likely than we to be concerned with the present only.

Closer to home and closer to the laboratory are data on the effects of social suggestion on perception. We shall see later how group influence can establish perceptual norms that determine the way an individual interprets the world (Chap. 18). The group that "sees" a stationary light move in a dark room (Sherif, 1936a) or that "sees" one line as shorter than another, when it actually is not shorter (Asch, 1951), exerts a powerful influence on the perceptions of the individual. Social pressure, or social suggestion, can sometimes restructure the individual's world.

A very lifelike example of the social factors in perception comes from a study of the reactions of Princeton and Dartmouth students to a very rough and tense football game between the two schools (Hastorf and Cantril, 1954). Groups of students at each school were asked a number of questions about the controversial game, questions concerning who was responsible and in what way for the "roughness" or "dirtiness" of the game. When asked which team "started it," 36 per cent of the Dartmouth students said that Dartmouth did; 86 per cent of the Princeton students laid the blame at Dartmouth's door; 34 per cent of the Dartmouth students saw the game as "rough and fair"; only 3 per cent of the Princeton students could make the same judgment, tending almost unanimously to see it as "rough and dirty" with the Dartmouth team responsible for the dirt. When later shown the complete movie of the game, Princeton students "saw," on the average, 9.8 rules infractions by Dartmouth players; Dartmouth students "saw" less than half that much illegality on the part of their players. (The research report on these matters does not include the datum on who won!)

In such a perceptual setting there are probably two factors operating to bias perception. First, each individual has his own private loyalty to his own team. Second, there is probably an added factor of bias produced by the groups and the pressure they exert on anyone who, in this tense situation, dares stoop to objectivity.

Other evidence of our tendency to see the world as others see it comes from the extensive literature on *suggestion*. If you suggest that I see a ghost in the corner or hear a mouse on the stairs, and if your prestige in my eyes is great, then I may actually see what you suggest I see. If I think you are an idiot child, I may be even less inclined to see ghosts and hear mice than if I were left to my own devices.

Researchers have traced down in considerable detail the workings of prestige suggestion (Lewis, 1940, 1941; Lorge, 1936; Kulp, 1934). One such experiment involved student responses to **Rorschach** inkblots under the conditions of suggestion (Coffin, 1941). The first group of students was given a "scientific" paper reporting that doctors, professors, manufacturers, and lawyers—all highly prestigeful people in the eyes of the students—tended to see the inkblots as wholes and to imagine animal rather than human or inanimate forms in the blots. The same group "learned" also that barbers, chauffeurs, and ditchdiggers tended to see small details and inanimate objects in the inkblots. The second group was given equally authoritative "information," but just the opposite of that given the first group. When, later, the two groups were exposed to the Rorschach stimuli, they responded quite differently. The first group saw wholes and animals, as the prestigeful professionals did. The second group saw details and inanimate objects, as the prestigeful professionals did. Of all the responses of the first group, for example, 39 per cent were whole responses. The second group gave whole responses—the alleged responses of ditchdiggers and barbers—in only 6 per cent of them. The first group gave 48 per cent of their responses in the animal category. The second group, believing that animal responses were characteristic of laborers, gave only 24 per cent of their responses in the animal category.

PERCEPTION AND REMEMBERING

The literature on symbolic factors in perception gives us many instances in which emotional or motivational factors "distort" perception, or arrange it so that the individual perceiver "sees" things in a way the theoretically objective observer would not. In a way each of us, within limits, reconstructs the world to his liking. This process of reconstructing or distorting is obvious enough even though we are in intimate touch with the sensory data. It becomes even more dramatic when we reconstruct from memory the events of the world. A number of writers (Allport and Post-

man, 1947; Bartlett, 1932) have observed that distortion is greater when memory or recall replaces face-to-face perception; they point out also the essential similarity between the interpretive processes of perception and the interpretive processes of memory. A number of experiments (Gibson, 1929; Bartlett, 1932) have shown how visual figures are distorted when subjects are asked to reproduce them after a period of time. The recall is particularly influenced if a label—a symbolic context—is associated with the visual presentation of the object.

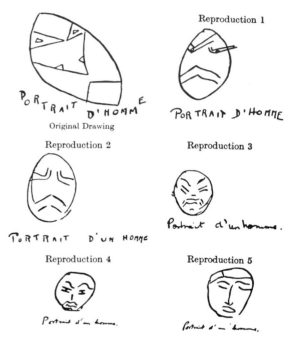

Figure 11–16. SERIAL DRAWINGS. *Distortions in perception and memory are seen clearly in serial reproduction. The first subject draws from memory the original figure (Reproduction I). The second sees Reproduction I and draws it from memory, and so on. By the fifth reproduction, there is clear evidence that the words have influenced the figure, giving it little resemblance to the original. (From Bartlett,* Remembering, *1932; by permission of Cambridge University Press.)*

The distortions of memory become particularly noticeable when the memory is passed through a number of distorting or potentially distorting individuals. Rumors, if they can be followed from their inception, present a good medium for the study of distortion of recall (and of perception). In one well-known study of rumor, the authors (Allport and Postman, 1947) report that as a rumor passes from nervous system to nervous system some predictable things happen to it:

1. *Leveling:* the rumor becomes shorter, more concise, more easily told; unnecessary details are eliminated; there are limits beyond which leveling will not go. The rumor reaches a stable length and form, and tends then to travel along without major change.

2. *Sharpening:* certain details will be selected and others eliminated. The rumor may be sharpened by giving it a local reference and by bringing it out of the past into the present. The rumor may be sharpened by giving it closure, by filling gaps, and thereby creating a neat and rounded story. Explanations may be added where needed to help the story make better sense.

3. *Assimilation:* the rumor will become assimilated with the intellectual and emotional context the listener brings to the hearing of the rumor. The rumor is made to fit the individual's ideas of a good story, is twisted so that it fits his own expectations. He also assimilates what he hears to his own linguistic habits, so that what he tells is what he heard, translated into his own personal language. The story also may assimilate to the self-interest of the listener or to his prejudice.

These phenomena of leveling, sharpening, and assimilation, here set down in connection with rumor, come somewhat close, perhaps, to describing many of the events that happen when the individual either perceives or recalls. Certainly, they are descriptive of the ways in which the organism makes the best sense he can out of his world.

THEORIES OF PERCEPTION

NEURAL THEORIES, BEHAVIORAL THEORIES, GESTALT THEORIES

In addition to the broadly inclusive adaptation-level theory, discussed below, there have

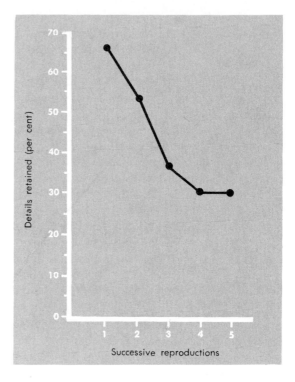

Figure 11–17. LEVELING. *In serial reproduction of verbal material, such as gossip or rumor, there is a rapid elimination of details. (From Allport and Postman, 1947,* The Psychology of Rumor, *Holt, Rinehart & Winston, Inc.;* © 1947 by Henry Holt & Co.)

been a number of somewhat more limited attempts to deal theoretically and systematically with perceptual phenomena (Broadbent, 1948; Hebb, 1949; Taylor, 1962; Gibson, 1929, 1963). Hebb (1949) proposes a neurologically oriented theory, which may account in part for such perceptual phenomena as constancy and for the role that learning plays in the individual's capacity to make discriminations. The key concept in this theory is that of the *cell assembly,* an organization produced on the basis of repeated stimulation of brain cells. Once a cell assembly is established, one can find *reverberating circuits,* neural circuits that can continue firing after input from sensory nerves has ceased. The firing of a single cell or of a few cells (perhaps stimulated by the sight of a portion of an object) can set off a response in a cell assembly that may involve a relatively widespread pattern of neurons.

One can begin to see how this theory can account for such phenomena as closure, form constancy, color constancy, and grouping. Hebb extends the theory to deal also with the known facts about perceptual development; cell assemblies, he maintains, develop sequentially in *phase sequences;* at any given time, the individual's perceptual performance is intimately dependent upon the number and variety of cell assemblies that have developed, sequentially, on the basis of past experience. This concept can be related to the studies of early sensory or perceptional deprivation; that is, such deprivation may prevent the organization of the first and basic cell assemblies, upon which later perceptual skills can sequentially be built. In the perceptual life of the normal organism, a sensory stimulus leads to the activation of interrelated, well-organized, and phase-sequential cell assemblies; complex perception, including perhaps novel or creative problem solving, is the result. The perceptually deprived individual cannot process information in the same way.

A different theoretical approach is that promulgated by the **Gestalt** psychologists. These theorists are inclined toward *nativism* in their formulations; they see the individual as equipped by nature to perceive an organized world. Consequently, in any actual instance of perception, the stimulus sets off an innately formed pattern of neurological events, which leads very naturally to the wholenesses and constancies of actual perception. Perceptual experience, in this view, is not built of bits and pieces of past experience, nor does the brain function on the basis of push-button connections between isolated stimuli and separate structures in the brain. The Gestalt psychologists prefer to think of visual fields and, in the brain, of systematic interactions among parts of the cortex. Only by such an emphasis, they hold, can we account for such a reality as that of the melody remaining the same regardless of the key in which it is played.

The more extreme **behavioristic** theorists (e.g., Taylor, 1962) grant nothing at all to nativism and very little to the significance of perceptual wholes and of organized conceptual patterns. According to them, the visual world is structured not by patterns in the brain but by the responses that can be made to that world. In this connection, the results of experiments on the perception of subjects who were required to wear distorting spectacles are cited (Kohler, 1962). The individual fitted with lenses that, in effect, turn his world upside down (by projecting a right-side-up image on the retina) will in time learn to move around skillfully in the inverted world and will in fact come to perceive that world as right side up. Responses, the argument runs, determine the perception. Although there is a plausibility in such a position, the extreme behavioristic approach still encounters grave difficulty in accounting for many perceptual phenomena that seem very real to us—such as the apparent movement we see when watching a series of still shots projected at a very rapid rate on a movie screen. Such apparent movement cannot be accounted for by eye movements or any other overt responses. Most psychologists who concern themselves with perception still feel it necessary to think of events and processes occurring *between* stimulus and the response.

ADAPTATION-LEVEL THEORY

Another theoretical formulation, one having a relevance for a wide range of perceptual and cognitive phenomena, is one that ascribes a central and unifying role to the general concept of adaptation. This theory, known as the adaptation-level theory (Helson, 1964), puts emphasis on the present and recently past level of activity of the organism as a prime determiner of what will be perceived.

The general idea of adaptation, central to this theory, is a concept first formulated by physiologists, who have long known that prolonged stimulation of a receptor or of a cell will produce a progressive decline in the rate of neural response and will finally lead to a complete cessation of response. This nonresponding state persists until there is some change in the level of stimulation, which will produce a renewed response. In sensory phenomena, then, adaptation may be viewed as a process that not only reduces sensitivity to prolonged stimulation but that, at the same time, tends to make the organism more sensitive to changes in the level of stimulation. In the present theory, the adaptation level of an organism at any given time is the "null" or "zero" point, a point illustrated by the "psychological zero" established through prolonged stimulation by one constant temperature. When the **psychological zero point** is set, then perceptions of heat or cold are produced by any change of the temperature stimulus away from that neutral point.

Starting with such a basic phenomenon, Helson builds his adaptation-level theory to have wide potential relevance not only for perceptual matters but for many aspects of behavior; for in his eyes attitudes, values, emotional behaviors, aesthetic judgments, and other behavioral processes all involve "modes of adaptation to environmental and organismic forces" (p. 37). Stimuli and patterns of stimuli, the theory points out, impinge on an organism already adapted to what has gone before. This general fact, Helson holds, must be considered in almost any study of almost any kind of living process. Certainly, it makes immediate sense that the organism's adaptation level has a great deal to do not only with the selective but also with other aspects of perception.

SUMMARY

1. For organized behavior to occur as the motivated organism interacts with its environment, there must be a selecting and an organizing of stimuli; perception is concerned with these two processes.

2. The organism selects certain physical stimuli to respond to and, functionally, eliminates others.

3. There is both a primitive and a symbolic organization of sensory data.

4. Attention is the selective principle; attention can be conceived in terms of set, or readiness to respond. There are motor sets, perceptual sets, and mental sets.

5. Situational and motivational factors help determine the organism's readiness to respond selectively. Also, there are characteristics of the stimulus that produce sets to perceive or to respond; these include the intensity, size, variability, and repetitiveness of the stimulus.

6. The primitive processes of organization occur as the organism takes into account a variety of stimulus factors; it perceives the world in terms of objects, groups, and so on.

7. Primitive organization can be seen in grouping, in closure, in the various constancy phenomena, and in the figure-ground effect.

8. The perception of depth and distance involves a taking-into-account of various sensory data, including importantly the data arising simultaneously from two eyes. Cues include shadow and brightness, relative clearness, motion parallax, linear perspective, retinal disparity, and convergence.

9. Research involving the deprivation of early sensory and perceptual experience indicates that learning plays an important role even in the more primitive forms of perception.

10. The organism stores up past experience, which functions, as apperceptive mass, to give perceptual meaning to present experiences. This context can be viewed as primarily emotional or as primarily intellectual.

11. The role of intellectual context in perception can be illustrated in a number of ways, including the relative speed with which familiar and unfamiliar words are recognized on tachistoscopic exposure.

12. The role of emotional or motivational context in perception is illustrated by the tend-

ency of hungry subjects to read food objects into amorphous stimuli, and to perceive food words rapidly.

13. Personality factors in perception can be seen (a) in the speed with which subjects perceive words related to their values, (b) in perceptual defense, (c) in the relation between poverty and the perceived size of coins, and (d) in the differences between field-dependent and field-independent perceivers.

14. There are many evidences of social influences on perception. These include the relation between language and perception, the role of group pressure on perception, and the influence of prestige suggestion.

15. The processes of perception and the processes of remembering are sometimes similar in their dependence on symbolic and contextual material.

16. Distortions of memory can be seen clearly in chain reproduction of either verbal or graphic materials. One can see processes of leveling, sharpening, and assimilation.

17. Hebb's theory of perception is a neural theory involving the concept of reverberating circuits and of learning cell assemblies and phase sequences for a variety of perceptual phenomena.

18. The Gestalt psychologists proposed a nativistic theory, in which the individual is inherently equipped to perceive an organized world. Gestalt theory emphasizes perceptual and neural fields rather than isolated molecular processes that become connected through experience.

19. Behavioristic theories of perception hold that the perceptual world is structured not by nativistic patterns in the brain but through response and learned patterns of responses.

20. The adaptation-level theory, a formulation having a relevance for a broad band of behavior, puts an emphasis on the present and recently past level of activity of the organism as a determiner of interpretations of the world.

RESEARCH REPORTS

ADAPTATION TO PERCEPTUAL DISTORTION [*]

It has been known for a long time that if subjects are required to wear prismatic lenses that distort the perceptual world in one way or another, they eventually will adapt so that they can find their way about in the world just about as well as if there were no distortion at all. The experiment under consideration here represents a step toward an analysis of the kinds of processes involved in such over-all adaptation to distortion. In the study, nine college students wore for 3 days, and eight other students wore for 42 days, some wedged prisms mounted in spectacle frames. The prisms produced various kinds of distortion, and the experimenters used a number of tests to measure the adaptation to the separate kinds of distortion. The first kind of distortion involved was an over-all displacement of the visual image of approximately 11°. Also there were produced (1) a curvature of vertical straight lines; (2) some spectral dispersion, producing colored fringes at the vertical contours of objects; and (3) a complex differential displacement of the visual image, varying in accordance with angle of regard and with the direction of head movement.

To test adaptation to the over-all displacement of the image—the 11° displacement of the visual image—the experimenters measured the accuracy with which a subject could localize the direction of targets. First, the subject was asked to touch a visual target displayed to him. He was asked next to listen to an audible click coming from behind a meter scale displayed in front of him and then to report the number from behind which the clicks emanated. These tests were administered before and immediately after putting on the prisms as well as periodically during the period the prisms were worn.

To measure adaptation to the convergence of horizontal lines above and below eye level, the subject was given a visual locus of one dot which he was told was to form the lower left-hand corner of a square, and was asked to move three other dots so as to complete a square. The success in constructing such a square could be measured pre-

* H. L. Pick, Jr., and J. C. Hay, Adaptation to prismatic distortion, *Psychon. Sci.*, 1964, 1, 199–200.

cisely and could be used as an indication of adaptation. To measure adaptation to the other kinds of distortion, the experimenters asked the subjects to select a prism that would just barely eliminate a particular kind of distortion they could perceive through the experimental prisms. The amount of adaptation that had occurred could thus be measured in terms of the amount of distortion needed to correct the apparent distortion in the subject's view of the world.

The experimenters were able to calculate, in comparable terms, the per cent of adaptation to the various kinds of distortion.

In making visual localizations of clicks coming from various directions, the 3-day subjects showed a 44.6 per cent adaptation. The test was not administered to the 42-day subjects. With respect to the touching of a visual target presented to them, the 3-day subjects showed an 85.8 per cent adaptation and the 42-day subjects a 90.1 per cent adaptation.

There was not nearly so much adaptation to the more intricate kinds of distortion involved in this experiment. As tested by the method in which the subject chose a distorting lens to "correct" existing distortions, the 42-day subjects showed only a 30 per cent adaptation to the distortion involved in the curvature of vertical straight lines, for example. And with respect to the tilting of horizontal lines with the up and down movement of the head, there was only a 14.6 per cent adaptation for the 42-day subjects.

These differences in the level of adaptation for various kinds of perceptual distortion present problems for further research.

SENSORY DEPRIVATION AND PERCEPTUAL FUNCTIONING [*]

There has been a good deal of research to indicate that isolation from sensory experience can influence the perceptual development of young organisms. It has also been demonstrated that periods of sensory deprivation for adults produce strange kinds of results. The research concerning us immediately here examines, among other things, the effects of periods of relatively prolonged periods of sensory deprivation on perceptual functioning.

In this study, fifteen male subjects were placed individually in an isolation chamber, where they were expected to stay for a period of two weeks. Of the fifteen, five failed to last the full two weeks, terminating their participation within the first four days. The remaining ten completed the fourteen-day period. During the entire time, they wore translucent goggles which admitted light but which excluded all pattern vision. Each subject also wore heavy gloves and a set of earmuffs through which came to him a constant flow of "white" noise, a noise similar to the constant whoosh one hears on a radio turned to high amplitude when there is no signal being broadcast. The subjects were not permitted to sing, or speak, or hum, or to engage in any other vocal activity. They were allowed to engage in whatever motor activity they chose.

EEG's were taken before isolation, and then during isolation at intervals of seven, ten, and fourteen days. Follow-up records were taken at intervals of one, two, seven, and ten days after termination. There was a general tendency for a change in the EEG over the period of isolation, with the mean occipital-lobe frequency declining with the increasing length of deprivation. There were also observed differences in effects on the motivation of the subjects; a number of subjects reported an inability to study or to engage in other activities for periods lasting up to eight days after the experimental session.

But there were no observed changes in such functions as depth perception and size constancy. Also, there were few reports of hallucinatory phenomena on the part of the subjects. Sensory deprivation of a two-week duration and in adulthood does not appear, then, to affect basic perceptual processes.

PERCEPTION OF VERBAL MATERIAL [*]

Of obvious importance for an understanding of reading skills and of considerable significance also for an understanding of the principles of perception is the question of the factors determining our perception of certain arrays of linguistic stimuli as unitary groups rather than as single units. It

[*] J. P. Zubek, Behavioral and EEG changes after 14 days of perceptual deprivation, Psychon. Sci., 1964, 1, 57–58.

[*] E. J. Gibson, C. H. Bishop, W. Schiff, and J. Smith, Comparison of meaningfulness and pronounceability as grouping principles in the perception and retention of verbal material, J. exp. Psychol., 1964, 67, 173–182.

has long been known that as an individual's reading speed increases, even to the remarkable heights achieved by excessively rapid readers, the individual perceives and understands in larger and larger units. The very slow reader will perceive every letter in a word and every word in a sentence. The rapid reader, by contrast, may perceive whole sentences or even paragraphs as units.

The present research deals with the relative contribution of pronounceability and meaningfulness to the grouping of verbal material into perceptual units.

Actually, the study goes on to deal with the role of both pronounceability and meaningfulness in the learning of verbal material; but for our purposes, the part of the research dealing with perception is most relevant.

In earlier work on the perception of words, it has been generally assumed that the meaningfulness of the word is the prime determiner of the speed or the ease with which it is perceived. Meaningful words, for example, are generally perceived more readily as units than are meaningless constructions. The present study attempts to separate the two factors of meaningfulness and pronounceability and to examine the contributions of each to the speed with which verbal materials are perceived as units.

For the experiment, the attempt was made to create equivalent lists, with each list composed of three types of trigrams—three types of three-letter nonsense units. The attempt was to find trigrams whose unitariness was constituted primarily by their being pronounceable as monosyllabic units, according to prevailing rules of English spelling and pronunciation. Also, the experimenters wanted other trigrams whose unitariness was constituted primarily by meaningfulness, with meaningfulness defined by the associations individuals could give to the whole unit or to parts thereof. Also, of course, there had to be control trigrams that were low in both pronounceability and in meaningfulness.

In the lists of trigrams actually used in the experiment, the trigrams KOR, TAV, and MIB, for example, were all rated as obviously high in pronounceability but, by the procedures employed, were rated as low in meaning. The trigrams RKO, TVA, and IBM are all obviously low in pronounceability were still rated relatively high in meaningfulness.

To control for letter shapes—so that the pronounceable list, the meaningful list, and the control list all had the same shapes to present to the perceivers—the same three letters in each trigram were arranged in a pronounceable form (as MIB above), an unpronounceable but meaningful form (as in IBM above), and in a control form that was low in both pronounceability and meaningfulness (here MBI). Similarly for the three letters T, O, and K: the pronounceable trigram was TOK; the meaningful was TKO; the control trigram, low in both meaningfulness and pronounceability, was OTK.

The perceptual thresholds were measured individually for each subject and for each word by varying the brightness contrast of the exposed field in relation to the brightness of the field both before and after exposure. For each trigram the time of exposure was maintained at a constant .25 seconds. The subject was seated in front of a projector at a distance of 8 feet from the screen. The groups of letters, typed in Roman capitals and prepared as slides, were projected one after another on the screen. The illumination necessary for the individual to perceive and write down accurately the exposed trigram was recorded for each item.

Although wide individual differences in the perceptual threshold for tachistoscopic recognition made it difficult to treat the data statistically, it was possible to convert individual measures into standard scores and to arrive at comparisons of mean thresholds for each trigram. The data indicate that the perceptual threshold for pronounceable trigrams was generally lower than that for the meaningful trigrams and that both pronounceable and meaningful trigrams were perceived more rapidly under standard conditions than were the control trigrams—the ones that were low in both pronounceability and meaningfulness. Looking at the results in another way, the experimenters reported that eleven of twelve pronounceable trigrams had lower thresholds than their meaningful counterparts, and all twelve pronounceable ones were lower than their control counterparts. If a low perceptual threshold, then, is an indicator of relative unitariness on perception, then pronounceability is more effective in creating a unity in a three-letter group than is meaningfulness. The researchers interpret these results to mean that in the perception of written language we must "code" the stimulus material into units of spoken language, which, naturally, comes in pronounceable units.

In later parts of the same experiment, the researchers found that both pronounceability and meaning led to more success in the learning and remembering words, and that, for remembering, the variable of meaningfulness seemed to be more significant than pronounceability.

SUGGESTED READINGS

Dember, W. N. *The psychology of perception.* New York: Holt, 1960.

Gibson, J. J. *The perception of the visual world.* Boston: Houghton Mifflin, 1950.

Ittleson, W. H. *Visual space perception.* New York: Springer, 1960.

Moncrieff, R. W. *The chemical senses.* New York: Wiley, 1946.

Smith, K. U., and W. M. Smith (with the assistance of Margaret F. Smith). *Perception and motion: An analysis of space-structured behavior.* Philadelphia: Saunders, 1962.

Taylor, J. G. *The behavioral basis of perception.* New Haven: Yale University Press, 1962.

Witkin, H. A., et al. *Psychological differentiation: Studies of development.* New York: Wiley, 1962.

OUTLINE / CHAPTER 12

I. PERSPECTIVES ON LEARNING

    A. Learning and the Psychological Process
    B. Biological Perspectives on Learning
    C. A Definition of Learning

II. SIMPLE LEARNING

    A. Classical Conditioning
        1. Conditions for Acquiring Conditioned Responses
        2. Phenomena of Classical Conditioning
            a. Extinction
            b. Spontaneous recovery
            c. Higher-order conditioning
            d. Stimulus generalization
            e. Response generalization
            f. Discrimination
    B. Instrumental Conditioning
        1. Instrumental and Classical Conditioning
        2. Laboratory Equipment for Instrumental Conditioning
        3. Kinds of Instrumental Conditioning
        4. Basic Phenomena of Instrumental Conditioning
            a. Acquisition
            b. Extinction
            c. Spontaneous recovery
            d. Generalization
            e. Discrimination
        5. Reinforcement
            a. Conditions of reinforcement
            b. Number of reinforcements
            c. Amount of reinforcement
            d. Time of reinforcement
            e. Partial reinforcement
    C. Summary: Simple Learning

III. LEARNING TO SOLVE PROBLEMS

    A. The Double-Alternation Problem
    B. Insightful Learning
    C. Learning to Learn

IV. THEORIES OF LEARNING

    A. Stimulus-Response Theories
    B. Cognitive Theories

V. LEARNING PRINCIPLES AND PERSONALITY DEVELOPMENT

VI. SUMMARY

VII. RESEARCH REPORT

CHAPTER 12

BASIC PROCESSES OF LEARNING*

PERSPECTIVES ON LEARNING

LEARNING AND THE PSYCHOLOGICAL PROCESS

The motivated organism senses its world, interprets it, responds to it, and then *responds to the consequences* of its own response. Once the organism has passed through this cycle, it is never again the same. Its first behavior has consequences; there is resultant comfort or relief or satisfaction. These consequences of its own behavior, registered and stored, become a part of the organism. It has gained experience. It is never again the same, and its be-

havior begins to show it. Tomorrow the organism interprets the world differently than it did today because *it* is different. It responds differently. It continues to register the consequences of its own behavior. It is well embarked on the spiraling, dynamic process of living, a process in which growth and change, over a period of time and with experience, plays a central role.

BIOLOGICAL PERSPECTIVES ON LEARNING

Organisms learn. Inanimate objects do not learn. Therein lies a momentous distinction, artfully drawn in the following quotation:

If some iron filings be sprinkled on a table and a magnet brought near them, they will fly through the air for a certain distance and stick to its surface. A savage seeing the phenomenon explains it as the result of an attraction or love between the magnet and the filings. But let a card cover the poles of the magnet, and the filings will press

---

° John Capaldi gave very significant help with the preparation of the first edition of this and of the following chapter. Hugh Poyner was a prime resource in the completion of the revised edition of the two chapters.

forever against its surface without its ever occurring to them to pass around its sides and thus come into more direct contact with the object of their love.

If now we pass from such actions as these to those of living things, we notice a striking difference. Romeo wants Juliet as the filings want the magnet; and if no obstacles intervene he moves toward her by as straight a line as they. But Romeo and Juliet, if a wall be built between them, do not remain idiotically pressing their faces against its opposite sides like the magnet and the filings with the card. Romeo soon finds a circuitous way, by scaling the wall or otherwise, of touching Juliet's lips directly. With the filings the path is fixed; whether it reaches the end depends on accidents. With the lover it is the end which is fixed; the path may be modified indefinitely.[1]

As far as we know, all animals learn. They do not often persist in behaving in precisely the same way in the face of the same external situation, at least not when some new behavior would be more advantageous to them. Some organisms, however, learn more than others, change more, and change more rapidly as the result of experience. Simple organisms such as the angleworm do not, as far as we can tell, have either the need or the capacity to learn a great deal. Built-in hereditary mechanisms seem to carry them along successfully through what we are inclined to view as a simple and untroubled life.

The self-sufficiency of instinctive mechanisms, however, is brought into question by evidence that instinctive patterns are modified by learning (Thorpe, 1956). The hunter wasp, for example, will lay eggs in several different burrows. But it must *learn* its way back to the burrows to care for its young. One writer (Deese, 1958) states, "There is great difficulty in separating the influence of instinct and learning in animals. Only now are we beginning to understand how these things interact in the natural world. Most animal behavior is a complicated interweaving of instinctive and learned components. Once an instinctive act has been released, it has opened the way for possible modification."[2]

Higher animal species, such as birds and fish, though they come equipped with an array of instinctive mechanisms to help them survive and reproduce in kind, still must profit from experience if they are to escape the predatory cat or the hungry heron. Psychologists (Smith and Geis, 1956) have demonstrated clearly that fish not only can learn but sometimes need to learn. Fish raised in hatcheries sooner or later learn that the approach of a shadow at the edge of the pool signals the presence of a food-bearing attendant. The fish rush to the surface, ready to eat. This response works well in the hatchery; but when the fish are transplanted to natural streams, where the approaching shadow may be that of a bear or crane or sportsman with predatory intent, the response turns out to be a very dangerous habit. Hatchery-bred fish disappear at a rapid rate during the few days after they are first placed in natural streams. To save the fish from some of nature's hazards, the psychologists devised a way to give them some survival training before releasing them from the hatchery. The procedure was to run a mild electric charge into the water every time a shadow appeared at its edge. The fish soon became educated. They learned now to shy away from moving objects at the edge of the water. When these sophisticated fish were put out into a natural environment, they were not such easy prey for predators and anglers.

All animals can and probably must learn. But nowhere is either the capacity or the necessity for learning so cardinally significant as in the human animal. The human neonate is relatively naked of ready-made mechanisms or instincts to insure his survival. He is born into what often impresses the young as an intolerably intricate culture with which he must make some manner of peace. He must learn and learn mightily, or his environment will overpower him. And though in the long months of infancy he is the most helpless of the

---

[1] From *Principles of Psychology*, by William James, 1890, pp. 6–7. Reprinted by permission of Holt, Rinehart and Winston, Inc., 1956.

[2] By permission from *The Psychology of Learning*, by James Deese, pp. 320–321. Copyright, 1958, McGraw-Hill Book Co., Inc.

helpless, he still has the innate capacity to learn—to learn almost anything his world and his elders demand of him.

What would his life be like if he did not have this capacity—if he stopped learning, say, on his second birthday? In the absence of learning, he would continue to grow and develop, provided he were fed, watered, protected from the elements, and kept free of disease. But his behavior would not change very much. When he reached college age, he would still have the simple and limited skills of the 2-year-old. He would walk to class, but precariously, and might still have periodic preferences for crawling. He probably would not arrive in class on time, for he has not learned the clock. Similarly, he would not have mastered the intricacies of toilet training; would not sit still very long, for he has not learned to control impulse or mobility; would understand only about twenty to forty words; could not take notes in class; and could ask only monosyllabic questions, if any at all. He probably would not have learned that clothing in this culture is regarded as desirable, and thus would be unable to select the diapers and rompers most in fashion this year. We would not be able, even should we wish, to use either hope of success or fear of failure to motivate his scholarly efforts; for he has not learned the symbols necessary for representing in the present any events not yet come to pass.

If all his classmates had also stopped learning at the age of 2, we could find relatively few differences among the individuals in our class. There would be physical differences and temperamental differences. And there would be some noticeable differences in the size and content of vocabulary, in the number and nature of habits, in fears and fondnesses. But there would be no Republicans, no Democrats, no liberals, no conservatives, no idealists, no realists, no bigots; for all of these aspects of motivation, attitude, and personality must be learned—sometimes laboriously and over a long period of time.

Such a fantasy might be elaborated much further. But enough of it. It has served its purpose by now. Learning is pervasive, and the consequences of its absence are profound.

The psychologist, in trying to understand and to state in scientific simplicity the nature of the process of adjustment, is forced into a deep concern with learning. Learning is intimately involved in almost every aspect of behavior he chooses to study. He seeks to analyze learning, to describe in precise and adequate terms the ways in which behavior changes as the result of experience. In this chapter, we shall be concerned with the attempts of psychologists to discover, to describe, and to account for the basic phenomena of learning. The big adventure in the study of learning is in seeking for the general principles underlying the almost infinitely varied behavioral changes that occur as the result of the individual's birth-to-death experience. In recapitulating this adventure we shall begin in this chapter by looking at a catalog of the behaviors we learn. Then we will turn to study of the phenomena of what can be called *simple learning*, seeking in the extensive research literature for those basic general principles that may help us to grasp—even to predict and control—the more complex learnings that occur in natural life.

A DEFINITION OF LEARNING

A good working definition of learning is as follows: *Learning is a relatively permanent change in behavior brought about as the result of experience.*

Such a definition, though it will not make all psychologists equally happy, will work reasonably well. Let us nudge it about a bit in order to appreciate its significance more fully. When we say that learning is a change in behavior, we tie the concept of learning to observable facts. We can see changes in behavior; and, if we are careful, we can determine which are relatively permanent changes. We can see behavior, and we can compare behavior on one occasion with behavior on another. The change—the observable fact—is learning, although learning in itself is a *construct* and is never directly observed. In this regard it is like the constructs of hunger, thirst, gregariousness, or intelligence.

When we say *relatively permanent* changes in behavior, we are making a distinction between *performance* and learning. Performance may vary from one time to another. A football team, on one Saturday, will demonstrate marvelous morale and energy and will rise up to smite a powerful foe. On the next Saturday, perhaps satiated with victory, it will perform very poorly in spite of the fact that every player has had a week in which to learn better the skills involved in the game. People will perform much better at one time than at another in typing, in playing golf, in juggling plates, or in reciting poetry. They *know* the same amount about their task but for one reason or another cannot always use this knowledge well. We must be very careful before we say that changes in performance are permanent changes due to learning. In order to distinguish between learning and impermanent changes in performance, we have to hold constant such things as motivation, incentive, the physiological state of the organism, and the stimulus situation. As we shall see, this can be arranged so that we can talk about learning and know with reasonable certainty what we are talking about.

Now, for *experience*—a term that includes a great variety of things: the reading of books and the practicing on the piano; the learning of new words, the exposure to new mathematical symbols, the repetitious muscular practice of simple physical tasks; and the sensory experiencing of events within the body. In short, experience can and must include everything in the past psychological history of the organism.

Learning, thus, is a construct by which we refer to observable and relatively permanent changes in behavior that are produced in the organism through some kind of contending with the environment.

SIMPLE LEARNING

In confronting the intricate business of learning, the experimental psychologist does not rush madly off at random, studying either learning in general or any instance of learning which may have practical importance. He follows a strategy of science, a strategy that leads him to *search first for simplicity*, to focus first on those instances of learning which can be (a) clearly defined, (b) brought into the laboratory, and (c) made amenable to precise measurement and quantification. He searches first for simplicity because he believes that a thorough exploration of the facts and relationships involved in the simplest forms of learning may lead to general theories and laws, which will give us an understanding of the highest forms of learning. Whether or not this strategy will work remains to be seen.

CLASSICAL CONDITIONING

The simplest of all forms of learning is that form known as *classical* conditioning. The basic fact of conditioning has been known for centuries and is firmly embedded in psychological folklore. It takes little professional training to find that the burned child fears the fire—and in the burned child's response to the sight of a fire, we see the core phenomenon of conditioning. The fact seems simple and natural—but only recently has anyone come to intimate intellectual grips with conditioning. When it is studied carefully in its various manifestations, conditioning turns out to be not so simple—nor even, perhaps, in an everyday view, very natural either.

The essential phenomenon in classical conditioning is that a *conditioned stimulus* (the sight of the fire) comes to evoke the *response* (fear) formerly reserved for the *unconditioned stimulus* (the actual heat of the fire). We can count on it that most organisms will innately respond to anything that actually burns. But to emote *before* being burned, to respond to the sight of the fire, is a learned accomplishment based on *some enduring change in the organism.* No plant, as far as we know, has ever achieved such a change—and certainly no brick or iron filing has done so. Organisms can become conditioned. And psychologists have thoroughly studied the conditions, circumstances, and consequences of conditioning. In their explorations they may have uncovered some of the dependable general principles of learning. We shall see.

There are many everyday examples of classical conditioning. One writer (Guthrie, 1938) reports the story of two farm boys who systematically reeducated the minister's horse. These boys, unhappy with their weekly assignment of grooming and feeding the horse while the minister visited their parents, conducted a learning experiment, the outcome of which they thought they would enjoy. For an hour, one boy held the horse between the shafts; his collaborator sat in the buggy repeatedly yelling "whoa" and immediately thereafter poking the horse with the point of a hay fork. It can be safely assumed that the horse's retraining produced some surprises for the minister.

Other and more practical examples of conditioning abound in everyday life. A child responds naturally to a slap on the hand. If the word "no" constantly accompanies the slap, his response to the slap will eventually be elicited by the word alone. The child naturally gives a fearful response to loud noises such as thunder; if these noises are associated with the dark, darkness itself will produce fear. Such conditioned responses are being built up every day of our lives. We are often unaware of them, but they can also be produced deliberately. For example, the fact that a child is wakened by the sound of a bell has been used in creating a method for curing bed wetting (Mowrer and Mowrer, 1938). The child sleeps on a special pad containing two pieces of screening. When moisture strikes the pad, an electric circuit is completed; a bell rings, awakening the child. Soon the stimuli from a distended bladder are evoking the response given to the bell, and the child has learned to awaken without artificial help.

In all these examples the form of learning is the same. The unconditioned stimulus, UCS (the bell, the thunder, the prod of the pitchfork) produces an unconditioned response, UCR (awakening, fear, jumping). The conditioned stimulus, CS (the stimuli from the bladder, darkness, "whoa")—when associated properly with the original unconditioned stimulus—leads to the conditioned response, CR (awakening, fear, jumping). A new stimulus comes to evoke an existing response. The new stimulus, a biologically inadequate stimulus to begin with, takes on behavioral effectiveness.

Conditions for Acquiring Conditioned Responses

Ivan Pavlov (1927), a Russian physiologist, was the first investigator to conduct systematic studies of conditioned responses. While studying digestive processes in animals, he became interested in the fact that laboratory animals, instead of salivating only after food was in the mouth, would frequently be set to salivating before the food reached them. This phenomenon, once Pavlov became curious about it, occupied the rest of his research life.

Figure 12–1. IVAN PAVLOV. *Pavlov, trained as a physiologist, became fascinated by what he called "psychic secretions" and spent the rest of his life studying conditioning.*

Pavlov began his conditioning work with dogs. He devised procedures for measuring very accurately the amount of salivation, built a soundproof room with timing devices so that he could control the stimuli reaching the dog and could time precisely the presentation of the food and the conditioned stimuli, such as lights or buzzers. The basic phenomenon he studied is the one we have already described:

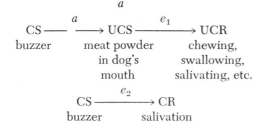

$$CS \xrightarrow{\ a\ } UCS \xrightarrow{\ e_1\ } UCR$$

As represented in the diagram, the buzzer is sounded; then, after a brief interval, meat powder is placed in the dog's mouth. The dog responds to the food in the usual manner; he salivates, chews, and swallows. The arrow e_1 here signifies that the food elicits a response that is automatic, that is unconditioned. The broken arrow a represents the fact that the sound of the buzzer is present when the food, the unconditioned stimulus, is present and while the unconditioned response is taking place, allowing the animal to *associate* the buzzer with the food and with his reaction to food. After repeated pairings of the buzzer—the CS—with the UCS (the food), the animal will act as if he expects the food to follow the buzzer; he will salivate at the sound of the buzzer alone (see arrow e_2 in the lower part of the diagram). The buzzer now *elicits* a response formerly elicited by food. A conditioned response, a part of the original unconditioned response, is established. It should be emphasized that the conditioned stimulus (the buzzer) must occur a fraction of a second *before* the unconditioned stimulus (the food), or conditioning will not take place.

Once we have devised arrangements for the experimental study of conditioning, we can systematically manipulate the various factors in the phenomenon and record precisely what

Figure 12–2. PAVLOV'S LABORATORY APPARATUS. *Such an arrangement allows for meticulous control of variables and the precise measurement of responses.*

happens, investigating such things as the best interval between the two stimuli, the number of trials necessary to establish a CR, what responses of what animals are amenable to con-

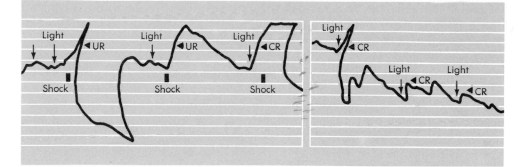

Figure 12–3. CONDITIONED GALVANIC SKIN RESPONSE. *An unconditioned galvanic skin response (GSR) occurs when an electric shock is applied (indicated by black bar). When the shock is repeatedly paired with a light (the arrow above), the GSR appears when the light alone (the conditioned stimulus) is applied. A conditioned response has been established. On the right above, we can see extinction in progress as the light is flashed repeatedly without any reinforcing shock.*

ditioning. We can quickly and roughly summarize an extensive research literature by saying that most CR's are learned best if the CS is presented very shortly before the UCS (about 0.5 seconds) and that almost any response of which the organism is capable can be elicited by almost any stimulus it can register.

Phenomena of Classical Conditioning

Extinction. A conditioned response may weaken or diminish, so that it does not occur every time the conditioned stimulus is presented. If this weakening or fading of the CR occurs simply with the passage of time (that is, if the conditioned stimulus is no longer presented), the weakening can be described as *forgetting*. But if the conditioned stimulus is repeatedly presented *without* the related presentation of the *reinforcing* unconditioned stimulus, the conditioned response will be *extinguished*. **Extinction** occurs, then, unless there is **reinforcement**, unless there is at least an occasional reassociation of the conditioned

with the unconditioned stimulus. Under ordinary conditions, the parson's horse will not continue into perpetuity to lunge forward when he hears "whoa"; if the reinforcing pitchfork is removed entirely from his life, the conditioned response will suffer eventual extinction.

The conditions for producing extinction are complex. The omission of the reinforcement is an active process; so is the substitution of a rewarding stimulus for the formerly painful one—or the replacing of a painful stimulus for a formerly rewarding one. Any one of these active developments has several possible consequences, any one of which can contribute to the disappearance of the conditioned response (Kimble, 1961). For example, the removal of the unconditioned stimulus may reduce motivation, it may build up an inhibitory state or a condition of fatigue, or it may initiate interfering responses which prevent the conditioned response from occurring. If the extinction involves the acquisition of a new response that is incompatible with the old, the phenomenon is known as *counter-conditioning;* if we wish to facilitate the speed of extinction of the parson's horse's response to "whoa," we we would do well not only to remove the pitchfork reinforcement but also to help the horse, through the application of a different reinforcer, learn a new response—or relearn the old one—to the conditioned stimuli.

Spontaneous recovery. We cannot always be sure that once a conditioned response is extinguished, it will stay extinguished. We can sound our dog's buzzer many times without presenting him any food; and we can reach a situation in which the dog, as far as we can tell, ignores the buzzer. But tomorrow he may inexplicably salivate again at the sound of the buzzer. The CR has *spontaneously recovered*. Whether a conditioned response once established ever completely disappears from the behavioral repertoire of an organism is not known. There might be, of course, a lifelong residue of some sort. We do know that a conditioned response which has been extinguished often reappears after periods of rest or disuse. Then, if there is no reinforcement, it is very likely to extinguish again.

A widely accepted theory of spontaneous recovery holds that it is due to the dissipation of the inhibitory state or the fatigue that builds up during extinction.

Higher-order conditioning. Higher-order conditioning occurs in the following way. If we establish firmly a conditioned response whereby a dog salivates at the sound of a buzzer, then we can pair the buzzer with another stimulus—say, a light—and the dog will give his response to the light. The buzzer, originally the conditioned stimulus, now acts

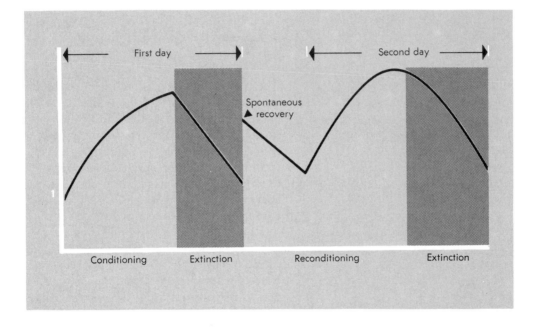

Figure 12–4. LIFE HISTORY OF A CONDITIONED RESPONSE. *The record above, read from left to right, presents in schematic form the life history of a classical conditioned response. The first gradual rise of the curve represents the increasing strength of the CR as the conditioned and unconditioned stimuli are repeatedly associated. Then comes extinction, when the US is no longer used to reinforce the CS. If there is a day's rest, spontaneous recovery will occur, followed by further extinction. When the US and CS are further paired, there is reconditioning, followed again by extinction if the unconditioned stimulus is removed.*

as if it were an unconditioned stimulus. By pairing the buzzer with a light, we produce *second-order conditioning*, whereby there is salivation at the flashing of a light, a light which has never itself been connected with food. Further, if we pair the light with a white square, the dog will salivate to the white square. This is *third-order conditioning*, apparently the limit to which a dog can aspire (see diagram).

In human beings, much higher-order conditioning probably occurs. Through this intricate procedure the burned child may give a fearful response to the sight of a fire, to the

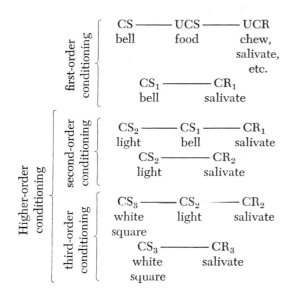

first-order conditioning

$$CS \text{—} UCS \text{—} UCR$$
$$\text{bell} \quad \text{food} \quad \text{chew, salivate, etc.}$$

$$CS_1 \text{—} CR_1$$
$$\text{bell} \quad \text{salivate}$$

Higher-order conditioning

second-order conditioning

$$CS_2 \text{—} CS_1 \text{—} CR_1$$
$$\text{light} \quad \text{bell} \quad \text{salivate}$$

$$CS_2 \text{—} CR_2$$
$$\text{light} \quad \text{salivate}$$

third-order conditioning

$$CS_3 \text{—} CS_2 \text{—} CR_2$$
$$\text{white square} \quad \text{light} \quad \text{salivate}$$

$$CS_3 \text{—} CR_3$$
$$\text{white square} \quad \text{salivate}$$

word *fire,* to furnaces in general, to fire houses, to pyrotechnics, and to oratory on the Fourth of July. Can a dislike of patriotic oratory be traced back, through the systematic working of higher-order conditioning, to an infantile burn? It sounds improbable, but such a tracing back has some plausibility about it, once we know that higher-order conditioning can and does occur.

Stimulus generalization. If the conditioned response occurred only to the precise stimulus originally involved, we might seriously doubt that classical conditioning could have general significance for understanding the more intricate kinds of human learning. However, once a conditioned response is established to a stimulus of a particular kind, the response will also occur to stimuli that are similar in some respect to the original stimulus. This is **stimulus generalization.** If we become conditioned to a light of a certain intensity, we will respond similarly to light of differing intensities. If we learn to blink or to change the heart rate at the sound of one particular tone, we will respond in very similar ways but to lesser extents to tones up or down the scale from the original one.

This aspect of conditioning, readily demonstrated in the laboratory, makes it increasingly likely that the mechanisms of conditioning have something to do with such things as the learning of prejudices, for example. A white man cannot have a prejudice against Negroes without having a response to a wide class of stimuli—to a wide assortment of Negroes. It is conceivable that the white man can learn a very negative response on the basis of experience with one Negro and then, through stimulus generalization, emit the same response to a wide variety of Negroes. Thus, a conditioned response can be set off by all objects or all people included under one general concept. If we learn to make a valid generalization—that is, if one response is given to all members of a rationally defined and logically constructed class of objects or events or people—we may be creating science. But if the class of objects eliciting the response is an irrationally or emotionally defined class, we may be described as demonstrating prejudice.

Perhaps no learning at all would occur without some kind of generalizing. Although no two stimuli or stimulus situations are ever exactly alike, they must be treated as if they were exactly alike in order to elicit the same response.

Response generalization. Not only will responses occur to stimuli that are similar to the original CS, but also, when the organism is prohibited from making exactly the learned response, he then will make a similar one. For example, a dog trained to lift a certain paw at the occurrence of the CS proceeded to lift another one when the educated paw was tied down (Bekhterev, 1932). If a human subject, with his palm turned down, is conditioned to extend his forefinger at the onset of the CS, and if the CS is then presented when his palm is turned upward, the response will be to reflex the finger that was formerly extended (Wickens, 1938).

Discrimination. Another significant aspect of conditioning phenomena is a process, essentially opposite to that of stimulus generalization, wherein different conditioned responses can be made to occur to stimuli that are only slightly different from one another. If a dog is trained to withdraw a paw from an electric grid at the sound of a tone, he will learn in

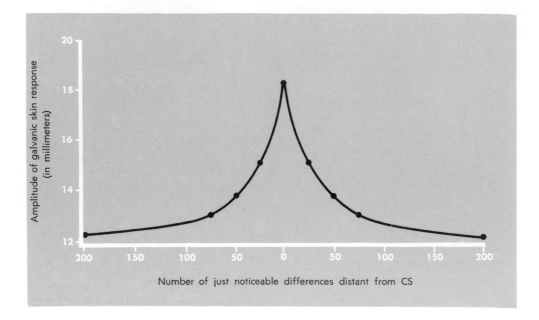

Figure 12–5. GENERALIZATION. *Once a conditioned response is established to one stimulus, it will be elicited by similar stimuli, with the strength of the response roughly proportional to the similarity of the stimuli. In the curve above, the amplitude of the conditioned GSR is related to tones differing in frequency from the original stimulus. Plotted on the baseline are just noticeable differences (jnd's) in psychologically equal degrees of difference between the original stimulus and the test stimulus. (Hovland, 1937; reproduced by permission of the* Journal of General Psychology.*)*

time that he needn't bother to move his paw at the sound of a tone very slightly different in pitch—provided the one tone is consistently reinforced while the other is not. We say that he has learned a discrimination.

Interim Stock-Taking

Classical conditioning is a comparatively simple form of learning and one readily amenable to intensive and thoroughgoing experimental examination. We know for sure that changes in behavior, more or less permanent changes, are produced through the pairing of conditioned stimuli with unconditioned stim-

uli. We know a great deal about the ways in which conditioning occurs and about the related phenomena of extinction, spontaneous recovery, discrimination, stimulus generalization, and higher-order conditioning. Do we have the basis yet for the formulation of laws of learning? Have we yet come to grips, through the experimental investigation of conditioning, with the core phenomena of learning? We possess a fairly impressive array of facts now about learning. But what can we say about *all* of learning? Very little. What can we say about the learning of conscience, for example? Or of personality traits? Or of intricate verbal and intellectual skills? Not much. But the exploration goes on. Let us follow it further.

INSTRUMENTAL CONDITIONING

Instrumental Conditioning and Classical Conditioning

Another distinguishable form of simple learning, perhaps a bit more complex than classical conditioning, is that form of learning described as instrumental conditioning, or operant conditioning. Where classical conditioning involves a change in the stimulus that evokes a response, instrumental conditioning involves a selection, from many responses, of the one that habitually will be given in a stimulus situation. As instrumental learning progresses, there is an increase in the frequency with which the reinforced response occurs in the presence of the stimulus.

The typical laboratory method of establishing instrumental conditioning is one in which we place a rat in a gadget that is rigged so that when the animal presses a bar he receives a pellet of food. When the rat first enters the box, completely uneducated about its workings, he will give a variety of responses that are normal for a rat in a gadget. He will sniff around, stand up to explore his environment, scratch and groom himself; he will manipulate almost anything manipulable. Sooner or later, essentially by accident, he can be counted on to hit the bar. He receives a pellet of food. This windfall does not make much of an impression on him at first; but eventually, if the rewards continue, he comes to press the bar with great vigor and regularity. The conditioned response—the pressing of the bar—becomes instrumental to his receiving a reward. The bar-pressing response becomes established as a new but predictable aspect of his behavior. He has learned. And in this process of learning, one response out of his whole repertoire of responses becomes gradually established, while the nonrewarding responses tend to fall by the wayside.

The instrumental conditioned response differs in significant ways from the classical conditioned response. In classical conditioning, the animal receives his reinforcing food whatever he does in the learning situation. His behavior has nothing to do with whether or not he is fed. The programmed series of events occurs without alteration. Sooner or later the CS will elicit the response that formerly occurred automatically to the UCS. In instrumental conditioning, by contrast, the behavior of the animal in the learning situation has everything to do with his receiving the reinforcing reward. His behavior is *instrumental* for reward. He gets nothing until he *emits* the proper response.

Classical conditioning requires the association of two stimuli, with one of them gradually

acquiring a significance it did not possess before. Instrumental conditioning, by contrast, involves the selection from among a repertoire of responses.

Instrumental conditioning takes place frequently in everyday life. If we wish, for example, to train a dog to speak or to roll over or to sit up, we follow the strategy of eliciting his natural array of responses in the learning situation and rewarding, when it occurs, the response we wish to stamp in. In training our children, we employ the same strategy, often without knowing it. The 3-year-old who, full of life, verve, and optimism, bounces into his parents' bedroom at 6 A.M. on Sunday morning can be counted on to emit a variety of behaviors, quite a few of which are not particularly rewarding either to him or to his parents. If his parents can arrange the proper rewards and are sufficiently clever not to allow disapproved behaviors to become rewarding, the child will eventually learn approved Sunday-morning behavior. He may even learn not only to amuse himself until the hour his parents regard as civilized, but also eventually to serve coffee and shirred eggs in bed. If bouncing and scrounging on the bed are rewarded, even once in awhile, the road to familial room service will be appreciably longer.

Laboratory Equipment for Instrumental Conditioning

Instrumental conditioning has proved particularly adapted to laboratory analysis. There are a number of devices widely used in research on this kind of learning. Historically, the first of such was E. L. Thorndike's (1898) *puzzle box*, which he used shortly before the turn of the century in some of the earliest systematic studies of animal learning. The puzzle box was a cage from which an animal (Thorndike used cats) could escape by turning a knob or pulling a string. Thorndike was interested primarily in the time it took his cats under various conditions to learn to escape from the box.

Another frequently used device is a *straight alley*, with a starting box at one end and a food box, or food holes, at the other. In such an apparatus the animal, after he is released from the starting box, may be required to traverse a runway and to discriminate between and then push aside one of two doors at the reward end of the runway. The experimenter, in addition to counting the number of trials it takes an animal to learn a given task, can measure the time it takes the animal to start and the time it takes him to traverse the whole runway or any part of it.

In recent years a device known as the Skinner box, after B. F. Skinner, its designer, has been widely used in laboratory studies. The Skinner box, fully equipped, is an automatic device for experimental work on animal learning. The animal, as we described earlier, is put in a box containing a bar to press, a string to pull, a button to peck, or some other object which, if appropriately dealt with, automatically supplies the animal with a measured bit of food. With such a device, particularly if it is rigged with timers and counters, the experimenter can place his animal in the box and leave him there to build up learning data while the experimenter goes off to teach his class or to write up last week's research.

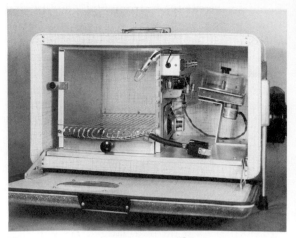

Figure 12–7. A SKINNER BOX. *The experimental rat is placed in the chamber at the left, where he can be stimulated in a variety of ways. His responses (pushing a lever, not shown), as well as the scheduling of stimuli and of rewards, can be automatically recorded.*

Figure 12–6. THORNDIKE PUZZLE BOX. *Early work on what is now called instrumental or operant conditioning was carried on by E. L. Thorndike through the use of puzzle boxes. The cat or other animal had to learn the instrumental response of pushing a lever in order to effect its desired escape from the box.*

One can see how the significant variables in learning can be controlled and measured when such devices as puzzle boxes and Skinner boxes are used. It is possible to record and control precisely such variables as the amount of food deprivation and the age or the previous experience of the animal before it is placed in the learning situation. Once the animal is in the box, almost every significant aspect of its behavior can be recorded exactly—the timing of its first and each subsequent pressing of the reward-giving bar, the frequency with which the bar is pressed during any given time, and so on. The properties of the learned response in which psychologists are interested include its *frequency,* or *response rate,* under known conditions of reward and its *resistance to extinction* when the reward is no longer administered. These properties, among others, are used as measures of the strength of the response.

Kinds of Instrumental Conditioning

There are four kinds of instrumental conditioning, all similar in that the learned response is instrumental in getting the organism biologically ahead. The simplest kind is called **primary reward conditioning.** The learned response is instrumental in obtaining a biologically significant reward, such as a pellet of food or a drink of water. In **escape conditioning** the organism learns a response that is instrumental in getting him out of some place he prefers not to be. **Avoidance conditioning** is the kind of learning in which a response to a cue is instrumental in avoiding a painful experience. A rat on a grid, for example, may avoid a shock if he quickly pushes a lever when a light signal goes on. **Secondary reward conditioning** is that in which there is instrumental behavior to get at a stimulus which has no biological utility itself but which has in the past been associated with a biologically significant stimulus. For example, chimpanzees will learn to press a lever to obtain poker chips, which they insert in a slot to secure grapes. Later they will work to accumulate poker chips even when they are not interested in grapes (Wolfe, 1936).

Basic Phenomena
of Instrumental Conditioning

Acquisition. As with classical conditioning, instrumental conditioning most often occurs gradually. On some occasions one-trial conditioning occurs, but most typically the learned response becomes only gradually fixed.

Extinction. Again as in classical conditioning, the learned instrumental response will generally tend to disappear if there is no reinforcement. There are some exceptions to this general principle, but it is relatively predictable that unrewarded conditioned responses, whether classical or instrumental, will tend to weaken or disappear.

Spontaneous recovery. The strange phenomenon of spontaneous recovery occurs for instrumental as well as for classical conditioning. Left unused and unrewarded, the response will probably reappear, at least for awhile, when the animal is placed again in the learning situation.

Generalization. As in classical conditioning, generalization appears again in instrumental conditioning. In one study (Grice and Saltz,

1950), for example, rats were trained to run down a maze and, at the end, to push open a small door located in the center of a white circle on a black background. During the training period, the white circle was of one specified size. After the rats had thoroughly learned this chore, the reward was removed so that extinction would occur. For the extinction runs, the size of the circle was changed. If the changed circle was very close in size to the original one, the reasoning went, the rats should extinguish slowly. If the circle was very different from the one for which the rats trained, the extinction should be relatively rapid. The number of responses before complete extinction, then, could be used as a measure of generalization. The results showed clearly the phenomenon of generalization (see Fig. 12–8). The animals responded to stimuli that were similar to but not the same as the stimulus on which they were trained. Furthermore, the tendency to respond was greater for stimuli that were most similar to the original. This phenomenon is known as the *generalization gradient,* and though the specific form and nature of the gradient may vary from experiment to experiment, it can be accepted as an established general phenomenon of all conditioning, whether classical or instrumental.

As in classical conditioning, the concept of generalization is most frequently used to apply only to stimulus generalization, but response generalization does occur in instrumental learning. If the learned instrumental response is blocked, an equivalent response may occur. If an animal for some reason cannot press a lever with a paw, he may use his nose or he may turn around and sit on it.

Discrimination. Again we find the phenomenon of discrimination in instrumental conditioning. It can be seen most clearly in an experiment whereby we train the animal to press a bar or to make any other desired response only when he gets a certain signal. We can see his increasing tendency to respond discriminately. He will, after training, not respond to signals that differ from the correct or rewarded one.

Discrimination is intimately involved in the

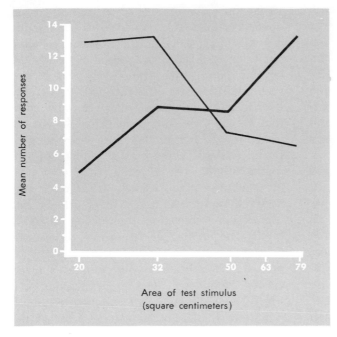

Figure 12–8. GENERALIZATION IN INSTRUMENTAL CONDITIONING. *The curves here present the results of one experiment in which rats were first trained to run down an alley and to obtain food by pushing open a small door. One group of rats was trained to run to a stimulus of 20 square centimeters; another group, to a stimulus of 79 square centimeters. The two groups were then tested, without reinforcement, on stimuli of different sizes. The lighter line above shows the number of responses during extinction of rats who trained on a 20-square-centimeter stimulus. As the stimulus is made larger, the number of responses decreases. The heavier curve shows similar results for rats trained on the 79-square-centimeter stimulus. As the stimulus becomes more like the original stimulus, the number of responses increases. Such curves depict what is known as the generalization gradient. (Grice and Saltz, 1950; reproduced by permission of the American Psychological Association.)*

process known as *shaping,* in which an animal's behavior is "shaped" by the experimenter through the use of the *principle of successive approximations.* If we are training a pigeon to peck a disk that opens a door that yields a grain of corn, we start by opening the door

ourselves, so that the pigeon can get in and eat from the food dish. The pigeon soon learns to eat from the dish and he builds up a favorable response to the door, particularly if it is opened. After this straightforward learning has occurred, then the trainer opens the door only when the pigeon is near the disk. When the bird learns that being near the disk is connected with the reward, the trainer can then raise the academic standards so that the pigeon must be within obvious pecking distance of the disk if he is to be fed. Next, the door is opened only if the bird actually pecks the disk. The pigeon thus becomes more discriminating or more refined in the behavioral response he makes.

Reinforcement

As in classical conditioning, reinforcement is a cardinally significant concept in understanding instrumental conditioning. In all conditioning, reinforced responses tend to be retained while unreinforced responses—though they may spontaneously recover, and though they may never be lost altogether—tend not to occur. That is the simple and core fact of reinforcement. The phenomena of reinforcement, however, are by no means simple.

An experiment on "superstitions" in pigeons

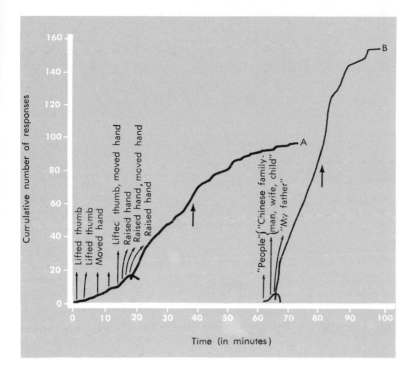

Figure 12–9. REINFORCEMENT OF VERBAL
RESPONSES. *In an experiment on reinforcement,
subjects were reinforced during an interview
every time they mentioned a member of their
own family. When the subject "scored a point"
by mentioning his family, the experimenter
raised his hand to signify the scoring. The
subjects were not aware of the rules of the
game, but the frequency with which they
mentioned members of their own families
increased significantly over a period of time.
The two curves above present the performance
of two individual subjects. (Verplanck, 1956;
reproduced by permission of the American
Psychological Association.)*

(Skinner, 1948) gives an unusual example of
the stamping-in effect of reinforcement. Skinner put his pigeons in a box and arranged his
machinery so that the food-giving door would
open every once in awhile no matter what the
pigeons were doing. In time the pigeons
learned a variety of "superstitions." One of
them would learn to bow to each side of the
box in order to get the door to open. Another
might learn to circle the box to the left. The
adventitiously given reinforcement would

eventually stamp in one ritual or superstition
for one pigeon and a different pattern of behavior for another. Perhaps there is an analogy
here to the human being who has learned that
walking under ladders brings on misadven-
ture or that stepping on every crack in a sidewalk is good luck. Someone at some time must
have encountered just the right reinforcement
to start such a superstition. After it has been
started, and passed down to us, we then may
keep it alive by selective remembering of
those reinforcing experiences that support the
superstition.

The functioning of reinforcement can be
seen in the informal experiment conducted by
a group of psychology students who decided
that on alternate days they would (a) laugh at
anything even remotely funny in the instructor's lecture and (b) not crack a smile whatever the instructor did. These experimenters—
or conspirators—reported that until the instructor caught on to the game there was great day-
to-day variation in the amount of humor or
attempted humor in the lectures. On days
when humor was reinforced, there were many
attempts to produce it. On the days when the
best jokes evoked stony silence, lectures soon

became grimly serious. Similar effects of reinforcement on verbal behavior have been produced less dramatically and more quantifiably, in laboratory investigation (Verplanck, 1956).

Conditions of reinforcement. To be precise in talking about reinforcement, we need to define it precisely—something we have not yet done. *A reinforcement is any event that will maintain or increase the strength of a response.* Such a definition is very much in line with our earlier discussions of reinforcement except that now we come face to face with the important concept of *strength of response,* which we mentioned earlier but did not deal with in detail.

The strength of a response is measured (or inferred, for strength is a construct) by several indicators: (a) *probability of occurrence* —a strong response is one that is very likely to occur every time the stimulus is presented; (b) *number of occurrences during a stated period of time*—the rat who presses Skinner's bar ten times a minute is demonstrating a stronger response than one who presses it only five times a minute; (c) *magnitude* of the response; (d) *latency* or reaction time of the response; and (e) its *resistance to extinction.*

Number of reinforcements. The strength of a response increases with the number of reinforcements of that response. In most instances of learning, a new response becomes gradually established. A number of experiments (Graham and Gagné, 1940) have shown that animals respond more quickly as the number of reinforced occurrences of a response increases. Other experiments have demonstrated that the magnitude of the response, up to a limit, increases with the number of reinforced trials (Hovland, 1937).

Amount of reinforcement. The amount of reinforcement as well as the number of reinforcements may affect the strength of the response. Rats will develop stronger responses in a Skinner box if they are rewarded by pellets containing higher concentrations of sugar (Harlow and Meyer, 1952). Such results, however, though very dependable, may not clearly

demonstrate that the larger or more desirable reward increases *learning* so much as it increases something else. These results may be demonstrating only that animals *perform* better for large rewards than they do for little ones. Performance and learning are not the same. The experimental literature, particularly that dealing with more complex learning tasks, suggests that animals' behavior *changes* no more rapidly for large rewards than for small, but that once behavior has changed, once learning has happened, behavior will be more vigorous or more dependable if larger rewards are involved. Such findings raise some key theoretical issues about the alleged necessity of reinforcement in learning. If larger rewards do not improve the rate of behavior change—learning—it may be that we have overestimated all along the role of reward in learning. It may be that the organism *performs* for the reward but that we need to separate mere performance from true learning. If obvious external reward is not necessary for learning, then our theory of learning must take on a form quite different from the way of thinking that ties learning to the biological simplicities of external reward and punishment.

Time of reinforcement. Generally speaking, the smaller the time between the response and the reinforcement, the more effective is the reinforcement in building the strength of the response. We know from everyday experience that the child will not learn to fear the radiator if it does not feel the burn until three hours after it has touched the hot iron. Nor will the dog learn not to puddle on the carpet if he is not punished for it until after father comes home. This seems to make immediate sense. But how can animals learn a response that is not rewarded for twenty minutes, and how can children learn a behavior today that will not be rewarded until tomorrow, or until they reach Heaven? To deal with such phenomena we must call on the concept of *secondary reinforcement* (which is another way of describing the phenomena of second-order conditioning, dealt with briefly in connection with classical conditioning), or *secondary reward conditioning,* described earlier.

The role of secondary reinforcement can be

seen clearly in an early experiment by Wolfe (1934). He had his rats confront a T-shaped maze with identical goal boxes at either end of the arm of the T. One goal box contained food, the other nothing. Just in front of each goal box was a door that the experimenter could raise, letting the rat through at any time he chose. Thus, the end of the maze became a retention chamber, in which the rat could be contained for varying lengths of time. It turned out that the rat could be held for as much as twenty minutes in the retention chamber and still learn to go to the end of the maze containing food. How can this be? We need not say to ourselves that the rat has an "idea" that the food is behind this particular door and hence will wait for it to open. We can rely instead on the more parsimonious notion of *secondary reinforcement*. Because the particular sights and smells of the end of the maze had always been there immediately before the food was given, the cues here became secondarily reinforcing—they became rewarding by association—and hence could sustain the rat during the waiting period. Apparently, these secondary reinforcers lose their potency after about twenty minutes unless they themselves are reinforced, for rats cannot "wait" more than twenty minutes for reinforcement and still learn.

The student can at least begin to see how secondary reinforcement and secondary reinforcers can operate in the learning of behavior for which the rewards are long delayed or, more intricately, are both delayed in time and symbolic in nature. One begins to see, for example, why children's behavior can be controlled by the words "Mother wants you to." In the course of the child's experiencing of the basic satisfactions of life, the mother is almost always there when food or warmth or dryness or fondling occurs. Mother becomes, by our theoretical model, a very powerful *secondary reinforcer*. Though not many mothers will be happy to conceive of themselves in such terms, they still may be able to accept this plausible way of accounting for much of the learning the child does later on. It gradually comes about that the presence of mother, the approval of mother, the symbolic representation of mother, or even the sound of the word itself takes on value as reinforcement. The presence of mother can make almost any associated stimulus a good thing. The approval of mother works mightily in selecting out those instrumental behaviors judged necessary for civilized existence. The word "mother" commercially associated with a loaf of bread helps, so advertisers think, in selling the bread.

Again we find in secondary reinforcement, and in higher-order conditioning, general principles that seem to have direct relevance for understanding the complex learned changes in behavior.

Partial reinforcement. In experiments on learning, the simplest and most usual procedure is to reinforce every correct response. Learning occurs most rapidly that way. But in the exploration of all facets of reinforcement, experimenters have tried out various *reinforcement schedules* in order to observe their effects on learning and on the occurrence of learned responses. This work has focused primarily on *partial reinforcement* as it affects resistance to extinction (see Fig. 12–10).

We know that any response that is no longer reinforced will tend to drop out. We also can observe in daily life that not all responses that seem very persistent are rewarded every time they appear. The chronic golfer does not make a satisfactory shot every time. In fact, he may be as often punished by a trek into the woods as he is rewarded by a shot to the green. But he keeps playing. The chronic gambler does not win on every hand. The burned child bumps cold radiators without losing his acquired fear, and the trained dog gets rewarded only occasionally when he sits up and speaks. But fears and habits persist—often in the face of vigorous attempts to remove them.

Laboratory work on partial reinforcement may use any one of many schedules. There may be *fixed-interval* or *periodic* reinforcement, whereby the animal is rewarded regularly every two or five or ten minutes after a response. There may be *fixed-ratio* reinforcement, whereby the reward comes after a certain number of responses. Or there can be *variable-ratio* reinforcement, with the reward coming one time, for example, after five re-

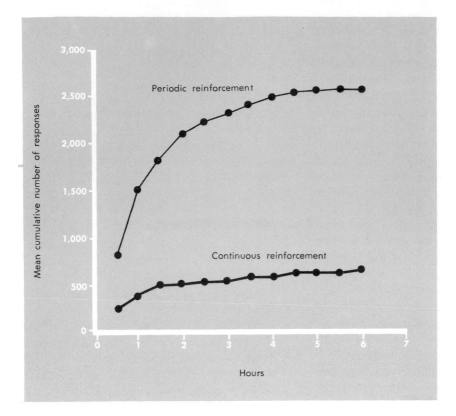

Figure 12–10. EFFECTS OF PARTIAL AND CONTINUOUS REINFORCEMENT. *The curves show the effects of partial reinforcement on resistance to extinction. The top curve shows the number of responses given after reinforcement was stopped, when the original 200 reinforcements were given on a variable-interval schedule. The bottom curve shows the number of responses during the extinction period when the animal was previously reinforced for 200 times, being rewarded each time he made a correct response. (Jenkins, McFann, and Clayton, 1950; reproduced by permission of the American Psychological Association.)*

sponses, next after ten responses, next after twenty, next after two, and so on.

Most of the extensive work on partial reinforcement has been done on responses already learned. Typically, the experimental animal or human subject will be trained by regular reinforcement to a measured degree of response strength and then observed when placed on a schedule of partial reinforcement.

Generally speaking, we know that the partially reinforced response has a tremendous resistance to extinction—and that this resistance goes up as the frequency of the customary reinforcement goes down. If we use the most effective schedule of reinforcement in training a rat to press a bar, the rat might well spend the rest of his life forlornly pushing the bar even when the experimenter has long since stopped reinforcement altogether and has moved to another university. Such laboratory phenomena throw some light on the lasting nature of natural habits—habits having a great resistance to extinction even when there is no visible reward whatsoever.

SUMMARY: SIMPLE LEARNING

Through the not so simple experimental study of simple learning, some tentative general principles of learning begin to come clear. Through classical conditioning, the organism can be conditioned to give a new response to any stimulus it can register. Through instrumental conditioning, it can learn to respond to a given stimulus with any behavior of which it is capable. These two general principles open the way for almost infinite change in behavior as the motivated organism contends with its environment.

The principle of *reinforcement* enables us to understand the dynamics of behavior change. This principle tells us about ways in which the consequences of present behavior, somehow recorded by the organism, influence future behavior. The reinforced conditioned stimulus comes to evoke a response formerly reserved for a biologically adequate stimulus. In instrumental conditioning, the reinforced response gains strength and in time is selected from among many possible responses.

There is *higher-order conditioning* and *secondary reinforcement*, taking the organism, as it continues to contend with its environment, further and further away from the biological simplicities of reward and punishment with which life and learning begin. There is *extinction*. Responses that are no longer reinforced tend to disappear from the organism's repertoire of behaviors. But these unreinforced responses, whether based on classical or instrumental conditioning, do *spontaneously recover*. And if a response is stamped into the organism by certain schedules of *partial reinforcement*, it may persist for very long periods without any reinforcement whatsoever. (We may wish to apply this analysis to other learning phenomena; and we may observe that probably some habits, attitudes, and values, once established, may last a lifetime in the absence of obvious and functional rewards.) The organism, with practice, learns *discrimination*, so that its responses fit more precisely the functionally adequate stimuli. It learns to respond the same way to whole classes of stimuli—i.e., there is *generalization*.

Our review of laboratory investigations of learning has led us to see certain fundamental processes involved in the change of behavior with experience. We set out upon this review with the stated aspiration of finding in the whole array of scientific research those simple principles that might have general relevance for all human learning. How well have we suc-

ceeded? There clearly are some general principles, firmly rooted in experimental evidence and obviously important for understanding the sort of everyday learning with which we are familiar. These principles must, of course, be regarded as tentative, for research continues, thinking is persistent, and tomorrow may bring new facts and new interpretations that will supplement or revise or perhaps forever replace the present ideas. But there *are* principles, principles that have a potential relevance for any learning anywhere. The principles of reinforcement, of generalization, and of discrimination, for example, apply with great generality to learning.

Can the principles of simple learning be applied in such a way as to account for all human learning? Very probably not. When we become curious about the learning of personality traits, or the learning of a conscience, or about the learning of all the intricacies of our native tongue, our principles of learning do not enable us either to describe or to account for all we see or all that we wonder about.

LEARNING TO SOLVE PROBLEMS

So far, in our concern with learning, we have concentrated on simple learning and the principles of conditioning. We have at least entertained the notion that, as knowledge advances, we may be able to account for the more complex forms of human learning in terms of the basic principles of conditioning.

Such an approach to learning has a bias about it. Many psychologists—and perhaps many students also—doubt that the more complex, symbolic, insightful, and creative learning that seems to characterize the human organism can ever be accounted for in terms of the repetitious association of stimulus with stimulus or stimulus with response or response with reinforcement.

There is an automaticity about conditioning phenomena that some psychologists feel does not apply to all learning. Principles that require of the organism no understanding or insight certainly will be stretched to account for the phenomena of insightful learning or problem solving. Perhaps we need less emphasis on habit and more emphasis on perception, knowledge, symbolic processes, and meaning.

THE DOUBLE-ALTERNATION PROBLEM

The nature of one theoretical dispute can be understood, perhaps, if we look for a moment at the behavior of animals faced with a *double-alternation* problem. A raccoon, placed in a maze-like apparatus, can learn to enter the box, take two turns to the right, and then two turns to the left in order to get his reward. Taking the two turns to the right does not seem so difficult. The more or less automatic processes of learning can account for that. But when he comes around to *the same point* at which he has turned right on two previous occasions, he now turns *left*. The sensory cues from the external environment are the same as they were for the two right turns. What cues tell the animal now to turn left? Can we deal with the problem in terms of simple associational principles, or do we assume that the raccoon is guided by some manner of cognitive *concept* of twoness? Is there meaning or perception or symbolization here that is different in nature from the automatic connections between stimuli and response? What does the animal "carry in his head" to help him handle his learning problem?

INSIGHTFUL LEARNING

The earliest and best-known experiments on what is called insightful learning were done by Wolfgang Köhler during World War I (Köhler, 1925). In observing chimpanzees, Köhler saw not Pavlov's painfully gradual learning of relationships but quick perceptions of relationships that allowed an animal to solve a problem—to acquire a new response—in one burst of insight.

A chimp in a cage, for example, sees and wants a piece of fruit outside his abode. He has a stick with which he tries to rake in the food. But the stick is too short. Outside the cage, closer than the fruit, is a longer stick. The chimp "thinks." Then quite suddenly he takes the short stick, goes to the side of the cage, rakes in the longer stick, takes the longer stick, and rakes in the fruit.

Pavlov, when he read Köhler's reports, immediately discounted the notion of sudden insight and was inclined to doubt that Köhler had observed carefully all the prior conditioning behind the chimp's final solution of the problem. Köhler sticks to the concept of insight—a sudden perception of a relationship.

LEARNING TO LEARN

There is evidence that insight, though it may represent a sudden breakthrough of perception or of intellect, occurs more readily under some circumstances than under others. It is not a bolt of lightning out of the psychological blue. Past experience with similar problems clearly increases the likelihood that crucial relationships will be seen and will be applied to solutions (Birch, 1945).

Of relevance for this matter is research demonstrating the occurrence of what is known as *learning* sets in monkeys. In certain circumstances monkeys appear to catch on to principles involved in a series of learning tasks; they do not continue to tackle each new problem in the same way they faced the old ones. Instead, with what appears to be insight, they *learn to learn*.

In one experiment, for example (Harlow, 1949), monkeys were given a long series of tasks involving discrimination. The first task might be to find whether a peanut is hidden under a triangle or under a square. In awhile, if the reward is always under the square, the monkey will learn to look under the square wherever it is placed with respect to the triangle. It may take him a number of trials to learn to play this particular game. When he has learned, the experimenter changes the task. Now the peanut may be under the triangle. This switch at first confuses the monkey, but he soon begins to learn the new rule. After handling a long series of such tasks, the monkey becomes very significantly quicker at making discriminations in a new situation. He

Figure 12–11. LEARNING TO LEARN. *Here a monkey is learning discrimination of form. When given a long series of discrimination tasks, in which he must learn which form hides the peanut, the animal develops a learning set. Later problems are solved much more quickly than early ones.*

seems to catch on to the general rules. After extended education in this kind of discrimination, he demonstrates what looks like insight in the face of new problems (see Fig. 12–12).

Research on problem solving in normal and feebleminded children has shown that the speed with which children learn to learn or establish learning sets varies with the level of intelligence (Stevenson and Swartz, 1958). Normal children rapidly "catch on" to the "rules of the game," while children extremely low in intelligence show little or no learning set although they are confronted with a long series of related problems.

Many college students, when asked what is at first a strange question about whether they "have yet learned to go to college," will give answers suggesting that they have learned to learn. They report that they can now learn more per hour of study, that they now know what to study, that they understand professors better. It may be that extended practice at college learning does bring about a learning of general principles or of general rules of the

game, so that seniors study more "insightfully" and more effectively than do freshmen.

We shall concern ourselves more intimately with problem solving in Chapter 14, where we deal with research on higher mental processes.

THEORIES OF LEARNING

In the foregoing pages we have examined many of the key concepts and basic relation-

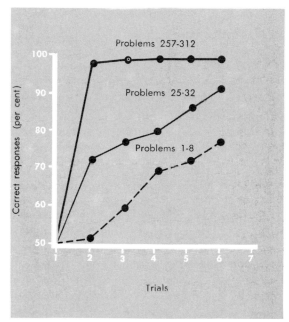

Figure 12–12. LEARNING SETS. *Here, monkeys are given a series of discrimination problems to solve. The task involves the discovery of which of two solid forms conceals a reward. At the beginning of the series the monkeys are naturally correct on the first trial 50 per cent of the time. By the sixth trial, they make the correct response 78 per cent of the time. By the time they come to the 257th problem, however, they are 98 per cent correct on the second trial. They seem to have learned that if the reward isn't under the first form they try, then it will be under the second, wherever it appears. The monkeys have learned to learn. (Harlow; 1949; reproduced by permission of the American Psychological Association.)*

ships in the field of learning. There has been no attempt to fit all these concepts and phenomena into one unified and unifying theory nor even to trace out the theoretical issues upon which psychologists vigorously and productively disagree ("productively," in that disagreements lead to research and to the advancement of knowledge). But not even an introductory look at learning can be complete without considering matters of learning theory.

The purpose of a scientific theory is to make available a system of abstract concepts and relationships that will guide the scientist in making predictions about the matters that interest him. Theoretical systems, in psychology and elsewhere, take many forms and make use in a variety of ways of the already available linguistic systems of logic, algebra, and calculus. The aim of the theoretical scientist is to state, in as precise a form as he can, the most inclusive possible generalizations of the facts and relationships he has observed. A theory is good if it facilitates prediction; or, to say it somewhat less baldly, a theory is good (though not necessarily "true") if it leads to the formulation of hypotheses that are both testable and worth the testing.

In the last thirty years, several notable attempts have been made to formulate general theories of learning. Two of these theories, S-R theories and cognitive theories, will concern us briefly here.

STIMULUS-RESPONSE (S-R) THEORIES

The oldest and still most widely espoused of the S-R theories is one associated with the name of Clark Hull (1943), who initiated it in the 1930s and whose students (including John Dollard, Ernest Hilgard, Neal Miller, Hobart Mowrer, and Kenneth Spence) have tested, extended, and revised and promulgated it. Another kind of S-R theory is connected with the name of W. K. Estes, its formulator and foremost promulgator.

Both of these theoretical formulations are S-R theories in that they both start with the assumption that stimuli and responses become linked through experience, and that learning, the unobserved factor—the **construct**—is responsible for the link. Both theories (as contrasted with cognitive theory) are also relatively atomistic or **molecular;** that is, they deal initially with single and simple S-R associations as "elements" in the construction of more complex chains and patterns of responses. Further, they are both *peripheral* theories; that is, they emphasize visible behavioral responses and also use other peripheral responses as integrators of learning—one response triggers others, each of which can be a stimulus for still others. There is no recourse to central or brain processes to serve as integrators of simple into complex responses.

It will not be appropriate here to try to present even an outline of the Estes theory, a highly mathematical formulation. There may be profit, however, in looking at some of the key features of the Hullian theoretical systems.

Hull's theory (1943, 1952), a highly formal system, relies heavily on deductive logic and mathematics. Hull was able to study the results of relatively simple laboratory experiments and to use those results inductively in developing a number of basic postulates. These postulates led to hypotheses, which led to experiments, which are still leading to the reexamination and re-formation of the original theory (Spence, 1956). We cannot here trace the intricacies of Hull's system, but it will be well for us to know about the two theoretical constructs that lie at the center of his thinking: *habit strength* ($_sH_r$, or learning) and *drive* (D, or **motivation**). According to Hull, H, habit strength, interacts multiplicatively with D, drive, to produce the "output potential" for responding. In simpler but still relatively adequate words, performance is a joint function of (1) how well an act is learned and (2) how highly motivated is the performer. Habit strength, Hull said, increases systematically with the number of rewarded responses. Relatedly, drive increases with, among other things, the duration of deprivation, so that the rat deprived of food for twenty hours, other things being equal, will perform more rapidly than one deprived for three hours. Perhaps the student can see how the refining, defining, testing, and reshaping of such general theoretical statements can lead to the advancement of knowledge.

COGNITIVE THEORIES OF LEARNING

Cognitive learning theorists (and the leading name among such theorists is that of E. C. Tolman) accept the same experimentally established facts that are available to the S-R theorists but choose a different interpretation. That, of course, is what a theory is—an interpretation. The cognitive theorists maintain that it is more fruitful to interpret the data of learning in terms of "central" rather than "peripheral" processes. Where the S-R theorists believe that a rat continues to run toward an unseen goal box because there are chained muscular responses and stimuli keeping him going, the cognitive theorist interprets in terms of central or brain processes such as *expectancies* or memories (Tolman, 1932) or purposive behavior (Hilgard, 1956). And where the S-R theorist thinks that what is learned are habits, the cognitive theorist says that "cognitive structures" are learned. Whereas all theorists of all kinds might agree that the simple concept of habit is adequate to account for the smooth-flowing performance of a well-learned act, the cognitive theorists are inclined to think that some learned form of "cognitive structure" is necessary to account for the use of alternative chains or patterns of responses, such as shown by an animal who runs a maze in alternative ways to reach the food box. The cognitive theorists are also inclined to account for problem solving in terms of cognitive restructuring or sudden insight rather than in terms of repetitive trial-and-error processes.

Theoretical controversy continues warmly, both among S-R theorists and between S-R theorists and their more cognitively oriented colleagues. And, of course, knowledge advances.

LEARNING PRINCIPLES AND PERSONALITY DEVELOPMENT

There have been a number of attempts to apply the basic principles of learning to the complex problems of personality development and social interaction. The earliest of these, in a brilliantly unsuccessful way, attempted to apply the principles of classical conditioning to phenomena of emotional and intellectual life and to problems of personality and personal conflict (Guthrie, 1938). Other writers, with great intelligence and perhaps some success, have applied principles of learning to problems of neurosis and psychotherapy (Shoben, 1949; Dollard and Miller, 1950; Mowrer, 1950; Wolpe, 1958). Others have used the basic principles of learning to account for the process whereby the child becomes a socialized member of his culture (Seward, 1954; Bandura and Walters, 1963), and whereby he develops his own personality (Rotter, 1954). We cannot here analyze or even summarize these attempts to relate scientifically sound laws of learning to the highly involved processes of living. It is accurate to report, however, that the attempts have scored enough intellectual success to lend a zest to the continuing search for a truly comprehensive science of learning.

An excellent example of the application of conditioning principles to matters of personality development is to be found in McClelland's (1951) analysis of the formation, in early childhood, of the generalized and persistent tendencies (conditions of the organism) which we have called psychological motives. McClelland's question is this: How is it that a child learns a general and a lasting motive rather than specific habits which may easily be extinguished? How does he come by an *achievement motive* rather than a small array of specific habits of doing well here and doing well there? Or how does he learn a general acquisitiveness when he might have learned instead a number of separate and specific responses toward specific objects? In Mc-

Clelland's view, the major differences between conditioned responses or habits, on one hand, and motives, on the other, are that motives are (a) *more general* and (b) *less amenable to extinction.* With respect to the achievement motive, for example, there are many and varied responses that are given to many and varied situations. All the responses have to do with achievement. There is the generality. Also there is the persistence, an apparent exemption from extinction. When the responses are not rewarded, they may grow stronger instead of fading away. Or when they are punished, they still show a strong resistance to extinction. We need to understand, then, McClelland holds, the aspects of childhood learning—for psychological motives seem to be learned early—that make for generality or *generalization* and for *resistance to extinction.*

To account for these two aspects of learning in childhood, McClelland cites, among others, the following factors and processes.[3]

1. *Lack of symbolic control.* Language helps the individual make precise discriminations about complex aspects of its environment. The child has no such control, no such capacity to make fine distinctions. Learning that occurs early in life, then, is characterized by great generalization. The child who finds one kind of response rewarding in one situation is very prone to make roughly similar responses in similar situations. He is thus on the way to the learning of general rather than specific responses.

2. *Generalized threats and promises.* Parental reinforcements, both positive and negative, are frequently very vague. If the child misbehaves, "something bad" will happen to him, or God will disapprove, or he will not get to Heaven. When the punishment is this vague, the child can do wrong and still not know whether he is punished. Prohibitions based on vague reinforcements, once they are learned, are difficult to unlearn. There is not a way to test reality so that extinction can occur if punishment does not happen. The same thing holds for vague rewards. The child cannot learn whether his behavior is really rewarded. Again, he cannot test reality enough for extinction to occur.

[3] From *Personality* by David C. McClelland, pp. 451–457. Adapted by permission of Holt, Rinehart and Winston, Inc. Copyright, 1951.

3. *Irregularity of learning conditions.* Here the principle of partial reinforcement is used to account for the persistence of responses. The child responds. He responds in a variety of ways in a variety of situations because of the lack of ability to discriminate. Reinforcement is irregular. Parents are inconsistent and vigilance is limited. The responses—the array of responses of the same general variety—do not extinguish.

4. *Inability to reproduce conditions of learning.* If we wish to extinguish a response in a cat, we put him in the original training situation and let him respond without reward. Soon the response will extinguish. The same sort of thing cannot be done with children because reinforcements or punishments can rarely be accomplished in the original learning situation. The child learns a response at a time when he is unable to distinguish clearly between himself and his environment. He doesn't know whether the rewards and pains associated with responses come from within or from outside. When later we try to recapture the original cues and conditions of learning in order to untrain a response, we find it impossible. Unlearning is very difficult, and the early responses persist.

To account in detail for the learning of a psychological motive or a trait of personality would require more than these four considerations. But perhaps it is possible to see in this kind of analysis the potential applicability of conditioning principles to problems of personality and motivation.

SUMMARY

1. As it is caught up in the psychological process, the organism responds to the consequences of its own behavior; it thereby learns.

2. The capacity to learn is a capacity of organisms and is not shared by inanimate objects: simple organisms, although they are creatures of instinct, learn; learning plays an increasingly significant role in survival as we ascend the evolutionary scale.

3. Learning is pervasive, especially in the life of human organisms; if human beings were

incapable of extensive learning, civilized life as we know it could not exist.

4. Learning is defined as a relatively permanent change in behavior brought about as the result of experience.

5. In studying learning, the psychologist has focused on simple learning in the hope that through experimental analysis he can discover simple and general laws of learning.

6. Classical conditioning, one form of simple learning, has been subjected to extensive laboratory study that has revealed facts concerning (a) conditions of acquisition, (b) extinction, (c) spontaneous recovery, (d) higher-order conditioning, (e) generalization, and (f) discrimination.

7. If a conditioned response is not reinforced by the associated presentation of the unconditioned stimulus, extinction will occur.

8. After a response has been extinguished through nonreinforcement, it characteristically shows spontaneous recovery.

9. The phenomena of conditioning include the making of a CR to stimuli that have been associated only with other CS's; this is higher-order conditioning.

10. The phenomena of conditioning also include the making of a CR to stimuli similar to, but not the same as, the original UCS; this is generalization. Under proper circumstances the organism also learns to make a CR to stimuli that are very similar to, but still different from, the original UCS; this is discrimination.

11. Classical conditioning involves the association of an unconditioned and a conditioned stimulus in such a way that the conditioned stimulus comes to elicit the unconditioned response. Instrumental conditioning, another form of simple learning, involves the selection, by reinforcement, of an emitted response from an array of emitted responses.

12. Through the use of specially designed laboratory equipment, various kinds of instrumental conditioning have been studied; these include primary reward conditioning, escape, avoidance, and secondary reward conditioning. The strength of a CR may be measured in terms of one or more criteria.

13. As in classical conditioning, the basic phenomena of simple learning apply to instrumental conditioning; there is gradual acquisition, extinction, spontaneous recovery, discrimination, and generalization.

14. In instrumental conditioning the conditions of reinforcement have been extensively studied; the strength of the CR varies with the number of reinforcements, the time of reinforcement, and the schedule of reinforcement.

15. Resistance to extinction for an instrumental CR is greater if there is partial reinforcement, with the strength of response greatest for a variable-ratio rather than a fixed-interval or a fixed-ratio schedule of reinforcement.

16. The principles of conditioning may not be able to account for problem-solving behavior or insightful learning; the learning of such a problem as the double-alternation problem may involve the formation of concepts; the solution of problems involving the use of tools seems to occur on the basis of sudden insight. Research on learning sets, however, shows that insight, or the application of principles to a learning task, may be based on protracted past experience.

17. Learning theorists try to devise systems of abstract concepts and relationships that will guide the making of predictions about learning. There are contrasting stimulus-response theories and cognitive theories of learning.

18. Stimulus-response theories deal initially with relatively simple and peripheral S-R associations and then state postulates or hypotheses concerning general and systematic relationships in learning phenomena. Cognitive theorists are less peripheral, less elementistic, and more inclined to interpret facts in terms of such cognitive and central constructs as expectancies or memories.

19. The principles of conditioning can be applied to the learning of motives, to the learning of persisting and general tendencies to respond. The young child appears to learn lasting motives rather than temporary habits because of generalization, the lack of symbolic sharpening of discrimination, the inability to reproduce the original learning situation, and the irregularity of both positive and negative reinforcement.

RESEARCH REPORT

VARIETIES OF CLASSICAL CONDITIONING [*]

I. The salt appetite of dogs was determined by allowing them to choose among several dishes of milk containing different amounts of salt solution. A rapid decrease in salt appetite was observed when 300–500 cc of 3–5 per cent salt solution was introduced into the stomach. Later, stomach distension produced by a rubber balloon into which 300–500 cc of water were poured preceded the introduction of the salt solution. These stomach distensions became conditioned reducers of salt appetite. The operational conditions in this experiment may be conceived in traditional learning terminology. Introduction of the salt solution represents the unconditioned stimulus (UCS); internal stimulation produced by stomach distension is the CS; and choice of the milk dish containing salt is the CR (Kassil, 1959).

II. Salivation of a 13-year-old boy was conditioned to verbal stimuli. Reinforcement (the UCS) followed the verbal stimulus "ten" but nonreinforcement followed the word "eight" until the boy had formed a clear pattern of CR's to "ten" and UCR's to the word "eight." Presumably, the UCS was a presentation of a very weak acid solution (i.e., lemon juice), which has the effect of producing salivation. When dogs are used in the traditional Pavlovian manner, the UCS is usually meat powder blown into the mouth of the hungry animal.

[*] The following research studies, all performed by Russian psychologists, are reported in English by G. Razran in: The observable unconscious and the inferable conscious in current Soviet psychophysiology: Interoceptive conditioning, semantic conditioning, and the orienting reflex, *Psychol. Rev.*, 1961, **68**, 81–147.

The boy was then presented with nineteen arithmetical problems in place of the previous conditioned stimuli, "eight" and "ten." Eleven of the problems had the answer "ten," and eight had the answer "eight." Results indicate that "answer ten" problems produced a median of seventeen drops of saliva in 30 seconds, whereas none of the "answer eight" problems produced more than three drops. This was true even when the "answer ten" problems had the number eight as a part of them (Shvarts, 1960).

III. It has been demonstrated that human subjects form blood coagulation following the administration of an electric shock. Using the sound

SAMPLE CONDITIONING RECORD

Arithmetical Operations Tested	No. drops of Saliva
5 + 5	16
83 − 73	15
56 ÷ 7	2
80 ÷ 8	17
99 − 91	3
88 ÷ 11	3
8 + 2	19
4 × 2	2

of a metronome as the CS and the shock as the UCS, Markosyan (1958) found that stable blood-coagulation responses could be formed. Furthermore, these CR's transferred from the sound of the ticking metronome to the word "metronome" and to phonetically related words. Razran reports that this experiment is important in disclosing evidence on the presence of semantic factors in such a function as blood coagulation, a function which Western hematologists, unlike the Russian ones, tend not to regard as within neural control. Further research will need to be carried out to decide the issue.

IV. A vasoconstrictive CR was formed in seven Russian university students using the word *skripka* (violin) as the CS. The vasoconstrictive response is an autonomic response to electric shock. Vasoconstriction means nothing more than the constriction of the blood vessels, producing heightened blood pressure. Three varieties of words were tested for CR transfer after stable CR's had developed to the CS word *skripka*. One variety was words related phonetically to the original CS; these were *skrepka* (paperclip), *strizhka* (hair cutting, shearing), and *skrytnost'* (reticence, secrecy). The other two transfer categories were semantically related words and totally unrelated words. Examples of the former variety are *smichok* (violin bow), *gitara* (guitar), *struna* (string), *arfa* (harp), *orkestr* (orchestra). Words in the unrelated category were, for example, *stakan* (glass), *lenta* (ribbon), and *voda* (water).

The results show that CR's transferred to all the semantically related words and to none of the unrelated words. One word in the phonetically related category transferred. It was *skrepka* (paperclip). (Vinogradova and Eysler, 1959.)

V. In a related study (Luria and Vinogradova, 1959), young school children were told to press a button when they heard the word *koshka* (cat),

when they pressed the button, the blood vessels in their fingers constricted. It was then determined whether the CR (vasoconstriction) would transfer to a large number of words semantically and phonetically related to the previous CS (*koshka*). Three groups of children served in this study: normal school children, feebleminded children, and extremely feebleminded children. No IQ scores are available, since the IQ is not used in Russia. Results indicated that the normal subjects transferred their CR's only to the semantically related words, the moderately feebleminded group manifested transfer to both semantically and phonetically related words, while the extremely dull group transferred only to phonetically related words.

SUGGESTED READINGS

Bandura, Albert, and R. H. Walters. *Social learning and personality development*. New York: Holt, Rinehart and Winston, 1963.

Deese, James. *The psychology of learning*. New York: McGraw-Hill, 1958.

Ferster, C. B., and B. F. Skinner. *Schedules of reinforcement*. New York: Appleton-Century-Crofts, 1957.

Hilgard, E. R. *Theories of learning*, 2nd ed. New York: Appleton-Century-Crofts, 1956 (1948).

Kimble, G. A. *Hilgard and Marquis' Conditioning and Learning*, 2nd ed. New York: Appleton-Century-Crofts, 1961.

Melton, A. W., ed. *Categories of human learning*. New York: Academic Press, 1964.

Miller, N. E., and John Dollard. *Social learning and imitation*. New Haven: Yale University Press, 1941.

Sanford, F. H., and E. J. Capaldi. *Advancing psychological science. Vol. II: Research in perception, learning, and conflict*. Belmont: Wadsworth Publishing Co., 1964.

Skinner, B. F. *Cumulative record: Enlarged edition*. New York: Appleton-Century-Crofts, 1961.

Spence, K. W. *Behavior theory and conditioning*. New Haven: Yale University Press, 1956.

OUTLINE / CHAPTER 13

I. APPROACHES TO THE INVESTIGATION OF LEARNING

II. ACQUISITION OF SKILLS

    A. Rate of Acquisition: Learning Curves
    B. Massed and Distributed Practice
    C. Learning by Wholes and by Parts
    D. Meaningfulness of Material
    E. Feedback, or Knowledge of Results
    F. Activity-Passivity

III. MOTIVATION AND LEARNING

    A. Extrinsic and Intrinsic Reinforcements
    B. Punishment and Learning

IV. TRANSFER OF TRAINING

    A. Transfer through Similarity
    B. Transfer through Techniques and Principles

V. FORGETTING

    A. Rate of Forgetting
    B. Forgetting Meaningful Material
    C. Overlearning and Forgetting
    D. Reminiscence
    E. Theories of Forgetting
        1. Interpolated Activity
        2. Retroactive Inhibition
        3. Distortion in Recall
        4. Motivated Forgetting

VI. TOWARD A TECHNOLOGY OF LEARNING

    A. Pigeons and Missiles
    B. Teaching Machines

VII. LEARNING AND THE CENTRAL NERVOUS SYSTEM

    A. Simple Learning: Conditioning
    B. Discrimination Learning
    C. Delayed-Response Learning
    D. Memory

VIII. SUMMARY

IX. RESEARCH REPORT

THE MANAGEMENT OF LEARNING*

APPROACHES TO THE INVESTIGATION OF LEARNING

In the last chapter we examined the psychologists' effort to create a systematic scientific understanding of some of the basic principles of learning. That effort has followed a strategy of science that characterizes many fields of research endeavor. The strategy has been a *reductionistic* one; the research workers have not started out by studying the full-blown learning of a college student in a trigonometry class or of a professional baseball pitcher perfecting his slider. The attempt has been to reduce learning to its simplest form

and to find the simplest and most basic underlying principles. The strategy has also been a rigorously *experimental* one. Phenomena are not casually observed or introspectively mulled over. They are experimentally researched through the use of sophisticated designs and rigorous controls. Also the strategy may be described as a highly *operational one,* in that constructs are operationally defined in terms of observed data, and theory is played close to the chest of experimental results. The goal of this enterprise is the description of the basic processes and the formulation of the basic principles that may underlie all learning of all organisms. The hope is that out of the true simplicities may be built a comprehensive understanding of the complexities.

The psychologist who devotes himself to the sort of research that has concerned us is in many ways the embodiment of the "pure scientist." Motivated by sheer curiosity, he learns

---

* John Capaldi assisted materially with the preparation of the first edition of this chapter. Hugh Poyner served as a prime consultant and resource person for the present version.

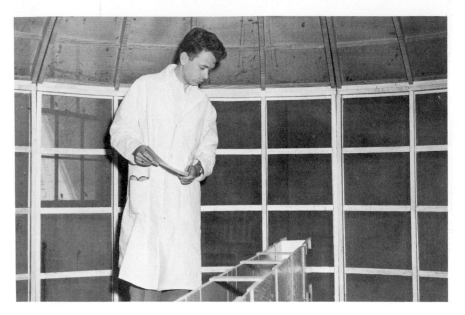

Figure 13–1. PSYCHOLOGIST AT WORK. *Most research psychologists who study learning do not concern themselves with problems of immediately practical utility; they study basic phenomena. Here a psychologist observes a rat in a maze. The room is domed in order to control cues from outside the maze.*

the highly technical language and methods of his field, he gets hunches, states hypotheses, runs experiments, learns something new about learning, and writes a scientific paper to add a little to the accumulating body of knowledge. He has no immediate concern for the practical problems of the parent, the teacher, the coach, or the trainer of animals. He is building a basic body of knowledge. As he discovers new facts and relationships, his efforts may turn out to have unexpectedly useful implications. Knowledge does get applied. But the "pure researcher" is not directly concerned with utility. He is building systematic knowledge. If he needs to justify his existence, he can point readily backward to the practical applications of basic research that already have been made, and he can point forward to the immense potential consequences for human affairs of a truly systematic science of learning.

There is, however, a research literature dealing with more immediately practical aspects of learning. This literature has a direct

relevance for those who wish to learn more and forget less. The research with which we will deal in this chapter, though just as scientific in method as any other, tends to be less reductionistic and less explicitly concerned with the building of the ultimate theory. It tends to look at learning from the outside, from a molar point of view, and to ask questions about the conditions under which skills are acquired, about the role of motivation and emotion in the acquiring of skills, about the relation of past experience to present learning, and about the nature and conditions of remembering and forgetting. These are the questions we will confront in the present chapter.

ACQUISITION OF SKILLS

A skill is an organized pattern of responses. The rat who learns a maze has acquired a skill, an organized sequence of responses. The pianist, the draftsman, the golfer, the typist— all have acquired skills or groups of skills. Over time, separate responses become connected into sequences and patterns. When we examine a skill from the outside, studying its more molar aspects, we naturally encounter questions about the rate at which skills are acquired and about the conditions affecting both the rate of learning and the ultimate quality of the skilled performance.

RATE OF ACQUISITION: LEARNING CURVES

Although we may learn the solution to an intellectual problem in a flash of understanding, skills, by contrast, require time. If we have a way to measure the amount of skill, then we can describe precisely the amount of skill gained per unit of practice. We can plot a **learning curve.** The acquisition of many different skills proceeds in similar ways. Many skills, in other words, have similar life histories.

If we are learning to type, we will find during the first few hours of practice that our improvements are relatively rapid. After a few practice sessions we increase, perhaps, from 100 correct strokes of the keys per half hour to 600 correct strokes during the same interval. This rapid rate of improvement will continue through 15 or 20 hours of practice. Then the rate of improvement tends to slow down. We may practice for many hours without scoring any appreciable gain in skill. Our learning curve has reached a **plateau.** If we do not give up practicing in the face of this failure to gain, we will eventually start improving again. New integrations or new organizations of responses occur, and we are off to new heights. If we continue to practice for a long time, however, we may reach a *physiological limit.* We will reach a level of skill that is as great as our particular nervous system can aspire to. **Nerve impulses** cannot travel at more than a certain speed, and neural connections cannot be made any more rapidly. (Figure 13–2 presents two forms of the "life history of a skill.")

Actually, we may doubt that any of us, in ordinary life, ever reaches a physiological limit. The regularity with which performance records are broken in competitive swimming and track, for example, suggests that last year's physiological limit is no more than last year's record. But when we deal with individual performance, there still is utility in the concept of a limit: your physiological limit may be higher than mine, but both the hare and

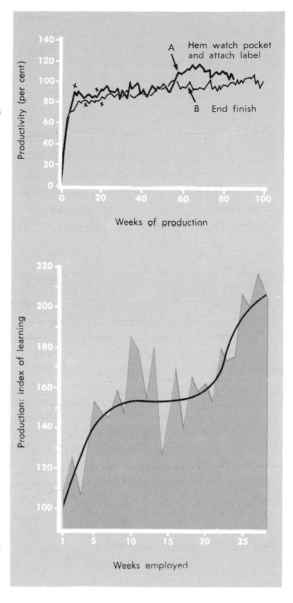

Figure 13–2. LEARNING CURVES. *The life history of a skill can be plotted on a learning curve. At top are learning curves for two jobs in a clothing factory. At bottom is a curve for new taxicab drivers. Each of these curves shows a period of rapid initial improvement, a plateau, and a further rise in skill. (*Top: Taylor and Smith, 1956; by permission of the American Psychological Association. Bottom: *From* Ghiselli and Brown, Personnel and Industrial Psychology, *Copyright 1955; by permission of McGraw-Hill Book Co.)*

the tortoise will, at least theoretically, face their built-in limitations.

The type of learning curve we have just described is encountered when we plot the life history of skills. Other kinds of curves do frequently appear, however, when we deal with other learning tasks. The *plateau* phenomenon does not appear in all learning of skills. If an individual maintains the same level of interest in the task, if he employs the same learning procedure throughout, and if he does not "bite off more than he can chew" in new assignments or new material, then he may avoid the plateau entirely. He often does. If he continues long enough at the practice of the skill, however, he may still reach his limit. And his ultimate limit is set by his physiology.

Any learning curve will show ups and downs from day to day. Such variations do not mean that the individual unlearns today what he learned yesterday or that tomorrow's higher score is necessarily due to more learning. Learning curves plot *performance*. Performance of a skill may vary with mood or health or motivation or other things. Learning is relatively *lasting change with experience over time.* We do not see learning; it is a construct that we infer from performance, and we need to exercise care in making the inference. All data that we regard as learning data are actually data on performance. But as we watch performance change over time, we can often, if we have controls for other factors affecting performance, accurately attribute the performance of learning to actual and lasting changes that are due to experience.

MASSED AND DISTRIBUTED PRACTICE

If you were going to take up piano playing, would it be better to practice hour after hour and day after day no matter what, or to distribute your efforts over a number of practice periods? Or, to ask the question more realistically, if you have ten hours to devote to practice, would it be better to practice for ten straight hours (**massed practice**) or to distribute practice so that you work an hour a day for ten days (**distributed practice**)?

The weight of the evidence favors distrib-

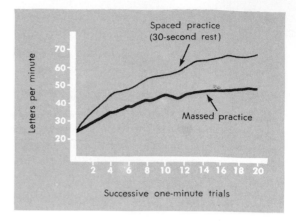

Figure 13–3. MASSED AND DISTRIBUTED PRACTICE *In the learning of simple motor skills (such as the printing of capital letters), spaced learning characteristically is more efficient than massed. Such results are not obtained, however, for very complex tasks or for tasks involving problem solving and inductive thinking.*

uted practice as the more effective for the learning of many sensorimotor and verbal materials—especially in the early stages of practice. (See Fig. 13–3 for a presentation of typical results.) Tasks involving inductive thinking or problem solving, however, seem to be handled better if the learner sticks to the job for relatively long periods, particularly during the first stages (Cook, 1934; Ericksen, 1942). Other evidence indicates that the advantage of distributed practice diminishes as the task becomes more complex (Riley, 1952). In learning lists of words, the advantage of distributed practice holds up for lists that are similar to one another but does not exist for lists where similarity is low from one to another (Underwood and Goad, 1951). These and related results show that the matter of massed versus distributed practice is by no means a simple one.

One investigator (Underwood, 1961) is inclined to the view that the differences between massed and distributed practice can be accounted for in terms of the **extinction** or nonextinction of *error tendencies*. When a subject is learning a series of **paired associates**—a list on which, say, the first stimulus word is "horse" and the first correct response word (the experimenter decides what is correct) is "moon"—any subject will bring with him to the experimental situation a variety of error tendencies that are set off by the stimulating "horse." He may have tendencies, of varying strengths, to say "buggy" or "barn" or "cow" or "power" or "Pferd" or any number of other things, depending on his own past experience with and present inclinations toward "horse." All of these potential responses are "wrong," by the experimenter's definition. All are sources of error and must be weakened or extinguished if the "correct" response is to be given consistently. In massed practice of lists of paired associates, these error tendencies may be only temporarily suppressed, tending to bounce back later to produce errors. In spaced learning, this line of reasoning goes, the error tendencies, being now relatively weaker than correct responses, are more likely to be extinguished. A research study bearing on this matter is reported at the end of the present chapter.

Until there is greater understanding of the problem, there can be no entirely safe and simple recommendation that distributed practice always be used or, even at a reduced level of generality, always used under certain specifiable conditions.

The most effective scheduling of practice and rest varies from task to task (Cook and Hilgard, 1949), but, generally speaking, an arrangement of relatively frequent and relatively short rest periods is likely to work best. The practice periods should not be so brief, however, that they do not allow for the practice of the whole series of responses involved in the pattern being learned.

LEARNING BY WHOLES AND BY PARTS

If the task is a long or involved one, such as learning a speech or learning to run an elaborate finger maze, the learner may choose either to divide the task into parts and tackle it a piece at a time or to go at the whole thing all at once. Which is better? This has turned out to be a remarkably involved question. Early researches tended to favor the "whole" method, and textbooks of a generation ago heartily recommended that learners practice the whole poem or whole speech all the way through. Now things are not so clear. Two authorities (McGeoch and Irion, 1952), after surveying and sorting the evidence on this matter, point out a number of factors bearing on the relative effectiveness of the part approach and the whole approach.

1. The effectiveness of the whole method varies with intelligence of the learner; the more intelligent can probably use it with greater profit.
2. The whole method becomes increasingly effective if practice is distributed rather than massed.
3. Practice with the whole method increases its effectiveness.
4. The whole method tends to work better than the part method for meaningful material.

The practical implication here seems to be that if you are bright and are learning meaningful material, then you will do well to employ the whole method, particularly if you will go on practicing its use—or, to say it differently, you should use units as large as you can handle.

MEANINGFULNESS OF MATERIAL

Meaningful material can be learned more readily than meaningless material. This statement, solidly backed by research findings, will probably surprise no one. There may be some profitable puzzling involved, however, if we explore for the meaning of "meaningfulness." There appears to be an element of sheer familiarity involved in those verbal materials we learn most readily. If we are given ten minutes to learn a list of three-letter words and equal time to learn a list of nonsense syllables, we will learn a good many more words than nonsense syllables. If the nonsense syllables have high association value, tending to "remind" us of familiar words, we will learn them more quickly than if they have no resemblance to anything familiar to us (McGeoch, 1930). Table 13–1 presents some data bearing on this point.

Table 13–1. LEARNING AND MEANINGFULNESS OF MATERIAL

MATERIAL LEARNED	NO. OUT OF TEN UNITS RECALLED
Three-letter words	9.11
100% syllables	7.35
53% syllables	6.41
0% syllables	5.09

When familiar three-letter words are learned, success in recall is high. When syllables having high association value (meaningfulness) are learned, recall is less successful but still more successful than for syllables of less association value or meaningfulness. The per cent figures above refer to the association value of the three groups of syllables used in the study. (Adapted from McGeoch, 1930.)

However, there is something other than familiarity or association value involved in meaningfulness. There is a factor of patterning or organization also. Given an assignment of learning 200 words of prose and 200 words of poetry, the subjects in one experiment took an average of 24 minutes to learn the prose and only 10 minutes to master the poetry (Lyon, 1914). The fact that the poetry is more patterned or organized seems to have made the difference.

In learning or in managing the learning of others, we will do well to work toward meaningfulness. If we can succeed in rendering the proper responses more available or more familiar, if we can tie them into a plan or a pattern of our—or the learner's—own devising, then learning will be facilitated.

FEEDBACK, OR KNOWLEDGE OF RESULTS

We would never achieve accuracy in archery if every arrow "fell to earth, I knew not where." There must be knowledge of results, or **feedback,** if the organism is to adjust its behavior on the basis of experience. The animal in the **Skinner box** would not learn to push the lever or press the button unless the feedback, in the form of reinforcement, were there.

The role of feedback in learning is clearly illustrated by an experiment (Greenspoon and Foreman, 1956) in which subjects were blindfolded, asked to draw a 3-inch line, and, after different intervals, given information on how they were doing. The subjects who were given immediate feedback showed the best learning. The longer the feedback was delayed, the poorer the learning. The subjects who were not told at all how they were doing showed very little improvement. The data in Figure 13–4, though based on a different experiment, illustrate the same point. One possible advantage of teaching machines and printed schedules for programmed instruction (developments that will concern us a little later) is the fact that they can be designed to give immediate feedback. The learner need not wait forever or even for a few minutes to find out whether his response was a good one.

ACTIVITY-PASSIVITY

In a classic study (Gates, 1917) it was demonstrated that students learned biographical material best when they spent only 20 per cent of their time reading and 80 per cent in reciting the material. For rote memory of nonsense syllables, the best distribution of time was also 20 per cent reading and 80 per cent in recitation. (See Fig. 13–5.) There is a good deal of evidence that vocalization assists learning, even when the tasks are not primarily verbal in nature. For example, children learn visual-discrimination tasks more rapidly if they "talk to themselves" (Weir and Stevenson, 1959), and adults learn a task more readily if they are required to tell, ahead of time, what their plan is (Ray, 1957). Such results, though they have a bearing on the matter of activity in learning, are probably more relevant for the general understanding of higher mental processes; we shall return to them in Chapter 14.

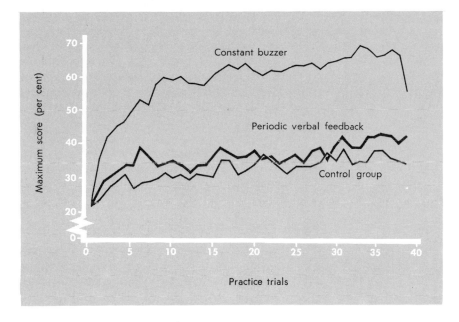

Figure 13–4. KNOWLEDGE OF RESULTS. *In this experiment subjects were given various kinds of "feedback," or knowledge of results, as they practiced on a gunnery trainer. The top curve represents the group given the sound of a buzzer whenever the subjects were on target. The middle curve represents the performance of the group that was given periodic verbal feedback. The control group (the bottom curve) was given no cues about the quality of performance. (Goldstein and Rittenhouse, 1954; by permission of the American Psychological Association.)*

With respect to the learner's active involvement in learning, a good general rule seems to be to *do something*—do something to make the material actively yours. Many experts who write on how to study recommend to college students a number of procedures that seem designed to help avoid passivity while cultivating an active involvement in the learning process. One author (Voeks, 1957), for example, gives among others the following items of advice to college students:

1. While studying, avoid too much relaxation of muscles.

2. Review immediately after class.
3. When reading, take an active, attentive stance toward the author.
4. Read with a set to find answers to your questions.
5. Think, find implications, find the principles and relationships; don't just memorize.
6. Practice making intelligent questions.
7. When appropriate, take copious lecture notes, especially on those statements you think are ridiculous or wrong.
8. Jot down questions that occur during lectures.
9. Be active, responsive, and attentive during class.
10. In studying for tests, ask yourself questions and try to answer them.
11. While reviewing, recite the details that should be remembered.[1]

All of these intelligent suggestions bear on the general matter of the learner's active involvement in the learning process. Learning is not a passive matter, and education does not occur by osmosis.

---

[1] From Virginia Voeks, *On Becoming an Educated Person: An Orientation to College*. Philadelphia: W. B. Saunders Co., 1957. By permission of the publisher.

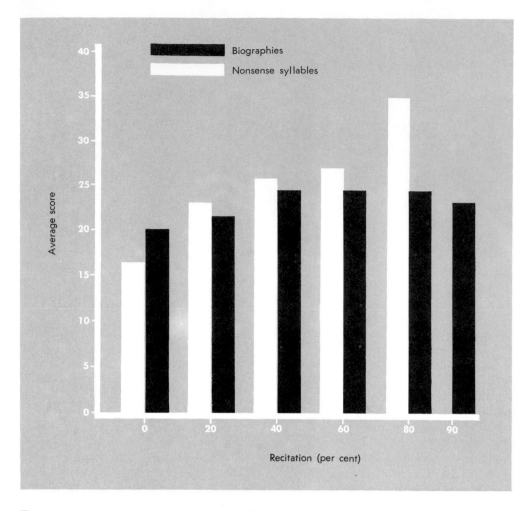

Figure 13–5. RECITATION AND LEARNING. *For learning nonsense syllables, efficiency is greatest when up to 80 per cent of available time is spent in recitation. Results for biographical material are similar but not so dramatic. (Gates, 1917.)*

MOTIVATION AND LEARNING

The principle of **reinforcement** has it that rewarded responses are stamped in while unrewarded responses either are not learned or tend to fade when reinforcement is withdrawn. We have seen that the principle does not operate with pristine simplicity in all learning situations. But the principle holds for a wide variety of situations and has a major bearing on the effectiveness of learning in life situations. Parents and teachers, who invest themselves in the learning of others, are in many respects managers of reinforcement. And their skill as managers has a good deal of consequence for their children and students.

EXTRINSIC AND INTRINSIC REINFORCEMENTS

In most of the laboratory research on learning and in a great many everyday attempts to control the learning of others, rewards for learning are *extrinsic*, are more or less artificially related to the learning to be achieved. If you learn to write well, you win a ribbon or a championship. If you wash the car, you earn a dollar. If you do exceptionally well in your classes, you earn a Phi Beta Kappa key. Ribbons, championships, dollars, and gold keys have no natural relationship to the learning itself. They are extrinsic rewards. *Intrinsic* rewards, by comparison, are those more closely connected with the activity itself. There is intrinsic reward in learning to write so as to enjoy corresponding with a friend or for the simple pleasure of putting words together in meaningful patterns. There is intrinsic reward in doing well in college for the pleasure of using one's head at its best or for the satisfaction of knowing more about the world.

In many of our efforts to manage the learning of others, we may fall back too easily on extrinsic rewards without exploring the subtle intrinsic factors involved in learning. The growing literature on the exploratory or curiosity **motive** in animals suggests, at least, that human learners at all levels may have more sheer curiosity than we give them credit for (see pp. 229–230). Perhaps more often than we think, learning is its own reward. One researcher has reported informally that a chimp who was supposed to learn a task in order to get a banana kept working at his assignment long after he had had his fill of bananas. He would go through his paces, successfully get the reward, then throw it away and be ready to start all over again.

In a less anecdotal manner, one theorist (Hunt, 1960) makes the case that intrinsic re-facilitate intrinsic pleasure in learning rather than to proffer pellets of grades or pats on the head or to hold out the distant but highly extrinsic hope of better jobs after graduation.

Whatever else may be said, there does seem to be some precariousness in the use of extrinsic **motivation** and some profit in the use of intrinsic rewards. Extrinsic rewards produce results. But let us think for a moment about what learning we may be arranging when we give our daughter a new dress for making an A or our son a car for passing all his classes. We may be removing any emphasis on the inherent importance of education or on the simple enjoyment of learning. We appear to indicate that the official results are the things that count. By making the official grade the important thing, we may even seem to be issuing a subtle invitation to get those grades by any available means, regardless of standards of honesty. Further, we may be reinforcing a youngster's tendency to live by parental standards (enforced in childhood by material considerations) rather than by his own. If a learner does engage in undesirable behavior while meeting the criteria for extrinsic reward, that undesirable behavior is, of course, reinforced.

An important aspect of prizes and honors is that they are things for people to do without. The one-in-a-hundred winner is pleased, and

Figure 13–6. INTRINSIC MOTIVATION. (*Courtesy, Austin [Tex.] American Statesman. Tm. Reg. U.S. Pat. Off.—All rights reserved. Copr. 1960 by United Feature Syndicate, Inc.*)

wards, such as those involved in play or in the pleasurable recognition of the almost familiar, may be more important in human affairs than has yet been recognized. Another psychologist (N. Sanford, 1962) has suggested that college teachers would do well to search for ways to

perhaps the reward has stamped in for him some desirable behaviors. But the 99 losers have all failed, and their mighty effort goes unreinforced. The effect on these also-rans should be considered in the use of extrinsic incentives. Also, of course, prizes and plaques and honors characteristically come too late, and too seldom, to be most effective in influencing performance.

Intrinsic rewards have few of the disadvantages of extrinsic rewards. The learner who wants a skill in order to use it, who seeks knowledge in order to apply it, or who learns for the pleasure of learning does not often need extrinsic reinforcement to keep effort high and learning effective. Skillful teachers, though they may need to use extrinsic rewards, work to increase the intrinsic motivations of the learner; or they work to convert the extrinsic to the intrinsic. They help the student see the need to learn, to grasp the meaningfulness of the material, to accept the learning task as his own task and not one imposed upon him. Many teachers report great pleasure at seeing college students, as they mature and feel their own intellectual power, begin to take responsibility for their own education—changing from reluctant participants in a cram-and-emetic process to become active users of the resources of the institution. These are the people who use the instructor, the textbook, and the library to accomplish their own educational goals. Many instructors, authors, and librarians like it that way.

PUNISHMENT AND LEARNING

Firmly rooted in our folklore is the idea that punishment is both necessary and proper in teaching children—or wayward adults—to behave in approved ways. The infrequently punished child is often regarded as spoiled, and parents who punish only sparingly may be viewed askance by any neighbor who has accepted the notion that sparing the rod spoils the child.

Punishment is administered in order to stop the occurrence of undesirable responses. We slap the dog to stop his jumping on the sofa. We spank the child to stop his paddling in his spinach or his slugging of his sister. We jail the criminal to teach him not to steal. How effective are these efforts to teach?

Punishment, the planned injection of noxious events, clearly does alter behavior. But the research literature shows punishment to have a number of effects that come as surprises to the average manager of other peoples' learning.

Edward L. Thorndike was the first psychologist to become disillusioned with what everybody knew about punishment and to take the problem to the laboratory (Thorndike, 1932a). On the basis of his research, he reached the surprising conclusion that *punishment really does not weaken the punished response*. In one of his studies, Thorndike (1932b) asked his subjects, who knew no Spanish, to guess which of five English words was the equivalent of a given Spanish word. If the subject chose the correct word, he was rewarded with a "right." If he erred, he was punished with a "wrong." As the experiment went on, it was possible to see whether the rewarding "right" increased correct behavior and the punishing "wrong" decreased erroneous behavior. Thorndike reported that although the rewarded responses, as expected, became stamped in, occurring with greater frequency as learning progressed, the punishment *did not decrease the frequency of wrong behavior*. More recent evidence on the same point is presented in Figure 13–7.

One of the strange aspects of punishment is that it may, under some circumstances, appear to be rewarding. One recent experiment (Lohr, 1959) showed that rats, given a choice of approaching food through either of two pathways, learned to prefer the route which required that they cross an electrified grill. (See Fig. 13–8.) In the circumstances of the experiment, the electrical shock came to be clearly associated with the attainment of food. So the shock, the punishment, seems to have become rewarding, since it reinforced the responses the animals made just before the reduction of hunger. We can say, if we empathize with the rats, that they chose the electrified side of the runway in order to be shocked in order to make the shocked jump in order to have their hunger reduced.

A similar state of affairs may arise in a human situation if the parent habitually follows punishment with a lavish display of guilt-produced affection. The punishment can appear to be rewarding in that it represents the road to attention and love. Children sometimes do seek out punishment; it represents for some the only attention they get. One psychologist tells the story of a neighbor's child who, when sent off to bed unsuccessfully several times, was finally threatened with dire consequences. The child reappeared at the top

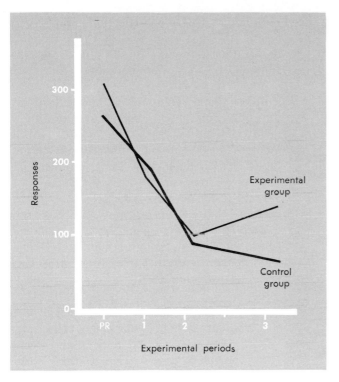

Figure 13–7. THE EFFECTS OF PUNISHMENT.
*Animals were trained to make operant
responses and were then left in the apparatus
for an hour. Animals in one group (the
experimental group) were shocked every time
they pressed the formerly rewarding lever
during minutes 5 to 20 while in the box. The
other group simply received no reinforcement.
The "punished" group did not extinguish as
rapidly as the "ignored" group. PR = periodic
rate of extinction. (Estes, 1944; by permission
of the American Psychological Association.)*

of the stairs and plaintively called down,
"Daddy, when are you coming to spank me?"

There is evidence that truly traumatic
avoidance conditioning may have a lasting
suppressive effect on a response (Solomon,
Kamin, and Wynne, 1953; Solomon and
Wynne, 1954) and additional evidence that
the emotional responses produced by punishment may be very resistant to extinction (Masserman, 1943). On the basis of an extensive
review of the literature on punishment, one
writer (Church, 1963) comes to two general
conclusions: (1) The amount of response suppression is greater when the noxious stimulus (the punishment) is associated with the
response rather than with a cue or stimulus
that is, in turn, associated with the response.
(2) Response suppression is greater, the
closer in time is the noxious stimulation to the
response.

The first conclusion seems to be in line with
the common-sense wisdom that we have to
make our own mistakes in order to learn.
Carried further, this principle would have it
that we do not learn not to do something until
we do it at least once and then suffer its consequences. There may be some truth here, but
there has to be doubt about the viability of
such a principle for subjects who, through
symbolic processes, can anticipate the consequences of an act without performing it. Experimental evidence bearing directly on the
first general point is furnished by a study
(Azrin, 1959) in which attempts were made to
teach two groups of pigeons to peck while a
blue light was on but not to peck while an
orange light shone. The members of one group
were shocked *whenever they pecked* while the
orange light was on. The second group was
shocked whenever the orange light was on,
whatever they did. The first group made fewer

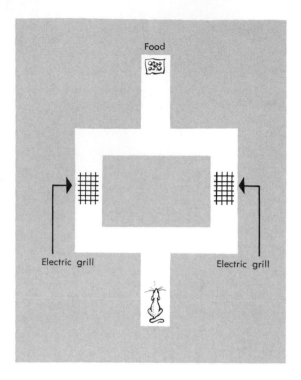

Figure 13–8. PUNISHMENT BECOMES REWARDING.
*Rats who preferred to approach food through
the right alley in this apparatus were given
a gradually increasing shock on repeated trials
in the maze. They continued to prefer the
shocking route to the food. Punishment, by
close association with reward, apparently
becomes rewarding. (From Lohr, 1959.)*

Punishment will more effectively suppress a response if it is associated with the response itself rather than with the stimulus or stimulus situation. And punishment is more effective if in time it is closely associated with the undesirable response. In addition, there is evidence that mild punishment can call attention to an incorrect response, which, without punishment, might be ignored (Stevenson, Weir, and Zigler, 1959). Such punishment-produced attention to errors can improve performance.

Punishment may also produce an emotional response that can have lasting and sometimes unpredictable consequences for behavior. Thus, punishment, though it may have a beneficial influence on behavior, may also have certain disadvantages:

1. While reward says, "Keep doing what you are doing," punishment says only, "Don't do this"; and it does not always even define precisely what "this" is, nor does it say what, on the positive side, should be done. The punished animal or child is a creature of the same motivations as before, but now he does not know what to do—except to be emotional.
2. Since a variety of responses are characteristically produced by punishment, the correct responses may be evoked and rewarded; but other responses to punishment—hatred, withdrawal, anxiety—may be the responses actually learned. The child who is punished for a failure in arithmetic may come to hate both the subject and its teacher. And he may learn ways both novel and unfortunate to express his feelings.
3. Punishment may become rewarding. When and if it does, the manager of learning can get distressingly lost.

"wrong" responses than did the second; for them the shock, the punishment, was associated directly with the response—not with the stimulus.

There is sound evidence too (Kamin, 1959) bearing on the second general point. It will not surprise many people that punishment is more effective if it is closely associated in time with the undesirable response. But some mothers still follow the policy of "just wait till Daddy comes home." And in training animals, we often punish the culprit at the time we discover the evidence, not at the more effective time at which the undesired response is made.

Punishment, then, can produce a temporary suppression of a response, during which new behavior can be learned, and traumatic punishment can have lasting effects on behavior.

Out of this analysis of punishment, we may distill some helpful hints for trainers of children and animals. First, it seems to be a sensible rule to reinforce approved responses rather than to punish disapproved ones. Second, if we do use punishment, we should combine reward and punishment whenever possible; while the punished response is in abeyance, we should arrange to have a proper response occur and be rewarded. Third, we should use punishment as informatively as possible; mild punishment will not often stir up great emotionality, and, if it is consistent and intelligent, it will point the way to right responses. Fourth, we should be hesitant to use punishment on very young children. Because they cannot discriminate, they generalize easily; they may be learning from the punishment many things the parent does not wish them to learn (McClelland, 1951). Fifth, we should associate the punishment with the undesired response itself, not with the stimuli. And sixth, we should administer the punishment now—instantly—rather than later.

TRANSFER OF TRAINING

According to the folklore of learning, the study of such subjects as Latin and algebra "trains the mind" so that the learning of other subjects will become easier. This belief, called the *theory of formal discipline*, was long ago taken to the laboratory for experimental examination (Thorndike and Woodworth, 1901). It was found faulty in many but not all respects. The learning of one relationship or of one subject or of one skill very often does permit one to learn other relationships and subjects and skills more easily and efficiently (Hebb, 1949). But **transfer of training, the influence of old learning on new, may be either favorable or unfavorable; there may be** *positive transfer* (transfer that facilitates learning) or *negative transfer* (transfer that interferes with subsequent learning).

There is no evidence to support the notion that hard exercise of the mind in learning one subject will increase the general power of a "learning faculty," so that any other subject can be mastered more readily. There *is* evidence that positive transfer will occur if there is a similarity between the two subjects and if there is a learning of *techniques* or *principles* in the first task that can be usefully applied to the second. Figure 13–9 presents data on the general phenomenon of transfer.

TRANSFER THROUGH SIMILARITY

A number of experiments have shown the role of similarity in the transfer of training. An early research (Thorndike and Ruger, 1923) tackled directly the alleged benefits of studying Latin. The researchers found that students who study Latin do indeed show an improved understanding of English, but *only of those English words having Latin roots.* There was no general improvement in use or understanding of Anglo-Saxon English.

Other studies have confirmed the principle of similarity, both for verbal and nonverbal learning. One experiment on 290 enlisted men in the Navy showed that practice on a paper-and-pencil model of an apparatus improved the learning of skills involving an actual apparatus (Gagné and Foster, 1949a). Another study (Duncan, 1953), involving the pressing of levers upon receiving light signals of various colors, showed not only a positive transfer from one task to another but also an increase of transfer with an increase of similarity between the two tasks.

In tracing down the details of this similarity matter, another experimenter worked with paired-associate learning, in which factors of similarity could be neatly controlled (Bruce, 1933). The subjects were first required to learn lists of paired words. The procedure was to flash one word—the stimulus—on the screen, then follow it soon thereafter with the word—the response word—with which it was paired. After going through the list of paired words a few times, the subject would look at the stimulus words and give the response word for each before the response word was flashed on the screen. When one list of paired associates had been learned, it was possible to examine the effect of that learning on the learning of subsequent lists. A second list could be learned more efficiently if the stimulus words were similar to the earlier ones while the responses were the same. Under these conditions the earlier learning gave positive transfer. If, however, the second series of pairs involved stimulus words identical to those in the first series but required entirely different responses, there was nega-

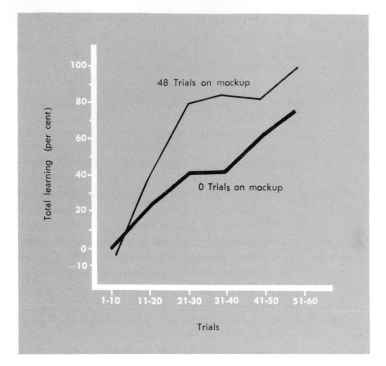

Figure 13–9. TRANSFER OF TRAINING. *In one experiment, groups of subjects were given different amounts of training on a printed mockup of a mechanical device and were then asked to learn to operate the actual device. The two curves above present a record of learning on the actual device by a group with no preliminary trials on the mockup and by a group with 48 trials on the mockup. The group with 48 trials on the "training device" learned the actual task much more efficiently. (Gagné and Foster, 1949b; adapted by permission of the American Psychological Association.)*

tive transfer. In this case, old connections interfered with the learning of new ones.

**TRANSFER THROUGH
TECHNIQUES AND PRINCIPLES**

It comes clear in the research on transfer that, in the learning of a second task, the gain from having learned a first one is often due to the carryover of a technique or principle from the first task to the second. We have seen that monkeys, given a long series of tasks, learn to

learn (Harlow, 1949). Human learners do at least as well.

The gain from transfer of techniques is illustrated by an experiment in *bilateral transfer*, transfer from practice with one hand to performance with the other. In this experiment subjects were required to practice, with one hand, the art of tossing a ball into the air and catching it in a cup. The ball was attached to the cup with a string. After practicing with one hand, the subjects performed better with the other hand than the subjects who had had no practice. The transfer seemed to be due to the subjects' getting an understanding of the best technique to employ. They learned, for example, that it was better to watch the ball than the cup and that the cup had to be held low in order best to catch the ball (Munn, 1932).

A classic experiment in transfer of principles (Judd, 1908) was carried out by having subjects shoot rifles at an underwater target. First, the target would be placed at one depth until the riflemen learned pretty well to hit it, in spite of the fact that they had to take into account the refraction of light waves by the water and the apparent distortion it produced. Then the target would be placed deeper under water. On this revised task some subjects scored no better than on the original task. There was no transfer. They went about it in a trial-and-error manner, just as they had on the original task. Other subjects, however, learned the principle of refraction of light as it enters water. For these enlightened riflemen there was transfer. Understanding the principle involved, they were able to apply earlier practice to the new situation.

The literature on transfer adds up to the not so surprising conclusion that the best way to learn a task is to practice *it* rather than ones similar to it. One learns English best by studying English. But transfer, nonetheless, does occur widely, and it is often important to facilitate its occurrence; for practice at simulated tasks is often more economical than practice at actual ones. An hour flying a simulated aircraft in a hangar is much less expensive and much less dangerous than flying a real plane. If practice on the simulated task improves performance on the real one, then there can be a real gain. For less dramatic learnings, even those we pursue for their own

inherent value, the more we can facilitate transfer through the grasping of techniques and principles, the better off we are. There is so much to learn and only a lifetime in which to learn it. The individual who learns to learn has a great advantage.

That transfer can be deliberately facilitated is demonstrated by a research in which college students were successfully taught to transfer learning from one task to another. There were three groups of students in the experiment. The control group took a group of tests involving memory for poetry, prose, Turkish-English vocabulary, history dates, orally presented consonants, and assorted facts. After three hours, with no planned activity intervening, they took the same tests. A second group, after taking the original tests, spent three hours memorizing similar materials. A third group spent three hours partly in memorizing similar materials and partly in being coached on some principles of learning—such as the use of the whole rather than the part approach, close attention to meaning, and silent recitation or self-testing. The control

Table 13–2. TRAINING FOR TRANSFER

| MATERIAL TO BE LEARNED | GROUP | AVERAGE SCORE | | PER CENT GAIN OR LOSS |
		FIRST TEST	SECOND TEST	
Facts (Substance)	Control	67.5	64.2	− 4.9
	Practice	64.0	61.0	− 4.7
	Training	64.0	72.2	+12.8
Dates	Control	7.6	9.8	+29.0
	Practice	7.2	9.9	+37.5
	Training	6.5	12.2	+87.7
Vocabulary	Control	16.2	16.1	− 0.6
(Turkish-	Practice	14.6	15.1	+ 3.4
English)	Training	13.6	21.1	+55.2

In this experiment the control group (N = 106) learned the indicated materials, took a test, did nothing until the second learning session. The practice group (N = 34) practiced learning poetry and nonsense syllables after the first test. The training group (N = 42), after the first test, was given information on some helpful principles and then given some practice. This group, coached for transfer, showed marked improvement on the second test; they had learned to learn. (Adapted from Woodrow, 1927.)

group, after three hours of doing what was officially nothing, showed no improvement on the second memory performance. The group that practiced using memory improved a bit. The coached group showed noteworthy gains, performing 30 per cent or more higher than the other two groups (Woodrow, 1927). See Table 13–2 for detailed results of this experiment.

With respect to transfer, the moral for the managers of learning is clear. *Teach for transfer*—if you want transfer. If you want the study of Latin to bear on an enriched understanding of English or French, teach for transfer. Point out the similarities, and work for the inculcation of general techniques and the grasping of general principles. If the learning of Latin or algebra or history or psychology is valuable for its own sake, then do not bother with transfer.

FORGETTING

The retention of past experience in some form is central to the very nature of learning. If there is no retention, there is no change in behavior and, by definition, no learning. Retention, however, is not always perfect. Nor is it an all-or-none matter. We have seen that conditioned responses tend to weaken if they are not reinforced. Skills fall apart if they are not used. And in the verbal and symbolic areas, we forget—sometimes less rapidly than we wish but most often more rapidly than we like. It may be that no experience, once registered in the nervous system, is ever fully eradicated. The evidence on memories that can be recaptured under hypnosis or through the direct stimulation of the brain (Penfield and Jasper, 1954) suggests that we somehow store up more of our past than we can consciously bring to light. The facts on conscious and deliberate recall, by contrast, reveal that memory is very short and highly fallible.

RATE OF FORGETTING

The rate at which we forget learned material depends on a number of factors, including the method used to measure it. For lists of nonsense syllables, with all lists learned equally well, the ability to *recall* the list, to reproduce it or recite it, falls off much more rapidly than the ability to *recognize* which syllables originally occurred on the list—indicating that there was a storage of something that could not actually be retrieved. In one experiment (Luh, 1922) subjects who learned a list of syllables were able, after an hour, to recall (retrieve) only 50 per cent of them. But they could recognize 95 per cent of them—indicating a storage of something that could not be actively retrieved (Fig. 13–10).

Whatever the method employed to measure the rate of forgetting (or the diminution of retention over time), the most rapid decrement of memory occurs during the period immediately after practice stops. Ebbinghaus (1913), the inventor of the nonsense syllable as a research device, performed a series of classic experiments in which he learned nonsense syllables well enough to recite a list once perfectly and then, after varying rest intervals, measured the time he took to relearn the list. He found he had forgotten 47 per cent of the material during the first 20 minutes, 66 per cent during the first day, and 79 per cent after 31 days. (Fig. 13–11.)

FORGETTING MEANINGFUL MATERIAL

Nonsense syllables, we have seen, are retained a relatively short time—a fact for which many subjects in learning experiments can be thankful. Generally, meaningful material tends to be retained longer. Of the various forms of meaningful material, poetry is remembered better than prose. Material learned on the basis of insight, such as the solutions of puzzles or the way to do a card trick, may be retained for a very long time (Guilford, 1952).

But that the factors and conditions involved in forgetting any kind of material are not simple matters is indicated by an analysis of two kinds of interference that can affect the recall or reproduction of previously learned material (Underwood and Postman, 1960). When subjects learn and later recite word (usually nonsense) lists, this view has it, one kind of interference is the presence of well-established

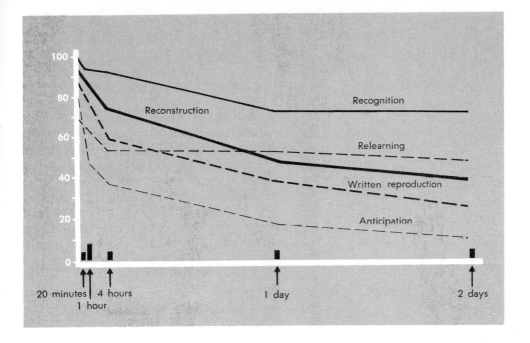

Figure 13–10. MEASURING RATE OF FORGETTING. *The graph above shows the per cent of a list of nonsense syllables retained after various intervals, with retention measured by different methods. Subjects were able correctly to recognize 80 per cent of the syllables after two days, but were able to reconstruct or recite less than 50 per cent. After the two-day interval, when subjects were given one word on the list and asked to anticipate the next one, they were able to respond correctly only about 10 per cent of the time. (Luh, 1922; reproduced by permission of the American Psychological Association.)*

letter-sequence habits, which must be overcome if a list containing novel combinations is to be learned. If we have to learn the word PTBY, for example, we could probably do better if we had gained linguistic experience with such sequences of letters; instead, because of our existing habits, we expect p to be followed by many letters other than t. What we "know," then, interferes with what we try to learn. A second kind of interference has to do with the *habitual sequences of units* in the material we are learning. When we come into a new learning situation, our linguistic habits have already become structured so that, for example, in the combination of the words "old" and "man," the sequence "old-man" is more habitual than the sequence "man-old." If we must learn the words in the latter sequence, our existing habits will interfere. Both these kinds of interferences must extinguish during the learning of new serial lists if the lists are to be reproduced properly. And even though they are extinguished so that the new material may be learned well enough to be reproduced once, the older responses will recover; and upon future attempts to reproduce the newer material, they will interfere again with correct recall or reproduction.

Such an analysis suggests that forgetting is an active rather than passive process and indicates that we must consider, if we are to understand the process of forgetting, not only the nature of the specific material to be learned—whether inherently very meaningful or not—but also the relations of that material to the nature of the habits the learner has acquired earlier.

OVERLEARNING AND FORGETTING

When Ebbinghaus learned his syllables well enough to recite a particular list once perfectly, he found that he forgot very rapidly. What would have happened had he learned a list more indelibly? Up to a certain point it

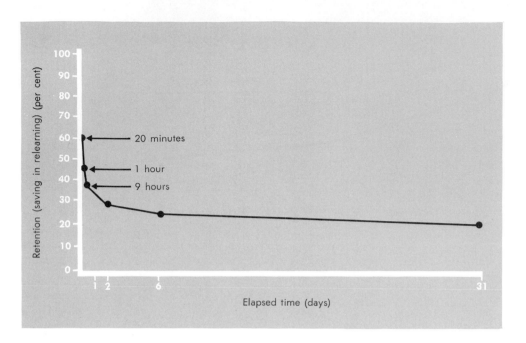

Figure 13–11. RAPIDITY OF FORGETTING. *For nonsense syllables the rate of forgetting is very rapid, particularly during the period immediately after learning. (From Estes, 1944; after Ebbinghaus, 1913.)*

seems that practice continued beyond the stage of one perfect recital might help memory. If it takes a subject four trials to learn a list so that he can repeat it once perfectly and we then make him practice for two more trials (giving him what is known as 50 per cent **overlearning**), he will retain after a day about 40 per cent of the list rather than about 25 per cent of it. If he has 100 per cent overlearning, practicing eight times rather than the four times necessary for one perfect recall, he will retain for a day about 50 per cent of the material, and so on (Kreuger, 1929).

REMINISCENCE

Although forgetting generally sets in as soon as practice stops, with a rapid fading of ability to recall, in some instances the learner can recall a *larger* amount after a period than he could recall immediately after he stopped practicing. This is the phenomenon known as *reminiscence*. It applies especially to motor learning and is most frequently found when the skill is incompletely mastered. Reminiscence is possibly related to the phenomenon of spontaneous recovery of an extinguished conditioned response, with both these strange phenomena being accounted for best, perhaps, in terms of the disappearance of the fatigue produced by practice. Reminiscence may be a factor in the superiority of distributed over massed practice in some tasks.

THEORIES OF FORGETTING

Learned material seems often to disappear from the nervous system, and developed skills disintegrate with disuse. Why? Do the neurons that record memories and patterns of movements change with time so that memory traces are lost? Or do materials and habits learned today become entwined with older habits and earlier memories, so that they cannot be disentangled from the mass and cannot now be separately recited or performed? There are some evidences bearing on these questions.

Interpolated Activity

If forgetting is an active process, involving the intermingling of new materials and habits with old, then we ought to remember better tomorrow what we learn today if, between today and tomorrow, we can *keep out* of the nervous system any materials that might interact with what we wish to remember. This kind of hypothesis has been tested by having subjects learn materials and then recall them (a) after periods of sleep and (b) after periods of normal activity. If forgetting is due to active interaction, then the sleeping subjects, having less "input" of potentially destructive materials, should remember better. They do (Jenkins and Dallenbach, 1924; Van Ormer, 1932). Subjects who learn a list of nonsense syllables recall them with appreciably greater success after periods of sleep than they do after periods of normal waking activity. One subject who slept eight hours after learning a list of nonsense syllables recalled 56 per cent of the words. The same subject, retested after eight hours of being awake, could recall only 9 per cent of the syllables (Jenkins and Dallenbach, 1924). Data from this experiment appear in Figure 13–12.

The same results hold for cockroaches. After learning to avoid the end of a training box in which they received a shock, one group of cockroaches was placed in a damp, dark passageway, remaining almost motionless; while another group was left in the regular cage, remaining relatively active. When all the roaches were required to relearn the skill of avoiding the shock, the inactive ones relearned more quickly (Minami and Dallenbach, 1946). Their second learning had not been affected adversely by interpolated activity. Human memory is also affected by interpolated activity. For example, if students learn lists of words and then, before recalling these words, are required to learn lists of synonyms of the words on the original list (following the design in Table 13–4), their recall of the original list is poorer than the recall shown by a control group of subjects whose second list is made up of words unrelated to those on the first list (McGeoch and McDonald, 1931).

Retroactive Inhibition

It begins to look as if any kind of activity or mental process occurring between the time of learning and the time of recall can interfere with recall—can promote forgetting. Such a sweeping generalization, however, is not accepted by experimental psychologists until it has been thoroughly explored. There has grown up an extensive literature on **retroactive inhibition,** a term given the phenomenon of the backward-working interference of new learning on learning that has occurred earlier.

If we were to run an experiment on retroactive inhibition, we might proceed the following way. We have two matched groups of subjects learn to the same degree of perfection a poem or list of nonsense syllables; then we set one group to learning additional materials

Table *13–3.* EXPERIMENTAL DESIGN FOR RESEARCH ON RETROACTIVE INHIBITION

	Stage 1	Stage 2	Stage 3
Experimental Group	Learn A	Learn B	Recall A
Control Group	Learn A	Rest	Recall A

The problem is to see, for the experimental group, whether the learning of B material acts retroactively on the learned A material to interfere with its recall. The control group must be treated like the experimental group in every way except that it rests in Stage 2. Obtained differences between the two groups in Stage 3 can be assumed to be due to the learning of B material— provided, of course, the two groups are equal at the beginning in learning ability.

while the other group does as much of nothing as can be arranged; after an interval we retest both groups on recall of the original material. If the busy group recalls less, we conclude that the intervening activity has exerted a disruptive influence on the earlier learning.

Following this experimental design, the details of retroactive inhibition can be explored thoroughly. In general it can be said that retroactive inhibition increases with the similarity of the intervening material to the original material. If the intervening material is quite different from the original material, there will

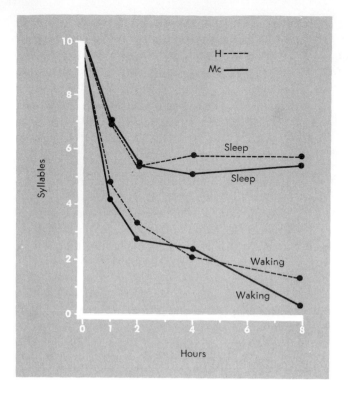

Figure 13–12. FORGETTING DURING SLEEP. *Each of two subjects, when tested after (a) a period of sleep and (b) a period of wakefulness, showed significantly greater recall of nonsense syllables after sleep. Such evidence shows forgetting to be an active rather than a passive process. (Jenkins and Dallenbach, 1924; reproduced, as corrected by personal communication from Dallenbach, by permission of the* American Journal of Psychology.*)*

Table 13–4. EXPERIMENTAL DESIGN FOR RESEARCH ON PROACTIVE INHIBITION

	Stage 1	Stage 2	Stage 3
Experimental Group	Learn A	Learn B	Recall B
Control Group	Rest	Learn B	Recall B

There has also been research on proactive inhibition, after the model presented here. The problem is to see whether A material, learned in Stage 1, proactively interferes with the recall of B material learned later. Under some conditions, it will.

be relatively little interference with recall. A practical implication of these results is that one should not study from 8 to 10 P.M. for an 8 A.M. French examination tomorrow and then get in a couple of hours of Spanish before going to bed.

Distortion in Recall

The research on retroactive inhibition yields additional evidence that forgetting is not a passive fading but an active process. The nature of the process can be further illuminated by the research on distortions of memory. In the chapter on perception, we saw some of the research on the dynamics of remembering; the individual's reconstruction or recall of an event may show the definite stamp of personal wish or idiosyncratic habit. In this connection the story is told about Charles Darwin's method of wisely watching his own tendency to recall selectively. Darwin kept a systematic set of notes on all evidence that seemed to run counter to his way of thinking; he observed that he had no difficulty whatsoever remembering facts *favorable* to his theory of evolution. We need not go further here into such matters except to point out that the facts about distortion of memory further support the notion that forgetting is a dynamic process.

Motivated Forgetting

The research on forgetting during sleep and on retroactive inhibition has dealt with the relatively intellectual aspects of forgetting and remembering. The literature on distortion in recall brings us closer to motivational matters; the attitudes of the individual get into the process of determining the form of his distorted memory. But what about other evidence on motivated forgetting? Do we really have "convenient" memories, tending to preserve intact those experiences that please us while forgetting things we find distasteful?

We do have a tendency to forget unpleasant events more rapidly than we do pleasant ones (Sharp, 1938), and we are more likely to remember materials that fit in pleasantly with our existing prejudices (Edwards, 1942). The effect of pleasantness and unpleasantness on memory is clearly demonstrated by a study in which college students, on the day they returned to school after the Christmas vacation, were asked (a) to write down all the experiences they had had during the Christmas vacation and (b) to rate the pleasantness and unpleasantness of each experience. The students, even then, recalled many more pleasant than unpleasant experiences. Perhaps this was due to selective recall, though the research could not show it. Six weeks later, however, selectivity was eminently clear. The pleasant experiences were recalled with considerable completeness, while those the students had labeled unpleasant were not then recalled nearly so well (Meltzer, 1930).

From our everyday experiences we can find instances of our forgetting things that we do not really want to remember. We may forget appointments with the dentist more often than appointments with the barber or hairdresser. We forget the names of our enemies and remember those of our friends. We forget our failures and reconstruct in great and succulent detail our successes.

Everyday slips of memory are akin to the phenomenon of **repression**, the complete blocking off from conscious life of the memory of threatening or painful experiences of the past. The concept of repression is centrally significant in the psychoanalytic theory of personality and shall concern us again when we deal with such matters. At the present it will be enough to understand how it can be that thoughts of extremely embarrassing or threatening events can be emotionally painful and hence can be—will be—shoved out of consciousness. The mechanism perhaps is similar to that of avoidance conditioning.

TOWARD A TECHNOLOGY OF LEARNING

The student who looks over the shoulder of the psychologist as he conducts basic experiments on the conditioning of animals may marvel at the patience and persistence of a man who pursues knowledge that has no connection with anything practical. Or he may choose to belittle this elaborate laboratory to-do about very minor matters. When we come to a study of the more practical problems of learning, as we have done in this chapter, the question of genuine utility may again be raised. What, really, is anybody going to do with knowledge about learning?

Perhaps a partial answer to such a question can be gained from a look at some developments in which principles learned in the laboratory are applied to the practical control of behavior. These developments show the distinct possibility that we can have what has been called a "technology of learning."

PIGEONS AND MISSILES

A first story has to do with the use of pigeons to guide military missiles. It is a story which, for security reasons, could only recently be told by its principal character—principal *human* character, that is (Skinner, 1960).

Late in the 1930s when World War II was threatening, one psychologist and his coworkers conceived the idea of using pigeons as tracking devices in missiles. The psychologists knew about the great capacities of the pigeon to make fine visual discriminations. And they knew, from laboratory work, about the ways in which the behavior of animals could be controlled through the precise arrangement of reinforcements.

Through a series of experiments they were able to devise a pigeon system of guidance that, on evidence, could outperform available electronic systems while involving much less space and weight.

The essential procedure was to train a pigeon to peck at an image of a target that was projected on a screen in front of him. As long as he pecked at the target, a system could be built that would connect his pecking to the guidance mechanisms of the missile. If the image of the target began to stray off to one side of the screen, so did the pigeon's pecking; and a feedback guidance system would turn the missile so that once more it was centered on the target. If the pigeon was to guide the missile to a particular target, he had to peck at an image or projection of that target and at no other. And he had to keep pecking, at a sufficient rate and for a sufficient time, to guide the missile from the time of its release to the time of impact.

Through a program of partial reinforcement, the pigeons could be trained to peck at a target for a long time after rewards were removed. And through discrimination training they could learn to follow and to peck a wide variety of targets. They were trained to ignore images of clouds or of flak, and to peck only at a specified land or sea target, wherever it appeared on the screen. In a laboratory mock-up, the pigeons were able to guide a missile to a particular street intersection in an aerial map of a particular enemy city. In order to increase the accuracy of pigeon guiding, the psychologists developed ways to use groups of three and of seven pigeons pecking simultaneously, with provisions to use the majority vote in case a minority started working on a wrong target. (Fig. 13–13.)

As the feasibility of the project became clear, the psychologists planned procedures for the rigid training of large numbers of pigeons. "We were proposing," Skinner writes, "to train certain birds for certain classes of targets, such as ships at sea, while special squads

Figure 13–13. PIGEONS AND MISSILES. *Three trained pigeons, working by majority rule and all pecking at the same target on the screens in front of them, could guide military missiles with great accuracy.*

were to be trained on special targets, photographs of which were to be obtained through reconnaissance. A large crew of pigeons would then be waiting for assignment, but we developed harnessing and training techniques which should have solved such problems quite easily" (Skinner, 1960, p. 32).

The project did not reach actuality, and not until after the war was it given military research support. Skinner writes, "The basic difficulty, of course, lay in convincing a dozen distinguished scientists that the behavior of a pigeon could be adequately controlled" (Skinner, 1960, p. 33).

TEACHING MACHINES

Continued and striking success in training animals to make precise discriminations and to perform elaborate skills led Skinner to explore the possible use of the principles of reinforcement in the learning of the basic human skills of arithmetic, spelling, and so on.

The present-day school systems, according to Skinner (1954), maintain *aversive controls:* the fear of punishment or disapproval is widely used to inculcate the basic skills of reading, writing, and arithmetic. "In this welter of aversive consequences," Skinner observes, "getting the right answer is in itself an

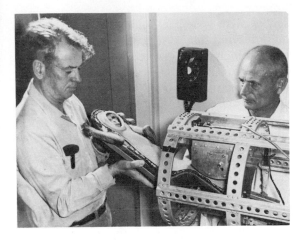

Figure 13–14. LEARNING AND SPACE TRAVEL. *Sam, the space-traveling monkey, was trained to avoid a shock by pulling a lever when given a signal. His behavioral reaction to the strains of space travel could then be recorded. Here Sam is in the biopack in which he made his space flight. The two psychologists here are Dr. Lynn Brown and Dr. Hugh Blodgett. They trained Sam and supervised the psychological aspects of his flight.*

insignificant event, any effect of which is lost amid the anxieties, the boredom, and the aggressions which are the inevitable by-products of aversive control" (pp. 90–91). Skinner also maintains that in the face of a need for immediate and frequent reinforcement to stamp in correct responses, the child receives only delayed and rare rewards from his overworked teacher. When the task, for example, is one of learning the great number of sequential steps needed for the mastery of arithmetic, the prevailing procedures are sadly at variance with our knowledge of ways to facilitate learning. Such a view of the modern classroom may be somewhat jaundiced, but few observers will feel that we now either possess or apply final knowledge about the learning process.

To overcome some of the difficulties he sees, Skinner (1958) has adapted a device used by one psychologist in the 1920s (Pressey, 1926, 1950) and proposes that it be employed widely in classrooms. It has been. And its use is increasing rapidly. The basic idea in this development is **programmed instruction,** a gen-eral term referring to any of a wide variety of carefully planned and sequentially presented series of items to be learned. The somewhat flashier term *teaching machine* is used to refer to devices, sometimes very complex and sometimes quite simple, for presenting stimulus material in the desired sequence and at the desired rate. Programs are microfilmed and loaded into a programming device, or presented in the form of a programmed textbook. In programmed textbooks, each frame, containing a question based on textbook information (the stimulus) usually is presented on successive pages, with the answer (response) to any one question placed next to the following frame. In this manner the learner goes through the book by completing successively more difficult frames. The learner must write down each response before checking the answer and proceeding to the next step. In this way, he takes an active role in the situation, and the value of feedback is more meaningful.

Those who work with programming and with teaching machines pretty well agree (Porter, 1958; Deterline, 1962; Jacobs, 1963; Trittipoe, Trittipoe, and Hahn, 1963) that there are certain essential steps in the programming process. First, there must be *input:* this most frequently consists of material arranged in a series of small steps designed to move the student gradually on to a new concept and new understanding. Second, there must be provision for *stimulus presentation* of the items or frames in the program; it is here that machines can be used, and the process can begin to become highly automated. Third, the stimulus that is presented must elicit the *desired response* from the learner. Fourth, there must be *immediate feedback* so that the learner knows whether he is right or wrong. And finally, there must be a *reinforcing* of correct responses and an *extinguishing* of incorrect ones; most often the feedback itself is an adequate reinforcer, for the learner who is informed that his response is correct is likely to feel quite rewarded.

A great number of programs and of machines for presenting them are now available and are being extensively used not only in schools but in military settings, in industry, in programs of remedial reading, and elsewhere.

Figure 13–15. TEACHING MACHINES. *When properly programmed, so that items are presented in the most desirable order, teaching machines can very effectively facilitate the learning of a variety of verbal and symbolic materials.*

Although teachers still have more favorable attitudes toward such conventional devices as flash cards than toward programmed instruction, and though they may positively blanch at mention of "automated teaching" (Tobias, 1963), there is abundant and increasing evidence that the programmed procedures do work. There is a growing research literature bearing on the general question of finding the most effective way to carry out each and all of the five steps mentioned earlier.

There is now no doubt that a wide variety of materials—varying from reading to arithmetic to complex industrial assembly jobs to algebra to calculus—can be programmed and pre-

sented in a machine, simple or complex, in an order and in a style that can be demonstrably conducive to highly efficient learning. The machines' immediate reporting of correct responses is reinforcing. Learning does occur. And if each learner has his own machine before him, he can work along at his own personal rate, with none to push him and none to hold him back. In a classroom equipped with teaching machines, the children can work away, with very little supervision, on the routine aspects of learning while the teacher can be free to spend his time and skills on the more intricate aspects of the classroom adventure.

An example of the kind of research that is occurring and that we can expect to lead to refinements in the design and use of programmed instruction is a study (Dick, 1963) in which two randomly composed groups of students were assigned to a 3,500-step program in modern algebra. Members of one group worked in pairs on the program, while members of the other worked alone. While there was no significant difference between the two groups when they took the final exam, the paired students scored significantly better when the two groups were retested after a year.

LEARNING AND THE CENTRAL NERVOUS SYSTEM

A great deal of research has been centered on the problem of finding the neural correlates of the psychological phenomena of learning, memory, and thinking. Where does learning occur? By what process? And memory? Is there a memory center? How are memories stored? And what are the brain processes involved in thought? These are the questions. As yet there are no definitive answers, but relevant data are accumulating.

SIMPLE LEARNING: CONDITIONING

Although the conditioned response is the simplest kind of learning, there is evidence that the giving of an old response to a new stimulus involves, in fairly elaborate ways, diverse segments of the brain. **Conditioning** can occur in the absence of a cortex. In human beings who have had to have the cortex removed, some evidence indicates that conditioning can still be established. The same goes for experimentally decorticated animals. But in the absence of a cortex, conditioning does not occur easily or normally. Although a decorticate animal can establish a connection between a new stimulus and a response, the response is not emitted as smoothly or as adaptively as it is when the cortex is intact (Culler, 1938).

Not a great deal is known about the details of the neural processes involved in any form of learning. It has been generally agreed among researchers, though without direct evidence, that learning somehow involves a change in synapse. Once an integrated pattern of behavior occurs, this view has it, there is some kind of "grooving" or some opening of neural pathways, so that the passage of impulses becomes easier the second time around.

Recent research demonstrating a *conditioned cortical electrical response* has thrown some light on (and created puzzles about) the neural events in learning. If a monkey is conditioned by using a flickering light as an unconditioned stimulus, and if the electrical activity in the cortex is recorded, it has been shown that there are two cortical responses when the conditioned stimulus—say, a tone—is presented. There is an electrical response *with a frequency the same as that of the flickering of the unconditioned stimulus*. In other words, the brain flickers when a tone is sounded. There is a separate electrical response of a diffuse nature in the visual sensory area (Morrell and Jasper, 1956). Similar electrical events occur in the reticular formation of the brain stem (Yoshii, Pruvot, and Gastaut, 1957). The discovery of these events may constitute a significant breakthrough in neurological research, but their significance is not yet clear. It has already been shown, for example, that the presence of an electrical conditioned response in the cortex does not necessarily mean that corresponding overt behavior will occur. In one experiment cats were conditioned to make a shock-avoiding response to a low-frequency flickering light; then, outside the avoidance apparatus, they were exposed to a pairing of the light and a tone until the conditioned cortical response occurred to the tone alone. When they were placed back in the apparatus, the cortical response occurred to the tone alone, but there was no avoidance of the shock (Chow, Dement, and John, 1957).

There is a good deal of additional evidence that the establishment of a conditioned response is not a simple chaining of specific neurons and that there is no simple one-to-one correspondence between electrical events in the brain and behavioral events in the world of adjustment.

DISCRIMINATION LEARNING

More complex than simple conditioning is learning involving fine sensory discriminations —such as the task of learning to respond to the relatively brighter of two lights or to a square rather than a triangle. Such learning cannot occur in the absence of the *sensory association centers* of the cortex. The learning of visual discriminations involves the *visual association center*, lying just in front of the primary visual projection areas. The learning of auditory discriminations involves the auditory association areas, contiguous with the auditory projection areas. And so on for the other senses.

If the visual cortex—the projection and association area—is destroyed, animals can still make crude discriminations concerning the presence or absence of a stimulus. A monkey so deprived, for example, can still catch a gnat in mid-air (Blum, Chow, and Pribram, 1950), and he can still respond differently to differences in brightness (Ettlinger and Wegener, 1958). Apparently, the more gross discriminations can be handled by subcortical centers. If the learning task involves more complex discriminations, however, the decorticate animal is helpless; it cannot make different responses to differences in complex patterns. For example, a chimpanzee was taught to discriminate (a) a cone from a pyramid and (b) a wedge from a pyramid on the basis of touch; he lost both discriminations when his parietal somesthetic association areas were removed. In time, he relearned the simpler discrimination of the cone from the pyramid (illustrating, incidentally, a capacity of some parts of the brain to take over functions of parts that are destroyed), but he was not able to relearn the wedge-pyramid chore (Ruch, Fulton, and German, 1938). Such a discrimination requires that the cortex be intact in those areas primarily concerned with the particular sense involved.

The sensory association areas are not the only areas involved in complex discrimination learning tasks, however. If the learning involves a sequence of behaviors or any delay between stimulus and response or any response to an absent stimulus, the frontal association areas are called into play. This matter can best be dealt with under the heading of delayed response.

DELAYED-RESPONSE LEARNING

Some animals, presumably because of the evolutionary development of a cortex, can handle problems involving a response to a stimulus not physically present. They can "remember" for awhile which door had a light over it and can go to that door even though the light has been turned off for some seconds or some minutes. It is well established that the capacity for such delayed response is primarily a frontal-lobe function (Jacobsen and Nissen, 1937) although other parts of the brain are also involved (Rosvold, Mishkin, and Szwarcbart, 1958). The frontal lobes appear to function in representing past events in the present, so that there can be an orderly organizing of sequences of behavior. Human beings who have undergone *lobotomy*, a cutting of pathways to the frontal lobes, often appear to be "free from the past," and cannot pursue a highly organized course of behavior. They can handle, for example, a complex grocery list and bring home everything the list says, but interruption or distraction may make them forget that they had planned to go to the grocery or to return home when

the shopping is done. One theorist (Pribram, 1960) holds that the frontal areas carry representations of the *intentions* of the organism. Without persisting intention, or set, the organism cannot organize incoming data into an orderly pattern or sequence.

MEMORY

There is extensive clinical data on the relation between brain damage and loss of memory, although there is no clear-cut picture at the moment of precisely what part of the brain, if any, is involved in what kind of memory—or loss thereof.

Disorders of memory are divided into three general classes. There are the aphasias, including various disorders of memory for linguistic function. Agnosia is the loss of memory for the meaning of objects; the subject may remember the word for a horse or bridge or clock but may have no meaningful context to bring to the interpretation of what the object is good for. Then there is apraxia—loss of memory for a series of motor responses such as those involved in swinging a golf club or driving a car.

With respect to memory disorders there are two general conclusions worth setting down here. First, a loss of memory is produced by damage to the association areas of the cortex, with the nature of the disorder at least approximately determined by the area of damage. Second, disorders in memory produced by brain damage need not be permanent; there is a principle of *equivalence of function* describing the capacity of remaining parts of the cortex to take over, in time, the functions formerly reserved for parts that are destroyed or removed.

SUMMARY

1. While much research on learning is reductionist in nature and theoretical in orientation, psychologists are also concerned with the more molar and more practical aspects of

learning, such as the conditions of effective acquisition and retention of learned material.

2. Most skills are acquired gradually, and their rate of acquisition can be plotted as learning curves.

3. A frequently seen learning curve shows a rapid initial rise in the rate of learning, a plateau, and then another rise toward a physiological limit.

4. In the learning of sensorimotor skills, distributed practice is generally more effective than massed practice. In verbal learning, the advantages of distributed practice are by no means clear-cut, with the effects of massed and distributed practice varying with such things as the complexity of the task and the similarity among units of material to be learned.

5. The method of learning by wholes instead of parts is frequently advantageous, but its effectiveness varies; it tends to increase with such factors as intelligence of the learner, amount of practice with the method, meaningfulness of the material, and distribution of practice.

6. Meaningful material is learned more readily than meaningless material.

7. Knowledge of results facilitates learning.

8. An active involvement, including verbalization, facilitates learning.

9. Learning may be facilitated either by extrinsic rewards (or external incentives) or by intrinsic rewards ("internal" satisfactions). Extrinsic rewards, though often effective, may sometimes reinforce undesirable behavior.

10. Punishment of erroneous behavior, though often effective in eliminating responses, may under some circumstances become rewarding, may result in undesirable emotional responses, is not always "informative."

11. Although there is no evidence to support the theory of formal discipline, there is transfer of training from one task to another; transfer occurs on the basis of *similarity*, and on the basis of *learned techniques* and *general principles*.

12. Forgetting is typically rapid during the time shortly after learning, less rapid during subsequent periods.

13. Forgetting is less rapid if the material is meaningful, if there is overlearning, and if there is no intervening activity between learning and recall.

14. The recall of learned material is affected by retroactive inhibition, with the amount of interference roughly proportional to the similarity of the interpolated material to the original material.

15. Motivational factors affect recall: pleasant experiences are recalled better than unpleasant ones; items that agree with our attitudes are recalled better than those that are dissonant.

16. The principles of conditioning are being applied to the development of a technology of behavior, including the design and operation of teaching machines.

17. Essential elements in the programming of material for a teaching machine include serialized input, provision for stimulus presentation, elicitation of desired response, immediate feedback, positive reinforcement of correct responses, and extinction of errors.

18. Simple learning can occur in the absence of a cortex, but it does not so occur easily or normally. The establishment of a conditioned response involves intricate neural events; it is not a simple chaining of neurons.

19. Discrimination learning cannot occur unless the sensory association areas of the cortex are intact; similarly, the frontal lobes of the cortex are necessary for learning that involves a delay between stimulus and response. Disorders of memory, including aphasias, agnosia, and apraxia, are produced by damage to the association areas of the cortex. Disorders may be rectified in time by equivalence of function.

RESEARCH REPORTS

MASSED AND DISTRIBUTED PRACTICE *

How does spaced practice facilitate the learning of verbal material? One theorist has it that such facilitation is due to the extinction of error tendencies that appear early in first phases of learning. Under massed training these error tendencies are only temporarily suppressed rather than extinguished.

As a case in point for this statement, the experiment reported here was carried out on college students. The experimenters presented the subjects with four lists of paired nonsense syllables, and each student was asked to memorize the pairs so that when shown the first member of the pair he could correctly anticipate the second member. Each list contained eight paired associates, and lists were presented five times each, in successive fashion, until the 32 pairs had been responded to. The measure of learning was the number of correct responses made to the first members of the pairs. To increase interference of response tendencies, each list had the same first member; but the second members of the pairs were different for each of four lists. Three groups learned the lists at three different rates: 4 seconds, 60 seconds, and 180 seconds between pair presentations.

The results indicate that error tendencies were suppressed in the massed-presentation procedure: i.e., there were consistently more correct anticipations of the second member of the pair over the five trials of each list for the 4-second group.

THE MANAGEMENT OF LEARNING: EFFECTIVENESS OF RESPONSE GUIDANCE †

It was 30 years or more ago that psychologists first became interested in the contribution of prompting or coaching to the effectiveness of learning. The present experiment attempts to compare the relative effectiveness of a procedure involving prompting with a procedure involving trial-and-error "confirmation" in the learning of a serial maze. The experiment also varied the practice-test ratio, so that half the subjects received

two practice trials and one test trial while the other half had a program of one practice trial and one test trial. The subjects in the experiment were forty undergraduate students; the apparatus was an electrical punch-board maze, through which the subjects were required to find a correct pathway.

All subjects received a total of thirty trials in the original learning session; they returned one week later and worked until they had relearned the maze so that they could run it two consecutive times without error. Half the subjects, during each practice trial, were allowed to trace out the pathway by trial and error and find the correct response at each point. This was the confirmation procedure. In it the subjects made their own errors and did their own learning. Under the prompting procedure, applying to the other half of the subjects, each subject was shown the correct response at each point and thus traced the pathway during each learning trial without making any errors. When a subject was given a test trial, the procedure was one in which he would trace the pathway through the maze without any prompting or any feedback; at the same time, the number of his errors and the time required to complete each trial was recorded.

The results of the experiment show that none of the major variables is significant in affecting the rate in which the maze is learned. Subjects learn just as well under prompting as they do under confirmation, and vice versa. They learn equally well if they are given two training trials and one test trial, or if they are given one learning trial and one test trial.

When it comes to the retention of the learning, however, the method of confirmation is superior. Although there were no differences in scores on the test for retention, between the two practice-test ratios the confirmation subjects were decidedly superior to the prompting subjects. In this task, then, coaching or prompting is a relatively ineffective strategy.

SHORT-TERM MEMORY *

The study reported here is concerned mainly with a method of testing short-term memory using children as subjects, but the study also presents results of interest to those who are concerned with substantive phenomena in this general area of learning.

* B. J. Underwood, R. Keppel, and R. Schulz, Studies in the distribution of practice: XXII. Some conditions which enhance retention, *J. exp. Psychol.*, 1962, **64**, 355–363.

† Adapted from J. R. Hawker, Training procedure and practice-test ratio in the acquisition and retention of a serial maze pattern, *Psychon. Sci.*, 1964, **1**, 97–98.

* From R. C. Atkinson, D. N. Hanson, and H. A. Bernback, Short-term memory with young children, *Psychon. Sci.*, 1964, **1**, 255–256.

In the present experiment, forty children, divided into two experimental groups of twenty subjects each, served as subjects. The first group contained children who were 3½ to 4½ years old, with a mean age of 4.16. The second group was made up of children whose age varied from 4½ to 5½, with a mean age of 5.09 years. Each group contained ten boys and ten girls. The material to be used in the experiment consisted of a set of eleven playing cards containing pictures of familiar animals. On each trial in the experiment, a set of eight cards was selected from the complete group of eleven, and each of these was shown, one at a time, to the subject. After each card was shown, it was placed face down on a table—so that, after all eight cards had been shown, they formed a row in front of the subject. After the last card was shown and laid down, a cue card, identical to one of the cards presented on that trial, was placed face up on the table; and the subject was asked to turn up the card which he thought matched the cue card. If, on the first trial, the child was incorrect, he was asked to continue to turn up cards until he located the correct one.

Each child was run for 32 trials. Basic data from this study are presented in the accompanying figure. In the figure, position 1 corresponds to the position of the last card displayed to the child; correspondingly, position 8 is the first card in the series. Results clearly show that the percentage of correct identification of the problem cards that match the cue cards was greater the more recently displayed was the problem card. It is also clear that the proportion of correct responses is a decreasing function of the number of items intervening between the presentation of a given problem item and of the cue card. Such a relationship

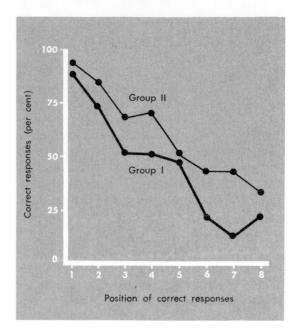

Percentage frequency of correct first-choice responses as a function of the position of the cue card.

holds pretty well throughout the range of the eight stimuli.

This study goes on to show the percentage of correct second-choice responses as a function of the position of the problem cards and also to give data on the time between the presentation of the cue card and of response, as this time varies with the position of the problem card. We need not concern ourselves in detail with these data; we simply mention the use of the variables as an indication of the kinds of relationships that are of interest to psychologists as they explore short-term memory.

SUGGESTED READINGS

Bartlett, F. C. *Remembering: A study in experimental and social psychology.* New York: Macmillan, 1932 (reprinted by Cambridge University Press, 1954).

Hilgard, E. R. *Theories of learning,* 2nd ed. New York: Appleton-Century-Crofts, 1956 (1948).

McGeoch, J. A. *The psychology of human learning,* 2nd ed. (revised by A. L. Irion). New York: Longmans, Green, 1952 (1942).

Underwood, B. J., and R. W. Schulz. *Meaningfulness and verbal learning.* Philadelphia: Lippincott, 1960.

OUTLINE / CHAPTER 14

CHAPTER 14

HIGHER MENTAL PROCESSES

The human **organism** clearly surpasses all others in its capacity to think. Through his conceptual capacity, man can recapture and reconstruct his past, using it in distilled form to solve present problems, to invent, to predict the future, to dream, to fantasy, to imagine events that have never occurred. His capacity to use his head contributes with unique significance to his pursuit of a human rather than merely an organismic existence.

When we study the behavior of lower animals, we find abundant evidence that they do change their behavior on the basis of experience. The earthworm conquers a maze, the cockroach learns to avoid a shock, the fish learns to withdraw from a shadow at the edge of a stream. When a motivated organism encounters blocks or barriers or problems, it proceeds with some degree of effectiveness to learn those new responses that get it where it wants to go. In lower animals, the adaptive changes in behavior come about very gradually and on the basis of repeated experience.

As we watch the behavior of higher organisms, we often see this gradual change of behavior with experience. Sometimes, even human problem solving takes on a form very similar to the simple repetitive pairing of stimulus and response or the simple trial-and-error approach that characterizes the learning of lower animals. But, with the higher animals, new elements appear to enter the process whereby the organism alters its behavior. Sometimes there appears to be a sudden change of behavior, a change that, as far as we can tell, is based on no simple responding to stimuli that are physically present and that involves no obvious amassing of repetitive experience.

The capacity of animals to respond on the basis of something other than cues that are immediately present has been investigated through experiments using a delayed-reaction procedure. In such experiments, the earliest of which was done more than half a century ago (Hunter, 1913), an animal is trained to go to the one of two or three openings that has a lighted bulb over it. Then, after the animal has mastered this assignment, going regularly to the lighted opening and finding a reward there, the rules are changed. The light over the reward-yielding door goes on, then goes off again, and stays off while the animal is restrained at the starting place. After a period of being restrained, the animal is released to see whether it can then go to the rewarding opening.

If the animal—or the child—can go to the correct door after a delay, the reasoning goes, he must be responding on the basis of some cue other than the external one. There has to be some representation of the absent light. Research has shown that laboratory rats can delay for about ten seconds and still make a correct response. Under comparable conditions, a 2½-year-old child can delay for about fifty seconds, while dogs can successfully delay up to three minutes. (Such experiments must be conducted, of course, so as to ensure that during the delay the animal is not maintaining an orienting position, is not steadily "pointing" at the correct opening.)

Many organisms, then, have the capacity to react to stimuli that are physically absent— or at least not physically present in the external environment. Such a capacity enters significantly into problem-solving behavior.

For higher animals, behavior in the face of problems seems to involve not only the capacity to respond to absent stimuli but also something more. Problem-solving behavior seems not so much a matter of random trial and error; not all behaviors that are possible in the problem situation actually occur. The organism appears to *approach its problems with a plan or a strategy or an insight.*

Actually, on this point, there may not be as much difference as common sense is inclined to suppose between animal learning and human learning. The naive cat in a puzzle box does not engage in completely random behavior. Nor is the rat in the maze, particularly if he has been in a maze before, just as

likely to emit one response as another. Past experience is probably always a factor in reducing randomness. In the more complex forms of human learning or problem solving, however, the absence of randomness is more clearly apparent. Hypotheses, strategies, and plans seem clearly to be the order of the day when the human organism confronts a problem.

PROCESSES BETWEEN STIMULUS AND RESPONSE

When we deal with these two aspects of problem-solving behavior—the absent external stimulus and the presence of a plan—we approach the complexities of higher mental processes. Our problem is no longer one of finding out what stimulus goes with what response but of exploring the processes that occur between stimulus and response. The dog turns his back on the ball we toss over the fence and carries some kind of representation of it with him as he detours around the neighbor's fence in order to fetch it. The human being does some thinking between the time his chess opponent makes a move and the making of his own.

We may say that the problem of understanding the higher mental processes is the problem of finding out what goes on between

Figure 14–1. REPRESENTATION FAILS. *When a young child turns its back on a chair, the chair "disappears." The child does not yet have the capacity to represent to itself an absent chair. So it adopts a strategy of looking directly at its target in order to approach it.*

the **stimulus** and **response.** We approach the problem here by asking, first, what is it in the organism that can represent the absent stimulus; then we shall consider available evidence on the nature and course of human thinking.

How may the human organism react to a world not physically present? What is stored in the nervous system that allows it to bring the past into the present and conceptually to rearrange its environment without lifting a finger? What, in other words, mediates behavior?

IMPLICIT MUSCULAR MOVEMENTS

It is conceivable that the nervous system stores up experience through a recording of past muscular movements, and that now, in the face of a problem, it "thinks" by reactivating muscular patterns of response. John B. Watson, the first behaviorist, maintained that this is just what happens, that thinking involves implicit muscular movements (Watson, 1924). He conceived these movements to be so minute as to be invisible, yet sufficiently real to serve a function in thinking, with an implicit movement producing sensory cues that in turn set off other implicit movements. These patterns of implicit movement, then, mediate between the initial stimulus and the eventual response.

There is evidence that higher mental processes do indeed involve implicit muscular movements. In one experiment, for example (Jacobson, 1932), a subject's arm was wired so that nerve impulses could be recorded. Systems of levers were also attached to his muscles, so that tiny movements would be magnified and thus made visible. When the subject was asked to think of moving his left arm or of throwing a ball, there was a flow of nerve impulses and also obvious movement in the muscles.

Watson also maintained that there are implicit movements in the vocal apparatus, the movements used to pronounce words; and that these movements are similarly used in thinking. As a matter of fact, he went so far as to maintain that thinking is largely if not entirely

a matter of subvocal talking. Although there is some evidence that thinking is accompanied by implicit movements in the vocal mechanism (Jacobson, 1932), few, if any, psychologists now will support the notion that thinking is *nothing but* implicit speech (Meehl, 1950; Cofer, 1961).

That muscular responses are not essential for thought is strongly suggested by a study (Smith, Brown, Toman, and Goodman, 1947) in which one of the experimenters injected himself with a form of curare, so that skeletal musculature was paralyzed so completely that he had to have artificial respiration and oxygen to survive. He could make no vocal responses. When the curare wore off, the subject reported that his mind had been perfectly clear. He had excellent recall for things said and done while he was paralyzed. He was able to solve problems as long as there was any means of communication left, such as a grunt or the lifting of a thumb. If thinking requires muscular activity, we would expect some disturbance of thought under conditions of paralysis.

We will examine later some of the evidence on the role of verbal activities in the thinking process; at the moment we leave it that speech may be related to thought and that thinking is accompanied by implicit movements in the throat.

IMAGES IN THINKING

A very likely notion is that we represent the world to ourselves through images of it, and that thinking involves a flow of imaginal materials through the **central nervous system.** Each of us has his own evidence that images are real. We all have them, and upon request most of us can call up visual or other images of our childhood home or of the faces of last night's companions.

Individuals differ widely in the kinds and qualities of their images; some, when asked to recall a familiar scene, can report very little detail. Others lead fuller imaginal lives, with their imagery extending into the world of sounds, smells, tastes, and kinesthesis.

There has been little recent interest in

imagery and in its possible role in problem solving. When psychology was much younger and much more involved with consciousness, however, the matter of images was of considerable consequence. Around the turn of the century, for example, a group of German psychologists, known as the Wurtzburg school, created a stir in psychological circles of that day by putting forward the notion that the individual can engage in imageless thought (Boring, 1929). These psychologists posed a variety of problems to their subjects and asked that the subject describe the kinds of images they had. As often as not, the subject could quickly solve the problem, such as naming an object (e.g., chair) that belongs to a general category (e.g., furniture) but then could report no imagery at all. So the door was opened to the idea that processes beyond conscious awareness enter into mental life.

Some people, most often children, have an extreme and rare kind of imagery, known as **eidetic imagery.** These individuals can look briefly at a scene and then apparently can project it on a wall and "read off" intimate details that cannot be recaptured in the images of an ordinary observer. One might test for eidetic imagery among children by having them look briefly at a complicated picture containing, say, a prominently displayed twelve-digit number; then the children can be asked to report the number, or better, to recite it backward.

There can be no doubt that we can represent the world through images of it. Perhaps the dog who turns his back on a ball or a bone in order to find it is carrying with him an image. We cannot know that, of course; for the dog cannot report on his introspections. Images do often accompany thought. Almost any individual who wrestles with a problem can report on a flowing series of images during his thoughtful period. But images are not necessary for thought. Any one of us can demonstrate that fact to ourselves by tackling a problem in algebra or trigonometry. The answer comes out most frequently without any reportable imagery.

CONCEPTS

We cannot make a case that the processes occurring between stimulus and response in a problem situation are (a) exclusively implicit muscular movements or (b) exclusively images. Thinking may involve both. It may, as far as we know, depend on neither. Recent research has demonstrated, by contrast, that **concepts** are intimately and vitally involved in thought processes. To deal with this research we need to understand clearly the nature of concepts, and the way in which they are learned.

The world is continuous, and the world is infinitely varied. We cannot, however, react always to continua, nor can we have a separate response for every individual member of a class of objects. There are continua from white to black, from idiot to genius, from dwarf to giant, from A student to F student. Though we may be wise to remember the continua, we often find it both convenient and necessary to categorize—to talk about a range of whites as if they were all the same, about all idiots or all A students as if they were the same; and we need sometimes to act as if idiots were clearly different from morons and a low A student different from the one who made a high B. We cannot always have a separate response for each professor or each chair or each brunette, although we know that each individual member of each of these classes is unduplicated. We could not contend with the behavior—the thousands of daily behaviors—of a friend if we were required to respond differently to every response he makes. We observe that some behaviors go with other behaviors; there is a similarity or connectedness. So we group many behaviors into a category and give the category a name such as extroversion or dominance or stupidity or acquisitiveness.

According to one team of researchers (Bruner, Goodnow, and Austin, 1956), if we used to the fullest our capacity to discriminate objects, we would be overwhelmed by the complexity of the environment and would, in effect, be "enslaved to the particular." They cite a number of advantages or achievements of categorizing. In addition to the reduction of complexity—such a reduction being a good thing unless it is carried too far—our categorizing also (a) enables us to place an object in a familiar class and thereby identify it; (b) reduces the necessity for constant learning, for we can place novel events or objects into existing categories; (c) provides direction for instrumental activity, for many of our categories imply an appropriate action; and (d) permits the ordering and relating of whole classes of events—for our categories are organized into systems, so that a whole and relevant system of categories may come into play as soon as our categorical response is made.

We do learn to categorize. We receive frequent **reinforcement** for adaptive categorizing. Perhaps also we learn to categorize because of an "effort after meaning" (Bartlett, 1932) or out of some form of cognitive need (Tolman, 1951; Woodworth, 1947); but we do learn to make a single response, of some degree of appropriateness, to many similar and grouped objects or people or behaviors. We learn to respond to whatever is common to all professors, to all chairs, to all brunettes, or to all Orientals. The outcome of categorizing experience is a concept, which for present purposes may be defined as *a learned response to a common property of a variety of stimuli.*

The Learning of Concepts

The way in which the organism learns a response to a common property of a variety of stimuli can be illustrated by a number of experiments in which animals have been trained to respond to classes of stimuli (Fields, 1932). A rat, for example, can learn to respond to triangles of various sizes and shapes, and to avoid circles. He learns, through the experimenter's judicious administration of reinforcement, to respond identically to many instances of triangularity. Through a slow process of conditioning, he has learned to respond to a common element in assorted stimuli. He has, in a simple way, learned a concept.

Human learning of concepts proceeds in similar ways. The child has many separate experiences with adults who in dress and manner are a good deal like his mother. He may soon demonstrate an approaching response to all of them. He has learned a concept—in this case, one his own true mother may find unsatisfactory. Generalization has carried him too far. So he must begin to discriminate between one womanly stimulus and others. It is a matter of reward and disappointment. He begins to make the discrimination when he finds out that only one of the large array of female stimulus objects yields proper reinforcement. Later he discovers that there are other mothers, even though he has only one. When he has learned to respond to the similarities among all mothers, then he has gained the abstract concept of mother or of motherhood. (For a simpler example, see Fig. 14–2.)

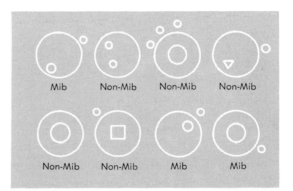

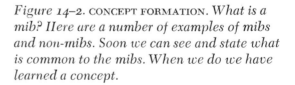

Figure 14–2. CONCEPT FORMATION. *What is a mib? Here are a number of examples of mibs and non-mibs. Soon we can see and state what is common to the mibs. When we do we have learned a concept.*

There has been a good deal of experimental investigation of the ways in which we learn concepts. In the earlier studies (Hull, 1921; Heidbreder, 1924) subjects were exposed to a variety of forms or objects and were asked to find and label similarities among them. One investigator (Heidbreder, 1946a, 1946b, 1947) was quite sure that the more concrete and perceptual concepts can be learned more readily than abstract ones; that one can more easily learn the concept of *table*, since tables are perceptually there, than the concept of *threeness*—the abstraction *threeness* being exemplified by three marbles or three trees or three of anything else. Later researches have shown this notion to be in error (Baum, 1954; Deterline, 1957). The abstract-concrete dimension is probably not the crucial one in the learning of concepts. More important is the number of conflicting responses aroused by the objects among which the similarity is to be seen. A table arouses relatively few responses or associations. Exposure to a number of specific tables, then, leads relatively quickly to a seeing of the common elements. Any instance of threeness, by contrast, three houses, three girls, three elephants, arouses many conflicting responses. So threeness is a more difficult concept to learn. The nature and variety of the responses we can make to separate objects or separate people or separate situations has a good deal to do with our learning of concepts.

The research literature in this area is growing rapidly. It has now been demonstrated, to cite some examples, that form and color concepts are learned most readily if the particular instances among which the similarity is to be found are all familiar to the learner (Forgus and Fowler, 1957). Another example is to be found in the fact that the concept *small* can be formulated more easily out of the stimulus words "gnat," "needle," "stone," and "canary" than can the concept *smelly* out of the stimulus words "sauerkraut," "hospital," "tobacco," and "gym" (Freedman and Mednick, 1958). Why should it be easy to see that "small" is the common element in the first list, while it is difficult to see that all of the second quartet of words are "smelly"? The crucial factor seems to be that one word of the first list strongly elicits the association "small." Seventy-six per cent of the time, when the word "gnat" is presented alone, the association response is "small." The "small hypothesis" becomes salient, is quickly tested and found correct. If we should insert a very obviously smelly word, such as "skunk," in the second

list, the concept of *smelly* would probably emerge quickly.

These and other researches on concept formation (Underwood and Richardson, 1956; Griffith, Spitz, and Lipman, 1959; Bousfield, 1953; Hovland and Weiss, 1953; and Bruner, Goodnow, and Austin, 1956) are tracing down in considerable detail the processes involved in the acquisition of concepts. For example, it has been shown that we learn concepts more readily from positive than from negative instances, from exposure to information about what something *is* rather than information about what it is *not* (Hovland and Weiss, 1953).

Concepts and Words

Throughout the discussion of concept formation, we have avoided the mention of words or of language. This was done for a purpose: to make very clear the difference between concepts and the linguistic **symbols** that are connected to them. Animals, even relatively lowly animals, can learn concepts, and such a capacity adds to the ability to solve problems. But animals lower than man do not come up to the human organism in the *capacity to have words symbolize concepts*. The rat or the chicken or the horse or the elephant can learn to make the same response to a variety of such stimuli as triangles; they can learn that there is a similarity among many sizes and shapes of triangles. But they cannot say "triangularity." They cannot readily symbolize by sound the similarity to which they can respond, and they cannot use the symbol to represent the concept in its absence. Such an accomplishment is a human accomplishment and one that is involved in man's vastly greater capacity to deal thoughtfully with the world.

Young children, before they can talk, closely resemble animals in the way they categorize and use concepts. And when they first begin to talk, their speech is largely a motor rather than an intellectual activity (Vygotsky, 1934; trans., 1962). But at about the age of 2, the development of speech becomes actively involved with the development of thought, and the child engages in a new and very human form of activity. When words become associated with concepts, concepts then can be used symbolically. A concept such as *triangle*, once a rote-learned and nonverbal response to a recurring aspect of geometric forms, can be given the name "triangle"; and this verbal response can be used as a symbol to stand for triangularity. Moreover, the verbal response "triangle" can now be connected with all the symbols and systems of symbols with which the individual has had experience. Specifically, everything that is "known" about triangles—their three sidedness, the variety of their shapes, etc.—can now be brought into the present situation. In other words, the particular symbol becomes a part of that intricate and interlocking array of symbols which, when shared by many people, constitute a language.

To gain anything approximating a thorough understanding of thought, we clearly need to understand the basic phenomena of language. Here we can only indicate the broad aspects of linguistic behavior and the general nature of the processes whereby language is acquired. A bit later we will examine in more detail the relation of linguistic behavior to the actual solving of problems.

In general terms we can say that learning to speak is not essentially different from learning any other response. Speech is often regarded as unique behavior, however, probably because of its uniquely enormous significance for the human organism, social and wordy creature that he is. Speech begins with the babbling of the infant. These emitted responses, occurring in a very great variety and with great frequency, are selectively reinforced, mainly by older people. Some sounds in some places lead to reinforcement; reinforcement increases the likelihood that those particular sounds will recur in a similar sequence in a similar situation. If the parents speak English, the child—who initially makes with equal happiness all the sounds of French, Bantu, Swahili, and all other known languages—soon comes to babble English babbles and

later to make English sounds in English sequences in the situations he encounters.

In addition to straightforward instrumental conditioning (involving both primary and secondary reinforcement), there may be as well a more elaborate form of imitative learning involved. Some learning theorists (Miller and Dollard, 1941) maintain that the child, through early reinforcement, learns deliberately to copy the behavior of those upon whom he is dependent, behavior that seems likely to lead to reward. Through learning, the young soon come to make the sounds of the culture into which they were born; and they make them at the times, in the places, and with the sequences and rhythms that lead to reinforcement—and to communication—in that particular environment.

Such an analysis, in all its sketchiness, deals only with speech as response, as emitted behavior. Speech, whether spoken or written, is also stimulus, of course; and the individual must learn what to make of the great variety of linguistic stimuli that come to him. In his dealing with linguistic stimuli, the child must learn what sounds are made by his elders in the presence of what stimuli. In other words, he learns the categories, concepts, and symbols of his culture. He may notice that those larger and older people with whom he lives point to people smaller than themselves and make the sound "child." He learns that boys, girls, Negroes, whites, small people, and very small people are all in some respect equivalent; and he comes to know that the sound "child" appropriately articulates the equivalence. Then, when one day he observes a small person and essays a "child" of his own, his reward comes quickly; and he is well on the way to both the understanding and the use of the meanings and shades of meaning that are current in his **culture**.

In learning the proper response to make to words he encounters, the child plays what one researcher has called a "word game" (Brown, 1962); that is, he observes the concrete instances upon which such a categorizing concept as "child" is used, and, as his skill and his vocabulary advance, he learns new words through their connection with words already familiar. He learns to use a dictionary and then can learn very efficiently through the direct verbal process of definition. Or he can learn a new concept by studying the **context** in which it occurs. Two experimenters (Werner and Kaplan, 1952, 1963), to demonstrate this contextual kind of learning, embedded artificial words in sentences and asked their young subjects, after a series of six sentences, to tell the meaning of the artificial word. For example, the child was given the word "contavish" and the following sentences containing it:

1. You can't fill anything with a contavish.
2. The more you take out of a contavish, the larger it gets.
3. Before the house is finished, the walls must have contavishes.
4. You can't feel or touch a contavish.
5. A bottle has only one contavish.
6. John fell into a contavish in the road.

Children could get the meaning of contavish from such contexts, and this ability increases with age. Also, older children showed less variability in their answers, demonstrating perhaps a growing familiarity with the contexts and meanings of adults who design contextual tests for children.

In another experiment (Riess, 1950), illustrating the subtlety of learned connections among words, subjects were first trained, through a paired presentation of a startlingly loud buzzer and a printed word, to give a conditioned galvanic skin response to certain printed words; then they were shown other printed words related in various ways to the original words. If the original word was "urn," the GSR will occur when the word "earn" is presented. The word "vase" will also produce a GSR from subjects who were conditioned on "urn." Thus, there are generalization phenomena in linguistic learning; and this tendency to generalize to synonyms increases with age. Children are more likely than adults to generalize to homonyms (words that sound alike, such as "urn" and "earn").

As this general linguistic learning progresses, the child learns not only the vocabulary of his culture, including a number of words his elders try to eradicate by negative reinforcement, but he learns also the connectional rules, the grammar, prevailing among those with whom he lives. And he can speak with his fellows; he can articulate thoughts, make predictions, express feelings; he can join with his fellows in the pooling of experience, in the division of labor, and in the deliberate evolution of a civilization.

SIGNIFICANCE OF VERBAL PROCESSES IN PROBLEM SOLVING

There have been a number of experiments showing the significance of language for prob-

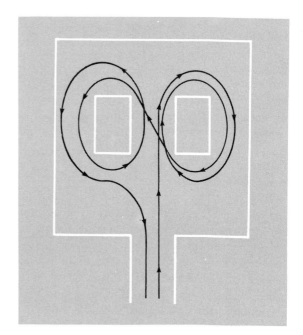

Figure 14–3. DOUBLE-ALTERNATION PROBLEM. *The double-alternation problem has been used in research on problem-solving behavior. The animal must learn to go twice around the right-hand box, then twice around the left-hand box in order to receive a reward. When he comes to the point where he must turn left, what cues can he use? It seems that he must employ some representation of twoness if he is to solve the problem.*

lem solving (Spiker, 1956; Ray, 1957; Gelfand, 1958). Perhaps the most clearly relevant one of these is that (Hunter and Bartlett, 1948) showing the effect of language on the solution of the familiar double-alternation problem. Before they can talk, children have great difficulty with the problem, performing not too much better than animals. When they can verbalize, however, the problem becomes easy. If they can say to themselves, "on the second time around, turn left," they in effect make the proper concepts immediately and implicitly present at the time they are needed. Symbols stand for the concepts. The symbols can be manipulated as mediating processes for the precise guidance of behavior, being there in great variety for use whenever needed. The verbal responses, standing for concepts, mediate problem-solving behavior. The stimulus situation is there.

LANGUAGE DIFFERENCES AND DIFFERENCES IN THOUGHT

A number of lines of evidence support the notion that the ways an individual perceives the world, categorizes it, and thinks about it are at least in part determined by the form and structure of his language. The Hopi Indians, for example (Whorf, 1940), having no past or future tenses, are said to be generally more oriented to the present than are people who speak a language of tenses. The Zuñi (Lenneberg and Roberts, 1956) have difficulty recognizing orange and yellow colors, apparently because they have only one name for the two colors. Among English-speaking students the ability to recognize previously seen color is related to the ready availability of a name for the color. Among the Hopi and the Navaho, objects are classified in ways that we regard as peculiar; the "strange" classification is apparently due to the structure of the language (Carrol and Casagrande, 1958). A number of other studies demonstrate that the availability of names, even artificially created nonsense names, helps in sorting—in seeing similarities and differences among various stimuli (Fenn and Goss, 1957; Lacey and Goss, 1959).

MEDIATION IN THINKING

The child in a double-alternation problem situation, when he must make a left turn after having made two right turns at the same place, can, without the benefit of words, employ the concept of twoness and with its help eventually learn to solve the problem. When he can say "two," either out loud or to himself, the solution is made easier. His behavior in the face of the problem is changed significantly because he can make *verbal-mediation responses*. His ability to respond with a verbal symbol, to make a response not immediately dependent on outside stimuli, makes it possible for him to solve the problem with human facility.

Since the early 1950s there has been a growing literature on the role of verbal mediation in human problem solving. We can here cite some examples of this research development. In one experiment (Ray, 1957) it was found that if subjects had to tell the experimenter ahead of time a plan of attack on a problem, they performed better than those who silently went about the job. Another study (Saltz and Newman, 1960) showed that subjects who learned the names of the component parts of a pressure regulator were better able to assemble the machine. Verbal responses, explicitly made, assist in problem solving.

The more detailed functioning of verbalized concepts in problem solving has been shown in a number of studies. In one experiment (Judson and Cofer, 1956) subjects were given sets of four words and asked to exclude the one that was different from the other three. For example, when the four words "skyscraper," "prayer," "temple," and "cathedral" are presented in this order, 40 per cent of the subjects will exclude skyscraper as different from the other three words. If the same words are presented "prayer," "skyscraper," "temple," and "cathedral," 70 per cent exclude skyscraper. Any one word can set off its own chain of verbal or conceptual responses; "skyscraper" coming first increases the likelihood that an architectural concept will evolve, while "prayer" sets up the probability that a religious concept will be hit upon. The same

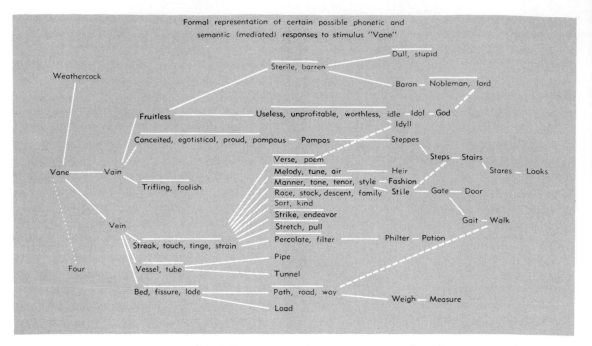

Figure 14–4. VERBAL MEDIATION. *Verbal mediation plays a significant role in higher mental processes. Here is a representation of the processes and associations that might be set off by the use of concept. (Cofer and Foley, 1942; by permission of the American Psychological Association.)*

experiment showed that subjects with strong religious interests, given the four words above, were likely to keep prayer and exclude skyscraper. Thus, the ready-made verbal-conceptual chains the individual brings with him into a problem situation may affect the solution he finds.

Along a similar line, it has been shown that the subjects can be "primed" for the solution of a problem if they are given lists of relevant concepts to learn beforehand (Judson, Cofer, and Gelfand, 1956). In this study, a subject was supposed to tie together the ends of two hanging ropes so placed that he could not possibly reach them both at the same time. The solution required the use of a weight on the end of one rope, so that the rope could be swung like a pendulum, bringing its end within reach of the subject, who, while holding the other rope, could then catch them both. All subjects before attempting the prob-

lem were required to learn a number of lists of words. One group learned a list composed of "rope," "swing," "pendulum," "clock," "time" in that order. Other groups had some exposure to the same words but in different contexts. The group most adequately "prepped" by these associated verbal responses excelled the others in solving the problem. The relevant concepts and the relevant connections among them, injected into the organism, enable it to solve problems.

These and related results suggest that the verbal responses and chains of verbal responses available to the individual have a significant role in the solution of problems. We perhaps can see that role more clearly as we try now to trace out the life history of a problem-solving activity.

THE THINKING PROCESS

On the basis of present knowledge it is obviously impossible to draw a detailed picture of what occurs when an individual confronts a problem. We face the necessity of inferring from observable behavior what are the processes that must occur between the presentation of the problem and the stating of the solution.

From our various lines of evidence we can, however, spell out a reasonably plausible—if hypothetical—account of the steps involved in finding a solution to a problem.

THERE MUST BE A PROBLEM

Thinking does not occur in a psychological vacuum. All learning, all problem solving begins when a motivated organism encounters some difficulty which must be overcome if it is to have its way. Although dreams and flights of fancy may occur in the absence of explicitly definable motivation, even these forms of mental activity are rooted in tensions of the organism. There must be a problem. The problems we deal with in our daily lives are of a very great diversity. Our problem may be a simple one of deciding whether to take a train or a plane, or a very abstruse one, such as trying to decide whether the universe is finite or infinite, steady in scope or continually expanding. But there must be a problem, or nothing much will occur between stimulus and response.

To add concreteness to our discussion of the problem-solving process, let us accept an actual problem and do what we can to trace out the course of our thinking about it. Problem: a man sat in a house, all sides of which faced south. He looked out of his window and saw a bear. What color was the bear?

Some students may be motivated to contend with this problem. If they are, we have the first necessary condition for thinking. Of course, some may solve it so easily and reduce tensions so quickly that the following paragraphs are not at all necessary—for the solution of the problem. The problem of understanding the nature of thinking remains, however, and the problem involving this bear may add usefully to our discussion along that line.

DEFINING THE PROBLEM

We define our problem and settle into it when the problem situation arouses in us an array of concepts that are more or less relevant. We have had experience with houses, men, windows, south, bears, and color. Each of these labeled concepts is aroused in us; and each, by past experience, is connected with other verbally labeled concepts arranged in our past experiences in a variety of contexts and embedded in grammatical habits. The concept *south*, for example, may bring up magnolias, plantations, slavery, desegregation, Alabama, and "the South shall rise again." The concept *house* may arouse the concepts *mansion, shack, cabin, woodsman, gun, bear.*

Such patterns of concepts, the result of previous learning, not only help define the problem but potentially move us toward a solution. If there are no concepts available, we of course cannot either define or solve the problem. If we know nothing of bears, for example, we are not equipped at all to solve the problem. We cannot solve problems in physics or calculus or psychology or arithmetic unless we have learned the concepts of these fields and the connections among them. Drills in arithmetic and the learning of technical vocabularies in introductory courses help equip us to solve future problems. In some problems the key concepts may not be available to consciousness; in personal problems of emotional adjustment, for example, key concepts may have been repressed. In such cases we may need a therapist to help uncover the buried concepts, making them available for the conscious solution of problems.

WEIGHING OF RELEVANCE

As soon as concepts begin to flow, we begin quickly to discard some as irrelevant and to retain others that seem to have greater likelihood of contributing to the solution. The arousal of the concept *house*, for example, may lead to the concept *White House*. But what is the probability that the White House has any connection with bears? More likely is a connection between *shack* and bears, in that both are found in the woods. So *shack* becomes a stronger concept now than White House or mansion or pagoda or penthouse.

If we are fixated on some concepts and, for personal reasons, are hostile to others, we are not equipped to weigh relevance and hence are less likely to solve the problem. If, in responding to *south,* we are attitudinally stuck with matters below the Mason-Dixon line, and cannot respond with the directional aspects of south, then we will not solve the problem. Of course, the statement of the problem itself, using the phrase "facing south," increases the likelihood that we will conceive of south as a direction rather than as a culture or a geographic area, for context has a major hand in determining which concepts will be aroused (Jenkins and Cofer, 1957).

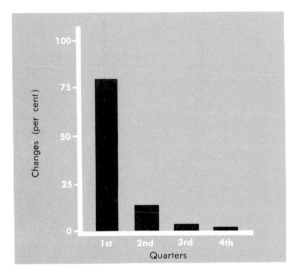

Figure 14–5. CREATIVE THOUGHT: EARLY STAGES. *Thought changes during four quarters of a creative task. A group of artists were asked to create a drawing to illustrate a poem. Study of their thought processes revealed that they changed their ideas frequently, during the early stages, apparently sifting through a number of possible alternative approaches. Such changes may be regarded as a definition of the problem and a sorting of relevant concepts. (Patrick, 1937; by permission of the* Journal of Psychology.)

FORMULATING HYPOTHESES

As concepts, verbally labeled and imbedded in contexts, begin to flow, we soon not only weigh them for relevance but begin also to have hunches (hypotheses) about which particular concepts are the key ones. In our particular problem, we may decide that the problem lies in the relation between the house and the bear. So we focus on these key elements in the puzzle, with the house concept and the bear concept becoming more salient. If, in the pursuit of this hypothesis, we hit simultaneously on polar and igloo, we are, of course, close to a solution. Or we may try other hypotheses, some of which may lead more quickly to a solution. A good hypothesis is that the bear and south are the key things to relate in a meaningful way. South, directional south, and *four sides facing south,* may lead sooner or later to the concept of south pole. From there it is not a long way, conceptually, to the north pole. So the house must be at the north pole. And bears at the north pole? White. The hypothesis, as it moves along, seems to hold up.

VERIFICATION

Our tentative hypotheses lead to firm hypotheses which can be tested. In essence, we have already tested and verified our emerging hypothesis that the bear is white. We might go a bit further, thinking the whole thing over again, checking out our concept of polar bear against our concept of a house at the north pole, to see whether everything jibes. It seems to. There is verification.

If, however, we are not sure about polar bears but have only a vague notion that they live in the Arctic and are white, then we use more explicit procedures of verification. We go to the encyclopedia to get some facts about bears. Until these facts are established, our solution is not verified.

In problems in science, the matter of verification is, of course, most often handled through experimental or other research procedures. Although the scientist may conduct research in order to find an hypothesis about what is puzzling him, most often his research is designed to test or verify a hunch or hypothesis he has formulated out of the interplay of the concepts of his field.

FACTORS INFLUENCING THOUGHT PROCESSES

In dealing in the foregoing paragraphs with the steps of thought process, we hit lightly upon a number of factors that can influence, for better or for worse, the success of our attempts to solve problems. There is experimental evidence bearing directly on a number of these, and the evidence deserves exploring.

KNOWLEDGE

Problems cannot be solved in the absence of knowledge. The individual must already possess the relevant concepts and be able to use them symbolically, or he is lost. We have seen evidence on the importance of having concepts available. The contrived availability of relevant concepts contributes to the solution of the two-rope problem (p. 412). Children who have verbally labeled concepts are better able to solve the double-alternation problem (p. 410). The existence in the language of a richly varied and precisely discriminating array of concepts assists in the solution of problems of sorting (p. 411). There are other and similar evidences in the literature (Welch and Long, 1940; Katona, 1940). Also we might regard the data on learning sets (Harlow, 1949) as bearing on the point; the problem-solving monkey, after long experience, seems to acquire concepts about the rules of the game; and these concepts are brought to bear on new problems. Further, when we say that transfer of training is facilitated by the learning of principles, we are saying, in essence, that the availability of concepts facilitates the solution of problems.

It seems true, also, that a factor in what we regard as highly creative or inventive thinking is sheer knowledge or sheer familiarity with the problem. Helmholtz (1896), the German physiologist, wrote: "It was always necessary first of all that I should have turned my problem over on all sides to such an extent that I had all its angles and complexities 'in

my head' and could run through them without writing. . . . To bring the matter to that point is usually impossible without long preliminary labor."

Many people faced with a perplexing problem or decision find apparent help in writing down all possible pro and con considerations bearing on the matter. Making the concepts thus clearly explicit seems to help get them "in the head" so that the problem-solving processes can go on.

After becoming thoroughly familiar with the relevant concepts, many creative thinkers report a period of *incubation* (Wallas, 1926), a period in which the problem slowly simmers, perhaps sometimes while the thinker is sleeping; or perhaps there are incubation processes at an unconscious level (Hadamard, 1945). Regarding the solution of a mathematical

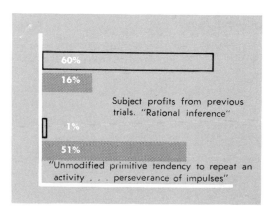

Figure 14–6. EMOTION AND THINKING. *Emotional excitement reduces the capacity to solve problems. The problem for the subjects in this experiment was to find their way out of a problem enclosure. The experimental group (shaded bars) was exposed to a variety of emotional experiences, including the sudden sounding of a klaxon horn and an unexpected dousing with cold water. Compared with the unexcited control group, the experimental group did poorly on the problem—among other things failing to profit from earlier experience and demonstrating a primitive tendency to repeat unprofitable responses. (Adapted from Patrick, 1934ab.)*

problem, Poincaré (1913) wrote, "Most striking at first is this appearance of sudden illumination, a manifest sign of long unconscious prior work. The role of this unconscious work in mathematical invention appears to me to be incontestible." But illumination will not come, and incubation is pointless unless first there are available the necessary concepts.

BIAS

There are a number of forms of bias that can affect the course of thinking, sometimes productively, often not. In a problem situation man does not behave like a thinking machine. He is possessed of all the fallibilities and all the gifts that human flesh is heir to. His attitudes, interests, emotions, and past experiences are there to help or hinder him in his search for a solution.

Emotional Bias

We saw earlier that students with strong religious interests tended to solve a problem one way while those without such an interest handled it another way (p. 412; Judson et al., 1956). In that particular instance, the religious solution was as good as any other; if it had not been, then the religious interest would have constituted a debilitating bias. An anti-religious attitude, of course, can achieve the same results.

Similar and more direct evidences come from a study (Thistlethwaite, 1950) in which students were asked to judge the correctness of logical syllogisms involving human affairs.

The subjects, from universities in various parts of the country, were given a "test of reasoning ability" composed of 72 arguments, and were asked to judge whether the conclusion, as written, followed logically from the statements or statement leading up to the conclusion. Half the test items were emotionally neutral, dealing with routine or trivial matters. The other half of the items were emotionally charged. Twelve dealt with Negroes, twelve with Jews, six with the "proper" role of women, and six with nationalistic slogans.

The following is an example of the invalid arguments dealing with Negroes.

Given: If production is important, then peaceful industrial relations are desirable. If production is important, then it is a mistake to have Negroes for foremen and leaders over Whites.
Therefore: If peaceful industrial relations are desirable, then it is a mistake to have Negroes for foremen and leaders over Whites.

Each subject could be given a distortion score on the basis of his excess of errors on the emotional items over the errors on the neutral items. All groups of subjects made more errors on the emotional items than on the neutral ones, with groups assumed to be more prejudiced showing greater distortion. On the 12 items concerning Negroes, for example, 247 Northern students had a mean distortion score of .41 while an equal number of Southern students showed significantly more distortion with a mean score of 1.18. (See Fig. 14–7.)

There are other evidences that bias—or freedom from it—contributes to the quality of thinking. Of general interest in this connection is a study of a number of students who were considered highly self-actualizing, self-fulfilling, and conspicuously healthy in their satisfaction of their basic needs (Maslow, 1957). One of the prime characteristics of these unusual people was their capacity to see the world clearly, freshly, and without bias or wish cluttering up their conceptions of reality. Of this group the researcher remarks:

One particularly impressive and instructive aspect of this superior relationship with reality is that self-actualizing people distinguish, far more easily than most, the fresh, concrete, and ideographic from the generic, abstract, and rubricised. The consequence is that they live more in the real world of nature than in the man-made mass of concepts, words, abstractions, expectations, beliefs, and stereotypes that most people confuse with the world. They are therefore far more apt to perceive what is there rather than their own wishes, hopes, fears, anxieties, their own theories and beliefs, or those of their cultural group (p. 2). *Also:* They do not cling to the familiar, nor is their quest for the truth a catastrophic need for

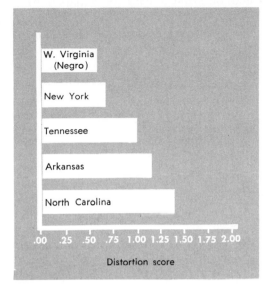

Figure 14–7. BIAS AND THINKING. *One study presented to subjects a number of propositions that appeared on the surface to be logical but that were, in actuality, illogical. The subject's prejudice leads him to accept the illogical as logical. The subject's departure from the logical can be computed as a distortion score. The above data present the relative distortion scores for groups of students from various states as they react to propositions concerning Negroes. The amount of distortion is least for Negro students from West Virginia, most for white students from North Carolina. (Adapted from Thistlethwaite, 1950; reproduced by permission of the American Psychological Association.)*

certainty, safety, definiteness, and order, such as we see in an exaggerated form . . . in the compulsive-obsessive neurotic. They can be, when the total objective situation calls for it, comfortably disorderly, sloppy, anarchic, chaotic, vague, doubtful, uncertain, indefinite, approximate, inexact, or inaccurate (all at certain moments in science, art, or life in general, quite desirable) (p. 3).[1]

---

[1] From A. H. Maslow in the Alfred Korzybski Memorial Lecture, New York, April, 1957; *General Semantics Bulletin* Nos. 20 & 21, 1957. By permission of the Institute of General Semantics, Lakeville, Connecticut.

Set

Another biasing effect is produced by the **set** or direction the individual employs in approaching the problem. The set can be established by the directions given a subject as he tackles a problem, or by factors in his own past experience. Set functions to increase the likelihood that certain concepts will be brought to the solution of the problem, whether they are relevant or not.

The effects of set can be demonstrated quite readily by a small exercise here. Let the reader think of a four-letter word ending in "any." The words "many" and "zany" come to mind. Now think of a four-letter word ending in "eny." If the reader will contend with this problem for awhile before he looks up the answer on the bottom of page 419, he will perhaps see intimately the phenomenon of mental set.

Many brain teasers and conundrums take such a form that our customary sets lead us astray. For example: "A farmer has 20 cows. All but 13 of them die. How many does he have left?" Anyone who answers 7 has been captured by a set. Or the problem: "There are two coins, one of which is not a nickel, totaling 30 cents. What are the coins?" or another: "Two men play five games of tennis. Each man wins five times. Explain." The set for the latter problem here activates the concept of a game *between* the two men. Until such a set is overcome, the solution is impossible.

The same effect can be produced and examined experimentally. In one study (Luchins, 1942) subjects were required to solve a series of problems using one formula. When new problems were presented, requiring a new approach, many of the subjects continued to apply the now maladaptive formula. Easier solutions were available but were not seen. (See Table 14–1.)

Another experimentally demonstrated effect of set (Duncker, 1945) involved the solution of a problem through the novel use of tools. One group of subjects were first required to use a tool in its ordinary way—e.g., pliers to

Table 14–1. SET AND PROBLEM SOLVING:
THE WATER-BOTTLE PROBLEM

Problem No.	Given as Measures Empty Jars Having the Indicated Gallon Capacities			Obtain the Required Gallons of Water in One Jar
1	21	127	3	100
2	14	163	25	99
3	18	43	10	5
4	9	42	6	21
5	20	59	4	31
6	23	49	3	20
7	15	39	3	18
8	28	76	3	25
9	18	48	4	22
10	14	36	8	6

The first few of the water-bottle problems can be solved by the use of the same formula. Somewhere down the list another procedure is better. On which problem does the existing set become a handicap? (From Luchins, 1942; reproduced by permission of the American Psychological Association.)

grip and unfasten a wire, or a paperclip to hold papers together. Then these subjects were presented with problems that could be solved only through using the tools in a novel way. The pliers had to be used to prop up a board and the paperclip unbent to serve as a hook. The subjects who first used the tool in its conventional way scored 61 per cent success on the problems requiring novel use. By contrast, subjects who had no practice with the conventional use of the tools scored 98 per cent success. The normal use of the tools apparently produced a set, a fixation, on one concept of the tool, preventing the ready arousal of the novel and more relevant concept.

There is evidence that individuals can be trained away from conventional sets and learn originality. One experiment first required that subjects take a test instructing them to think of unusual uses for familiar objects. Then they were required to take the same test again, with the instruction that they give responses they hadn't given before. They did. Such practice at giving original responses increased the originality of responses on later tests that were not immediately related to the first. Practice at giving the same response given before cut

Table 14–2. SET AND PROBLEM SOLVING

	Problem	No. Subjects	Per Cent of Problems Solved
Without Practice	Gimlet	10	100
	Box	7	100
	Pliers	15	100
	Weight	12	100
	Paperclip	7	86
After Practice of Conventional Use	Gimlet	14	71
	Box	7	43
	Pliers	9	44
	Weight	12	75
	Paperclip	7	57

Subjects who practice the conventional use of tools develop sets which interfere with solution of problems requiring a novel use of tools. (From Duncker, 1945; reproduced by permission of the American Psychological Association.)

Figure 14–8. SET IN A MAZE. *After subjects had learned to solve the left-hand maze while blindfolded, they were given a series of mazes like that on the right. Many continued to use the now inefficient zigzag path. (Luchins, 1942; mission of the American Psychological Association.)*

down on later originality (Maltzman, Bogartz, and Breger, 1958).

Most psychological writers tend to regard set as a bad thing—an inflexibility that prevents creative thinking. Yet a great deal of education may be regarded as the inculcation of sets. We teach our students to handle new phenomena, new problems in the ways that have been found effective in the past. Perhaps the virtue of the educated man is that he has a richer variety of sets than his untutored neighbor. He can approach any problem from a number of different directions. Nevertheless, his sets, varied though they may be, are still rooted in the cultural past. They keep him in contact with his past and present environment but may prevent the completely novel approach necessary for creative invention. Galileo somehow overcame the prevailing sets of his time when he refused to believe that objects of different weight necessarily fall with different velocity. And Darwin's view of the continuity of life required that he break loose from the prevailing set wherein organisms were perceived as a motley array of discrete forms.

Perhaps, during the so-called incubation period of problem solving, maladaptive sets weaken a bit, so that all relevant concepts have a chance to enter into the solution. It has been demonstrated that if time elapses between the acquisition of a wrong set and the actual work on a problem, the set weakens or disappears so that problem solving can proceed (Adamson and Taylor, 1954). It may be a good practical procedure to back off from a problem that seems insoluble, to put it aside for awhile. In the interval the old sets fade and new ones arise, which will allow more relevant concepts to enter into the thinking process.[2]

STRATEGIES IN PROBLEM SOLVING

We made the point earlier that human beings, in the face of problems, do not behave randomly. They act as if they have been there before. They have relevant concepts which cut down on the randomness of behavior. They may also have definite strategies, sometimes without knowing it, about the way to solve problems of a particular kind.

In dealing with our problem of the white bear, we might have followed any one of several strategies. We might have taken each term in the statement of the problem and followed it into the depths of association to be sure that all relevant concepts were activated and available. Or we might have taken the strategy that a selected three of the items in the puzzle were the key ones and that what was needed was to search for all concepts that related meaningfully to each of these three. Or we might have taken a wild gamble by picking one concept as a likely one and by concentrating exclusively on concepts related to that one.

We approach our problems on the basis of our knowledge or belief about what has paid off in the past. Reinforcement has determined that. We approach the new problem with an expectancy or with a learning set rooted in our prior experience.

In one experiment demonstrating the operation of strategies in problem solving (Goodnow and Pettigrew, 1955), subjects were required to learn the way a laboratory slot

[2] Answer to problem on page 417: The word ending in *eny* is *deny*.

machine, a "two-armed bandit," paid off. The subjects were given chips and instructed to insert them, one at a time, in the machine. They could then pull either the right- or left-hand lever, one of which was sure to pay off each time. The experimenter could control the system of payoff. The subject was paid in actual cash if he was ahead of the game at the end of the experimental runs.

For one group of subjects, at the beginning of the experiment, the machine was set so that the left-hand lever paid off 100 per cent of the time. These subjects learned in a hurry the strategy of "sticking with a winner." It took them only about nine trials to learn to ignore the right lever and work only the left. The subjects were then confronted with a change in rules without being told what was happening. Each lever paid off now on a random 50-50 basis. Their established strategy was now no good. But they tended to stick with it in the face of a changed problem. They continued frequently to pull the left lever a second time after it paid off once. After 70 trials of this 50-50 arrangement, the rules were changed again, so that one lever paid off 100 per cent of the time. Now the "stick with a winner" strategy was a good one. The subjects adopted it with great alacrity, taking only 2 trials, on the average, to settle again into the strategy that had paid off so handsomely at the beginning of the experiment.

A second group started off by trying to beat a system in which each lever paid off randomly 50 per cent of the time. This group obviously had difficulty with strategy. They could not long follow a strategy of sticking with a winner, for to pull again the lever that had just paid off would not be consistently rewarding. They might have followed a strategy of win and shift, but that would not have paid off consistently either. When the rules changed on this group, so that one of the levers started paying off 100 per cent of the time, there was considerable difficulty in hitting upon the obviously profitable strategy— that of sticking with a winner. They learned this strategy only after an average of 16 trials.

This experiment illustrates not only the existence of problem-solving strategies but the persistence of a strategy that has proved rewarding.

A similar experiment (Bruner, Goodnow, and Austin, 1956) showed that subjects when faced with a complicated problem of probability developed several distinct forms of strategy. Some worked out a logical strategy— which, though it had the sound of effectiveness, was a poor strategy in this particular case. There were simply more aspects to the problem than could be kept in mind and handled logically. Others adopted a strategy of *conservative focusing;* they would concentrate on one attribute of the problem at a time and proceed cautiously from there. There were some who fell into the strategy of *focus gambling;* these strategists would take a relatively wild fling at the problem, having no hesitancy to guess in spite of relatively great chances of failure.

Perhaps each of us has his own strategies for handling the problems he encounters. In a particular situation we estimate as best we can our chance of winning, and we play our conceptual cards accordingly. In general terms, each of us probably has problem-solving traits. We may be cautious, conservative, and slow, fearing mistakes more than we anticipate success. Or we may be intuitive jumpers into the middle of things, giving free rein to a confusing flow of concepts in the optimistic expectation that the answer will come. Some of us may follow the strategy of courting input—of cultivating initial confusion—feeling that the more aspects of the problem we can learn about, whether of apparent relevance or not, the greater our chance of finding the inventive solution. Or we may follow Helmholtz's strategy of very thorough preparation in those concepts known to be relevant. Or we may follow the strategy of ignoring the whole problem in the hope that it will go away.

OTHER KINDS OF HIGHER MENTAL PROCESSES

Throughout the present chapter we have concentrated on problem solving. This focus on directly adaptive behavior has kept us on the topic of the more reality-oriented and the more rational processes that intervene between the presentation of a problem and the terminal behavior that solves it. Such problem-solving activity is referred to as **directed thinking;** it is aimed at a goal and it frequently gets somewhere. Not all higher mental processes, however, can be regarded as either reality-oriented or rational. Perhaps little of our thinking, since we are notoriously prone to bias and distortion, is truly rational. But some higher mental processes are clearly more in touch with both reality and reasonableness than are others. Fantasy and dreams, for example, though they may have characteristics in common with problem-solving processes and may make good psychological sense when interpreted by a psychoanalyst, are somehow cut loose from the exigencies of reality and are unfettered by logic or orderliness. Such processes, relatively free of control and directions, are referred to as **associative thinking.**

AUTISTIC THINKING

Problem-solving behavior may be described as purposive. Its aim is to change something in the world of reality so that the organism likes things better. **Autistic thinking,** by contrast, is relatively aimless—at least from a practical point of view. The motivated organism, unable to do much about its needs, takes flight into fancy, into a world of daydreams, where, through the free flow of images and concepts, the life of wish replaces the life of actuality. This autistic thought, however, is by no means *psychologically* aimless.

Autism is close in form and nature to what we call imagination. We may say that autism is imagination self-determined. Someone may ask us what would happen if we were left on the planet Mars without a bit of food or a stitch of clothes and had to get along with the natives. We can imagine it. And in so doing we might spin out a tale which, touching reality only here and there, can be published as science fiction. And perhaps imaginative flights of fancy also play a role in creative thinking and invention. The scientist often

finds himself imagining "what would happen if." In the following of such a fancy, in the deliberate cultivation of hypotheses contrary to fact, he may come upon new and unexpected ways to perceive reality.

Pure autism, if there is any such thing, is not concerned with reality, with eventual adjustments to the world. It is self-generated and self-contained. And it is perfectly natural. Perhaps we all daydream. Certainly there is no harm in it, and we do not concern ourselves about it until we see signs that an individual begins to substitute an autistic world for the one most of us regard as real.

DREAMS

Dreams have much in common with the autistic thinking of our waking hours, except that dreams are perhaps still less bound by the real and the possible. The laws of nature can be readily dreamed away so that we can soar with the eagle or transport ourselves instantly to other times, other lands, other worlds.

It was Sigmund Freud's theory (Freud, 1900) that all dreams represent wish fulfillment. The dreams of children, he maintained, are often directly and simply the expression of wishes, while adult dreams, though born also of primitive wish, come in disguised form. The adult's mental life is characterized by conflict, by opposing wishes, by the necessity to fool himself. So the adult's dreams come in disguised form, often with more civilized and tolerable concepts symbolically standing for concepts we do not choose to face up to. It was Freud's contention that the inner dynamics of the personality can be revealed through an analysis of dream life; but to make such an analysis requires patient exploration into the individual's own system of concepts. It is necessary to find out what is connected with what and what explicit content is symbolizing what concepts lying latently behind. This is a job for a psychoanalyst.

On a different level of analysis, there has been some recent experimental work on dreams and dreaming. It has been determined, for example, that the EEG (electroencephalograph) can be used to learn both about the depth of sleep and about dreaming, and that eye movements during sleep also have a connection with dreaming (Dement and Kleitman, 1957). If the individual is awakened when the EEG indicates light sleep and when there are also eye movements occurring, he is very likely to report that he was dreaming. There is good evidence from a study of these two indicators that the individual dreams about a fifth of the time he is asleep. Most dreams, though the individual can report at least their presence when awakened, are not remembered the next day.

Another fact about dreaming has a potential bearing on the functional significance of this kind of associative activity; if a person is kept from dreaming during one night (by being awakened every time he starts to dream), he will dream more continually the following night. If he is awakened just as frequently, but between dreams, there is no increase in dreaming on the following night (Dement, 1960).

PATHOLOGICAL THINKING

There has been a good deal of attention to the distorted thought processes of **psychotic** patients, but as yet there is little systematic knowledge in this area. One writer (McKellar, 1957) describes psychotic thinking as characterized by discontinuities. Whereas in normal thinking there is an inhibition of irrelevant or purely subjective concepts, the psychotic has no such control of the irrelevant and so appears to be thinking in a disjointed and sometimes almost random way. One subject, under the influence of **mescaline**, describes this aspect of psychotic thinking; she described herself as "so busy chasing hares off the pathway through the woods that I lost the main path" (McKellar, pp. 99–100). Another writer describes such thinking as "polyphony and not one voice" (Stekel, 1924).

Another investigation (Von Domarus, 1929) suggests that in **schizophrenic** thought there is a tendency to believe that if the same thing can be predicted of several things, then those several things are identical. Thus, in **schizoid** logic, the following syllogism holds true:

> I am a virgin.
> The Virgin Mary was a virgin.
> Therefore, I am the Virgin Mary.

Such observations of psychotic thinking are suggestive and may lead to productive research in the area. At the moment we do not possess much knowledge of pathological thought processes. Nor, for that matter, of the fascinating ways of childhood thought.

SUMMARY

1. When higher organisms encounter problems, their behavior appears to have two characteristics not seen in the behavior of the simpler organism; there is the capacity to react to external stimulus not physically present, and there appears to be more of a plan or strategy in the search for solutions.

2. In the attempt to discover what it is that occurs between stimulus and response in a problem situation, there has been exploration for the nature of the representation of physically absent stimuli. There is evidence that implicit muscular movements are involved. There is evidence that implicit speech is involved. Imagery is also involved, but it is not necessary for thinking.

3. Concepts, whether or not they involve implicit muscular movement or images, are intimately involved in thought processes.

4. A concept is a learned response to a common property of a variety of stimuli; concepts enable us to categorize the infinite variety of objects in the world.

5. Animals can learn a single response to the common property of a variety of stimuli such as assorted triangles; they learn concepts. The learning of concepts involves both generalization and discrimination.

6. Researches on concept formation in human beings have shown that concepts are learned most easily (a) if there are few conflicting responses to single instances of the concept, (b) if single instances are all familiar, (c) if the array of instances contain one instance strongly eliciting the relevant response, (d) if instances are positive rather than negative.

7. Animals can learn concepts, but they cannot approach the human capacity to use words to symbolize concepts; man uses symbols which are commonly shared and organized into a grammar.

8. There are a number of lines of evidence showing the significance of symbolically labeled concepts in problem solving; for example, children who can verbalize gain in their ability to solve a double-alternation problem.

9. Differences in linguistic habits lead to differences in the ability to solve problems of sorting and discrimination.

10. Verbal mediation refers to the use of a symbolic verbal response, often implicit, between the original stimulus and the response. There are a number of researches showing the function of verbal mediation in problem solving: (a) the explicit statement of a plan facilitates solutions; (b) the explicit labeling of parts of a problem facilitates solution; (c) subjects can be verbally primed for a solution.

11. The thinking process, at one level of description, involves (a) the presence of a problem, (b) a definition of the problem, involving the arousal of relevant concepts, (c) a weighing of relevance or probabilities, and (d) verification.

12. The effective solution of problems involves knowledge; often there is an incubation period followed by a flash of illumination.

13. Bias can in various ways interfere with the solution of problems; emotional bias can bring in irrelevant concepts and can overcome logic; the bias of set, or a preformed readiness to respond in ways not adaptive for the problem at hand, can delay or prevent solutions.

14. There are a number of experimental demonstrations of the functioning of set; generally speaking, procedures found effective on old problems are applied, sometimes uselessly, to the solution of new problems. Subjects can be trained away from conventional sets.

15. Experimental subjects learn to employ strategies in the approach to problems. Old and rewarding strategies, operating as sets, tend to interfere with the trying of new strategies.

16. The term "higher mental processes" includes not only rational problem solving but also autistic thinking, dreaming, and pathological thought.

17. Autistic thinking refers to fantasy and to imaginative productions that are not primarily concerned with reality or the solution of problems; dreams have much in common with autistic thinking in that they are motivated but not bound by reality; pathological thinking, characterized by discontinuities and illogicality, occurs in psychosis.

RESEARCH REPORTS

THE LEARNING OF CONCEPTS *

Because of the key role of the use of concepts in many kinds of problem solving, there is considerable significance in research on the relative difficulty with which known concepts are learned. This experiment attempted to examine the difficulty of concept attainment as that difficulty varies with the complexity of concepts. The concepts used as problems in the experiment varied from what seemed to be relatively simple ones to combined concepts of relatively great complexity. Actually, the concepts used involved no more than two features, but these two features were combined in a number of relatively complex ways. Table 1 lists the attributes employed in the research and furnishes examples of each of them.

---

* Ulric Neisser and Paul Weene, Hierarchies in concept attainment, *J. exp. Psychol.*, 1962, **64**, 640–645.

In the left column of the table there are such notations as *A·B,* used to indicate what is known as *conjunctive concepts*. This notation can be read as "*A* and *B*" and means "both *A* and *B*." There are also *disjunctive concepts,* in both everyday life and this experiment. In this research, they are indicated by the notation *AvB.* (This notation can be read, "Either *A* or *B* must be present.") The two features, *A* and *B*, can be combined in any of a variety of ways, with some combinations —like those at the bottom of the table—posing more inherent difficulty than others.

It was the hypothesis of the experimenters that Level II concepts are more difficult to learn than those at Level I, and that those of Level III are more difficult to learn than those of Level II.

The stimulus objects presented to the subjects (twenty college-age students) were strings of four consonants, with each string presented on a 4 x 6 filing card. Only the letters *J, Q, V, X,* and *Z* were used. There were 625 distinguishable stimulus cards altogether. The subjects were to look at each of these stimulus cards and to judge whether or not the card was an instance of the concept for which he was looking. The subject

Table 1. TYPES OF ATTRIBUTES THAT CAN BE DEFINED BY PRESENCE OR ABSENCE

OF TWO FEATURES

Name and Symbolic Designation	Description of Positive Instance	Example
Level I		
Presence (*A*)	*A* must be present	Vertebrate: must have a backbone
Absence (—*A*)	*A* must not be present (complement of presence)	Invertebrate: must not have a backbone
Level II		
Conjunction (*A·B*)	Both *A* and *B* must be present	Good quality: both material and workmanship must be first class
Disjunction (*AvB*)	Either *A* or *B* or both must be present	Allergenic: a food which contains either tomatoes or strawberries (for example)
Exclusion (*A·—B*)	*A* must be present and *B* not present	Eligible for driver's license: must have passed test and not have committed felony
Disjunctive absence (—*Av—B*)	Either *A* or *B*, or both, must be absent (complement of conjunction)	Poor quality: either material or workmanship is not first class
Conjunctive absence (—*A·—B*)	*A* and *B* must both be absent (complement of disjunction)	Nonallergenic: a food which contains neither tomatoes nor strawberries (for example)
Implication (—*AvB*)	Either *A* is absent, or *B* is present. If *A* is present, then *B* must be present; thus, *A* implies *B* (complement of exclusion)	Ineligible for driver's license: must either have not passed test or have committed felony
Level III		
Either/or (*A·—B*)v (—*A·B*)	Either *A* or *B* must be present, but not both together	Negative product: either factor negative, but not both
Both/neither (*A·B*)v (—*A·—B*)	Both *A* and *B* must be present, unless neither is (complement of either/or)	Positive product: both factors may be negative, or neither, but not just one

started out, in every instance, by having no idea of what concept he was looking for. He began to get evidence as to what the concept might be, since each time he was asked to guess whether or not the card represented an instance of what he was looking for (for example, Q and Z were present, but not J), he was given a "yes" or "no" reinforcement. Eventually, he was able to verbalize the nature of the concept for which he was looking. A subject was judged to have attained the concept when he had made 25 consecutive correct responses with only a single error.

A tabulation of the results indicated quite clearly that concepts at the three levels differed in the ease of attainment. Concepts at the first level—the concepts involving the presence or absence of a single item—were relatively easily obtained. During the first run of problems, the subjects took a median of 11 trials to attain the concept involving the presence of an item and only 7 trials to attain the concept involving the simple absence of an item. The more complex concepts at Level II yielded medians varying from 13 to 29 trials. The concepts at Level III were obviously more difficult. For example, take the concept stated as "Either A or B must be present but not both together"; on their first exposure to this problem, it took the subjects a median of 68 trials to attain the concept.

In their discussion of the reasons for the relative difficulty of the more complex concepts, the experimenters report that they consider it not a matter of the logical elimination of those hypotheses that compete with the correct one. To test this kind of statement, the experimenters programmed a computer so that it could, by rote and logic, arrive at the correct solution of the experimental problems. The computer, as logical as it was, found that Level II problems took no longer than problems involving the simple attributes at Level I. And the concepts at Level III take the fewest trials of all. It seems clear that human subjects do not attain concepts through a process of logical elimination.

The researchers also entertain the notion that the difficulty of attaining high-level concepts might be due to the difficulty of the verbal formulation of them. Although they do not entirely reject this hypothesis, they are inclined to favor a formulation which says that the attainment of concepts at high levels of complexity involves a familiarity with and use of concepts at a lower level of complexity; in other words, there is a hierarchicality involved in attainment of concepts.

SPECIFIC CUES OR PERCEPTUAL REORGANIZATION? *

One theory of problem solving has it that problem solution occurs when a cue from one behavioral chain becomes contiguous with a response from a different chain; such contiguity leads to a connection between cue and response, and this in turn leads to solution. This is the associationistic view of problem solving. Another theory says that there is no such simple connection involved in problem solving but that the finding of a solution involves perceptual reorganization of a fairly intricate and involved kind. The present study concerns this controversy and examines the connection between (a) the immediate availability of a relevant cue and (b) the solving of a problem.

The problem involved was the candle problem, used in a number of experiments in psychology, in which the subject is given a candle, some matches, and a box filled with thumb tacks and is asked to find a way to fix the candle on a wall and to light it so that it burns properly. In order to solve the problem, the subject must empty the tacks out of the box and then use the tacks to fasten the box to the wall. Once this is done, the candle can be set on the box and lighted. What interferes with the solution of the problem is what is known as the *functional fixedness* of the match box. It normally is fixed in the observer's perception as a match box, not as a bracket to hold a candle. In order to solve this problem, then, one must overcome the functional fixedness of this particular object.

The present experiment states two alternative hypotheses: (1) that the problem solution will occur at the time of the initial contact with the box; (2) that the problem solution will occur at the time of some subsequent contact with the box.

In order to examine the tenability of these alternative hypotheses, the experimenter used ten male undergraduates from psychology courses in Princeton University as subjects; each was confronted with the candle problem described above. Each subject was given instructions about the nature of the problem and the objects available to him for its solution. Each was also told that a prize of ten dollars would be awarded for the fastest solution to the problem. The subject was fitted with opaque goggles so that he could not

---

* Sam Glucksberg, Functional fixedness: Problem solution as a function of observing responses, *Psychono. Sci.*, 1964, 1, 117–118.

see any of the objects and had to work from tactile cues alone. He was observed carefully as he felt the objects and as he found the solution; the time of getting to the solution was recorded. If he had not found a solution within 15 minutes, he was regarded as a failure and his score was recorded as such. In the course of the experiment, all manual contacts with the match box were scored as "observing responses." These could be clearly subdivided as "exploratory" and as "adventitious." If the subject touched the box and seemed to explore it, that was exploratory. If he touched the box accidentally, that was scored as an adventitious contact with the box.

Of the ten subjects, eight solved the problem within the 15-minute period. Seven of the eight who solved the problem did so immediately after touching the box adventitiously; most often they touched the box while reaching for a tack in an attempt to fasten the candle on the wall. Most of them suddenly gave up the attempt to fasten the candle on the wall and proceeded to empty the tacks from the box and to fasten the box to the wall—thereby solving the problem.

The data from the experiment showed very clearly that the solution of the problem does not occur at the first contact with the box. The subject who solved the problem almost immediately had four exploratory contacts with the box and one accidental one, solving the problem quickly after the accidental contact. The individual taking the longest time to solve the problem, 7.02 minutes, had seventeen contacts with the box, four of which were exploratory and thirteen of which were adventitious. After the fifteenth contact with the box, an adventitious one, the solution came to him. These observing responses, whether exploratory or adventitious, seem very regularly to come immediately before solution of the problem.

SUGGESTED READINGS

Ashby, W. R. *Design for a brain,* 2nd ed. New York: Wiley, 1960 (1952).

Brown, R. W. *Words and things.* Glencoe, Ill.: Free Press, 1958.

Bruner, J. S., Jacqueline J. Goodnow, and G. A. Austin. *A study of thinking.* New York: Wiley, 1956.

Humphrey, George. *Thinking: An introduction to its experimental psychology.* New York: Wiley, 1951.

Hunt, E. B. *Concept learning: An information processing problem.* New York: Wiley, 1962.

——————, Eugene Galanter, and K. H. Pribram. *Plans and the structure of behavior.* New York: Holt, 1960.

Miller, G. A. *Language and communication.* New York: McGraw-Hill, 1951.

PART FIVE

BEHAVIOR OF THE WHOLE ORGANISM

OUTLINE / CHAPTER 15

I. THE PERSON AND THE PSYCHOLOGICAL PROCESS

II. DEFINITION OF PERSONALITY

III. APPROACHES TO THE STUDY OF PERSONALITY

    A. Typologies
        1. The Humoral Typology—Hippocrates
        2. Kretschmer's Typology
        3. The Trouble with Typologies
    B. Descriptions of Temperament
        1. The Dimensions of Body Build
        2. Temperamental Variables
    C. Descriptions of Stylistic Traits
    D. Descriptions of Motivational Traits
    E. The Factor-Analytic Approach
    F. Cognitive Approaches
    G. Concept of Self
    H. The Psychoanalytic Approach
        1. Sigmund Freud
        2. Criticisms of the Psychoanalytic Movement
        3. Adler, Jung, and the Neo-Freudians

IV. DEVELOPMENT OF PERSONALITY

    A. The Role of Learning in Personality Development
    B. Culture and Personality
    C. Learning and Social Class
    D. Learning in the Family
    E. Individual Learning

V. THE PROBLEM OF PREDICTING INDIVIDUAL BEHAVIOR

VI. SUMMARY

VII. RESEARCH REPORTS

CHAPTER 15

PERSONALITY

THE PERSON AND THE PSYCHOLOGICAL PROCESS

If we stand off and watch the human **organism** as it contends with its **environment,** we very naturally see the organism as a unitary entity. We see it as a whole, as an organized system with its own over-all characteristics. It lives and moves and has its being as a unit.

If we are psychologists, our curiosity and our scientific strategy might lead us to move closer to this entity, so that we can concentrate on one or more of the subprocesses or subsystems of the whole organism. In our efforts to understand the organism, we might direct our curiosity to the subsystems involved in sensing; and we might spend the rest of our lives in complete and productive fascination with the ways in which the organism

visually registers outside events. Or we might come down with an interest in the processes of learning, saying to ourselves that a complete understanding of these processes will, in the long run, contribute most to man's understanding of man. Or we might spend the next forty years investigating the ways in which motivational processes interact with perceptual processes.

Other psychologists, however, follow the strategy of studying the person as an organized entity. They wish to see it in its entirety, to observe its structure and functions, to describe its characteristics and to account for the organized and persisting behaviors of the whole human system. These are the psychologists who study personality. And they are the psychologists with whom most introductory students are in greatest sympathy; for most nonpsychologists, by preference and by habit of thought, find the whole psychological system more interesting than any of its psychological segments. Many students would be quite happy to devote the whole introductory course to the study of personality, leaving to the wayward curiosity of professional researchers such intricate matters as retinal function, pitch discrimination, perceptual organization, physiological motivation, and schedules of reinforcement.

So far, in developing the "plot" of the present book, we have concentrated most heavily on the psychologist's research attacks upon what we have regarded as segments of the psychological process. We took time out from this major plotline to deal with the *methods* the psychologist uses as he goes about his work. We also looked, in a nonsegmental way, at the biological development of the human organism. And we dealt at some length with intelligence, one well-known attribute of the whole organism. Mostly, however, we have dealt with segments or subprocesses. We have seen that any one subprocess is related to other subprocesses; perception depends upon sensation, and learning involves perception, and motivation is intimately related to learning, and so on. But we have not yet followed the psychologist as he takes the more distant or the more **molar** view and tries to make scientific sense out of the behavior of the whole psychological system. We now do so. We study personality.

DEFINITION OF PERSONALITY

If we observe over a period of time the behavior of a number of human individuals, we will be almost forced to a number of conclusions. First, we may notice that each individual behaves, from one situation to another, *in ways that are consistent*. If his behavior appears to us confident today, it is likely to appear confident tomorrow. If he behaves intelligently on one problem that confronts him, he is likely to behave intelligently on a variety of problems. Even his interests are relatively stable (Fig. 15–1). There are consistent and *enduring attributes of his behavior*.

Second, we will probably come to the conclusion that there is a *system*, an *organization*, in the behaviors of the individual. He does not appear to be merely a bundle of separate attributes tied together by a skin. As we observe him, we readily and perhaps necessarily see long-term directions, over-all goals and aspirations—*patterns of behavior* in which some enduring attributes are subordinate to others. And perhaps, too, we find a consistent, unifying, and articulate philosophy of life. We conceive of the person as a psychological system, a system in which behaviors here are somehow in touch with behaviors there, and behaviors today are systematically related to behaviors yesterday and tomorrow.

Our third observation will probaby be that each individual we observe behaves in a way that seems *unique*. No two individuals, even identical twins, behave in precisely the same way over any period of time.

We put these three general observations together in the high-level **construct** of personality—the *unique organization of enduring attributes* of the individual. Such a definition of personality will enable us, perhaps, to talk reasonably consistent sense about the behavior of the person. But anyone can see the enormous difficulties here for a truly scientific approach. On the matter of uniqueness, there obviously can be trouble for the scientist. Some maintain that science, with its established strategies and tactics, is ill-equipped to deal with uniquenesses, that it takes more naturally to similarities.

There will be less difficulty in dealing with enduring attributes—although, as we have seen in our attempts to talk sense about intelligence, the problems here are by no means simple if we really wish to adhere rigorously to the rules of objective observation, precise definition, and quantitative report. Few, if any, enduring general attributes of the organism's behavior have so far been as well defined and as successfully measured as the attribute of intelligence; and even with respect to intelligence we still encounter difficulties of definition, reliability, and validity.

When we come to deal with organization,

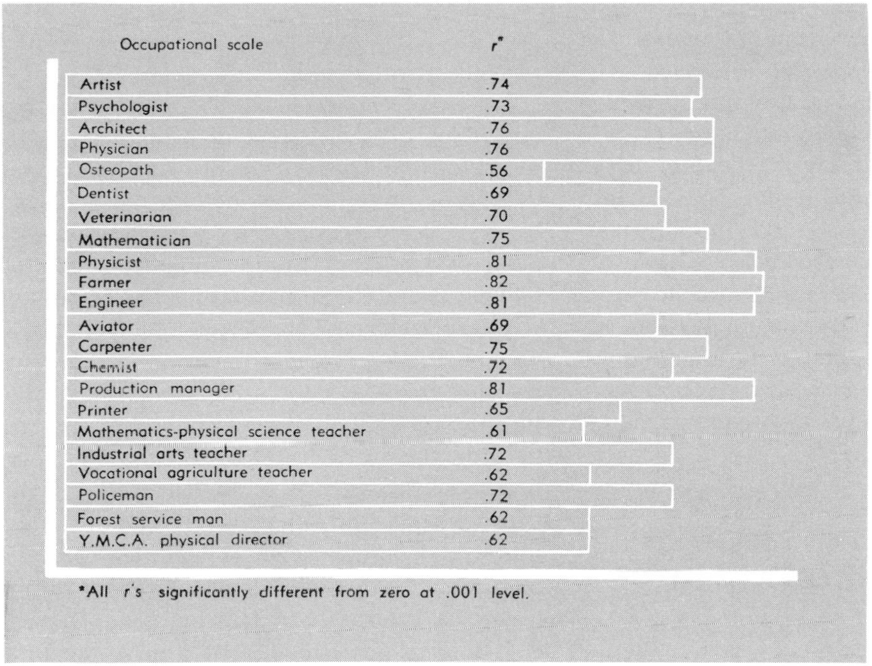

Occupational scale	r^*
Artist	.74
Psychologist	.73
Architect	.76
Physician	.76
Osteopath	.56
Dentist	.69
Veterinarian	.70
Mathematician	.75
Physicist	.81
Farmer	.82
Engineer	.81
Aviator	.69
Carpenter	.75
Chemist	.72
Production manager	.81
Printer	.65
Mathematics-physical science teacher	.61
Industrial arts teacher	.72
Vocational agriculture teacher	.62
Policeman	.72
Forest service man	.62
Y.M.C.A. physical director	.62

*All r's significantly different from zero at .001 level.

Figure 15-1. ENDURING ATTRIBUTES OF PERSONALITY. *The relative stability of interests illustrates the enduring nature of personality. Standard scores on the Strong Vocational Interest Blank obtained at one testing correlate with the same scores obtained after a ten-year interval. The length of the light bars in the figure is proportional to the magnitude of the correlation for the various categories of interest. For example, those showing a pattern of interest similar to that of physicists at the first testing show a very similar pattern* ($r = .81$) *after ten years. (Powers, 1956; adapted by permission of the American Psychological Association.)*

things again become difficult. Of course, no one who has ever looked from inside out at his own personality will doubt for a minute that organization is there. Nor are we likely to deny that the behavior of a Tolstoy or a Churchill or a Schweitzer or of our best friend is highly organized—with all behaviors, all attributes, somehow blending together into a wholeness. But the wholeness of personality, the patterning of a life, is a matter sometimes handled with more apparent ease by poets, biographers, and novelists than by anyone

aspiring to adhere consistently to the canons of science.

However, psychologists have not all been overwhelmed by the obvious difficulty of dealing with the unique organization of enduring attributes of the human organism. We shall examine some of their efforts and some of the outcomes of their research.

On the matter of definition, then, we reiterate that personality is a high-level construct referring to the unique organization of enduring attributes of the individual. Before we go on to look at substantive matters of personality, two additional points need to be made about our definition. First, it is nonsense to talk about the "amount of personality," as many people are inclined to do. By our definition, every individual has a personality—a unique organization of attributes. Personalities differ in many ways, but not in amount. Some personalities are more attractive to more people than are others. Lively and attractive people are the ones who are often seen as having "a lot of personality." It is much more accurate and more meaningful to avoid such an evaluative term and to say, if possible, *why* a given personality is attractive or unattractive.

A second point: our definition makes almost inevitable a *comparative approach*. Although we might spend a lifetime studying the unique organization of attributes of the single individual, most of our dealing with human attributes is, and perhaps has to be, comparative. We compare the intelligence or the aggressiveness or the independence of one personality with the same attributes in other people or in a known population of other people. And, in spite of the uniqueness of the personality, we compare attributes or dimensions or traits that are common to many personalities.

APPROACHES TO THE STUDY OF PERSONALITY

In studying the whole human system, as in studying any segment of it, we study behavior. This is all we have—to begin with, anyway. Behavior is the raw data with which we work and out of which we hope to create scientific sense. When we direct our attention to the whole human system, we tend to see the larger, more *molar* behavior. We are not likely to care much about the more molecular and delicate behaviors involved in fine visual discrimination or in retroactive inhibition while performing a laboratory task. We look instead at the general directions the whole person takes, or at his responses to large slices of his environment or at the major goals toward which he seems to be heading. And, of course, we then employ constructs to describe and summarize our data or, if we use more dynamic motivational constructs, to "explain" the behavior we see.

The psychologist's attempts to study personality will sometimes take him into paths not dreamed of by common sense. In many ways, however, the psychologist in pursuing his enterprise is doing very much what we all do, or try to do, when we characterize our friends and make predictions about their behavior. Perhaps we can appreciate more fully the psychologist's study of personality if we can see the similarities between his approaches and those prevailing wherever people talk about people.

We saw earlier (Chap. 5) that when any one of us puts the label of brilliance or stupidity on our friend Irma, we are with some degree of precision conducting a psychological test. We observe Irma's behavior, assign a label or construct to the similarities in that behavior, and then compare Irma's behavior with the behavior of others. The psychologist, when he assigns an intelligence score to Irma, is doing essentially the same thing, except that he follows a set of very demanding rules regarding the ways he observes and the ways he interprets. He encumbers his effort with considerations of objectivity, reliability, validity, and norms; he must consider carefully matters of parsimony and definition in the use of the interpretive construct "intelligence."

When we come to the study of personality, similar procedures are followed both by the layman and by the psychologist. Of course, the study of personality involves a much greater variety of behaviors than does the study of intelligence. This naturally makes for much greater complexity, for human behavior is both enormously complex and, at least in superficial appearance, staggeringly varied. But this is the sort of complexity that each of us, whether part-time or full-time psychologist, tries to reduce to meaningful simplicity.

We saw in the last chapter that in a very varied world we use categories to avoid or to reduce chaos. Similarly, our daily attempts to understand our friends often involve a simplification of the complex. During any day or week, any individual we may be interested in understanding will give forth thousands and thousands of responses. We would find it both impossible and intolerable to observe and record every one of these responses as if it were a separate and unitary bit of behavior. If we are to escape chaos, we must bring order and simplicity into the intricate world of our friends' behavior. And we must, if we can, bring the kind of order and simplicity that enables us to predict what behavior will occur this afternoon and tomorrow, for we have only a limited tolerance for surprise. We do not really want our friends behaving in unexpected ways. So in our search for order and simplicity, we observe, often with great perspicacity, that each bit of behavior is not a separate thing unto itself but that some behaviors can be meaningfully grouped with other behaviors. We see, going back to Irma, that behavior in the presence of numbers has something in common with vocabulary and with responses to a problem in perceptual organization. We move toward the construct of intelligence. This move is a very significant step toward useful simplification—and toward prediction.

When we turn to other kinds of behavior, we encounter a similar need for simplification and similar—but perhaps more troublesome—problems in bringing it about. We say, for example, that Conrad is shy. Sometimes we make this characterization in a quick and cavalier way, without bothering to slow ourselves down by concern for rules of either observation or interpretation. But sometimes our characterizations are quite sound. They do enable us to predict the behavior of our friends well enough to keep surprise within tolerable limits. These keen characterizations probably come about in somewhat the following manner. We observe Conrad in a variety of situations over a period of time. We see him, for instance, with a group of students in the coffee shop. He says very little. He speaks only when he is spoken to, and even then he speaks hesitantly. Can we say now that he is shy, or should we conclude that we are seeing only today's mood? We cannot say. We observe further. We see Conrad turn down invitations to parties. We see that he has no dates. We see that he spends a great deal of time in his room and on long lonesome walks. We see that he blushes when a girl speaks to him. When anyone talks with him, he casts down his eyes and seems to make implicit withdrawal responses as if he were on the point of running. All these and other behaviors seem to us related. And out of many hundreds of personality words we have at our disposal, we choose the word "shy" as the best summary construct. Conrad's behavior is consistently shy.

Conrad *is* shy, we say. And in so saying, we go beyond the mere description of what behaviors go with what behaviors—what behaviors occur together in a consistent pattern. We also imbue Conrad's system with some kind of lasting condition that produces the behaviors we see. We predict that this condition will lead to shy behaviors in situations that have not yet occurred and not yet been observed. And we are often correct.

There are, of course, a number of factors that can render our characterizations of our friends both useless to us and insulting to our friends. We reviewed many of these difficulties when we examined the problem of applying, with proper precision, the construct of intelligence. In the area of personality, we encounter similar pitfalls. We easily lose objectivity, fail to consider reliability, insult the **law of parsimony,** and fail to define our constructs in terms of observable events. What I see as withdrawing behavior, you may choose to regard as thoughtful behavior. What you interpret as shyness, I may classify as principled choice of companions. And what we both agree is shyness may better be termed integrity—or perhaps **schizophrenic** tendency.

We have said that in many ways the psychologist's study of personality parallels the processes of everyday classification and "explanations" of the behavior of whole human beings. The scientific study of personality may be described as the attempt to see *what behaviors occur together in consistent patterns —and why.* As he makes this study, the psychologist observes very carefully what behaviors go with what behaviors. He seeks to find the best terms to describe the consistent patterns of behavior he sees, and he goes on to see whether he can define those constructs and systems of constructs and make the best and most inclusive sense in accounting for the behavior he sees.

Psychologists have taken a variety of stances in their attempts to describe and account for the unique organizations of human attributes. In considering some of these approaches to personality, we shall deal first and briefly with the early attempts to deal with personality *types*—the attempts to describe in simple and all-inclusive terms the cardinal integrating or ruling themes of individual personalities. Then we shall turn to several of the more modern attempts to examine what behaviors consistently go with what behaviors and shall end with a look at the psychoanalytic view of the inner dynamics lying behind certain significant behaviors of the whole organism. Perhaps as we travel this sometimes tortuous road, the student will find ideas, concepts, and points of view that will enrich his own lifelong efforts to describe, understand, and predict personalities—including his own.

TYPOLOGIES

In the history of man's attempts to understand and predict his fellow man, there have appeared a number of systems of description that can be called *typologies*. A typology is a descriptive system in which all men are classified into a limited number of categories or types, with each typological term supposedly describing a central or overriding characteristic of all aspects of the individual's life.

The Humoral Typology—Hippocrates

As early as 400 B.C. Hippocrates wrote about the "humors" of the body and the effects of these "humors" on personality (Fig. 15–2). His system had it that the body is made up of four primary properties or humors—blood, black bile, yellow bile, and phlegm. In each body, he held, one of these properties or humors is the dominating one. And the character or temperament of the person reflects the dominant humor, as follows:

Body Humors	Character or Temperament
Blood	Sanguine (hopeful)
Black bile	Melancholic (sad)
Yellow bile	Choleric (irritable)
Phlegm	Phlegmatic (apathetic)

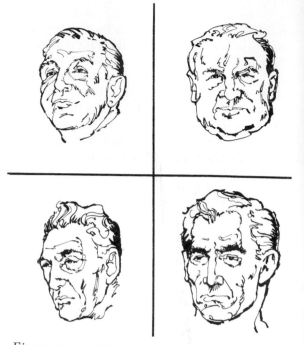

Figure 15–2. A HUMORAL APPROACH. *Hippocrates classed all men into four typological categories—the sanguine, the phlegmatic, the melancholic, and the choleric.*

Although Hippocrates' notion of body humors was a new and radical departure for his day, it hardly is in line with modern physiological knowledge. And though his description of temperament in many cases showed keen awareness of aspects of personality, no modern observer would link behavior traits and humors. Perhaps, however, when Hippocrates described one of his contemporaries as phlegmatic or sanguine in type, he achieved as much accuracy as we do when we say that one of our friends is the "shy type" or the "extroverted type." Perhaps both Hippocrates and we go too far in our attempts to see the simplicities of togetherness among the complexities of behavior. We shall see in a moment some of the dangers in typological thinking.

Kretschmer's Typology

Another and much more recent typological system was developed by Ernst Kretschmer (1925), a German investigator, who built his descriptive system around body build. Out of his observations of patients in mental hospitals came his conviction that different kinds of mental symptoms tend to be found in different kinds of bodies. Any given body, he said, can be typed as **asthenic** (thin and frail), **pyknik** (short, soft, rounded), **athletic** (muscular), or **dysplastic** (not together with itself—that is, of one type in one segment and another type somewhere else). The asthenic type, if he becomes mentally ill, tends to develop symptons of *dementia praecox* (now called schizophrenia). The normal versions of these symptoms—such as introversion, withdrawal, idealism, and formalism—are supposed to be found in normal people with asthenic bodies. Pyknik types tend to develop manic-depressive symptoms; and such traits as fluctuating moodiness, joviality, extroversion, realism, and objectivity—traits which appear in exaggerated form in manic-depressive insanity—are supposed to characterize normal people with pyknik physiques.

The Trouble with Typologies

Typological systems, whether based on Hippocratic humors or Kretschmerian physiques, have some built-in difficulties that seriously hamper their usefulness for the description of personality. Of course, we cannot now accept the notion of four bodily humors. Hippocrates' idea of four types of personality, while having a plausibility, is also not scientifically tenable nor practically useful. Kretschmer's idea of a relation between body build and personality is probably a sound one, in essence; but when he, like Hippocrates, casts all bodies and all personalities into types, he commits what seems to be an insult to the nature of human variability.

When one looks at a population of millions of individuals and tries to place all individuals in a few all-or-none categories, he forces on nature an oversimplified and artificial scheme. Even if an individual can, with some degree of accuracy, be described as basically the phlegmatic type, the manic-depressive type, or, in more modern terms, the egghead type or the introverted type or the aggressive type, such a description is inadequate—first, because it essentially ignores hundreds of other attributes of the individual, selecting only one or a few to use in ticketing him; second, because it assumes that two individuals tossed into the same typological pot are the same, both in respect to the single attribute and, more grievously still, in respect to all other attributes.

DESCRIPTIONS OF TEMPERAMENT

The typological approaches to personality attempted to deal, in one swoop of insight, with the entire personality—to draw, with a few strokes of the brush, a finished portrait of the human individual. More recent studies focus observations, descriptions, and, where possible, techniques of measurement, on more limited and more definable attributes of the human system. One such development, led by William Sheldon (1942) and his co-workers, grew directly out of Kretschmer's work and seeks to define a number of what may be called *temperamental traits* and to examine, more precisely than Kretschmer could, the relations between these traits and certain aspects of the physique. This development can illustrate for us, first, the distinction between *temperamental* traits and other traits of personality and, second, the difference between a typological approach and a *dimensional* approach to descriptions of personality. It also, of course, can give us some facts about what behaviors consistently occur together in the life of the individual.

The Dimensions of Body Build

Sheldon, in his curiosity about the often noticed relation between body structure and behavior, achieved one advantage over earlier investigators by freeing himself from the typological habit of thought and by seeking to define instead the basic *dimensions of body build*. He reasoned that, instead of a number of mutually exclusive types of bodies, perhaps there are a number of basic *dimensions* or *variables*, which, if they are defined as continua, can be used to describe accurately any physique (Fig. 15–3). Following this line of thought, Sheldon defined what he conceived to be three primary variables of body build and devised a way of giving any individual physique a score on each one of these variables. His first variable he called

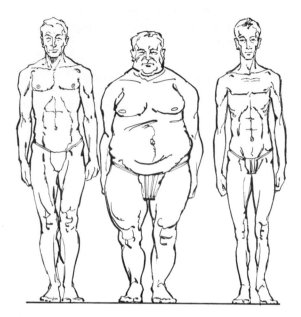

Figure 15–3. SHELDON'S DIMENSIONS. *Any individual can be rated on each of three primary dimensions of physique.*

endomorphy. The person high in endomorphy is similar to Kretschmer's pyknik type. There is a roundness of body contours, a softness, a central concentration of mass, and so on. Through a fairly elaborate series of measurements, Sheldon could give any individual a score on a seven-point scale of endomorphy. The body extremely high in endomorphy would get a score of 7; the body having little or no endomorphy scored 1. The second variable, similarly scaled, is **mesomorphy.** High mesomorphy entails a squareness and muscularity of body, with a prominence of bones and connective tissues. *Ectomorphy,* the third variable or component, is characterized by elongation of body, fragility and delicacy of structure, and relatively little subcutaneous or connective tissue.

With these three components defined and scaled, it became possible to give any physique

a rating on each of three scales. A person low in endomorphy, high in mesomorphy, and low in ectomorphy would be described as a 2–6–2, for example. A rating of 5–4–2 would describe a rounded but relatively muscular and sturdy individual, and so on. The three measurements constitute the individual's **somatotype.**

Temperamental Variables

After they could describe physique with reasonable accuracy and reliability, the investigators went on to tackle the problem of the relation between body and behavior. They defined three *temperamental variables:* **viscerotonia** (related to endomorphy), **somatotonia** (related to mesomorphy), and **cerebrotonia** (related to ectomorphy). The viscerotonic trait, as its label implies, represents a tone or flavor of temperament that is rooted in the viscera. The somatotonic trait and the cerebrotonic trait imply a tonicity centered in the muscles and in the brain, respectively.

The following description of an extreme case[1] illustrates one basic temperamental trait with which Sheldon worked, and indicates the sort of description Sheldon formulated.

Aubrey: Extreme Viscerotonia

Aubrey is 22—a fat, round-faced, good-natured young man of medium stature. He derives from old American stock, with some German and Irish admixture, and has lived for nearly all his life in a small midwestern community. Although the family is fairly well established and industrious, Aubrey is far from industrious. He has always been lazy, shiftless, and irresponsible. But he is exceedingly good-natured. He is of that sociable, easygoing, placid sort that is never disliked and is usually forgiven for shortcomings. He has never been guilty of serious misdemeanor or delinquency. His IQ, tested at three different times in his school career, has in each instance fallen between 100 and 115. His health has been fairly good.

The boy is the second in a family of four children. Early childhood was essentially normal, although he was slow to learn. The school record

---

[1] From W. H. Sheldon and S. S. Stevens, *The Varieties of Temperament,* pp. 97, 121, 147. Copyright 1942 by Harper & Brothers, New York. Reprinted by permission of publisher.

was consistently mediocre, but he was never kept back a grade. He went to a Midwestern state university for nearly two years, and there also his grades were passing but mediocre. After two years he dropped out of college ostensibly to work in his father's hardware store, but the father states that Aubrey's slovenly and wasteful habits render him a liability rather than an asset.

Aubrey is extremely generous, not only with his own property, but especially with his father's. He assumes no responsibility, overeats and oversleeps, and appears to be altogether unconcerned about his future. The specific trait which most disturbs the father is his tendency to attract loafers. Aubrey is always surrounded by a more or less worthless group of hangers-on. When he is at the store, the "laziest and most worthless young rabble of the town collect there like flies around the sugar barrel."

In considering the notion that temperamental traits are related to dimensions of physique, we are, of course, going beyond the mere description of what behaviors go with what behaviors and are touching upon explanatory matters. The relation between bodily dimensions and behavioral traits at least suggests that the enduring attributes we see here are due to basic physiological processes of the organism, the same physiological processes that produce the structure of the body. Should we demonstrate such a relationship, we would be making progress toward an explanation of the unique organization of enduring attributes. We cannot at the moment, however, explain clearly the relationships Sheldon describes. Perhaps body chemistry does determine both physique and temperament. But equally likely is the notion that attributes of the inherited physique determine not only what the person can do but what he and those he lives with expect him to do (see case of Shorty, pp. 71–72). At any rate, we can put it down now that both physique and temperament have a significance for the study of personality.

DESCRIPTIONS OF STYLISTIC TRAITS

The unique and organized human system is characterized not only by persisting temperamental attributes but also by what can be termed *stylistic* or *expressive* traits. Observers of individuality have long and often noted that the human being, whatever he is doing, goes about life with his own personal style. Ernest Newman (1928), for example, writes about Franz Shubert and Beethoven: "Shubert's letters are the true counterpart of his music; the style is simple—melodic and diatonic, we may almost call it—without any involutions or complexities. . . . The uncouth insufficiency of some of Beethoven's first sketches for a musical work has its counterpart in the general shapelessness of his literary style" (pp. v–vi).

Although matters of personal style—of writing, of composing music, of talking, or of behaving in any situation—might be judged too delicate and too ineffable to show forth with clarity in quantitative psychological research, a number of successful attempts have been made to examine the enduring expressive attributes of personality, the enduring *adverbial* attributes having to do not with what adjustments are made but with the manner, the style, in which they are carried forward.

In one systematic study of what was called *expressive movement* (Allport and Vernon, 1933), a group of subjects were required to carry out several dozen different tasks, performance on which could be measured. The tasks included such chores as reading aloud, counting aloud, walking outdoors, strolling indoors, estimations of distances, drawing of circles to estimate the size of certain objects, estimations of angles, estimations of weight, and others. These investigators found a marked tendency for the individual to perform the same task in the same manner on two different occasions. The average uncorrected repeat reliability was .68 for the 49 measures employed in the study.

The investigators also found consistency of expressive movement when the same task was performed with different muscle groups. The average of 92 correlation coefficients between different muscle groups on measures of such things as speed, pressure, and distance was .76 after short intervals and .62 after longer intervals of a day or more. It seems that handwriting and footwriting, for example, are both *personality* writing.

When the experimenters examined all their

Figure 15–4. EXPRESSIVE BEHAVIOR. *Each of many individuals reacting to the same situation does so with his own characteristic pattern of expressive behavior.*

measures for the presence of general expressive traits, they found what to them was satisfactory evidence that there are indeed tendencies for the individual's expressive movements to be similar in many kinds of activities. They report, for instance, that there are statistically significant intercorrelations among the following variables:

Ratings on voice intensity
Fewness of parallel lines drawn on page
Ratings on movement during speech
Writing pressure
Overestimation of weights
Finger pressure on stylus
Tapping pressure
Underestimation of distance between hands
Verbal slowness
Ratings on forcefulness
Overestimation of angles

Pressure of resting hand
Unoccupied space in drawing figures

The investigators regard this interrelated group of measures and ratings as constituting an expressive factor of *emphasis*. The emphatic individual, then, tends to be emphatic in these indicated ways in a wide variety of tasks. Similar statements can be made with respect to the other general expressive traits delineated by these investigators—the centrifugal trait and the areal trait.

Other researchers tend to confirm the presence of consistent and enduring stylistic traits. In studies of handwriting, for example, there is clear evidence not only of distinctive individuality of a consistent kind but indications also that in handwriting the sensitive observer can find cues about other traits of personality. In one experiment, college students, faculty members, and graphologists (experts, sometimes self-appointed, in handwriting) were given samples of handwriting from ten subjects and were asked to match the handwriting with carefully prepared personality sketches of the same subjects. By chance alone, the judges would be expected to be correct one out of ten times. The college students scored 1.77; the faculty group, 1.80; and the graphologists, 2.41 (Powers, 1930). The fact that all groups exceeded chance, even to this small degree, suggests that personality is at least to some extent revealed in handwriting. But that practicing graphologists can give full and accurate personality diagnoses on the basis of analyses of handwriting seems very doubtful.

The whole array of evidence for the existence of general and consistent expressive or stylistic traits has been used (Allport, 1937) to argue for the unitary organization of personality. If, in a wide variety of adjusting situations, the individual demonstrates similar expressive behavior, then, the argument runs, we must assume the existence of large unitary determiners in the structure of the personality, determiners that work themselves out into behavior in numerous but consistent and congruent ways.

DESCRIPTIONS OF MOTIVATIONAL TRAITS

Both temperamental and stylistic traits bear on the *how* of behavior rather than on the *what* or *why*. If we can define and measure expressive and temperamental traits, we know about the style and flavor of adjusting behaviors. We will not know what **adjustments** the organism is making or trying to make. To study the goals and directions, the aspirations and strivings of the individual, we need to know about his personal motivating conditions. There have been a number of attempts to describe and catalog the motivating traits of the individual personality (personal motives), which impel it to directed action.

One of the best-known and most thorough of these attempts is that of H. A. Murray and his associates (1938). This protracted project involved an intensive study, using a wide variety of techniques, of a number of normal personalities. Describing the procedure and the attempt to list the dynamic traits of individuals, Murray writes:

From these and other sorts of facts we have attempted to infer the operation of one of a class of hypothetical brain tensions (drives or needs). Some psychologists may prefer to regard each variable as a mere label to denote a category into which a great number of behavioral patterns have been arbitrarily placed. Even to these, if we have been successful in putting together what belongs together, the classification may be of some use.[2]

Among the procedures used to define and describe "needs" or dynamic traits were (1) questionnaires dealing with the subject's reports on his own behavior, and (2) lists of sentiments to which the subject was asked to respond. A subject who agreed to the following questionnaire items, for example, would be rated high in the *need for autonomy,* one of the basic traits the study dealt with.

1. I am unable to do my best work when I am in a subservient position.
2. I become stubborn and resistant when others attempt to coerce me.
3. I often act contrary to custom or to the wishes of my parents.
4. I argue against people who attempt to assert their authority over me.
5. I try to avoid situations where I am expected to conform to conventional standards.
6. I go my own way regardless of the opinions of others.
7. I am disinclined to adopt a course of action dictated by others.
8. I disregard the rules and regulations that hamper my freedom.
9. I demand independence and liberty above everything.
10. I am apt to criticize whoever happens to be in authority (Murray, p. 158).

The subjects were also asked to record their agreement or disagreement with a wide array of sentiments or general statements about people and life. A marked tendency to agree with the following sentiments would constitute additional evidence of a strong *need for autonomy.*

---

[2] From *Explorations in Personality: A Clinical and Experimental Study of Fifty Men of College Age* by Henry A. Murray and others, p. 144. Copyright 1938 by Oxford Univer. Press, Inc., New York. Reprinted by permission of the publisher.

1. He shall be the greatest who can be the most solitary, the most concealed, the most divergent.
2. A man can learn as well by striking out blindly on his own as he can by following the advice of others.
3. The greatest fortunes are for those who leave the common turnpike and blaze a new trail for themselves.
4. The superior individual has no respect for government.
5. Society everywhere is in conspiracy against the manhood of every one of its members.
6. As men's prayers are a disease of the will, so are their creeds a disease of the intellect.
7. Whoso would be a man must be a nonconformist.
8. There is a time in every man's education when he arrives at the conviction that imitation is suicide.
9. The state is made for the individual; the individual is not made for the state.
10. A member of an institution is no more nor less than a slave.
11. Adherence to convention produces the worst kind of citizen.
12. A man must make his own decisions, uninfluenced by public opinion.
13. A member of a group is merely an unnecessary duplicate.
14. The individualist is the man who is most likely to discover the best road to a new future (Murray, pp. 158–159).

Out of these and other methods of investigation—methods for discovering what behaviors go with what behaviors—the following list of needs, or personal motives, was constructed:

dominance—desire to control sentiments and behavior of others.
deference—willingness to follow an admired leader.
autonomy—need to go one's own way, uninfluenced and uncoerced.
aggression—need to attack with anger in face of opposition or annoyance or insult.
abasement—need to submit, to accept and enjoy pain or blame or criticism, to surrender, to resign oneself to fate.
achievement—need to accomplish something difficult, to master or manipulate physical objects; to overcome obstacles.
sentience—need to seek and enjoy sensuous impressions.
exhibition—need to make an impression, to be seen and heard, to excite, amaze, entertain or shock people.
play—the need to do things for fun without further purpose.
affiliation—the need to cooperate, to please people, to associate with people.
rejection—need to be separated from undesirable people, the need to snub or exclude or ignore or jilt.
succorance—need to be helped, the need to be given aid or love or protection.
nurturance—to help, love or protect the helpless, the weak; to give sympathy.
infavoidance—to avoid humiliation, embarrassment or belittlement.
defendance—to defend against attack, to avoid criticism or blame, to vindicate oneself.
counteraction—to make up for failure by trying harder, to overcome humiliation by renewed effort, to overcome weaknesses.
harmavoidance—to avoid pain, illness, injury, or death, to be cautious.
order—to put things in order, to keep things clean, orderly, organized, tidy, and precise.
understanding—need to understand relationships, to understand for the sake of understanding.
sex—erotic attitude (Murray, pp. 144 ff.).

In addition to these motivational traits, the Murray group described an array of other aspects of personality they found necessary for dealing meaningfully with the whole individual. These added traits, mainly of a temperamental or expressive kind, include the following:

conjunctivity—coherence and integration in behavior.
disjunctivity—lack of coherence and integration.
impulsion—tendency to respond quickly and without reflection.
emotionality—frequency, intensity and duration of emotions.
creativity—ingenuity, intuition, quick learning.
intensity—zest, forcefulness, eagerness.
endurance—duration of direct action.
projectivity—egocentricity in perception, tendency to see in others one's own fears, wishes, etc.

objectivity—tendency to see conditions as they actually exist.

extraception—tendency to be determined by concrete physical conditions and objective fact.

intraception—tendency to be determined by diffuse subjective feelings.

narcism—love of oneself with disrespect for others (Murray, pp. 146 ff.).

This whole approach to personality represents an attempt, as we have seen, to discover which behaviors of individuals tend to be related to other behaviors, and to infer the relatively enduring conditions—Murray conceives these conditions to be "brain tensions" —that lie behind the relatedness in behavior. Presumably, with the Murray needs defined in terms of behavior, any personality can be given a rating or score or assessment on each of the dynamic needs and thereby can be given a personality profile describing his unique array of personal motives. Further, it becomes theoretically possible to move beyond both the description of congruent patterns of behavior and the cataloguing of personal motives of varying strengths that underlie the behaviors, and to begin to explore for ways in which all these factors are uniquely organized in the life of an individual.

Also, once a congruence has been discovered in many behaviors of the individual, and once it has been assigned a meaningful construct, we can focus on that attribute of the total system in order to see how it may best be measured, how it came about, and how it interrelates with other attributes. We saw earlier (Chap. 8), for example, that some of the recent work on the need for achievement illustrates what does and can happen when a construct is articulated and defined.

The student who learns Murray's array of personality constructs and who, on the basis of careful observations of behavior, can apply the constructs with reasonable accuracy will probably find himself thinking about personality in ways that are quite strange to him. It is not possible to say that this list is *the* definitive list of dynamic traits of human personality, and it is not now possible to measure each of these constructs with anything approaching

high precision; however, this array of constructs represents the outcome of a long and arduous attempt on the part of a group of psychologists to discover the basic congruences or togethernesses in behavior, to assign constructs to these congruences, and to seek for the best theoretical ways of accounting for the organized behavior of the whole human system. The employment of these constructs and these approaches can undoubtedly lead to increased understanding of personality.

THE FACTOR-ANALYTIC APPROACH

Another attempt to find the basic ways in which behaviors are related to behaviors comes from the application of the statistical technique known as *factor analysis*. This procedure, as we saw in connection with our study of intelligence testing, can take a wide variety of tests and ratings and, through proper techniques, reduce multiplicity to simplicity by finding the primary factors underlying all the tests and ratings.

One such study (Cattell, 1957), employing data from a wide variety of test results and ratings of actual behavior, yielded a list of fifteen bipolar "source traits." The first "source trait" or factor is described as follows, with the general trait name at the top and the related traits and behaviors listed beneath.

Cyclothymia	vs.	Schizothymia
Easygoing		Obstructive, cantankerous
Adaptable (in habits)		Inflexible, "rigid"
Warmhearted, attentive to people		Cool, indifferent
Frank, placid		Close-mouthed, secretive, anxious
Emotional, expressive		Reserved
Trustful, credulous		Suspicious, "canny"
Impulsive, generous		Close, cautious
Cooperative, self-effacing		Hostile, egotistical
Subject to personal emotional appeals		Impersonal
Humorous		Dry, impassive

Cattell sees this trait, defined here on the basis of statistical analysis of tests and ratings as constituting an essential verification of Kretschmer's descriptions of the manic-depressive and the schizophrenic personalities. Here, of course, the evidence that these various behaviors tend to occur in patterns is more precise than Kretschmer's clinical observations, and the trait is conceived and defined as a continuum rather than in typological terms. But Cattell sees in the factor-analytic approach a clarification and a validation of Kretschmer's rich clinical observations concerning the manic-depressive pattern—here the cyclothymic—and the schizoid pattern—here the schizothymic—of behaviors in normal personalities.

The student may also notice here a similarity to Sheldon's variables of temperament. The individual high in cyclothymia Sheldon would probably describe as viscerotonic. And Cattell's schizothymia seems close to Sheldon's cerebrotonia. The fact that three different investigators, each employing his own methods but each searching for basic patterns of behavior, see very similar patterns may be taken as evidence that here we are close to describing a fundamental way in which behaviors tend to relate with other behaviors in a consistent pattern. Perhaps it will become possible to create very precise ways in which to measure individuals with respect to this trait and then to study it—its psychological or physiological determinants, its relation with other traits or patterns, and its place and function in the total organization of the personality.

COGNITIVE APPROACHES

A leading personality theorist (N. Sanford, 1963) has pointed out that there has been a recent upsurge of interest in cognitive aspects of personal functioning, aspects that can be differentiated from the motivational variables with which Murray and many others have dealt. These cognitive aspects or variables have a relatively intimate bearing on intellectual as differentiated from motivational life. Psychologists who may be described as cognitive in approach may focus their attention on the relatively simple variables of *opinion* and *attitude* as they function in individual life,

or they may study more intricate aspects of what has been termed cognitive style (Janis, Hovland, et al., 1959; Witkin et al., 1962; Witkin, 1964; Rokeach, 1960), or they may build a whole and comprehensive theory of personality in which cognitive processes are at the very heart (Kelly, 1955, 1963).

These and related approaches to the study of personality have a kinship, of some degree of directness, to an older and more general historical development known as *cognitive theory*. The cognitive theorists, in turn, are historically and attitudinally related to the **Gestalt** psychologists; they join with the Gestalt theorists in an emphasis on perception and cognition (rather than on response alone), and in their concern that the reality of wholes and organizations be not destroyed by the atomizing inclinations of behavior theorists.

Stated in the simplest terms, the cognitive theorists believe that the way an individual sees and thinks about the world has a cardinal significance for what he does in it and about it. This approach, like some others, can perhaps be clarified by a knowledge of the enemies it keeps. A leading cognitive theorist has pointed out (Scheerer, 1964) that cognitive theorists attempt primarily to understand the ways in which man understands his world, and believe that acts of behavior have **molar** qualities different from the physiological processes that make them up. They deny that psychologists can explain whole and complex events in terms of simpler elements or parts; they deny that psychological science can be built or that personality can be understood in terms merely of peripheral connections between stimuli and responses; they deny that learning cannot take place without the reinforcing reduction of some primary drive or deficit.

One can see a consonance between the cognitivists' general stand and a number of lines of more specific research in the area of personality. The large volume of research on authoritarianism, for example, although this line of study had its official roots in psychoanalytic theory, has resulted in an increased interest in the individual's general view of the world and the people in it (Adorno, Levinson, Frenkel-Brunswick, and Sanford, 1950). The authoritarian individual (one who scores high on the California F Scale), for example, is described as showing a high degree of *projectivity;* he has a tendency to believe that wild and dangerous things go on in the world; that "the most important thing a child should learn is obedience to his parent"; and that "there must always be war and conflict" (Sanford, 1950). The attitudinal terms on the F Scale and on related tests do go together to form patterns. Authoritarianism, although theoretically rooted in the deep motivational processes of the personality, can be viewed as a general attitude or a general ideology or as a general dimension of the individual's cognitive system.

Closer to the cognitive orientation is the work, growing historically out of the studies of authoritarianism, on *dogmatism* (Rokeach, 1960). This variable is conceived as a consistent and measurable dimension of the individual's cognitive functioning, and the *dogmatism scale* has been constructed to measure what is conceived to be the individual's openness or closedness of mind. With intelligence equal, individuals who score high in dogmatism take longer to solve a laboratory problem requiring that some old and habitual assumptions be overcome while novel "belief systems" be cultivated. The "closed" subjects also perform poorly on a task involving perceptual synthesis, and, as compared with those more "open" and less dogmatic, are less accepting of unconventional music; the "closed" and "open" subjects are equally approving of selections from Brahms, but the "closed" ones balk at Schönberg.

Another developing line of research deals with the relation between the individual's perceptual proclivities and other attributes of personality. We touched earlier (p. 334) upon the work of Witkin and his associates, in which there was a delineation of the personality characteristics of "field-dependent" and "field-independent" perceivers. This work, particularly as extended, has as much relevance for the study of personality as for the study of perception. It has been shown that the individual's field dependency in perception relates to a variety of behaviors, including performance on certain subtests of intelligence tests, on the **Rorschach,** and on other personality tests (Witkin et al., 1962). Also there are indications that the individual's perceptual tendencies relate to such a variable as the adaptive-flexibility dimension of cognitive functioning: field-independent perceivers perform better than field-dependent perceivers in solving a tricky intellectual problem (Witkin, 1964). This kind of finding has led to the definition of dimensional aspects of cognitive style, designated as *analytic* at one extreme and as *global-field* at another. The investigators view this general dimension as significant for understanding the ways in which the individual thinks not only about objects in his environment but also about his own body and his own self.

As mentioned above, George Kelly has formulated a new and comprehensive theory of personality, designated the *psychology of personal constructs,* in which the cognitive processes of construing and anticipating events are fundamental to life and living. Central to this theory is the view of man not so much as a creature of appetites, tissue tensions, and animal impulses but as a scientist—man mightily motivated to make cognitive sense out of his world. As man gives expression to his powerful scientist-like impulses, he creates *personal constructs,* through which he attempts to bring order to his universe; and employs *construction systems,* some public and widely shared, some strictly personal and noncommunicable. The individual's constructs and systems of constructs serve as the basis for his predicting or anticipating events. If the constructs and organizations of constructs meet certain standards of adequacy, the individual functions well. If these cognitive processes are faulty, the individual has trouble. The theoretical system relies on such matters as the nature and necessity of dichotomous constructs, and on the difficulty, perhaps of pathological proportions, one can encounter if one half of an *inherently* dichotomous construct is lost to functional awareness. There then are matters of *alternative constructs,* of the *range of convenience* of constructs, the *permeability* of constructs, the compatibility and incompatibility of systems and subsystems of constructs, and so on. The reader perhaps can register something of the flavor and scope of this still relatively novel, relatively jarring, and thoroughly cognitive view of the human individual.

CONCEPT OF SELF

In trying to increase the understanding of personality, psychologists have assayed a variety of approaches. They have looked for and found some consistent and enduring traits of style. They have searched for and scored at least a limited success in the search for temperamental traits. Through a number of procedures, they have explored for consistent and meaningful motivational traits and for cognitive dispositions that could serve as elements of personality. These searches have led to the advancement of knowledge, but no one can make a case that the knowledge is final or that the varied searches should be called off. They will continue, and they will continue to be accompanied by still other searches with still different approaches. We will examine, at least briefly, some other attacks upon the problems of personality. The first of these additional approaches is concept of self.

One way in which the personality, with all its many-faceted diversity, seems to be given unity is through its *concept of self*. The young child, as he begins to store up experience with the world, has no initial way of telling the difference between himself and the world around him. He soon learns, however, that the parts of the body closest to him are *his*. If they are hurt, *he* is hurt. As life goes on, this self-awareness grows and becomes both differentiated and integrated, eventually forming an organized *concept of self*. One way of saying it is that a construct of self is formulated out of all the data coming to the individual. The environment, working through both its animate and inanimate educators, teaches the child that he is a unit, and a unit having a certain pattern of attributes. He begins to see the changing world from the standpoint of a constant self.

He may learn a highly favorable view of himself if his parents and colleagues react favorably to him. Or he may downgrade himself if his world of people, with justification or not, reacts to him with constant disapproval and reproach.

Once the concept of self is formed and integrated, it tends to preserve itself in as favorable light as possible. There seems to be something of a psychological **homeostasis** at work, so that behavior is adjusted and the world interpreted in ways that preserve the self-concept. The individual will not often do things that "are not like me." To find oneself doing surprising things is a shock, a shock that is avoided as much as possible. If the individual encounters, in the judgments of his friends or in the world's indifference to his own accomplishments, evidence that jars his perception of himself, he can be counted on to defend his self-image, sometimes in strange and wonderful—and irrational—ways (see **defense mechanisms**, Chap. 16). Of course, the individual is in constant and sometimes serious difficulty if his self-concept is greatly at variance with the image of him that exists in the minds of his associates.

In the view of some psychologists, the concept or construct of self, formed over time out of the rewarding and punishing experiences with the world, serves as a unifying and organizing factor in the behavior of the whole system. It keeps molecular bits of behavior in line with perceived general attributes; and it preserves itself, sometimes by guiding behavior, sometimes through distorting perceptions of outside events.

The theoretical approach that emphasizes the role of the self has been gaining increasing prominence in recent thinking and research on personality. A leading exponent of "self-psychology" is Carl Rogers (1951), who has not only spelled out the theory but has designed a psychotherapeutic procedure called **client-centered therapy** around it. Rogers maintains that out of the experience of interacting with the environment, the individual forms an organized pattern of perceptions of the "I" and the "me" and attaches values to these self-characteristics. As he lives his life, the individual encounters many additional experiences that are perceived accurately and brought into an organized relationship to the self. Other experiences are ignored or are distorted because they are inconsistent with the structure of the self. Ways of behaving that are consistent with the structure of the self are adopted and inconsistent behaviors are avoided. The individual is well adjusted when all experiences can be assimilated into a consistent relationship with the self. There is trouble when the individual denies to awareness significant experiences that cannot be tolerated by the structure of the self. Client-centered psychotherapy is a process whereby the individual learns to examine experiences and to revise the structure of the self so as to establish a consistent and meaningful relationship with these formerly distorted and denied experiences.

THE PSYCHOANALYTIC APPROACH

The psychoanalytic theory of personality, originated by the Viennese physician and psychologist Sigmund Freud, is perhaps the most widely known of all modern theories of personality. In order to approach this theory in perspective, we may do well here to review briefly the nature of the approaches we have already seen.

All study of personality begins with the study of behavior. When the attempt is made to view a wide array of behaviors and to find out which behaviors commonly and consistently occur in patterns, the approach may be said to be purely *descriptive*. When we examine expressive movement, for example, and find that emphatic movements are made by the same individuals in many situations over a period of time, we are describing an emphatic trait or an emphatic pattern of behaviors. In so doing we are not imbuing the organism with any tensions or conditions or forces that produce emphatic behavior. We simply describe as accurately as we can what we see—a lasting and consistent pattern of behaviors. When we deal with such ideas as the need for achievement, or the need for deference, however, we go beyond mere de-

scription. The procedure then is to observe patterns of behavior, as in the descriptive approach, but to infer what conditions of the organism *lie behind* and *produce* the consistent pattern of lasting behavior we see. This is referred to as a *dynamic* approach rather than a descriptive approach. Such an approach, however far it may go in precision and insight, has a general similarity to the common-sense approach all of us use. We all want to predict the behavior of our friends, and, by habit of thought, we tend to do so in terms of motivational or dynamic conditions we infer them to "have." No laymen and not many psychologists are satisfied with mere descriptions—not even the highly technical and elaborate descriptions that result from factor analysis. There is a desire for explanation in terms of inner conditions, inner forces. In consistency with this yen, the approach of Murray and his colleagues attempts to delineate the inner dynamic forces that produce the patterned behavior we see.

Some approaches to personality are relatively *elementistic*, whether they emphasize descriptive or dynamic patterns of behavior. The catalogs of both Murray and Cattell, if they were left as mere lists of commonly occurring and consistent patterns of behavior, would be elementistic catalogs. And the spelling out of elements does not allow us either to describe or account for over-all organization.

The approach of Rogers, placing major emphasis on the role and structure of the self, is by no means an elementistic approach. There is a seeing of the organism as a whole. But there is not a direct interest in seeing and dealing with *all* the consistent patterns of behavior of the individual. There is a focus of attention on those behaviors related most directly to the structure and functioning of the self and, more narrowly, on those behaviors having a bearing on the adjustment or maladjustment of the individual.

Now, what about psychoanalysis? It is a *dynamic* approach to personality in that it is by no means interested in the mere description of what behaviors consistently go with what behaviors. It is *not* an elementistic approach.

It has little connection with the search for the basic common traits of individuals. It seeks to spell out the dynamic drama occurring within the organized—or disorganized—human system. It is, like the Rogers approach, *selective*. It is concerned primarily with those behaviors having a significant bearing on the centrally dynamic forces of the personality and, at least in its historical conception, with those behaviors and behavior patterns relating to symptoms of mental disturbance.

In describing the psychoanalytic theory of personality, we shall depart a long way from common sense. We shall also have to leave behind some of the psychology with which we have been contending, for psychoanalysis does not attempt to deal with all aspects of behavior or all the subprocesses of the psychological system. This other-worldliness of the approach was described by one psychologist (Allport, 1937) as follows:

> Psychoanalysis is not an eclectic movement; it has made no contact with other branches of psychology. The somewhat fantastic metaphors it employs show how little it has profited from the antecedent labors of psychological science. Much is known to general psychology about the unconscious operations of the mind, the processes of remembering, forgetting, dreaming, inhibiting, learning, reasoning, self-knowledge, and even about the mechanisms of motive and desire, and all of this knowledge psychoanalysis should but does not employ. No school of psychology can afford such splendid isolation.[3]

In the more than twenty years since this passage was written, there has been increased contact between the psychoanalytic theory and general psychology. The theory, to some extent, however, still stands apart. But the theory still stands, and our purpose here is to look at its outlines, including its "somewhat fantastic metaphors" and to see where it carries us in our search for an understanding of the human personality.

Sigmund Freud

The psychoanalytic movement was initiated when Sigmund Freud began to puzzle about

³ From *Personality, A Psychological Interpretation*, by G. W. Allport, p. 13. Reprinted by permission of Holt, Rinehart and Winston, Inc. Copyright, 1956.

the symptoms of emotionally disturbed patients who came to him for medical treatment. Particularly, what were called *hysterical symptoms* fascinated him. One patient, for example, would come down with a paralyzed arm, with the paralysis obviously due to no neurological cause. (Before Freud's time, these symptoms were labeled "hysterical" because they were observed in women and thought to be due to disturbances in the womb.) Another patient would have **glove anesthesia** (Fig. 15–5), an inability to feel anything over the whole area of the skin normally covered by a glove. Freud knew that the sensory nerves in the hand did not distribute themselves in the shape of the glove; hence there was again no evidence of neurological damage. Instead of falling into the moralistic position that these symptoms were "fake," Freud stuck to the general conviction that they were very genuine and that they somehow were necessary for the preservation of the system in which they occurred. This naturalistic cause-and-effect conviction led him to encumber himself with a wide variety of factual material about his patients.

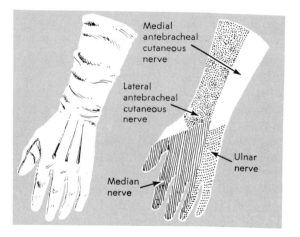

Figure 15–5. HYSTERICAL SYMPTOMS. *Freud described as hysterical those physical symptoms for which there are no organic causes. The drawing on the right shows the areas covered by the four sensory nerves serving the hand and lower arm. If any one of these nerves were cut, there would be anesthesia over a limited area. The drawing at left shows a pattern of "glove anesthesia."*

He collected *life-history data,* having the feeling that present symptoms were somehow rooted in the past experience of his patients. He searched through many hours of his patients' **free associations,** looking for repeated themes and recurring connections in the speech of his patients as they put words to all the thoughts passing through their minds. He collected data on *dreams,* and began to formulate the conclusion that in dream life there is a representation, though strangely disguised, of the inner dynamics of the personality. He collected data on verbal slips, on lapses of memory, on accidents and misadventures, beginning to convince himself that all these departures from intended behavior somehow made sense in the over-all pattern of the individual's adjustment.

In the face of this vast and initially jumbled array of behavioral data, Freud created his system of constructs that constitute the core of the psychoanalytic theory. He could not escape the conviction that in every personality there is an area of untamed, untrammeled, animal-like motivation. He conceived it to be there at birth—an instinctive, universal set of violent urges. This pattern of primitiveness he termed the **id.** He thought he saw two different kinds of urges in the id. There were urges to live, to create, to love. These forces he called the **life wish,** and he used the term **libido** to symbolize that part of the life wish concerning sexual or other affiliative relations with people. Freud also saw evidence of hostile and destructive impulses lying behind behavior. These, in his spelling out of the drama of personality dynamics, he called the **death wish.** This construct, apparently important to Freud as he viewed the aggressions of World War I, has not been of central significance in recent psychoanalytic thinking.

In young children, according to Freud's constructions, the id seems to rule life with a primitive directness. The young child, without restraint or regret, seeks its pleasures and vents its destructive impulses on the world. But, in time, controls develop. At first, immoral, asocial, and officially disapproved behavior is inhibited only in the presence of disapproving and punishing adults. Later on, the individual interiorizes these external controls. They become his own controls. This system of controls Freud called the **superego,** defining this construct as the moral principle, the principle of propriety, control, decency, and ethicality in the personality.

The third basic construct that seemed necessary to Freud to account for the behaviors he saw was that of **ego.** He found in his patients, as we have seen, an array of primitive and unreasoning urges, on the one hand, and rigid and sometimes equally unreasoning controls on the other. He also saw the capacity to deal intelligently and rationally with reality. This reality principle he called the *ego,* conceiving this factor to be something of an intelligent administrator concerned with finding ways in which the system could maintain an integral survival in the face of the conflicting demands of the id and the superego and in the face of an environment that has an irrefutable reality about it.

Three principal characters, then, walk on the stage of the lifelong drama within the confines of the personality. There is the Calaban, the Old Adam, the id; there is the rigid, uncompromising epitome of rectitude, the superego; and there is the weak but nimble compromiser and arranger, the ego. The central theme of the play is *conflict.* Freud saw an everlasting and irreconcilable conflict between good and evil, between superego and id. And he conceived of much of this conflict occurring beyond the conscious awareness of the ego. As the drama unfolds, the ego is required forever to contend with currents and countercurrents, many of which it cannot fully understand.

The concept of unconsciousness occupies a central place in Freud's theory. He, as an outside observer, saw many behaviors which either completely mystified his patients or were explained by them in terms he himself regarded as either very superficial or beside the mark entirely. It was his view that personal life, like the iceberg, lies mostly beneath the conscious surface. Though most psychologists accept the reality of unconscious processes in the personal system, the idea of unconsciousness, carrying with it the implication of irrationality of much of behavior, is strange if not repulsive to many people whose self-images will not tolerate such an "uncomplimentary" concept.

We already have seen a number of evidences supporting the notion that many behaviors occur beyond, or without, conscious awareness. Perhaps here, by illustration, we can see the kinds of data that led Freud to the conviction that the concept of unconscious processes is necessary for the understanding to the dynamics of behavior.

Case of Mrs. W.

Mrs. W., a 34-year-old housewife with four children and a husband she says she "simply adores," says to her friends many times a day how fortunate she is to have such a family. They are all "living dolls" and she says she has real pity for childless couples. "There is never a dull moment at our house," she says. "It's such a pleasure to help young people grow up. I'd never take a job that takes me away from home."

Mrs. W. is also a member of the board of the League of Women Voters, the president of one PTA and a member of the finance committee of another, a highly dependable member of a bridge club, a twice-a-week golfer, an active member of the Junior League and an occasional volunteer secretary for the local Mental Health Association. She is rarely or never home when the children come in from school. She's *so* busy. She frequently persuades her husband to take the whole family out to dinner since she is "really a very poor cook." When the family has dinner at home the food is often precooked meals, requiring only warming up. Upon being interviewed she demonstrates little knowledge of what her children are interested in, how they are progressing at school, or even where they are at any given time.

In such a case one might expect a strong unconscious resentment at having to play the role of mother and housewife, a resentment and perhaps a hostility that is covered up by excessively loud protestations of conscious enjoyment of family life.

What seems to be happening in such a case is that negative or hostile feelings toward her family are there but are intolerable to a person whose self-image is one of a loving and fully realized American mother and wife. The unacceptable impulses are *repressed*, denied

to consciousness, but they nevertheless seem to be there, influencing behavior.

Case of John B.

John B., a 26-year-old unmarried engineer, lives with his parents. Outwardly he is a fond and dutiful son to his father. He will on any appropriate occasion state his open admiration for his father's history of self-made success, his father's ability as an after-dinner speaker, his father's skill as a bartender, golfer, amateur chef, and gardener. But for the last three years he has forgotten, once entirely and twice for a day, his father's birthday. Last Christmas he gave his father a box of cigars of a brand his father has frequently said he did not like. Recently he borrowed his father's golf clubs and left them at the 18th hole, where they were rained on. When his father takes an automobile trip, John warns him at great length and in gory detail about the accidents he might have unless he drives very carefully.

Do we need the notion here of an unconscious dislike of the father, expressing itself not openly but in hidden and symbolic ways? Probably so.

In its complete form the psychoanalytic theory is a good deal more elaborate than the segments of it we have presented here. But perhaps we have its essence and can, in the next chapter, examine the ways in which the theory applies to conflict, frustration, neurosis and psychosis—the kinds of behavioral matters the theory was designed to deal with.

Criticisms of the Psychoanalytic Movement

Although the psychoanalytic theory is now widely accepted, particularly among those who study and treat the emotionally disturbed, it remains a controversial theory, particularly in the minds of those who wish to gain an understanding of the entire psychological system of the normal person. Among the criticisms frequently and sometimes violently leveled against the psychoanalysts are the following:

1. The theory was created out of a preoccupation with pathology; it remains in doubt that such

a theory can best deal with the normal personality.

2. The theory overemphasizes the unconscious processes in behavior. Normal people may be on much better speaking terms with their own motives than Freud gives them credit for.

3. The theory was created on the basis of the emotional disturbances among middle-class people in Vienna a half-century ago. There is no good evidence that the theory holds equally well for other kinds of people in other cultural settings.

Adler, Jung, and the Neo-Freudians

In spite of the fact that the psychoanalytic theory is accused of being doctrinaire and "party-line" in its rigid adherence to true Freudian doctrine, there have been from the beginning of psychoanalytic thought a number of creative defectors or "deviationists." Well known among the early adherents who moved conceptually away from Freud was Alfred Adler (1920), who rejected Freud's insistence on the prime significance of instinctual drives and built a dynamic theory on other bases. Adler would have little to do with Freud's emphasis on sexual strivings. Instead, he gave prime importance to the child's **organ inferiority** and to the accompanying feelings; he viewed the dynamics of living as the individual's lifelong attempt to contend with the powerful and early feelings of inferiority. Carl Jung was another of Freud's early colleagues who first went along with him and then broke away into theoretical formulations of a markedly different kind. Jung's ideas (1939), like Freud's, were clearly of a dynamic kind, and he also embraced the concept of unconscious processes. But he evolved an elaborate and unique theoretical system resting on the concept of innate ideas and symbols (**archetypes**), springing from the **collective unconscious.**

In recent years there have been a number of influential personality theorists (referred to as **Neo-Freudians**) who have adhered to some of the basic tenets of Freudian theory but who have departed in a variety of respects from the original doctrine. (It perhaps should be pointed out that Freud himself was a neo-Freudian; for, on the basis of his own experience, he changed his theoretical formulations a number of times during his lifetime.) Perhaps the most significant revisions in psychoanalytic theory have been changes (1) that give more emphasis to social factors in both the development and functioning of personality and (2) that endow the ego with a more significant role than Freud gave it in the conduct of life's vital affairs. The writings of Horney (1939), Sullivan (1953), Fromm (1947), Kardiner (1939), and others exemplify a modern psychoanalytic tendency to view personality as social. Hartmann, Kris, and Lowenstein (1947) endow the ego with more functional effectiveness than Freud ever granted. Some of these theorists and these theories will concern us again when we come to deal with psychosis and neurosis (Chap. 17).

DEVELOPMENT OF PERSONALITY

Where does personality come from? Or, to use a more careful phrasing, how do we account for the development of a vast variety of unique organizations of attributes? However we choose to view the adult personality and whatever approach we take to a study of it, we are still faced with the question of what determiners produce the patterns of behavior we see and the underlying patterns of dynamic forces we assume to be there. We of course cannot pursue this question at much length or depth here but perhaps we can develop a general format for constructive thinking about developmental matters.

In very general terms we can say that any psychobiological system, with its present unique organization of attributes, is a product of its biological and psychological history. The system began existence as a unique organism which, through growth and maturation, came into its own particular biological inheritance. At birth, with its unique endowment, it began to engage in the psychological process of sensing, interpreting, responding, and of changing its behavior on the basis of its own particular experience. At the present time, we see the resultant psychobiological entity, with its own personal pattern of motives and emotions, its own personal ways of interpreting the world and its own characteristic ways of responding to it. The present organization of the system has evolved over time as the motivated biological organism has engaged, in accordance with its own capacities and in response to its own changing needs, in the psychological process of interacting with its environment.

From such a broad view we must say that we already have studied the development of personality. We have studied the heredity and the biological development of the human organism. We have studied the motives, both physiological and social, of men; and we have seen how motives—and the ways of satisfying motives—can be learned. We have studied emotions, have seen their function in the psychological process and have dealt with ways in which the organism learns what to be emotional about. We have studied perception, seeing the ways the system interprets its world. And we have studied learning, seeing the principles and mechanisms involved in the change of behavior with experience. In all these matters our primary aim has been to understand the similarities among all human organisms. We have sought for general principles of behavior, general principles applicable to all human organisms. But in the study of similarities and generalities we do not by any means exclude a consideration of differences and uniqueness. Now that we have switched our focus from similarities to differences, turning from a search for general principles to the search for ways of understanding the single individual, we should be able to do so from a well-educated stance. A knowledge of the general must add to our study of the particular, for the individual personality, though we may wish now to emphasize its uniqueness, remains an organism subject to all the laws and principles governing human behavior. Our ultimate view of the unique organization of your attributes or mine *must not* run counter to the facts and principles of heredity, maturation, emotion, motivation, perception, learning, and cognition. More

positively, our view of personality, both of its development and of its present functioning, can be vastly improved and clarified through our knowledge of the human organism's behavior as it engages in the psychological process.

THE ROLE OF LEARNING IN PERSONALITY DEVELOPMENT

When we talk about personality development we are, of course, talking about the development of behavior. Although, as we have seen, both heredity and the biological factors of growth and maturation are involved in the development of behavior, the behaviors which excite our greatest interest in our study of personality are behaviors *that have been learned.* Hence the principles of learning play a cardinally important role in our attempts to describe and understand how you and I came to be the sort of organized systems we are today. Our goals, our hopes, our fears, our aspirations, our insecurities, our interests, and our attitudes—though they all have been and are influenced by hereditary and physiological factors—*have been learned.*

We cannot here trace out again the detailed story of the mechanisms by which traits or personal motives, or interests or attitudes, are learned. In general terms, the student may profit by a quick review of the basic general principles applying to the change of behavior through experience. Motivated behavior, we can say, leads to varied behavior. Some behaviors lead to rewards. They are reinforced. Motivated tension is reduced and the behavior that reduces it is retained. Other behaviors are, from a motivational point of view, ineffective. They lead to no reward or to negative rewards. Such behaviors tend to disappear from the array of the organism's activities. The organism has learned. It has learned personality attributes. In the interlocking operation of motives, learning, and symbolic processes, there are the phenomena of reinforcement, discrimination, and generalization. Out of this intricate and interwoven process emerges the array of personal motives, personal ways of perceiving the world and behaving in it—the personally unique organization of attributes.

It may be possible, at least eventually, to account for all of human learning in terms of the general principles growing out of laboratory research on the learning process. Certainly a knowledge of these principles, as presently defined, can aid enormously in anybody's attempt to understand how behavior of the whole human being comes to be organized into consistent and enduring patterns. However, for thinking and research at the molar level of approach, the concept of **identification** is a useful one as a supplement to such principles as reinforcement and generalization. The process of identification is defined as one whereby the *individual takes on the behavior of another significant individual and behaves as if he were that other individual.*

We see the *process of identification* most clearly in the child's relation to its parents. During its first year or two of life the child's position in the world is one of very great dependency. He is not required to do anything to earn either the satisfactions for his physiological needs or the love of his parents. Later, as he grows older, external pressures are applied in the interest of having the child learn the approved ways of civilization. He must show more mature behavior if he is to gain satisfaction. He is denied approval until he performs as people of his age level are supposed to perform. He must control his bladder and bowels, he must dress himself, he must eat with spoons from plates, he must go off and sleep in his own room. If he doesn't do these things he isn't loved. In the face of these bothersome pressures upon him, he notices that adults quite easily gain the gratifications which he must earn by hard labor. This discovery does not by any means increase his affection for his parents, of course, but it does tell him, in some vague and unconscious way, that there is profit in behaving like a grownup. So, if he is a boy, he *identifies* with his father, seeming to say to himself that if he behaves like his father he will gain the gratification his father gains. Then he can be independent,

Figure 15–6. IDENTIFICATION. *A youngster identifies with parents, older siblings, heroes. He "tries on" the behavior of those older than himself, thereby finding out whether the more mature patterns of behavior are rewarding.*

then he can be important, then he can eat what and when he pleases, and then he doesn't have to go off at night and sleep alone in his own crib. And because his father's standards of behavior become his own standards, he is relieved of the necessity of troublesome rebellion. He begins to talk with his father's intonations, to walk like his father, and in games with other children he tries with all his might to win the opportunity to "be the daddy." He gets practice, through play, in behaving like his father. Similar processes can be observed as girl children relate with their mothers. Later, there may be identification with teachers, with other family adults, or with heroes of movies, television dramas, or literature. The processes of identification are powerful in bringing about the child's learning of the ways of his family, his class, his culture. We shall return in the next chapter (p. 481) to a view of identification as an adjustmental process and shall, in dealing with social psychology, see it in yet another context (Chap. 18). Here we simply define the process and point out its probable significance for personality development.

Particularly in the psychoanalytic theory of personality is identification stressed, for that view of adult behavior places cardinal importance on learning experience during the early years of life.

CULTURE AND PERSONALITY

Closer to the molar level of analysis that seems presently most useful in the study of personality is a consideration not of the processes of learning but of *what* the individual learns. The mechanisms of learning can tell us *how* the individual learns what he learns, but from the standpoint of personality it may be more profitable to talk about the *content* of learning and to do such talking on the basis of observing the conditions under which particular habits or attitudes or values or motives are implanted in the individual personality.

One way to analyze the content of learning and the conditions under which personality is learned is to examine the relation between the individual's learned behaviors and the learned behaviors prevalent in the culture in which the individual lives. Most generally, the individual learns the behaviors that are approved by his elders. If he is born into a tribe of Crow Indians, for example (McAllester, 1941), he probably will have a pervasive fear of water. He will not eat food that comes from water, he will tell you tall tales about frightening water monsters, and he will be mightily insulted if water is thrown upon him. This un-American orientation to water probably has something to do with the practice among Crow parents of pouring water down the noses of children in order to quiet them when they cry. Throughout his life, the Crow individual receives **reinforcement** from his elders and his peers whenever he behaves toward water in the culturally sanctioned manner.

Child-rearing practices vary significantly from culture to culture and have an obvious bearing on the kind of adult personalities produced. Along this line, one anthropologist (Williams, 1965) has listed six established

patterns of parental behavior that lend a distinct character to socialization among the Dusun, a people of Borneo. These six patterns (and we can see how child-rearing practices in any culture might be examined with respect to these patterns) are as follows:

1. A pattern of assumptions about the nature of children.
2. A pattern of rewards and punishments.
3. A pattern concerning work responsibilities or freedom from work.
4. A pattern of supernatural sanctions to control behavior.
5. A pattern of judgments of the child as a nonadult or nonperson.
6. A pattern of affective bonds to parents and grandparents.

With respect to the first pattern, the Dusun hold to what the standard American parent might regard as the sour and jaundiced view that children are noisy, sickly, violent, quarrelsome, wasteful, characterless beings prone to destructiveness and thievery.

Similarly distinctive patterns can be spelled out under each of the other five rubrics above. Perhaps more than one of the patterns finds expression in the lullabies the Dusun mothers sing to their young. One of these deals with the soul of the dead who carries a big stick and big knife and comes to beat the baby: sleep, sleep, sleep. Another pictures a hawk flying about looking for prey, looking for something to snatch up in his claws, and ends by calling down the hawk to snatch up the baby (Williams, 1965).

This anthropological researcher also reports that Dusun mothers, after such lullabies and when the baby is just on the verge of sleep, will frequently sound a loud and startling "huh" in the baby's face, whereupon the baby falls almost instantly asleep. (The ethnologist also observes that the adult Dusun will frequently fall asleep in reaction to stress. In a lull during a battle or upon a stressful development during proceedings in court, the soldier or the witness may drift off into sleep. It is easy to speculate about the connection between the infant training and the adult behavior.)

Figure 15–7. CULTURE AND PERSONALITY. *The individual learns in accordance with the organized system of rewards and punishments in his culture. The American boy tends to learn one kind of personality, the Saudi Arabian another.*

We can conceive of a culture as an organized system of positive and negative reinforcements which, when administered by other, generally older members of the culture, succeed in producing "civilized" behavior in the new arrival.

LEARNING AND SOCIAL CLASS

Each social class in a society will tend to have its own particular set of approved behaviors and, through the effective operation of positive and negative reinforcements, and through processes of identification, will teach those behaviors to most members of the class. Among the lower-class families in America,

for example (Warner, 1953), there seems to be a premium on immediate gratification of impulses. Food is to be immediately eaten and money to be spent. Among middle-class families, by contrast (Havighurst and Taba, 1949), there is much greater emphasis on long-time planning for the future, on delayed reward. Food is to be treated wisely, and money is to be saved. The lower and middle classes also differ significantly with respect to sexual behavior. In the lower classes there are fewer and different inhibitions and strong inclinations toward immediate and casual sexual gratification. In the middle class, sexual activity is encompassed about by many controls; courtship is a highly prescribed and ritualized procedure, and sexual relationships are viewed in horror except within the proper matrimonial conditions.

The individual is under tremendous pressure to learn and to make his own behavior conform to the attitudes and standards prevalent in his social class.

Figure 15–8. SOCIAL CLASS AND PERSONALITY. *To illustrate the role of class membership on personality, one might imagine how well an upper-middle-class American youngster, the same age as the one pictured here, would react to—and survive in—this kind of environment.*

LEARNING IN THE FAMILY

The parents, as the administrators of direct rewards and punishments, have a highly significant hand in determining what behaviors will be learned and what general stance the individual will take in his adjustment to life.

There is a large and growing literature showing the ways in which parental behavior and the atmosphere in the home produce personality effects in children. Sometimes the effects can be direct and relatively simple matters of reinforcement. The child may be either rewarded or punished for outgoing and friendly behavior, for example. If rewarded, if encouraged to approach people and expect warmth from them, outgoing behavior will be stamped in. If friendliness is punished, it may disappear, with social hesitancy taking its place.

Often, the learning of the child cannot be dealt with in terms of simple reinforcement phenomena. One study, for example (Levy,

1943), demonstrated a relation between overprotection on the part of the mother and something that appeared to be a pervasive anxiety on the part of the children. The mothers in the study, whether dominatingly overprotective or indulgently overprotective, tended to keep their children always in sight, psychologically tied to the maternal apron strings. There was frequent physical contact between mother and child, including continued bathing and dressing long past the age at which the children could have been independent in such matters. If the child were even mildly sick, there was ostentatious and protracted nursing.

The children of these overprotective mothers tended to demonstrate definite effects of their experience. The children of the domineeringly overprotective mothers tended to be anxiously submissive, shy, withdrawn. The children of the indulgently overprotective mothers showed equal anxiety but expressed it in terms of tyrannical or dominating behavior toward their peers, leading to little friendship and much isolation. They were disobedient and demanding in their relations with adults. We shall see later the kinds of adjustment that may produce overprotectiveness in the mother and may flavor the child's learning situation in ways of which neither he nor his mother is aware.

INDIVIDUAL LEARNING

We have seen before that we cannot understand a human individual completely by knowing his culture, his class, his family, or any other group to which he belongs, or any gross category into which we may place him. Though his personality is developed in some kind of accordance with the learning demands placed on him by his culture, class, family, and by other groups to which he belongs, he remains a unique organism and his learning is often a highly individual affair. To know fully about the development of any single personality, then, we would need to understand how he, in his own unique way, has seen, interpreted, responded to, and learned about the world in which he has lived.

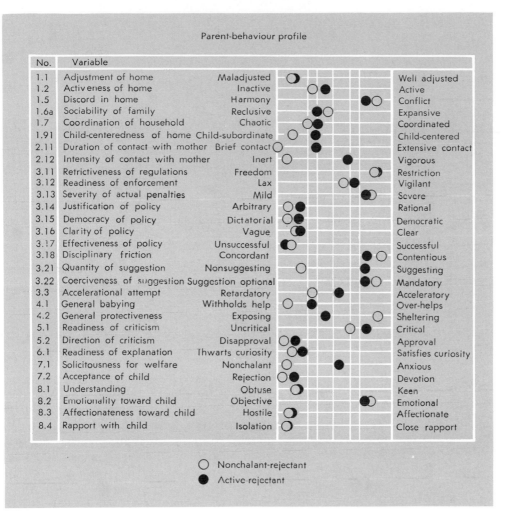

Figure 15–9. PATTERNS OF PARENTAL BEHAVIOR. *This form, with its accompanying rating scales, has been used to study the patterns of parental behavior in actual homes. The individual family can be rated on each of the continua indicated on the right side of the chart. The open circles above represent the ratings of one family described as nonchalant-rejectant. The solid circles represent ratings of another family described as active-rejectant. Evidence shows that the child's personality is clearly affected by these parental patterns. (From Baldwin, 1948, reproduced by permission of the Society for Research in Child Development.)*

THE PROBLEM OF PREDICTING INDIVIDUAL BEHAVIOR

Both for the layman and the scientist one prime reason for studying personality is to gain an increased ability to predict individual behavior. For practical purposes, prediction is obviously important. We want to know whether we should associate with or hire or marry an individual. For scientific purposes, prediction is equally important in that successful prediction serves as a validation of observations, hypotheses, and theories. All the approaches to personality we have examined in the foregoing pages attempt to predict behavior by observing, analyzing, and conceptu-

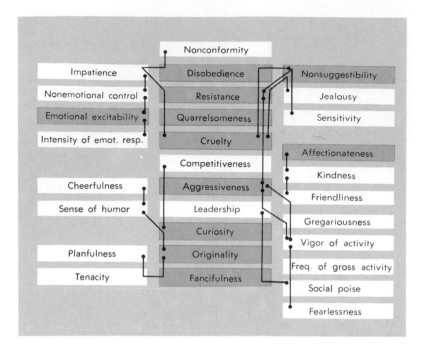

Figure 15–10. THE PERSONALITY CONSEQUENCES
OF PARENTAL PRACTICE. *If the home atmosphere
is characterized by high control and low
democracy, the child will be relatively low in
traits named in the shaded areas. Variables
touched by any single line are intercorrelated
with r's of .50 or more. (Data from Baldwin
et al., 1945; by permission of the American
Psychological Association.)*

alizing individual behaviors or persisting individual motives. The prevailing notion is that
patterns of behavior, once established, will occur again and again. But none of the approaches explicitly attempts to deal with the
situations in which behavior will recur or occur. There may be serious question about the
accuracy that can be achieved by such a focus
on the individual, a focus that does not deal
with the nature of the situations the individual confronts or will confront. To say, with
whatever accuracy, that an individual has a
need for deference or a strong superego is not
to say that either of these conditions of the organism will produce certain specific behaviors
on every possible occasion. On many occasions, yes. But on precisely *what* occasions,

in *what kinds* of situations? We cannot say.
In our everyday predictions of people, we
probably do a fairly good job of viewing the
individual in a situation, and we do, with
some success, predict how an individual will
behave in situations not yet occurred. But
generally speaking, in our focus on the individual, we are not very keen in analyzing the
nature of the situations in which personality
reveals itself through behavior. A case can be
made that prediction of behavior cannot be
very keen or accurate until we find a way to
study the *individual in a situation.*

Although we cannot now consider the more
situation-oriented approaches to personality,
we should point out that they do exist and are,
in one variant or another, leading to what may
be highly productive research (Lewin, 1935;
Rotter, 1954).

SUMMARY

1. Some psychologists prefer to study separate segments of the psychological process;
others wish to regard the psychological sys-

tem as a whole and to study it as a unitary phenomenon.

2. If we observe the behavior of a whole person, we see consistent and enduring attributes, organization, and uniqueness; personality is defined as the unique organization of enduring attributes of the human individual.

3. In the scientific study of personality, as in our everyday attempts to understand individuals, a frequent aim is to see what behaviors occur with what behaviors, and why. We wish general descriptions and, if possible, general explanations in terms of underlying factors.

4. In the attempt to see clearly what behaviors occur with what behaviors there have been studies of types, of temperaments, of expressive traits, and of dynamic traits.

5. Hippocrates' humoral typology and Kretschmer's character typology, based on types of physique, represent attempts to describe in simple and all-inclusive terms the entire personality; typologies present certain inherent difficulties, mainly in that they oversimplify.

6. The work of Sheldon represents an attempt to relate body build to temperament through a dimensional rather than a typological approach. The dimensions of physique—endomorphy, mesomorphy, and ectomorphy—relate to the temperamental dimensions of viscerotonia, somatotonia, and cerebrotonia.

7. Stylistic traits are "adverbial" traits, dealing with the ways in which behavior occurs rather than with goals or motives; studies of expressive behavior have demonstrated the existence of consistent and general stylistic traits, such as an emphatic trait.

8. Motivational traits—or personal motives—refer to the dynamic conditions or factors in the personality that are inferred to lie behind observed behaviors. H. A. Murray and his associates have defined and investigated a large array of motivational traits.

9. The factor-analysis procedure, applied to a wide variety of ratings and test results, has yielded a large number of clusters of behaviors that may constitute basic traits of personality; these factor-analytic results and others add to our knowledge of personality; but probably we do not yet have the "final" or the "best" way to describe what behaviors occur with what behaviors.

10. Cognitive theorists focus on variations in opinion or attitude, or on "cognitive style." Research in this area includes studies of authoritarianism, dogmatism, and perceptual proclivities; and George Kelly's "psychology of personal constructs."

11. The self-concept, emphasized by Carl Rogers, is seen as playing a unifying role in behavior; the individual is guided by his self-concept and when faced with evidence that is inconsistent with his self-concept will face discomfort and may distort his perception of reality.

12. The psychoanalytic approach to personality is dynamic rather than descriptive, is nonelementistic, is selective.

13. Freud, examining data from the life histories, free associations, and dreams of emotionally disturbed patients, invented a system of constructs to account for personality functioning; he created the primitive id, consisting of the libido or life-wish and the death-wish, the superego, or the principle of controlled propriety, and the ego, or the principle of realistic intelligence.

14. Central to Freud's dynamic theory are the ideas of conflict and of unconscious motivation.

15. The psychoanalytic theory has been criticized on the grounds that it is preoccupied with pathology, that it overemphasizes unconscious processes, that it is closed to experimental examination, that it is based on the study of a peculiar population of individuals, that it is not eclectic.

16. Freud's followers Alfred Adler and Carl Jung later broke away from him. Adler stressed organ inferiority rather than sexual strivings. Jung developed a system involving archetypes and the collective unconscious. Twentieth-century Neo-Freudians give more stress than did Freud to social factors and the role of the ego.

17. A thorough study of the development of personality would involve much of the material on development, motivation, emotion, perception, and learning that we have already dealt with in this book, except that now the focus would be on the individual rather than on human beings in general.

18. Learning, of course, plays a central role in the development of personality, for in large measure we learn our personalities; the concept of identification is a key one in understanding personality development, and a study of personality development in various cultural, social, and familial settings can reveal, in a molar way, a great deal about the content of personal learning.

19. The problem of predicting individual behavior is made difficult by the fact that we cannot predict the situation that will confront the individual.

RESEARCH REPORTS

RESEARCH ON EXPRESSIVE BEHAVIOR [*]

This study deals with the perceived consistency of expression in various kinds of "writing" that are produced by different sets of muscles of the same individual. Hence, the study is very much in the tradition of early research on expressive movement. This study proceeds on the hypothesis that if an individual's handwriting expresses primarily an imagined design, which the individual effectuates by available efferent mechanisms, then it will have elements in common with the various expressions of his imagined design, whatever the set of muscles or mechanisms involved in producing the design.

The experimenter investigated this kind of relationship by eliciting from each of three male and three female "writers" 16 samples of written material. These samples of "writing" consisted of two samples done in each of the following manners:

1. Normal writing with the dominant hand.
2. Dominant hand, eyes closed.
3. Nondominant hand.
4. With a pencil strapped to the foot on the dominant side.
5. With a pencil held in plastic grip in the mouth.
6. Moving a clipboard and paper against a pencil held in a clamp.
7. With a pencil held in a harness projecting from the chest.
8. Using the dominant hand but behind the back.

Each writer wrote eight commonplace expressions, such as "My country, 'tis of thee"; and each of these commonplace expressions was written twice in each of the ways listed above. Then the samples of writing were submitted to judges, 15 male and 15 female employees of a state hospital; a judge was first given the normal handwriting sample of two writers, and was asked to look over the other samples of writing from each of these two subjects and then to match the other samples with the samples produced in the normal manner, so that all the specimens from one person would be together. The results obtained by these judges could be compared with chance expectation.

In every instance of writing, whatever the mode of its production, samples were matched to an extent apparently greater than chance alone would allow; but not all matchings were *significantly* greater than chance. The ones where matching was most successful involved the matching of the normal handwriting with writing by foot, writing by the nondominant hand, and writing with the eyes closed.

These results led the researcher to the conclusion that "a complex, habitual motor pattern, of which handwriting is the commonest example, is a function of the person's imagined design, but only to the extent that existing neuromuscular mechanisms will sustain its effective expression" (p. 86).

---

[*] Joseph Lyons, Recognition of expressive patterns as a function of their mode of production, *J. consult. Psychol.*, 1964, **28**, 85–86.

HOW ENDURING ARE ENDURING ATTRIBUTES? *

Personality theorists are naturally interested in determining whether or not personality traits measured or delineated at one time are to be found at another and much later time. They are also interested in (a) the bearing of any given personality trait on the general adjustment of an individual, (b) the relation of a given trait to other traits, and (c) the change in any patterning of traits as the personality develops. Similarly, personality theorists are interested in the way in which the individual learns and enacts the role behaviors that are required of him in his society. Everyone has to learn to enact a sex role, either masculine or feminine; and the way the individual learns to enact this role has a bearing on the reinforcements that will come to him from an approving or disapproving society.

The present study attempts to examine the long-term consequences of an individual male's high or low masculine identification during adolescence. Subjects for the present study—selected from among 100 males who were participating in a protracted longitudinal growth study—were 14 male subjects, now in their late 30's, who had had highly masculine interests during their late teens; and 12 subjects, also in their late 30's, who were known to have had relatively feminine interests during their late teens. The two groups did not differ significantly in intelligence or in social-class status. For the present study each of the subjects was interviewed from two to six hours by a highly trained clinical psychologist, who wrote a detailed report on the sessions and, in addition, made a total of 86 impressionistic ratings of the subjects' status on such matters as self-expressiveness, sociability, poise, emotional tensions, drives, cognitive attributes, and a series of other "manifest traits." For these ratings the psychologists used a seven-point scale. It was not possible in this study to secure data on reliability of these ratings, but the researcher points out that the interviewer had no knowledge, prior to the interviews, of the developmental histories of the individuals nor any access to available data that were gathered in connection with the growth study. It was possible to make quantitative comparisons between the more masculine subjects and the more feminine subjects on each of the 86

impressionistic ratings. (The masculinity and femininity scores were those attained by the individuals on the test of masculinity-femininity administered twenty years before the present study began.)

In summary, the experimenter reported that those who had had relatively feminine interest patterns as adolescents manifested more of the "emotional-expressive" role characteristics as adults; they were rated as more dependent but more social in orientation. By contrast, those with highly masculine adolescent patterns possessed, both in their late teens and in their late 30's, more active and "instrumental" characteristics; on both occasions they showed greater self-sufficiency, less social orientation, and, in adulthood, less introspectiveness. These results, then, indicate a relatively persistent and long-lasting attribute of the personality structure.

However, there was not much congruence over time with respect to other characteristics of personality. During adolescence, the researcher reports, the highly masculine subjects possessed more self-confidence and more feelings of adequacy than did the more feminine group; but as adults, the more masculine students were lacking in qualities of leadership, in dominance, in self-confidence, and in self-acceptance. It seems as if the highly masculine pattern was more socially rewarded in adolescence than in adulthood and led to more self-confidence then than it did later in mature life. These highly masculine subjects had been socially successful as adolescents and perhaps were well adjusted, but then they failed to develop those attributes of sociability and outgoingness that may be essential for the achievement of good relationships in adulthood. The more feminine subjects, by contrast, seemed to "improve" with time. Those who were more feminine as adolescents seemed to develop during that time a social orientation and perhaps the social skills that lead to later social and vocational success and to later feelings of adequacy and belongingness.

OPEN-MINDEDNESS AND PROBLEM SOLVING *

A number of attributes of the individual have been shown to bear on both the success and the

* Paul H. Mussen, Long-term consequents of masculinity of interests in adolescence, *J. consult. Psychol.*, 1962, **26**, 435–440.

* Frank Restle, Martha Andrews, and Milton Rokeach, Differences between open- and closed-minded subjects on learning-set and oddity problems, *J. abn. soc. Psychol.*, 1964, **68**, 648–654.

style with which he confronts problems. In recent years there has been a growing interest in a variable, *dogmatism*, which has a bearing on what is described in the literature as open-mindedness and closed-mindedness. This variable has been measured by a dogmatism scale, described on page 443.

The present study tests the hypothesis that subjects with closed minds will differ from open-minded subjects in the success with which they handle certain intellectual problems—namely, that open-minded subjects will evaluate information on its own merits and seek for *principles* in solving a problem, while closed-minded people, by contrast, will seek for the hints and cues given by authorities.

In this experiment, open-minded and closed-minded subjects (as diagnosed by an accepted test) confronted two kinds of problems: (1) a problem in which the subjects were required for solution to look closely to the authority figure in the situation, the experimenter; (2) a problem involving the learning of a principle rather than the learning of the preferences, or the probable preferences, of an authoritative experimenter.

The subjects in the experiment were 240 introductory psychology students, as well as 400 freshmen, newly arrived in the fall of 1960 at Michigan State University. All of these subjects were given the Dogmatism Scale, and two groups of 40 were chosen—one group from the lowest 15 per cent and the other from the highest 15 per cent of the distribution of scores on the scale. In the open group, there were 25 males and 15 females and, in the closed group, 29 males and 11 females. Each subject was brought into the experimental situation and presented with a series of 8 x 12 cards, which represented problems he was to solve. On each of the cards there were three stimulus forms cut from construction paper. Each form was made up of one of five distinct straight-line shapes, one of four colors, and one of two sizes. Each of the cards contained a form (A) on the right side of the card, another form (B) on the left side of the card, and then one of those two forms repeated in the middle of the card. Thus, on any given card presented to the subject, the forms A and B could be arranged in any one of four different ways: *AAB, ABA, BBA,* or *BAB.* The two forms on any one card differed in two of the three dimensions of shape, color, and size. The set of stimulus cards contained 30 pairs of forms (30 different A's and 30 different

B's). Each of the 30 pairs was then arranged in the four possible ways described above, so that there were 30 decks of four cards each. When an experimenter presented a card to the subject, the subject pointed either to the right or to the left and was then reinforced verbally by "yes" or "no." Through a trial-and-error procedure of this sort, he had to learn the solution.

For the first part of the experimental procedure, the subjects had to find out which of the two end forms the experimenter had arbitrarily chosen to be correct on a card. In this part of the experiment, the middle form was simply a source of irrelevant cues. After the subject had learned the first correct response, the experimenter suddenly changed the rules, so that whatever form he had decided upon as originally correct became suddenly wrong. The subjects then had to reorient themselves to a reversal of the rules. Throughout this part of the experiment, there was no principle to follow, only cues to the experimenter's arbitrary decision about what was correct.

In the next part of the experiment, the part involving a "problem of oddities," the subjects were presented the same cards, but their task was to point out, by the same trial-and-error procedure, which of the three forms was the odd one.

When the results were tabulated, it was clear that the open-minded subjects solved the oddities problem faster than did the closed-minded subjects. As expected, the open-minded subjects sought for and found the principle involved, a principle that was independent of the arbitrary will of the experimenter himself. These open-minded subjects had difficulty in solving the original set of problems, where it was necessary to find out which form had been arbitrarily selected as the right one. Apparently, the open-minded subjects, even in facing a problem where there was no principle, began looking for a rational principle that could guide their behavior. By contrast, the closed-minded subjects did better at solving the problem involving the discovery of the arbitrary rules. They did not do very well in finding the principle that would enable them to solve rapidly the problem of oddities.

The order in which the problems were presented to the subjects significantly affected their performance. For open-minded subjects who solved first the oddities problem, the mean total errors was 4.45. If these same subjects were given the other problem first, their error on the oddities problem was 11.25. By contrast, the closed subjects scored 11.50 errors when the oddities problem was given first, and 13.25 errors on the oddities problem when the other problem was given first.

The authors argue, but not on the basis of data from experimental controls, that differences in anxiety or intelligence cannot properly account for the obtained results.

SUGGESTED READINGS

Allport, G. W. *Pattern and growth in personality.* New York: Holt, Rinehart and Winston, 1961.

Freud, Sigmund. *A general introduction to psycho-analysis.* New York: Boni and Liveright, 1920 (reprinted by Washington Square Press, 1960).

Gordon, Jesse E. *Personality and behavior.* New York: Macmillan, 1963.

Hall, C. S., and Gardner Lindzey. *Theories of personality.* New York: Wiley, 1957.

Kagan, Jerome, and H. A. Moss. *Birth to maturity: A study in psychological development.* New York: Wiley, 1962.

Kelly, G. A. *The psychology of personal constructs.* Vol. I. *A theory of personality.* New York: Norton, 1955.

Rogers, C. R. *On becoming a person: A therapist's view of psychotherapy.* Boston: Houghton Mifflin, 1961.

Rokeach, Milton. *The open and closed mind: Investigations into the nature of belief systems and personality systems.* New York: Basic Books, 1960.

White, R. W. *Lives in progress: A study of the natural growth of personality.* New York: Dryden Press, 1952.

OUTLINE / CHAPTER 16

I. THE ADJUSTING INDIVIDUAL

   A. Criteria of Effective Adjusting
   B. The Problem of Frustrated, Multiple, and Conflicting Motives

II. FRUSTRATION

   A. Direct Reaction to Frustration
   B. Other Reactions to Frustration

III. CONFLICT

   A. Kinds of Conflict
     1. Conflicting Habits
     2. Conflicting Cognitions
     3. Conflicting Motives
   B. Field-of-Force Analysis of Conflict
     1. Approach-Approach Conflict
     2. Avoidance-Avoidance Conflict
     3. Approach-Avoidance Conflict
     4. Double Approach-Avoidance Conflict
   C. Sources of Conflict
     1. Intra-individual Sources
     2. Conflicting Values
     3. Role Conflicts
   D. Tension-Producing Nature of Conflict
   E. Ego Involvement in Frustration and Conflict
   F. Unconscious Factors in Conflict and Frustration
   G. Conflict and Anxiety
   H. Defensive Reactions to Frustration and Conflict
     1. Rationalization
     2. Reaction Formation
     3. Compensation
     4. Fantasy
     5. Projection
     6. Identification
     7. Displacement
     8. Regressive Responses
     9. Repression of Entire Conflict

IV. SUMMARY

V. RESEARCH REPORTS

CHAPTER 16

ADJUSTING

THE ADJUSTING INDIVIDUAL

Human individuals, as organized systems, seek the goals that will satisfy their patterns of physiological and psychological **motives;** they seek to adjust, to achieve a working relationship with the **environment.** And in this chapter we seek to study the process of adjusting—to study the success with which goals are achieved, the form and flavor of goal-seeking behavior, and the events that ensue when goal-seeking behavior is delayed or blocked.

From the time of the **functionalists,** who thrived about a half a century ago, psychologists have been interested in the phenomena of adjusting, in understanding the processes whereby the individual contends with and survives in his environment. In one sense, of course, all psychological science is concerned with the phenomena of adjusting, for all psychology deals in some way with the interactions of the individual with the environment. But some present-day psychologists, mainly those who ply the more molar approaches to behavior, are interested in learning about the ways in which an individual, as an organized system, meets the demands of his environment.

Questions and assertions concerning human adjustment come at different levels of abstractness. Many people in our society, some very learned and some not, are willing to ask questions and to make statements about an ideal personality structure or the truly human adjustment of human beings, about the nature of the good life, about the characteristics of the good person. Psychologists, as scientists, are by no means especially equipped to make assertions about such matters. To talk scientifically about the factually true or about the theoretically tenable is not the same, in form or in spirit, as talking about the everlastingly good. The goodness or badness of life or of the individuals who lead it are matters requiring ethical or philosophical or religious treatment. The scientist, as scientist, can contribute substantive knowledge and alternative interpretations of data to those who wish to make evaluative assertions about good men leading the good life, but ethical or philosophical or theological evaluations are beyond the realm of science.

Psychologists can and do concern themselves, however, with over-all dimensions of human adjustment and, as *applied* scientists, can and do make attempts to change adjustment for the better. The practicing psychologist, as an applied scientist, can and does, for example, help diagnose cases of emotional disturbances and does help prescribe and carry out treatments designed to change the nature of the disturbed individual's adjustment. The psychologist can do these things because our Western society regards as poor the adjustment of such a one as the homicidal psychotic, and there is social approval for professional intervention in the adjustment of such individuals.

The psychologist as pure scientist can also involve himself in the problem of emotional disturbance; once there is an objective description and definition of behavior tendencies involved in homicidal paranoia (see p. 505), the psychological researcher can, without making any value judgments, follow his interests and ply his research skills. He can try to find out, for example, what earlier experiences have led up to the present adjustmental phenomena.

In human and social terms, a paranoid adjustment is poor adjustment. But in strictly scientific terms, one form of adjustment is as good as another. The deluded psychotic in the mental hospital has reached one way of interacting with his environment, while the popular and respected president of the senior class has evolved another form of adjustment. There is no doubt which form of adjustment would be regarded, in most cultures of the world, as the better. But from a scientific

point of view, both adjustments are equally in evidence and equally deserving of study.

Although there is no universal agreement that the individual who is emotionally or behaviorally or mentally disturbed should be referred to as "mentally ill" (p. 490), the individual's adjustment *can* be described and, with some degree of accuracy, labeled. Nor is there much disagreement that efforts should be made to change the disturbed individual's manner of adjusting. These are matters that will concern us in the next chapter.

When it comes to describing and labeling the nature of the adjustment of the individual who is clearly not disturbed, some very complex intellectual problems arise. And when it comes to matters of "good adjustment" or "good personality," especially if these characterizations carry the implication that we ought to labor to make everybody "well adjusted," serious ethical questions arise. Psychologists have nevertheless talked and written about such matters as the nature of effective personal functioning and have tried to describe dimensions of the mature personality. In this chapter we will look first at some of the literature dealing at this level with problems of adjustment. Then we will confront, at what is a more compatible level for many psychologists, the less abstract adjustmental processes involved when the individual is thrown into frustration or conflict.

CRITERIA OF EFFECTIVE ADJUSTING

Many personality theorists have attempted, each in terms congruent with his own theoretical system, to describe the characteristics of the individual who is functioning with conspicuous adequacy. The characteristics and behavior of such an individual have been described in various ways. But, as one theorist (Jahoda, 1958) has pointed out, there are a number of common and recurring themes in the writing of those personality theorists who concern themselves with the quality of human adjustment. It may be profitable to examine these themes.

1. *Realistic and accepting attitudes toward oneself*. Many theorists of personality agree

that the mature personality or the fully effective individual or the successfully adjusting
individual is characterized by a certain orientation to himself as a person. Gordon Allport
(1937), a leading personality theorist, regards
self-objectification as a key criterion of the
mature personality. According to Allport, the
mature individual can view himself with perspective and humor, can see his own actual
objectives in relation to possible objectives,
and can compare his opinion of himself with
the opinions others hold of him. Carl Rogers
(1961) emphasizes *self-acceptance* and *accuracy of self-perception* as characteristics of
"fully functioning persons." Roger's fully functioning person is free from pretensions or
phoniness, and, as he grows, is capable of
realizing his own potential. Erik Erikson
(1963, 1964), along a consonant line, emphasizes that the developing individual needs a
sense of identity, a belief that he, and other
people as well, can maintain some degree of
sameness and continuity over a period of
time.

2. *Continued growth, development, and
self-actualization.* In addition, according to
many personality theorists (Carl Rogers,
1961; Fromm, 1947, 1955; Maslow, 1950), the
best-adjusted individual continues to grow
throughout life, to move toward "self-realiza-
tion" or "self-actualization." The term "self-
actualization," first used in the psychological
literature (Goldstein, 1940) to refer to a process seen as occurring in every organism, was
described as something of a master motive
that initiates behavior and dominates life.

One writer (Maslow, 1950) selected for
study a group of conspicuously successful and
effective undergraduates and then set down a
number of traits that appeared consistently in
their behavior. He found that these students
generally had some notion of progress toward
selfhood, progress toward becoming what one
can become. These students Maslow described
as "*self-actualizing*" individuals. Another
theorist (Sanford, 1962) describes growth as
a continual process, in which the individual
is increasingly able to *differentiate,* to make
finer and finer distinctions about more and
more aspects of himself and the world; and to

integrate, to organize experiences more inclu-
sively into functioning wholes of separate
systems and subsystems. No theorist has ever
emphasized stagnation or rigidity as characteristics of the fully effective individual.

3. *Integration.* The process of organizing
discrete responses, habits, subsystems, and
systems into larger systems has been regarded
as a key aspect of growth but has also been
described separately as a criterion of full maturity. The psychoanalytic theorists frequently
refer to the idea of a *balance* among, or *integration* of, the forces of **ego, superego,** and **id.**
It was Freud's own notion, expressed in the
oft-quoted statement "Where id was, there
shall ego be," that personal integration is
achieved by the gradual growth of ego, so that
it, as a rational principle, could establish control over the blind forces of unreason, whether
those forces are found in the id or in the
superego. In one form or another the principle of integration seems to be prominent in
the views of other theorists. Allport (1937),
for example, talks of a *unifying philosophy
of life.* Such a philosophy, according to Allport, serves as a framework to give meaning
to life and to supply a sense of direction to
one's major activities. Rogers (1961), in seeking to describe the "fully functioning person,"
also talks about a movement toward integrated
self-direction and away from a slavish adherence to the wayward expectations of others.
No personality theorist recommends inconsistency or disorganization as a desirable quality of a successfully adjusting individual.

4. *Individual autonomy.* Many personality
theorists emphasize that the effectively functioning or mature personality has *autonomy.*
Maslow (1950) points out that his self-actualizing people are relatively free from the demands of either the physical or the social environment. They are able somehow to be true
to themselves and to tolerate social rejection
in the interest of being free and autonomous
in their own way. Maslow describes these
people as resistant to enculturation; they can
adopt critical attitudes toward the sacred cows
of their own cultures. Rogers also emphasizes
movement toward autonomous self-direction,
as we have seen, and an increased freedom

from adherence to expectations of others. Most of the **ego psychologists** (e.g., Hartmann, 1951) emphasize as desirable a growth toward autonomy. Similarly, Fromm (1947, 1955) stresses that the effective individual, the one who achieves a "productive orientation to life," must escape from a "receptive orientation" and move into something more autonomous and creative. To all of these theorists, then, the fully effective individual *acts* on the basis of processes occurring within himself; he does not merely *react* passively to other people or to outside events. Rather than accommodating himself to outside demands, he assimilates outside events into his own ongoing processes.

5. *Clear perception of reality*. Almost every theorist who deals at all with the general quality of adjusting emphasizes that the adjusted person must have a clear perception of reality. Certainly no theorist recommends delusion as the basis of effective or successful or adequate or mature or healthy functioning.

6. *Mastery of the environment*. According to many theorists, effective adjusting requires successful "coping" with the environment. If the individual is to function effectively, if he is to contend successfully with the various demands of an environment, he must have a realistic and functioning armamentarium of skills and insights and knowledge.

THE PROBLEM OF FRUSTRATED, MULTIPLE, AND CONFLICTING MOTIVES

At any given stage of his life history, the human being may be regarded as an organized system with patterns of motivational tendencies and arrays of learned responses, which in the past have served with some success to satisfy his motives. Given these facts, the organism's life of adjusting would be a simple process (1) if motives became aroused one at a time, (2) if the world were such a wonderful place that an infinitely varied array of satisfactions were there for the taking, and (3) if the individual's available array of habits enabled him to make precisely the proper response for the quick and easy connection of motive with satisfaction.

It does not take a psychologist to point out that none of these conditions is met in ordinary human existence. The individual must lead his life in a world by no means ideally tailored to the needs of the single unique personality. There are barriers and pitfalls and shortages; also, because other people are always around, there are also reluctancies, contrary-mindednesses, competitions, resentments, aggressions, and hostilities. Further, it can be counted on that the world will change, so that yesterday's firm habits and last week's cherished mode of existence are disturbingly inadequate for today's demands. Motivated behavior is blocked, and goals are often either very difficult to reach or are altogether unobtainable; frustration is pervasive and perhaps inevitable.

The life of adjusting is further complicated by the reality that motives do not become activated singly. A number of motivating conditions are very likely to operate simultaneously; and each one, with some degree of insistence, makes its own demands. Often, we are motivated at the same time toward two opposing goals or two mutually exclusive end states. Sometimes, as the psychoanalysts have pointed out, conflicting motives may be at the very core of the personality and may exert urgent pressures upon the system and, to complicate matters further, may create anxieties and other tensions that can affect our comfort and our lives while still remaining beyond the reach of consciousness.

In the following pages we deal with the organism's behavior when motives are blocked and with its reactions to conflicting motives.

FRUSTRATION

When many millions of people, each one seeking satisfaction for his own pattern of needs, live in a world that does not readily bend itself to human desire, we find very frequent blocking, or **frustration,** of human motives. Perhaps the inevitability of frustration may be regarded as a prime principle of life. Certainly, frustration is frequent; and the way an individual handles his frustrations has an important bearing on the general comfort and effectiveness with which he lives.

In the following paragraphs, we shall see what are the frequent and normal reactions to the frequent and normal frustrations of everyday life.

DIRECT REACTIONS TO FRUSTRATION

Emotionality

As we have seen earlier (Chap. 9), when one of his motives is blocked, the frustrated individual will probably become emotional. In Western cultures, he will most likely become angry. In other cultures, he may show different emotions; there is evidence, for example (Bateson, 1941; Belo, 1935), that the Balinese do not always respond angrily to frustration; the extremely frustrated Balinese man may shut himself away from all contact with other people and "pout" for days, going without food and water all this while.

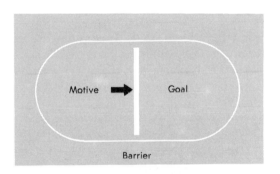

Figure 16–1. A SCHEMA OF FRUSTRATION. *Motivated behavior directed toward a goal encounters barriers, either physical or psychological. Frustration is the result.*

Increased Strength of Motives

The emotional responses that do arise when an operating motive is blocked may serve to increase the strength of the motive and to redouble the efforts to get ahead with the blocked line of activity (Wright, 1937; Child, 1946).

Experiments have shown that these increased efforts are affected by the timing of the frustrating experience. If rats who are running a maze are presented with a barrier shortly before the goal is reached, they will be more likely to persist in the goal-seeking behavior (show more resistance to **extinction**) than if the barrier is placed at a distance from the goal (Lambert and Solomon, 1952). Similarly, if college students asked to learn a maze are told that their performances will be compared with that of students all over the country and, then, if all subjects are stopped and told that their performance is lagging behind the average, those stopped near the end of the maze are less likely to give up the attempt than those stopped at the middle or the beginning of the maze (Adelman and Rosenbaum, 1954). If the frustration arises when the individual is close to the goal, persistence remains high and effort continues.

We might describe individuals who continue this effort as showing, at least in this situation, a high degree of **frustration tolerance,** in that they experience a good deal of frustration without a disruption of behavior. Such frustration tolerance may be situationally determined, as in the experiments above, or may be a result of the protracted experience an individual has had with frustration. Some individuals may have learned, through reinforcing experience, that persistence pays off.

Apathetic Responses

Another common reaction to continued or repeated frustration is **apathy,** or the cessation of responses. Apathy may be thought of, at least figuratively, as a generalized extinction of unrewarding responses. A general apathetic response has been observed among the inmates of concentration camps; there frustration is pervasive, and all attempts to combat it are thwarted and hence extinguished.

Variety of Responses

It can be counted on also that the frustrated organism will demonstrate a variety of responses in the frustrating situation. The apparent impossibility of reaching the desired goal through the plying of old habits may reduce the organism to a trial-and-error approach to the old problem. The student who is frustrated by a low grade may revise his study habits, trying a new approach to his goal. The moneyless boy goes out to catch foul balls in order to get into the baseball park. The scientific investigator whose first idea did not work conducts a variety of experiments that throw additional light on his problem. Necessity may indeed be the mother of some inventions; frustration can promote learning. The intelligent confrontation of the frustrating situation may lead to highly successful **detour behavior.**

Aggression

An additional and equally direct reaction to frustration is the aggressive response. A case can be made that any frustration produces an angry impulse to **aggression,** but the impulse does not always lead to overtly aggressive behavior. Other responses, including rational problem-solving activity, may occur first. But often there is a direct and sometimes violently irrational attack upon the frustrating agent. The child, ignoring the odds against him and unmindful of the consequences of his acts, may physically attack the parent who inter-

rupts his play or denies him the cookie he wants just before mealtime. Or there may be less violent and less immediately culpable aggressive responses on the part of the child who is often and severely frustrated by his parents; he may express his aggression by wetting the bed or by refusing to eat, thereby causing his parents to worry in a way that must furnish the child with a great deal of satisfaction.

OTHER REACTIONS TO FRUSTRATION

The most direct and most potentially useful reactions to frustration are problem-solving behaviors or successful detour behaviors. The barrier is circumvented, the blocked motive is satisfied, tension is reduced. The direct attack upon the barrier, though it may sometimes lead to useful results, is not likely to be as often successful—particularly when the barrier is animate and has the capacity to fight back. But perhaps direct attack does serve to reduce the tension produced by frustration.

Still other responses to frustration are **regression,** or the falling back on childish behaviors, and **displacement,** the attack on some

Figure 16–2. DISPLACED AGGRESSION IN THE LABORATORY. *Rats can be trained, through instrumental-conditioning procedures, to fight one another in order to obtain a reward. After a rat has learned such an aggressive response, and when he is placed in a cage with a rubber doll rather than another rat, he will fight the doll.*

person or object having nothing to do with the frustrating. These responses, which are most likely to occur when neither detour behavior nor direct attack can solve the problem, do not seem as positive or as clearly useful to the organism. If the frustration is not relieved, tension—often very threatening and anxious tension—persists. The organism must

NONFRUSTRATION

House with a lot of windows

FRUSTRATION

Experimenter: "What is that?"
Subject: "Just something."

Age 4-5-6

Figure 16–3. REGRESSED DRAWING. *The top drawing is one done by a child in a normal free-play situation. The same child, when frustrated, produced the regressed drawing at the bottom. (Barker, Dembo, and Lewin, 1941; reproduced by permission of the State University of Iowa.)*

do something about it. It must relieve the tension. It must defend its own integrity. These *defensive responses* to persisting and anxious tension will be discussed after we have dealt with conflict and the ways in which conflicting motives can produce tensions and stresses with which the organism must contend.

CONFLICT

Psychologists employ this term **conflict** to refer to the arousal of two or more behavior tendencies that are inherently incompatible. A situation often arises in which the organism, human or otherwise, is equally inclined to make two responses or to adopt two modes of behavior when only one response or one mode of behavior is possible. Or the organism may encounter an environmental situation that evokes two or more responses, each of which is equally strong but neither of which can gain ascendancy over the other.

KINDS OF CONFLICT

It is possible to describe three kinds of conflicts an organism is likely to encounter in the process of contending with its environment. The simplest kinds of conflicts are those involving conflicting habits; there are also conflicting cognitions and conflicting motives. Every individual has had experience, most often unpleasant, with each of these kinds of conflict.

Conflicting Habits

The phenomenon of conflicting habits can be demonstrated if we train a laboratory animal to make one response to a square stimulus and another response to a circular one. If we then place the trained animal in a situation where he "wants" to respond but we adjust the lighting so that he cannot determine whether the stimulus is square or round, then the animal is in conflict. He has available two habitual responses, equally "ready" and equally strong; and neither can be made overt. In such a situation the animal may become disturbed, unpredictable, aggressive, and otherwise "neurotic" (Cook, 1939; Liddell, 1944).

Many human individuals also experience conflict between or among habits. For example, in the activity of speaking, we encounter many points, as we go from one sentence to another, at which two or more alternative responses are equally strong; when this happens, we may be thrown into a temporary paralysis or may do a bit of stuttering or at least say a sort of frozen "uh" while one response or another gets the upper hand. We will see in a moment that there can be experimental analyses of human behavior in situations that stimulate conflicting habits.

Conflicting Cognitions

Cognitive conflict involves, in simplest terms, a conflict of ideas. To say it more precisely, cognitions are in conflict when one of them, instead of following directly from the other, follows from the *obverse of the other* (Brehm and Cohen, 1962). A man cannot, for example, hold simultaneously to the idea (a) that he is meticulously honest and (b) that he has just lied to a child. When two cognitions are in such conflict, the individual experiencing the conflict is said to be undergoing cognitive dissonance, and it is predictable that he will do something to remove himself from what he very clearly finds to be an undesirable if not intolerable situation.

Cognitive dissonance and its consequences may be illustrated by a research study of the behavior of a group of people (Festinger, Riecken, and Schachter, 1956), religiously oriented, who believed that they were receiving through their leaders communications coming from the Gods, communications stating that a catastrophic flood would overwhelm most of the world and that only members of that particular group would be saved when flying saucers came to rescue them from the rising waters of the flood. On the day of the predicted flood, the chosen few were stationed at the proper places waiting for the vehicles of the Gods to carry them away to safety. When the saucers did not arrive at the time first predicted, this development naturally produced a dissonance. If the people believed it true that the Gods were sending the saucers, then they found it difficult to believe that the Gods had failed to send the saucers on time. There was dissonance here that had to be reduced; the development was interpreted as a test set up by the Gods to see if true believers could withstand uncertainty. Subsequent word was received that the flying saucers would come at a later time. Then, when they did not come as predicted, and when several other predictions about their arrival were also proved wrong, and when grave doubt began to arise concerning the coming of the catastrophic flood, the true believers had a genuine problem. They were in

a stage of apathetic puzzlement until they came by the happy construction, conveyed to them as if it were a message from the Gods, that because of the faith and steadfastness of the followers, the Gods had decided to spare the world, to call off the flood, and to rearrange the divine plan for the true believers. This construction, this cognition, relieved the dissonance. But to keep it effective in relieving dissonance, it had to be built up to more credible proportions. Consequently, the true believers exerted strong efforts, through news releases and through missionary work, to publicize the great event that had transpired and to win more converts to the cause. Through investing additional efforts in consonant cognitions, they reduced dissonance and prevented it from taking on destructive proportions.

The phenomenon of cognitive dissonance can also be illustrated in laboratory situations; in one experiment, for example (Festinger, 1957, 1962), college students were first induced to make statements that were against their personal beliefs and then, through a manipulation of experimental variables affecting dissonance, were influenced to revise their beliefs toward consonance with the statements they had been induced to make. In this procedure each subject, just after completing a very dull and repetitious "experiment," was offered a sum of money to tell another waiting subject (a "planted" colleague of the experimenters) that the experiment in which he was about to participate was very enjoyable, interesting, and pleasant—a report clearly at variance with the actual beliefs of the subject who had just completed the dull regimen. Some students were paid one dollar for their services; others were paid twenty dollars for the same performance. Later, the two groups of subjects were interviewed about what they regarded as the true level of interest and pleasantness of the first part of the experiment. Upon this later examination, the students who were given only one dollar for reporting a statement that ran counter to their beliefs had changed their beliefs; they were significantly more favorable toward the experiment than were the students who were paid twenty dollars. Apparently, according to the experimenters, students who make a statement contrary to their beliefs, and who receive very little reward for making such a statement, then must act as if their original statement is relatively true; it makes no sense to them to find themselves lying for so little reward. So they must convince themselves that they weren't lying. The students who gained twenty dollars, while they may have had a problem of conscience, did not have much of a problem with their cognitions; they could conceive that they were making mildly untrue statements but that the twenty-dollar reward made quite permissible a little lying.

Conflicting Motives

The third general kind of conflict, motivational conflict, has been given the most attention for the longest time by psychologists. Although cognitive conflicts do take on a motivational form in that they lead to both cognitive and behavioral responses, the more directly motivational conflicts are more familiar to us in everyday life. Many of us are familiar with the basic conflict between the desire to achieve and the fear of failure. Many soldiers know very intimately and shudderingly about the violence of the conflict in which there is a strong fear of death but also a powerful fear of being judged a coward. And there is the college student who wishes with all his heart to pass a course and will adopt almost any means to do it but who has a strong revulsion to the idea of cheating. These are the lifelike motivational conflicts with which most of us have had some experience.

FIELD-OF-FORCES ANALYSIS OF CONFLICT

The varieties of conflict can be classified not only in terms of their psychological ingredients—habits, cognitions, or motives—but, as Kurt Lewin (1935) postulated, in terms of the plus and minus influences exerted on an individual in a motivational "field of force." Perhaps with profit we can employ Lewin's mode of analysis.

Approach-Approach Conflict

Approach-approach conflict arises when there are tendencies to move toward two different goals at the same time. This relatively happy kind of conflict has been produced experimentally by the following procedure (Hovland and Sears, 1938). Subjects are seated with a 6-inch-square sheet of paper before them. They are trained to draw a diagonal line *toward* a green light when it is flashed at one top corner of a paper and to draw a line *from* a red light when it is flashed at the other top corner. We may think of the subjects as motivated to make these two different responses under the proper circumstances. The approach-approach conflict arises when *both* corners of the paper have green lights. (See Fig. 16–4.)

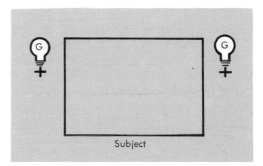

Figure 16–4. APPROACH-APPROACH CONFLICT. *The subject is required to make two contradictory approaching responses. (Hovland and Sears, 1938; by permission of the* Journal of General Psychology.)

Such a situation demands two "green" responses at the same time. Two green responses cannot occur at the same time. Something has to give. Actually, the subjects had little difficulty with this simple positive-positive, green-green problem. Most of them (58 per cent) simply responded by drawing a line to one corner and letting the matter rest there. In more highly charged conflicts, the same response can be seen. Shall I accept admission to Harvard or to Yale? Shall I take political science or business law? Shall I date the sparkling Marie or the sultry Sandra? When we are in such fortunate choice situations, we generally make our choice without great strain, and we generally are able to convince ourselves after a time—our ability to reconcile ourselves to our actions being what it is—that the choice we made was the good one. Few of us, looking back on past approach-approach conflicts, are inclined to think we made the wrong decision, particularly if our lives have gone along pretty well. If there was strong motivation leading us toward both horns of the dilemma, however, we may sometimes find the denied course of action inserting itself into our fantasies about what might have been.

There are other solutions to the experimental approach-approach conflict, each also serving as a paradigm for behavior in life's conflicts. Twenty-one per cent of the subjects in the experimental situation described above chose the response of *alternation*. They first drew a line to one green light and then to the other. The choice is not an all-or-none matter but one merely of scheduling. We date Sandra tonight and Marie tomorrow (unless, of course, dating Sandra obliterates all interest in Marie). Many of our daily conflicts can be handled satisfactorily by programming or scheduling our activities.

Twelve per cent of the subjects in the conflict experiment chose a *compromise* solution: they gave up both green lights and drew a line straight up the middle of the page. In real life we also sometimes employ this solution. If we are inventive and if we are fully aware of our own inclinations, we can probably find compromise courses of action yielding rewards that include both of the apparently conflicting original goals. We can sometimes have our cake and eat it too. The choice between Marie and Sandra may result in a happy marriage to Sue, who sometimes sparkles with gaiety but who, on occasion, can be very sultry also. And, besides, Sue is the best cook of the three.

A fourth type of response, given by 9 per cent of the subjects in the approach-approach situation, was that of *freezing*. They gave no response at all, really acting like the theoretical jackass—who starved to death while standing

exactly equidistant from two piles of hay. Such responses are not frequent in everyday affairs. Our attention wanders, perhaps, bringing us psychologically closer to one goal so that it looks like the better of the two. If so, action occurs and the conflict is solved.

Avoidance-Avoidance Conflict

If our trained experimental subjects were simultaneously given two red lights at the two corners of the page, they would be placed in a situation requiring two conflicting *withdrawal* responses (Fig. 16–5). In this situation, the most frequent response, given by nearly half the subjects, was that of *freezing* or *blocking*. They did nothing. Others used the *compromise* response described earlier, drawing a line from the top to the bottom of the page halfway between the two red lights.

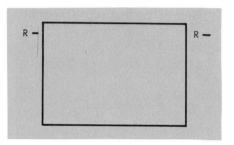

Figure 16–5. AVOIDANCE-AVOIDANCE CONFLICT. *In this situation the subject is required to make two simultaneous withdrawing responses. (Hovland and Sears, 1938; by permission of the* Journal of Experimental Psychology.)

We encounter many of these **avoidance-avoidance conflicts** in the process of living. We must wash the greasy dishes or face parental ire. We must apologize to our roommate or feel ashamed if we do not. We must perform a hateful job or go bankrupt. We must kowtow to an authoritarian boss or live in the doghouse.

A quite frequent response in actual life to these disagreeable avoidance-avoidance situations, as we will see, is **withdrawal.** We get out of there—a solution not available to the subjects in the conflict experiment. We may withdraw physically, if possible. We may run away from home or leave college. Or we may, as we shall see, withdraw psychologically by running away from reality. There may also be a *blocking* of response. Perhaps much so-called laziness in human life is produced by **avoidance-avoidance conflicts**. Unable to do anything very adaptive about either of two equally disagreeable courses of action, the organism just sits there and gets itself labeled as lazy by people who do not understand the debilitating effects of conflicts.

Approach-Avoidance Conflict

If our experimentally trained line-drawers are given a green light and a red light at the same time and at the same corner of the paper, they are caught in the conflicting tendency to make two opposing and incompatible responses to the same corner (Fig. 16–6).

This situation is equivalent to wishing to dance with a girl who we fear may haughtily refuse, or of attending an exciting movie which costs more than the budget will stand. On a deeper level, the **approach-avoidance conflict** may be seen in those situations where our basic motives "tempt" us toward primitive satisfactions but our conscience, the superego, gives us a stern and puritanical nay. At a simple level, the most frequent solution to the approach-avoidance conflict is *alternation*. We approach, then avoid. Such a solution is rarely possible in actual situations, and even if possible it is rarely effective. The choice of either alternative before us generally involves an unrecoverable cost. If we go to the movie, the money is gone. If we save our money, the movie is gone. If we approach the girl, we live with our anxiety in her presence. If we stay away from her, we are ashamed of our cowardice. If we follow our primitive impulses, guilt will haunt us. If we bow to the dictates of conscience, we deprive ourselves of satisfaction and perhaps live in jealousy of those who are sufficiently free of conscience to engage in the unconflicted enjoyment of "sin."

An especially trying aspect of approach-avoidance conflict is the fact that an individual may find it impossible to leave the psychological field in which the conflict occurs. The

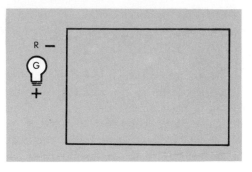

Figure 16–6. APPROACH-AVOIDANCE CONFLICT. *In this situation, the subject is required to approach and avoid simultaneously. (Hovland and Sears, 1938; by permission of the* Journal of Experimental Psychology.)

dynamics of the situation have been illustrated by experiments in which rats are alternatively shocked and fed at one end of a runway (Miller, 1959) and then are placed at the far end of the runway. A rat who has had this experience will not now go to the shock-food place in the runway. He will, however, move away from the far end. At any given place in the maze, he will have both approach tendencies and avoidance tendencies. Both these tendencies weaken with increased distance from the goal, but because the strength of the avoidance tendency diminishes more rapidly with distance than does the approach tendency, the rat will at first move toward the food-shock place and will continue to move until there is a stable equilibrium of approach and avoidance tendencies; and there he is and there he is likely to stay—caught in a field of balanced forces. Incidentally, if the rat is placed near the crucial end of the maze, he will retreat a certain distance from it. Miller (1957) and his associates, through an ingenious combination of experiment and theory building, have been able to predict with great accuracy the behavior of rats in this and related conflict situations.

In our achievement-oriented culture a frequent—and frequently debilitating—approach-avoidance conflict is one involving the desire to achieve on one hand and the fear of failure on the other. Very often we find ourselves in situations where we wish with all our might we could make the team, win the race, pass the examination, attend the senior ball, pin the campus queen, or date the football star; but, haunted by a fear of failure, we may be thrown into such paralytic anxiety that we are unable to do anything adaptive about our aspirations. The tension produced by such a conflict leads to a variety of behaviors, some of which come under the heading of *defensive reactions*, to be discussed later. Some reactions seem more straightforward. In one research (Atkinson and Litwin, 1960), for example, it was shown that students who had a high score on a fear-of-failure test left college examinations early. Apparently, they found the examining situation so tension producing that they removed themselves from it at the earliest possible moment—thereby increasing, perhaps, the likelihood of failure.

Another experiment (Atkinson, Bastion, Earl, and Litwin, 1960) demonstrated that people with strong fear of failure would, in a laboratory game, take either very high or very low risks. In playing the game, the subjects were asked to throw a ring around a peg that could be placed at varying distances from the thrower. If a subject threw the ring around a distant peg, he would receive a very high score. If he threw it around a near peg, the score was low. Pegs at middle distances gave intermediate scores. The individuals who scored high on a fear-of-failure test rarely chose to throw at the middle pegs. They either played it very safe by dropping the ring around the close low-score pegs or else they "shot the works" by trying to hit the most distant and highest-scoring pegs. In both cases, these people were handling the conflict in such a way as to minimize the trauma of failure. By playing things safe, they reduced the likelihood of achieving a high score—as well as the likelihood of complete failure. By going for the long-shot, they could tolerate failure because even the best performers were likely to fail at this task; and if the best performers were likely to fail, then failure was made tolerable. It may be that a good deal of our wilder "shoot-at-the-moon" and "go-for-broke" behaviors are rooted in a pervasive fear of failure and in our attempts to make failure bearable.

Double Approach-Avoidance Conflict

The most involved kind of conflict is one in which there are two courses of action, each of which has both pleasant and unpleasant consequences. In the line-drawing conflict experiment we have been describing, this kind of situation was simulated when both red and green signals appeared at both top corners of the paper (Fig. 16–7). This situation requires the subject to respond all at once in two different ways in two different directions. It paralyzes him. In the experiment, only about one quarter of the subjects were able to give any kind of response. The others simply sat there, presumably loaded with stress and tension.

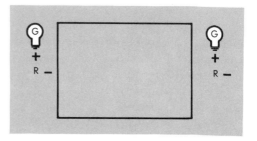

Figure 16–7. DOUBLE APPROACH-AVOIDANCE CONFLICT. *Here the subject is required simultaneously to approach and to avoid each of two stimulus objects. (Hovland and Sears, 1938; by permission of the* Journal of Experimental Psychology.)

In normal living, we encounter these more elaborate conflicts perhaps more frequently than we do the simpler ones. For example, consider the beauty-contest winner who has an opportunity to start a movie career, but who, in the process of growing up in a happy middle-class family, has become strongly attracted to the role of housewife and mother. The goals appear now mutually exclusive. She wants both but cannot have both. This may not appear on the surface to be a very serious conflict, even if we add the factor that our beauty is very close to becoming engaged to a man who attracts her strongly. But let's look further into the matter. We see that each horn of the dilemma presents its own dilemma. She wants the movie career, but she is very frightened by the prospect of leaving home and relating with strangers, whose morals she suspects, in Hollywood. She also wants marriage—soon. She wants to marry her chosen man. But marriage, too, has its psychological bugaboos. She fears sex. Her upbringing has taught her that sex is evil, a fascinating but nonetheless abhorrent evil. She knows what is "required" of married women, but she has nightmares in which her dread of—and fascination with—sex comes to haunt her.

Even were she fully conscious of all aspects of this motivational mish-mash, she would need to be a genius at hedonic calculus in order to "know her own mind" and to act in the most adjustive manner. If some aspects of it are unconscious or are misrepresented in her awareness, then she has genuine trouble. Conflict produces tension. The psychological system can tolerate only so much tension. Adjustments, sometimes strange and not very adaptive adjustments, will be made.

SOURCES OF CONFLICT

We can analyze conflict with respect to the psychological variables involved (habits, cognition, or motive), and we can classify conflict in accordance with Lewin's plus-minus dimensions, as immediately above. We can also, and with some profit, describe conflicts in terms of their sources. Although all conflicts may, in the last analysis, involve tendencies within the individual, some conflicts may be described as more inherently *intra-individual* while others stem more directly from *conflicting values* in the culture or from the individual's involvement in *conflicting social roles*.

Intra-individual Sources

We have seen earlier (Chap. 15) that the idea of conflict is central to the psychoanalytic theory of man. The **id**, the primitive urges of the organism, is seen as inevitably and inexorably in conflict with the **superego**, the internalized rules of civilized propriety. The ego functions, sometimes with success, to mitigate the clashes between primitive drives and civilizing controls. The general cast of the individual personality as well as the form of civilization is determined, the theory holds, by the dynamic conflict between these two forces.

Conflicting Values

Another source of conflict lies in the array of conflicting values that characterize culture. The individual must learn the values, sentiments, and attitudes that his elders hold to be proper. If there were complete consistency in the patterns of values the individual is required to learn, life would be relatively simple. But there are inconsistencies, and they can throw the learner into serious conflict. Our own culture teaches us, for example, that "early to bed, early to rise, makes a man healthy, wealthy, and wise"; it also teaches us that "early to bed and early to rise" will not only make us miss all the best parties but will reduce the likelihood of our meeting and marrying the boss's daughter, which is the real way to wealth—which can make us wise and healthy.

On a more serious level, we can consider the values and sentiments we are supposed to learn in Sunday school as they contrast with the values and sentiments we are supposed to learn if we work for a hard-driving used-car dealer. Or perhaps closer to home, there is a conflict between the pressure in the college environment that demands good academic performance and the pressure that requires almost full-time participation in social or athletic activities. Some cultures, some environments, some particular situations are more conflict-producing than others.

Role Conflicts

As members of society, individuals learn to enact roles, to engage in organized patterns of activities that their elders and their peers expect of them. The boy must learn the role of a boy, and the girl that of a girl. There are patterns of behavior—a role—for father, for mother, for doctor and lawyer and Indian chief. Each of us learns a succession of roles in the process of growing up, and each of us learns a pattern of roles as we pursue our individual lives in a social setting. Generally speaking, each of us comes to enact various roles that fit reasonably well our abilities and inclinations. But we can also experience *role strain* (Goode, 1960) or out-and-out role conflict (Merton, 1957) or a lack of basic congruence between role and self (Sarbin, 1964). Many students have experienced conflict between the role of a minor and the role of an adult. Parents sometimes contribute to the conflict by expecting conformity to incompatible standards: "Act like an adult, dear, but drive with both hands and be home by ten o'clock." More serious is the conflict of role involved when a military officer, who was recently, say, a civilian social worker devoted to alleviating misery, has to order an infantry platoon to march to almost certain death. And there is Arthur Miller's salesman, who moved inexorably into despair and death because his role as a salesman was intolerably incongruent with his conception of himself.

THE TENSION-PRODUCING NATURE OF CONFLICT

Of great significance for the adjustment of the personal system is the fact that conflict produces tension—tension that may persist for a long time and that may lead to varied, not always useful, behaviors. The tensions that spring from conflict are illustrated clearly in an experiment designed to produce conflict in cats (Masserman, 1943). Cats were first put in cages and trained to lift the lid of a food box whenever they received a signal. The cats readily learned this assignment and some variations upon it. If, while the cat was in the box but not eating, he was hit by a blast of air, he would show signs of a normal fear and an ordinary desire to avoid the blast. These responses were not violent and soon tended to fade. But if the cat was given a strong blast of air just at the moment it began eating, the responses were dramatically different. The experimenter reports that the cats, when caught

in the conflict between approaching the food and avoiding the blast, showed very strong emotional responses—frantic mewing, erection of the hair, dilation of the pupils, and increased heart rate. After a few exposures to this trying situation, the cats would show signs of a strong disinclination to come anywhere near the situation. They would fight to stay out of the apparatus; once in it, they would tremble, crouch, and try to hide; when given the signal for the now psychologically contaminated food, they would try desperately to escape. Some cats, the report goes, developed what appeared to be ritualistic behaviors; they would engage in excessive washing of their fur. Some formerly docile cats turned restless; others, generally lively by temperament, became passive, sometimes demonstrating a rigid posture which they held for many minutes after facing the conflict situation. Some of the cats persistently refused to eat even when they were removed entirely from the experimental situation, and some seemed to show a general personality change; the friendly might become aggressive, and the more boisterous inert.

Other researchers (Cook, 1939; Liddell, 1944; Brown, 1942; Bijou, 1943) have demonstrated, in less dramatic but more systematic ways, the reality of conflict in animals and have begun to explore the variables that seem to make conflict conducive to breakdown and "experimental neurosis." Generally speaking, when an animal is put in a situation from which it cannot escape and is forced to make discriminations beyond its capacity, it shows a general disruption of behavior, sometimes so severe that the animal is no longer useful as an experimental subject.

EGO INVOLVEMENT IN FRUSTRATION AND CONFLICT

Whatever the particular form of the conflict, and whatever the grievousness of the frustration, the resulting tensions are generally much more severe if there is present what is known as **ego involvement.** Each of us has a *concept of self.* Each of us does what he can to maintain a satisfyingly favorable concept of ourselves. Whenever a frustration or conflict threatens our image of ourselves, tension can be counted on to mount. If I conceive of myself as the possessor of high intelligence, destined for scholarly achievement, then the inability to pass a course that ought to be easy is a particularly thorny burden. I am required, perhaps, to revise my image of myself, an assignment as tough as any undertaken by human kind. We frequently get ourselves into a psychological bind by overestimating our capacities; upon such a misperception of self, we then build a *level of aspiration* beyond the achievement that can, in all good sense, be expected. The ego-involved discrepancy between aspiration and achievement is a frequent producer of human misery. There is painful failure and agonizing reappraisal ahead for the student who, perhaps on the basis of an uncritical swallowing of his parents' misplaced ambitions for him, aspires to a medical career while lacking the aptitude to pass medical courses. The small-town choir singer who heads for Broadway with a large vision and a small talent represents the heart-rending material out of which soap operas are made. When the acids of reality eat away at a glowing and tenderly artistic self-image, there is great personal misery and psychological contortion.

There is also frequent ego involvement, of course, in conflict. We may find ourselves in a situation where any conceivable course of action will roughen up our self-esteem. And we may find ourselves with impulses the very existence of which we do not wish to admit. If, in my own estimation, I am a sturdily upright, meticulously moral, highly and articulately principled fellow, no one would expect me to accept the existence in my own system of impulses to mayhem, manslaughter, murder, or rape. But the psychoanalysts say that such impulses are there, and that with proper provocation they may threaten to burst forth into action, the very thought of which is enough to send me into a conflictful tizzy.

In many frustrating and conflictful situations, then, we can expect an ego involvement that (a) increases the emotional tensions and (b) helps determine the responses the individual will make. A man will go to great lengths to preserve his image of himself. Any situation that turns up evidence inconsistent with that image will be a threatening situation—particularly if the evidence demands that the self be seen in a less favorable light. We have made the point earlier that we do not often enjoy being surprised by the behavior of our friends. Even less tolerable to us are surprises about ourselves. We probably have some resistance even to surprisingly favorable evidences about ourselves. When someone observes that we have a hidden talent or undeveloped capacity, we are sometimes inclined to take this not as a compliment but as an accusation—to be rejected—that we are not on good speaking terms with our own abilities and that we have failed to develop ourselves properly. If the surprising evidence has an uncomplimentary tenor, our disturbed resistance is, of course, very much greater. Ego involvement, then, in either frustration or conflict, increases tension in the psychological system.

UNCONSCIOUS FACTORS IN CONFLICT AND FRUSTRATION

We have seen in a number of contexts already the possibility or the likelihood that one segment or another of a conflict may be influential in producing tension but may be beyond the consciousness of the conflicted individual. Impulses or motives of which we are not proud are candidates for **repression**—for motivated forgetting. It is the psychoanalytic position that all of our id impulses, instinctively rooted in the very core of human existence, never really abate and never submit wholly to civilized harnessing. In the attempt, necessary in an organized social existence, to break the spirit of the primitive impulses and to turn into socially approved channels the energies of the organism, we develop superego controls; and we develop egos with which we confront the world—egos which, when they conceive themselves, put the best of possible constructions on what they see. The self-image is of a civilized person, possessed of attributes of decency and propriety. The ego preserves itself. It protects its view of itself from evidence, sometimes very powerful evidence when viewed objectively, which, if accepted, would create a dissonance in the image. We have seen in many instances (Chap. 11) that each of us is possessed of the human tendency to see the world not as it is, but as we are. And the research on attention has shown how selective we can be in filtering the stream of worldly energies impinging on the organism. We have seen also that forgetting is an active rather than a passive process, often clearly assuming the form of a motivated process (Chap. 13).

From these evidences it is not a very large intellectual leap to the idea that the conscious organism, viewing its world and watching its own behavior in it, reading the evidences arising from the urgings and tensions within its own system, will arrange for itself a safe and filtered view of what it sees in the mirror as well as of what it sees in the outside world. The psychological system preserves its integrity as best it can; and if there is a choice between integrity, or even the illusion of integrity on one side, and fully accurate perceptions on the other, then accuracy and objectivity lose out, being with apparent cheerfulness left as innocuously good things for the scientists to maunder about.

We are, then, often unaware of one or more of the motives that are participating in the conflict. We may, in fact, be unaware of all of the forces involved in the conflict, consciously knowing only of the resultant tension and unhappiness. If that is so, the term *unconscious conflict* becomes appropriate.

CONFLICT AND ANXIETY

We have seen that experimental animals caught in a conflict show definite and often extreme signs of emotional tension. Thwarted motives—whether the thwarting agent is another motive, a personal incapacity, or an environmental barrier—do not go away. The system remains under tension unless an appropriate goal is reached. And more than that, the blocking of motives leads to the arousal of emotions which add to the general level of tension or stress. This combination of unresolved motivational tension and the accompanying emotional responses is referred to as *anxiety.* Subjectively, anxiety appears to be a mixture of dread and hope, with there being no great clarity as to just what is dreaded or precisely what is hoped for. But it is very clear to the anxious individual that his system is under stress. It is even clearer that it is a vastly unpleasant state to be in. The individual who is unable, for example, to decide whether to resign his steady job and strike out on his own, or to keep his job in the face of low pay and a domineering management, will find himself in an emotional stew, in which he dreads the consequences of anything he does but simultaneously gets glimmers of hope regarding the possible outcomes of any course of action. As long as he is caught in the conflict, the vague and very uncomfortable state persists. The bitter and paralyzing pangs of anxiety are also known to the person who is tempted to cheat on an examination but who is unable either to commit the act or to remove himself from the tempting situation. Highly charged anxiety grips a Hamlet who tries to decide, amid a welter of conflicting passions and haunting doubts, whether or not he will kill his father's brother.

In many cases, human anxiety seems to feed upon itself, growing more violent and intolerable the longer it persists. For when the human individual finds himself unable to do a single adjustive thing about a conflict, he experiences the stark feeling of helplessness. Such a feeling of helplessness is itself unbearable to the self-image of anyone who conceives of himself as a decisive individual able to control his own life and work out his own fate. This ego involvement in the whole situation makes it all the more unbearable and increases the likelihood that the individual will resort to sometimes strange and desperate means just to alleviate the anxiety, means which may contribute nothing to the solution of the problem that led originally to the anxiety. The anxiety itself becomes the enemy of the system, and the system must contend with it or run the risk of disintegration.

In many respects it would make sense to

regard anxiety as a strong and general avoidance motive, one that has been learned in a way similar to any of the psychological motives we have dealt with earlier, and one that now functions, as do other psychological motives, with some apparent freedom from its past history. It has a directionality—it leads to movement away from the stimulating situation. It has accompanying emotional responses; and the anxious individual gripped by the motive can engage in a variety of behaviors in the presence of a goal—which is the reduction of anxiety.

DEFENSIVE REACTIONS TO FRUSTRATION AND CONFLICT

When faced with conflict situations of a simple and conscious sort, the organism may, as we have seen, behave in some relatively simple and relatively sensible ways. It may *choose one alternative* and ignore the other—sometimes without either great pain or great loss. It may *alternate*. It may *compromise*. All of these responses may get it somewhere. The response of *withdrawing* may be the better part of valor in some situations, but it is an ostrich approach unless the conflict actually does go away while the head is in the sand. But, of course, the conflict will not, cannot, evaporate if it arises out of two or more ineradicable forces in the personality. The response of *freezing* or *blocking*, which we have also described, cannot impress anyone as doing very much to satisfy either of the conflicting motives. However, while the organism sits in frozen inactivity, the environment may change in ways that will enable the organism to live again.

We can make the case that these foregoing behaviors in the face of conflict, though few of them may impress us as highly creative, can serve in a positive manner to satisfy the individual's motives. They can, with varying degrees of success, move him ahead toward his goals. There are other responses, however, that do not appear to contribute at all to the positive satisfaction of motives. These responses serve only the purpose of defending the organized system against disruptive forces

—against intolerable anxiety and against events that would have a disruptive effect on the self-image. Fairly often in the lives of any of us—as many-faceted systems in a demanding world—we find ourselves in situations where we are forced to give up, at least temporarily, the ongoing, integrated, progressively more skillful seeking of our goals and take time out to defend ourselves, to pull the system back together, to patch up a hurting ego, or to contend directly with a debilitating anxiety. These *defensive reactions* or **defense mechanisms** shall concern us for the remainder of the present chapter.

Some of the defensive reactions we see in others and, often with less accuracy and much less frequency, in ourselves may appear, from the point of view of common sense, to be strange indeed. But when we take the view that the intricate psychological system that is the human personality *must* at all cost defend itself, *must* maintain its organization, its structure, its integrity as a system, then there is sense in the strange and wonderful defensive behaviors of which we are capable.

Rationalization

Rationalization is the process of finding *good* reasons to replace real reasons. When there is anxiety, produced by either frustration or conflict, the individual can frequently find some alleviation of this bother through certain kinds of talking to himself. Benjamin Franklin in his autobiography gives an example of both the essence and the function of rationalization.

I believe I have omitted mentioning that, in my first voyage from Boston, being becalm'd off Block Island, our people set about catching cod, and hauled up a great many. Hitherto I had stuck to my resolution of not eating animal food, and on this occasion consider'd, with my master Tryone, the taking every fish as a kind of unprovoked murder, since none of them had, or ever could do us any injury that might justify the slaughter. All this seemed very reasonable. But I had formerly been a great lover of fish, and, when this came hot out of the frying pan, it smelt admirably well. I balanc'd some time between principle and inclination, till I recollected that, when the fish were opened, I saw smaller fish taken out of their stomachs; then thought I, "If you eat one another, I don't see why we mayn't eat you." So I din'd upon cod very heartily and continued to eat with other people, returning only now and then occasionally to a vegetable diet. So convenient a thing it is to be a *reasonable creature*, since it enables one to find or make a reason for everything one has a mind to do.

Man is perhaps just as inventive in finding ways to fool himself as he is in any other field of human activity. Whenever his self-concept is in jeopardy, his mental agility comes quickly to the rescue to find ways of twisting reality into a form palatable to his pervasive taste for self-esteem. He fails in a task he was sure he could accomplish and tells himself how little he really tried. He wins second prize in a contest in which he has exerted his last-ditch effort and elaborates to himself and his friends how much he values the 79-cent cup he won. He tongue-lashes his wife and then salves his conscience by saying what a terrible day he has had. He bitterly resents his own pint-size body but bravely talks about—and believes in —the relationship between the smallness of packages and the quality of the contents. We all rationalize, sometimes half in jest, sometimes in complete and serious self-deception. Such a gambit never solves the underlying problem, but it may help hold things together until such a time as the real battle can be joined.

Reaction Formation

If two motives are in conflict, the system may respond by doing all it can to build up the strength of one of the motives, usually the more acceptable one, so that the other motive is safely contained. This response to conflict is called **reaction formation**. The member of the Watch and Ward Society, for example, may engage in elaborate behaviors calculated to convince himself and everyone else of his great and pristine purity. If there is enough evidence of purity, then no one, including the member himself, can possibly believe that impure motives reside in a system so dedicated to the pursuit of purity. The individual may still find some outlet for the contained motives, however, through reading all the salacious books that come out. Somebody has to decide whether they are fit for public consumption.

Another example is the mother who, though she has strong negative feelings for her children, embarks on a loud and visible campaign of ostentatious mothering. She does everything possible for her children, devoting so much time and effort to their welfare that she becomes a leading candidate for mother of the year. Such reaction formation succeeds in hiding her hostilities toward her children. But the hostilities still do not go away. They may be expressing themselves in the smothering effect of overmothering.

Compensation

The term **compensation** is used to describe the overemphasis of one type of behavior in order to cover up felt deficiencies in other areas. The self-image may suffer deeply at failure in a chosen endeavor, but is at least somewhat restored to a tolerable state by evidence at competence somewhere else. There can be *direct compensation,* such as that seen where the sexually inadequate male engages in frenzied sexual and pseudosexual exploits in order to show his virility. Such exploits and such a preoccupation may succeed in convincing himself and others that he really is a man. The frail child who practices boxing and courts the reputation of "tough guy" in his neighborhood may be doing the same kind of compensatory thing.

Indirect compensation refers to the *investment of increased energy in the pursuit of a substitute goal.* The boy who feels keenly his lack of recognition as a scholar has added zest to bring to football. The third-string halfback may build his self-esteem by added attention to his course work.

Compensation, through self-deception, may serve a useful purpose not only by helping contain anxiety but also by reducing the strength of the originally frustrated motive.

The term **sublimation** refers to a reaction very similar to compensation. Freud held that the energy of frustrated sexual urges was often drained off and at least partially gratified through aesthetic activity. This drainage theory, however, particularly when applied to a basic physiological motive, is not widely credited.

Fantasy

Tensions and anxieties can sometimes be ameliorated through **fantasy,** through the imaginary escape from the real world into one where the trammeled ego can play the untrammeled hero, winning in fancy the success and glory denied it in the grubby actualities of life. There is probably no harm in fantasy, especially if it is pursued with self-consciousness. Much literature grows out of fantasy. But when the fantastic world begins to replace the real one, then we worry that tension has built up beyond tolerable limits. Confusion between the world of fancy and the world of fact is a sign of severe mental disorder (see pp. 502–506).

Projection

Projection is a mechanism to alleviate conflict through seeing in others the motives about which one is anxious. By seeing others as hostile, for example, the hostile individual is able to rail against hostility with all his might—thereby, in the strange realm of conflict, hoping to keep his own motives either in check or disguised or both. By seeing others as sexual sinners, I am licensed to rue their imagined behavior, to cluck and gasp, and sometimes to punish them severely, thereby telling myself, in ways I fervently but unconsciously hope will be effective, what will happen to me if I follow my own wayward impulses. Goethe once wrote (incidentally, 100 years before Freud, who coined the term *projection*), "It is not hard to observe that in this world man feels most free from his sins and most blameless when he can comfortably expiate on the same shortcomings in others."

Identification

When the individual is frustrated by, or has conflicting feelings toward, a highly respected individual the reaction may be that of **identification,** a process of becoming the same as the other individual or of trying to be like the other individual.

We saw in the last chapter that identification occurs very frequently on the part of children as they deal with parents, who are the source of most of the good things of life and who—especially as the child grows a bit older—withhold gratifications. Adults can respond in similar ways. The salesman who has strong hostile impulses toward his boss may be observed to talk like the boss, think like the boss, and in fantasy to see himself in the role of boss. Such identification serves for the adult the same functions it does for the child. It makes impossible the expression of frighteningly hostile impulses toward the boss. The salesman says, in effect, "I *am* the boss. I can't hate me." Also the identification with the boss represents an adoption of the boss's standards and practices. Once these are adopted as one's own, the need for rebellion and resistance is removed and the troublesome young buck identifies his way into middle-aged conservatism. Perhaps on-the-job identification in hierarchical business structures preserves the mores and folkways of business much as the child's identification with his parents and other significant figures preserves the norms and niceties of the larger society.

Displacement

Frequently the frustrated organism, instead of attacking the immediate cause of its difficulty, will vent its anger on other and safer objects that come readily to hand. This **displacement** of aggression can be seen most directly in the behavior of children. After a few years of experience with the ways of civilization, children rarely engage in direct attack on their parents, who, as the enforcers of social proprieties, are the source of many frustrations (as well as the dispensers of most of the good things of life). It is not only physically unsafe but also very poor psychological strategy to bite the hand that feeds. So the frustrated child turns his aggression elsewhere. He picks on his brothers and sisters—preferably, with sensible primitive simplicity, his *younger* brothers and sisters. He may take out his roughness on his neighbors and colleagues. Or he may engage in cruelty to animals. It would be a plausible hypothesis that if we could measure the amount of parentally produced frustration in a hundred homes, and then count the frequency with which the children in each home aggress against one another or against neighbor children, we would find a significant positive correlation between the two measures.

In adult behavior, too, we find misplaced aggression. The man who has had a tough day at the office, suffering the disapproval of his boss and irritations at the hands of his co-workers, walks into the house at night with his glandular dander up. He kicks the cat, damns the dog, yells at the children for doing things they do with impunity every day. And, because familiarity breeds aggression at least as much as it does contempt, he probably will find occasion to express some kind of disapproval of his wife. "Why in the world do you wear that ridiculous-looking outfit?" he asks. Or he shouts with both feeling and inaccuracy, "You're *always* eating apples in bed!"

One theory of **scapegoating**—the visiting of one's sins on a sacrificial "goat"—rests on the assumption of displacement of aggression. The frustrated majority group, for example, either unable to find the true cause of its troubles or afraid to attack it, directs its hostility toward safe and visible members of a minority group. According to such a theory, in times of stress and deprivation we would expect an increase in aggression against minority groups. And we would expect the most pervasively frustrated members of the majority group to mount the most vigorous attacks upon the minority.

There is some evidence in support of such a displacement theory of lynching. One set of researchers (Dollard et al., 1939) compiled data, for the years between 1882 and 1930, on

Figure 16–8. SCAPEGOATING. *Often, when there is no direct outlet for the aggression growing out of frustration, the aggression will be displaced, perhaps being vented on a scapegoat. Many instances of racial conflict may represent the displacement of aggression on the part of the "superior" group.*

(1) the annual per acre value of cotton for fourteen Southern states and (2) the number of lynchings per year. There was a correlation of —.67 between the market price of cotton and the number of lynchings. It does appear that aggression is not so likely to occur when times are good and frustration is reduced.

Regressive Responses

In the face of grievous frustration and conflict the individual may resort, under some circumstances, to behaviors of a more childish variety than those generally employed in his adjustments (see Fig. 16–3). This is **regression** —the reactivation of behaviors which in earlier and simpler stages of development served an adjustmental purpose.

The regressive reaction was demonstrated very clearly in a classic experiment (Barker, Dembo, and Lewin, 1941) on frustration in children. In this study children were first observed carefully while they were engaging in normal and routine activities in a playroom. Then a partition was removed, revealing a fascinating array of new toys which the children were allowed to play with. Next, the children were separated by a wire screen from the new toys. Frustration. Some children attacked the barrier; others appealed to the adults for help. Some tried to withdraw from the entire situation by leaving the room. Others went back to the old toys, but their activities then, according to the ratings of the experimenters, were on the average the *kind of play engaged in by children 18 months younger.* Table 16–1 presents in detail some data from this study.

Adults, when frustrated, also sometimes show regressive behaviors: childlike pouting, running home to mother, temper tantrums. Perhaps the adult playing of practical jokes on disliked or irritating or powerful people is a combination of regression and aggression— having much in common with the act of putting a tack in teacher's chair or a garter snake in mother's purse.

Repression of Entire Conflict

We have seen that unpleasant motives (unacceptable to the ego, in psychoanalytic terms) tend to be forced from consciousness. Behaviors which the outsider interprets in terms of primitive (id) impulses, the ego itself misinterprets or ignores. The ego may similarly find intolerable all evidence of component forces in conflict. In psychoanalytic terms, both the id impulses and the rigid superego restraints may be hidden from consciousness through repression. The conflict persists, however, keeping the system under pressure so that anxiety, felt but not understood, still persists and other symptoms and mechanisms are needed.

The repression of the entire conflict can be most clearly seen in instances where the present anxiety stems from a conflictful event occurring long ago but now entirely repressed,

Table 16–1. FRUSTRATION AND REGRESSION: EFFECTS OF FRUSTRATION ON CONSTRUCTIVENESS OF PLAY

Subject	Constructiveness Rating during Free Play	Constructiveness Rating during Frustration	Difference (Fru — FPl)
1	5.50	4.00	−1.50
2	4.50	6.00	+1.50
3	4.50	1.00	−3.50
4	7.00	7.00	0.00
5	5.50	4.50	−1.00
6	6.50	5.50	−1.00
7	5.50	6.50	+1.00
8	5.00	2.50	−2.50
9	5.50	5.50	0.00
10	5.50	7.00	+1.50
11	6.50	6.00	−0.50
12	6.50	2.00	−4.50
13	6.50	5.50	−1.00
14	6.50	6.50	0.00

When children are frustrated, they tend to engage in play of a less constructive and more infantile type. The table gives constructiveness ratings on the play of 14 children as (a) they play freely and (b) they play in a frustrating situation. (Adapted from Barker, Dembo, and Lewin, 1941; by permission of the State University of Iowa.)

repressed because both the incident itself, involving conflict, and any memories of it are vastly unpleasant to the conscious self. Freud found many evidences of such unconscious conflicts in his patients. The present defensive symptoms were often related to repressed childhood incidents of a conflictful nature which, under present circumstances, threaten to re-enter consciousness—an eventuality the ego tries to prevent at all costs. (Such "metaphors" do indeed seem "fantastic" sometimes, but they are undoubtedly convenient and highly plausible. And they are clearly the best terms we have for dealing with conflict.)

Perhaps the ideally mature and completely integrated person never wastes a minute defending his ego or contending with conflictful anxiety. Perhaps he, with complete and unselfconscious and insightful effectiveness, quickly resolves the inevitable conflicts and effectively invents ways to move ahead toward an evolving integration of his life in spite of the frustrations he encounters. But such an ideal person does not exist, except in someone's imagination—and no two people will quite agree on the details of such an imagined ideal. It might be possible, however, to define a continuum that begins with the idea of positive adjusting on one end and extends to the complete helplessness of self-defeating adjustment on the other. With a reasonable amount of oversimplification, we could place each member of a population somewhere on such an adjustmental continuum. Few, if any, could be placed close to the completely positive end. All of us some of the time engage in self-deception and defense in order to contend with the inevitable frustrations and conflicts. Some of us, perhaps with greater general sturdiness coupled with insight, use defense mechanisms only once in awhile and perhaps rarely get into the situations which make necessary the more drastic kinds of defensive contortions. Some of us, however, encounter such violent conflicts and such grievous anxieties that the system begins to break down or the more distorting defenses become necessary. Then we would be classed as *neurotic*. If breakdown is more complete, so that we become helpless or dangerous to ourselves or potentially harmful to our fellows, then we would be described as *psychotic*. On such a continuum, of course, there is no clear line of distinction between normalcy and neurosis or between neurosis and frank mental illness.

The next chapter will concern itself with neurosis and psychosis, and with the therapies employed in their treatment.

SUMMARY

1. The study of adjusting is the study of the success and of the form of behavior involved when the motivated individual pursues goals, contends with frustrations, and is caught up in conflict.

2. From the purely scientific point of view, one form of adjustment is as good as another; as applied scientists, however, psychologists do attempt to change adjustment in ways that are approved by the adjusting individual and by his society.

3. Personality theorists, concerned with the nature of good adjustment or of the mature personality, have set down a number of criteria: (a) realistic and accepting attitudes toward self, (b) continuing growth or self-actualization, (c) integration, (d) autonomy, (e) clear perception of reality, and (f) environmental mastery.

4. Motives do not become activated singly, and not all motives can be satisfied; hence, conflict and frustration occur. Adjusting often involves reactions to conflict and frustration.

5. When motivated behavior is blocked, when there is frustration, the organism will show emotionality, a variety of responses, and aggressive impulses. He may or may not demonstrate frustration tolerance, intelligent detour behavior, or overt attack on the frustrating agent.

6. When two or more opposing or irreconcilable motives are aroused, the organism is in conflict; conflict entails a very considerable tension.

7. There are a number of distinguishable kinds of conflict; there is conflict of habitual

responses, conflicting cognitions which produce dissonance, and conflicting motives.

8. The field-of-force analysis of conflicts delineates approach-approach, approach-avoidance, avoidance-avoidance, and double approach-avoidance conflicts.

9. Some personal conflicts have their origin in intra-individual factors, others in conflicting social values, others in conflicting social roles that the individual enacts.

10. The simpler responses to conflict include alternation, freezing or blocking, compromise, and withdrawal.

11. The tension produced by frustration or conflict is more severe if there is ego involvement; an ego-involved discrepancy between level of aspiration and level of achievement can produce severe tension.

12. One or more of the motivating forces in conflict may be repressed; many conflicts operate wholly or partially at an unconscious level.

13. Severe and persisting tension produced by conflict is termed anxiety; the psychological system will take steps to alleviate anxiety even if the steps do nothing to resolve the original conflict.

14. In contrast to direct and creative behaviors in the face of conflict or frustration are the defensive reactions, reactions that may not resolve conflict or satisfy frustrated motives but that do defend the psychological system.

15. Rationalization, a frequent defensive reaction, is a process of interpreting our own behavior in ways to make it more acceptable to the self; it is said to be a process of finding good reasons to substitute for real reasons.

16. Reaction formation is a reaction in which the more acceptable of conflicting motives is exaggerated.

17. Compensation is the overemphasis on one type of behavior in order to cover up felt deficiencies in other areas; there can be direct or indirect compensation.

18. Fantasy can serve as an escape from the reality of conflict or frustration.

19. Projection involves a seeing in others the motives about which we ourselves are anxious.

20. Identification is the process of taking on the identity of a powerful and frustrating other person.

21. Displacement is the indirect or misdirected expression of aggression; scapegoating may be regarded as an indirect expression of aggression.

22. Regression is the reactivation of behaviors which in earlier stages of development proved satisfying.

RESEARCH REPORTS

CHILD-REARING PRACTICES AND ANTI-SEMITISM *

A persisting and tenable theory of anti-Semitism has it that an individual with frustrated aggressive tendencies will, under some circumstances, displace the aggression on scapegoat targets—demonstrating negative attitudes toward members of various outgroups. In this study, Weatherley examined a related hypothesis: namely, a child who is severely punished for displaying aggression will develop internal barriers against direct, overt expressions of aggression; more specifically, children who have been subjected to harsh discipline for childhood aggression will demonstrate anti-Semitism.

In the present research the subjects were 39 non-Jewish undergraduate college women enrolled in elementary psychology courses, and their mothers. The 39 students were given two measures of anti-Semitism: (1) a standard anti-Semitism scale and (2) a rating procedure in which the students were asked to record in quantitative manner their reactions to four names (presented in systematically varied order): "Samuel Goldblatt," "Herbert Rosen," "James Brooks," and "Kenneth Taylor."

The mothers were contacted by mail and asked to answer questions concerning the way they had handled their daughters' aggression in childhood—for instance, the extent to which a mother had permitted her daughter to express verbal aggres-

---

* Donald Weatherley, Maternal response to childhood aggression and subsequent anti-Semitism, *J. abn. soc. Psychol.*, 1963, **66**, 183–185.

sion toward other children and toward parents. On the basis of the responses to these questions, each mother was given a *permissiveness* score. One of the questions dealt with the severity of punishment the daughters received for expressing prohibited aggression; each mother was given a *punitiveness* score on the basis of her response to this item. The experimenter made a combination of the punitiveness and permissiveness scores for each mother, thereby formulating a "general *sternness* score" by subtracting each mother's permissiveness score from her punitiveness score.

The results of this study are presented in the accompanying table.

CORRELATIONS BETWEEN MEASURES OF MOTHERS' RESPONSES TO CHILDHOOD AGGRESSION AND DAUGHTERS' ANTI-SEMITISM MEASURES

Mother variables	Daughter variables	r
Permissiveness	A-S scale score	−.247
Permissiveness	Jewish-name evaluation	−.156
Punitiveness	A-S scale score	+.256
Punitiveness	Jewish-name evaluation	+.328*
Sternness	A-S scale score	+.333*
Sternness	Jewish-name evaluation	+.338*

* *Significant at the .05 level of confidence.*

As can be seen from these data, the degree of permissiveness reported by mothers shows no significant relation to either of the measures of the daughter's anti-Semitism; the direction on the correlation, however, was in line with the hypothesis. The punitiveness of the mothers was significantly related to both indices of the daughters' anti-Semitism. The mothers' sternness was also significantly related to both measures of anti-Semitism. The sterner the mother, the more likely the daughter to agree with unfavorable statements about Jews and to attribute negative connotations to Jewish-sounding names.

In support of the general conclusion that stern discipline for aggression leads to displacement and hence to anti-Semitism, the researcher points out that the daughters of stern mothers do not differ from daughters of less stern mothers in their general evaluation of non-Jewish-sounding names; they do not dislike people in general.

The researcher points out that these data do not furnish conclusive evidence that the discipline described is in itself causative; perhaps, stern discipline for aggression was accompanied by a carefully taught authoritarian ideology that includes negative orientation on Jews and other minority groups.

COGNITIVE CONFLICT AND PROJECTION [*]

For some time it has been a well-established theory that when an individual projects onto others some unwanted and denied trait of his own, he is likely to select as targets for his projection the members of disliked outgroups such as Negroes or Jews. The present experiment, which examines this theory, also demonstrates ways in which cognitive conflict (dissonance) can be produced and the effects of such dissonance on behavior and perception.

In this experiment, the subjects were given false but convincing—and naturally dissonant—information that they themselves possessed homosexual tendencies. The experimental group, given this dissonance treatment, was then asked to rate the degree of homosexuality possessed by a target person, represented by a voice on a tape recorder; for one group this person was identified as a member of his own social category—a student having the same major as he, and at the same academic level; for another group, the voice was represented as that of a convicted criminal.

After this recording was completed, all subjects were asked to complete a form, on which each rated his own homosexuality and that of the individual making the recording. For this rating there was a six-point scale, running from "completely lacking in homosexual tendencies" to "very strong homosexual tendencies." Similar scales elicited the subjects' impressions of the friendliness, generosity, and over-all favorableness of the impression of the individual who was making the recording.

At the end of the session, each subject was asked to compare himself with the individual who made the recording with respect to similarity in general, to estimate the prevalence of homosexuality in the population at large, and to describe his own personal attitude toward homosexuality.

When the results were tabulated, it was clear that the experimental subjects ascribed to themselves more homosexuality than did the individuals in the control group. In the over-all ratings of the audible student and criminal, all subjects rated the student more favorably than they did the criminal. On the question of general similarity to the student and to the criminal, all subjects were inclined to consider themselves more similar to the student than to the criminal. On the basis of these data, then, it could be said that if the subjects who had been given dissonant informa-

[*] Dana Bramel, Selection of a target for defensive projection, *J. abn. soc. Psychol.,* 1963, **66**, 318–324.

tion about themselves tended to see the student as more homosexual than the criminal, they were projecting on individuals *who were similar to themselves,* who were favorably judged, and who were members of their own social class.

Analysis of the results indicates a difference in the projective tendencies of the control and the experimental group. The experimental subjects, convinced of their own homosexual tendencies, rate the recorded student at 2.97 on a six-point scale of homosexuality; the control subjects rate

the same student at 1.94. The difference between the two figures is statistically significant. For the experimental group, there is also a statistically significant tendency to rate the student higher than the criminal in homosexuality. These data seem to show that under circumstances in which an individual cannot deny an unfavorable trait, that individual will tend to project that trait onto individuals who are seen as similar to himself. The following table presents the data in more detail.

MEANS AND STANDARD DEVIATIONS OF RATINGS OF OWN HOMOSEXUALITY,
AND PERCEIVED SIMILARITY TO AND ATTITUDE TOWARD STIMULUS PERSON

| | CONDITION | | | |
| | STUDENT | | CRIMINAL | |
VARIABLE	No Dissonance (N = 17)	Dissonance (N = 31)	No Dissonance (N = 16)	Dissonance (N = 33)
Similarity				
M	1.53	1.29	.84	1.03
SD	.62	.73	.57	.47
Over-all impression (three scales)				
M	4.16	3.99	3.27	3.66
SD	.50	.90	.86	.85
Own homosexuality				
M	1.88	2.74	2.12	2.67
SD	.93	1.00	.96	1.05

SUGGESTED READINGS

Berkowitz, Leonard. *Aggression: A social psychological analysis.* New York: McGraw-Hill, 1962.

Carroll, Herbert A. *Mental hygiene: The dynamics of adjustment,* 4th ed. Englewood Cliffs, N. J.: Prentice-Hall, 1964.

Jahoda, Marie. *Current concepts of positive mental health.* Monograph Series No. 1. Joint Commission on Mental Illness and Health. New York: Basic Books, 1958.

Jourard, S. M. *Personal adjustment: An approach through the study of healthy personality,* 2nd ed. New York: Macmillan, 1963.

Lehner, G. F., and Ella Kube. *The dynamics of personal adjustment,* 2nd ed. Englewood Cliffs, N. J.: Prentice-Hall, 1964.

Shaffer, L. F. *The psychology of adjustment: An objective approach to mental hygiene.* Boston: Houghton Mifflin, 1936 (reprinted 1944).

Sutherland, R. L., W. H. Holtzman, E. A. Koile, and Bert K. Smith, eds. *Personality factors on the college campus: Review of a symposium.* Austin, Tex.: Hogg Foundation for Mental Health, 1962.

Yates, A. J. *Frustration and conflict.* New York: Wiley, 1962.

OUTLINE / CHAPTER 17

I. THE PROBLEM OF MENTAL DISORDER

    A. Kinds and Prevalence of Disorders
    B. Is Mental Illness Illness?

II. VARIETIES OF NEUROTIC BEHAVIOR

    A. Anxiety Reaction
    B. Dissociative Reaction
    C. Conversion Reaction
    D. Phobic Reaction
    E. Obsessive-Compulsion Reaction
    F. Depressive Reaction
    G. Nature and Genesis of Neurotic Behavior: A Case Study

III. THEORIES OF NEUROSIS

    A. Freudian and Neo-Freudian Theories of Neurosis
    B. The Self-Concept Theory of Neurosis
    C. Neurosis as Sin: The Mowrer Theory
    D. The Dollard-Miller Theory of Neurosis

IV. HEREDITARY FACTORS IN NEUROSIS

V. PSYCHOTHERAPY WITH NEUROTICS

    A. Psychoanalytic Therapy
    B. Directive Therapy
    C. Nondirective Therapy
    D. Role Therapy
    E. Behavior Therapy
    F. Group Therapy
    G. Effectiveness of Psychotherapy

VI. PSYCHOSIS

    A. Kinds of Psychoses
      1. Organic Psychosis
      2. Functional Psychosis
    B. Biological Factors in Psychosis
    C. Psychological Theories of Schizophrenia
    D. Treatment of Psychosis
      1. Drug Therapy or Chemotherapy
      2. Shock Therapy
      3. Psychosurgery
      4. Psychotherapy
      5. Milieu Therapy

VII. SUMMARY

VIII. RESEARCH REPORTS

CHAPTER 17

NEUROSIS, PSYCHOSIS, AND PSYCHOTHERAPY*

THE PROBLEM OF MENTAL DISORDER

In the last two chapters we have been dealing with attempts to gain a scientific understanding of the organized human system as it confronts its **environment.** In the chapter on personality we dealt with some of the psychologists' attempts to characterize the integrated human system—to describe the ways in which its behaviors are organized and to find the underlying organizing principles. In the chapter on adjusting we studied the ways in which the whole system contends with problems of frustration and conflict as it lives and moves and has its being in a complicated world.

Frustration and conflict, of course, represent trouble for a motivated psychological system. Sometimes this trouble is faced successfully, even creatively. But often, in the face of barriers and confusion, the organism is thrown into such a state of **anxiety** that it must, at least temporarily and in some measure, give up the positive, ongoing, creative processes of adjusting and take steps to defend itself, to hold itself together in the face of disruptive pressures. At such times, in the face of disappointment, failure, confusion, and ambivalence, most of us fall back at least occasionally on one or more of the **defense mechanisms.** Such is life. And because many of us much of the time engage in defensive behavior, we regard defensive responses as normal. **Rationalization, compensation, projection, reaction formation,** and other mecha-

* Austin Grigg gave significant assistance in the preparation of this chapter by drafting a large section of it and by critical examination of the whole. Some of the case materials, disguised, come from his clinical files. Demetrios Papageorgis helped very materially in the work on the revised version of this chapter.

nisms do seem to hold us together; and they do not totally incapacitate us for forward movement. We concern ourselves now with the more disruptive forms of adjusting.

KINDS AND PREVALENCE OF DISORDERS

When the reactions of the system to the strain of frustration and conflict become so severe as to cause grave psychological discomfort and serious incapacitation, then we say that the system is a **neurotic** one. There is no clear line of distinction between normal difficulties and neurotically incapacitating difficulties, just as there is no clear line of distinction between white and gray. So the definition of neurosis cannot be a very precise one. In general terms we can define neurosis as *a serious discomfort or incapacitation that is not due to organic causes*. Thus, neurotic behavior is distinguished from normal behavior on the not entirely satisfactory basis of degree of seriousness.

The distinction between neurotic behaviors and the even more seriously disruptive **psychotic** behaviors is also not clear. The term psychotic is used to refer to disturbances that are more serious, more completely incapacitating than are neurotic states. But there are other distinctions also. Psychosis is characterized by one or more of the following symptoms, none of which applies to neurosis: (a) a lasting deterioration in intellectual functions, (b) severe disturbances of mood (such as extreme apathy), and (c) persistent distortions of reality (such as **delusions**). These symptoms of psychosis we will deal with a bit later (p. 502).

It has been estimated that one out of every ten Americans has some kind of emotional disorder (National Committee, 1957) and, on any day, up to 800,000 of these are in mental hospitals (Joint Commission, 1961). Further, it is a good estimate that on any given day in the year, half the hospital beds in the country are occupied by psychiatric patients. There can be no doubt then about the grim seriousness of the problem of mental disorder. In this chapter we will look first at some of the conceptual and historical issues involved in

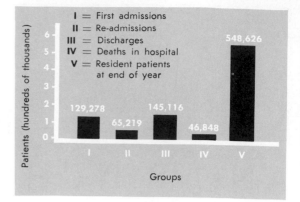

Figure 17–1. PATIENTS IN PUBLIC MENTAL HOSPITALS. *At the end of 1957, there were 548,626 resident patients in public mental hospitals. In addition to this number, approximately 280,000 individuals are clients during a year in mental-health clinics. Also at any time there are many thousands in private mental hospitals. These figures give support to the contention that mental illness is the nation's number-one health problem. (Data in the chart are from Public Health Service Publication No. 543, revised 1958.)*

dealing with the problem; then will go on to examine some of the forms of neurosis and psychosis; will look at the evidence on causes of such disturbances; and, finally, will study at least briefly some of the forms of treatment used in dealing with neurosis and psychosis.

IS MENTAL ILLNESS ILLNESS?

It has not been very long, in the course of human history, since the days when people who behaved peculiarly were judged to be possessed by devils and, as recently as the colonial days in this country, were sometimes burned as witches. Gradually, there was more humanity and humaneness in the way emotionally disturbed individuals were perceived and were treated. In this country the first institution expressly for the mentally disturbed was founded in Williamsburg, Virginia, in 1773 (Deutch, 1938). And at about the same time, Dr. Benjamin Rush, now known as the father of American psychiatry, was vigorously

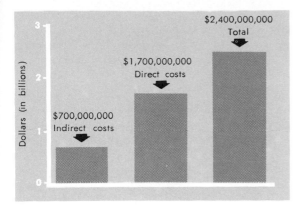

Figure 17–2. THE COST OF MENTAL ILLNESS. *The indirect cost of mental illness is the dollar value of labor lost in 1952 by resident patients in mental institutions. Direct costs include the actual expenditures per year in America on the care and treatment of the mentally ill. (Adapted from Fein,* Economics of Mental Illness. *Copyright 1958; permission of Basic Books, Inc., Publishers.)*

promulgating the humane treatment of "the insane." Even among the more enlightened and the more humane, however, there remained what we today would regard as great harshness both in conceiving of and in caring for those who were in emotional or behavioral difficulty. In 1844, of the thirteen physicians who met to organize the American Psychiatric Association, six came from institutions officially labeled "lunatic asylums"; only two were from institutions bearing the "hospital" label (Ridenour, 1961).

In the history of man's humanity to man, many will agree that there were great steps forward when the mentally or emotionally disturbed came to be regarded as ill rather than bedeviled or bewitched, when they were placed in lunatic asylums rather than prisons, and, later, when they were treated in hospitals rather than in lunatic asylums. Some observers today, however, maintain that the next great step will come when we begin to regard mental illness as a myth (Szasz, 1961) and seek for new and nonmedical ways both to conceptualize and to treat disturbed individuals. A number of writers have argued (Szasz, 1961; Mowrer, 1960) that there is error and perhaps even inhumanity in retaining the term "mental illness" and in holding to the medical analogy that is implied. "Illness" suggests a disease that affects the body. And, traditionally, anyone having an illness must be patient—or *a* patient—while being treated. To think in terms of illnesses and patients, the argument runs, leads to confused thinking, since relatively few psychological disorders are known to be associated with diseases of, or damage to, the **central nervous system.** Although there are "organic psychoses" and acute or chronic "brain syndromes" associated with brain damage, no known neural or physical malfunctioning is associated with the vast majority of disorders described as either psychosis or neurosis. These are *functional*—as opposed to structural or somatic—disorders. It may not be appropriate to use the word "illness" to refer to inefficient or uncomfortable or socially disapproved patterns of behavior. And it may be similarly inappropriate to use the term "patient" for an individual who perhaps should not assume a passive role when he has much active work to do if he is to learn more satisfactory ways of meeting his environment.

Still other writers (Smith, 1959; Jahoda, 1955, 1958; Sanford, 1956) have been disillusioned with the term "mental health." Pronouncing the term an essentially negative one —a problem-oriented one that implies nothing more constructive than the absence of mental illness—these writers emphasize positive, striving behavior or "creative health"; but they do not fully define the positive state or describe procedures for bringing it about. There can be no denying, however, that since 1908— when, under the leadership of Clifford Beers, the first organization of citizens for mental health (Deutch, 1938) was founded—the public has become increasingly concerned about problems of mental disorder and inclined to take more positive steps—steps to prevent disorder or to promote positive adjusting. It is difficult at the moment to demonstrate that such concerns have led to significant success in advancing human welfare. But

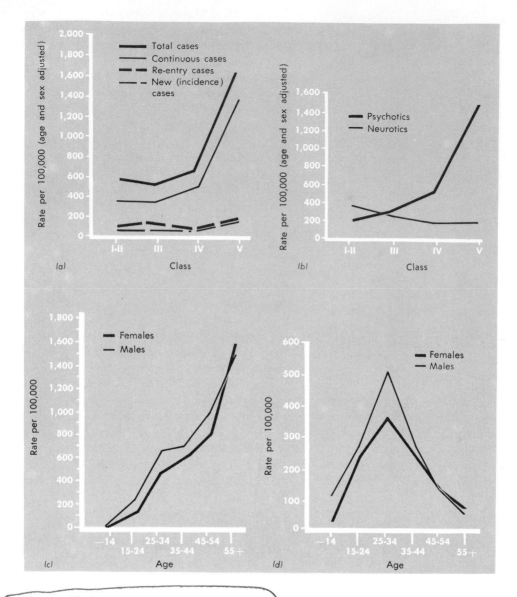

Figure 17—3. DATA ON THE PREVALENCE OF MENTAL ILLNESS. *In a study of mental illness in New Haven, it was found (a) that prevalence of psychosis is greater among the lower than among the upper socioeconomic classes; (b) that neurosis is less prevalent in the lower classes; (c) that the prevalence of psychosis for both men and women is greater as age advances; (d) that the prevalence of neurosis is greatest in the age range 25—34. In the figures above, Classes I—II represent the highest socioeconomic groups, Class V is the lowest. (Figures a and b reprinted with permission from Hollingshead and Redlich,* Social Class and Mental Illness, *copyright 1958, John Wiley & Sons, Inc.; Figures c and d reprinted with permission from Hollingshead in* Readings in Social Psychology, *edited by Maccoby et al., copyright 1958, Holt, Rinehart and Winston, Inc.)*

there is a growing tendency to recognize that the factors producing behavior disorders are complex and wide ranging (Langner and Michael, 1963; Srole et al., 1962) and that the control of deviant or disturbed behavior demands much more than the traditional medical approach, in which there is an emphasis on the one-to-one, doctor-patient relation: the resources of the whole community may be needed if progress is to be made in reducing the toll taken by emotional and behavioral difficulties.

VARIETIES OF NEUROTIC BEHAVIOR

Whether or not we regard emotional disorder as illness and whether or not we wish to stress the social factors in producing and controlling peculiar behavior, there are patterns of disordered behavior that can be labeled and described. Even though any individual, disturbed or not, is unique—so that we might expect every neurosis to have upon it the personal stamp of uniqueness—we *can* make crude classifications of neurotic individuals. Such classifications are usually based on the nature of the most prominent symptoms. For our purposes here, we shall use the systems of classification employed in the *Diagnostic and Statistical Manual of Mental Disorders* of the American Psychiatric Association (1955).

ANXIETY REACTION

This reaction is characterized by the fearful expectation, or nonspecific fear, that something terrible is about to happen. The fear is not restricted to definite situations or objects, and it is not controlled by any specific psychological defense mechanism.

An example of this reaction is that of a businessman who reported that unexplained attacks of fear would come over him as he was walking from the parking lot to his office. Later, these attacks of panic would occur at restaurants, in his office, in movies, and elsewhere. He also developed certain reactions such as cold sweating, palpitations of the heart, and feelings of dizziness.

DISSOCIATIVE REACTION

Dissociative reaction is characterized by some loss of contact with reality. It is held to be a result of extreme **repression** of certain aspects of reality—now so painful to the individual that he defensively pushes entire episodes of his life out of his awareness. The repressed impulse that gives rise to the anxiety is thought to be discharged into various symptoms such as stupor, amnesia, dream state, or multiple personality.

This reaction is illustrated by the woman who, after unhappy family conflicts, reported that she began to feel as if she were an observer of her own life, that she did not feel real. Later, she would have transient periods of forgetting who she was, or what she had set forth to do.

CONVERSION REACTION

In **conversion reactions,** the impulse that causes extreme anxiety is "converted" into functional symptoms in organs or parts of the body. Here are classified so-called hysterical blindness, hysterical deafness, hysterical paralysis, certain tremors, and various aches and pains that are purely psychological in origin and that have some practical or symbolic significance in the life of the individual.

This reaction is exemplified by the case of a male concert pianist who had conflicts about playing a piano for a living rather than working in robust, aggressive occupations as his brothers did. He later developed a defensive "hysterical" paralysis of his hands. Here the symptoms actually removed him from the conflictful occupation; this is termed a "secondary gain" of the symptoms.

PHOBIC REACTION

In cases of **phobia,** the prevailing view has it, the anxiety becomes detached from some specific object or event, and through **displacement** (or through **stimulus generalization**) the fear recurs in response to some symbolic idea or situation. There is usually repression of some event perceived as catastrophic, and then a displacement of the anxiety to some circumstance or object partially associated with the original fear. Fear of high places, of animals, of closed places, of crowds, and of dirt, are commonly encountered phobias.

A secretary became faint whenever she heard water running, as from a dripping faucet. Later, she could not tolerate any sounds suggesting running water. She was found to be suffering from repression of a very catastrophic early childhood experience in which she became trapped for several hours under a waterfall.

OBSESSIVE-COMPULSIVE REACTION

The **obsessive-compulsive** individual may experience recurring unwanted ideas (obsession) or feel compelled to carry out undesired or ridiculous acts (compulsion). So-called handwashing mania, kleptomania, and ritualistic touching ceremonials are classified here.

A preacher displayed an obsession when he complained to a psychiatrist that, as he got into the pulpit each week, a very offensive joke would race through his mind, and he was afraid he might "slip" and tell the story. A good example of compulsion would be the morbid stealing or shoplifting (kleptomania) by a person who actually has ample funds to purchase the objects.

DEPRESSIVE REACTION

The **depression** here is precipitated by an actual event in the environment, usually some loss, with resulting feelings of guilt and self-depreciation. The reaction is sometimes termed "reaction depression" because careful study of the afflicted individual will reveal that the depression is an exaggerated reaction to an actual depression-arousing event.

Following the death of her son in the war, a mother became so depressed that even three months after the tragedy she was unable to perform housework, was dull and lethargic, began to refuse food, became morbidly guilty about having been a poor mother when the son was alive. She constantly derided herself and began to have prolonged crying spells.

NATURE AND GENESIS OF NEUROTIC BEHAVIOR: A CASE STUDY

The brief illustrative cases under each of the foregoing headings above can serve, perhaps, to give meaning to the technical terms (all of which, incidentally, are current in literature and mass communication and many of which are often carelessly or erroneously used). The following case, presented in somewhat more detail, will illustrate more concretely the nature and the genesis of neurotic behavior.

Miss X, an attractive graduate student, came to the Counseling Center with complaints of headaches and nausea, which apparently had no physiological cause. Her story was an interesting one in that she was raised on a farm by a very strict father who quoted the Bible to prove that men are more valuable than women. An only daughter in a family of four boys, she had been a tomboy, but did not understand that this was most likely an attempt to win her father's esteem as if by saying, "See, I'm really like a boy." Miss X wore very loosely fitting clothes to her counseling interviews. When the therapist suggested to her that perhaps she was dressing in such a manner to try to hide that she was really a woman, she denied this, and insisted that this was simply her style of dressing, that she felt tight clothes were vulgar. When the therapist suggested that clothes properly sized were not vulgar, she became hostile and exclaimed that he was being like all men; as she complained, her headache became intense and she became ill. In later interviews, she revealed that she had once run away from home because she had felt sexual desires for boys when in high school, and her father had warned that sexual desires of women had brought sin and evil into the world. Her headaches had begun recently after she had accepted the attentions of a male graduate student, had gone to meals and to a movie with him.

The therapist brought out other childhood memories that suggested she had learned early to regard all feminine aspects of herself as dangerous and evil, and that she had devoted much energy to the attempt to win her father's acceptance but was always rebuffed by him. As she related her story, through several interviews, she began to see for herself the pattern in which she became hostile and angry when adolescent boys flirted with her. Finally she told the therapist: "Perhaps you may be right; I wonder if I am trying to hide that I am a woman and that I am attractive to men." She later admitted attraction to her college date and admitted that her headaches and nausea became worse after having been with him. Eventually, she came to realize that she became anxious whenever a boy expressed interest in her as a girl, and whenever she felt attraction to him. She bought a properly fitted dress for Easter and was ashamed at first to wear it in public. The dress was not a tight one, but it did reveal a very feminine physique.

It seems clear that the patient had exhibited **conversion** reactions—headaches and nausea—that were defenses against the anxiety and guilt aroused by the recognition of sexual feelings and by the insight that she was a feminine person capable of attracting men. Incidentally, this patient returned for an interview many months later with the complaint that she was a "frigid" wife.

THEORIES OF NEUROSIS

In the last chapter we dealt, though somewhat indirectly, with the outlines of a theory of neurosis. The theory has also injected itself somewhat in the foregoing description of neurotic reactions. We saw that the blocking of motives, either by **frustration** or by **conflict**, produces tension. Such tension often takes the form of anxiety. The system must deal with the anxiety, for it finds intolerable such a state of tension, particularly when the tension threatens to engulf the whole self. The system employs defense mechanisms in its effort to handle anxiety and to maintain an acceptable view of itself. The tension, the anxieties, and the defense mechanisms become more difficult to deal with when there is an element of **repression** involved, when the nature of the inner struggle is denied to consciousness.

The same general conceptualization applies to neurotic reactions; for, as we have pointed out, neurotic reactions may be viewed as more serious forms of normal reactions. We now turn to a more thorough examination of the various theories that attempt, in general terms, to account for the disruption, including neurotic disruptions, in what we regard as the more positive problem-solving, motive-satisfying processes of living.

FREUDIAN AND NEO-FREUDIAN THEORIES OF NEUROSIS

Freud's theory of neurosis, having much in common with his theory of all human functioning, viewed neurosis as the consequence of a conflict between, on one hand, primitive **motivation** residing in the **id** and, on the other, society's prohibitions which in the adult personality have been personally absorbed to constitute the **superego.** The **ego,** the conscious intelligence of the individual, carries the burden of solving the conflict between the two opposing forces in the personality. "Goaded on by the id," Freud said, "hemmed in by the superego and rebuffed by reality, the ego struggles to cope with its economic task of reducing the forces and influences which work in it and upon it to some kind of harmony" (Freud, 1933, p. 109). Neurotic symptoms result, according to Freud, when the ego, in allegiance to reality, suppresses some force in the id. The suppressed force, admitting to only temporary defeat, still strives for expression; sometimes in disguised form, it erupts into behavior, producing the superficially strange but psychologically meaningful symptoms of neurosis.

It was central to Freud's theory that the conflicts and experiences of early childhood are the crucial events in producing adult neuroses. The basic form of the psychological drama within the personality is established early in life, often as the result of particularly strong childhood experiences. Adult experiences serve to reactivate the hidden tensions of the past, producing distorted ideas and behaviors, each of which serves in some degree to defend the system against its own tensions.

Freud later introduced a number of revisions of his general theory. He faced new facts and gained new insights. Since his day, a number of people, now termed *Neo-Freudians,* have taken theoretical positions that are somewhat at variance with the original Freudian principles.

Karen Horney, one of the Neo-Freudians, takes the position that neurosis results from the child's hostile feelings toward parents who are emotionally rejecting in their attitudes toward the child (Horney, 1945). When the child feels rejection, Horney holds, he has immediate impulses to hostility and aggression. But such impulses seriously threaten the child, because cultural **taboos,** some of which the child has adopted as his own, are very sternly opposed to open attack on parents. So the child represses his hostile impulses, and, as part of his defense mechanism, he acquiesces to his parents. He learns never to assert himself, and in many cases becomes overcompliant. Thus, the perfect little lady or gentleman, so approved in some families, may be the product of rejecting parents; the rejection has produced hostile impulses, which, through the mechanism of reaction formation, lead to overcompliance and eventually perhaps to neurosis. The overcompliant child, the theory goes, fails to seek expression for many of his natural impulses, and spends much of his energy fighting against his own supposedly dangerous and evil wishes.

Harry Stack Sullivan, another Neo-Freudian theorist, takes a stance that again has much in common with Freud's views and yet carries a different emphasis (Sullivan, 1953). Sullivan centers his theory on the idea that the child (a) must learn what to expect from many "significant others," including the parents, and (b) must have a satisfying relationship with his parents if the learning of expectancies is to occur naturally and healthfully. If there is an upsetting relationship with the parents, then the child engages in a form of anxious **overlearning**—an overlearning that actually prevents highly discriminative learning. For example, such a child may learn to expect to find his mother's domination in his high school teacher or, later, in his wife. This inability to see others clearly, or the tendency to expect behaviors that will not in reality occur, clutters up many aspects of adult life. The man who expects his boss, on the basis of no objective evidence whatever, to behave in a domineering or patronizing way, as his father had behaved toward him, will have great difficulty understanding or relating with an actual boss. Neurosis, Sullivan says, is brought on when the individual, caught by habits of inhibition and misperception, is cast into an adult world full of potentially gratifying opportunities which he cannot accurately perceive. He still is so psychologically engrossed in solving childhood problems that he copes with present situations in what are essentially childish ways.

There are, in spite of some obvious differences, a number of common elements in the theories of Freud, Horney, and Sullivan. Each theorist emphasizes conflict between motivational impulses on one hand and the demands of civilization, however misperceived, on the other. Each stresses the importance of childhood experience. And each sees adult neurosis as brought on by an event or events that somehow reactivate the emotional struggle of childhood. None of these theories, however great their plausibility and however keen the clinical insights upon which they are based, is as firmly grounded in demonstrable scientific facts and relationships as the experimental scientist would like.

THE SELF-CONCEPT THEORY OF NEUROSIS

We had a glance in Chapter 15 at Rogers' theory of personality and of personality disturbance. According to Rogers, emotional disturbance occurs when the individual cannot reconcile present experience with his existing concept of himself. When there is a discrepancy between his established view of himself and data coming to him either from the outside world or from within his own skin, there is pain, guilt, and anxiety.

Rogers stresses growth and flexibility as signs of good mental health. The healthy individual can face all new experiences and can find ways of incorporating them into a consistent way of life. By contrast, the maladjusted person is inflexible and presently incapable of growth. He lives in accordance with rigid personal constructs, based upon ways he has construed experience in the past. He is characterized by stasis and fixity (Rogers, 1958).

NEUROSIS AS SIN: THE MOWRER THEORY

Sharply contrasting to the Freudian and Neo-Freudian theories of neurosis is Hobart Mowrer's view (1959) that neurosis is produced when the individual suffers guilt from impulses or behaviors that run counter to his conscience. The psychoanalytic theory tends to trace neurosis to a too-severe superego generated when the individual takes unto himself the harsh conscience of oversevere parents. The stern and forbidding superego, the Freudian theory goes, brings about a repression of primitive impulses. The individual recovers from neurosis when he can accept his primitive impulses. Mowrer reverses all this, saying that the self-hatred involved in emotional disturbances comes not from the introjection of harsh parental attitudes but from the actual behavior of the individual, who experiences justified guilt from his own bad or sinful behavior. Recovery from the misery of self-hatred occurs when the individual changes his attitudes and his actions, so that he justifiably feels he deserves something better. Along this line Mowrer writes:

As long as one remains, in old-fashioned religious phraseology, hard-of-heart and unrepentant, just so long will one's conscience hold him in the vice-like grip of "neurotic" rigidity and suffering. But if, at length, an individual confesses his past stupidities and errors and makes what poor attempts he can at restitution, then the superego (like the parents of an earlier day—and society in general) forgives and relaxes its stern hold; and the individual is once again free, "well" (Mowrer, 1960).

Mowrer, as we have seen, follows this line of thinking to raise doubts about the propriety of using the term "illness" in connection with mental disturbances. He is inclined to agree with Szasz (1961), who says ". . . mental illness is a myth, whose function it is to disguise and then render more palatable the bitter pill of moral conflicts in human relations" (p. 118). If mental disturbance is more appropriately regarded as sin than as illness, Mowrer reasons, then it is not a medical problem, as the psychiatrists maintain, but a moral problem. And if it is a moral problem, the whole psychoanalytic tendency to "accept" the disturbed individual as the victim of inevitable psychic forces is then in serious error.

Not many psychologists or psychiatrists are inclined to agree with Mowrer's position; but, as we have seen earlier, there is an increasingly strong tendency among those who work in the mental-health field to doubt the value of the conventional and medically oriented concept of mental illness.

THE DOLLARD-MILLER THEORY OF NEUROSIS

The theories of Freud, Horney, and Sullivan are products of keen minds steeped in the clinical approach to human problems and exposed to a variety of actual cases. There are other theories of neurosis that are products of keen minds steeped in the traditions of *experimental* science and exposed to a variety of actual cases. The two kinds of theories are not necessarily dissonant, but they do differ in approach and flavor.

The best-known and perhaps most complete theory of the latter variety is put forward by Dollard and Miller (1950) and is rooted in experimental psychology of the kind we cited in the sections of the preceding chapter dealing with conflicts.

This theory, in brief recapitulation, may be described as follows. The situation leading to neurosis is one in which the individual is embroiled in an **approach-avoidance conflict.** There are two or more motives, requiring incompatible behaviors, operating simultaneously. This conflict throws the individual into a state of highly charged psychological paralysis; he is not able to make either of the two responses. This inability to respond leads to anxiety, which further enhances the individual's helpless inability to respond. The unsatisfied motives increase in strength, producing a chronic state of tension characterized by high motivation and anxiety. In this state, anxiety-producing thoughts occur; and the cognitive processes, negatively reinforced, are avoided. Soon *all* anxiety-producing thoughts are avoided—are repressed—and the individual's superficial comfort is improved. But if repression occurs, the individual is unable to find adequate solutions to his conflict; repression denies him access to the very data he needs to solve his problems intelligently. He still feels impulses, but he cannot now label them; they impress him as mysterious.

So there is the neurosis. The individual has an anxiety-laden conflict that prevents action. Repression prevents effective thinking. His behavior in such a state will not be of a kind to advance his integral adjustment.

HEREDITARY FACTORS IN NEUROSIS

Most theories of neurosis stress learning. The general view among both the clinically and the experimentally inclined theorists is that the individual has learned his way into his neurotic difficulties. But is there a biological and inherited predisposition to neurosis? Do some people, because of inherited characteristics, learn more easily than others the neurotic solution to problems? The evidence on the point is not clear.

One investigator (Slater, 1943), after studying the case histories of 2,000 neurotic British soldiers, concluded that there is a tendency for neurosis to run in families. Members of some families seem to require less environmental stress than others to produce neurotic breakdown.

Such results, of course, are open to two possible interpretations. Even if neurosis does run in families, is it because of a common heredity or because the children are exposed to parents whose behavior toward them tends to produce neuroses? That the latter is a significant factor is indicated by research (Ingham, 1949; Henry, 1951) showing that neurotic parents, by their behavior toward their children, do indeed incline their children toward neurotic development. Psychological factors undoubtedly are involved in the development of neurosis; the role of biological or hereditary factors is as yet unknown.

PSYCHOTHERAPY WITH NEUROTICS

There are a number of forms of therapy used by psychiatrists and clinical psychologists in the attempt to help the neurotic find solutions to his problems.

PSYCHOANALYTIC THERAPY

The most widely known—and most frequently misunderstood—form of psychotherapy is the one originated by Freud, and, with various adjustments and revisions, employed today by practicing psychoanalysts. This technique of therapy is based on the psychoanalytic theory and places great emphasis on uncovering repressed childhood experiences assumed to lie behind adult neuroses.

In **psychoanalysis,** the therapist employs a number of techniques designed to help the patient recall past experiences and to reveal the way he interprets his world. There is *free association,* in which the patient is asked to relax and to put words to whatever comes to his mind, letting ideas flow with no regard for logic or coherence. Psychoanalysts also sometimes employ *dream analysis,* on the theory that the person's inner dynamics are revealed, in disguised and symbolic form, in his dream life. While the analyst is collecting all these data about life history and inner dynamics—data upon which he, and eventually the analysand, will base a "theory" of the case—the analyst plays a passive role. He is there—an observant, highly sophisticated listener.

During this process the patient establishes a special relationship with the therapist. He begins to *transfer* to the analyst his feelings for and expectations about significant figures in his past life. He may respond to the analyst, for example, as if the analyst were his own father. By studying this **transference,** the analyst learns more about the individual's relationships with others. In this transference situation, the analysand can re-experience, now in a safe and adult situation, some of the significant events, feelings, and relationships of his past.

When the analyst has gained an adequate picture of the significant events in the life of the individual and when he understands the individual's conflicts, defense mechanisms, and relationships with others, the analyst can begin to *interpret.* He wants to have the analysand see clearly and objectively how he has been reacting to events and to people and how he has been perceiving himself. The hoped-for end result is the individual's ability to understand himself more clearly, to deal with his feelings more healthfully, to establish more satisfying relationships with others, and to pursue with more effectiveness his life's goals.

Psychoanalysis is a protracted process. The neurotic individual may spend two or three years seeing his analyst for three 50-minute hours per week. It is also a very expensive process, for psychoanalysts are most frequently medically trained people who have spent long postgraduate years in psychoanalytic training (including the process of being psychoanalyzed themselves by a training analyst).

DIRECTIVE THERAPY

A form of treatment termed, without complete appropriateness, **directive therapy** is a somewhat simpler, less protracted, and more direct approach to the problems of the disturbed individual. In directive therapy, the psychiatrist or clinical psychologist tries, through diagnostic tests and interviews, to learn all he can about the past of the patient and about his present adjustments. The technique of free association is not employed, and the relationship between client and therapist does not become as intense as in full-fledged psychoanalysis.

When he himself understands the nature and source of the client's difficulty, the therapist works actively to help the client understand the relation between past events and his present feelings and present behavior, and to grasp a psychological "theory" of his present difficulties.

NONDIRECTIVE THERAPY

Nondirective or **client-centered therapy** is an approach growing directly out of Carl Rogers' theory of personality. It is Rogers' view that psychological disturbances arise when the individual is not able to incorporate into a consistent and acceptable view of the self significant data coming to him from his own inner processes or from the external world. The aim of nondirective therapy is to have the individual arrive at a workably accurate and acceptable conception of the self. To achieve this aim, the therapist works

to have the client accept the primary responsibility for the conduct of the therapy sessions and for the learning or relearning that must occur. The therapist aims to establish an accepting relationship with the client, one in which the client feels free to be and act himself. There is an avoidance of interpretation or explanation. The therapist's function is to understand the client, to feel with him, to see the world through the client's eyes, and to *reflect* these feelings so that the client knows he is understood and accepted. In such a situation, a very rare one in everyday human experience, the client is in a position to learn new perspectives on himself and his world.

Rogers (1957) describes the following six conditions as necessary for constructive personality change in the therapeutic situation.

1. There must be psychological contact between therapist and client.
2. The client must be suffering some anxiety, must be feeling a discrepancy between his self-image and some actual experiences.
3. The therapist must be genuinely and freely himself when relating with the client.
4. The therapist must, without any reservations, genuinely accept the client.
5. The therapist must be so sensitively aware of the client's experiences that they seem to be the therapist's own experiences.
6. The therapist must be able to communicate to the client that he fully understands all of the client's feelings.

ROLE THERAPY

George Kelly (1955) has proposed a novel approach to psychotherapy with neurotics, called **fixed-role therapy.** Here, the client writes a characterization of himself; then, after careful study of this characterization, the therapist, in collaboration with other clinicians, writes a new sketch. This new sketch is actually a role, like a role in a play. Its general format is similar in many respects to the present personality of the patient, but also contains some sharp contrasts. The therapist and the patient discuss the role; during the therapy hour, they practice it; and then the patient is urged to act, during the days following the interview, as though he were the person in the role. The theory is that, as the patient assumes the mask of a new role, he will test new hypotheses (**constructs**) and thus is enabled to experiment with changes in his behavior, some of which he will find rewarding. The rewarding or satisfying behaviors are kept as part of the revised personality of the client. This concept of treatment for neurosis is an outgrowth of Kelly's theory of personality, called *the psychology of personal constructs*, which holds that a person conducts himself according to the ways in which he anticipates events, and that a person develops ideas (constructs) which he uses to predict events on the basis of his experiences with others and with himself. Some people develop a very flexible and permeable system of constructs; others develop rigid, inflexible construct systems and thus are confined to very few alternative possibilities for solving dilemmas.

BEHAVIOR THERAPY

In recent years psychologists and psychiatrists have placed increasing emphasis on the application of learning theory to the understanding and treatment of behavior disorders. The basic thesis of a variety of recent approaches is that neuroses, as well as other disorders, represent configurations of *learned* responses that have become thoroughly habitual. Effective treatment is sought through the specific use of techniques—techniques for relearning—derived from the basic principles of **conditioning: extinction, stimulus generalization,** and so forth.

Joseph Wolpe (1958) is a systematic and articulate user of such principles. He calls his technique *psychotherapy by reciprocal inhibition.* Basically, he attempts to remove the anxiety that prior learning has attached to useful and desirable responses. The individual is asked to think or to behave in ways that make him moderately anxious, but under circumstances that are incompatible with the arousal of severe anxiety. Thus, a person may think about objects that provoke his irrational fears while at the same time he is in a state of complete relaxation. The relaxation inhibits the anxiety. Systematic repetition of this procedure results in the reduction of anxiety to such a level that it no longer interferes with the behavior. Relaxation is not the only type of response that Wolpe found can inhibit anxiety: assertive and sexual responses also have the same anxiety-inhibiting effect; and eating can be used to "cure" animals of their experimental "neuroses."

Wolpe has published accounts of successful results with certain cases; and he believes that reciprocal inhibition occurs in other methods of therapy and is responsible for the success of the therapy. He also believes that people who have improved without professional help (the so-called "spontaneous-remission" cases) have benefited from unintentional, but fortunate, reciprocal inhibition.

The contrast between behavior therapy and the more traditional forms of psychotherapy illustrates a live controversy in present-day psychology. Eysenck (1960), a proponent of the former approach, points out several differences in the two kinds of therapy: (1) Traditional, and especially psychoanalytic, therapy considers transference relations as essential for its success, whereas behavior therapy views transference phenomena as sometimes helpful but not essential. (2) Traditional therapy views the mere treatment of symptoms as potentially harmful, since new and perhaps more serious symptoms will replace the old ones unless underlying causes are removed; behavior therapy views the treatment of symptoms, provided certain conditions are met, as leading to total recovery. (3) Interpretation of behavior and dreams is important in traditional therapy; behavior therapy views it as irrelevant. (4) Traditional therapy emphasizes the past and the historical development of the neurotic condition; behavior therapy views the development of symptoms in the person's history as largely irrelevant and focuses instead on habits existing at the time of treatment. (5) In behavior therapy faulty learning replaces the traditional role of repression and the unconscious in the formation of symptoms. (6) Behavior therapy is based on a more consistent and empirically tested theory—learning theory.

GROUP THERAPY

Psychiatrists and clinical psychologists most often employ individual psychotherapy in treating the neurotic person; however, there is a growing interest in **group therapy,** a form of treatment that places several disturbed people in a group situation with the therapist in attendance. Many of the neurotic's symptoms are activated by the stress of interpersonal relationships, and the group-therapy situation is a kind of miniature sample of the stresses of socializing. Various workers have claimed quite different rationales for group therapy, but the major difference between group and individual therapy is as follows: in group therapy the patient learns to share his feelings, his conflicts, his characteristic reactions with others while in a situation where others will respond to his actions at that moment; in individual therapy, the patient may not be as pushed by his therapist to examine each and every reaction (Bach, 1954; Schilder, 1938; Slavson, 1947). Group approaches are also being tried with psychotic patients.

EFFECTIVENESS OF PSYCHOTHERAPY

Each of these therapeutic approaches, although they may differ in both theory and technique, rests on the assumption that the neurotic person is suffering from a distortion of his feelings and of his perceptions of himself and of others; that this distortion is a result of previous learning; and that, under

Figure 17–4. GROUP PSYCHOTHERAPY. *Group psychotherapy places several disturbed individuals in a social setting with a psychologist. The individual in the group expresses his feelings so that group members may respond at the moment. Procedure may involve psychodrama—the acting out of realistic scenes—and other special procedures. (Courtesy of Dr. George R. Bach, Institute of Group Psychotherapy.)*

proper circumstances, relearning can occur so that the individual can begin to see himself more clearly, to perceive the world more accurately, and to find a way of behaving that will bring more satisfaction and less pain.

How effective is psychotherapy in the treatment of neurosis? There is a large and controversial literature on this important question, but there are now few straightforward answers. Not many psychologists doubt that troubled individuals do derive benefit from psychotherapy. Many clients do appear to undergo definite changes in behavior as a result of therapeutic experiences. But it is not now possible to say with certainty how many of what kinds of neurotics are helped to what extent by what form of therapeutic experience. As long as it remains very difficult to define "good mental health" or to recognize clearly what is "recovery," it will be very difficult to assess the exact effects of psychotherapy. It remains equally difficult, of course, to assess the effect, or the "effectiveness" of any complex human experience. Many people "know," for example, that a liberal education is effective. But few can demonstrate it. How could one assess either the "therapeutic" or educational effectiveness of a course in introductory psychology?

Research on the effectiveness of psychotherapy has encountered at least two major difficulties. First, there is the difficulty of settling on the criteria to be used in judging effectiveness. And second, there is the equally crucial difficulty of setting up a control group so that research results can be meaningfully interpreted.

On the question of criteria, there are disagreements among both therapists and researchers concerning the definable goals of therapy. Is it to be scored as successful when specific symptoms, such as sexual frigidity or a specific phobia, are removed, or should there be a restructuring of a whole personality so that debilitating symptoms of some different sort will not appear? If a client reports that he feels better, do we accept that as evidence that therapy is effective? Can we put credence in a change, after therapy, in scores on personality tests or in ratings given by uninvolved therapists? There is at present no agreement on the answers to such questions.

Similar and equally grievous problems arise around the need for control groups in conducting research on psychotherapy. Not only is it technically difficult to find groups that can be properly matched with experimental groups, but even if such groups could be found, many therapists would refuse, on ethical grounds, to deny any suffering person the possible benefits of therapy.

In the light of these difficulties it is not surprising that we have only inconclusive evidence on either the effectiveness of psychotherapy or on the relative effectiveness of any particular kind of psychotherapy. It is also not surprising that one psychologist (Eysenck, 1961) suggests that psychotherapy should not be practiced at all until its effectiveness is demonstrated; nor is it surprising that practitioners of psychotherapy should be outraged at such a suggestion.

In addition to questions about the effectiveness of psychotherapy, psychologists and others have recently concerned themselves with the social and ethical aspects of psychotherapy as a technique of exerting influence on human individuals and, potentially at least, of bringing about a variety of changes in behavior. What is the difference between psychotherapy and "brainwashing"? Such a question is being asked and confronted (Frank, 1961). And to what extent, and through what justification, does the psychologist or psychiatrist become a social engineer? These questions, too, are being dealt with articulately (Szasz, 1963).

PSYCHOSIS

Psychotic reactions are not always easily distinguished from neurotic reactions. We can make a distinction, although an imprecise one, on the basis of seriousness. Disorders properly labeled psychotic are more seriously disruptive of normal psychological functioning than are neuroses. The psychotic person is sometimes defined as one who cannot function adequately in ordinary society, or as a person who is dangerous to himself or to others. But there are other and perhaps more meaningful distinctions. Neurosis does not entail a deterioration in intellectual capacity. Psychosis sometimes does. Neurosis does not entail dramatic disturbances of mood or drastic distortions of emotional responses. Psychosis often does. In addition, some forms of psychotic behavior, termed *organic psychoses,* are associated with damage to the **central nervous system.** In contrast, most if not all neuroses are believed to fall into the *functional* category—disorders that are most likely the products of learning and that lack demonstrable central nervous system pathology.

Perhaps the clearest distinction between neurosis and psychosis is that neurosis does not involve a "break with reality" while psychosis often does. The neurotic individual, though he may misperceive some aspects of the world, still knows that he himself is out of step, and the world exists for him in just about the form it exists for others. The psychotic, by comparison, may create a private world having little in common with that perceived and inhabited by most of us.

The extreme distortions of reality are perhaps the most significant and the most obvious symptoms of psychosis. The psychotic patient may have both **hallucinations and delusions.**

Hallucinations are defined as *false perceptions*—perceptions occurring in the absence of sensory experience. The psychotic patient, alone in his room, may "see" his mother standing before him and engage her in conversation. Another may hear voices that reach his ear alone, or he may feel vibrations which no one else can register. Such hallucinations are very rare in normal or neurotic individuals.

Where hallucinations are false perceptions, delusions are defined as *false beliefs.* The psychotic patient may, for example, believe that he is God and may build around this belief a consistent delusional system into which all of his distorted perceptions fit.

The following case of a young paranoid psychotic illustrates the interplay of hallucination and delusion in mental illness.

During high school, the patient had begun to take long walks alone, began missing meals, often stared out of his window, and, in general, began to exhibit signs of withdrawal. His parents did not become worried, for they interpreted such behavior as the blossoming of a scholarly way of life. After he was admitted to the mental hospital, his mother recalled that on several occasions she had heard him talking to someone in his room when no one was there, but that she had assumed he was studying aloud.

When he was hospitalized, the patient spoke of having had a study companion who would appear through the walls of his room. He also told of getting secret instructions from this companion while taking tests. He exhibited disturbing hallucinations during his early hospitalization and felt that he was being subjected to irradiation effects, and also that pigeons which appeared at his window ledge were attempting to speak to him. After 17 electroconvulsive shock treatments, his hallucinations and delusions failed to appear, and he became more rational. After six months of psychotherapy, during which extreme hostility to the mother and jealousy of an older brother were brought out, he was sufficiently free of symptoms to be allowed to return home.

We should note again that delusions are not only absent in certain psychotic individuals, but also are not uncommon among neurotic and normal people. Many of us maintain cherished beliefs despite overwhelming evidence that they are unfounded, and it has also been reported (Festinger, Riecken, and Schachter, 1956) that sometimes, rather than abandon erroneous beliefs, people may engage in some fairly extreme cognitive contortions to reduce dissonance; and they may vigorously attempt to convince other people of the validity of their own strange beliefs. The difference with respect to delusions between normal individuals and psychotics is one of degree and social consequence: psychotic delusions tend to be more bizarre, they exercise a greater control over the individual's intellectual life, and are more likely to influence what he says and does.

KINDS OF PSYCHOSES

As with neuroses, it is always a unique individual who develops psychosis. The forms his disturbance may take are greatly varied. But we can still classify, with some degree of precision, an array of symptoms commonly classed as psychotic. First of all, as mentioned, we can distinguish between the *organic psychoses,* which are associated with demonstrable pathology of the central nervous system, and the _functional psychoses,_ accompanied by no demonstrable brain pathology and believed to be largely products of experience and learning. This distinction, however, is not absolute. Organic psychotics are recognized by their history, and by such factors as intellectual deterioration, neurological symptoms, and physical diseases; however, their delusions, hallucinations, and other psychotic behaviors are often indistinguishable from the corresponding behaviors of functional psychotics. It is widely held that psychotic symptoms in general represent attempts by unique individuals to adjust to stress; the stress in question may be a brain disease or injury or may arise solely from extreme environmental factors. Since a considerable number of psychotic symptoms are means of adjustment, we can logically and psychologically expect that the choice of the specific symptoms, whether the psychosis is functional or organic, will depend more on the individual's personality than on the specific nature of the stress. Despite the similarity between many organic and functional symptoms, however, the organic psychotic will very often display additional symptoms reflecting a deficit in brain function; for example, damage to the inhibitory areas of the cerebral cortex may result in an inability to control and organize behavior.

Psychoses are also classified as _acute_ or _chronic._ An acute psychosis, which may be either functional or organic, is of relatively sudden onset and subsides after a period of time, usually following treatment but sometimes without it. In contrast, chronic psychoses are of long duration and the patient may show no recovery or only an incomplete recovery. The acute-chronic distinction, however, is not always as clear as it may seem: acute psychotics have been known to become chronic, and chronic psychotics have been known to show relatively sudden improvement only to return to serious psychotic behavior a little later. In spite of shortcomings, however, both the acute-chronic distinction and the functional-organic one have been found useful over the years. It is also true that each of these distinctions fits certain patients and certain conditions better than it fits others.

Organic Psychoses

Psychotic conditions that are related to organic disturbance may arise from a variety of causes. Organic psychoses are classified on the basis of the organic disturbance that contributes to the psychotic condition. Thus, we have psychoses associated with central nervous system syphilis, the most common variety of which is called **general paresis.** This disorder is characterized by a progressive deterioration of intellectual and behavior functions, eventually leading to death unless treated. The incidence of general paresis has been decreasing since the discovery that penicillin is effective in treating syphilis, although an alarming number of cases of what by now is a preventable disorder are still found. The main symptom of paresis is the progressive destruction of all mental functions (Bruetsch, 1959). The onset is usually slow and difficult to detect. The psychotic symptoms vary from patient to patient: some patients show only a gradual intellectual deterioration; others may show delusions, excitement, and depression.

Organic psychotic behavior is also sometimes caused by brain deterioration that results from _senility._ Again the symptoms are extremely varied, with simple deterioration, delusions, and depression likely to occur. With the increase in life expectancy, an increasing number of hospitalized patients suffer from senile psychosis. Other organic psychoses may be the result of injury to the brain, arteriosclerosis, encephalitis, vitamin deficiencies, or poisons. Among the psychotic reactions produced by poisons are the psychoses resulting from alcoholism. Acute alcoholic psychoses, such as **delirium tremens** (DT's) and acute alcoholic hallucinosis, are caused by the direct effect of alcohol on the brain. Chronic alcoholic psychoses, which include several varieties, are usually only indirectly caused by alcohol and often represent the result of a nutritional deficiency.

Functional Psychoses

Functional psychoses are classified on the basis of configurations of symptoms. The main categories include various manic or depressive reactions, several varieties of schizophrenia, and paranoia and paranoid states.

Involutional psychotic reaction. This reaction is characterized by depression, agitation, delusional ideas, and somatic concerns and typically occurs during the involutional (post-menopausal) period, in an individual without previous history of psychotic depression.

Manic-depressive reactions. These are the psychotic reactions characterized by extreme fluctuations in mood, from great excitement and frenetic activity to deep and inert depression. There are also usually illusions, delusions, and hallucinations. There is a definite tendency for recurrence of the illness.

Psychotic depressive reaction. Somewhat more severe than a neurotic depressive reaction, this reaction is characterized by severe depression, delusions, and hallucinations. This reaction, like all forms of schizophrenia, involves a break with reality (actually a split from reality—not, as is commonly said, a "split personality").

Schizophrenia, simple type. The simple schizophrenic reaction involves a gradual retraction of interests and external attachments and is characterized by impoverished human relationships.

Schizophrenia, hebephrenic type. Classified here are patients who show unpredictable giggling, silly behavior and mannerisms, delusions, hallucinations, and marked regression to earlier modes of behavior.

Schizophrenia, catatonic type. These patients exhibit waxy rigidity, stupor, mutism, marked inhibition. If, for example, the arm of a catatonic is raised and extended by someone else, the arm may remain for an hour in the position given it. This kind of rigidity may shift, however, and the patient may become excessively agitated or excited.

Schizophrenic, paranoid type. Here there is unrealistic thinking with bizarre delusions of persecution and/or grandeur, usually a hostile attitude, and often hallucinations.

Schizophrenic, acute undifferentiated type. This reaction is characterized by confusion, emotional upset, anxiety, delusions. Usually the symptoms disappear in a few weeks.

Schizophrenic, chronic undifferentiated type. This is a classification used for patients who are obviously schizophrenic but who are so mixed in their symptoms that they do not fit clearly into one of the more specific categories.

Schizophrenic, schizo-affective type. This reaction is characterized by bizarre, disjunctive or disconnected thinking, and with pronounced elation or depression.

Schizophrenic, childhood type. Psychotic reactions in childhood are classified here, especially if autism, a tendency to break away from reality and to live in a dream world, is a prominent feature.

Schizophrenic, residual type. This term is used for patients who have improved sufficiently from a schizophrenic reaction to return to the community, although they continue to show disturbance in thinking and in social interactions.

Paranoia. Here are classified those patients with logical delusions of persecution or grandeur. Their delusions are not bizarre; to a stranger who lacks the actual facts, they may even seem very plausible.

Paranoid state. A temporary form of paranoid disorder, usually occurring when the individual is under great stress.

These classifications are not as well defined in reality as they appear on paper. Still, in the absence of concrete knowledge as to causation and specific treatment, they serve as convenient sources of statistics and as means of more or less effective communication between professionals. From time to time there have been well-reasoned pleas for a revision of the classification system. For example, Kantor, Wallner, and Winder (1953) are among those who have proposed that at least two varieties of what is called "schizophrenia" can be distinguished: *reactive schizophrenia*, characterized by relatively sudden onset, adequate prepsychotic adjustment, and good prognosis (or probability of cure); and *process schizophrenia*, a long-standing disorder, with slow onset, poor prepsychotic adjustment, and poor prognosis. Organic involvement is also suggested as likely in the latter category. These new attempts at classification are at present used in research work, while in practical everyday situations we are more likely to encounter the traditional labels.

One final general category of behavior disorders that should be mentioned here, although there is no wide agreement that it is properly classed as psychotic, falls under the label *character disorder.* This term is equivalent to the older label *psychopathic personal-*

ity, which is now largely abandoned. Individuals placed in this category have at least average intelligence but show repeated failures in constructive undertakings and persistent antisocial behavior in the face of little or no provocation. They are irresponsible, unable to accept blame, incapable of forming meaningful and lasting relationships, incapable of learning from experience, and lacking in insight (Cleckley, 1959). More often than not, these individuals lack honest motivation for treatment.

BIOLOGICAL FACTORS IN PSYCHOSIS

All the functional psychotic reactions listed above are described as **psychogenic**—as produced by psychological rather than organic factors. There is a good deal of evidence, however, that biological and hereditary factors play a prominent role in the development of psychotic behavior. Earlier, in our examination of hereditary factors in development (Chap. 3), we saw evidence suggesting a definite hereditary factor in schizophrenia (Kallmann, 1938). There is similar evidence that manic-depressive reactions tend to run in families and to be based on an hereditary predisposition. It was found in one study (Kallmann, 1953), for example, that if one of a pair of identical twins develops a manic-depressive psychosis, the chances are 90 in 100 that the other twin will develop the same psychosis.

Research on the physiological and biochemical factors in schizophrenia is beginning to accumulate a body of evidence that may eventually lead to successful chemical treatment of this most frequent of psychoses. At the moment, however, the state of knowledge and alleged knowledge in this field is confused and confusing. In 1948 one writer (Bellak), after reviewing some 3,200 published research reports dealing with organic factors in schizophrenia, concluded that there is no consistently positive evidence that organic factors have anything to do with schizophrenia. Ten years later, the same author wrote: "probably in the vast majority of schizophrenias the ontogenetic developmental data, particularly psychogenic factors such as conceptualized in psychoanalytic theory, suffice to account for the schizophrenic syndrome" (Bellak, 1958, p. 62).

That biochemical processes are involved somehow in psychosis, however, is suggested by several lines of research in which chemical substances have been used to produce what appear to be psychotic reactions in human subjects. These substances—including a lysergic acid derivation (called LSD), mescaline, dimethyl tryptamine, Sernyl, and others —are called **psychotomimetic** or **psychodelic** drugs; they are believed by some to mimic psychotic reactions.

When a volunteer subject is given one of these psychotomimetic drugs, he may have hallucinations, suffer violent changes in mood, have difficulty in paying attention, and show some derangement of verbal behavior. The subject may also report feelings of estrangement and disturbing shifts in the way he perceives his own body.

The response of subjects to these substances is not highly predictable. It is also possible that the nature of the response is determined by the personality characteristics of the subject or by his **set** toward the experimenter.

The similarity of these chemically induced reactions to the reactions of psychotic patients has led some investigators toward a reaffirmed belief that the "true answer to mental illness" lies in biochemical research and that soon we shall see a great scientific breakthrough that will enable us to cure schizophrenia. Not all researchers, however, share this optimism, being inclined to discount the similarity between these experimentally produced states and genuine psychosis.

PSYCHOLOGICAL THEORIES OF SCHIZOPHRENIA

Sigmund Freud was the first to develop a psychological theory of psychosis, viewing the psychotic reaction as a form of extreme regression in which the individual withdraws from present reality and employs behaviors and perceptions that characterized him as a child. Under extreme stress, Freud held, the ego withdraws from reality, tending to remodel its world, to distort it, to symbolize it until it becomes a less intolerable environment in which to exist. Intellectual deterioration, so frequently observed in psychosis, Freud saw as regression—a return of the ego to the primitive undifferentiated state of early infancy.

Freud's theory, a broad and inclusive formulation, is a theory of psychosis in general, a theory in which psychosis is an extreme form of adjustment. Other theories of psychosis tend to focus on schizophrenia, but tend to agree with Freud in seeing the malady as a way of adjusting to life's pressures. A number of recent studies have described the nature of the early psychological experiences that seem to lead to schizophrenia. Several studies show, for example, that the early home life of schizophrenic patients is characterized by a great deal of nagging, scolding, and criticism (Mark, 1953; Gerard and Siegel, 1950; Freeman and Grayson, 1955; Tietze, 1949).

Out of these and related studies there evolves a general theoretical picture of a child —rejected, criticized, and confused—learning a pervasive feeling of worthlessness. He fails to develop any self-esteem or sense of personal identity. He learns to expect disapproval. The child detaches himself emotionally from this forbidding world in a desperate attempt to avoid further hurt. He is on the road to full-blown schizophrenia.

The following case illustrates adult psychosis that is probably rooted in the kinds of childhood experiences described in a number of studies of the psychological history of schizophrenia.

Mr. Y was a junior in college. His fraternity brothers reported that he had begun to seclude himself in his room, would not take his meals with the rest of the fraternity, began to accuse some of his fraternity brothers of "stealing" his ideas for term papers and of copying his "superior" notes. At the student clinic, he was found to have

delusions that many people were jealous of his superior mind, that there was a plot to take his ideas and to use his class notes so that others could do as well as he was doing. He also was afraid of one particular fraternity brother whom he accused of having homosexual interests.

His family reported that he had always been well behaved but rather aloof, had liked heavy literature and philosophical reading, and had not dated often. His parents, involved in their own careers, had apparently not devoted much recreational attention to the boy, although they did keep him under heavy pressure to excel in school. An older brother, a straight-A student, had been the family favorite, and the patient had often been punished for not being conscientious about his lessons.

Most present students of schizophrenia, although their formulations differ in some respects, tend to agree that the disorder represents a learned and desperate attempt to solve stressful problems. Most theorists agree also that the learning that leads to schizophrenic adjustment begins early in life, and involves stressful parent-child relationships. Arieti (1955), for example, presents a graphic picture of the rejected child—anxious and hostile, withdrawing into seclusion in order to avoid the interpersonal contacts he cannot enjoy or understand. In such a picture, the role of the mother is of special significance. In the life of the pre-schizophrenic child, according to Arieti, there is frequently a domineering, nagging, and hostile mother, who gives neither the child nor a weak and dependent husband any chance for self-assertion. Or there may be a tyrannical father, who imposes his harsh rule on both wife and child so that there can be no expression of mother-child affection. Either situation leads naturally to withdrawal, anxiety, hostility, and sometimes to schizophrenia.

TREATMENT OF PSYCHOSIS

There are four major kinds of treatment that are, or have been recently, used on psychotic patients. These are (1) drug therapy, (2) shock therapy, (3) psychosurgery, and (4) psychotherapy.

Drug Therapy or Chemotherapy

Many kinds of drugs are employed in the treatment of the mentally ill. (Clinical psychologists, of course, do not employ drugs in dealing with emotionally disturbed individuals. Sometimes, however, they work in collaboration with psychiatrists or other physicians who do.) Some drugs are used to facilitate communication with the patient, especially in instances where there is difficulty in the recall of painful or traumatic experiences. Such drugs are more likely to be useful in treating neuroses, but they may be used also on psychotic individuals. Certain of these drugs, such as Sodium Pentothal and Sodium Amytal, are sometimes used to produce a state of half-sleep, during which *narcoanalysis* can be attempted. In narco-analysis the patient, in a state of "twilight sleep," can often be easily induced to talk about experiences which, in full consciousness, he finds too painful to confront. The psychotherapist is then able to get more complete information about the individual's difficulties and may progress toward helping him make psychological peace with the intolerable tensions.

This method of treatment has been found especially successful in alleviating acute anxiety states and dissociative reactions of recent origin—reactions that are actually more neurotic than psychotic. Extensive use was made of this method in treating cases of so-called "war neurosis" (Grinker and Spiegel, 1945).

Of more recent origin, and presently extensively used are the so-called *psychoactive* drugs, sometimes inaccurately referred to as "tranquilizing" drugs. Actually, tranquilizers are only one general category of these drugs. It is not possible to attempt an extended discussion of each one of the large and rapidly growing number of psychoactive drugs; we can, however, at least mention some of the more widely used ones. The so-called "tranquilizers" are sometimes considered to be agents that reduce excitement and to do so without the clouding of consciousness that is characteristic of some earlier narcotics; however, the tranquilizing drugs do more than reduce excitement; they facilitate communication, reduce delusions and hallucinations, and promote social adjustment (Berger, 1960).

Among these tranquilizers we may distinguish several subgroups. One of these groups are the phenothiazine derivatives, including (1) phenothiazine, (2) chlorpromazine (Thorazine), and (3) thioridazine (Mellaril). Another group is derived from the root of the Indian snakeroot plant and are known as the Rauwolfia alkaloids, with reserpine (Serpasil) perhaps the best-known example. A third group consists of the so-called diphenylmethanes and includes hydroxizine (Atarax). The substituted propanediol derivatives include the well-known meprobamate (Miltown, Equanil). Finally, the substituted amide group includes pentabarbital (Nembutal).

A second major group of psychoactive drugs consists of the *energizers,* or *stimulants,* or *antidepressants.* These labels again serve to create confusion regarding the psychological properties of these drugs. At least three subgroups may be distinguished. There are the analeptics (antidepressives), which produce hyperexcitability and include amphetamine (Benzedrine) and dextro-amphetamine (Dexedrine). Another group includes the monoaminoxidase inhibitors that include iproniazid (marsalid). A third group is made up of the acetylcholine precursors.

It is now quite clear that all these drugs affect the behavior of many mental patients. Since the beginning of their extensive use in the early 1950s, there have been definite increases in the discharge rates of mental hospitals. A greater number of mental patients, because of drugs, are able to return to their homes and to lead relatively normal lives. Not much is yet known, however, about the physiological or neurological effects of the drugs. It is clear that they do not *cure* mental illness. They—the "tranquilizers" in particular—tend mainly to make patients more docile. Since their advent, many mental hospitals have removed the bars from their windows and the locks from their doors. Fewer mental hospitals now are snakepits. From a coldly analytical view, however, it is not now possible to say exactly what has been the contribution of the new drugs to this development. Perhaps the effect is a direct chemical one. But it is also a tenable hypothesis that the more humane attitudes and more human treatments that accompanied the advent of the drugs might alone have produced in many cases the calmer and "saner" behavior on the mental wards.

Shock Therapy

A frequently used treatment in psychosis involves the production in the patient of violent reactions similar to convulsions or to epileptic seizures. The most widely used methods in this area include (1) the injection of insulin, and (2) the administration, through electrodes placed on the head, of an electric shock best known as ECT or **electroconvulsive therapy.**

Insulin. Insulin shock, used most often on schizophrenic patients, places the patient in a coma that may last for several hours. When consciousness is regained, the patient most generally seems to be in very "sane" contact with reality for periods lasting up to an hour. During this period the patient can be treated by psychotherapy. Over a period, involving repeated shocks and repeated periods of psychotherapy, the patient may show definite signs of improvement. This method of treatment, introduced by Manfred Sakel (1938), is expensive and time-consuming; consequently, its use is not widespread.

Electroconvulsive Therapy. The history of convulsive shock therapy (not the same as insulin shock) began with the use of a drug, Metrazol, that chemically induced convulsions followed by loss of consciousness. The idea originated in the belief, now known to be erroneous, that epilepsy and schizophrenia are antagonistic to each other. Metrazol-induced convulsions were dangerous and very unpleasant to the patients, and it was with some relief that this method was supplanted by the use of electrical shock, introduced in 1938

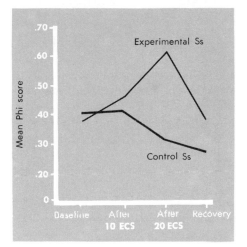

Figure 17–5. EFFECTS OF ELECTROCONVULSIVE SHOCK. *The experimental subjects were given twenty electroconvulsive shocks; the control subjects, none. The phi score is essentially a measure of the subject's present reference to immediately preceding events in solving an experimental problem. Shock appears to increase the individual's reference to immediately past events and to decrease reference to events relatively long past. (Goodnow, Rubenstein, and Shanks, 1959; by permission of the American Psychological Association.)*

by Cerletti and Bini (Cerletti, 1950). Since its introduction, shock treatment has been used very extensively but not without opposition. Although it is effective, especially in cases of depression, the advent of the new drugs has reduced the frequency of shock therapy as well as the use of other physical methods of treatment.

There is little or no knowledge as to *why* shock therapy of any kind is effective. Perhaps it has beneficial effects through actual physiological or neurological changes, or it may be effective through purely psychological mechanisms; perhaps the patient gets well in order to avoid the repeated trauma of shock, or perhaps the pain involved represents a therapeutically useful punishment for patients who have overriding feelings of guilt. Future research will clarify this matter.

Psychosurgery

Surgery performed on the brain of mental patients, including the operation known as lobotomy, is by far the most drastic of the treatments. These surgical operations were first performed by the Portuguese surgeon Egas Moniz; the idea was introduced in this country by Freeman (Freeman and Watts, 1950).

Lobotomy, now used only rarely, involves an operation in which there is a cutting of connections between the prefrontal lobes of the brain and the lower brain centers. The prefrontal areas of the brain are the centers in which are mediated the higher or more symbolic mental processes. Permanently disconnecting these centers from the centers of emotion serves to reduce the imaginative creation of intolerable fears and anxieties. After lobotomy, the patient is somewhat unemotional and, presumably, is able to live a less violent and more adjusted emotional life. However, the operation produces irreversible changes in the nervous system, and sometimes there are resultant personality changes of an extreme kind; the individual who loses his fears may also lose the capacity to plan or to control a sequence of behavior.

Psychotherapy

Freud originally believed that psychotherapy could not be used effectively on psychotics; they were too far regressed for the method to produce any results. Recent evidence, however, indicates some success for psychotherapy on psychotic individuals (Arieti, 1955; Rosen, 1953; Fromm-Reichman, 1950).

In dealing with a psychotic, the therapist tries to communicate that he wants to understand the patient, does accept him as a human being, does have a feeling for his fears, and does want to be with him. Over a long period of time the patient may respond to such genuine overtures and may make tentative efforts to establish a relationship with his therapist. When this occurs, the patient may be led on to a learning experience that will help him deal with his inner turmoil and eventually face again the real world.

In very recent years there have been a number of attempts to use *group therapy* with psychotic patients. In many mental hospitals psychologists and psychiatrists are exploring the possibilities of therapeutic groups.

Milieu Therapy

In recent years there has been a significant increase in research on social and institutional factors—the milieu—that bear on the well-being of mentally disturbed individuals. There now seems little room for doubt that characteristics of mental institutions help determine whether an individual will be ready for discharge at an early or late date and also whether or not he will have to return to the hospital. For example, there is solid evidence that (a) the size of a mental hospital, (b) staff-inmate ratio, and (c) measurable aspects of the hospital environment are all significantly related to an individual's likelihood of getting out of the hospital soon and staying out a long time (Gurel, 1964; Ullman, 1964; Cohen, 1964; Davis, 1964). The smaller the hospital, the less conventional and authoritarian its atmosphere, and the more staff per hundred inmates, the more favorable is the prognosis for the hospitalized individual.

Other studies have manipulated, with telling therapeutic effect, one or more aspects of the hospital environment. In one experiment (Johnson et al., 1965; Morton, 1965), chronic neurotics were given a month-long laboratory course in group dynamics and interpersonal relations—the kind of course formerly available only for undergraduate psychology majors and industrial executives. At the end of thirty days, more than half of these "students," after having been in the hospital for an average of five years, were discharged. Another research succeeded in changing, toward the more active and more involved, the role of ward attendant (Ellsworth, 1961) and thereby raised very significantly the discharge rate of those who

Figure 17–6. LIFE HISTORY OF A MENTAL PATIENT. *These photographs of the life history of a mental patient were made by the Medical Illustration Service of the Veterans Administration Hospital, Houston, Texas. Appreciation is hereby expressed to Mrs. Ellamae Breckenridge, Director of the Medical Illustration Service, and to Mr. Robert B. Southworth, photographer. Great appreciation also goes to Dr. Alex D. Porkorny, Chief of Psychiatry and Neurology; to Dr. Robert B. Morton, Chief, Psychology Service; and to the members of their staffs who took time from their duties to participate in this photographic project. Special thanks are expressed to Dr. Phillip Hanson, staff member of the Psychology Service, who posed as a patient in the series of photographs. And by no means least, there is gratitude to Dr. Lee D. Cady, Director of the Houston VA Hospital, for opening his excellent institution to this illustration project.*

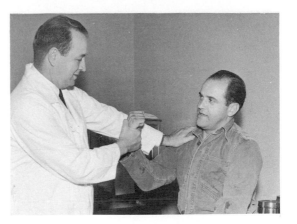

2. The patient is given a physical and neurological examination. The examining physician is Dr. Alex Porkorny.

3. The patient is given a psychological evaluation. Here, Dr. George Faibish, clinical psychologist, administers a test.

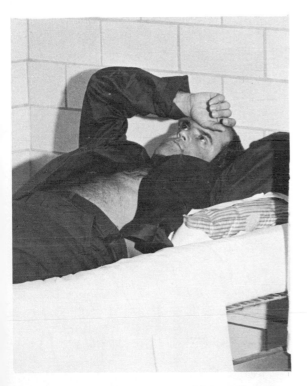

1. After being admitted, issued hospital garb, and assigned to a ward, and after an initial physical examination, the patient is assigned a bed and temporarily left to himself.

4. Medication. Tranquilizing drugs are widely used in mental hospitals.

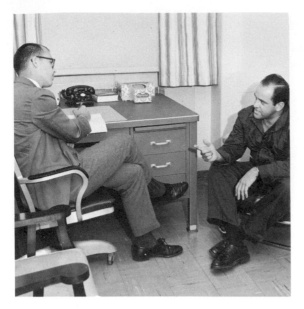

5. *Individual therapy. After the psychological evaluation and after the psychiatrists, psychologists, and psychiatric nurses have met with the patient to assess his status and to plan his treatment, he is assigned for individual therapy with a clinical psychologist. The psychologist here is Dr. Dale Johnson.*

6. *Group therapy. The patient is soon assigned to group therapy, where, under the supervision of a therapist, he begins therapeutic interaction with other patients. In his present state the patient shows little evidence of interest in the activities of the group. The therapist here, in white coat, is clinical psychologist Dr. Marian Yeager.*

7. *Social interaction. As he improves under therapy, the patient begins to interact socially with others.*

8. *Occupational therapy. The patient, under the guidance of an occupational therapist, undertakes simple creative work.*

9. *Group therapy continues. As time passes, the patient becomes a more active participant.*

10. Social life on the ward. As he improves, the patient takes more interest in the activities of others; participates in ward self-government.

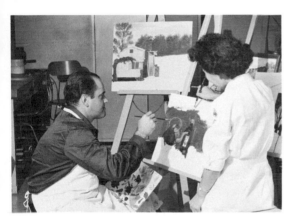

11. Occupational therapy continues. The patient is now given more challenging and complex tasks.

12. Evaluation by Industrial Rehabilitation Board. Board members meet to assess the patient's progress, capacities, and occupational prospects.

13. Industrial therapy assignment. Having "passed" the Rehabilitation Board, the patient is assigned work of increasing complexity and responsibility.

14. Discharge. Having attained maximum benefit from the hospital, the patient is ready for discharge. Here he is being taken for an interview with a prospective employer. The Vocational Rehabilitation specialists, with full information about the patient's experience, abilities, and interests, facilitate occupational placement and return to community life.

had been diagnosed as chronic schizophrenics. Other studies (Fairweather, 1964) make it appear that almost anything that can be done to "dehospitalize" a mental institution, to increase the level and quality of human interaction, and to remove the individual from the passive role of patient will contribute to the individual's return to normal functioning.

SUMMARY

1. In contending with problems of adjustment, the individual may react in ways that are described as normally defensive, as neurotic, or, in more severe cases, as psychotic.

2. Neurosis may be defined as a serious discomfort or incapacitation that is not due to organic causes. Psychosis is a more serious disorder that may involve lasting intellectual deterioration, severe disturbances of mood, and persistent distortions of reality.

3. Although none will doubt the discomfort, the severity, and the reality of mental or emotional disorder, a number of recent writers maintain that it is both therapeutically and scientifically wrong to define such disorder as illness.

4. Each neurotic individual behaves in his own way, but there can be a crude classification of neurotic reactions; the classification includes dissociation, conversion, phobic, anxiety, depressive, and obsessive-compulsive reactions.

5. The Freudian and Neo-Freudian theories of neurosis emphasize (a) a relation between neurotic symptoms and anxiety and (b) the importance of childhood experiences.

6. The Freudian theory of neurosis has it that the ego represses id forces, which then express themselves in neurotic symptoms; Horney emphasizes childhood rejection, re-

pression of hostile impulses, and overcompliance; Sullivan emphasizes overanxious, undiscriminating learning and childish coping with adult problems.

7. The Rogerian theory of neurosis holds that anxiety and neurotic symptoms arise when the individual is confronted with experiences he cannot reconcile with his self-image.

8. Mowrer sees neurosis as self-hatred created by "sin" or failure to live up to superego demands; the Dollard-Miller theory holds that neurosis arises out of approach-avoidance conflict, in which anxiety prevents action and repression prevents effective thinking.

9. There is some evidence that neurosis tends to run in families, but no evidence that there is an hereditary factor.

10. Psychoanalytic therapy, a protracted process, involves the techniques of free association and dream analysis and the processes of transference and interpretation.

11. Directive therapy is a briefer form of treatment, in which the therapist works on the basis of his expert knowledge to help the client see relationships between present behavior and past experience.

12. In nondirective or client-centered therapy there is no direction, no interpretation; an understanding therapist reflects feelings in such a way that the client can revise his image of himself.

13. Role therapy, growing out of the psychology of personal constructs, assists the client in playing roles that change the way he construes himself and others.

14. Behavior therapy, based on the thesis that neurosis is learned, is a technique designed to facilitate the learning of new responses to replace the troublesome neurotic responses. A well-known form of behavior therapy is based on the principle of reciprocal inhibition.

15. Group psychotherapy encourages the client to share his feelings with others in a situation where he can learn from the immediate reactions of others.

16. Because clearly sound and relevant data are very difficult to obtain, there is only inconclusive evidence on the effectiveness of psychotherapy with neurotic individuals. There can be little doubt, however, that disturbed individuals derive comfort from therapeutic procedures and that they will continue to seek the services of therapists.

17. Psychoses, defined as severe disorders of psychogenic origin without clearly defined physical cause or structural change in the brain, are often characterized by (a) intellectual deterioration, (b) drastic disturbance in mood, and (c) breaks with reality entailing hallucinations and/or delusions. Psychosis may be chronic or acute; it may be organic or functional.

18. A standard classification of psychotic reactions includes 15 definable syndromes or reaction patterns.

19. There is evidence of an hereditary predisposition to psychosis; the evidence on biological or chemical factors is inconclusive; psychological studies suggest that whatever the hereditary or biochemical factors, the child's early experiences in the home are significant for producing psychotic reactions.

20. Methods for treating psychosis include chemotherapy, shock therapy, psychosurgery, psychotherapy, and milieu therapy.

21. Chemotherapy includes the use of sleep-inducing drugs, of tranquilizers, and of antidepressants; many of the tranquilizers render patients more manageable, more open to communication.

22. Shock may be administered by insulin or by electric currents; electroshock is now more frequently used; shock treatment is often combined with psychotherapy.

23. Psychosurgery, including lobotomy, is the most drastic form of treatment of psychosis and is now practiced only in rare instances.

24. Psychotherapy, including group therapy, has had at least limited success with psychotic patients.

25. There has been a recent emphasis on the therapeutic manipulation of the hospital environment; milieu therapy aims to use the hospital organization and the social atmosphere to exert helpful influence on the mentally disturbed.

RESEARCH REPORTS

EFFECTS OF DRUGS IN SCHIZOPHRENIA [*]

The so-called "tranquilizing" drugs were used long before anyone knew much about either the physiology or neurology involved in their functioning. They were used on what is called an "empirical" basis, and caused what was judged to be a useful docility in patients. However, little knowledge has been available about the particular way in which the drugs affect the emotional or intellectual lives of people who take them. The present research was designed to reveal some precise effects of phenothiazines, one class of tranquilizing drugs, on intellectual functioning.

The subjects, 24 white male schizophrenic patients (ages 21–55) at the State Hospital in Danville, Kentucky, were not mentally deficient or suffering from brain damage; all had been in the hospital for at least six months before the experiment began, and none had received either psychosurgery, or electroshock therapy during the previous three months. The mean age of the group was 48.9 years, and most of the patients had been schizophrenic for many years. All agreed to participate in the experiment.

Some of the subjects were first tested before they began taking chlorpromazine (the phenothiazine primarily used in the experiment) and

---

[*] L. J. Chapman and R. R. Knowles, The effects of phenothiazine on disordered thought in schizophrenia, *J. consult. Psychol.*, 1964, **28**, 165–169.

were tested again after they started taking the drug. Others were tested for the first time while they were taking the drug and were given the second test after being taken off the drug, with a placebo substituting for the drug.

Two types of tests were given to examine three categories of intellectual functioning. One was designed to measure *excessive breadth of concepts*. In this test, each subject was given a pile of thirty cards, each of which named an object that fell into one of three categories. For example, on one test the cards named ten fruits, ten vegetables, and ten objects of sports equipment, and the subject was told to sort the cards into two boxes, the fruit cards into one (labeled "fruit") and everything else into the other.

It was possible in this test for the subject to sort on a broader category than that of fruit. He might sort according to the concept of "edibles," a category obviously broader than only fruit. If he began by placing vegetables with fruits in the same category, the experimenter interpreted this as indicating an error of *excessive breadth* of the concept of fruit. If the subject put sports-equipment cards in with the fruit cards, his error was termed a *random* error, possibly indicating a decrease in general intellectual alertness.

The second set of intellectual tests was designed to measure *excessive narrowing of concepts*. In this test, similar cards were used, but the test was one of exclusion. The subject was asked to put in one box all the things that a person could eat and, in another, the nonedible items. Thus, to be correct, he would put fruits and vegetables in the same box. If he put in only fruits and excluded vegetables, his errors were defined as excessive narrowing of the concept.

The measure, of *intellectual apathy,* or loss of alertness, was made by counting the random errors that entered into the performance of the two tests.

The experimenters thought, on the basis of earlier research into the thought processes of schizophrenics, that the drug might succeed in reducing errors thought to be characteristically "schizophrenic"—those caused by excessively broad interpretations of concepts.

Their expectations were realized to a degree, even though test results showed that total errors were slightly higher while the patients were on the drugs. The increase was not statistically significant; however, there were significant differences in the kinds of errors the subjects made

while on and off phenothiazine. Random errors were higher during use of the drugs. The experimenters interpret this to mean that phenothiazines cause a decline in intellectual efficiency.

In errors of excessive breadth of concepts, believed characteristic of schizophrenic thinking, there was a statistically significant reduction while patients were on the drug. Errors of excessive narrowing of concept, the researchers report, showed no significant change. The experimenters concluded that phenothiazine therapy produces a general decline in intellectual efficiency while reducing the typically schizophrenic errors due to excessive breadth of concepts.

COHESIVE GROUPS OF SCHIZOPHRENICS [*]

The research concerning us here is a contribution to a growing literature dealing with the effects of social influences on the behavior of mentally disturbed individuals. The attempt of the present study was to arrange small-group situations in which individuals' performances under maximum staff supervision could be compared with performance under minimal staff supervision. The subjects were thirty hospital inmates diagnosed as chronic schizophrenics with no record of organic involvement; all were under 55 years of age. They were placed in six groups of five members each, with the groups matched for age, length of hospitalization, education, and "verbal fluency" of the members. Their mean age was 42.36 years; formal education, 10.51 years; and their mean stay in the hospital was 6.4 years. An analysis of data on the six groups before the experiment showed no significant differences among the six groups with respect to age, education, or length of hospitalization.

Each group was assigned to police one of six identical dormitory units. The study continued for a period of seven weeks, and every day each group was instructed and began its work by making all the beds. The groups continued to work for fifty minutes toward the completion of eleven specific jobs assigned to them, including washing windows, cleaning the sills, wiping chairs, and sweeping floors.

At the beginning of the experiment, each pa-

[*] M. J. Lerner and G. W. Fairweather, Social behavior of chronic schizophrenics in supervised and unsupervised work groups, *J. abn. soc. Psychol.*, 1963, **67**, 219–225.

tient was interviewed and informed of his assignment to his work group. This involved a change of an hour in his preexisting daily schedule. Each was told that the idea behind the change was that the patients were now assuming responsibility for maintaining their own quarters. All seemed to accept this new assignment with characteristic passivity.

All members of the six groups appeared regularly at the dormitory for their daily meetings. Three groups were under minimal staff supervision; three under maximum supervision. Under minimal conditions, the staff member explained the cleaning tasks, informed subjects where they could get equipment they needed and then retired to a chair just outside the door. He made the suggestion that the members of the group should make all beds before doing any other cleaning, but other than that the subjects were left to their own devices. When the subjects would approach the supervisor to ask for information or for evaluation or advice, the supervisor listened but usually did not help. As a matter of fact, he chose not to help them in any very direct way. Most of the time he sat outside of the work area reading a newspaper.

The experimenter conducting maximal supervision, on the other hand, suggested directly that the patients begin work by making the beds and then, throughout their work period, gave additional direct suggestions on procedures necessary for the subjects to complete their work faster and better. The staff member made suggestions, designed to be as helpful as possible, at the rate of about one every two minutes. He applied no coercion but actively played the role of someone there to integrate the activity of everybody through appropriate recommendations. He neither evaluated work nor commented on the quality of behavior of the individual subject.

At the end of each work period, the staff member rated each individual member and each group as a whole on a number of attributes. As a check on the reliability of the ratings the staff psychologist, using the same rating scale, also observed the same groups on five days during the course of the experiment. Comparison of these two sets of ratings indicated high reliability—97 per cent of all judgments on the eleven-point rating scales were within one point of each other. Ratings were made on (1) amount accomplished, (2) quality of work, (3) verbal interaction, (4) group morale, (5) attitudes to the leader, (6) dependency on

leader, (7) the number of minutes required by the group to make all beds, (8) the number of tasks completed of the eleven assigned.

During the seven weeks of the experiment, all six groups improved their performance; the time necessary to complete the making of all beds, for example, decreased a statistically significant amount for all groups. Generally speaking, the groups given maximal supervision showed more consistent improvement over the seven weeks than did the minimally supervised groups. They were statistically superior in the number of days in which they completed all assigned tasks, and they showed a steady improvement in the amount accomplished throughout the seven weeks. They gave no signs of forming a cohesive group.

The minimally supervised groups showed more tendency to become a cohesive group over the seven week period; by comparison with the other groups, they showed both more independence from the leader and an increasing number of instances of independence as the experiment continued. Also, they more often displayed positive feelings for one another. In comparison with the maximally supervised groups there was a high level of verbal interaction; however, all groups showed a continuous drop in verbal interaction over time (apparently as they grasped better the conditions of the work and understood more clearly the role that each individual had assumed with respect to the performance of the assigned tasks). There were a number of indications of a consistent pattern of group process and of group cohesiveness for each of the minimally supervised groups. The longer each of the three groups worked together, the less was the dependence on the supervisor, the higher the rated morale, and the better the performance at making the beds. As their dependency on the supervisor decreased, their attitudes toward the supervisor became less positive. Also, an increase in the feeling for other group members was noted.

It was the observation of the experimenters that each of the minimally supervised groups evolved for itself a distinctive pattern, one that was continued throughout the experiment. One of these unsupervised groups developed a true leader who gave directions, divided the work, and generally integrated activities of all the members during the initial weeks. Over a period of time this leader's role gradually diminished, and he eventually gave it up entirely. The second of the supervised groups developed a pattern in which there was infrequent interaction and apparently little sign that members were aware of one and another. However, each member of this group adopted the same norm which involved an intense concentration on cleaning activities. The third group developed a pattern in which they began by working very well to make the beds but then would get involved in talking and joking in a manner described as borderline psychotic. They showed more signs than any of the other groups of wanting relationships with one and another and had active interaction without much concern for getting jobs done.

The experimenters, on the basis of this study, concluded that chronic schizophrenics can develop into cohesive groups and that such development has a significance not only for events inside the hospital but for the possibility of discharging patients as cohesive groups into their communities.

VERBAL CONDITIONING IN THERAPY [*]

Both those who formulate theories of abnormal behavior and those who undertake the treatment of disturbed individuals are interested not only in childhood experiences but also in the capacity of the individual to recall those experiences. This experiment (Craddick and Stern, 1964) was an attempt to investigate the effectiveness of both continuous and partial reinforcement in the production of memories of childhood events.

The subjects in the experiment were 25 students, 14 of whom were females and 11 males. The procedure was, first, to tell each subject: "I'm doing a study on memory and I want you to tell me as many things concerning people and events as you can remember that occurred before the age of 10." Then the experimenter, by nodding his head and saying "good," would reinforce, on prearranged schedules, each "correct" response—one in which the subject mentioned a member of his own family.

Each of the 25 subjects was assigned to one of three groups. Group I received reinforcement during the training period every time a "correct" response was given for the main part of the experiment. Group II received reinforcement for

---

[*] R. A. Craddick and Michael R. Stern, Verbal conditioning: the effect of partial reinforcement upon the recall of early memories, *J. abn. soc. Psychol.*, 1964, **68**, 353–355.

every fifth "correct" response (a 4 to 1 ratio of reinforcement) emitted by the subject. Group III received no reinforcement for the entire session. Each interview with each subject lasted 25 minutes. The first five minutes of the session was designated as a pre-training period during which the subject began to tell the experimenter the memories he could recall; the experimenter refrained from any reinforcing behavior. The second period, designated a training period, lasted 10 minutes. During this time both Groups I and II received reinforcement, Group I receiving reinforcement for every correct response, and Group II receiving reinforcement on a 4 to 1 ratio for "correct" responses. Group III received no reinforcement during this training period. The third period, an extinction period, lasted 10 minutes for all three groups. During this period no reinforcement was administered to anybody. A terminal interview showed that none of the 25 subjects knew the "rules" of this procedure or the specific behavior the experimenter was reinforcing.

An analysis was made of the memories given during the first five minutes of nonreinforcement. The data indicated that before the experiment began there were no differences among the three groups in the relevant frequency with which family members were mentioned.

A study of the data during the ten-minute training period showed that both the continuously reinforced and the periodically reinforced groups increased, to a statistically significant extent, the relative frequency of family memories given. Group III, the control group, showed a decline in relative frequency of family memories.

During the third period, the ten-minute extinction period, the two experimental groups showed more resistance to extinction than did the control. Both groups continued to give relatively frequent mention of family memories. Group II, on a schedule of periodic reinforcement, showed greater resistance to extinction than did Group I.

On the matter of the relative effectiveness of continuous versus partial reinforcement, the results of the experiment are not clear. During the ten-minute training period, Group I subjects received an average of 11.3 reinforcements, while Group II subjects received an average of 2.4 reinforcements. Since the amount of learning is related to the number of reinforcements as well as to the schedule of reinforcement, it is not possible to make a direct comparison of the effectiveness of these two forms of reinforcement during an interval as short as ten minutes. The experimenters conclude that if there had been an equal number of reinforcements, then the schedule of partial reinforcement would probably have been superior. One may also draw the conclusion that the therapist, by following the proper techniques of reinforcement, can induce an individual to produce an increased number of childhood memories.

SUGGESTED READINGS

Axline, Virginia M. *Dibs: In search of self. Personality development in play therapy.* Boston: Houghton Mifflin, 1964.

Dollard, John, and N. E. Miller. *Personality and psychotherapy: An analysis in terms of learning, thinking, and culture.* New York: McGraw-Hill, 1950.

Kaplan, Bert, ed. *The inner world of mental illness: A series of first-person accounts of what it was like.* New York: Harper and Row, 1964.

Rogers, C. R. *Counseling and psychotherapy: Newer concepts in practice.* Boston: Houghton Mifflin, 1942.

Stein, M. I., ed. *Contemporary psychotherapies.* New York: Free Press, 1961.

White, R. W. *Ego and reality in psychoanalytic theory: A proposal regarding independent ego energies.* New York: International Universities Press, 1963.

OUTLINE / CHAPTER 18

I. EVIDENCES OF SOCIAL INFLUENCE
- A. Cultural Differences
- B. Group Influence on Voting
- C. Social Influence in Simple Tasks and Simple Judgments
- D. Social Influence in Conformity and Nonconformity Behavior
- E. Social Influence on Food Habits

II. THE FUNCTIONS OF SOCIETY

III. SOCIAL NORMS AND THE INDIVIDUAL
- A. Perceptual Norms
- B. Norms for Behavior
- C. Children's Learning of Norms
- D. Group Norms in an Industrial Setting

IV. SOCIAL ROLES AND INDIVIDUAL BEHAVIOR
- A. Definition and Scope of Social Roles
- B. The Learning of Roles

V. ATTITUDES

VI. SMALL-GROUP PHENOMENA
- A. Uniformities of Interaction in Small Groups
  1. Universal Problems of Face-to-Face Groups
  2. The Life History of a Group
  3. Kinds of Interactions
  4. Role Differentiation
- B. Other Research on Small Groups

VII. LEADERSHIP
- A. The Search for Leadership Traits
- B. Leadership and Dimensions of the Group
- C. Leadership and the Needs of Followers
- D. Leadership and Group Functioning
  1. Two Basic Kinds of Group Functions
  2. Distribution of Functions among Members of the Group
- E. A Tentative View of Leadership

VIII. OTHER FIELDS OF RESEARCH IN SOCIAL PSYCHOLOGY

IX. SUMMARY

X. RESEARCH REPORTS

CHAPTER 18

SOCIAL PSYCHOLOGY*

Social psychology is concerned with the study of individual behavior in a social setting.

In a general sense it might be said that all of psychology is social psychology, for the human organism lives and moves and has its being in a social world. It must interact with other human **organisms** on the day of its birth and throughout its life. But in the psychological study of man, the social approach is neither always necessary nor always desirable. The psychologist concerned with **sensation**, for example, does not care whether the light waves reaching the eye of his subject are reflected from a human face or from a paper disk—just so he knows the wavelength, the amplitude, and the complexity of the stimulus. Similarly, the psychologist studying the effects on learning of a variable-ratio schedule of **reinforcement** regards it as unimportant whether the reinforcement is a pellet of bubble gum, a tapping toe, or a motherly pat on the head. And the psychologist studying temperament or expressive movement may not care at all whether the behavior he sees is socially approved or socially frowned upon. When the goal is an understanding of a general principle of behavior or a tracing out of the complete process between **stimulus** and **response**, it is a matter of indifference whether the stimuli have social origins or the responses social consequences.

But the social psychologist *is* social in his orientation. While he wants to know all he can about the general principles of motivation, sensation, perception, and learning, he wishes primarily to understand how these matters operate in a social setting when the *organized human individual interacts with other whole individuals,*

* Eugene Burnstein assisted materially with the first edition of this chapter by drafting some sections of it and by a critical reading of the whole.

Perhaps it would clarify the approach of social psychology if we could return to the first chapter of this book and read it again in the light of what we have learned about the human individual and the psychological process. We can say now a great deal about the ways in which the uniquely organized and motivated psychological system senses, interprets, responds to, and learns about its world. We know something about each of the segments of the psychological process and about the ways these segments are organized so as to constitute personality. Now, going backward through the categories we employed in Chapter 1, let us place the individual system successively in a family, a religious group, a racial group, a socioeconomic group, a national group, and so on. We would not now be placing him merely in a succession of social categories. We would be confronting him with an *interlocking series of learning situations*. Whatever his age, whatever the present structure of his personality, he would have to contend with the system of rewards and punishments that prevails in his social **environment**. And he would have to learn, in accordance with the principles of sensing, perceiving, learning, and thinking, to gain satisfaction for his **motives** by behaving in ways that allow him to survive in *this* family, in *this* class, in *this* society. If we put him in the home of a white, Baptist, middle-class lawyer, he will contend with one pattern of rewards and punishments. If we place him in the lower-class home of a Negro construction worker, the patterns of reinforcement are quite different. Wherever we place him, he remains an individual, possessed of unique attributes. And whatever he has to learn, he will do so according to the psychological principles of learning. But *what* he learns—his ruling social motives, his ways of interpreting the world, his ways of responding to it—all of this will vary in accordance with dimensions and demands of the social setting in which he lives.

The social psychologist is interested in what the whole individual learns—and does—in response to variations in the social environment. In order to advance this scientific interest, the social psychologist studies not only the be-

Figure 18–1. BEHAVIOR IN SOCIAL SETTINGS. *Social psychology is a study of individual behavior in social settings. The individual is engaged in almost constant interactions with others. Much of his personality is socially formed, and his present behavior is socially influenced.*

havior of the individual but also the social environment itself and the ways in which human individuals interact with it.

In our present approach to social psychology, we shall first examine a few selected evidences of social influence on individual behavior, then survey briefly some aspects of the structured social environment in which individuals live, and then outline some of the psychological mechanisms involved as the individual makes his way in a social world, ending our introduction to social psychology with a consideration of some of the phenomena in the socially important processes of leadership.

EVIDENCES OF SOCIAL INFLUENCE

CULTURAL DIFFERENCES

Perhaps the most dramatic evidence of social influence can be gained from looking at the behavior of two individuals who were brought up in different cultures. Two human infants, possessed of very similar inherent capacities, starting life with the same physiological mo-

tives and the same limited ability to do anything about them, will sense, interpret, respond, and learn through the operation of the same psychological mechanisms. But in a few months the two will be behaving in quite dissimilar ways. And by the time they are adults, they are worlds apart in motives, habits, attitudes, and values. They see the world differently, speak about it in a different language, have vastly different expectations about their survival in it and their departure from it. Such cultural differences in behavior illustrate very impressively the role of social influences on the individual. Of course, such a general illustration does not tell us very specifically about the influences themselves or the ways in which they are exerted on the individuals.

We can make this idea more concrete if, in imagination, we take a well-endowed 12-year-old boy from a tenant farm in Alabama and have him suddenly trade environments with an equally able 12-year-old son of a Boston banker. In spite of the fantasies of wealth and power the young Alabaman may have had, he probably would not like his Bostonian environment. His speech, his clothes, his sleeping and eating habits would make him conspicuous and uncomfortable. He would have few, if any, interests in common with his Boston contemporaries; for dancing school, music lessons, ice skating, and children's symphonies would not hold much charm for him. He might not even show much loyalty to the baseball Red Sox, the hockey Bruins, or the basketball Celtics. Similarly, the present Alabama life of the transplanted young Bostonian would be incompatible with his past. He would have no competence at plowing, feeding poultry, slopping hogs, or hunting squirrels. His interest in swimming in the creek or rafting on the river would be less than overpowering. He would not understand more than three quarters of what was said to him and would have equal trouble in communicating with others.

Figure 18 2. SOCIAL AND CULTURAL DIFFERENCES. *How would a 12-year-old boy from an upper-class Boston family react to this home environment?*

This social-cultural point is illustrated by a study of differences in husband-wife relationships in two different cultures. In this study, interpersonal relations between couples with a European background were compared with the relations between husbands and wives from a Middle Eastern background (Foa, 1964).

Although the two groups of couples were living essentially side by side in Israel at the time of the study, there were still cultural differences between them with respect to interpersonal behavior. For couples from the Middle Eastern culture, there is more permissive reaction to the husbands' rejecting behavior than among those from the Western background; these Middle Eastern couples reflect the accepted Middle Eastern practice that allows the male to beat his wife and his children, without such beating being interpreted as a lack of affection. Among the couples from the Western background, by contrast, any evidence of aggression is likely to put a great strain on domestic relations. In the West, a man cannot beat his wife at noon and expect to reestablish a mutually affectionate relationship by dusk. Another cultural difference affecting personal relations between husband and wife involves the number of domestic chores considered properly assigned to husband or to wife. Generally the husband's share of such tasks is smaller in the Middle Eastern culture, where the husband's role and the wife's are more differentiated and more independent of one another than in the Western world. Wives from a Middle Eastern culture, though living in Israel, do not expect from their husbands much help around the house.

GROUP INFLUENCE ON VOTING

The culture to which a man belongs will influence him in very many ways. So also will the subcultures within the over-all culture. We can see the latter kind of influence exerting itself in the voting behavior of individuals.

Two men walk into voting booths. One man quickly pulls the lever on the left, while the second man, after some hesitation, pulls the right-hand lever. We know, from our study of learning, that lever-pulling responses occur in accordance with well-established principles of reinforcement. But where is the reinforcement here? There clearly is no immediate pellet of reward for either of the voters, and neither has had any operant training in lever pulling. We must, if we follow this model, look for a pattern of reinforcement in the past experience of each voter. So, in our effort to understand the patterns of reinforcement operating in the voting booths, we look at the social groups to which each voter belongs.

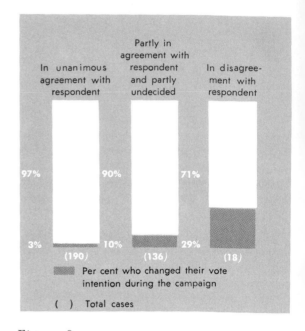

Figure 18–3. FAMILY HOMOGENEITY AND VOTE CHANGING. *The more closely a family agrees on political preference, the less likely is a member of that family to change his vote during a campaign. If a voter's family disagrees with him, he shows an increased tendency to change his vote. These data may be taken as evidence of the effect of social pressure on voting behavior. (Lazarsfeld, Berelson, and Gaudet, Copyright 1944; by permission Duell, Sloan and Pearce, Inc.)*

A study of voting behavior in the 1940 Presidential election (Lazarsfeld, Berelson, and Gaudet, 1944) revealed a high level of family similarity in political preferences; in interviews conducted three months before the election, 78 per cent of the second voters in two-voter households independently stated the same Presidential preference as the first voter. In some instances the second voter would not state a preference, but in only 2 per cent of the cases did the second voter state a preference *opposite* to that of the first voter. When voting day came closer, the agreement between two voters in the same household was even higher. Ninety-six per cent of the second voters interviewed reported voting the same way the first voter did. If we want to make bets, then, on the way an individual will vote, and we already know the vote of the only other voter in the household, we could win our bets 96 per cent of the time.

Further evidence of family similarity in voting comes from the same study. There was disagreement between husband and wife, on the average, in only one out of 22 couples. When a parent and a son or daughter were paired, only one out of twelve pairs were in disagreement. The data in Figure 18–3 give further evidence of family influence on voting behavior. Figures 18–4 and 18–5 present evidence on other social influences on voting behavior.

It seems fairly clear that whatever are the factors that lead to political preference—expressed in the pulling of levers in the voting place—these factors tend to run in families. If we were to push further our analysis of **socioeconomic** factors in voting, we would find that families in one socioeconomic class tend to share one preference while families in another class share another preference. And families oriented to membership in labor unions share preferences that differ from those of white-collar workers or professional people.

The social act of pulling a lever in a voting booth has a good deal in common with a similar lever-pulling act on the part of a rat or a monkey or a child in a learning situation in the laboratory. But the act of voting, in spite of its apparent simplicity, is a very complex act; an elaborate pattern of experience lies behind it, and the rewards it brings the voter are social and symbolic satisfactions of an intricate kind. To have a full understanding of this act, we need to know the basic principles

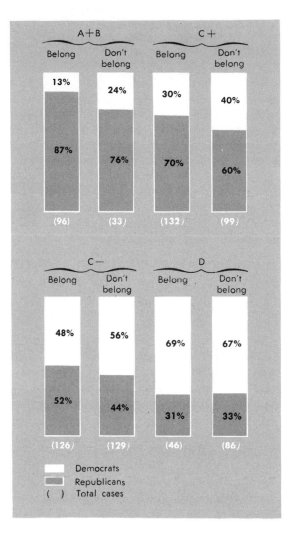

Figure 18–4. GROUP MEMBERSHIP AND VOTING. *The shaded areas represent the per cent of the four socioeconomic classes who voted Republican in the 1940 Presidential election. Socioeconomic status (SES) was determined by interviewers' assessments of the home, possessions, appearance, and manner of a subject. Ratings were from A (highest SES) to D (lowest). For each class of the three higher classes, those who belong to social or similar organizations are more inclined to vote Republican than are those who do not belong to such groups. It seems that increased contact with members of a group increases the likelihood of voting as that group does. (Lazarsfeld et al., Copyright 1944; by permission of Duell, Sloan and Pearce, Inc.)*

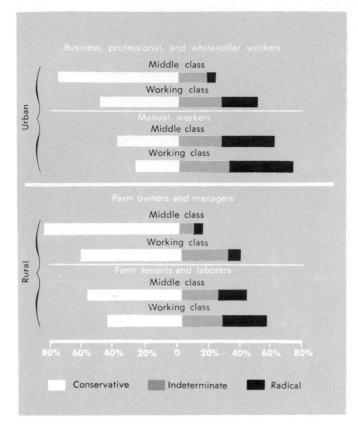

Figure 18–5. GROUP DIFFERENCES IN CONSERVATISM-RADICALISM. *The members of a social class or stratum show similarities in political attitudes. On a measure of radicalism-conservatism in attitudes, members of the middle class, whether rural or urban and whatever their occupation, tend to be much more conservative than members of the working class. Here is additional evidence of social influence on individual psychological processes. (Centers, Copyright 1949; reproduced by permission of the Princeton University Press.)*

of learning. But we need also to understand the phenomena of social influence. We need to see the behavior of the individual not only in terms of the basic dimensions of the psychological process but also against a background of social influence.

SOCIAL INFLUENCE IN SIMPLE TASKS AND SIMPLE JUDGMENTS

In one of the earliest experiments in social psychology (Allport, 1924) it was demonstrated that the mere presence of other individuals has a measurable effect on performance. If subjects are placed in isolated rooms and assigned simple tasks such as canceling vowels on a printed page or doing simple problems in multiplication, each subject will work along in his own manner and at his own speed. If nothing in the experiment is changed except that now several subjects are seated around the same table working at the tasks, performance changes. In the social situation, speed increases very predictably. But accuracy may be affected either way, up or down. With respect to simple behavior, then, there is often a **social facilitation** of individual response.

The same experimenter found that the "together" situation also affected judgmental processes. Where asked to judge the pleasantness of odors and the heaviness of weights, the "together" subjects tended to make more moderate or conventional judgments than they did when working alone.

A later group of researchers (Taylor, Thompson, and Spassoff, 1937) duplicated some of the conditions of these experiments, except that they imposed a much more onerous task on their subjects. They required their subjects to spend four hours, at first alone and then in groups, pushing a machine nut through a series of grooves, using a stylus. The subjects made appreciably better scores alone than they did in the together situation. What goes on? The results here appear to contradict the earlier ones in a very similar situation. A likely interpretation is that when the subjects spent four hours together on a disagreeable task, they acted on the opportunity to declare a rebellion—perhaps an unspoken rebellion—against the psychologists who were setting the task. At any rate, the group itself exerted influence on individual performance. Mere togetherness is influential. But *interaction* with a group may be more so—and may be influential in a variety of directions.

SOCIAL INFLUENCE IN CONFORMITY AND NONCONFORMITY BEHAVIOR

Another clear illustration of social influence on the individual was demonstrated in a simple and ingenious experiment (Lefkowitz, Blake, and Mouton, 1955) involving behavior of pedestrians at a city traffic light. Under normal conditions on one street corner, only one per cent of 742 observed pedestrians crossed the street against a clearly lighted traffic signal spelling out in neon the word *Wait*. If the conditions were changed by having a male graduate student, dressed in scuffed shoes, patched pants, and a denim shirt, walk across the street in violation of the signal, 4 per cent of the pedestrians joined in the violation. If the same student, now dressed in a well-pressed suit, white shirt, and a hat, violated the signal, then 14 per cent of the pedestrians joined in the violation.

Those who exult in individuality and nonconformity may wish to observe that only 14 per cent gave in to conformity pressure.

An experiment dealing with the signing of a petition illustrates similarly the existence and strength of social influence (Blake, Mouton, and Hain, 1956). A number of students passing one spot on the campus were asked to sign the following petition: "We, the undersigned students of the University of Texas, request that University officials place lights on Littlefield Fountain to add to the beauty of the Memorial." The petition carried no previous signatures. Under one experimental condition, fifteen students were asked to sign the petition after having seen another person (a "stooge") sign it. Fourteen of these students signed without hesitation. Fifteen others were asked to sign after having seen another person refuse to sign it. Only four of the fifteen signed. (Table 18–1.)

Table 18–1. REACTIONS OF SUBJECTS TO DIFFERENT BEHAVIOR OF AN ASSISTANT

REACTIONS OF ASSISTANT	REACTIONS OF SUBJECTS	
	Sign	*Refuse*
Sign	14	1
Absent	8	7
Refuse	4	11
Total	26	19

When strangers are asked, with an intermediate degree of insistence, to sign a petition, their behavior varies with the behavior of an assistant. If the assistant, hearing the request, signs the petition, the stranger is likely to sign also. If the assistant refuses, so will the stranger. (Blake, Mouton, and Hain, 1956.)

Additional evidence of the power of group influences is given by an experiment designed to see whether group pressure can influence the actual and overt action of an individual, as well as the kind of perceptual and linguistic response involved in the studies cited above (Milgram, 1964). In this study there were eighty subjects—forty in a control group and forty, matched for age and occupational status, in an experimental group. Each of the subjects was included in a team of three individuals, two of whom were confederates of the experimenter. This team was asked to observe and to judge the performance of a fourth individual as he carried out an assigned laboratory task. Whenever this fourth individual made a mistake, it was up to the team to "teach" him by administering an electric shock. In the experimental group the two confederate subjects suggested an increasingly high level of shock for the erring performer. The experimenter observed whether or not the naive subject resisted the pressure to increase the voltage levels. Members of the control group were treated the same as the experimental subjects except that there was no pressure on them to increase the amount of shock administered to the erring individual. The experimental subjects, as compared with the control group, demonstrated a remarkable willingness to administer high levels of allegedly educative shock; whereas the uninfluenced subjects administered shocks of three or four units of intensity, the influenced subjects administered shocks averaging as high as fourteen units of intensity.

SOCIAL INFLUENCES ON FOOD HABITS

Another example of the functioning of group norms comes from research designed to find the most effective way, in the face of the meat shortages of World War II, to persuade people toward the economically sensible and clearly healthful consumption of beef hearts, kidneys, and sweetbreads (Lewin, 1943). Normally, people in our society have considerable aversion to these meats, connecting them with the negatively toned idea of animals' entrails and regarding them as food fit only for the poor and the nutritionally desperate. The prevailing norms in our society at large, then, work against the use of these beef orts.

In the efforts to persuade women to cook these meats, two methods were used. One method was the conventional one of giving lectures designed to be convincing. Three groups of women were told expertly about the relation between nutritional problems and the war effort, were given solid data on the nutritional value of the three meats, and were given helpful hints about their tasty preparation.

In three other groups a skilled discussion leader initiated group talk about the same topic, with the individuals in the group encouraged to discuss "how housewives like themselves" might handle the problems that would arise if such foods were put on the family table. Helpful suggestions and recipes were offered the group only after the members had become involved and interested in the problems and obstacles. At the end of the meeting, the groups were asked to indicate by a show of hands how many were willing to try one of the three meats during the following week.

A follow-up study showed that 3 per cent of the lectured women served one of the three meats they had never served before, whereas 32 per cent of the members of the discussion groups made the plunge into culinary novelty. (Table 18–2.)

Although this study does not make clear exactly *what* exerts the influence, social influence clearly is present. Actually, there is evidence (Bennett, 1955) that the influential factor is group decision, not group discussion itself.

The research on voting behavior, the experiments showing group influences on simple performance, and the research on conformity and nonconformity behavior demonstrate clearly that groups influence individuals, that social factors in the environment need to be understood if we are to have the fullest understanding of human behavior. We shall return later to the study of group influences, but first it will be well to think a bit about the nature of the social environment in which individuals live.

Table 18–2. GROUP INFLUENCE ON
FOOD HABITS

	Group Decision	Lecture
Per cent of individuals serving one or more of the three meats	52	10
Per cent of individuals serving a meat they had *never* or *hardly ever* served before	44	3
Per cent of individuals serving a meat they had *never* served before	32	3
Per cent of participants serving one or more new meats who had *never* served *any* of the three meats before the experiment	29*	0†
Number of participants	44	41

* Out of a total of 14 participants
† Out of a total of 11 participants

The reaching of a decision on the basis of group discussion results in greater change in food habits than listening to a lecture. The decision in the group apparently results in a substitution of a new norm for an old one. (Data from The Problem of Changing Food Habits, *Bulletin 108, National Research Council, 1943.)*

THE FUNCTIONS OF SOCIETY

If we are to see most clearly the ways in which the human individual interacts with his social environment, we need to understand the nature of that environment—the environment to which he must respond and of which, for other individuals, he constitutes a part.

With the possible exception of feral children (children deserted by their human parents and reared by animals), every human individual lives in a human society. If we en-

dow the human infant with mature perspectives and then look at the world through his eyes, society is seen as a thing outside, an enormously intricate thing which the individual must somehow learn about and join up with if he wishes to survive in comfort. Each of us, by the time we read books, has learned about society, has made some manner of peace with it, has taken into himself as his very own many of its rules and regulations. We find it difficult now to see clearly our social environment, for we take it almost as much for granted as the air we breathe. Perhaps the following description of the *functions of society*—of any society—can help us gain some perspective on our own social environment and lead us on to an understanding of the individual's interaction with a social world (Aberle et al., 1950).

Every society provides for an adequate relationship to the environment. No society can survive unless it finds ways to manipulate its physical environment or so adjust to it that a sufficient number of members of the society can live. Man is a biological organism. He must have food and shelter. Also, on a different plane, no society can survive unless it has ways of preventing its own absorption or destruction by another society. So there must be procedures for defense. In time of peace, the society defends its own rights and its own integrity through diplomacy. In time of physical threat or in actual warfare, military mechanisms are employed. Every society does something about the physical and social world in which it exists.

Every society has provisions for sexual recruiting and functioning. Every society must have enough adult members to perform the necessary social functions. To ensure that there are enough members, there must be assurance that reproduction will occur at least at a minimal and necessary rate. If the society has more members than is conducive to its best functioning, there may be mechanisms to limit the increase in population. There may be birth control, infanticide, or geronticide.

Every society has procedures, sometimes very elaborate, for regulating sexual recruitment, for controlling sexual competition and for setting what it regards as the proper conditions for reproductive activities.

Every society has provisions for role differentiation and role assignment. Every society, in performing such functions as contending with its physical environment, defending itself, maintaining its own form of organization, and distributing benefits to its individual members, finds that there are a number of definable activities that must be performed by individuals. In our own society, for example, the food must be produced, the factories manned, the army organized, the churches led, the courts presided over, the government staffed, the garbage hauled, and so on. In order that these and hundreds of other acts be performed and their performers properly rewarded, the society spells out a variety of *roles* which are assigned to individuals. A role may be defined as a *pattern of behavior expected of an individual.* The judge of the criminal court, for example, is expected to have a certain array of knowledge and a certain way of behaving. The judge has these expectancies of himself, also, for he and society share a definition of what the proper judge is and does. He cannot be illiterate or ignorant of the law. He cannot be prejudiced. And in the details of his demeanor, there are expectancies which must not be insulted. The proper judge does not, in the middle of a trial, do a clog dance for the amusement of the jury.

When this role of judge is assigned, on the basis of accepted procedures, to an individual, that individual must take on an array of behaviors that are in accord with expectancies. The same kind of thing occurs throughout any society. Patterns of behavior are defined as appropriate for the fulfillment of social function. The butcher, the baker, the candlestick-maker, the minister, the teacher, the industrialist, the laborer, the foreman, the sergeant, the private, the general, the doctor, the mortician—all are acting out social roles that have been in some way assigned them in the interest of carrying forward society's business. If any of these individuals gets too far out of the social role defined for him, he will be forcefully brought back into line or removed from the role.

Every society has a system of communication. No society can exist without shared, symbolic modes of communication. Without communication there can be no common values, no division of labor, no role-differentiation, no success in inducting new members into the society. The more intricate the society, the more varied and elaborate the communications procedures and instruments become. In the more complex societies, the existence of a face-to-face language is not enough.

Elaborate mechanisms are invented to facilitate rapid and distant contact. Our own society could not function at its present level of complexity on a smoke-signal system for long-distance communication.

Every society has an array of shared cognitive orientations. There must be a commonly shared way of viewing and interpreting significant aspects of the world. A society is in trouble, for example, if one segment sees the existing political system as a dictatorship, another as an oligarchy, while another views it as a democracy in which voting is both free and effective. At a lower level of abstraction, we can see the difficulties that would arise if you think paper money is worthless while I regard it as valuable—or if you regard my sacred cow as your source of sirloin steaks.

Every society has a shared and articulate set of goals. Unless most members of a society seek the same general goals, there will be no unitary organization. Individuals may differ widely in their pattern of individual goals, but unless there is some openly agreed upon communality of goals —perhaps as general as the goal that the society shall preserve itself—there is no society.

Every society has a system for regulating means for the pursuit of goals. If the society's goals include the preservation of political democracy, then it prescribes the means for obtaining that goal—voting regulations, rules of candidacy, legislative and administrative structures, and so on. If the society's goal is the greatest good for the greatest number, then it may say that the masses may not be destroyed to advance the welfare of the few. If its goal is the preservation of the sanctity of individual life, then the physician may not kill anyone he thinks not suited for human existence. On a more concrete level, the society may accept the gaining of wealth as a legitimate goal for an individual, but there are firm rules prohibiting fraud and controlling the use of force in the efforts to gain wealth.

Every society regulates affective expression. There must be ways to communicate likes and dislikes and to keep destructive or disruptive emotional expression within tolerable limits. There are rules of politeness, gentlemanliness, decency, and good sportsmanship. People do not laugh at funerals or make love in the middle of Main Street. Men do not weep in public. Women do not cuss like troopers.

Every society provides for socialization. The society must train its young into its ways if it is to survive. There must be a learning of the communication system, of the approved ways of viewing the world, of the permissible and forbidden goals, of approved and disapproved means of pursuing goals, of proper and improper expression of emotion. The new member must also learn his role and what are his responsibilities and rights in the role he plays in the over-all structure. He must also learn what to expect and to permit in viewing other members in other roles.

Figure 18–6. THE FUNCTIONS OF SOCIETY: SOCIALIZATION. *Every society socializes its new members. School (here a Venezuelan school) is a primary means of socialization.*

Every society has a system of control over disruptive forms of behavior. In any society there will be some scarcity and, hence, some frustration. And the socialization of new members will not always be complete. Fraud, unfair competition, unacceptable use of force and other breaches of vital rules and regulations will occur. There must be means for controlling disruptive behaviors when they occur. There may be informal controls, such as gossip and ridicule. There are also formal controls—policemen, courts, and jails.

The authors of this list of functions maintain that every viable society must and does perform each of these functions in some manner and some degree. If this be so, then it follows that each of us, if we conceive of ourselves as unsocialized and independent entities—which of course we are not, except at birth—is constrained constantly by the demands of a society that is preserving itself. The list of functions can serve at least two purposes for us here. First, we can use the list to illustrate both the fact and the complexity of a social environment. Second, we can, if we wish, use this list of functions in our attempt to gain some concrete understanding of precisely the kind of social environment in which we live. Each student might, with profit and perhaps some disturbance, assess his own relation to his own society by examining the ways in which he has experienced the impact of each of these societal functions. Also, the imaginative student may derive some intellectual pleasure by using this set of rubrics to describe the college or university society with which he is now, perhaps with some stress, relating.

SOCIAL NORMS AND THE INDIVIDUAL

The individual lives in a social setting. From his first breath he is in contact with other individuals. For awhile, he is dependent on them for the preservation of his life. Later he is dependent on them for the molding of his personality and character—for their ways become his ways and their life his. As we see the individual taking on the ways of his fellows and his eventual conforming to their preferences, we might be able to account for what we see in terms of the laws and principles of individual psychology. But the social psychologist prefers more general, more **molar** approaches to the phenomena of social influence.

In trying to see where the social psychologist can lead us, we have, in this chapter, examined some assorted examples of social influence on individual behavior. The group does affect the behavior of the individual. After we saw some instances of social influence, we turned to a general survey of the social environment, setting down ten functions of a society. The point in examining these functions is that each one of them represents an area in which the group, the society, exerts influence on the individual. The society functions as an organized entity. As it does so, it has its way with the individual. It teaches him, sets standards for him, defines the limits within which his behavior must be contained. It does all this through mechanisms that are consonant with the principles of motivation, perception, and learning which we earlier have seen. But at a more general level of analysis it does this also through the definition and enforcement of **social norms,** and through the definition and enforcement of social **roles.** We shall consider each of these concepts briefly in order to get at least a glimpse of what the social psychologists are doing and thinking.

A *social norm* is a **construct,** just as intelligence and the achievement motive are constructs. The social scientist looks at behavior in groups, in the large society and in smaller units; and he formulates the notion that social behavior can best be understood if we think in terms of *social norms,* in terms of *standards* or *rules that are defined and enforced in group situations.* It is partially through the operation of norms, the social scientist tells us, that individual behavior is brought into line with the group's need to function and to survive.

Any society or subgroup in a society will have some explicit rules about what is correct behavior and what is incorrect. Such rules serve to restrict or to facilitate the behaviors of the individual in such a way as to enhance what the whole society, or subgroup thereof, regards as the general welfare. Many separate norms may arise with respect to any one of the general societal functions described above. On the matter of sexual recruitment, for example, the prevailing norm is that there shall be no reproduction except within the bonds of matrimony. With respect to the more abstract matter of our society's goals, a rule or norm is that no individual may subvert the government by selling military secrets to an outsider. With respect to the expression of affect, the norm is that gentlemen do not use profanity in the presence of ladies nor express violent anger during a church service.

Such norms are enforced on the individual by other members of the group. Correct behavior is approved by one kind or another of reinforcement. Incorrect behavior is punished. The group's administration of rewards and punishment controls the behavior of the individual—if it needs controlling. The group's administration of rewards and punishments to young people, an administration delegated by society principally to parents and teachers, produces the socialization of the newer members of the society.

Through defining, teaching, and enforcing its norms, the group influences the individual. We need to see, then, how norms come about, and we need to examine ways in which norms affect the behavior of individuals. We can proceed profitably by examining three researches on the formation and operation of norms.

PERCEPTUAL NORMS

The first research is an experimental one involving what is known as the **autokinetic phenomenon** (Sherif, 1936ab). If a subject is placed in a totally dark room and shown a single point of light, the light will move *autokinetically;* that is, it will appear to move—although, in fact, it remains stationary. The subject is asked to report how much the light moves. The original experiment proceeded in two ways. First, the subjects were asked to make their judgments alone and were then brought into a group situation. In the other approach, different subjects made their first judgments in the group situation and then moved into isolation to see how much the light moved.

When the subjects were alone in the presence of this light, which they were sure actually moved, they had to set up their own individual "norms" or ranges of apparent movement. One person would report large movements through a number of trials; another would always see relatively limited movement. When these individuals are then brought into a group situation, where other subjects are calling out their estimates of movement, there is a strong tendency for individual judgments to move toward a homogeneous norm. The extreme individuals become much less deviant, beginning to see the light move the way the majority of the group sees it. In this individual-to-group sequence, a group norm generally develops after four group sessions.

When the other sequence is followed, when judgments are first made in the group situation, the subjects *almost at once show a uniformity of judgment,* and the uniformity through four sessions is always greater than that found in the other situation. The group, then, quickly establishes a norm. It defines the "correct" way this part of the world shall be seen. If, after participating in the group judgment, the individuals are next placed in isolation to make their judgments, they then see the movement as the group saw it. They carry the group norm with them into non-group situations. (See Figure 18–7.) The group's way of viewing the world has become *interiorized,* taken into the way of life of the individual. Few, if any, of the subjects were aware of their conformity to the group norm. Perhaps this is a good illustration of the way in which our views of the world are fixed by social influences while we remain unaware of what is happening to us.

NORMS FOR BEHAVIOR

Not only does the group establish *perceptual norms*—thereby influencing the way the individual sees the world; it also establishes **behavioral norms** defining and enforcing standards of correct behavior. Take the simple matter of behavior in the face of traffic laws. The data in Figure 18–8 represent a distribution of behaviors at a traffic light (Allport, 1934).

The same kind of curve describes time of arrival at class, time of arrival at appointments, and so on. One can easily visualize the social pressures that produce these uniformities in behavior. On one side of the norm, a too-early arrival may be not only personally inconvenient but may be socially disapproved also. The parking lot is not yet open, or it is still full from the last shift. The university may not want large groups of students jamming the hall outside the classroom in which an earlier class is in session. The social penalties for late

arrival are clear. The management or the professor will do what is possible—and a good deal is—to ensure on-time arrival. Of course, in most situations, no open exercise of social enforcement is necessary. We are all trained to be on time. We have interiorized the general on-time norm. If we are late, we feel at least a little bit guilty; if some other member of the group is late, we are likely to put some pressure on him, for to see him getting away with behavior which our own conscience forbids us is disturbing to us. Frequently, we pressure others to behave in accordance with our own interiorized standards of propriety.

CHILDREN'S LEARNING OF NORMS

Every group, whether a whole society or a less intricate organization, sees to it that new members become *socialized* by learning the approved ways of perceiving, thinking, and behaving.

In his description of the ways in which children of various ages approach the game of marbles, Jean Piaget, a famous Swiss psychologist, has given us clear examples of the learning of norms (Piaget, 1932). Young children of 6 years or less, while they love to "play marbles," have no conception of rules or of fairness or of scoring. They just play. If they play together, any two children may be playing two entirely different games. If one is asked whether he won, he is not able to say with certainty whether he has or not, except he generally thinks he has. There are no group norms in force. The relations to the world are **autistic**—determined largely by the wishes and preferences of the individual. Older children, by contrast, have very definite notions about fairness and about the proprieties. They tend first to regard rules as absolute and rigid and vitally necessary. Things must be done exactly right, or the game isn't fair. Piaget describes this as the *absolute* orientation to norms. Later, by the age of 11 or 12, children have learned that rules, though necessary to avoid squabbling and disagreement, may be changed if the group agrees on the change. Players may argue and scrap about what are good rules to use, but they do eventually agree

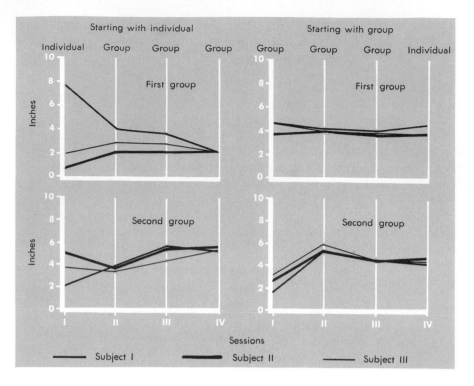

Starting with individual

Individual Group Group Group

First group

Inches

Starting with group

Group Group Group Individual

First group

Second group

Inches

Second group

Sessions

——— Subject I   ▬▬▬ Subject II   ——— Subject III

Figure 18–7. PERCEPTUAL NORMS. *When asked to judge how much a motionless light moves, solitary subjects vary widely in the amount of autokinetic movement seen (see the left side of the two graphs on the left above). If they then are put in groups, their judgments quickly conform to group norms. If subjects judge first in a group situation (as in the two right-hand graphs), their later solitary judgment remains similar to the group norms. (Adapted from Sherif, 1936b; by permission of Harper & Row.)*

on rules, sometimes quite inventive ones, and they play away. This more relaxed attitude toward norms is described as the *relative* orientation.

Piaget also gives us observations of the way children learn and accept general norms of right and wrong behavior. Young children, in an *absolutistic* way, tend to think that punishment should be meted out in proportion to the enormity of the crime, regardless of intent or responsibility. The child who accidently breaks a dozen plates should be punished more severely than one who breaks only one.

By the age of 8 or 9, however, more sophistication appears. There is less tendency to regard norms as absolute rules for behavior and more tendency to accept them as complicated and relative matters. The 9-year-old, for example, has learned that the punishment should be relative to the intent or the provocation of the criminal. For example, he sees it as worse for the well-fed child to steal food than it is for a poor and hungry child.

Children, then, do learn group norms, and they do interiorize them, so that the group rules do not have to be enforced by external power or external authority but are accepted by the individual as his own rules for interpreting the world and for behaving in it. In terms we have used earlier, the individual gains a **superego**.

GROUP NORMS IN AN INDUSTRIAL SETTING

Working groups of various kinds set and enforce norms that control the behavior of individual workers. The "rate buster," the individual who works harder than the group is willing to work, turns up in many settings and is, most generally, brought into line by

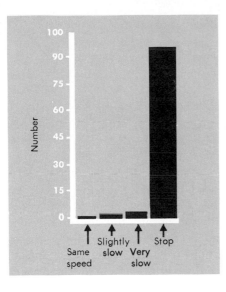

Figure 18–8. NORMS PRODUCE CONFORMITY.
*A quantitative description of conformity
behavior, sometimes referred to as "J-curve
behavior." The data above describe the normative behavior of motorists at a stop light. The
vast majority of motorists conform to the norm
by stopping. A few show various kinds of
nonconformist behavior. The same kind of
curve results when we plot the time of arrival
at work or similar behaviors. (Allport, 1934;
reproduced by permission of the* Journal of
Social Psychology.)

other members of the group. A clear illustration of the operation of a group norm and
the pressure exerted on the "rate buster" is
given in Figure 18–9. In this case, all members of the group were paid on a piecework
basis, so that the more units an individual
produced, the more he was paid. The group
had established a norm as to what constituted
a reasonable rate of output. They apparently
were convinced that if they produced more,
management would pay less per piece. One
member of the group started exceeding the
group norm by pressing garments at a faster
rate. When this "rate busting" became obvious
to the group, the individual was quickly
whipped back into line. Later, this group was

broken up, so that only the "deviant" operator
was left at the original job. With group pressure removed, the individual operator immediately began working at a markedly faster
rate and after a few days was doing almost
twice as much work as the group norms allowed. Not all group norms, then, continue to
influence behavior in the absence of the group.
It remains a problem why group-based perceptual norms influence later individual behavior while group-based work norms do not.
Perhaps the reader will have hypotheses. *In
groups,* however, group work norms remain
powerful.

This kind of control of output is seen in
many work situations. In college groups, for
example, the student who works particularly
hard on his courses is seen as a "rate buster"
(or "greasy grind" or "eager beaver"), and
social pressure is exerted to bring him down to
the group norm so that the world is safe for
"gentlemanly C's."

Against this kind of background two researchers (Coch and French, 1948) designed
an experiment to study the effects on productivity of different ways of handling the often
difficult problem of introducing change of
routine in a factory situation. In many situations, change in industrial routine has an ad-
verse effect on both productivity and labor
turnover. Workers frequently show resentment against a management that changes their
jobs and often develop feelings of frustration
and hopelessness. The research with which we
are concerned here explored the effects of
group decision by the workers themselves on
the ease and effectiveness with which a change
in a clothing factory was brought about. The
change, made necessary by the fact that the
kind of pajamas produced for several years
was no longer selling at a profit, demanded
that the workers learn a new set of routines
and adjust to a new piece rate.

One group of workers (the control group)
was called together and, in the traditional way,
told about the change and the necessity for it.
A new piece rate was announced and explained. Three experimental groups were each
involved, in slightly different ways, in a discussion of the change. They were given a

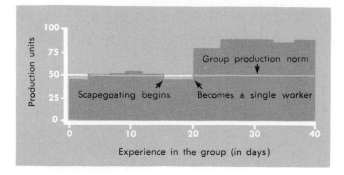

Figure 18–9. GROUP NORMS AND INDIVIDUAL BEHAVIOR. *Daily production records of one presser in a clothing factory. As a group member, his production record is relatively low. If it gets too high, the group brings pressure on the individual to conform. Later, when the individual works alone, free of the group norm, production soars. (Coch and French, 1948; reproduced by permission of the authors.)*

complete background on the facts of the market that made the change necessary. The plan for new routines and a new piece rate was presented and discussed. The groups approved the plan and made a number of helpful suggestions about ways the changeover could be made most effectively.

When production was measured after the change, the control group did learn the new rate of piece-work pay, but they went on producing at essentially their old rate. Old norms prevailed. The workers showed obvious distrust of the company and expressed hostility to the supervisors. During the first forty days after the change, 17 per cent of this group quit their jobs.

In each of the experimental groups, the picture was quite different. The changeover was made with only a slight drop in productivity; and, after a very few days, productivity climbed to levels appreciably higher than those prevailing on the old job. During forty days, no member of either of the three experimental groups quit his job. These groups showed little resentment of management and worked well with their supervisors.

In the new situation, norms were still op-

erating in each of the four groups, and we can be sure that individual members were kept in line with the norms. But the groups who participated in the discussion of the change set higher norms than the group that did not. For the control group, the old resentments against a distant and money-grabbing management were still operating in the new situation. Fearful and hostile interpretations of the situation make it natural that production be restricted by a low group norm, and that every member of the group be pressured to conform to the low group standard. The experimental groups, feeling less hostile to the company, were free to set and maintain higher production records.

In high-morale groups, where the success of the group contributes to the welfare of each of its members, the slacker rather than the rate buster becomes the object of the group's hostility and is brought *up* to the group norm.

Aside from its relevance for an understanding of group norms, this research bears on the general phenomenon of the dispersion of power or responsibility in a group. We return to this matter a bit later.

SOCIAL ROLES AND INDIVIDUAL BEHAVIOR

The group, in order to survive and function, defines and enforces standards of proper and improper behavior. These standards are referred to as social norms. We have seen some of the ways in which social norms influence the behavior of the individual, and ways in which social norms, originally existing "outside" the individual, become *interiorized* to form a part of what we may call the social conscience or **superego** of the individual, rendering him a properly socialized member of the group. The construct *norm* serves the social scientist well in his attempts to describe and account for social influences on the individual.

Social scientists need and use other constructs also in their attempts to deal with social behavior and to understand the relations between the individual and his social world. Foremost among these is the construct of *social role*, which we can define as *an organized pattern of behavior expected of an individual who occupies a certain position in a social group.*

DEFINITION AND SCOPE OF SOCIAL ROLES

All societies, large or small, simple or complex, define certain patterns of behavior that are necessary for the functioning of the society and assign these patterns of behavior to individuals. These prescribed patterns of behavior are social roles. Every society evolves its own array of roles in order to advance its goals, maintain its own form of organization and order, socialize its young, and so on. Every individual in the society is assigned—or sometimes, by his own efforts, assumes—a role, or more generally a *pattern* of roles, whereby he makes his contribution to the group and earns the rewards that society gives him.

For illustrative purposes, let us examine the most conspicuous role in American society—that of President of the United States. There are elaborate procedures whereby this role is assigned to an individual. The whole panoply of Presidential politics is involved. Once the role is assigned, then it almost completely takes over the behavior of the individual incumbent. There is, of course, an elaborate array of official duties. Perhaps even more engrossing and demanding are all the things, by precedent and practice, the President is expected to do. These expectancies demand everything from the greeting of visiting heads of government to the tossing of the first ball on the opening day of the baseball season.

The President's every act is watched by millions, all of whom are ready and willing to judge whether the act is truly Presidential in flavor. The role captures the individual. And this one cardinally significant role takes obvious precedence over the other roles of the individual incumbent. A President on the day of his election may also be a husband, a father, an elder in his church, a member of various fraternal and social organizations, and a dependable member of a weekend foursome at the golf club. All these and other roles must now be subjugated to the primary role.

Not many of us will assume or be assigned social roles as conspicuously demanding as the role of President. But the President's functioning as an individual in society is not too different from the situation facing each of us. Even should we assume the role of village idiot, we must conform to a pattern of behavior that is defined in the minds—in the expectancies—of the villagers. Each of us must find a way to combine our various roles into a workable pattern.

In many everyday groups the role structure is eminently clear. The left guard on the football team has clearly defined assignments; in addition, he is under some pressure to walk, talk, and look like a left guard rather than a halfback. The quarterback's role is defined perhaps with even more clarity. Not only must he perform certain physical acts at certain times, but he must behave in such a way that his teammates know him to be calmly in command of every tactical and strategic eventuality.

A modern hospital operates on the basis of an interlocking pattern of roles, each clearly defined and carefully assigned to individuals who are, by skill and temperament, in some degree equipped to assume them. The roles of the physician, the surgeon, the radiologist, the anesthesiologist, the head nurse, the registered nurse, the student nurse, the attendant, and the orderly are each precisely defined and all interwoven into a functional pattern. Each role has its responsibilities, its skills, and its privileges clearly defined. And any individual who gets out of role is subject to social pressure, sometimes of a very harsh kind. The nurse who gives an unauthorized shot of morphine or the orderly who gives any kind of shot of anything is not long tolerated. Each person in such a social structure knows what is expected of him. He knows what to expect of himself. Others know what they expect of him. In his social role, then, he is entwined in a pattern of expectancies and positive and negative sanctions.

In our social existence, each of us has to play a variety of roles. Each of us, early in life, has to begin to learn our sex role—how to act like a girl or a boy. First we must learn to act like little boys and little girls, then to act like big boys or big girls, and later, often without much opportunity to practice, we must suddenly take on the ways of grown men or women. The boy learns the role of brother, older or younger, of cub scout, boy scout, eagle scout. He learns the role of doctor's son or carpenter's son or minister's son, continually exploring the expectancies of the social world, sometimes finding them to his liking, sometimes chafing against their restraints. Eventually he learns the roles of husband, of father, of breadwinner, of responsible citizen, of doctor or lawyer or salesman or business executive. He learns to act and dress and live in accordance with the patterns of roles he has assumed. His female counterpart, of course, leads an equivalent life of roles.

Laboratory observations of small groups have demonstrated clearly that even when total strangers are put together and assigned a group task, there develops a variety of specialized roles. One person becomes, for example, the "encourager" for the group. He spends his efforts at keeping morale high. In times of stress, his fellows expect him to be encouraging; and by his own behavior and the expectancies of his fellows, he stays with a certain role. If he suddenly changes his role to that of "hostile critic," he will probably be disappointed with himself and rejected by his peers.

As an example of the dramatic potency of role enactment, one writer (Sarbin, 1954) defines certain hypnotic phenomena in terms of role enactment and then cites convincing evidence that such hypnotic role enactment in-

fluences somatic processes. In one experiment, for example (Lewis and Sarbin, 1943), subjects who had had no food for 15 hours and who had swallowed a device for recording stomach contractions were hypnotized and asked to "act as if" they were having a normal breakfast—to take on the role, we can say, of a recently fed individual. Subjects who had shown a susceptibility to deep hypnosis showed an inhibition of stomach contractions —"hunger pangs"—at the time they would normally be having them. The writer (Sarbin) goes on to cite evidence that a change in sex-role identification under hypnosis can influence problem-solving performance; that is, girls who adopt a masculine role are better at solving the kinds of problems at which boys generally excel.

THE LEARNING OF ROLES

The literature gives us a very little experimental analysis of the learning of roles. Such learning obviously begins early in life and is, as one theorist has pointed out (Sarbin, 1954), carried on both through *intentional instruction* and through *incidental learning*. With respect to intentional learning, the elders in a society very deliberately instruct the young in ways to behave in role. With some consistency, parents, teachers, and others reinforce the child, through administering punishment or reward, for performance of unitary and meaningful patterns of behavior. Also, in the area of incidental learning, the individual child will "pick up" whole patterns of behavior from his peers or from his elders; he will retain those patterns which lead to positive reinforcement, while nonreinforced or negatively reinforced patterns will be dropped from his repertoire.

Along with the learning of patterns of overt behavior, the individual learns *patterns of expectancies*. The little boy not only learns the whole patterns of behaviors that his culture regards as properly boy-like; he learns also to expect the same pattern from other boys. And when other boys depart from the expected pattern, they are brought back into line through one form or another of social reinforcement. The young boy who is termed "sissy" will probably soon eliminate girl-like responses from his pattern of behavior. Similarly, boys learn to expect that girls will be girls and will exert influence to see that girls are indeed girlish. And, of course, girls are similarly involved in role learning and teaching.

An early theorist (Mead, 1934) pointed out that childhood play is an important process in the learning of social roles. In their play, children gain experience in the enactment of roles and in the exercise of social expectations, and they learn to shift roles, to take on the roles of assorted others. It is Mead's notion that such shifting of roles is a significant part of the process of socialization.

The experimental analysis of role learning may be expected to advance when the basic concepts of imitation and of **identification** are more thoroughly analyzed and understood. There has been promising work along this line (Bandura and Walters, 1963), but at present there is no systematic psychology of role learning.

ATTITUDES

In attempts to analyze the relation between the individual and his social environment, the concepts of *social norm* and *social role* have been widely used. Both concepts can be clearly useful in seeing the ways in which the social world affects the individual to control his perceptions and his behavior and, as socialization advances, to shape his very personality. A third concept of cardinal significance for social psychology is that of **attitude**. An attitude is defined as a *readiness to respond positively or negatively to objects or symbols in the environment.*

The concept of attitude, as compared to the concepts of *norm* and *role,* focuses more directly on the individual and his own orientation to aspects of his environment. As the individual lives out his life responding to norms and assuming roles, he learns a pattern of *attitudes,* or readinesses to respond, to the specific objects and symbols in his social world.

Often we want to examine in detail the ways in which the individual orients himself to particular segments of his social environment. in the study of social psychology in an industrial setting, for example, we want to know not only about the group norms that are in force, and not only about the way a particular individual handles the role of foreman, but also how the individual foreman personally orients himself to management, to the company, to the union, and perhaps to the political world. So we study his attitudes toward these aspects of his world, and in studying his attitudes we round out the picture of the relation between the individual and his social world.

The concept of attitude is, of course, a motivational construct. It has references to forces within the individual system that will lead to overt behavior. In this respect, an attitude is similar to a motive. Both are constructs, inferred from observable behavior, dealing with forces or conditions within the individual system. The attitude construct, however, is *more specifically related to environmental objects* than is the construct of motive. We thus speak of the *motive* of hunger, but the *attitude* toward artichokes or hamburgers; or we speak of the achievement motive, but attitudes toward success or toward particular jobs.

A great achievement of social psychologists has been in the definition and measurement of attitudes. As with intelligence, the clear definition of a variable and the availability of procedures for its relatively precise measurement can lead to great advancement in knowledge of behaviors.

There is in existence now an enormous and growing literature on the formation and change of attitudes. While we cannot try here to summarize or epitomize the vast array of research data, we can give some recent specimens of it.

Some of the most recent work in this area, and in many ways the most fascinating, has to do with the relation of **cognitive dissonance** to attitude change. We can here summarize two illustrative experiments.

One informative and suggestive experiment (Aronson and Carlsmith, 1963) involves the behavior of children in the face of threats of differing magnitude. The experimenters used as subjects children approximately 4 years of age, each of whom was individually brought into a playroom where there was a table displaying five attractive toys. While the child was in the room, before and after the actual beginning of the experimental procedure, he was observed through a one-way mirror. After the child had played briefly with each of the five toys, the experimenter succeeded in getting the child to express his relative preference for each of them. Then the experimenter put four toys at various places on the floor and placed on the table the toy that had come out to be second-highest in preference. The experimenter then set up one of three different situations. The first arrangement put the child in a "no-threat" situation; the experimenter told him that he could play with any of the toys in the room until the experimenter came back, but the experimenter took the second-ranked toy with him as he left the room. In the second condition, the experimenter told the child he could play with any toy in the room except the one on the table—the second-ranked one; and he was threatened with drastic punishment if he did play with the forbidden toy. The third, a "mild-threat" condition, was the same as the foregoing except that there was only a mild punishment threatened for playing with the toy on the table. The child was observed through the one-way mirror. After ten minutes the experimenter returned to the playroom, allowed each child to play briefly with each of the five toys, and then obtained a second expression of the child's relative preference for each toy. When the results were tabulated, a majority of the children in the "no-threat" conditions rated the absent toy higher at the end of the experiment than at the beginning.

One interpretation of this experiment (Festinger and Freedman, 1964) cites these data as evidence that forbidden fruit is likely to become more attractive. When the children were given a strong threat and hence refrained from playing with the forbidden toy, there was some tendency for them to increase their evaluation of the forbidden stimulus. In no case out of 22 children was there a decrease in the evaluation of the forbidden toy. The mild-threat condition, however, is the one showing the real influence of dissonance. In this condition the children were given only a mild threat, but they still did not play with the forbidden toy. This condition yielded a significant decrease in the attractiveness of the forbidden toy. In dissonance theory, compliance with a mild threat would be dissonant with the belief that the forbidden fruit was strongly attractive; it simply makes no sense to deny a pleasure unless there is a genuine reason for the denial. So, if there is not a genuine reason, a reason is created to "explain" the behavior. If nonmeaningful compliance occurs, the theory has it, then there must be some readjustment of something. The readjustment these children tended to make resulted in a diminution of the attractiveness of the forbidden fruit. Some cognitive theorists (Festinger and Freedman, 1964) suggest that data such as these have at least a relevance for the internalization of moral values and socialized behaviors. If a child, the argument goes, complies with moral dictates on the basis of mild threats alone or on the basis of no threat whatsoever, then, in order to keep dissonance reduced, he must believe that the adjured line of activity was not very attractive; or he may go the other way and hold that it was awfully important, for some personal reasons, that he refrain from committing the "immoral" act. Either of these adjustments will reduce dissonance and will give the child a cognitive structure that is consonant with approved moral dictates.

An allied and somewhat similar experiment (Brehm and Cohen, 1962) involved student attitudes toward the city police who were involved in quelling a student riot at Yale University. During the riot the New Haven police, in the students' eyes, had behaved very poorly. The students in the experiment were asked to participate in the research because the experimenter "very much needed their help" and were asked to write a strong, forceful, and thoughtful essay that was definitely against their own personal positions and in favor of the police side of the story of the riots. The students were then offered money for completing the essays. The amounts varied from $10 to 50 cents from one group to another. After the essays were completed, the students were given an attitude scale, on which they were asked to record their feelings about the justification of the acts of the police. Whereas all of the essays had been ostensibly in favor of the police and very much against the students' own personal positions, the elicited attitudes toward the police showed a definite and systematic variation with the amount of the reward. The students who received the least reward for the essay were much more positive in their attitudes toward the police than were those who received the largest reward. The experimenters maintain that these results cannot be accounted for except through dissonance theory: the individual who complied with the request but received only a small reward was faced with a dissonant situation requiring that something change; what changed was the attitude toward the police. As that attitude became less negative, it became less dissonant with the sentiments in the essay and less dissonant with the awareness that the student, receiving only 50 cents, had been writing for something other than money alone.

A third experiment, showing how an individual's attitudes relate simultaneously to his other personal attributes and to ways in which the external world is construed, can illustrate another approach to the exploration of this area. This experiment (Feather, 1964) concerned itself with the influence of (1) the individual's attitude strength, (2) his critical ability, and (3) his intolerance of inconsistency on the way in which the individual construed some statements relevant to his attitude. Each subject in the experiment was administered (1) an attitude scale selected to measure the strength of his general attitude toward religion; (2) a test of critical ability, leading to a score for the ability to find logical errors in attitudinally neutral statements; and (3) a test of intolerance of inconsistency, a test yielding a measure of the degree to which the subject felt threatened by ambiguous situations. Then all subjects were exposed to an array of syllogistically arranged arguments concerning religion. For example, one syllogism was as follows:

A charitable and tolerant attitude towards mankind helps to bring people together in love and harmony. Christianity always helps to bring people together in love and harmony. Therefore, a consequence of Christianity is a charitable and tolerant attitude toward mankind (Feather, p. 130).

It was the experimenter's hypothesis that the individual would tend to evaluate such syllogisms in a way consistent with his own attitudes and, further, that the tendency to do so would increase with the strength of the attitude. Both phases of this hypothesis were confirmed, particularly with subjects whose attitudes were strongly favorable to religion. The stronger their attitude, the more likely they were to interpret the argument as supporting their attitudes. A second hypothesis stated that the higher the critical ability of the subject, the lower will be his tendency to interpret arguments as consistent with his attitudes. This hypothesis was confirmed. So was a third one, stating that the individual who is intolerant of inconsistency will be more inclined to find arguments, regardless of their logicality, consistent with his own attitudes.

There is here additional evidence that we tend to see the world "not as it is but as we are"; and we have an indication that the more extreme the attitude, the more likely it is to influence our construction of the world. This experiment also suggests that not all construing of the external world is completely distorted by the biases of the construer; a critical cast of mind and a tolerance of ambiguity can contribute to a freedom from bias.

SMALL-GROUP PHENOMENA

In the remainder of this chapter, we shall deal extensively with selected aspects of recent research on small groups. While a general description of the nature of society and of the concepts of norm, role, and attitude give us useful background for a social psychology, the scientific explorer is not satisfied with general descriptions or rough sketches of significant features of the terrain. He wants to get down to hard facts and to details of process. He can sometimes do this through the close and often experimental study of small groups in laboratory situations. In some respects a small group may serve as a microcosm—a small replica—of the larger society. For example, if we bring six total strangers into the laboratory and assign them a problem to solve, we can observe at first hand many of the ten functions of society. We can see the individual's orientation to the group goal. We can see the group's definition of means whereby the goal is to be reached. We can see one group defend itself against other groups. We can see intimately the processes of communication. We can see the formation of both perceptual and behavioral norms and perhaps the group efforts to control deviation. We might, if we wished, bring in a new member to an established group and observe the processes whereby the newcomer is socialized. And we can observe the ways in which roles are differentiated and assigned, with one or more persons assuming or being assigned the leadership role while others take on other roles that contribute in various ways and in varying degrees to group functioning.

Laboratory research has been devoted to a number of these aspects of group functioning. We shall here describe some general findings coming from one protracted series of studies, shall mention briefly some of the kinds of research on small groups and then shall concentrate for a while on the problem of leadership.

UNIFORMITIES OF INTERACTION IN SMALL GROUPS

One investigator (Bales, 1952) has formulated a number of general hypotheses—which we can regard as general descriptions—of events occurring in each one of a great number of face-to-face groups in which there is a definite task to perform and a requirement that the group reach a joint decision. A review of these general hypotheses, or tentative descriptions, can add to our understanding of social psychology and perhaps to our ability to observe, for both pleasure and profit, the many groups of which we all are and will be members.

Universal Problems of Face-to-Face Groups

Bales observes that any face-to-face group —whether it is a children's play group, a discussion group, a committee, a planning group, a therapy group, or any other—faces similar problems. These problems must be handled with some effectiveness if the group is to do a group task.

First there are *problems of communication*. Individuals in the group must communicate with one another if there is to be any joint decision or joint action. Communication problems in face-to-face groups come in three forms. There is the communication problem of *orientation*. The group members must have a common way of viewing the situation, must have shared cognitive orientations. Each member of the group starts out with some uncertainty and confusion about what the situation is all about. But each member also has relevant facts to offer and relevant observations to make. Through communication, the workable common orientation is evolved.

Related to the problem of orientation, according to Bales, is the problem of *evaluation*, the problem of reaching a common judgment as to the value of doing whatever the group may be contemplating. How important is the problem? What are the consequences if we do not do anything about it? Such questions arise in every group and must be handled through communication.

Then every group confronts problems of *control*, which must be handled through communication. The behavior of individual members of the group must be controlled if there is to be joint action. Any joint action will require the suppression of some individual preferences and will involve the frustration of somebody. Individuals influence one another in the interest of finding the common agreement. This influence is exerted through communication.

A second variety of problem confronting any face-to-face group concerns matters of *organization and maintenance*. The group must have some kind of structure and must avoid disintegration. In every group there will be some shuffling about until problems of leadership are solved and until there is some decision about what are to be the roles of each member. Each group establishes some prestige system within itself. These problems create tensions which the group must somehow handle if it is to avoid falling apart.

The Life History of a Group

Where any face-to-face group begins to function, all these problems exist and must be handled. It is Bales' observation that as groups move through time they follow certain predictable *phases* (see Fig. 18–10). First, they deal with *problems of orientation*. Each group needs to decide first "what it's all about," to settle cognitively into the situation. If the Dean appoints six students to a Committee on Academic Integrity, the first meeting of the committee will probably be devoted to general questions about why the Dean appointed such a committee, what he expects from it, what is the general nature of the problem, and exactly what is academic integrity anyhow.

Once problems of orientation are solved, the group tends to move on to *problems of evaluation*—problems of "how do we feel about it." Once we understand what the Dean has in mind—once know that when he says "academic integrity," he is worried about cheating on exams—then we must decide how we feel about the general situation of having a group of students concern themselves with the honesty of other students. Is the problem important? Is it likely that this group can do anything effective about it?

If the group moves successfully through this phase, evolving a common feeling that the problem is important and that this committee can indeed do something effective about it, then there is movement on to *problems of control*—problems of "what do we do about it." Alternative courses of action are suggested, and individual members begin to persuade

one another, to argue, to compromise, to invent.

During all these three phases the group encounters problems of organization and maintenance. Disagreements and uncertainties create anxieties and antagonisms. These become greater as the group moves from orientation through evaluation to control. As the group continues, there is an increasing frequency of negative reactions on the part of members—they aggress against one another, express wishes that they had never been placed on the committee in the first place, withdraw into silence and show other negative or hostile behaviors. But there still can be progress. And if the group does reach a consensus, there is a great show of release of these tensions in laughing, joking, and back-slapping.

Kinds of Interactions

Bales found that in the many face-to-face groups he observed, individual behaviors could be classified into four general categories —and that behavior in each of the categories tended to occur with about the same frequency in a wide variety of groups. For example, in all groups some individuals some of the time show what Bales terms *expressive-integrative acts*. This category of behavior includes the giving of help, the praising of another member, joking to release tension, agreeing with someone, and demonstrating solidarity. In group after group, about 25 per cent of all individual behaviors fall into this category.

The other categories of interaction were as follows:

Instrumental task-relevant acts. This category includes behaviors that move the group toward a solution of its chosen problem. Answering questions, giving suggestions, giving opinions, giving clarification or explanations all fall into this category. Of all the behaviors in groups 56 per cent are of this type.

Instrumental task-relevant acts of asking questions. Included here are requests for orientation, requests for suggestions, for opinions. Of all interactions in groups, 6.9 per cent fall into this category.

Negative expressive-integrative acts. This

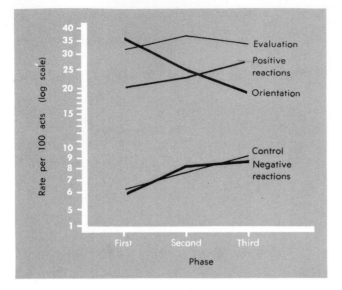

Figure 18–10. LIFE HISTORY OF A GROUP.
Relative frequency of kinds of interaction as a
group progresses through three phases of its
history. As the group moves from the initial
phase to the terminal phase, for example, there
is a decrease in orienting reactions and an
increase in instances of control. Data here are
based on study of 22 sessions of small groups.
(Bales and Strodtbeck, 1951; reproduced by
permission of the American Psychological
Association.)

category includes statements of disagreement, of tension or antagonism and withdrawal. This category includes 11.2 per cent of the total interaction in Bales' groups.

We now begin to get a rounded picture of events in face-to-face groups. (See Fig. 18–11 for a summary presentation of interaction data.) Such groups, when facing an actual task requiring a concerted attack, encounter problems of communication and of organization. These problems evoke a variety of individual behaviors. The individual behaviors can be classed into the four categories just described. Over a period of time, with these behaviors occurring, the group moves from a phase of orientation to a phase of evaluation and on to a phase of control. All of these events and processes, Bales concludes, can be observed in any face-to-face group of which

we are members or which we may wish to study in the laboratory. Figure 18–12 presents the whole array of observational categories.

Role Differentiation

Bales goes on to observe the processes of *role differentiation* as another universal aspect of face-to-face groups. As the group continues over time to contend with its problems, Bales reports, individual members begin to "specialize" in certain kinds of behavior. One member begins to concern himself primarily, for example, with the social and individual problems of the group; and his behavior is predominantly of the expressive-integrative type. He may have few ideas about how to get the task done, but he does a great deal to hold the group together, to keep tension within tolerable limits, to reduce anxiety, and to make everybody feel as if he were somebody. Soon this member finds that this is the way he is "supposed" to act. Other members expect these behaviors of him. He now has a role in the group. He cannot now, without great strain, suddenly switch to the role of the grumpy isolate or hostile minority member. The same kind of process goes on in spelling out the role of the sterner and more task-oriented leader. Thus does role differentiation —a social division of labor—come about.

As roles become differentiated, some roles

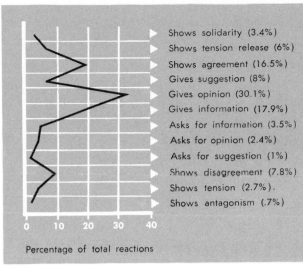

Shows solidarity (3.4%)
Shows tension release (6%)
Shows agreement (16.5%)
Gives suggestion (8%)
Gives opinion (30.1%)
Gives information (17.9%)
Asks for information (3.5%)
Asks for opinion (2.4%)
Asks for suggestion (1%)
Shows disagreement (7.8%)
Shows tension (2.7%).
Shows antagonism (.7%)

Percentage of total reactions

Figure 18–11. PSYCHOLOGICAL EVENTS IN SMALL GROUPS. *The data here are based on 71,838 observations of 24 groups in 96 different sessions. The profile of behavior here may be regarded as typical of many small groups. Of all the reactions of group members, for example, 30.1 per cent fall in the class of giving opinions while less than 1 per cent show overt antagonism. (Bales, 1955; by permission of the* Scientific American.)

appear to have more to do than others with the welfare and progress of the group. These roles are more highly regarded than the roles that seem to contribute little or nothing either to the happiness or the success of the group. The more highly regarded roles are generally referred to as *leadership roles.* Against the background picture of the events occurring in groups we are now about ready to tackle the phenomenon of leadership. But before doing so, let us pursue a bit further Bales' analysis of role differentiation.

Bales had members of his groups rank the other members on (1) amount of activity shown in the group, (2) the number of valuable ideas contributed, and (3) the amount the individual was liked by members of the group. It turned out that people who were ranked high on activity tended also to be given a high rank on valuable ideas. But these active and valuable members were not generally well liked. Over a number of meetings it was observed that if the individual member rose in activity and value, he tended to go down in the affection of his colleagues. It appears that making active and valuable contributions to the group is a way to gain status and lose friends (see Fig. 18–13).

When one individual in a group assumes the role of active contributor to progress, a second person often will rise to another kind of leadership role. This second person, Bales observes, tackles the social-emotional problems of the group, engaging in the expressive-integrative behaviors described a moment ago. The first leader moves usefully ahead and is given respect. The second leader holds the group together and is accorded affection. Here we have a picture of a double-headed leadership in a group. There is a complementary pair of roles that arises out of the nature of the problems facing the group. This is an approach to leadership to which we shall return.

OTHER RESEARCH ON SMALL GROUPS

Bales' material on life in small groups has a value in giving us a general background for understanding some general group processes. There have been many other research attacks upon small-group phenomena, each having a distinctiveness and each deserving more space than is available here. There has been research

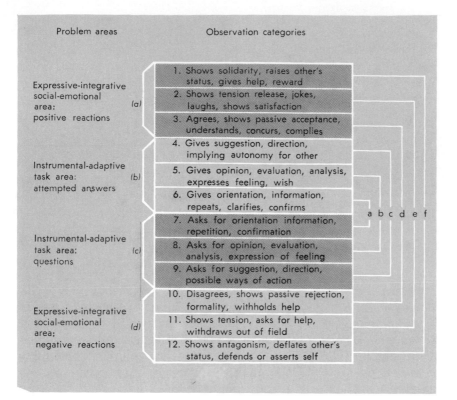

Figure 18–12. KINDS OF INTERACTIONS IN SMALL GROUPS. *A set of twelve categories used in the observation of small groups in action. The categories connected by lettered lines at right constitute functioned pairs. The categories are also grouped into four problem areas, indicated by the letters at left. The nature of the interaction in any stage of almost any small group can be described by tabulating the frequency of behaviors falling into each of these categories. Also the typical "profile" of interaction of an individual member of a group can be described. (Bales and Strodtbeck, 1951; reproduced by permission of the American Psychological Association.)*

attention to problems of communication in small groups: What patterns of communication are most conducive to high effectiveness and/or high morale? The problems of decision making have also received extensive study. Under what conditions do groups reach quick and/or wise decisions? There is a growing literature on such problems as the

conditions of group creativity, on the phenomena of power structure in groups, on problems of conformity and deviant behavior in groups, on perception in group settings, on cohesiveness, on cooperation and competition, on intergroup relations. A rich, varied, significant, and in many respects an experimental social psychology is coming into existence.

LEADERSHIP

We have seen some of the ways in which a group in society, through the definition and enforcement of norms and roles, exerts influence on the individual and brings him into the ways of functioning which the group finds adaptive. We have seen, in somewhat more intimate detail, the pressures and challenges involved as individuals interact in small groups. We have seen indications that groups, as they go about their business, differentiate and define certain roles and assign them to individuals. One role—or one array of roles—that is differentiated in almost every group has

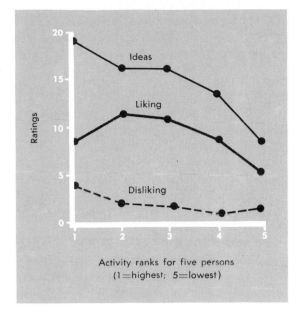

Ratings

Ideas

Liking

Disliking

Activity ranks for five persons
(1=highest; 5=lowest)

Figure 18–13. PRODUCTIVITY AND POPULARITY
IN GROUPS. *When group members rate one
another on (1) activity, (2) ideas contributed
to the group, (3) being liked, and (4) being
disliked, the results show that popularity and
active contribution to the group are not
positively related. The individual ranked most
active is ranked high on ideas but is only
moderately liked and has the highest of the
five ranks on being disliked. The data suggest
that emphasis on getting the job done may win
respect but lose friends. (Bales, in* Working
Papers in the Theory of Action, *Parsons, Bales,
and Shils, eds., 1953; by permission of The
Free Press.)*

to do with what we commonly call leadership.
For the remainder of this chapter, we shall
concern ourselves, in moderate depth, with
matters of leadership.

In recent years there has been a great deal
of attention, on the part of both the general
public and the social scientist, to the problems
and phenomena of leadership. Perhaps the
wide dispersion of leadership and responsibility in a democratic society helps create both
a common-sense and a research preoccupation
with the problem of what is good leadership
and who is a good leader. Certainly if we had

a thoroughly feudal social structure, in which
all leadership was in the hands of those born
to the role, there would be little point in worrying about ways to select or train leaders, or
ways in which the self-made man might learn
to lead a corporation or a political party or a
city council.

THE SEARCH FOR LEADERSHIP TRAITS

There have been many research attempts to
define the personal attributes that are associated with leadership. In our everyday view
of social realities we tend easily to assume
that a man is a leader because he has certain
skills and drives that set him apart from other
men. We are more likely to believe that men
make history than that history makes men.
But the facts do not lend much support to the
contention that leaders lead because they have
certain traits of leadership.

There have been thousands of literary attempts and hundreds of research attempts to
spell out leadership traits. This total effort
has added up to very little. One investigator
(Bird, 1940) made an extensive examination
of all available research literature on the subject and compiled a long list of the traits which
had been found, in one situation or another,
to set leaders apart from followers. There
could be no denying that most of the researches were properly conducted and that in
each one leaders and followers did actually
differ with respect to measurable traits. But
only 5 per cent of the total list of leadership
traits turned up in as many as four of the
research reports.

A more recent survey of this literature (Stogdill, 1948) yields similar results. There are a
few traits that do, in a number of different
situations, distinguish between leaders and
followers. In many situations, for example,
leaders do excel their followers in intelligence,
dependability, responsibility, social participation, and socioeconomic status. This, however,
constitutes a fairly meager array of traits, and
there is doubt about the relevance of any one
of these traits in all leadership situations.
Leaders, for example, are often more intelligent than their followers, but this does not

hold in all leadership situations; and in some situations the intelligence of the leader may be totally irrelevant.

A reasonable conclusion from the research on leadership traits is (1) that certain minimal abilities may be required of all leaders, (2) that these abilities are widely distributed among nonleaders, and (3) that the traits or behaviors that constitute effective leadership in one group or situation may not be the same traits or behaviors that will be necessary in a different group or situation. The leader of a team of atomic physicists needs intelligence, but in the leader of a team of sand hogs sheer intelligence may be relatively unimportant.

LEADERSHIP AND DIMENSIONS OF THE GROUP

The paucity of returns from the search for leadership traits led to other approaches to the phenomena of leadership. One attack was based on the idea that the behavior of a leader is meaningfully related to the dimensions of the group in which leadership occurs (Hemphill, 1950). The notion here was that a group can be regarded as a unitary entity and described, much like a human personality, in terms of a few basic traits or dimensions. And once the group is described—given a profile, as it were—then it would be possible to see what kind of leadership behavior actually occurs in what kind of group. By having a number of subjects describe in detail (a) groups to which they had belonged and (b) the behavior of leaders of these groups, it became possible to relate the observed behavior of leaders to the characteristics of the groups. Some meaningful relationships were discovered. For example, with respect to the simple dimension of size, it became quickly apparent that "good" leaders of large groups behave quite differently from "good" leaders of small groups.

LEADERSHIP AND THE NEEDS OF FOLLOWERS

Another approach to leadership takes off from the general idea that it is the function of the leader to do something about the needs of the followers. The follower, the reasoning goes, is the one who must accept or reject leadership. This acceptance or rejection will depend on the followers' psychological needs in the particular group situation and whether the leader is seen as one who is likely to do something to satisfy these needs. If the followers in one group, for example, need warm paternal support and approval, they will accept a leader who is able to furnish this kind of psychological income for the group members. The stern, task-oriented leader will be rejected, if possible. In another situation the followers' primary need, it may be, is to get out of an emergency situation alive. Where there is such an urgent need for group action, no follower will worry about the approving warmth of the leader; the coldly hostile individual will be accepted as leader if he has ideas that will save the lives of the group members.

The general idea in this approach is that the needs of the followers in any group situation can be assessed, perhaps profiled, and this assessment will define what the leader must do if he is to "fit" the situation. There follows a suggested list of followers' needs, a list that can presumably be used to describe the pattern or profile of needs maintaining in any group (Sanford, 1951b).

1. *The need for material support.* The need to be fed, clothed, "paid off" by authority.
2. *The need for ego support.* The need to have the leader increase my self-esteem, my feeling of importance.
3. *The need for love support.* The need to have the leader love "me," the need for an atmosphere of approval.
4. *The need for affiliation with one's fellows.* The need to have warm relations with other members of the group; this need is related to a concern for the welfare of one's fellow members and a desire for the leader to facilitate interpersonal relations.
5. *The need for submission.* The need to submit to a strong leader; tendency to feel safe when authority is very strong, protective, directive.
6. *The need for structure.* The need to know what is going on, what the problem is, where "we" are headed, how to get there.

7. *The need for conformity.* The need to stick to in-group values and procedures, associated with the need to have others do likewise.
8. *The need to advance group goals.* The need for the group with which the individual is identified to succeed in carrying out its function.

This approach was employed in a study of the public orientation to Franklin D. Roosevelt (Sanford, 1951a). A representative sample of 963 citizens of Philadelphia were asked in 1950 (a) whether they thought Roosevelt was a good leader and (b) why. Ninety-six per cent thought he was a good leader and gave their reasons. When asked to name the great person, living or dead, they admired most, 42 per cent of the same population named Roosevelt and gave their reasons why. An analysis of the reasons given for accepting Roosevelt as a good leader yielded the following data.

Reason for Thinking Roosevelt a Good Leader	Per cent Giving Such Response
Warm personal characteristics	19.5
National accomplishments and benefits to specific groups	28.1
Competence and personal strength	21.1
Other traits of personality and character	9.8
International accomplishment	1.5
Other	20.0

These data were interpreted to mean that in the national situation of 1950 the American citizen perceived Roosevelt as a warm human being who liked people, as a powerful individual possessed of great competence, and as an individual who "paid off" in terms of practical benefits to the citizens. The public orientation to Roosevelt suggests that (a) the need for material support, (b) the need for warm approval, and (c) the need to submit to strength are salient needs of the American voter and will influence the choice of national political leaders. As the international situation becomes more tense, the reasoning goes, there will be a greater need for strength and com-petence and less need for warm approval. In periods of economic stress there will be a greater emphasis on matters of material support and perhaps less on personal warmth. The pattern of needs of the followers, a pattern that varies from group to group and from time to time in the same group, this general hypothesis says, will influence the choice of leader and will determine what will be acceptable leadership behavior.

LEADERSHIP AND GROUP FUNCTIONING

The approach to leadership emphasizing group dimensions and the approach emphasizing the needs of the followers are both departures from the search for universal traits of leadership. And both approaches move toward an emphasis on the group itself as a factor in determining leadership. They both say, in effect, that leadership is something that happens in a group. Neither approach has yielded as yet a rounded and systematic understanding of leadership phenomena.

The more recent researches on leadership have emphasized one or another aspect of group functioning as a significant determiner of leadership phenomena. In reviewing Bales' work, we ended with the general notion that there are two highly active and visible roles that become differentiated in face-to-face groups: (1) the role of the idea giver and problem solver and (2) the role of the integrative comfort-giving maintainer of morale. Both roles may be regarded as leadership roles. And when we do so regard them, we are seeing leadership from the standpoint of group functioning.

In one of a series of experiments (Carter and Nixon, 1949b), one-hundred high school students were brought into the laboratory where each one, paired off with another student who was initially a stranger to him, was asked to work on each of three tasks. First the pair of students was asked to perform an *intellectual task* involving the plotting of data on a board. Then, in two different pairings, each student was asked to work on a *clerical task*, involving the sorting of some cards, and a *mechanical task*, requiring the assembly of a giant Tinker-Toy kind of apparatus. Each pair of students was carefully observed from behind a one-way glass, and each individual was given a rating on leadership behavior on each of the tasks. The observers found they could achieve good inter-judge reliability in rating leadership behavior in these three situations. Table 18–3 presents the basic data from the study.

The initial question in this research was that of the generality of leadership traits. In essence the reasoning had it that if a student is characterized by general leadership traits, then these traits will show themselves in each of the three situations; he will "take charge," show initiative, make suggestions in all three situations. Such was not exactly the case. Where leadership ratings for the intellectual task were compared with similar ratings on a clerical task, there was a .48 correlation. The correlation was .18 between leadership in the intellectual task and leadership on the mechanical test, and .32 between the clerical task and the mechanical task. These figures suggest that leadership behavior is by no means solely a function of the personality of the individual but must be understood in terms of the situation in which leadership occurs. The same study carried further the consideration of situational versus personal factors in leadership behavior. The investigators obtained ratings of leadership potential on each of their subjects from (a) their teachers or supervisors and (b) their acquaintances. They also obtained a score for each subject on general

school activity. None of these ratings or scores related very closely to the ratings of actual leadership in the actual situation.

Of further relevance for the question of situational versus personal determiners of leadership behavior, the same investigators gave a group of subjects an extensive battery of tests of ability, interests, and personality variables in the attempt to see whether the results were related to ratings of actual leadership performance in the three situations and to other criteria of leadership (Carter and Nixon, 1949a). They found some tests which seemed to relate somewhat with all the criteria of leadership while others related meaningfully to leadership in one situation but not to that in another. An interest in music, for example, was related negatively (1) to observers' ratings of leadership performance in three different situations, (2) to supervisors' ratings of leadership ability, (3) to ratings by acquaintances, and (4) to the activity score. An interest in persuasive activities, by comparison, relates positively to ratings of leadership performance on the intellectual task but shows very little or even a negative relation to any of the other ratings or scores.

These studies and others lead to the general point of view that in understanding the phenomena of leadership we need to consider both (a) the group functions that are to be performed and (b) the personal attributes— the abilities, interests, and traits—of the individual who is designated, or who assumes, the leadership position.

Table 18–3. CORRELATION BETWEEN WORK-TASK LEADERSHIP SCORES AND OTHER CRITERIA OF LEADERSHIP

Work-Task	Work-Task Scores and Supervisor's Rating		Work-Task Score and Rating by Acquaintances	Work-Task Score and School-Activity Score
	School 1	School 2		
Intellectual	.31	.45	.13	.13
Clerical	.17	.27	−.25	.02
Mechanical	.14	.35	.05	.22

(Adapted from Carter and Nixon, 1949b.)

Two Basic Kinds of Group Functions

Bales' analysis, reviewed earlier, suggested that any group confronts two different, if interlocking, problems as it goes through its life history. Every group probably has the problem, in one form or another, of *achieving some particular goal*. Every group probably also has the problem of *maintaining or strengthening the group itself*.

In handling the first problem, the group needs a member or members who can clarify goals, initiate action, keep attention focused on goals, formulate plans, supply expert information, and evaluate the quality of the work done. Most groups seem to find a member or members who, with some success, fall into this goal-oriented pattern of activity and who are regarded as respected leaders.

In dealing with the second problem, that of group maintenance, an individual or individuals very frequently can be seen to assume the job of straightening out interpersonal relations, defending minority rights, arbitrating disputes, giving comfort to individual members, and increasing togetherness or interdependence.

In any group that is initially leaderless, it is Bales' observation, there will be a tendency for these two roles to become differentiated and assigned to two different individuals. In many everyday groups we can see this pattern of dual leadership. In many family groups, for example, we can see this kind of complementariness in the leadership roles of the two parents. Perhaps the father is the goal-oriented taskmaster while the mother is the solver of the social-emotional problems that tend to tear the family apart. Or it can be the other way around. In military organizations, the commanding officer plays one or the other of these two roles while his executive officer complements him in the other. In most cases, the goal-oriented standard setter is the respected man without friends, while the social-emotional leader is not highly respected but has many friends among the members of the group. In political affairs, it has been observed, it is almost impossible that the man most able to handle the technical problems of his office can be elected to that office; social-emotional skills are more likely to appeal to voters. Franklin Roosevelt, as we have seen, was perceived by the voters as being both technically competent and personally warm. But there was greater emphasis among his admirers on his personal warmth—a personal warmth that apparently has not been found in all able aspirants to the Presidency.

There are a number of lines of evidence reinforcing the notion that the necessity for a group to handle certain problems is a significant factor in determining leadership phenomena. In one research, for example (Heyns, 1948), the designated leaders of experimental groups deliberately failed to perform certain obvious leadership functions. In such cases, another group member stepped into the breach and saw that the function was performed. In a related study (Kahn and Katz, 1952) it was shown that in groups where the official foremen of industrial groups failed to provide adequate leadership, informal leaders stepped in to see that jobs were done. Along a similar line, there are many instances in military history where the appointed leader either failed to do his job or was killed, and where some enlisted man, formerly regarded as unprepossessing indeed, stepped forward to take command. All these evidences, both of a research and an anecdotal nature, may indicate that leadership behavior is best understood by first understanding group dynamics.

Distribution of Functions among Members of the Group

To say, as we have above, that there are two kinds of functions that must be performed in every group is not to say that these functions must be performed by only two individuals. Or that these two functions are the only functions that must be performed.

In some groups, the functions that are seen as most important are assigned to particular individuals, and things are arranged so that other individuals may not perform them. Only the commanding officer may command. Only

Figure 18–14. LEADERSHIP STYLES. *The traits of leaders vary widely. What traits, if any, are common to Kennedy and Castro? Does the leader make history or history the leader?*

the quarterback may give technical leadership in a football game. Many organizations make it eminently clear that individuals in the lower reaches of status are not expected to contribute to the policy or planning functions of the organization. Too many decision-making cooks, this view of organization has it, spoil the broth. Power and responsibility must be concentrated "at the top."

Another view of social organization, by contrast, holds that a concentration of the more responsible group functions in the hands of a few undermines the morale of the other members. To limit responsibility and to curtail full participation, this view has it, creates hostility between members and leaders, reduces enthusiasm, and destroys the creativity of the group.

In a classic study in this area (Lewin, Lippitt, and White, 1939), a number of boys' clubs were exposed to experimentally created "social climates" or "styles of leadership," and their behavior was observed during and after the meetings of their clubs. Each group of boys was exposed to each of three kinds of leadership. In the *autocratic climate,* the leader directed all activities of the boys, making the decisions about what would be the

project of the day and telling each boy what he would do as his part of the group's function. In the *democratic climate,* the leader would help the group itself determine its policies through group discussion; the boys themselves would decide who would work with whom and how the various tasks would be assigned. In a third climate, the *laissez-faire* one, there was little or no leadership. The boys were completely free to organize themselves or not. The leader took no part in discussion and supplied information only when asked.

The autocratic and democratic groups showed the clearest contrasts. In the autocratic groups the boys showed either definite hostility or marked apathy. In one experiment, there was thirty times as much hostility expressed in the autocratic group as in a comparable democratic one, with much of the hostility being shown in "picking" on scapegoats. When the autocratic leader had left the room, aggressive behavior would break out in all directions. After the meeting, the boys would often destroy the things they had made under the direction of the autocratic leader. In the democratic groups there was much less aggression and more apparent pride in the results of their work. Nineteen out of twenty boys preferred the democratic leader to the autocratic one.

In a related research on college students (Flanders, 1951) it was shown that if a teacher behaves in a directive and autocratic way, students will express more hostility to one another and to the teacher, will show more apathy and more tendency to withdraw than is the case with a more accepting, "democratic" teacher.

One way of interpreting these results is in terms of the wider dispersion of responsible functions among the members of the more democratic groups. Each member of such a group feels his own utility and responsibility; everybody is somebody. Hence morale is high. A related experiment appears to bear on the point. In an experiment (Pepitone, 1952) in which all group members were performing exactly the same task, some members were surreptitiously told by the experimenter that the jobs they were doing were of very special significance for the group. Those who thereby felt their behavior more important for the group developed greater feelings of responsibility to the group and were willing to devote more energy to it.

Such evidence does not justify the conclusion, however, that the "democratic" form of distributing leadership functions is always most effective. One investigator reports, for example, that concentration of leadership in the hands of a few produces lower morale but more efficient performance—at least over short periods of time (Bavelas, 1942).

A TENTATIVE VIEW OF LEADERSHIP

Research on leadership continues. At the moment we can, with what appears to be good sense, take the view that leadership is best thought about in terms of a fit or congruence between the problems faced by a group and the personal attributes of certain individual group members. The research on leadership traits does not encourage us to think that some individuals are "born leaders" and hence will naturally assume the leader's role whatever the situation. The literature tells us that we must take into account the situation in which leadership occurs. We must consider the dimensions of the group or the followers' needs or the dynamics of group functioning if we are to understand leadership. Whenever leadership occurs, its effectiveness or its acceptability in the group will relate both to the aspects of the situation and to the attributes of the individual or individuals.

OTHER FIELDS OF RESEARCH IN SOCIAL PSYCHOLOGY

The purpose of this chapter has been to move toward (1) a general understanding of social psychology as a field of research and (2) a working knowledge of some of the key concepts in the field. In pursuing these goals we have touched upon many research findings in many specific areas of investigation. But we have by no means surveyed the field of social psychology. A number of areas of both theoretical and practical significance have not been included. We here merely mention some of these excluded areas, so that the student can get at least a rough idea of the scope and variety of research concerns of social psychologists.

We no more than touched upon the matter of *attitude measurements*. This field of research, particularly when it expands to include matters of attitude formation and attitude change, is large and well explored. So is the related field of *public-opinion measurement*, in which there exists both a highly developed technology and a massive body of substantive knowledge. Then there is the socially significant matter of *prejudice*. Much is known about the roots and forms of prejudice and methods for containing its socially disruptive power. Finally, there is the problem of *delinquency*, about which there is an increasing body of knowledge.

SUMMARY

1. Social psychology is the study of individual behavior in a social setting, or of the

interaction of the whole individual with other whole individuals.

2. There are many evidences of social influences on the behavior of the individual; there are many aspects of culturally determined similarities in many segments of personality; there are group similarities and differences in voting behavior; there are social influences in the performance of simple tasks and in making judgments; there are social influences producing conformity.

3. The social psychologist finds it desirable to study the social environment in which behavior occurs. He can do this through examining the functions of society. All societies perform certain functions in order to ensure their own survival and integrity; these functions include provision for (a) an adequate relationship with the environment, (b) sexual recruiting and functioning, (c) role differentiation and assignment, (d) shared cognitive orientation, (e) a system of communication, (f) shared goals, (g) regulated means for pursuing goals, (h) regulation of affect, (i) socialization of new members, and (j) control of disruptive behavior.

4. Key concepts for the social psychologist are those of social norms, social roles, and social attitudes.

5. Social norms are standards or rules that are devised and enforced in group situations: there are perceptual norms, illustrated by the research on the autokinetic phenomena; and behavioral norms, illustrated by research on conformity behavior.

6. Children, in learning norms, can be observed to pass through autistic and absolutistic orientation and on to a relativistic one.

7. Researches on industrial and other working groups have demonstrated the operation of group norms; the procedures of decision making bear on the formulation and effectiveness of group norms.

8. A social role is an organized pattern of norms concerning the behavior of individuals who perform certain functions in the group.

All groups define roles and, through expectancies, see that roles are performed.

9. An attitude is a readiness to respond positively or negatively to objects or symbols in the environment. There has been much research on attitudes, their measurement and operation, but only specimens of that research are reviewed in the present chapter. These deal with the effect of cognitive dissonance on behavior.

10. Small groups have been extensively studied by social psychologists because they are amenable to experimental investigations and because the small group may constitute a microcosm.

11. Small groups of many kinds show uniformities in functioning; many groups face problems of communication, including problems of orientation, evaluation, and control; they also face problems of organization and maintenance.

12. As it lives through its life, the small group first faces problems of orientation, then problems of evaluation, then problems of control.

13. In many small groups the same kinds of interactions occur with about the same frequency; there are expressive-integrative acts, instrumental task-relevant acts, questioning task-relevant acts, and negative expressive-integrative acts.

14. Small groups differentiate and define a variety of roles; two leadership roles frequently differentiated are (a) the role of the idea-giving, task-oriented person and (b) the role of the comfort-giving and morale-oriented person.

15. The search for leadership traits has not been conspicuously successful; the traits of leaders in one situation are not the traits that appear in leaders in another situation. There is some relationship between the behavior of the leader and the dimensions of the group in which leadership occurs. There may be profit in thinking about leadership in terms of the followers' needs that vary from situation to situation.

16. Probably the most productive view of leadership is one in which it is seen against a background of group functioning; the skills and attributes that the group needs or that the followers want vary from one situation to another. Two kinds of leadership functions appear in many group situations: (a) the function of idea giving or problem solving and (b) the function of maintaining morale.

17. Organizations and groups vary widely with respect to the distribution of leadership functions. Autocratic groups, with high concentration of leadership or power, and democratic groups, with wide distribution of power, function differently.

RESEARCH REPORTS

GROUP INFLUENCE ON INDIVIDUAL BEHAVIOR [*]

It has been asserted that a group almost always exerts a conservative influence on an individual, so that solutions to problems in group settings are likely to be duller, more routine, less creative, and less risky than are solutions found by individuals. It has been argued, for example, that the widespread use of committees and teams in the management of business and other enterprises always and inexorably limits the degree of boldness and risk taking. The present study attempted (1) to evaluate experimentally the effect of the group influence on the willingness of individuals to take risks; (2) to examine the role of individual influence on the risk-taking decisions of a group; (3) to determine whether there are sex differences in response to group influence on risk taking; (4) to determine whether a member's compliance with the group decision with respect to risk taking extends to his acceptance of risky decisions when he responds later as an individual; and (5) to determine how long-lasting are the group effects, if any, on individual behavior.

The experiment involved fourteen all-male groups and fourteen all-female groups of college students, with six subjects assigned to each of the twenty-eight groups. At the beginning of the experiment, subjects were administered a questionnaire containing descriptions of twelve hypothetical situations, responses to which could be scored on the basis of indications of the subjects' willingness to take risks.

A specimen item on this questionnaire was as follows: "An electrical engineer may stick with his present job at a modest but adequate salary, or take a new job offering considerably more money but no long-term security." Answers to this and eleven other items could be scored with respect to magnitude of the risk the subject was willing to take. Earlier researchers had indicated that this scale gave a reliable index of personal tendency to take risks and that the scale had satisfactory construct validity.

At the beginning of the experiment, the six subjects in any group were requested to read the instructions to the questionnaire and then, after being instructed about the meaning of the items, to respond to all twelve items. The six subjects were then asked to move together in a discussion group. They were each given another copy of the questionnaire and, under careful instructions, were now asked to discuss each question and to arrive at a unanimous decision on each. Most groups were able to come to unanimous decisions, although they were occasionally deadlocked concerning the desirable amount of risk to take with respect to one of the twelve items on the scale.

After this discussion was finished, the experimenter asked the group members to spread apart for some further individual work and to take their questionnaires with them. He then asked them to go back over the twelve items of the questionnaire and to indicate their own personal decisions. It was the experimenters' hypothesis that these ratings on an individual basis would indicate whether the discussion process had influenced covert individual acceptance as well as public compliance.

After this discussion was finished, the experimenter asked the individuals, each subject was asked to rank everyone in the group, including himself, on how much each individual had influenced the final group decision. Then each subject was asked to make a similar rating of how much he would like to become better acquainted with each member of his group. (Each group was composed of people who had not had a prior opportunity to become acquainted with one another.) The subjects were all sworn to secrecy, on the grounds that the experiment would be continued and would involve

[*] Michael A. Wallach, Nathan Kogan, and Daryl Bem, Group influence on individual risk taken, *J. abn. soc. Psychol.*, 1962, **65**, 75–86.

other group problems on the campus. Then, to round things off, a representative sample of the subjects came back, two to six weeks later, to take the questionnaire again, on an individual basis.

The control group of the experiment was formed in the same way as were the experimental groups and was treated in much the same way. Members of the control group were given an original individual-questionnaire session and a second individual-decision session in which they were asked to reconsider their earlier responses to the questionnaire. They did not participate in any discussion of the proper degree of risk to take.

SIGNIFICANCE OF CONSERVATISM DIFFERENCE BETWEEN MEAN OF PRE-DISCUSSION INDIVIDUAL DECISIONS FOR A GROUP'S MEMBERS AND GROUP'S CONSENSUAL DECISION: MALES

Item	Mean difference [a]	Number of groups [b]	t
All combined	−9.4	14	6.46§
1	−1.0	14	4.34§
2	−0.2	14	<1.00
3	−1.1	13	2.19*
4	−1.8	13	6.18§
5	+0.1	13	<1.00
6	−1.2	13	3.35†
7	−2.0	14	9.64§
8	−1.1	14	1.97
9	−1.0	10	3.67†
10	−0.4	13	<1.00
11	−1.1	12	4.37‡
12	+0.8	11	2.34*

[a] A negative difference signifies a risky shift, a positive difference signifies a conservative shift.
[b] Number of groups for an item is less than fourteen when one or more groups deadlocked on that item. Any deadlocked item is, of course, not included when scores for all items combined are calculated.
* $p < .05$.
† $p < .01$.
‡ $p < .005$.
§ $p < .001$.

The table gives the results of the experiment for the fourteen groups of male subjects. The left-hand column of the table presents the individual items on the questionnaire as well as the total mean score on the test of risk taking. The mean differences registered in the second column are differences between risk scores before and after group decision; minus signs represent an increased willingness to take risks. The third column indicates the statistical significance of the differences from prediscussion to post-discussion situations, with respect to total items and to the separate

items. It is clear that after group decision there is increased willingness to take risks.

The same results obtained for the female groups, indicating that the results cannot be accounted for on the basis of a group facilitation of a male role, which might be construed to involve a bold and risky orientation to decisions.

When the same kind of analysis was made of the control groups, on two separate responses to the questionnaire, there were no significant differences between the first and second sessions in the degree of expressed riskiness.

With respect to influence of individual members, the data indicate that members of any given group agree, to an extent considerably larger than chance expectation, in their ratings of the influence of individual members. They similarly agreed on the popularity of group members—on whether or not they would like to become better acquainted with an individual.

When the average rated influence of individuals is correlated with the risk-taking scores for the same subjects, there are positive r's of significant magnitude. While a degree of rated influence on an individual correlated with the rated popularity of that individual, the procedure of partial correlation showed that the popularity of an individual is not related to the degree of risk taking. The experimenters do not know exactly how to interpret this relationship. It may be due to the fact that high risk takers exert more influence simply because the group turns out to move toward greater risk taking; they may be leaders after the fact. Or it may be that high risk takers are those who are more likely to take more initiative in social situations.

When a random sample of the original subjects were brought back after two to six weeks for a "post post-discussion" session, it became clear that the results produced as a result of the group discussion persisted over this length of time. The risk-taking propensities of these people at this delayed session were still significantly different from those displayed before the group discussion.

ATTITUDE CHANGE THROUGH PRESTIGE SUGGESTION *

It is a frequently encountered hypothesis that the higher the prestige of an individual making a suggestion, the greater the likelihood that the

---

* Donald H. Blandford and Edward E. Sampson, Induction of prestige suggestion through classical conditioning, J. abn. soc. Psychol., 1964, 69, 332–337.

suggestion will be accepted and will lead to a change of attitude. The present research uses prestige suggestion, through a procedure involving experimental conditioning, to change attitudes toward nonsense words used as stimuli.

In format and design, the experiment replicated an earlier one performed by other investigators. In the earlier experiment, six nonsense syllables, YOF, XEH, LAJ, WUH, QUG, GIW, were presented on a screen; and, contiguously with each presentation, a word, with either favorable, neutral, or negative connotation, was pronounced orally by the experimenter, with the subjects required to repeat each word aloud immediately following the experimenter's pronouncing it. It was earlier demonstrated that a nonsense syllable that is repeatedly associated with positive words will come to elicit a positive response from subjects. Similarly, a syllable associated with negative words will later elicit a negative reaction.

The subjects in the present experiment were eighty students, forty males and forty females, from courses in elementary psychology. They were given some early training in "learning" nonsense syllables and in the related "learning" of lists of auditorily presented words. For the key part of the experiment, after a training period that familiarized them with the procedure but disguised the purpose of the experiment, the individuals were presented with the six nonsense syllables cited above, each separately projected visually onto a screen. Each time a nonsense syllable was projected, the experimenter pronounced the name of a well-known individual, who, on the basis of previous ratings by undergraduate students, was known to be either positive or neutral or negative in tone. There were 18 critical positive names, 18 critical negative names, and 72 noncritical names (familiar to the students but relatively neutral). Two of the nonsense syllables were selected, without the subjects' awareness, as the critical nonsense syllables. Every time the syllable YOF was projected, the experimenter pronounced a positive name, such as Winston Churchill, John F. Kennedy, George Washington, or Albert Einstein. Every time the nonsense syllable YEX appeared, one of the negative names was pronounced: e.g., Joseph Stalin, Jimmy Hoffa, Adolph Hitler, Hermann Göring. When any one of the other nonsense syllables was projected, one of the neutral names was pronounced. The subject ostensibly was required to learn both the nonsense syllables and the names.

When each of the six syllables had been pre-

sented eighteen times, the subjects were asked to work on a booklet containing seven pages, with each page requesting that he rate, on a number of seven-point positive-negative scales, his reactions to each of the nonsense syllables. The crucial data consisted of his ratings of the two nonsense syllables YOF and XEH.

An analysis of the data indicated a strong conditioning effect between the nonsense syllables and the positive and negative names associated with them. YOF had been associated eighteen times with eighteen "good" names; YOF became good. YEX was associated eighteen times with bad names, and YEX became a bad word. The subjects were not aware of what was happening to them in the experiment.

Both males and females showed the conditioning effect, but females seem to be more extremely affected by the prestige of the name. Compared to men, they rated a nonsense syllable more negatively when it was associated with negative names and more positively when it was associated with positive names.

RESEARCH ON MALE AND FEMALE ROLES [*]

The individual must learn his role if he is to participate actively and functionally in society. A vital role is the sex role. In the literature one can find a number of statements that the adolescent, as he moves from childhood toward adulthood, must establish his adult sex role in order to have a feeling of ego identity. He must perceive himself as essentially the same person from one time to another and in a variety of situations; he must have evidence that others perceive him as essentially the same person over time; and he must build up a confidence that his perception of himself corresponds to others' perception of him. If he does all of this, he—or she—will move with confidence and comfort into the proper pattern of roles, including the sex role.

The present study attempts to throw empirical light on these assertions by examining the relation between the masculinity of behavior of late adolescent males and the perceived role consistency of those males. The study also deals with similar phenomena in female behavior, but less confidently.

There were two measures employed in this study. First was a measure of masculinity-femi-

[*] Alfred B. Heilbrun, Jr., Conformity to masculinity-femininity stereotypes and ego identity in adolescents, *Psychol. Reports* (1964), 14, 351–357.

ninity, a measure composed of a standard Adjective Check List, which asks the individual to check a variety of self-descriptive adjectives. The 54 adjectives on this list had been properly scaled and standardized on a college population. High scores on the scale indicate higher masculinity for both sexes, while lower scores indicate greater femininity. Role consistency (RC) was measured by having each subject rank himself on twenty descriptive adjectives; the subject was asked to imagine himself in a series of eight interpersonal situations and in each one to rate each of the adjectives from most to least characteristic of himself. For example, each S was to rank himself with respect to "Humorous," in the following situations: with someone in whom there is a sexual interest, with an acquaintance he doesn't care much about, with an employer, with a child, with a mother or mother figure, with a father figure, with a close male (or female) friend, with someone he or she would like to know better. The performance on this test could be given a quantitative designation, ranging between .00 and 1.00, with higher values indicating greater perceived role consistency over a variety of interpersonal situations. The experimenter regarded scores on this test as a direct measure of one aspect of what has been defined as *ego identity*—the aspect bearing on the individual's perception of himself as the same person from one time to another and from one situation to another.

The subjects, 54 male and 61 female volunteers from undergraduate classes at the University of Iowa, took both of the above tests. For an analysis of the results, the males were divided into two groups: those who fell above the college-male mean on masculinity-femininity, and those who were below the mean. The females were separated into three groups: (1) those falling at least a half sigma below the college mean on masculinity-femininity (highly feminine), (2) those with scores at least a half sigma above the mean (low

in femininity), and (3) those falling in between (moderately feminine).

Results showed that highly masculine males were higher in RC than were the males who were low in masculinity, and these results are statistically significant. Females who were either high or low in femininity had higher scores on RC. They could either be high in femininity or low in femininity and have more perceived consistency of role. But those who were in the middle range with respect to femininity had lower scores on the RC instrument.

These results seem to be explicable in terms of social reinforcements for role behaviors. The experimenter was inclined to the interpretation that highly masculine behavior on the part of late-adolescent boys conforms to approved social patterns and hence leads to social reinforcement; also, this behavior tends to be the same from situation to situation and is likely to be perceived by the individual himself as the same from situation to situation. Social reinforcement, then, stabilizes the self-image of the more masculine adolescent boy. The results for the females in this study are more difficult to interpret, but perhaps can be dealt with in terms of the changing role of women in society. It is still possible for them to be highly feminine in a traditional kind of way and to win social rewards; and, through the reinforcing effect of repeated rewards, they work out a consistent self-concept. Or they can be relatively active and masculine and still be socially rewarded, and in this way work out a satisfying and consistent pattern. But girls in between the more masculine and the more feminine perhaps mix elements of both patterns into their behavior and hence have a somewhat confused image of themselves.

(For evidence on the future consequences for personality of the adolescent's consistent and masculine self-concept, see the research reading presented at the end of the chapter on Personality.)

SUGGESTED READINGS

Cartwright, Dorwin, and Alvin Zander. *Group dynamics: Research and theory,* 2nd ed. Evanston, Ill.: Row, Peterson, 1960.

Hovland, C. I., and I. L. Janis, eds. *Personality and persuasibility.* New Haven: Yale University Press, 1959.

Hsu, F. L. K., ed. *Psychological anthropology: Approaches to culture and personality.* Homewood, Ill.: Dorsey, 1961.

Krech, David, R. S. Crutchfield, and E. L. Ballachey. *Individual in society: A textbook of social psychology.* New York: McGraw-Hill, 1962.

Lazarsfeld, P. F., Bernard Berelson, and Hazel Gaudet. *The people's choice: How the voter makes up his mind in a presidential campaign,* 2nd ed. New York: Columbia University Press, 1948.

Maccoby, Eleanor E., T. M. Newcomb, and E. L. Hartley, eds. *Reading in social psychology,* 3rd ed. New York: Holt, 1958.

Sanford, F. H., and E. J. Capaldi. *Advancing psychological science. Vol. III: Research in developmental, personality, and social psychology.* Belmont, Calif.: Wadsworth, 1964.

Schachter, Stanley. *The psychology of affiliation: Experimental studies of the sources of gregariousness.* Stanford, Calif.: Stanford University Press, 1951.

GLOSSARY *

A

ABCISSA. The horizontal or base reference axis of a two-dimensional chart or graph.

ABSOLUTE THRESHOLD. The lowest intensity of a stimulus that can be sensed under optimal conditions of observation; in reference to neural transmission, the minimal intensity that can produce an impulse.

ACCOMMODATION. Automatic adjusting of shape of the lens of the eye in order to focus the image of an object on the retina.

ACETYLCHOLINE. A chemical substance that probably facilitates the passage of a nerve impulse from one neuron to another.

ACHIEVEMENT. Actual performance; used in reference to scores on tests, to performance in school, and to performance on laboratory tasks.

* A number of the definitions included here are adaptations from H. B. English and A. C. English, *A Comprehensive Dictionary of Psychological and Psychoanalytical Terms* (New York: Longmans, Green & Co., Inc., 1958).

ACHIEVEMENT MOTIVE. An inferred condition of the organism, leading it to strive for high standards of performance.

ACHIEVEMENT TEST. A measure of proficiency level or performance in a given subject matter or field.

ACQUISITIVENESS. A condition of the organism which leads that organism to acquire objects having no apparent biological utility.

ACROMEGALY. An overgrowth of the hands, arms, jawbone, feet, and chest; caused by oversecretion of pituitary growth hormone.

ADAPTATION. The change of sensitivity with changing conditions of stimulation.

ADDITIVE COLOR MIXTURE. The mixture of lights with wavelengths of different hues being added together.

ADJUSTING. The process whereby the whole organism gains satisfactions for its motives.

ADJUSTMENT. The relationship between the motivated organism and the environment.

ADOLESCENCE. The period from the beginning of puberty to the attainment of maturity.

ADRENAL ANDROGENS. Hormones secreted by the adrenal cortex regulating the development of secondary sex characteristics, primarily of the male.

ADRENAL GLANDS. Ductless endocrine glands located at upper end of kidneys.

ADRENAL MEDULLA. Inner core of the adrenal gland; secretes hormones adrenaline and nor-adrenaline.

ADRENALIN(E). Hormone secreted by the adrenal medulla; causes various bodily changes, including an increase in blood sugar, a rise in blood pressure, and an increased pulse rate.

AERIAL PERSPECTIVE. Term used to refer to the cue of clearness, or the lack of it, in perceiving depth and distance.

AFFERENT. Incoming; used primarily in connection with nerve fibers and impulses.

AFFILIATIVENESS (AFFILIATIVE NEED). The need to be associated with another person or persons.

AFTERIMAGE. Prolongation, renewal, or reversal of a sensory experience after the stimulus has been removed.

AGGRESSION. A general term applying to hostile or attacking behavior or to impulses of a hostile variety.

AGNOSIA. Loss of memory for the meaning of objects, usually due to brain injury.

ALL-OR-NONE LAW. The principle that a nervous impulse is either evoked at full strength or not at all.

ALPHA RHYTHM. Electrical rhythm, of about ten oscillations per second, typical of the brain during normal wakefulness.

AMOEBA. One of the simplest of single-celled organisms.

AMPULLA. An enlargement at the base of each semi-circular canal, containing hairlike structures.

AMYGDALA. A division of the brain located in the lower frontal lobe of the cortex; functions as a center for control of emotional and motivational process.

ANALYSAND. A person undergoing psychoanalysis.

ANDROGEN. Male hormone regulating sexual development.

ANIMISM. The doctrine or belief that various classes of objects—or all objects—have souls or wills of their own.

ANOXIA. Lack of sufficient oxygen.

ANTHROPOLOGY. In general terms, the study of man; the anthropologist may study the physi-cal or cultural aspects of man or may focus on man's earliest existence.

ANTHROPOMORPHISM. The ascribing of human characteristics to nonhuman objects.

ANVIL. One of three bones in the middle ear (the others are the hammer and the stirrup) which, as a system of levers, transmit vibrations from the eardrum to the inner ear.

ANXIETY. Generalized feelings of worry and apprehension, present in many conflict situations and in neurosis.

ANXIETY REACTION. Abnormal reaction pattern characterized by extremely fearful expectations or apprehensions.

APHAGIA. Loss of appetite.

APHASIA. A disturbance of linguistic functioning, usually caused by brain damage; may be either sensory or motor or both.

APPROACH-APPROACH CONFLICT. A conflict arising where there are tendencies to move toward two different goals at the same time.

APPROACH-AVOIDANCE CONFLICT. Conflict in which a person is both attracted to and repelled by the same object or situation.

APRAXIA. Loss of memory for a series of motor responses.

APTITUDE. Potential capacity to learn, inferred from performance.

ARCHETYPE. The original model or type.

ASSOCIATION. A working connection between a stimulus or stimulus situation and a particular response.

ASSOCIATION AREAS. General term for areas of cerebral cortex involved in such complex functions as learning and memory.

ASSOCIATION FIBERS. Short fibers serving as internal connectors within the cortex.

ASSOCIATIONISM. In learning, the theory that learning is a process of forming associative bonds or connections between stimuli and responses. In the history of psychology, the theory that mental life is structured through the lawful association of ideas.

ASSOCIATIVE THINKING. Relatively free and undirected thinking, as in free association or dreams.

ASTHENIC. One of Kretschmer's body types, characterized by a frail, thin physique, supposedly showing a tendency to dementia praecox or schizophrenia.

ASTIGMATISM. A defect in the curvature of the lens and/or the cornea, so that the image of any object is distorted.

ATHLETIC. One of Kretschmer's body types; the square and muscular physique.

ATTITUDE. An enduring, learned readiness to behave in a consistent way toward a given object or class of objects.

ATTITUDE SCALE. A method of measuring attitudes, so that the strength of positive or negative readiness to respond can be assessed.

AUDITION. The sense or act of hearing.

AUDITORY. Pertaining to the sense of hearing.

AUDITORY CANAL. The canal leading from the outside of the head to the eardrum.

AUTISTIC THINKING. Thinking which is determined primarily by the individual's needs or desires; daydreaming.

AUTOKINETIC PHENOMENON. The apparent movement of a single stationary point of light in a dark room.

AUTONOMIC NERVOUS SYSTEM. The part of the nervous system that regulates bodily activities (e.g., visceral changes) occurring during emotions; the two parts of the autonomic system are the sympathetic and the parasympathetic.

AVOIDANCE-AVOIDANCE CONFLICT. A conflict arising when one is placed in a situation requiring two opposite withdrawal responses.

AVOIDANCE CONDITIONING. A response to a cue that is instrumental in avoiding a painful experience.

AXON. Long fiber leading from the cell body of the neuron, terminating in endbrushes.

B

BABINSKI REFLEX. Automatic upward extension of the toes, when the sole of the foot is lightly stroked.

BASAL METABOLISM. The energy expenditure necessary for minimum vital functioning of the body.

BASILAR MEMBRANE. A delicate membrane in the cochlea of the inner ear; functions in translating vibrations into neural impulses.

BASKET NERVE ENDINGS. Structures at the roots of hairs on the body—sense organ for pressure or touch.

BEHAVIOR. Observable activities of an organism.

BEHAVIORAL NORMS. Socially accepted and enforced standards of behavior.

BEHAVIORAL SCIENCE. Any science concerned with the behavior of man and the lower organisms; includes social anthropology, psychology, sociology, and some aspects of biology, economics, political science, and history.

BEHAVIORISM. Viewpoint maintaining that psychology should be limited to the study of objectively observable behavior.

BIMODAL CURVE. Graphic representation of the distribution of measures in which the cases cluster around two extremes or modes rather than around a single mode in the middle.

BINOCULAR. Pertaining to the use of the two eyes at the same time.

BINOMIAL THEOREM. A theorem concerning the algebra of chance and involving the expansion of the binomial $(q + p)^n$, which can yield an approximation to the normal probability curve.

BLIND SPOT. Area in the retina, where the optic nerve enters, where there is no vision; an area in the visual field in which there is no vision.

BODY-TYPE THEORIES. Theories that attempt to relate the individual's body build to attributes of his personality.

BRAIN POTENTIALS. Brain waves; minute rhythmic electrical discharges given off by the cerebral cortex; measured by the electroencephalograph.

BRIGHTNESS. Quality of visual sensation determined by the amplitude (intensity) of the light waves.

BRIGHTNESS CONSTANCY. Phenomenon in perception in which the organism sees an object as having a constant brightness even though the physical illumination changes. Snow, for example, is white at night.

C

CARDIAC MUSCLE. Heart muscle, resembling striated muscles.

CASTRATION. Surgical removal of the testes.

CELL BODY (NEURON). Single cell—the fundamental unit of a structure of nerve tissue.

CENTILE SCORE. Point below which a given per cent of the cases of a distribution fall; the median is the fiftieth centile.

CENTRAL NERVOUS SYSTEM. The part of the nervous system that includes the brain and the spinal cord.

CENTRAL TENDENCY. Tendency of measures, especially in normal distributions, to mass around the center of the distribution; the mean, median, and mode are measures of central tendency.

CEPHALOCAUDAL SEQUENCE. The head-to-tail sequence in growth.

CEREBELLUM. A division of the brain, whose function is the receiving and relaying of both incoming and outgoing messages having to do with motor coordination.

CEREBRAL CORTEX. A large mass of gray matter, part of the telencephalon, lying in folds near the interior surface of the skull; the part of the brain involved in higher mental processes.

CEREBROTONIA. One of Sheldon's temperamental variables; characterized by unsociability, susceptibility to pain, unadventurousness; associated with the ectomorph.

CHLORETONE. Trade name of drug chlorobutanol, a hypnotic, sedative, and anticonvulsant.

CHROMOSOMES. Small bodies that contain genes responsible for hereditary traits, occurring in pairs in organic cells.

CILIARY MUSCLES. Muscles of accommodation attached to the lens, adjusting the shape of the lens according to the distance of an object so that the object is in focus on the retina.

CLASSICAL CONDITIONING. Simple learning in which a neutral stimulus, by association with a biologically adequate stimulus, comes to evoke responses formerly given only to the biologically adequate stimulus.

CLIENT-CENTERED THERAPY. A process whereby the individual learns to examine experiences and to revise the structure of self so as to establish a consistent and meaningful relation with past experience. Carl Rogers is its chief proponent.

CLINICAL PSYCHOLOGY. A branch of psychology that deals with the psychological knowledge and practice employed in helping a client who has some behavior or mental disorder.

COCHLEA. Spiral bony tube in the inner ear; contains the basilar membrane and other delicate structures involved in hearing.

COCHLEAR CANAL. The middle canal of the three canals in the cochlea.

COEFFICIENT OF CORRELATION. A numerical statement of the strength of the tendency of two or more variables to vary concomitantly.

COGNITIVE DISSONANCE. The condition that exists when one holds beliefs or attitudes that disagree with each other.

COLLECTIVE UNCONSCIOUS. That part of the individual's unconscious which is held by some theorists to be inherited and which the individual shares with other members of the species.

COLLOID. Any substance in a state of fine dispersion.

COLOR BLINDNESS. Visual defect in which the individual is unable to distinguish between hues that appear different to people with normal vision.

COLOR CONSTANCY. Phenomenon in which colors of an ordinary object are relatively independent of changes of illumination or of other viewing conditions.

COLOR WHEEL. A schematic diagram showing relationships among hues.

COMMISSURAL FIBERS. Long fibers that connect one side of the cortex with the other.

COMPENSATION. A term used to describe the overemphasis on one type of behavior in order to cover up felt deficiencies in other areas of behavior.

COMPLEMENTARY COLORS. Two colors that are opposite on the color wheel and that, when combined, yield gray.

COMPLEXITY. One of the physical characteristics of a light wave or sound wave. In vision, it is related to saturation; in hearing, to timbre.

COMPROMISE. A response to frustration, in which the individual partially gives in to each of two conflicting tendencies.

CONCEPT. A learned response to a common property of a variety of stimuli; concepts can serve to mediate problem-solving behavior and, when labeled, can be used as symbols.

CONDITIONED RESPONSE. A learned response to a stimulus not originally capable of producing the response.

CONDITIONED STIMULUS. A previously neutral stimulus which, through association with an unconditioned stimulus, has become capable of producing a conditioned response.

CONDITIONING. A general term, referring to simple learning, in which a new stimulus comes to evoke an old response or one response is selected out of an array of responses; includes classical conditioning and instrumental (or operant) conditioning.

CONDUCTION DEAFNESS. Deafness produced when vibrations are not conducted adequately to the cochlea.

CONES. One of the two kinds of receptor cells in the retina, sensitive to both hue and brightness; primarily most effective in daylight conditions.

CONFLICT. The state of being simultaneously motivated by incompatible or mutually exclusive tendencies.

CONNECTORS. Biological structures, primarily nerve cells, that connect receptors with effectors.

CONTEXT. Surrounding conditions that influence our perceptions or cognitions.

CONSTRUCT. A concept, defined in terms of observable events, used to summarize or to account for regularities or relationships in data.

CONTROL. Deliberate arrangement of experimental or research conditions so that observed effects, if any, can be directly traced to a known variable or variables.

CONVERSION REACTION. Neurotic reactions in which extreme anxiety is "converted" into functional symptoms in organs or parts of the body—e.g., hysterical blindness, deafness, paralysis.

CORNEA. The transparent outside layer of the front of the eye.

CORPUS CALLOSUM. The part of the brain that connects the two hemispheres of the cerebrum.

CORRELATION (COVARIATION). The tendency to concomitant variation. The degree to which two (or more) variables vary together.

CORTEX. See CEREBRAL CORTEX.

CORTICALIZATION. The progress in evolutionary development of cortical control over the functions of the remainder of the nervous system.

CRANIAL NERVES. The twelve nerves, some sensory and some motor, that connect directly with the brain.

CRETINISM. Retarded development caused by thyroid deficiency during infancy or early childhood. Often accompanied by mental deficiency.

CROSS-SECTIONAL METHOD. The study of the relationship between variables, such as age and intelligence, in two or more groups simultaneously available; contrasts with the longitudinal method, in which the relationship is studied in the same group over a period of time.

CULTURE. The pattern of customs, norms, and traditions characteristic of a people or a social group.

CUTANEOUS SENSE. Any of the senses whose receptors lie in or near the skin.

D

DARK ADAPTATION. Increase in sensitivity of the eye when the eye remains in the dark.

DEATH WISH. Psychoanalytic term for the hostile and destructive impulses lying behind behavior.

DECIBEL. A logarithmic unit for measuring sound intensity.

DEFENSE MECHANISM. A reaction to frustration or conflict that defends the person against anxiety.

DELUSIONS. False beliefs, usually of grandeur or persecution; often diagnostic of psychosis.

DENDRITES. Branched fibers occurring at receiving end of a neuron.

DENDRITIC POTENTIAL. The electrical charge constituting the "constant state of excitation" of the dendrites.

DEPENDENT VARIABLE. The variable in which the changes are dependent on the changes in the independent variable or variables.

DEPRESSIVE REACTION. Neurotic behavior resulting in depression, produced by an actual event such as the loss of a loved one.

DEPTH PERCEPTION. Perception of three-dimensionality and of the distance of objects.

DESCRIPTIVE STATISTICS. Statistics used for the purpose of describing rather than analyzing arrays of data.

DETERMINISM. Belief that the feelings and actions are determined by factors beyond one's control; belief that all behavior is due to natural causes and hence is predictable.

DETOUR BEHAVIOR. Any indirect action that leads toward a goal when direct progress is obstructed.

DEUTERANOPE. A partially color-blind person who cannot distinguish red and green.

DIAGNOSTIC TEST. A test designed to discover and describe emotional or behavioral problems.

DICHROMATISM. A form of partial color blindness, in which there is sensitivity to only two colors, blue and yellow.

DIENCEPHALON. A division of the brain, containing the thalamus, hypothalamus, mammillary bodies, pituitary gland, and optic tracts.

DIFFERENTIAL THRESHOLD. The smallest difference between two stimuli that can be sensed.

DIMETHYL TRYPTAMINE. See PSYCHOTOMIMETIC DRUGS.

DIRECTED THINKING. Thought processes governed by a formulated goal.

DIRECTIVE THERAPY. Therapy in which the therapist tries, through diagnostic tests and interviews, to learn all he can about the patient's past and present adjustments, and thence to prescribe a course of action or remedy.

DISCRIMINATION. Differential response to two stimuli.

DISCRIMINATION DEAFNESS. Deafness (formerly called nerve deafness) due to damage either of nerves themselves or to delicate mechanisms in the cochlea.

DISPERSION. Scatter or variability of observations or measures; measured most often by the standard deviation.

DISPLACEMENT. The transfer of emotion from the person or object causing the emotion to another person or object considered "safer."

DISSOCIATIVE REACTION. Neurotic reactions to stress, in which entire episodes of life are repressed, as in amnesia, fugue, multiple personality.

DISTRIBUTED PRACTICE. Practice, in verbal or motor learning, that is arranged in relatively brief spaced periods.

DOMINANCE. Tendency to seek control over others.

DOMINANT GENE. A gene that produces an observable effect in the offspring when present, even though the gene pair also contains a recessive gene.

DOUBLE APPROACH-AVOIDANCE CONFLICT. A conflict in which each of two conflicting courses of action has its own positive and negative aspects.

DUCTLESS GLANDS. Glands that secrete their substances directly into the blood stream; endocrine glands.

DUPLICITY THEORY OF VISION. Theory based on the knowledge that there are two kinds of receptors differentially distributed in the retina.

DWARFISM. Underdevelopment produced by a deficiency of the pituitary growth hormone early in life.

DYSPLASTIC. One of Kretschmer's body types; not together with itself, having one type of build in one segment and another type somewhere else.

E

EARDRUM. A thin membrane separating the external auditory canal from the middle ear.

ECTOMORPHY. One of Sheldon's dimensions of body build, characterized by fragility and linearity; associated with cerebrotonic temperament.

EFFECTORS. The cells and structures with which the organism responds; include muscular and glandular cells.

EFFERENT. Outgoing, as in efferent nerve fibers running to the effectors.

EGO. In psychoanalytic theory, the rational problem-solving aspect of the personality; functions to reconcile the demands of the id with those of the superego; generally, the concept of *self*.

EGO INVOLVEMENT. Perception of a situation as having the possibility of threatening or enhancing one's self-concept.

EGO PSYCHOLOGY. A form or "school" of psychoanalytic psychology; puts more emphasis than does classical psychoanalysis on the significance and potency of the ego.

EIDETIC IMAGERY. Extremely detailed and realistic imagery; more common in children than in adults.

ELECTROENCEPHALOGRAPH (EEG). Instrument for recording the brain potentials or brain waves from the cerebral cortex.

ELECTROMAGNETIC RADIATION. A general term referring to a variety of physical changes in the environment; term includes light waves, radio waves, X rays, and cosmic rays.

ELECTROSHOCK. A form of convulsive therapy for mental illness; electric current passed through the brain produces instant unconsciousness and convulsions.

ELEMENTISTIC APPROACH. Analysis in terms of elementary units rather than patterns of organization.

EMBRYO. An unborn organism in early stages of development; for human beings, the embryonic period begins at conception and extends for a period of two months.

EMOTION. A complex response involving conscious experience and internal and overt physical responses, and tending to facilitate or to interfere with motivated behavior.

EMPIRICAL. Founded on proved, directly experienced facts such as those gained from experiment.

EMPIRICISM (BRITISH). In the history of psychology, the philosophical position that emphasized the importance of sense data for mental life.

ENCEPHALIZATION. The tendency for the major ganglion or connection center to be located at the head end of the organism.

ENDOCRINE GLANDS. See DUCTLESS GLANDS.

ENDOLYMPH. Liquid in the semicircular canals of the ampullae; related to sense of movement and sense of position in space.

ENDOMORPHY. One of Sheldon's dimensions of body build; characterized by a tendency toward roundness and softness; believed to be associated with viscerotonic temperament.

ENVIRONMENT. The sum of the external factors and conditions potentially capable of influencing an organism.

ENZYME. An organic catalyst substance serving to regulate certain processes in metabolism.

ESCAPE CONDITIONING. A form of instrumental conditioning, in which the organism learns a response that will enable him to get out of a place he prefers not to be in.

ESTROGEN. Female hormone produced by the ovaries; important for the development of both primary and secondary sexual characteristics of the female.

ETHNOCENTRISM. The tendency to exalt the superiority of the group to which one belongs and to judge outsiders by the standards of one's own group.

EVOLUTION. The theory that present animal and plant species have evolved or developed by descent, with modification, from other pre-existing species.

EXOCRINE GLANDS. Glands that secrete through ducts—e.g., salivary glands, tear glands.

EXPANSIVE. Free and unrestrained in feeling and imagination, and in verbal or bodily expressions.

EXPERIMENT. A definite arrangement of conditions under which events to be observed shall take place, with a view to determining relations between or among observed events.

EXPERIMENTAL DESIGN. The plan of an experiment with the aim of ensuring that obtained results can be meaningfully interpreted.

EXPERIMENTAL NEUROSIS. A severe disturbance of behavior produced by placing an animal in a situation where it must make impossible discriminations or face conflicts impossible to resolve.

EXPERIMENTAL PSYCHOLOGY. The investigation of psychological phenomena by experimental methods.

EXTENSOR. A muscle involved in stretching.

EXTINCTION. The procedure and/or the effect of presenting a conditioned stimulus without reinforcement; in general terms, the disappearance of a conditioned response.

EXTRINSIC MOTIVATION. The use of incentives that are capable of arousing action but have no inherent relationships to the task to be performed.

EXTROVERSION. An interest in and response to things outside oneself, rather than a concern with one's own thoughts and feelings.

EXTROVERT. Person who is interested in things outside himself, rather than in his own thoughts and feelings.

F

FACTOR ANALYSIS. The statistical technique of identifying and measuring the underlying variables, or factors, involved in a complex ability or trait or in a large variety of measures.

FACTORS. Functional units statistically derived, involved in a complex ability or trait, or in a large variety of measures.

FANTASY. A defensive withdrawal reaction, in which the individual escapes through daydreaming.

FARSIGHTEDNESS. A condition in which distant objects can be seen relatively more clearly than near ones.

FEEBLE-MINDEDNESS. A general term describing individuals who are mentally deficient. The term *mental deficiency* is preferred.

FEEDBACK. Returned information concerning the consequences of an act or event.

FETAL PERIOD. Period from two months after conception until birth.

FETUS. The unborn human organism from two months after conception until birth.

FISSURE OF ROLANDO. Vertical groove in the side of each hemisphere of the cortex; separates the frontal and parietal lobes; also known as the central fissure or central sulcus.

FISSURE OF SYLVIUS. Horizontal groove in the lateral surface of each hemisphere of the cortex; separates the temporal from the frontal and parietal lobes; also called the lateral fissure.

FLEXOR. A muscle involved in bending.

FOVEA. Central area of retina containing greatest density of cones but no rods; area of clearest daylight vision.

FRAME OF REFERENCE. A subjective standard or system of standards against which incoming experience is evaluated.

FRATERNAL TWINS. Twins who develop from two separate fertilized eggs; simultaneous siblings.

FREE ASSOCIATION. A technique used in psychoanalytic therapy requiring the client to give his mind free rein and to put into words every thought and feeling coming to him.

FREE-FLOATING ANXIETY. A chronic state of fear or foreboding which is unrelated to any specific situation but which can be activated by a wide variety of situations and activities.

FREE NERVE ENDINGS. Nerve endings that are not connected with any special receptor structures; found in skin, blood vessels, and other parts of the body; serve as receptors for pain and probably for pressure.

FREQUENCY. In audition and vision, the number of cycles per unit of time in a periodic vibration; in statistics, the number of cases or the number of measures in a given category or set; generally, the number of times a specified event occurs.

FREQUENCY DISTRIBUTION. A distribution showing the number of times a given measure occurs in a sample.

FRONTAL LOBE. Division of the cerebral cortex lying in front of the fissure of Rolando and above the fissure of Sylvius; functions primarily as center for complex associations.

FRUSTRATION. (1) The blocking of, or interference with, ongoing motivated behavior. (2) The emotional state resulting from being blocked, thwarted, or defeated.

FRUSTRATION TOLERANCE. The capacity to control emotional responses to frustration and to invest increased energy in adaptive pursuit of the goal.

FUNCTIONAL AUTONOMY. The tendency of a motive to become independent of the primary biological need from which it originated.

FUNCTIONALISM. Historical point of view in psychology which emphasized the study of the organism's total adjustment to its environment.

G

GALVANIC SKIN RESPONSE. Increase in voltage and/or change in electrical resistance of the skin occurring as a result of the autonomic influence on the sweat glands.

GANGLION (*Pl.* GANGLIA). A collection of nerve cells and synapses.

GANGLIONIC ORGANIZATION. An organization into a collection of nerve cells, synapses.

GENERALIZATION. In conditioning, the giving of the same response to new but similar stimuli or stimulus situations.

GENES. Elements, carried in the chromosomes, that determine the transmission of hereditary characteristics.

GENETICS. Branch of biology concerned with heredity and the transmission of hereditary characteristics.

GESTALT PSYCHOLOGY. An approach to psychology emphasizing organization, patterning, wholeness rather than elementistic analysis; opposed both to structuralism and behaviorism.

GIANTISM. Overdevelopment of the skeletal system caused by oversecretion of the pituitary growth hormone early in life.

GLOVE ANESTHESIA. An hysterical symptom involving an inability to feel anything over the whole area of the skin normally covered by a glove.

GOAL. Substance, object, or end state capable of satisfying a motive and toward which motivated behavior is directed.

GOLGI TENDON ORGAN. A nerve ending found at the juncture of tendon and muscle, and believed to be sensitive to tension.

GONADS. The sex glands (testes in male and ovaries in female).

GREGARIOUSNESS. Generally, descriptive of the tendency of organisms to seek out their kind and to live in groups; as a psychological motive, an inferred condition of the organism leading it to seek out the presence of others and to feel satisfaction in the company of others.

GROUP THERAPY. A form of psychological treatment, in which a number of emotionally disturbed people meet in a group with a therapist and, through social interaction, gain therapeutically useful experiences.

H

HABIT. Generally, almost any product of learning; more specifically, a learned stimulus-response sequence.

HALLUCINATIONS. False perceptions or perceptions occurring in the absence of sensory experience. Diagnostic of certain mental disorders.

HALO EFFECT. The influence of a general impression of a person on ratings or estimates of specific traits of that person.

HAMMER. The first of three connected bones in the ear which transmit vibrations from the eardrum to the oval window of the cochlea.

HEREDITY. Transmission of characteristics, from parents to offspring; also, genetic endowment.

HOLISTIC PSYCHOLOGIST. Psychologist who emphasizes the wholeness of the individual and the unity and organization of behavior.

HOMEOSTASIS. The maintenance of an optimal constancy or equilibrium in organic functioning.

HORMONES. Secretions of the ductless (endocrine) glands.

HUE. Quality of color sensation determined by the frequency or wavelength of the stimulus.

HUMORAL THEORY. Oldest known characterological theory, developed by Hippocrates, which states that human nature can be ascribed to the four "humors" or fluids of the body—blood, black bile, yellow bile, and phlegm.

HYPEROPIA. A condition in which light rays come to focus behind the retina instead of directly on it. Commonly called *farsightedness.*

HYPERPHAGIA. Pronounced overeating.

HYPNOSIS. An artificially produced trancelike state in which there is greatly increased suggestibility to the hypnotist.

HYPOTHALAMUS. A structure in the diencephalon serving as a primary brain center for autonomic functions.

HYPOTHESIS. A tentative explanation of a relationship.

HYSTERIA. Neurotic reaction in which there are physical symptoms that have no organic basis; a conversion reaction.

I

ID. In psychoanalytic theory, the primitive, instinctual part of the personality; characterized by unrestrained, untamed motivational impulses.

IDENTICAL TWINS. Twins who develop from the same fertilized egg (ovum) and have identical hereditary characteristics.

IDENTIFICATION. A process whereby the individual takes on the behavior of another significant individual and behaves as if he were that individual.

IDEOLOGY. An accepted system of ideas, beliefs, and attitudes.

IDIOT. A person with an IQ of 20 or less.

IMAGE. A representation in consciousness of sensory experience in the absence of the relevant sensory stimulation.

IMBECILE. A person with an IQ between 20 and 50.

IMPRINTING. Very rapid learning occurring in some animals at certain crucial stages of development.

INDEPENDENT VARIABLE. The variable that is manipulated or treated in an experiment to see what effect changes in that variable bring about in the variables regarded as dependent upon it.

INHIBITION. In connection with neural transmission, the phenomenon in which one chain of communication is stopped by the initiation of another.

INNER EAR. The internal portion of the ear, containing the cochlea, the vestibular sacs, and the semicircular canals.

INSIGHT. Understanding and evaluation of one's own mental processes; at a more general level, self-knowledge, accurate appraisal of one's own motives and abilities.

INSTINCT. An unlearned behavior pattern that appears in full form when there is an adequate stimulus.

INSTRUMENTAL (OPERANT) CONDITIONING. Simple learning in which one response, through reinforcement, is selected out of many responses to become instrumental in receiving a reward.

INSULIN SHOCK. Treatment in which an injection of insulin is used to produce convulsions and coma; used on some schizophrenic patients who, after shock, can sometimes participate in psychotherapy.

INTELLIGENCE. What intelligence tests test; a construct defined in terms of performance of a variety of tasks involving verbal comprehension, reasoning, manipulation of numbers, space visualization, and other factors; generally and loosely, complex mental ability.

INTELLIGENCE QUOTIENT (IQ). A measure of intelligence based on the ratio of mental age to chronological age. For the computation of IQ, mental age is measured by comparing an individual's score on an intelligence test with the scores of others of his same chronological age. His mental age and chronological age are the same if he makes an average score for his age group; his IQ is then 1.00, or 100, by the convention of removing the decimal. If his mental age is greater than his chronological age, his IQ is above 100.

INTENSITY. One of the physical characteristics of light and sound waves; in vision, related to the psychological dimensions of brightness; and in hearing, loudness; also spoken of as amplitude.

INTERVAL SCALE. A scale based on differences between two items or reference points.

INTRINSIC MOTIVATION. Motivation to work for rewards that are inherently related to the matter to be learned or the task to be performed.

INTROSPECTION. Technique of observing conscious

processes and states, as they relate to stimulus situations.

INTROVERT. A person who tends to withdraw into himself, to avoid other people, to value thoughts and feelings above action and objects.

INVOLUNTARY MUSCLES. Generally, the smooth muscles of organs and glands, not amenable to voluntary control.

IRRADIATION. The phenomenon in which an increase in the strength of the stimulus leads to the involvement of additional nerve fibers.

J

J-SHAPED CURVE. A distribution curve in the shape of a J or reversed J, in which many cases fall at the mode while the remainder fall on only one side of the mode, this number decreasing with the distance from the mode.

K

KINESTHESIS. An inclusive term for the muscle, tendon, and joint senses; referring to judgments about the movements and positions of the various parts of the body.

KRAUSE'S END BULB. One of the special structures of the skin; thought to be one kind of receptor for cold stimuli.

L

LANDOLT RINGS. An array of circles of various sizes and thickness of line, containing breaks of varying widths; used in testing visual acuity.

LATERAL GENICULATE BODY. Subdivision of the thalamus relaying messages from the eye.

LAW OF PARSIMONY. The use of the simplest kind of construct that involves the fewest unwarranted assumptions and still deals adequately with the data.

LEARNING. Relatively permanent changes in behavior that result from past experience (past response, practice).

LEARNING CURVE. A graphical representation of progress in learning; the graphic "life history of a skill."

LEARNING SET. A learned set to learn, observed when subjects become increasingly skillful in solving problems, each of which is new but all of which are of the same general type; a form of transfer of training.

LENS. The transparent structure of the eye which focuses light rays on the retina.

LEVEL OF ASPIRATION. The level of performance to which a person aspires.

LEVEL OF PERFORMANCE. The level of actual achievement rather than the level of aspiration.

LIBIDO. In psychoanalytic theory, a term symbolizing that part of the life wish concerning sexual or other affiliative relations with people.

LIE DETECTOR. See POLYGRAPH RECORDER.

LIFE WISH. In psychoanalytic theory, the urge to live, to create, to love.

LIMBIC SYSTEMS. Three functional circuits extending from the cortex downward to lower brain centers; one has to do with olfactory functions, one is undefined as to function, and the third —beginning at the septal area and extending downward to the amygdala—functions to facilitate and control emotion and motivation.

LINEAR PERSPECTIVE. The perception of faraway objects as close together and of nearby objects as far apart. Significant factor in depth perception.

LOBOTOMY. A brain operation in which the connections between the prefrontal areas of the brain and the lower brain centers are cut; formerly used in treating some forms of chronic psychosis but now used very rarely.

LONGITUDINAL METHOD. A method of study wherein the changes in the same person or persons are studied over a considerable period of time. Contrasts with cross-sectional method.

LOUDNESS. The sensed or psychological intensity of sound, determined by the amplitude of the sound wave.

LSD. See PSYCHOTOMIMETIC DRUGS.

M

MAMMILARY BODIES. Two small rounded bodies in the hypothalmus.

MASOCHIST. An individual characterized by a perversion in which erotic or sexual excitement is derived from being subjected to pain, whether by oneself or another.

MASSED PRACTICE. Practice which is continuous or in which trials follow one another without intervals between.

MATURATION. Development, resulting in changes in behavior, due to hereditary factors rather than to learning.

MAZE. A learning device consisting of runways with correct pathways and blind alleys.

MEAN. A measure of central tendency, also known as the average, calculated by dividing the sum of all the values by the number of cases in a statistical series.

MECHANICAL-APTITUDE TEST. A test designed to predict how well a person can learn to perform tasks involving the understanding and manipulation of mechanical devices.

MEDIAL GENICULATE BODY. Subdivision of the thalamus, relaying auditory messages.

MEDIAN. A measure of central tendency; the middle score of a sample, separating the upper half of the cases from the lower half.

MEISSNER CORPUSCLES. Small elliptical bodies in the hairless portions of the skin, containing nerve endings believed to be receptors for pressure or touch.

MEL. Unit of pitch.

MEMORY SPAN. Amount of material that can be repeated accurately after a single presentation.

MENTAL AGE (MA). The level of intellectual development; measured by comparing the child's performance on an intelligence test with the performance of children of the same chronological age.

MENTAL DEFICIENCY. Subnormal intellectual development.

MENTAL RETARDATION. The slowing up or suppression of intellectual development.

MESCALINE. Drug sometimes used in therapy, primarily to induce regression to childhood experiences. It also can produce symptoms like those of mental illness.

MESENCEPHALON. A division of the brain, often called the midbrain, the small bridge between the lower brain centers and the diencephalon.

MESOMORPHY. One of Sheldon's dimensions of body build, characterized by predominance of muscle and bone; believed to be associated with the somatotonic temperamental trait.

METABOLISM. A general term referring to the assimilation of food, storage and use of energy, the removal of waste.

METENCEPHALON. A division of the brain containing principally the cerebellum and the pons.

METRAZOL. A drug producing violent convulsions, formerly used in shock therapy.

MICROCOSM. A small replica of a large system.

MIDDLE EAR. A cavity containing a system of bones that link the eardrum to the cochlea.

MIGRAINE. A psychosomatic disorder marked chiefly by severe headaches accompanied by nausea.

MILLIMICRON. A unit of measurement used with electromagnetic radiations, including light waves. Symbol: mμ

MODE. A measure of central tendency; the most common value or class of values in a distribution.

MODEL. A mathematical, logical, or mechanical replica of a relationship or a system or a sequence of events so designed that a study of the model can yield some understanding of the real thing; e.g., electronic model of the brain.

MOLAR APPROACH. A way of studying behavior best defined in relative terms as contrasting with the molecular approach; may emphasize large rather than small units of behavior, a psychological rather than a physiological analysis, ends and goals rather than detailed responses.

MOLECULAR APPROACH. A way of studying behavior best defined in relative terms as contrasting with the molar approach; may emphasize physiological mechanisms rather than psychological variables, small rather than large units of behavior, separate responses rather than goals.

MONGOLOID. A type of feeble-mindedness characterized by Mongolian facial features; possibly caused by some condition affecting metabolism during prenatal development.

MONOCULAR. Pertaining to the use of one eye.

MONOZYGOTIC TWINS. Twins that develop from a single fertilized egg, thereby having identical heredity; identical twins.

MORON. A person with an IQ of 50–70.

MOTION PARALLAX. The cue to depth of distance perception involving the apparent movement of objects in the field of vision as the point of view is shifted laterally.

MOTIVATION. A general term referring to energizing states of the organism which direct it toward goals.

MOTIVE. An inferred condition of the organism serving to direct that organism toward a certain goal.

MOTOR NEURON. A neuron conducting impulses away from the central nervous system toward a muscle.

MUTATION. An abrupt change in the nature of a gene so that it reduplicates itself in a new form.

MYELENCEPHALON. Often called the medulla, connects the spinal cord to the brain; it contains centers that control breathing, heartbeat, and blood pressure.

MYELIN SHEATH. White coating found on most axons and dendrites of the nerve cells; not found on cells in "gray matter" of the brain.

MYOPIA. Nearsightedness; a condition of the eye in which the light rays focus in front of the retina instead of directly upon it.

N

NARCOSIS. Use of sleep-producing drugs in therapy.

NEED. In H. A. Murray's system, a motivational trait of the individual; for example, the need for autonomy, the need for achievement, the need for dependency, and, in the most general sense, any psychological or physiological condition of the organism serving as a motive.

NEED FOR ACHIEVEMENT (NEED ACHIEVE-MENT or *N ACH*). A condition of the organism leading it to seek high standards of excellence in performance.

NEGATIVE TRANSFER. The phenomenon in which slower learning in one situation is due to earlier learning in another situation.

NEO-FREUDIAN. Follower of Freud who departs in various ways from the latter's doctrines.

NEONATE. New-born infant.

NERVE FIBER. *See* AXON and DENDRITES.

NERVE IMPULSE. Electrochemical excitation passing along a nerve fiber or chain of nerve cells.

NERVOUS SYSTEM. The brain, spinal cord, and nerves.

NEUROLOGY. The scientific study of the brain and nervous system.

NEURON. A cell, consisting of dendrite, a cell body, and an axon; the basic structural unit of the nervous system.

NEUROSIS. A serious disorder of behavior that is not due to organic causes.

NEUROTIC. Tendency toward or characterized by neurosis.

NONDIRECTIVE THERAPY. Psychotherapy in which the patient takes the initiative in seeking to express his feelings and to gain insight, with the therapist serving as an accepting, understanding auditor. Also called *client-centered therapy*. Originated by Carl Rogers.

NONSENSE SYLLABLE. A meaningless but pronounceable combination of letters, used chiefly in memory experiments.

NORM. In psychological measurement, a standard against which individual performance can be quantitatively assessed; the norms for a psychological test describe the performance on that test of a known population of subjects, so that an individual's score can be compared with the scores of that population. In social psychology, a socially defined and enforced standard concerning the way the individual should interpret the world and/or behave in it.

NORMAL CURVE (NORMAL-DISTRIBUTION CURVE or NORMAL FREQUENCY CURVE). A symmetrical bell-shaped distribution curve in which few cases fall at either extreme, and with the greatest frequencies falling at or close to the mean; properties of the curve are used widely in making statistical inferences from samples.

NUCLEUS. A central part of a cell body.

NYSTAGMUS. A quick, jerky movement of the eyes.

O

OBJECTIVITY. (1) Freedom from bias; judgment unaffected by feeling. (2) In a test, the degree to which two or more persons can score a subject's responses and get the same results.

OBSESSION. Compulsive reaction; neurotic reaction characterized by recurring unwanted ideas (obsession); the feeling of strong urge to carry out undesired or ridiculous acts (compulsion)—e.g., handwashing, kleptomania.

OCCIPITAL LOBE. Portion of the cerebral cortex located at the back of the brain; primary center for vision.

OLFACTION. The sense of smell.

OLIGOPHRENIA. A form of mental deficiency produced by metabolic disorder.

OPERANT CONDITIONING. *See* INSTRUMEN-TAL CONDITIONING.

OPERATIONISM. A principle maintaining that the meaning of a term or variable is based on the operations used to measure or define it; in general terms, an emphasis on empirical or sense data in scientific research.

OPTIC NERVE. Nerve that carries impulses from the retina to the brain.

ORDINAL SCALE. A scale indicating order or succession; usually involves a procedure whereby persons, objects, or events are ranked according to the amount of some attribute.

ORDINATE. The vertical reference axis of a two-dimensional chart or graph.

ORGAN OF CORTI. A delicate structure in the

cochlea containing the receptor cells for hearing.

ORGAN INFERIORITY. The doctrine that real or imaginary defect or inferiority of any organ may cause a feeling of inferiority.

ORGANISM. A living being capable of maintaining itself as a system.

OSSICLES. In hearing, a chain of small bones in the middle ear that transmit the movements of the eardrum to the oval window of the cochlea; includes the hammer, the anvil, and the stirrup.

OTOLYTHS. Small solid objects in the fluid of the labyrinth of the inner ear; involved in the sensing of position and balance.

OUTER EAR. The visible part of the hearing mechanism.

OVARIES. Female sex glands.

OVERLEARNING. Learning in which practice proceeds beyond the point where the act can just be performed with the required degree of excellence.

OVUM. A cell in the ovary of the female which, when fertilized by the male sperm, normally develops into a new individual.

P

PAIRED-ASSOCIATE LEARNING. Learning to associate pairs of stimuli, most often verbal; the subject is required to respond with one word or syllable when presented with a stimulus word or syllable.

PANCREAS. An endocrine gland that secretes insulin; located along lower wall of the stomach.

PARAMECIUM. A single-celled animal.

PARASYMPATHETIC NERVOUS SYSTEM. A subdivision of the autonomic nervous system; it is concerned with the routine maintenance of the normal bodily functions.

PARATHYROID GLANDS. Endocrine glands located next to the thyroid glands of the neck, secreting hormones that regulate calcium and phosphorus balance in the body.

PARIETAL LOBE. A division of the cerebral hemisphere lying behind the central fissure of Rolando and in front of the occipital lobe and extending laterally about four-fifths of the way around the cortex.

PARSIMONY, LAW OF. See LAW OF PARSIMONY.

PERCEPTION. A process whereby the organism selects, organizes, and interprets sensory data available to it.

PERCEPTUAL NORMS. In social psychology, socially defined and enforced standards for perceiving the environment.

PERFORMANCE TEST. A test emphasizing nonverbal responses.

PERILYMPH. One of the fluids in the inner ear. See also ENDOLYMPH.

PERIPHERAL NERVOUS SYSTEM. Cell bodies and nerve fibers outside the spinal cord and brain.

PERSONALITY. The unique organization of enduring attributes of the human individual.

PHOBIA. An excessive and irrational fear; a neurotic reaction thought to involve a displacement of anxiety from a specific object or event so that the anxious response is now aroused by an object or event having only a symbolic connection with the original fear-producing situation.

PHYSIOLOGICAL PSYCHOLOGY. The study of the physiological correlates of sensation, perception, motivation, learning, etc.

PITCH. A dimension of auditory sensation varying systematically but not simply with the frequency of the physical stimulus.

PITCH SCALE. A curve showing the systematic relationship between stimulus frequency and perceived pitch.

PITUITARY GLAND. Endocrine gland, located in the center of the head, directly involved in growth; secretes (a) growth hormone, which controls normal growth in childhood, and (b) a number of "middle-man" hormones, which act directly upon other endocrine glands.

PLACE THEORY. In hearing, the theory that stimuli of different frequencies set off responses in different places in the cochlea, thereby giving cues for pitch discrimination.

PLATEAU. A flat place on a learning curve, indicating no improvement in performance in spite of continued practice.

POLYGRAPH RECORDER. A device for recording simultaneously the subject's blood pressure, breathing pattern, and galvanic skin response; commonly called a lie detector.

PONS. Structure in the brain located in front of the cerebellum; part of the metencephalon and primarily a transmission center.

POPULATION. A designated part of a universe from which a sample is drawn.

POSITIVE TRANSFER. More efficient learning in one situation produced by previous learning in another.

POSITIVISM. Philosophical point of view maintaining

that science is limited to observed facts and what can be rigorously deduced from facts.

PRAGMATISM. The philosophical doctrine that the meaning of anything derives from its practical consequences, that action is the test of truth.

PREJUDICE. A prejudgment; an emotionally toned attitude or readiness to respond favorably or unfavorably to objects, people, or classes; most frequently it refers to negative prejudgment.

PRENATAL PERIOD. Period between conception and birth, normally about 280 days in human beings.

PRESBYOPIA. A form of farsightedness occurring with advancing age and due chiefly to hardening of the lens of the eye.

PRIMARY COLORS. Basic colors which cannot be produced by mixing other colors but which can, in mixture, produce all other colors. For mixture of light, primary colors are red, green, and blue; for pigment, red, yellow, and blue. Psychological primaries, as distinct from physical primaries, are those colors that appear irreducible—red, yellow, green, and blue.

PRIMARY MENTAL ABILITIES. The relatively independent abilities, identified through factor analysis, that make up "general intelligence." According to Thurstone, they include spatial, numerical, and reasoning abilities, perceptual speed and rote memory.

PRIMARY MENTAL DEFECTIVES. Persons mentally deficient but having no history of disease or injury that might have caused such deficiency.

PRIMARY REINFORCEMENT. In classical conditioning, the presentation of the unconditioned stimulus (or reward) immediately following the conditioned stimulus; in instrumental learning, the presentation of a reward immediately following the instrumental response; contrasts with secondary reinforcement.

PRIMARY REWARD CONDITIONING. The simplest kind of instrumental conditioning wherein the learned response is instrumental in receiving direct reinforcement.

PROACTIVE INHIBITION. The interfering effect previous learning can have upon the retention of material learned subsequently. (See also Retroactive Inhibition.)

PRODUCT-MOMENT CORRELATION (or PEARSONIAN r). The most usual method of computing correlation; involves computations of relations between actual scores rather than between ranks on two measures.

PROGESTIN. Female hormone secreted by the ovaries; prepares the uterus for the support of the fetus.

PROGRAMMED INSTRUCTION. Instruction in which material is presented in a sequence of steps, or "frames," each ending with an item that the subject or student must answer correctly before proceeding to the next.

PROJECTION. A defense mechanism to alleviate conflict by seeing in others the motives or attributes about which one is anxious.

PROJECTION FIBERS. Nerve fibers, both sensory and motor, connecting receptors and effectors with the cortex.

PROJECTIVE TESTS. Psychological tests requiring the subject to view ambiguous or unstructured stimuli and to interpret what he sees; in theory, the person's individual way of viewing the stimuli represents a projection of his own needs and fears and yields data of use in personality assessment and clinical diagnosis.

PROPOSITIONAL LANGUAGE. Speech in which the relations of the words to each other yield a new meaning not given by mere addition of the distinct words.

PROTANOPE. A partially color-blind person who cannot distinguish red and green and who also has difficulty with brightness discrimination.

PROTOPLASM. A semifluid colloidal substance of which all living cells are composed.

PROXIMAL AND DISTAL SEQUENCE. In development, the tendency for organs and functions near the center of the organism to develop earlier than those farther away.

PSYCHIATRY. A medical specialty concerned with the diagnosis and treatment of mental illness.

PSYCHOANALYSIS. A theory of, or an approach to, psychology; emphasizes dynamic conflicts within the personality and unconscious motivational processes. Originated by Sigmund Freud. Also, a form of psychotherapy involving free association, dream analysis, transference, and the uncovering of unconscious conflicts.

PSYCHOGENIC. Pertaining to reactions that are produced by psychological rather than organic factors.

PSYCHOGRAPH. A graphic representation of an individual's scores on psychological tests and/or ratings on personality variables; can constitute a profile of traits, interests, and abilities.

PSYCHOLOGICAL MOTIVE. Inferred condition of the organism, a condition probably learned and not directly related to physiological needs, that serves to direct the organism toward certain goals; e.g., achievement motive, status motive, acquisitive motive.

PSYCHOLOGICAL PRIMARY COLORS. Those colors—red, yellow, green, and blue—which appear pure and irreducible. Not the same as physical primaries.

PSYCHOLOGICAL ZERO POINT. Point at which neither warmth nor cold is experienced; point of indifference; usually about 90 degrees Fahrenheit, but can vary according to the temperature to which the organism has become adapted.

PSYCHOLOGY. The science seeking to describe, understand, and predict the behavior of organisms.

PSYCHOMETRY. The measurement of psychological variables, most often referring to tests of intelligence or other attributes of persons.

PSYCHOPHYSICS. Scientific study of the functional relations between physical events and sensory or perceptual events. In Fechner's original terms, the science of the relationship between body and mind.

PSYCHOSIS. Severe mental disorder involving drastic changes in personality functioning, often including mental deterioration, hallucinations, and delusions.

PSYCHOSOMATIC ILLNESS. Physical symptoms, often including actual damage to tissues, produced by prolonged emotional disturbance rather than by physical or organic factors.

PSYCHOTHERAPY. Psychological methods used in treating psychological disorders.

PSYCHOTOMIMETIC DRUGS. Chemicals, including LSD, mescaline, and others, which have been used to produce psychotic-like reactions in human subjects.

PUBERTY. Stage of physical maturation when reproduction first becomes possible.

PUPIL. Transparent opening in the iris of the eye through which light enters; expands and contracts reflexively to control amount of light striking the retina.

PURE TONE. A sound produced by a physical stimulus composed of only one vibratory frequency.

PURKINJE EFFECT. The apparent darkening of some hues more than others when there is a reduction in level of illumination; in duplicity theory, a shift from cone to rod vision.

PYKNIK. One of Kretschmer's body types, characterized by a short, soft, rounded physique; Kretschmer held that the pyknik type shows a tendency to manic-depressive behavior.

R

RANDOMNESS. Occurring by chance, haphazard; referring to events or behavior that occurs by chance.

RANGE. In statistics, the distance from the highest to the lowest score or value in a distribution.

RATIONALIZATION. A defense mechanism whereby seemingly logical or "good" reasons are devised to replace real reasons; justification of behavior which the person would otherwise find disturbing to his self-concept or self-esteem.

REACTION FORMATION. A defense mechanism in which the individual consciously builds up one motive in order to contain or "overpower" a conflicting or repressed motive.

REACTION TIME. The interval between a stimulus and a response.

RECALL. In learning, a widely used method of measuring retention; the method measures the completion and accuracy with which a subject can reproduce something learned earlier.

RECEPTOR. A specialized structure which can register changes in physical energy and translate physical events into neural events.

RECESSIVE GENE. One of a pair of genes whose hereditary effect is masked when it is paired with a dominant gene.

RECIPROCAL INNERVATION. The automatic process whereby there is simultaneous excitation of one set of motor neurons and inhibition of another, making coordinated movement possible.

RECOGNITION. A method of measuring retention, in which the subject is required only to recognize rather than to recall or reproduce correct responses.

RECRUITMENT. In neurophysiology, a process whereby a repeated stimulus will set off a response when a single stimulus will not.

REFLEX. Specific, automatic, stimulus-response connection involving few nerve connections and only a small part of the body.

REFRACTORY PHASE. A brief period after the discharge of a nervous impulse when the neuron is insensitive to stimulation so that it either will not react at all or requires an unusually strong stimulus to evoke another impulse.

REGRESSION. A return to earlier and less mature forms of behavior; one of the reactions to frustration.

REINFORCEMENT. In classical conditioning, the association of the biologically adequate unconditioned stimulus with the conditioned stimulus; in instrumental conditioning, the rewarding of the correct response.

RELIABILITY. The tendency of a test or measurement to agree with itself when it measures twice or more some entity or attribute believed not to have changed in the interval between measurements.

RELIABILITY, SPLIT-HALF; REPEAT. The stability of a measure or of a test; it may be examined through split-half or test-retest procedures.

REPRESENTATIVE SAMPLE. A sample selected or constructed so that all significant characteristics of the population from which it is drawn are proportionally present in the sample.

REPRESSION. A psychoanalytic term for the removal from or denial to consciousness of thoughts or memories that are anxiety producing.

RESONANCE THEORY. In hearing, Helmholtz's theory that the basilar membrane is tuned like a harp, so that different "strings" are set to resonating to different stimulus frequencies.

RESPONSE. Any organic event set off by a stimulus.

RETENTION. A measure of learning in terms of the amount correctly remembered.

RETICULAR FORMATION. Network of cells deep in the center of the brain, extending from lower to higher centers; has significant function with respect to the alertness or lethargy of the organism.

RETINA. The sensitive membrane, located at the back of the eyeball, containing rods and cones.

RETINAL DISPARITY. The difference between the two images on the two retinas of two eyes, produced by the fact that each eye views an object from a slightly different angle; important for depth perception.

RETROACTIVE INHIBITION. In learning, the interference of later learning with earlier learning; more precisely, the phenomenon in which the recall of material or performance of acts once learned is interfered with by learning done after the original learning.

REVERBERATION. A neural process in which an incoming impulse travels over a neural network and comes back to restimulate the neuron originally bringing the impulse.

REWARD. An object or a situation that can serve to reinforce a response, to satisfy a motive, or to afford pleasure.

RHINENCEPHALON. The olfactory bulb and a portion of the forebrain in the lateral fissure.

RODS. Cylindrical receptor cells of the retina sensitive to brightness but not to wavelength; the receptors for night vision, although they function in daylight also.

ROLE. In social psychology, socially defined pattern of behavior expected of an individual assigned a certain social function, such as that of judge, clergyman, or teacher.

ROLE THERAPY. Therapy in which the therapist and client determine a role for the client to play, with the notion that, as the patient experiments with a new role, he can learn new and more rewarding ways of seeing the world and behaving in it.

RORSCHACH TEST. A projective test utilizing ten cards, printed with bilaterally symmetrical inkblots, to which the subject responds by telling what he sees on each card.

ROTE MEMORY. Memory requiring no thought or understanding or involved associative processes.

RUBRIC. A heading; hence, a division or classification.

RUFFINI CORPUSCLE. A specialized receptor in subcutaneous tissues, probably sensitive to warmth.

S

SADIST. An individual who tends to associate sexual satisfaction with the infliction of pain upon another.

SAMPLING. The selection of a sample of individuals or measurements from the total population to be studied; may involve elaborate selection procedures if inferences from the sample are to be sound.

SATURATION. Quality of color sensation determined by the complexity of the light waves reaching the eye; the more complex the waves, the more white or gray the light and the more "washed out" or less saturated the color.

SCAPEGOATING. A defense mechanism involving the displacement of aggression to a safe and convenient group or class; e.g., the frustrated child beats his smaller brother or some "inferior" child in the neighborhood.

SCHIZOID. Pertaining to schizophrenia, a form of mental illness in which there is, among other symptoms, "a break with reality."

SCHIZOPHRENIA. One of the psychoses, characterized by a "splitting off" from reality; frequently involves hallucinations, delusions, withdrawal, and serious disturbances of emotional life.

SCIENTIFIC METHOD. The method that emphasizes the gaining of knowledge through systematic and objective observation, precise recording and report, the stating and the testing of hypotheses, and the formulation of tentative general principles.

SECONDARY MENTAL DEFICIENCY. Mental deficiency due to disease, brain injury, or accident of development.

SECONDARY REINFORCEMENT. The reinforcing effect of a stimulus that has been previously paired with a primary reinforcement.

SECONDARY REWARD CONDITIONING. Secondary reinforcement in instrumental conditioning.

SELF-INVENTORY. A list whereon a subject checks the traits or attributes or attitudes or interests he believes to be characteristic of himself.

SEMICIRCULAR CANALS. Canals, found near the cochlea in each ear, containing receptors sensitive to changes in the position of the head.

SENSATION. Psychological event occurring when receptors are stimulated.

SENSORY NEURON. A neuron transmitting nervous impulses from sense organs into the central nervous system.

SEPTAL AREA(S). Part of the brain, lying underneath the central frontal part of the cortex.

SERIAL LEARNING. The learning of a series of words or syllables one at a time so that on successive showings the subject can anticipate the item that comes next.

SERNYL. See PSYCHOTOMIMETIC DRUGS.

SET. Readiness to respond in a certain way to some stimulus situation; there are motor sets, perceptual sets, and mental sets.

SEX-LINKED CHARACTERISTIC. A hereditary characteristic controlled by a gene carried on the sex-determining chromosome; color blindness is an example.

SHOCK THERAPY. A treatment for psychosis involving the production in the patient of violent convulsions similar to epileptic seizures; shock typically produces coma followed by brief period of rationality.

SIBLING. A brother or sister.

SKEWED CURVE. A *frequency curve* that is twisted to one side or another, so that it extends farther to one side of the mode than the other. Skewness is said to be toward the longer tail; it is positive when the longer tail of the curve is of cases greater than the mode, negative when the longer tail is less than the mode.

SKEWNESS. See SKEWED CURVE.

SKIN SENSES. The senses of pain, warmth, cold, and pressure, the receptors for which are located in the skin.

SKINNER BOX. A small box equipped with a lever or other device, which an animal must operate to get reinforcement; used in instrumental conditioning.

SMOOTH MUSCLE. Muscle that has no stripe; smooth muscles control movements of digestion and bring about expansion and contraction of blood vessels.

SNELLEN CHART. A chart of block letters used to test visual acuity.

SOCIAL FACILITATION. Increased motivation and effort arising from the stimulus provided by other people; now often called social reinforcement.

SOCIAL NORM. Standards or rules for perception or behavior that are defined and enforced in group situations.

SOCIAL PSYCHOLOGY. A field of specialization concerned with individual behavior in social settings.

SOCIALIZATION. Learning to behave in a manner prescribed by one's society.

SOCIOECONOMIC STATUS. An individual's position in a society. Generally described in terms of membership in one of the socioeconomic classes which, in turn, are generally defined in terms of wealth and occupation.

SOMATIC NERVOUS SYSTEM. The system of nerve cells and fibers serving the sense organs and skeletal muscles; distinct from the autonomic nervous system.

SOMATOTONIA. A dimension of temperament defined by Sheldon, characterized by love of adventure, physical exertion, extroversion, action; associated with mesomorphy in body build.

SOMATOTYPE. Sheldon's term to describe physique; includes primarily the rating on each of three components or dimensions of body build.

SOMESTHESIS. The "sense of body," including sense of the skin and kinesthesis or sense of movement.

SOUND WAVE. The traveling series of condensations and rarefactions of particles set up by a vibrating source, characterized by a certain frequency, amplitude or intensity, and complexity.

SOURCE TRAIT. A term used by Cattell to describe the primary factors of personality.

SPAN OF ATTENTION. The number of distinct objects that can be perceived in a single "very brief" presentation.

SPERM. Male germ cell.

SPERMATOZOAN. A mature sperm cell ready to fertilize an egg.

SPINAL CORD. The cordlike neural structure encased in the backbone; serves as pathway for impulses to and from the brain and as a connection center for reflexes.

SPINAL NERVES. The 31 pairs of nerves connecting at intervals in the spinal cord.

SPONTANEOUS RECOVERY. The spontaneous reappearance of a conditioned response following extinction.

STANDARD DEVIATION (σ). The most commonly used measure of dispersion in a distribution, representing a specified distance along the base line of a distribution curve.

STANDARDIZATION. The process of testing a population to obtain norms or standards with which the score of an individual can be compared.

STANDARDIZED INTERVIEW. A structured interview in which certain questions are asked in the same way and in the same order of all interviewees.

STARTLE PATTERN. An extremely rapid reaction to a sudden unexpected stimulus, apparently very much the same for all individuals.

STATISTICAL INFERENCE. A statement about a population or populations made on the basis of observation or measures of a sample.

STATISTICS. Mathematical and logical procedures for dealing with variable data.

STATUS. *See* SOCIOECONOMIC STATUS.

STATUS SEEKING. A condition of the organism leading it to seek a status that is equal to or better than that of other members of the group to which the organism belongs.

STEREOTYPE. A relatively rigid and oversimplified concept of an aspect of reality, especially of persons or social groups.

STIMULUS (*Pl.* STIMULI). In most general terms, any event or situation that leads to response; more specifically, a physical event or energy change having the capacity to affect a receptor.

STIMULUS GENERALIZATION. Description of the fact that after a subject learns to make a certain response to a certain stimulus, other similar but previously ineffective stimuli will also elicit the conditioned response.

STIRRUP. The last of three interlocking bones in the middle ear which together transmit vibrations from the eardrum to the oval window of the cochlea.

STRESS. Strong, unpleasant emotional tension.

STRIPED (or STRIATED) MUSCLE. Microscopically striped muscles, involved principally with the movements of the skeleton.

STRUCTURALISM (STRUCTURAL PSYCHOLOGY). In the history of psychology, the "school" that studied, mainly through introspective methods, the structure of mind; the structuralist's focus was on sensation and perception.

STYLISTIC TRAITS. Traits describing the manner in which behavior occurs rather than the goals to which it is directed.

SUBLIMATION. A defense mechanism in which a blocked motive is given an indirect and socially acceptable outlet; used most often to refer to indirect expression of socially unacceptable sexual motives.

SUBMISSIVE. Manifesting a personal trait leading to the acceptance of the domination of others.

SUMMATION. In reference to neural function, the phenomenon whereby two or more impulses arriving within a short interval will succeed in bridging a synapse when one impulse will not.

SURVEY. In reference to psychological research, a method calculated to get comparable data, usually by interview or questionnaire, from a wide and accurately described sample of individuals.

SUPEREGO. In psychoanalytic terms, that part of the dynamic personal system concerned with civilized control of behavior; the conscience.

SYMBOL. In the broadest sense, anything that stands for something else.

SYMPATHETIC NERVOUS SYSTEM. A division of the autonomic system primarily concerned with emergency or emotional states.

SYNAPSE. The place at which the dendrites of one nerve fiber connect, across a space, with the axon of another.

SYNAPTIC SUMMATIONS. The phenomenon in which two or more neural impulses arriving within a brief period of time lead to a bridging of the synapse when one impulse from a single fiber may not succeed in bridging it.

T

"T" STATISTIC. Referring to procedures, usually involving small samples, for estimating significance of statistical findings.

TABES DORSALIS. Disease involving destruction of nerves carrying sensations from muscles to brain; involves serious impairment of control of muscular movements.

TABOO. A strongly enforced norm of a society; most frequently used to refer to behaviors that must not occur.

TACHISTOSCOPE. An instrument for providing a very brief time exposure of visual material such as pictures, letters, or digits.

TASTE BUDS. Small receptor structures, principally on the tongue, sensitive to chemical stimulation and giving rise to sensations of taste.

TELENCEPHALON. Highest part of the brain; consisting principally of the two hemispheres of the cerebrum, the two olfactory bulbs, and the corpus callosum.

TELEPHONE THEORY. The theory that the auditory nerve, reacting to events in the inner ear, acts like a telephone line carrying frequency messages to the brain, with sensed pitch being delineated by the arriving frequency.

TEMPORAL LOBE. Division of the cerebral hemisphere below the fissure of Sylvius and underneath areas of skull designated as temples; contains centers for hearing, speech perception, and related associations.

TESTES. Male sex glands.

TESTICULAR ANDROGENS. Male sex hormones produced by the testes.

THALAMUS. Structure lying beneath the telencephalon at the center of the brain, a relay center between the lower part of the brain and nervous system on one hand and the cerebrum on the other.

THEMATIC APPERCEPTION TEST (TAT). Projective technique in which the subject is asked to make up stories about a series of relatively unstructured pictures; the themes that appear in his stories are viewed as expressions of his personality needs.

THEORY. A statement of the relations believed to prevail in a comprehensive body of facts; a general principle tentatively accepted.

THERAPIST. One skilled in the employment of treatment techniques.

THERAPY. Treatment of an illness.

THINKING. Processes occurring between the presentation of a stimulus and the emergence of an overt response, involving an interplay of concepts, symbols, or mediating responses rather than direct manipulation of environmental objects.

THRESHOLD. The smallest amount of a stimulus that can elicit a response. *See* ABSOLUTE THRESHOLD.

THYROID GLAND. An endocrine gland that produces thyroxin; located in the neck.

TIMBRE. Quality of auditory sensation determined by the complexity of the sound wave.

TRAIT. A construct applied to a number of behaviors that seem to occur together and seem to constitute a relatively enduring general attribute of the individual's behavior.

TRANQUILIZERS. Drugs that have a quieting, calming effect on mental patients.

TRANSFER OF TRAINING. Change in learning in one situation due to prior learning in another situation; can be positive (with second learning improved by the first) or negative (where the reverse holds).

TRANSFERENCE. In psychoanalytic therapy, the process in which the patient or client transfers to the therapist responses formerly made to other significant people, usually parents.

TYMPANIC CANAL. A canal in the cochlea.

TYPOLOGY. A descriptive system in which all men are classified into a limited number of categories or types.

U

UNCONDITIONED RESPONSE. Response occurring without any learning to an unconditioned or biologically adequate stimulus.

UNCONDITIONED STIMULUS. A stimulus biologically adequate to elicit a response; unlearned or "natural" stimulus.

UNCONSCIOUS MOTIVES. Those motives inferred from the person's behavior but which he himself cannot report upon.

U-SHAPED CURVE. A distribution curve in which there are relatively few measures in the middle ranges, relatively many at the two extremes.

V

VAGUS NERVE. One of the twelve cranial nerves, the only one to extend beyond the cranium; serves the heart, blood vessels, and viscera.

VALIDITY. The capacity of a test to predict what it was designed to predict, stated most generally in terms of the correlation between scores on the test and scores or measures of performance on the criterion.

VARIABLE. One of the varying factors being studied in experimental or other research.

VESTIBULE. A bony cavity in the labyrinth of the inner ear; involved in sensing of acceleration and of position in space.

VIRILISM. Accentuation of masculine characteristics caused by overactivity of the adrenal cortex.

VISCEROTONIA. One of Sheldon's dimensions of temperament, characterized by fondness of food, amiability, love of comfort; associated with endomorphy of body build.

VISIBLE SPECTRUM. Narrow range of electromagnetic wavelengths to which the eye is sensitive, extending from approximately 400 to approximately 800 millimicrons.

VISUAL ACUITY. The ability of the human visual mechanism to distinguish small objects or spatial separations or intervals.

VOLLEY THEORY. Theory in hearing; states that nerve fibers operate in groups and that various groups send relays of impulses along the auditory nerve.

VOLUNTARY MUSCLES. The striped or striated muscles involved in skeletal movement, voluntarily or otherwise.

W

WAVELENGTH. Linear distance from a point on one wave to the corresponding point on the next wave; applies to physical stimuli for vision and for hearing.

WEBER-FECHNER LAW. Mathematical formulations describing relationships between changes in the stimulus and corresponding changes in sensation.

WHITE NOISE. A sound stimulus containing all frequencies; heard as a "whoosh."

WITHDRAWAL. A defense mechanism involving either physical or psychological flight from a conflictful or frustrating situation.

Y

YOUNG-HELMHOLTZ THEORY. Theory that the human eye contains three kinds of cones, each kind responding to one of the three primary colors of light.

Z

ZYGOTE. Cell formed by the union of the male and female germ cells.

REFERENCES AND INDEX TO AUTHORS OF WORKS CITED *

A

Aberle, D. F., et al. (1950) "The functional prerequisites of a society." *Ethics*, 60:100–111. **529**

Adamson, R. E., and D. W. Taylor. (1954) "Functional fixedness as related to elapsed time and to set." *J. exp. Psychol.*, 47:122–126. **419**

Adelman, H. A., and G. Rosenbaum. (1954) "Extinction of instrumental behavior as a function of frustration at various distances from the goal." *J. exp. Psychol.*, 47:429–432. **467**

Ader, R., and M. L. Belfer. (1962) "Prenatal maternal anxiety and offspring emotionality in the rat." *Psychol. Reports*, 10:711–718. **74**

Adler, A. (1925; 1st ed., 1920) *The practice and theory of individual psychology.* London: Routledge and Kegan Paul. **449**

Adolph, E. F. (1950) "Thirst and its inhibition in the stomach." *Amer. J. Physiol.*, 161:374–386. **225**

Adorno, T. W., E. Frenkel-Brunswick, D. J. Levinson, R. N. Sanford. (1950) *The authoritarian personality.* New York: Harper. **443**

Alexander, F. (1934) "The influence of psychological factors upon gastro-intestinal disturbances." *Psychoanal. Quart.*, 3:501–539. **268**

Allport, F. H. (1924) *Social psychology.* Boston: Houghton Mifflin. **526**

———. (1934) "The J-curve hypothesis of conforming behavior." *J. soc. Psychol.*, 5:141–183. **533, 535**

Allport, G. W. (1937) *Personality: A psychological interpretation.* New York: Holt, Rinehart and Winston. **439, 446, 465**

———. (1954) "The historical background of modern social psychology." In G. Lindzey, ed. *Handbook of social psychology.* Reading, Mass.: Addison-Wesley. 1:3–56. **18, 33**

———, and L. Postman. (1947) *The psychology of rumor.* New York: Holt, Rinehart and Winston. **336, 337**

———, and P. E. Vernon. (1933) *Studies in expressive movement.* New York: Macmillan. **435**

———, and G. Lindzey. (1951) *A study of values, a scale for measuring the dominant interests in personality.* Boston: Houghton Mifflin. **144**

American Psychiatric Association. (1955) *Diagnostic and statistical manual of mental disorders.* Washington, D.C.: A.P.A. **493**

---

* The numbers in **bold face** at the end of each reference indicate the page(s) in the text on which a given reference is cited or discussed.

Anand, B. K., and J. R. Brobeck. (1951) "Hypothalamic control of food intake in rat and cat." *Yale J. Biol. Med., 24*:123–140.   **219**

Anastasi, A., N. Cohen, and D. Spatz. (1948) "A study of fear and anger in college students through the controlled diary method." *J. genet. Psychol., 73*:243–249.   **261, 262**

Andersson, B., P. A. Jewell, and S. Larsson. (1958) "An appraisal of the effects of diencephalic stimulation of conscious animals in terms of normal behavior." In G. E. Wolstenholme and V. M. O'Conner, eds., *Neurological basis of behavior.* London: Churchill. Pp. 76–89.   **218**

———, and S. M. McCann. (1955) "A further study of polydipsia—evoked by hypothalamic stimulation in the goat. *Acta physiol. Scand., 33*:-333–346.   **224**

Arieti, S. (1955) *Interpretation of schizophrenia.* New York: Robert Brunner.   **507, 510**

Aronson, E., and J. M. Carlsmith. (1963) "The effect of the severity of threat on the devaluation of forbidden behavior." *J. abn. soc. Psychol., 66*:584–588.   **539**

Arthur, G. A. (1947) *Arthur Point Scale Tests. Revised form II: Manual for administering and scoring the tests.* New York: Psychological Corporation.   **139**

Asch, S. E. (1951) "Effects of group pressure upon the modification and distortion of judgments." In H. Guetzkow, ed., *Groups, leadership and men.* Pittsburgh: Carnegie Press.   **335**

Ashley, W. R., R. S. Harper, and D. L. Runyon. (1951) "The perceived size of coins in normal and hypnotically induced economic states." *Amer. J. Psychol., 64*:564–572.   **332**

Atkinson, J. W. (1950) "Studies in projective measurement of achievement motivation." Unpublished doctoral dissertation, Univ. Michigan.   **235**

———. (1958) *Motives in fantasy, action, and society.* Princeton, N.J.: Van Nostrand.   **146, 232**

———, J. R. Bastian, R. W. Earl, and G. H. Litwin. (1960) "The achievement motive, goal setting and probability preferences." *J. abn. soc. Psychol., 60*:27–37.   **474**

———, and G. H. Litwin. (1960) "Achievement motive and test anxiety conceived as motive to approach success and motive to avoid failure." *J. abn. soc. Psychol., 60*:53–62.   **474**

Atkinson, R. C., D. N. Hanson, and H. A. Birnbach. (1964) "Short-term memory with young children." *Psychon. Sci., 1*:255–256.   **400–401**

Azrin, N. H. (1959) "Punishment and recovery during fixed-ratio performance." *J. exp. Anal. Behav., 2*:301–305.   **383**

B

Bach, G. R. (1954) *Intensive group psychotherapy.* New York: Ronald.   **501**

Baker, C. T., L. W. Sontag, and V. L. Nelson. (1958) "Individual and group differences in the longitudinal measurement of change in mental ability." *Monogr. Soc. Res. Child Devel., 23*: 11–85.   **186**

Baldwin, A. L. (1948) "Socialization and the parent-child relationship." *Child Devel., 19*:127–136.   **455**

———, J. Kalhorn, and F. H. Breese. (1945) "Patterns of parent behavior." *Psychol. Monogr. 58* (Whole No. 268).   **456**

Bales, R. F. (1952) "Some uniformities of behavior in small social systems." In G. E. Swanson, T. M. Newcomb, and E. L. Hartley, eds., *Readings in social psychology.* New York: Holt, Rinehart and Winston. Pp. 146–159.   **542**

———. (1955) "How people interact in conferences." *Sci. Amer., 192*:31–35.   **545**

———, and F. L. Strodtbeck. (1951) "Phases in group problem solving." *J. abn. soc. Psychol., 46*: 485–495.   **544, 546**

Ball, R. S. (1938) "The predictability of occupational level from intelligence." *J. consult. Psychol., 2*: 184–186.   **196**

Bandura, A., and R. H. Walters. (1963) *Social learning and personality development.* New York: Holt, Rinehart and Winston.   **539**

Bard, P. (1934) "On emotional expression after decortication with some remarks on certain theoretical views." Part I: *Psychol. Rev., 41*: 309–329. Part II: *Psychol. Rev., 41*:424–449.   **264**

Bare, J. K. (1949) "The specific hunger for sodium chloride in normal and adrenalectomized white rats." *J. comp. physiol. Psychol., 42*:242–253.   **221**

Barker, R., T. Dembo, and K. Lewin. (1941) "Frustration and regression, an experiment with young children." *Univ. Iowa Stud. Child Welf., 18*: No. 1., 314.   **469, 482, 483**

Bartlett, F. C. (1932) *Remembering.* New York and London: Univ. Cambridge Press.   **366, 407**

Bateson, G. (1941) "The frustration-aggression hypothesis and culture." *Psychol. Rev., 48*:350–355.   **467**

Baum, M. H. (1954) "Simple concept learning as a function of intralist generalization." *J. exp. Psychol., 47*:89–94.   **408**

Bavelas, A. (1942) "Morale and training of leaders." In G. Watson, ed., *Civilian morale*. New York: Reynal and Hitchcock. Pp. 143–145. **553**

Bayer, E. (1929) "Beiträge zur Zweikomponenten-theorie des Hungers." *Z. Psychol., 112:*1–54. **221**

Bayley, N. (1940) "Mental growth in young children." *Yearbk. Nat. Soc. Stud. Educ., 39:*11–47. **185, 186**

———. (1949) "Consistency and variability in the growth of intelligence from birth to eighteen years. *J. genet. Psychol., 75:*165–196. **195**

Beach, F. A., and L. Jordan. (1956) "Sexual exhaustion and recovery in the male rat." *Quart. J. exp. Psychol., 8:*121–133. **228**

———, A. Zitrin, and J. Jaynes. (1956) "Neural mediation of mating in male cats: I. Effects of unilateral and bilateral removal of the neocortex." *J. comp. physiol. Psychol., 49:*321–327. **227**

Beck, L. H., and W. R. Miles. (1947) "Some experimental and theoretical relationships between infrared absorption and olfaction." *Science, 106:*511 *abstr.* **307**

Beck, S. J. (1944) *Rorschach's test*. New York: Grune & Stratton. Vols. I and II. **145**

Beidler, L. M. (1961) "Mechanisms of gustatory and olfactory receptor stimulation." In W. A. Rosenblith, ed., *Sensory communication*. New York: Wiley; Cambridge, Mass.: MIT Press. Pp. 143–157. **306**

Békésy, C. (1928) "Zur Theorie des Hörens. Die Schwingungsform der Basilarmembran." *Physik. Zsch., 29:*793–810. **291**

Bekhterev, V. M. (1932) *General principles of human reflexology*. New York: International. **353**

Bellak, L. (1948) *Dementia praecox, the past decade's work and present status: A review and evaluation*. New York: Grune & Stratton. **506**

———. (1958) *Schizophrenia: A review of the syndrome*. New York: Logos Press. **506**

Bellows, R. T. (1939) "Time factors in water drinking in dogs." *Amer. J. Physiol., 125:*87–97. **224**

———, and W. P. Van Wagenen. (1939) "The effect of resection of the olfactory, gustatory, and trigeminal nerves on water drinking in dogs with and without diabetes insipidus." *Amer. J. Physiol., 126:*13–19. **224**

Belo, J. (1935) "The Balinese temper." *Charact. and Person., 4:*120–146. **467**

Benedict, R., and G. Weltfish. (1943) *Races of mankind*. New York: Public Affairs Comm. **202, 203**

Bennett, E. B. (1955) "Discussion, decision, commitment, and consensus in 'group decision.'" *Human Relations, 8:*251–273. **528**

Bennett, G. K. (1947) *Hand-tool dexterity test: Manual*. New York: Psychological Corporation. **142**

———, et al. (1957) *College qualification tests*. New York: Psychological Corporation. **138**

———, et al. (1959) *Differential aptitude tests, manual*, 3rd ed. New York: Psychological Corporation. **142**

Bentz, V. J. (1953) "A test-retest experiment on the relationship between age and mental ability." *Amer. Psychologist, 8:*319–320. **188**

Berger, F. M. (1960) "Classification of psychoactive drugs according to their chemical structures and sites of action." In L. Uhr and J. G. Miller, eds., *Drugs and behavior*. New York: Wiley. **508**

Berlyne, D. E. (1955) "The arousal and satiation of perceptual curiosity in the rat." *J. comp. physiol. Psychol., 48:*238–246. **230**

Bermant, G. (1961) "Response latencies of female rats during sexual intercourse." *Science, 133:*1771–1773. **228**

Bexton, W. H., W. Heron, and T. H. Scott. (1954) "Effects of decreased variation in the sensory environment." *Canad. J. Psychol., 8:*70–76. **109**

Bijou, S. W. (1943) "A study of 'experimental neurosis' in the rat by the conditioned response technique." *J. comp. Psychol., 36:*1–20. **476**

Binet, A., and T. Simon. (1905) "Methodes nouvelles pour le diagnostic du niveau intellectual des anormaux." *L'année Psychol., 11:*191–244. **134**

———, and ———. (1911). *A method of measuring the development of the intelligence of young children* (trans. C. G. Town). Lincoln, Ill.: The Courier Co. **134**

Birch, H. G. (1945). "The relation of previous experience to insightful problem-solving." *J. comp. Psychol., 38:*367–383. **364**

Bird, C. (1940) *Social psychology*. New York: Appleton-Century-Crofts. **547**

Bishop, G., and M. H. Clare. (1952) "Cites of origin of electric potentials in striate cortex." *J. Neurophysiol., 15:*201–220. **106**

Blake, R. R., J. S. Mouton, and J. D. Hain. (1956) "Social forces in petition-signing." *Southwestern soc. sci. Quart., 36:*385–390. **527**

Blandford, D. H., and E. E. Sampson. (1964) "Induction of prestige suggestion through classical conditioning." *J. abn. soc. Psychol.*, 69:332–337. **556–557**

Blum, J. S., K. L. Chow, and K. H. Pribram. (1950) "A behavioral analysis of the organization of the parieto-temporo-preoccipital cortex." *J. comp. Neurol.*, 93:53–100. **397**

Boring, E. G. (1929) *A history of experimental psychology.* New York: Century. **18, 313, 406**

Bousfield, W. A. (1953) "The occurrence of clustering in the recall of randomly arranged associates." *J. genet. Psychol.*, 49:229–240. **408**

Bovard, E. W. (1958) "The effects of early handling on viability of the albino rat." *Psychol. Rev.*, 65:257–271. **85**

Bowlby, J. (1951) "Maternal care and mental health." *Bull. World Health Organ.*, 3:355–534. **86**

Brady, J. V. (1958) "Ulcers in the 'executive monkey.'" *Sci. Amer.*, 199:362–404. **266**

Bramel, D. (1963) "Selection of a target for defensive projection." *J. abn. soc. Psychol.*, 66:318–324. **486–487**

Brattgard, S. (1952) "The importance of adequate stimulation for the chemical composition of retinal ganglion cells during early post-natal development." *Acta Radiologica,* Supp. 196. **326**

Brehm, J., and A. R. Cohen. (1962) *Explorations in cognitive dissonance.* New York: Wiley. **470, 540**

Bridges, K. M. B. (1932) "Emotional development in early infancy." *Child Devel.*, 3:324–341. **270**

Bridgman, P. W. (1927) *The logic of modern physics.* New York: Macmillan. **42**

———. (1945) "The prospect for intelligence." *Yale Rev.*, 34:444–461. **31**

Broadbent, D. E. (1948) *Perception and communication.* New York: Pergamon Press. **337**

Brookhart, J. M., and F. L. Dey. (1941) "Reduction of sexual behavior in male guinea pigs by hypothalamic lesions." *Amer. J. Physiol.*, 133:551–554. **226**

Brown, J. S. (1942) "Factors determining conflict reactions in difficult discriminations." *J. exp. Psychol.*, 31:272–292. **476**

Brown, R. (1962) "Models of attitude change." In I. R. Brown et al. *New directions in psychology.* New York: Holt, Rinehart and Winston. **409**

Bruce, R. H. (1941) "An experimental analysis of social factors affecting the performance of white rats. I: Performance in learning a simple field situation." *J. comp. Psychol.*, 31:363–377. **221**

Bruce, R. W. (1933) "Conditions of transfer of training." *J. exp. Psychol.*, 16:343–361. **385**

Bruetsch, W. L. (1959) "Neurosyphilitic conditions." In S. Arieti, ed., *American handbook of psychiatry.* New York: Basic Books. 1003–1020. **504**

Bruner, J. S. (1957) "On perceptual readiness." *Psychol. Rev.*, 64:123–152. **107, 327, 332**

———. (1962) *On knowing: Essays for the left hand.* Cambridge, Mass.: Belknap Press of Harvard Univ. Press. **197**

———, and C. C. Goodman. (1947) "Value and need as organizing factors in perception." *J. abn. soc. Psychol.*, 13:33–44. **47, 333**

———, J. J. Goodnow, and G. A. Austin. (1956) *A study of thinking.* New York: Wiley. **406, 408, 420**

———, and L. Postman. (1947) "Emotional selectivity in perception and reaction." *J. Pers.*, 16:69–77. **334**

Bryce, J. (1908) *The American commonwealth.* New York: Macmillan. **15**

Bühler, C. (1931) *Kindheit und Jugend.*, 3rd ed. Leipzig: Hirzel. **78**

Burtt, H. E. (1938) *Psychology of advertising.* Boston: Houghton Mifflin. **320**

Butler, R. A., and H. M. Alexander. (1955) "Daily patterns of visual exploratory behavior in the monkey." *J. comp. physiol. Psychol.*, 48:247–249. **230**

C

Cannon, W. B. (1918) "The physiological basis of thirst." *Proc. Roy. Soc. London*, B, 90:283–301. **223**

———. (1927) "The James-Lange theory of emotions and an alternative theory." *Amer. J. Psychol.*, 39:106–124. **264**

———, and A. L. Washburn. (1912) "An explanation of hunger." *Amer. J. Psychol.*, 29:441–454. **217**

Carmichael, L. (1926) "The development of behavior in vertebrates experimentally removed from the influence of external stimulation." *Psychol. Rev.*, 33:51–58. **81**

Carnap, R. (1956) "The methodological character of theoretical concepts." In H. Feigl and M. S. Scriver, eds., *Minnesota studies in the philosophy of science.* Minneapolis: Univ. Minnesota Press. **43**

Carrol, J. B., and J. B. Casagrande. (1958) "The function of language classifications in behavior." In E. Maccoby, T. M. Newcomb, and E. L. Hartley, eds., *Readings in social psychology.* New York: Holt, Rinehart and Winston. Pp. 18–31. **411**

Carter, L., and M. Nixon. (1949a) "Ability, perceptual, personality and interest factors associated with different criteria of leadership." *J. Psychol.*, 27:377–388. **550**

——, and ——. (1949b) "An investigation of the relationship between four criteria of leadership ability for four different tasks." *J. Psychol.*, 27:245–261. **549, 550**

Cason, H. (1930) "Common annoyances: A psychological study of everyday aversions and irritations." *Psychol. Monogr.*, 182:1–218. **262**

Cassirer, E. (1933) *Le langage et la construction du monde des objets. Psychologie du langage.* Paris: Felix Alcan. **7**

Cattell, J. McK. (1890) "Mental tests and measurements." *Mind*, 15:373–380. **124, 133**

——. (1903) "A statistical study of eminent men." *Pop. Sci. Mon.*, 62:359–377. **200**

Cattell, P. (1937) "Stanford-Binet IQ variations." *School and Society*, 45:615–618. **130**

Cattell, R. B. (1957) *Personality and motivation structure.* Yonkers, N. Y.: World. **441**

Centers, R. (1949) *The psychology of social classes.* Princeton: Princeton Univ. Press. **526**

Cerletti, U. (1950) "Old and new information about electroshock." *Amer. J. Psychiat.*, 107:87–92. **509**

Chapanis, A. (1949) *Human factors in undersea warfare.* Washington, D. C.: National Research Council. **298**

Chapman, L. J., and R. R. Knowles. (1964) "The effects of phenothiazine on disordered thought in schiozophrenia." *J. consult. Psychol.*, 28:165–169. **515–516**

Chauncey, H., and J. E. Dobbin. (1963) *Testing: Its place in education today.* New York: Harper & Row. **150**

Chesire L., M. Saffir, and L. I. Thurstone. (1933) *Computing diagrams for the tetrachoric correlation coefficient.* Chicago: Univ. Chicago Press. **173**

Child, I. L. (1946) "Children's preference for goals easy or difficult to obtain." *Psychol. Monogr.*, 60 (Whole No. 280). **467**

Chow, K. L., W. C. Dement, and E. R. John. (1957) "Conditioned electrocorticographic potentials and behavioral avoidance responses in the cat." *J. Neurophysiol.*, 20:484–493. **397**

Church, R. M. (1963) "The varied effects of punishment on behavior." *Psychol. Rev.*, 70:369–402. **383**

Cleckley, H. M. (1959) "Psychopathic states." In S. Arieti, ed., *American handbook of psychiatry.* New York: Basic Books, 567–588. **506**

Coch, L., and J. R. P. French, Jr. (1948) "Overcoming resistance to change," *Hum. Rel.*, 1:512–532. **535, 536**

Cofer, C. N. (1961) "Experimental studies of the role of verbal processes in concept formation and problem solving." *Ann. N.Y. Acad. Sci.*, 9:94–107. **405**

——, and M. H. Appley. (1964) *Motivation: Theory and research.* New York: Wiley. **219, 223, 230**

——, and J. P. Foley, Jr. (1942) "Mediated generalization and the interpretation of verbal behavior. I: Prolegomena." *Psychol. Rev.*, 49:512–540. **412**

Coffin, T. E. (1941) "Some conditions of suggestion and suggestibility: A study of certain attitudinal and situational factors influencing the process of suggestion." *Psychol. Monogr.*, 53 (No. 4). **336**

Cohen, A. (1964) Paper read at American Psychological Association, Los Angeles. **510**

College Entrance Examination Board. (1956) *Scholastic Aptitude Test.* Princeton, N.J.: CEEB. **138**

Commager, H. S. (1947) *America in perspective.* New York: Random House. **15**

Conel, J. L. (1939) *The postnatal development of the human cerebral cortex. I: The cortex of the newborn.* Cambridge, Mass.: Harvard Univ. Press. **83**

Conrad, H. S., and H. E. Jones. (1940) "A second study of familial resemblance in intelligence: Environmental and genetic implications of parent-child and sibling correlations in the total sample." *39th Yearbk. Nat. Soc. Stud. Educ.*, Part II, pp. 97–141. **179**

Cook, B. S., and E. R. Hilgard. (1949) "Distributed practice in motor learning: Progressively increasing and decreasing rests." *J. exp. Psychol.*, 39:169–172. **377**

Cook, S. W. (1939) "The production of 'experimental neurosis' in the white rat." *Psychosom. Med.*, 1:293–308. **469, 476**

Cook, T. W. (1934) "Massed and distributed practice in puzzle solving." *Psychol. Rev.*, 41:330–355. **376**

Corbit, J. D., and E. Stellar. (1964) "Palatability, food intake, and obesity in normal and hyperphagic rats." *J. comp. physiol. Psychol.*, 58:63–67. **247–248**

Cox, C. M. (1926) *The early mental traits of three hundred geniuses.* Stanford, Calif.: Stanford Univ. Press. **192–193**

Craddick, R. A., and M. R. Stern. (1964) "Verbal conditioning: The effect of partial reinforcement upon the recall of early memories." *J. abn. soc. Psychol.*, 68:353–355. **518–519**

Crawford, J. E., and D. M. Crawford. (1949) *Small Parts Dexterity Test.* New York: Psychological Corporation. **142**

Cronbach, L. J. (1960) *Essentials of psychological testing*, 2nd ed. New York: Harper. **138**

Culler, E. A. (1938) "Recent advances in some concepts of conditioning." *Psychol. Rev.*, 45:134–159. **397**

D

Dallenbach, K. M. (1927) "The temperature spots and end-organs." *Amer. J. Psychol.*, 39:402–427. **309**

Darlington, C. D. (1948) *Conway memorial lecture on the conflict of society and science.* London: Watts. **49**

Davis, C. M. (1928) "Self-selection of diet by newly weaned infants." *Amer. J. Dis. Child.*, 36:651–679. **219**

Davis, H. (1947) *Hearing and deafness: A guide for laymen.* New York: Holt, Rinehart and Winston. **286**

Davis, J. E., Jr. (1964) "Empirical dimensions of psychiatric hospital organization." Paper read at American Psychological Assoc., Los Angeles. **510**

Davis, J. T., and F. Taylor. (1959) "The role of adsorption and molecular morphology in olfaction: The calculation of olfactory thresholds." *Biol. Bull.*, 117:222–238. **307**

Davis, W. A., and R. J. Havighurst. (1948) "The measurement of mental systems (Can intelligence be measured?)" *Sci. Mon.*, 66:301–316. **201**

DeCharnes, R. C., H. Morrison, W. R. Reitmani, and D. C. McClelland. (1955) "Behavioral correlates of directly measured achievement motivation." In D. C. McClelland, ed., *Studies in motivation.* New York: Appleton-Century-Crofts. **233**

Deese, J. (1958) *The psychology of learning.* New York: McGraw-Hill. **346**

Delgado, J. M. R., W. W. Roberts, and N. Miller. (1954) "Learning motivated by electrical stimulation of subcortical structures in the monkey brain." *J. comp. physiol. Psychol.*, 49:373–380. **110**

Dember, W. N. (1964) Birth order and need affiliation. *J. abn. soc. Psychol.*, 68:555–557. **249**

———, R. W. Earl, and R. W. Paradise. (1957) "Response by rats to differential stimulus com-

plexity." *J. comp. physiol. Psychol.*, 50:514–518. **230**

Dement, W. (1960) "The effect of dream deprivation." *Science*, 131:1705–1707. **422**

———, and N. Kleitman. (1957) "The relation of eye movement during sleep to dream activity: An objective method for the study of dreaming." *J. exp. Psychol.*, 53:339–440. **422**

Dempsey, E. W., and D. McK. Rioch. (1939) "The localization in the oestrus responses of the female guinea pig." *J. Neurophysiol.*, 2:9–18. **226**

Dennis, W. (1960) "Causes of retardation among institutional children: Iran." *J. genet. Psychol.*, 96:47–59. **89, 183**

Derbyshire, A. J., and H. Davis. (1935) "The action potentials of the auditory nerve." *Amer. J. Physiol.*, 113:476–504. **290**

Deterline, W. A. (1957) "Verbal responses and concept formation." *Psychol. Rep.*, 3:372. **408**

———. (1962) *An introduction to programed instruction.* Englewood Cliffs, N.J.: Prentice-Hall. **395**

De Tocqueville, A. (1956) *Democracy in America*, rev. ed. New York: Knopf. **15**

Deutch, A. (1938) *The mentally ill in America.* New York: Doubleday & Co., Inc. **490, 491**

Deutsch, J. A., and D. Deutsch. (1963) "Attention: Some theoretical considerations." *Psychol. Rev.*, 70:80–90. **223**

Dewey, J. (1911; rev. ed., 1948) *Reconstruction in philosophy.* Boston: Beacon Press. **49**

Dick, Walter. (1963) "Retention as a function of paired and individual use of programed instruction." *Programed Instruction*, 2:17–23. **396**

Dollard, J., and N. E. Miller. (1950) *Personality and psychotherapy: An analysis in terms of learning, thinking and culture.* New York: McGraw-Hill. **367, 497**

———, et al. (1939) *Frustration and aggression.* New Haven: Yale Univ. Press. **482**

Dragstedt, L. R., H. Ragins, and S. O. Evans. (1956) "Stress and duodenal ulcer." *Ann. Surg.* 144:450–463. **268**

Draper, G., C. W. Dupertuis, and J. L. Caughey, Jr. (1944) *Human constitution in medicine.* New York, London: Hoeber. **268**

Duncan, C. P. (1953) "Transfer in motor learning as a function of degree of first-task learning and inter-task similarity." *J. exp. Psychol.*, 45:1–11. **385**

Duncker, K. (1945) "On problem-solving" (trans.

from 1935 original). *Psychol. Mongr.*, 58:111–113. **417, 418**

Dvorak, B. J. (1947) "The new USES general aptitude test battery." *J. appl. Psychol.*, 31:372–376. (Includes U.S. Employment Service Pegboard test.) **142**

E

Ebbinghaus, H. (1913) *Memory, a contribution to experimental psychology.* New York: Columbia Univ. Press. **388, 390**

Edwards, A. L. (1942) "The retention of affective experiences; a criticism and restatement of the problem." *Psychol. Rev.*, 49:43–53. **393**

Ellis, H. (1904) *A study of British genius.* London: Hurst & Blackett. **200**

Ellson, D. G. (1952) *A report of research on detection of deception.* Report of research performed by Indiana University under contract No. N6ONT–18011 with ONR. **260.**

Ellsworth, R. B. (1961) Psychiatric aide-role project, 2nd Interim report. Veterans Administration Hospital, Fort Meade, S.D. (mimeographed). **510**

Ericksen, S. C. (1942) "Variability of attack in massed and distributed practice." *J. exp. Psychol.*, 31:339–345. **376**

Erickson, M. H. (1030) "Experimental demonstration of the psychopathology of everyday life—unconscious resentment expressing itself in masked forms through a smoke screen of overcompensatory courtesy." *Psychoanal. Quart.*, 8:338–353. **240**

Erikson, E. H. (1963) *Childhood and society,* 2nd ed. New York: Norton. **465**

———. (1964) *Insight and responsibility.* New York: Norton. **465**

Estes, K. W. (1944) "An experimental study of punishment." *Psychol. Monogr.*, 57 (No. 263):40. **383, 390**

Ettlinger, G., and J. Wegener. (1958) "Somaesthetic alternation discrimination and orientation after frontal and parietal lesions in monkeys." *Quart. J. exp. Psychol.*, 10:177–186. **397**

Evans, C. L. (1956) *Starling's principles of human physiology,* 12th ed. London: J. and A. Churchill. **98**

Eysenck, H. J. (1960) *Behaviour therapy and the neuroses.* New York: Pergamon Press. **500**

———. (1961) "The effects of psychotherapy." In H. J. Eysenck, ed., *Handbook of abnormal psychology.* New York: Basic Books. Pp. 697–725. **502**

F

Fairweather, G. W. (1964) *Social psychology in treating mental illness: An experimental approach.* New York: Wiley. **514**

Feather, N. T. (1964) "Acceptance and rejection of arguments in relation to attitude strength, critical ability, and intolerance of inconsistency." *J. abn. soc. Psychol.*, 69:127–136. **541**

Feigl, H. (1951) "Principles and problems of theory construction in psychology." In *Current trends in psychological theory.* Pittsburgh: Univ. Pittsburgh Press. **30**

Fein, R. (1958) *Economics of mental illness.* Joint Commission on Mental Illness and Health. Monogr. Series No. 2. New York: Basic Books. **491**

Fenn, J. D., and A. E. Goss. (1957) "The role of mediating verbal responses on the conceptual sorting behavior of normals and paranoid schizophrenics." *J. genet. Psychol.*, 90:59–67. **411**

Fenz, W. D. (1964) "Conflict and stress as related to physiological activation and sensory, perceptual, and cognitive functioning." *Psychol. Monogr.*, 78:585. **273–275**

Fernberger, S. W. (1950) "An early example of a 'hidden-figure' picture." *Amer. J. Psychol.*, 63:488. **334**

Fessard, A. (1926) "Les temps de réaction et leur variabilité, étude statistique." *L'année Psychol.*, 27:215–224. **158**

Festinger, L. (1957; reissued 1962) *A theory of cognitive dissonance.* Stanford, Calif.: Stanford Univ. Press. **470**

———, and J. L. Freedman. (1964) "Dissonance reduction and moral values." In P. Worchal and D. Byrne, eds., *Personality change.* New York: Wiley. Pp. 220–243. **540**

———, H. W. Riecken, and S. Schachter. (1956) *When prophecy fails: A social and psychological study of a modern group that predicted the destruction of the world.* New York: Harper & Row. **470, 503**

Fields, P. E. (1932) "Studies in concept formation. I: The development of the concept of triangularity by the white rat." *Comp. Psychol. Monogr.*, 9:1–70. **407**

Fischer, L. K. (1952) "Hospitalism in six-month-old infants." *Amer. J. Orthopsychiat.*, 22:522–533. **86**

Flanders, N. A. (1951) "Personal-social anxiety as a factor in experimental learning situations." *J. educ. Res.*, 45:100–110. **552**

Foa, U. G. (1964) "Cross-cultural similarity and difference in interpersonal behavior." *J. abn. soc. Psychol.*, 68:517–522. **524**

Ford, C. S., and F. H. Beach. (1952) *Patterns of sexual behavior*. New York: Hoeber. **226, 227**

Forgus, R. H., and H. Fowler. (1957) "The order of dominance in concept attainment as affected by experience." *J. Psychol.*, 77:105–108. **408**

Frank, J. D. (1961) *Persuasion and healing*. Baltimore: Johns Hopkins Press. **502**

Freedman, J. L., and S. A. Mednick. (1958) "Ease of attainment of concepts as a function of response dominance variance." *J. exp. Psychol.*, 55:463–466. **408**

Freeman, F. N. (1939). *Mental tests, their history, principles and application*. Boston: Houghton Mifflin. **138**

Freeman, R. V., and H. M. Grayson. (1955) "Maternal attitudes in schizophrenia." *J. abn. soc. Psychol.*, 50:45–52. **507**

Freeman, W., and J. W. Watts. (1950) *Psychosurgery*, 2nd ed. Springfield, Ill.: Thomas. **510**

French, E. G. (1958) "Development of a measure of complex motivation." In J. W. Atkinson, ed., *Motives in fantasy, action, and society*. Princeton, N.J.: Van Nostrand. **233**

———, and F. H. Thomas. (1958) "The relation of achievement to problem-solving effectiveness." *J. abn. soc. Psychol.*, 56:45–48. **235**

Freud, S. (1900; rev. ed., 1937) *Interpretation of dreams* (trans. A. A. Brill). London: Allen & Unwin; New York: Macmillan. **421**

———. (1915; rev. ed., 1957) *The standard edition of the complete works of Sigmund Freud*, Vol. 14. London: Hogarth. **43**

———. (1933) *New introductory lectures on psychoanalysis* (trans. W. J. H. Sprott). New York: Norton. **495**

Fromm, E. (1947) *Man for himself*. New York: Holt, Rinehart & Winston. **449, 465, 466**

———. (1955) *The sane society*. New York: Holt, Rinehart & Winston. **465, 466**

Fromm-Reichman, F. (1950) *Principles of intensive psychotherapy*. Chicago: Univ. Chicago Press. **510**

Fuster, J. M. (1958) "Subcortical effects of stimulation of brain stem on tachistoscopic perception." *Science*, 127:150. **109**

G

Gagné, R. M., and H. Foster. (1949a) "Transfer of training from practice on components in a motor skill." *J. exp. Psychol.*, 39:47–68. **385**

———, and ———. (1949b) "Transfer to a motor skill from practice on a pictured representation." *J. exp. Psychol.*, 39:342–354. **386**

Galton, F. (1869) *Hereditary genius*. London: Macmillan. **124**

———. (1888) *Proc. Roy. Soc. London, XLV*. **124**

Gardner, E. (1958) *Fundamentals of neurology*, 3rd ed. Philadelphia: W. B. Saunders. **96**

Garth, T. R. (1925) "A review of racial psychology." *Psychol. Bull.*, 22:343–364. **201**

Gates, A. I. (1917) "Recitation as a factor in memorizing." *Arch. Psychol.*, No. 40. New York: The Science Press. **378, 380**

Gelfand, S. (1958) "Effects of prior associations and task complexity upon the identification of concepts." *Psychol. Rep.*, 4:567–574. **411**

Gelhorn, E., and G. N. Loofbourrow. (1963) *Emotions and emotional disorders: A neurophysiological study*. New York: Harper & Row. **268**

Gerard, D. L., and J. Siegel. (1950) "The family background of schizophrenia." *Psychiat. Quart.*, 24:46–53. **507**

Gerard, R. W. (1963) "The material basis of memory." *J. verb. Learning and verb. Behavior, 2*: 22–33. **118–119**

Gesell, A., and C. Amatruda. (1947) *Development diagnosis: Normal and abnormal child development. Clinical methods and pediatric applications*. New York: Hoeber. **76**

Getzels, J. W., and P. W. Jackson. (1962) *Creativity and intelligence: Explorations with gifted children*. New York: Wiley. **198**

Ghiselli, E. E., and C. W. Brown. (1955) *Personnel and industrial psychology*. New York: McGraw-Hill. **375**

Gibson, E. J., C. H. Bishop, W. Schiff, and J. Smith. (1964) "Comparison of meaningfulness and pronounceability as grouping principles in the perception and retention of verbal material." *J. exp. Psychol.*, 67:173–182. **341–343**

———, J. J. Gibson, O. W. Smith, and H. Flock. (1959) "Motion parallax as a determinant of perceived depth." *J. exp. Psychol.*, 58:40–51. **324**

———, and R. D. Walk. (1956) "The effect of prolonged exposure to visually presented patterns on learning to discriminate them." *J. comp. physiol. Psychol.*, 49:239–242. **84**

Gibson, J. J. (1929) "The reproduction of visually perceived forms." *J. exp. Psychol.*, 12:1–39. **336, 337**

———. (1963) "The useful dimensions of sensitivity." *Amer. Psychologist, 18*:1–15. **337**

Glucksberg, S. (1964) "Functional fixedness: Problem

solution as a function of observing responses." *Psychon. Sci.*, 1:117–118. **425–426**

Goddard, H. H. (1911) "A revision of the Binet scale." *Training Sch. Bull.*, 8:56–62. **134**

Goldfarb, W. (1955) "Emotional and intellectual consequences of psychologic deprivation in infancy." In E. Hoch and J. Zubin, eds., *Psychopathology in childhood*. New York: Grune & Stratton. Pp. 105–119. **185, 205–206**

Goldstein, K. (1940) *Human nature in the light of psychopathology*. Cambridge, Mass.: Harvard Univ. Press. **465**

Goldstein, M., and C. H. Rittenhouse. (1954) "Knowledge of results in the acquisition and transfer of a gunnery skill." *J. exp. Psychol.*, 48:187–196. **379**

Goode, W. J. (1960) "A theory of role strain." *Am. sociol. Rev.*, 25:483–496. **476**

Goodenough, F. L. (1926) *Measurement of intelligence by drawings.* Yonkers-on-Hudson, New York: World. **130**

Goodman, L. (1932) "The effect of total absence of function upon the optic system of rabbits." *Amer. J. Physiol.*, 100:46–63. **326**

Goodnow, J. J., and T. F. Pettigrew. (1955) "Effect of prior patterns of experience upon strategies and learning sets." *J. exp. Psychol.*, 49:381–389. **419**

———, I. Rubenstein, and B. L. Shanks. (1959) "The role of past events in problem solving." *J. exp. Psychol.*, 58:461–464. **509**

Gordon, H. (1923) *Mental and scholastic tests among retarded children, physically defective, canal boat and gypsy children and backward children in ordinary elementary schools. An inquiry into the effects of schooling on the various tests.* London: Board of Education. Pamphlet No. 44. **183**

Gorer, G. (1948) *The American people.* New York: Norton. **15**

Gough, H. G. (1953) "Minnesota multiphasic personality inventory." In A. Weider, ed., *Contributions toward medical psychology.* New York: The Ronald Press. II:545–567. **144**

———. (1955) "Factors related to differential achievement among gifted persons." Paper presented at American Psychological Association symposium on the gifted child. **195**

———. (1957) *California personality inventory.* Palo Alto, Calif.: Consulting Psychologists Press. **145**

———. (1964) "Identifying the creative person." Talk given at a meeting of the American Society of Value Engineers, Los Angeles, Calif. **198**

Graham, C. H., and R. M. Gagné. (1940) "The acquisition, extinction and spontaneous recovery of a conditioned operant response." *J. exp. Psychol.*, 26:251–280. **360**

Granit, R. (1959) "Neural activity in the retina." In *Handbook of physiology*, Vol. I. Washington, D.C.: American Physiological Society. **304**

Green, B. F., Jr. (1963) *Digital computers in research: An introduction for behavioral and social scientists.* New York: McGraw-Hill. **124**

Greenspoon, J., and S. Foreman. (1956) "Effect of delay of knowledge of results on learning a motor task." *J. exp. Psychol.*, 51:226–228. **378**

Gregerson, M. I. (1932) "The physiological mechanism of thirst." *Amer. J. Physiol.*, 101:44–45. **223**

Grice, G. R., and E. Saltz. (1950) "The generalization of an instrumental response to stimuli varying in the size dimension." *J. exp. Psychol.*, 40:702–708. **357, 358**

Griffith, A. V., H. S. Upshaw, and R. Fowler. (1958) "The psychaesthenic and hypomanic scales of the MMPI and uncertainty in judgments." *J. clin. Psychol.*, 14:385–386. **149**

Griffith, B. C., H. H. Spitz, and R. S. Lipman. (1959) "Verbal mediation and concept formation in retarded and normal subjects." *J. exp. Psychol.*, 58:247–251. **408**

Grinker, R. R., and J. P. Spiegel. (1945) *War neurosis.* Philadelphia: Blakiston Co. **508**

Guetzkow, H., and B. H. Bowman. (1946) *Men and hunger, a psychological manual for relief workers.* Elgin, Ill.: Brethren Publishing House. **222**

Guilford, J. P. (1952) *General psychology.* Princeton, N.J.: Van Nostrand. **388**

———. (1950) "Creativity." *Amer. Psychologist*, 5:444–454. **197**

Gurel, L. (1964) "Correlates of psychiatric hospital effectiveness." Paper read at American Psychological Association, Los Angeles. **510**

Guthrie, E. R. (1938) *The psychology of human conflict.* New York: Harper. **349, 367**

H

Hadamard, J. (1945) *An essay on the psychology of invention in the mathematical field.* Princeton, N.J.: Princeton Univ. Press. **415**

Haldeman-Julius, E. (1928) *The first hundred million.* New York: Simon & Schuster. **332**

Hall, C. S. (1938) "The inheritance of emotionality." *Sigma X Quart.*, 26:17–27. **74**

Harlow, H. F. (1949) "The formation of learning sets." *Psychol. Rev.*, 56:51–65. **364, 365, 386, 415**

———. (1960a) "Of love in infants." *Nat. Hist.*, 69:18–23. **263**

———. (1960b) "Primary affectional patterns in primates." *Amer. J. Orthopsychiat.*, 30:676–684. **230**

———. (1962) "The heterosexual affectional system in monkeys." *Amer. Psychologist*, 16:1–9. **87**

———, M. K. Harlow, and D. R. Meyer. (1950) "Learning motivated by a manipulation drive." *J. exp. Psychol.*, 40:228–234. **230**

———, and D. Meyer. (1952) "Paired comparison scales for monkey rewards." *J. comp. physiol. Psychol.*, 45:73–79. **360**

———, and R. R. Zimmerman. (1959) "Affectional responses in the infant monkey." *Science, 130:* 421–432. **87**

Harrell, T. W., and M. S. Harrell. (1945) "Army general classification test scores for civilian occupations." *Educ. psychol. Measmt.*, 5:229–239. **196**

Harriman, A. E. (1955) "Provitamin-A selection by vitamin-A depleted rats." *J. genet. Psychol.*, 86:45–50. **219**

Hartmann, H. (1951) "Ego psychology and the problem of adaptation" In D. Rapaport, ed., *Organization and pathology of thought.* New York: Columbia Univ. Press. **466**

———, E. Kris, and R. Loewenstein. (1947) "Comments on the formation of psychic structure." In T. French et al., eds., *The psychoanalytic study of the child*, Vol. 2. New York: International Universities Press. **449**

Hartry, A. L. (1962) "The effects of reserpine on the psychogenic production of gastric ulcers in rats." *J. comp. physiol. Psychol.*, 55:719–721. **272–273**

———, P. Keith-Lee, and W. D. Morton. (1964) " 'Planaria: Memory transfer through cannibalism' reexamined." *Science, 146:*274–275. **117–118**

Hastorf, A., and H. Cantril. (1954) "They saw a game: A case study." *J. abn. soc. Psychol.*, 49:129–134. **335**

Hathaway, S. R. (1964) "The MMPI: Professional use by professional people." *Amer. Psychologist, 19:*204–210. **145**

Havighurst, R. J., and F. H. Breese. (1947) "Relation between ability and social status in a midwestern community. II: Primary mental abilities." *J. educ. Psychol.*, 38:241–247. **199**

———, and J. L. Janke. (1944) "Relations between ability and social status in a midwestern community. I: Ten-year-old children." *J. educ. Psychol.*, 35:357–368. **180**

———, and H. Taba. (1949) *Adolescent character and personality.* New York: Wiley. **453**

Hawker, J. R. (1964) "Training procedure and practice-test ratio in the acquisition and retention of a serial maze pattern." *Psychon. Sci., 1:*97–98. **400**

Hayes, C. (1951) *The ape in our house.* New York: Harper. **82, 83**

Hebb, D. O. (1937a) "The innate organization of visual activity. I: Perception of figures by rats reared in darkness." *J. genet. Psychol., 51:* 101–126. **326**

———. (1937b) "The innate organization of visual activity. II: Transfer of response in the discrimination of brightness and darkness and size by rats reared in total darkness." *J. comp. Psychol.*, 24:277–299. **326**

———. (1949) *Organization of behavior: A neuropsychological theory.* New York: Wiley. **78, 107, 184, 325, 337, 385**

———. (1955) "Drives and the C.N.S. (conceptual nervous system)." *Psychol. Rev.*, 62:243–254. **78, 109, 111**

———. (1958) *A Textbook of psychology.* Philadelphia: Saunders. **263**

———. (1959) "A neuropsychological theory." In S. Koch, ed., *Psychology: A study of a science. I: Sensory, perceptual, and physiological formulations.* New York: McGraw-Hill. Pp. 622–643. **178**

Hegge, T. G. (1944) "The occupational status of higher-grade mental defectives in the present emergency: A study of parolees from the Wayne Co. Training School at Northville, Mich." *Amer. J. ment. Defic.*, 49:86–98. **191**

Heidbreder, E. (1924) "An experimental study of thinking." *Arch. Psychol.*, II, No. 73. New York: Science Press. **407**

———. (1946a) "The attainment of concepts. I: Terminology and methodology." *J. genet. Psychol.*, 35:173–189. **407**

———. (1946b) "The attainment of concepts. II: The problem." *J. genet. Psychol.*, 35:191–223. **407**

———. (1947) "The attainment of concepts. III: The process." *J. Psychol.*, 24:93–138. **407**

Heilbrun, A. B., Jr. (1964) "Conformity to masculinity-femininity stereotypes and ego identity in adolescents." *Psychol. Rep.*, 14:351–357. **557–558**

Heisenberg, W. (1958) *Physics and philosophy.* New York: Harper. **11**

Helmholtz, H. von. (1896) *Vorträge und Reder*, 5th Auf. Vol. I. Braunschweig: F. Vieweg und Sohn. **415**

Helson, H. (1964) *Adaptation-level theory: An ex-*

perimental and systematic approach to behavior. New York: Harper & Row. **338**

Hemphill, J. K. (1950) "Relations between the size of the group and the behavior of 'superior leaders.'" *J. soc. Psychol.,* 32:11–22. **548**

Henry, J. (1951) "Family structure and the transmission of neurotic behavior." *Amer. J. Orthopsychiat.,* 21:800–818. **498**

Hering, E. (1878; trans. 1964) *Outlines of a theory of the light sense* (trans. L. M. Hurvich and D. Jameson). Cambridge, Mass.: Harvard Univ. Press. **303**

Hernández-Péon, R., H. Scherrer, and M. Jouvet. (1956) "Modification of electric activity in cochlear nucleus during 'attention' in unanesthetized cats." *Science, 123:*331–332. **321**

Hess, E. H. (1958) "'Imprinting' in animals." *Sci. Amer., 198:*81–90. **86, 87**

———. (1962) "Ethology: An approach toward the complete analysis of behavior." In R. Brown, E. Galanter, E. Hess, and G. Mandler, eds., *New directions in psychology.* New York: Holt, Rinehart & Winston. Pp. 157–266. **86**

Hetherington, A. W., and W. W. Ranson (1940) "Hypothalamic lesions and adiposity in the rat." *Anat. Rec.,* 78:149–172. **219**

Heyns, R. W. (1948) "Effects of variation in leadership on participant behavior in discussion groups." Unpublished dissertation, Univ. Michigan. **551**

Hickman, C. P. (1955) *Integrated principles of zoology.* St. Louis: C. V. Mosby. **5**

Hilden, A. H. (1949) "A longitudinal study of intellectual development." *J. Psychol.,* 28:187–214. **186**

Hildreth, G. H., et al. (1951) *Metropolitan Achievement Tests: Manual for interpreting.* Yonkers-on-Hudson, N.Y.: World Book Co. **143**

Hilgard, E. R. (1956) *Theories of learning.* New York: Appleton-Century-Crofts. **367**

Hilgard, J. R. (1932) "Learning and maturation in preschool children." *J. genet. Psychol.,* 41:36–56. **82**

Hobson, J. R. (1947) "Sex differences in primary mental abilities." *J. educ. Psychol.,* 47:36–56. **199**

Hogben, L. (1937) *Mathematics for the millions.* New York: Norton. **48**

Hoisington, L. B. (1928) "Pleasantness and unpleasantness as modes of bodily experience." In M. L. Reymert, ed., *Feelings and emotions, the Wittenberg Symposium.* Worcester, Mass.: Clark Univ. Press. Chap. 20. **254**

Hollingshead, A. B. (1958) "Factors associated with prevalence of mental illness." In E. E. Maccoby, T. M. Newcomb, and H. L. Hartley,

eds., *Readings in social psychology.* New York: Holt, Rinehart and Winston. Pp. 425–436. **492**

———, and R. C. Redlich. (1958) *Social class and mental illness.* New York: Basic Books. **492**

Holt, E. B. (1931) *Animal drive and the learning process.* New York: Holt, Rinehart and Winston. **216**

Holtzman, W. H. (1961) *Inkblot perception and personality.* Austin, Tex.: Univ. Texas Press. **146**

Holway, A. H., and E. G. Boring. (1941) "Determinants of apparent visual size with distance variant." *Amer. J. Psychol.,* 54:21–37. **323**

Honzik, M. R., J. W. Macfarlane, and L. Allen. (1948) "The stability of mental test performance between two and eighteen years." *J. exp. Educ.,* 17:309–324. **186**

Hooker, D. (1943) "Reflex activities in the human fetus." In R. G. Baker, J. S. Kounin, and H. F. Wright, eds., *Child behavior and development.* New York: McGraw-Hill. **67**

Horney, K. (1939) *New ways in psychoanalysis.* New York: Norton. **449**

———. (1945) *Our inner conflict: A constructive theory of neurosis.* New York: Norton. **495**

Hovland, C. I. (1937) "The generalization of conditioned responses. I: The sensory generalization of conditioned responses with varying frequencies of tone." *J. genet. Psychol.,* 17:125–148. **354**

———, and R. R. Sears. (1938) "Experiments on motor conflict. I: Types of conflict and their modes of resolution." *J. exp. Psychol.,* 23:477–493. **471, 472, 473, 474**

———, and W. Weiss. (1953) "Transmission of information concerning concepts through positive and negative instances." *J. exp. Psychol.,* 45:175–182. **408**

Howard, T. C. (1962) "Conditioned temperature drive in rats." *Psychol. Rep.,* 10:371–373. **248–249**

Howes, D. H., and R. L. Solomon. (1951) "Visual duration threshold as a function of word-probability." *J. exp. Psychol.,* 41:401–410. **328**

Hull, C. L. (1921) "Quantitative aspects of the evolution of concepts: An experimental study." *Psychol. Monogr.,* 28 (Whole No. 123). **407**

———. (1943) *Principles of behavior.* New York: Appleton-Century-Crofts. **366**

———. (1952) *A behavior system.* New Haven: Yale Univ. Press. **366**

Hunt, J. McV. (1960) "Experience and the development of motivation: Some reinterpretations." *Child Devel.,* 31:489–504. **381**

———. (1961) *Intelligence and experience.* New York: Ronald Press. **68, 78, 185, 189, 191**

Hunter, W. S. (1913) "The delayed reaction in animals and children." *Behav. Monogr., 2.* **404**

———, and S. C. Bartlett. (1948) "Double alternation behavior in young children." *J. exp. Psychol., 38:558–567.* **411**

Hurlock, E. B. (1953) *Development psychology.* New York: McGraw-Hill. **270**

I

Ingham, H. V. (1949) "A statistical study of family relationships in psychoneurosis." *Amer. J. Psychiat., 106:91–98.* **498**

J

Jacobs, P. I. (1963) "Item difficulty and programed learning." *Programed Instruction, 2:21–36.* **395**

Jacobsen, C. F., and H. W. Nissen. (1937) "Studies of cerebral function in primates. IV: The effects of frontal lobe lesions on the delayed alternation habit in monkeys." *J. comp. physiol. Psychol., 23:101–112.* **398**

Jacobson, E. (1932) "Electrophysiology of mental activity." *Amer. J. Psychol., 44:677–694.* **405**

Jahoda, M. (1955) "Toward a social psychology of mental health." In A. M. Rose, ed., *Mental health and mental disorder.* New York: Norton. **491**

———. (1958) *Current concepts of positive mental health.* Joint Commission on Mental Illness and Health. Monogr. Series No. I. New York: Basic Books. **464, 491**

James, W. (1890) *Principles of psychology.* New York: Holt, Rinehart and Winston, 1956. **346**

Janis, I. L., C. I. Hovland, et al. (1959) *Personality and persuasibility.* New Haven: Yale Univ. Press. **442**

Janke, L. L., and R. J. Havighurst. (1945) "Relations between ability and social status in a midwestern community. II: Sixteen-year-old boys and girls." *J. educ. Psychol., 36:499–509.* **180**

Jastrow, J. P. (1894) "Exposition d'anthropologie de Chicago-testes psychologique etc." *Année Psychol., 1:522–526.*

Jaynes, J. (1956) "Imprinting: The interaction of learned and innate behavior. I: Development and generalization." *J. comp. physiol. Psychol., 49:201–206.* **86, 87**

———. (1957) "Imprinting: The interaction of learned and innate behavior. II: The critical period." *J. comp. physiol. Psychol., 50:6–10.* **86, 87**

Jenkins, J. G., and K. M. Dallenbach. (1924) "Oblivescence during sleep and waking." *Amer. J. Psychol., 35:605–612.* **391, 392**

Jenkins, P. M., and C. N. Cofer. (1957) "An exploratory study of discrete free association to compound verbal stimuli." *Psychol. Rep., 3: 599–602.* **414**

Jenkins, W. O., H. McFann, and F. L. Clayton. (1950) "A methodological study of extinction following periodic and continuous reinforcement." *J. comp. physiol. Psychol., 43:155–167.* **362**

Jersild, A. T., F. V. Markey, and C. L. Jersild. (1933) "Children's fears, dreams, wishes, day-dreams, dislikes, pleasant and unpleasant memories." *Child Devel. Monogr.* No. 12. **260, 261**

Jervis, G. A. (1954) "Phenylpyruvic oligophrenia (phenylketonuria)." *A. Res. nerv. ment. Dis. Proc., 33:259.* **191**

———. (1959) "The mental deficiencies." In S. Arieti, ed., *American handbook of psychiatry,* Vol. II. New York: Basic Books. **191**

Johnson, D. L., et al. (1965) "Follow-up evaluation of human relations training for psychiatric patients." In W. Bennis and E. Schein, eds., *Human relations laboratory training theory and practice.* New York: Wiley. **510**

Joint Commission on Mental Illness and Health. (1961) *Action for mental health.* New York: Basic Books. **490**

Jones, H. E., and H. S. Conrad. (1933) "The growth and decline of intelligence: A study of a homogeneous group between the ages of ten and sixty." *Psychol. Monogr., 13:223–298.* **188**

———, and ———. (1954) Unpublished data cited in H. E. Jones, "The environment and mental development." In L. Carmichael, ed., *Manual of child psychology.* New York: Wiley. **180**

Judd, C. H. (1908) "The relation of special training to general intelligence." *Educ. Rev., 36:28–42.* **386**

Judd, D. B. (1951) "Basic correlates of the visual stimulus," In S. S. Stevens, ed., *Handbook of experimental psychology.* New York: Wiley. **299**

Judson, A. J., and C. N. Cofer. (1956) "Reasoning as an associative process. I: 'Direction' in a simple verbal problem." *Psychol. Rep., 2:469–476.* **411**

———, ———, and S. Gelfand. (1956) "Reasoning as an associative process. II: 'Direction' in problem solving as a function of prior reinforcement of relevant responses." *Psychol. Rep., 2:501–507.* **412, 416**

Jung, C. G. (1939) *The integration of personality.* New York: Farrar & Rinehart. **449**

K

Kahn, R. L., and D. Katz. (1952) "Some recent findings in human-relations research in industry." In G. E. Swanson, T. M. Newcomb, and E. L. Hartley, eds., *Readings in social psychology.* New York: Holt, Rinehart and Winston. Pp. 650–665. **551**

Kallmann, F. J. (1938) *The genetics of schizophrenia.* New York: J. J. Augustin. **506**

———. (1953) *Heredity in health and mental disorder: Principles of psychiatric genetics in the light of comparative twin studies.* New York: Norton. **71, 72, 506**

Kamin, L. J. (1959) "The delay of punishment gradient." *J. comp. physiol. Psychol.,* 52:434–437. **384**

Kantor, R. E., J. M. Wallner, and C. L. Winder. (1953) "Process and reactive schizophrenia." *J. consult. Psychol.,* 17:157–162. **505**

Kardiner, A. (1939) *The individual and his society: The psychodynamics of primitive social organization.* New York: Columbia Univ. Press. **449**

Kassil, V. G. (1959) "Conditioned reflex influence of the receptors of the stomach in higher animals." *Dokl. Akad. Nauk SSSR,* 129:464–467. **370**

Katona, G. (1940) *Organizing and memorizing.* New York: Columbia Univ. Press. **415**

Kellogg, L. A., and W. N. Kellogg. (1933) *The ape and the child.* New York: McGraw-Hill. **82**

Kelly, G. A. (1955) *The psychology of personal constructs.* New York: Norton. **30, 442, 499**

———. (1963) *A theory of personality.* New York: Norton. **442**

Kerr, D. B., F. Haugen, and R. Melzack. (1955) "Responses evoked in brain stem by tooth stimulation." *Am. J. Physiol.,* 183:253–258. **229**

Keys, A., et al. (1950) *The biology of human starvation.* Minneapolis: Univ. Minnesota Press. **217, 222, 329**

Kimble, G. A. (1961) *Hilgard & Marquis' Conditioning and learning.* New York: Appleton-Century-Crofts. **351**

Kinsey, A. C., et al. (1948) *Sexual behavior in the human male.* Philadelphia: Saunders. **226, 227**

———, et al. (1953) *Sexual behavior in the human female.* Philadelphia: Saunders. **228**

Klineberg, O. (1935) *Negro intelligence and selective migration.* New York: Columbia Univ. Press. **202, 203**

———. (1938) "Emotional expression in Chinese literature." *J. abn. soc. Psychol.,* 33:517–520. **256**

———. (1954) *Social psychology,* 2nd ed. New York: Holt, Rinehart and Winston. **242**

Klopfer, B., and D. M. Kelley. (1942) *The Rorschach technique.* Yonkers-on-Hudson, N.Y.: World Book Co. **145**

Klüver, H., and P. C. Bucy. (1937) "'Psychic blindness' and other symptoms following bilateral temporal lobectomy in Rhesus monkeys." *Amer. J. Physiol.,* 119:352–353. **264**

Köhler, W. (1925) *The mentality of apes.* New York: Harcourt, Brace & World. **7, 8, 364**

Kohler, I. (1962) "Experiments with goggles." *Sci. Amer.,* 206:62–72. **338**

Kretschmer, E. (1925) *Physique and character,* 2nd ed. (trans. W. J. H. Spratt). New York: Harcourt, Brace & World. **434**

Kreuger, W. C. F. (1929) "The effect of overlearning on retention." *J. exp. Psychol.,* 12:71–78. **390**

Kryter, K. D. (1950) "Effects of noise on man." *J. Speech hear. Dis.,* Supp. No. I, p. 18. **262**

Kuder, G. F. (1953) *Kuder Preference Record–Vocational: Manual,* and *Kuder Preference Record–Personal: Manual.* Chicago: Science Research Associates. **143**

Kulp, D. H. (1934) "Prestige as measured by single experience changes and their permanency." *J. educ. Res.,* 27:663–672. **336**

Kulpe, O. (1904) "Versuche über Abstraktion." *Berlin I Kongr. exper. Psychol.,* 56–68. **319**

L

Lacey, H., and A. E. Goss. (1959) "Conceptual block sorting as a function of number, pattern of assignment and strength of labeling responses." *J. genet. Psychol.,* 94:221–232. **411**

Ladd-Franklin, C. (1929) *Colour and colour theories.* New York: Harcourt, Brace. **304**

Lambert, W. W., and R. L. Solomon. (1952) "Extinction of a running response as a function of block point from the goal." *J. comp. physiol. Psychol.,* 45:269–279. **467**

Landis, C., and W. A. Hunt. (1939) *The startle pattern.* New York: Farrar & Rinehart. **256**

Langner, S., and T. Michael. (1963) *Life stress and mental health: The Midtown Manhattan Study,* Vol. II. New York: Free Press. **492**

Lashley, K. S. (1938) "The thalamus and emotion." *Psychol. Rev.,* 45:42–61. **255**

Laski, H. J. (1948) *The American democracy*. New York: Viking. **15**

Lawrence, D. H., and W. A. Mason. (1955) "Intake and weight adjustment in rats to changes in feeding schedule." *J. comp. physiol. Psychol.*, 48:267–271. **221**

Lazarsfeld, P. F., B. Berelson, and H. Gaudet. (1944) *The people's choice*. New York: Duell, Sloan & Pearce. **524, 525**

Lee, E. S. (1951) "Negro intelligence and selective migration: A Philadelphia test of the Klineberg hypothesis." *Amer. soc. Rev.*, 16:227–233. **202**

Lefkowitz, M., R. R. Blake, and J. S. Mouton. (1955) "Status factors in pedestrian violation of traffic signals." *J. abn. soc. Psychol.*, 51:704–706. **527**

Lejeune, J., et al. (1959) "Étude des chromosomes somatiques de neuf enfants mongoliens." *C. R. Acad. Sci. Paris*, 248:1721–1722. **191**

Lenneberg, E. H., and J. M. Roberts. (1956) "The language of experience: A study in methodology." *Int. J. Amer. Linguistics*, Suppl. 22 (memoir 13). **411**

Leonard, W. E. (1927) *The locomotive God*. New York: Appleton-Century-Crofts. **269**

Lerner, M. J., and G. W. Fairweather. (1963) "Social behavior of chronic schizophrenics in supervised and unsupervised work groups." *J. abn. soc. Psychol.*, 67:219–225. **516–518**

Levine, R., I. Chein, and G. Murphy. (1942) "The relation of the intensity of a need to the amount of perceptual distortion: A preliminary report." *J. Psychol.*, 13:283–293. **330**

Levy, D. M. (1943) *Maternal overprotection*. New York: Columbia Univ. Press. **454**

Lewin, K. (1935) *A dynamic theory of personality*. New York: McGraw-Hill. **456, 471**

——. (1943) "Forces behind food habits and methods of change." *Bull. Nat. Res. Coun.*, 108:35–65. **528**

——, R. Lippitt, and R. White. (1939) "Patterns of aggressive behavior in experimentally created 'social climates.' " *J. soc. Psychol.*, 10:271–299. **552**

Lewis, H. B. (1940) "Studies in the principles of judgments and attitudes. II: The influence of political attitude on the organization and stability of judgments." *J. soc. Psychol.*, 11: 121–146. **336**

——. (1941) "Studies in the principles of judgments and attitudes. IV: The operation of 'prestige suggestion.' " *J. soc. Psychol.*, 14:229–256. **336**

Lewis, J. H., and T. R. Sarbin. (1943) "Studies in psychosomatics: The influence of hypnotic

stimulation on gastric hunger contractions." *Psychosom. Med.*, 5:125–131. **538**

Li, C. L., C. Cullen, and H. H. Jasper. (1956) "Laminar microelectrode analysis of cortical unspecific recruiting response and spontaneous rhythms." *J. Neurophysiol.*, 19:131–143. **106**

Licklider, J. C. R. (1951) "A duplex theory of pitch perception." *Experientia*, 7:128–134. **291**

Liddell, H. S. (1944) "Conditioned reflex method and experimental neurosis." In J. McV. Hunt, ed., *Personality and the behavior disorders*. New York: Ronald. Pp. 389–412. **469, 476**

Lindholm, B. W. (1962) "Critical periods and the effects of early shock on later emotional behavior in the white rat." *J. comp. physiol. Psychol.*, 55:597–599. **85**

Lindquist, E. F. (1948) *Iowa tests of educational development: General manual*. Chicago: Science Research Associates. **143**

Lindsley, D. B. (1948) "Emotions and the electroencephalogram." In M. L. Reymert, ed., *The second international symposium on feelings and emotions*. New York: McGraw-Hill. **261**

——. (1951) "Emotion." In S. S. Stevens, ed., *Handbook of experimental psychology*. New York: Wiley. Pp. 473–516. **108, 109, 258, 264**

Lockman, R. F. (1964) "An empirical description of the subfields of psychology." *Amer. Psychologist*, 19:645–653. **53–54**

Lohr, T. F. (1959) "The effect of shock on the rat's choice of a path to food." *J. exp. Psychol.*, 58: 312–318. **382, 384**

Lorenz, K. (1957) "Companionship in bird life." In C. H. Schiller, ed., *Instinctive behavior: The development of a modern concept*. New York: International Universities Press. **86**

Lorge, I. (1936) "Prestige, suggestion, attitudes." *J. soc. Psychol.*, 7:386–402. **336**

——. (1945) "Schooling makes a difference." *Teach. Coll. Rec.*, 46:483–492. **183**

Lowell, E. L. (1952) "The effect of need for achievement on learning and speed of performance." *J. Psychol.*, 33:31–40. **235**

Lowell, F. E. (1941) "A study of the variability of IQ's in retest." *J. appl. Psychol.*, 25:341–356. **188**

Luchins, A. A. (1942) "Mechanization in problem solving, the effect of *Einstellung*." *Psychol. Monogr.*, 54 (Whole No. 248). **418, 419**

Luh, C. W. (1922) "The conditions of retention." *Psychol. Monogr.*, 31 (Whole No. 142). **388, 389, 417, 418, 419**

Lyon, D. O. (1914) "The relation of length of material to time taken for learning and optimum distribution of time." *J. educ. Psychol.*, 5:1–9, 85–91, 155–163. **378**

Lyons, J. (1964) "Expressive patterns as a function of their mode of production." *J. consult. Psychol.*, 28:85–86. **458**

Mc

McAllester, D. (1941) "Water as a disciplinary agent among the Crow and Blackfoot." *Amer. Anthrop.*, 43:593–604. **452**

McCarthy, D. (1944) "A study of the reliability of the Goodenough drawing test of intelligence." *J. Psychol.*, 18:201–216. **130**

McClelland, D. C. (1951) *Personality.* New York: William Sloane Associates. **367, 368, 385**

———. (1958) "The use of measures of human motivation in the study of society." In J. W. Atkinson, ed., *Motives in fantasy, action and society.* Princeton, N.J.: Van Nostrand. **236, 238**

———. (1961) *The achieving society.* Princeton, N.J.: Van Nostrand. **232, 237, 239**

———, and J. W. Atkinson. (1948) "The projective expression of needs. I: The effect of different intensities of the hunger drive on perception." *J. Psychol.*, 25:205–222. **330**

———, ———, R. A. Clark, and E. L. Lowell. (1953) *The achievement motive.* New York: Appleton-Century-Crofts. **146, 232, 233, 234, 236, 237**

———, and G. A. Friedman. (1952) "A cross-cultural study of the relationship between child-training practices and achievement motivation appearing in folk tales." In G. E. Swanson, T. M. Newcomb, and E. L. Hartley, eds., *Readings in social psychology.* New York: Holt, Rinehart and Winston. **234**

———, and A. M. Liberman. (1949) "The effect of need for achievement on recognition of need-related words." *J. Pers.*, 18:236–251. **235**

McConnell, J. V. (1962) "Memory transfer through cannibalism in planarians." *J. Neuropsychiat.*, 3:S42–48. **113–117**

McDougall, W. (1908) *An introduction to social psychology.* London: Methuen. **216**

McGeoch, J. A. (1930) "The influence of associative value upon the difficulty of nonsense-syllable lists." *J. genet. Psychol.*, 37:421–426. **378**

———, and A. L. Irion. (1952) *The psychology of human learning*, 2nd ed. New York: Longmans, Green. **377**

———, and W. T. McDonald. (1931) "Meaningful relation and retroactive inhibition." *Amer. J. Psychol.*, 43:579–588. **391**

McGinnies, E. (1949) "Emotionality and perceptual defense." *Psychol. Rev.*, 56:244–251. **334**

McGregor, D. (1960) *The human side of the enterprise.* New York: McGraw-Hill. **241, 242, 243**

McKellar, P. (1957) *Imagination and thinking: A psychological analysis.* New York: Basic Books. **422**

MacLean, P. D. (1960) "Psychosomatics." In *Handbook of physiology.* Washington, D.C.: Amer. Physiol. Soc. Pp. 1723–1744. **264**

———. (1964) "Psychosomatic disease and the 'visceral brain,' recent developments bearing on the Papez theory of emotion." In R. L. Isaacson, ed., *Basic readings in neuropsychology.* New York: Harper & Row. Pp. 181–211. **306**

McLellan, F. C. (1939) *The neurogenic bladder.* Springfield, Ill.: Thomas. **83**

McNemar, G. (1942) *The revision of the Stanford-Binet scale: An analysis of the standardization data.* Boston: Houghton Mifflin. **180, 199**

M

Magoun, H. W. (1963) *The waking brain*, 2nd ed. Springfield, Ill.: Thomas. **229**

Maltzman, I., W. Bogartz, and L. Breger. (1958) "A procedure for increasing word association originality and its transfer effects." *J. exp. Psychol.*, 56:392–398. **419**

Mark, J. C. (1953) "The attitudes of the mothers of male schizophrenics toward child behavior." *J. abn. soc. Psychol.*, 48:185–189. **507**

Markosyan, A. A. (1958) "The interaction of signal systems in the process of blood coagulation." *Zh. vyssh. nervn. Deyatel.*, 8:161–167. **370**

Marquis, D. P. (1931) "Can conditioned responses be established in the newborn infant?" *J. genet. Psychol.*, 39:479–492. **74**

Masland, R. L. (1958) "The prevention of mental retardation: A survey of research." *Amer. J. ment. Def.*, 62:991–1112. **191**

Maslow, A. (1950) "Self-actualizing people: A study of psychological health." *Personality Symposia*, 1.16. **465**

———. (1954) *Motivation and personality.* New York: Harper. **241**

———. (1957) "Two kinds of cognition and their integration." *Gen. Semantics Bull.*, Nos. 20 and 21. Lakeville, Conn.: Inst. General Semantics. **416, 417**

———. (1962) *Toward a psychology of being.* Princeton, N.J.: Van Nostrand. **465**

Mason, W. A., and P. C. Green. (1962) "The effects of social restriction on the behavior of Rhesus monkeys. IV: Responses to a novel environment and to an alien species." *J. comp. physiol. Psychol.*, 55:363–368. **84**

Masserman, J. H. (1943) *Behavior and neurosis: An experimental psychoanalytic approach to psychological principles.* Chicago: Univ. Chicago Press. **255, 383, 476**

———. (1946) *Principles of dynamic psychiatry.* Philadelphia: W. B. Saunders. **255**

Mead, G. H. (1934) *Mind, self and society.* Chicago: Univ. Chicago Press. **6, 539**

Mead, M. (1935) *Sex and temperament in three primitive societies.* New York: Morrow. **13**

Meehl, P. E. (1950) "On the circularity of the law of effect." *Psychol. Bull.*, 47:52–75. **405**

Meltzer, H. (1930) "Individual differences in forgetting pleasant and unpleasant experience." *J. educ. Psychol.*, 21:399–409. **393**

———. (1933) "Students' adjustment in anger." *J. soc. Psychol.*, 4:285–309. **262**

Melzack, R. (1954) "The genesis of emotional behavior: An experimental study of the dog." *J. comp. physiol. Psychol.*, 47:166–168. **270**

Mendelsohn, G. A., and B. Griswold. (1964) "Differential use of incidental stimuli in problem-solving as a function of creativity." *J. abn. soc. Psychol.*, 68:431–436. **206**

Menzel, E. W., Jr., R. K. Davenport, and C. M. Rogers. (1963) "The effects of environmental restriction upon the chimpanzee's responsiveness to objects." *J. comp. physiol. Psychol.*, 56:78–85. **85**

Merton, R. K. (1957) *Social theory and social structure.* New York: Free Press. **476**

Meyers, W. J. (1962) "Critical period for the facilitation of exploratory behavior by infantile experience." *J. comp. physiol. Psychol.*, 55:1099–1101. **85**

Miles, W. R., and L. H. Beck. (1949) "Infrared absorption in field studies of olfaction in honeybees." *Proc. Nat. Acad. Sci.*, 35:292–310. **307**

Milgram, S. (1964) "Group pressure and action against a person." *J. abn. soc. Psychol.*, 69:137–143. **528**

Miller, D. C. (1937) *Sound waves: Their shape and speed.* New York: Macmillan. **282**

Miller, G. A. (1958) From a speech presented at the University of Texas. **30**

———. (1962) *Psychology: The science of mental life.* New York: Harper & Row. **18, 20, 49**

———. (1964) *Mathematics and psychology.* New York: Wiley. **124**

———, E. H. Galanter, and K. H. Pribram. (1960)

Plans and the structure of behavior. New York: Holt, Rinehart and Winston. **107**

Miller, N. E. (1957) "Experiments on motivation: Studies combining psychological, physiological and pharmacological techniques." *Science, 126:* 1271–1278. **224**

———, and J. Dollard. (1941) *Social learning and imitation.* New Haven: Yale Univ. Press. **409**

———, R. I. Sampliner, and P. Woodrow. (1957) "Thirst-reducing effects of water by stomach fistula vs. water by mouth measured by both a consummatory and an instrumental response." *J. comp. physiol. Psychol.*, 50:1–5. **225**

Miller, W. S. (1950) *Miller Analogies Test: Manual.* New York: Psychological Corporation. **138**

Minami, H., and K. M. Dallenbach. (1946) "The effect of activity upon learning and retention in the cockroach, *periplaneta Americana.*" *Amer. J. Psychol.*, 59:1–58. **391**

Minnesota Multiphasic Personality Inventory, copyright by the University of Minnesota, published by The Psychological Corporation. **144**

Mitchell, P. H. (1948) *A textbook of general physiology,* 4th ed. New York: McGraw-Hill. **104**

Moltz, H., and L. A. Rosenblum (1959) "Imprinting and associative learning: The stability of the following responses in Peking ducks (*anas platyrhynchous*)." *J. comp. physiol. Psychol.*, 51:580–583. **87**

Montgomery, K. C., and J. A. Monkman. (1955) "The relation between fear and exploratory behavior." *J. comp. physiol. Psychol.*, 48:132–136. **230**

Montgomery, M. F. (1931) "The role of the salivary glands in the thirst mechanism." *Amer. J. Physiol.*, 96:221–227. **223**

Moran, L. J., and R. B. Mefferd, Jr. (1959) "Repetitive psychometric measures." *Psychol. Rep.*, 5:269–275. **149–150**

Morgan, C. L. (1891; 2nd ed., 1899) *Introduction to comparative psychology.* London: W. Scott. **42**

Morgan, C. T., and J. D. Morgan. (1940) "Studies in hunger. II: The relation of gastric denervation and dietary sugar to the effect of insulin upon food-intake in the rat." *J. genet. Psychol.*, 57:153–163. **217**

———, and E. Stellar. (1950) *Physiological psychology,* 2nd ed. New York: McGraw-Hill. **258**

Morgan, H. H. (1951) "An analysis of certain structured and unstructured test results of achieving and non-achieving high ability college students." Unpublished doctoral dissertation, Univ. Michigan. **235**

Morley, D. W. (1954) *The evolution of an insect society.* London: Allen and Unwin. **9**

Morrell, F., and H. H. Jasper. (1956) "Electrographic studies of the function of temporary connections in the brain." *EEG clin. Neurophysiol.*, 20:574–587. **397**

Morris, C. W. (1956) *Varieties of human value.* Chicago: Univ. Chicago Press. **14**

Morton, R. B. (1965) "Patient training laboratory." In W. Bennis and E. Schein, eds., *Human relations laboratory training theory and practice.* New York: Wiley. **510**

Moruzzi, G., and H. W. Magoun. (1949) "Brain stem reticular formation and activation of the EEG." *EEG clin. Neurophysiol.*, 1:455–473. **108**

Mountcastle, V. B. (1961) "Some functional properties of the somatic afferent system." In W. A. Rosenblith, ed., *Sensory communication.* New York: Wiley; Cambridge, Mass.: MIT Press. Pp. 403–435. **309**

Mowrer, O. H. (1936) "Maturation vs. 'learning' in the development of vestibular and optokinetic nystagmus." *J. genet. Psychol.*, 48:383–404. **326**

———. (1950) *Learning theory and personality dynamics: Selected papers.* New York: Ronald. **367**

———. (1959) "Changing conceptions of the unconscious." *J. nerv. ment. Dis.* 129:222–234. **496**

———. (1960) "Sin, the lesser of two evils." *Amer. Psychologist*, 15:301–304. **491, 497**

———, and Mowrer, W. M. (1938) "Enuresis—a method for its study and treatment." *Amer. J. Orthopsychiat.* 8:436–459. **349**

Munn, N. L. (1932) "Bilateral transfer of learning." *J. exp. Psychol.*, 15:343–353. **386**

Murray, H. A. (1938) *Explorations in personality.* New York: Oxford Univ. Press. **145, 439**

———. (1943) *Thematic Apperception Test: Manual.* Cambridge, Mass.: Harvard Univ. Press. **145**

Mussen, P. H. (1962) "Consequents of masculinity of interest in adolescence." *J. consult. Psychol.*, 26:435–440. **458**

———, and H. K. Naylor. (1954) "The relationship between overt and fantasy aggression." *J. abn. soc. Psychol.*, 49:235–240. **149, 459**

N

Nafe, J. P. (1934) "The relation of warmth and cold to vaso-constriction and dilation." *Psychol. Bull.*, 31:709–710. **309**

———. (1937) "An experimental study of the affective qualities." *Amer. J. Psychol.*, 38:725–743. **254**

National Committee against Mental Illness. (1957) *What are the facts about mental illness?* Washington, D.C.: National Committee against Mental Illness. **491**

National Research Council Bull. 108. (1943) *The problem of changing food habits.* Washington, D.C.: National Research Council, Natl. Acad. Sci. **529**

Neisser, U., and P. Weene. (1962) "Hierarchies in concept attainment." *J. exp. Psychol.*, 64:640–645. **424–425**

Newman, E. (1928) Introduction to O. P. Deutsch, ed., *Franz Schubert's letters and other writings.* London: Faber & Gwyer. **437**

Newman, H. H., F. F. Newman, and K. J. Holzinger. (1937) *Twins, a study of heredity and environment.* Chicago: Univ. Chicago Press. **179, 181, 182**

Nissen, H. W., K. L. Chow, and J. Semmes. (1951) "Effects of restricted opportunity for tactual, kinesthetic and manipulative experience on the behavior of a chimpanzee." *Amer. J. Psychol.*, 64:485–507. **84, 326**

Northrop, F. S. C. (1946) *The meeting of east and west.* New York: Macmillan. **14**

O

O'Kelley, L. I., and J. L. Falk. (1958) "Water regulation in the rat. II: The effects of preloads of water and sodium chloride on the bar-pressing performance of thirsty rats." *J. comp. physiol. Psychol.*, 51:22–25. **224**

Olds, J. (1955) "Physiological mechanisms of reward." In "Current theory and research in motivation, a symposium." *The Nebraska symposium on motivation.* Vol. III. Lincoln: Univ. Nebraska Press. **110**

———. (1956) "Pleasure centers in the brain." *Sci. Amer.*, 195:104–116. **111**

———, and P. Milner. (1944) "Positive reinforcement produced by electrical stimulation of septal area and other regions of rat brain." *J. comp. physiol. Psychol.*, 47:419–427. **110**

Osgood, C. E. (1952) "The nature and measurement of meaning." *Psychol. Bull.* 49:197–237. **33**

Otis, A. S. (1937, 1939) *Otis Quick-Scoring Mental Ability Tests. Manuals: Gamma, Alpha, Beta.*

Yonkers-on-Hudson, N.Y.: World Book Co. **138**

Outhit, M. C. (1933) "A study of the resemblance of parents and children in general intelligence." *Arch. Psychol.*, 149:1–60. **180**

Owens, W. A., Jr. (1953) "Age and mental abilities: A longitudinal study." *Genet. Psychol. Monogr.*, 48:3–54. **188**

P

Papez, J. W. (1937) "A proposed mechanism of emotion." *Arch. Neurol. Psychiat.*, 38:507–544. **264**

Parsons, T., R. F. Bales, and E. A. Shils. (1953) *Working papers in the theory of action.* Glencoe, Ill.: Free Press. **547**

Patrick, C. (1937) "Creative thought in artists." *J. Psychol.*, 4:35–73. **414**

Patrick, J. R. (1934a) "Studies in rational behavior and emotional excitement. I: Rational behavior in human subjects." *J. comp. Psychol.*, 18:1–22. **415**

———. (1934b) "The effect of emotional excitement on rational behavior in human subjects." *J. comp. Psychol.*, 18:153–195. **415**

Pavlov, I. P. (1927) *Conditioned reflexes* (trans. G. Vanup). New York: Oxford Univ. Press. **349**

Penfield, W., and H. Jasper. (1954) *Epilepsy and the functional anatomy of the brain.* Boston: Little, Brown. **388**

———, and T. Rasmussen. (1950) *The cerebral cortex of man.* New York: Macmillan. **107, 108**

Pepitone, E. A. (1952) "Responsibility to the group and its effects on the performance of members." Unpublished doctoral dissertation, Univ. Michigan. **553**

Pfaffman, C. (1960) "Taste and smell." In S. S. Stevens, ed., *Handbook of experimental psychology.* New York: Wiley. Pp. 1143–1177. **306**

———, R. P. Erickson, G. P. Frommer, and B. P. Halpern. (1961) "Gustatory discharges in the rat medulla and thalamus." In W. A. Rosenblith, ed., *Sensory communication.* New York: Wiley; Cambridge, Mass.: MIT Press. Pp. 455–473. **306**

Piaget, J. (1932) *The moral judgment of the child.* New York: Harcourt, Brace & World. **533**

Pick, H. L., Jr., and J. C. Hay. (1964) "Adaptation of prismatic distortion." *Psychon. Sci.*, 1:199–200. **340**

Pielstick, N. L., and A. B. Woodruff. (1964) "Exploratory behavior and curiosity in two age and ability groups of children." *Psychol. Rep.*, 14:831–839. **249–250**

Pinneau, S. A. (1955) "The infantile disorders of hospitalism and anaclitic depression." *Psychol. Bull.*, 52:429–452. **86**

Poincaré, H. (1913) "Mathematical creation." In G. B. Halstead, trans., *The foundations of science.* New York: Science Press. **416**

Porter, D. (1958) "Teaching machines." *Harvard Grad. Sch. Ed. Assn. Bull.*, No. III. **395**

Postman, L., J. Bruner, and E. McGinnies. (1948) "Personal values as selective factors in perception." *J. abn. soc. Psychol.*, 43:142–154. **331**

———, and B. H. Schneider. (1951) "Personal values, visual recognition and recall." *Psychol. Rev.*, 58:271–284. **332**

Powers, E. (1930) *Graphic factors in relation to personality.* Hanover, N.H.: Dartmouth College Library. **439**

Powers, M. K. (1956) "Permanence of measured vocational interests of adult males." *J. appl. Psychol.*, 40:69–72. **431**

Premack, D. (1959) "Toward empirical behavior laws. I: Positive reinforcement." *Psychol. Rev.*, 66:219–233.

President's Panel on Mental Retardation. (1963) *Mental retardation: A national plan for a national problem. Chart Book.* Washington, D.C.: U.S. Dept. Health, Education and Welfare. **190**

Pressey, S. L. (1926) "A simple apparatus which gives tests and scores—and teaches." *Sch. and Soc.*, 23:373–376. **395**

———. (1950) "Development and appraisal of automatic devices providing immediate scoring of objective tests and concomitant self-instruction." *J. Psychol.*, 29:417–447. **395**

Pribram. K. H. (1960) "A review of theory in physiological psychology." *Ann. Rev. Psychol.*, 11:1–40. **105, 398**

Price, R. (1954) *The rich sardine.* New York: Simon and Schuster. **327**

Primac, D. W., A. F. Mirsky, and H. E. Rosvold. (1957) "Effects of centrally acting drugs on two tests of brain damage." *AMA Arch. Neurol. Psychiat.*, 77:328–332. **109**

Printers' Ink. (1932) "Peeled eye department." Sept. 29. 15. **321**

Public Health Service Publication No. 543 (rev. 1958). **490**

R

Rasmussen, E. W. (1936) "Social facilitation in albino rats." *Acta psychol. Hague.*, 4:275–294. **221**

Ray, W. S. (1957) "Verbal compared with manipulative solution of an apparatus problem." *Amer. J. Psychol.*, 50:429–444. **378, 411**

Razran, G. (1961) "The observable unconscious and the inferable conscious in current Soviet psychophysiology: Interceptive conditioning, semantic conditioning, and the orienting reflex." *Psychol. Rev.*, 68:81–147. **370–371**

Reger, R. (1962) "Repeated measurements with the WISC." *Psychol. Rep.*, 11:418. **205**

Restle, F., M. Andrews, and M. Rokeach. (1964) "Differences between open- and closed-minded subjects on learning-set and oddity problems." *J. abn. soc. Psychol.*, 68:648–654. **459**

Révész, G. (1937) "The problem of space with particular emphasis on specific sensory spaces." *Amer. J. Psychol.*, 50:429–444. **322**

Ribble, M. A. (1944) "Infantile experience in relation to personality development." In J. McV. Hunt, ed., *Personality and the behavior disorders.* New York: Ronald. **86**

Richter, C. P. (1943) *Total self-regulatory functions in animals and human beings.* Harvey Lect. 38:63–103. **220**

Ridenour, N. (1961) *Mental health in the U.S.: A 50-year history.* Cambridge, Mass.: Harvard Univ. Press. **491**

Riesen, A. H. (1949) "The development of visual perception in man and chimpanzee." *Science,* 106:107–108. **84, 326**

———. (1950) "Arrested vision." *Sci. Amer.,* 183:16–19. **326**

———. (1951) "Post-partum development of behavior." *Chicago Med. Sch. Quart.,* 13:17–24. **84, 326**

Riesman, D. (1955) *The lonely crowd.* New York: Doubleday. **14**

Riess, B. F. (1950) "The isolation of factors of learning and native behavior in field and laboratory studies." *Ann. N.Y. Acad. Sci.,* 1093–1102. **410**

Riley, D. A. (1952) "Rote learning as a function of distribution of practice and the complexity of the situation." *J. exp. Psychol.,* 43:88–95. **376**

Rogers, C. R. (1951) *Client-centered therapy: Its current practice, implication and theory.* Boston: Houghton Mifflin. **444**

———. (1957) "The necessary and sufficient conditions of therapeutic personality change." *J. consult. Psychol.,* 21:95–103. **499**

———. (1958) "A process conception of psychotherapy." *Amer. Psychologist,* 13:142–149. **496**

———. (1961) *On becoming a person.* Boston: Houghton Mifflin. **465**

Rokeach, Milton. (1960) *The open and closed mind.* New York: Basic Books. **442, 443**

Romanes, G. J. (1912) *Animal intelligence.* New York: Appleton-Century-Crofts. **230**

Rorschach, H. (1942) *Psychodiagnostics* (trans. P. Lemkau, and B. Kronenberg). Berne: Hans Huber. **145**

Rosen, J. (1953) *Direct analysis: Selected papers.* New York: Grune & Stratton. **510**

Ross, S., and R. F. Lockman. (1963) *A career in psychology.* Washington, D.C.: American Psychological Association. **55**

———, and ———. (1964) "Survey of graduate education in psychology: Some trends for the last decade." *Amer. Psychologist,* 19:623–628. **54–55**

Rosvold, H. E. (1959) "Physiological psychology." *Ann. Rev. Psychol.,* 10:415–454. **227**

———, M. Mishkin, and M. K. Szwarcbart. (1958) "Effects of subcortical lesions in monkeys on visual discrimination and single alternation performance." *J. comp. physiol. Psychol.,* 51:437–444. **398**

Rotter, J. B. (1954) *Social learning and clinical psychology.* Englewood Cliffs, N.J.: Prentice-Hall, **367, 456**

Ruch, T. C., J. F. Fulton, and W. J. German. (1938) "Sensory discrimination in the monkey, chimpanzee and man after lesions of the parietal lobe." *Arch. Neurol. Psychiat.,* 39:919–937. **398**

Ruggles, R., and Allport, G. W. (1939) "Recent applications of the A-S reaction study." *J. abn. soc. Psychol.,* 34:518–528. **127**

S

Sadacca, R., H. N. Ricciuti, and E. O. Swanson. (1956) *Content analysis of achievement motivation protocols: A study of scorer agreement.* Princeton, N.J.: Educational Testing Service. **235**

Sakel, M. (1938) "The pharmacological shock treatment of schizophrenia." *Nerv. ment. Dis. Monogr.* No. 62. **509**

Saltz, E., and S. E. Newman. (1960) "The effect of prior learning of symbols on performance in reasoning." *Amer. J. Psychol.,* 73:91–99. **411**

Sanford, F. H. (1950) *Authorization and leadership: A study of the follower's orientation to leadership.* Philadelphia: Institute for Research in Human Relations. **32**

———. (1951a) "Public orientation to Roosevelt." *Pub. Opinion Quart.,* 15:189–216. **549**

———. (1951b) "Leadership identification and acceptance." In H. Guetzkow, ed., *Groups, leadership and men.* Pittsburgh: Carnegie Press. **548**

———. (1956) "Creative health and the principle of habeas mentem." *Amer. J. Pub. Health,* 46:139–148. **491**

Sanford, R. N. (1936) "The effects of abstinence from food upon imaginal processes: A preliminary experiment." *J. Psychol.,* 2:129–136. **222**

———. (1962) "Implication of personality studies for curriculum and personnel planning." In W. Holtzman et al., *Personality factors on the college campus: Review of a symposium.* Austin, Tex.: Hogg Foundation. Pp. 6–7. **50, 381, 465**

———. (1963) "Personality: Its place in psychology." In S. Koch, ed., *Psychology: A study of a science.* New York: McGraw-Hill. V:488–592. **22, 442**

Sarason, S. B., and T. Gladwin. (1958) "Psychological and cultural problems in mental abnormality: A review of research." *Amer. J. ment. Defic.,* 62:1115–1307. **191**

Sarbin, T. R. (1954) "Role theory." In G. Lindzey, ed., *Handbook of social psychology.* Cambridge, Mass.: Addison-Wesley. **538**

———. (1964) "Role theoretical interpretation of psychological change." In P. Worchal and D. Byrne, eds., *Personality change.* New York: Wiley. **476**

Saul, L. J. (1939) "Hostility in cases of essential hypertension." *Psychosom. Med.,* 1:153–161. **268**

Schachter, S. (1959) *The psychology of affiliation.* Stanford: Stanford Univ. Press. **239**

Scheerer, C., ed. (1964) *Cognition: Theory, research, promise.* New York: Harper & Row. **442**

Schilder, P. (1938) *Psychotherapy.* London: Kegan Paul; New York: Norton. **501**

Schreiner, L., and A. Kling. (1956) "Rhinencephalon and behavior." *Amer. J. Physiol.,* 184:486–490. **255**

Scottish Council for Research on Education. (1949) *The trend of Scottish intelligence.* London: London Univ. Press. **199**

Searle, L. V. (1949) "The organization of hereditary maze-brightness and maze-dullness." *Genet. Psychol. Monogr.,* 39:279–325. **69**

Seay, B., B. K. Alexander, and H. Harlow. (1964) "Maternal behavior of socially deprived Rhesus monkeys." *J. abn. soc. Psychol.,* 69:345–354. **89–90**

Seward, J. P. (1954) "Learning theory and identification. II: Role of punishment." *J. genet. Psychol.,* 84:201–210. **367**

Shaffer, L. F. (1947) "Fear and courage in aerial combat." *J. consult. Psychol.,* 11:137–143. **254**

Sharp, A. A. (1938) "An experimental test of Freud's doctrine of the relation of hedonic tone to memory revival." *J. exp. Psychol.,* 22:395–418. **393**

Sheldon, W. H., and S. S. Stevens. (1942) *The varieties of temperament.* New York: Harper. **435, 436**

Sherif, M. (1936a) "A study of some social factors in perception." *Arch. Psychol.,* No. 187. **47, 335, 532**

———. (1936b) *The psychology of social norms.* New York: Harper. **532, 534**

Sherman, M., and C. B. Key. (1932) "The intelligence of isolated mountain children." *Child Devel.,* 3:279–290. **183**

Shipley, T. E., and J. Veroff. (1952) "A projective measure of need for affiliation." *J. exp. Psychol.,* 43:349–356. **239**

Shirley, M. M. (1933) *The first two years: A study of twenty-five babies. Vol. II. Intellectual development.* Minneapolis: Univ. Minnesota Press. **77**

Shoben, E. J., Jr. (1949) "Psychotherapy as a problem in learning theory." *Psychol. Bull.,* 46:366–392. **367**

Shvarts, L. A. (1960) "Conditioned reflexes to verbal stimuli." *Vop. Psikhol.,* 6:86–98. **370**

Siegel, A. I. (1953) "Deprivation of visual form definition in the ring dove. I: Discriminatory learning." *J. comp. physiol. Psychol.,* 46:115–119; "II: Perceptual-motor transfer." 46:249–252. **326**

Sivian, L. J., and S. D. White. (1933) "On minimum audible sound fields." *J. Acoust. Soc. Amer.,* 4:288–321. **287**

Skeels, H. M. (1938) "Mental development of children in foster homes." *J. consult. Psychol.,* 2:33–43. **182**

———, and H. B. Dye. (1939) "A study of the effects of differential stimulation on mentally retarded children." *Proc. Amer. Assoc. ment. Def.,* 44:114–136. **183**

Skinner, B. F. (1948) " 'Superstition' in the pigeon." *J. exp. Psychol.,* 38:168–172. **359**

———. (1954) "The science of learning and the art of teaching." *Harv. educ. Rev.*, 24:86–97. **394**

———. (1958) "Teaching machines." *Science, 128:* 969–977. **395**

———. (1960) "Pigeons in a pelican." *Amer. Psychologist, 15:*28–37. **393, 394**

Skodak, M. (1939) "Children in foster homes: A study of mental development." *Univ. Iowa Stud. Child. Welf., 16* (No. 1): 156. **182**

———. (1950) "Mental growth of adopted children in the same family." *J. genet. Psychol., 77:*3–9. **182**

———, and H. M. Skeels. (1945) "A follow-up study of children in adoptive homes." *J. genet. Psychol., 66:*21–58. **182**

———, and ———. (1949) "A final follow-up study of one hundred adopted children." *J. genet. Psychol., 75:*85–125. **182**

Slater, E. (1943) "The neurotic constitution: A statistical study of two thousand neurotic soldiers." *J. Neurol., Neurosurg., Psychiat., 6:* 1–16. **498**

Slavson, S. R. (1947) *The practice of group therapy.* New York: International Universities Press. **501**

Smith, E. M., H. O. Brown, J. E. P. Toman, and L. S. Goodman. (1947) "The lack of cerebral effects of d-tubo-curarine." *Anesthesiology, 8:*1–14. **405**

Smith, M. B. (1959) "Research strategies toward a conception of positive mental health." *Amer. Psychologist, 14:*673–681. **491**

Smith, M. E. (1926) "An investigation of the development of the sentence and the extent of vocabulary in young children." State University of Iowa, *Univ. Iowa Stud. Child Welf., 3* (No. 5). **79**

Smith, O. H., Jr., and A. D. Geis. (1956) "Comparative psychology in wildlife conservation." *Amer. Psychologist, 11:*183–187. **346**

Solarz, A. K. (1958) "Effects of hydration on the running and drinking performance of thirsty rats." *J. comp. physiol. Psychol., 51:*146–151. **225**

Solomon, R. L., and D. W. Howes. (1951) "Word frequency, personal values and visual deviation thresholds." *Psychol. Rev., 58:*256–270. **334**

———, L. J. Kamin, and L. C. Wynne. (1953) "Traumatic avoidance learning: The outcome of several extinction procedures with dogs." *J. abn. soc. Psychol., 48:*291–302. **383**

———, and L. Postman. (1952) "Frequency of usage as a determinant of recognition thresholds for words." *J. exp. Psychol., 43:*195–201. **329**

———, and L. C. Wynne. (1954) "Traumatic avoidance learning: The principles of anxiety conservation and partial irreversibility." *Psychol. Rev., 61:*353–385. **383**

Spelt, D. K. (1948) "The conditioning of the human fetus in utero." *J. exp. Psychol., 38:*338–346. **74**

Spence, K. W. (1956) *Behavior theory and conditioning.* New Haven, Conn.: Yale Univ. Press. **366**

Spiker, C. C. (1956) "Stimulus pretraining and subsequent performance in the delayed reaction experiment." *J. exp. Psychol., 52:*107–111. **411**

Spitz, R. A. (1953) "Psychoanalytische Begriffsbildung und physiologisches Denkmodell." *Schweiz Psychol. Anwend., 12:*24–39. **85, 183**

———. (1955) "Reply to Dr. Pinneau." *Psychol. Bull., 52:*453–459. **86, 183**

Srole, L., et al. (1962) *Mental health in the metropolis: The Midtown Manhattan Study,* Vol. I. New York: McGraw-Hill. **492**

Stekel, W. (1924) "The polyphony of thought." In D. Rapaport, ed., *Organization and pathology of thought.* New York: Columbia Univ. Press. **422**

Stendler, C. B. (1954) "Possible causes of overdependency in young children." *Child Devel., 25:* 125–146. **66**

Stevens, S. S. (1951) "Mathematics, measurement and psychophysics." In S. S. Stevens, ed., *Handbook of experimental psychology.* New York: Wiley. **49, 129**

———. (1957) "On the psychophysical law." *Psychol. Rev., 64:*153–181. **314**

———. (1959) "The quantification of sensation." *Daedalus, 88:*606–621. **314**

———, and H. Davis. (1938) *Hearing, its psychology and physiology.* New York: Wiley. **283**

———, and E. Newman. (1936) "The localization of actual sources of sound." *Amer. J. Psychol., 48:*297–306. **289**

———, and J. Volkmann. (1940) "The relation of pitch to frequency: A revised scale." *Amer. J. Psychol., 53:*329–353. **288**

Stevenson, H. W., and J. D. Swartz. (1958) "Learning set in children as a function of intellectual level." *J. comp. physiol. Psychol., 51:*755–757. **365**

———, M. M. Weir, and E. F. Zigler. (1959) "Discrimination learning in children as a function of motive-incentive conditions." *Psychol. Rep., 5:*95–98. **384**

Stewart, N. (1947) "A.G.C.T. scores of army personnel grouped by occupation." *Occupations*, 26:5–41. **197**

———. (1955) *Statistical studies of selected service testing*. Princeton, N.J.: Educational Testing Service. **203**

Stogdill, R. M. (1948) "Personal factors associated with leadership: A survey of the literature." *J. Psychol.*, 25:35–71. **547**

Stolz, H. R. (1940) "Shorty comes to terms with himself." *Progr. Educ.*, 17:405–411. **72**

Strong, E. K. (1915) Research Bulletin, Association of National Advertisers. **320**

———. (1951) *Vocational Interest Blank for Women: Manual; for Men: Manual*. Stanford, Calif.: Stanford Univ. Press. **143**

Sullivan, E. T., E. W. Clark, and E. W. Tiegs. (1951) *California Test of Mental Maturity (CTMM)*. Los Angeles, Calif.: California Testing Bureau. **138**

Sullivan, H. S. (1953) *The interpersonal theory of psychiatry*. New York: Norton. **449, 496**

Szasz, T. S. (1961) *The myth of mental illness*. New York: Hoeber. **491, 497**

———. (1963) *Law, liberty and psychiatry*. New York: Macmillan Co. **502**

T

Taylor, C. W., ed. (1964) *Widening horizons in creativity*. New York: Wiley. **198**

Taylor, J. G. (1962) *The behavioral basis of perception*. New Haven: Yale Univ. Press. **337, 338**

———, and P. C. Smith. (1956) "An investigation of the shape of learning curves for industrial motor tasks." *J. appl. Psychol.*, 40:142–149. **375**

Taylor, J. H., C. E. Thompson, and D. Spassoff. (1937) "The effects of conditions of work and various suggested attitudes on production and reported feelings of tiredness and boredness." *J. appl. Psychol.*, 21:431–450. **527**

Terman, L. M., et al. (1918) *The Stanford revision and extension of Binet-Simon scale for measuring intelligence*. Baltimore: Warwick & York. **134**

———, and M. A. Merrill (1937; rev., 1960) *Stanford-Binet intelligence scale*. Boston: Houghton Mifflin. **136, 137, 185, 186, 187, 189, 190**

———, and ———. (1937) *Measuring intelligence: A guide to the administration of the new revised Stanford-Binet tests of intelligence*. Cambridge, Mass.: The Riverside Press. **136, 137, 185**

———, and M. H. Oden. (1947) *The gifted child grows up*. Stanford, Calif.: Stanford Univ. Press. **194, 195**

———, and L. E. Tyler. (1954) "Psychological sex differences." In L. Carmichael, ed., *Manual of child psychology*, 2nd ed. New York: Wiley. Pp. 1064–1115. **199**

Thistlethwaite, D. (1950) "Attitude and structure as factors in the distortion of reasoning." *J. abn. soc. Psychol.*, 45:442–458. **416, 417**

Thompson, G. G. (1962) *Child psychology: Growth trends in psychological adjustment*, 2nd ed. Boston: Houghton Mifflin. **74**

Thompson, W. R. (1957) "Influence of prenatal anxiety on emotionality in young rats." *Science*, 125:698–699. **73, 74**

———, and W. Heron. (1954) "The effects of restricting early experience on the problem-solving capacity of dogs." *Canad. J. Psychol.*, 8:17–31. **85, 184**

Thorndike, E. L. (1898) "Animal intelligence." *Psychol. Monogr.*, Supp. 2 (Whole No. 8). **355**

———. (1932a) "Reward and punishment in animal learning." *Comp. Psychol. Monogr.*, 8 (Whole No. 39). **382**

———. (1932b) *The fundamentals of learning*. New York: Teachers College, Bureau of Publications. **382**

———, and G. J. Ruger. (1923) "The effect of first-year Latin upon knowledge of English words of Latin derivation." *Sch. and Soc.*, 18:260–270. **385**

———, and Woodworth, R. S. (1901) "The influence of improvement in one mental function upon the efficiency of other functions." *Psychol. Rev.*, 8:247–267, 384–395. **385**

Thorndike, R. L. (1933) "The effect of the interval between test and retest on the constancy of the I.Q." *J. educ. Psychol.*, 24:543–549. **186**

———. (1940) "Constancy of the I.Q." *Psychol. Bull.*, 37:167–186. **185, 186**

Thorpe, W. H. (1956) *Learning and instinct in animals*. Cambridge, Mass.: Harvard Univ. Press. **346**

Tiegs, E. W., and W. W. Clark. (1951) *California Achievement Tests: Manuals of Direction for primary, elementary, intermediate, advanced batteries*. Los Angeles, Calif.: California Testing Bureau. **143**

Tietze, T. (1949) "A study of mothers of schizophrenic patients." *Psychiatry*, 12:55–65. **507**

Tinbergen, N. (1951) *The study of instinct*. London: Oxford Univ. Press. **260**

Tobias, Sigmund. (1963) "Teachers' attitudes toward programed instructional terms." *J. of Programed Instruction*, 2:25–29. **396**

Tolman, E. C. (1932) *Purposive behavior in animals and man.* New York: Appleton-Century-Crofts. **367**

——. (1951) "A psychological model." In T. Parsons and E. A. Shils, eds., *Toward a general theory of action.* Cambridge, Mass.: Harvard Univ. Press. Pp. 279–361. **407**

Torrance, E. P. (1960) "Educational achievement of the highly intelligent and the highly creative: Eight partial replications of the Getzels-Jackson study." *Research Memorandum,* BER-60-18. Minneapolis: Bureau of Educational Research, University of Minnesota. **198**

——. (1962) *Guiding creative talent.* Englewood Cliffs, N.J.: Prentice-Hall. **198**

Travers, R. M. W. (1949) "Significant research on the prediction of academic success." In W. T. Donohue, C. H. Coomb, and R. M. W. Travers, eds., *The measurement of student adjustment and achievement.* Ann Arbor: Univ. Michigan Press. Pp. 147–190. **195**

Trittipoe, W. J., T. G. Trittipoe, and C. P. Hahn (1963). "The effectiveness of three programed-learning frame styles." *J. of Programmed Instruction,* 2:35–43. **395**

Tryon, R. C. (1940) "Genetic differences in maze learning in rats." *39th Yearbk. Nat. Soc. Stud. Educ.* Bloomington, Ill.: Public School Publishing Co. I:111–119. **69, 70**

Tschukitschew. (1930) "The action of insulin on the motility of the gastro-intestinal tract." *Amer. J. Physiol.,* 91:467–474. **218**

Tyler, L. E. (1956) *The psychology of human differences,* 2nd ed. New York: Appleton-Century-Crofts. **188, 195, 200, 202**

U

Ullmann, L. P. (1964) "Psychiatric hospital effectiveness: Replication on a sample three years removed." Paper read at American Psychological Association, Los Angeles. **510**

Underwood, B. J. (1961) "Ten years of massed and distributed practice." *Psychol. Rev.,* 78:229–247. **376**

——, and D. Goad. (1951) "Studies of distributed practice. I: The influence of intra-list similarity in serial learning." *J. exp. Psychol.,* 42:125–134. **376**

——, R. Keppel, and R. Schulz. (1962) "Studies in the distribution of practice. XXII: Some conditions which enhance retention. *J. exp. Psychol.,* 64:355–363. **400**

——, and L. Postman. (1960) "Extraexperimental sources of interference and forgetting." *Psychol. Rev.,* 67:73–94. **388**

——, and J. Richardson. (1956) "Verbal concept learning as a function of instructions and dominance level." *J. exp. Psychol.,* 51:229–238. **408**

U.S. Department of Labor, Bureau of Employment Security, USES. (1958) Technical report on standardization of General Aptitude Test Battery. *Tech. Rep. B-381,* July. **142**

V

Van Alstyne, D. (1929) "The environment of three-year-old children: Factors related to intelligence and vocabulary tests." *Teach. Coll. Contrib. Educ.,* No. 366. **184**

Van Ormer, E. B. (1932) "Retention after intervals of sleep and of waking." *Arch. Psychol.,* No. 137. New York: Columbia Univ. Press. **391**

Veblen, T. (1945) *The theory of the leisure class.* New York: Wiley. **15**

Verney, E. B. (1947) "The antidiuretic hormone and the factors which determine its release." *Proc. Roy. Soc. London,* B, 135:25–106. **224**

Veroff, J. (1957) "Development and validation of a projective measure of power motivation." *J. abn. soc. Psychol.,* 54:1–8. **239**

Verplanck, W. S. (1956) "The operant conditioning of human motor behavior." *Psychol. Bull.,* 53:70–83. **359, 360**

Vinogradova, O. S., and N. A. Eysler. (1959) "The manifestations of verbal connections in the recording vascular reactions." *Vop. Psikhol.,* 2:101–116. **371**

Voeks, V. (1957) *On becoming an educated person: An orientation to college.* Philadelphia: Saunders. **379**

Von Domarus, E. (1929) *Das Denken und seine Krankhaften Störungen.* Leipzig: Kabitzch. **422**

Von Frisch, K. (1950) *Bees: Their vision, chemical senses and language.* Ithaca, N.Y.: Cornell Univ. Press. **6**

Von Senden, M. V. (1932) *Raum- und Gestaltauffassung bei operierten Blindgeborenen vor und nach Operation.* Leipzig: Barth. **84, 325**

Von Uexküll, J. (1934) "A stroll through the worlds of animals and men." In C. H. Schiller, ed., *Instinctive behavior.* Pp. 5–80. New York: International Universities Press. **278**

Vygotsky, L. S. (1962) *Thought and language.* Cam-

bridge, Mass.: MIT Press; New York: Wiley.
408

W

Wall, P. A. (1961) "Two transmissions systems for skin sensations." In W. A. Rosenblith, ed., *Sensory communication*. New York: Wiley; Cambridge, Mass.: MIT Press. Pp. 475–495. **309**

Wallach, M. A., N. Kogan, and D. J. Bem. (1962) "Group influence on individual risk taking." *J. abn. soc. Psychol.*, 65:75–86. **555–556**

Wallas, G. (1926) *The art of thought*. New York: Harcourt, Brace & World; London: J. Cape. **415**

Warner, L. H. (1927) "A study of sex behavior in the white rat by means of the obstruction method." *Comp. Psychol. Monogr. 4.* **228**

Warner, W. L. (1953) *American life*. Chicago: Univ. Chicago Press. **453**

Washburn, M. F., D. Deyo, and D. Marks. (1924) "Studies from the psychological laboratory at Vassar College. XLIV: A further study of revived emotions." *Amer. J. Psychol.*, 35:113–120. **263**

Watson, J. B. (1924) *Psychology from the standpoint of a behaviorist*, 3rd ed. Philadelphia: Lippincott. **405**

Weatherley, D. (1963) "Maternal response to childhood aggression and subsequent anti-Semitism." *J. abn. soc. Psychol.*, 66:183–185. **485–486**

Weaver, K. S. (1949) "A provisional standard observer for low level photometry." *J. opt. Soc. Amer.*, 39:278. **298**

Weaver, W. (1955) "Science, mankind's servant." Summary of presidential address, AAAS. *Sci. Newslt.*, 69:19. **31**

Wechsler, D. (1949) *Wechsler Intelligence Scale for Children: Manual*. New York: Psychological Corporation. **138**

———. (1955) *Wechsler Adult Intelligence Scale: Manual*. New York: Psychological Corporation. **138**

———. (1958) *Measurement and appraisal of adult intelligence*, 4th ed. Baltimore: Williams & Wilkins. **136**

Weddell, G. "Studies related to the mechanism of common sensibility." In W. Montagna, ed., *Advances in biology of skin. I: Cutaneous innervation*. Pp. 112–160. New York: Pergamon Press. **309**

Weininger, O. (1956) "The effects of early experience on behavior and growth characteristics." *J. comp. physiol. Psychol.*, 49:1–9. **85**

Weir, M. W., and H. W. Stevenson. (1959) "The effect of verbalization in children's learning as a function of chronological age." *Child Devel.*, 30:143–149.

Welch, L., and L. Long. (1940) "The higher structural phases of concept formation of children." *J. Psychol.*, 9:59–95. **378, 415**

Welker, W. I. (1956) "The effects of age and experience on play and exploration of young chimpanzees." *J. comp. physiol. Psychol.*, 49: 233–226. **230**

Wellman, B. L. (1940) "Iowa studies on the effects of schooling." *39th Yearbk. Nat. Soc. Stud. Educ.*, II:377–399. **183**

Wenger, M. A. (1936) "An investigation of conditioned responses in human infants." *Univ. Iowa Stud. Child. Welf.*, 12:7–90. **74, 75**

Werner, H., and B. Kaplan. (1952) "The acquisition of word meanings: A developmental study." *Monogr. Soc. Res. Child Devel.*, 15:190–200. **410**

———, and ———. (1963) *Symbol formation: An organismic developmental approach to language and the expression of thought*. New York: Wiley. **410**

Wever, E. G., and C. W. Bray. (1930) "The nature of acoustic response." *J. exp. Psychol.*, 13:373–387. **290**

White, R. W. (1959) "Motivation reconsidered: The concept of competence." *Psychol Rev.*, 66:297–333. **239**

———. (1963) *Ego and reality in psychoanalytic theory: A proposal regarding independent ego energies*. New York: International Universities Press. **239**

Whitehead, A. N. (1925) *Science and the modern world*. New York: Macmillan. **48**

Whorf, B. L. (1940) "Science and linguistics." *Tech. Rev.*, 44:229–231, 247–248. **335, 411**

Wickens, D. (1938) "The transference of conditioned excitation and conditioned inhibition from one muscle group to the antagonistic muscle group." *J. exp. Psychol.*, 22:101–123. **353**

Wilder, C. E. (1937) "Selection of rachitic and antirachitic diets in the rat." *J. comp. Psychol.*, 24:547–577. **219**

Williams, R. M., Jr. (1951) *American society*. New York: Knopf. **15**

Williams, T. R. (1965) *The Dusun: A Borneo society*. New York: Holt, Rinehart & Winston. **452**

Winkelmann, R. K. (1960) "Similarities in cutaneous nerve end-organs." In W. Montagna, ed.,

Advances in biology of skin. I: Cutaneous innervation. Pp. 48–62. New York: Pergamon Press. **309**

Winterbottom, M. R. (1953) "The sources of achievement motivation in mothers' attitudes toward independence training." In D. C. McLelland, et al., eds., *The achievement motive.* New York: Appleton-Century-Crofts. **233**

Wispe, L. G., and N. C. Drambarean. (1953) "Physiological needs, word frequency and visual duration thresholds." *J. exp. Psychol., 46*:25–31. **330**

Witkin, H. A. (1964) "Origins of cognitive style." In C. Sheerer, ed., *Cognition: Theory, research, promise.* New York: Harper & Row. Pp. 172–205. **442**

———, et al. (1954) *Personality through perception: An experimental and clinical study.* New York: Harper. **334**

———, et al. (1962) *Psychological differentiation: Studies of development.* New York: Wiley. **335, 442**

Wolf, S., and H. G. Wolff. (1942) "Evidence on the genesis of peptic ulcer in man." *J. Amer. Med. Assn., 120* (No. 9). **267, 268**

Wolfe, J. B. (1934) "The effect of delayed reward upon learning in the white rat." *J. comp. Psychol., 17*:1–21. **361**

———. (1936) "Effectiveness of token rewards for chimpanzees." *Comp. Psychol. Monogr., 12* (No. 60). **357**

Wolfenstein, M. (1951) "The emergence of fun morality." In A. Maslow, ed., "American culture and personality." *J. soc. Issues., 7*:15–25. **14**

Wolpe, J. (1958) *Psychotherapy by reciprocal inhibition.* Stanford: Stanford Univ. Press. **367, 500**

Woodrow, H. (1927) "The effect of type of training upon transference." *J. educ. Psychol., 18*:159–172. **387, 388**

Woodworth, R. S. (1941) "Heredity and environment: A critical survey of recently published material on twins and foster children." *Soc. Sci. Res. Council Bull. 47.* **181**

———. (1947) "Reinforcement of perception." *Amer. J. Psychol., 60*:119–124. **407**

Wrenn, C. C. (1949) "Potential research talent in the sciences based on intelligence quotients of Ph.D.'s." *Educ. Rec., 30*:5–22. **195**

Wright, H. F. (1937) "The influence of barriers upon strength of motivation." *Contr. Psychol. Theory, 1* (No. 3). **467**

Wright, R. T., C. Reid, and R. Evans. (1956) "Odour and molecular vibration. IV: New theory of olfactory stimulation." *Chem. & Indust.,* London. Pp. 973–977. **307**

Wrightsman, L. S., Jr. (1964) "Measurement of philosophies of human nature." *Psychol. Rep., 14*:743–751. **55–56**

Y

Yerkes, R. M. (1921) "Psychological examining in the U.S. Army." *Memoirs: Nat. Acad. Sci., 15*:1–890. **138, 188, 196, 201**

———. (1943) *Chimpanzees: A laboratory colony.* New Haven: Yale Univ. Press. **8**

Yonge, K. A. (1956) "The value of the interview: An orientation and pilot study." *J. appl. Psychol., 40*:25–31. **147**

Yoshii, N., P. Pruvot, and H. Gastaut. (1957) "Electrographic activity of the mesencephalic reticular formation during conditioning in the cat." *EEG clin. Neurophysiol., 9*:595–608. **397**

Young, P. T. (1962) "Methods for the study of feeling and of emotion." In D. K. Candland, ed., *Emotion.* Princeton: Van Nostrand. Chap. 6. **255**

Yule, G. U., and M. G. Kendall. (1958) *An introduction to the theory of statistics.* London: Griffin. **160, 162**

Z

Zeigler, H. P., and H. Leibowitz. (1957) "Apparent visual size as a function of distance for children and adults." *Amer. J. Psychol., 70*:106–109. **323**

Ziegler, W. A. (1939) *Minnesota Rate of Manipulation Test.* Minneapolis: Educational Testing Bureau. **142**

Zubek, J. P. (1964) "Behavioral and EEG changes after 14 days of perceptual deprivation." *Psychon. Sci., 1*:57–58. **341**

INDEX OF SUBJECTS

Adjustment (*continued*)
conflict and, 469–484 (*see also* Conflict)
criteria of, 464–466
defense responses, 467–469, 477–484 *passim*
detour behavior, 8, 184–185, 467
displacement, 468, 481–482, 493
environment and heredity and, 68–69, 71–72
fantasy, 421, 481
freezing response, 472
to frustration, 466–469, 477–484 *passim*
homeostasis (*see* Homeostasis)
identification as technique of, 481
integration criterion, 465
learning as process of (*see* Learning)
motivation and, 466
neurotic reactions, 493–496 (*see also* Psychopathology)
pain and (*see* Pain)
physiology of (*see* Nervous system; Physiology)
projection technique, 481, 486–487
psychopathology, 468
by psychosis, 507 (*see also* Psychopathology)
rationalization technique, 479–480
reaction formation, 480
regression, 482–484, 486
repression, 393, 448, 477, 483–484, 493
sensation (*see* Sensation)
sublimation, 481
withdrawal responses, 472–473
Adler, Alfred, 449
Adolescence (*see* Childhood)
Adrenal gland, 81, 258
Aerial perspective, 324
Affect (*see* Emotion)
Afferent fiber, 106
Affiliation motive, 239, 249–250
Agassiz, Louis, 24
Age (*see also* Childhood; Infancy):
and intelligence, 186
and perception, 323–324
and sex motive, 226
and taste acuity, 306
and vision, 323–324
Aggression, 240, 468, 481–482
Agnosia, 398
Agoraphobia, 265
Alcoholic psychoses, 504
Allport, Gordon, 464
Alternation response, 472, 473
American culture, 14–15
American Psychiatric Association, 491
American Psychological Association, 51
Amoeba, 4
Ampulla, 309
Amygdala, 101
Ancestry (*see* Heredity)
Androgens, 81, 226
Anesthesia, 446
Anger, 258, 261–262, 268–269

Animals and insects:
audition, 279, 289
communication, 6–7
conceptualization by, 407, 408
conditioned response, 113–118 *passim*, 349–350, 355–357, 360–362, 383–384, 407
culture of, 9–10
delayed-response learning, 398, 404
early development, 66, 84–85, 89–90
emotion, 255, 260, 263, 264, 467
exploratory behavior, 229–230
hunger, 217–221 *passim*, 247–248
insight, 364–365
instincts, 67–68, 216
intelligence, 184–185
learning, 346, 381
learning sets, 364–365
memory, 113–118, 391
nervous system, 104–105
perception, 326
problem seeking, 230
problem solving, 364–365
punishment effects, 382
reasoning, 8–9
sensory experience and deprivation, 84–85, 89, 263, 277–278, 279, 397–398
sex motive, 226, 228
smell, 279, 306, 307
social relations, 9–10, 86–87
tactility, 84
temperature motive, 248
thirst, 223–225 *passim*
ulcer development, 272–273
vision, 84, 279
Animism, 12
Annoyance, 262
Ant culture, 9–10
Anthropology, 15
Anthropomorphism, 42
Anti-Semitism, 485–486
Anxiety:
and affiliation motive, 239
conflict and, 472–484 *passim*, 493–502 *passim*
definition, 478
in neurosis, 493–502
overprotection and, 454
prenatal influences, 73–74
Apathy, 467
Aphagia, 219
Aphasia, 108, 398
Apperceptive mass, 326
Applied psychology, 44–46, 374, 464
Apraxia, 398
Aptitude tests, 141–142 (*see also* Achievement)
Archetypes, 449
Army Alpha Test, 188
Army General Classification Test, 196
Arousal (*see* Motivation; Motives; Stimuli)
Arthur Point Scale Performance Test, 139

Defense mechanisms, 468–469, 477–484 *passim* (*see also* Adjustment)
Degree of certainty, 168–169
Delayed-response learning, 398, 403–404
Delerium tremens, 504
Delusions, 503
Dementia praecox (*see* Schizophrenia)
Dendrites, 97
Dendritic potential, 106–107
Dependency, 65–67, 261, 346–347 (*see also* Childhood; Infancy)
Dependent variable, 39
Depression, 494, 505
Deprivation of sensory experience, 84–89 *passim*, 109, 205–206, 263, 270, 326, 341
Determinism, 11–12, 41–42, 67–68 (*see also* Science; Theory)
Detour behavior, 8, 184–185, 467
Deviation IQ, 136
Dewey, John, 20
Diagnostic testing and interviewing, 37, 138, 145, 146–147
Dichromatism, 304
Diencephalon, 100–101
Differential Aptitude Tests (DAT), 142
Differentiation of responses (*see* Perception; Sensation)
Directed thinking, 421
Discrimination deafness, 285
Discrimination of stimuli, 353–354, 397–398, 405–406 (*see also* Sensation)
Dispersion measures, 161–163
Displacement, 468, 481–482, 493
Dissociative reaction, 493
Distribution data (*see* Statistics; Variation)
Division of labor (*see* Role)
Dogmatism, 443, 460
Dollard-Miller theory of neurosis, 497
Dominant traits, 64–65
Double-alternation problem, 364, 411
Dreams, 421–422, 447, 498
Drives (*see* Motives)
Drugs, 506, 508, 515–516
Duct and ductless glands, 79, 95
Duplicity theory of vision, 298–300
Dwarfism, 80
Dynamic psychology, 21, 445
Dysplastic physique and personality, 435

E

Ear, 283–285, 309–310
Ebbinghaus nonsense syllables, 388
Ectomorphy, 436
Education:
    and intelligence, 183, 202
    motivation and, 235–236
    punishment in, 382–385 *passim*
    reinforcement of, 382–396 *passim*

Education (*continued*)
    set and, 419
    sex differences, 199–200
Effectance motive, 239
Effector cells, 95, 280
Efferent neurons, 106
Ego, 447, 449, 465 (*see also* Defense mechanisms; Self-concept)
Ego involvement, 476–477
Ego psychology, 466
Eidetic images, 406
Electrical activity of nervous system, 106–107, 111
Electrocardiograph (EKG), 259
Electroencephalograph (EEG), 106, 260, 421–422
Electromagnetic waves, 292–304 *passim*
Electroshock treatment, 509
Emotion, 253–275 (*see also* Attitudes)
    activation theory of, 264
    adrenal functions and, 81
    and aggression, 467
    anger, 258, 261–262, 268–269
    annoyance, 262
    and anxiety, 478
    apathy, 467
    arousal of, 261–263
    and behavior, 253–254, 256–258
    brain functions in, 101, 255, 258–260 *passim*
    cultural factors, 256
    definition, 254–260
    development of, 66, 76, 260–261, 263, 270–271
    distortion and disruption by (*see* Psychopathology)
    energizing role of, 81, 253–254, 256–257, 258
    and expressions and gestures, 256
    fear, 260–261, 265–266, 269
    frustration and, 261–262, 467
    happiness, 262–263
    hunger and, 222
    of infant, 66, 76, 260–261, 263, 270–271
    and intellectual functioning, 273–275, 416–417
    learning of, 256, 261, 265, 269, 270
    love, 263
    maturity of, 271
    motives and, 253–254
    and pain, 257
    and perception, 273–275, 328–336
    personality and, 269–270
    phobias, 265–266
    physiological theory of, 263
    physiology of, 105–106, 110–111, 258–260, 267–269 *passim*
    prenatal influences, 73–74
    psychosomatic reactions, 266–269, 272–273
    and sensation, 273–275
    sensory deprivation and, 85–89 *passim*, 205–206
    theories of, 263–264
    and tissue damage, 266–269 *passim*
Emotional maladjustment (*see* Psychopathology)
Empirical validity, 131
Empiricism, 124–132 (*see also* Science)
    British school of, 18

Empiricism (*continued*)
casual vs. controlled observation, 35–43
and construct development, 125–126 (*see also* Constructs)
experimental approach, 18–19, 25–26, 31 (note), 38–39, 153–175
"facts," 36, 39–40, 43, 126
objectivity, 33–50 *passim*, 125–128 *passim*
reliability (*see* Reliability)
specificity of observation, 44
in test construction, 145
testing and measuring (*see* Testing and measuring)
validity (*see* Validity)
Endocrine glands, 79, 95
Endomorphy, 436
Energy level, 253–254, 256–257, 258
Environment (*see also* Stimuli):
adjustment to (*see* Adjustment)
cultural factors (*see* Culture; Values)
heredity vs., 68–69, 71–72
and intelligence, 179–185, 187, 201–203 *passim*
interaction with, 4, 16–17, 345, 404–410
and personality, 187
selective response to, 317–321
sensory experience of, 277–315 (*see also* Sensation)
social aspects of (*see* Norms; Role; Social interaction)
stress, 266–269 *passim*
Erikson, Erik, 465
Escape conditioning, 357
Estes, W. K., 366
Estrogen, 81, 226
Evolution, 63
Exocrine glands, 95
Experimental approach, 18–19, 25–26, 31 (note), 38–39, 153–175
Experimental behavior, 30–32, 499–500
Exploration motive, 229–230, 249–250, 381
Expressive behavior and traits, 6–7, 146–147, 256, 260–261, 265–266, 269, 437–439, 458, 459
Extinction of conditioned response, 351, 357
Eye color, 64
Eyes, 292–304 *passim*, 422 (*see also* Vision)

F

Face validity, 126, 131
Factor analysis, 139–140, 441–442
Facts, 36, 39–40, 43, 126
Failure (*see* Achievement motive; Frustration)
Fantasy, 421, 481
Farsightedness, 293
Fear, 260–261, 265–266, 269
Fechner, Gustav, 18, 26, 313–314
Feeblemindedness, 80, 183, 190–191, 192
Feedback, 378, 395
Feelings (*see* Emotion; Sensation)
Fetus development, 73–75
Field-of-forces analysis, 471–475

Fissure of Rolando, 102, 107, 108
Fissure of Sylvius, 102, 108
Fixed-role therapy, 499–500
Food selection, 219–223 *passim*, 528–529
Forgetting, 388–393 (*see also* Memory; Repression)
Form discrimination, 296–297
Foster-children intelligence studies, 182
Fovea, 293
Free association, 498
Freedom and determinism, 11–12, 41–42, 67–68
Free nerve endings, 308–310 *passim*
Freezing, 472
Frequency distributions, 158 (*see also* Statistics; Variation)
Frequency theory of hearing, 289
Freud, Sigmund, 21, 421, 445–449 *passim*, 465, 495, 506–507, 510 (*see also* Psychoanalytic approach)
Frontal lobes, 101
Frustration, 466–469 (*see also* Conflict)
and anger, 261–262
defense reactions, 479–484
tolerance of, 467
unconscious factors, 477–478
Functionalist psychology, 19–20, 463

G

Galton, Sir Francis, 124
Galvanic skin response, 259, 351
Ganglion, 99
Gastric secretion, 267–269 *passim*
General Aptitude Test Battery (GATB), 142
Generalization (*see also* Concepts; Inference; Symbolic representations):
of learning, 364–365
of motives, 367–368
of stimuli, 353, 406–407
General paresis, 504
Genes, 64–65 (*see also* Heredity)
Genius (*see* Intelligence)
Gestalt psychology, 20–21, 338, 442
Gesture, 6–7 (*see also* Expressive behavior and traits)
Giantism, 80
Glands:
and infant development, 79–81
and sex characteristics, 80, 81
and sex motive, 226
types and functions (*see* Physiology)
Glove anesthesia, 446
Goal orientation, 413, 421 (*see also* Motivation; Problem solving)
Goddard, H. H., 134
Golgi tendon organs, 310
Granit color theory, 304, 305
Graphology, 438–439
Gratification (*see* Frustration; Motivation; Motives; Rewards)
Greek society, 237

Inference (*continued*)
   experimental design and, 163–169
   from statistical data, 163–169
Inherited traits (*see* Heredity)
Inkblot tests, 145, 146, 336
"Inner-directedness," 465–466
Insect behavior (*see* Animals and insects)
Insight, 364 (*see also* Problem solving)
Instinct, 6, 67–68, 216, 346, 447
Instrumental conditioning, 354–363
Insulin shock treatment, 509
Integrated response, 76, 93–96 *passim*, 106–107, 310, 429–432 *passim*, 447, 465
Intellect and intellectual functioning (*see also* Intelligence; Problem solving):
   achievement (*see* Achievement)
   emotion and, 273–275
   higher mental processes, 103–425
   impairment of, 109, 504
   lobotomy effects on, 264, 510
   mental set, 319
   and perception, 328
   psychosis and, 490, 504
Intelligence, 177–207 (*see also* Learning; Thinking)
   age and, 186
   of animals, 184–185
   and behavior, 191–199
   biochemical factors, 111, 191
   change in, 183, 185–189
   and creativity, 196–199
   cretinism, 80
   cultural influences, 136
   definitions, 139, 178–179, 179–190
   distribution in the population, 189–190
   education and, 183, 202
   environmental aspects, 179–185, 205–206
   factorial studies of, 139–140, 179–185
   folklore of, 177–178
   foster-children studies, 182
   gifted children, 192–195
   group tests, 138–139, 140
   hereditary and biological factors, 69–71, 80, 170–182
   and learning, 365
   mental deficiency, 80, 183, 190–191, 192, 365
   and occupational success, 196
   performance tests, 139
   personality and, 186–188, 194–196 *passim*
   race and, 200–203
   regional differences, 201–203
   reliability of tests of, 134, 136, 139, 140, 185–186
   sensory deprivation and, 85, 205–206
   sex differences, 186, 199–200
   testing of, 124, 133–140, 179–180, 181–182
   validity of tests of, 140–141, 191–199 *passim*
Interaction (*see* Social interaction)
Interest tests, 143–144
Interiorization of norms, 533 (*see also* Socialization)
Inter-observer reliability, 96
Interpolated stimuli, 390–391

Interpretation (*see also* Inference):
   of motivation, 243–244
   in perception, 126–127, 317–343 *passim*
   in science, 43, 46, 47–49 *passim*, 164–166
   of test scores, 123–147 *passim*
Interval scales, 129
Intervening variable, 40–41
Interviews, 37, 146–147
Introspection, 19, 26
Involuntary muscles, 95
Involutional psychotic reaction, 505
IQ scores, 136 (*see also* Intelligence)
Irrationality, 358–359, 447–448 (*see also* Psychopathology)
Irritability of protoplasm, 4, 97, 103–104

J

James-Lange theory of emotion, 263
James, William, 19–20, 24–26
Jastrow, Joseph, 124, 133
J-curve distributions, 159
Jung, Carl, 449
"Just noticeable differences," 313

K

Kinesthesis, 310–311, 325
Kleptomania, 494
Knowledge, 378, 395, 415–416
Koffka, Kurt, 20
Köhler, Wolfgang, 20, 364
Krause end bulbs, 309
Kretschmer's personality typology, 434–435, 442
Kuder Preference Record, 143

L

Ladd-Franklin color theory, 304, 305
Landolt rings, 300
Language (*see also* Audition; Communication; Concepts; Constructs; Symbolic representations):
   brain functions in, 108, 398
   of children, 78–79, 408–411 *passim*
   concepts and, 408–410
   conflict and, 469
   and culture preservation, 11
   learning aspects, 78–79, 118, 385–386, 407–411, 445
   mathematics as mode of, 48–49, 123–124 *passim*
   perception factors, 335, 341–342, 411
   propositional, 7
   public and private meanings, 46–48
   rules of, 7
   in science, 38, 39–43, 46–47 (*see also* Constructs)
   skill in, 385–386
   stylistic patterns, 437, 447
   transfer of training in, 385–386, 415

Motives (*continued*)
 hostility, 240–241
 and human nature, 243–244
 hunger, 217–223
 pain, 228–229
 primary motives, 213, 216–230
 projection of (*see* Projection)
 repression of, 393, 448, 477, 483–484, 493
 self-actualization, 465
 sex, 225–228
 social factors, 220, 221, 223
 strength of, 467
 temperature, 248
 thirst, 223–225
Motor behavior:
 bilateral transfer, 368
 brain functions in, 100, 103, 107–108
 coordination of, 310
 of infant, 75–77 *passim*
 skill acquisition, 375–380
 tests of, 142
Motor learning, 374–380, 390
Motor set, 318–319
Movement, 309–310, 320–321
 and visual perception, 324
Mowrer theory of neurosis, 496–497
Müller-Lyer illusion, 321–322
Murray, H. A., 439–441
Musculature, 95, 405 (*see also* Motor behavior; Motor set)
Myelencephalon, 99
Myelin sheath, 97

N

Narcoanalysis, 508
National character, 14–15
Naturalism, 11–12, 36–37, 41–42
Navaho Indians, 234
Nearsightedness, 293
Need, 213
Neo-Freudian theories, 449, 495–497
Neonate, 61–68 (*see also* Infancy)
Nerve cells, 96–97
Nervous system and neural process, 93–119 (*see also* Physiology)
 apperceptive mass, 326
 of audition, 285–292 *passim*
 autonomic system, 99, 101, 258
 basket nerve endings, 307
 brain, 99–111, 260
 central nervous system, 98, 99–101, 280, 321, 396–398, 404, 491, 502–503
 cerebral cortex, 99–111 *passim*, 255, 264, 397
 chemical factors, 111
 in conditioning, 396–397
 connectors, 95
 damage to, 105, 108, 109, 111, 191, 310, 398, 487, 502–503

Nervous system and neural process (*continued*)
 effectors, 95, 280
 electrical activity, 97–98, 106–107, 111
 electroencephalograph phenomena, 106–107
 and emotion, 110, 255, 258–260, 263–264
 evolution of, 103–105
 free nerve endings, 308–310 *passim*
 ganglia, 99
 Golgi tendon organs, 311
 in hunger, 217–219
 impulse transmission, 97–98, 106–107, 111
 integrative functions, 106–107
 kinesthesia, 310–311, 325
 Krause end bulbs, 309
 in learning, 81–83, 375, 396–398
 limbic systems, 105–106, 110–111, 264
 in linguistic functions, 108, 398
 lobotomy, 264, 510
 in memory, 118–119, 390–392 *passim*, 398
 and motivation, 106, 110
 and movement, 310
 nerve-cell structure, 96–97
 optic nerve, 292
 in pain, 229, 308
 and perception, 321–330 *passim*
 peripheral system, 98
 in psychological process, 21–22, 94, 105, 107–111
 receptors, 95, 224, 280, 292, 304–305, 307–310 *passim* (*see also* Sensation)
 in reflexes, 67, 96, 255–256, 264
 reticular formation, 105
 retinal disparity, 325
 rhinencephalon, 255
 Ruffini cylinders, 309
 semicircular canals, 309–310
 in sensory response, 95, 397–398 (*see also* Sensation)
 in sex motivation, 226–227
 in smell, 306, 307
 somatic system, 98–99
 spinal cord, 99
 symbol storage, 8
 sympathetic and parasympathetic functions, 99, 258
 synaptic transmissions, 98, 106
 in thinking functions, 405
 in thirst, 223–225 *passim*
 thyroid functions and, 80
 vagus nerve, 99, 268
Neurological view of psychological process, 21–22, 94, 107–111, 337–338
Neurology (*see* Nervous system; Physiology; Sensation)
Neuron, 96–97
Neurosis, 490, 493–502 (*see also* Psychopathology)
Newtonian color laws, 303
Nondirective therapy, 499
Normal distribution, 126, 159, 189 (*see also* Statistics)
Norms and normative behavior (*see also* Values):
 and achievement, 526–527, 535–536
 conformity (*see* Conformity)

Norms and normative behavior (*continued*)
cultural basis of, 13–15, 422–424
and data's significance, 128–129
enforcement of, 424–426, 535–536
"inner-directedness" vs., 465–466
interiorization of, 533 (*see also* Socialization)
male and female roles, 13, 14, 229, 424, 538, 556–557
in role behavior (*see* Role)
in sex behavior, 227–228 *passim*, 453
in small groups, 424–426, 531–536 *passim*
social determination of, 449–455 *passim*
and standardization of tests, 128–129, 134
in voting, 424–426
Nutrition factors, 73
Nystagmus, 310

O

Objectivity, 33–50 *passim*, 125–128 *passim* (*see also* Empiricism)
interpretation vs., 39–40, 47–48
vs. personal perception, 47
and problem solving, 34–35
vs. projection (*see* Projection)
publication and, 46–47
reliability and (*see* Reliability)
Observation (*see* Empiricism; Experimental approach; Methodology; Testing and measuring)
Obsessive-compulsive reaction, 494
Occipital lobes, 101
Occupation and intelligence, 196
Olfactory receptors and functions, 101, 105, 278, 306–307
Operant conditioning, 354–363
Operational definitions, 42, 126–128 *passim*, 139, 178, 373
Opinion, 40
Optic tracts, 100 (*see also* Vision)
Ordinal scale, 129
Organ of Corti, 284
Organic view, 5, 21, 22
Organism, 4–6
arousal needs of, 109
development of, 61–91
homeostasis of functioning of, 5, 211–212
integrated behavior of, 76, 93–95, 310, 429–432 *passim* 444
"wisdom of," 345
Osmoreceptors, 224
Ossicles, 284
Overlearning, 389–390, 496
Ovum, 63

P

Pain, 110, 228–229, 257, 308
Paramecium, 5

Paranoia, 505 (*see also* Psychopathology)
Parasympathetic nervous system, 99
Parietal lobes, 102
Partial reinforcement, 361–362
Passive movement sensation, 324
Pathology (*see* Psychopathology)
Pavlov, Ivan, 349–350, 364
Pearsonian *r*, 170, 172, 173
Peirce, C. S., 20, 25
Peptic ulcers, 267–268
Perception, 317–343 (*see also* Sensation)
achievement motive and, 235
adaptation to distortion in, 340–341
age and, 323–324
apperceptive mass, 326
attention and, 317–318
attitudes and, 327, 331–334
autokinetic phenomena, 47, 532
binocular cues, 325
brain functions in, 321
closure, 322
constancy phenomena, 322–323
context factors in, 321–336
convergence, 325
culture and, 335–336
defense mechanisms and, 334
depth and distance, 324–325
emotion and, 273–275, 328–336
Gestalt approach to, 21, 338
grouping of impressions, 322
hallucinations, 503
hunger and, 222–223, 329–331
illusions, 321–322
insight, 364
intellectual factors, 328
learning and, 17, 325–326, 345
linguistic influences, 335, 341–342, 411
and memory, 336–337
monocular cues, 324–325
motivation and, 222–223, 228, 320, 328–336
of movement, 324
neurological processes in, 321–330 *passim*
neurosis and, 496
objectivity of (*see* Objectivity)
organic need and, 329–331
organization aspects of, 321–337
of peripheral stimuli, 205–206
personality and, 334, 416–417, 442–443
of perspective, 324–325
and problem solving, 417–419, 425–426
projection in, 329–330 (*see also* Projection)
psychopathology and, 496
reality and, 466
retinal disparity, 325
selection aspect, 222–223, 317–321
of self, 444–445, 464–465, 476–478 *passim*, 480, 496, 499
sensory deprivation and, 326, 341
set in, 317–321, 417–419
sex motive and, 228

Prediction (*continued*)
  in perception, 332
  of personality and behavior, 445, 455–456
  process and, 445
  of school success, 195
  statistics and (*see* Statistics)
  testing and (*see* Testing and measuring)
  theory as basis of, 445
  validation by, 131
Prejudice, 353, 393, 485–486
Prenatal influences, 73–75
Presbyopia, 293
President's Commission on Mental Retardation, 190
Pressure sensitivity, 307–308
Prestige (*see* Status)
Primary colors, 302–303
Primary motives, 213, 216–230
Primary reward conditioning, 356–357
Primitive organization processes, 321–326
Principle of successive approximations, 358
Probability (*see* Statistics)
Problem-seeking motive, 230
Problem solving, 363–365, 403–425
  association in, 377–378, 412, 419, 425–426
  characteristics of process of, 34–50, 139–140
  computers, 124
  conditioning and, 363–364
  creativity and, 196–199 *passim*, 205–206
  detour behavior, 8, 184–185, 467
  directed thinking, 121
  and intelligence, 178
  learning and, 363–365, 404
  motivation and, 268, 367–368
  perception and, 425–426
  personality and, 421, 459–461
  reasoning, 8–9
  sets and, 364–365
  verbal processes and, 140, 410–412
Process, study of, 43–48 *passim*
Product-moment procedure, 170, 172, 173
Progestin, 81
Programmed instruction, 394–396
Projection, 481
  and authoritarianism, 443
  conflict and, 486–487
  and creativity, 198
  testing techniques, 145–146, 149, 232–233
Projection fibers, 103
Propositional language, 7
Protoplasm, 4–5
Proximal-distal sequence, 76
Psychiatry, 51 (*see also* Psychotherapy)
Psychoactive drugs, 508
Psychoanalytic approaches, 21
  criticism of, 448–449
  neo-Freudian views, 449, 495–497
  neurosis, theory of, 495–496
  personality theory, 444–449, 452, 463
  repression, theory of, 477–478
  therapy, 498–499

Psychological motives, 191–217 (*see also* Motivation; Motives)
Psychological primary colors, 302–303
Psychological process, 16–22, 43–48 *passim*
  and biological development, 83–88
  brain functions and structures in, 21–22, 94, 105, 107–111
  conflict (*see* Conflict)
  of emotion (*see* Emotion)
  homeostasis in, 444
  identification, 451–452, 459, 481, 539
  learning, 345–371 (*see also* Learning)
  motivation (*see* Motivation; Motives)
  neurological approach to, 21–22, 94, 107–111, 337–338
  perception (*see* Perception)
  of personality (*see* Personality)
  sensation (*see* Sensation)
  social factors, 521–558 (*see also* Socialization)
  unconsciousness, 447–448 (*see also* Unconsciousness)
Psychological tests (*see* Tests and measurements)
Psychologists, 50–51, 54–55
Psychology, 50–53
  applied psychology, 44–46, 374, 464
  behaviorism, 20
  careers in, 50–51
  content of, 4–16 *passim*, 17–18
  descriptive vs. dynamic approach, 21, 445
  field-of-forces analysis, 471–475
  fields of, 53–54
  functionalism, 19–20, 463
  Gestalt approach, 20–21, 338, 442
  history of, 18–23, 124
  holistic vs. segmental approaches, 21, 22, 442, 445–446
  laboratory study, 18
  lay views of, 30–53 *passim*
  methodology of (*see* Methodology)
  neurological approach, 21–22
  personal-constructs theory, 443–444
  physiological approach, 21–22, 94, 263–264
  prediction and process in, 43–48 (*see also* Prediction; Psychological process)
  psychoanalytic approaches, 21 (*see also* Psychoanalytic approaches)
  research in (*see* Research)
  situation orientation, 456
  social psychology, 521–558
  structuralism, 18–19
  tests and measurements in (*see* Testing and measuring; Tests and measurements)
  theory (*see* Theory)
Psychometrics (*see* Tests and measurements)
Psychopathic personality, 505–506
Psychopathology, 265–269, 464, 489–519
  alcoholic psychoses, 504
  autism, 421
  anxiety reaction, 493 (*see also* Anxiety)
  biological and hereditary factors, 71, 498, 506